PREFACE

State-of-the-art supercomputers are introduced in this text. Major design issues and typical applications requirements of high-performance computer systems are presented with milestone systems development achievements as reported in the open literature. The tutorial covers the following aspects of supercomputers: systems architecture, technology bases, large-scale computations, vector processing, language extensions, compiling techniques, commercial and exploratory systems, parallel algorithms, resource allocation, important applications, dataflow and very large-scale integration (VLSI) computing, and future trends in supercomputing.

The text is designed for scientists, systems designers, programmers, and educators and for those who are involved in the research, development, and application of high-performance computers. It is intended as a tutorial text for novices as well as a major reference for computer professionals.

The text is divided into five parts in which the designs and applications of various supercomputers are discussed. At the beginning of each part, a tutorial guide is provided. At the end of the text, an up-to-date bibliography is attached. The selected articles report major developments in recent years.

Part I introduces the area of supercomputing and two generations of supercomputer development. Part II is devoted to vector supercomputers, which are either pipelined or array structured. Language extensions and vectorizing compilers are introduced.

Part III covers multiprocessing supercomputers that have been produced commercially or are currently being developed at various research communities. Major design issues of multiprocessor systems are covered. Part IV presents some parallel algorithms and representative applications of modern supercomputers.

Part V consists of three chapters covering dataflow projects, VLSI and wafer-scale integrated (WSI) computing structures, and future perspectives of supercomputers. Additional references are listed in the attached bibliography which contains literature published up to the second quarter of 1984.

In addition to providing information on the algorithms for parallel processing, vectorization, and multiprocessing principles, the text also provides functional descriptions and performance evaluations of the following supercomputer systems: Control Data's Cyber 205, Cray Research's Cray 1 and Cray X-MP, Fujitsu's Facom VP-200, Burroughs Scientific Processor (BSP), Goodyear Aerospace's MPP, Denelcor's HEP, the S-1 multiprocessor, the Cedar multiprocessor, the NYU Ultracomputer, the Erlangen multiprocessor, and the supercomputers developed in Japan. These are current-generation supercomputers. The earlier models, TI-ASC, Illiac IV, and Star-100, are not discussed here because they are no longer being produced.

Possible future supercomputers are also elaborated upon, including the HEP-2, Cray 2 and 3, ETA-GF10, Japan's national supercomputer project, the United States strategic computing project, and various dataflow and VLSI systems. In addition to the use of supercomputers for numerical analysis, their potential uses for knowledge engineering and artificial intelligence (AI)-oriented applications are also assessed.

Forty-five reprints of papers are included in this tutorial. Literature guides are given in various parts of the tutorial. Readers should refer to the attached bibliography for additional references. We intend to update this reference listing in future editions. To assist those readers who need more information beyond the scope of this tutorial, we list the following books as suggested further readings:

Kuhn, R. H. and Padua, D. A. (1981). **Tutorial on Parallel Processing,** *IEEE Computer Society Press, Silver Spring, Maryland.*

Hockney, R. W. and Jesshope, C. R. (1981). **Parallel Computers,** *Adam Hilger Ltd., Techno House, Redcliff Way, Bristol, England BS1 6NX.*

Hwang, K. and Briggs, F. A. (1984). **Computer Architecture and Parallel Processing,** *McGraw-Hill Book Co., New York.*

Kuck, D. J. (1978). **The Structures of Computers and Computations,** *John Wiley & Sons, Inc., New York.*

Stone, H. (1980). **Introduction to Computer Architecture,** *Science Research Associates, Inc., Chicago.*

Siewiorek, D. P., Bell, C. G., and Newell, A. (1982). **Computer Structures: Principles and Examples,** *McGraw-Hill Book Co., New York.*

Rodrigue, G. (1982). **Parallel Computations,** *Academic Press, Inc., New York.*

Evans, D. J. (1982). **Parallel Processing Systems,** *Cambridge University Press, Cambridge, England.*

I wish to use this opportunity to thank all the authors who have contributed to this tutorial text. The area of supercomputers and scientific computations grows rapidly. I apologize to those authors whose valuable papers were not included due to the page limitation set by the Computer Society Press. In future editions, we intend to replace the older articles by more recent ones. Authors are encouraged to contact the editor in this regard.

In particular, I wish to thank Robert H. Kuhn, Faye A. Briggs, Chuan-Lin Wu, Tse-yun Feng, Daniel Gajski, George Paul, Ken Kennedy, Steve Chen, A. H. Sameh, John Rice, Sidney Fernbach, Garry Rodrigue, and H. T. Kung for their timely inputs which helped improve the contents of this text. The help from Mr. Z. W. Xu in updating the bibliography is gratefully acknowledged. I wish also to express my special appreciation to Jill Comer of Purdue University and Margaret Brown of IEEE Computer Society Press for their assistance in the production of this text.

Kai Hwang
August, 1984

Table of Contents

TUTORIAL
SUPERCOMPUTERS: DESIGN AND APPLICATIONS

KAI HWANG

IEEE CATALOG NUMBER EHO219-6
LIBRARY OF CONGRESS NUMBER 84-81316
IEEE COMPUTER SOCIETY ORDER NUMBER 581
ISBN 0-8186-0581-2

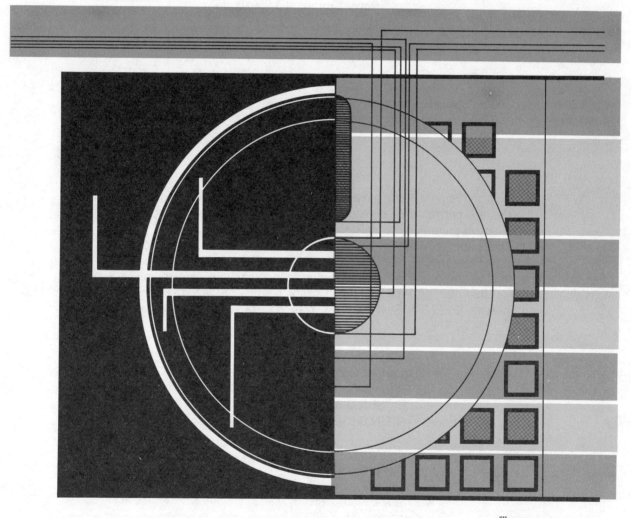

 IEEE COMPUTER SOCIETY

 1884 1984 THE INSTITUTE OF ELECTRICAL AND ELECTRONICS ENGINEERS, INC.

IEEE
COMPUTER
SOCIETY
PRESS

Published by IEEE Computer Society Press
1109 Spring Street
Suite 300
Silver Spring, MD 20910

IEEE Catalog Number EHO219-6
Library of Congress Number 84-81316
IEEE Computer Society Order Number 581
ISBN 0-8186-0581-2 (Paper)
ISBN 0-8186-4581-4 (Microfiche)

Order from: IEEE Computer Society
Post Office Box 80452
Worldway Postal Center
Los Angeles, CA 90080

IEEE Service Center
445 Hoes Lane
Piscataway, NJ 08854

The Institute of Electrical and Electronics Engineers, Inc.

Part I: Introduction

Chapter 1: Modern Supercomputers

PART I

INTRODUCTION

Supercomputers are the fastest computers available at any specific time. Dr. Sidney Fernbach (1981) said once: "Today's large computers (mainframes) would have been considered supercomputers 10 to 20 years ago. By the same token, today's supercomputers will be considered state-of-the-art standard equipment 10 to 20 years from now." Supercomputers are playing a major role in advancing human civilization.

Demands for the use of supercomputers in solving complex problems increase rapidly in the areas of structural analysis, weather forecasting, fusion energy research, petroleum exploration, aerodynamic simulations, electronic circuit design, remote sensing, medical diagnosis, artificial intelligence, expert systems, advanced automation, military defense and weapons design, genetic engineering, and socioeconomics.

These demands apply to a wide range of science, technology, and engineering applications, that require the processing of huge volumes of data and demand enormous computational power. This introductory section characterizes the basic requirements of supercomputing. These requirements set forth the system design objectives and application spectrum.

Bill Buzbee (1983) of Los Alamos Scientific Laboratory has identified the value of supercomputing in three important directions. First, supercomputers aid in **knowledge acquisition** via the treatment of complexity within a reasonable time. Knowledge examples include logical inference, expert systems, partial differential equations, and extraordinary phenomena such as fusion, geophysics, oceanography, atmospheric science, and material science.

Second, supercomputers provide **computational tractability** in instrumentation, predictive simulations, energy resource explora-

tion, general circulation modeling, weapons effects, atmospheric testing, etc. Third, supercomputers **promote productivity**, as in systems optimization, computer-aided design and manufacture (CAD/CAM), VLSI circuit design, etc. A large range of supporting services are being engendered via supercomputing.

The mainstream use of computers is experiencing a trend of four ascending levels of sophistication (Hwang and Briggs 1984). We started with the use of computers for **data processing**, in which number crunching is the major task performed. The next level is for **information processing**, in which related data items are processed in a structured manner. Most of today's computers are still being used for data and/or information processing.

Neil Lincoln (1982) of ETA Systems, Inc., defines a supercomputer as a system that is only one generation behind the computing requirements of leading-edge efforts in science and engineering. This leads to the role of using supercomputing for knowledge processing and intelligence applications in the future.

Japanese computer scientists have predicted that the use of computers for **knowledge processing** will be the major thrust in the 1990s. Semantic meanings are added into information items in knowledge processing. Thus nonnumeric symbol manipulations are demanded in knowledge-based information processing.

Ultimately, we wish to use future computers for **intelligence processing**, in which new knowledge can be acquired through computer learning from large-scale, accumulated knowledge databases. Presently, we are entering the knowledge-processing era. It is still too remote for an intelligent computer to communicate with humans in speech, written languages, pictures, and images and to perform creative thinking through logical inference.

Based on today's technology, we classify a computer as a super machine if it can perform hundreds of millions of floating-point operations per second (100 Mflops) with a word length of approximately 64 bits and a main memory capacity of millions of words (Norrie 1984).

The demand of computational speed is increasing sharply in recent years. "We have problems that would take 500 to 1,000 hours to solve on today's supercomputers," said David Nowak at Lawrence Livermore National Laboratory, where a cluster of seven supercomputers is used for nuclear weapons research.

Without supercomputers, many of the aforementioned challenges cannot be realized within a reasonable time. Generating timely results is crucially important in meeting the present and future demands.

Chapter 1: Modern Supercomputers

1.1: Evolution of Modern Supercomputers by Kai Hwang
1.2: Second Generation of Vector Supercomputers by E.W. Kozdrowicki
and D.J. Theis

4

CHAPTER 1
MODERN SUPERCOMPUTERS

In this introductory chapter, an overview of modern supercomputers is provided. The evolution of supercomputing systems is reviewed in Section **1.1**. Supercomputers manufactured in the United States, Japan, and other countries are briefly introduced. The peak performances of these machines are compared. Several future target systems are mentioned.

In section **1.2**, Kozdrowicki and Theis (1980) provide a detailed comparison of three modern supercomputers, namely Cray Research's Cray 1, Control Data's Cyber 205, and the BSP. Concurrent scalar processing and increased parallelism in vector processing are the major advances in supercomputer systems. These two introductory sections will prepare the reader for a successful study of the subsequent chapters.

1.1 Evolution of Modern Supercomputers

Modern supercomputers have so far experienced two generations of development. The first generation of vector supercomputers was marked by the development of the Star-100, TI-ASC, and the Illiac IV in the 1960s. By 1978, there were seven installations of ASC, four installations of Star-100, and only one Illiac IV system at various user sites.

Both the Star-100 and ASC systems are equipped with multiple pipelined processors to achieve parallel vector processing. The Star-100 has a memory-to-memory architecture with two pipeline processors. The ASC can handle up to three-dimensional vector computations in the pipelined mode. The peak speed of both systems is around 40 Mflops.

All these first-generation machines are now no longer in production. The second or current generation started with the creation of the Cray 1 in 1976. Seymour Cray was America's premiere supercomputer designer who designed the Cray 1 and the basic architecture of Control Data's Cyber 205.

State-of-the-art supercomputers can be characterized as belonging to one of three architectural classes: **pipelined computers, array processors,** and **multiprocessor systems.** All these supercomputer classes emphasize parallel processing in different forms. A pipelined computer performs overlapped computations to exploit temporal parallelism. An array processor uses multiple arithmetic/logic units to achieve spatial parallelism. A multiprocessor system has multiple instruction streams over a set of interactive processors with shared resources (memories, databases, etc.) These three parallel approaches to computer system design are not mutually exclusive.

In fact, most existing computers are now pipelined; some also assume an array or a multiprocessor structure. The fundamental difference between an array processor and a multiprocessor system is in that the processing elements in an array processor operate synchronously under a common controller, whereas the processors in a multiprocessor system may operate asynchronously with separate controllers. Array processors have mostly special-purpose applications, whereas multiprocessors offer much higher flexibility for general purpose applications.

Presently, pipelined uniprocessor systems are dominating the marketplace in either business or scientific applications. Pipelined computers are more cost-effective, and their operating systems are well developed to achieve better resource utilization and thus higher performance.

Array processors are most often custom designed for specific applications. The performance-to-cost ratio of such special-purpose machines might be low. Programming on an array processor is much more difficult because of to its rigid architecture.

Multiprocessor systems are the most flexible in exploiting arbitrarily structured parallelism. Pipelined multiprocessor systems represent the state-of-the-art design in parallel processing computers. Many of the supercomputer manufacturers are taking this route in upgrading their high-end models.

Both pipelined and array supercomputers are designed mainly for vector processing of large arrays of data. Presently, most of the commercially available vector supercomputers are pipelined machines owing to their cost-effectiveness. Besides using multiple pipelines in uniprocessor systems, supercomputer manufacturers are also challenging multitasking through the use of multiple processors.

The speedup of using an n-processor system over a uniprocessor system has been theoretically estimated to be within the range $(\log_2 n, n/\ln n)$. For an example, the speedup range is less than 6.9 for $n=16$. Most of today's commercial multiprocessors have only 2 to 4 processors in a system.

Dr. John Worlton of the Los Alamos Scientific Laboratory has assessed "The designers of supercomputers will do better at exploiting concurrency in the computing problems, if they use a small number of fast processors instead of a large number of slower processors." This implies that the use of a small number of processors will be more cost-effective, based on today's technology and mechanisms for resource management. By the late 1980s, we may expect systems of 8-16 processors. Unless the technology changes drastically, we will not anticipate massive multiprocessor systems until the 90s.

The peak speed of a computer system is defined as the maximum computation rate that can be theoretically achieved by full utilization of all functional units with a continuous supply of data to and from the memory hierarchy. Such a peak speed may never be attainable in real life, benchmark experiments. However, it shows the absolute maximum capability of a machine. The average speed of a machine, although very difficult to estimate accurately, is usually only a fraction of the peak speed.

We briefly introduce the space of modern supercomputers in Figure 1. The peak speeds of nine existing systems are compared in terms of millions of operations per second. The numbers in parentheses are peak speeds or ranges of peak speed. The year when each system was first introduced is marked. There are

five systems developed in the United States, namely Cray Research's Cray 1 and Cray X-MP, Control Data's Cyber 205, Denelcor's HEP-1, and Goodyear Aerospace's MPP.

The speed performances are based on 64-bit floating-point operations, except that the MPP has a peak speed ranging from 6.5 G integer (8-bit) operations to 216 Mflops of 32-bit results. In the last two years, three supercomputers were announced in Japan. These machines have peak speeds ranging from 500 Mflops to 1300 Mflops. According to absolute hardware speed, the NEC SX-2 system is by far the fastest supercomputer ever built. China's Galaxy was announced in 1984 as a 120 Mflops vector processor.

Of these nine systems, the MPP is the only single-instruction-stream, multiple-data-stream (SIMD) array processor that handles a single instruction stream over possibly 2^{14} data streams. Denelcor's HEP-1 is a multiple-instruction-stream-multiple-data-stream (MIMD) multiprocessor system with as many as 16 processors. The Cray X-MP is a dual-processor system with each central processing unit (CPU) modified from the Cray 1s. The rest are all pipelined uniprocessor systems having multiple functional pipelines that can operate on multiple streams of data having various formats.

Several future systems are indicated in the upper right corner of Figure 1. These are systems possibly to be extended from the existing supercomputers. At least 1 Gflops is anticipated in these future systems. Most of these future supercomputers will be multiprocessors.

The ETA-GF10 is a 10 Gflops supercomputer currently under development by ETA Systems, Inc., which will extend the structure of Cyber 205 to 8 processors. The S-1 is a 16-processor system currently under development at Lawrence Livermore National Laboratory.

The Japanese national supercomputer project is targeted to be a 10 Gflops machine. The U.S. Strategic Computing project demands a supercomputer that can perform 1 Tflops (10^{12} floating-point operations per second). These supercomputers are planned to appear within the next decade.

Supercomputers can aid in knowledge acquisition, provide a wide range of supporting

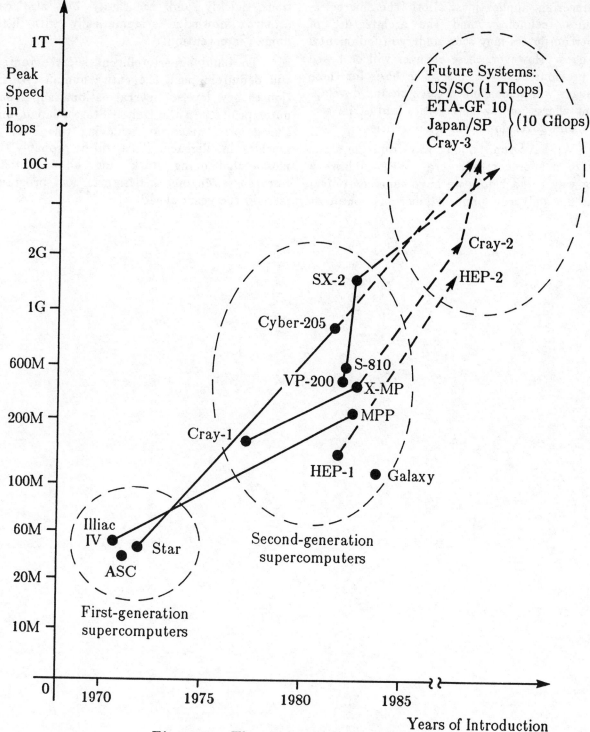

Figure 1.   The space of supercomputers.

services, advance scientific exploitations, and create high technology in modern civilization. By early 1984, only about 120 supercomputer installations are extant worldwide. This number of installations is small compared with

the widespread use of personal computers in recent years.

Supercomputers are crucial and indispensable to many scientific, technologic, and engineering applications. Both the microelectronics technology and the architecture of supercomputers may soon undergo fundamental changes. However, these changes will be based on previous achievements. The basis for these changes will be continued research and development efforts among universities, industrial sectors, and government research agencies.

We have come a long way from the stone age to a supercomputer era. We still have a long way to go before we have supercomputers that not only can perform laborious computations quickly and accurately but also can acquire knowledge systematically with little human intervention.

To build superintelligent supercomputers will definitely push the entire human civilization to new levels. Several national supercomputer projects in the United States, Japan, and Europe are aimed at achieving this level of machine intelligence. This will be probably the most challenging task for all scientists, researchers, engineers, designers, and programmers in the years ahead.

Integral scalar processing and increased parallelism are major advances in supercomputer evolution. Three second-generation machines—BSP, Cyber 205, and Cray-1—are here described and compared.

Second Generation of Vector Supercomputers

Edward W. Kozdrowicki
Douglas J. Theis
The Aerospace Corporation

In a 1974 article, * we compared the characteristics and capabilities of the first generation of vector supercomputers, Control Data Corporation's Star-100 and Texas Instruments' ASC—for string array and advanced scientific computer, respectively. At that time, before the first generation of vector supercomputers gave way to the second, the Star-100 had four installations and the ASC seven.

The second generation of vector supercomputers began in 1975 when Cray Research, Inc., announced the Cray-1. First installed in 1976, the Cray-1 computer has demonstrated high reliability, high-speed secondary storage, complete interfacing to many front-end computers, and has an extensive amount of useful software support. As of September 1980 there were 20 Cray-1 machines at user facilities. The Control Data Corporation Cyber 203 was announced in 1976, and the Burroughs Scientific Processor in 1977. In 1980 CDC announced its Cyber 205, a significantly improved version of the Cyber 203 (only one Cyber 203 was delivered). Both Burroughs and CDC have orders for 1980-1981 deliveries of their machines.

The architectures of these machines have unique differences as well as similarities, yet all three were specifically designed for vector array processing. The BSP is an advanced array architecture which evolved from Burroughs' significant experience in designing and building the Illiac IV and the PEPE—parallel elements of processing ensemble—machine for the Army's Advanced Ballistic Missile Program. (Only one Illiac IV was ever put into production, at the Ames NASA Research Center at Moffet Field, California.) The Cyber 205 is an all-LSI version of the 203, a much improved design that also used newer technology parts to upgrade CDC's basic Star-100 architecture. Cray-1, of course, is a new architecture devel-

oped by Seymour Cray when he started his own company. Since Cray was the principal architect of the CDC 6600 and CDC 7600, the Cray-1 has some evolutionary similarities which are traceable to those designs. Thus, each of these three supercomputers is the result of 15 to 20 years of design evolution.

Characteristics of supercomputers

A supercomputer is generally characterized by three main features: (1) high computational speed, (2) large main memory, and (3) fast and large secondary memory. The high computational speed is of obvious desirability. A large main memory is useful in processing large amounts of data as units and in operating large, complicated programs from main memory without time-consuming overlay procedures.

Secondary memory is important in many scientific jobs because the data simply will not fit in main memory. In such cases, secondary storage may be regarded as an overflow of main memory. Many scientific programmers have reported spending the bulk of their effort in optimizing such data transfers between memories—i.e., on input/output. Cray and CDC have solved their secondary memory problem with highly sophisticated disk systems. Burroughs plans to use a 64M-word solid-state file memory for secondary memory, and has thereby expressed its intention to produce the first supercomputer capable of truly practical, efficient processing of scientific programs with data spaces in the tens of millions of words.

In 1977 Auerbach Publishers suggested that the Cray computer would be initially limited to a small circle of scientific users in nuclear research, seismic analysis, and weather modeling. Now, models for aerodynamics, com-

* D.J. Theis, "Special Tutorial: Vector Supercomputers," *Computer*, Vol. 7, No. 4, April 1974, pp. 52-61.

Reprinted from *Computer*, November 1980, pages 71-83. Copyright © 1980 by The Institute of Electrical and Electronics Engineers, Inc.

puter-assisted tomography, human organ modeling, fusion power, and such exotic ideas as artificial intelligence experimentation are being prepared for supercomputers. But as scientists refine their models in the 1980's, still another order of magnitude of computational capability will be demanded. Fusion power models, for example, need 1000 times the power of today's most advanced computer.

The most obvious architectural improvement of second-generation supercomputers over the first is the inclusion, as an integral design element, of a scalar processor for nonvector operations. In addition to being a vector supercomputer, these second generation machines do well for scalar operation benchmarks. In fact, the Cray-1 is the world's fastest scalar computer, a distinction which it will hold for some time since there are no announcements of any planned computer with a faster cycle time. By fastest scalar computer, we mean that its basic cycle time of 12.5 nanoseconds is the fastest of any computer. The Cray-1's closest competitor, for many years, has been the CDC 7600 or, more recently, the Cyber 176, which has a 27.5-nanosecond cycle time. The new Cyber 205 will be the second-fastest machine, with a cycle time of 20 nanoseconds. The BSP has a cycle time of 160 nanoseconds, eight times slower than the Cyber and 12.8 times slower than the Cray. Furthermore, the BSP requires two cycles to produce any result, making it 25.6 times slower than the Cray hardware.

But raw hardware speed alone does not make a supercomputer. Cray is clearly pushing current hardware limitations, producing complete operation segments in the time it takes an electric pulse, flowing at the speed of light (.98351 feet/nanosecond), to travel a distance of only 12.27 feet. Indeed, the Cray computer is specifically designed to be small because of these distances; the machine is less than five feet in diameter and less than seven feet tall (56½" × 77"). The CDC 7600, also designed by Seymour Cray, is so distance-critical that wires hanging from module to module are actually cut to precise lengths.

Cray speeds seem to have reached a current practical limit, but it is difficult to predict what the logic speed of future technologies will uncover. Those interested in showing the uncomputability of some meta-astronomical quantities (e.g., chess at 10^{120} combinations) have even theorized logic that operates on molecular dimensions (i.e., that a logical operation performed in the time it takes an electric pulse to traverse the dimension of a molecule ($\approx 1 \times 10^{-11}$ feet)). The dimension of subatomic particles might be carrying computational speeds a little far. Actually, such theorizing may not even be in the right direction. The human brain is a highly superior computational device, yet operates on millisecond logic 100,000 times slower than the Cray-1. It would be unfair to look at the above figures and conclude that the BSP is 25 times slower than the Cray. In fact, Burroughs deliberately uses slower logic to accomplish certain goals, mainly effective use of parallelism.

Even though vector supercomputers have very fast scalar computation speeds, it must be emphasized that the importance, utility, and success of all three machines are directly related to the execution of very large programs with a high degree of parallelism. To better understand the concepts of parallelism, it is necessary to consider the basic definition for computational speed now commonly accepted by scientific programmers for numerical analysis work. The accepted term is millions of floating point operations per second, or MFLOPS. Consider the following program segment:

$$DO\ I\ =\ 1, 1\ 000\ 000$$
$$Y\ (I)\ =\ A(I)\ *\ B(I)\ +\ C(I)$$
$$END\ DO$$

Each pass through this DO loop accomplishes two useful floating point operations. Therefore, any computer that could execute this DO loop one million times in one second would be computing at a rate of two million floating point operations per second, or at 2 MFLOPS. This measurement refers specifically to actually accomplished useful operations.

Clearly, with each pass through this DO loop, much more work is actually done than one multiplication and one addition. The operands must be fetched from main memory storage and inserted into intermediate registers before they can be fed to the units that actually perform the floating point operation. The index, labeled I, must be incremented, and some procedure must determine completion of the entire DO loop. Generally, about five individual operations must take place to complete one useful floating point operation. In early machines, each of these presumed five operations took place individually and in sequence. Later machines, such as the CDC 6600, introduced some degree of simultaneity. Current supercomputers can execute all five of these presumed operations concurrently, and such parallel concurrent operation can be sustained for large percentages of the total time. It is this effective performance of many operations in parallel that makes the second generation of supercomputers great.

As an example of parallel instruction execution, consider the following DO loop:

$$DO\ I\ =\ 1, 64$$
$$Y\ (I)\ =\ A(I)\ *\ B(I)$$
$$END\ DO$$

On the Cray-1, the above DO loop would be executed and actually produce one answer every 12.5 nanoseconds or each clock period. This rate would be sustained from the time the first answer is produced until the 64th answer is produced. For this period of time the Cray would be computing at a rate of

$$1000/12.5\ ns/answer\ =\ 80\ MFLOPS$$

For the Cyber 205 the corresponding figure would be

$$1000/20\ ns/answer\ =\ 50\ MFLOPS$$

although, in some instances, it can operate two pipes to give a possible corresponding 100 MFLOP rate. The BSP would divide this DO loop into four groups of 16. The 16

The Cray-1 (shown above, with disk controller) has a 12.5-nanosecond cycle time (for both scalar and vector operations), the world's fastest. From its introduction in 1975 through September 1980, the Cray-1 has been installed at 20 user facilities. The LSI circuitry of the CDC Cyber 205 is compared at right with the equivalent logic from the Star-100. The Cyber 205 provides four million words of central memory and can perform up to 100 million floating point operations per second (32-bit words). The Burroughs Scientific Processor (below) has a 64M-word solid-state file memory for secondary memory, enabling it to handle programs with data spaces in the tens of millions of words. (Photos courtesy Cray Research, Inc., Control Data Corporation, and Burroughs Corporation)

parallel processing elements, all operating in lock step, would compute at a rate of

$$1000/320 \text{ ns/answer} \times 16 \text{ PEs} = 50 \text{ MFLOPS}$$

Note that the corresponding computational rate, for all practical purposes, is very high on all three supercomputers.

It must be emphasized that the above computation rates are burst rates measured from the time the first answer appears until the 64th answer appears. It takes extra time to set up the operation, and if the length of the DO loop is greater than 64, the entire operation must be grouped in successive segments since 64 is the maximum vector on the Cray and on the Cyber 205. This procedure does not apply to the BSP.

We next present separately what each manufacturer did to efficiently implement parallel architectural capabilities, achieving from tens to over a hundred million floating point operations per second. Following some concluding remarks on overall architectural approaches, a series of annotated tables (Tables 1-10) provides some basis for evaluating these machines on certain common parameters.

The Burroughs Scientific Processor

The Burroughs Scientific Processor is the culmination of extensive experience in parallel processing architectures, both in hardware and software. The BSP is an SIMD—serial instruction multiple data—architecture with 16 arithmetic elements—AEs—driven synchronously by a single instruction stream. The BSP's instruction set (109 in the AE) is designed around the concept of linear vectors of variable length. Special control hardware accommodates vector lengths which are not integral multiples of the number of AEs. The basic arithmetic instruction execution times are 320 nanoseconds (two machine cycles) times 16 arithmetic elements for a maximum rate of 50 MFLOPS where all 16 AEs execute synchronously. The AEs are implemented with hardwired primitive operators in a microprogrammed fashion where the control word is 100 bits wide. The AE has both floating arithmetic capability (48 bits, 36 bits mantissa and 10 bits exponent) as well as considerable nonnumeric operators for control, testing, and editing functions. Each AE has double-length registers to provide hardware double precision capability.

The BSP architecture (Figure 1) provides four levels of parallelism in order to fully use the AEs. The 16 AEs comprise the major portion of the parallel processor. The control processor, the brain of the BSP, has a small, efficient operating system in CP memory. The control and maintenance unit supports all BSP control communications with the front-end B7800. The CMU has access to critical data paths and registers of the BSP, and thus can perform state analysis and circuit diagnostics under control of maintenance software running in the system manager. All work job requests, loading, and maintenance functions are done there. The scalar processing unit has a non-I/O Fortran optimizer processor which assembles instructions for the parallel processor control unit. The PPCU receives vector operation output from the SPU and trans-

Table 1.
Instruction repertoire types.

BSP		CYBER 205		CRAY-1	
Scalar	Vector	Scalar	Vector	Scalar	Vector
All of those listed under Vector, plus:	Arithmetic	Load and Store	Arithmetic	Register Entry	Register Entry
	Logical	Arithmetic	Compare	Inter Register Transfers	Inter Register Transfers
Register	Relational	Index	Search	Shift	Shift
Load and Store	Search	Increment and Test	Move	Merge	Arithmetic
Input/Output	Compare	Bit	Normalize	Arithmetic	Normalize
Special Instructions for operating system and generation of vector macro instructions for the parallel processor section (ref: BSP Block Diagram)	Test and Select	Normalize	Data Type Conversion	Logical Operations	Logical Operations
	Minimum and Maximum	Data Type Conversion	Sparse Vector	Memory/ Register Transfers	Memory/ Register Transfers
	Shift and Extract	Branch	String (byte and bit)		
	Type Convert	Logical	Vector Macros	Branch	Branch
	Character Conversion	Monitor Call	Dot Product	Population Count	Population Count
	Branching		Polynomial Evaluation	Normalize	Merge
	Expand and Merge		Average Difference	Input/Output	
	Random Read and Store		Average	Executive Mode	
	Dot Product		Adjacent Mean	Program Real-Time Clock Control	
	Recurrence		Vector Logical		
	Reduction		Mask/Merge		
			Gather/Scatter		

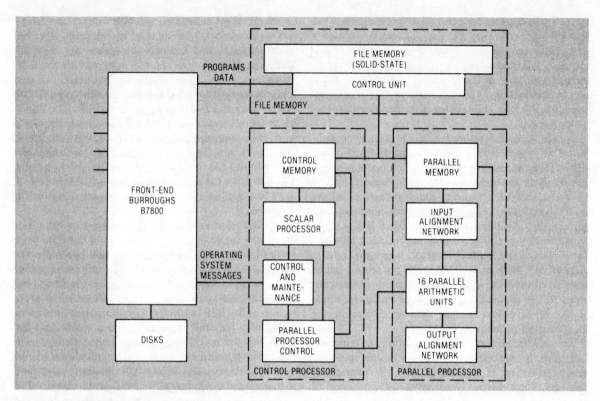

Figure 1. Burroughs Scientific Processor.

Table 2.
CPU organization.

	BSP	CYBER 205	CRAY-1
Instruction Word Length(s)	48-bits	32-bits, 64-bits	16-bits, 32-bits
Clock Period	320 ns	20 ns	12.5 ns
Programmable Addressable Registers	(16) 48-bits (16) 120-bits	(256) 64-bits	(72) 24-bits (584) 64-bits
Instruction Stack	262K (48-bit) Words in Control Processor	64 Words	64 Words
Hardware Look-ahead/Overlap	Consists of Instructions in Control Processor	16-32 Instructions	256 Instructions
Functional (e.g. Aritthmetic) Units	16 + 1 (AEs + CP)	11 (6 Vector: 2 FL PT, 1 String; 5 Scaler: ADD/SUB, MULT, LOG, SHIFT, DIV/SQ)	12
Pipeline Segments	4 × 16 (Where each stage contains 16 variables for a total of 64 pipeline slots)	Up to 26	Up to 14 segments with a result every clock
Maximum Vector Results Rate	320/16 = 20 ns	20/2 = 10 ns (2 Pipes)	12.5 ns

Notes to Table 2:

BSP. The instruction stack of the BSP really is the 256K word control processor memory for all the program instructions and data that will be executed in the parallel processor. There is also a push-down stack for subroutine entry and exit operations.

The BSP has two other important features, residue check on all arithmetic operations, and instruction retry on all instructions including all vector instructions.

forms it into optimized control steps for execution in the parallel processor. The SPU also provides the necessary queues and controls to synchronize the AEs in the parallel processor subsystem. The PPCU does this by storing the starting address of all the templates which are sequences of microinstructions. There are some 80 templates implemented in PROMs, and each template provides some vector operation.

Data input/output is through the file memory controller—FMC—and file memory, which are designed to provide the large capacity, high throughput operation necessary to sustain the high computational processing rates of the 16 parallel AEs. This secondary storage unit of the BSP is composed of solid-state devices—not disks—for performance. The FMC handles multiple I/O requests from the file memory and the parallel memory, all under the control of the control processor. Aggregate transfer rates of up 12.5M words (75M bytes) per second can be handled via the FMC. Conflict-free memory access is provided by the alignment networks (see Figure 1), which consist of hardware crossbar switches connecting the parallel memory banks to the AEs.

The parallel memory, in reality an array of 17 memory units directly supporting the AEs, is organized to permit simultaneous access to almost any 16 consecutive elements. These can be referenced as rows, columns, or diagonals in an array. This memory, consisting of 512K words for each unit or 8M words total, has an overall transfer bandwidth of 100M words per second.

The BSP software control and user interface is done via the master control program. MCP residence is split between the B7800 and the BSP's control processor. The B7800 provides the extended Fortran compiler and a vectorizer in addition to a work flow language to prescribe task procedures (like JCL) for doing BSP jobs. The compiler (with its two optimizers), linking editor, and vectorizer are reentrant. All the programs for the BSP must be written in Fortran. Operationally, the B7800 MCP runs in the foreground environment, where BSP production work is stored, new applications are developed in-

teractively from terminals, and BSP outputs are edited and reported. In the background environment, the BSP MCP manages and controls the queue for the BSP workload. Users cannot directly interact with the BSP operations, and are therefore constrained to the foreground environment. For these reasons only a B7800 can be used as a front-end host to the BSP. The BSP's MCP (which executes in the CP) interprets the user's work-flow-language requests, schedules BSP tasks based on priority, supplies data associated with tasks not contained in the file memory, and provides checkpointing capability. On the average, approximately 20 percent of the B7800 host time is required to manage and control the BSP's MCP.

The BSP Fortran compiler has several important vectorization capabilities to convert serial Fortran code strings into vector constructs. Burroughs has added extensions to the BSP Fortran to allow addressing within elements (as scalars) and in combinations (as arrays) for performing manipulations and computations on these arrays to utilize BSP hardware execution capabilities more efficiently. The BSP Fortran generates vector code for most recursive and IF statements; these constructs were previously handled as scalar. The compiler even has an option for regenerating serial ANSI standard source code to make programs compatible and transportable to other systems, and for comparison purposes during program development. Results from benchmarks indicate that BSP Fortran-based applications run 50 to 100 times faster than those run on a B7800 in the foreground.

Control Data Corporation's Cyber 205

The Cyber 205 is the latest version of CDC's improved Star-100. In an earlier model, the Cyber 203, significant additions to the basic Star-100 included the scalar operations unit and the LSI single-error-correction double-error-correction memory technology upgrade, along with a memory interface design that permitted instructions to be issued every 20 nanoseconds (the Star-100 requires 40 nanoseconds). The addition of the scalar processor unit provided instructions that were fully compatible with the vector stream processor unit but independent of parallel operations. The major improvements of the Cyber 205 (Figure 2) over the 203 are that it is an all-LSI machine with larger memory capabilities, it has added vector instructions such as vector link and shift, and it is supported by the NOS-based operating system.

The scalar processor receives and decodes all instructions from central memory. Since the scalar processor contains the central instruction control, it directs decoded vector/string instructions to the vector or string processor for execution. It also provides orderly buffering and execution of the load and store instructions. The instruction stack in the scalar processor accommodates eight virtually addressed words (eight 64-bit words), which consist of 64 instructions (64-bit), 128 instructions (32-bit), or a combination of both. The instruction issue pipe is then capable of issuing at a rate of one instruction every 20 nanoseconds. With independent vector and scalar instruction controls operating on a single instruction stream, the

Table 3.
CPU computation rates.

	BSP	CYBER 205	CRAY-1
32-bit Operands			
Addition	-	200×10^6/s	80×10^6/s
Multiplication	-	200×10^6/s	80×10^6/s
Division	-	25×10^6/s	25×10^6/s
		(Square root also)	(Reciprocal approx)
48-bit Operands			
Addition	50×10^6/s	-	-
Multiplication	50×10^6/s	-	-
Division	14×10^6/s	-	-
64-bit Operands			
Addition	-	100×10^6/s	80×10^6/s
Mulitiplication	-	100×10^6/s	80×10^6/s
Division	-	12.5×10^6/s	25×10^6/s
		(Square root also)	(Reciprocal approx)
96-bit Operands			
Addition	12.5×10^6/s	-	-
Multiplication	10.0×10^6/s	-	-
Division	6.7×10^6/s	-	-
	(Reciprocal approx)		

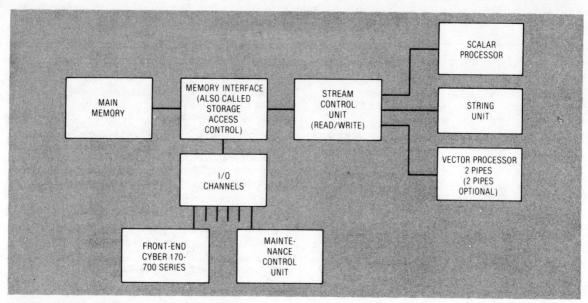

Figure 2. Control Data Corporation's Cyber 205.

Table 4.
Overall operating system characteristics.

	BSP	CYBER 205	CRAY-1
Resident (i.e., Kernel) Main Memory required	30K Words (48-bits)	64K Words (64-bits) 8K Words Inner Kernel with Disk Overlays	48K Words (64-bits)
Reentrant System Routines/Compilers (i.e., single copy shared by all users)	BSP executes only one job at a time (7800 Programs reentrant)	Yes/Yes	Yes/No
Job Switchover Response Time (Instruction-to-Instruction)	Executes to Completion	3 μs (exchange jump)	5.125 μs
User Interface Support	Work Flow Language (Integrates front-end with BSP operations)	JCL, special monitor instructions	JCL, Monitor, Macro, and Library
Maintenance	Complete control of maintenance diagnostics from a remote terminal	Maintenance control unit is dedicated I/O station which provides monitoring, error logging, recovery of hardware faults, diagnostics, and dead start.	The maintenance control unit is a 16-bit minicomputer internal to Cray-1 to provide system initialization, recovery operations and performance data logging.
Special Comments	All system functions are executed in front-end B7800	Majority of operating system virtually addressable (i.e. automatically moved in and out of 64K Words)	Cray-1 has its own operating system (48K Words) exclusive of 1MW main memory. It is a table-driven, multiprogramming system with several priority scheduling algorithms options.

Notes to Table 4:

BSP. Many operating system functions are executed in the front-end B7800 for the BSP. The BSP is unique in how and when file movement occurs between the B7800 and the BSP. Files are pre-loaded and post-dumped from the file memory in parallel with the job currently running on the BSP. All I/O for the job executing on the BSP is from file memory and overlapped with computation executing in the parallel processor.

Cyber 205. The job switchover time calculation is based on the all-LSI machine as 3 microseconds; it was 6.2 microseconds on the Cyber 203.

Cray-1. The priority scheduling algorithms can be optimized for CPU bound, I/O bound, or a combination of expected loading conditions.

The Test Station is a separate minicomputer from the maintenance control unit.

The COS operating system is always one partner in any exchange sequence for job switchover. All interrupts are done in hardware and the new instruction issue occurs only after proper terminations are made.

Table 5.
Fortran IV characteristics/features.

	BSP	CYBER 205	CRAY-1
Standard Compatibility	ANSI 66	ANSI 66 (77 Development)	ANSI 66 (77 imminent)
Levels of Optimization	2 (Global, code level) plus another level of H/W optimization	3 (options in scalar such as instruction scheduling, algebraic, register optimization)	2 (Scheduler, On-Off)
Extension functions (or options) to utilize vector capabilities	Array Extensions (where, pack, unpack, if, then else), and vectorizer analyses data dependencies and generates parallel code executable constructs	Vector arithmetic, vector compare, order; min-max index; dot product; gather, scatter; control store bit map. Option-automatic vectorization.	AUTOMATIC, Compiler override, Directives available. Compiler executes in CRAY-1 itself and it has automatic vectorization with programmer override in both directions.
Diagnostic Levels	3	Many	3 (Subsystem, Board, and Chip)
Debug/Test Statements	Debug, Dump, Monitor, Statistics, Trace, XREF	Dump, Snap, Trace Debug, Breakpoint	Debug, Dump, XREF Symbol Table, Flowtrace
Special I/O Statements	Encode-Decode, BUF-IN, BUF-OUT	Encode-Decode BUF-IN, BUF-OUT, Advise, Time-step	Encode-Decode, BUF-IN, BUF-OUT

Table 6.
Central memory organization.

	BSP	CYBER 205	CRAY-1
Memory Word Length	48 bits (+8 bits SECDED)	64 bits (+7 bits SECDED/32-bit Half Word)	64 bits (+8 bits SECDED)
Memory Access Increment (i.e. effective data path width)	4 Words (Control Processor), 16 Words (Parallel Processor)	512 bits (i.e., Sword = 8 Words)	64 bits
Address Field	24 bits	48 bits	24 bits
Standard Working Hardware (Capacity) Configuration	262K Words (CP) + 1M Words (PP) + 8M Words File Memory	1M Words	1M Words
Incremental Hardware Additions	1M Words, 4M Words in File Memory	1/2 M, 1M, 2M Words	1/4, 1/2, 1M Words
Maximum Hardware Capacity	16M Words (Parallel)	4M Words	4M Words
Maximum Virtual Capacity	16×10^6 Words (2^{24} Words)	4×10^{12} Words (2^{42} Words)	16×10^6 Words (2^{22} Words)

Table 7.
Central memory characteristics.

	BSP	CYBER 205	CRAY-1
Memory Cycle Time	160 ns (16 words @ 10 ns)	80 ns	50 ns
Memory Word Length	48 bits (+8 SECDED bits)	64 bits (each 32 bits has 7 SECDED bits)	64 bits (+8 SECDED bits)
N-way Interleave	16 banks	32 Banks	16 Banks
Maximum Bandwidth (Words/sec)	100×10^6 (48-bit Words)	400×10^6 (64-bit Words) with 4 MW capacity	320×10^6 (64-bit Words) (80×10^6 per Bank $\times$ 4 Banks)
Maximum Bandwidth	4.8×10^9	25.6×10^9	20.48×10^9 (4×80 MW/s $\times 64$ bit Words)

Note to Table 7:

Cyber 205. The memory is bipolar, 80-nanosecond cycle time with 4-word interleave resulting in 20-nanosecond effective cycle times. It has the provision for more memory banks.

scalar processor can execute scalar instructions in parallel with most vector instructions if there are no memory references generated by the scalar instruction. Three exceptions are load and store, vector start-up which uses registers, and certain vector instructions which result in scalar sums. The scalar processor contains five independent floating-point functional units. These are pipelined units capable of accepting new operands every 20 nanoseconds.

The vector processor contains two floating-point pipeline arithmetic units. The stream unit manages the data streams between central memory and the vector pipelines. A pipelined arithmetic unit (i.e., pipe) provides a vector addition, subtraction, multiplication, division, or square root with capability for two 32-bit or one 64-bit result. The Cyber 205 system has two pipelines where the clocking is 20 nanoseconds per 64-bit result without chaining or linking, and CDC has developed an option providing two additional pipes for a total of four. The string unit processes the control vectors during streaming operations. It provides the capability for BCD and binary arithmetic, address arithmetic, and boolean operations.

Main memory capacity is available with up to 4M words. It is a bipolar memory running at 80 nanoseconds with 4-word interleave for an effective cycle time of 20 nanoseconds per word. Memory on the Cyber 205 is accessed by the superword (eight 64-bit words) for vector operations and by the halfword or full word for scalar operations. The central memory is a virtual memory system. It has advanced memory management features such as key and lock for memory protection and separation,

hardware mapping from virtual to physical address, user program/data sharing capability, small page sizes (1K, 2K, 8K words) as well as a large page size (65K words), and an ordered page table to minimize operating system overhead. The page table is an ordered list of the associative words necessary to define the pages in absolute memory. The associative unit in the scalar processor contains the page table virtual-addressing mechanism. The associative unit is capable of comparing the associative register contents with the space table entries in one minor cycle, at the ratio of two entries every 20 nanoseconds. The memory interface is divided into several units to facilitate more parallel memory operations (e.g., the LSI scalar unit can do virtual to physical address translation through the associative unit while the memory access is going through a different part of the memory interface unit).

The Cyber 205 has 16 input/output channels, each 16 bits wide. The I/O system consists of stations which are themselves 16-bit word minicomputers similar to those in the Star-100. Up to 10 disk stations can be put on the Cyber 205. Each station can accommodate eight disk drives (currently CDC 819 double-density 600M-byte). Practically speaking, a typical user would have two stations on four channels with eight disk drives, and a larger user would have three stations on six channels with 16 disk drives. Note the station architecture is integral to the architecture. The Cyber 205 has 50M-bit/second serial line interfaces and network access devices to support the use of networking Cyber 205s with CDC's loosely-coupled network architecture.

Table 8.
Physical hardware/electronics.

	BSP	CYBER 205	CRAY-1
Size (W × D × H, in ft.)	20 × 19 × 7.2 3 ft. clearance above required for maintenance (2M Words + 6M Words File Mem.)	18 × 27.5 × 6 (1 M Words)	8.8 (diam.) by 6.5 (high) (4M Words)
Weight (Mainframe with Memory)	7.2 tons	8 tons (1M Words)	5.25 tons (1M Words)
Cooling	Air and water	Freon, water exchanger outside	Freon/water
Plug-in Modules	N.A.*	1760	1700 (×2 DIES)
Module/Card Types	N.A.*	8	115
PC Cards (Boards)	4 Layers	15 Layers (150 chips/BD)	5 Layers
Circuitry (equiv. no. of transistors)	1M Gates + Memory	10.5M (1420 transistors/chip)	2.5M
Chip Types	N.A.*	26 (7303 chips total)	4
Logic	CML-Current Mode Logic	ECL, 6 picojoules 168 gate chips	ECL, 1 ns per gate delay
High Density Logic	MSI	LSI-20 ns	SSI

* N.A. = INFORMATION NOT AVAILABLE

Notes to Table 8:

Cyber 205. The 15-layer PC boards have one additional resistive layer where a resistor is etched directly below a path for termination to achieve the 6 picojoule speed-power product (i.e., the switching is approximately 600 picoseconds).

Cray-1. There are only four basic chip types used to build the Cray-1. These are SSI ECL chips. The only LSI is the 4K × 1 ECL RAMs. The Cray-1 generates about four times as much heat per cubic inch as the CDC 7600.

November 1980

The same operating system software developed for the Star-100 (with modifications for improvements) is run on the Cyber 205. Software support for the Cyber 205 consists primarily of the operating system, the language processors, and the maintenance aids. The major attribute of the Cyber 205 operating system is based on an efficient file concept where all executable code exists as files. The interactive user as well as batch user programs consist of a file name followed by the appropriate parameters. The operating system recognizes three file ownership categories: public, shared files, and private. It also fully supports the virtual memory hardware by properly allocating storage between main memory and mass storage so that information/files can move back and forth, and by setting page-table values so that hardware can translate virtual addresses to absolute ones. The multitasking approach inherent in this structure allows job processing on a priority basis with input/output done implicitly by the operating system, or explicitly by reads and writes so that users can control execution of certain time-dependent tasks.

The resident portion of the operating system consists of the kernel and the pager. The kernel handles time slicing of active jobs and message communication, and the pager does the memory allocation and page swapping. User jobs, privileged user tasks, and virtual system tasks communicate messages to the kernel through hardware interrupts. The pager communicates with the kernel by setting pointers in the queueing structure without using external interrupts. The kernel communicates with the front-end computer and/or peripheral station by setting pointers or station channel flags. Messages provide all communications between these elements.

The primary language processors on the Cyber 205 are extended Fortran IV and the CDC Meta assembler. Both are available for interactive or batch programming. The Fortran was originally developed to ANSI X3.9-1966 with extensions for the Cyber 205 architecture that retained basic compatibility across the CDC family of large-scale Cyber machines. The Cyber 205 Fortran compiler provides code optimization, loop collapsing into vector instructions whenever possible, effective utilization of the large Cyber 205 register file, and acccessibility to virtually all of the Cyber 205 instructions. Programmers can write in traditional Fortran, allowing the compiler to optimize and collapse loops where possible, or may use the extensions which permit direct access to the vector and string-manipulation hardware capabilities.

Cray Research's Cray-1

The Cray-1 was designed to extend the independent functional (pipelined) unit concepts of Seymour Cray's

Table 9.
Input/output configuration.

	BSP	CYBER 205	CRAY-1
Class of Front-End Processor Unit	B7800	Cyber 170 Series, IBM 303X	IBM, CDC, UNIVAC, others
Major Subsystems	Control Unit Channel Buffers	Station (control unit and buffer memory) for high-performance disk and/or tapes	I/O subsystem, Device Controller
Basic Design Approach	Independent	Independent	Integral/Independent-Option
Processor Word Length	Not applicable	16 bits	16 bits
Memory Cycle Time	Not applicable	320 ns	50 ns
Max. Transfer Rate for Std. Chan	1.5M bytes per sec	50M bits per sec	50M bits per sec
Max. Transfer Rate on Direct Access Chan./Port	Not applicable	50M bits per sec on 16 Chns. (total 800M bits per sec)	850M bits per sec
Max. Configuration of Chns./Ports	28 per processor (up to 4 processors)	16 Chans.	12 Std. bidirectional I/O Chans. + Memory Port + I/O subsystem with 16 Std. bidirectional I/O Chans.

Notes to Table 9:

BSP. The speed of execution in the BSP is independent of I/O operations which are strictly in and out of the file memory staged from the front-end B7800.

Cyber 205. Most station control units use a 200 nanosecond memory, not 1.1 microsecond as was used in the Star-100. CDC is now evaluating use of the network access device for input-ouput handling.

Cray-1. The input-output processor is the Cray-designed minicomputer (previously called the "A" processor) not to be confused with the front-end computer.

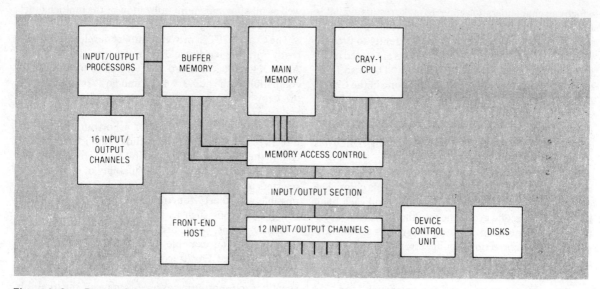

Figure 3. Cray Research Incorporated's Cray-1.

CDC 6600 and CDC 7600 architectures, and to add vector processing capability as an integral part of the machine. Figure 3 shows the block diagram of the overall Cray-1. *

* The new designation for the Cray-1 is the Cray-1S.

The Cray-1 executes 225 operation codes as either 16-bit or 32-bit instructions. Operations codes provide for fully integrated and segmented functional units for both scalar and vector processing at a 12.5-nanosecond clock rate. There are 13 distinct functional units within the CPU

Table 10.
Peripheral characterisitics.

	BSP	CYBER 205	CRAY-1
Disc/Memory Unit	Not Applicable	Model CDC 819-1/819-21	Model CDC 819-1/819-21
Capacity		300M bytes/600M bytes	300M bytes/600M bytes
ARE Access Time		50 ms	50 ms
Transfer Rate		38.7M bits/s	38.7M bits/s
No. of Units		Up to 8 Drives/Contr	Up to 8 Drives/Contr
		Up to 10 Controllers	Up to 32 Controllers
Front-end Computer	Burroughs 7800	CYBER 170-750	IBM 3033
Disc/Drum Memory Unit	Model 9494-44/9373-21	Models 885/844-41	Models 3350
Capacity	402M bytes/5.9M bytes	692M Chars/237M Chars	572M bytes
Ave. Access Time	34 ms/5 ms	25 ms/30 ms	25 ms
Transfer Rate (/sec)	1.2M bytes/1.2M bytes	1.2M Chars/1.1M Chars	1.2M bytes
No. of Units	Up to 200/Up to 40	Up to 8 Drives/Controller	Up to 8 Drives/Controller
Magnetic Tape Unit	Model 9495-24	Model 679-7	Model 3420 Mod 8
Density (BPI)	1600/6250	1600/6250	1600/6250
Speed (IPS)	Up to 200	Up to 200	Up to 200
Transfer Rate	1.25 to 200	1.5M bytes/s	1.25M bytes/s
Record Method	PE/GCR	PE/GCR	PE/GCR
Line Printer	Model 9246-20	Model 580-200	Model 3800/3211
Speed (LPM)	Up to 2000	2000	20,000/2,000
Chars/line	132	136	136/132
		(48 Chars Nominal)	
		at 2000 LPM)	
Card Reader	Model 9112	Model 405	Model 3505
Speed (CPM)	1400	1200	1200
Columns		80	80
Card Punch Unit	Model 9213	Model 415	Model 3525P3
Speed (CPM)	300	250	300

Note to Table 10:

BSP. The disk and drum storage units for the BSP have SECDED error detection and correction capability as a standard feature. In addition to having this complement of peripherals, the host B7800 system can support up to eight data communication processors which in turn can accommodate up to several hundred data communication terminals.

which can chain operation codes to make results available for another functional unit at the next clock period. All the functional units can operate concurrently to provide parallelism where the intermediate results are stored in the large number of internal CPU registers. This also facilitates compiling operations which are done in the Cray-1 itself. Floating point instructions provide for addition, subtraction, multiplication, and reciprocal approximation for division. Internal character representation is in ASCII with each 64-bit word accommodating eight bytes or characters.

Main memory has a capacity of up to 4M 64-bit words and consists of 4K ECL Fairchild or Motorola chips. The main memory is configured in 16 banks, and each bank has a 50 nanosecond cycle time resulting in a 320M word-per-second bandwidth. Main memory uses a SECDED —single-error-correction double-error-detection—technique with eight check bits per memory word.

The Cray-1 can be used as a stand-alone machine, but augmentation with a front-end computer such as an IBM 370, CDC Cyber, or Univac 1100 are definitely recommended. Connection requires a channel adapter (provided by Cray) between the front-end computer channel and the Cray-1 main memory.* The front-end computer distance limitation is 300 feet using parallel wire cables at a maximum rate of 64M bits per second. The other method for getting into and out of the Cray-1 is the input/output subsystem. The I/O subsystem consists of two, three, or four I/O processor stations. The I/O processor is a Cray-designed 16-bit minicomputer which has a 50-nanosecond cycle time (bipolar memory), with up to 64K 16-bit-word capacity. A large buffer memory buffers between the I/O subsystem and the Cray-1 main memory port. Each port has a maximum bandwidth of 850M bits per second. The device control unit uses one of the 12 bidirectional standard channels (each capable of 50M bits per second) for CDC 819 disk memory. A typical large Cray-1 system can accommodate up to 32 double-density (600M-byte capacity) high-performance 819 on-line disks (using eight controllers).

Software products provided with the Cray-1 are the Cray operating system, an ANSI Fortran compiler called the CFT, and a full line of utility and diagnostic routines. Other Cray supplied and supported software includes a macro assembler, a relocatable overlay loader, file manager, source program maintenance facility, text editor, and program debug aids.

The operating system environment consists of the front-end computer, the front-end channel adapter commands, data format conversions, and the COS. The front-end operating system controls batch job entries and read/write operations to magnetic tapes, supports unit record equipment, and controls the spooling of jobs to/from the Cray-1. COS is a batch operating system capable of supporting up to 63 jobs in a multiprogramming environment and a table-driven operating system that automatically supports roll-in and roll-out. It provides data set management of files for the creation and maintenance of temporary and permanent data sets as well as making maximum utilization of the multichannel access to disk storage.

The Cray-1 CFT, a proven compiler developed concurrently with the hardware design, is compatible with the ANSI X3.9-1966 standard and very close to being fully compatible with the X3.9-1978 standard. It compiles on the Cray-1 and generates up to 150,000 lines of object code per minute to match the hardware capabilities. CFT analyzes the innermost loops of a Fortran program to direct vectorizable sequences without additions or special calls in the language. It then generates code to take advantage of the segmentation and availability of intermediate registers to exploit the very-high-speed vector operations possible with the 13-functional-unit architecture. Other compiler options such as assembly code listings, cross reference maps, and programming debug aids are available. As an example of a debug aid, CFT has a capability called Flowtrace which enables the programmer to obtain a complete analysis of the execution time spent in each subroutine as a percentage of the total job execution time.

The Cray-1 assembler—called CAL—provides the programmer with symbolic instructions for all hardware functions. The user can augment CAL with pseudo-operations used to define macro instructions for a particular application. Cray provides a complete set of scalar and vector versions of all standard Fortran library routines. Also supplied are the Basic Linear Algebra Subroutines, a comprehensive set of mathematical routines (FFTs, matrix and linear algebra, etc.) tailored for high performance on the Cray-1.

Conclusion

Improvements in the second generation of vector supercomputers include such hardware features as extensive use of LSI memory chip technology, improved memory management to enhance throughput performance, better designs to link and chain execution strings within the CPU, and much higher effective-speed I/O operations integrated into the architecture. Improved software items are a result of both better-working hardware and better compilers. Optimal use of hardware performance and assurance of the efficient generation of code by the compiler vectorizer and optimizer have been evaluated via benchmarks and results analysis. These results allowed significant improvements in software tools, and a more solid system.

The Burroughs BSP, with its 16 arithmetic processors, has major architectural differences from the more conventional Cyber 205 and Cray-1, which are relatively similar with their combined vector and scalar CPU organizations. However, the Cyber 205 and Cray-1 differ, especially in the operation of their internal arithmetic units and in the I/O linkage/operation to the front-end computer. Another major difference is the all-LSI chip technology of the Cyber 205 as opposed to the Cray-1, which uses SSI parts except for the LSI 4K ECL RAM chips in memory. As noted in our April 1974 article on vector supercomputers, advanced high-performance implementations can be achieved with old or new chip

---

* The physical connection between the front-end computer and the Cray-1 is completely specified in Reference 7, pp. 3.6-1 ff.

COMPUTER

technologies. This emphasizes the importance of an architecture that minimizes bottlenecks, makes the most of a balanced design approach, and provides maximum overall throughput performance capabilities.

The key to evaluating these machines is a comparision of the strengths and limitations of their architectures. Tables 1-10 compare the functional characteristics of the three machines and provide a measure of the sizing and timing throughput capabilities inherent in each machine. The application of a particular set of requirements to these comparisons provides a good starting point for analysis of the models' peformance and their suitability to user needs. ∎

5. *The Cray-1 Computer System,* Cray Research, Inc., Pub. No. 2240008B, 1976, 12 pp.

6. *The Cray-1 Computer, Hardware Reference Manual,* Cray Research, Inc., Pub. No. 224004, May 1979.

7. *The Cray-1S Series of Computers,* Cray Research, Inc., Pub. No. 2240008C, 1979, 24 pp.

8. *Cray-OS Version 1 System Programmer's Manual,* Cray, Research, Inc. Pub., No. 2240012, Sept. 1979, Vol. 1, 2, and 3.

9. *Cray-1 Fortran (CFT) Reference Manual,* Cray Research, Inc., Pub. No. 2240009, Dec. 1979.

10. *Cray-1 Library Reference Manual,* Cray Research, Inc., Pub. No. 2240014, Dec. 1979.

References

Burroughs

1. Carl Jensen, "Taking Another Approach to Supercomputing," *Datamation,* Vol. 24, No. 2, Feb. 1978, pp. 159-172.

2. *BSP—Burroughs Scientific Processor,* Burroughs Corp., Pub. No. 4001564, June 1977, 28 pp.

3. *BSP-Overview, Perspective, Architecture,* Burroughs Corp., Pub. No. 61391A, Feb. 1978, 31 pp.

4. *BSP-File Memory,* Burroughs Corp., Pub. No. 61391B, Feb. 1978, 13 pp.

5. *BSP-Fault-Tolerant Features,* Burroughs Corp., Pub. No. 61391C, Feb. 1978, 18 pp.

6. *BSP-Control Program,* Burroughs Corp., Pub. No. 61391D, Feb. 1978, 23 pp.

7. *BSP-Implementation of Fortran,* Burroughs Corp., Pub. No. 61391E, Feb. 1978, 19 pp.

8. *BSP-Parallelism-the Design Strategy for the BSP,* Burroughs Corp., Pub. No. 61411, Dec. 1978, 15 pp.

9. *BSP-Floating Point Arithmetic,* Burroughs Corp., Pub. No. 61416, Dec. 1978, 27 pp.

10. *B7000/B6000 Work Flow Language Reference Manual,* Burroughs Corp., Pub. No. 5001555, June 1978.

Control Data Corporation

1. M.J. Kascic, *Vector Processing on the Cyber 200,* Control Data Corp., 1979, 38 pp.

2. *CDC Cyber 200/Model 203 Technical Description,* Control Data Corp., no date, 43 pp.

3. *CDC Cyber 200 Operating System 1.4 Reference Manual,* Control Data Corp., Pub. No. 60457000, Vol. 1 of 2, 1979.

4. *CDC Cyber 200 Fortran Language 1.4 Reference Manual,* Control Data Corp., Pub. No. 60456040, 1979.

Cray Research

1. Lee Higbie, "Applications of Vector Processing," *Computer Design,* Vol. 17, No. 4, Apr. 1978, pp. 139-145.

2. Paul M. Johnson, "An Introduction to Vector Processing," *Computer Design,* Vol. 17, No. 2, Feb. 1978, pp. 89-97.

3. Wesley P. Peterson, *Cray-1 Basic Linear Algebra Subprograms for CFT Usage,* Cray Research, Inc., Pub. No. 2240208, 1979.

4. Richard M. Russell, "The Cray-1 Computer System," *Comm. ACM,* Vol. 21, No. 1, Jan. 1978, pp. 63-72.

E.W. Kozdrowicki has been a member of the technical staff at The Aerospace Corporation for three years, specializing in computer architecture. He spent four years at the Bell Telephone Company's Engineering Research Center in Princeton, working on automated analog circuit testing. Prior to that, he did research on automated chess (COKO, the Cooper-Koz chess program) at the University of California at Davis, where he taught electrical engineering and computer science. He received his PhD in 1967 from the University of Washington.

D.J. Theis is the director of the Computer Architecture Department of The Aerospace Corporation. His responsibilities include definition of real-time computer requirements, analysis of computer system configurations with the appropriate timing and sizing of hardware and software, and evaluation of computer state-of-the-art technologies. Theis was formerly a senior consultant with Hobbs Associates; and from 1962-1967 was a senior engineer for North American Space and Information Division in the Computer and Simulation Center on the Apollo Program. He had responsibilities in developing the real-time simulators for the Apollo rendezvous and reentry missions. He holds a BS in engineering from UCLA and an MSEE from the University of Southern California, and is a registered electrical engineer in the state of California. An author of several articles on memory technology, minicomputers, and microprocessors, Theis has been a member of the Computer Society since 1959.

Part II: Vector Supercomputers

Chapter 2: Pipelined Supercomputers
Chapter 3: Array Processors
Chapter 4: Language and Software Supports

PART II
VECTOR SUPERCOMPUTERS

Vector processing computers have appeared in either pipelined machines or array processors. These vector supercomputers are described in the following three chapters. Chapter 2 is devoted to pipelined supercomputers. Systems to be covered include the Cyber 205, Cray X-MP, Facom VP-200, and NEC SX-2. Chapter 3 presents two recently designed array processors, the BSP and MPP, and several papers on interconnection networks and parallel memory systems for array/vector processing. The articles presented in Chapter 4 discuss language extensions and vectorizing compilers needed for either pipelined or array supercomputers.

Applied science and high technology require the performance of large-scale, predictive simulations on supercomputers. Many of these simulations are described in partial differential equations. These are, in turn, described as large simultaneous linear equations and eigenvalue problems, which are processed as vector operations.

The efficiency of a vector processing supercomputer is primarily determined by its capability to handle vectors, arrays, and matrices. Continuous-field problems, such as those in fluid dynamics, meteorology, and geophysics, are solved on a supercomputer by the use of a finite difference method. A finite set of discrete grid points, in 2-dimensional to 4-dimensional space (i.e. the spatial dimensions plus the fourth dimension of time), is often used to approximate a continuous field.

The accuracy of the simulation depends on the grid size or the resolution of the field. At each grid point, there may be several state variables to be processed. The number of floating-point operations to be performed per grid point varies from a magnitude expressed in tens to one expressed in hundreds.

Over a huge mesh or grid of elements, differential equations are applied to produce element-stiffness matrices. These multidimensional matrices may vary with time. All the time-dependent matrices represent a system of simultaneous equations. This large-scale system of equations is then solved for the unknown variables by the supercomputer.

The solution of a large-scale scientific problem involves three interactive disciplines: **theories, experiments, and computations.** Theoretical scientists develop mathematical models that computer engineers solve numerically; the numerical results may then suggest new theories. Experimental scientists provide data for computational scientists, who applying the principles of their discipline can model processes that are difficult to approach experimentally.

The use of supercomputers to solve these problems has the advantages of being cheaper, faster, and more accurate, subject only to the constraints of computational speed and memory capacity.

Superproblems need supercomputer for their solution. Most vector supercomputers are pipelined. According to ways data arrays are retrieved in a vector processor, we classify pipelined supercomputers into two classes: one is the **memory-to-memory** architecture, in which source operands and intermediate and final results are retrieved directly between the pipelines and the main memory. The information of base address, offset, increment, and vector length must be specified in order to transfer streams of data between the main memory and the pipelines. Vector instructions in TI-ASC, CDC Star-100, and Cyber 205 have a memory-to-memory format.

The other machine architecture has a **register-to-register** operation, in which operands and results are loaded from the main memory to a large number of vector or scalar registers before they can be used by the pipelines. Vector instructions in the Cray 1, Cray

Table 1.　Specification of several pipelined supercomputers.

Features	Cray-1 (Cray Research)	VP-200 (Fugitsu)	SX-2 (NEC)	Cyber-205 (Control Data)
Architecture and instruction set	Register-to-register, 128 instructions	Register-to-register, 277 instructions	Register-to-register, 155 instructions	Memory-to-memory, 256 instructions
Vector registers	4 Kbytes	64 Kbytes	80 Kbytes	Unused
Main Memory	32 Mbytes	256 Mbytes	256 Mbytes	32 Mbytes
Functional Units in Vector/Scalar Processors	12 unifunction pipes for vector, scalar, FLP, and FXP operations	6 vector pipes for arithmetic, logic, masking, and access. Mask unit and scalar unit.	4 sets of vector pipes (16 parallel units). Mask unit and scalar unit.	Up-to-4 vector processors with 6 pipes in each separate string unit and scalar unit
Basic pipeline clock period	12.5 nsec	7.5 nsec	8 nsec	20 nsec
Maximum speed (theoretical peak)	160 Mflops	500 Mflops	1300 Mflops	200-800 Mflops
Software and Language	Cray Fortran (CFT) with vectorization and pipeline chaining	Fortran 77/VP with automatic vectorization and tuning	Fortran 77/SX with automatic vectorization and high-level pipeline chaining	Cyber 200 Fortran with automatic vectorization
Front-end host machine	IBM/MVS, CDC/NOS, Univac/EXEC	facom 200 Series with MSP/MVS	NEC ACOS series or standalone operations	Cyber 170 series, IBM 303X

X-MP, Hitachi S-810, NEC SX-2, China's Galaxy, and Fujitsu VP-200 all have a register-to-register structure.

Table 1 summarizes the key architectural features of four representative vector supercomputers. All these four systems are used as back-end machines attached to a host computer, which handles the input/output (I/O) and system management functions. The hardware and software capabilities of these machines are quite comparable.

Details of the Fujitsu VP-200 can be found in the article by Miura and Uchida (1983) in Section 2.3. Both the Cray 1 and Cyber 205 are well described by Kozdrowicki and Theis (1980) in Section 1.2. Lincoln's article in Section 2.1 is devoted to Cyber 205. Bucher's article in Section 2.4 assesses the speed performance of Cray 1. The article by Hwang, Su, and Ni (1981) compares various vector supercomputer architectures and characterizes vectorization techniques.

It is instructive to make a few comparisons between these vector supercomputers. All have separate scalar processors that can run in parallel with the vector processors. This concurrent vector/scalar processing capability is very important for general-purpose applications.

Register-to-register architectures demand the use of large register files. The memory-to-memory architecture as used in the Cyber 205 demands a higher memory bandwidth. Vectorizing compilers are developed in these Fortran-based machines.

The Cyber 205 has a separate string unit for handling masked vector operations on four identical vector processors. This is especially useful for sparse matrix computations. The four identical vector pipelines in the Cyber 205 are used on a round-robin basis for handling long vectors.

The Cray 1 has short vector start-up delays whereas the Cyber 205 has longer ones. This implies that the Cyber 205 is more efficient for processing long vectors than it is for handling short ones.

The three Japanese machines are all similar to the Cray 1 in regard to architecture, although each system has some claimed improvements of its own. Fortran 77 has been used in these vector machines. The major improvements in the Japanese supercomputers over the US counterparts include the use of larger main memory (from 32 Mbytes to 256 Mbytes), more vector registers used (from 4 Kbytes to 80 Kbytes), a separate mask unit for controlling sparse matrix computations, multiple memory-access pipes between vector/scalar pipelines and the main memory, and extensive vectorization features developed in the Fortran 77 compilers.

As an example, the 1.3 Gflops supercomputer, the SX-2 system, by the NEC Corpora-

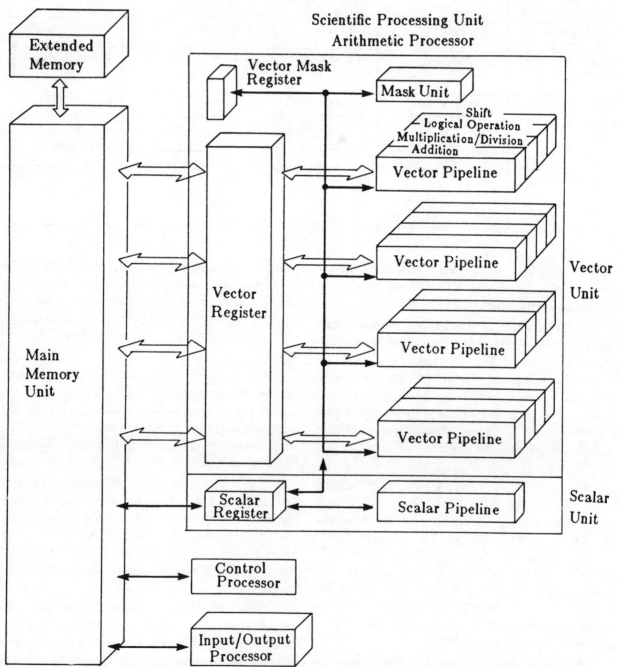

Figure 2.   The system configuration of NEC SX supercomputer with a maximum speed of 1.3 Gflops.

tion is depicted in Figure 2. The system is equipped with four sets of vector pipelines and a separate scalar pipeline. Four vector arithmetic units are in each vector pipeline set. This enables a maximum of 16 parallel vector operations to be performed, using a maximum of 80 Kbytes of vector registers. By employing high-speed metal oxide semiconductor (MOS) static random access memories (RAMs) in a 512-way interleaved memory, the SX system is capable of supplying as many as 11 Gbytes of data to these pipelines per second.

Like the Cray 1, the SX system also provides high-level, automatic chaining of a sequence of dependent vector operations. The mask unit is pipelined for sparse matrix computations and implementing conditional vector operations. High-speed scalar pipelines and scalar registers are used in the scalar processor.

The NEC machine uses large-scale integration (LSI) logic circuits with a density of 1,000 gates per chip, with a delay of only 250 psec per gate. The cache memory and vector registers are made of 1 Kbit bipolar memory LSIs with a 3.5 nsec access time. Liquid-cooled, high density, LSI packaging is used to have 36 LSI chips mounted on a ceramic substrate of only 10 cm^2. This allows 36,000 gates on a single package, very similar to the thermal conduction module (TMC) technology developed by IBM in its 3081 series.

The usefulness of a supercomputer is not entirely determined by its hardware capabilities. In fact, the efficiency relies to a large extent on the availability of supersoftware, which while easy to use, is capable of obtaining the maximum parallelism from the hardware. First, a sophisticated automatic vectorizer is needed to convert DO loops into vector code. Vectorization should be done even for complicated loops containing IF statements, intrinsic functions, and list vectors. Optimal or dynamic register allocation and code optimization by program flow-analysis are desired.

Tools are needed to support vectorization. For example, the NEC SX system offers several software tools: the ANALYZER/SX analyzes a program's dynamic and static characteristics; the VECTORIZER/SX, can, when used interactively, improve the vectorization ratio; and the OPTIMIZER performs such optimization tasks as in-line expansion of user functions and subroutines.

High-speed I/O operations are demanded in supercomputers. As extended memory unit can be used to augment the main memory. High-speed I/O channels and the support of stand-alone and loosely coupled systems are also often desired.

Besides pipelining, parallel computers structured as a mesh of processing elements for SIMD operations have been challenged to meet the demand of supercomputing. Most SIMD computers are special-purpose systems. Figure 3 shows the family tree of SIMD array processors.

The size of the machines increased from 8x8 processing elements (PEs) in the Illiac IV to 128x128 PEs in the MPP over a period of about 10 years. The distributed array processor (DAP) is developed by International Computer Limited in England. The DAP can be constructed in groups of 16 PEs in various sizes, ranging from 32x32 to 256x256. A good description of DAP can be found in the book by Hockney and Jesshope (1981). The peak speeds of the array processors are indicated in the brackets, under ideal programming and resource allocation conditions.

The Illiac IV was the first major array supercomputer developed in the late 1960s. The BSP was the commerical attempt by Burroughs Corporation in the production of scientific machines. Because of marketing reasons, the BSP was suspended before it was fully completed.

In 1979, Burroughs proposed to extend the BSP to a 512-PE array processor updating 521 memory modules. The Phoenix project was proposed as a multiple-SIMD array processor consisting of 16 Illiac IV arrays with a total of 1024 PEs (Feierbach and Stevenson 1978).

Both Burroughs and Phoenix systems are now being proposed for funding as machines that will operate at speeds measured in terms of Gflops. The article by Kuck and Stokes in Section 3.1 presents a comprehensive report on BSP. The prime memory system used in BSP

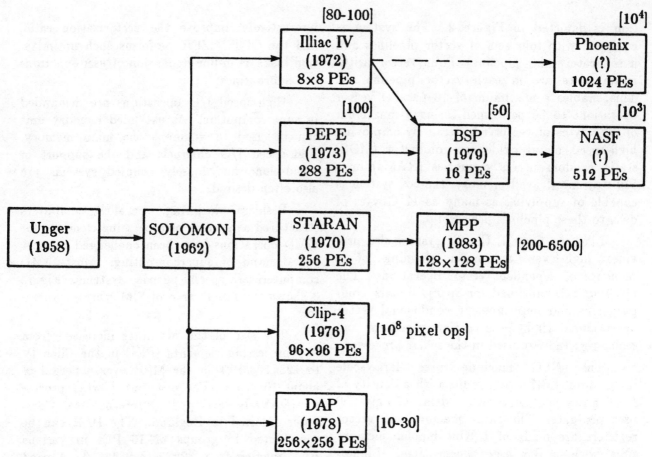

Figure 3. The family tree of SIMD array processors. (Numbers in brackets are peak performance in Mflops.)

is reported by Lawrie and Vora (1982) in Section 3.5.

Along the line for bit-plane array processing, the MPP was developed to process satellite imagery at the NASA Goddard Space Flight Center. A mesh of 128x128 = 18,384 bit-slice microprocessors is used in parallel in the MPP. The system is also an attached back-end machine.

The MPP can perform variable-length arithmetic operations. It has a microprogrammable controller, which can be used to define a quite flexible instruction set for vector, scalar, and I/O operations. Custom-designed VLSI chips are used to implement each 4x2 PE subarrays in the 128x128 mesh (Figure 4). Bipolar RAMs are used to implement the bit-slice memory planes. The projected speed of MPP ranges from 6.5 Gflops integer operations (8 bit wide) to 216 Mflops of 32-bit results. The Clip 4 is another bit-slice array processor developed in London for image processing

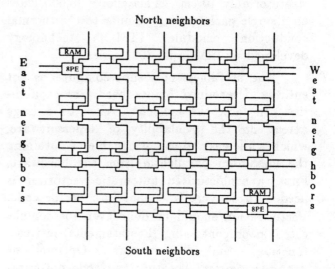

Figure 4. The interconnection of processing elements (PEs) and random access memory (RAMs) in the MPP array. (Courtesy of Goodyear Aerospace Corp., 1980.)

applications (Duff 1983). Details of MPP can be found in Batcher's article in Section 3.2.

Theoretically, the performance of an array processor should increase linearly with the increase of the number of PEs in the array. However, this linear speedup is very difficult to achieve owing to the constraints of programming language and data structure and to the lack of efficient resource management system for large-scale, reconfigurable, multi-array SIMD computers.

Further research and development are required for the maturation of array processing technology. Various interconnection structures for SIMD and MIMD computers can be found in the articles by Feng in Section 3.3 and by Wu and Feng in Section 3.4.

An intelligent compiler must be developed to detect the concurrency among scalar instructions that can be realized with pipelined or array processors. A vectorizing compiler would regenerate the parallelism that was lost in the use of sequential languages. It is desirable to use high-level programming languages with rich parallel constructs on vector processors.

Four stages have been recognized in Figure 5 for the exploitation of parallelism in advanced programming. The parameter in parentheses indicates the degree of parallelism

explorable at each stage: Parallel Algorithm (A), High-level Language (L), Efficient Object code (O), and Target Machine code (M).

The degree of parallelism refers to the number of independent operations that can be performed simultaneously. A fast algorithm should contain a high degree of parallelism (A). We also need to develop parallel languages to express parallelism (L). Unfortunately, no parallel language standards have yet been universally accepted. At present, most users still write their source code in sequential languages.

In sequential languages like Fortran, Pascal, and Algol, we still have $L = 1$. The natural parallelism in a machine is determined by the hardware. For example, the Cray 1 had $O = M = 64$ or 32. In the ideal situation with well-developed parallel-constructed user languages, we should expect $A \geq L \geq O \geq M$, as illustrated in Figure 5a.

At present, the parallelism in an algorithm is lost when it is expressed in a sequential high-level language. To promote parallel processing in machine hardware, an intelligent compiler is needed for the regeneration of parallelism lost in using serial codes. This regeneration process is called vectorization, as illustrated by Figure 5b.

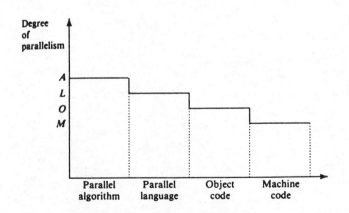

(a) The ideal case of using parallel algorithm/language.

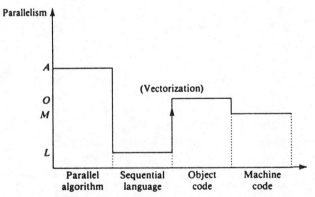

(b) The case of using vectorizing compiler and sequential language.

Figure 5. Parallelism regeneration using a vectorizing compiler with sequential high-level language.

The process of replacing a block of sequential code by a few vector instructions is called **vectorization.** The system software that regenerates this parallelism is known as a **vectorizing compiler.** We need parallel constructs in high-level languages so they can be easily translated into vector code by the vectorizer.

In Chapter 4, George Paul (1982) of IBM presents the VECTRAN and the proposed vector-array extensions to ANSI Fortran for scientific and engineering computations. The structure of an advanced retargetable vectorizer, called PARAFRASE, is presented by Kuck et al. (1984) in Section 4.2.

Arnold (1983) compared (Section 4.3) the performance of several vectorizers and presented some results on optimization of vector operations on the Cyber 205. A program, PFC, to convert FORTRAN to parallel form is introduced by Allen and Kennedy (1984) in Section 4.4. Since most existing vector machines are Fortran based, these Fortran vectorizers should be useful to many contemporary vector machine users.

Chapter 2: Pipelined Supercomputers

IEEE TRANSACTIONS ON COMPUTERS, VOL. C-31, NO. 5, MAY 1982

Technology and Design Tradeoffs in the Creation of a Modern Supercomputer

NEIL R. LINCOLN

Abstract—Supercomputers, which derive their title from the relative power they possess in any given period of computer life cycle, possess certain qualities which make their creation unique in the general milieu of computational engines. The interaction of technology, architecture, manufacturing, and user demands gives rise to compromises and design decisions which challenge the supercomputer developer. The nature of some of these challenges and their resolution, in the case of the production of the Control Data CYBER 205, is discussed in this paper in an attempt to elevate supercomputer development from the mystique of being an art to the level of a science of synergistic combination of programming, technology, structure, and packaging.

Index Terms—Architecture, parallelism, pipeline, supercomputer, technology, vector processor.

INTRODUCTION

A CLASS VI computer has been informally defined as a processor possessing scalar processing speeds in excess of twenty million floating point operations per second (20 Mflops) and vector (or parallel) execution in excess of 100 Mflops. The number of potential customers for a Class VI computer was conservatively estimated to be between 50 and 100 separate installations in 1981. At that time, two machines were in existence in that category, the CRAY-1 and the Control Data CYBER 205. Even as those estimates were announced, computer users in the aerospace and petroleum industries were claiming that performance at those levels is inadequate to meet the needs of key applications in their particular disciplines. The term "supercomputer," as applied to the most powerful computing machines in existence, thence became defined as that computer which is only one generation behind the computational needs of certain key industries. Obviously, there are many "key industries" whose demands for computational power are escalating faster than the performance capabilities of our computing systems.

The rationale for higher and higher performance in one class of computer is essentially as follows.

1) The cost/performance for a supercomputer applied to certain classes of problems is superior to that of more modest systems. This is particularly true when the applications require a great deal of on-line storage, I/O bandwidth, central memory, arithmetically intensive computations, or some combination of these.

2) The need for machines to solve three-dimensional models

of oil fields, reactors, fluid flows, and structures in production environments implies central memory systems on the order of 8 to 32 million words of storage and auxiliary storage (other than disk) ranging from 32 to 256 million words, where a word is 64 bits in length. Algorithms have now been refined and informational needs have progressed to the point where improvement of three-dimensional modeling is becoming a necessity in many disciplines, rather than a luxury or research curiosity. The scaling of memory requirements when one moves from two- to three-dimensional solutions is a dramatic example of the separation of supercomputer systems from standard or medium scale systems. A two-dimensional system having dimensions of 100 points by 100 points, with each point represented by six independent variables, requires only 60 000 words of memory to hold the initial database. When this system is extended into the third dimension, memory requirements become 6 000 000 words for just the initial database!

3) Three-dimensional computations also require a massive increase in the amount of arithmetic which must be performed to arrive at a solution. If a two-dimensional model has been yielding adequate production results after one hour of CPU time, the three-dimensional version could require 100 h to achieve comparable results. The computational capability must then be increased in a supersystem to match the memory capacities for three-dimensional models.

4) Many applications on supercomputers possess huge amounts of input and result data which, despite massive central and auxiliary storage systems, must be moved through the machine at high rates in order to exploit the computational power of the machine. Thus, a supercomputer must provide extreme I/O bandwidths and connectivity to match the attached peripherals and the demands of the central processor.

The motivation for a user to procure a supercomputer is rarely item 1) above, but rather the need to fit an increased model size or computing speed requirement. The motivation for a manufacturer to produce a supercomputer is to realize sufficient sales and profit to justify launching an expensive and risky development effort.

Once the decision has been made to commence a large-scale supercomputer project, the architecture, technology, design approach, and production methodology choices must be made. These elements of the project are interrelated in many subtle ways with the final outcome being a necessary compromise between the constraints of each discipline and the opportunities offered by advances in the state of the art of each arena. The

Manuscript received July 5, 1981; revised December 17, 1981.

The author is with the Control Data Corporation, Arden Hills, MN 55112.

Reprinted from *IEEE Transactions on Computers*, Volume C-31, Number 5, May 1982, pages 349-362. Copyright © 1982 by The Institute of Electrical and Electronics Engineers, Inc.

purpose of this paper is to discuss major decisions made in the Control Data CYBER 200 project in an attempt to illuminate the processes involved for future developers.

THE GENERAL CYBER 200 ARCHITECTURE

In 1975, when the CYBER 200 project commenced, the overall concept of this supercomputer was taken from the STAR-100 architecture which had its origin in 1964. In that year, at the urging of the Atomic Energy Commission, various manufacturers began research into new and somewhat radical machine structures leading to the Burroughs ILLIAC IV array processor and the Texas Instruments Advanced Scientific Computer (ASC) and the Control Data STAR-100 vector processors. The major features of the STAR-100 which are considered its basic architecture are as follows.

1) Massive, High-Speed Central Memory: In particular, any generation of the machine was expected to possess the maximum amount of memory permitted by extant technology and engineering judgment. For the first STAR-100, a high-density core memory with a maximum of one million words was considered the limit of that technology. The speed of this memory was focused on the overall system bandwidth established at 12.8 billion bits/s.

2) High-Speed Memory-to-Memory Vector Operations: In current supercomputer terminology, a vector is a contiguously stored string of data, unrelated to the mathematical significance of such an order. Given a Fortran declaration

DIMENSION $A(4,4)$, $B(4,4,4)$

and the normal Fortran memory allocation system, the entire array A could be considered a vector of length 16, and B could be a vector of length 64 if all the data were to be processed as a unit with all elements independent of one another. If every other plane of the B array were to be processed, one could view the data as being in four vectors, each of length 16 elements (see Fig. 1). The requirement for contiguous storage of data in memory arises from the engineering solution to achieving high bandwidth (Fig. 2) but the conceptual notion of dealing with problem solutions in vector form has value in its own right, and is being exploited by mathematicians in the development of new algorithms [1]–[7].

In the case of the STAR-100, the data in vector form are read from central memory and sent to the arithmetic units with the results returned to memory upon completion of the operation; hence the term "memory-to-memory" when applied to this architecture. This system also appeared in the TI ASC which, while quite similar in functionality to the STAR-100, could create vectors out of noncontiguously stored data at a consequent degradation in machine performance. The remaining vector machine of note, the CRAY-1, provides arithmetic functions similar to those of the STAR-100 and ASC, but its vectors are read from a set of high-speed registers, which themselves must be loaded from and unloaded to central memory at different points in the processing.

In all three instances the arithmetic units were constructed as pipelines (see Fig. 3). Since the data arriving at these units are usually contiguous, every segment in a pipeline will be performing useful work except at the very beginning and end

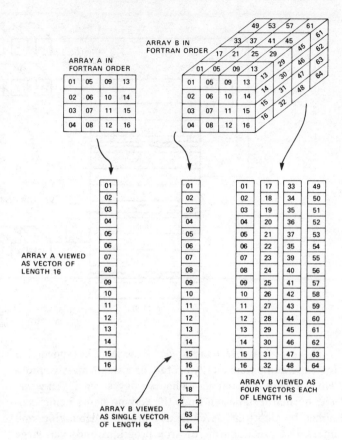

Fig. 1. Fortran arrays as vectors.

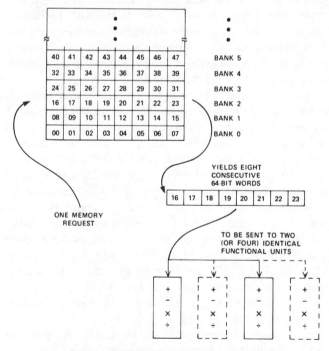

Fig. 2. CYBER 200 memory organization.

of a vector operation (as the pipeline fills and empties). From an engineering point of view this makes very efficient use of the circuitry employed, at a cost of some time to "get the operation rolling" (first result returned to memory or registers) due to the length (in number of clock cycles) of the pipeline.

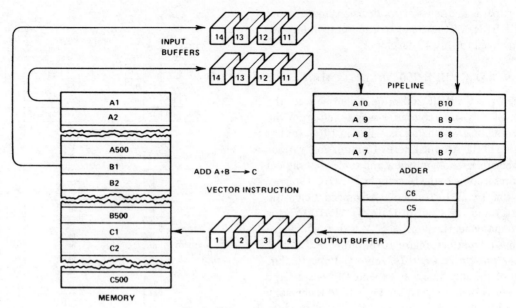

Fig. 3. Vector pipeline concept.

3) Vast Virtual Memory Space: Experience has shown that few supercomputers totally operate on a single massive problem in a dedicated manner 24 hours a day, seven days a week. The normal installation finds the waking hours being consumed by algorithm development, program debugging, and interactive execution of research programs and even large production programs. The evening and midnight hours are usually more structured, with one or more major programs monopolizing the machine's resources and with, perhaps, a modest amount of interactive debugging being pursued in a background mode. These different forms of operation present problems to operating system designers, operations personnel, and even applications programmers.

In a fixed-memory allocation system the user must be aware of the resources being consumed by a particular program at all times. For example, a programmer, preparing a set of run parameters for a job to be run at night, may need to verify several passes of that process before committing the entire ensemble to the hands of the midnight crew. If this job truly consumes the total resource at midnight with that set of parameters, then it will demand that same resource during the prime time daylight hours even though the effort is primarily debugging. In a fixed memory scheme this means that all other users are denied access while the major job is being tested, or at the very least, while jobs are swapped to and from the CPU with consequent loss of turnaround efficiency.

A virtual memory system has a place in a supercomputer as a tool to do the following.

a) Assist in Memory Management: The operating system can commit and decommit arbitrary blocks of real memory without having to ensure the physical contiguity of a user's workspace. This reduces overhead for actions such as accumulation of unused space, which could be quite costly in large memory systems (on the order of eight million words).

b) Provide Identically Appearing Execution of All Jobs (Ignoring the Turnaround Time, Of Course) Regardless of What Resources are Required or Available: This means that a program's DIMENSION statements and input parameters can

remain unchanged whether or not a four hour run is being contemplated or a simple debugging run of a particular phase is intended.

c) Eliminate Working Space Constraints from Algorithm Development: Mathematicians/programmers can begin developing an algorithm as if they had available an infinite workspace in which to put data and temporary results. Once the algorithm is developed, the introduction of "ADVICE" from the programmer on how to handle paging of the information can be introduced into the code to optimize the performance of the system, and to eliminate the oft-feared thrashing that can occur in virtual memory machines moving data to and from real central memory.

The STAR-100 was given a monolithic virtual space of 32 trillion bytes, which could be considered essentially infinite for most applications. This scheme of virtual storage was a "workspace" scheme rather than a "segmented memory" scheme. The latter was employed on the IBM series computers wherein the virtual memory was used to link and structure data files. Fig. 4 illustrates the STAR-100 virtual memory scheme.

4) Concurrent Input–Output and Arithmetic Processing: If a supercomputer must stop its high performance processing while input–output (I/O) operations are being performed, then for many applications, the effective speed of the machine can be reduced to less than a quarter of its theoretical capacity. This fact is particularly evident in areas such as seismic processing where few calculations are performed for every data element, but in which the amount of data flowing through the machine is enormous. The STAR-100 was architected to ensure that the peak pipeline rates could be sustained regardless of the amount of I/O activity. This activity could reach peaks of 600 Mbits/s total for 12 channels.

5) Employment of "Iverson" or APL Operations as an Adjunct to the Standard Arithmetic Operations of ADD, SUBTRACT, MULTIPLY, DIVIDE, and SQUARE ROOT: It becomes quite clear that the ability to effectively vectorize a problem and make optimal use of a vector structure, such as

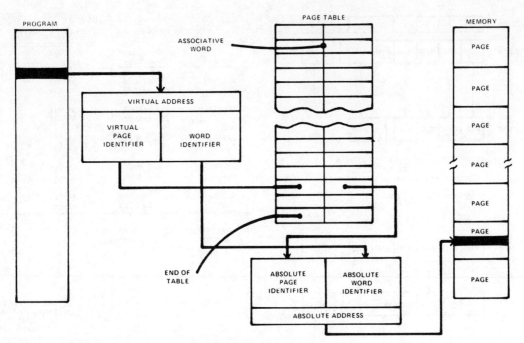

Fig. 4.   STAR-100 virtual memory scheme.

the STAR-100, is dependent on the availability of means for data "mapping" or restructuring to produce vectors from otherwise nonvector constructs. Iverson, in *A Programming Language* [8], provided a conceptual basis and notational scheme for these mapping functions. The functions of COM-PRESS, MASK, MERGE, SCATTER, and GATHER were derived from this book and incorporated into the STAR-100; in addition, many of the reduction operations SUM, PRODUCT, and INNER PRODUCT were implemented in STAR hardware.

A most significant contribution of the APL concept was the notion that strings of binary bits (called bit vectors) could be used to carry information about vectors and applied to those vectors to perform some key functions (see Fig. 5). Since the bit strings became key to the vector restructuring concept, a means had to be provided to manipulate bit vectors as well as numeric vectors; thus was added the "string" functional unit to the hardware ensemble, and the name String Array (or STAR) processor was born.

It is interesting to note that all other vector and array processors of the past few years (including the Burroughs Scientific Processor) adopted forms of the Iverson functions.

SPECIFIC ARCHITECTURE OF THE CYBER 200/205

Architects learn from the construction experience of each of their creations. The same is true of supercomputer engineers for whom experience during the construction and usage of a current generation computer acts as guidance for the next generation. The lessons learned from the STAR-100 were not, in the main, architectural in nature but were of an engineering character. For example, the emphasis placed on the performance of the various vector instructions for the STAR-100 was quite literally based on instinctive estimates of the value of such functions. The processing rates for various instructions are given in Table I. Note that the throughput rates for the Iverson functions, including the SCATTER/GATHER operation, are

from 6 to 50 times slower than the arithmetic functions of ADD, SUBTRACT, and MULTIPLY. These ratios were the accidental consequences of decisions related to economics and schedules during the design of the STAR-100, and were not inherent in the architecture of the machine itself. As production programs were fully developed for the STAR-100, it became obvious that the nonarithmetic functions had to proceed at arithmetic speeds to prevent them from becoming a bottleneck to machine performance. The CYBER 205 column of Table I illustrates the design decisions made for this new machine as a result of the STAR experience.

The design of a new supercomputer is influenced by the experiential base provided by its predecessor. This base is first translated into a set of "design objectives" which serve as goals for the designer. In a sense, these represent architectural decisions because they guide the overall direction of the CPU engineering; however, they do not affect the structure of the machine in ways that are visible to the user and which must be dealt with by the operating system and compilers. Three major changes were made in the architecture of the STAR-100 to yield the CYBER 205.

1) In the STAR-100, the operation of the scalar unit was coupled with the vector unit such that only one type of operation could be performed at a time. This feature became built into the architecture in that the register file, which could house 256 64-bit operands for processing by the scalar unit, was also made a part of the virtual memory over which vector operations could function (see Fig. 6). This meant that the register file could behave as the source and destination for vector arithmetic operations, and at other times could provide operands for scalar arithmetic and vector setup. The difficulties inherent in checking for potential conflicts between scalar usage and vector usage of the register file made it necessary to interlock these two units, allowing only one function at a time.

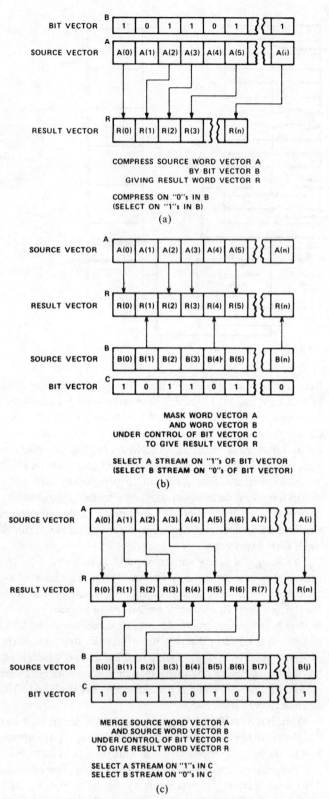

Fig. 5. Bit vectors for Iverson functions. (a) Example of COMPRESS. (b) Example of MASK. (c) Example of MERGE.

TABLE I
VECTOR PROCESSING RATES (KEY INSTRUCTIONS)

Operation	STAR-100 Peak Rate	Operand Size	CYBER 200 Peak Rate
ADD/SUB	50 MFLOPS 100 MFLOPS	64-bit 32-bit	200 MFLOPS 400 MFLOPS
MULTIPLY	25 MFLOPS 100 MFLOPS	64-bit 32-bit	200 MFLOPS 400 MFLOPS
DIVIDE/ SQUARE ROOT	12.5 MFLOPS 25 MFLOPS	64-bit 32-bit	64 MFLOPS 122.4 MFLOPS
COMPRESS/ MERGE	4.2 MOPS 4.2 MOPS	64-bit 32-bit	200 MOPS 400 MOPS
GATHER/ SCATTER	.78 MOPS .78 MOPS	64-bit 32-bit	33 MOPS 33 MOPS

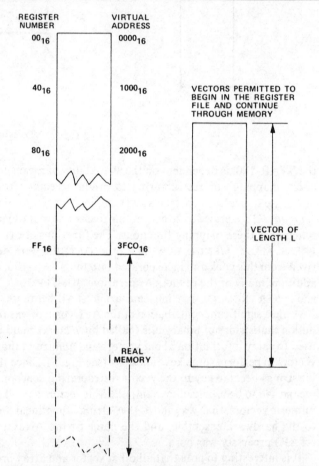

Fig. 6. STAR register file as virtual memory.

The ability to run both vector and scalar units in parallel became highly desirable as a vast array of user programs were being run through the STAR machine during its development. The result was a decision, made very late in the STAR-100 design effort, to eliminate the register file from the virtual memory space so that future models could, in fact, provide parallelism of the various functional units. Although this decision came too late for the STAR-100 to utilize the inherent parallelism, it was made with the intention that a later but compatible machine could benefit. The impact of this decision was rather momentous. First, many memory-to-memory string operations were originally used to provide register logical operations such as AND, OR, EXCLUSIVE-OR, and SHIFT. Once the register file was removed from virtual memory, a complete set of register-to-register logical and shift operations had to be added to the command repertoire. Second, the compiler and operating system had to undergo substantial modifications to incorporate the newly added instructions and to eliminate a number of philosophical constructs related to the placement of the registers in virtual memory.

With the roadblock of the register file allocation eliminated, the designers of the CYBER 205 could concentrate on the functional parallelism of the scalar and vector units. The technology of the STAR-100, which could be termed small scale integration (SSI), made it necessary to share a good deal of logic between the vector and scalar functional elements. The arithmetic portions of the machine were completely shared in this manner. Parallel operation of these units became an engineering possibility with the advent of high-speed large scale integration (LSI). Thus, the architecture of the CYBER 205 became inextricably linked with the technology to be used for its implementation. The increased density and reduced parts count provided by this LSI made possible a substantial enlargement of functional components, among which were dual arithmetic systems, one scalar and one vector.

2) The virtual memory system provided two units of physical memory allocation (called pages). The smaller unit contains 4096 bytes and is called small page. The size of this page was chosen because it appeared to be a convenient size for interactive users. The larger unit, called large page, contains 524 288 bytes. This large page was intended for major production jobs that would consume most of the machine resources. Since 1974, 40 Mbit/s disk storage units and data trunks have been available for paging of virtual memory to and from the central memory. The time required to access a single page on rotating mass storage includes system software and disk "seek" time. The movement of 4096 byte pages in single units thus becomes quite inefficient, since the transfer time of 800 μs becomes swamped by the 16 000 μs positioning time of the disk. In addition to the above factors, it became evident early in the life of the STAR-100 that basic program modules and data blocks would be larger than 4096 bytes; hence, the large page was included.

To fit a variety of operating environments, the CYBER 200 family was provided with a range of small page sizes beginning with 4096 bytes and ending with 65 536 bytes. The large page size of the STAR-100 was retained since it appeared to be optimum for large production programs. The reason for offering more than one small page was to maintain compatibility at the outset with the STAR-100 and its 4096 byte page, while providing more efficient transfer units, depending upon the needs of a particular environment. As in the decision to provide dual arithmetic units in the CYBER 205, the availability of LSI as a circuit element made providing several different page sizes in the associative register system an engineering reality.

3) The input–output system employed in the STAR-100 was of the "star network" type with node-to-node communication between the CPU and attached peripherals. Management of the peripherals was accomplished by a high-speed, 16 bit miniprocessor called a buffer controller. The STAR computer possessed 12 40 Mbit/s channels, which for large applications was barely sufficient. Fig. 7 illustrates the star network connection of the STAR-100 and attached peripherals, and contrasts this with the CYBER 205. Note that the connectivity of the CYBER 205 is potentially much greater than that of its predecessor. In addition, data transfers between elements of the CYBER 205 system can bypass the front end

elements; in the STAR-100, data rates between permanent file storage and the CPU are limited by the capacity of the front end processor, which typically is on the order of 1–4 Mbits/s.

The change from a point-to-point interconnection to a network form of I/O, which is called the Loosely Coupled Network (LCN), was a major switch for hardware and software alike on the CYBER 205. Transmission of data is accomplished on a high-speed, bit-serial trunk to which 2 to 16 system elements can be coupled. The method of establishing a link is based on "addresses" in the serial message which can be recognized by the hardware trunk coupler, called the Network Access Device (NAD) (see Fig. 8). The most significant aspect of this decision has been the philosophical departure from dedicated peripherals to shared peripherals which are accessed on a "party line" basis. Once this change has been incorporated in the system software, the actual transmission media and hardware form of NAD is invisible to the user, thus permitting the employment of light pipe and microwave transmission as the cost and practicality permit, without change to system software or user programs.

The availability of a technological base was again responsible for the choice of the LCN as the I/O subsystem of the CYBER 205. Key elements here were: 1) the existence of highly reliable 50 Mbit MODEM's, 2) high-speed TTL logic circuits permitting cycle times in the NAD of 100 ns, and 3) memory capacities of 65 536 16-bit words with a bandwidth of 150 Mbits/s. System software, an often neglected technology, has had to mature to the state where a vast network and its operations, maintenance, and performance could become a reality. In effect, network schemes have been under hardware development since 1970 but the software development, to the point of a mature, stable, and deliverable commodity, has required even greater time and manpower.

TECHNOLOGY, THE FUNDAMENTAL ELEMENT IN SUPERCOMPUTERS

The STAR-100 was constructed with the most advanced semiconductor technology available in 1966–1970, called transistor current switch (TCS). This family preceded the introduction of the successful Motorola-MECL 10K family of high-performance, moderate power, small scale integration circuits (containing from three to ten simple gates), and was essential to meeting the performance levels required of the STAR. The beginning point for a supercomputer development is the acquisition of the fastest, densest technology available in a given generation (about six to ten years) of circuitry. The clock cycle of a fast computer is then determined by the speed of the basic gate and the time delay of all the interconnections between circuits (see Fig. 9) constituting two consecutive ranks of data latches (flip-flops).

The designer's desire is obviously highest speed and capacity; these are limited by a factor called the "speed–power product" of a single gate. In order to achieve faster switching times, thereby permitting use of a higher clock rate for a given silicon technology gate, greater power is required, resulting in higher heat dissipation. As these gates are aggregated into large

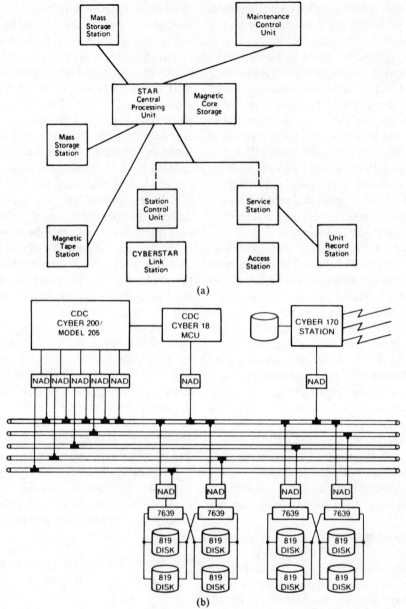

Fig. 7. Input–output configurations. (a) STAR-100 network. (b)
CYBER 200 network.

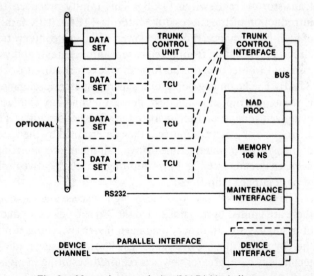

Fig. 8. Network access device (NAD) block diagram.

MULTI BOARD MODULE

INTERCONNECT	≈ 40%
CIRCUITRY	≈ 60%

SINGLE MODULE

INTERCONNECT	≈ 25%
CIRCUITRY	≈ 75%

Fig. 9. Distribution of propagation time.

ensembles on a piece of silicon about 0.1 inch square, the heat buildup can cause the device to become inoperable or to have a seriously shortened lifetime. Each new generation of technology incorporates improvements in lithography and silicon processing which reduce the speed-power product in dramatic stages. Unfortunately, this reduction is matched by equally dramatic increases in demands for density to meet larger gate counts for supercomputers. The result is a necessary com-

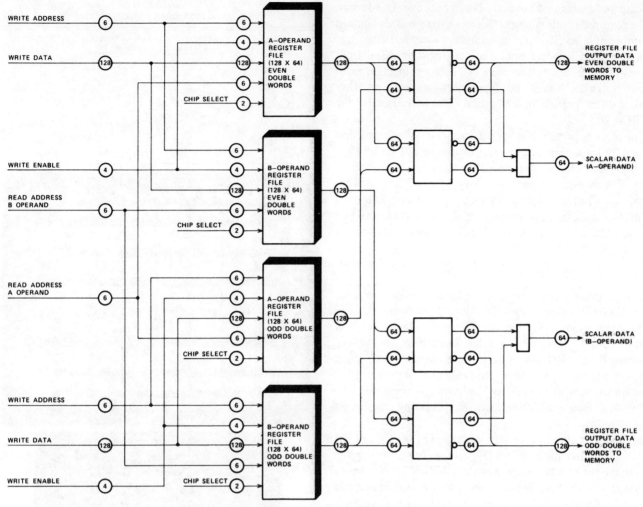

Fig. 10. CYBER 205 register file.

promise between the designer's desires and the practicalities of powering and cooling the requisite high-performance circuits.

MEMORIES, ONE SEGMENT OF TECHNOLOGY

The CYBER 205 possesses a memory hierarchy which was necessitated by the range of cost, performance, power, and density characteristics of available technology, and the need for speed on one hand and large capacity on the other. The most crucial memory, in terms of dictating the clock rate of the CPU, is the register file; until all input operands are fetched and a result is stored away in the file, no new instruction can be issued to the CYBER 205 functional units. This issue rate was targeted at one instruction per clock cycle, thus imposing high demands on the register file technology. The first key technology search for the CYBER 205 project was for a "chip" containing as many bits of data as possible, with the ability to read two operands and write one operand in a clock cycle (whose target was 13.3 ns). No such circuit existed in the inventory or laboratories of any semiconductor vendor in 1975. The chip nearest to possessing these qualities was a 4 bit wide by 16 bit deep chip with separate read and write address registers; this chip could read one operand and write one operand in about 8–10 ns.

Since this compromise chip was not capable of supporting two operand reads and one operand write in a clock cycle, it was decided to build a register file subsystem with the 4 × 16 bit chip, but duplicating the entire file to provide for the two simultaneous operand reads needed to meet CYBER 205 goals (see Fig. 10). A special development could have been initiated to create a totally new chip to meet the project goals, but the 18 month minimum lead time and the risk of not meeting performance goals dictated the use of standard products from the semiconductor catalog. It should be noted that in 1975 the 4 × 16 bit chip was an entry in a catalog, which means almost two years had already transpired for it to achieve production status; in addition, in 1981, it still possessed some undesirable design attributes.

The second most crucial memory technology was that needed for a high-speed, dense random access memory (RAM) device which could be used for the microcode control that was to be distributed throughout the CYBER 205. Since the clock cycle of the CYBER 205 was targeted at 13.3 ns, such a microcode memory had to have an access time on the order of 8–10 ns so that the resulting control signals could be transmitted to key functional elements in the CPU. A 1 bit by 256 bit chip was chosen for this function.

A number of other functional elements in the CYBER 205, like I/O buffers and vector unit buffers, employ the same 256 bit chip and associated auxiliary board package. In addition to the required memory chips, these auxiliary boards contain a number of other SSI circuits for memory support circuitry, such as address decode, fanout, and data registers. Aside from a specific use in controlling the 1 × 256 bit chip as an associative instruction stack and the support logic role, no other small scale integration logic was used in the mainframe of the CYBER 205.

The most important but least risky memory logic was that needed for the mainframe memory consisting of 1 bit by 1024 bit, high-speed RAM chips, with a maximum access time of 37 ns. These chips dissipate between 0.5 and 0.75 W; this necessitated a radical cooling system approach since large assemblages of memory, on the order of one or two million 64 bit words, were to be housed in a compact chassis close to the high-speed scalar unit.

LSI, The Key Technology

The electronic element which is the keystone of performance in the CYBER 205 is a newly developed, high-powered, large scale integration (LSI) circuit. This device provides 168 emitter coupled logic (ECL) gates which have an average switching time of 600–800 ps. It resulted from a research effort begun by Control Data's Advanced Design Laboratory in 1972 in conjunction with several key semiconductor vendors. The technology choices which were made in creating this circuit were as follows.

1) LSI was chosen over the available SSI because of the need to minimize parts counts (for reliability reasons) while increasing the number of gates in the CYBER 200 to almost double that of the STAR-100. A secondary consideration was the improved performance possible by reducing interconnect distances between gates when on the same chip. Table II gives the relative transmission speeds of various interconnect media, and highlights the desirability for a high degree of integration. Finally, LSI was chosen as the technology basis for the CYBER 200 because such is the direction of the semiconductor industry. Although high-powered LSI was in its developmental infancy in 1974–1976, it seemed clear that design and manufacturing techniques would mature quickly and substantial flow of reliable parts would be available from several vendors by the time the CYBER 200 was to reach its peak manufacturing volume.

2) ECL technology was chosen since it offered the highest performance available in 1974–1976, and exhibited extremely stable switching characteristics. These qualities are achieved at the cost of relatively large power dissipation per gate. This limits the total number of gates that can be integrated on a single silicon die and then be effectively cooled when packaged. A lower powered and consequently much slower technology such as metal oxide semiconductors (MOS) can achieve densities of tens of thousands of gates, as in microprocessor chips such as the Z80, 8080, and 6800. The term LSI applied to ECL family circuits, when evaluated in light of these factors, should include 168 ECL gates as being LSI in the 1980's. Power requirements of even this level of integration make extraordinary demands on creative packaging and cooling of the parts, individually and collectively.

TABLE II
PROPAGATION DELAY VERSUS MEDIUM

Medium	Delay (ps/micron)	Typical Length (microns)	Typical Delay(ps)
Interconnect (On Chip)	2.4×10^{-2}	12.5×10^2	30
PC Board (Teflon Glass)	1.2×10^{-2}	1500×10^2	1800
Coax (Foam)	0.4×10^{-2}	9000×10^2	3600
Light	0.33×10^{-2}	–	–

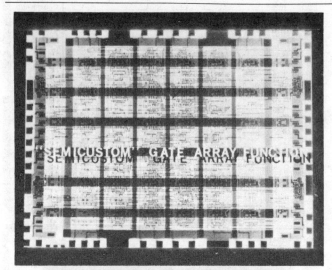

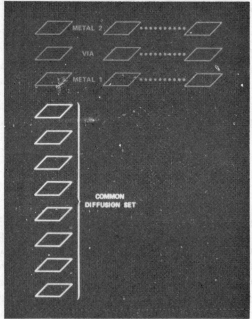

Fig. 11. Gate array concept.

3) The gate array concept (Fig. 11) became the technological base for the circuitry. The alternative methodology would have been to create totally different custom arrays (see Fig. 12), where each diffusion layer would differ between parts. The advantages of the gate array technique are as follows.

a) Lower Start-Up Cost on a Per-Part Basis: The most important feature of the gate array approach is that all layers imposed upon the silicon, except for two layers of metal and a layer of "via," are all common. This means that a large

Fig. 12. Fully custom LSI.

number of fundamental type chips can be mass produced and stored, or held, until a unique metalization is laid down at a later date.

b) Shorter Turnaround Time in Producing New or Modified Parts: The ability to store the basic part until a later date, and then introduce changed metal masks, reduces the development and processing time for a newly developed type or a type modification.

c) Vendor Willingness to Participate in the Project: Another property of the gate array scheme is the utilization of standard wafer processing techniques at the semiconductor manufacturer's plant. The disruption of a commercial silicon facility's operation must be drastically minimized; otherwise, semiconductor business decisions will weigh in favor of the standard (guaranteed profit making) product lines at the expense of more challenging and economically risky efforts.

The disadvantages of this approach are as follows.

i) Performance and Density are Not Optimal for the Same Silicon Area and Technology: The use of the gate-matrix structure means that the densest gate structure per square millimeter of silicon cannot be attained. The generality of the matrix structure ensures that all of the silicon surface cannot be utilized productively.

ii) The Long Term Unit Cost Per Circuit for Custom Designed Devices is Lower. Once the development cost and time have been amortized, a custom device, because it utilizes less silicon for the same job, will cost less than a gate array device, if the volume of production is high enough. In the case of supercomputers, where the final volumes of parts are predictably small, this disadvantage is minimal.

iii) The Ability of Competitors to Duplicate Gate Array Parts is Enhanced, Since the "Personality" of a Given Part is Determined by So Little Metalization.

In any event, the decision to utilize an LSI family designed specifically for the CYBER 205 created some additional problems, and gave rise to some engineering challenges. The STAR-100 was built from SSI parts mounted 60 to a two-sided circuit board. Each of these boards could exist as a unique type, with its personality determined by the types, quantities, and placement of chips on the board, as well as the routing of the foil paths between chips and to the board's connector pins. The

engineers on the STAR-100 were reasonably free to design as many types of boards (modules) as they needed, each one requiring only a different layout, documentation package, and separate exposure plates for the metal paths. The utilization of this scheme resulted in over 300 different types of boards being created in about three years design time.

The amount of logic that could be organized onto a CYBER 200 gate array could, in many cases, be roughly equivalent to that included on a STAR module. When faced with the possibility of producing 300–400 different chip types (of low volume) for the CYBER 205, semiconductor vendors reacted with horror and outright resistance to such a project. The reasons for this are manifold but include the following.

1) A major bottleneck in a semiconductor vendor's operation is the mask shop, wherein the precision masks are generated for each type of component being produced by the vendor. The constant development of new parts and the improvement of existing parts for the "bread and butter" standard products of a vendor create a large demand for the resources of a mask shop. The introduction of "special request" masks from projects such as the CYBER 205 can cause great perturbations in product schedules and possibly jeopardize critical product developments. Any new part types demanded by the CYBER 205 project would have to be processed within the excess capacities of a typical mask shop. This might limit engineers to perhaps 8–20 types.

2) The process of testing arrays at the conclusion of the manufacturing cycle requires fixtures, tester firmware, and documentation for each unique entity. Management of this operation for a vast number of types becomes quite arduous and costly.

3) If a large number of part types is permitted, most will be highly specialized to a particular machine design and, thus, unavailable as general purpose devices that could be made part of a standard product line. This means that no part type will ever be manufactured in great volume, and even though manufacturing costs are passed on to the consumer, the financial return to the semiconductor vendor for low volume elements may not justify the resource commitment needed to manage the development and production facilities.

From the consuming project point of view, to permit a great variety of special parts is not necessarily desirable either. If a complete kit of parts, so to speak, to produce a CYBER 205 were to contain 300 types of chips, then a failure in any one of the 300 production lines could blockade the manufacturing and checkout of machines on the assembly line.

As a consequence of these considerations, the CYBER 205 engineering group had to limit the number of different types of LSI chips created to 14 for the scalar unit; and no more than an additional 11 types could be used for the vector and I/O units of the machine. This meant that additional engineering time was consumed in the aggregation of certain designs into a single part type. The design activity then demanded considerable interaction within the design team to achieve common part types which could be used in different ways and in different areas of the machine. Only three chip types became so unique that their use was impossible in some universal capacity: the multiply chip, the associative register chip, and the result address register chip (which is used to control instruction issue in the scalar unit).

A significant result of the CYBER 205 design project was that despite the compromises required by the chip type constraints listed, the overall performance of the machine was not degraded from what might have been possible had a larger number of types been available. This conclusion was reached after the machine was completed and design alternatives were reviewed in detail.

PACKAGING AND COOLING, THE UNHERALDED TECHNOLOGY

The circuit family chosen for the CYBER 205 possessed many pleasant attributes for design engineers but exhibited one challenging characteristic: high power dissipation. The average power per chip was about 5 W. To maintain a desirable junction temperature of 55° C at this dissipation level demanded some creativity from the packaging and cooling engineers. The solution finally obtained was to bring a liquid coolant (Freon) into contact with each and every chip. Air cooling was discarded early as an alternative since each printed circuit board was designed to hold 150 arrays and thus would be emitting 750 W in less than a square foot of chassis area. Other conductive techniques, using metal heat transfer paths, also yielded thermal resistances too high to manage. The reason for this is that any liquid coolant system cannot create exposed surfaces cooler than a nominal dew point in today's standard machine room. If this were not so, then a very low temperature medium could be used as a cooling agent, overcoming deficiencies in the thermal pathing.

Fig. 13 shows the basic circuit package of the CYBER 205 with the Freon tube running underneath the chip which has a heat spreader mounted on its base. The basic LSI package shown here is the culmination of the tradeoffs between density and cooling capability, gate count and interconnectability. The connector interfaces 52 gold-plated contacts to each LSI array, with the bottom contact pressure being provided by the spring clip which covers the assemblage. The spring clip also provides force to ensure good mating between the heat spreader and the liquid coolant tube. While more contact pins are desired by designers, board technology and tester complexity act as constraints. While it is desirable to pack more chips on a board, printed circuit technology (hole and foil densities) and power and cooling considerations limit this area of the technology.

THE CYBER 205 MAINFRAME

The functional and performance objectives of a machine like the CYBER 205 are arrived at through a process of matching demands with technological and manufacturing reality. A first step in this process consists of estimating the probable minimum clock period possible for the architecture and technology combination. The CYBER 205 was designed to be implemented in three stages: 1) an enhancement to the memory and scalar units of the STAR-100, 2) a replacement of the STAR-I/O system, and 3) an evolution to a totally LSI-based mainframe. This approach dictated that the LSI scalar unit would have to operate at an integral subdivision of the STAR-100 clock cycle of 40 ns. The choices are limited. At one-half the clock cycle (20 ns) the overall performance of a CYBER 200 machine would be a marginal improvement for the investment made, if the STAR-100 structure were retained intact. At one-third the clock cycle of the STAR-100 (13.33 ··· ns) the speed of the machine would be easily comparable to the nearest competitor (the CRAY-1) at 12.5 ns. At one-fourth the clock rate (10 ns) the technology would strain to achieve the performance, let alone possess any reasonable margin for manufacturing variants. The clock cycle target was then set at 13.33 ··· ns as a possible goal, to be proven by the viability of a final design.

A set of design ground rules containing average gate delays and the mean transmission times for circuits was then used in the design of what were considered to be the "hard spots" (long paths) of a STAR type architecture. The major hard spots included the following.

1) The instruction issue path begins with the time to translate an operation code, proceeds with the reading of two operands from the register file (if available), and ends with the loading of a new instruction into the primary instruction register.

2) The memory fetch cycle consists of translating the instruction, computing a memory address, transforming the address from virtual to real in the associative registers, sending the request to the central memory system, and returning the requested data to the register file.

3) The time required to set up memory addresses for vector instructions, resolve any conflicts between all memory requests, and move input and output vector data to and from central memory is critical to start-up and throughput potential of the high-speed arithmetic units. With the initial (and as yet unproven with actual parts in 1976) ground rules, the 13.33 ··· ns clock cycle became a marginal possibility. The decision was made to design the major subsystems to operate at the aggressive 13.3 ns cycle. In particular, the register file and the central memory were designed, built, and tested at that speed. The engineering staff then endeavored to design all other components to operate at that clock rate. Given the possibility that the next slower clock cycle (20 ns) would become the CYBER 200 fundamental clock, it became necessary to seek structural changes which would increase the overall machine performance beyond the automatic factor of two yielded by the clock improvement. The goals then set for the mainframe were established, assuming a 20 ns clock cycle, and created to provide competitive performance characteristics at that speed. These goals by functional unit were based on relative performance targets set for the CYBER 205 computer. The design implications of these goals were much more complicated in the following areas.

1) The STAR-100 was capable of issuing instructions at a maximum rate of one every two (40 ns) clock cycles. The limiting factor of this rate was, originally, the ability to read only one operand per cycle out of the register file of the STAR-100, while two operands were required for most instructions. As stated previously, the Advanced Design Laboratory technologists obviated this problem, thus challenging the engineers to utilize the new register file. The consequence

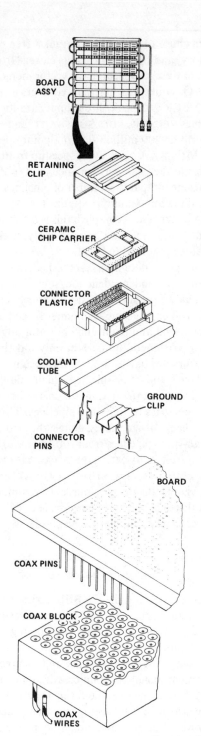

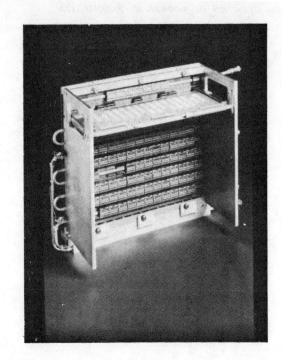

Fig. 13. CYBER 200 packaging and cooling technology.

of this effort was the discovery that the final designs of the STAR-100 scalar arithmetic elements assumed the slower rate and thus were inadequate to the new challenge. The effect of this relevation was an increase of engineering investment over that planned on the basis of estimates which included translation of existing designs into a new technology. A short stop or loop back path, which returns pipeline results back to the inputs of arithmetic units before they arrive at the register file, improved the issue potential of the scalar processor.

2) Start-up time of vector operations includes the instruction translation time, and the delay imposed by fetching and aligning the input streams and by aligning and moving output streams to memory. Fig. 14 illustrates the impact of start-up time on the effective performance of the CYBER 205 architecture. A major improvement in the overall performance of this type of memory-to-memory vector architecture requires careful attention to start-up time. In addition to the raw improvement in clock speed, the designers were directed to other methods for reducing the delay in vector initiation. Given the STAR-100 as a basis, the actions of address setup and management of vector arithmetic control lines required substantial speedup. In addition, providing separate and independent functional units in each of the scalar and vector processors permits execution of those functions in parallel. Hence, the

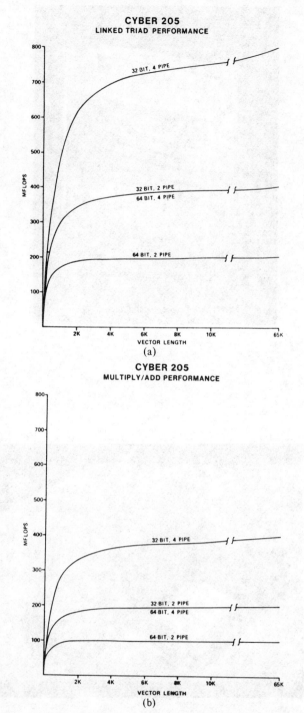

Fig. 14. Effect of start-up time on CYBER 205 vector performance. (a) Multiply/add performance. (b) Linked triad performance.

"apparent" start-up time becomes smaller than what the hardware provides. This feature, in the best cases, results in parallel execution of both scalar and vector floating-point operations with a consequent increase in overall performance.

3) The STAR-100 guaranteed the attainment of peak vector rates by "slotting" input–output requests around the memory demands of the vector streams. From this demand arose an extremely complex design which attempted to cope with the 32-minor-cycle (1.28 μs) bank busy time and the random arrivals of bulk (524 288 byte) I/O transfers. CYBER

205 designers chose to give input–output a free entry to the central memory, and found that it was easier (from an engineering point of view) to schedule the vector memory requests around the I/O requests rather than vice versa.

4) The CYBER 205 peak throughput rate for simple operations, such as VECTOR, ADD, SUBTRACT, and MULTIPLY, was specified to be 200 million floating point operations per second (200 Mflops). A clock cycle speedup from 40 to 20 ns would only bring the peak performance to 100 Mflops in 64 bit mode. This meant that the number of pipelines would have to be doubled in the maximum configuration. The increase in hardware components to accomplish this is offset for the most part by the utilization of the LSI gate array, making such a large assemblage practical to build.

5) Once the overall design was established, the CYBER 205 engineers realized the independent add, subtract, multiply, and divide units could be produced at little additional cost, whereas in the STAR-100 engineering economies forced a sharing of hardware (back-end and front-end shift and alignment networks) among arithmetic units. Not only did this permit a more straightforward partitioning of the design, but a simple interunit linkage could be established which would permit the execution of two separate arithmetic operations on a single vector during one pass through the pipelines. This design attribute would then, for some cases, double the arithmetic result rate of the high-speed pipelines from 200 Mflops to 400 Mflops for LINKED 64 bit ADD-MULTIPLY/MULTIPLY-ADD and some other operations such as SHIFT, LOGICAL, and VECTOR COMPARE. Again, this design approach was made possible only through the employment of large-scale circuit integration which reduces parts counts to acceptable manufacturing levels.

CONCLUSIONS

The process of creating the CYBER 205 has involved the blending of technological and architectural evolution with state-of-the-art power, packaging and cooling, and manufacturing techniques to yield a practical and reproducible computer system. The requirements and desires evident in large-scale computational environments are tempered with the reality of engineering and manufacturing practices. If this were not so, the world would be seeing massive processors with trillions of words of memory and processing power on the order of trillions of floating point operations per second. Parts counts, interchassis wiring, and power and cooling considerations dominate the production of real, usable supercomputers, with technology and architecture becoming necessary, but secondary, considerations. A high performance memory system of eight million 64 bit words, for example, depends on the availability of circuits containing at least 16 000 bits each, with access times in the range of 35-45 ns. The central processor architecture must provide the address busing for such a large assemblage of memory. The entire ensemble must be manufacturable and maintainable or the architectural and technological achievements are wasted.

It is the realization that these sobering pragmatics set limits on achievable computational power which gives rise to the

IEEE TRANSACTIONS ON COMPUTERS, VOL. C-31, NO. 5, MAY 1982

cautionary "There ain't no magic" poster which hangs in the CYBER 205 development laboratory. If, in fact, there is no "magic bullet" which will yield new and extraordinary supercomputer power, what can be expected in the future?

In the next five years (1982–1986), a new generation of supercomputer will emerge, driven by customer demands and other competitive pressures. If the current supercomputers (CRAY-1 and CYBER 205) are termed "Class VI computers," then one might call their successors "Class VII" machines. Memory capacities will be two to four times greater than now possible, and processing speeds will be improved from 2.5 to 20 times current rates. These goals will be achieved by employing another generation of silicon technology, with emphasis on larger scales of integration rather than exotic technologies such as Josephson junction or gallium arsenide. Larger aggregates of ECL gates on a silicon die will mean higher power, and thus will demand innovative packaging and cooling systems with continued reliance on liquid coolant techniques. The consequent reductions in size and parts counts in an LSI system make it possible to increase redundancy and maintenance features, as well as the number of functional units. The result will be higher powered, more efficient, lower cost, and more reliable supercomputers in the coming generation.

The major element of this next generation will be a continued evolution of architectures involving parallelism. Vector processors, multiprocessors, and similar parallel structures will be required to keep pace with the demand for computational power. The exploitation of these architectures, through new algorithms, operating systems, and compiler technology, is the key to achieving the goals of the next generation consumer. The practicality of such software development is another challenge . . . and another story.

REFERENCES

[1] M. J. Kascic, "A direct Poisson solver on STAR processor," in *Proc. LASL Workshop Vector and Parallel Processing*, 1978, LA-7491-C.

[2] ——, "Application of vector processors to the solution of finite difference equations," *Soc. Petroleum Eng. AIME*, SPE 7675, 1979.

[3] ——, "Vector processing, problem or opportunity," presented at IEEE COMPCON'80, 1979.

[4] ——, "Vector processing and vector numerical linear algebra," in *Proc. 3rd GAMM Conf. Numerical Methods in Fluid Mechanics*, DFVLR, Koln, Germany, Oct. 1979.

[5] ——, "Vector processing on the CYBER 200," in *Infotech State of the Art Report "Supercomputer,"* Infotech Int. Ltd., Maidenhead, England, 1979.

[6] ——, "Vector processing for high energy physics," in *Computer Physics Comm. 22*. Amsterdam, The Netherlands: North-Holland, 1981.

[7] ——, "Tridiagonal systems and OCI on the CYBER 200," *SIAM*, Oct. 1981.

[8] K. E. Iverson, *A Programming Language*. New York: Wiley, 1962.

[9] P. D. Jones, N. R. Lincoln and J. E. Thornton, "Whither computer architecture," in *Proc. IFIP Cong. 71*. Amsterdam, The Netherlands: North-Holland, 1972.

[10] N. R. Lincoln, "It's really not as much fun building a supercomputer as it is simply inventing one," in *Proc. Symp. High Speed Computer and Algorithm Organization*. New York: Academic, Apr. 1977.

[11] ——, "A safari through the Control Data STAR-100 with gun and camera," in *Proc. AFIPS Nat. Comput. Conf.*, June 1978.

[12] R. Stokes and R. Cantarella, "The history of parallel processing at Burroughs," in *Proc. Int. Conf. Parallel Processing*, 1981.

[13] G. H. Barnes *et al.*, "The ILLIAC IV computer," *IEEE Trans. Comput.*, vol. C-17, Aug. 1968.

[14] R. L. Davis, "The ILLIAC IV processing element," *IEEE Trans. Comput.*, vol. C-18, Sept. 1969.

[15] D. H. Lawrie *et al.*, "Glypnir—A programming language for ILLIAC IV," *Commun. Ass. Comput. Mach.*, vol. 18, no. 3, 1975.

[16] R. M. Russell, "The CRAY-1 computer system," *Commun. Ass. Comput. Mach.*, vol. 21, no. 1, 1978.

[17] N. R. Lincoln, "Supercomputer development—The pleasure and the pain," presented at IEEE COMPCON '77, 1977.

Neil R. Lincoln, photograph and biography not available at the time of publication.

Large-scale and High-Speed

Multiprocessor System

for

Scientific Applications

(Revised from the presentation made in NATO Advanced Research Workshop on High Speed Computing, Kwalik, Editor, W. Germany, June, 1983)

CRAY X-MP-2 Series

Steve Chen
Cray Research, Inc.

Overview of CRAY X-MP System

1. General-purpose multiprocessor system for multitasking applications.

   - Run independent tasks of different jobs on multiple processors. Program compatibility (with CRAY-1) is maintained for all tasks.

   - Run related tasks of single job on multiple processors.

     - Loosely-coupled tasks communicating through shared memory.

     - Tightly-coupled tasks communicating through shared registers.

   - Small overhead of task initiation for multitasking, $O(1\mu s)$ to $O(1ms)$, depending on granularity of the tasks and software implementation techniques.

   - Flexible architecture concept for processor clustering.

     - All processors are identical and symmetric in their programming functions, i.e., there is no permanent master/slave relation existing between all processors.

     - A cluster of k processors $(0 \le k \le p)$ can be assigned to perform a single task, where $p = 2$ is the number of physical processors in the system.

     - Up to $p + 1$ processor clusters can be assigned by the operating system.

     - Each cluster contains a unique set of shared data and synchronization registers for the inter-communication of all processors in a cluster.

     - Each processor in a cluster can run in either monitor or user mode controlled by the operating system.

     - Each processor in a cluster can asynchronously perform either scalar or vector operations dictated by user programs.

     - Any processor running in monitor mode can interrupt any other processor and cause it to switch from user mode to monitor mode.

     - Built-in detection of system deadlock within the cluster.

   - Faster exchange for switching machine state between tasks.

   - Hardware supports separation of memory segments for each user's data and program to facilitate the concurrent programming.

2. General-purpose multiprocessor system for compute-bound and I/O-bound applications.

   - All processors share a central bipolar memory (4MW), organized in m=32 interleaved memory banks (twice that of CRAY-1). All banks can be accessed independently and in parallel during each machine clock period. Each processor has four parallel memory ports (four times that of CRAY-1) connected to this central memory, two for vector fetches, one for vector store, and one for independent I/O operations. The multiport memory has built-in conflict resolution hardware to minimize the delay and maintain the integrity of all memory references to the same bank in the same time, from all processor's ports. The interleaved and efficient multiport memory design, coupled with shorter memory cycle time, provide a high-performance and balanced memory organization with sufficient bandwidth (eight times that of CRAY-1) to support simultaneous high-speed CPU and I/O operations.

   - New, large, CPU-driven Solid-state Storage Device (SSD) is designed as an integral part of the mainframe with very high block transfer rate. This can be used as a fast-access device for user large pre-staged or intermediate files generated and manipulated repetitively by user programs, or used by the system for job "swapping" space and temporary storage of system programs. The SSD design with its large size (32MW), very fast data transfer speed (maximum rate 10 Gb/sec, and typical rate 1000 MB/sec, 250 times faster than disk), and much shorter access time (less than .5 ms, 100 times faster than disk), coupled with the high-performance multiprocessor design, will enable the user to explore new application algorithms for solving bigger and more sophisticated problems in science and engineering which they could not attempt before.

   - The I/O Subsystem, which is an integral part of the CRAY X-MP-2 System, also contributes to the system's overall performance. The I/O Subsystem (compatible with CRAY-1/S) offers parallel streaming of disk drives, I/O buffering (8MW max. size) for disk-resident and Buffer Memory-resident datasets, high-performance on-line tape handling, and common device for front-end system communication, networking, or specialized data acquisition. The IOP design enables faster and more efficient asynchronous I/O operations for data access and deposition of initial and final outputs through high-speed channels (each channel has maximum rate 850 Mb/sec, and typical rate 40 MB/sec, 10 times faster than disk), while relieving the CPUs to perform computation-intensive operations.

3. General-purpose multiprocessor system for scalar and vector applications.

   - All processors are controlled synchronously by a central clock with improved cycle time = 9.5 ns (vs. 12.5 ns of CRAY-1).

   - The scalar performance of each processor is improved through faster machine clock, shorter memory access time, and larger instruction buffers (twice that of CRAY-1).

   - The vector performance of each processor is improved through faster machine clock, parallel memory ports, and hardware automatic "flexible chaining" features. These new features allow simultaneous memory fetches, arithmetic, and memory store operations in a series of related vector operations (this contrasts to the "fixed chaining" and uni-directional vector fetch/store in CRAY-1). As a result, the processor design provides higher speed and more balanced vector processing capabilities for both long and short vectors, characterized by heavy register-to-register or heavy memory-to-memory vector operations.

   - The processor design is well-balanced for processing both scalar and vector codes. The overall effective performance of each processor in execution of typical user programs with interspersing scalar and vector codes (usually short vectors) is ensured through fast data flow between scalar and vector functional units, short memory access time for vector and scalar references, as well as small start-up time for scalar and vector operations. As a result of this unique design characteristic, the machine can perform very well in real programming environments using standard compiler, without resorting to enormous amount of hand-coding or even restructuring of the original application algorithms. Certainly, as the code is more vectorized, and the vector length is becoming longer, an even better performance can be achieved.

CRAY X-MP-2 DATA FLOW

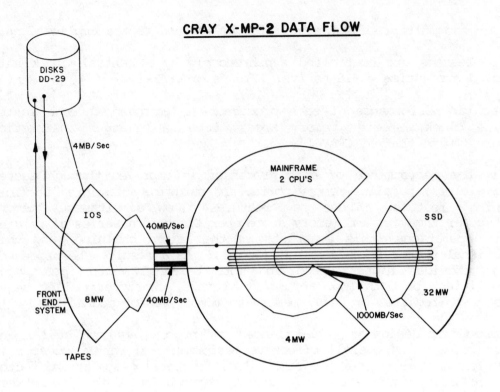

CRAY X-MP-2 OVERALL SYSTEM ORGANIZATION

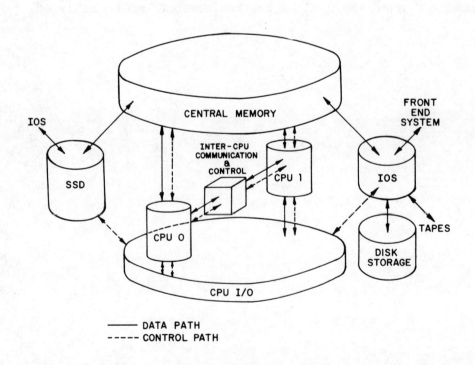

SSD CONCEPT

```
CPU           I/O           I/O
 &          _____       _____
DISK  USER          USER          USER
      _____       _____       _____


CPU      I/O     I/O     I/O     I/O
 &      _____   _____   _____   _____
SSD   USER    USER    USER    USER    USER
      _____   _____   _____   _____   _____
```

SSD

Used as disk

FUNCTIONS   as extension of central memory

DUE to very short access time: < .5 ms

     very fast transfer rate: 1000 MB/SEC

APPLICATION for BIGGER, MORE COMPLEX

     problems, which was NOT achievable

     before

SSD USAGE

Add one JCL card for each temporary
file used.

EXAMPLE:

```
    JOB, --.
    ACCOUNT, --.
    CFT.

→   ASSIGN, DN=FT01, DV=SSD-0-20.

    LDR.
    /EOF
     ⋮
    WRITE(1) A,B,C
    REWIND(1)
    READ(1) A,B,C
     ⋮
    /EOF
```

- NO PROGRAM CHANGES REQUIRED
- FORMATTED OR BINARY I/O
- BLOCKED OR UNBLOCKED I/O
- RANDOM OR SEQUENTIAL I/O

TWO DIMENSIONS OF PARALLELISM

MULTITASKING

HIGHER level parallelism
Independent ALGORITHMS
JOB/PROGRAM/LOOP oriented
SINGLE and MULTI-JOB performance

LOWER level parallelism
Independent OPERATIONS
STATEMENT oriented
SINGLE JOB performance

SEQUENTIAL   VECTORIZATION
(SCALAR)   (VECTOR)

MULTITASKING VS. VECTORIZATION
FOR THE CRAY X-MP-2

-Vectorization offers a speedup of up to 10-20 over scalar processing, depending on actual code and vector length

- Total speedup over scalar processing
   = SPEEDUP (MULTITASKING)*SPEEDUP (VECTORIZATION)
   e.g. = Sp*(10-20)=18-38 : ASSUMING Sp=1.8-1.9

- Multitasking offers an additional speedup of Sp ≤ 2 , depending on task size and relative multitasking overhead

- A general guideline: first, partition tasks at the highest possible level to apply multitasking, and then vectorize each task as much as possible

VECTOR COMPUTATIONS

$$\bar{A} = \bar{B} + s * \bar{D}$$

FETCH $\bar{B}$ $\}$ CRAY-1 1ST CHAIN

FETCH $\bar{D}$

MULTIPLY $\}$ CRAY-1 2ND CHAIN

ADD

STORE $\bar{A}$ $\}$ CRAY -1 3RD CHAIN

CRAY X-MP-2
ONE CHAIN

NOTES:

1. Using 3 memory ports per processor

2. Hardware automatically "chains" through all five vector operations such that one result per clock period can be delivered

3. Support conditional vector operations: Gather/scatter, Compressed Index

VECTOR LOOP FAMILIES
BENCHMARK TIMINGS ON X-MP-2

	1-CPU		
	SHORT VECTOR (VL = 8)	MEDIUM VECTOR (VL - 128)	LONG VECTOR (VL - 1024)
A=B	1.1	1.8	2.1
A=B+C	1.2	2.2	2.7
A=B*C	1.5	2.6	3.3
A=B/C	1.5	1.9	2.0
A=B+C+D	1.5	2.7	3.2
A=B+C*D	1.4	2.9	3.6
A=B+s*D	1.3	3.0	4.0
A=B+C+D+E	1.3	2.3	2.7
A=B+C+D*E	1.6	2.5	2.9
A=B*C+D*E	1.3	2.5	3.1
A=B+C*D+E*F	1.5	2.1	2.2
	1.5	2.5	3.0

(Unit based on compiler
generated code running on 1/S)

NASTRAN BENCHMARK

(mins)

Computer System	Memory Used	CPU Time	I/O Time	Total Time	Relative Performance
IBM 3081	Virtual	720	180	900	1.0
CRAY 1/M	1/4 MW	137	81	218	4.1
CRAY 1/M	1/2 MW	123	56	179	5.0
CRAY 1/M	3/4 MW	119	53	172	5.2
CRAY 1/M	1 3/4 MW	118	49	167	5.4
CRAY X-MP with 32MW SSD (1-CPU)	1 3/4 MW	84	20	104	8.7

*72,000 degrees of freedom

* ~ 17 X two job system throughput

SCIENTIFIC LIBRARY (CAL) BENCHMARK TIMINGS ON X-MP-2

CODE	(1-CPU X)/1S SPEEDUP FACTOR	
SSUM	1.36	
SDOT	2.26	
SAXPY	4.04	
FOLR (*)	5.93	(3.40)
FOLRN (*)	7.32	(1.94)
GATHER	2.55	
SCATTER	2.48	
MXM	1.33	
MXMA	1.42	
MINV	2.18	
CFFT2	2.16	
CRFFT2	2.12	
RCFFT2	2.11	

(*) New vector algorithms used on X only;
the number in ( ) indicates the speedup
when vector algorithms are applied to
both the X and S

GENERAL LINEAR ALGEBRA (FORTRAN) BENCHMARK TIMING ON X-MP-2

CODE	(1-CPU X)/1S SPEEDUP FACTOR
SGEFA	2.77
SGECO	2.75
SGESL	2.84
SGEDI	2.63
TRED2	3.08
TRED1	2.08
TRBAK1	3.27

MULTITASKING ON THE
CRAY X-MP-2 MULTIPROCESSOR

OFFERS:

– An opportunity for numerical analysts to
  explore new and faster parallel algorithms

– The exploitation of another dimension of
  parallelism beyond vector processing

– A convenient way for programmers to
  express concurrency in their programs

– A natural way for scientists and engineers
  to view their problems

– Improved performance at several levels

MULTITASKING – EXPLOITING
PARALLELISM AT SEVERAL LEVELS

(Conceptual Examples)

1. Multitasking at the job level (1)

```
CPU - 0        CPU - 1
  |              |
JOB 1          JOB 2
```

2. Multitasking at the job-step level (2)

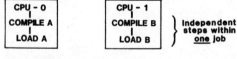

```
CPU - 0        CPU - 1
  |              |
COMPILE A      COMPILE B
  |              |
LOAD A         LOAD B
```
} Independent steps within one job

3. Multitasking at the program level (3)

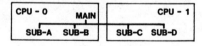

```
CPU - 0      MAIN        CPU - 1
SUB-A   SUB-B      SUB-C   SUB-D
```

4. Multitasking at the loop level (4)

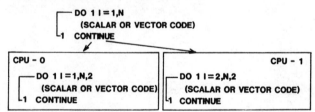

```
        DO 1 I=1,N
          (SCALAR OR VECTOR CODE)
      1  CONTINUE

CPU - 0                              CPU - 1
    DO 1 I=1,N,2                       DO 1 I=2,N,2
      (SCALAR OR VECTOR CODE)            (SCALAR OR VECTOR CODE)
  1  CONTINUE                        1  CONTINUE
```

NOTES: 1. SW support available now
        2. Need further feasibility study
        3., 4. SW support for user-directed multitasking available now

MULTITASKING OF VECTOR CODE

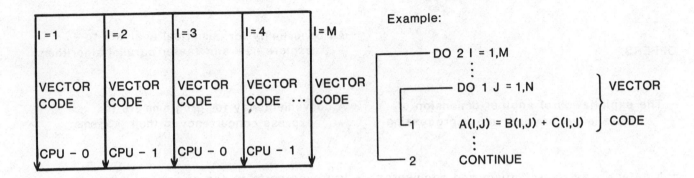

Example:

```
      DO 2 I = 1,M
         .
         .                            }
         DO 1 J = 1,N                   VECTOR
   1        A(I,J) = B(I,J) + C(I,J)  }  CODE
         .
         .
      2  CONTINUE
```

MULTITASKING OF SCALAR CODE

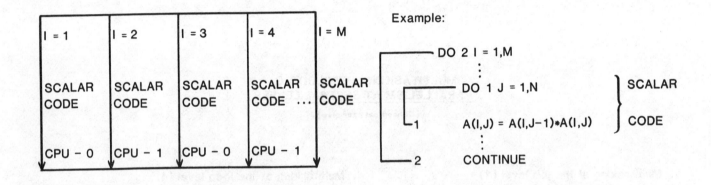

Example:

```
      DO 2 I = 1,M
         .
         .                            }
         DO 1 J = 1,N                   SCALAR
   1        A(I,J) = A(I,J-1)*A(I,J)  }  CODE
         .
         .
      2  CONTINUE
```

MULTITASKING BY PROCESSOR PIPELINING

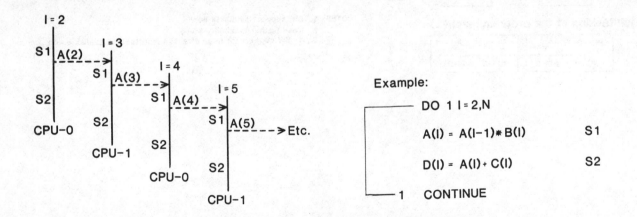

Example:

```
      DO 1 I = 2,N
         A(I) = A(I-1)*B(I)      S1
         D(I) = A(I) + C(I)      S2
      1  CONTINUE
```

56

X-MP-2 MULTITASKING PERFORMANCE

- Multitasking <u>is running</u> on the X-MP.

- Multitasking has been demonstrated with PIC code, SPECTRAL code and MG3D code.

- For two processors the speedup is 1.8 – 1.9 over one processor.

- Parallelism is at a <u>high level</u> – program modification is <u>minimal.</u>

- Multitasking overhead with the X-MP hardware/software is negligible.

CRAY X-MP-2 OVERALL PERFORMANCE

1-CPU RATE$_1$ (PEAK 210 MFLOPS)

    MINIMUM: 1.25

    TYPICAL: 1.5 – 2.5

    MAXIMUM: 4

2-CPU RATE$_2$ (PEAK 420 MFLOPS)

    MINIMUM: 2.5

    TYPICAL: 3 – 5

    MAXIMUM: 8

I/O RATE$_3$

	ACCESS TIME	TRANSFER RATE
DISK	1	1
SSD	.01	250

NOTES: 1. Unit based on compiler generated code running on 1/S. TYPICAL refers to small-to-medium size vectors encountered in typical programs

2. Assuming two CPU's are dedicated to multitasking of a single large job

3. Unit based on measured time per sector

PIC

- A particle-in-cell simulation program for electro/magneto static interaction between collisionless beams of plasma

- Parallelism occurs in the independent tracking of particles, and the evaluation of total charge distribution

- Multitasking accounts for 96% of the execution time of a model experiment involving 37,000 particles, and 50 time steps

- 1-CPU execution time = 22.5 seconds on X-MP

- 2-CPU execution time = 12.1 seconds on X-MP

Actual 2-CPU speedup = 1.86 over 1-CPU

SPECTRAL

- This is a benchmark code for short term weather forecast

- Parallelism occurs on the latitude level, i.e., the outermost loop inside each time step

- Multitasking accounts for 98% of the execution time of a model experiment involving a global grid structure with 160 latitude by 192 longitude points, and 200 time steps

- 1-CPU execution time = 380.8 seconds on X-MP

- 2-CPU execution time = 201.2 seconds on X-MP

Actual 2-CPU speedup = 1.89 over 1-CPU

MG3D

- A seismic 3-D migration code to construct underground reflector structure.

- Parallelism occurs in the decoupled frequency domain at each depth level, after Fourier Transform over time.

- Multitasking accounts for 98% of the execution time of a model experiment involving 200 x 200 traces, with 1024 time samples for each trace, and 1000 depth level.

  - Total computation = 1.5×10^{12} FLOPS

  - Total I/O = 40×10^9 Words

- 1-CPU execution time = 23.8 hours with disk

  = 3.58 hours with SSD

  (6.6 times speedup over 1-CPU with disk)

- 2-CPU execution time = 1.89 hours with SSD

  (12.6 times speedup over 1-CPU with disk)

Actual 2-CPU speedup = 1.89 over 1-CPU

(Preliminary version of this paper has been submitted to Proceedings of NATO Advanced Research Workshop on High Speed Computing, which is to be published as NATO ASI Series, Vol. F7, Springer-Verlag, 1984.)

FACOM VECTOR PROCESSOR SYSTEM:VP-100/VP-200

Kenichi Miura and Keiichiro Uchida
Mainframe Division
Fujitsu Limited
Kawasaki, Japan

1. Introduction

In 1982 Fujitsu announced two models of the FACOM Vector Processor System, VP-100 and VP-200, for large scale scientific and engineering computations. These machines both employ the pipeline architecture with multiple pipeline units which can operate concurrently. The maximum performances of VP-100 and VP-200 are 267 MFLOPS and 533 MFLOPS, respectively. VP-200 allows up to 256M bytes of the main storage. In developing the FACOM Vector Processor, we have also incorporated several advanced features of vector processing, in order to achieve very high average performance for FORTRAN programs in wide range of scientific and engineering applications. This paper describes our design approach, technologies, architecture and software of the FACOM Vector Processor System, with an emphasis on the implementation of the advanced features from the view points of hardware and software.

2. Design Approach of FACOM Vector Processor System

Development of the supercomputers have been mainly motivated by

Revised from *Proceedings of NATO Advanced Research Workshop on High Speed Computing*, Kawalik (Editor), Volume F7, 1984. Copyright © 1984 by Springer-Verlag. Reprinted with permission.

the needs to perform large scale simulations of physical models such as hydrodynamics, numerical weather prediction and nuclear energy researches. As the extremely powerful computational capabilities of the supercomputers attracted attentions from various branches of science and industry, however, the market started to proliferate; structural analysis, VLSI design, oil reservoir simulations, nuclear plant simulations, utilities and quantum chemistry, just to name a few. This trend, in return, has created demands for supercomputers which can handle various kinds of users' programs efficiently.

Prior to designing the FACOM Vector Processor System, we have analyzed more than 1,000 FORTRAN programs in the typical application areas. The main purposes of this study were to clarify the common characteristics encountered in the scientific and engineering computations, and to obtain useful feedbacks to the architecture and the compiler design. The detailed results of this study have been published [1]. We just summarize here the conclusions which we have obtained from this study.

Although high speed components, high degree of parallelism and/or pipelining and large-sized main memory are the basic requirements to stretch the computational capabilities of a supercomputer, the following advanced features in architecture are also important for such a machine to be versatile enough for wide range of applications;

(1) Efficient processing of DO loops which contain IF statements,
(2) Powerful vector editing capabilities,
(3) Efficient utilization of the vector registers,
(4) Highly concurrent vector-vector and scalar-vector operations.

These advanced features greatly increase the so-called "vectorization ratio" for practical application programs. Subsequent sections will describe how we have developed FACOM Vector Processor System along the line of this approach; especially how we have incorporated technology, architecture and software (i.e., Fujitsu's vectorizing compiler FORTRAN77/VP) in implementing the above features.

3. Technology

We have fully utilized Fujitsu's latest technologies in the
FACOM Vector Processor. The gate-array logic LSI's contain 400 gates
per chip, and some special functional LSI's such as the register files
contain 1,300 gates. Signal propagation delay per gate of the LSI's
is 350 pico seconds for both types. The high-speed memory LSI's
containing 4K bits per module with an access time of 5.5 nanoseconds
are used where extreme high speed is necessary. Up to 121 LSI's can
be mounted on a 29cm by 31 cm 14-layered printed circuit board called
MCC (Multi Chip Carrier). Logic LSI's and memory LSI's can be mixed
on the same MCC. 13 such MCC's are mounted horizontally in a $(50 \text{ cm})^3$
cube, called stack. We have employed the forced air cooling technique
throughout the system. These technologies have all been well-proven
with Fujitsu's FACOM M-380 mainframes. It is with these technologies
that we could realize a 7.5 nanosecond clock for the vector unit and
15 nanosecond clock for the scalar unit.

As for the main storage, we have employed 64K bit MOS Static RAM
LSI's with 55 nanosecond chip access time. The main storage unit for
VP-200 can accommodate as large as 256M bytes with such high density
devices.

4. Architecture

This section describes the structure and basic functions of the
Vector Processor System. Advanced features will be separately
described in sections 5. The FACOM Vector Processor System consists
of the scalar unit, the vector unit and the main storage unit (Fig.1).

4.1. Scalar Unit

The scalar unit fetches and decodes all the instructions.
There are 277 instructions, of which 195 are scalar type and 82 are

vector type. When an instruction is scalar type, it is executed in the scalar unit, otherwise issued to the vector unit. The scalar unit is equipped with 16 general purpose registers, 8 floating point registers, and 64k bytes of cache memory.

4.2. Vector Unit

The vector unit mainly consists of six functional pipeline units, Vector Registers and Mask Registers. The functional pipeline units are: Add/Logical Pipe, Multiply Pipe, Divide Pipe, Mask Pipe and two Load/Store Pipes. The first three pipes are for arithmetic operations, any two of which can operate concurrently. All the floating-point arithmetic operations are performed in full-precision (64 bits). The operands and the results for all the vector arithmetic operations are assumed to be in the 256 Vector Registers. Two Load/Store Pipes take care of data transfer between the main storage and the Vector Registers; they are both bidirectional.

For VP-200, the throughputs of Add/Logical Pipe and Multiply Pipe are 267 MFLOPS each, whereas that of the Divide pipe is 38 MFLOPS. Hence 533 MFLOPS maximum throughput, when the Add/Logical and the Multiply pipes are linked together. Each of the two Load/Store Pipes has the data bandwidth of 32 bytes/15 nanoseconds, or equivalently, 267 M words/second in either direction. This rate matches the the maximum throughputs of the arithmetic pipelines. The total capacity of the Vector Registers is 64K Bytes, with the basic hardware vector length of 32 full-precision words. Vector Registers of this capacity can greatly reduce the data traffic to and from the main storage unit. As for VP-100, the throughputs of the pipeline units and the total size of Vector Registers are half of the figures given above.

In order to control conditional vector operations and vector editing functions, bit strings (called mask vectors) are also provided. 256 Mask Registers (16-bits each for VP-100 and 32 bits each for VP-200) store mask vectors, and Mask Pipe performs logical operations associated with the mask vectors. More about these will be described in section 5.

4.3. Main Storage Unit

As described earlier, the maximum capacity of the main storage is 256 M Bytes for VP-200, with 256-way interleave, or 128 M Bytes for VP-100, with 128-way interleave, respectively. Possible modes of vector accesses are contiguous, constant-strided and indirect addressing using list vectors.

5. Advanced Features in architecture

This section describes how the advanced features, as listed in section 2, have been implemented in the FACOM Vector Processor System from architectural point of view.

5.1. Conditional Vector Operations

The results of the application program study indicates that the conditional statements are frequently encountered within DO loops. The upwind differencing is a typical example. The FACOM Vector Processor System provides three different methods to efficiently execute vector operations involving certain conditional branches: masked arithmetic operations, compress/expand functions and vector indirect addressing.

In the case of the masked arithmetic operations, Add/Logical Pipe generates mask vectors which indicate the TRUE/FALSE values of conditional statements, and the arithmetic pipeline units take such mask vectors via Mask Registers as the control inputs. The arithmetic pipeline units store the results back to Vector Registers only for the vector elements having "1"'s in the corresponding locations of the mask vector: old values are retained, otherwise (Fig. 2a). Note that for a given vector length, the execution time of a masked arithmetic operation is constant regardless of the ratio of TRUE values to the vector length (called "true ratio").

63

Two other methods utilize the vector editing functions, which we will describe in the following subsection. In short, those vector elements which meet the given condition are brought into new vectors prior to vector arithmetic operations. In contrast to the masked operation, the execution time of a conditional arithmetic operations with these two methods depends on the true ratio.

5.2. Vector Editing Functions

The FACOM Vector Processor System provides two kinds of editing functions: compress/expand operations and vector indirect addressing. These functions can be used not only for the conditional vector operations, but for sparse matrix computations and other data editing applications.

Vectors on Vector Registers can be edited by compress and expand functions using Load/Store Pipes as data alignment circuits; no access to the main storage is involved in these cases. Compressing a vector A under a mask M means that the elements of A marked with "1"'s in the corresponding locations of the mask vector M are copied into another vector B, where these elements are stored in contiguous locations with their order preserved (Fig. 2b). Expanding a vector means the opposite operation.

In the vector indirect addressing, on the other hand, a list vector J on Vector Registers holds the indices for the elements of another vector A stored in the main memory, which is to be loaded into vector B defined on Vector Registers. Namely, $B(I)=A(J(I))$ (Fig. 3c). This is a very versatile and powerful operation, since the order of the elements can be scrambled in any manner. The data transfer rate for vector indirect addressing, however, is lower than that for the contiguous vectors, due to possible bank and/or bus conflicts.

5.3. Dynamically Reconfigurable Vector Registers

One of the most unique features of the FACOM Vector Processor System is the dynamically reconfigurable Vector Registers. The results of our study indicate that the requirements for the length and

the number of vector registers vary from one programs to another, or
even within a program. To make the best utilization of the total
capacity of 64K bytes for VP-200, for example, the Vector Registers
may be concatenated to take the following configurations:
32(length)x256(total number), 64x128, 128x64,......,1,024x8. The
length of Vector Registers for the currently executed vector
instruction is specified by a special register, and it can be altered
by an instruction in the program.

5.4. High Level Concurrency

The FACOM Vector Processor System allows concurrent operations
at various levels (Fig. 3). In the vector unit, five functional pipeline units can operate concurrently: two out of three arithmetic
pipes, two Load/Store Pipes and Mask Pipe. Furthermore, vector
operands associated with consecutive instructions can flow
continuously through each of the arithmetic pipes. This implies that
the start-up time for vector operations can be effectively masked out.

The vector unit and the scalar unit can also operate concurrently.
Without such feature, the scalar operations between the vector operations could cause considerable performance degradation. Serialization
instructions are provided to preserve the data dependency relations
among instructions.

6. <u>Vectorizing Compiler--- FORTRAN77/VP</u>

A vectorizing compiler, FORTRAN77/VP, has been developed for the
FACOM Vec. Processor System. FORTRAN77 has been chosen as the
language for this machine, so that the large software assets can
become readily available. In order to obtain high vectorization ratio
for wide range of application programs, FORTRAN77/VP compiler
vectorizes not only the simple DO loops but nested DO loops and the
macro operations such as the inner product efficiently. It also
detects and separates the recurrences. These general techniques have

been reported in Ref. [1]. We will discuss, in the following four subsections, the techniques which are related to the advanced features in sections 2 and 5. We will also discuss other unique features of FORTRAN77/VP in the final subsection.

6.1. Vectorization of IF Statements

The results of our study indicate that the true ratio of conditional statements widely varies from one case to another. In fact, the true ratio and the relative frequency of load/store instruction executions over the total instruction executions within a DO loop are the two key parameters in selecting the best among the three methods described in 5.1. If the true ratio is medium to high, the masked arithmetic operation is the best; otherwise, the compress/expand method is the best when the frequency of load/store operations is low, and the indirect addressing the best when such frequency is high. The FORTRAN77/VP compiler analyzes each DO loop, compares the estimated execution times for all three methods and selects the one which yields the shortest time.

6.2. Vector Editing Functions

When vector compress/expand functions are used for conditional vector operations, two steps are usually involved: mask vector generation, and actual operations. Frequently used mask patterns may be stored in Mask Registers to skip the first step. When the indirect addressing is used for the same purpose, on the other hand, three steps are involved: mask vector generation, index list vector generation from the mask vector, and actual data transfer between the Vector Register and the main storage. In this case, index vectors rather than the mask vectors may be stored for frequently used access patterns.

6.3. Optimal Register Assignments

In order to best utilize the dynamically reconfigurable Vector Registers, the compiler must know the frequently used hardware vector length for each program, or even within one program the vector length

may have to be adjusted. When the vector length is too short, load/
store instructions will have to be issued more frequently, whereas if
it is unnecessarily long, the number of available vectors will decrease
and resulting in frequent load/store operations again. In general, the
compiler puts a higher priority on the number of vectors rather than
the length in determining the register configuration.

6.4. Pipeline Parallelization

The compiler performs the extensive dataflow analysis of the
FORTRAN source programs and schedules the instruction stream, so that
the vector arithmetic pipeline units are kept as busy as possible.
This process includes the reordering of instruction sequence, balanced
assignments of two Load/Store Pipes, and insertion of serialization
instructions wherever necessary.

6.5. Other Features of Software

Ease of use is another key objective of the compiler. FORTRAN77
/VP provides debugging aids, a performance analyzer, an interactive
vectorizer, and a vectorized version of the scientific subroutine
library (called SSL II/VP). One of the unique features is the interactive vectorizer. This software is a tuning tool for improving the
vectorization ratio of user programs via TSS terminals. Fig. 4 shows
an example of a page on CRT screen. Programmers can provide the
compiler such useful information as the estimated true ratios of the
conditional statements, the estimated hardware vector lengths through
the interactive vectorizer.

7. Performance Measurements

Some results of the benchmarking of FACOM vector Processor
System are summarized in Table 1 and in Table 2. Table 1 shows the
scalar and vector performances (in MFLOPS) of VP-100 and VP-200 for
the 14 Livermore kernels. It should be noted that none of the

original loops have been modified for this measurement. Table 2 compares the scalar and vector execution times (in Seconds) of some application programs which have been developed by Fujitsu. The first three are either taken from subroutine packages or part of programs, and two others are complete programs. They are all written in FORTRAN. Some other results of benchmarking of FACOM Vector Processor System have also been reported in Ref. [2].

8. Conclusions

In this paper we have outlined technologies, architecture and software of the FACOM Vector Processor System, VP-100/VP-200. We have pointed out the advanced features, which will significantly improve the average performance for the practical application programs, and also described how such features have been implemented in hardware and software. We have also shown some results of benchmarking of VP-100 and VP-200, which are very promising. We are now conducting researches on various kinds of vector algorithms tailored for the FACOM VP100/200 architecture, which can provide nearly maximal performances for specific applications. Some such examples are Linear Equation Solver and FFT.

The first FACOM Vector Processor System (VP-100) was installed at the Institute of Plasma Physics at Nagoya University, in December, 1983. We expect several more shipments in 1984.

Acknowledgements

The authors wish to express their thanks to Messrs. Y.Tanakura and S. Kamiya of Software Division, Mr. M. Shinohara of the Mainframe Division, and Dr. T.Matsuura of Systems Engineering Division for valuable discussions and comments.

References

1) S. Kamiya et. al. :Practical Vectorization Techniques for The "FACOM VP", Information Processing 83, R.E.A. Mason(ed.), pp.389-394, Elsevier Science Publishers B.V., 1983.

2) R.Mendez: SIAM News, Vol.17, No. 2 (March 1984)

Table 1.   PERFORMANCE MEASUREMENTS OF VP-100/VP-200
(14 Livermore Kernels)

Loop No.	Scalar	Vector VP-100	VP-200	Loop No.	Scalar	Vector VP-100	VP-200
1	10.1	187.1	331.4	8	13.3	86.1	90.4
2	11.1	104.7	180.4	9	12.7	160.8	260.8
3	7.8	174.7	338.2	10	7.8	50.0	85.9
4	5.7	73.9	88.1	11	4.8	4.8	4.8
5	10.0	10.0	10.0	12	4.8	59.1	115.3
6	9.5	9.5	9.5	13	2.5	6.0	6.2
7	14.0	189.2	331.0	14	5.8	12.9	13.8
Arithmetic Average					8.6	80.6	133.3

(Units: MFLOPS)

Table 2. PERFORMANCE MEASUREMENTS OF SOME APPLICATION PROGRAMS ON VP-200

Program No.	Description of Programs	Computation Time		Performance Ratio
		Scalar (Sec.)	Vector (Sec.)	
1	Matrix Multiplication (Order: 100)	307.66	4.08	75.4
2	Linear Equation Solver (Order: 100) (Order: 256)	.141 2.27	.01 .056	14.1 40.6
3	Self-sorting Type FFT (4096 points, radix 2)	---	.000973	(227 MFLOPS)
4	Molecular Dynamics (High Density Liquid)	144.22	9.97	14.5
5	Simplified Marker and Cell (Poiseuille Flow)	137.0	15.8	8.7

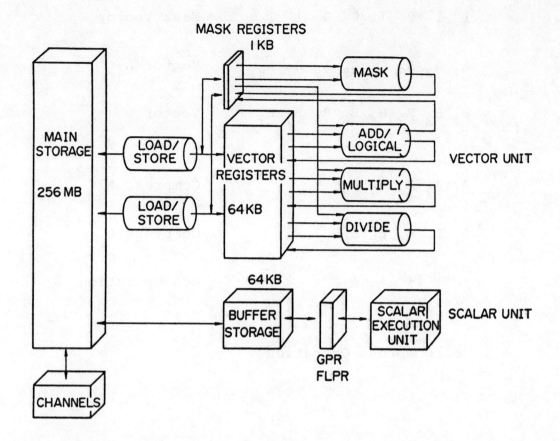

Figure 1.   FACOM Vector Processor Block Diagram

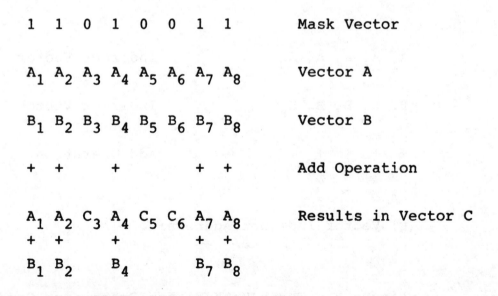

(a) Masked Operation

Figure 2.   Three Methods for Conditional Vector
Operations

```
1  1  0  1  0  0  1  1          Mask Vector

A₁ A₂ A₃ A₄ A₅ A₆ A₇ A₈         Vector A

B₁ B₂ B₃ B₄ B₅ B₆ B₇ B₈         Vector B


A₁ A₂ A₄ A₇ A₈                  Compress A

B₁ B₂ B₄ B₇ B₈                  Compress B

+  +  +  +  +                   Add Operation
```

(b) Compress Operation

```
1  1  0  1  0  0  1  1          Mask Vector


1  2  4  7  8                   List Vector J Generation


A₁ A₂ A₄ A₇ A₈                  Indirect Vector Load A

B₁ B₂ B₄ B₇ B₈                  Indirect Vector Load B

+  +  +  +  +                   Add Operation
```

(c) Vector Indirect Addressing

Figure 2. Three Methods for Processing Conditional
           Vector Operations (Continued)

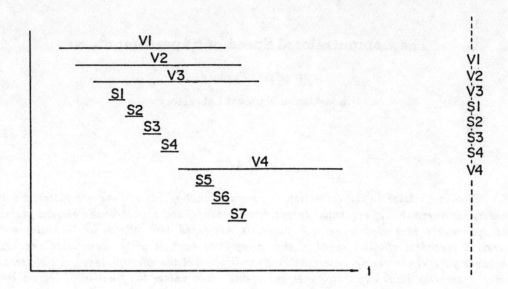

Figure 3. Concurrent Processing of Scalar and
Vector Instructions

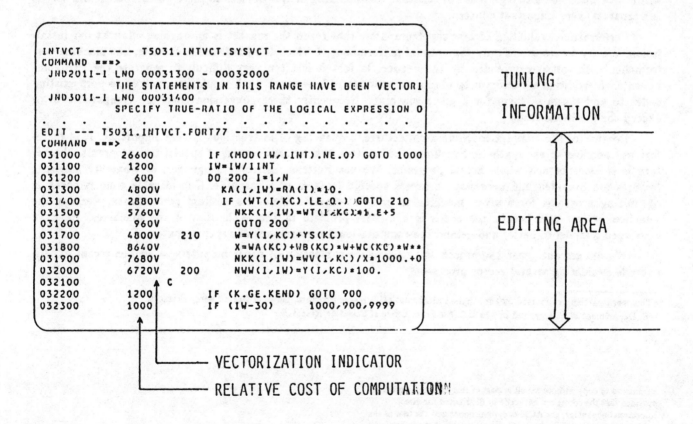

Figure 4.   Interactive Vectorizer

The Computational Speed of Supercomputers

Ingrid Y. Bucher*

Los Alamos National Laboratory

ABSTRACT

Problems related to the evaluation of computational speeds of supercomputers are discussed. Measurements of sequential speeds, vector speeds, and asynchronous parallel processing speeds are presented. A simple model is developed that allows us to evaluate the workload-dependent effective speed of current systems such as vector computers and asynchronous parallel processing systems. Results indicate that the effective speed of a supercomputer is severely limited by its slowest processing mode unless the fraction of the workload that has to be processed in this mode is negligibly small.

1. Introduction

The performance evaluation of supercomputers, i.e., number-crunching mainframes capable of performing millions of floating-point operations per second, is a complex task. This is due to today's complex architecture of these machines, all of which are capable of executing multiple tasks or instructions in parallel. We restrict our discussion to measuring computational speeds of single tasks that consume practically all resources of the machine, a mode of operation that is very important for large scientific computations. I/O performance will not be discussed although it is obvious that the matching of I/O devices to the high computational speeds is a separate, very important concern.

Performance evaluation of new supercomputers that reach the market is an ongoing effort at our installation. We try to assess not only the optimal performance of which the hardware is capable, but machine performance with software provided by the vendor. In fact it is often very difficult to separate the two components. In addition we attempt to obtain an estimate of how much work would be involved to port existing codes to and optimize them for a given machine. Frequently these conversion costs are comparable to or exceed the hardware costs.

Because of the complex machine architectures, sequencing of instructions is very important. It is therefore not possible to use synthetic benchmark codes. Our benchmarks consist of special test programs, characteristic sections of and whole actual programs. We use Fortran, assembly languages, or whatever language features are provided and necessary to access specific features of a machine. Considerable time is spent in optimizing programs for a given machine to gain information about its optimal performance. Because the selection of test and benchmark codes is a critical problem in the evaluation of the machines, we have developed a model to better understand the computational performance of supercomputers.

We discuss our general approach to performance evaluation of supercomputers as well as recent experiences in evaluating several vector processors.

*This work partially supported by the Applied Mathematical Sciences Program, Office of Basic Energy Sciences, U.S. Department of Energy, and by the U.S. Air Force Office of Scientific Research.

"The Computational Speed of Supercomputers" by I.Y. Bucher from *The Proceedings of ACM Sigmetrics Conference on Measurement and Modeling of Computer Systems*, August 1983, pages 151-165. Copyright 1983 by The Association for Computing Machinery, Inc., Reprinted by permission.

2. Architecture, Parallelism, and Amdahl's Law.

Today's supercomputers come in a variety of architectures. Using Flynn's taxonomy [1], we distinguish

(a) *Single Instruction-Multiple Data Stream Machines* (SIMD). These machines consist either of an array of processors operating in lock-step like the Illiac IV and the BSP previously produced by Burroughs, or are pipelined vector processors like the CRI Cray-1S, the CDC Cyber-205, the Fujitsu VP, the Hitachi S-810 and S-820, and the NEC ACOS 1000. They are capable of performing identical operations on arrays of data at very high speed. We will call this mode of processing *synchronous parallel processing*.

(b) *Multiple Instruction-Multiple Data Stream Machines* (MIMD) consisting of several processors each processing its own instruction stream. We call this mode of operation *asynchronous parallel processing*. An example of this type of machine is the Denelcor HEP-1.

(c) *Multiple Vector Processors*. Examples are the Cray X-MP with two vector processors connected to a common fast memory and the not yet announced Cray-2. These machines will be capable of both synchronous and asynchronous parallel processing.

It is reasonable to assume that the next generation of supercomputers will be characterized by several speeds, three of which seem of particular importance:

(1) *The sequential speed* S_{seq}, characterizing the rate at which a machine can process code that has to be processed in sequential mode, either for reasons of logic or because it is too costly to vectorize or parallelize it.

(2) *The synchronous parallel speed* S_{syn}, characterizing the rate at which a machine can process code that lends itself to vectorization or synchronous parallel processing with small granularity. This speed is dependent on the vector length and on other characteristics of the workload.

(3) *The asynchronous parallel speed* S_{asyn}, characterizing the rate at which the machine can process code that is unsuitable to vectorization or synchronous parallel processing but can be parallel processed asynchronously in large chunks, as for example Monte Carlo and Particle-In-Cell (PIC) simulations. The asynchronous parallel speed will depend on the number of processors available, the percentage of the tasks that can be parallelized, the amount of communication including overhead, the number of synchronization steps, and the choice of algorithm. It might be considerably lower than its upper limit, the product of sequential speed and the number of processors.

Let

F_{seq} be the fraction of the workload that can be processed in sequential mode only,

F_{syn} be the fraction that can be either vectorized or processed by synchronous parallelism, and

F_{asyn} the fraction that can be parallelized asynchronously;

then the time required to run this workload is proportional to

$$T = \frac{F_{seq}}{S_{seq}} + \frac{F_{syn}}{S_{syn}} + \frac{F_{asyn}}{S_{asyn}} \equiv \frac{1}{S_{eff}} \tag{1}$$

where S_{eff} is the workload-dependent, effective speed of the machine. Equation (1) is an extension of a relation known as Amdahl's Law [2, 3]. It implies that the slowest of the execution speeds will critically influence the effective speed unless the weight factor F associated with it is negligibly small.

The weight factors F_{seq}, F_{syn}, and F_{asyn} in Eq. (1) have to be determined empirically from the workload and adjusted by projections of how the workload will evolve in the future. It is important to note that the choice of machine might influence future characteristics of the workload, for example, a machine with high asynchronous speed might encourage more Monte Carlo simulations. Work on the characterization of our workload is being reported elsewhere [4].

The choice of metric for Eq. (1) is important, and so far no really satisfactory solution has been found for supercomputers. It is desirable to use a measure that characterizes the amount of computational work and is independent of machine architecture and compiler optimization. The number of instructions issued is a completely misleading figure for powerful vector machines because a lot of work can be accomplished in a single vector instruction, up to 130 000 floating-point operations on the Cyber-205. MIPS (millions of instructions per second) for highly optimized vector code are lower on the Cray-1S in vector mode than in scalar mode; the opposite is of course true of execution speeds. The generally accepted metric is number of floating-point operations for the amount of computational work and millions of floating-point operations per second (MFLOPS) for the execution speeds. This metric is excellent for machines with slow floating-point arithmetic but not for supercomputers that often execute floating-point operations faster than other instructions. We use MFLOPS as our metric; however, it should be kept in mind that much useful work done by number-crunching machines is not included in this measure. Logical operations, integer arithmetic, jumps, and table look-ups are examples that are usually difficult to separate from computational overhead that is dependent on machine and compiler construction. Due to the highly parallel architecture of each processing unit, these operations may often be performed in parallel with the floating-point work.

The measurement of sequential speeds S_{seq}, vector speeds S_{syn}, and asynchronous speeds S_{asyn} for vector computers and parallel processors has been the topic of several of our studies [5,6,7]. The following sections outline our basic approach.

3. Measurement of Synchronous Parallel Speed (Vector Speed)

Today's commercially successful computers with synchronous parallel processing capabilities are vector computers. Their vector processing units are capable of performing operations on arrays at very high speed in a pipelined fashion.

The time required to perform operations on vectors of length N is a linear function of N given by

$$T = T_{start} + N*T_{el} \ , \tag{2}$$

where T_{start} is the startup time for the vector operation and T_{el} is the time per result element. We prefer the above form of the relation to the equivalent one used by Hockney and Jesshope [8]:

$$T = (N_{half} + N)*T_{el} \ , \tag{3}$$

where

$$N_{half} = \frac{T_{start}}{T_{el}}$$

is the vector length for which the operation reaches half of its asymptotic speed for long vectors. Obviously, low values for T_{start}, T_{el}, and N_{half} are desirable design goals for high-performance processors. However, in comparing two machines, N_{half} can be misleading. The Cray X-MP, for example, has shorter startup and element times for its vector operations than the Cray-1S and therefore clearly has the superior vector processor However, the vector length N_{half} at which it reaches half of its maximum processing speed is considerably higher than that of the Cray-1S.

The vector execution speeds are given by

$$S_{syn} = \frac{N}{T} = \frac{1}{T_{el} + T_{start}/N} \ . \tag{4}$$

Two basic types of vector architectures can be distinguished based on their mode of memory access. We discuss in detail our measurements on one machine of each type, the Cyber-205 and the Cray-1S.

The Cyber-205 and the Cray-1S have many features in common. Both contain a scalar processor subdivided into several functional units capable of performing a variety of operations in parallel with each other and with the vector pipes. Both machines contain pipelined vector arithmetic processors. The Cray vector processor is subdivided into multiple units permitting multiple results each cycle. The Cyber-205 can have one, two, or four vector pipelines, each capable of producing one result each cycle. The cycle times are 12.5 ns for the Cray-1S and 20 ns for the Cyber-205. Most measurements on the Cyber-205 were performed on 2-pipe machines.

Although the Cyber-205 vector instructions reference memory directly, the Cray-1S has 8 vector registers, each 64 words long, usually making it unnecessary to store intermediate results in memory. Ease of access to the vector registers combined with concurrent execution of vector operations accounts for the high speed of the Cray-1S when each operand does not have to be fetched from memory or each result stored. The Cray processes long vectors in sections of length 64, the Cyber-205 in sections of up to 65,536. If the Cyber-205 is to achieve peak result rates, the vectors must be contiguous in memory. For the Cray-1S, vectors must have a constant stride (distance between memory locations), but the stride need not be 1. Thus, on the Cray in contrast to the Cyber-205, columns and rows of a matrix can be accessed with equal efficiency. For many repetitive computations, however, data are not stored in memory in a regular pattern; for example, they may be extracted from or stored into tables or may be associated with operations on irregular domains. For both machines, operands stored at irregular locations in memory must be gathered, and the results may have to be scattered back into memory. These processes slow down operations on both machines. The Cyber-205 has vector instructions to gather operands from memory locations specified by an index vector into a temporary vector array and to scatter results from a temporary array into memory locations specified by an index vector [9]. The Cray-1S performs gathers and scatters in scalar mode only. Gather and, in particular, scatter operations have to be treated with great caution in a parallel environment. Frequently, their parallel execution may lead to incorrect results as in tally updates for Monte Carlo and PIC simulations.

A simple set of programs was written to measure the speed of 64-bit floating-point operations as a function of vector length. Typically, one million operations were timed, irrespective of vector length.

3.1. Vector Operations for Vectors Stored in Contiguous Locations

Vector execution rates for the Cyber-205 and the Cray-1S are presented in Table I.

For the Cyber-205, the average time T required to perform a vector operation on a vector of length N $< 65,537$ is given by Eq. (2). For the vector add, T is plotted as a function of the vector length N in Fig. 1 along with results obtained for the Cray-1S. The linear relationship of Eq. (2) is evident. Table II presents values for T_{start} and T_{el} derived from the measured data for the Cyber-205 vector unit with two pipes. For more complex operations than those listed in Table II, startup and element times are the sums of startup and element times of the elementary operations involved.

Table I. Cyber-205 and Cray-1 Vector Operations - Rates for Vectors Stored in Consecutive Locations (in MFLOPS)

Operation	Cyber-205 Vector Length				Cray-1 Vector Length			
	10	100	100	10000	10	100	1000	10000
V=V+ S	9	50	91	99	7	25	33	34
V=S*V	9	50	92	99	7	25	33	34
V=V+ V	9	50	91	99	6	19	23	23
V=V*V	9	50	92	99	6	19	23	23
V=V+ S*V	12	78	173	197	12	31	36	36
V=V*V+ S	12	78	173	197	12	36	44	45
V=V*V+ V	9	50	91	99	11	25	29	29
V=S*V+ S*V	10	64	133	148	17	54	66	67
V=V*V+ V*V	9	51	91	99	15	37	42	42

$V = vector$
$S = scalar$

Table II. Time Required to Perform a Vector Operation on the Cyber-205

Operation	Number of Floating-Point Operations per Result	T_{start} (in ns)	T_{el} (in ns)
add v:=v+s or v:=v+v	1	1020	10
mult v:=v*s or v:=v*V	1	980	10
triad v:=v+s*v or v:=s+v*v	2	1580	10

For the Cray-1S, the average time T to process a vector of length N is a more complicated relationship than Eq. (2) because vectors of length N > 64 are stripmined in sections of length 64. This is evident from Fig. 1 by the steep rise in processing time T each time the vector length exceeds an integer multiple of 64 For N equal to multiples of 64, T is a linear function of N and can be represented by

$$T_{cray} = T_{startout} + N*(T_{startstrip}/64 + T_{el})\qquad(5)$$

where $T_{startout}$ is the startup time for the outer loop, $T_{startstrip}$ is the startup time, which could not be over-lapped with the vector operations, for each strip of length 64, and T_{el} is the time required to process one result element. These startup times are often associated with more than one floating-point operation per result element. In Table III, values for $T_{startout}$, $T_{startstrip}$, and T_{el} are listed for the Cray-1S and the CFT compiler version 1.09. For the operations programmed requiring one memory reference per vector operand, T_{el} was determined by the speed with which the Cray-1S can access its memory; namely, in the absence of bank conflicts, one load or store operation per 12.5-ns clock cycle. There are two exceptions for which the compiler generated less than optimal code. $T_{startout}$ and $T_{startstrip}$ are compiler dependent. The minimum values of $T_{startstrip}$ are given by the startup times of vector memory reference and arithmetic operations and are close to

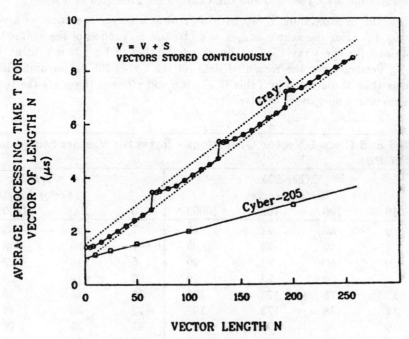

Fig. 1. Average processing time for vector of length N as a function of vector length N. Vectors are stored contiguously.

the values measured. However, inspection of the compiler-generated assembly code indicates that the value of $T_{startout}$, the startup time of the outer loop, could have been reduced by better compiler optimization. For DO loops containing more than one Fortran statement, the outer loop overhead remains the same, thus reducing the overhead per floating-point operation. It might appear from above results that the speed of the Cray-1S is severely limited by its ability to access memory. Actually in real codes the average number of memory accesses is considerably lower than in the operations timed above, even for compiler-generated code [10].

Table III. Cray-1, CFT Compiler Version 1.09 Time Parameters for Vector Operations[a] (in nanoseconds)

Operation	Number of Floating-Point Operations per Result	$T_{startout}$	$T_{startstrip}$	T_{el}
V=V+S	1	900	275	25.0
V=S*V	1	900	288	25.0
V=V+V	1	900	326	37.5
V=V*V	1	900	339	37.5
V=V+S*V	2	900	326	50.0 (min 37.5)
V=V*V+S	2	900	442	37.5
V=V*V+V	2	900	378	62.5 (min 50.0)
V=S*V+S*V	3	900	442	37.5
V=V*V+V*V	3	900	531	62.5

[a]See Eq. (5).

3.2. Vector Operations for Vectors Stored with Constant Stride

Arithmetic on vectors stored not in consecutive memory locations but with a constant stride is more complicated for the Cyber-205 [9] than for the Cray-1S. Basically, there are two options:

(i) Perform the arithmetic on the entire vector; that is, all numbers fetched from contiguous locations; then store selected results under the control of a bit vector. This option is optimal for small strides. For optimal speed, this process has to be coded with special language features, which is cumbersome. For this option, speeds were measured that are consistent with those obtained by dividing the results of Table I by the stride.

(ii) Do periodic gathers followed by the arithmetic operation and a subsequent periodic scatter. Both periodic gather and scatter are vector operations on the Cyber-205. This option yields the fastest results for large strides.

Execution rates measured for the Cyber-205 with periodic gather-scatters and for the Cray-1S are presented in Table IV. The corresponding results for the average time T required to process vectors of length N are plotted for the addition of a scalar to a vector in Fig. 2. Equations (2) and (5) hold for both machines. For the Cyber-205 the additional required vector operations required the following times:

each periodic gather: $T_{start} = 750$ ns, $T_{el} = 25$ ns;

each periodic scatter: $T_{start} = 1300$ ns, $T_{el} = 24$ ns.

Due to poor compiler optimization, startup times for the outer loop are somewhat higher than those for contiguous operations on the Cray-1S.

Table IV. Cyber-205 and Cray-1 Vector Operations - Rates for Vectors Stored with a Constant Stride[a] (in MFLOPS)

	Cyber-205 Vector Length			Cray-1 Vector Length		
Operation	10	100	1000	10	100	1000
V=V+ S	3	10	13	6	23	33
V=S*V	3	10	13	5	23	32
V=V+ V	2	8	10	5	18	23
V=V*V	2	8	10	5	17	23
V=V+ S*V	4	15	19	9	29	25
V=V*V+ S	4	15	19	9	34	44
V=V*V+ V	3	11	13	9	24	29
V=S*V+ S*V	5	19	26	14	51	65
V=V*V+ V*V	3	12	16	12	35	41

[a]$Stride = 49$

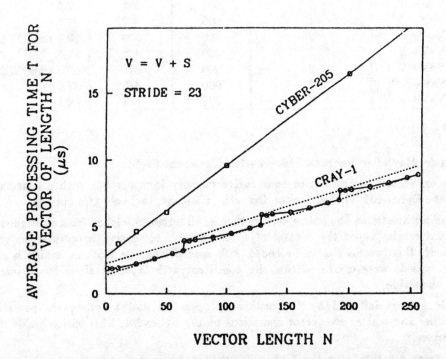

Fig. 2. Average processing time for vector of length N as a function of vector length N. Vectors are stored noncontiguously with constant stride.

3.3. Operations Involving Random Gathers and Scatters.

This section discusses speeds of arithmetic operations for which operands or results or both are stored at irregular locations in memory. For our tests these locations were specified by an index to arrays of the form

$$INDEX = J(I) + K \quad ,$$

where J is an integer array properly initialized (e.g., by a random number generator), I is the loop count, and K is an arbitrary integer constant.

Although the Cyber-205 has vector instructions for random gather and scatter operations, its compiler has so far not been able to generate efficient code for these instructions. Results of a program coded with special language features and CDC vector syntax along with results obtained for the Cray-1S with functions that were optimized in Cray Assembly Language (CAL) are presented in Table V.

Random gathers and scatters, which proceed in vector mode on the Cyber-205, are characterized by the following times:

random gather: $T_{start} = 1300$ ns, $T_{el} = 32$ ns;

random scatter: $T_{start} = 1100$ ns, $T_{el} = 31$ ns;

Random gathers and scatters on the Cray-1S proceed at much lower speed because, contrary to the Cyber-205, these operations are performed in the scalar unit.

It has to be pointed out that for some important applications vector instructions cannot be used for gather and scatter operations because they would lead to incorrect results. Rates for scalar random gathers and scatters on the Cyber-205 are lower than those for the Cray-1S.

Table V. Cyber-205 and Cray-1 Vector Operations Involving Random Gathers and Scatters (in MFLOPS)

Operation	Cyber-205 Vector Length				Cray-1 Vector Length			
	10	100	1000	100000	10	100	1000	100000
V=V(IND)+ S	3	12	18	19	2	6	6	7
V(IND)=V*V	3	13	19	20	2	3	3	3
V(IND)=V(IND)+ V*V	3	13	20	20	3	4	4	4
V=V+ V*V(IND)	4	17	28	30	5	10	11	11

$V = vector$
$S = scalar$
$IND = index vector of random integers$

3.4. Effective Vector Speed S_{syn}

Our measurements indicate that we have to distinguish three vector speeds at which today's vector computers process vectorizable code:

S_{syn1}, the vector speed for operands and results stored in contiguous memory locations,
S_{syn2}, the vector speed for operands and results stored noncontiguously but with constant stride,
S_{syn3}, the speed for operands and results stored in memory in a random fashion.

All three speeds depend on the vector length.

The effective synchronous processing speed is workload dependent and can be computed from a relation similar to that of Eq. (1):

$$\frac{1}{S_{syn}} = \frac{F_1}{S_{syn1}} + \frac{F_2}{S_{syn2}} + \frac{F_3}{S_{syn3}} . \tag{6}$$

where F_1, F_2, and F_3 are the fractions of the vectorizable workload corresponding to the speeds described above.

Data for the average vector length and the fractions of vector loads and stores involving contiguous memory locations and noncontiguous memory locations with constant stride can be obtained by dynamic counts on running codes [10]. It is difficult to measure the fraction of random gather and scatter operations on the Cray, and because the Cyber-205 compiler still does not recognize random scatter-gathers, it is futile to attempt measurements on code produced by it. Estimates by code developers indicate the amount of vectorizable code fetched from and stored into random locations is several percent. We will assume it is 2%.

For the Cray, the number of loads and stores per floating-point operation greatly influences its vector speed. Preliminary measurements indicate that 0.6 to 1.0 loads and 0.2 to 0.5 stores were observed per floating-point operation for vector codes that we consider typical. It will therefore be assumed that the Fortran statement

$$V1(I) = S1*V2(I) + S2*V3(I)$$

produces typical code and, further, that two such statements are contained in a typical DO loop, reducing the startup time for the outer loop per floating-point operation by a factor of 2 for the Cray.

Table VI contains values for vector speeds of vector computers currently available on the U.S. market for a workload similar to that running at our Laboratory; Table VII for a more ideal workload. It is interesting to note how much effective speeds are degraded by only small admixtures of slow components.

Table VI. Characteristic Vector Speeds for Several Vector Processors[a]
Vector Length = 100 (in MFLOPS)

Machine	S_{syn1} Vector Speed for Contiguous Vectors	S_{syn2} Vector Speed for Constant Stride	S_{syn3} Vector Speed for Random Memory Access	S_{syn} Effective Vector Speed
Cyber-205 (two vector pipes)	64	19	12	41
Cray-1S	58	56	5	46
Cray-1M	55	53	4	44
Cray X-MP (one of two processors)	107	101	6	79

[a] *The workload is characterized by the following parameters:*

Fraction of vector operations involving contiguous vectors	*78%*
Fraction of vector operations involving constant strides	*20%*
Fraction of vector operations involving random memory access	*2%*

Table VII. Characteristic Vector Speeds for Several Vector Processors[a]
Vector Length = 500 (in MFLOPS)

Machine	S_{syn1} Vector Speed for Contiguous Vectors	S_{syn2} Vector Speed for Constant Stride	S_{syn3} Vector Speed for Random Memory Access	S_{syn} Effective Vector Speed
Cyber-205 (two vector pipes)	119	25	17	76
Cray-1S	66	65	5	66
Cray-1M	63	63	4	63
Cray X-MP (one of two processors)	133	132	6	133

[a]*The workload is characterized by the following parameters:*

Fraction of vector operations involving contiguous vectors	*85%*
Fraction of vector operations involving constant strides	*15%*
Fraction of vector operations involving random memory access	*0%*

4. Measurements of Sequential Speed S_{seq}

To measure the sequential speed of vector processors, it is not sufficient to time repetitive scalar operations. These operations can, with adequate compiler optimization, make use of the parallel and pipelined features of the scalar processors and therefore generally run much faster than truly sequential code that does not lend itself to vectorization. Inspection of execution rates of our benchmark programs indicates that vectorizable codes run faster, even when executed in the scalar unit, than nonvectorizable codes.

We have selected one of our benchmark programs, BMK21A, that performs a radiation transport calculation using Monte Carlo techniques in a nontrivial geometry to measure sequential speed. Its execution speed on the Cray-1S is close to that of nonvectorizing parts of large production codes. Execution speeds of BMK21A for several vector computers are listed in Table VIII. We will assume that these speeds are representative of the sequential processing speeds of these machines.

Table VIII. Sequential Execution Speeds S_{seq} for Vector Computers for BMK21A (GAMTEB)

Machine	S_{seq} IN MFLOPS
Cyber-205	3.3
Cray-1S	4.2
Cray-1M	4.1
Cray X-MP (one of two processors)	5.4

5. Measurement of Asynchronous Parallel Speed S_{asyn}

It appears unlikely that advances in semiconductor technology or even the transition to Josephson junction technology will bring the speedup of two orders of magnitude needed for scientific computing within the next decade. It is therefore safe to assume that the next generation of supercomputers will achieve most of their speedup by more parallelism, probably in the form of several scalar or vector processors operating in parallel asynchronously and connected to a common memory. Communication overhead and Amdahl's law will limit the number of cooperating processors to probably not more than 16.

A small group at our Laboratory addressed two questions in recent studies:

(i)   Can scientific computations be parallelized asynchronously in large chunks?

(ii)   How frequent and time-consuming are necessary communications between parallel processes?

The answer to the first question is positive. We have studied three kinds of tasks that seem fairly representative of the work at our Laboratory: Monte Carlo simulations, a PIC code, and the solution of partial differential equations. We observe that:

*   Physical problems are naturally parallel. Asynchronous parallelization of codes seems to be conceptually simpler than vectorization.

*   Most of the computational work of all three codes could be parallelized at the subroutine level. This is very important. Because we do not expect compilers to recognize this type of parallelism in the near future, changing codes by hand must not be too time consuming.

*   The work could be evenly distributed between any number of processors. This is important for achieving maximum efficiency. Typically, each processor is executing the same code, although not all may choose the same path through it.

The study of the second question brought some valuable insights. We ran the PIC code on an array of eight Floating Point Systems 120B array processors connected to a Univac 1100 as a host. Although communications between processes were infrequent and short, operating system overhead to initiate communications was disastrous [6]. Experiments on a 4-processor Univac 1100/84 [7] and a single processor of the HEP, which is capable of handling up to 8 processes without interference, were more successful.

Let F_{asyn} be the fraction of a code that can be processed in parallel mode on an arbitrary number of P processors, with the remainder F_{seq} of it to be processed sequentially, then execution time T is proportional to

$$\frac{1}{S_{eff}} = \frac{F_{asyn}}{P*S_{seq}} + \frac{F_{seq}}{S_{seq}} + P*T_{comm} \ .$$

The execution time is a linear function of 1/P if and only if the communication overhead T_{comm} is negligible. The execution times for the PIC code on the Univac 1100/84 are plotted in Fig. 3 as a function of the reciprocal of the number of processors. The relation is linear, indicating that communication overhead was negligible and that the code was 90% parallelized. We believe that most of the remaining 10% can be parallelized as well. Runs on the HEP with up to eight processes yield similar results.

The connection of each processor to a common memory is an important architectural feature, especially for Monte Carlo computations and partial differential equations. Efficient synchronization hardware accessible to the user program is another important requirement. With these features our preliminary results indicate that, for a small number of processors, speedup factors nearly equal to the number of processors are achievable.

6. Effective Processing Speed S_{eff}

Using the results of previous sections and Eq. (1), we compiled characteristic speeds of several commercially available supercomputers and some hypothetical machines in Tables IX and X for two workloads with differing characteristics. The machines in quotes are hypothetical machines. Numbers in parentheses are best estimates or postulated numbers for hypothetical computers.

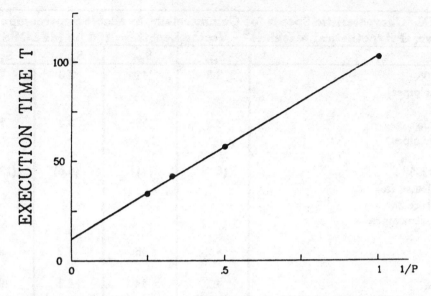

Fig. 3. Execution time T of PIC code on one to four processors of UNIVAC 1100/84 as a function of the reciprocal of the number of working processors P.

Inspection of Tables IX and X indicates that the effective execution rates of present vector computers are considerably lower than the advertised maximum speeds, even for the ideal workload of Table X. Real workloads have characteristics close to the parameters of Table IX. Measurements for our workload on the Cray-1S indicate that the effective speed is approximately 10 MFLOPS, in agreement with the result of Table IX.

Figure 4 is a three-dimensional representation of the effective speed of vector computers as a function of vectorization F_{syn} and the ratio of sequential to vector speeds S_{seq}/S_{syn}. The vector speed S_{syn} is normalized to 1 in the plot. For small values of S_{seq}/S_{syn}, very high degrees of vectorization are required to reach even half of the maximum speed.

7. Conclusions

We can draw the following conclusions.

- The effective speed of modern supercomputers is strongly workload dependent. It is necessary to know the workload well in order to decide which machine will process it most efficiently.

- The slowest characteristic processing speed will affect the effective speed critically unless the fraction of the workload associated with that speed is negligibly small. It acts like a bottleneck. The most effective way to speed up a machine is to increase this speed or to decrease the fraction of work associated with it. Both solutions are often very difficult.

- Speeding up the fastest characteristic speed of a supercomputer will markedly improve its effective speed only if the fraction of the workload running at that speed is close to 1. If this is not the case, installation of additional vector pipes on a vector computer is not useful.

- Performance modeling will not replace benchmark runs. However it will help to select benchmarks more intelligently.

Table IX. Characteristic Speeds for Commercially Available Supercomputers and Several Hypothetical Machines[a] **- Vector Length = 100 (in MFLOPS)**

Machine	S_{seq}	S_{syn}	S_{asyn}	S_{eff}
Cyber-205 (2 vector pipes)	3.3	41	3.3	7.4
Cyber-205 (4 vector pipes)	3.3	58	3.3	7.6
"Cyber-205" with twice as fast scalar processor and 2 vector pipes	(6.6)	(41)	(6.6)	(13.3)
Cray-1S	4.2	46	4.2	9.2
Cray-1M	4.1	44	4.1	9.0
Cray X-MP (1 processor)	5.4	79	5.4	12.2
Cray X-MP (2 processors)	5.4	(158)	(10.8)	(16.8)
"Cray X-MP" (4 processors)	5.4	(316)	(21.6)	(20.7)

[a] *The workload is characterized by the following parameters:*

Fraction of workload that has to be processed sequentially	F_{seq}	*20%*
Fraction of workload that can be vectorized	F_{syn}	*60%*
Fraction of workload that can be parallel processed asynchrously	F_{asyn}	*20%*

86

Table X. Characteristic Speeds for Commercially Available Supercomputers and Several Hypothetical Machines[a] - Vector Length = 500 (in MFLOPS)

Machine	S_{seq}	S_{syn}	S_{asyn}	S_{eff}
Cyber-205 (2 vector pipes)	3.3	76	3.3	14.1
Cyber-205 (4 vector pipes)	3.3	109	3.3	14.7
"Cyber-205" (2 vector pipes and twice as fast scalar box)	(6.6)	(76)	(6.6)	(24.5)
Cray-1S	4.2	66	4.2	16.7
Cray-1M	4.1	63	4.1	16.3
Cray X-MP (1 processor)	5.4	133	5.4	23.2
Cray X-MP (2 processors)	5.4	(266)	(10.8)	(32.5)
"Cray X-MP" (4 processors)	5.4	(532)	(21.6)	(40.6)

[a]*The workload is characterized by the following parameters:*

Fraction of workload that has to be processed sewquentially	F_{seq}	*10%*
Fraction of workload that can be vectorized	F_{syn}	*80%*
Fraction of workload that can be parallel processed asynchrously	F_{asyn}	*10%*

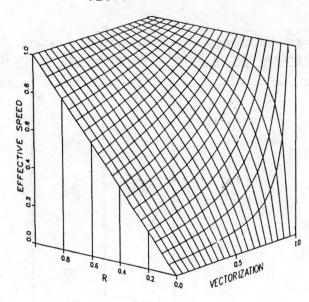

Fig. 4. Effective speed of vector processors as a function of vectorization
F_{syn} and the ratio $R = S_{seq}/S_{syn}$ of sequential and vector speeds.

ACKNOWLEDGMENTS

The author wishes to thank Tom Jordan for sharing some of his wisdom during many stimulating discussions and David Kuck for several helpful suggestions

REFERENCES

[1]   Flynn, M. J., IEEE Trans. Comp., *C-21* (1972) 948-960.

[2]   Amdahl, G. M., AFIPS Conf. Proc., *30* (1967) 483-485.

[3]   Worlton, J., A Philosophy of Supercomputing, Los Alamos National Laboratory report LA-8849-MS (1981).

[4]   Bucher, I. Y., Martin, J., Methodology for Characterizing a Scientific Workload, Proc. CPEUG 1982, to be published.

[5]   Bucher, I. Y., Moore, J., Proc. CMG XII (1981), 252-261.

[6]   Bucher, I. Y., Buzbee, B. L., Frederickson, P., Proc. 1981 Internat. Conf. Parallel Processing (1981) 166-167.

[7]   Hiromoto, R., Proc. 1982 Internat. Conf. Parallel Processing (1982) 243-244.

[8]   Hockney, R. W., Jesshope, C. R., Parallel Computers, Adam Hilger (1981).

[9]   CDC Cyber 200 Model 205 Computer System, Control Data Corporation, Publication 60256020 (1980).

[10] Martin, J., Bucher, I. Y., Warnock, T. T., Workload Characterization for Vector Computers: Tools and Techniques, to be published (1982).

Chapter 3: Array Processors

The Burroughs Scientific Processor (BSP)

DAVID J. KUCK, MEMBER, IEEE, AND RICHARD A. STOKES

Abstract—The Burroughs Scientific Processor (BSP), a high-performance computer system, performed the Department of Energy LLL loops at roughly the speed of the CRAY-1. The BSP combined parallelism and pipelining, performing memory-to-memory operations. Seventeen memory units and two crossbar switch data alignment networks provided conflict-free access to most indexed arrays. Fast linear recurrence algorithms provided good performance on constructs that some machines execute serially. A system manager computer ran the operating system and a vectorizing Fortran compiler. An MOS file memory system served as a high bandwidth secondary memory.

Index Terms—Conflict-free array access, high-speed computer, parallel computer, pipeline computer, scientific computing, vectorizing compiler.

I. INTRODUCTION

FROM the beginning of the Burroughs Scientific Processor (BSP) design activity, we attempted to develop a system with high performance and reliability that is practical to manufacture, easy to use, and produces high quality numerical results. It is not possible to substantiate the success or failure in achieving these goals because the product was cancelled before user installations were realized. However, a full prototype system was operational for several months on customer benchmarks and demonstrated the practicality of the architecture. A number of points of technical merit have surfaced and are presented herein.

Because of the market place for which the BSP was intended, we chose Fortran as the main programming language for the machine. This choice leads to a need for array-oriented memory and processor schemes. It also leads to various control mechanisms that are required for Fortran program execution. To design a cost-effective and user-oriented system, more than programming languages must be considered; characteristics of the types of programs to be run on the machine must be carefully considered. We have throughout the design effort paid attention to the syntax of Fortran and also the details of "typical" scientific Fortran programs.

In the past 10 years several high performance systems have been built, including the pipelined CDC STAR (CYBER-205) [12], CRAY-1 [22], MU5 [24], and TI ASC [29], as well as Burroughs Illiac IV (BBKK68) and PEPE [9], the Goodyear Aerospace STARAN [21], and the ICL DAP [10], all parallel

machines. While parallelism and pipelining are effective ways of improving system speed for a given technology (circuit and memory family, etc.), they both have shortcomings. Some pipelines perform better, the longer the vectors are that they have to process. The performance of other pipeline systems depends on vector lengths matching high-speed register set sizes. Parallel systems perform best on vectors whose length is a multiple of the number of processors available. Either type of system performs adequately if vector sizes are very large relative to the machine, but as these systems are used in wider application areas, short vector performance becomes more important. Other limitations of most pipeline processors have been that the arithmetic operations to be pipelined can reasonably be broken into only a limited number of segments and that overlapping of several instructions in one pipeline leads to unreasonable control problems.

Another important characteristic of high performance machines is the level of the language they execute. The CDC STAR and TI ASC, for example, have in their machine languages scalar and very high-level vector instructions, while ILLIAC IV, on the other hand, has a traditionally very low level machine language. A high-level machine language that is well matched to source programs can make compilation and control unit design easier and also helps ensure high system performance. A difficulty of array instructions can be that the setup time for instructions effectively stretches the pipeline length out intolerably.

System Overview

In the BSP we have combined parallelism and pipelining, and have provided array instructions that seem well matched to user programs. The machine has a five segment, memory-to-memory data pipeline, plus earlier instruction-setup pipeline segments. The data pipeline executes instructions that represent whole array assignment statements, recurrence system evaluations, etc., in contrast to most machines in which one or two arithmetic operations may be pipelined together. The BSP has 17 parallel memories, 16 parallel processors, and two data alignment networks. Since most instructions can be set up in the control pipeline preceding the data pipeline, instruction setup overhead should be insignificant in most cases. Thus, we have attempted to balance those architectural features that can provide good speedups with various overheads that can degrade or ruin system performance.

Another important factor in most supercomputers is I/O speed. If a very high speed processor is connected to standard disks, system performance may collapse because of I/O bound computations. The BSP has a high performance semiconductor

Manuscript received June 5, 1978; revised December 3, 1981. This work was supported in part by the National Science Foundation under Grant US NSF MCS77-27910 and the Burroughs Corporation, Paoli, PA.

D. J. Kuck is with the Department of Computer Science, University of Illinois, Urbana, IL 61801.

R. A. Stokes is with the Burroughs Corporation, Paoli, PA 19301.

90

Reprinted from *IEEE Transactions on Computers*, Volume C-31, Number 5, May 1982, pages 363-376. Copyright © 1982 by The Institute of Electrical and Electronics Engineers, Inc.

file memory. This is used as a backup memory and to provide a smooth flow of jobs to and from the BSP.

Certain technological decisions were dictated by a Burroughs parallel development of a standard circuit and packaging design called Burroughs Current Mode Logic (BCML). A relatively long clock period was established in order to reduce the number of pipeline segments (for both data flow and instruction setup), avoid the complexities of high frequency clock distribution, and to facilitate manufacturing and testing the machine. The memory cycle time, the time to align 16 words between memories and processors (in either direction), and the time for many processor operations are all one 160 ns clock period; two clocks are required for floating-point addition and multiplication. In terms of these major events per clock, we attempted to lay out an array instruction set whose performance in the final system could be easily estimated during the design period.

A very important point in predicting system performance, and hence rationally choosing between design alternatives, is the determinacy of the system's behavior. We attempted to remove as much uncertainty as possible by several design choices. First, a parallel memory system was designed that provides conflict-free access to multidimensional arrays for most of the standard access patterns observed in programs. For cost reasons a parallel memory is required to achieve adequate bandwidth, and our design guarantees that for most instructions the effective bandwidth will be exactly at its maximum capacity. Since array elements are accessed in a different order from that in which they are processed, data alignment networks are needed along the path from memory to the processors and from the processors back to memory. These alignment networks also operate in a conflict-free way for most common operations. Finally, to guarantee that the memory-to-memory data pipeline is seldom broken, an array instruction set was designed. For example, a single BSP instruction can handle a whole assignment statement (with up to five right-hand side arguments) nested in one or two loops. The instruction can represent a number of 16 element slices of the operands, as long vector operations are automatically sliced and the slices overlapped in the memory-to-memory pipeline. Furthermore, as one vector assignment statement instruction ends, the next one can be overlapped with it in the pipeline. So for short vector operations there is usually no problem in keeping the pipeline full, since several different Fortran level instructions may be in operation at once.

Thus, for a wide class of instructions it was possible to predict the system performance (up to the clock speed) very early in the design process (1973). Furthermore, it has been possible during the later stages of design to make tradeoffs in these terms. Array instructions have also been very beneficial in allowing logic designers and compiler writers to communicate with each other about their own design efforts and to make tradeoffs in concrete performance terms.

A Fortran compiler has been implemented that vectorizes ANS Fortran programs, thus allowing old programs to be run without expensive reprogramming efforts. Vector extensions to Fortran are also provided to allow users to "improve" certain parts of old programs, if desired, or to write new programs in efficient ways. The vectorizer not only handles array operations, it also substantially speeds up linear recurrences—as found, for example, in processes that reduce vectors to scalars (e.g., inner product, polynomial evaluation, etc.)—and effectively handles many conditional branches within loops.

For some applications, numerical stability is a serious problem. The BSP does high quality (approximate $R*$) rounding of its 36-bit mantissas and also provides double precision hardware operations. Furthermore, interrupts are generated for standard floating-point faults. Error detection and correction are provided throughout the system and automatic instruction retry is provided to ease the burden on the user in some cases.

The BSP and its file memory form a high-speed computing system that may be viewed as standing inside a computational envelope. This envelope is serviced by a *system manager* that can be a Burroughs B6700, B6800, B7700, or B7800. This front-end general-purpose system provides the following:
- compilation of BSP programs,
- archival storage for the BSP,
- data communication and time-sharing services to a user community,
- other languages and computation facilities.

Thus, a typical user will interactively generate compiled program and data files on the system manager, pass them to the BSP for execution, and have results returned via the system manager with permanent files maintained on the system manager's disks. Most job scheduling and operating system activities for the BSP are carried out on the system manager, so the BSP is dedicated to high-speed execution of user application programs.

II. SYSTEM OVERVIEW

Fig. 1 shows a block diagram of the BSP and the system manager. The BSP itself consists of three major parts: the control processor, the parallel processor, and the file memory. In this section some characteristics of these parts of the BSP will be presented. In subsequent sections we will give more details about how they operate.

A. Control Processor (CP)

The control processor is a high-speed element of the BSP that provides the supervisory interface to the system manager in addition to controlling the parallel processor and the file memory. The CP consists of a scalar processor unit, a parallel processor control unit, a control memory, and a control and maintenance unit.

The CP executes some serial or scalar portions of user programs utilizing an arithmetic element (similar to one of the 16 arithmetic elements in the parallel processor) that contains additional capabilities to perform integer arithmetic and indexing operations. The CP also performs task scheduling, file memory allocation, and I/O management under control of the BSP operating system.

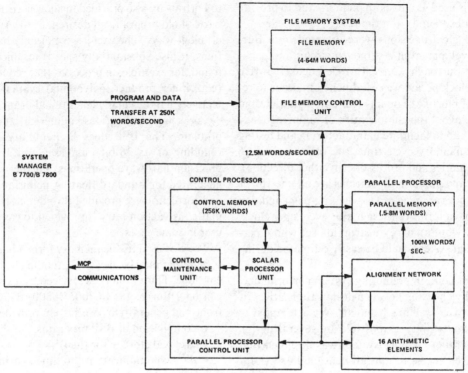

Fig. 1.   BSP system diagram.

Scalar Processor Unit (SPU): The scalar processor unit processes all operating system and user program instructions that are stored in control memory. It has a clock frequency of 12.5 MHz and is able to perform up to 1.5 million floating-point operations/s. All array instructions and certain scalar operations are passed to the parallel processor control unit, which queues them for execution on the parallel processor.

Parallel Processor Control Unit (PPCU): The PPCU receives array instructions from the scalar processor unit. The instructions are validated and transformed into microsequences that control the operation of all 16 arithmetic elements in the parallel processor. Vectors of any length are handled automatically by the PPCU hardware, relieving the programmer and compiler of this burden.

Control Memory (CM): The control memory is used to store portions of the operating system and all user programs as they are being executed. It is also used to store data values that are operands for those instructions executed by the scalar processor unit. The control memory is a 4K bit/chip NMOS memory with a 160 ns cycle time. Capacity of the memory is 256K words; each word consists of 48 data bits and 8 bits for error detection and correction. Four words are accessed simultaneously, giving a minimum effective 40 ns access time per 48 bit word.

Control and Maintenance Unit (CMU): The control and maintenance unit serves as the direct interface between the system manager and the rest of the control processor for initialization, communication of supervisory commands, and maintenance. It communicates with the input/output processor of the system manager. The CMU has access to critical data paths and registers of the BSP, so that it can perform state

analysis and circuit diagnostics under control of maintenance software running on the system manager.

B. Parallel Processor (PP)

The parallel processor performs array-oriented computations at high speeds by executing 16 identical operations simultaneously in its 16 arithmetic elements. Data for the array operations are stored in a parallel memory (PM) consisting of 17 memory modules. Parallel memory is accessed by the arithmetic elements through input and output alignment networks. A memory-to-memory data pipeline is formed by the five steps (fetch, align, process, align, store) and overlap in the pipeline provides significant performance benefits.

Parallel Memory (PM): The parallel memory is used only to hold data arrays for the parallel processor and consists of 17 memory units, each of which may contain from 32K to 512K words, making a total of from 0.5 to 8 million words. It is a 4K bit/chip NMOS memory with a 160 ns cycle time as in the control processor memory. Each word contains 48 data bits and 8 bits for error detection and correction. The maximum rate of data transfer between the PM and the arithmetic elements is 10^8 words/s. The organization of the PM permits simultaneous access to most commonly referenced components of an indexed array, such as rows, columns, or diagonals. For some operands the compiler must choose between allocating storage in PM or CM, and performance can suffer if this is not done properly.

The Alignment Networks (AN): The BSP has two alignment networks: the input alignment network for data fetching and the output alignment network for data stores. Both units contain full crossbar switching networks as well as hardware for broadcasting data to several destinations and for resolving conflicts if several sources seek the same destination. This permits general-purpose interconnectivity between the arithmetic array and the memory storage modules. It is the combined function of the memory storage scheme and the alignment networks that supports the conflict-free capabilities of the parallel memory. The output alignment network is also used for interarithmetic element switching to support special functions such as the data compress and expand operations and the fast Fourier transform algorithm.

Arithmetic Elements (AE): At any time all of the arithmetic elements are executing the same instruction on different data values. The arithmetic elements operate at a clock frequency of 6.25 MHz and are able to complete the most common arithmetic operations in two clock periods. Each arithmetic element can perform a floating-point add, subtract, or multiply in 320 ns, so the BSP is capable of executing up to 50 million floating-point operations/s. Each arithmetic element can perform a floating-point divide in 1280 ns and extract a square root in 2080 ns.

C. File Memory (FM)

The file memory is a high-speed secondary storage device that is loaded by the system manager with BSP tasks and task files. These tasks are then queued for execution by the control processor. The FM is also used to store scratch files and output files produced during execution of a BSP program. It is the only peripheral device under the direct control of the BSP; all other peripheral devices are controlled by the system manager.

The FM utilizes high-speed semiconductor memory as its storage medium; it combines a 1 ms access time with a 12.5M word/s transfer rate. Since it is entirely semiconductor, the reliability of the file memory is much greater than that of conventional rotating storage devices.

III. LANGUAGES AND THEIR TRANSLATION

The BSP can be regarded as a high performance Fortran machine, although many of the ideas in the design are useful for various languages. In this section we present some details of the vector form language seen by the PPCU and discuss how vector forms can be obtained from Fortran programs by a vectorizing compiler. The essential elements of many numerical algorithms are represented by these vector forms and numerical programs in most languages could be reduced to the same set of vector forms. However, the large collection of Fortran programs existing in the numerical computation community has dictated that the primary language of the BSP be Fortran. Nevertheless, vector extensions to Fortran are provided so that users may write new programs in a more convenient language than Fortran, and also to allow faster translation and possibly faster executable BSP code. We conclude this section with a sketch of the BSP vector Fortran extensions.

A. Vector Forms

The parallel processor control unit sequences the five stages of the data pipeline: fetch, align, process, align, store (FAPAS). In this pipeline several instructions corresponding to Fortran statements may be in execution at one time. To clarify this process, several definitions are required; these will lead to an understanding of the parallel processor control unit and compiler.

The BSP has a total of 64 *vector forms* that may be grouped in the following four types:

1) array expression statements,
2) recurrence and reduction statements,
3) expand, compress, random store, and fetch, and
4) parallel memory transmissions to and from control memory and file memory.

Array expression statements include indexing and evaluating right-hand side array expressions ranging from monad to pentad (five right-hand side operands), plus the assignment of the resulting values to parallel memory. A separate vector form exists for each possible parse of each right-hand side expression. The array operations are performed in an element by element fashion and allow scalars and array variables of one or two dimensions to be mixed on the right-hand side. For example,

$$DO\ 5\ I = 1, 30$$
$$DO\ 5\ J = 7, 25$$
$$5\qquad X(I, J) = (A(I, J + 1) * 0.5 + B(I + 1, J))$$
$$* X(I, J + 1) + C(J)$$

would be compiled as a single vector form. This vector form can be regarded as a six-address instruction that contains the four array arithmetic operation specifications and the assignment operation.

Recurrence vector forms correspond to assignment statements with data dependence loops. For example,

$$DO\ 3\ I = 1, 25$$
$$3\qquad Y(I) = F(I) * Y(I - 1) + G(I)$$

has a right-hand side that uses a result computed on the previous iteration. This recurrence produces an array of results, while others lead to a scalar result and are called *reductions*. For example, a polynomial evaluation by Horner's rule leads to the reduction

$$P = C(O)$$
$$DO\ 5\ I = 1, 25$$
$$5\qquad P = C(I) + Y * P.$$

Both of these are recurrences that can be represented by a linear system of the form $x = Ax + b$, where A is a lower triangular matrix with a single band, one diagonal below the main diagonal, and x is an unknown vector. We will refer to a linear recurrence of dimension n and order m as an $R\langle n, m \rangle$ recurrence, where n is the dimension of the matrix A and $m + 1$ is the bandwidth of matrix A. Thus, the above program leads to an $R\langle 25, 1 \rangle$ system. Fast efficient algorithms exist for solving such systems and the $R\langle n, 1 \rangle$ solver of [7] and [23] for small n and the $R\langle n, 1 \rangle$ solver of [6] for large n have been built into the BSP. For wider bandwidth recurrences the column sweep algorithm [15] is more efficient and it is used in the BSP. However, the user is not concerned with any of these considerations, since the vector forms described have array control unit hardware for their direct execution, as we shall see shortly.

Note that all recurrences would have to be executed serially without these algorithms. With them, $R\langle n, m\rangle$ systems ($1 < m \leq 16$ will obtain speedups proportional to m. For $m = 1$ and n of moderate size (say, 50 to 100), a speedup of 5 to 6 can be obtained, with greater speedups for large n. By speedup we mean time reduction compared to a hypothetical BSP with just one AE.

The third type of vector forms involves various sparse array operations. For example, in the case of a Fortran variable with subscripted subscripts, e.g., $A(B(I))$, no guarantee can be made concerning conflict-free access to the array A. In this case the indexing hardware generates a sequence of addresses that allows access to one operand per clock and these are then processed in parallel in the arithmetic elements. These are called *random store* and *random fetch* vector forms. Sparse arrays may be stored in memory in a compressed form and then expanded to their natural array positions using the input alignment network. After processing, the results may be compressed for storage by the output alignment network. These are called *compressed vector operand* and *compressed vector result* vector forms and they use control bit vectors that are packed, such that one 48 bit word is used for accesses to three 16 element vector slices.

A list illustrating the above three classes of vector forms is found in Table I. The mnemonics and comments should give an idea of what these vector forms do.

The fourth class of vector forms is used for I/O. Scalar and array assignments are made to control memory and parallel memory depending on whether they are to be processed in the scalar processor unit or the parallel processor, respectively; however, it is occasionally necessary to transmit data back and fourth between these memories. Transmissions to file memory are standard I/O types of operations.

These four types of vector forms comprise the entire set of array functions performed by the BSP. At the vector form level, the array processor may be regarded as arbitrarily large; thus, vector code generation is simplified in the compiler because it can transform Fortran programs into objects that map easily into vector forms, as we shall see shortly. However, in most Fortran programs some parameters are not defined at compile time (e.g., loop limits), so some run-time source language processing remains. This is carried out by the scalar processing unit of the control processor, and when it is finished the parallel processor is controlled by a template sequencing mechanism (see Section IV-D).

Vector forms are very high-level instructions with many parameters. For example, an array expression statement vector form corresponds to an assignment statement parse tree and leads to the execution of up to four operations on operands that may be combinations of scalars and one- or two-dimensional arrays. The following is a sketch of how the scalar processing

unit (SPU) initiates the execution of a vector form in the parallel processor control unit (PPCU).

Consider a triad vector form

$RBV, Z = (A \; op_1 \; B)op_2 \; C, OBV$

where Z, A, B, and C are vector descriptors, op_1 and op_2 are operators, and RBV and OBV are optional result and bit-vector descriptors, respectively. Bit vectors may be used to specify the elements of an array to be operated on or stored; they are optional (but not shown) for a number of the entries in Table I. In executing the triad, the SPU issues the following sequence of instructions that describe the vector form to the PPCU:

VFORM TRIAD, op_1, op_2
OBV
RBV
VOPERAND A
VOPERAND B
VOPERAND C
VRESULT Z.

The VFORM instruction contains bits that name the first template (see Section IV-D) to be executed, specify actual operator names, indicate the presence of bit-vectors, and specify the program countercontents; it also contains other synchronization and condition bits. The OBV and RBV descriptors give the bit-vector starting addresses and lengths. The VOPERAND and VRESULT instructions give the start of the vector relative to an array location, the location of the array, the volume of the array, the skip distance between vector elements to be accessed, and optionally the skip distance between the start of subsequent vectors in a nested pair of loops. The VFORM instruction is preceded by a VLEN instruction that specifies the level of loop nesting and array dimensions. At this point, all source language parameters have been bound and run-time source language processing ends. The remaining processing done by the PPCU, e.g., array bounds checking, is the same for all operations. We shall return to a discussion of template sequencing in Section IV.

B. Fortran Vectorizer

In ordinary Fortran programs it is possible to detect many array operations that easily can be mapped into BSP vector forms. This is accomplished in the BSP compiler by a program called the Fortran vectorizer. We will not attempt a complete description of the vectorizer here, but we will sketch its organization, emphasizing a few key steps. For more discussion of these ideas, see [15], [17], and [4].

First, consider the generation of a program graph based on data dependences. Each assignment statement is represented by a graph node, and directed arcs are drawn between nodes to indicate that one node is to be executed before another. Algorithms for data dependence graph construction are well known [1], [4] and will not be discussed here. It should be observed that some compilers have used naive algorithms, for example, checking only variable names. The BSP algorithm does a detailed subscript analysis and thus builds a high quality graph with few redundant arcs, thereby leading to more array operations and fewer recurrences.

TABLE I

Vector Forms

MONAD	It accepts one vector set operand, does one monadic operation on it and produces one vector set result.	$Z \leftarrow op\ A$
DYAD	It accepts two vector set operands, does one operation on them and produces one vector set result.	$Z \leftarrow A\ op\ B$
VSDYAD	It is similar to the DYAD except that operand B is a scalar.	$Z \leftarrow A\ op\ B$
EXTENDED DYAD	It accepts two vector set operands, does one operation and produces two vector set results.	$(Z1,Z2) \leftarrow A\ op\ B$
DOUBLE PRECISION DYAD	It accepts four vector set operands (i.e., two double precision operands), performs one operation and produces two vector set results.	$(Z1,Z2) \leftarrow (A1,A2)$ $op\ (B1,B2)$
DUAL-DYAD	It accepts four vector set operands, does two operations and produces two vector set results.	$Z \leftarrow A\ op_1\ B$ $Y \leftarrow C\ op_2\ D$
TRIAD	It accepts three vector set operands, does two operations and produces one vector set result.	$Z \leftarrow (A\ op_1\ B)\ op_2\ C$
TETRAD1	It accepts four set operands, does three operations and produces one vector set result.	$Z \leftarrow ((A\ op_1\ B)op_2\ C)$ $op_3\ D$
TETRAD2	It is similar to the TETRAD1 except for the order of operations.	$Z \leftarrow (A\ op_1\ B)op_2$ $(C\ op_3\ D)$
PENTAD1	It accepts five vector set operands, does four operations and produces one vector set result.	$Z \leftarrow (((A\ op_1\ B)op_2\ C)$ $op_3\ D)op_4\ E$
PENTAD2	It is similar to the PENTAD1 except for the order of operations.	$Z \leftarrow ((A\ op_1\ B)op_2$ $(C\ op_3\ D))op_4\ F$
PENTAD3	It is similar to the PENTAD1 except for the order of operations.	$Z \leftarrow ((A\ op_1\ B)op_2\ C)$ $op_3\ (D\ op_4\ E)$
AMTM	It is similar to the MONAD and is used to transmit from parallel memory to control memory.	$Z \leftarrow op\ A$
TMAM	It accepts 6 vector set operands from control memory to transmit to parallel memory.	$Z \leftarrow A1(0,0),\ A2(0,0)$ $A3(0,0),\ A4(0,0),$ $A5(0,0),\ A6(0,0)$
COMPRESS	It accepts a vector set operand, compresses it under a bit vector operand control and produces a vector set result.	$X \leftarrow A,\ BVO$
EXPAND	It accepts a vector operand, expands it under a bit vector control and produces a vector set result.	$X \leftarrow V,\ BVO$
MERGE	It is the same as the EXPAND except that the vector set result elements corresponding to a zero bit in BV are not changed in the parallel memory.	$X \leftarrow V,\ BVO$
RANDOM FETCH	It performs the following operation $Z(j,k) \leftarrow U(I(j,k))$, where U is a vector and I is an index vector set.	
RANDOM STORE	It performs the following operation $X(I(j,k)) \leftarrow A(j,k)$, where X is a vector and I is an index vector set.	
REDUCTION	It accepts one vector set operand and produces one vector result given by $X(i) \leftarrow A(i,0)\ op\ A(i,1)\ op\ A(i,2)\ op\ A(i,3)\ \dots\ A(i,L)$, where op must be a commutative and associative operator.	

95

TABLE I (CONTINUED)

DOUBLE-PRECISION REDUCTION	It accepts two vector set operands (one double-precision vector set) and produces two vector results (one d.p. vector) given by $(X_1(i),X_2(i)) \leftarrow (A_1(i,0),A_2(i,0))$ op $(A_1(i,1), A_2(i,1))$ op ... $(A_1(i,L), A_2(i,L))$, where op must be a commutative and associative operator.
GENERALIZED DOT PRODUCT	It accepts two vector set operands and produces one vector result given by $X(i) \leftarrow \{A(i,0)$ op$_2$ $B(i,0)\}$ op$_1$ $\{A(i,1)$ op$_2$ $B(i,1)\}$ op$_1$ ... $\{A(i,L)$ op$_2$ $B(i,L)\}$, where op$_1$ must be a commutative and associative operator.
RECURRENCE-1L	It accepts two vector set operands and produces one vector result given by $X(i) \leftarrow (\{...\{(B(i,0)$ op$_1$ $A(i,1))$ op$_2$ $B(i,1)\}$ op$_1$ ...$\}$ op$_1$ $A(1,L))$ op$_2$ $B(i,L)$ where op$_2$ can be ADD or IOR and op$_1$ can be MULT or AND.
PARTIAL REDUCTION	It accepts one vector set operand and produces one vector set result given by $Z(i,j) \leftarrow Z(i,j-1)$ op $A(i,j)$, where op must be a commutative and associative operator.
RECURRENCE-1A	It accepts two vector set operands and produces one vector set result given by $Z(i,j) \leftarrow \{Z(i,j-1)$ op$_1$ $A(i,j)\}$ op$_2$ $B(i,j)$, where op$_1$ can be MULT or AND and op$_2$ can be ADD or IOR.

As an example, consider the following program:

```
DO 5 I = 1, 25
1      A(I) = 3 * B(I)
          DO 3 J = 1, 35
3              X(I, J) = A(I) * X(I, J − 1) + C(J)
5      B(I) = 2 * B(I + 1).
```

A dependence graph for this program is shown in Fig. 2, where nodes are numbered according to the statement label numbers of the program. Node 1 has an arc to node 3 because of the $A(I)$ dependence and node 3 has a self-loop because $X(I, J − 1)$ is used one J iteration after it is generated. The crossed arc from node 1 to node 5 is an antidependence arc [16] indicating that statement 1 must be executed before statement 5 to ensure that $B(I)$ on the right-hand side of statement 1 is an initial value and not one computed by statement 5. Arcs from above denote initial values being supplied to each of the three statements: array B to statements 1 and 5, and array C to statement 3. The square brackets denote the scope of loop control for each of the DO statements.

Given a data dependence graph, loop control can be distributed down to individual assignment statements or collections of statements with internal loops of data dependences. In our example there is one loop (containing just one statement) and two individual assignment statements. After the distribution of loop control, the graph of Fig. 2 may be redrawn as shown in Fig. 3.

The graph of Fig. 3 can easily be mapped into BSP vector forms. Statements 1 and 5 go into array expression statement vector forms directly since they are both dyads. Had they had more than five right-hand side variables, their parse trees would have been broken into two or more array expression statement vector forms and joined by a temporary array assignment. Statement 3 can be split into 25 independent re-

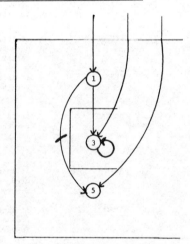

Fig. 2. Data dependence graph.

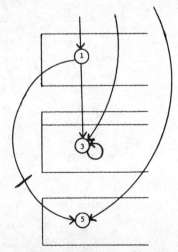

Fig. 3. Graph with distributed loop control.

currence systems, each with a bandwidth of 1 caused by the $J - 1$ to J dependence, resulting in 25 independent $R\langle 35, 1\rangle$ systems, each of which maps into a recurrence vector form. Alternatively, it can be computed as a series of 35 array expression statement vector forms (triads). The maximum speed choice is made based on the loop limits.

The above cases are rather simple constructs, but they are typical of those found in existing Fortran programs. Several kinds of more complex cases are possible. If arrays with subscripted subscripts occur, they are compiled using the random fetch or store vector forms mentioned earlier. If recurrences with nonlinear right-hand sides occur, e.g., $X(I) = A(I) * X(I - 1) * X(I - 2) + B(I)$, then serial code is compiled. To this point we have ignored conditional statements inside loops, another problem that in the past has caused serial code to be compiled.

A number of IF statements can in fact be handled in parallel in the BSP. For a theoretical discussion of various types of IF's, see [14], where examples and measurements of the frequency of various types of IF's are presented. It turns out that many of the commonly found IF's can be handled in the BSP by using standard vector forms which include bit vectors. In this way, certain IF statements can be combined with assignment statements in a single vector form. For example, consider the following program:

DO 1 $I = 1, 92, 2$
DO $J = 1, 46$
1   IF$(A(I, J).LT.0)$ $B(I, J) = A(I, J) * 3.5$.

This loop can be mapped into a single array expression statement vector form with bit-vector control that performs the parallel tests and makes the appropriate assignments to $B(I, J)$. By using loop distribution, many of the IF's found in ordinary Fortran programs can be transformed into such vector operations that allow substantial speedups on the BSP. Of course, there is also a residual set of IF's that must be compiled as serial code.

A traditional objection to array computers was that too many of the statements found in ordinary programs could not be vectorized and would have to be executed in a traditional sequential manner. In the BSP a combination of software and hardware innovations has led to a system that avoids most of these traditional objections. Of primary software importance are the distribution of loop control, fast algorithms to solve linear recurrences, and the vectorization of IF statements. Also of key importance is a good test for data dependence between subscripted variables, the appropriate introduction of additional subscripts to variables of lower dimension than their depth of loop nesting, and the transformation of scalar expressions inside loops as well as their substitution into subscripts. After a source program has been mapped into vector forms it is ready for execution.

C. Fortran Language Extensions

To provide users with language conveniences for writing new programs and to allow rewriting old programs that are difficult to vectorize automatically, several language extensions are being provided in the BSP software. Some of these extensions are also part of the proposed new ANS Fortran. The extensions may be categorized in four cases as array description, array operation, control, and I/O statements; we shall deal with them in that order, providing only a quick sketch of the ideas.

Arrays may be declared with the colon notation, using positive and negative subscripts, e.g., REAL $A(0:3, 0:3, -3:3)$ declares a $4 \times 4 \times 7$ array. Portions of declared arrays may be renamed for easy reference using an ARRAY statement as the following example shows:

REAL $A(100, 100)$
ARRAY ROW $2(J = 1:100) = A(2, J)$,
DIAG$(I = 1:100) = A(I, I)$

identifies ROW 2 as a vector consisting of the second row of A and DIAG as the main diagonal of A. No storage is allocated or data are moved by an ARRAY statement, only additional array descriptors are created.

Array operations can be specified in various ways. If A and B are declared arrays, then $A = 0$ sets all elements of A to zero and $B = B + 1$ adds 1 to all elements of B. If A is two-dimensional, then $A(*, 0) = 2$ sets column zero of A to 2. Arithmetic, relational, and logical operators may be applied to pairs of arrays that are congruent, in which case element by element operations are performed. Furthermore, bit-vectors may be used to control array operations by use of the WHERE statement as follows. Assume that A and B are 500 element vectors then

$$\text{WHERE}(A.GE.0)\ B = B + A$$

is equivalent to

DO 10 $I = 1, 500$
10   IF $(A(I).GE.0)$ $B(I) = B(I) + A(I)$.

This is generalized to a block-structured WHERE DO that contains a sequence of OTHERWISE statements and ends with an END WHERE. PACK and UNPACK statements are provided to allow sparse arrays to be compressed and expanded, respectively; multidimensional arrays may be packed into vectors based on logical tests. There is also an IF-THEN-ELSE construct and an END DO that does not require a label in its DO statement. For scalars or congruent arrays, the exchange statement

$$A == B$$

exchanges A and B in memory.

A collection of intrinsic functions is also provided, one set generalizes the standard scalar intrinsics to arrays (e.g., transcendental functions of the elements of an array) and the other set provides some standard array operations (e.g., dot product, matrix product, max of an array, etc.).

User programs can control I/O without supervisor intervention and without buffering by using the DIRECT statement which names an array that appears in a following READ statement. Execution of statements after the READ continues simultaneously with the input until the DIRECT named variable is encountered on the right-hand side of an assignment statement, at which point execution is suspended until the READ is completed.

IV. SYSTEM OPERATION

In this section we give more details of the overall system operation. First, the parallel memory and its conflict-free structure are discussed (Section IV-A), and this is followed (Section IV-B) by the alignment networks that stand between the parallel memory and the arithmetic elements, which are discussed in Section IV-C. Section IV-D ties these components of the parallel processor together by detailing the template sequencing as carried out by the parallel processor control unit.

This also relates back to Section III-A, where it was pointed out that source programs are first mapped by software into vector forms which in turn are mapped by hardware into a sequence of templates. The template sequencing mechanism is one of the key points in achieving high system utilization through pipelining and overlap of vector forms in the BSP. This section concludes with a discussion of the high performance file memory used for secondary storage in the BSP.

A. Parallel Memory

The BSP parallel memory consists of 17 memory modules, each with a 160 ns cycle time; and since we access 16 words per cycle, this provides a maximum effective 10 ns memory cycle time. This is well balanced with the arithmetic elements which perform floating point addition and multiplication at the rate of $(320\,\text{ns}/16\text{ operations}) = 20(\text{ns/operation})$, since each operation requires 2 arguments and temporary registers are provided in the arithmetic elements. Note that only array accessing (including I/O) uses parallel memory, since programs and scalars are held in control memory. Thus, perfect balance between parallel memory and floating-point arithmetic may be achieved for triad vector forms since three arguments and one result (four memory accesses) are required for two arithmetic operations. For longer vector forms, since temporaries reside in registers, only one operand is required per operation, so there is substantial parallel memory bandwidth remaining for I/O.

The total memory size ranges from 0.5 to 8 million 48 bit words. Eight parity bits provide single error correction and double error detection.

The main innovation in the parallel memory of the BSP is its 17 modules. In past supercomputers it has been common to use a number of parallel memory modules, but such memory systems are vulnerable to serious bandwidth degradation due to conflicts. For example, if 16 memories were used and a 16 × 16 array were stored with rows across the units and one column in each memory unit, then column access would be sequential.

Various storage schemes have been invented to avoid such memory conflicts. For example, arrays may be skewed [16] so that rows and columns can be accessed without conflict, and other related skewing schemes may be found with other useful properties. However, it is easy to show [5] that in general it is impossible to access rows, columns, and diagonals of square arrays without conflict if any power of two number of memory modules is used. Of course, various ad hoc procedures may be contrived, e.g., different skewing schemes for different arrays, but in the long run these are a compiler writer's (or user's) nightmare. A uniform, conflict-free procedure carried out by the hardware would be far superior for users of the system.

Early in the design of the BSP we decided to build the best possible parallel memory in this respect, and thereby avoid as many software implementation and performance problems as possible. For this reason we settled on a 17 memory module system that would provide conflict-free array access to most common array partitions, and yet have little redundant memory bandwidth since only one memory unit is unused per cycle.

With 17 memory modules it is clear that conflict-free access to one-dimensional arrays is possible for any arithmetic sequence index pattern except every 17th element. For two-dimensional arrays with a skewing distance of 4, conflict-free access is possible for rows, columns, diagonals, back-diagonals, and other common partitions, including arithmetic sequence indexing of these partitions [5]. The method extends to higher numbers of dimensions in a straightforward way.

One mundane characteristic of some Fortran programs can cause a problem here, namely, the use of COMMON in subroutine parameter passing. If used in the most general ways, this forces the storage of arrays in a contiguous way across parallel memory. In this case conflict-free access can still be guaranteed to any arithmetic sequence of physical memory addresses, as long as the difference between addresses is not a multiple of 17. This may force some array dimensions to be adjusted slightly for conflict-free access to all of the desired patterns.

To access parallel memory a set of 16 memory addresses must be generated. Assume that addresses are to a linear address space, i.e., multidimensional arrays have been mapped into a one-dimensional array, and that the array is stored across the memory modules beginning with module 0, through module 16, continuing in module 0, and so on. Then to access address α we must generate a *module number* μ and an *index* i in that module. These are defined by[1]

$$\mu = \alpha(\text{mod } 17)$$

$$i = \left\lfloor \frac{\alpha}{16} \right\rfloor$$

since there are 17 memory modules and we access 16 numbers (one for each AE) per memory cycle. Notice that this wastes $\frac{1}{17}$ of the address space, a minor penalty for the conflict-free access it provides. Address generation hardware for the memory system is somewhat complex, but can be done in parallel for a sequence of addresses in one clock using the scheme described in [18]. This hardware also generates indices to set the alignment networks appropriately for each memory access.

B. Alignment Networks

The separation of data alignment functions from processing and memory activities is another departure of the BSP from most previous computers. As discussed earlier, the BSP has an input alignment network (IAN) connecting parallel memory to the arithmetic elements, and an output alignment network (OAN) connecting the arithmetic elements either to themselves or to parallel memory. Alignment of the elements of two arrays is sometimes required by the parallel memory and sometimes required by program or algorithm constraints, as the following examples illustrate.

Suppose we want to add together two rows of a matrix, element by element. The origins of the rows will in general be stored in different memory modules, so one row must be shifted relative to the other to align them for addition. Now if we want to add the odd elements of one row to the elements of another row (half as long), the first row will have to be "squeezed" as well as shifted to align proper pairs of operands. Similar alignment problems arise in row-column, column-diagonal, etc., pairings. Since we must store arrays consistently in parallel memory, the output alignment network is used to satisfy

[1] We use $\lfloor x \rfloor$ to denote the integer part of x.

98

the storage requirements and indexing patterns of the variable on the left-hand side of each assignment statement.

The above uses of the alignment networks hold for recurrence and reduction vector forms. In these cases, data may be aligned after fetching via the IAN, but now the OAN is useful between processing steps. As a simple example, consider the summation of 32 numbers. This may be done in five steps, each step consisting of an addition followed by an output alignment network mapping of the AE's into the AE's in the form of a tree, which reduces the 32 numbers to one in $\log_2 32$ steps. Similarly, other reduction operations may be carried out using the OAN; these include such operations as finding the maximum or minimum of a set of numbers. Notice that for any such operations the reduction to a set of 16 numbers is carried out using all 16 processors, and after that the number of processors used is halved on each step.

In solving more general linear recurrences, a vector of results is produced, e.g., an $R\langle n, 1\rangle$ system leads to n results. Again, the OAN is used for an AE to AE mapping of intermediate results. Other important algorithms also require data alignment between operations; the FFT [20] and the Batcher merge and sort algorithms [2] are examples. These and other algorithms can be implemented directly in the BSP using microprogrammed AN sequencing patterns. Each alignment operation takes one clock in a FAPAS pipeline sequence. In array expression statement vector forms most are overlapped, while in recurrence vector forms the later alignments must be alternated with arithmetic.

In the course of some of the above algorithms, certain vector positions are vacated during the course of the computation, e.g., reduction operations reduce a vector to a scalar. An effective way of handling this is to have the IAN introduce *null elements* into the computation at appropriate points. In AE operations null elements are handled as follows:

$$\text{operand} \leftarrow \text{null } \theta \text{ operand}$$
$$\text{operand} \leftarrow \text{operand } \theta \text{ null}$$
$$\text{null} \leftarrow \text{null } \theta \text{ null}$$

for any operator θ. Memory modules block the storing of a null. Nulls are also used when a vector length is not equal to a multiple of 16, so the last slice of the vector is padded out with nulls by the IAN.

The alignment networks are constructed from multiplexers and are generalizations of crossbar switches. In addition to the permutation functions of crossbars, the alignment networks can also broadcast an input element to any selected set of destinations. Furthermore, the random store and fetch vector forms, as well as the compress and expand operations, use the alignment networks to carry out their mappings. Control of the AN's is closely related to PM control. As was pointed out in Section IV-A, memory addressing information and AN control indices are generated by the same hardware control unit.

The two alignment networks have similar control in that they are both source initiated; conceptually, for the IAN the memories specify which AE to transmit to and for the OAN, the AE's specify which memory they want to store to. In certain cases, e.g., random store and fetch, the AE's actually generate memory addresses as suggested here, whereas in the standard array expression statement or recurrence vector forms all of the addressing is carried out by a special control unit hardware. Conflict resolution hardware is provided to sequence certain alignments in several steps. For more AN details, see [18].

C. Arithmetic Element

The 16 arithmetic elements are microprogrammed, being sequenced by the parallel processor control unit using a wide (128 bit) microcode word. Besides the arithmetic operations expected in a scientific processor, the BSP has a rich set of nonnumeric operations that include field manipulation, editing, and Fortran format conversion operators. Floating-point addition, subtraction, and multiplication require two 160 ns clocks each, floating-point division requires 1280 ns, and the square root operation requires 2080 ns; the latter two use Newton–Raphson iterations that start with ROM values selected in each AE [11].

Single precision floating-point arithmetic is carried out using normalized signed magnitude numbers with 36 bits of mantissa and 10 bits of exponent, providing about 11 decimal digits of precision with a range between approximately 5.56×10^{-309} and 8.99×10^{307}. Four guard digits are retained within the AE and R* rounding is carried out using these four bits. Given that most alignment shifts are small [25], this should provide a good approximation of full R* rounding. Double-precision operations are carried out in the hardware (a double length product is always generated) about four times slower than single precision. The range of double precision numbers is the same as for single precision, and the precision is twice as great. Characters are stored as 8 bit EBCDIC bytes, packed six to a word.

Although they are not seen by users, each AE has a file of 10 registers, in addition to the standard registers used in the course of various operations. These are very convenient for holding intermediate results in the course of evaluating vector forms. The register assignment is done within the vector forms and the number of registers necessary to ensure high system performance was thus decided when the machine was designed. This is in contrast to building a machine first and then studying register allocation as a later compiler design question.

To add to the system reliability each AE contains residue checking hardware to check the arithmetic operations. Two-bit, modulo 3, residue calculations are carried out for each exponent and mantissa. To enhance the diagnosability of the entire system, the AE's (actually the AE-alignment network interfaces) contain Hamming code generators, detectors, and correctors for the data path loop from the AE's through the alignment networks and memory, and back to the AE's. This allows control information to be included in the Hamming code in order to check for failures in the control hardware of the parallel memory and alignment networks as well as the data paths mentioned above. The eight parity bits allow single error correction and double error detection. Most double-bit parity failures and all residue check failures lead to an instruction retry (see Section IV-D).

D. Template Sequencing

The execution of a vector form must be broken into a sequence of elemental array sequences called templates. This is done by the parallel processor control unit which issues a sequence of (one or more) *templates* to execute each vector form. The template provides the control framework in which vector forms are executed. Because it is desirable to overlap the execution of these template in the FAPAS pipeline, appropriate matching must be found in one template to accommodate the next template. For example, the fetching of operands for the next template may occur before the storing of the results from the previous template. In terms of such matching, *template families* have been defined with respect to the interface characteristics of their front and back templates. Each is said to have a front and back family number.

During execution the PPCU chooses templates on the basis of the vector form and the family numbers. For example, in executing a dyad followed by a triad, the PPCU will match the front family of the first triad template with the back family of the last dyad template. Then (assuming that there are more than 16 triad operations to perform) a second triad template will be chosen by matching its front family with the back family of the first triad template. Within three templates this reaches a cycle of one or two templates that repeats until the end of this particular vector form execution.

It is important to realize that the FAPAS overlap between templates as well as the arithmetic element register allocation for each one is done at machine design time. This leads to an *a priori* understanding of the machine's performance over a wide range of computations and also allows more vector operation overlap than might be possible otherwise, since all possible template combinations have been considered at machine design time.

This is in contrast to most previous high performance machines, wherein such overlap attempts are made at compile time or execution time. For example, in the CDC 6600 [27] and its successors, the control unit SCOREBOARD attempts run-time overlap and this is aided by compile-time transformations [26]. In the IBM 360/91 an overlap mechanism was built into the processor [28] in an effort to sequence several functional units at once. Most previous high performance machines seem to have overlap mechanisms that combine compile-time and run-time (control unit and processor) overlap decisions in ways similar to these. In some cases, however, certain common functions can be chained together (e.g., multiply and add for inner product in the CRAY-1), although in the CRAY-1, for example, intricate run-time considerations dictate whether or not chaining is possible [8].

The five-stage FAPAS pipeline may have four templates in process at once, and five more templates may be in various stages of setup in the PPCU pipeline that precedes execution. The amount of such overlap that exists at any moment depends, of course, on the width of individual templates. However, it is clear from an analysis of the templates that for most of the common Fortran constructs a very high percentage of processor and memory utilization can be expected in the BSP. Notice that there is overlap between templates of one vector form as well as overlap between different vector forms.

Due to the fact that the BSP executes a very high-level array language, complex hazard checking can be performed. As was mentioned in the discussion of template families, one template's fetches may begin before a previous template's store has been executed. In some cases, two previous stores may be pending while a third template's fetch is executed. This leads to *data dependence hazards* that must be checked before executing such memory accesses, i.e., if a fetch is for data that are to be stored by a previous template, the fetch must be delayed until after the store. Such hazard checking is carried out for up to two stores before a fetch by a combination of software and hardware in the BSP.

To clarify the above ideas, consider the following example program:

    DO 1 I = 1, 40
  1    $Y(I) = A(I) + B(I)$
    DO 2 I = 1, 90
  2    $Z(I) = (C(I) + D(I)) * E(I).$

This would be compiled as a dyad vector form followed by a triad; the dyad would be executed using $3 \left(= \left\lceil \frac{40}{16} \right\rceil \right)$ templates and the triad using $6 \left(= \left\lceil \frac{90}{16} \right\rceil \right)$ templates. Fig. 4 shows a FAPAS pipeline timing diagram for the execution of these templates.

In Fig. 4 notice that three distinct dyad templates are used:[2] dyad (2, 3), dyad (3, 6), and dyad (6, 7). The last memory cycle on clock 3 is provided for a previous template—some waste can be expected when beginning or ending a computation—but otherwise all memory cycles are occupied until clock 8. Notice also that after processing begins, the first three templates use $\frac{2}{3}$ of the processor clocks until clock 12.

The triad processing begins with three distinct templates: triad (2, 4), triad (4, 8), and triad (8, 8). It then continues in a steady state with triad (8, 8) templates. Except for one last clock at the dyad interface, the triad templates operate with total utilization of both the parallel memory and the parallel processor. Generally speaking, longer templates achieve very high utilization of the system hardware.

The total number of clocks required to execute this sequence of templates is 39, and since the original program contains 220 floating-point operations, the effective speed of this computation is greater than 35 million floating-point operations/s (Mflops). Assuming processing overlap at the beginning and end of this sequence, only 36 clocks are required for processing and on this basis a rate of more than 38 Mflops is achieved.

The use of vector forms and templates allows the easy implementation of a number of desirable features. The basic idea is that templates can be regarded as global microinstructions (the PPCU is microprogrammed) or "macroinstructions" that sequence the entire parallel processor. Consequently, even with

---

[2] The parenthesized numbers are the front family and back family identification numbers. The back family number of one must match the front family number of the next.

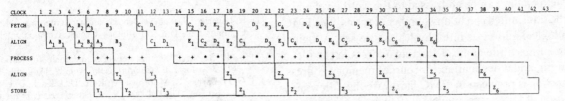

Fig. 4.   Triad template sequencing.

a set of overlapped templates in progress, it is easy to delay the entire parallel processor. This is easiest to think of in terms of Fig. 4. For example, if an error occurs, a vertical slice is made through Fig. 4 at the end of some clock period and all further steps may be deferred until the interrupt is handled. Also, longer operations than addition and multiplication (i.e., division or square root) can simply be handled by extending the process step for sufficiently many clocks and deferring all other tracks in the FAPAS diagram, resuming them when the longer operation is complete; double precision is implemented in a similar manner. Furthermore, instruction retry is facilitated by this ability to break the FAPAS sequence at any step and back up to the beginning of a vector form, since memory stores are prevented in case of an error.

The distinction between data pipelining and overlap here and in other machines should be clear at this point. The BSP pipelines each template through the five FAPAS segments, in contrast to traditional pipelining of arithmetic operations; the individual operations being decomposed are array assignment statements, recurrences, etc., in the BSP. A sequence of templates can be likened to a sequence of additions in an arithmetic pipeline. On the other hand, most modern machines are overlapped in the sense that memory and arithmetic can be performed simultaneously, based on run-time lookahead. In the BSP the analogous process is overlap between vector forms, as was illustrated in Fig. 4.

Run-time lookahead schemes are limited by data hazards, jumps, and various other resource conflicts. By complex analysis of source programs, much more simultaneity is possible. For the BSP, many IF and GOTO statements are replaced by bit-vector modifications of vector forms, so even these difficulties of standard run-time lookahead schemes are often avoided.

Globally, the PPCU may be viewed as accepting a single stream of array instructions, namely, vector forms, and producing five streams of array instructions to sequence the FAPAS segments. Thus, in the terminology of [16], the BSP array processor is a SIAMEA (single instruction array/multiple execution array) machine. Of course, the scalar processor unit also may execute instructions from a given Fortran program simultaneously with the parallel processor.

E. File Memory

The BSP file memory consists of two sections, the file storage units and the file memory controller. This is the secondary memory of the BSP, with longer term storage being provided on conventional disks and other I/O devices attached to the system manager (see Fig. 1).

During the BSP design phase several semiconductor technologies showed promise as high-speed secondary memory devices, in competition with conventional head-per-track disks. Charge-coupled device (CCD) and random access memory (RAM) chips were considered because they provide very attractive characteristics, they were well along in development, and their price outlook seemed likely to be competitive with head-per-track disks. As a result, an MOS RAM was chosen to provide the BSP file memory with a very low latency and a high transfer rate, which is expected to perform with good reliability and maintainability at a reasonable cost.

The file storage unit is built with semiconductor high density memory devices that provide a transfer rate of two words every 160 ns with a maximum latency of less than 1 ms. Nonaddressed modules are operated at $\frac{1}{4}$ that clock rate to conserve power, yet provide the refresh needed for the volatile devices. Each file storage unit is organized in 4 M ($M = 2^{20}$) word sections and may contain 4 sections for a total of 16 M words of 48 data bits plus 8 parity bits. Two words are accessed in

$$ \text{parallel for a transfer rate of } 112 \text{ bits}/160 \text{ ns} = \frac{2 \text{ words}}{160 \text{ ns}} = 12.5 $$

$\times 10^6$ word/s. A file memory system may contain up to 4 file memory units for maximum file memory capacity of 64 M (64×10^6) words. Thus, the file memory provides a backup storage of one to two orders of magnitude the size of parallel memory.

Consider the file memory in relation to a typical BSP computation. For example, a block of 32K words may be read at an overall effective rate of about 10^7 words/s. Since the BSP operates at a maximum of 50 Mflops, this means that only 5 floating-point operations need be performed per I/O word to balance the I/O and processing rates. To sustain this, output must be considered as well so the ratio becomes 10 floating-point operations per I/O word, for balance. These ratios seem well within the range of most large scientific calculations (whose ratios often range up to 100 or more).

The file memory stands between the BSP and the system manager. The file memory controller can transmit data to and from the BSP parallel memory or control memory as well as the system manager I/O processor (see Fig. 1), the latter at the 0.25×10^6 words/s maximum channel speed of the system manager. I/O instructions are passed between the BSP control processor and the file memory controller.

The file memory controller (FMC) contains buffer areas to match the file memory speed with that of the system manager. I/O requests from the BSP and system manager are queued in the FMC in a 32 entry queue. Normally, the slower system manager receives highest priority and the BSP requests are handled in a first-in, first-out manner.

The file memory can be addressed to the word level and a block to be transmitted can be any number of words. The FMC converts logical addresses into physical addresses. A logical address contains a file name, a starting address in the file, a block length, and a destination (or source) memory address. File protection is provided by FMC hardware that allows any combination of four access modes: system manager READ or WRITE and BSP user program READ or WRITE. When operating in problem state, BSP I/O instructions can be executed with no supervisor program intervention at all for error-free transmissions. Synchronization bit registers are provided that allow BSP user programs to test for I/O completion without supervisor program intervention. The FMC also contains hardware for I/O instruction retry for all errors not automatically corrected. Thus, a number of situations that might traditionally have required slow, operation system intervention are handled by FMC hardware in the BSP.

Task switching within the BSP takes less than one-half second, but the speed of flow of jobs from the system manager, through file memory, and into the parallel memory and control memory, depends on many details of individual jobs.

V. Conclusion

We have outlined the organization of the BSP, a high performance scientific computer. Its key features include high quality, fast arithmetic, conflict-free access to arrays in parallel memory, separate data alignment networks, a pipelined control unit that sequences a high-level data pipeline and can overlap the execution of its vector form language, and a semiconductor file memory for secondary storage. Many error-checking and correcting features are included throughout the system to enhance its reliability and maintainability. Software was provided on a system manager computer that handles most operating system functions and has a Fortran vectorizing compiler that can also handle vector extensions.

The BSP system design effort began in early 1973, and led to an operational prototype machine in 1978. The maximum system speed is 50 million floating-point operations/s. The system performed as a "class 6" computer by running the Department of Energy LLL loops at speeds in excess of 20 Mflops. In fact, its average speed is almost identical to the average speed of the CRAY-1 on these benchmarks. A major design goal was a system that could achieve a high sustained performance over a wide variety of scientific and engineering calculations using standard Fortran programs. It is estimated that 20–40 Mflops could be achieved for a broad range of Fortran computations.

Acknowledgment

The authors are grateful to the entire BSP design team for years of work in the development of this system.

References

[1] U. Banerjee, "Data dependence in ordinary programs," M.S. thesis, Dep. Comput. Sci., Univ. of Illinois, Urbana-Champaign, Rep. 76-837, Nov. 1976.

[2] K. E. Batcher, "Sorting networks and their applications," in *Proc. AFIPS Spring Joint Comput. Conf.*, vol. 32, 1968, pp. 307–315.

[3] G. H. Barnes, R. M. Brown, M. Kato, D. J. Kuck, D. L. Slotnick, and R. A. Stokes, "The ILLIAC IV computer," *IEEE Trans. Comput.*, vol. C-17, pp. 746–757, Aug. 1968.

[4] U. Banerjee, S. C. Chen, D. J. Kuck, and R. A. Towle, "Time and parallel processor bounds for Fortran-like loops," *IEEE Trans. Comput.*, vol. C-28, pp. 660–670, Sept. 1979.

[5] P. Budnik and D. J. Kuck, "The organization and use of parallel memories," *IEEE Trans. Comput.*, vol. C-20, pp. 1566–1569, Dec. 1971.

[6] S. C. Chen, D. J. Kuck, and A. H. Sameh, "Practical parallel band triangular system solvers," *ACM Trans. Math. Software*, vol. 4, pp. 270–277, Sept. 1978.

[7] S. C. Chen and D. J. Kuck, "Time and parallel processor bounds for linear recurrence systems," *IEEE Trans. Comput.*, vol. C-24, pp. 701–717, July 1975.

[8] "The CRAY-1 computer," *Preliminary Reference Manual*, Cray Res. Inc., Chippewa Falls, WI, 1975.

[9] P. H. Enslow, Ed., *Multiprocessors and Parallel Processing*. New York: Wiley-Interscience, 1974.

[10] P. M. Flanders, D. J. Hunt, S. F. Reddaway, and D. Parkinson, "Efficient high speed computing with the distributed array processor," in *High Speed Computer and Algorithm Organization*. New York: Academic, 1977, pp. 113–128.

[11] D. D. Gajski and L. P. Rubinfield, "Design of arithmetic elements for Burroughs scientific processor," in *Proc. 4th Symp. Comput. Arithmetic*, Santa Monica, CA, 1978, pp. 245–256; also in *Proc. 1978 LASL Workshop Vector and Parallel Processors*, Los Alamos, NM, 1978.

[12] R. G. Hintz and D. P. Tate, "Control data STAR-100 processor design," in *Proc. IEEE COMPCON 1972*, Sept. 1972, pp. 1–4.

[13] D. J. Kuck, "ILLIAC IV software and application programming," *IEEE Trans. Comput.*, vol. C-17, pp. 758–770, Aug. 1968.

[14] ——, "Parallel processing of ordinary programs," in *Advances in Computers*, vol. 15, M. Rubinoff and M. C. Yovits, Eds. New York: Academic, 1976, pp. 119–179.

[15] ——, "A survey of parallel machine organization and programming," *ACM Comput. Surveys*, vol. 9, pp. 29–59, Mar. 1977.

[16] ——, *The Structure of Computers and Computations*, Vol. I. New York: Wiley, 1978.

[17] D. J. Kuck, Y. Muraoka, and S. C. Chen, "On the number of operations simultaneously executable in Fortran-like programs and their resulting speed-up," *IEEE Trans. Comput.*, vol. C-21, pp. 1293–1310, Dec. 1972.

[18] D. H. Lawrie and C. R. Vora, "Multidimensional parallel access computer memory system," U.S. Patent No. 4,051,551, Sept. 27, 1977.

[19] ——, "The prime memory system for array access," *IEEE Trans. Comput.*, vol. C-31, this issue, pp. 435–442.

[20] M. C. Pease, "An adaptation of the fast Fourier transform for parallel processing," *J. Ass. Comput. Mach.*, vol. 15, pp. 252–264, Apr. 1968.

[21] J. A. Rudolph, "A production implementation of an associative array processor—STARAN," in *Proc. 1972 AFIPS Fall Joint Comput. Conf.*, vol. 41, 1972, pp. 229–241.

[22] R. M. Russell, "The CRAY-1 computer system," *Commun. Ass. Comput. Mach.*, vol. 21, pp. 63–72, Jan. 1978.

[23] A. H. Sameh and R. P. Brent, "Solving triangular systems on a parallel computer," *SIAM J. Numer. Anal.*, vol. 14, pp. 1101–1113, Dec. 1977.

[24] F. H. Sumner, "MU5—An assessment of the design," in *Proc. IFIP Congress, Information Processing 1974*. Amsterdam, The Netherlands: North-Holland, 1974, pp. 133–136.

[25] D. W. Sweeney, "An analysis of floating-point addition," *IBM Syst. J.*, vol. 4, no. 1, pp. 31–42, 1965.

[26] J. F. Thorlin, "Code generation for PIE (Parallel Instruction Execution) computers," in *Proc. AFIPS Spring Joint Comput. Conf.*, 1967, pp. 641–643.

[27] J. E. Thornton, *Design of a Computer, the Control Data 6600.* Glenview, IL: Scott, Foresman, and Co., 1970.

[28] R. M. Tomasulo, "An efficient algorithm for exploiting multiple arithmetic units," *IBM J. Res. Develop.*, vol. 11, pp. 25-33, Jan. 1967.

[29] W. J. Watson, "The TI ASC-A highly modular and flexible super computer architecture," in *Proc. 1972 AFIPS Fall Joint Comput. Conf.*, 1972, pp. 221-228.

pirical analysis of real programs, and the design of high-performance processing, switching, and memory systems for classes of computation ranging from numerical to nonnumerical. The latter work includes the study of interactive text processing and database systems, from the point of view of both the computer and the user.

Dr. Kuck has served as an Editor for a number of professional journals, including the IEEE TRANSACTIONS ON COMPUTERS, and is presently an area editor of the *Journal of the Association for Computing Machinery.* Among his publications are *The Structure of Computers and Computations,* vol. I. He has consulted with many computer manufacturers and users and is the founder and president of Kuck and Associates, Inc., an architecture and optimizing compiler company.

David J. Kuck (S'59-M'69) was born in Muskegon, MI, on October 3, 1937. He received the B.S.E.E. degree from the University of Michigan, Ann Arbor, in 1959, and the M.S. and Ph.D. degrees from Northwestern University, Evanston, IL, in 1960 and 1963, respectively.

From 1963 to 1965 he was a Ford Postdoctoral Fellow and Assistant Professor of Electrical Engineering at the Massachusetts Institute of Technology, Cambridge. In 1965 he joined the Department of Computer Science, University of Illinois, Urbana, where he is now a Professor. Currently, his research interests are in the coherent design of hardware and software systems. This includes the development of the PARAFRASE system, a program transformation facility for array and multiprocessor machines. His recent computer systems research has included theoretical studies of upper bounds on computation time, em-

Richard A. Stokes was born in the Bronx, NY, on June 30, 1931. He received the A.B. degree in mathematics from St. Michael's College, Winooski, VT, and the B.S.E. degree in computer science from George Washington University, Washington, DC.

Following military service he joined the National Security Agency where he was involved in the early application of magnetic cores and transistor to computer design. In 1960 he joined the Martin Company as project leader in the development of CRT graphic displays. In 1964 he joined the Burroughs Corporation, Paoli, PA, as a Staff Engineer working on the design of the B 8501 computer. Later he became Lead Engineer in the development of the Illiac IV computer. In 1976 he was made General Manager of the plant responsible for the design and manufacture of the BSP. He holds several patents in computer design including the B 8501, the Illiac IV, and BSP.

Design of a Massively Parallel Processor

KENNETH E. BATCHER

Abstract—The massively parallel processor (MPP) system is designed to process satellite imagery at high rates. A large number (16 384) of processing elements (PE's) are configured in a square array. For optimum performance on operands of arbitrary length, processing is performed in a bit-serial manner. On 8-bit integer data, addition can occur at 6553 million operations per second (MOPS) and multiplication at 1861 MOPS. On 32-bit floating-point data, addition can occur at 430 MOPS and multiplication at 216 MOPS.

Index Terms—Array processing, bit-slice processing, computer architecture, image processing, parallel processing, satellite imagery.

INTRODUCTION

In this decade, NASA will orbit imaging sensors that can generate data at rates up to 10^{13} bits per day. A variety of image processing tasks such as geometric correction, correlation, image registration, feature selection, multispectral classification, and area measurement are required to extract useful information from this mass of data. The expected workload is between 10^9 and 10^{10} operations per second.

In 1971 NASA Goddard Space Flight Center initiated a program to develop ultra high-speed image processing systems capable of processing this workload. These systems use thousands of processing elements (PE's) operating simultaneously (massive parallelism) to achieve their speed. They exploit the fact that the typical satellite image contains millions of picture elements (pixels) that can generally be processed at the same time.

In December 1979 NASA Goddard awarded a contract to Goodyear Aerospace to construct a massively parallel processor (MPP) to be delivered in the first quarter of 1982. The basic elements of the MPP architecture were developed at NASA Goddard. This correspondence presents the design of the MPP system. The major components are shown in Fig. 1. The array unit (ARU) processes arrays of data at high speed and is controlled by the array control unit (ACU), which also performs scalar arithmetic. The program and data management unit (PDMU) controls the overall flow of data and programs through the system and handles certain ancillary tasks such as program development and diagnostics. The staging memories buffer and reorder data between the ARU, PDMU, and external (host) computer.

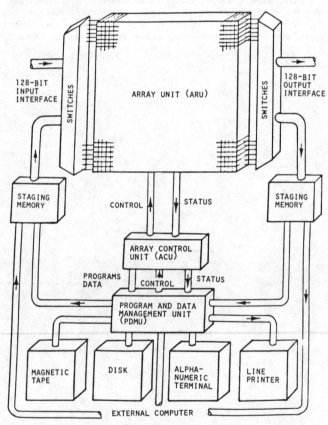

Fig. 1. Block diagram of the massively parallel processor (MPP).

Manuscript received August 6, 1979; revised April 9, 1980. This work was partially funded by NASA Goddard Space Flight Center under Contracts NAS5-25392 and NAS5-25942.

The author is with the Digital Technology Department, Goodyear Aerospace Corporation, Akron, OH 44315.

Reprinted from *IEEE Transactions on Computers,* Volume C-29, Number 9, September 1980, pages 836-840. Copyright © 1980 by The Institute of Electrical and Electronics Engineers, Inc.

Array Unit

Logically, the array unit (ARU) contains 16 384 processing elements (PE's) organized as a 128 by 128 square. Physically, the ARU has an extra 128 by 4 rectangle of PE's that is used to reconfigure the ARU when a PE fault is detected. The PE's are bit-serial processors for efficiently processing operands of any length. The basic clock rate is 10 MHz. With 16 384 PE's operating in parallel, the ARU has a very high processing speed (see Table I). Despite the bit-serial nature of the PE's, even the floating-point speeds compare favorably with several fast number crunchers.

Routing Topology

Each PE in the 128 by 128 square communicates with its nearest neighbor; up, down, right, and left—a topology similar to Illiac IV and some other array processors. Alternative routing topologies such as the flip network [1] or one of its equivalents [2] were investigated. They have the ability to shift data over many PE's in one step and allow data to be accessed in many different directions [3]. Certain paths in the alternative topologies have long runs that complicate their layout and limit their cycle rate. When the number of PE's interconnected is only 256 as in the STARAN® computer, this is no problem; when 16 384 PE's are interconnected, it is a severe problem.

Most of the expected workload does not use the routing flexibility of the alternative topologies. The ability to access data in different directions is important when arrays of data are input and output; it can be used to reorient the arrays between the bit-plane format of the ARU and the pixel format of the outside world.

These considerations lead to the conclusion that the ARU should have a two-dimensional nearest neighbor routing topology such as Illiac IV since it is easy to implement and matches the two-dimensional nature of satellite imagery. The problem of reformatting I/O data is best handled in a staging memory between the ARU and the outside world.

Around the edges of the 128 by 128 array of PE's the edges can be left open (e.g., a row of zeros can be entered along the left edge when routing data to the right) or the opposite edges can be connected. Cases were found where open edges were preferred and other cases where connected edges were preferred. It was decided to make edge-connectivity a programmable function. A topology-register in the array control unit defines the connections between opposite edges of the PE array. The top and bottom edges can either be connected or left open. The connectivity between the left and right edges has four states: open (no connection), cylindrical (connect the left PE of each row to the right PE of the same row), open spiral (for $1 \leq n \leq 127$, connect the left PE of row n to the right PE of row $n - 1$), and closed spiral (like the open spiral, but also connect the left PE of row 0 to the right PE of row 127).

The spiral modes connect the 16 384 PE's together in one long linear array. One can pack several linear arrays of odd sizes (e.g., lines with thousands of image pixels per line) in the ARU and process them in parallel.

Redundancy

The ARU includes some redundancy so that a faulty PE can be bypassed. Redundancy can be added to a two-dimensional array of PE's by adding an extra column (or row) of PE's and inserting bypass gates in the routing network. When a faulty PE is discovered, one disables the whole column containing the faulty PE and joins the columns on either side of it with the bypass gates.

® Registered service mark of the Goodyear Aerospace Corporation, Akron, OH 44315.

TABLE I
SPEED OF TYPICAL OPERATIONS

Operations	Execution Speed*
Addition of Arrays	
8-bit integers (9-bit sum)	6553
12-bit integers (13-bit sum)	4428
32-bit floating-point numbers	430
Multiplication of Arrays (Element-by-Element)	
8-bit integers (16-bit product)	1861
12-bit integers (24-bit product)	910
32-bit floating-point numbers	216
Multiplication of Array by Scalar	
8-bit integers (16-bit product)	2340
12-bit integers (24-bit product)	1260
32-bit floating-point numbers	373

*Million Operations per Second

The PE's in the ARU are implemented with two-row by four-column VLSI chips, thus, it is more convenient to add four redundant columns of PE's and bypass four columns at a time. The PE array has 128 rows and 132 columns. It is divided into 33 groups, with each group containing 128 rows and four columns of PE's. Each group has an independent group-disable control line from the ACU. When a group is disabled, all its outputs are disabled and the groups on either side of it are joined together with 128 bypass gates in the routing network.

When there is no faulty PE, an arbitrary group is disabled so that the size of the logical array is always 128 by 128. Application programs are not aware of which group is disabled and need not be modified when the disabled group is changed. They always use the logical address of a PE to access PE dependent data. The logical address of a PE is a pair of 7-bit numbers X and Y showing its position in the logical array of enabled PE's. A simple routine executed in 27 μs will load the memory of each PE with its logical address.

When a faulty PE is discovered, its data cannot be trusted so the normal error recovery procedure is to reconfigure the ARU to disable the column containing the fault and then to restart the application program from the last checkpoint or from the beginning.

Bit-Serial Processing

The data arrays being processed have a wide range of element lengths. A spectral band of an input pixel may have a resolution of 6 to 12 bits. Intermediate results can have any length from 6 to more than 30 bits. Single-bit flag arrays are generated when pixels are classified. Some computations may be performed in floating point. Thus, the PE's should be able to process operands of any length efficiently.

Conventional computers typically use bit-parallel arithmetic units with certain fixed-word lengths such as 8, 16, or 32 bits. Operands of odd lengths are extended to fit the standard word sizes of the machine. Some of the hardware in the memory and the arithmetic unit is wasted storing and processing the extensions.

Bit-serial processors process operands bit by bit and can handle operands of any length without any wasted hardware. Their slower speed can be counteracted by using a multitude of them and processing many operands in parallel.

There is a wide variety of operand lengths and a prevalence of low-precision operands in the expected workload. Thus, bit-serial processors are more efficient in the use of hardware than bit-parallel processors.

Processing Elements

The initial MPP design had PE's using downshifting binary counters for arithmetic [4], [6], [7]. The PE design was modified to use a full adder and shift register combination for arithmetic. The modified design performs the basic arithmetic operations faster. Each of the PE's has six 1-bit registers (*A, B, C, G, P,* and *S*), a shift register with a programmable length, a random-access memory, a data bus (*D*), a full adder, and some combinatorial logic (see Fig. 2). The basic cycle time of the PE is 100 ns.

Logic and Routing: The *P*-register is used for logic and routing operations. A logic operation combines the state of the *P*-register and the state of the data bus (*D*) to form the new state of the *P*-register. All 16 Boolean functions of the two variables *P* and *D* are implemented. A routing operation shifts the state of the *P*-register into the *P*-register of a neighboring PE (up, down, right, or left).

Arithmetic: The full adder, shift register, and registers *A, B,* and *C* are used for bit-serial arithmetic operations. To add two operands, the bits of one operand are put into the *A*-register, one at a time, least significant bit (LSB) first; corresponding bits of the other operand are put into the *P*-register; the full adder adds the bits in *A* and *P* to the carry bits in the *C*-register to form the sum and carry bits; each carry bit is stored in *C* to be added in the next cycle; and each sum bit is stored in *B*. The sum formed in *B* can be stored in the random-access memory and/or in the shift register. Two's complement subtraction is performed by adding the one's complement of the operand in *P* to the operand in *A* and setting the initial carry bit in *C* to 1 instead of 0.

Multiplication is a series of addition steps where the partial product is recirculated through the shift register and registers *A* and *B*. Appropriate multiples of the multiplicand are formed in *P* and added to the partial product as it recirculates. Division is performed with a nonrestoring division algorithm. The partial dividend is recirculated through the shift register and registers *A* and *B* while the divisor or its complement is formed in *P* and added to it.

Floating-point addition compares exponents; places the fraction of the operand with the least exponent in the shift register; shifts it to the right to align it with the other fraction; adds the other fraction to the shift register; and normalizes the sum. Floating-point multiplication is a multiplication of the fractions, a normalization of the product, and an addition of the exponents.

Masking: The *G*-register can hold a mask bit that can control the activity of the PE. Unmasked logic, routing, and arithmetic operations are performed in all PE's. Masked operations are only performed in those PE's where the *G*-register equals 1.

Several operations may be combined in one 100 ns instruction. Logic and routing operations are masked independently of arithmetic operations so one can combine a masked routing operation with an unmasked arithmetic operation or vice versa. This feature proves to be quite useful in a number of algorithms.

Storage: The random-access memory stores 1024 bits per PE. Standard RAM integrated circuits are used to make it easy to expand storage as advances occur in solid-state memory technology. The ACU generates 16-bit addresses so ARU storage can be expanded to 65 536 bits per PE. Thus, the initial complement of 2 Mbytes of ARU storage can be expanded sixty-fourfold if technology allows it.

Parity error detection is used to find memory faults. A parity bit is added to the eight data bits of each 2 by 4 subarray of PE's. Parity bits are generated and stored for each memory write cycle and checked when the memories are read. A parity error sets an error

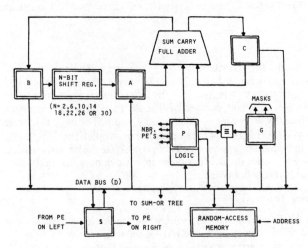

Fig. 2. One processing element

flip-flop associated with the 2 by 4 subarray. A tree of logic elements gives the ACU an inclusive-or of all error flip-flops (after some delay). By operating the group-disable control lines, the ACU can locate the group containing the error and disable it.

Sum-Or Tree: The data bus states of all enabled PE's are combined in a tree of inclusive-or elements called the sum-or tree. The output of this tree is fed to the ACU and used in certain operations such as finding the maximum or minimum value of an array in the ARU.

Input/Output: The *S*-register is used to input and output ARU data. While the PE's are processing data in the random-access memories, columns of input data are shifted into the left side of the ARU (Fig. 1) and through the *S*-registers (Fig. 2) until a plane of 16 384 bits is loaded. The input plane is then stored in the random-access memories in one 100 ns cycle by interrupting the processing momentarily in all PE's and moving the *S*-register values to the memory elements. Planes of data are output by moving them from the memory elements to the *S*-registers and then shifting them out column by column through the right side of the ARU. The shift rate is 10 MHz; thus, up to 160 Mbytes/s can be transferred through the ARU I/O ports. Processing is interrupted for 100 ns for each bit plane of 16 384 bits transferred—less than 1 percent of the time.

Packaging

Standard 4- by 1024-bit RAM elements are used for the PE memories. All other components of a 2 by 4 subarray of PE's are packaged on a custom VLSI CMOS/SOS chip. The VLSI chip also contains the parity tree and the bypass gates for the subarray.

Each $8\frac{1}{2}$ in by 14 in printed circuit board contains 192 PE's in a 16 by 12 array. A board contains 24 VLSI chips, 54 memory elements, and some support circuitry. Eleven boards make up an array slice of 16 by 132 PE's.

Eight array slices (88 boards) make up the ARU. Eight other boards contain the topology switches, control fan out, and other support circuitry. The 96 boards of the ARU are packaged in one cabinet (the leftmost cabinet in Fig. 3). Forced-air cooling is used.

ARRAY CONTROL UNIT

Like the control units of other parallel processors, the array control unit (ACU) performs scalar arithmetic and controls the PE's. It has three sections that operate in parallel (see Fig. 4): PE control, I/O control, and main control. PE control performs all array arithmetic of the application program. I/O control manages the flow of data in and out of the ARU. Main control performs all scalar arithmetic of

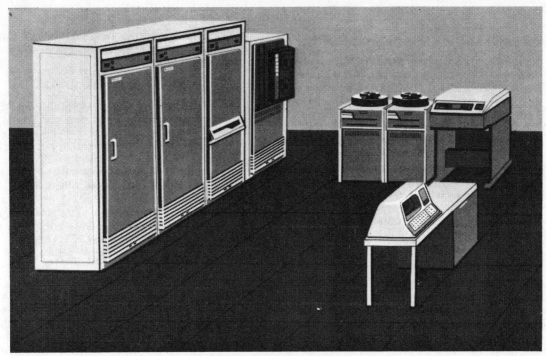

Fig. 3.   MPP physical configuration.

the application program. This arrangement allows array arithmetic, scalar arithmetic, and input/output to be overlapped for minimum execution time.

PE Control

PE control generates all ARU control signals except those associated with I/O. It contains a 64-bit common register to hold scalars and eight 16-bit index registers to hold the addresses of bit planes in the PE memory elements, to count loop executions, and to hold the index of a bit in the common register. PE control reads 64-bit-wide microinstructions from PE control memory. Most instructions are read and executed in 100 ns. One instruction can perform several PE operations, manipulate any number of index registers, and branch conditionally. This reduces overhead significantly so that little, if any, PE processing power is wasted.

PE control memory contains a number of system routines and user-written routines to operate on arrays of data in the ARU. The routines include both array-to-array and scalar-to-array arithmetic operations. A queue between PE control and main control queues up to 7 calls to the PE control routines. Each call contains up to 8 initial index-register values and up to 64 bits of scalar information. Some routines extract scalar information from the ARU (such as a maximum value) and return it to main control.

I/O Control

I/O control shifts the ARU S-registers, manages the flow of information in and out of the ARU ports, and interrupts PE control momentarily to transfer data between the S-registers and buffer areas in the PE memory elements. Once initiated by main control or the PDMU, I/O control can chain through a number of I/O commands. It reads the commands from main control memory.

Main Control

Main control is a fast scalar processor. It reads and executes the application program in the main control memory. It performs all scalar arithmetic itself and places all array arithmetic operations on the PE control call queue. It contains 16 general-purpose registers, three registers to control the ARU group-disable lines, 13 registers associated with the call queue, 12 registers to receive scalars from PE control, and six registers to monitor and control the status of PE control, I/O control, and the ARU.

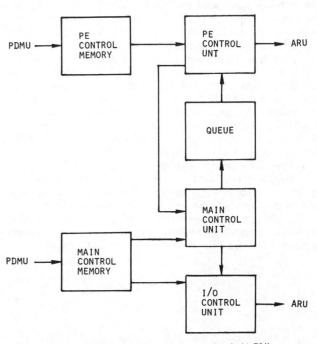

Fig. 4.   Block diagram of array control unit (ACU).

PROGRAM AND DATA MANAGEMENT UNIT

The program and data management unit (PDMU) controls the overall flow of programs and data in the system (Fig. 1). Control is from an alphanumeric terminal. The PDMU is a minicomputer (DEC PDP-11) with custom interfaces to the ACU control memories and registers and to the staging memories. The operating system is DEC's RSX-11M real-time multiprogramming system.

The PDMU also executes the MPP program-development software package. The package includes a PE control assembler to develop array processing routines for PE control, a main assembler to develop application programs executing in main control, a linker to form load modules for the ACU, and a control and debug module that loads programs into the ACU, controls their execution, and facilitates debugging. This package is written in Fortran for easy movement to the host computer.

STAGING MEMORIES

The staging memories reside between the wide I/O ports of the ARU and the PDMU. They also have a port to an external (host) computer. Besides acting as buffers for ARU data being input and output, the memories reorder arrays of data.

Satellite imagery is normally stored in pixel order in the PDMU and other conventional computers. That is, line 1 pixel 1 followed by line 1 pixel 2, etc., followed by the pixels of line 2, line 3, etc. The imagery might be band-interleaved (all spectral bands of a pixel stored together) or band-sequential (band 1 of all pixels followed by band 2 of all pixels, etc.).

Arrays of data are transferred through the ARU ports in bit-sequential order. That is, the most (or least) significant bit of 16 384 elements followed by the next bit of 16 384 elements, etc. Reordering is required to fit the normal order of satellite imagery in the PDMU or the host. Thus the staging memories are given a reordering capability.

The staging memories are packaged together in a large multidimensional-access (MDA) or corner-turning memory. Items of data flow through a substager which is a smaller MDA memory. Input data items from the ARU, PDMU, or host are reformatted in the substager into patches which are sent to the large staging memory. Output data patches from the large staging memory are reformatted in the substager for transmission to the ARU, PDMU, or host.

The large staging memory uses 1280 dynamic RAM integrated-circuits for data storage and 384 RAM's for error-correcting-code (ECC) storage. (A 6-bit ECC is added to each 20-bit word.) Initially, the boards will be populated with 16K bit RAM's for a capacity of 2.5 Mbytes. Later, as memory technology advances, the 16K bit RAM's can be replaced with 64K bit RAM's or 256K bit RAM's to increase the capacity of 10 Mbytes or 40 Mbytes.

The substager can access the main stager at a 320 Mbyte per second rate (thirty-two 20-bit words every 250 ns). The accesses can be spread across the main stager in a variety of ways. Patches of data in various orientations can be read or written conveniently.

The substager has a smaller memory with 1-bit words. It assembles input data into patches for the main staging memory and disassembles patches of data from the main staging memory for output.

The main staging memory and the substager are controlled by a control unit that can be programmed to input and output imagery in a wide variety of formats.

HOST INTERFACE

The MPP to be delivered to NASA will use a DEC VAX-11/780 for a host computer. The staging memories of the MPP are connected to a DR-780 high-speed user interface of the VAX-11/780. Imagery can be transferred over this path at the rate of the DR-780 (at least 6 Mbytes/s). To allow control of the MPP by the host, the custom interface of the MPP is switched from the PDMU to the host. The switching is simplified by the fact that both the PDMU (a DEC PDP-11) and the host (a DEC VAX-11/780) have a DEC UNIBUS. The transfer of system software to the host is simplified by writing much of it in Fortran and using the compatibility mode of VAX to execute those portions written in PDP-11 code.

CONCLUSIONS

The massively parallel processor is designed to process satellite imagery at high rates. Its high-processing speed, large memory capacity, and I/O reformatting capabilities should make it useful in other applications. Preliminary studies indicate that the MPP can support such diverse application areas as general image processing, weather simulation, aerodynamic studies, radar processing, reactor diffusion analysis, and computer-image generation.

The modular structure of the MPP allows it to be scaled up or down for different applications. The number of processing elements in the ARU can be adjusted to support different processing rates. The sizes of the ARU and staging memories are also adjustable. Host computers other than the VAX-11/780 can be accommodated. The PDMU functions can be absorbed by the host or alternatively, the PDMU can act as the host (since the PDMU is in the PDP-11 and VAX family, a wide variety of PDMU capacities and configurations are feasible).

As part of their ongoing program to develop space-borne image processors, NASA Opaque Goddard is pursuing the design of a miniaturized version of the MPP [5].

REFERENCES

[1] K. E. Batcher, "The flip network in STARAN," in *1976 Proc. Int. Conf. Parallel Processing*, pp. 65–71.

[2] H. J. Siegel and S. D. Smith, "Study of multistage SIMD interconnection networks," in *Proc. 5th Annu. Symp. Comput. Architecture*, Apr. 1978, pp. 223–229.

[3] K. E. Batcher, "The multi-dimensional-access memory in STARAN," *IEEE Trans. Comput.*, vol. C-26, pp. 174–177, Feb. 1977.

[4] L-W Fung, *A Massively Parallel Processing Computer; High-Speed Computer and Algorithm Organization*, D. J. Kuck *et al.*, Ed. New York: Academic, 1977, pp. 203–204.

[5] D. H. Schaefer, "Massively parallel information processing systems for space applications," presented at AIAA Comput. Aerospace Conf. II, Oct. 1979.

[6] L. W. Fung, "MPPC: A massively parallel processing computer," Goddard Space Flight Center, Greenbelt, MD, GSFC Image Systems Section Rep., Sept. 1976.

[7] Request for Proposal, RFP GSFC-5-45191/254 (Appendix A).

Concurrent processing depends on interconnection networks for communication among processors and memory modules. Various network topologies and switching strategies are covered here.

A Survey of Interconnection Networks

Tse-yun Feng
The Ohio State University

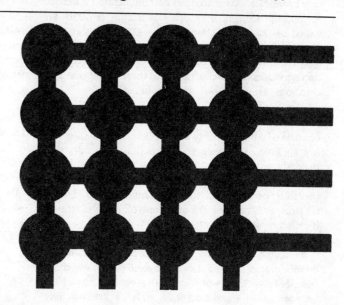

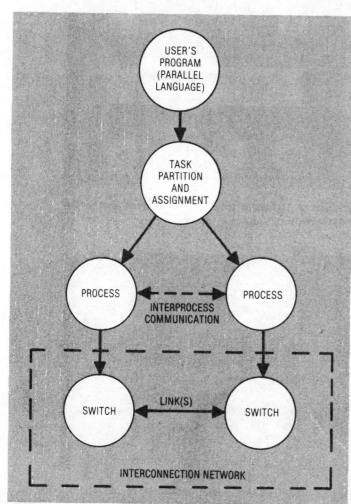

Figure 1. An overview of concurrent processing systems.

Concurrent processing of data items is considered a proper approach for significantly increasing processing speed.[1] In many real-time applications—such as image processing and weather computation, which need an instruction execution rate of more than one billion floating-point instructions per second—concurrent processing is unavoidable. And now, with the advent of LSI technology, it is economically feasible to construct a concurrent processing system by interconnecting hundreds—even thousands—of off-the-shelf processors and memory modules.

A basic concurrent processing system is shown in Figure 1. Processes, generated by compiling and partitioning a user's program, are assigned to individual processors, and an interconnection network implements interprocess communication. A general model of the hardware system is shown in Figure 2. The interconnection network facilitates communication not only among the *n* processors and the *m* memory modules but also between the processors and memory modules.

Many interconnection networks have been reviewed in other surveys.[2-9] In this article we consider interconnection networks from a practical design viewpoint. We examine design decisions that are essential in choosing a cost-effective communication network, survey the various topologies and communication protocols, and discuss connection issues related to concurrent processing.

Design decisions

In selecting the architecture of an interconnection network, four design decisions can be identified.[10] They concern operation mode, control strategy, switching method, and network topology.

EHO219-6/84/0000/0109$01.00 © 1981 IEEE

Operation mode. Two types of communication can be identified: synchronous and asynchronous. Synchronous communication is needed for processing in which communication paths are established synchronously for either a data manipulating function[11] or a data/instruction broadcast. Asynchronous communication is needed for multiprocessing in which connection requests are issued dynamically. A system may also be designed to facilitate both synchronous and asynchronous processing. Therefore, typical operation modes of interconnection networks can be classified into three categories: synchronous, asnychronous, and combined.

Control strategy. A typical interconnection network consists of a number of switching elements and interconnecting links. Interconnection functions are realized by properly setting control of the switching elements. The control-setting function can be managed by a centralized controller or by the individual switching element. The latter strategy is called distributed control; the first strategy is called centralized control.

Switching methodology. The two major switching methodologies are circuit switching and packet switching. In circuit switching, a physical path is actually established between a source and a destination. In packet switching, data is put in a packet and routed through the interconnection network without establishing a physical connection path. In general, circuit switching is much more suitable for bulk data transmission, and packet switching is more efficient for short data messages. Another option, integrated switching, includes capabilities of both circuit switching and packet switching. Therefore, three switching methodologies can be identified: circuit switching, packet switching, and integrated switching.

Network topology. A network can be depicted by a graph in which nodes represent switching points and edges represent communication links. The topologies tend to be regular and can be grouped into two categories: static and dynamic. In a static topology, links between

two processors are passive and dedicated buses cannot be reconfigured for direct connections to other processors. On the other hand, links in the dynamic category can be reconfigured by setting the network's active switching elements.

The cross product of the set of categories in each design decision—{operation mode} × {control strategy} × {switching methodology} × {network topology}—represents a space of interconnection networks. Obviously, the cross product contains some uninteresting cases, but a network designer can obtain a meaningful subspace by exercising a practical view of engineering technology.

Topologies

Network topology is a key factor in determining a suitable architectural structure, and many topologies have been considered for telephone switching connections.[12] Here, we review those proposed or used for connections in tightly coupled multiple-processor systems (see Figure 3).

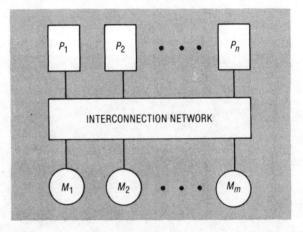

Figure 2. Hardware model of concurrent processing systems.

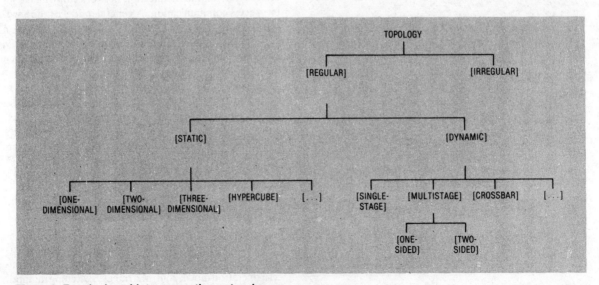

Figure 3. Topologies of interconnection networks.

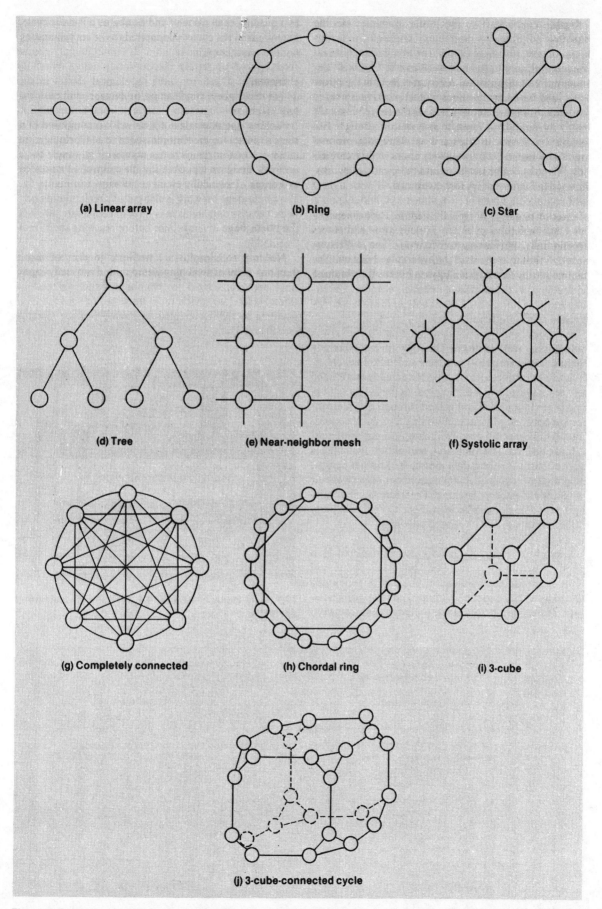

Figure 4. Examples of static network toplogies: (a) one dimensional; (b-f) two dimensional; and (g-j) three dimensional.

Static. Topologies in the static category can be classified according to dimensions required for layout —specifically, one-dimensional, two-dimensional, three-dimensional, and hypercube as shown in Figure 3. Examples of one-dimensional topologies include the linear array used for some pipeline architectures (Figure 4a).[13] Two-dimensional topologies include the ring,[14,15] star,[16] tree,[17] near-neighbor mesh,[18] and systolic array.[13] Examples are shown in Figure 4b-f. Three-dimensional topologies include the completely connected,[19] chordal ring,[20] 3-cube,[21] and 3-cube-connected-cycle[22] networks depicted in Figure 4g-j. A D-dimensional, W-wide hypercube contains W nodes in each dimension, and there is a connection to a node in each dimension. The near-neighbor mesh and the 3-cube are actually two- and three-dimensional hypercubes, respectively. The cube-connected-cycle is a deviation of the hypercube. For example, the 3-cube-connected-cycle shown in Figure 4j is obtained by replacing each node of the 3-cube by a 3-node cycle. Each node in the cycle is connected to the corresponding node in another cycle.

Dynamic. There are three topological classes in the dynamic category: single-stage, multistage, and crossbar (see Figure 5).

Single-stage. A single-stage network is composed of a stage of switching elements cascaded to a link connection pattern. The shuffle-exchange network[23] is a single-stage network based on a perfect-shuffle connection cascaded to a stage of switching elements as shown in Figure 5a. The single-stage network is also called a recirculating network because data items may have to recirculate through the single stage several times before reaching their final destination.

Multistage. A multistage network consists of more than one stage of switching elements and is usually capa-

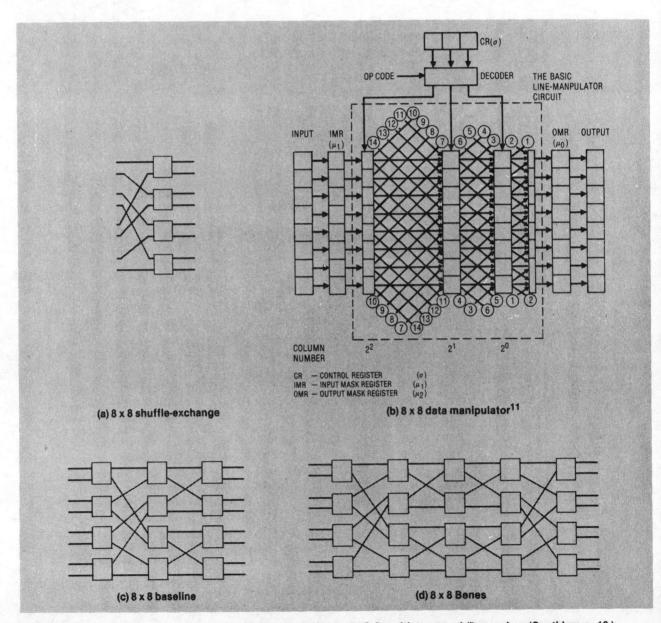

(a) 8 x 8 shuffle-exchange

(b) 8 x 8 data manipulator[11]

(c) 8 x 8 baseline

(d) 8 x 8 Benes

CR — CONTROL REGISTER (σ)
IMR — INPUT MASK REGISTER (μ_1)
OMR — OUTPUT MASK REGISTER (μ_2)

Figure 5. Examples of dynamic network topologies: (a) single stage; (b-i) multistage; and (j) crossbar. (Cont'd on p. 16.)

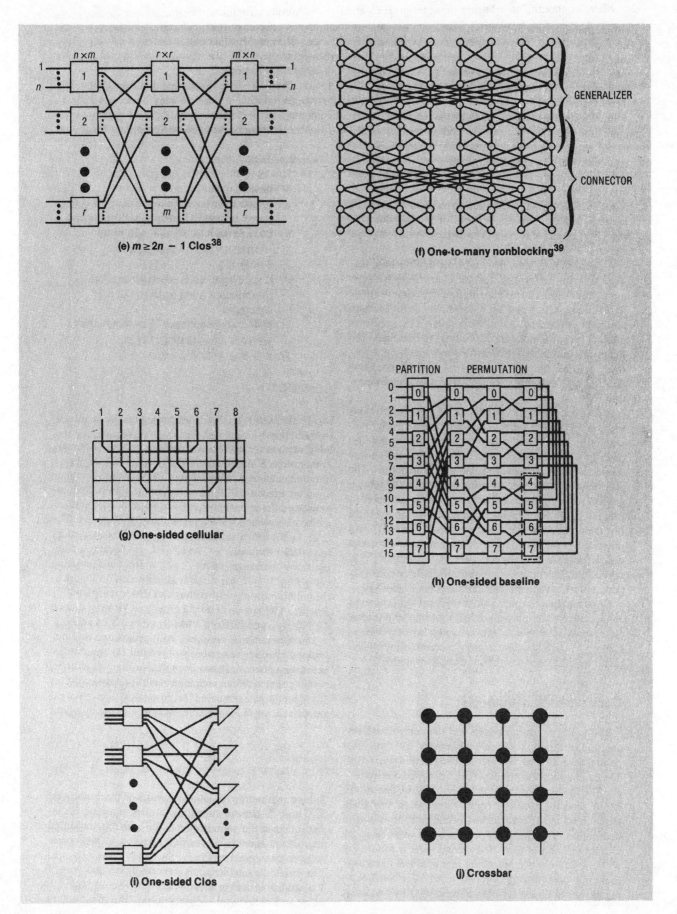

(e) $m \geq 2n - 1$ Clos[38]

(f) One-to-many nonblocking[39]

GENERALIZER

CONNECTOR

(g) One-sided cellular

PARTITION   PERMUTATION

(h) One-sided baseline

(i) One-sided Clos

(j) Crossbar

Figure 5 (cont'd from p.15). Examples of multistage and crossbar (j) dynamic network topologies.

ble of connecting an arbitrary input terminal to an arbitrary output terminal. Multistage networks can be one-sided or two-sided. The one-sided networks, sometimes called full switches, have input-output ports on the same side. The two-sided multistage networks, which usually have an input side and an output side, can be divided into three classes: blocking, rearrangeable, and nonblocking.

In blocking networks, simultaneous connections of more than one terminal pair may result in conflicts in the use of network communication links. Examples of this type of network, which has been extensively investigated, include data manipulator,[24] baseline,[25,26] SW banyan,[27] omega,[28] flip,[29] indirect binary n-cube,[30] and delta.[31] A topological equivalence relationship has been established for this class of networks in terms of the baseline network.[25,26] A data manipulator and a baseline network are shown in Figure 5b and 5c.

A network is called a rearrangeable nonblocking network if it can perform all possible connections between inputs and outputs by rearranging its existing connections so that a connection path for a new input-output pair can always be established. A well-defined network, the Benes network[12] shown in Figure 5d, belongs to this class. The Benes rearrangeable network topology has been extensively studied for use in synchronous data permutation[32-35] and asynchronous interprocessor communication.[36,37]

A network which can handle all possible connections without blocking is called a nonblocking network. Two cases have been considered in the literature. In the first case, the Clos network[38] shown in Figure 5e, a one-to-one connection is made between an input and an output. The other case considers one-to-many connections.[39] Here, a generalized-connection network topology is generated to pass any of the N^N mapping of inputs onto outputs where N is the number of inputs or outputs (see Figure 5f). In a one-sided network (or full switch), one-to-one connection is possible between all pairs of terminals.[40,41] A cellular implementation, a base-line topology construction, and a Clos construction are shown in Figure 5g-i.

Crossbar. In a crossbar switch every input port can be connected to a free output port without blocking. Figure 5j shows a schematic which is similar to one used in C.mmp.[42] A crossbar switch called a versatile line manipulator has also been designed and implemented.[43,44]

Communication protocols

The switching methodology and the control strategy are implemented in switching elements (or switching points) according to required communication protocols. The communication protocols can be viewed on two levels. The first level concerns switching control algorithms which generate necessary control settings on switching elements to ensure reliable data routings from source to destination. The first-level protocols are referred to as routing techniques here. The second level is concerned with the link control procedure that provides the hand-shaking process among switching points. The handshaking process is a basic function implemented by switching elements.

Routing techniques. The routing techniques depend on the network topology and the operation mode used. More or less, each multiple-processor system needs a routing algorithm. Here, we use several well-defined routing algorithms for examples.

Near-neighbor mesh. Bitonic sort has been adapted by several authors[45-47] for the routing of an $n \times n$ mesh-connected, single instruction-multiple data stream system. The procedure developed by Nassimi[47] is as follows:

Procedure SORT (n,n)
 1) K ← S ← 1
 2) **While** K < n do
    a) consider the $n \times n$ processor array as composed of many adjacent $K \times 2K$ subarrays
    b) **do** in parallel for each $K \times 2K$ array
       HORIZONTAL_MERGE(K, 2K)
    c) S ← S + 1
    d) Consider the $n \times n$ processor array as composed of many adjacent $2K \times 2K$ subarrays
    e) **do** in parallel for each $2K \times 2K$ subarray
       VERTICAL_MERGE(2K, 2K)
    f) S ← S + 1; K ← 2 * K
  end
end SORT

The HORIZONTAL_MERGE sorts a bitonic sequence arranged in two arrays with the increasing sequence on the left array and the decreasing sequence on the right array, or vice versa. Similarly, the VERTICAL_MERGE sorts a bitonic sequence arranged in two arrays with the increasing sequence on the upper array and the decreasing sequence on the lower array, or vice versa. A complete example of sorting a 4×4 array is shown in Figure 6. The order into which a subarray gets sorted is determined by the SIGN function, " + " and " − ", used during a comparison-interchange where " + " is for nondecreasing order and " − " is for nonincreasing order. In Figure 6, the initial values given go through an HM sort on two 1×1 arrays, a VM sort on two 1×2 arrays, an HM sort on two 2×2 arrays, and finally a VM sort on two 2×4 arrays.

Shuffle-exchange network. Both centralized and distributed routings have been worked out for the shuffle-exchange network. It has been shown that the shuffle-exchange network can realize an arbitrary permutation in $3(\log_2 N) - 1$ passes where N is the network size.[48] An example is shown in Figure 7 for the following permutation:

$$p = \begin{pmatrix} 0 & 1 & 2 & 3 & 4 & 5 & 6 & 7 & 8 & 9 & 10 & 11 & 12 & 13 & 14 & 15 \\ 14 & 12 & 5 & 7 & 15 & 8 & 9 & 13 & 4 & 3 & 10 & 6 & 1 & 0 & 2 & 11 \end{pmatrix}$$

The control setting developed consists of three matrices, $\overline{F}$, $\overline{S}$, and $\overline{T}$. Among these three control matrices, $\overline{S}$ is independent of the permutation and $\overline{F}$ and $\overline{T}$ are modified matrices obtained by performing some prescribed operations on the control matrix for the Benes binary network. The detailed transformation is shown in Wu and Feng.[48] The shuffle-exchange network can also be constructed to adapt to a distributed control scheme. The construction

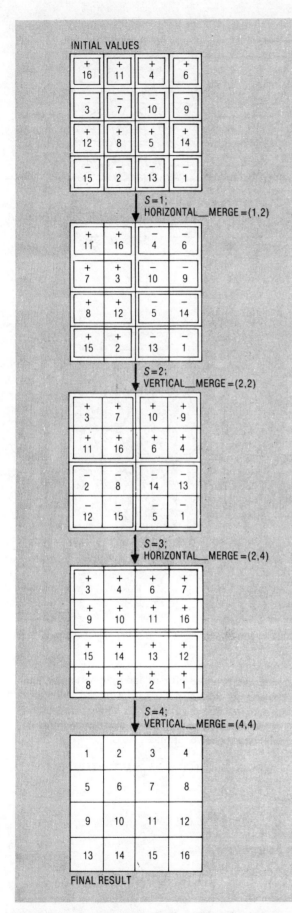

INITIAL VALUES

$S=1$;
HORIZONTAL__MERGE = (1,2)

$S=2$;
VERTICAL__MERGE = (2,2)

$S=3$;
HORIZONTAL__MERGE = (2,4)

$S=4$;
VERTICAL__MERGE = (4,4)

FINAL RESULT

Figure 6. A complete example of sorting a 4 x 4 array.

can be considered as a sorting network, and the binary codes of the destination names are used as the values to be sorted.[23,49] Figure 8 illustrates an example for 2^n elements where $n = 4$. Each of the n^2 steps in this scheme consists of a perfect-shuffle followed by simultaneous operations performed on 2^{n-1} pairs of adjacent elements. Each of the latter operations is either "0" (no operation, straight connection), " + " (comparator module which sends the larger value to the lower link), or " − " (a reverse comparator module). The sorting proceeds in n stages of n steps each: during stage s, for $s \leq n$, we do $n-s$ steps in which all operations are "0", followed by s steps in which the operations consist alternately of 2^t " + " followed by 2^t " − " for $t = 1, 2, \ldots, s$. During the last stage, all operations are " + ".

Data manipulator. A centralized control scheme is designed for implementing data manipulating functions such as permuting, replicating, spacing, masking, and complementing.[11] To implement a data manipulating function, proper control lines of the six groups ($U_1^{2^i}, U_2^{2^i}, H_1^{2^i}, H_2^{2^i}, D_1^{2^i}, D_2^{2^i}$) in each column must be properly set through the use of the control register and the associated decoder. A "duplicate spaced substrings down" operation is illustrated in Figure 9. The two substrings to be duplicated are AB and EF. For this operation the control line groups $D_1^{2^i}$ and $H_1^{2^i}$ or $H_1^{2^i}$ and $H_2^{2^i}$ are activated, depending on whether the control bit is 1 or 0 as determined by substring length. In this example, the substring is 2; thus, only the control bit for column 2^1 has a value of 1, all others are 0's. Thus, in columns 2^2 and 2^0, $H_1^{2^i}$ and $H_2^{2^i}$ are activated, and in column 2^1, $D_1^{2^i}$ and $H_1^{2^i}$ are activated. With this control pattern, the substrings can be generated at the output register.

A distributed control scheme has also been developed by McMillen and Siegel.[50] It uses a routing tag which contains $2n$ bits and is of the form $F = (f_{2n-1} \cdots f_{n+1} f_n f_{n-1} \cdots f_1 f_0)$. The n low-order bits represent the magnitudes of the route, and the n high-order bits represent the sign corresponding to the magnitudes. In stage i, a given switching element examines bits i and $n+i$ of the routing tag. If $f_i = 0$, the straight link is used, regardless of the value of f_{n+i}. If $f_i = 1$, bit $n+i$ is examined. If $f_{n+i} = 0$, the $+2^i$ link is used; if $f_{n+i} = 1$, the -2^i link is used. The source processor generates its own routing tag. For example, in a data manipulator of $N = 2^4$, if the source is 13 and the destination is 6, one possible value for F is 00000111. The path traversed is straight, $+2^2$, $+2^1$, $+2^0$. Multiple paths exist between a source-destination pair. For example, an alternative routing tag from source 13 to destination 6 is (0001 1001). The example is shown in Figure 10. A general rule to calculate the routing tag is shown as

$$D = S + (-1)^{f_{2n-1}} (f_n 2^{n-1}) + (-1)^{f_{2n-2}} (f_{n-1} 2^{n-2})$$

$$+ \ldots (-1)^{f_n} (f_0 2^0)$$

where S and D are the addresses of the source and the destination, respectively.

Baseline network. Routing techniques for baseline networks described here are also useful for other topological-

115

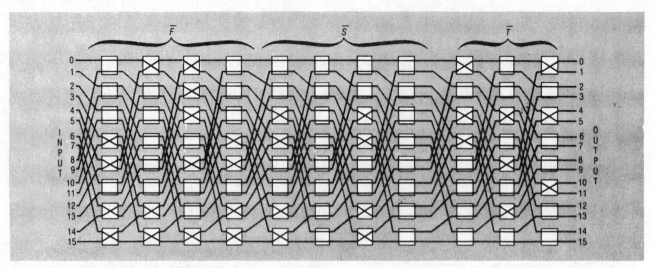

Figure 7. An example for universal realization of permutations.[48]

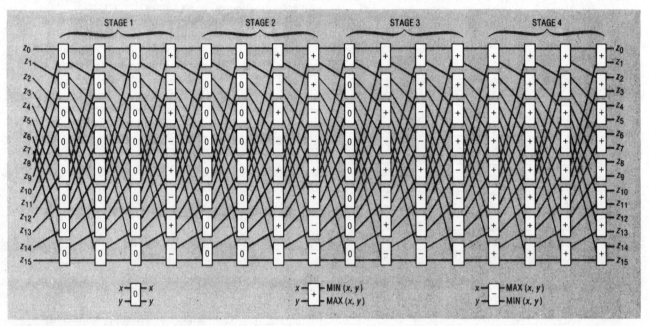

Figure 8. Sorting with shuffle-exchange. (Adapted from *The Art of Computer Programming, Vol. 3: Sorting and Searching* by D. E. Knuth; Addison-Wesley, Reading, Mass., © 1973.)

ly equivalent blocking multistage networks.[25] Basically, two types of routing are available: recursive routing and destination tag routing.[25,28,51] The recursive routing algorithm determines the control pattern according to permutation names. For some permutation, useful in parallel processing, the control pattern can be calculated recursively on the fly as the data pass through the network. Six categories of such permutations have been identified. For our purpose, we describe one here and show the recursive routing algorithm. The flip permutation function[29] is described as follows:

$$F_k^{\{n\}} \ (0 \le k < 2^n): p(X^r \oplus k) = X \text{ and } p(X \oplus k) = X^r$$

where X^r is the number whose binary representation is the reverse of X. Let $k = 2k_1 + k_0$ and $[L;R]$ denote the cascaded matrix whose left part and right part are L and R, respectively. Also let $V^{(n-1)}(b)$ be the 2^{n-1} bit vector whose components are all equal to b. The control pattern $K^{(n)}$ of the flip function can then be expressed in terms of the following recursive formula:

$$K^{(n)}(F_k^{\{n\}}) = [V^{(n-1)}(k_0); K^{(n-1)}(F_k^{\{n\}})],$$

where

$$K^{(1)}(F_k^{\{n\}}) = [V^{(n-1)}(k)].$$

For example, assuming

$$p = \begin{pmatrix} 0 & 1 & 2 & 3 & 4 & 5 & 6 & 7 \\ 1 & 5 & 3 & 7 & 0 & 4 & 2 & 6 \end{pmatrix}$$

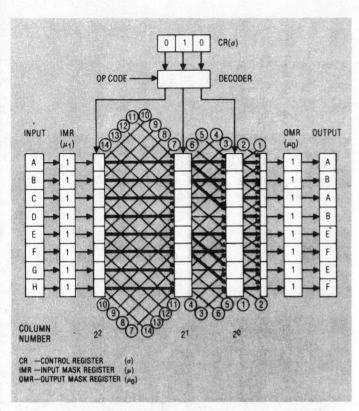

Figure 9. Duplicate spaced substring down on data manipulator.[11]

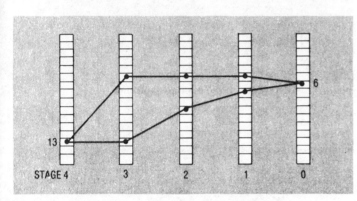

Figure 10. Distributed routing on the data manipulator.

p can be described by

$$F_4^{(3)}: p(X^r \oplus 4) = X.$$

Accordingly, we have

$$K^{(3)}(F_4^{(3)}) = [V^2(0); V^{(2)}(0); V^{(2)}(1)].$$

Hence

$$K^{(3)}(p) = \begin{bmatrix} 0 & 0 & 1 \\ 0 & 0 & 1 \\ 0 & 0 & 1 \\ 0 & 0 & 1 \end{bmatrix}$$

The destination tag routing uses the binary representation

of the destination as a routing tag. Let the source terminal link and destination terminal link be A and Z, respectively. Also, let the binary representation of Z be $z_{n-1}z_{n-2}\ldots z_0$. Starting at A, the first node to which A is connected is set to switch A to the upper link if $z_{n-1}=0$ or the lower link if $z_{n-1}=1$. The second node in the path is again set to switch A to the upper link if $z_{n-2}=0$ or the lower link if $z_{n-2}=1$. This scheme is continued until we get the proper destination. For example, in Figure 11, $A=2$ and $Z=11$ (i.e., $z_3z_2z_1z_0=1011$). Switching element 1 of the left-most stage switches A to the lower link because $z_3=1$. At the next stage, switching element 4 switches A to the upper link because $z_2=0$. Again, switching element 4 in the third stage and switching element 5 in the right-most stage both switch A to the lower links because $z_1=z_0=1$. If we consider Z as the source and A as the destination, using the binary representation of A as the routing tag and repeating the same routing procedure will lead us to choose the same path. This routing tag algorithm will connect the only path available between a source and a destination and is extremely suitable for a distributed control scheme. A conflict resolution scheme[25] has also been developed for implementing destination tag routing in terms of centralized control.

Benes network. Sequential routing algorithms[34,52] need $O(N \log N)$ steps where N is the network size. Many researchers have worked toward improving this time complexity in terms of parallel processing technique,[53] heuristic method,[37] or recursive formula.[35] Here, we demonstrate the very basic routing algorithm, called the looping algorithm. The basic principle, in terms of the permutation to be realized by the Benes binary network shown in Figure 5d, is

$$p = \begin{pmatrix} 0 & 1 & 2 & 3 & 4 & 5 & 6 & 7 \\ 3 & 7 & 4 & 0 & 2 & 6 & 1 & 5 \end{pmatrix}$$

The loop algorithm starts recording the permutation, p, as shown in Figure 12. The two output numbers of a switching element in the output stage are shown in the same column, and the two input numbers of a switching element in the input stage are shown in the same row. We then choose an arbitrary entry in the chart as a starting point. For example, electing to start at row 23 and column 01, we then look for a same-row or column entry to form a loop and, in Figure 12, choose row 23 and column 45. The process continues until we obtain a loop by re-entering row 23 and column 01. The loop's member entries are then assigned "a" and "b" alternately. The second loop can be formed in the same way. Then, we assign input and output lines named "a" to subnetwork a and those named "b" to subnetwork b. The control of the input and output switching elements must be set as depicted in Figure 13. This looping algorithm can be applied recursively to the two subnetworks.

Construction of interconnection networks. Interconnection networks are usually designed so they can be constructed of a single type of modular building block called a switching element. The switching element realizes communication protocols which specify the control strategy and the switching methodology.

The logic design of switching elements has been explored in many projects,[54-56] including recent LSI implementations.[10,57] Here, we describe in more detail three designs that have been implemented and are operational.

Flip network 2 × 2 switching element. The flip network uses centralized control and circuit switching.[29] The 2 × 2 switching element can be set by a control line into a direct-connection or crossed-connection state. Assume that I_0, I_1, O_0, O_1, and C represent the two inputs, the two outputs, and the switching element control. The switching element's output function can be expressed as follows:

$$O_0 = \overline{C} I_0 + C \cdot I_1, \text{and}$$

$$O_1 = \overline{C} I_1 + C \cdot I_0$$

where $C = 0$ means straight connection and $C = 1$ crossed connection (see Figure 14).

Dimond 2 × 2 switching element. A switching element with two input and output ports, called Dimond for dual interconnection modular network device,[58] allows modular construction of interconnection networks. A packet of messages (containing routing information) arriving at a Dimond is switched to a designated output port, where it is stored in a register. Figure 15 shows an implementation of Dimond which requires one control clock for all interconnected switching elements. The central clock has two phases. In the first clock phase, it is determined which inputs have to be copied into which registers. The copy allowances so determined are stored in four flip-flops: C_{00}, C_{01}, C_{10}, and C_{11} (C_{01} is the allowance for copying in_0 into reg_1). In addition, output signals of copy acknowledgments ($cack_0$ and $cack_1$), internal control signals ($cross_0$, $fill_0$, and $fill_1$) are generated. More precisely, we have the following:

$$C_{00} = creq_0 \cdot \overline{des_0} \cdot \overline{stat_0} \cdot (\overline{creq_1} + des_1 +, \overline{prio}) ;$$

$$C_{01} = creq_0 \cdot des_0 \cdot \overline{stat_1} \cdot (\overline{creq_1} + \overline{des_1} + \overline{prio}) ;$$

$$C_{10} = creq_1 \cdot \overline{des_1} \cdot \overline{stat_0} \cdot (\overline{creq_0} + des_0 + prio) ;$$

$$C_{11} = creq_1 \cdot des_1 \cdot \overline{stat_1} \cdot (\overline{creq_0} + \overline{des_0} + prio) ;$$

$$Cack_0 = C_{00} + C_{01} ;$$

$$Cack_1 = C_{10} + C_{11} ;$$

$$Cross = C_{00} + C_{11} ;$$

$$Fill_0 = C_{00} + C_{10} ;$$

$$Fill_1 = C_{01} + C_{11} ;$$

where *prio* is the priority line indicating the index (0,1) of the input served first in the event of conflict, and des_0 and des_1 are destination lines for in_0 and in_1. In the second clock phase, two actions are performed concurrently. Inputs are copied into the output register, if required, and

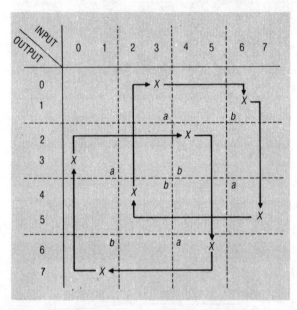

Figure 12. An example of the looping algorithm.

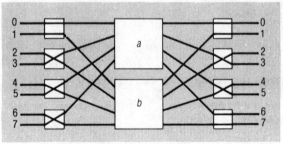

Figure 13. Control setting result from the first iteration of the looping algorithm.

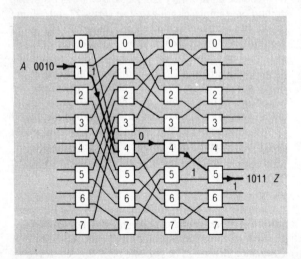

Figure 11. Distributed routing on a baseline network.

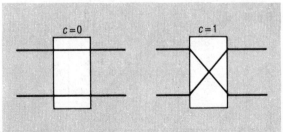

Figure 14. A 2 x 2 switching element.

the status flip-flops, $stat_0$ and $stat_1$ (status of reg_0 and reg_1, respectively) are adapted. Precisely, we have the following:

$$Fill_0 \rightarrow reg_0 = cross \cdot in_0 + \overline{cross} \cdot in_1 \quad ;$$

$$Fill_1 \rightarrow reg_1 = \overline{cross} \cdot in_0 + cross \cdot in_1 \quad ;$$

$$Fill_0 \cdot rel_0 \rightarrow stat_0 = 1 \quad ;$$
$$rel_0 \rightarrow stat_0 = 0 \quad ;$$

$$Fill_1 \cdot \overline{rel_1} \rightarrow stat_1 = 1 \quad ;$$
$$rel_1 \rightarrow stat_1 = 0 \quad .$$

The information-available lines are connected to the status flip-flops:

$$infa_0 = stat_0 \quad ;$$

$$infa_1 = stat_1 \quad .$$

The interconnection of two Dimonds is shown in Figure 16, which depicts the relation of handshaking lines.

64×64 *switching element.* A centralized-control and circuit-switching 64×64 versatile data manipulator[11] (see Figure 17) is operating in conjunction with the Staran computer at the Rome Air Development Center.[44] The

data manipulator operates under the control of the Staran computer's parallel input-output unit. The contents of the input and output masks, of the address control register, and of the input and output control registers, as well as the data to be manipulated, are entered via the 256-bit wide PIO buffer interface. The manipulated data leave the data manipulator via the same interface. The data manipulator's instruction repertoire allows one to load the various address registers and masks and to start and stop data manipulation. Self-test is performed by loading address and input-data registers, allowing verification of correct operation without assistance from the Staran computer. There are 64×64 cells in the basic crossbar circuit. The output gate of cell (i,j) is controlled by the ith address control register through a decoder. The decoder has 64 outputs to control the 64 output gates in a basic-crossbar-circuit row.

Connection issues for concurrent processing

Two approaches—array processing and multiprocessing—have been tried to provide processing concurrency. Since array processors, which consist of multiple processing elements and parallel memory modules under one control unit, can handle single instructions and multiple data streams, they are also known as SIMD computers. Existing examples include Illiac IV and Staran. An overall SIMD machine organization[59] is shown in Figure 18. The N processing elements, or PEs, are connected by two interconnection networks to the M parallel memory modules. The control unit in the center provides control over PEs and memory modules.

Array processors allow explicit expression of parallelism in user programs. The compiler detects the parallelism and generates object code suitable for execution in the multiple processing elements and the control unit. Program segments which cannot be converted into parallel executable forms are executed in the control unit; program segments which can be converted into parallel executable forms are sent to the PEs and executed synchronously on data fetched from parallel memory modules under the control of the control unit. To enable synchronous manipulation in the PEs, the data are permuted and arranged in vector form. Thus, to run a program more efficiently on an array processor, one must develop a technique for vectorizing the program (or algorithm). The interconnection network plays a major role in vectorization.

The second approach for concurrent processing uses multiprocessing. The multiprocessor can handle multiple instructions and multiple data streams and hence is called an MIMD processor. Examples of the MIMD architecture include HEP,[60] data flow processor,[61] and flow model processor.[62] A configuration of MIMD architecture[62] is shown in Figure 19. The N processing elements are connected to the M memory modules by an interconnection network. The activities are coordinated by the coordinator. Unlike the control unit in an array processor, the coordinator does not execute object code; it only implements the synchronization of processes and smooths out the execution sequence. Again, the compiler

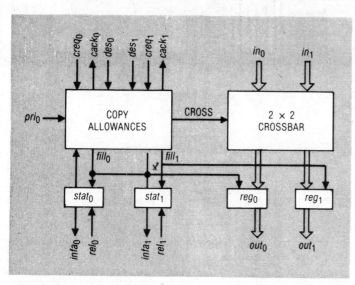

Figure 15. A 2 x 2 dual interconnecting modular network device— Dimond[58]—for packet switching.

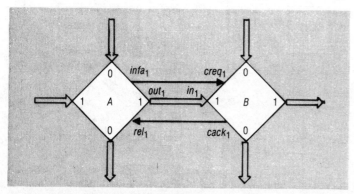

Figure 16. Connecting two Dimonds.[58]

COMPUTER

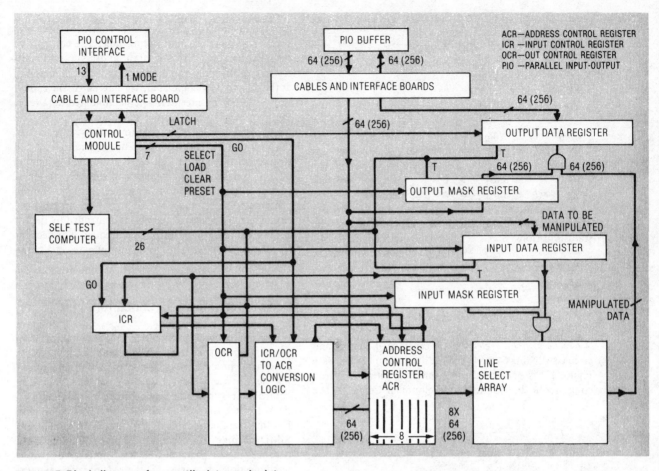

Figure 17. Block diagram of a versatile data manipulator.

must be designed to partition a computation task and assign each piece to individual processing elements. Effective partitioning and assignment are essential for efficient multiprocessing. The criterion is to match memory bandwidth with the processor processing load, and the interconnection network is a critical factor in this matching.

Below, we address some problems and results regarding the role of the interconnection network in concurrent processing.

Combinatorial capability. In array processing, data are often stored in parallel memory modules in skewed forms that allow a vector of data to be fetched without conflict.[63-65] However, the fetched data must be realigned in prescribed order before they can be sent to individual PEs for processing. This alignment is implemented by permutation functions of the interconnection network, which also realigns data generated by individual PEs into skewed form for storage in the memory modules.

In the computer architecture project, one should question whether the interconnection network chosen can efficiently perform the alignment. The rearrangeable network and the nonblocking network can realize every permutation function, but using these networks for alignment requires considerable effort to calculate control settings. A recursive routing mechanism has been provided for a few families of permutations needed for parallel processing[35]; however, the problem remains for the realization

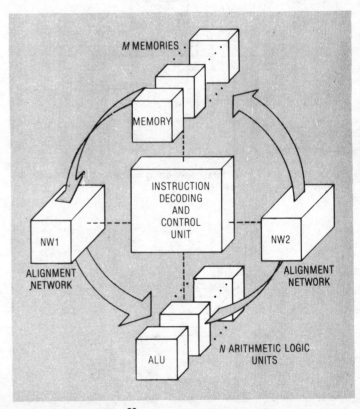

Figure 18. SIMD model.[59]

of general permutations. Many articles[45,51,66,67] concentrating on the permutation capabilities of single-stage networks and blocking multistage networks have shown that these networks cannot realize arbitrary permutations in a single pass. Recent results show that the baseline network can realize arbitrary permutations in just two passes[51] while other blocking multistage networks, such as the omega network, need at least three passes.[66] As mentioned previously, the shuffle-exchange network can realize arbitrary permutations in $3(\log_2 N) - 1$ passes where N is the network size.[48]

Task assignments and reconfiguration. Consider a parallel program segment using M memory modules and N processing elements. During execution, data is usually transferred from memory modules to processing elements or vice versa. It is also necessary to transfer data among processing elements for data sharing and synchronization. Simultaneous data transfers through the intercon-

nection network, which implements the transfers, may result in contention for communication links and switching elements. In case of conflict, some of the data transfers must be deferred; consequently, throughput decreases because the processing elements which need the deferred data cannot proceed as originally expected. To minimize delays caused by communication conflicts, program codes must be assigned to proper processing elements and data assigned to proper memory modules. The assignment of data to memory modules, called mapping,[68] has recently been extended to include assignment of program modules to processing elements.[69]

A configuration concept has been proposed to better use the interconnection network.[51] Under this concept, a network is just a configuration of another one in the same, topologically equivalent class.[25] To configure a permutation function as an interconnection network, we can assign input/output link names in a way that realizes the permutation function in one conflict-free pass. The problem of assigning logical names that realize various

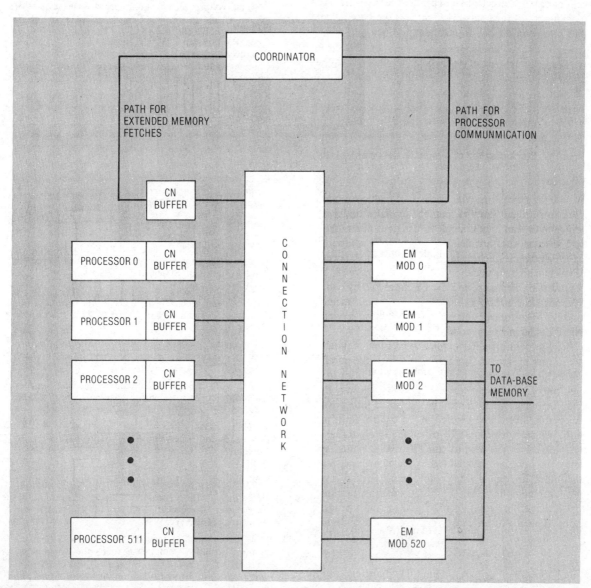

Figure 19. MIMD model.

permutation functions without conflicts is called a reconfiguration problem. It has been shown that, through the reconfiguration process, the baseline network can realize every permutation in one pass without conflicts.[69] This implies that concurrent processing throughput could be enhanced by proper assignment of tasks to processing elements and data to memory modules.

Partitioning. In partitioning—that is, dividing the network into independent subnetworks of different sizes—each subnetwork must have all the interconnection capabilities of a complete network of the same type and size. Hence, with a partitionable network, a system can support multiple SIMD machines. By dynamically reconfiguring the system into independent SIMD machines and properly assigning tasks to each partition, we can use resources more efficiently.

Several authors have noted the importance of partitioning.[30] One recent study[70] shows that single-stage networks, such as the shuffle-exchange and Illiac networks, cannot be partitioned into independent subnetworks, but blocking multistage networks, such as the baseline and data manipulator, can be partitioned.

Bandwidth of interconnection networks. The bandwidth can be defined as the expected number of requests accepted per unit time. Since the bus system cannot provide sufficient bandwidth for a large-scale multiprocessor system and the crossbar switch is too expensive, it is particularly interesting to know what kind of bandwidth various interconnection networks can provide.

The analytic method has been used to estimate bandwidth.[31,71,72] However, one cannot obtain a closed-form solution, and the analytic model is sometimes too simplified. Just for example, one result showed that for a blocking multistage interconnection network of size 256×256, the bandwidth is 77 requests (per memory cycle) and for a crossbar switch of the same size, the bandwidth is 162. However, the crossbar costs about 20 times as much as the multistage network, and with buffering (packet switching), the performance of the multistage network is quite comparable to the crossbar switch.[71]

Numerical simulation, also used to estimate the bandwidth,[71] can simulate actual PE connection requests by analyzing the program to be executed. The access conflicts in the network and memory modules can be detected as shown by Wu and Feng.[25] Using the simulation method, Barnes[73] concluded that the baseline network is more than adequate to support connection needs of a proposed MIMD system which can execute one billion floating-point instructions per second.

Reliability. Reliable operation of interconnection networks is important to overall system performance. The reliability issue can be thought of as two problems: fault diagnosis and fault tolerance. The fault-diagnosis problem has been studied for a class of multistage interconnection networks constructed of switching elements with two valid states.[74] The problem is approached by generating suitable fault-detection and fault-location test sets for every fault in the assumed fault model. The test sets are then trimmed to a mimimal or nearly minimal set. Detecting a single fault (link fault or switching-element fault) requires only four tests, which are independent of network size. The number of tests for locating single faults and detecting multiple faults are also workable.

The second reliability problem mainly concerns the degree of fault tolerance.[75] It is important to design a network that combines full connection capability with graceful degradation—in spite of the existence of faults. ■

Acknowledgment

The author wishes to acknowledge the original contribution of Dr. C. Wu in preparing this article.

References

1. T. Feng, editor's introduction, special issue on parallel processors and processing, *Computing Surveys,* Vol. 9, No. 1, Mar. 1977, pp. 1-2.

2. C. V. Ramamoorthy, T. Krishnarao, and P. Jahanian, "Hardware Software Issues in Multi-Microprocessor Computer Architecture," *Proc. First Annual Rocky Mountain Symp. Microcomputers,* 1977, pp. 235-261.

3. K. J. Thurber, "Interconnection Networks—A Survey and Assessment," *AFIPS Conf. Proc.,* Vol. 43, 1974 NCC, pp. 909-919.

4. K. J. Thurber, "Circuit Switching Technology: A State-of-the-Art Survey," *Proc. Compcon Fall 1978,* Sept. 1978, pp. 116-124.

5. K. J. Thurber and G. M. Masson, *Distributed-Processor Communication Architecture,* Lexington Books, Lexington, Mass., 1979, 252 pp.

6. H. J. Siegel, "Interconnection Networks for SIMD Machines," *Computer,* Vol. 12, No. 6, June 1979, pp. 57-66.

7. H. J. Siegel, R. J. McMillen, and P. T. Mueller, Jr., "A Survey of Interconnection Methods for Reconfigurable Parallel Processing Systems," *AFIPS Conf. Proc.,* Vol. 48, 1979 NCC, pp. 387-400.

8. G. M. Masson, G. C. Gingher, and Shinji Nakamura, "A Sampler of Circuit Switching Networks," *Computer,* Vol. 12, No. 6, June 1979, pp. 32-48.

9. T. Feng and C. Wu, *Interconnection Networks in Multiple-Processor Systems,* Rome Air Development Center report, RADC-TR-79-304, Dec. 1979, 244 pp.

10. C. Wu and T. Feng, "A VLSI Interconnection Network for Multiprocessor Systems," *Digest Compcon Spring 1981,* pp. 294-298.

11. T. Feng, "Data Manipulating Functions in Parallel Processors and Their Implementations," *IEEE Trans. Computers,* Vol. C-23, No. 3, Mar. 1974, pp. 309-318.

12. V. Benes, *Mathematical Theory of Connecting Networks,* Academic Press, N.Y., 1965.

13. H. T. Kung, "The Structure of Parallel Algorithms," in *Advances in Computers,* Vol. 19, M. C. Yovits, ed., Academic Press, N.Y., 1980.

14. D. J. Farber and K. C. Larson, "The System Architecture of the Distributed Computer System—the Communications System," *Proc. Symp. Computer Comm. Networks and Teletraffic,* Brooklyn Polytechnic Press, Apr. 1972, pp. 21-27.

15. C. C. Reames and M. T. Liu, "A Loop Network for Simultaneous Transmission of Variable Length Messages," *Proc. Second Symp. Computer Architecture,* Jan. 1975, pp. 7-12.

16. S. I. Saffer et al., "NODAS—The Net Oriented Data Acquisition System for the Medical Environment," *AFIPS Conf. Proc.,* Vol. 46, 1977 NCC, pp. 295-300.

17. J. A. Harris and D. R. Smith, "Hierarchical Multiprocessor Organization," *Proc. Fourth Symp. Computer Architecture,* Mar. 1977, pp. 41-48.

18. G. H. Barnes et al., "The Illiac IV Computer," *IEEE Trans. Computers,* Vol. C-17, No. 8, Aug. 1968, pp. 746-757.

19. E. M. Aupperle, "MERIT Computer Network: Hardware Considerations," in *Computer Networks,* R. Rustin, ed., Prentice-Hall, Englewood Cliffs, N.J., 1972, pp. 49-63.

20. B. W. Arden and H. Lee, "Analysis of Chordal Ring Network," *IEEE Trans. Computers,* Vol. C-30, No. 4, April 1981, pp. 291-295.

21. H. Sullivan, T. R. Bashkow, and K. Klappholz, "A Large Scale Homogeneous, Fully Distributed Parallel Machine," *Proc. Fourth Symp. Computer Architecture,* Nov. 1977, pp. 105-125.

22. F. P. Preparata and J. Vuillemin, "The Cube-Connected Cycles: A Versatile Network for Parallel Computation," *Comm. ACM,* Vol. 24, No. 5, May 1981, pp. 300-309.

23. H. S. Stone, "Parallel Processing with the Perfect Shuffle," *IEEE Trans. Computers,* Vol. C-20, No. 2, Feb. 1971, pp. 153-161.

24. T. Feng, *Parallel Processing Characteristics and Implementation of Data Manipulating Functions,* Rome Air Development Center report, RADC-TR-73-189, July 1973.

25. C. Wu and T. Feng, "On a Class of Multistage Interconnection Networks," *IEEE Trans. Computers,* Vol. C-29, No. 8, Aug. 1980, pp. 694-702.

26. C. Wu and T. Feng, "On a Distributed-Processor Communication Architecture," *Proc. Compcon Fall 1980,* pp. 599-605.

27. L. R. Goke and G. J. Lipovski, "Banyan Networks for Partitioning Multiprocessing Systems," *Proc. First Annual Computer Architecture Conf.,* Dec. 1973, pp. 21-28.

28. D. H. Lawrie, "Access and Alignment of Data in an Array Processor," *IEEE Trans. Computers,* Vol. C-24, No. 12, Dec. 1975, pp. 1145-1155.

29. K. E. Batcher, "The Flip Network in STARAN," *Proc. 1976 Int'l Conf. Parallel Processing,* Aug. 1976, pp. 65-71.

30. M. C. Pease, "The Indirect Binary n-Cube Microprocessor Array," *IEEE Trans. Computers,* Vol. C-26, No. 5, May 1977, pp. 548-573.

31. J. H. Patel, "Processor-Memory Interconnections for Multiprocessors," *Proc. Sixth Annual Symp. Computer Architecture,* Apr. 1979, pp. 168-177.

32. A. Waksman, "A Permutation Network," *J. ACM,* Vol. 9, No. 1, Jan. 1968, pp. 159-163.

33. A. E. Joel, Jr., "On Permutation Switching Networks," *B.S.T.J.,* Vol. 67, 1968, pp. 813-822.

34. D. C. Opferman and N. T. Tsao-Wu, "On a Class of Rearrangeable Switching Networks—Part I: Control Algorithm; Part II: Enumeration Studies of Fault Diagnosis," *B.S.T.J.,* 1971, pp. 1579-1618.

35. J. Lenfant, "Parallel Permutations of Data: A Benes Network Control Algorithm for Frequently Used Permutations," *IEEE Trans. Computers,* Vol. C-27, No. 7, July 1978, pp. 637-647.

36. T. Feng, C. Wu, and D. P. Agrawal, "A Microprocessor-Controlled Asynchronous Circuit Switching Network," *Proc. Sixth Annual Symp. Computer Architecture,* 1979, pp. 202-215.

37. Y-C. Chow, R. D. Dixon, T. Feng, and C. Wu, "Routing Techniques for Rearrangeable Interconnection Networks," *Proc. Workshop on Interconnection Networks,* Apr. 1980, pp. 64-69.

38. C. Clos, "A Study of Nonblocking Switching Networks," *Bell System Tech. J.,* Vol. 32, 1953, pp. 406-424.

39. C. D. Thompson,"Generalized Connection Networks for Parallel Processor Intercommunication," *IEEE Trans. Computers,* C-27, No. 12, Dec. 1978, pp. 1119-1125.

40. J. Gecsei, "Interconnection Networks from Three-State Cells," *IEEE Trans. Computers,* Vol. C-26, No. 8, Aug. 1977, pp. 705-711.

41. Y-C. Chow, R. D. Dixon, and T. Feng, "An Interconnection Network for Processor Communication with Optimized Local Connections," *Proc. 1980 Int'l Conf. Parallel Processing,* Aug. 1980, pp. 65-74.

42. W. A. Wulf and C. G. Bell, "C.mmp—A Multimicroprocessor," *AFIPS Conf. Proc.,* Vol. 41, 1972 FJCC, pp. 765-777.

43. T. Feng, *The Design of a Versatile Line Manipulator,* Rome Air Development Center report, RADC-TR-73-292, Sept. 1973.

44. W. W. Gaertner, *Design, Construction,and Installation of Data Manipulator,* Rome Air Development Center report, RADC-TR-77-166, May 1977, 80 pp.

45. S. E. Orcutt, "Implementation of Permutations Functions in an Illiac IV-Type Computer," *IEEE Trans. Computers,* Vol. C-25, No. 9, Sept. 1976, pp. 929-936.

46. C. D. Thompson and H. T. Kung, "Sorting on a Mesh-Connected Parallel Computer," *Comm. ACM,* Vol. 20, No. 4, Apr. 1977, pp. 263-271.

47. D. Nassimi and S. Sahni, "Bitonic Sort on a Mesh-Connected Parallel Computer," *IEEE Trans. Computers,* Vol. C-28, No. 1, Jan. 1979, pp. 2-7.

48. C. Wu and T. Feng, "Universality of the Shuffle-Exchange Network," *IEEE Trans. Computers,* Vol. C-30, No. 5, May 1981.

49. D. E. Knuth, *The Art of Computer Programming, Vol. 3: Sorting and Searching,* Addison-Wesley, Reading, Mass., 1973.

50. R. J. McMillen and H. J. Siegel, "MIMD Machine Communication Using the Augmented Data Manipulator Network," *Proc. Seventh Symp. Computer Architecture,* June 1980, pp. 51-58.

51. C. Wu and T. Feng, "The Reverse-Exchange Interconnection Network," *IEEE Trans. Computers,* Vol. C-29, No. 9, Sept. 1980, pp. 801-811; also *Proc. 1979 Int'l Conf. Parallel Processing,* pp. 160-174.

52. S. Anderson, "The Looping Algorithm Extended to Base 2^t Rearrangeable Switching Networks," *IEEE Trans. Comm.,* Vol. COM-25, No. 10, Oct. 1977, pp. 1057-1063.

53. G. Lev, N. Pippenger, and L. G. Valiant, "A Fast Parallel Algorithm for Routing in Permutation Networks," *IEEE Trans. Computers,* Vol. C-30, No. 2, Feb. 1981, pp. 93-100.

54. D. H. Lawrie, *Memory-Processor Conneciton Networks,* UIUCDCS-R-73-557, University of Ilinois, Urbana, Feb. 1973.

55. *Numerical Aerodynamic Simulation Facility Feasibility Study,* Burroughs Corporation, Mar. 1979.

56. U. V. Premkuma, R. Kapur, M. Malek, G. J. Lipovski,

and P. Horne, "Design and Implementation of the Banyan Interconnection Network in TRAC," *AFIPS Conf. Proc.,* Vol. 49, 1980 NCC, pp. 643-653.

57. M. A. Franklin, "VLSI Performance Comparison of Banyan and Crossbar Communication Networks," *IEEE Trans. Computers,* Vol. C-30, No. 4, Apr. 1981, pp. 283-290.

58. P. G. Jansen and J. L. W. Kessels, "The DIMOND: A Component for the Modular Construction of Switching Networks," *IEEE Trans. Computers,* Vol. C-29, No. 10, Oct. 1980, pp. 884-889.

59. D. J. Kuck, "A Survey of Parallel Machine Organization and Programming," *Computing Surveys,* Vol. 9, No. 1, Mar. 1977, pp. 29-59. Also in *Proc. 1975 Sagamore Computer Conf. Parallel Processing,* pp. 15-39.

60. B. J. Smith, "A Pipelined, Shared Resource MIMD Computer," *Proc. 1978 Int'l Conf. Parallel Processing,* pp. 6-8.

61. J. B. Dennis, "Data Flow Supercomputers," *Computer,* Vol. 13, No. 11, Nov. 1980, pp. 48-56.

62. S. F. Lundstrom and G. Barnes, "A Controllable MIMD Architecture," *Proc. 1980 Int'l Conf. Parallel Processing,* pp. 19-27.

63. D. J. Kuck, "ILLIAC IV Software and Application Programming," *IEEE Trans. on Computers,* Vol. C-17, No. 8, Aug. 1968, pp. 758-770.

64. K. E. Batcher, "The Multi-Dimensional Access Memory in STARAN," *IEEE Trans. Computers,* Vol. C-26, No. 2, Feb. 1977, pp. 174-177.

65. D. H. Lawrie and C. Vora, "The Prime Memory System for Array Access," *Proc. 1980 Int'l Conf. Parallel Processing,* pp. 81-87.

66. A. Shimer and S. Ruhman, "Toward a Generalization of Two- and Three-Pass Multistage, Blocking Interconnection Networks," *Proc. 1980 Int'l Conf. Parallel Processing,* pp. 337-346.

67. T. Lang and H. S. Stone, "A Shuffle-Exchange Network with Simplified Control," *IEEE Trans. Computers,* Vol. C-25, No. 6, Jan. 1976, pp. 55-65.

68. H. T. Kung and D. Stevenson, "A Software Technique for Reducing the Routing Time on a Parallel Computer with a Fixed Interconnection Network," in *High Speed Computer and Algorithm Organization,* Academic Press, N.Y., 1977, pp. 423-433.

69. C. Wu and T. Feng, "A Software Technique for Enhancing Performance of a Distributed Computer System," *Proc. Compsac 80,* Oct. 1980, pp. 274-280.

70. H. J. Siegel, "The Theory Underlying the Partitioning of Permutation Networks," *IEEE Trans. Computers,* Vol. C-29, No. 9, Sept. 1980, pp. 791-801.

71. D. M. Dias and J. R. Jump, "Analysis and Simulation of Buffered Delta Networks," *IEEE Trans. Computers,* Vol. C-30, No. 4, Apr. 1981, pp. 273-282.

72. D. A. Padua, D. J. Kuck, and D. H. Lawrie, "High-Speed Multiprocessors and Compilation Techniques," *IEEE Trans. Computers,* Vol. C-29, No. 9, Sept. 1980, pp. 763-776.

73. G. H. Barnes, "Design and Validation of a Connection Network for Many-Processor Multiprocessing Systems," *Proc. 1980 Int'l Conf. Parallel Processing,* pp. 79-80.

74. C. Wu and T. Feng, "Fault Diagnosis for a Class of Multistage Interconnection Networks," *Proc. 1979 Int'l Conf. Parallel Processing,* pp. 269-278.

75. J. P. Shen and J. P. Hayes, "Fault Tolerance of a Class of Connecting Networks," *Proc. Seventh Symp. Computer Architecture,* 1980, pp. 61-71.

Tse-yun Feng is a professor in the Department of Computer and Information Science, Ohio State University, Columbus. Previously, he was on the faculty at Wayne State University, Detroit, and Syracuse University, New York. He has extensive technical publications in the areas of associative processing, parallel and concurrent processors, computer architecture, switching theory, and logic design, and has received a number of awards for his technical contributions and scholarship.

A past president of the IEEE Computer Society (1979-80), Feng was a distinguished visitor (1973-78), and has served as a reviewer, panelist, or session chairman for various technical magazines and conferences. He also initiated the Sagamore Computer Conference on Parallel Processing and the International Conference on Parallel Processing.

He received the BS degree from the National Taiwan University, Taipei, the MS degree from Oklahoma State University, Stillwater, and the PhD degree from the University of Michigan, Ann Arbor, all in electrical engineering.

Reprinted from *IEEE Transactions on Computers*, Volume C-29, Number 8, August 1980, pages 694-702. Copyright © 1980 by The Institute of Electrical and Electronics Engineers, Inc.

On a Class of Multistage Interconnection Networks

CHUAN-LIN WU, MEMBER, IEEE, AND TSE-YUN FENG, FELLOW, IEEE

Abstract—A baseline network and a configuration concept are introduced to evaluate relationships among some proposed multistage interconnection networks. It is proven that the data manipulator (modified version), flip network, omega network, indirect binary n-cube network, and regular SW banyan network ($S = F = 2$) are topologically equivalent. The configuration concept facilitates developing a homogeneous routing algorithm which allows one-to-one and one-to-many connections from an arbitrary side of a network to the other side. This routing algorithm is extended to full communication which allows connections between terminals on the same side of a network. A conflict resolution scheme is also included. Some practical implications of our results are presented for further research.

Index Terms—Array processing, computer architecture, conflict resolution, interconnection networks, MIMD machine, multiple-processor systems, network configurations, parallel processing, routing techniques, SIMD machine.

I. INTRODUCTION

SOME multistage interconnection networks have specifically been proposed or implemented for parallel processing systems [1]–[3]. These networks include the data

Manuscript received April 15, 1978; revised Janary 3, 1980. This work was supported by the Rome Air Development Center under Contract F 30602-76-C-0282.

The authors are with the Department of Computer Science, Wright State University, Dayton, OH 45435.

manipulator (modified version) [1], flip network [4], indirect binary n-cube network [5], omega network [6], and regular SW banyan network with spread and fanout of 2 ($S = F = 2$) [7], [8]. Each of these networks consists of a set of N input terminals, a set of N output terminals, $\log_2 N$ stages of logic cells, and a set of control lines. The set of N input terminals and the set of N output terminals are two disjoint sets of terminals. All of these networks are capable of connecting an arbitrary input terminal to an arbitrary output terminal. But simultaneous connections of more than one terminal pair may result in conflicts in the communication path within the logic cells.

This paper evaluates relationships among these interconnection networks, provides related routing techniques, and presents a conflict resolution scheme. Practical implications of our results are also discussed for some important design issues such as packet switching communication [9]. In Section II, we define a baseline network which can serve as a reference for evaluating the relationships among most existing interconnection networks, and compare the baseline network to the existing networks mentioned in the above paragraph. Section III describes a simple routing procedure which can result in the same connection path no matter which side of the terminals is chosen as the input side and the other side as the output side.

The routing procedure also includes a scheme for conflict resolution. Section IV extends the routing procedure to allow one-to-one connections between all pairs of terminals. The conclusion is presented in Section V.

II. Isomorphic Topology

In the first part of this section, a baseline network is introduced. Then a topological equivalence of several multistage interconnection networks is given.

A. Configuration of a Baseline Network

The performance of an interconnection network is determined largely by its configuration. By the *configuration* of an interconnection network we mean the topology and the label of the components of the network. Here we define the *topology* in terms of three of the four variable parameters for designing a data manipulator [1]. These three parameters are the number of communication paths of each switching element, the number of columns (or stages), and the interconnection paths (or links) between switching elements. In this paper we consider $\log_2 N$ stages of 2×2 switching elements, i.e., switching elements, each with two input and two output terminals, and describe the connectivities of the interconnection paths between switching elements using a set of mathematical rules, called *topology describing rules,* derived directly from the structure definition of the network. Fig. 1 shows a 2×2 switching element which has capabilities of direct and crossed connections. The *logical names* of the components of a network can be used to unambiguously identify each link and each switching element in the network by applying some mapping rules on their physical names. A *physical name* is given to each switching component (stage, element, link) for identifying its relative location in the network in order to describe its topology.

Now we introduce a baseline network which can serve as a reference for evaluating other existing multistage networks. The topology of the baseline network can be generated in a recursive way. Fig. 2 shows the first iteration of the recursive process in which the first stage contains one $N \times N$ block and the second stage contains two $(N/2) \times (N/2)$ subblocks, C_0 and C_1. The process can recursively be applied to the subblocks in each iteration until the $N/2$ subblocks of size 2×2 are reached. To complete the process, $(\log_2 N) - 1$ iterations are needed. There are $\log_2 N$ stages of the switching elements and $(\log_2 N) + 1$ levels of the links. There is a similarity between this baseline network and Batcher's bitonic sorting network [10]. It is, therefore, possible to design a switching element for both purposes. A network of $N = 16$ is illustrated in Fig. 3.

The physical names are assigned as follows. The stages are labeled in a sequence from 0 to $(\log_2 N) - 1$ with 0 for the leftmost stage and $(\log_2 N) - 1$ for the rightmost stage. Similarly, the levels of links are labeled in a sequence from 0 to $\log_2 N$. In each stage, each switching element is named by a codeword of $l = (\log_2 N) - 1$ binary bits, $p_l p_{l-1} \cdots p_1$, which is the binary representation of its location in the stage. Each link in each level is named by a codeword of $l + 1$ binary bits, $p_l p_{l-1} \cdots p_0$, which is coded according to the following scheme. The first l leftmost bits, $p_l p_{l-1} \cdots p_1$, are the same as the binary representation of the switching element to which the link is

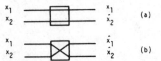

Fig. 1. A switching element. (a) Direct connection. (b) Crossed connection.

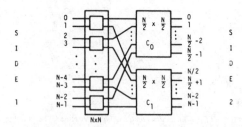

Fig. 2. Recursive process to construct the baseline network.

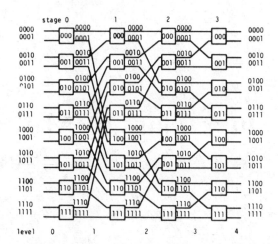

Fig. 3. A baseline network with name representation.

connected on one of two right terminals of the switching element (or left terminals for the case of level 0); the last bit, p_0, is equal to 0 if the link is connected to an upper terminal of the switching element and p_0 is equal to 1 if the link is connected to a lower terminal. For an example of the binary representation of the physical names of the switching elements and the links, see Fig. 3. Throughout the rest of this paper, the binary representations of physical names of a switching element in stage i and a link in level i are thus assigned $(p_l p_{l-1} \cdots p_1)_i$ and $(p_l p_{l-1} \cdots p_0)_i$, respectively. In the baseline network, the physical name is also used as its logical name. However, logical names other than physical names will be developed in the latter sections for other networks.

The topology describing rules of the baseline network are defined by

$$\beta_i^0[(p_l p_{l-1} \cdots p_1)_i] = (p_l \cdots p_{l-i+1} 0 p_{l-i} \cdots p_2)_{i+1},$$
$$\text{for link } (p_l p_{l-1} \cdots p_1 0)_{i+1}, 0 \le i < l \quad (1)$$

and

$$\beta_i^1[(p_l p_{l-1} \cdots p_1)_i] = (p_l \cdots p_{l-i+1} 1 p_{l-i} \cdots p_2)_{i+1},$$
$$\text{for link } (p_l p_{l-1} \cdots p_1 1)_{i+1}, 0 \le i < l. \quad (2)$$

The β_i's describe the interconnections by mapping a switching element in stage i to two switching elements in stage $i + 1$, one element per link "out of" the switching element in stage i.

B. Equivalent Networks

Some equivalence relationships among networks have been described in the literature [4]–[6]. However, these descriptions have not formally been proven. A partial comparative study also appears in the literature [11]. In this subsection, an equivalence relationship will be defined and will be used as a parameter for evaluating other multistage interconnection networks.

Let $\{\alpha_i^0, \alpha_i^1 \mid 0 \leq i < l\}$ and $\{\beta_i^0, \beta_i^1 \mid 0 \leq i < l\}$ be two sets of topology describing rules of two multistage interconnection networks N_1 and N_2, respectively. Network N_1 is topologically equivalent to network N_2 if there is a set of one-to-one and onto mapping rules (γ_i) on $(p_l p_{l-1} \cdots p_1)_i$ such that

$$\beta_i^0 \gamma_i [(p_l p_{l-1} \cdots p_1)_i] = \gamma_{i+1} \alpha_i^0 [(p_l p_{l-1} \cdots p_1)_i] \quad (3)$$

and

$$\beta_i^1 \gamma_i [(p_l p_{l-1} \cdots p_1)_i] = \gamma_{i+1} \alpha_i^1 [(p_l p_{l-1} \cdots p_1)_i] \quad (4)$$

for $0 \leq i < l$. If two networks are topologically equivalent, we also say that they show an isomorphic topology. We use the image of γ_i as a logical name, $(b_l b_{l-1} \cdots b_1)_i$, and denote the relation as $(b_l b_{l-1} \cdots b_1)_i = \gamma_i [(p_l p_{l-1} \cdots p_1)_i]$. On the right-hand side of (3), $\alpha_i^0 [(p_l p_{l-1} \cdots p_1)_i]$ is the physical name of the switching element in stage $i + 1$ which has link $(p_l p_{l-1} \cdots p_1 0)_{i+1}$ as a communication path and $\gamma_{i+1} \alpha_i^0 [(p_l p_{l-1} \cdots p_1 0)_i]$ is the logical name of this switching element. On the left-hand side of (3), $\gamma_i [(p_l p_{l-1} \cdots p_1)_i]$ is the logical name of the switching element in stage i which has link $(p_l p_{l-1} \cdots p_1 0)_{i+1}$ as a communication path. Similar arguments can be made for (4). Hence, (3) and (4) just imply a condition that there exists a logical name scheme for network N_1 such that the connectivities of the interconnection paths labeled with logical names in network N_1 can be described by the topology describing rules of network N_2.

The following theorems on the isomorphic topology are proven by showing that (3) and (4) hold. In each proof, we also show an example network labeled with logical names.

Theorem 1: The regular SW banyan network with $S = F = 2$ or the indirect binary n-cube network defined by

$$\alpha_i^0 [(p_l p_{l-1} \cdots p_1)_i] = (p_l \cdots p_{i+2} 0 p_i \cdots p_1)_{i+1},$$
$$\text{for link } (p_l p_{l-1} \cdots p_1 0)_{i+1}, 0 \leq i < l \quad (5)$$

and

$$\alpha_i^1 [(p_l p_{l-1} \cdots p_1)_i] = (p_l \cdots p_{i+2} 1 p_i \cdots p_1)_{i+1},$$
$$\text{for link } (p_l p_{l-1} \cdots p_1 1)_{i+1}, 0 \leq i < l \quad (6)$$

is topologically equivalent to the baseline network.

Proof: The following mapping rule, γ_i, is used to show the equivalence:

$$\gamma_i [(p_l p_{l-1} \cdots p_1)_i] = (p_l \cdots p_i p_l \cdots p_{i+1})_i,$$
$$\text{for } 0 \leq i < l. \quad (7)$$

It can be seen that the mapping rule provides a one-to-one and onto relationship between the physical and logical names. The logical name assignment $(b_l b_{l-1} \cdots b_1)_i = \gamma_i [(p_l p_{l-1} \cdots p_1)_i]$ on a regular SW banyan network with $S = F = 2$ or an indirect

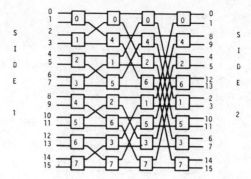

Fig. 4. A banyan ($S = F = 2$) or indirect binary n-cube network structure with new configuration.

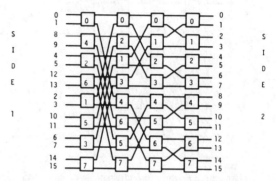

Fig. 5. A modified data manipulator with configuration.

binary n-cube network is shown in Fig. 4.

From (1), (5), and (7) we have

$$\gamma_{i+1} \alpha_i^0 [(p_l p_{l-1} \cdots p_1)_i] = \gamma_{i+1} [(p_l \cdots p_{i+2} 0 p_i \cdots p_1)_{i+1}]$$
$$= (p_1 \cdots p_i 0 p_l \cdots p_{i+2})_{i+1} \quad (8)$$

and

$$\beta_i^0 \gamma_i [(p_l p_{l-1} \cdots p_1)_i] = \beta_i^0 [(p_1 \cdots p_i p_l \cdots p_{i+1})_i]$$
$$= (p_1 \cdots p_i 0 p_l \cdots p_{i+2})_{i+1} \quad (9)$$

for $0 \leq i < l$. By (8) and (9), we show that (3) holds. Similarly, using (2), (6), and (7), we can also show that (4) holds.

Q.E.D.

Theorem 2: The modified data manipulator defined by

$$\alpha_i^0 [(p_l p_{l-1} \cdots p_1)_i] = (p_l \cdots p_{l-i+1} 0 p_{l-i-1} \cdots p_1)_{i+1},$$
$$\text{for link } (p_l p_{l-1} \cdots p_1 0)_{i+1}, 0 \leq i < l \quad (10)$$

and

$$\alpha_i^1 [(p_l p_{l-1} \cdots p_1)_i] = (p_l \cdots p_{l-i+1} 1 p_{l-i-1} \cdots p_1)_{i+1},$$
$$\text{for link } (p_l p_{l-1} \cdots p_1 1)_{i+1}, 0 \leq i < l \quad (11)$$

is topologically equivalent to the baseline network.

Proof: The following mapping rule, γ_i, is used to show the equivalence:

$$\gamma_i [(p_l p_{l-1} \cdots p_1)_i] = (p_l \cdots p_{l-i+1} p_1 \cdots p_{l-i})_i,$$
$$\text{for } 0 \leq i \leq l. \quad (12)$$

It can be seen that the mapping rule is one-to-one and onto. The logical name assignment on a modified data manipulator of $N = 16$ is shown in Fig. 5.

From (1), (10), and (12), we have

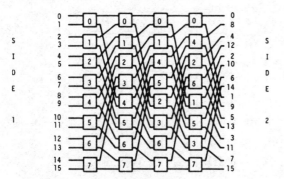

Fig. 6. A flip network structure with new configuration.

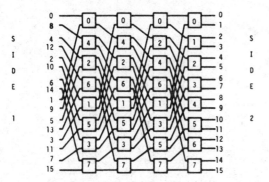

Fig. 7. An omega network structure with new configuration.

$$\gamma_{i+1}\alpha_i^0[(p_l p_{l-1} \cdots p_1)_i]$$
$$= \gamma_{i+1}[(p_l \cdots p_{l-i+1}0p_{l-i-1} \cdots p_1)_{i+1}]$$
$$= (p_l \cdots p_{l-i+1}0p_1 \cdots p_{l-i-1})_{i+1} \quad (13)$$

and

$$\beta_i^0 \gamma_i[(p_l p_{l-1} \cdots p_1)_i] = \beta_i^0[(p_l \cdots p_{l-i+1}p_1 \cdots p_{l-i})_i]$$
$$= (p_l \cdots p_{l-i+1}0p_1 \cdots p_{l-i-1})_{i+1} \quad (14)$$

for $0 \le i < l$. By (13) and (14), we show that (3) holds. Similarly, using (2), (11), and (12), we can also show that (4) holds.
Q.E.D.

Theorem 3: The flip network defined by

$$\alpha_i^0[(p_l p_{l-1} \cdots p_1)_i] = (0p_l p_{l-1} \cdots p_2)_{i+1},$$
$$\text{for link } (p_l p_{l-1} \cdots p_1 0)_{i+1}, 0 \le i < l \quad (15)$$

and

$$\alpha_i^1[(p_l p_{l-1} \cdots p_1)_i] = (1p_l p_{l-1} \cdots p_2)_{i+1},$$
$$\text{for link } (p_l p_{l-1} \cdots p_1 1)_{i+1}, 0 \le i < l \quad (16)$$

is topologically equivalent to the baseline network.

Proof: The following mapping rule, γ_i, is used to show the equivalence:

$$\gamma_i[(p_l p_{l-1} \cdots p_1)_i] = (p_{l-i+1} \cdots p_l p_{l-i} \cdots p_1)_i,$$
$$\text{for } 0 \le i \le l. \quad (17)$$

It can be seen that the mapping rule is one-to-one and onto. The logical name assignment on a flip network of $N = 16$ is shown in Fig. 6. From (1), (15), and (17), we have

$$\gamma_{i+1}\alpha_i^0[(p_l p_{l-1} \cdots p_1)_i] = \gamma_{i+1}[(0p_l p_{l-1} \cdots p_2)_{i+1}]$$
$$= (p_{l-i+1} \cdots p_l 0 p_{l-i} \cdots p_2)_{i+1} \quad (18)$$

and

$$\beta_i^0 \gamma_i[(p_l p_{l-1} \cdots p_1)_i] = \beta_i^0[(p_{l-i+1} \cdots p_l p_{l-i} \cdots p_1)_i]$$
$$= (p_{l-i+1} \cdots p_l 0 p_{l-i} \cdots p_2)_{i+1} \quad (19)$$

for $0 \le i < l$. By (18) and (19), we show that (3) holds. Similarly, using (2), (16), and (17), we can also show that (4) holds.
Q.E.D.

Theorem 4: The omega network defined by

$$\alpha_i^0[(p_l p_{l-1} \cdots p_1)_i] = (p_{l-1}p_{l-2} \cdots p_1 0)_{i+1},$$
$$\text{for link } (p_l p_{l-1} \cdots p_1 0)_{i+1}, 0 \le i < l \quad (20)$$

and

$$\alpha_i^1[(p_l p_{l-1} \cdots p_1)_i] = (p_{l-1}p_{l-2} \cdots p_1 1)_{i+1},$$
$$\text{for link } (p_l p_{l-1} \cdots p_1 1)_{i+1}, 0 \le i < l \quad (21)$$

is topologically equivalent to the baseline network.

Proof: The following mapping rule, γ_i, is used to show the equivalence:

$$\gamma_i[(p_l p_{l-1} \cdots p_1)_i] = (p_i \cdots p_1 p_{i+1} \cdots p_l)_i,$$
$$\text{for } 0 \le i < l. \quad (22)$$

It can be seen that the mapping rule is one-to-one and onto. The logical name assignment on an omega network of $N = 16$ is shown in Fig. 7.

From (1), (20), and (22), we have

$$\gamma_{i+1}\alpha_i^0[(p_l p_{l-1} \cdots p_1)_i] = \gamma_{i+1}[(p_{l-1}p_{l-2} \cdots p_1 0)_{i+1}]$$
$$= (p_i \cdots p_1 0 p_{i+1} \cdots p_{l-1})_{i+1} \quad (23)$$

and

$$\beta_i^0 \gamma_i[(p_l p_{l-1} \cdots p_1)_i] = \beta_i^0[(p_i \cdots p_1 p_{i+1} \cdots p_l)_i]$$
$$= (p_i \cdots p_1 0 p_{i+1} \cdots p_{l-1})_{i+1} \quad (24)$$

for $0 \le i < l$. By (23) and (24), we show that (3) holds. Similarly, using (2), (21), and (22), we can also show that (4) holds.
Q.E.D.

Theorem 5: The reverse baseline network defined by

$$\alpha_i^0[(p_l p_{l-1} \cdots p_1)_i] = (p_l \cdots p_{i+2}p_i \cdots p_1 0)_{i+1},$$
$$\text{for link } (p_l p_{l-1} \cdots p_1 0)_{i+1}, 0 \le i < l \quad (25)$$

and

$$\alpha_i^1[(p_l p_{l-1} \cdots p_1)_i] = (p_l \cdots p_{i+2}p_i \cdots p_1 1)_{i+1},$$
$$\text{for link } (p_l p_{l-1} \cdots p_1 1)_{i+1}, 0 \le i < l \quad (26)$$

is topologically equivalent to the baseline network.

Proof: The following mapping rule, γ_i, is used to show the equivalence:

$$\gamma_i[(p_l p_{l-1} \cdots p_1)_i] = (p_i \cdots p_1 p_l \cdots p_{i+1})_i,$$
$$\text{for } 0 \le i \le l. \quad (27)$$

It can be seen that the mapping rule is one-to-one and onto. The logical name assignment on a reverse baseline network of $N = 16$ is shown in Fig. 8.

From (1), (25), and (27), we have

$$\gamma_{i+1}\alpha_i^0[(p_l p_{l-1} \cdots p_{l-1})_i] = \gamma_{i+1}[(p_l \cdots p_{i+2}p_i \cdots p_1 0)_{i+1}]$$
$$= (p_i \cdots p_1 0 p_l \cdots p_{i+2})_{i+1} \quad (28)$$

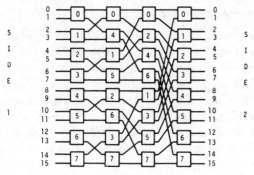

Fig. 8. A reverse baseline network with configuration.

and

$$\beta_i^0 \gamma_i [(p_l p_{l-1} \cdots p_1)_i] = \beta_i^0 [(p_l \cdots p_1 p_l \cdots p_{i+1})_i]$$
$$= (p_l \cdots p_1 0 p_l \cdots p_{i+2})_{i+1} \quad (29)$$

for $0 \le i < l$. By (28) and (29), we show that (3) holds. Similarly, using (2), (26), and (27), we can also show that (4) holds.
Q.E.D.

The networks described in Theorems 1–5 and any other similar networks form a topologically equivalent class of multistage interconnection networks. The proofs of Theorems 1–5 also provide rules, (7), (12), (17), (22), and (27) for the logical name assignment on the switching elements. The logical name of each link in the network can be obtained from the logical name of the adjacent switching element according to the rules set up in Section II-A.

Corollary 1: If network N_1 is shown to be topologically equivalent to network N_2 by using the set of one-to-one and onto mapping rules (γ_i) (i.e., $N_1 \xrightarrow{\gamma_i} N_2$), then $N_2 \xrightarrow{\gamma_i^{-1}} N_1$.

The fact of Corollary 1 is obvious since the γ_i's are one-to-one and onto and hence the (γ_i^{-1}) exist.

Corollary 2: If $N_1 \xrightarrow{\gamma_i} N_2$ and $N_2 \xrightarrow{\delta_i} N_3$, then $N_1 \xrightarrow{\delta_i \gamma_i} N_3$.

Proof: Assume that the topology describing rules of N_1, N_2, and N_3 are $\{\alpha_i^0, \alpha_i^1 | 0 \le i < l\}$, $\{\beta_i^0, \beta_i^1 | 0 \le i < l\}$, and $\{\xi_i^0, \xi_i^1 | 0 \le i < l\}$, and the logical names of switching elements on N_1 and N_2 are $(a_l a_{l-1} \cdots a_1)_i$ and $(b_l b_{l-1} \cdots b_1)_i$, respectively. By the definitions, we have

$$\beta_i^j \gamma_i [(a_l a_{l-1} \cdots a_1)_i] = \gamma_{i+1} \alpha_i^j [(a_l a_{l-1} \cdots a_1)_i] \quad (30)$$

and

$$\xi_i^j \delta_i [(b_l b_{l-1} \cdots b_1)_i] = \delta_{i+1} \beta_i^j [(b_l b_{l-1} \cdots b_1)_i] \quad (31)$$

for $0 \le i < l$ and $j = 0$ or 1. From (31), we have

$$\xi_i^j \delta_i \gamma_i [(a_l a_{l-1} \cdots a_1)_i] = \delta_{i+1} \beta_i^j \gamma_i [(a_l a_{l-1} \cdots a_1)_i] \quad (32)$$

for $0 \le i < l$ and $j = 0$ or 1. Substituting (30) into (32), we have

$$\xi_i^j \delta_i \gamma_i [(a_l a_{l-1} \cdots a_1)_i] = \delta_{i+1} \gamma_{i+1} \alpha_i^j [(a_l a_{l-1} \cdots a_1)_i]$$
$$(33)$$

for $0 \le i < l$ and $j = 0$ or 1. Equation (33) shows that N_1 and N_3 are topologically equivalent. Q.E.D.

Using the symmetrical and transitive properties which are shown in Corollaries 1 and 2, respectively, we can describe the following corollary.

Corollary 3: The indirect binary n-cube network, the regular SW banyan network with $S = F = 2$, the modified data manipulator, the flip network, the omega network, the reverse baseline network, and the baseline network are all topologically equivalent.

There are several implications of the topological equivalence. The first implication is that the dual physical/logical naming scheme allows us to reduce the difference between networks that were developed or laid out differently on a two-dimensional space. Furthermore, given a network whose topology belongs to the isomorphic class, it is possible to rename the inputs and outputs so that this network can directly simulate any network topology in the class. The only difference between two isomorphic networks is thus from their control structure which can be defined as states of each switching element and the way to set these states. Siegel [11] takes the control structure into account in his comparison study. Our results abstract from the control structure and provide a set of isomorphic relationships among the control structures of networks in the class. Therefore, the third implication is that a network which simulates an isomorphic network can directly use routing information (the way to set the switching element states for interconnection functions) developed on the simulated network. Some other implications will become more obvious after we go through the following sections.

III. ROUTING TECHNIQUES

In this section, we shall discuss some routing techniques for the class of multistage interconnection networks. Since routing techniques also depend on the control structure of a network under investigation, we assume that the control structure considered in this section has a capability to individually set the state of each switching element. We also assume that each switching element has the direct and crossed connection capability, as shown in Fig. 1, for any mapping connection (one-to-one connection) from one terminal on one side to another terminal on the other side. For the case of a one-to-many connection from one terminal on one side to many terminals on the other side, we assume that each switching element has the broadcast capability as proposed for the omega network [6] in addition to the capability of the direct and crossed connection. We first develop a *binary tree coding method* which provides a labeling scheme to facilitate a simple routing algorithm according to the concept of reducible sets [12]. A *destination-tag routing method* proposed for the omega network [6] shows an equivalent concept of the reducible sets. However, the original configuration of the omega network restricts the destination tag routing method in one-way communications from a set of inputs to a set of outputs. The binary tree coding method can result in the same connection path no matter which side of the terminal is chosen as the input side and the other as the output side so that no distinction needs to be made between the inputs and the outputs.

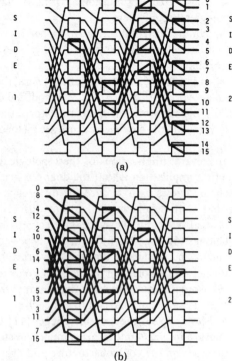

Fig. 9.   Binary tree coding of omega network. (a) Right side.
(b) Left side.

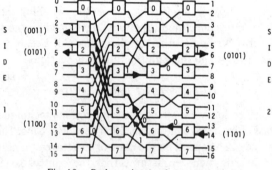

Fig. 10.   Path routing (path 1—; path 2—).

A. Labeling Scheme for the Terminal Link

The label assigned to a terminal link as shown in the logical name assignment in the previous section can be considered as the address of the processing unit attached to that terminal link. However, we will describe a shortcut scheme which can be used to label the terminal link without going into the mapping rules. A binary tree can be formed by choosing any one of the switching elements in stage 0 as the root and iteratively considering the adjacent switching elements in the next stage as the nodes of the binary tree. There are two outgoing links from the root and every node in the binary tree. The label of each terminal link on side 2 can be obtained by assigning weight 0 for the upper outgoing link and 1 for the lower one and concatenating the weight along the path from the root to the terminal link. There are N binary trees which can be formed for labeling purposes and each tree results in the same labels. Fig. 9(a) shows an example for an omega network. For labeling terminal links on side 1, a binary tree can be similarly formed by using one of the switching elements in the rightmost stage as the root [see Fig. 9(b)].

B. Routing Algorithm

A simple algorithm follows from the binary coding of the terminal links. In the algorithm, each terminal link is assigned to a binary tree using the adjacent switching element as the root. For each connection request from the source terminal link to the destination link(s), the routing algorithm sets up a subtree of the binary tree assigned to the source terminal link according to the binary representations of the destination labels. For a simple demonstration, we first consider the one-to-one connection request. Let source terminal link A labeled by $a_l a_{l-1} \cdots a_0$ on side 1 be connected to destination terminal link Z labeled by $z_l z_{l-1} \cdots z_0$ on side 2. Starting at A, the first node (root of the tree) to which A is connected is set to switch A to the upper link if $z_l = 0$ or the lower link if $z_l = 1$. The second node in the path is again set to switch A to the upper link if $z_{l-1} = 0$ or the lower link if $z_{l-1} = 1$. This scheme is continued until we get the proper destination. The path connected is one part of the binary tree assigned to source A. An example is shown by path 1 in Fig. 10. If we consider Z as the source terminal link and A as the destination terminal link, the same procedure will lead us to choose the same path. At this point, properties of the completeness and homogeneity of the routing algorithm will be proven.

Theorem 6—Completeness: The binary tree coding method can set up any mapping connection from one terminal on one side of a network to another terminal on the other side. *Homogeneity:* The binary tree coding method will lead to the same path between these two terminals no matter which end terminal is chosen as the source terminal so that no distinction needs to be made between the inputs and the outputs.

Proof—Completeness: Since the binary representation of a destination terminal on both sides is the same as the codeword formed by concatenating the weight of the link in the path from the source terminal to the destination terminal, we can see that any source terminal on one side can be connected to an arbitrary terminal on the other side by using the routing algorithm. Hence, the routing algorithm can connect the terminal pair specified in any connection request. *Homogeneity:* The homogeneity can be proven by showing that the two sets of the switching elements, respectively, in the two paths set up in opposite directions are identical. Assume again that a source terminal $A = a_l a_{l-1} \cdots a_0$ on side 1 is to be connected to a destination terminal $Z = z_l z_{l-1} \cdots z_0$ on side 2. From (1) and (2), we can see that the first switching element in the path from A to Z is $(a_l a_{l-1} \cdots a_1)_0$, the second one is $(z_l a_l a_{l-1} \cdots a_2)_1$, and the third one is $(z_l z_{l-1} a_l a_{l-1} \cdots a_3)_2$. In general, the set of the switching elements which are in the connected path is

$$S_1 = \{(z_l \cdots z_{l-i+1} a_l a_{l-1} \cdots a_{i+1})_i \mid \quad 0 \le i \le l\}. \quad (34)$$

Similarly, the topology describing rules, (25) and (26), of the reverse baseline network can be used to compute the set of in-path switching elements if we choose Z as the source and A as the destination. Considering that Z is on side 1 of the reverse baseline network, we can see that the first switching element is $(z_l z_{l-1} \cdots z_1)_0$, the second one is $(z_l z_{l-1} \cdots z_2 a_l)_1$, and the third one is $(z_l z_{l-1} \cdots z_3 a_l a_{l-1})_2$. In general, the set of in-path switching elements becomes

$$S_2 = \{(z_l z_{l-1} \cdots z_{j+1} a_l a_{l-1} \cdots a_{l-j-1})_{l-j} \mid$$
$$0 \le j \le l\}. \quad (35)$$

Since, in the baseline network, $j = l - i$, we have $S_1 = S_2$ by (34) and (35). This result shows that the two sets of the switching elements, respectively, in the two paths set up in opposite directions are identical. Q.E.D.

The one-to-one connection request is considered to be a special case of the one-to-many connection request. For a one-to-many connection request, there are as many source–destination pairs as the number of destination terminals specified in the request. The switching element set and the link set of the subtree for a one-to-many connection request can be obtained by unioning respective sets of each individual source–destination path. An example is shown in path 2 in Fig. 10 in which a subtree is set up for the one-to-two connection request of source–destination pairs from terminal 13 on side 2 to terminal 3 and terminal 5 on side 1.

C. Conflict Resolution

Since simultaneous connections of more than one terminal pair of a network in the isomorphic class may result in conflicts in the use of connection links of the network, an effort should be taken to avoid this kind of conflict situation. In SIMD environment, parallel algorithmic processes usually need simultaneous one-to-one connections. Designing a parallel algorithmic process which needs only conflict-free simultaneous one-to-one connections is one way to avoid conflicts. However, we cannot guarantee that we can have this kind of ideal parallel algorithmic processes in all problem solutions. The problem is thus to work out an efficient way for realizing simultaneous one-to-one connections if these connections are not conflict-free. On the other hand, in an MIMD environment, connection requests are likely to occur dynamically and asynchronously. Conflicts must be resolved on the fly by the network. So far there is no systematic way for the conflict resolution. Here we provide a conflict resolution algorithm. However, as a first trial, our algorithm is a fairly static approach and we do not claim optimum for it.

The sharing of a common link by two or more independent subtrees is called a *conflict*. Our algorithm detects any conflicts and resolves the conflicts by deferring some connection requests in the given request set so that all the connection requests that remain show no conflicts. Before we can detect the conflicts, we should compute the set of links which must be connected in a subtree for a connection request. In the proof of Theorem 6, we have shown, in (34), that the in-path switching element in stage i for the mapping from $a_l a_{l-1} \cdots a_0$ on side 1 to $z_l z_{l-1} \cdots z_0$ on side 2 can be expressed as $(z_l \cdots z_{l-i+1} a_l \cdots a_{i+1})_i$. Hence, the in-path link in level $i + 1$ can be expressed as $(z_l \cdots z_{l-i+1} a_l \cdots a_{i+1} z_{l-i})_{i+1}$. For the sake of clarity, the binary representations for the links are converted into decimal numbers. For example, the ordered set of links for the mapping shown in path 1 in Fig. 10 is expressed as follows:

$$P = \begin{pmatrix} 1 & 1 & 0 & 0 \\ 0 & 1 & 0 & 1 \end{pmatrix} = \begin{pmatrix} 12 \\ 5 \end{pmatrix} = \{12, 12, 7, 6, 5\}.$$

TABLE I
A CONFLICT TABLE

Conflict Link / Link Set	Level 1		Level 2		Level 3
	1	6	2	4	5
{0, 1, 5, 6}	X				
{1, 1, 4, 5}	X			X	X
{2, 3, 4, 5}				X	X
{3, 2, 1, 3}					
{4, 4, 2, 0}			X		
{5, 5, 7, 7}					
{6, 6, 2, 1}		X	X		
{7, 6, 3, 2}		X			

Now we are able to detect the conflicts. We shall demonstrate the scheme by an example. It contains eight connection requests:

$$P = \begin{pmatrix} 0 & 1 & 2 & 3 & 4 & 5 & 6 & 7 \\ 6 & 5 & 5 & 3 & 0 & 7 & 1 & 2 \end{pmatrix}.$$

The conflicts for request set P are shown in Table I. The entries of the conflict table are filled in this way. If an ith link set (row) contains a jth conflict link (column), then the $i - j$ entry of the table is filled with an X. Otherwise, it is left unfilled. In the conflict table, each column has at least two X's. In this example, there are conflicts at some links of levels 1, 2, and 3, and there is no conflict in level 0. The conflicts resolution problem then reduces to the choice of a minimal or nearly minimal set of deferred rows such that after deleting those rows, each column has one and only one X. There are many ways to choose the "deferred set." We shall show a possible way in the conflict table. First, we can weigh each link set by adding the number of X's on that link set row and the number of X's on the columns in which the link set being considered has an X. For example, there are three X's on link set row $\{1, 1, 4, 5\}$, which indicate that the conflicts occur at link 1 of level 1, link 4 of level 2, and link 5 of level 3. As shown in Table I, there is another X on each column of these three conflict links. Hence, the weight of row $\{1, 1, 4, 5\}$ is equal to 6. Then we can choose the link set with the highest weight as one member of the deferred set, mark the chosen one with a $\sqrt{}$, and delete entries in that row. In Table I, the link ordered set of $\{1, 1, 4, 5\}$ happens to have the highest weight, 6. We choose $\{1, 1, 4, 5\}$ as the one to be deferred, mark it, and delete the entries in that row. Now a reduced conflict table can be constructed by deleting all the columns with a single X since the link associated with each of these columns is conflict-free after the connection request of the deleted row is deferred. In the reduced table, Table II, columns labeled with 1 in level 1, with 4 in level 2, and with 5 in level 3 have been deleted since they are conflict-free after $\{1, 1, 4, 5\}$ is deferred. The same cycle can be repeated on the reduced table until there is no conflict column. In Table II, $\{6, 6, 2, 1\}$ is chosen to be deferred. The link sets marked with $\sqrt{}$ form a deferred set. The link sets other than those in the deferred set are conflict-free and can be passed by the network.

131

TABLE II
A Reduced Table of Conflict Resolution

Conflict Link / Link Set	Level 1		Level 2		Level 3
	1	6	2	4	5
{0, 1, 5, 6}	X				
✓ {1, 1, 4, 5}	X			X	X
{2, 3, 4, 5}				X	X
{3, 2, 1, 3}					
{4, 4, 2, 0}			X		
{5, 5, 7, 7}					
{6, 6, 2, 1}		X	X		
{7, 6, 3, 2}		X			

TABLE III
Result of Conflict Resolution

Conflict Link / Link Set	Level 1		Level 2		Level 3
	1	6	2	4	5
{0, 1, 5, 6}	X				
✓ {1, 1, 4, 5}	X			X	X
{2, 3, 4, 5}				X	X
{3, 2, 1, 3}					
{4, 4, 2, 0}			X		
{5, 5, 7, 7}					
✓ {6, 6, 2, 1}		X	X		
{7, 6, 3, 2}		X			

Fig. 11. A full switch.

Table III shows the result of the conflict resolution for the example. There are two requests that should be deferred in the example.

IV. FULL COMMUNICATION

The capability of *full communication* of a network is meant to be the ability of the network to connect one of its terminals to other terminals at either side of the network. To achieve the full communication capability, a three-state switch can be introduced [13], as shown in Fig. 11. The mapping requests made on the baseline network with the three-state switches can be classified into four types: 1) side 1 to side 2; 2) side 2 to side 1; 3) side 1 to side 1; 4) side 2 to side 2. The routing procedure for the first two types has been discussed in the previous section. In this section, we only discuss the remaining two types.

Assume that the two terminals $A = a_l a_{l-1} \cdots a_0$ and $Z = z_l z_{l-1} \cdots z_0$ are on the same side, say side 1. Define $c_l c_{l-1} \cdots c_0 = a_l a_{l-1} \cdots a_0 \oplus z_l z_{l-1} \cdots z_0$ where $\oplus$ is a bit-by-bit EX-CLUSIVE OR operation. A routing procedure to connect A and Z is given by the following theorem.

Theorem 7: Assuming $c_i = 1$ and $c_j = 0$ for all $j > i$, there are exactly 2^i possible shortest paths defined to include states of switching elements to connect A and Z and the number of links in the shortest path is exactly equal to $2(i + 1)$.

Proof: Since A and Z are on the same side of the network, there is at least one switching element in the third state, as shown in Fig. 11(c), in the path connecting A and Z. To count how many paths which can connect A and Z, we can count the number of switching elements which can be in the third state in the path. From (34), the set of switching elements in stage k which can be reached from A can be expressed as

$$S_A^k = \{(d_{k-1} d_{k-2} \cdots d_0 a_l a_{l-1} \cdots a_{k+1})_k | \quad d_j = 0 \text{ or } 1; \\ 0 \le j \le k - 1\}. \quad (36)$$

Similarly, the set for Z is

$$S_Z^k = \{(d_{k-1} d_{k-2} \cdots d_0 z_l z_{l-1} \cdots z_{k+1})_k | \quad d_j = 0 \text{ or } 1; \\ 0 \le j \le k - 1\}. \quad (37)$$

The shortest connection path should be the one in which the only one third-state switching element T should be the one in S_A^k and S_Z^k with minimum k. Since $c_i = 1$ and $c_j = 0$ for all $j > i$, $a_l = z_l, \cdots, a_{i+1} = z_{i+1}$ and $a_i \ne z_i$. By (36) and (37), the minimum k to make a common element in S_A^k and S_Z^k is the one which makes $a_l a_{l-1} \cdots a_{k+1} = z_l z_{l-1} \cdots z_{k+1}$. Thus, $k = i$. Hence,

$$T = (d_{i-1} d_{i-2} \cdots d_0 a_l a_{l-1} \cdots a_{i+1})_i \quad (38)$$

where $d_j = 0$ or 1 and $0 \le j \le i - 1$. There are 2^i possible values for T since d_j can be 0 or 1 for $0 \le j \le i - 1$. So there are 2^i possible shortest paths which can connect A and Z. The number of links which connect T and A or Z is equal to $i + 1$ so that the length of the shortest path is $2(i + 1)$.   Q.E.D.

Theorem 7 demonstrates a routing procedure for the full communication. An example is shown in Fig. 12. First, we compute i using an EXCLUSIVE OR operation on the logical names of two terminals, A and Z, on the same side, which should be connected. In the example, i is equal to 2. Next we can compute the set of the third-state switching elements in the paths:

$$\{(d_{i-1} d_{i-2} \cdots d_0 a_l a_{l-1} \cdots a_{i+1})_i | \\ d_j = 0 \text{ or } 1; 0 \le j \le i - 1\}. \quad (39)$$

By (39), the set of the third-state switching element in the example is $\{(d_1 d_0 0)_2 | d_0 = 0 \text{ or } 1; d_1 = 0 \text{ or } 1\}$. Third, we can compute some of the 2^i possible shortest paths by using A and Z as the source terminals and $(d_{i-1} d_{i-2} \cdots d_0 a_l a_{l-1} \cdots a_{i+1})_i$ as the destination switching element. However, in the implementation phase, a scheme should be set up to determine which one in the 2^i possible shortest paths should be computed. There is a total of 2^2 possible shortest paths for connecting A and Z in the example. Finally, one of the possible paths can be chosen by applying the procedure for the conflict resolution as described in the previous section. Fig. 12 shows a connecting path in which switching element $(010)_2$ is in the third state.

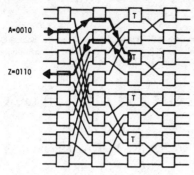

A=0010

Z=0110

Fig. 12. An example of full communication. (*T* is the third-state switching element in a possible path.)

V. CONCLUSION

We have presented a mathematical model for better describing multistage interconnection networks. In the mathematical model, we propose a concept of configuration. It is then proven that a class of isomorphic multistage interconnection networks can be obtained by properly permuting switching elements and associated links of a reference network, called the baseline network, within the same stage. The class of isomorphic multistage interconnection networks includes the indirect binary *n*-cube network, the modified data manipulator, the flip network, the omega network, the regular SW banyan network with $S = F = 2$, the reverse baseline network, and the baseline network. Routing techniques for the class of isomorphic networks are also developed. Specifically speaking, we have developed a homogeneous routing algorithm which allows one-to-one and one-to-many connections from an arbitrary side of a network to the other side. This routing algorithm is also extended to full communication which allows connections between terminals on the same side of a network. A conflict resolution scheme is included in the routing techniques.

There are at least two important practical implications from our results. Since those multistage interconnection networks which have been proposed from significantly different viewpoints are topologically equivalent, the difference among them comes from their configurations. Therefore, we can simulate different configurations on a network in the isomorphic class. The second implication comes from the fact that our mathematical model facilitates the possibility of calculating the set of switching elements (or links) on a connection path on the basis of knowing the names of two terminals to be connected. This fact essentially lays a groundwork for developing a fault-diagnosis scheme, logic partitioning for LSI implementation, and a scheme for packet switching communication. Exploiting these two practical implications will be a good topic for further research.

REFERENCES

[1] T. Feng, "Data manipulating functions in parallel processors and their implementations," *IEEE Trans. Comput.*, vol. C-23, pp. 309–318, Mar. 1974.

[2] H. J. Siegel, "Analysis techniques for SIMD machine interconnection networks and the effects of processor address masks," *IEEE Trans. Comput.*, vol. C-26, pp. 153–161, Feb. 1977.

[3] K. J. Thurber, "Interconnection network—A survey and assessment," in *Proc. AFIPS 1974 Nat. Comput. Conf.*, pp. 909–919.

[4] K. E. Batcher, "The flip network in STARAN," in *Proc. 1976 Int. Conf. Parallel Processing*, pp. 65–71.

[5] M. C. Pease, III, "The indirect binary *n*-cube microprocessor array," *IEEE Trans. Comput.*, vol. C-26, pp. 458–473, May 1977.

[6] D. K. Lawrie, "Access and alignment of data in an array processor," *IEEE Trans. Comput.*, vol. C-24, pp. 1145–1155, Dec. 1975.

[7] G. J. Lipovski and A. Tripathi, "A reconfigurable varistructure array processor," in *Proc. 1977 Int. Conf. Parallel Processing*, pp. 165–174.

[8] L. R. Goke and G. J. Lipovski, "Banyan networks for partitioning multiprocessing systems," in *Proc. 1st Annu. Comput. Architecture Conf.*, Dec. 1973, pp. 21–28.

[9] H. Sullivan, T. R. Bashkow, and K. Klappholz, "A large scale homogeneous, fully distributed parallel machine," in *Proc. 4th Annu. Symp. Comput. Architecture*, Nov. 1977, pp. 105–125.

[10] K. E. Batch, "Sorting networks and their applications," in *1968 Spring Joint Computer Conf., AFIPS Conf. Proc.* Washington, DC: Spartan, 1968, pp. 307–314.

[11] H. J. Siegel and S. D. Smith, "Study of multistage SIMD interconnection network," in *Proc. 5th Annu. Symp. Comput. Architecture*, Apr. 1978, pp. 223–229.

[12] D. Opferman and N. Tsao-Wu, "On a class of rearrangeable switching networks," *Bell Syst. Tech. J.*, vol. 50, pp. 1579–1618, May–June 1971.

[13] J. Gecsei, "Interconnection networks from three-state cells," *IEEE Trans. Comput.*, vol. C-26, pp. 705–711, Aug. 1977.

Chuan-lin Wu (M'80) received the B.S. and M.S. degrees in electrical engineering from Chiao Tung University, Taiwan, China. In December 1978 he completed Ph.D. requirements in the Department of Electrical and Computer Engineering, Wayne State University, Detroit, MI, under the supervision of Prof. Tse-yun Feng and received an Assistant Professor appointment from the same department.

In September 1979 he joined the Department of Computer Science, Wright State University, Dayton, OH, where he is currently an Assistant Professor. His research interests include parallel processing, computer architecture, database machines, and computer communication.

Dr. Wu is a member of Phi Tau Phi and the Association for Computing Machinery.

Tse-yun Feng (S'61–M'67–SM'75–F'80) received the B.S. degree from the National Taiwan University, Taipei, Taiwan, the M.S. degree from Oklahoma State University, Stillwater, and the Ph.D. degree from the University of Michigan, Ann Arbor, all in electrical engineering.

He was on the Faculty of the Department of Electrical and Computer Engineering, Syracuse University, Syracuse, NY, from 1967 to 1975, and Wayne State University, Detroit, MI, from 1975 to 1979. He is now a Professor and Chairman of the Department of Computer Science, Wright State University, Dayton, OH. He has extensive technical publications in the areas of associative processing, parallel and concurrent processors, computer architecture, switching theory, and logic design, and has edited four *Sagamore Computer Conference Proceedings* (including *Parallel Processing* published by Springer-Verlag). He has also been an invited speaker to various organizations and served as a consultant or reviewer to several companies and publishers.

Dr. Feng has received a number of awards and honorary recognitions for his technical contributions and scholarship. He was a Distinguished Visitor of the IEEE Computer Society from 1973 to 1978. He is also active professionally. He is presently the President of IEEE Computer Society, a member of IEEE Technical Activities Board, a member of AFIPS Board of Directors, and Director of Northeast Consortium for Engineering Education, among others. He has served as a reviewer, panelist, or session chairman for various technical magazines and conferences. He also initiated the Sagamore Computer Conference on Parallel Processing and the International Conference on Parallel Processing.

Reprinted from *IEEE Transactions on Computers*, Volume C-31, Number 5, May 1982, pages 435–442. Copyright © 1982 by The Institute of Electrical and Electronics Engineers, Inc.

The Prime Memory System for Array Access

DUNCAN H. LAWRIE, SENIOR MEMBER, IEEE, AND CHANDRA R. VORA, MEMBER, IEEE

Abstract—In this paper we describe a memory system designed for parallel array access. The system is based on the use of a prime number of memories and a powerful combination of indexing hardware and data alignment switches. Particular emphasis is placed on the indexing equations and their implementation.

Index Terms—Array access, Burroughs Scientific Processor (BSP), conflict-free array memory, memory system, parallel computer system, SIMD computer memory.

I. Introduction

THERE have always been certain application areas which require computation power far beyond what technology can deliver, despite the remarkable technological advances made in the past. Today these applications include airframe design, weather prediction, seismic analysis, and physics research, to name just a few. In order to achieve this computation power, computer designers have had to rely on innovative computer organization. The main approach taken in the 1960's and 1970's was to exploit vector processing rather than to only increase the speed of scalar computation. This was done by using either pipeline or parallel computer structures.

Pipeline computers have been the primary commercially successful approach to date, as evidenced by the CRAY-1. These organizations achieve their performance by breaking each basic operation (multiply, add, etc.) into a number of segments. For example, addition can be divided into: 1) mantissa alignment, 2) one or more steps of mantissa addition, and 3) rounding and post normalization. A series of additions can then be sequenced through these segments in less time than it would take to do each addition separately.

A parallel processor consists of a large number of arithmetic units combined into a single machine sharing a common memory system. Theoretically, the performance improvement is limited only by the amount of inherent parallelism in the application rather than by the number of processors (or segments) that can be built.

In practice, however, a number of factors have contributed to the less than optimal performance of parallel machines. One factor is the design of a memory system (a problem shared by high-speed pipeline designs). Given that the processor ensemble is capable of very high computation speeds, a memory

Manuscript received July 2, 1981; revised December 16, 1981. This work was supported by the Burroughs Corporation, Paoli, PA, the Department of Computer Science, University of Illinois at Urbana-Champaign, and the National Science Foundation under Grant US NSF MCS77-27910.

D. H. Lawrie is with the Department of Computer Science, University of Illinois at Urbana-Champaign, Urbana, IL 61801.

C. R. Vora was with the Burroughs Corporation, Paoli, PA 19301. He is now with the Data General Corporation, Westboro, MA 01581.

system must be capable of supporting these speeds. This is done by providing parallel (i.e., interleaved) memories. If the data for each parallel operation are evenly and completely distributed over M memories, then all memories can deliver a word during each memory cycle, and the design problem is simply to supply enough memories to provide sufficient bandwidth to match the processors' requirements. But if the data are not evenly distributed, significant degradation can occur due to memory access contention.

The problem discussed in this paper is the design of a memory system that can access, in parallel, the required sections of an array, e.g., a row, column, diagonal, etc. A number of these memory systems have been discussed in the literature. In [2] Batcher discusses a scheme for allowing access to words, bit slices, or "byte" slices of a two-dimensional bit array. Feng described another scheme for accessing various "slices" of data in [7]. Other work described in [20], [21], [10], [11], [14], [18], [13], and [16] has also treated the problem of array access and alignment, but because these designs use a power of two memories and restricted alignment networks, they all have restrictions either on the kinds of "slices" available without memory access conflicts or in the data alignment capabilities. (See [18] for a survey of this work.)

In [3] Budnik and Kuck observed that if the number of memory modules is a prime number, then access to any "linear" array slices can be achieved without conflict (provided that the memory ordering of the desired array elements is relatively prime to the number of array elements). For example, assume that we want to access every other element of a column of an array stored in column major order. If the number of memories M is a power of two, then two parallel accesses would be required to access M elements. But if M is a prime number (>2), only one parallel access would be required (see Fig. 2). This observation turns out to be quite useful. However, the problem of addressing this type of memory turns out to be difficult due to the need to do integer divisions and modulo operations in the addressing hardware. In this paper we will discuss these problems in more detail, and will present a feasible implementation of the prime memory system.

Since many of the ideas in this paper have been incorporated in the design of the Burroughs Scientific Processor (BSP), we will describe some of the details of the memory, alignment, and indexing hardware of this machine. The BSP is a high performance computer designed to be especially effective on vector processing applications, without significantly impairing its performance on scalar computations. A complete description of the BSP is beyond the scope of this paper. However, in order to illustrate the ideas in this paper, we will present a brief overview of the architecture. As can be seen in Fig. 1, the BSP consists of 16 processing units, 17 memories, two alignment networks, and a central control and scalar processing unit. Total memory can be as large as eight million words. The control unit includes a fully functional scalar processing unit which can be be overlapped with vector operations, and additional memory (256K max words) for scalar data and program storage. Additional components of the system include a high-speed file memory, disks, and a front-end computer. (See [9] for further details.)

The BSP is designed to facilitate vector operations utilizing the 16 processing elements. Special hardware is included in the control unit to perform vector addressing and alignment control, and these operations can be overlapped with vector and scalar processing.

The alignment networks shown in Fig. 1 are in reality crossbar switches controlled by *source tags*. (That is, each output port of the network can supply a "tag" which specifies the number of the input from which it needs data.) While in general, crossbar switches are too expensive for large arrays of processors, due to the relatively small number of processors in the BSP it was determined that crossbar switches were the most cost-effective form of switch capable of performing all the designed alignments.

In particular, the functions such as compress, expand, and merge, require a random aligning pattern which only the crossbar switch could perform efficiently in the allocated time. Other forms of switches were investigated, e.g., the Swanson networks [21], Omega switch [13], Barrel Shift network, etc., but these switches do not perform all the functions needed in the allocated time, and they become cost-effective only with a large number of ports.

II. THE STORAGE SCHEME AND ASSOCIATED EQUATIONS

By a storage scheme we mean the set of rules which determine the module number and address within that module where a given array element is stored. For the present, we will restrict our attention to two-dimensional arrays. However, generalization of these storage schemes is trivial for higher dimensioned arrays.

Fig. 2 shows an 8 × 8 array stored in 5 memory modules using column major storage. (In order to simplify the equations below, we assume that all arrays are indexed starting at zero unless indicated otherwise.) Notice that any 5 consecutive elements of a row, column, diagonal, etc., all lie in separate modules and thus can be accessed in parallel, i.e., without conflict. For example, the second through sixth elements of the first row are stored in module numbers 3, 1, 4, 2, 0, and at addresses 2, 4, 6, 8, 10, respectively.

We begin with some definitions. Let M be the number of memory modules and P be the number of processors, where we assume $P \leq M$ and M is prime. There are two *storage equations* $f(i, j)$ and $g(i, j)$ which determine the module number and address, respectively, of element (i, j) of the array. In our case we have the following equations:

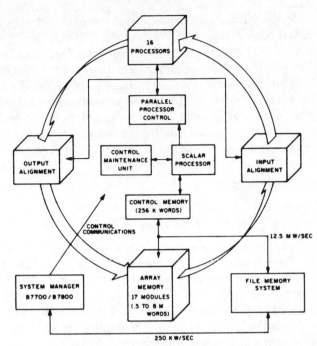

Fig. 1. Block diagram of the Burroughs Scientific Processor.

Memory Module Number

Address	0	1	2	3	4
0	00	10	20	30	x
1	50	60	70	x	40
2	21	31	x	01	11
3	71	x	41	51	61
4	x	02	12	22	32
5	42	52	62	72	x
6	13	23	33	x	03
7	63	73	x	43	53
8	34	x	04	14	24
9	x	44	54	64	74
10	05	15	25	35	x
11	55	65	75	x	45
12	26	36	x	06	16
13	76	x	46	56	66
14	x	07	17	27	37
15	47	57	67	77	x

Fig. 2. Example of a 8 × 8 array stored column major in 5 memory modules.

$$f(i, j) = [j * I + i + \text{base}] \bmod M \qquad (1)$$

$$g(i, j) = [j * I + i + \text{base}]/P \qquad (2)$$

where we assume the array is dimensioned (I, J), "base" is the base address of the array, and P the number of processors is the greatest power of two less than M. Notice that these equations require a mod M operation where M is a prime number. They also require an integer divide by P operation. However, P is a power of two which makes this divide easily implementable. This simplification is made possible by the "holes" shown in Fig. 2. (A hole is an unused memory location.)

Clearly, the number of holes in each row of the memory is equal to $M - P$ in general. For example, if $M = 37$ and $P = 32$, then $5/37$ of the memory is wasted. These holes could be filled with other data, e.g., scalar data, but a cleaner solution is available at the expense of an increase in the complexity of the indexing equations. The necessary modifications will become apparent in Section III when we discuss the partitioning of the equations and the indexing hardware.

Next we define a *linear P-vector* or simply a *P-vector*, to be a P element set of the elements of the array formed by linear subscript equations

$$V(a, b, c, e) = \{A(i, j): i = ax + b,$$
$$j = cx + e, \quad 0 \le x < P \le M \quad (3)$$

where again we assume the array is dimensioned $A(I, J)$. Thus, if $a = b = 0$ and $c = e = 1$, then the P-vector ($P = 5$) is the second through sixth elements of the first row of A: $A(0, 1)$, $A(0, 2), \cdots, A(0, 5)$. If $a = c = 2$ and $b = e = 0$, then the P-vector ($P = 4$) is every other element of the main diagonal of A: $A(0, 0), A(2, 2), \cdots, A(6, 6)$. Notice that the elements of the P-vector are ordered with index x.

Next we define the *index equations* for the P-vector V. We define $\alpha(x)$ to be the address in module $\mu(x)$ of the xth element of the P-vector. Thus, combining (1)–(3) above, we get

$$\mu(x) = f(ax + b, cx + e)$$
$$= [(cx + e) * I + (ax + b) + \text{base}] \bmod M$$
$$= [dx + B] \bmod M \quad (4)$$

where $d = a + cI$ and $B = b + eI + \text{base}$. We define d to be the *order* of the P-vector and B to be the initial or base address. Next, we get

$$\alpha(x) = g(ax + b, cx + e)$$
$$= [(cx + e) * I + (ax + b) + \text{base}]/P$$
$$= [dx + B]/P. \quad (5)$$

It is easy to show that if d is relatively prime to the number of memory modules, then access to the P-vector can be made without memory conflict. (See [3] and [13] for a proof.)

Since it is most convenient to be able to generate the address $\alpha(x)$ in memory $\mu(x)$, we solve for x in terms of μ and get

$$x(\mu) = [(\mu - B)d'] \bmod M \quad (6)$$

where $d \cdot d' = 1 \bmod M$. Substituting this into (5), we get

$$\alpha(\mu) = \{(a + Ic)[(\mu - B)d' \bmod M] + b + eI + \text{base}\}/P$$
$$= \{d[(\mu - B)d' \bmod M] + B\}/P. \quad (7)$$

For example, consider the 5-vector $V(0, 0, 1, 1)$, i.e., the second through sixth elements of the first row of $A(8 \times 8)$. We have $B = 8$ and $d = 8$; thus

$$\mu(x) = [(x) * 8 + 8] \bmod 5$$
$$\alpha(x) = [(x) * 8 + 8]/4$$

and since $d' = 2$ (i.e., $2 * 8 = 1 \bmod 5$), $B = 8$, and $M = 5$, we get

$$\alpha(\mu) = \{8[2(\mu - 8) \bmod 5] + 8\}/4.$$

Thus,

$$\mu(x) = (3, 1, 4, 2, 0)$$
$$\alpha(x) = (2, 4, 6, 8, 10)$$

and

$$\alpha(\mu) = (10, 4, 8, 2, 6).$$

Notice that the proper addresses in memories $0, 1, \cdots, 4$, are $10, 4, 8, 2, 6$, respectively. We use the $\mu(x)$ equation in the xth processor to determine the module number of the memory containing the xth element of the desired N-vector. At the same time, addressing hardware in memory μ uses the $\alpha(\mu)$ equation to determine the necessary address of the desired element. We use $\alpha(\mu)$ instead of $\alpha(x)$ because this eliminates the need to route the addresses from the processors through the switch.

This process is reasonably straightforward, except that it is not obvious that the hardware can do the necessary calculations efficiently. In Section III we will describe how we partition the equations into parts that can be done separately by special hardware in the CU, AU, and memory addressing box.

III. INDEXING HARDWARE

The BSP consists of a control unit, 16 processors, 17 memories, and two alignment networks as shown in Fig. 1. Vector instructions in the BSP are designed to allow processing on vectors of arbitrary length. The control unit automatically sequences vector operations as a series of *superword* operations where a superword consists of 16 or less vector elements. For example, a vector instruction which specifies a vector of length 53 would be sequenced as three superwords of 16 elements, followed by a superword of 5 elements.

Associated with every array is an *array descriptor* (AD), shown in Fig. 3(a). The two values in the AD describe the base address and total volume (words) of the array and are used for addressing and bounds checks on the array. Every vector instruction refers to at least one and as many as six *vector operands*. Each vector operand is referenced through a *vector set descriptor* (VSD), shown in Fig. 3(b). The VSD actually describes a set of vectors from a given array. B is the address of the first element of the first vector in the set. This vector is ordered with distance d and contains L elements. The first element of the second vector in the set is the (signed) distance D from the first element of the first vector. There are K vectors in the set. Thus, the VSD describes a two-dimensional set of data.

For example, the VSD ($B = 1, d = 8, LL = 8, D = 2, K = 4$) describes the odd-numbered rows of the array $A(8, 8)$ shown in Fig. 2. Similarly, VSD ($B = 0, d = 1, LL = 8, D = 16, K = 4$) describes even numbered columns and VSD ($B = 0, d = 0, LL = 8, D = 1, K = 8$) describes a two-dimensional set of data $X(i, j)$, where $X(i, j) = A(i, 0), 0 \le i, j < 8$, and $A(i, j)$ is the array shown in Fig. 2.

The above parameters are not all stored together. The first step in preparing a vector instruction is to compute the above parameters, together with other values needed for addressing

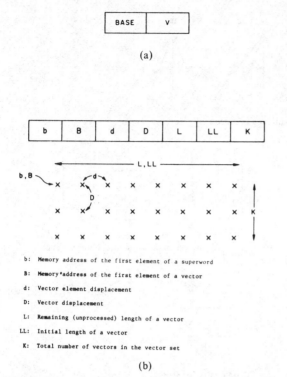

(a)

(b)

b: Memory address of the first element of a superword

B: Memory address of the first element of a vector

d: Vector element displacement

D: Vector displacement

L: Remaining (unprocessed) length of a vector

LL: Initial length of a vector

K: Total number of vectors in the vector set

Fig. 3. (a) Array descriptor. (b) Vector set descriptor (VSD).

and alignment. This is greatly facilitated by special-purpose indexing hardware.

The purpose of the indexing hardware is to generate alignment tags and memory addresses for vector access. Consider first the input alignment network. To access a superword, processor p must generate an input alignment tag IAT, which specifies the memory module number of the pth element of the superword, i.e., $\mu(p)$. At the same time, the address of the pth element $\alpha(p)$ is generated in memory $\mu(p)$. Notice that each processor could generate the required address using (5), and then route this address to the proper memory through the output alignment network. However, by using (7) we avoid the extra routing operation.

The output alignment network works similarly. Memory $\mu(p)$ is to receive the pth element of a superword, and thus generates an output alignment tag OAT whose value is computed from (6) above. Each memory also computes the required address $\alpha(\mu)$ for storing the output.

The alignment, indexing, and memory systems are also responsible for a number of other functions as follows:

1) processor to processor routing, without going to memory,

2) handling of nonlinear P-vectors through the use of tags and addresses computed by the processor, or stored in special ROM memories or main memory,

3) handling bit vectors used for sparse vector operations and conditional vector expressions,

4) padding short superwords and with null elements,

5) providing for broadcase of scalar data from the control unit or main memory.

We will discuss these functions in a later section. For now we will restrict our attention to accessing linear P-vectors.

A. Linear P-Vector Access

Let us assume for the moment that we are interested in access to a single superword with initial base address B and with order d. If the superword is to be *fetched* from the memory, then for each memory μ, we must generate an address [see (4)–(7)]

$$\alpha(\mu) = \{B + p(\mu) \cdot d\}/P \tag{8}$$

where

$$p(\mu) = \{(\mu - B)d' \bmod M\} \tag{9}$$

and for each processor p, we must generate an IAT

$$\mu(p) = (B + d * p) \bmod M. \tag{10}$$

However, if the superword is to be *stored* in the memory, then for each memory μ we must generate an address given by (8) and (9) and for each memory μ we must also generate an OAT

$$p(\mu) = [(\mu - B)d'] \bmod M. \tag{11}$$

Thus, M − addresses and P − IAT's or M − OAT's are required to access a superword. In the next section we will show how the generation of these values can be simplified.

1) Recursive Generation Technique: Consider (10). Substituting $(p + k)$ and $(p - k)$ for p, we get

$$\mu(p \pm k) = [B + d * (p \pm k)] \bmod M$$
$$= [\mu(p \pm k \mp 1) \pm d] \bmod M. \tag{12}$$

Equation (12) implies that $\mu(p + k)$ can be generated from $\mu(p)$ with modulo M addition/subtraction operations instead of a multiply followed by a modulo M addition. Extending the notion, from any $\mu(p)$ all tags can be generated recursively with appropriate modulo M additions or subtractions. In practice, primary $\mu(p)$ for several values of p are generated using (10), and secondary $\mu(p)$ for the remaining values of p are generated using (12). The number of primary $\mu(p)$ versus the number of secondary $\mu(p)$ calculated can be determined by a simple hardware versus time tradeoff.

The same technique can be applied to generate output alignment tags and memory addresses. The equation for the OAT's is

$$p(\mu \pm k) = [p(\mu \pm k \mp 1) \pm d'] \bmod M. \tag{13}$$

For memory addresses, the equation is

$$\alpha(\mu \pm k) = (B + \{[p(\mu \pm k \mp 1) \pm d'] \bmod M\}d)/P. \tag{14}$$

2) BSP Implementation: For the BSP, $P = 16$ and $M = 17$. The base address B is a 23-bit value. Element displacement d is a 23-bit signed quantity. For timing and hardware considerations, 4 initial memory addresses, 4 IAT's, and 4 OAT's are generated by using multiplications and modulo and normal additions. Other addresses and tags are generated by using binary adders. To use the binary adders, the equations de-

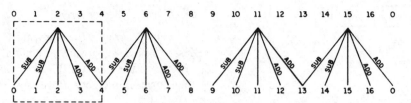

Fig. 4. Primary and secondary address generation.

scribed in the previous section were further simplified as follows. Let $\delta = d \bmod M$, and notice that $\mu(p) < M$. For IAT's, we get

$$\mu(p + k) = \mu(p) + k\delta - cM \qquad (15)$$

where c is a correction factor such that $cM \le \mu(p) + k\delta < (c + 1)M$. For example, assume that $M = 17$. We might generate primary $\mu(p)$ for $p = 1, 4, 7, 10, 13, 16$ from (10). Secondary $\mu(p)$ for the remaining values of p would be generated as follows from (15):

$\mu(p + 1) = \mu(p) + \delta$ corrected by -17 if $\mu(p) + \delta \ge 17$

$\mu(p - 1) = \mu(p) - \delta$ corrected by $+17$ if $\mu(p) + \delta < 0$.

Equations for OAT's are the same as above except δ is replaced by d'. For memory address generation, the equations are as follows. Let

$$A(\mu) = B + p(\mu) \cdot d \text{ so that } \alpha(\mu) = A(\mu)/P.$$

Then

$$\begin{aligned}A(\mu + k) &= B + d \cdot p(\mu + k) \\ &= B + d([d'(\mu + k - B)] \bmod M) \\ &= B + d([p(\mu) + kd'] \bmod M) \\ &= A(\mu) + kdd' - dcM \end{aligned}$$

where

$$cM \le p(\mu) + kd' < (c + 1)M. \qquad (16)$$

Address generation in the BSP is performed as follows. Primary $A(\mu)$ are generated for $\mu = 2, 6, 11,$ and 15 as shown in Fig. 4. Then secondary values are generated for $k = \pm 1, \pm 2$. Notice that $A(\mu)$ for $\mu = 4$ and 13 are each generated twice. This redundancy is used to check the hardware integrity by comparing duplicated values. (In addition, modulo 3 checks are performed on all additions to further verify hardware integrity.)

A primary $A(\mu)$ generator is shown in Fig. 5. $B \bmod M$ and d' are each 5-bit quantities (since $M = 17$) and are supplied by the Central Index Unit (to be discussed in the next section). The quantity $d'(\mu - B) \bmod M$ is supplied by a 1024×5 bit ROM. (The ROM contents differ for each primary μ.)

A secondary address generator for $A(\mu + 2)$ is shown in Fig. 6. Notice that in (16) a test is required to determine the quantity added to (or subtracted from) $A(\mu)$. This test depends on the quantity $p(\mu) + 2d' = d'(\mu - B) \bmod M + 2d'$ [see (16)]. $d'(\mu - B) \bmod M$ (available from the primary address generator) and d' are each 5-bit quantities and are used as address inputs to a 1024×2 ROM. The output of the ROM determines the test result and is used to multiply the necessary

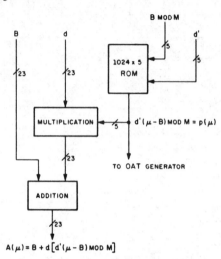

Fig. 5. A primary address generator.

additive factor for the final adder. The other secondary address generators for $A(\mu + 1)$, $A(\mu - 1)$, and $A(\mu - 2)$ are similar to the one shown in Fig. 6. However, the $A(\mu \pm 1)$ generators only need 2-way multiplexers and a one-bit wide decision ROM. (Through further simplification, these decision ROM's can be reduced to 512 words, so that the total decision ROM for four secondary generators is just 6×512 bits.) The primary and its four associated secondary address generators are all grouped together physically.

Generation of IAT's and OAT's is essentially the same or simpler than address generation. Only the values and number of bits change. One group of hardware, described above, generates the addresses, and a similar group of hardware generates both the IAT's and OAT's. Both groups of hardware form part of the Central Index Unit that will be described next.

3) The Central Index Unit: One of the components of the control unit is the Central Index Unit (CIU). The purpose of the CIU is to: 1) perform automatic indexing of multiple superwords of up to two-dimensional arrays, 2) generate input and output alignment tags, and 3) generate 4 initial memory addresses and indexing constants. The CIU can be divided into 4 major sections: 1) Descriptor Store Unit, 2) Descriptor Processing Unit, 3) IAT and OAT generators, and 4) Memory Address and Indexing Constant Generators. Fig. 7 shows the organization of the above sections. The IAT, OAT, and address generators were described in the previous section.

The descriptor store unit scores up to 16 vector set descriptors (VSD). A simplified descriptor's contents are shown in Fig. 3(b).

A superword access requires an Indexing Event in the CIU.

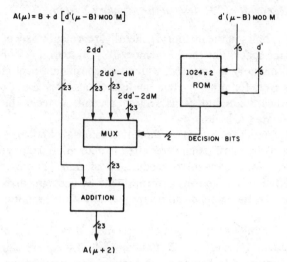

Fig. 6. Secondary address generation for $A(\mu \pm 2)$.

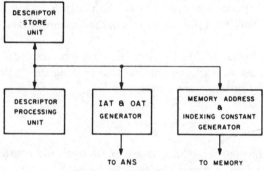

Fig. 7. Central index unit.

During this event the descriptor is updated by the Descriptor Processing Unit to reflect the access. The processing depends upon the kind of descriptor as well as the data values within the descriptor. For example, suppose we have a two-dimensional vector set operand (e.g., $K > 1$). The processing will be as follows.

If the length L is longer than a superword (P), then the descriptor values are updated as follows. These updates are performed after each superword access is initiated.

$$b \leftarrow b + d * P$$
$$B \leftarrow B$$
$$L \leftarrow L - P$$
$$K \leftarrow K.$$

However, if the length L of the last access was equal or less than a superword (P), then the next superword should come from the next vector in the vector set. The appropriate update equations are as follows.

$$b \leftarrow B + D$$
$$B \leftarrow B + D$$
$$L \leftarrow LL$$
$$K \leftarrow K - 1.$$

These actions cause the length to be reset to the initial length

(LL) and increment the base address (B) to the base of the next vector in the set.

As an example of the use of vector set description, consider the following Fortran program segment.

DIMENSION $X(100, 200)$, $Y(300, 400)$, $Z(200, 100, 100)$
DO 1 I = 2, 100, 2
   DO 1 J = 1, 100
1      $X(I, J) = Y(2 * I - 1, I + J) * Z(I + J, I, J)$

This entire segment would be performed by a single BSP instruction which would refer to three VSD's. These VSD's would be initially constructed as shown in Fig. 8(a). (Assume that the base of the X array is x. Similarly for Y and Z.) In this case all values shown in the VSD's (except the base addresses) could be computed at compile time.

Fig. 8(b) shows the state of the VSD's after the first superword operation has been issued. Fig. 8(c) shows their state after the operation is issued for the last superword ($N = 4$) of the first vector. At this point, b and B indicate the first word of the second vector.

4) Automatic Padding of Short Superwords: As mentioned earlier, not all superwords in a vector operation are a full 16 words. Internally in the BSP System, the Arithmetic Elements (AE's) recognize a "NULL" operand. In the BSP word format, bit #48 is used as a tag to indicate a valid or NULL operand. The AE treats the NULL operand in the following manner:

NULL operand (op) Valid operand = Valid operand
NULL operand (op) NULL operand = NULL operand.

The array memory also recognizes the NULL operand and inhibits a store when a NULL operand is encountered. The control unit automatically causes the alignment networks to pad short superwords by selecting NULL operands during input and output alignment events.

B. Other Functions of the Alignment, Indexing, and Memory System

As we mentioned above, the AIM system is also responsible for a number of other functions. In order to facilitate the smooth flow of data through the vector processing elements, forms of data other than linear N-vectors must be handled more or less automatically. These functions will be discussed next.

1) Scalar Data in Vector Operations: Scalar data can be combined with vector data in two ways, depending on whether the scalar data are located in scalar memory (e.g., for $A * B(*)$) or in the array memory (e.g., for $B(1) * C(*)$).

If the data are located in scalar memory, then it is handled as follows. One of the CIU descriptors will represent a "vector set" consisting of a replicated scalar value. The scalar value is included in the VSD descriptor fields. The CIU recognizes this and transfers the scalar value (instead of the IAT's) directly to the input alignment network. The control unit forces the network to select this value instead of data coming from the memory.

From Array Memory, a scalar word can be broadcast to all AE's by simply making the vector displacement field d equal

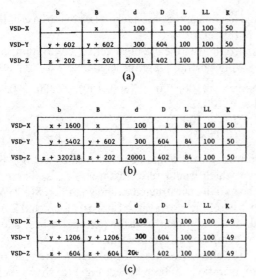

Fig. 8. (a) Initial VSD's. (b) VSD's after first superword. (c) VSD's after seventh superword.

C. Removal of "Holes" in the Memory System

The holes in the memory, generally, represent waste of the storage space. For the 17 memory BSP System, 1/17 of the total memory is not used, which was considered negligible. However, for other system configurations, this could be a significant amount. This section presents a technique to eliminate the holes.

Referring to (5) and (7), note that removal of holes means a divide by M function is required to determine the physical address for each memory module. Artzy *et al.* [1] presented an efficient method to perform divide by constant divisors. However, the method can be applied only if the remainder is zero.

Referring to (7), note that $A(\mu) \bmod M = \mu$. Thus, if we subtract μ from $\{d[(\mu - B)d' \bmod M] + B\}$, a zero remainder is guaranteed. Also, this subtraction does not change the quotient. Thus, the algorithm to efficiently divide by M is a subtraction by μ followed by a multiplication by a predetermined number, followed by taking the 2's complement of the result.

In addition to this, the simplification schemes discussed in earlier sections can be applied, thus making the "hole-less" memory system more efficient.

IV. CONCLUSION

In this paper we have shown one design for a conflict-free array access memory. This design is based on the use of a prime number of memories. Crucial to this design is the simplification of the indexing equations which allow most of the mod M operations and much of the other index calculations to be done with ROM's and other simple hardware. These simplifications were discussed in Section III, along with a brief discussion of some of the necessary indexing hardware. Further details can be found in [12].

The design of this memory system fits nicely in the context of the Burroughs Scientific Processor [19], [9]. The vector machine instructions on this computer can encompass two levels of loop nesting, and the indexing hardware carries out the necessary addressing and alignment calculations automatically, once the initial vector set descriptors have been set up. One of the major problems with large vector computers has been that indexing overhead and memory access conflicts have a significant effect on overall vector performance. By using the prime memory system and indexing hardware described in this paper, the BSP is able to execute vector instructions efficiently.

The performance of this SIMD machine depends to a large extent on its ability to access arrays in a deterministic, conflict-free way. Future supercomputers will undoubtedly tend more toward MIMD operation. In MIMD machines we must depend more on the probabilistic behavior of the memory system. That is, we must be concerned less with deterministic array access and more on the average time required to deliver data. Other work [4], [15], [6], [5] has shown that memory and communication schemes can be designed for use in MIMD

to zero. The CIU performs the broadcast by making all tags equal to the memory module from which the scalar is to be broadcast.

2) Scalar Data from the AE's: There are some cases where scalar data produced by the AE are required by the CU. This case is handled by forcing the output alignment network to route the required data item to the CU.

3) Vector Element Conflict: In the memory storage scheme, if $d \bmod M = 0$, all the elements of the linear vector lie in the same memory module. This is referred to as a vector element conflict condition. In this case the access to the memory has to be sequential. In the BSP System this condition is handled by forcing superword size equal to 1. Thus, the BSP System automatically adapts to this case without any software or other interruption.

4) Inner and Outer Loop Optimization: Consider the following Fortran program segment.

```
DO 10 I = E, F, G
DO 10 J = P, Q, R
10    A(I,J) = B(I,J) + C(I,J)
```

This program can be performed in a single BSP vector operation using Vector Set Descriptors having $K = \left\lceil \dfrac{F - E}{G} \right\rceil + 1$ parallel vectors, each having a length equal to $L = \left\lceil \dfrac{Q - P}{R} \right\rceil + $ 1. Clearly, the last superword length in each vector is equal to the remainder $L/16$. The remaining AE's will be idle. This will be repeated K times in the above case.

If the remainder $K/16$ is greater than the remainder $L/16$, it is faster to execute the above program segment with inner and outer loops interchanged. This is exactly what happens in the BSP to maximize performance. Hardware detection of the fastest loop order is made from the parameters L and K of a VSD. Of course, not all loops can be interchanged, and a software check is made to allow the above optimization.

environments. Supercomputers will have to depend on a combination of parallel, pipeline, and MIMD techniques, together with complex memory systems.

ACKNOWLEDGMENT

A number of people have contributed to this work. The overall design of BSP is due primarily to D. Kuck and R. Stokes. Special thanks go to R. Cantarella, who made many significant contributions to the BSP design and especially to the alignment, indexing, and memory system. O. Gupta and R. Gupta also made contributions.

REFERENCES

[1] E. Artzy, J. A. Hinds, and H. J. Saal, "A fast division technique for constant divisors," *Commun. Ass. Comput. Mach.*, vol. 19, pp. 98–101, Feb. 1976.

[2] K. E. Batcher, "The multidimensional access memory in STARAN," *IEEE Trans. Comput.*, vol. C-26, pp. 174–177, Feb. 1977.

[3] P. Budnik and D. J. Kuck, "The organization and use of parallel memories," *IEEE Trans. Comput.*, vol. C-20, pp. 1566–1569, Dec. 1971.

[4] D. Chang, D. J. Kuck, and D. H. Lawrie, "On the effective bandwidth of parallel memories," *IEEE Trans. Comput.*, vol. C-26, pp. 480–490, May 1977.

[5] P-Y. Chen, D. H. Lawrie, D. A. Padua, and P-C. Yew, "Interconnection networks using shuffles," *IEEE Computer*, vol. 14, pp. 55–64, Dec. 1981.

[6] D. M. Dias and J. R. Jump, "Packet switching interconnection networks for modular systems," *IEEE Computer*, vol. 14, pp. 43–53, Dec. 1981.

[7] T-Y. Feng, "Data manipulation functions in parallel processors and their implementations," *IEEE Trans. Comput.*, vol. C-23, pp. 309–318, Mar. 1974.

[8] D. D. Gajski and L. R. Rubinfield, "Design of arithmetic elements for Burroughs Scientific Processor," in *Proc. 4th Symp. Comput. Arithmetic*, 1978, pp. 245–256; also in *Proc. 1978 LASL Workshop Vector and Parallel Processors*, 1978.

[9] D. J. Kuck and R. Stokes, "The Burroughs Scientific Processor (BSP)," *IEEE Trans. Comput.*, vol. C-31, this issue, pp. 363–376.

[10] T. Lang, "Interconnections between processors and memory modules using the shuffle-exchange network," *IEEE Trans. Comput.*, vol. C-25, pp. 496–503, May 1976.

[11] T. Lang and H. S. Stone, "A shuffle exchange network with simplified control," *IEEE Trans. Comput.*, vol. C-25, pp. 55–65, Jan. 1976.

[12] D. H. Lawrie and C. R. Vora, "Multidimensional parallel access computer memory system," U.S. Patent 4 051 551, Sept. 27, 1977.

[13] D. H. Lawrie, "Access and alignment of data in an array processor," *IEEE Trans. Comput.*, vol. C-24, pp. 1145–1155, Dec. 1975.

[14] S. E. Orcutt, "Implementation of permutation functions in ILLIAC IV-type computers," *IEEE Trans. Comput.*, vol. C-25, pp. 929–936, Sept. 1976.

[15] J. H. Patel, "Performance of processor-memory interconnections for multiprocessors," *IEEE Trans. Comput.*, vol. C-30, pp. 771–780, Oct. 1981.

[16] H. D. Shapiro, "Theoretical limitations on the use of parallel memories," Ph.D. dissertation, Dep. Comput. Sci., Univ. of Illinois, Urbana-Champaign, Rep. No. 75-776, Dec. 1975.

[17] H. J. Siegel, "Controlling the active/inactive status of SIMD machine processors," in *Proc. 1977 Int. Conf. Parallel Processing*, Aug. 1977, p. 183.

[18] ——, "Interconnection networks for SIMD machines," *IEEE Computer*, vol. 12, pp. 57–65, June 1979.

[19] R. A. Stokes, "Burroughs Scientific Processor," in *High Speed Computer and Algorithm Organization.* New York: Academic, 1977, pp. 85–89.

[20] H. S. Stone, "Parallel processing with the perfect shuffle," *IEEE Trans. Comput.*, vol. C-20, pp. 153–161, Feb. 1971.

[21] R. C. Swanson, "Interconnections for parallel memories to unscramble *p*-ordered vectors," *IEEE Trans. Comput.*, vol. C-23, pp. 1105–1115, Nov. 1974.

Duncan H. Lawrie (S'66–M'73–SM'81) is currently an Associate Professor of Computer Science at the University of Illinois at Urbana-Champaign. He has been active in the area of parallel computation systems since 1966, when he worked on the Illiac IV computer. Since then he has contributed to the design of several other machines, including most recently the Burroughs Scientific Processor. He specializes in research and consulting in the area of design, construction, and use of very large computing systems.

Dr. Lawrie has served as a referee for the IEEE TRANSACTIONS ON COMPUTERS as well as several national conferences. He was Program Co-Chairman for the Symposium of High-Speed Computer and Algorithm Organization, the 9th International Conference on Parallel Processing, a member of the Program Committee for the Workshop on Interconnection Networks, and Program Co-Chairman for the 1980 International Conference on Parallel Processing. He is a member of Tau Beta Pi, Eta Kappa Nu, Sigma Xi, the Association for Computing Machinery, and the American Association of University Professors.

Chandra R. Vora (S'76–M'78) received the B.S.E.E. degree from M.S. University of Baroda, Baroda, India, and the M.S. degree in electrical sciences from the State University of New York in 1973.

Currently, he is a Project Engineer in the Technical Products Division of Data General Corporation, Westboro, MA. Previously, he was with the Burroughs Corporation, where he was involved in the design and development of the Burroughs Scientific Processor. His interests include parallel distributed processing, multiprocessors systems, and microprocessors. He holds several U.S. patents in the computer system design field.

Chapter 4: Language and Software Supports

VECTRAN and the Proposed
Vector/Array Extensions to ANSI FORTRAN
for Scientific and Engineering Computation

George Paul

Computer Sciences Department
IBM T.J. Watson Research Center
Yorktown Heights, New York 10598

ABSTRACT

In the early 1970's, VECTRAN was developed within IBM as an experimental language extension to FORTRAN to study and facilitate the introduction of vector/array and parallel processing algorithms into scientific and engineering application programs. An experimental prototype compiler was written for VECTRAN containing IBM FORTRAN IV as a proper subset in 1973. VECTRAN first appeared in the public literature in 1975 in the form of a language manual.

Since its publication VECTRAN has been used as a functional model for the development of several vector/array extensions to FORTRAN including the new proposals by the American National Standards Institute X3J3 Committee for the future ANSI FORTRAN Standard. In this paper the vector/array processing functional extensions proposed for inclusion in ANSI FORTRAN are compared with VECTRAN and their use illustrated in common numerical algorithms.

FOREWORD

This paper purposely follows the logical presentation and exposition given in reference [2] for VECTRAN to illustrate both the functional model provided by VECTRAN for the development of the proposed ANSI language extensions for arrays and the differences both in syntax and in function between VECTRAN and the proposed extensions. This paper can be read in conjunction with reference [2], side by side, for a rapid overview of differences or stand-alone by itself.

The syntax used for the proposed extensions herein is that currently used within the ANSI X3J3 Committee for working purposes only. This syntax may be changed by the committee prior to publication of the future standard for public review or for adoption as a new standard, to provide greater consistency and regularity in the language.

The purpose of the publication of this paper is to disseminate the current work and thinking of the ANSI X3J3 Committee to as broad a user audience as possible for early review and should not be construed as representing support for, or approval of the proposed extensions by the IBM Corporation.

I. INTRODUCTION

In the early 1970's, VECTRAN [1, 2] was developed in the IBM Houston Scientific Center as an experimental language extension to FORTRAN to study and facilitate the introduction of vector/array and parallel processing algorithms into scientific and engineering application programs. An experimental prototype compiler was written for VECTRAN containing IBM FORTRAN IV [3] as a proper subset in 1973. This implementation and development of VECTRAN was based on the ANSI X3.9-1966 FORTRAN Standard [4].

VECTRAN first appeared in the public literature in 1975 in the form of a language manual [1]. Since its publication VECTRAN has been used as a functional model for the development of several vector/array extensions to FORTRAN including the new proposals by the American National Standards Institute X3J3 Committee for the future ANSI FORTRAN Standard. In this paper the vector/array processing functional extensions proposed for inclusion in ANSI FORTRAN are compared with VECTRAN and their use illustrated in common numerical algorithms using the proposed syntax for the future ANSI FORTRAN.

II. VECTRAN FUNCTIONAL REQUIREMENTS AND DESIGN CONSIDERATIONS

Several design prerequisites and functional requirements were specified for the design/implementation of the VECTRAN language/compiler. Among the functional requirements specified for VECTRAN, the authors felt that to be viable the language must go beyond the use of unsubscripted array names in expressions and the simple semantic extension of current operators and library functions to operate distributively, element by element upon the scalar components of arrays. Consequently the following five requirements were set forth for the language. The language must provide:

   i)   a convenient means to specify rectangular subarrays and general sections of arrays
   ii)   a direct facility to manipulate both arrays and subarrays as entities on either side of assignment statements
   iii)   array-valued functions and the use of array-valued expressions as arguments to subprograms
   iv)   an array oriented operator set including matrix and reduction operators

v) facilities to support sparse matrix algorithms employing both logical arrays and index vectors as means to specify the structure and compressed storage addressing mechanisms.

Among the design prerequisites specified, the authors felt that two considerations -- performance and compatibility, should dictate the language and compiler design. Consequently the following guidelines among others were set forth. The language/compiler should:

i) maintain an object-time orientation and provide for early binding (compilation) wherever possible and avoid constructs which would require late binding (interpretation) at object-time
ii) provide for subset containment, i.e., the new features where not utilized should not adversely affect performance
iii) be upward compatible with existing FORTRAN (FORTRAN '66) and be immediately comprehensible as an extension to FORTRAN

In general these requirements and design prerequisites have been carried over into the specifications of the proposals for the new standard with the following exceptions:

i) new infix operators for matrix computation, reductions and array manipulation have not been introduced and instead these operations have been introduced solely as new intrinsic library functions to simplify the concept of conformability in the parsing and analysis of expressions.
ii) the object-time orientation has been relaxed to allow array sections to occur in expressions in which their conformability may not be determined at compile time.

Finally the introduction of lower bounds in array declarations and the introduction of the character data type into the ANSI X3.9-1978 FORTRAN Standard [5] has forced syntactic and functional extensions beyond the simpler *unit origin* orientation of arrays found in VECTRAN and FORTRAN '66.

III.   NEW CONCEPTS

The present FORTRAN concept of an array is limited only to view arrays as a set or aggregate of data items (scalars) identified by a single symbolic name. This notion allows only the use of individual elements of an array in expressions, and expressions must always represent a single scalar value. In order to broaden this narrow view of arrays, VECTRAN introduced the concept of an *array value* and its ancillary notions of *atomicity, range* and *conformability* and the concepts of *elemental* and *transformational* operators and functions. The proposed ANSI extensions also incorporate these notions or new concepts into FORTRAN, but the VECTRAN concepts of *range* and *conformability* have been simplified because of the absence of transformational operators in the proposed ANSI extensions. The property of an array or array-valued expression referred to in VECTRAN as *range* is referred to as *shape* in the proposed new extensions.

A.   Array Values and Atomicity

VECTRAN introduced the concept of an *array value* and defined this concept in a manner analogous to the relationship defined traditionally in FORTRAN between arrays and scalar data items. An *array value* is defined to be an aggregate of scalar values. In VECTRAN and in the proposed ANSI extensions entire arrays, subarrays (sections) and/or subsets of arrays as well as elements of arrays may be used in expressions. Furthermore an expression may represent either an array value or a scalar value.

Individual scalar values bear the same relation to the array value they compose as subscripted variables do to the array name. In VECTRAN and in the proposed extensions all array values are rectilinear, and an array value may be referred to as a single *atomic* entity, as it is conceptually in mathematics. The use of an array name in an expression refers to the entire array value, and it is not simply an abbreviation for a sequence of scalar values. In an assignment statement involving array values, the array value specified by the right-hand-side expression is conceptually totally evaluated prior to assignment. Hence the *atomicity* of array-valued expressions is maintained. This model of array computation is analogous to that used in APL.

B.   Shape and Conformability

As indicated above the conceptual property of all arrays and array-valued expressions referred to as *range* in VECTRAN is referred to as *shape* in the proposed ANSI extensions. *Shape* refers to both the *rank* or number of dimensions in the array and the *extent* or number of elements along each dimension of the array.

Array-valued entities or expressions are judged to be *conformable* if they have the same *shape.*

A scalar entity or expression is defined to be *conformable* with an entity of any *shape.*

Conformability is purely a compile-time concept in VECTRAN, allowing the VEC-TRAN processor (compiler) to determine the legality of expressions wholly at compile time. In the proposed ANSI extensions *conformability* is both a compile-time and an object-time concept, and the legality of expressions may only be determined at object time in some cases. Similarly *rank* and *shape* are both compile-time and object-time concepts in the proposed extensions, and *rank* and *shape,* like *mode,* propagate through expressions.

C.   Elemental and Transformational Operators/Functions

In VECTRAN an operator or function is said to be *elemental* if it operates distributively on each element of its array-valued argument(s) independently, and if its result has the same *range* (*shape*) as its argument(s).

In VECTRAN an operator or function which is not *elemental* is said to be *transformational.* Typically the elements of the result of a *transformational* operator or function are each computationally dependent on several or all elements of the operands, and/or the array-valued result has a *range* (*shape*) which is different from its operands. Matrix multiply, reduction operators and matrix transposition are examples of transformationals.

Both of these concepts are included in the proposed ANSI extensions using the same terminology, however, the proposed ANSI extensions do not include any transformational infix operators at this time.

IV.   ARRAY IDENTIFIERS

In VECTRAN the range of an array-valued data item could be specified by the user by means of a RANGE statement. The RANGE statement was a new declaration statement introduced in VECTRAN which could be used in lieu of, or in conjunction with the DIMEN-SION or type statement. In VECTRAN if an explicit RANGE statement did not appear for an array-valued object, its shape or range was determined from the dimension data provided for the array thus preserving upward compatibility with FORTRAN.

Although the concept of conformability has carried over into the proposals for the future ANSI standard, the RANGE declaration statement has not been adopted. This has introduced a different interpretation for the semantics associated with unsubscripted array identifiers and in the relaxation of compile-time determination of conformability found in VECTRAN. As in VECTRAN, declared arrays and subarrays may be identified as follows:

A. Unsubscripted Array Identifiers

Array names may be used without subscripts in arithmetic or logical expressions to designate array-valued entities. When utilized in this manner in the proposed ANSI extensions, the unsubscripted array name references the whole array as declared or dimensioned in the storage allocation. In VECTRAN unsubscripted array names reference only those elements in a subarray which lay in the currently defined range. These elements are referred to as belonging to the *principal subarray* of the referenced array.

B. Sections of Arrays

In addition to unsubscripted array names, sections of arrays may be used as array-valued data items. In the proposed ANSI extensions, sections are specified using a different syntax from that originally proposed in VECTRAN. Sections may include, for example, any part of any row or column, etc. of a declared array, and sections are designated syntactically using a *colon* or *triplet* notation analogous to the character string notation of the 1978 FORTRAN standard. Briefly the *triplet* notation consists of three parameters separated by colons. These parameters correspond semantically to the three parameters of the DO-loop. That is, the first parameter corresponds to the starting point or origin of the section in the dimension specified; the second parameter, to the end-point or last element and the third parameter, to the index or stride between elements. This notation is illustrated in Figure 1 below.

$$REAL\ A(1:7,5:19)$$
$$M = 7$$
$$N = M/2 + 1$$

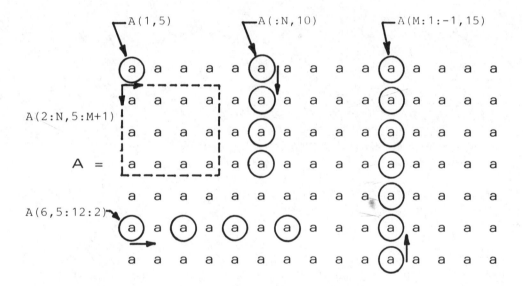

Figure 1

In VECTRAN a section was designated by the use of an asterisk (the section selector symbol) as a subscript selector. The asterisk implied that all elements of the designated dimension within the object-time range were to be used in the expression. For example, G(*,K) implied that all elements (rows) within the active range of the K'th column of the matrix G were to be used. This notation corresponded to an origin and length specification of the section which facilitated conformance checking as opposed to the starting-point and end-point specification adopted in the ANSI proposal. VECTRAN further extended the

147

section concept by defining shifted sections designated by placing an additive expression to the immediate right of the asterisk or subscript selector specifying the section. The shifted section designation was read to mean that the origin (the first element of the section in the specified dimension) of the section was to be the first element of the array in the specified dimension offset by plus or minus the value of the expression. VECTRAN also allowed converse sections, sections with a negative index or stride, to be designated by placing a minus sign to the immediate left of the asterisk or section selector symbol.

The concept of sections as specified in VECTRAN or as specified in the proposed ANSI extensions provides the user with a very powerful notational tool by which general rectilinear subarrays may be directly specified and operated upon. As in VECTRAN, expressions in the proposed ANSI extensions are fully evaluated prior to assignment of the computed result. Consequently operations between arrays or sections of arrays may be carried-out and array-valued results assigned without ambiguity or loss of data integrity.

The following program excerpt is taken from a subroutine which performs the Levinson algorithm [6] for the solution of a system of linear equations in which the matrix of coefficient values has the Toeplitz form. This algorithm is commonly used to compute Wiener matched filters.

```
      SUBROUTINE LEVIN ( M, F, G, R )
      INTEGER M
      REAL R(:), F(:), G(:), WORK(1:M)
          .
          .
          .
C
C  SOLVE LOOP
C
      DO (K = 1,M-1)
         H = -BETA/ALPHA
         IF ( K .GT. 1 ) THEN
            WORK(2:K) = WORK(2:K) + H*WORK(K:2:-1)
         END IF
         WORK(K+1) = H*WORK(1)
         ALPHA = ALPHA + H*BETA
         BETA = DOTPRODUCT (WORK(1:K+1),R(K+2:2:-1))
         Q = (G(K+1) - GAMMA)/ALPHA
         F(K+1) = Q*WORK(1)
         F(1:K) = F(1:K) + Q*WORK(K+1:2:-1)
         GAMMA = DOTPRODUCT (F(1:K+1),R(K+2:2:-1))
      REPEAT
```

The four lines indicated by the solid right arrows utilize either sections, shifted sections, converse sections or some combination of these array identifiers. (Note, these arrows are utilized purely for illustration herein, and are not part of the input syntax.) The first such line, utilizes both the shifted section WORK(2:K) and its converse section WORK(K:2:-1) in the same expression, and stores the resulting vector back into WORK(2:K). This line offers both an excellent example of the use of shifted and converse sections and of the importance of maintaining atomicity in the evaluation of array-valued expressions. In this example, a vector temporary is created to preserve data integrity. The second and fourth lines utilize the vector inner product intrinsic library function, DOTPRODUCT, as well as sections. The third line, like the first, computes the sum of a vector plus a scalar times a vector.

In these examples the compiler may determine conformability of each of the four array expressions at compile time by symbolic manipulation since the range of each of the sections used was specified consistently in terms of the DO-loop parameter, K, and a stride of unit magnitude was used in each case.

C.   Vector-Valued Subscripts

VECTRAN introduced vector-valued subscript quantities as legitimate subscript selectors to facilitate sparse matrix manipulation and to provide a convenient means of indirectly addressing and manipulating arrays via tables. Vector-valued subscripts have likewise been adopted in the proposed ANSI extensions. The syntax used in VECTRAN and in the ANSI proposal is identical.

Vector-valued subscripts are utilized in much the same manner as scalar-valued subscripts. Vector-valued subscripts, however, denote the selection of a set of array elements (in the order specified by the vector subscript selector) rather than a specific individual array element. Note, an array subscripted by vector-valued subscript quantities cannot be used in either VECTRAN or in the proposed ANSI extensions directly as an argument to a subprogram because of the indexing procedures invoked to address the array, but expressions containing arrays with vector-valued subscripts may be utilized as arguments to subprograms, or both the array name and subscript vectors may be passed as separate arguments to a subprogram which may then utilize the subscript vectors to reference the array.

Suppose Z is an array of 5x7 elements, and U and V are vectors of 3 and 4 elements, respectively. Furthermore, assume:

$$U = 1\ 3\ 2$$
$$V = 2\ 1\ 1\ 3$$

then, Z(3,V) consists of the elements of the third row of Z in the order:

$$Z(3,2)\ Z(3,1)\ Z(3,1)\ Z(3,3),$$

and Z(U,2) consists of the column elements:

$$Z(1,2)\ Z(3,2)\ Z(2,2),$$

and finally Z(U,V), of the elements:

$$Z(1,2)\ Z(1,1)\ Z(1,1)\ Z(1,3)$$
$$Z(3,2)\ Z(3,1)\ Z(3,1)\ Z(3,3)$$
$$Z(2,2)\ Z(2,1)\ Z(2,1)\ Z(2,3).$$

Sections may also be used in conjunction with vector-valued subscript selectors, for example, Z(U,1:7) consists of the elements:

$$Z(1,1)\ Z(1,2)\ Z(1,3)\ Z(1,4)\ Z(1,5)\ Z(1,6)\ Z(1,7)$$
$$Z(3,1)\ Z(3,2)\ Z(3,3)\ Z(3,4)\ Z(3,5)\ Z(3,6)\ Z(3,7)$$
$$Z(2,1)\ Z(2,2)\ Z(2,3)\ Z(2,4)\ Z(2,5)\ Z(2,6)\ Z(2,7).$$

When a vector-valued subscript is used in a subscripted array, the number of elements in the resulting section along the dimension selected by the vector-valued expression is determined by and is equal to the number of elements in the vector-valued expression.

By the above examples, the reader can easily see that vector-valued subscripts permit the user to access the elements of arrays in any desired order, and indeed the ordering specified need not be one to one with the array referenced. Consequently, the use of vector-valued subscripts permit the referenced array to be augmented by any specified repetition --in any sequence-- of the array elements.

V.   IDENTIFICATION OF SECONDARY ARRAYS

The section notation in VECTRAN allowed only the designation of contiguous arrays or subarrays. Consequently VECTRAN further extended the user's capability to define and manipulate sections of arrays which are regularly ordered, but which might be composed of elements which are non-contiguous or which might belong to skewed sections of the array such as the diagonal of a matrix by means of the IDENTIFY statement. The proposed ANSI extensions allow sections to be composed of non-contiguous array elements using the third parameter of the triplex or colon notation to specify a stride other than unity. However, skewed sections may not be designated using the triplex notation. Consequently for this and other reasons the proposed ANSI extensions also include a proposal for an IDENTIFY statement. As we shall see, the IDENTIFY statement is also useful to facilitate the implementation of algorithms involving storage mappings for banded or triangular matrices, etc.

A.   Dynamic Equivalence and Virtual Arrays

The IDENTIFY statement IS AN EXECUTABLE STATEMENT which allows the user to dynamically equivalence an identified secondary (*virtual*) array with selected elements of a primary (*real*) array or with the elements of another identified secondary array.

The IDENTIFY statement is perhaps the most powerful semantic extension to FORTRAN in either VECTRAN or the proposed ANSI extensions. IDENTIFY allows the user to readily manipulate non-contiguous data, skewed sections and other similar subscripted arrays directly by array name in the same manner as any explicitly declared array.

The IDENTIFY statement consists of four principal parts:

i)   a declaration of the subscript bounds for the identified secondary (*virtual*) array
ii)   the variable name to be associated with the identified (*virtual*) array.
iii) the variable name of the host array, (*real* or *virtual*)
iv)   a selection mapping which specifies which elements of the host array are to be equivalenced with the *virtual* array name, and the subscript order in which these elements are to be referenced in the *virtual* array.

It is important to note, that neither execution of the IDENTIFY statement nor subsequent reference to the identified array cause duplication or creation of a new array. Execution of the IDENTIFY merely causes the addressing parameters for the identified array to be evaluated and associated with the new array name. Subsequence reference to the identified array invokes the standard addressing mechanisms with no additional overhead. An identified array is an *equivalenced* array and program reference to either the host array name or the identified array name may be used to change the value in main storage of the array elements.

The IDENTIFY statement differs in two important aspects from the EQUIVALENCE statement.

i)   The EQUIVALENCE statement specifies a static equivalence relation which is in effect throughout the program execution. The IDENTIFY statement dynamically establishes at its point of execution an equivalence relation which may be altered through the course of the program execution. Indeed reference to an identified array invokes the mapping parameters last associated with the identified array name in order of program execution. (The rank of an identified array, however, must remain the same throughout the program unit.)

150

ii) The EQUIVALENCE statement establishes an equivalence between arrays, array elements or scalar variables with respect to a *fixed point* in the program's address space in storage. All other elements are equivalenced by virtue of their position in storage relative to this point. The IDENTIFY statement may be utilized to identify the virtual array name with selected elements of the host array; these elements are specified via a linear index mapping. The equivalence thus established is independent of storage association.

B.   Index Mapping Parameters and the Subscript Mapping Mechanism

Prior to defining the IDENTIFY statement, it is convenient to first define and discuss addressing procedures invoked by FORTRAN to reference arrays [7] . FORTRAN stores arrays in ascending address locations in main storage with the value of the first subscript quantity of an array increasing most rapidly, and the value of the last subscript quantity increasing least rapidly.

Consequently given a primary array A of rank R, dimensioned $N_1 xN_2 x ...xN_R$, and given that the length of each element of A is L bytes; the address of the array element $A(I_1 , I_2 , ..., I_R)$ is given by:

$$ADDR (A(I_1 , I_2 , ..., I_R)) = BA + L*((I_1 -1) + (I_2 -1)*N_1 + (I_3 -1)*N_1 *N_2 + ...)$$

$$= BA + (I_1 *M_1 + I_2 *M_2 + I_3 *M_3 + ... +I_R *M_R)$$
$$- (M_1 + M_2 + ... + M_R)$$

Where:

BA is the byte address of the first element of A.

$(M_1 , M_2 , ..., M_R)$ is a set of multipliers determined from the storage allocation (dimension) of A, and the length in bytes of each element of A, (i.e., $M_1 = L$, $M_2 = L*N_1$, $M_3 = L*N_1 *N_2$, ..., etc.).

The byte address, BA, and the set of multipliers $(M_1 , M_2 , ..., M_R)$ are the index mapping parameters for the array A. The function ADDR is the subscript mapping function for A.

Let B be a secondary array of rank S, which is identified as a *regular,* rectilinear section of A. (By *regular,* we mean that for each dimension, the elements of B have equal spacing.) The array B may also be described by a subscript mapping function:

$$ADDR (B(J_1 , J_2 , ..., J_S)) = BA' + (J_1 *M_1 ' + J_2 * M_2 ' + ...+ J_S *M_S ')$$
$$- (M_1 ' + M_2 ' + ...+ M_S ')$$

The multipliers M_j ' may no longer be as simply related to the dimension data as in the former case however.

Upon execution of the IDENTIFY statement, the selection mapping specifying the equivalenced elements is examined and the index mapping parameters for the identified array are evaluated, stored and associated with the virtual array name. Subsequent program references to the identified array name invoke the above (normal) array indexing procedures using these parameters. Clearly, the host array may in turn be an identified array as this process is simply a transformation of the index mapping parameters.

C.   The IDENTIFY Statement

General Form

$$\text{IDENTIFY } (b_1 ,b_2 ,....,b_N) \; v \; (i_1 ,i_2 ,....,i_N) = r \; (m_1 ,m_2 ,....,m_M)$$

Where:

v is the identified or *virtual* array name and has rank N.

r is the host array name and has rank M.

$i_1 ,i_2 , ...,i_N$ is a set of one to seven unsubscripted integer variable names, separated by commas, which are to be used as dummy subscript variables in none or more of the linear mapping expressions defining v. The order in which the dummy subscript variable names appear in the list defines the ordinal order of the mapping of v onto a subset of r. The number of dummy subscript variable names appearing in the list defines the rank of v.

$b_1 ,b_2 , ...,b_N$ is a set of one to seven bounds declarators separated by commas. The number of bounds declarators must equal the number of dummy subscript variables declared for v, i.e. must equal the rank of v. Each bound declarator is of the form $[\, l: \,] \, u$ in which l is a lower bound specification and u is an upper bound specification for the dummy variable corresponding to the bound declarator by its position in the list. If the specification for l is omitted, the lower bound is assumed to have the value one. Each lower or upper bound specification must be a scalar-valued integer expression.

$m_1 ,m_2 , ...,m_M$ is a set of one to seven scalar-valued integer expressions, separated by commas, each of which is linear in the dummy subscript variables. The set of expressions $(m_1 ,m_2 , ...,m_M)$ taken together define the mapping of v onto r in terms of the dummy subscript variables. The number of expressions in the list must equal the rank of the host or parent array, r.

The identified array name, v, must not have been previously declared as an array name except possibly in another IDENTIFY statement in the program unit, nor may v and r be the same name.

The type of the identified virtual array is that of the host array. The first appearance of an identified array name in an executable statement must be on the left-hand-side of the equals sign in an IDENTIFY statement.

The first occurrence (in statement order) of the identified array name in an IDENTIFY statement defines its rank throughout the program. The rank is implicitly declared by the number of entries in the list of dummy subscript variables, $(i_1 ,i_2 , ...,i_N)$. The rank declared for v in any subsequent use must equal the initially declared rank of v, although any or all of $r \; (i_1 ,i_2 , ...,i_N)$, $(b_1 ,b_2 , ...,b_N)$ and $(m_1 ,m_2 , ...,m_M)$ may be different in any subsequent IDENTIFY statement.

When an IDENTIFY statement is executed (b_1 ,b_2 , ...,b_N) and (m_1 ,m_2 , ...,m_M) are evaluated. Subsequent changes to the value of any variable used in their evaluation have no effect on the shape of v or on the mapping unless the IDENTIFY statement is re-executed.

Further, the dummy subscript variables (i_1 ,i_2 , ...,i_N) are utilized only in a formal sense; values assigned to the variables, (names), elsewhere in the program unit are unaltered by the occurrence of these variables, (names), in the IDENTIFY statement.

The scalar-valued subscript quantities appearing in (m_1 ,m_2 , ...,m_M) must each be at most linear integer-valued expressions in one or more of the implicit dummy subscript variables, (i_1 ,i_2 , ...,i_N), but may contain other variables and constants.

The host array, r, may be an explicitly declared *real* array or a previously identified *virtual* array.

The array r may have at most rank seven; similarly, the rank of v may be at most seven.

The scalar subscript quantities, (m_1 ,m_2 , ...,m_M), along with the dummy subscript variables, (i_1 ,i_2 , ...,i_N), specify the selection mapping of the identified array. The order in which the dummy subscript variables appear in the list, (i_1 ,i_2 , ...,i_N), defines the specific ordering in which the virtual array v is to be defined and referenced. If a dummy subscript variable included in the list (i_1 ,i_2 , ...,i_N) is not utilized in the list of scalar subscript quantities, (m_1 ,m_2 , ...,m_M), replication of the host array r is implied. If the mapping of the virtual array is such that two or more virtual array elements map to a single array element in the host array, then the virtual array may be referenced, but not defined or redefined.

Once defined by an IDENTIFY statement, identified arrays may be utilized in exactly the same manner as any declared *real* array. In particular, an identified array may be subscripted or sectioned, and an identified array or section of an identified array may be passed as an argument to a subprogram in the same manner as a declared *real* array.

When an identified array or section of an identified array is passed as an argument to a subprogram, only elements within the identified virtual array or array section are passed to the subprogram. If the mapping of the virtual array is such that two or more virtual array elements map to a single array element in the host array, the virtual array is treated as an expression when used as an actual argument.

Consider the following examples. The following statements dynamically equivalence the upper and lower diagonals of the 7x7 matrix X as the vectors XU and XL, indicated by circles and squares respectively, and equivalence the skew diagonal, as the vector Y, indicated by triangles.

```
REAL X(1:7,1:7)
        .
        .
K = 6
L = 4
        .
        .
IDENTIFY (1:4) XU(I) = X(I,I+1)
IDENTIFY (1:K) XL(I) = X(I+1,I)
IDENTIFY (1:L) Y(J)  = X(8-J,2*J-1)
        .
        .
```

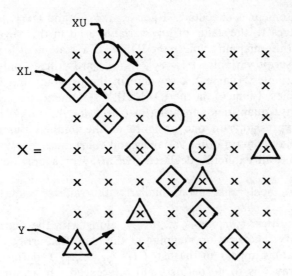

Figure 2

Once identified as above the four elements of XU and Y may be added element by element and the results assigned to the first four elements of XL simply by the statement:

$$XL(1:4) = XU(1:4) + Y(1:4)$$

Note that the section selectors on XU and Y could simply have been suppressed, since each of these vectors have been declared to consist of only four elements. Note also that the reference to these virtual arrays invokes exactly the same subscript addressing procedures that would be invoked if they had been explicitly declared one dimensional arrays, and in fact is more efficient than referencing these same elements as elements of the two dimensional array, X, because the identified arrays are one dimensional.

As a second example let us assume that we wish to solve a set of linear algebraic equations

$$L y = b$$

in which L is a lower triangular matrix which has been stored row-wise into a linearized array, LL, such that

$$L(1,1) = LL(1)$$
$$L(2,1) = LL(2)$$
$$L(2,2) = LL(3)$$
$$L(3,1) = LL(4)$$
$$L(3,2) = LL(5)$$
$$\cdot$$
$$\cdot$$
$$\cdot$$

etc.

Then the following program excerpt is taken from a subroutine which computes the forward solution of the system of equations.

```
SUBROUTINE FORWRD (N,LL,Y,B)
REAL LL(:),Y(:),B(:)
INTEGER N,OFFSET
        .
        .
        .
OFFSET = 0
Y(1) = B(1) / LL(1)
DO (K=2,N)
    OFFSET = OFFSET+K-1
    IDENTIFY (1:K) ROWK(I) = LL(OFFSET+I)
    Y(K) = (B(K) - DOTPRODUCT (ROWK(1:K-1),Y(1:K-1)))/ROWK(K)
REPEAT
        .
        .
        .
```

VI. OPERATORS AND FUNCTIONS

As indicated above among the functional requirements set forth for VECTRAN was the need for user-defined array-valued functions and for an extension to the operator set and intrinsic library of FORTRAN to provide new operators and functions for matrix computation and reduction operations as well as extending the semantics of all existing FORTRAN arithmetic and logical operators and intrinsic library functions to imply that the operation or function is applied distributively element by element to array-valued arguments.

While generally satisfying the same objectives the proposed ANSI extensions do not add any additional new arithmetic or logical infix operators syntactically into the language. As in VECTRAN the semantics of all existing FORTRAN arithmetic and logical operators and intrinsic library functions are extended to imply that the operation or function is applied distributively to array-valued arguments, i.e. these operators and functions are defined to be elemental, but all new arithmetic and logical operations for array or matrix computations including reductions have been solely confined to the intrinsic function library.

Both VECTRAN and the proposed ANSI extensions include new library functions for:

i)   arithmetic and logical operations between array-valued arguments and reduction operations
ii) manipulation of arrays within expressions
iii) utility functions

as well as allowing the user to define array-valued function subprograms with scalar and/or array-valued arguments.

A. New Arithmetic and Logical Functions

Among the new transformational array-valued arithmetic intrinsic library functions proposed in the new ANSI array extensions are matrix multiplication, MATMUL, and Hermitian vector inner product, DOTPRODUCT. Among the new arithmetic reductions are sum and product reductions, SUM and PRODUCT, and functions to determine the algebraic maximum (minimum) scalar value contained within an array-valued argument, MAXVAL and MINVAL. These reduction functions optionally may be applied selectively to act upon any chosen dimension of an array (i.e. row-wise, column-wise, etc.) and a mask option is also included which confines these reduction operations to those elements of their array-valued arguments corresponding to elements in a conformable logical expression which have the value .TRUE.. In addition MAXLOC and MINLOC functions have been proposed to be included in the extensions, but these functions and their masked versions have not yet been adopted by X3J3. These functions return the subscript location of the algebraic maximum and minimum value respectively.

Among the logical reduction functions are the Boolean AND and OR reductions (named respectively ALL and ANY), the COUNT function which returns the integer value of the number of occurences of .TRUE. within a logical array and the functions FIRSTLOC and LASTLOC which return the location in a logical array of the first and last occurrences (in subscript order) of the value .TRUE..

B. New Array Manipulation Functions

Among the new array manipulation functions provided in the proposed extensions are functions for Hermitian matrix transposition - TRANSPOSE. Also included are functions to merge two conformable arrays under the control of a conformable logical array - MERGE, to augment the rank of an array - SPREAD, to replicate an array in a specified dimension - REPLICATE, to create a diagonal matrix from a vector - DIAGONAL, and to change the shape of an array - RESHAPE.

Two functions, originally included in VECTRAN as new statements, are included: 1) to compress the elements of an array corresponding, to .TRUE. values in a conformable logical mask and assign these elements in subscript order to a vector, and 2) conversely to expand the elements of a vector and assign these values in subscript order to those elements of an array corresponding to .TRUE. values in a conformable logical mask array. The functions are respectively called PACK and UNPACK as they were in VECTRAN.

Three additional intrinsic functions are provided CSHIFT, EOSHIFT and PROJECT. These functions respectively circularly shift the elements of an array-valued argument parallel to a specified dimension, perform an end-off shift of an array-valued argument parallel to a specified dimension filling in the vacated positions with a specified value, and lastly return a *projection* of an array-valued argument corresponding to a conformable logical mask. There are no corresponding analogs to these three functions in VECTRAN.

C. New Utility Functions

Among the new utility functions proposed for arrays are RANK which determines the number of dimensions within an array, SHAPE which returns the number of elements in one or all of the dimensions, SIZE which determines the total number of elements within an array and LBOUND and UBOUND which determine respectively the lower and upper bounds of one or all dimensions of an array.

VECTRAN included analogs for many of these functions above in either intrinsic function or operator forms.

The following program excerpt is taken from a subroutine which implements the conjugate gradient algorithm [8]. This program illustrates the use of several of the library functions described above.

```
        SUBROUTINE CONJG (N,A,B,X,ERR)
➡       REAL A(N,N) , B(N) , X(N)
➡       REAL P(N) , R(N) , S(N) , LAMDA
C
C   INITIALIZATION
C
        I = 0
➡       R(1:N) = B(1:N) - MATMUL (A(1:N,1:N),X(1:N))
➡       P(1:N) = R(1:N)
C
C   CONJUGATE GRADIENT ITERATION LOOP
C
        DO
➡          S(1:N) = MATMUL (A(1:N,1:N),P(1:N))
➡          LAMDA = DOTPRODUCT (P(1:N),S(1:N))
➡          ALPHA = DOTPRODUCT (R(1:N),P(1:N)) / LAMDA
➡          X(1:N) = X(1:N) + ALPHA*P(1:N)
           IF ( I .GT. N-1 ) EXIT
➡          R(1:N) = R(1:N) - ALPHA*S(1:N)
➡          BETA = - DOTPRODUCT (R(1:N),S(1:N)) / LAMDA
➡          P(1:N) = R(1:N) + BETA*P(1:N)
           I = I + 1
➡          ERR = DOTPRODUCT (R(1:N),R(1:N))
        REPEAT
        RETURN
        END
```

VII. THE LOGICAL WHERE STATEMENT AND THE WHERE BLOCK

Two new control constructs are included in the proposed ANSI extensions for arrays; they are the logical WHERE statement and the WHERE block. The logical WHERE statement corresponds to the conditional assignment statement called WHEN in VECTRAN. The new control constructs provide the user with a convenient means of computing and assigning results selectively to arbitrarily shaped subsets of elements within an array under logical mask control.

A. The WHERE Block

The syntax of the WHERE block construct is illustrated below.

General Form

    WHERE (*lexpr*)
        wblock
    OTHERWISE
        oblock
    END WHERE

Where:

lexpr is an array-valued logical expression.

wblock consists of all of the executable statements that appear following the block WHERE statement up to, but not including, the next OTHERWISE or END WHERE statement. All of the executable statements in *wblock* must be array assignment statements. In each array assignment statement, both the target array and the source expression must be conformable with the shape of *lexpr*. No statement in *wblock* may be the terminal statement of a DO. *wblock* may be empty.

oblock consists of all of the executable statments that appear following the OTHERWISE statement up to, but not including, the END WHERE statement. All of the executable statements in *oblock* must be array assignment statements. In each array assignment statement, both the target array and the source expression must be conformable with the shape of *lexpr*. No statement in *oblock* may be the terminal statement of a DO. *oblock* may be empty.

Let us first consider an example in which the block WHERE is used in conjunction with array-valued assignment statements.

Assume,

$$
I (1{:}3,1{:}4) = \begin{array}{cccc} 3 & 2 & 4 & 9 \\ 4 & 5 & 1 & 8 \\ 2 & 7 & 6 & 5 \end{array}
$$

$$
J (1{:}3,1{:}4) = \begin{array}{cccc} 1 & 2 & 0 & 1 \\ 2 & 1 & 0 & 2 \\ 0 & 1 & 2 & 0 \end{array}
$$

then the statements,

```
WHERE (J(1:3,1:4) .NE.0)
   I(1:3,1:4) = I(1:3,1:4) /J(1:3,1:4)
OTHERWISE
   J(1:3,1:4) = 1
END WHERE
```

yield the results,

$$
I(1:3,1:4) = \begin{array}{cccc}
3 & 1 & 4 & 9 \\
2 & 5 & 1 & 4 \\
2 & 7 & 3 & 5
\end{array}
$$

$$
J(1:3,1:4) = \begin{array}{cccc}
1 & 2 & 1 & 1 \\
2 & 1 & 1 & 2 \\
1 & 1 & 2 & 1
\end{array}
$$

Note, the definition of the WHERE block does not preclude possible implementations in which the divisions by those original elements of J which are equal to zero might take place, possibly for a parallel processor. However, any machine check or interruption arising from such computations must not be reported back to the program.

B.   The Logical WHERE Statement
      The syntax of the logical WHERE statement is illustrated below.

General Form

   WHERE (*lexpr*) *stmt*

Where:

   lexpr is an array-valued logical expression.

   stmt is an array assignment statement in which both the target array and the source expression must be conformable with the shape of *lexpr*.

VIII. SUBPROGRAMS

As stated in Section II, two of the functional objectives of VECTRAN were to provide the user with a means of defining array-valued function subprograms and to allow the user to utilize array-valued expressions as arguments to functions and subroutines. These objectives have also been expressed for the future FORTRAN extensions.

A.   Array-Valued Arguments

In general array identifiers (with the exception of vector-subscripted arrays) and array-valued expressions may be used as arguments to function or subroutine subprograms (except for statement functions) in either VECTRAN or the proposed ANSI extensions. This includes all array names (explicitly declared or identified) and their sections. As noted above although vector-subscripted arrays may not be utilized as actual argument, they may be components of an array-valued expression which is an actual argument, or both the array name and the subscript vector(s) defining the subscripted array may be passed as actual arguments -- thus allowing the subscripted array to be *recreated* within the subprogram.

B.   Extensions to User-Supplied Functions

VECTRAN extended FORTRAN function definitions in two ways. First VECTRAN allowed the user to declare a scalar external function subprogram to be elemental which implied that this function subprogram could be applied distributively element by element to array-valued arguments and that the *result* of this function is an *array* conformable with its arguments. However, only intrinsic functions may be elemental in the proposed ANSI extensions.

Second VECTRAN allowed the user to define external array-valued functions by extending the syntax of the FUNCTION statement to include explicit specification of the assigned range (shape) for the array-valued function. Note the name of the referenced array-valued external function was also required to appear in a RANGE declaration statement in the calling VECTRAN program to permit the VECTRAN compiler to determine the conformability of the result of the array-valued function in the expression in which it was referenced.

An extension to allow the user to define external array-valued functions is also included in the proposed ANSI extensions. An array-valued function is distinguished from a scalar-valued function in the ANSI extensions by the appearance of an array declaration for the function name in the function subprogram. The actual shape returned by a reference to the function is determined by evaluation of each of the dimension-bound expressions within the array declaration of the function name at the time of reference of the function. Values involved in the determination of the shape may become redefined during the execution of the function, but this will not affect the shape.

The following example illustrates how a user might define a vector-valued function to linearly interpolate the function values corresponding to a vector of input values using vector-valued subscripts.

```
        REAL FUNCTION INTRP (N, X, YTBL)
C
C   GIVEN A VECTOR, X, OF N DATA POINTS, AND THE TABLE
C   OF FUNCTION VALUES, YTBL, OF Y(X), THIS FUNCTION
C   RETURNS A VECTOR OF LINEARLY INTERPOLATED VALUES
C   FROM YTBL CORRESPONDING TO THE VALUES OF X.
C   YTBL IS ASSUMED TO CONSIST OF THE VALUES:
C           Y(X), X = 1,2,...,M
C
        INTEGER N, M, IX (N)
        REAL X(:), YTBL (:), INTRP(N), DELX (N)
        M = SIZE (YTBL)
        IX = INT (X)
        WHERE ((IX.GE.1) .AND. (IX .LT.M))
            DELX = X - REAL (IX)
            INTRP = YTBL (IX) + DELX * (YTBL(IX+1) - YTBL (IX))
        OTHERWISE
            INTRP = HUGE (X)
        END WHERE
        RETURN
        END
```

IX.   SUMMARY

The proposed ANSI extensions provide a broad general purpose functional capability to FORTRAN for processing arrays without greatly expanding the syntax of FORTRAN.

The extensions are designed to be implementable on a broad range of machine architectures and do not specifically reflect any particular machine design. They may be implemented on a scalar, pipelined vector, or parallel processor.

The underlying computational model by which these extensions were developed is that of parallel, independent computation of each component or element of an array expression. No temporal sequentialness is generally implied, however, spatial sequentialness (subscript order) is exposed for obvious reasons in functions such as the PACK and UNPACK, etc.

Finally the extensions as described here are only a *snapshot* taken at the time of this writing of the development process within the X3J3 committee. They do not represent a completed design. The syntax used here is largely *illustrative only* and very likely will be changed prior to formal publication of the proposals for public review or adoption by ANSI. The semantics and detailed rules governing the usage of these extensions is under continuous development and review by the X3J3 committee. Considerable effort is still anticipated to review and redefine these extensions as required for regularity and orthogonality with the remainder of the FORTRAN language and for economy of language. The X3J3 committee would welcome your comments or criticisms about these and other extensions being proposed.

REFERENCES

1. G. Paul and M. Wayne Wilson, "The VECTRAN Language: An Experimental Language for Vector/Matrix Array Processing," IBM Palo Alto Scientific Center report G320-3334 (August 1975).

2. G. Paul and M. Wayne Wilson, "An Introduction to VECTRAN and Its Use in Scientific Applications Programming," Proc. of 1978 LASL Workshop on Vector and Parallel Processors, Tech. Report LA-7491-C, Los Alamos Scientific Laboratory (September 1978).

3. IBM System/360 and System/370 FORTRAN IV Language, form GC28-6515.

4. American Standard FORTRAN X3.9-1966, American Standards Association, Inc., New York (1966).

5. American National Standard - Programming Language FORTRAN X3.9-1978, American National Standards Institute, Inc., New York (1978).

6. N. Wiener, Extrapolation, Interpolation and Smoothing of Stationary Time Series, Appendix B by Norman Levinson, John Wiley & Sons, Inc., New York (1949), pp. 129-139.

7. M. Wayne Wilson, "Flexible Subarray Facilities for Classical Programming Languages," IBM Houston Scientific Center report G320-2426 (November 1973).

8. A. Ralston and H.S. Wilf, Mathematical Methods for Digital Computers, "The Solution of Linear Equations by the Conjugate Gradient Method," by F.S. Beckman, John Wiley and Sons, Inc., (1965), pp. 62-72.

The Structure of an Advanced
Retargetable Vectorizer

David J. Kuck (1), Robert H. Kuhn (2),
Bruce Leasure (3), and Michael Wolfe (3)

Abstract

This paper describes the structure of the PARAFRASE restructurer which is an optimizing compiler preprocessor for high-speed architectures. PARAFRASE is retargetable to a wide range of high speed machine architectures: Single Execution stream Array (SEA), Multiple Execution stream Scalar (MES) and Multiple Execution stream Array (MEA). This paper concentrates on register-to-register pipelined processors, a type of SEA architecture. This class of high speed machine is the most common parallel processor in the marketplace. PARAFRASE consists of a sequence of source-to-source passes divided into front-end, intermediate, and back-end subsequences. Typical passes are described from the *front-end sequence* which optimizes the source language program towards parallel architectures in general: SEA, MES, and MEA. Typical passes are also described from the *intermediate sequence* which optimizes programs for SEA but not exclusively register-to-register pipelined architectures. Finally, typical passes are described from the *back-end sequence* which targets the code for register-to-register pipelined architectures. The point is that PARAFRASE is structured in rings of optimizations that focus in on particular high speed machine architectures. The form of data flow analysis that is used in PARAFRASE, the *data dependence graph* is described. Data dependence graphs are defined and are contrasted with conventional data flow analysis. The algorithms used to construct data dependence graphs are described for both local and global intraprocedural analysis. Although we can not give unbiased runtime performance figures because there are so many machines in this class that the vectorized code could be run on, the performance of PARAFRASE on benchmark numerical codes is described. The measures used are architecturally correct and the paper concludes with: a discussion of what this vectorizer misses and why, a discussion of what is achievable from any vectorizer, and advice on how to design vector machines with software in mind. (Note this paper is a slightly abridged version of the original paper.)

1. Introduction

High-speed register-to-register pipelined processors such as the Cray X-MP (64 bit words) or the FPS AP-120B (36 bits words) are capable of burst performance ranging from 300 to 12 megaflops, respectively. However, their performance running standard numerical Fortran programs is often a decimal order of magnitude below this rate. This implies that either standard numerical Fortran does not contain enough parallelism to utilize these processors or that the Fortran compilers for these machines are not producing optimal code for them. Previous work [KuMC72] and [KBCD74] (see also [KSCV84]) indicates that the former is not the case. Several *vectorizers*, optimizing compilers or preprocessors for high-speed machines, have been developed by industry for this purpose. They include: The MCA vectorizer [Mysz78], the Cray Research Fortran compiler, the Fortran compiler for the TI ASC [Wede75], the vectorizer for the Burroughs BSP, the Fortran compiler for the Cyber 205 and the vectorizers for the new Fujitsu and Hitachi vector supercomputers. In this paper, we describe a vectorizer, called PARAFRASE. Our work on PARAFRASE has resulted in a commercial product called KAP which is being implemented by Kuck and Associates, Inc. and is compared to another commercially available vectorizer, VAST by Pacific Sierra Inc. [Brod81], in [Arno82].

Except for a few references to more general parallel processors, the scope of this paper is limited to register-to-register pipelined processors. There are two reasons to consider this special case. First, these processors are rapidly becoming more popular. And second, although the PARAFRASE system optimizes code for many parallel processors, it is helpful to limit the scope of this paper to a readily understandable architecture so that the design of PARAFRASE is itself readily understandable. Pipelined mainframe processors have been produced or are being designed by a number of vendors. In addition, there are about 15 so-called array processors [KaCo81] on the market. These machines are designed for attach-

(1) Department of Computer Science, University of Illinois Urbana, Illinois 61801

(2) Gould Laboratories, Gould Inc., 40 Gould Center, Rolling Meadows, Illinois 60008

(3) Kuck and Associates, Inc., Champaign, Illinois 61820

EHO219-6/84/0000/0163$01.00 © 1980 IEEE

ment to smaller host machines and most of these are pipelined.

As a class, register-to-register pipelined processors have architectures which present unique opportunities for an optimizing or vectorizing compiler such as PARAFRASE. We feel that the following features define a target architecture in sufficient detail to form the basic requirements of a vectorizing compiler for these pipelined processors:

- The registers in pipelined architectures may be managed in a different way than the registers in a serial processors because they are *vector registers.*

- Pipelined processors often provide more sophisticated *indexing hardware* which has some impact on code for loop control.

- Taking advantage of *overlapping functional units* and *chaining* on the Cray 1 (or linking on the CYBER 205) can substantially decrease the running time of a program.

- Replacing conditional statements by *control* or *mask vectors* increases the amount of vectorizable code.

- Generating *vector instructions* improves performance. Generally, the longer the vector operations, the better.

As an example of the distinction between vectorizing for a register-to-register pipelined machine and vectorizing for a memory-to-memory pipelined machine consider the last point. For register-to-register pipelined machines, a long vector operation will be done in stripes the size of the vector register, plus one reduced size vector operation, with length equal to the remainder of the vector operation length divided by the vector register size. The longer the vector operation is, the smaller the effect of the reduced size operation is. For memory-to-memory pipelined machines, the longer the operation the smaller the effect of pipeline fill and drain time. In this case, both machines have the same vectorization goal but for architecturally different reasons. In general, for memory-to-memory pipelined machines some of these restrictions can be lifted and we can conclude that a compiler for the register architecture should perform well for the memory based architecture.

The structure of the PARAFRASE vectorizer is designed for flexibility. It consists of a sequence of Fortran-to-Fortran optimization passes. Each optimization accepts a Fortran source program and emits a semantically equivalent Fortran program. The principal advantage of making each optimization Fortran-to-Fortran is that the sequence of optimizations can be (and frequently is) changed from run to run in experimental studies. In this way, PARAFRASE can be restructured to include optimizations suitable for other than the *Single Execution* stream *Array* architectures (SEA) discussed here. Two examples are virtual memory hierarchies [AbKL79], and multiprocessors [KuPa79] (*Multiple Execution* stream *Scalar* architectures, MES). Producing Fortran output is not considered to be a disadvantage because Fortran is so unstructured that the emitted code can be relatively close to the assembly language of most pipelined machines. Only a few extensions to Fortran are necessary. They are: that loops can be marked as *vector loops,* and that statements can be *masked* by control vectors. Thus, without loss of parallelism, the output of the vectorizer can be translated into vector machine code by a non-optimizing Fortran compiler which is generally provided by the vendor. Although each vendor has a different dialect of vector Fortran, a degree of portability is achieved in this manner. In addition, producing Fortran output allows the user to see how PARAFRASE vectorized his program.

Two methods of improving the performance of high-speed processors, besides vectorizing, are being investigated by other researchers. One is vector programming languages, see [PaWi78], [Perr79], and [ANSI82] for examples. The other involves hand coding kernel operations, see [Dong78] and [LHKK79] for examples. This can be particularly effective when used with sophisticated simulators, such as [OrCa78] which detect where the machine is wasting cycles. However, no one method, neither vectorization nor these two, obviates the need for the others. Vector languages can profit from optimization because they are designed primarily for usability and secondarily for code efficiency. Large application codes cannot be entirely hand coded due to software development costs. In addition, a large existing code can not be recoded for each new machine the user buys.

The rest of this paper is divided into four sections. In Section 2, the basic data flow constructs used by all the optimizations are defined. In Section 3, we present a catalog of optimizations used by the vectorizer. In Section 4, some performance statistics are given. Section 5 contains some conclusions and future goals for PARAFRASE.

2. Data Dependence Analysis

In Section 3, a catalog of optimizations will be presented. Many of the optimizations require information about how data flows through the source program. In this vectorizer, as in most optimizers, certain data flow constructs are used in a manner which is independent of the particular optimization being applied. In this section we define the data flow constructs used by PARAFRASE.

Data flow information is generated on two levels of complexity: *Local information* involving only pairs of statements in the program, and *global information* involving information flow through an entire subroutine. Local flow analysis is called *data dependence testing* and is defined first. Global flow analysis is called *pi partitioning* and is described after that.

Data dependence testing is used to gather data flow information between pairs of statements.

Definition: Let Si and Sj be an ordered pair of statements. If: (1) there exists a control flow path from Si to Sj and (2) there exists at least one set of loop index values such that a variable assigned in statement Si is used in statement Sj then, Sj is *flow dependent* on statement Si. If conditions (1) and (2) hold except that Si uses the variable and Sj assigns the variable then Sj is *anti-dependent* on Si; or if (1) and (2) hold except that Si and Sj are both assignments to the variable, then Sj is *output dependent* on Si.

A test for condition (1) is called a *prior test* in that one is testing whether statement Si is executed prior to statement Sj. A test for condition (2) is called an *intersection test*. Figure 2.1 represents the dependence graph for Example 3, in Section 3 before and after optimization. The number in each node corresponds to the statement labels in Example 3.

Some optimizations only need the data dependence graph for local data flow information. Others, however, require global data flow information. The global data flow information supported by PARAFRASE is *pi partitioning*.

Definition: A *pi block* is a maximal set of statements cyclically connected by data dependence. A *pi partition* is a partition of the statements in a subroutine into pi blocks. A *partial ordering graph* is the cover of the data dependence graph with respect to the pi partitioning. That is, for each data dependence in the data dependence graph, say between Si and Sj, there exists an arc in the partial ordering graph between the pi blocks containing Si and Sj.

A pi block may or may not contain a cycle of data dependences. If it does, the pi block is called a *recurrence*. A recurrence pi block can be viewed as a strongly connected component in the data dependence graph. Note that each of the cycles in the data dependence graph is contained within some pi block; thus the type of graph connecting the pi blocks is acyclic and can be called a partial ordering graph. Figure 2.2 shows the data dependence graph, the pi blocks, and the partial order graph for Example 6.b in Section 3. Statements 4, 5, and 53 are strongly connected forming a recurrence pi block. Each of the other statements is an independent pi block. A recurrence represents a set of statements in a loop that

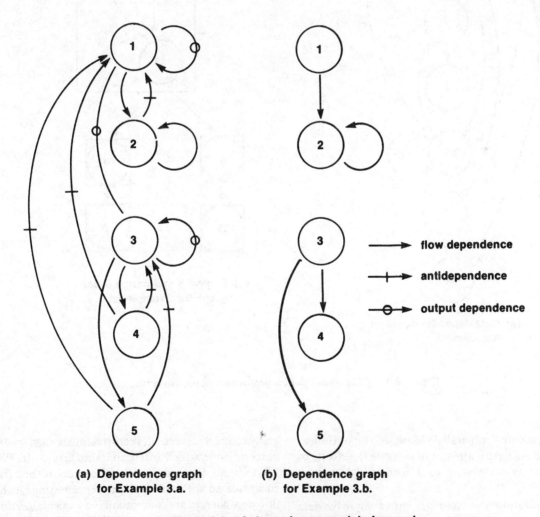

(a) Dependence graph for Example 3.a.

(b) Dependence graph for Example 3.b.

→ flow dependence

-+→ antidependence

-o→ output dependence

Figure 2.1.   A dependence graph before and after optimization.

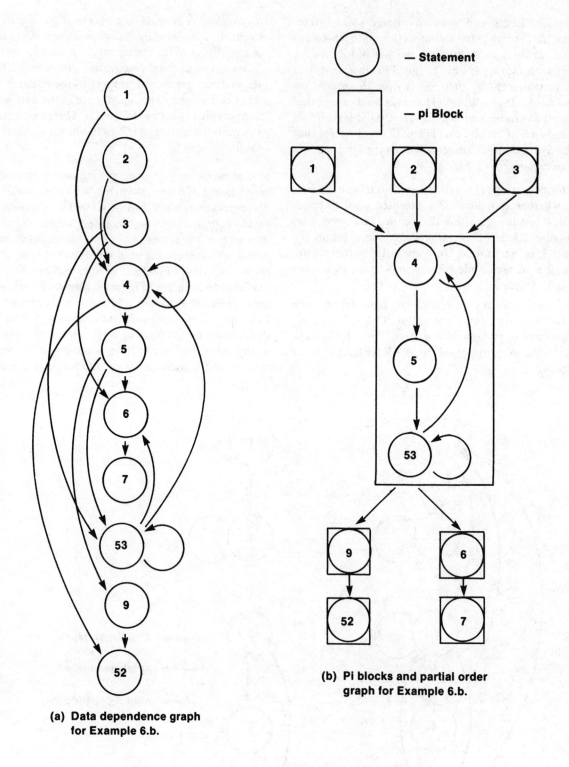

— Statement

— pi Block

(a) Data dependence graph for Example 6.b.

(b) Pi blocks and partial order graph for Example 6.b.

Figure 2.2.   Data dependence graph and pi partitioning.

cannot be executed in parallel. Many of the optimizations in PARAFRASE attempt to mitigate the effects of a recurrence by translating to a form which can be speeded-up.

The optimizations in a vectorizer must analyze the data flow due to arrays carefully because, first, many optimizations attempt to map arrays, not scalars, to the target architecture and, second, vectorization is most fruitful on numeric code which often contains arrays. In PARAFRASE, all of the data flow information for arrays is encapsulated within data dependence testing. Although flow dependences are conceptually equivalent to *definition-use chains* in *data flow analysis* ([Hech77] and [MuJo81]) and although others have attempted to use the data flow analysis framework for vectorization [Schn72], we find it inadequate for two reasons:

(1) Data flow analysis ignores all flow of control information other than the form of the flow graph on the grounds that any other control information may be undecidable. However, most of the array subscripts in numeric code are dependent on loop indices and constants which can be analyzed at compile time.

(2) Data flow analysis treats all of the elements of an array ensemble. This too frequently leads to a very conservative estimate of data dependence. For example, if an array of N elements has elements 2 through N assigned in statement Si and statement Sj reads the first element, then no flow dependence exists from statement Si to Sj.

PARAFRASE performs fast tests [Bane76] which permit a more accurate, less conservative, dependence graph to be constructed. Ultimately, vectorizers which employ such tests are solving the problem of finding the existence of solutions of Diophantine equations, linear systems with integer solutions. For example, PARAFRASE uses the tests described in [Bane76]; the TI ASC vectorized used the tests described in [Coha72]. These tests are outside the data flow analysis framework. Although the tests vectorizers perform provide more information than data flow analysis, they are not expensive computationally. If a variable occurs in m statements, $0(m^2)$ dependences may exist between these statements. However, in practice the maximum m is usually much smaller than the number of statements in a program. Also, experience indicates that the number of dependences tests is closer to linear in m. Further the prior test reduces the number of dependence tests considerably. Global flow analysis by pi partitioning can be computed by using Tarjan's $0(n \log n)$ depth first strongly connected component algorithm described in [Tarj72]. The complexity of this form of data flow analysis is almost as low as the expected linear complexity of some data flow analysis algorithms.

3. A Catalog of Optimizations for the Analyzer

Frequently optimizers and vectorizers consist of a set of modules each of which makes one pass over the users code. Each transformation pass is called an optimization. Collectively the set of available optimizations is called the *catalog*. In this section, the optimizations in the catalog used to vectorize code for a register-to-register pipelined machine are described in distinct subsections. (More optimizations are available in PARAFRASE for other architectures. Some of these have been reported in [AbKL79] and [KuPa79].) The examples used in this section to illustrate the optimizations performed by the catalog are all taken from a package of two Fortran programs. The package is a Geophysical Fluid Dynamics Laboratory (GFDL) weather forecasting code, a benchmark of 1500 cards.

3.1 Induction variable substitution (Front-end)

A scalar that is incremented by a constant on each iteration of the loop, such as A and B in Example 2a is called an *induction variable*. (Example 1 was removed from this abridged version.) Induction variable substitution replaces the right-hand side of an induction variable assignment by a linear function of the index variable as shown in Example 2b.

Induction variable substitution can improve the source program performance in two ways. First, if the induction variable is used in an array subscript, dependence testing is simplified without increasing execution time because pipelined processors often have sophisticated memory indexing hardware. Second, even if the induction variable is not used in a subscript, substitution removes a linear recurrence, see Section 2, as illustrated in Example 2a and 2b. In 2a, the statement A=A+2 and B=B+1 are trivial linear recurrences which can be executed efficiently on pipelined processors by indexing hardware. Induction variable substitution is the inverse of reduction in strength [AhU173] which would transform Example 2b to 2a. Reduction in strength may be used for conventional architectures when multiplication is slower than addition to evaluate subscripts quickly. For conventional architectures the linear recurrence generated can be evaluated serially with no performance penalty. Induction variable substitution may not always improve the quality of the code generated but it puts the source program into a standard form for subsequent optimizations.

```
Example  2a:   Source   program   before   induction
variable  substitution

FUNCTION ORDLEG (abridged)
...
ANG = FN * THETA
S1 = 0
C4 = 1
A = -1
B = 0
DO 27 KK = 1, N1, 2
    K = KK - 1
    IF (K .EQ. N) C4 = C4 /2
    S1 = S1 + C4 * DCOS(ANG)
    A = A + 2
    B = B + 1
    ANG = THETA * (FN - K - 2)
    C4 = C4 * (A * (FN - B + 1) / (B * (FN2 - A)))
    CONTINUE
```

```
Example 2b:  Program transformation after induction
variable  substitution

FUNCTION ORDLEG (abridged)
...
ANG = FN * THETA
S1 = 0
C4 = 1
A = -1
B = 0
DO 27 KK = 1, N1, 2
    K = KK - 1
    IF (K .EQ. N) C4 = C4 /2
    S1 = S1 + C4 * DCOS(ANG)
    A = KK
    B = KK / 2 + 1
    ANG = THETA * (FN - K - 2)
    C4 = C4 * (A * (FN - B + 1) / (B * (FN2 - A)))
27 CONTINUE
```

3.2 Scalar renaming (Front-end)

Consider a program which assigns, reads, reassigns, and rereads a scalar such as EM in Exmaple 3a. There is an avoidable sequentiallity in this program caused by the fact that the first use of EM must occur before the second assignment which will overwrite the value of the first assignment. Scalar renaming avoids this sequentially when possible by generating a compiler temporary EMa for the second assignment and its uses as shown in Example 3b.

3.3 Scalar forward substitution (Front-end)

A scalar that is assigned a value and subsequently is used in a subscript is a candidate for scalar forward substitution. In Example 4a, scalars K10 and K11 are forward substituted as shown in Example 4b. The purpose of scalar forward substitution is to provide more information for data dependence testing. It is especially beneficial if the expression forward substituted is dependent on the loop indices (as in Example 4a) or an induction variable expression. In Example 4a it is not clear to a compiler whether the statement inside the I loop is a recurrence or not without knowing the values of K10 and K11. Scalar forward substitution makes these values known in the sense that dependence testing can now detect the recurrence in this case.

Example 3a: Source program before renaming scalar

```
      SUBROUTINE PARMTR (abridged)
      ...
      ENTRY LGNDRE
      ...
      DO 24 M = 2, MLIM
1       EM = M - 1
2       ALP(M,1) = DSQRT( HALF * (TWO * EM + ONE)
                 * (ONE - X ** 2) / EM ) * ALP(M - 1,1)
24      CONTINUE

      DO 20 M = 1, MX
3       EM = WGHT * (M - 1)
4       POLYDX(M,1) = (EM * ALP(M,1))
5       POLYDY(M,1) = (-EM * ALP(M,2) * EPSI(2,M))
      ...
20      CONTINUE
```

Example 3b: Program transformation after scalar renaming

```
      SUBROUTINE PARMTR (abridged)
      ...
      ENTRY LGNDRE
      ...
      DO 24M = 2, MLIM
1       EM = M - 1
2       ALP(M,1) = DSQRT( HALF * (TWO * EM + ONE)
                 * (ONE - X ** 2) / EM ) * ALP(M-1,1)
24      CONTINUE
      ...
      DO 20 M = 1, MX
3       EMa = WGHT * (M - 1)
4       POLYDX(M,1) = (EMa * ALP(M,1))
5       POLYDY(M,1) = (-EMa * ALP(M,2) * EPSI(2,M))
      ...
20      CONTINUE
```

3.4 Dead code elimination (Front-end)

A statement which assigns a value to a variable which is not used again in the program or to a variable which is overwritten before it is used has no effect on the semantics of the program. It is *dead code* and can be eliminated. It is unusual to find source programs which contain dead code, but dead code often enters the program as a result of previous optimizations. For example, scalar forward substitution often leaves dead code in a program. (A related anecdote concerns benchmarks which are sometimes an exception to this rule. Since benchmark codes are not intended to answer any question except how fast a machine runs, benchmark programs sometimes do not output the result variables of a program. In this case the entire program is dead code eliminated making the PARAFRASE vectorized benchmark run very fast indeed.) Example 4c shows Example 4b after dead code elimination. Dead code elimination is a conventional optimization in that it is even useful for conventional architectures.

Example 4a: Source program before scalar forward substitution

```
      SUBROUTINE NEXTRW (abridged)
      ...
      DO 40 KK = 2, MK
        K10 = 10 - KK
        K11 = 11 - KK
        DO 40 I = NISTRT, NIEND
          GP6(I,K10) = GP6(K,K11) + QLOG(K10)
                 * ( VT6(I,K11) + VT6(I,K10) )
40      CONTINUE
```

Example 4b: Program transformation after scalar forward substitution

```
      SUBROUTINE NEXTRW (abridged)
      ...
      DO 40 KK = 2,MK
        K10 = 10 - KK
        K11 = 11 - KK
        DO 40 I = NISTRT, NIEND
          GP6(I,10 - KK) = GP6(I,11 - KK) + QLOG(10 - KK)
                 * ( VT6(I,11 - KK) + VT6(I,10 - KK) )
40      CONTINUE
```

Example 4c: Program transformation after dead code elimination

```
      SUBROUTINE NEXTRW (abridged)
      ...
      DO 40 KK = 2,MK
        DO 40 I = NISTRT,NIEND
          GP6(I,10 - KK) = GP6(I,11 - KK) + QLOG(10 - KK)
                 * ( VT6(I,11 - KK) - VT6(I,10 - KK) )
40      CONTINUE
```

3.5 Scalar expansion (Front-end)

Consider a program which assigns a value to a scalar inside a loop. There is an avoidable sequentiallity in this program similar to the one described under scalar renaming above. Each iteration of the loop must be performed sequentially so that the scalar can be read before being reassigned. This can be avoided by replacing the scalar by a compiler generated array with one element for each iteration of the loop that we wish to execute in parallel. Scalar expansion also allows the loop enclosing the scalar assignment to be distributed more effectively by loop distribution (see Section 3.9). Example 3c shows how a scalar renamed program, Example 3b, is scalar expanded. The expanded scalars are EM and EMa. Most vectorizing compilers provided a more limited optimization. The term *scalar promotion* is sometimes used in this context.

Expanding scalars requires additional storage which is dependent upon the number of iterations of the loops enclosing the scalar assignment. A complementary optimization, *compiler array shrinking,* is performed in the back-end optimization sequence if the sequentiality forced by not expanding is found unavoidable for other reasons or if more parallelism than the architecture needs was found.

Example 3c: Program after scalar expansion

```
      SUBROUTINE PARMTR (abridged)
      ...
      ENTRY LGNDRE
      ...
      DO 24 M = 2,MLIM
1        EM(M) = M - 1
2        ALP(M,1) = DSQRT( HALF * (TWO * EM(M) - ONE)
                 * (ONE - X ** 2) / EM(M) ) * ALP(M-1,1)
24       CONTINUE
      ...
      DO 20 M = 1,MX
3        EMa(M) = WGHT * (M - 1)
4        POLYDX(M,1) = (EMa(M) * ALP(M,1))
5        POLYDY(M,1) = (-EMa(M) * ALP(M,2) * EPSI(2,M))
      ...
20       CONTINUE
```

3.6 If removal (Intermediate)

The term "if removal" refers to a translation which removes conditionals from loops and replaces them with semantically equivalent manipulations of control vectors. Here, for simplicity we will consider conditional execution structures with 2 branches. More complex conditionals are handled in a similar way. With this assumption *if removal* is divided into two cases: when the scope of the conditional is nested within the loop surrounding it, and when the conditional branches out of that loop. The transformations for the two cases are described in order.

Removing conditionals with scope nested with loop

(1) The conditional is replaced by an assignment to a compiler generated control vector, FV(i), storing the value of the conditional for each iteration of the loop.

(2) The statements on the true branch are masked by the control vector; statements on the false branch are masked by the complement of the control vector.

(3) For multiple conditionals, the control vectors are AND'ed together at conditionals (the divergence of program flow paths) and OR'ed together at converging flow paths.

(4) Simplify control vector mask expressions for nested conditionals.

Example 5a illustrates this type of conditional. The transformed program is shown in Example 5b.

Removing conditionals that branch out of a loop

(1) The conditional statement is replaced by an assignment to a control vector, FV(i).

(2) Another control vector, ME(i), contains .TRUE. for all iterations of the loop that are not executed because the exit branch is taken. ME(1) is set to .FALSE. because the loop is executed at least once. ME(i + 1) is set to ME(i) .OR. FV(i), i.e., the exit was taken before this iteration or the exit condition holds on this iteration.

(3) The statements before the conditional are masked by ME(i); the statements after the conditional are masked by another control vector, MX(i), set to .NOT. (ME(i) .OR. FV(i)) which contains .TRUE. for all loop iterations actually executed except for the exit iteration.

Example 5a: Source program with nested conditional before if removal

```
      SUBROUTINE MRADJ (abridged)
      DO 100 I = ISTART,IEND
         DO 90 K = 1,MK
            IF (RM7(I,K) .GE.0) GO TO 90
            RADJ(1) = RM7(I + 1,K)
            IF (K .NE. 1) GO TO 20
            RADJ(4) = RM7(I,K + 1)
            GO TO 40
20          IF (K .NE. MK) GO TO 30
            RADJ(2) = RM7(I,K - 1)
            GO TO 40
30          RADJ(4) = RM7(I,K + 1)
40          CONTINUE
            SUMR = (RADJ(1) + RADJ(3)) * DQ(K)
                 + RADJ(2) * DQKM + RADJ(4) * DQKP
90       CONTINUE
100   CONTINUE
```

Example 5b: Program with nested conditional after if removal

```
      SUBROUTINE MRADJ (abridged)
      DO 100 I = ISTART,IEND
         DO 90 K = 1,MK
            FVI(J,K) = RM7(K,K) .GE.0
            RADJ(1) = RM(I + 1,K)  WHEN(.NOT.FV1(I,K))
            FV2(I,K) = (K .NE. 1) .AND. .NOT. FV1(I,K)
            RADJ(4) = RM7(I,K + 1) WHEN(.NOT.FV1(I,K))
            FV3(I,K) = (K .NE. MK) .AND. FV2(I,K)
            RADJ(2) = RM7(I,K - 1) WHEN(.NOT.FV3(I,K))
            RADJ(4) = RM7(I,K + 1) WHEN(FV3(I,K))
            SUMR = (RADJ(1) + RADJ(3)) * DQ(K)
                 + RADJ(2) * DQKM + RADJ(4) * DQKP
                              WHEN(.NOT.FV1(I,K))
90       CONTINUE
100      CONTINUE
```

(4) The statements below the loop and before the target of the conditional are branched around if the exit condition ever held. This is tested by a call to the intrinsic function ANY(FV,1,n) which tests elements 1 through n of the control vector FV.

Examples 6a and 6b illustrate this algorithm.

Example 6a: Source program with conditional branching
out of loop before if removal

```
      SUBROUTINE PARMTR (abridged)
      WGHT = ELP
      X = .5 * DLOG(1 - DC(L) * * 2)
      DO 53 M = 1, MX - 1
         WGHT = WGHT + X + ALP(M + 1,1)
         IF (WGHT + ALP(M + 1,2) .LT. EM GO TO 52
53       MVL(L) = M + 1
      GO TO 50
52    IF (WGHT .LE. EL) STOP 99
50    RETURN
```

Example 6b: Program with conditional branching out of
loop after if removal

```
      SUBROUTINE PARMTR (abridged)
1     WGHT = ELP
2     X = .5 * DLOG(1 - DC(L) * * 2)
3     ME(1) = .FALSE.
      DO 53 M = 1, MX - 1
4        WGHT = WGHT + X + ALP(M + 1,1) WHEN(.NOT. ME(M))
5        FV(M) = ( WGHT + ALP(M + 1,2) ) .LT. EM
6        MX(M) = .NOT. (ME(M) .OR. FV(M))
7        MXV(L) = M + 1
53       ME(M + 1) = ME(M) .OR. FV(M)
9     IF (ANY(FV,1,MX - 1))  GO TO 52
      GO TO 50
52    IF (WGHT .LE. EL) STOP 99
50    RETURN
```

3.8   Boolean recurrence translation (Intermediate)

Removing conditionals from loops generates recurrences if the conditional branches out of the loop. In some cases, these recurrences are Boolean linear recurrences which can be solved by an intrinsic subroutine which is tuned to the architecture of the target machine. For example, when the conditional in Example 6a is removed, a recurrence including the exit control vector statement, ME(M + 1) = ME(M) .OR. FV(M) in Example 6b, is detected. This statement by itself is a Boolean linear recurrence which would be subject to this translation. However, in Example 6b the recurrence also includes the first two statements in the loop making this translation inappropriate.

3.9   Loop distribution (Back-end)

A multiple statement DO loop is broken down into several smaller loops by *loop distribution* [KuMC72]. Loops are distributed around one or more statements. The limiting condition is that a loop cannot be distributed around individual statements in a recurrence. Loop distribution has two effects. First, if a loop can be distributed around a single statement and if the statement can be executed in parallel, then a vector operation has been formed. Second, loop distribution can be used to increase the locality of the program by referencing all of the elements of the arrays referenced in one distributed loop before executing the next distributed loop. Loop distribution may reorder the statements in the loop when data dependences do not prohibit it, and in nested loops, distribution is performed from the inside-out. Examples 7a and 7b illustrate loop distribution. The dependence graph of the program is shown in the left column.

3.10   Loop fusion (Back-end)

A pair of loops with identical iteration sets can sometimes be combined into one loop [ArCo72] and [AbKL79]. Fusion may have the effect of increasing the number of variables referenced in the loop. Fusion is beneficial in decreasing memory-register traffic for a register-to-register machine in the case when fused loops share references to variables or in the case in which the individual loops do not reference enough variables to use all of the registers available on the machine. On the other hand, exceeding the number of registers available leads to allocation of temporaries and additional memory references loading and storing the temporaries. PARAFRASE fuses loops until the number of variables referenced is less than the number of registers available and fusing another loop will exceed that number. Finding the optimum fusion which minimizes the number of loops after fusion is a difficult problem; the heuristic PARAFRASE uses does not find the optimum fusion for all cases but it is relatively fast. Example 7c shows Example 7b after *loop fusion* assuming that 4 vector registers are available.

Example 7a: Source program before loop distribution

```
      SUBROUTINE CONST (abridged)
      DO 10 K = 1,MK
1        Q(K) = (3. - 2. * SIGMAX2(K))
            * SIGMAX2(K) * SIGMAX2(K)
2        TDTKO(K) = TDTK / Q(K)
3        SIGMAX1(K) = SIGMAX2(K) + DELTA
4        SQX(K) = (3. - 2. * SIGMAX1(K))
            * SIGMAX1(K) * SIGMAX1(K)
      ...
5        SIGMAX2(K + 1) = SIGMAX1(K) + DELTA
10    CONTINUE
```

Example 7b: Transformed program after loop distribution

```
      SUBROUTINE CONST
      DO 11 J = 1,MK
3        SIGMAX1(K) = SIGMAX2(K) + DELTA
5        SIGMAX2(K + 1) = SIGMAX1(K) + DELTA
11    CONTINUE
      DO 12 K = 1,MK
1        Q(K) = (3. - 2. * SIGMAX2(K))
            * SIGMAX2(K) * SIGMAX2(K)
12    CONTINUE
      DO 13 K = 1,MK
2        TDTKO(K) = TDTK / Q(K)
13    CONTINUE
      DO 14 K = 1,MK
4        SQX(K) = (3. - 2. * SIGMAX1(K))
            * SIGMAX1(K) * SIGMAX1(K)
14    CONTINUE
```

Example 7c: Transformed program after loop
fusion (5 registers)

```
      SUBROUTINE CONST (abridged)
      DO 11 K = 1,MK
3        SIGMAX1(K) = SIGMAX2(K) + DELTA
5        SIGMAX2(K + 1) = SIGMAX1(K) + DELTA
1        Q(K) = (3. - 2. * SIGMAX2(K))
            * SIGMAX2(K) * SIGMAX2(K)
11    CONTINUE
      DO 12 K = 1,MK
2        TDTKO(K) = TDTK / Q(K)
4        SQX(K) = (3. - 2. * SIGMAX1(K))
            * SIGMAX1(K) * SIGMAX1(K)
12    CONTINUE
```

3.11 Loop blocking (Back-end)

Loop blocking splits loops in the program into a pair of nested loops so that array sections the size of the vector registers can be accessed in parallel. When a loop is blocked, the outer loop in the pair of loops in called the *block loop;* the inner loop is called the *strip loop*. When loops are nested, loops are selected for blocking depending on whether the loop index accesses an array or not. The loop that indexes the most arrays is blocked first, and so forth, until all the arrays have at least one block loop. A loop that is not used to index any array is called an *unused index loop*. There is no need to block unused index loops. Examples 8a and 8b show a program before and after loop blocking. Here and subsequently we assume that vector registers have 64 elements. The *DO ITER* loop is an unused index loop. The *DO* 50 K loop and the *DO* 60 K loop are loops with less than 64 iterations. They are not blocked and are considered to be strip loops. Some vectorizing compilers refer to blocking of innermost loops as *strip mining*.

3.12 Interchange block loops (Back-end)

This optimization attempts to move at least one strip loop inside all block and unused index loops. The validity of loop interchanging is determined by rules such as those found in [Wolf78]. In a multiple loop nest, more than one way to interchange loops may be valid. In these cases, PARAFRASE selects a loop interchange according to the following rules in priority order:

- Recurrences should not be across the inner loop, to maximize the number of vector operations.

- Storage references should be minimized. They may be reduced further by subsequent *register load-store floating*, see below.

- The number of stride-one storage references should be maximized.

Example 8c shows how the loops in Example 8b were interchanged. The *DO* 50 K strip loop was interchanged with the *DO* 50 IS strip loop to make PSQPH(I,K) a stride-one reference. The *DO* 60 K strip loop could not be interchanged with the *DO* 80 IS strip loop because of other statements within these loops which have been elided.

Example 8a: Source program before loop blocking

```
      SUBROUTINE INNER1 (abridged)
      ...
      DO 50 I = 1, IEND
        DO 50 K = 1,9
          PSQPH(I,K) = PS7(I) * QPH(K)
50      CONTINUE
      DO 80 ITER = 1,MAXIT
        DO 80 I = 1,IEND
          DO 60 K = 1,9
            TKPH = .5 * (T7(I,K) + T7(I,K + 1))
            IT(I,K) = MAXO( 1,
                     MIN1( TMAX, TKPH - TBASE ) )
60        CONTINUE
          ...
80      CONTINUE
```

Example 8b: Program transformation after loop blocking

```
      SUBROUTINE INNER1 (abridged)
C*** Compiler generated statement function
C*** to compute the number of blocks.
      IBLOCK(I,J) = (I + J - 1) / J
C***
      DO 50 IB = 1, IBLOCK(IEND,64)
        DO 50 IS = 1,MIN(64,IEND - IB * 64)
          I = 64 * (IB - 1) + IS
          DO 50 K = 1,9
            PSQPH(I,K) = PS7(I) * QPH(K)
50        CONTINUE
      DO 80 ITER = 1, MAXIT
        DO 80 IB = 1, IBLOCK(IEND,64)
          DO 80 IS = 1,MIN(64,IEND - IB * 64)
            I = 64 * (IB - 1) + IS
            DO 60 K = 1,9
              TKPH = .5 * (T7(I,K) + T7 (I,K-1))
              IT(I,K) = MAXO( 1,
                       MIN1( TMAX,TKPH-TBASE ) )
60          CONTINUE
            ...
80        CONTINUE
```

Example 8c: Program transformation after interchanging blocked loops.

```
      SUBROUTINE INNER (abridged)
C*** Compiler generated statement function
C*** to compute the number of blocks.
      IBLOCK(I,J) = (I + J - 1) / J
C***
      DO 50 IB = 1, IBLOCK(IEND,64)
        DO 50 K = 1,9
          DO 50 IS = 1,MIN(64,IEND - 64 * IB)
            I = 64 * (IB - 1) + IS
            PSQPH(I,K) = PS7(I) * QPH(K)
50        CONTINUE
      DO 80 ITER = 1,MAXIT
        DO 80 IB = 1,IBLOCK(IEND,64)
          DO 80 IS = 1,MIN(64,IEND - 64 * IB)
            I = 64 * (IB - 1) + IS
            DO 60 K = 1,9
              TKPH = .5 * (T7(I,K) + T7(I,K + 1))
              IT(I,K) = MAXO( 1,
                       MIN1( TMAX, TKPH - TBASE ) )
60          CONTINUE
            ...
80        CONTINUE
```

3.13 Assign Registers (Back-end)

This replaces a reference to an array by a reference to a register. If the array reference occurred on the left-hand side, a register store is generated. If the array reference occurred on the right-hand side, a register fetch is generated. Managing vector registers has already been simplified by the loop distribution and loop fusion optimizations. Example 8d shows how registers were allocated for Example 8c. PARAFRASE generates identifiers RVi to denote vector registers. Each statement within the loops labelled *STRIP* represents a vector instruction except those which compute index expressions. (Generation of efficient code for index expressions has been explored but the subject is difficult to discuss for the class of register-to-register vector machines as a whole.)

If the value loaded into or stored from a register is in a loop in which it is invariant, the load or store is *floated*, moved outside the loop. This is a form of general *loop invariant floating* [A1Co72].

Example 8d: Assign Registers after transformation

```
      SUBROUTINE INVERT (abridged)
C*** Compiler generated statement function
C*** to compute the number of blocks.
      IBLOCK(I,J) = (I + J - 1) / J
C***
      DO 50 IB = 1, IBLOCK(IEND,64)
      DO 51 K = 1,9 STRIP
         RV1(K) = QPH(K)
51       CONTINUE
      DO 50 K = 1,9
      DO 50 IS = 1,MIN(64,IEND-64*IB) STRIP
         I = 64 * (IB - 1) + IS
         RV0(IS) = PS7(I)
         RV0(IS) = RV0(I) * RV1(K)
50       CONTINUE
      DO ITER = 1, MAXIT
      DO 80 I = 1, IEND
      DO 80 K = 1,9 STRIP
         RV1(K) = T7(I,K)
         RV2(K) = T7(I,K+1)
         RV3(K) = RV2(K) + RV1(K)
         RV1(K) = .5 * RV3(K)
         RV2(K) = RV1(K) - TBASE
         RV3(K) = MIN1(TMAX,RV2(K))
         RV4(K) = MAX0(1,RV3(K))
         IT(I,K) = RV4(K)
80       CONTINUE
```

4. Vectorizer Performance

Measuring the performance of a retargetable vectorizer such as PARAFRASE is difficult. The performance of vectorized programs is dependent upon the input data to the program and upon variations in machine architecture and operating environment. (The operating system, microcode efficiency on microcoded pipeline processors, and even the host processor operating system can all have significant impacts.) However, non-vectorized statements in the innermost loop are frequently the bottleneck in pipelined processing. A relatively dependable measure of performance then is the fraction of innermost loop statements that are vectorized.

Amdahl's argument that the speedup of a program is limited to the reciprocal of the time the pipeline processor spends executing non-vectorized code [Amda67] exhibits itself here. For the GFDL benchmark codes used in the

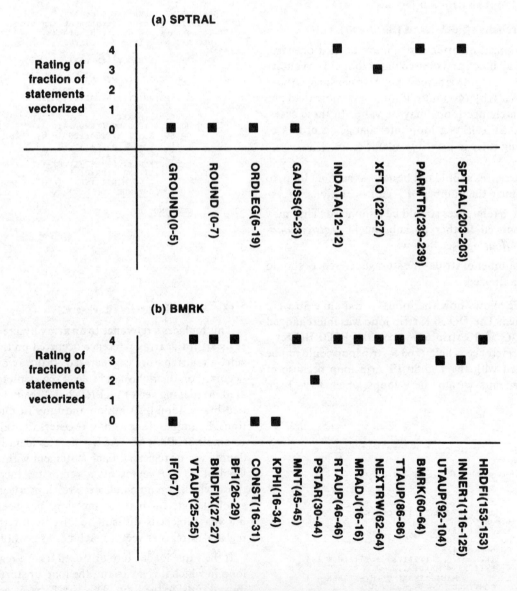

Figure 4.1 Fraction of innermost loop statements vectorized for GFDL

172

examples of Sections 3 and 4, Figure 4.1 shows the fraction of vectorized inner loop statements versus subroutines, ranked in increasing size. The GFDL benchmark is divided into two programs: SPTRAL, Figure 4.1(a) and BMRK, Figure 4.1(b). The fraction of statements vectorized has been quantized to rate each program on a 5 point scale with 4 indicating entirely (or almost entirely) vectorized and 0 indicating about 50% or less of the executable statements vectorized. The size of each subroutine is in parentheses after the subroutine name; first the number of source statements within loops is listed, then the total number of source statements is listed.

This benchmark's performance is typical of most codes we have vectorized. (See also [KSCW84].) When ranked in order of program complexity it becomes apparent that very small subroutines tend to vectorize poorly because they contain few or no loops. On the other hand, very large subroutines may have a tendency to vectorize poorly too. The phenomenon manifest is that while each statement presents a small risk of non-vectorizability of an entire loop, the aggregate risk in large loops is not negligible. Loop distribution attempts to distribute large non-vectorizable loops into smaller vectorizable and non-vectorizable components. However, frequently the non-vectorizable part is larger than it needs to be because imperfect information is available at compile time. Once one unknown subscript of a variable occurs in the loop, any other references to that variable must be assumed to depend on the unknown subscript. In addition, once a part of the loop does not vectorize, the vectorizer fuses otherwise vectorizable statements into the loop to make the best of a bad situation. That is, if a loop is going to run serially, a fall back strategy is to gain parallelism by keeping all of the functional units busy by jamming other operations into the loop.

The effect of the vectorizer as a whole is a result of a complex series of optimizations. To characterize the effect of individual optimizations, we vectorized GFDL several times removing a different optimization from each run. The results on one GFDL code are shown in Figure 4.2. The optimizations removed were: scalar renaming, scalar expansion, IF removal, loop interchange, and recurrence detection. On this set of subroutines, scalar renaming and recurrence detection had no significant effect on any particular subroutine. Scalar expansion, if removal, and loop interchange did have a significant effect on at least one subroutine. It is interesting to observe that the performance change is usually major, a drop in rating of at least one or two points, and that for the most part different subroutines were effected by each optimization.

The dramatic change in performance caused in isolated subroutines can be explained in terms of Amdahl's argument by observing that the derivative of speedup with respect to the fraction of innermost loop statements vectorized is an inverse quadratic. This tends to emphasize the "knee" of such curves. This phenomenon justifies our approach to vectorization. An optimization tool kit should be set up to facilitate the construction and inclusion of optimizations targeted at particular source language constructs which may occur relatively infrequently. Also note that this phenomenon does not appear in compiler optimizations making rare such dramatic changes in performance. Thus, the fact that the removal of scalar renaming and recurrence detection did not noticably change performance does not mean that these optimizations should not be included in a vectorizer. But rather that this particular GFDL benchmark did not need these two vectorizations.

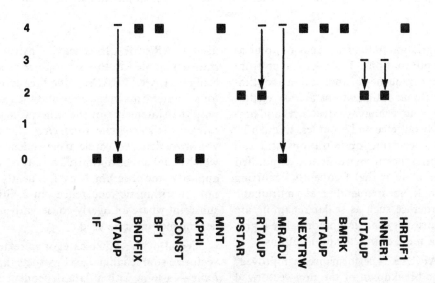

Figure 4.2. BMFK without scalar expansion, loop interchange, or IF removal

Table 4.1 Optimization frequency in BMRK.

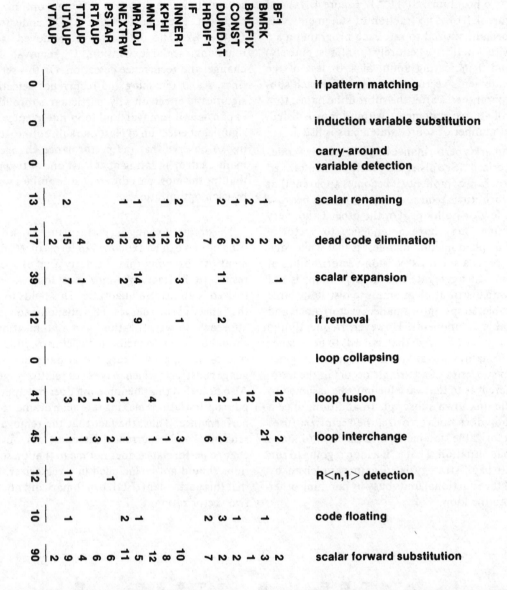

Optimization	Total	BF1	BMRK	BNDFIX	CONST	DUMDAT	HRDIF1	IF	INNER1	KPHI	MNT	MRADJ	NEXTRW	PSTAR	RTAUP	TTAUP	UTAUP	VTAUP
if pattern matching	0																	
induction variable substitution	0																	
carry-around variable detection	0																	
scalar renaming	13		2					1	1	1	2	2	1	2				1
dead code elimination	117	15	4	2	6	12	8	12	25	12	7	6	2	2	2	2		
scalar expansion	39		7				1	2	14	3	11							1
if removal	12							9	1	2								
loop collapsing	0																	
loop fusion	41	3	2	1	2	1	4	12	12	1	2	1						
loop interchange	45	1	1	3	2	1	1	3	21	6	2	2						
R<n,1> detection	12					11			1									
code floating	10		1					2	1	2	3	1						1
scalar forward substitution	90	2	9	4	6	6	11	5	12	8	10	7	2	2	1	3	2	

There is a large variation in the frequency of application of individual optimizations. Table 4.1 (taken from [KKLW80]) shows the frequency of application of optimizations in BMRK. Some optimizations are targeted at frequently·occurring source language structures and others are more narrowly targeted and occur less frequently. The less frequently occurring optimizations still can make a dramatic difference in performance as pointed out above. Another point is that frequently occurring optimizations which do not frequently make a dramatic difference in performance such as scalar renaming are still significant because they can act to normalize a program for subsequent more dramatic optimizations.

How could PARAFRASE's performance be improved? Table 4.2 shows the breakdown of the non-vectorized statements in one GFDL code. The categories shown for non-vectorizability are those reported by the vectorizer itself. (PARAFRASE is heavily instrumented; all of the statistics quoted in this section are generated automatically by PARAFRASE.) The breakdown is given once for all statements in the code and then again considering only the statements in the innermost loop. The major category is *Recurrences detected* which means that the vectorizer detected a cycle of dependences within the loop which could not be optimized by any of the optimizations applied to the program. Most frequently the recurrence is not an arithmetic recurrence but a difficult to analyze subscript where an overly conservative estimate of data dependence must be used.

Several of the other categories relate to difficult to vectorize source language constructs in the program. *IF loop* — a loop with a data dependent number of iterations (e.g.,WHILE loop). *CALL in loop* — it is very difficult to optimize subroutine calls. (Experiments con-

Table 4.2. Nonvectorizability statistics.

Subroutine	vector operation total	nonvector total	Nonvectorizable reason given							innermost loop statements nonvectorizable reason given						
			recurrence detected	IF loop	CALL in loop	Carry around variable	Input Output	Enclosed Recurrence	IF skip	recurrence detected	IF Loop	CALL in loop	Carry around variable	Input Output	Enclosed Recurrence	IF skip
IF(no loops)	0	0														
VTAUP	25	0														
BNDFIX	27	0														
BF1	26	3	3							0						
CONST	16	15				15							15			
KPHI	46	23	2	13	7				1	2	13	3				0
MNT	45	0														
PSTAR	30	16	16							14						
RTAUP	46	0														
MRADJ	16	38	38							0						
NEXTRW	62	2	2							2						
TTAUP	86	4	4							0						
BMRK	60	47	4				43			4				0		
UTAUP	92	18	12					6		12					0	
INNER1	116	10	10							9						
HARDIF1	153	0														
Total	816	176	91	13	7	15	43	6	1	43	13	3	15	0	0	0

ducted for interprocedural vectorization can be found in [Huso81].) *Input-Output* usually the semantics of IO imply a sequential stream of data. (IO is usually done in parallel asynchronously by IO processors anyway.) *IF skip* — is generated on a conditional branch around a loop.

Other categories refer to algorithm structures which are difficult to vectorize. *Carry around variable* — refers to a program construct to handle periodic boundary conditions in a differential equation. *Enclosed recurrence* — is an outer loop containing a recurrence, the outer loop can not be vectorized if the inner loop can not. (Before serializing such a loop, the vectorizer attempts to interchange the inner and outer loops to see if better code could be generated.)

Progress can and is being made on reducing the number of statements in each of these categories, and it should be noted that when a set of loops does not vectorize, PARAFRASE fuses the loop together if possible to avoid serial loop overhead and performs conventional optimizations. Thus, if a totally non-vectorizable pro-

gram was input, the program would, after the sequence of optimization attempts would be restored to its original form at worst. To summarize Table 4.2 the majority of non-vectorized statements are not innermost loop statements. In all, 18% (176 of 992 statements) of the statements were not vectorized. Counting innermost loop statements only, where most of the computational time is spent, only 7% of the statements did not vectorize.

In conclusion, it should be pointed out that computer architects have evaluated proposed arthitectures before implementation using PARAFRASE. Using a compiler to count the frequency of use of instructions and to evaluate ease of code generation before investing in an emulator is now widely acknowledged to be the way machines should be designed. The modular structure of PARAFRASE makes it ideal for such evaluation studies. Consider for example the salient architectural features in a vector register machine as they were outlined in the introduction. Throughout the paper we have described how the optimizations performed improve the code generated for such a machine. Here we make some architectural observations based on the statistics generated for the GFDL benchmarks. From statistics generated by PARAFRASE, allowing 16 vector registers of any type (e.g. double precision data was counted as only 1 vector register) is sufficient for nearly all programs. For example, in GFDL no program had to reuse a register. In addition, the number of registers needed correlates well with the number of statements in the subroutine, as expected. Control vector code generated seems to indicate that relatively few control vector registers are needed for efficient operation. For example, in one subroutine, 9 IF's were removed generating 8 control vector operations but only one control vector register was used. Linear recurrences occur relatively frequently, an average of one per subroutine. It is interesting to note that linear recurrences can frequently be avoided by the application of other optimizations. For example, loop interchanging was effective in moving the linear recurrence outside the innermost loop 4 times in one GFDL subroutine and 3 times in another GFDL subroutine.

5. Summary

The point of this paper has been that the proper structure for a vectorizer for high speed machines is a sequence of passes which can be thought of in terms of subsequences which successively target into the desired architecture. One analogy is that of a ring structure.

1. The outermost ring, the front-end, transforms the source for a more or less general high speed architecture.

2. The next inner ring, the intermediate sequence, transforms the source for, in this case, a Single Execution stream Array (SEA) architecture. An alternate ring would be used for another architectural class such as multiprocessors.

3. The next inner ring, the back-end, transforms the source code for, in this case, a register-to-register pipelined machine.

4. The next inner ring would be the compiler provided by the vendor. From practical, sometimes bitter, experience this compiler supports its own extensions to the high level language being compiler and is thus even more specific to the target machine than the back-end ring.

5. The innermost ring of course is the machine itself.

With the pass structure of PARAFRASE the user can: pick and choose optimizations from any ring to suit the particular machine being targetted, or construct a different ring for a different architectural class. Each pass may use any of a set of data dependence analysis tools which are tuned to analyze programs for high speed architectures. These tools differ from conventional data flow analysis for good reason. Although they differ with regard to information extracted, they do not differ significantly in execution speed from conventional data flow

analysis. Finally, we have shown here that the quality of code produced by the vectorizer is excellent.

Where then does one go from here? From a software point of view, one can hope for: faster vectorization, better vectorization, or more interactive vectorization.

1. Faster vectorization is not worth the effort. Although compilers take a substantial fraction of the computing dollar, a vectorizer tends to be run less frequently than a compiler during software development, and PARAFRASE is already very fast. (Several hundred cards per minute.) For example, it may be tempting to collapse several optimizations into a single pass to gain speed, our advice is that the software engineering overhead caused by poorly structured code makes this unjustifyable. Further, due to well known lower bound arguments, one can not hope for algorithms that are much faster.

2. Better vectorization on the other hand has been and continues to be a worthwhile subject. This was argued in the previous section. Substantially better vectorization can be achieved by considering either a new source language domain or a new target language domain. Examples of new source language domains are: interprocedural optimization as part of a software environment, e.g. an ADA environment, or a conceptually different semantic model for a HOL, such as applicative or logic based AI languages. New architectural classes are examples of new target language domains. For example, we are developing an ultra high speed machine called CEDAR which is in the Multiple Execution stream Scalar class. Another new target language domain that we have had some success with is hardware description languages for VLSI designs.

3. Regarding better interactive interfaces, several interactive features have been developed within PARAFRASE. They are not described in this paper. Assertion capability and algorithm restructuring advice are two important examples. Another important interface not described here is an interactive database of PARAFRASE analysis results which is used in machine architecture studies.

References

[AbKL79] W. Abu-Sufah. D. J. Kuck, D. H. Lawrie, "Automatic Program Transformations for Virtual Memory Computers," *Proc. of the Nat'l Computer Conference,* Vol. 48, pp. 969-975, AFIPS Press, 1979.

[Acke79] W. B. Ackerman, "Data Flow Languages," *Proc. of the Nat'l Computing Conf.,* Vol. 48, pp. 1087-1095, AFIPS Press, 1979.

[AhU173] A. V. Aho and J. D. Ullman, *The Theory of Parsing, Translation, and Compiling*, Prentice-Hall, 1973.

[AhU177] A. V. Aho and J. D. Ullman, *Principles of Compiler Design*, Addison-Wesley, 1977.

[AlCo72] F. E. Allen and J. Cocke, "A Catalog of Optimizing Transformations," *Design and Optimization of Compilers*, R. Rustin, Ed., Prentice-Hall, pp. 1-30, 1972.

[Amda67] G. M. Amdahl, "Validity of the Single Processor Approach to Achieving Large Scale Computing Capabilities," *AFIPS SJCC*, Vol. 30, pp. 483-485, 1967.

[Arno82] C. N. Arnold, "Performance Evaluation of Three Automatic Vectorization Packages," *Proc. of 1979 Int'l Conf. on Parallel Processing*, pp. 235-242, 1982.

[Bane76] U. Banerjee, "Data Dependence in Ordinary Programs," Department of Computer Science, University of Illinois at Urbana-Champaign, *UIUCDCS-R-76-837*, 1976.

[Brod81] B. Brode, "Precompilation of Fortran Programs to Facilitate Array Processing," *IEEE Computer*, pp. 46-51, Sept. 1981.

[Coha73] W. L. Cohagan, "Vector Optimization for the ASC," *Proc. of the 7th Annual Conf. on Information and System Sciences*, pp. 169-174, 1973.

[Dong78] J. J. Dongarra, "Some Linpack Timings on the Cray-1," *Proc. of the 1978 Los Alamos Scientific Lab. Workshop of Vector and Parallel Processing*, pp. 58-75, Sept. 1978.

[ANSI82] American National Standard Institute X3J3, "Fortran 8X—Proposals Approved for Fortran," *Committee Document S6.81*, May 1982.

[Hech77] M. S. Hecht, *Data Flow Analysis of Computer Programs*, Elsevier North-Holland, 1977.

[Huso82] C. A. Huson, "An In-Line Subroutine Expander for Parafrase," MS Thesis, Department of Computer Science, University of Illinois at Urbana-Champaign, *UIUCDCS-R-82-118*, Dec. 1982

[KBCD74] D. J. Kuck et al, "Measurement of Parallelism in Ordinary Fortran Programs," *IEEE Computer*, Vol. 7, No. 1, pp. 37-46, Jan. 1974.

[KaCo81] W. J. Karplus and D. Cohen, "Architectural and Software Issues in the Design and Application of Peripheral Array Processors," *IEEE Computer*, pp. 11-17, Sept. 1981.

[KKLW80] D. J. Kuck, R. H. Kuhn, B. Leasure, and M. Wolfe, "The Structure of an Advanced Vectorizer for Pipelined Processors," *Proc. of COMPSAC 80*, pp. 709-715, 1980.

[KSCV84] D. J. Kuck, et al, "The Effects of Program Restructuring, Algorithm Change, and Architectural Choice on Program Performance," To be presented at The 1984 Int'l Conf. on Parallel Processing.

[Kuck76] D. Kuck, "Parallel Processing in Ordinary Programs," *Advances in Computing*, Vol. 15, pp. 119-179, M. Rubinoff and M. C. Yovits, Eds., Academic Press, 1976.

[KuMC72] D. J. Kuck, Y. Muraoka, and S. C. Chen, "On the Number of Operations Simultaneously Executable in Fortran-like Programs and Their Resulting Speed-Up," *IEEE Trans. on Computers*, Vol. C-21, No. 12, pp. 1293-1310, Dec. 1972.

[KuPa79] D. J. Kuck and D. A. Padua, "High-Speed Multiprocessors and Their Compilers," *Proc. of the 1979 Int'l Conf. on Parallel Processing*, pp. 5-16, Aug. 1979.

[Leas76] B. R. Leasure, "Compiling Serial Languages for Parallel Machines," Department of Computer Science, University of Illinois at Urbana-Champaign, *UIUCDCS--R-76-805*, 1976.

[LHKK79] C. L. Lawson, et al, "Basic Linear Algebra Subprograms for Fortran Usage," *ACM Trans. on Math. Software*, pp. 308-323, Sept. 1979.

[MuJo81] S. S. Muchnick and N. D. Jones, Eds., *Program Flow Analysis: Theory and Applications*, Prentice-Hall, 1981.

[Mysz78] M. Myszewski, "The Vectorizer System: Current and Proposed Capabilities," Massachusetts Computer Associates, *CA-7809-1511*, Sept. 1978.

[OrCa78] D. A. Orbits and D. A. Calahan, "A Cray-1 Simulator and Its Application to Development of High-Performance Codes," *Proc. of the 1978 Los Alamos Scientific Lab. Workshop of Vector and Parallel Processing*, pp. 42-56, Sept., 1978.

[Owen73] J. L. Owens, "The Influence of Machine Organization on Algorithms," *Complexity of Sequential and Parallel Numerical Algorithms*, Academic Press, pp. 111-131, 1973.

[PaWi78] G. Paul and M. W. Wilson, "An Introduction to Vectran and Its Use in Scientific Applications Programming," *Proc. of the 1978 Los Alamos Scientific Lab. Workshop of Vector and Parallel Processing*, pp. 176-204, Sept. 1978.

[Perr79] R. H. Perrott, "A Language for Array and Vector Processors," *ACM Trans. on Programming Languages and Systems,* Vol. 1, No. 2, pp. 176-195, Oct. 1979.

[Schn72] P. B. Schneck, "Automatic Recognition of Vector and Parallel Operations in a Higher Level Language," *Proc. of the ACM 25th Anniversary Conf.,* pp. 772-780, 1972.

[Tarj72] R. Tarjan, "Depth-First Search and Linear Graph Algorithms," *SIAM Journal of Computing,* Vol. 1, pp. 146-160, 1972.

[TeEn68] L. G. Tesler and H. J. Enea, "A Language Designed for Concurrent Processes," *Proc. of the AFIPS Conf.,* Vol. 32, pp. 403-408, 1968.

[Wolfe78] M. J. Wolfe, "Techniques for Improving the Inherent Parallelism in Programs," Department of Computer Science, University of Illinois at Urbana-Champaign, *UIUCDCS-R-78-929,* 1978.

[Wolf82] M. J. Wolfe, "Optimizing Supercompilers for Supercomputers," Department of Computer Science, University of Illinois at Urbana-Champaign, *UIUCDCS-R-82-1105,* Oct. 1982.

CLIFFORD N. ARNOLD
SOFTWARE RESEARCH
CONTROL DATA CORPORATION
ARDEN HILLS, MINNESOTA

ABSTRACT. Vector optimization is defined as generating the best object code for a given vector computation for a given machine. In this paper an analytical performance model is developed for both scalar and vector source code as executed on the Control Data CYBER 205. The accuracy of these models is typically within 30% for scalar code and within 10% for vector code. If the compiler can generate more than one version of code for a given parallel computation, then performance estimates from these models can be used to choose which version should be executed. Sixteen FORTRAN kernels with two or more versions of source code were used as a benchmark to test this method. Thirteen kernels were "vector optimized" correctly. The three kernels not properly optimized had an average performance penalty of 17%. Using the set of kernels as a benchmark, vector optimization improved its performance by more than a factor of four, and obtained 98% of the improvement possible had all kernels been correctly optimized.

I.   INTRODUCTION

Automatic vectorization is the process by which a serial or scalar version of source code is analyzed by a piece of software to discover the code's inherent parallelism. The result is a transformation of the original code which expresses the parallelism discovered by the analysis. This can take many forms, for example rewritten source code using a parallel dialect, machine dependent object code, and many expressions in a variety of languages in between. A lot of work has gone into automatic vectorization software, both in the computer industry and in academia. Performance analysis of three such software packages is reviewed in [1]. There the concept of vector optimization was introduced; "The goal of vector optimization is to generate the best object code for a given vector computation (for a given computer)." Little study has been done in this area, which is unfortunate. As users of vector computers in the field know all too well, code vectorization to a higher level of parallelism can in some cases slow the computation down.

This paper addresses the following question. As information pertaining to the vectorizability of a kernel is increased, will a kernel always run at least at the same speed as before with the possibility of being sped up many times? Clearly the scalar (original) version of the code can be used, thus guaranteeing the same execution speed as before vectorization. To make vectorization analysis worth the trouble, a vector optimization tool needs to determine correctly when to choose the scalar version of the code and when to choose the vector version. In many cases more than one vector version is possible, and in such cases a decision among these versions also needs to be made. Figure 1 below illustrates the issue. Three different possible code solutions are depicted with their performance assumed to be a function of some data dependent parameter set.

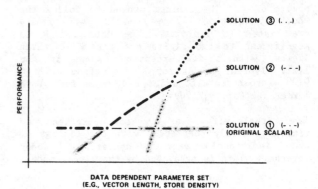

FIGURE 1.   Performance Profile of Three Code Versions of the Same Kernel

Vector optimization would hopefully choose the bold face line. If it did not successfully do that, it would successfully avoid the shaded areas.

I have applied a simple but surprisingly successful model to estimate the timings of different solutions based on their respective source code versions alone. These estimates are then used to make the optimization decisions. In this paper I describe the timing model for vector performance (Section II) and scalar performance (Section III) for the CYBER 205. Validation of the model against 16 kernels from the Livermore Loops (3) as run through several vectorizers (see [1]) is described in Section IV. Results are discussed in Section V.

Reprinted from *The Proceedings of the 1983 International Conference on Parallel Processing*, 1983, pages 530-536. Copyright © 1983 by The Institute of Electrical and Electronics Engineers, Inc.

II. MODELING VECTOR PERFORMANCE OF THE CYBER 205

Assume the time to execute a vector operation is a linear function of the vector length n:

$$\text{time} = S + R * n \qquad (1)$$

Equation (1) is rewritten by Hockney and Jesshope [2] as:

$$t = (n + n_{[1/2]})/r_{[\infty]} \qquad (2)$$

where $r_{[\infty]}$ is the asymptotic performance (MFLOPS) at infinite vector length and $n_{[1/2]}$ is the vector length required to achieve half the asymptotic performance. Note that t is then in microseconds. The coefficients in Equation (1) are defined in terms of $r_{[\infty]}$ and $n_{[1/2]}$ as noted below:

$$R = 1/r_{[\infty]} \text{ (microsec/result)}$$
$$S = n_{[1/2]}/r_{[\infty]} \text{ (microsec)} \qquad (3)$$

R and S were measured for 34 vector instructions using vector lengths ranging from 2 to 8192 in powers of 2. The timings proved to follow the model of Equation (1) very well. The results are listed in Table 1. The data for R is significant to two digits and for S to three digits, with a few exceptions shown in the list. Typical values for R range from 0.01 to 0.03 microsec/result, and for S range from 1 to 3 microsec ($n_{[1/2]}$~100).

Test kernels with several vector operations had timings entirely consistent with the timings of the individual vector operations added together. This is predicted by the linear model.

III. MODELING SCALAR PERFORMANCE OF THE CYBER 205

Initially Equation (1) was also applied to scalar loops where n was the trip count of the loop. Over a hundred short test kernels were timed. Though the resulting timings were linear, it was found that R was not constant for a given instruction in different loop contexts. This should not be surprising. For example, if loads and stores for an add operation can be overlapped by a multiply operation in the same loop, the rate is clearly different than if no overlap can be scheduled. R for an add operation was found to range from 0.42 microsec/result to 0.08 microsec/result depending on the context of the loop. Figure 2 shows the dependence of R on the number of operations (I) in the loop. For adds and multiplies this can be fitted well by:

$$R = 0.08 * \exp(1.61/I) \qquad (4)$$

$$t(\text{scalar loop}) = S + R * n * I \qquad (4a)$$

For divide and square root, R is constant:

$$R = 1.1 \text{ microsec/result} \qquad (5)$$

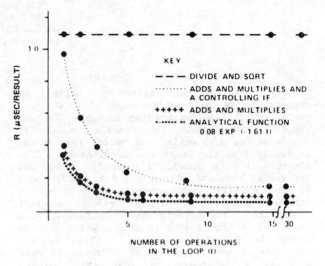

FIGURE 2. R in Scalar Loops

More testing showed R to also be a function of whether the operands were in memory or in the scalar register file (256 registers). All dimensioned variables (indexed operands) are in memory whereas as many scalar variables as possible are in the register file, for which operations are significantly quicker. Thus Equation (4) was fitted to include register to register operations:

$$R_{[scalar]} = (0.08 - 0.03*(J/(J+K)))$$
$$* \exp(1.61/I) \qquad (6)$$

where J is the number of scalar references and K is the number of indexed references in the loop. (Note: I ~ J+K).

The behavior of S and R is surprisingly simple for scalar loops. S is always less than 1.0 microsec, and usually about 0.25 microsec. Each IF statement in the loop (assuming no nested IFs) adds 0.7/I microsec/result to R and has no effect on S. For nested structures, like nested Do Loops, simply evaluate the inner most loop first and then have it act as an in-line routine with its characteristic I, J, K and S added to the other statements in the next level of the nest structure.

Initially it seemed unlikely that the scalar unit could be timed as simply as noted above. The FORTRAN compiler's scalar optimizer and the hardware were essentially being treated as a black box. It is interesting and curious to suggest that it can be timed empirically without knowledge of its detailed operation. Investigators might want to try this for other machines.

TABLE 1. INSTRUCTION TIMING
MODEL FOR C205 VECTOR OPERATIONS

Operation	S (microsec)	R (microsec/result)	n[1/2]= S/R
ASSIGNMENT	1.00	0.010	100
ADD (Floating Pt.)	1.00	0.010	100
MULTIPLY (Floating Pt.)	1.04	0.010	104
DIVIDE (Floating Pt.)	1.60	0.031	52
ADD (Integer)	1.04	0.010	104
MULTIPLY (Integer)	3.72	0.040	93
DIVIDE (Integer)	2.50	0.041	61
Q8VINTL	0.95	0.020	48
Q8VGATHR (Index List)	1.50	0.027 to 0.081	53
COMPARE (Floating Pt.)	1.35	0.010	135
Q8SSUM	2.50	0.020	125
Q8VSCATR (Index List)	1.38	0.025 to 0.081	55
* Q8SDOT	2.65	0.020	133
Q8VMASK	1.90	0.010	190
Q8VCMPRS	1.38	0.010	138
Q8VEXPND	1.45	0.010	145
Q8VGATHP (Periodic)	0.83	0.029	29
Q8VSCATP (Periodic)	1.50	0.024	125
Q8SMAX	1.50	0.020	75
VSQRT	1.55	0.030	52
* LINK ([S(+)V](+)V)	2.84	0.010	284
* LINK ([V(+)V](+)S)	2.60	0.010	260
VIFIX	1.05	0.010	105
VFLOAT	1.05	0.010	105
Q8VMKO(Z)	1.04	0.0013	800
BIT COMPARE	1.22	0.00125	976
WHERE (Logical)	0.20	0.0 #	
WHERE (Expression)	1.00	0.0 #	
STACKLIB TRIADS	5.-16.	0.144	35 to 111
STACKLIB DIADS	2.- 4.	0.113 to 0.128	18 to 35
Q8VMERG	1.50	0.010	150
VEXP	24.	0.5 to 0.6	40 to 48
(REAL)**REAL	24.	0.05 to 0.06	400 to 480
VSIN	19.	0.28 to 0.42	45 to 68
Q8VCTRL	1.10	0.010	110

*   Each result takes two (2) floating point operations.

\#   The WHERE statement only has start-up time. The time per result is zero. If there is an expression in the WHERE statement its timing must be calculated separately and then the WHERE statement start-up added to it.

(+) This signifies either the multipication or addition operator in the Link instruction. In a given Link on the Cyber 205 there can not be more than one add or multiply. There are other types of operators which can be Linked, but these were not timed.

IV. PERFORMANCE MODEL VALIDATION

A test base of 18 FORTRAN kernels from the Lawrence Livermore Laboratory [3] were used just as in [1]. For each loop there were at least two different source code versions, scalar and vector, and for loops 2, 4, and 18 there were two or more vector versions. Kernels 16 and 17 were discarded because the unknown data dependent branching probabilities made these loops impossible to time. Note that the same was not true of Loop 15 which has many IF statements in the original code.

Using Equations (1), (4a), (5), and (6) and Table 1, the test base kernels were timed using the source code versions alone. Scalar times converted to MFLOPS are listed in Table 2. These are compared to the actual timings with the relative error noted. On the average the predicted performance is 15% too high. More interesting is the spread in the relative error. In statisics this is called the "sample varience" or "standard deviation," and is annotated as "sigma." For this sample the scalar timings have a sigma of about 31%. Thus, over a performance range of 1.7 to 22.4 MFLOPS, scalar timings can be predicted repeatedly to within +31% using a very simple three parameter equation (S, J, and I). Figure 3 shows the distribution of errors in a histogram format.

Vector timings, converted to MFLOPS are listed in Table 3. The triple entries represent three different vector lengths where typically the second length is twice the first, and the third vector length is twice the second (see [1]). Note that performance is well predicted over a large span of vector lengths and over a

performance range of 3.4 to 168 MFLOPS. Loops 2a, 4, 8, 13, 14, 15, 18 are examples of kernels that are tricky timing exercises requiring index list gathers and scatters, partial vectorization, bit vector operations, WHERE blocks, multiple nested loops, and up to 73 timing equations (Loop 15).

Figure 4 shows in a histogram format the distribution of errors for this test base in vector mode. Loop 13 is a statistical "outlier" at more than the 3 sigma level, implying that it is not a statistical anomaly but a technical one not satisfied by the model. Therefore it should not be used in the sample for calculating the sample mean or variance. With that loop eliminated, Loop 14 is a statistical outlier at the 2 sigma level, suggestive, but not a compelling reason to delete it from the sample. Ignoring Loop 13, the average predicted performance is about 5% too high. The spread in the relative error (sigma) is less than 10%.

Loops 13 and 14 both involve random indexing through memory. My timings for Q8VGATHR and Q8VSCATR assumed a "well behaved list," and they likely are not that well behaved. More tests showed the performance could degrade by a factor of 3 in R in the worst case. Thus a range in R is shown in Table 1. These ranges more than make up for the error in the predictions of Loops 13 and 14. A good working value of R for these two instructions is 0.035 microsec/result. Making this correction to the performance predictions of these loops brings these estimates into line with their actual performance.

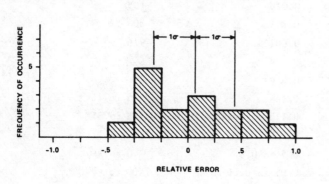

FIGURE 3. Histogram of Relative Error for Scalar Loop Timing Predictions

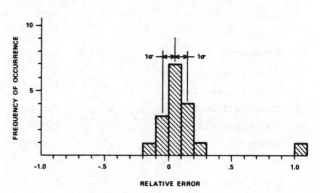

FIGURE 4. Histogram of Relative Errors for Vector Code Timing Predictions

TABLE 2.   C205 PERFORMANCE MODEL — Scalar Code

Kernel No.	Predicted (MFLOPS)	Actual (MFLOPS)	Relative Error
1	11.1	9.6	15.6%
2	11.0	12.3	-10.6%
3	6.4	5.9	8.5%
4	5.4	3.3	73.6%
5	9.6	7.9	21.5%
6	8.5	5.2	62.5%
7	15.1	17.0	-11.2%
8	15.2	22.4	-32.1%
9	13.6	13.0	4.6%
10	11.7	8.6	36.0%
11	2.5	1.7	47.0%
12	2.5	2.9	-13.8%
13	4.7	3.1	51.6%
14	4.7	5.5	-14.5%
15	3.8	3.4	11.8%
18	7.3	8.3	-12.0%
			$14.9 \pm 31.3\%$

TABLE 3.   C205 PERFORMANCE MODEL — Vector Code

Kernel No.	Predicted (MFLOPS)	Actual (MFLOPS)	Relative Error
1	89.7, 116.6, 137.2	94.4, 122, 138.9	-3.5%
2a	12.3, 16.9, 20.8	12.5, 16.2, 19.8	$2.6\% \pm 3.6\%$
2b	65.4, 79.1, 88.3	64.6, 76.9, 87.2	1.8%
3	65.4, 79.1, 88.3	64.6, 76.9, 87.2	1.8%
4a	13.5, 22.9, 30.0	12.2, 21.5, 29.1	4.8%
4b	9.5, 16.1, 21.1	8.7, 15.3, 20.4	6.0%
5	5.8, 6.2, 6.5	5.1, 5.7, 5.9	10.9%
6	6.1, 6.5, 6.7	5.4, 6.1, 6.4	8.1%
7	93.6, 127.6, 155.8	113, 146, 168	-12.3%
8	3.2, 18.1, 18.9	3.4, 15.9, 16.6	$7.3\% \pm 11.4\%$
9	52.0, 79.6, 108.5	54.4, 81, 110	-2.5%
10	22.4, 30.5, 37.1	22.7, 30.0, 36.1	$1.0\% \pm 2.1\%$
11	7.6, 7.9, 8.1	8.0, 8.5, 8.6	-6.0%
12	71.4, 83.3, 90.9	62, 75, 83	11.9%
13	7.7, 8.8, 9.4	3.9, 4.4, 4.5	102%
14	6.2, 6.5, 6.6	5.0, 5.3, 5.2	24.5%
15	21.4, 29.2, 35.7	18.4, 25.6, 30.3	16.1%
18a	44.1, 54.4, 61.6	42.3, 50.4, 55.6	7.7%
18b	38.3, 47.4, 53.8	35.0, 42.4, 47.3	11.7%
18c	4.2, 4.2, 4.2	4.2, 4.2, 4.2	0%
All 16 Kernels			$9.7\% \pm 23.2\%$
All 16 Kernels except #13			$4.8\% \pm 8.4\%$

V. RESULTS

For 9 of the 16 kernels in this test base (kernels 1, 2, 3, 7, 9, 10, 11, 12, and 15), vector optimization clearly discriminates among the possible source code choices. The likelihood of an error being made in any of these choices is quite small. The differences in their respective scalar and vector performance predictions far exceeds the sum of their expected errors, in all cases by more than 2 sigma and in most by more than 3 sigma. Of these 9 kernels, kernels 2, and 15 were subtle timing exercises (Section IV).

Making the proper choice of source code for kernels 4, 5, 6, 8, 13, 14 and 18 is not so straightforward. Figure 5 shows the probability of making an error in code choice for a kernel as a function of the separation of the performance estimates. An error is made when the code version with the faster time estimate turns out to be the slower running version. In Figure 5, M1 and M2 are the respective performance estimates of two choices of source code for the same kernel. Kernels 2a, 4ab, 5, 6, 8, 13, 14 and 18ab are noted on the figure as examples. The average overestimation of vector performance (5%) and scalar performance (15%) has been factored out in these cases. The standard errors, S1 and S2, for scalar and vector estimates are 31% and 10% of their respective estimates (Mv and Sv for the vector estimate and Ms and Ss for the scalar one). Out of these 8 examples, it is expected that one (rounding to the nearest integer) will be wrong. In fact, three of them are (kernels 6, 8, and 14). The slower versions are 15%, 29%, and 4% slower than their faster estimates not chosen. It should be noted that the scalar speed of kernel 8 is unusually fast (rumor has it that the compiler was tuned on this particular piece of code).

Given an incorrect choice of the version of source code, statistics predicts how much error will likely cost in performance. Where Figure 5 shows the probability of making an error, Figure 6 shows the probability of the size of the penalty as a function of the separation of the estimates. This assumes that the error has been made. Kernels 6, 8, and 14 are included as examples. This "penalty" function is fairly flat with the average penalty for a large sample of incorrect choices typically in the range of 5% to 20%. The top curve represents the 90% confidence interval of the penalty. Therefore the probability that the penalty lies below that line is 90%.

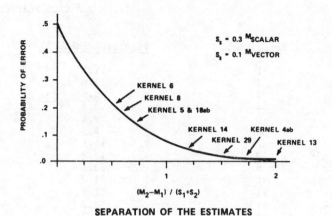

FIGURE 5. Probability of Choosing the Wrong Source Code Version

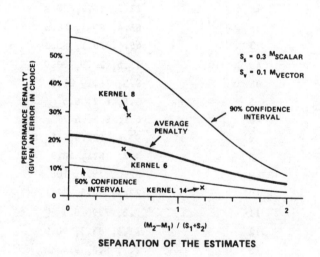

FIGURE 6. Performance Penalty when the Wrong Code Version is Choosen

VI.   Conclusions

The analytical timing model presented in this paper estimates the performance of scalar kernels with a standard deviation of 30%. The performance of vector kernels is more accurately predicted with standard deviation being 10%. In many cases these errors are insignificant compared to the difference in predicted timings for two coded versions (e.g. scalar versus vector) of the same kernel. In such cases vector optimization is eminently safe and useful. One class of kernels that will repeatedly fall into this category on the CYBER 205 are the kernels whose vector performance is predicted to exceed 25 MFLOPS. The test base showed some slower kernels for which vector optimization also clearly discriminated the faster version.

When vector optimization chooses between two versions of a kernel whose performance difference is comparable to the expected errors, the probability of making an error in choice is no longer negligible. When choosing between scalar and vector code, the chance of error is 8% when the performance difference is 40% of the average estimate. The chance of error grows to 42% when the performance difference is 10%. When choosing between two vector versions, the probability of error is 0.5% at a performance difference of 40% of the average estimate, and 22% at a performance difference of 10%. When an error is made the typical performance penalty incurred ranges from 5 to 20%. Rarely (less than 10% of the time) would the penalty exceed 50%. These conclusions assume that the errors in timing predictions obey Normal Distribution statistics. This assumption looks correct for the vector timing predictions, but is suspect for the scalar ones. This code sample implies that high performance scalar code is selectively underestimated, while the slow performance scalar code is selectively overestimated. Perhaps the analytical timing model for scalar performance needs a nonlinear term to better match the high and low performance extremes. I think this last point forces more interpretation than is really in the data. The model needs to be tested on more code, preferably real applications, and I intend doing this in the future.

The bottom line for this experiment is that out of 16 kernels, 9 have clear vector optimization choices from among two or more choices. Of the remaining 7 harder to discriminate versions 3 are chosen incorrectly for an average penalty of 17%. Weighting all 16 kernels equally, the mean scalar performance is 8.1 MFLOPS while the mean vector performance is 32.1 MFLOPS (for the shortest vector lengths), 41.6 MFLOPS (for the middle vector length), and 48.3 MFLOPS (for the longest vector lengths). Vector optimization yields a mean performance of 37.7, 47.2, 54.7 MFLOPS respectively for these vector lengths. If scalar code is chosen in all cases except where the best vector performance estimate exceeds the scalar one by 40% (less than 8% chance of slowing the code by choosing vector) then such a vector optimization algorithm would yield an average performance of 37.7, 48.0, 55.1 MFLOPS. If the vector optimization decisions had been all correct (that is, best effort), the mean performance for this test base would have been 37.7, 48.1, and 55.2 MFLOPS.

The vector optimization algorithm presented here should be easy to implement in a compiler or other automatic vectorization software.

VII.   References

[1] C. N. Arnold, Performance Evaluation of Three Automatic Vectorizer Packages, International Conference for Parallel Processing 1982, Bellaire, Michigan, August 1982.

[2] R. W. Hockney, C. R. Jesshope, Parallel Computers, Adam Hilger Ltd, Bristol, UK, 1981.

[3] F. McMahon, 1972, Unpublished. (Available from C. N. Arnold on request)

PFC: **A Program to Convert Fortran to Parallel Form**

John R. Allen
Ken Kennedy

Department of Mathematical Sciences
Rice University
Houston, Texas 77251

Abstract

The recent success of vector computers like the Cray-1 and array processors such as those manufactured by Floating Point Systems has increased interest in making vector operations available to the Fortran programmer. The Fortran standards committee is currently considering extensions to Fortran which will permit the programmer to explicitly specify vector and array operations. The proposed standard is usually referred to as *Fortran 8x*.

This paper describes *PFC* (for Parallel Fortran Converter), a system that translates sequential programs written in Fortran to Fortran 8x, replacing loops by array operations wherever possible. Central to the theory underlying PFC is the concept of *dependence*. In another work [Kenn 80], we developed a test for dependence between statements which distinguished dependences that arise due to the iteration of different loops.

In this work, we show how that test is incorporated into a powerful program for recognizing parallelism. By using a careful implementation strategy, combined with judicious choice of data abstraction mechanisms, we have been able to implement a flexible and sophisticated software system while maintaining reasonable efficiency. In fact, our implementation outperforms one of our previous efforts by a factor of more that ten.

The resulting program is an interesting case study of the application of theoretical techniques to a practical implementation problem.

1. Introduction

With the advent of successful vector computers like the Cray-1 [Cray 76, Russ 78] and the popularity of array processors like the Floating Point Systems AP-120 [FPS 78, Witt 78], there has been increased interest in making vector operations available to the Fortran programmer. One common method is to supply a "vectorizing" Fortran compiler [Cray 80] as depicted in Figure 1. Here standard Fortran is accepted as input and, as a part of the optimization phase of the compiler, an automatic vectorization stage attempts to

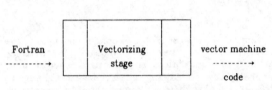

Figure 1: A Vectorizing Compiler

convert the innermost loops to vector operations. The code generator can then produce vector machine code for these operations.

This scheme has several advantages. Programmers need not learn a new language since the Fortran compiler itself takes on the task of discovering where vector operations may be useful. This also means that there should be no major conversion effort required to bring old code across to the new machine.

In practice, however, there are drawbacks to this system. Because exploiting parallelism in programs is a subtle intellectual activity, the compiler just isn't good enough to do a truly thorough job of recognizing vector operations. As a result, the programmer must assist by recoding loops to trick the compiler into recognizing them as vector operations. Indeed, the Cray Fortran manual [Cray 80] has several pages devoted to such recoding methods. In this environment, the programmer is once again obligated to rewrite his programs for a new machine, not because the compiler will not accept the old program, but because the compiler is unable to convert that program into suitably efficient code. During a number of visits to Los Alamos Scientific Laboratory, which has several Crays, we have observed the widespread sentiment that every Fortran program will need to be rewritten if it is to be acceptably efficient on the Cray-1.

This leads us to the question: if we are forced to rewrite Fortran programs into vector form anyway, why not write them in a language that permits explicit specification of vector operations while still maintaining the flavor of Fortran? Many such languages have been proposed. Vectran [PauW 75, PauW 78] is one of the earliest and most influential of such proposals, although there have been numerous others [Burr 72, DoE 79, Weth 79]. In fact, it seems clear that the next ANSI standard for Fortran, which we shall refer to as *Fortran 8x*, will contain explicit vector operations like those in Vectran [Paul 80, ANSI 81].

Suppose then, that instead of a vectorizing Fortran compiler we were to provide a Fortran 8x compiler for use with a vector machine. This would allow the programmer to bypass the implicitly sequential semantics of Fortran and explicitly code vector algorithms in a language designed for that purpose. However, a problem remains: what do we do about old code?

One answer is to provide a translator that will take Fortran 66 or 77 as input and produce Fortran 8x as output. This would lead to the system depicted in Figure 2. An advantage of this system is that, since the translation from Fortran to Fortran 8x is done only once or twice, the translator need not be as efficient as a vectorizing stage embedded in a compiler must be. Therefore, the translator might attempt substantially more ambitious program transformations, perhaps using techniques from program verification and artificial intelligence. This should enable a more effective translation.

A second advantage is that if the translator fails to discover a potential vector operation in some critical program region, the programmer can correct the problem directly in the Fortran 8x version rather than trying to recode the input so that the translator will recognize it. This is particularly important since there are some loops which, because of the underlying structure of the problem being solved, can be directly converted to vector form without error, even though the inherently sequential semantics of Fortran makes them difficult or impossible for a translator to convert. Such loops are often easy to recode as explicit vector

statements in Fortran 8x.

This paper reports on a project at Rice University to develop an automatic translator from Fortran to Fortran 8x. The Rice project, based initially upon the research of Kuck and others at the University of Illinois [Kuck 77, Kuck 78, KKLW 80, KKLP 81, Mura 71, Leas 76, Bane 76, Towl 76, Wolf 78], is a continuation of work begun at IBM Research in Yorktown Heights, NY. Our first implementation was based on the Illinois Parafrase Compiler [Wolf 78, KKLW 80], but the current version is a completely new program, although many of the transformations are the same as those performed by Parafrase. Other projects which have influenced our work are the Texas Instruments ASC compiler [Coha 73, Wede 75], the Cray-1 Fortran compiler [Higb 79], and the Massachusetts Computer Associates Vectorizer [Leve 77, Mysz 78].

The paper is organized into seven sections. Section 2 introduces Fortran 8x and gives examples of its use. Section 3 presents a theoretical overview of the translation process. Section 4 discusses program transformations which are preliminary to applying the dependence test; Section 5 presents details on how the test is used for each pair of statements; and Section 6 shows how the resulting dependence information is applied. Section 7 introduces auxiliary transformations that can enhance the opportunities for vectorization. Finally, Section 8 describes the current state of the Rice implementation and discusses future plans.

In a related project, we are implementing a compiler that will accept the output of the translator as input. That project will be reported upon in another paper. Other related papers discuss the theoretical underpinnings of our project [Kenn 80, Alle 83], and a method for handling conditional statements [AKPW 83].

2. Fortran 8x Array Operations

It is difficult to describe any language whose definition is still evolving, much less write a language translator for it. Nevertheless, we need some language as the basis for our discussion. In this section, we will describe one potential version of the language, which is similar to what the ANSI X3J3 committee is considering. This version is an extension of 1977 ANSI Fortran to include the proposed features for support of array processing and most of the proposed control structures for the language.

One of the major enhancements proposed in the latest Fortran standard is array assignments. If X and Y are two arrays of the same dimension, then

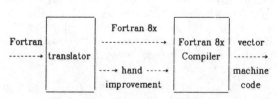

Figure 2: A Vector Translator

$$X = Y$$

copies Y into X element by element. In other words, this assignment is equivalent to

$$X(1) = Y(1)$$
$$X(2) = Y(2)$$
.
.
.
$$X(N) = Y(N)$$

Scalar quantities may be mixed with vector quantities using the convention that a scalar is expanded to a vector of the appropriate dimensions before operations are performed. Thus,

$$X = X + 5.0$$

adds the constant 5 to every element of array X.

The semantics of array operations in Fortran 8x are *simultaneous*; that is, the operation must be executed as though all values on the left side of the assignment are simultaneously stored. This requirement has a significant effect on the execution of statements such as

$$X = X/X(2)$$

Array semantics require that the store to X(2) occur at the same time as the stores to all other elements of X; as a result, the original value of X(2) is used throughout the operation. The result is the same as

$$T\ \ \ \ \ = X(2)$$
$$X(1) = X(1)/T$$
$$X(2) = X(2)/T$$
.
.
.
$$X(N) = X(N)/T$$

This important semantic distinction will have a significant impact on the translation process.

Quite often, one only wishes to work with a section of an array, rather than the whole array. In Fortran 8x, this may be accomplished by using *triplet* notation. For example, the following code

$$A(1:M:1,I) = B(J,1:M:1)$$

assigns the first M elements of the Jth row of B to the first M elements of the Ith column of A. Note that M may contain a value much smaller than the actual upper bound of either of these arrays. Triplet notation essentially represents a DO loop that is run simultaneously -- the first member is the starting element; the second the ending element; and the final member the stride. In a further analogy to DO loops, an implicit stride of 1 is assumed when no third

member is specified. Thus, the above assignment is equivalent to

$$A(1:M,I) = B(J,1:M)$$

In order to perform array assignments in irregular locations, Fortran 8x will permit an array assignment to be controlled by a condition array. The WHERE statement masks assignments such as the following:

$$WHERE\ (A.GT.0.0)\ A = A + B$$

This statement specifies that the vector sum of A and B be formed but the store back to A take place only in positions where A was originally greater than zero. The semantics of this statement are such that it behaves as if all of the components of the respective arrays are involved in the computation of the right hand side, but that stores take place only in the positions where the controlling conditions are true.

With this introduction to Fortran 8x, we can now proceed to describe the translation process in PFC.

3. The Translation Process

Fundamental to the translation of sequential programs to vector form is the concept of *dependence*. The reason for this is that dependence precisely captures the difference between statements which can be correctly rewritten in vector form and statements which cannot be correctly rewritten. For example, the following sequential assignment

```
        DO 10 I = 1,100
            X(I) = X(I)+Y(I)
    10 CONTINUE
```

uses only the *old* values of its input operands, and hence can be correctly rewritten as

$$X(1:100) = X(1:100) + Y(1:100)$$

If the previous example is changed just slightly into

```
        DO 10 I = 1,100
            X(I+1) = X(I) + Y(I)
    10    CONTINUE
```

it cannot be directly converted to a parallel assignment. This loop computes a value on one iteration which it then uses on a later iteration; as a result, its semantics are not equivalent to those of a vector assignment. A statement such as this which depends upon itself is called a *recurrence*.

In general, any statement that does not depend upon itself either directly or indirectly through a chain of statements may be correctly rewritten in vector form. However, for this assertion to hold, dependence must be enhanced so that it recognizes all order dependent operations within a program. Kuck and his students have defined three types of dependence that can affect vector translation [Kuck 78, Towl 76]:

Definition: If control flow within a program can reach statement S_2 after passing through S_1, then S_2 *depends on* S_1 if

(1) S_2 uses the output of S_1 (*true dependence*, written $S_1 \delta S_2$).

$$S_1: X = \Big\}_\delta$$
$$S_2: \quad = X$$

(2) S_2 might wrongly use the output of S_1 if they were reversed in sequence (*antidependence*, written $S_1 \delta^{-1} S_2$).

$$S_1: \quad = X \Big\}_{\delta^{-1}}$$
$$S_2: X =$$

(3) S_2 recomputes the output of S_1, and if they were reversed, subsequently executed statements might use the wrong value of that output (*output dependence*, written $S_1 \delta^0 S_2$).

$$S_1: X = \Big\}_{\delta^0}$$
$$S_2: X =$$

□

When attempting vectorization, we must consider all three types of dependence.

Once a full dependence graph has been constructed for a program, the task of identifying which statements can be rewritten into array assignments is equivalent to the problem of finding strongly connected regions in the dependence graph. However, this simple approach to vectorization may cause us to miss many cases of partial vectorization. Consider the example in Figure 3. In this example, statement (1) depends upon itself, so one might assume that all vectorization is impossible. This is not true. While the statement cannot be

```
        DO 10 I = 1, N
          DO 10 J = 1, N
            DO 10 K = 1, N
(1)           X(K,J,I) = X(K,J,I-1) + D
        10 CONTINUE
```
Figure 3

vectorized in all three loops, it can be vectorized in two loops. The problem with our view of dependence is that it is too monolithic -- a recurrence at any level inhibits vectorization at all levels.

For this reason, we introduce a *layered* view of dependence, in which a dependence is directly attributed to the loop whose variation gives rise to it. We intend to examine this idea as it applies to our example, but first we need to define our concept of layered dependence.

Definition: Suppose two statements

$$S_1: X(f(i_k)) = R$$
$$S_2: L = F(X(g(i_k)))$$

(where R and L denote arbitrary right and left hand sides respectively and F denotes an arbitrary expression in its argument) are contained in the same loop at nesting level k, and suppose that i_k is the loop induction variable at that level. (By convention, nesting levels are numbered from the outside in, so the outermost loop will be at level 1.) Then S_2 *depends on* S_1 *at level k*, written

$$S_1 \delta_k S_2$$

if there exist integers j_1, j_2 such that

$$1 \leq j_1 < j_2 \leq N_k$$

where N_k is the upper bound of the level-k loop, and such that

$$f(j_1) = g(j_2)$$

□

In other words, if S_1 computes a value on one iteration of the loop at level k that is used as input by S_2 on a later iteration of that loop, then S_2 depends on S_1 at level k.

In Figure 3, the loop on I is at level 1, the loop on J at level 2, and the loop on K at level 3. The dependence of (1) on itself is carried only by the I loop -- that is, every dependence crosses the I loop. Since this dependence is at level 1, we write

$$S_1 \delta_1 S_1$$

The important aspect of layered dependence comes from the fact that a dependence at level k will be broken as long as we run the k outer loops sequentially [Alle 83]. Thus, in Figure 3, if we run the I loop sequentially, we break the recurrence. As a result, the inner loops may be run in vector, giving

```
    DO 30 I = 1, N
      X(1:N, 1:N, I) = X(1:N, 1:N, I-1) + D
30 CONTINUE
```

All this suggests the following recursive scheme for parallel code generation.

(1) Find all strongly-connected regions in the dependence graph.

(2) For any statement S not in a strongly-connected region, generate parallel code in as many dimensions as possible.

(3) For every strongly-connected region R, generate a sequential DO loop to surround it and try to generate parallel code for the statements in R using a dependence graph in which the top-level dependences have been cast out. If parallel code can be generated for such a statement, it will be parallel in one fewer dimension.

The parallel code generation routine *codegen*, more precisely specified in Figure 4, is almost exactly the one implemented in PFC. It can be easily shown that this procedure will generate statements which are parallel in the maximum number of inner dimensions consistent with the given dependence graph.

The last theoretical aspect necessary to perform the translation is a test for dependence at level k. Such a test is provided in the following theorem.

Theorem: Assume the statements

$$S_1: \ X(f(i_1,i_2,...,i_{n_1})) = R$$
$$S_2: \ L = F(X(g(i_1,i_2,...,i_{n_2})))$$

occur together in at least k loops. (Here S_1 is contained in n_1 loops and S_2 is contained in n_2 loops.) If all loops are *normalized* to run from 1 to an upper bound N_i in steps of 1, and if f and g are linear functions of the loop induction variables, i.e.

$$f(i_1,i_2,\cdots,i_{n_1})=a_0+\sum_{j=1}^{n_1}a_ji_j \ \text{ and}$$

$$g(i_1,i_2,\cdots,i_{n_2})=b_0+\sum_{j=1}^{n_2}b_ji_j$$

then $S_1 \ \delta_k \ S_2$ only if

a) *gcd test*:

$$gcd(a_1-b_1, \ a_2-b_2, \ \cdots,a_{k-1}-b_{k-1},$$
$$a_k,\cdots,a_{n_1}, \ b_1,\cdots,b_{n_2}) \qquad | \ b_0-a_0$$

b) *Banerjee inequality*:

$$-\ b_k-\sum_{i=1}^{k-1}(a_i-b_i)^-(N_i-1)$$

$$-(a_k^-+b_k)^+(N_k-2)$$

$$-\sum_{i=k+1}^{n_1}a_i^-(N_i-1)-\sum_{i=k+1}^{n_2}b_i^+(N_i-1)$$

$$\leq\sum_{i=0}^{n_2}b_i-\sum_{i=0}^{n_1}a_i$$

$$\leq-b_k+\sum_{i=1}^{k-1}(a_i-b_i)^+(N_i-1)$$

$$+(a_k^+-b_k)^+(N_k-2)$$

$$+\sum_{i=k+1}^{n_1}a_i^+(N_i-1)+\sum_{i=k+1}^{n_2}b_i^-(N_i-1)$$

$\square$

A proof of this theorem may be found elsewhere [Kenn 80].

This test provides a precise, though not exact, test for dependence between two statements. It is complicated, but its computation can be speeded up in a number of ways. However, before it can be applied to a program, the program must be *normalized*; that is, loops must run from 1 to an upper bound in increments of 1, and subscripts must be converted to linear functions of loop induction variables. After normalization, dependence analysis may be invoked to construct the dependence graph for the program. Finally, parallel code generation can use the dependence graph to convert the program to an equivalent parallel form.

The next three sections describe how this process is implemented in PFC. The first section deals with program normalization; the second with dependence analysis; and the final one with parallel code generation.

4. Subscript Standardization

In order to perform accurate dependence testing, a program must be converted into normal form. The STANDARD phase of PFC is responsible for this task. Two different transformations are used to normalize programs. First, *DO loop normalization*, which is performed by the module STDDNRM transforms all DO loops to run from 1 to an upper bound in increments of 1. Next, *induction variable substitution* is performed by the module STIVSUB to convert typical programming practices into a form more amenable for vectorization.

```
procedure codegen (R,k,D);
    /* R is the region for which we must */
    /*    generate code                  */
    /* k is the minimum nesting level of */
    /*    possible parallel loops        */
    /* D is the dependence graph among   */
    /*    statements in R                */

    find the set {S₁, S₂,...,Sₚ} of maximal
       strongly-connected regions in the
       dependence graph D restricted to R
       (use Tarjan's algorithm);

    construct R_π from R by reducing each
       Sᵢ to a single node and  compute D_π,
       the graph naturally induced on R_π by D;

    let {π₁, π₂,...,πₘ} be the nodes of R_π
       numbered consistent with D_π
       (use topological sort);

    for i ← 1 to m do
        if πᵢ is strongly-connected
        then
              generate a level-k DO;

              let Dᵢ be the dependence graph of
                 all edges in D internal to πᵢ
                 with level k+1 or greater;

              codegen (πᵢ, k+1, Dᵢ);

              generate the level-k CONTINUE;

        else
              generate a parallel statement for
                 πᵢ in ρ(πᵢ)-k+1 dimensions,
                 where ρ(πᵢ) is the number of
                 loops containing πᵢ

    od
end
```

Figure 4. Parallel code generation routine.

Suppose the translator is presented with the following code segment.

```
       DO 20 I = 1,100
(1)        KI = I
       DO 10 J = 1,300,3
(2)        KI = KI+2
(3)        U(J) = U(J)*W(KI)
(4)        V(J+1) = V(J)+W(KI)
    10   CONTINUE
    20 CONTINUE
```

The eventual aim to to convert statements (3) and (4) into vector form, if that does not violate

their semantics. The following sections trace through the standardization process as applied to this code.

4.1. *DO Loop Normalization*

The first step in subscript standardization, DO loop normalization, is relatively straightforward. STDDNRM simply walks through the *abstract syntax tree* (henceforth referred to as AST) that represents the program, transforming loops as it encounters them. Whenever it finds a DO statement, it saves the control variable of that loop in an array called the LCD, which is indexed by nesting level. Since STDDNRM intends to replace the DO statement with a standardized version, it creates a variable to control the new loop. The name of this variable, which is artificially generated by concatenating '&' with the nesting level of the statements in the loop, identifies it as a loop induction variable and makes it easy to determine the level of iteration it controls.

The standardized DO statement is now simple to generate. Both the lower bound and the increment are known to be 1; the new upper bound is simply:

(upper_bnd - lower_bnd + step) / step

For example, STDDNRM will convert the second DO loop in the example to

DO 10 &2 = 1, 100

Altering the DO loop requires that references to the old induction variable be replaced with an expression in the new induction variable. In order to perform this transformation, STDDNRM stores both the old loop control variable and the replacement expression in the LCD. The replacement expression is generated as follows:

*lower_bnd + step * (new_loop_var - 1)*

Although this expression appears complicated, the use of a powerful integer simplifier STDSIMP usually reduces such expressions to a very managable form. Whenever STDDNRM passes a variable in a loop, it checks that variable against all entries in the LCD. If the variable is found, it is replaced with the corresponding replacement expression. In our example, statements (3) and (4) become

U(3*&2-2) = U(3*&2-2)*W(KI)
V(3*&2-1) = U(3*&2-2)*W(KI)

The replacement process is straightforward, except that some care must be taken to replace all induction variables in a deeper DO statement before generating any new expressions from it.

Upon leaving a loop, STDDNRM performs two actions. First, it creates an assignment statement to the old loop variable, giving it the value it normally would have had upon termination of the loop. This guards against later sections of code using this variable. Second, it erases the entry in the LCD for that loop, guaranteeing that later uses of the old loop control variable will not accidentally be replaced. The completely normalized example is as follows:

```
     DO 20 &1 = 1,100
        KI = I
        DO 10 &2 = 1,100
           KI = KI+2
           U(3*&2-2) = U(3*&2-2)*W(KI)
           V(3*&2-1) = V(3*&2-2)+W(KI)
 10     CONTINUE
        J = 301
 20  CONTINUE
     I = 101
```

The transformations performed by STDDNRM do not produce semantically equivalent programs in all cases. For instance, branches out of a loop might cause the old loop control variable to be undefined at the branch target, since it is undefined throughout the execution of the standardized loop. This situation is indicative of a fundamental problem in vectorization -- namely determining the effects of control flow on data dependence. PFC handles control flow changes by a process known as *IF conversion* [AKPW 83, Alle 83]. While IF conversion can correctly account for any type of control change, it can be a very expensive process that may increase execution time in many cases. As a result, IF conversion is an option that may be invoked in PFC. When it is not in effect, PFC restricts its vectorizing efforts to what we call *extended basic blocks* -- sections of code that contain no branches other than DO loops. Within extended blocks, all transformations produce semantically equivalent code, and the problems caused by branches are avoided.

4.2. *Induction Variable Substitution*

Because of limitations imposed by early standards of Fortran, *auxiliary induction variables* are quite common in many programs. An auxiliary induction variable is a variable which is incremented or decremented by a constant amount on every iteration of the loop. In the following example,

```
        KI = 101
        DO 100 I = 1, 100
           KI = KI - 1
           A(KI) = A(KI) - I
 100    CONTINUE
```

KI is an auxiliary induction variable used to avoid a loop induction variable with a negative increment. If subscripts are to be converted to linear functions of loop induction variables so that dependence testing can be applied, then auxiliary induction variables must be replaced by appropriate expressions. STIVSUB is the module in PFC that effects this transformation.

Initially, STIVSUB was designed only to substitute for auxiliary induction variables. However, the method we devised for handling substitution was very easily generalized to perform limited constant propagation, expression folding, code motion, and dead code elimination. This has contributed tremendously to the amount of vectorization achievable in PFC, because it eliminates many symbolic subscripts in the program. Symbolic dependence testing in PFC is much slower and far less accurate than dependence testing which only involves known constants. Additionally, by eliminating some dead code, STIVSUB decreases the running time of dependence analysis, which dominates the cost of vectorization.

Induction variable substitution is accomplished in two passes over the code. The first pass creates two lists: one of all the variables used as inputs in the block of code and one of all the variables produced as output. Information stored in the *input list* includes

(1)   the variable's symbol table location,

(2)   a pointer to the variable's predecessor in the tree (so that it can be replaced),

(3)   a pointer to the expression that must be simplified if this variable is replaced,

(4)   the relative statement number of the statement in which the reference occurs, and

(5)   the nesting level of that statement.

The *output list* holds

(1)   the variable's symbol table location,

(2)   a pointer to the predecessor of the statement in which the variable is defined (so that the definition can be deleted if the assignment turns out to be dead),

(3)   the relative statement number of the statement, and

(4)   the nesting level of the statement.

In both lists, the variables are stored in the order that they are encountered when walking the AST.

If STIVSUB encounters a nested DO statement while building up its lists, it invokes itself recursively on that loop before continuing. Thus, complete substitution for any nested loops will be accomplished before substitution is attempted for the present loop. Consider our previously normalized example:

```
(1)        DO 20 &1 = 1,100
(2)          KI = I
(3)          DO 10 &2 = 1,100
(4)            KI = KI+2
(5)            U(3*&2-2) = U(3*&2-2)*W(KI)
(6)            V(3*&2-1) = V(3*&2-2)+W(KI)
      10     CONTINUE
(7)          J = 301
      20   CONTINUE
           I = 101
```

When STIVSUB is called on this section of code, it initially builds up variable lists for statement (1) and (2). At that point, it would recursively invoke itself on statement 3, performing all substitution on the inner loop before returning to attempt substitution on the outer loop. Upon the return of the second invocation, the induction variable KI will have been replaced in the inner loop, giving

```
        DO 20 &1 = 1,100
          KI = I
          DO 10 &2 = 1,100
            U(3*&2-2)=U(3*&2-2)*W(KI+2*&2)
            V(3*&2-1)=V(3*&2-2)+W(KI+2*&2)
      10    CONTINUE
          KI = KI + 200
          J = 301
      20  CONTINUE
          I = 101
```

Note that all references to the auxiliary induction variable KI have been replaced within the inner loop, and a new assignment has been generated to give KI the correct value in the outer loop. At this point STIVSUB would continue building lists for the rest of the program. Note that the initial invocation of STIVSUB would not have to build up the input output lists for statements 3,5, and 6, because the recursive invocation would have returned the lists for the code it modified. The initial invocation can simply merge the returned lists into its own, thereby avoiding the expense of walking code a second time.

Once the data lists are built for a section of code, the substitution process is a straightforward two-phase procedure that is applied to every member of the output list defined at the outermost nesting level under consideration. The first phase finds definitions of variables that are *loop invariant* or whose only varying component is a loop control variable. The information necessary for determining this is very conveniently available in the data lists. In our example, the initial assignment to KI is just such a variable and would be forward substituted by STIVSUB, giving

```
DO 20 &1 = 1,100
  DO 10 &2 = 1,100
    U(3*&2-2) = U(3*&2-2)*W(2*&2+&1)
    V(3*&2-1) = V(3*&2-2)+W(2*&2+&1)
10  CONTINUE
  KI = &1 + 200
  J = 301
20 CONTINUE
  I = 101
```

With this substitution, the remaining definitions of KI and J also fit the pattern, and would be moved out of the loop:

```
DO 20 &1 = 1,100
  DO 10 &2 = 1,100
    U(3*&2-2)=U(3*&2-2)*W(2*&2+&1)
    V(3*&2-1)=V(3*&2-2)+W(2*&2+&1)
10  CONTINUE
20 CONTINUE
  J = 301
  KI = 300
  I = 101
```

Rules governing expressions that may be propagated are quite complex, and may be found elsewhere [AllK 82].

The second phase of analysis finds and substitutes for actual auxiliary induction variables. Once again, given the information in the data lists, this process is a very straightforward pattern matching scheme. However, the full rules for substitution are too complex to be discussed here, and may be found elsewhere [AllK 82].

After STIVSUB has completed its work, a global data flow analysis pass is made over the entire program. The use-def chains obtained from this pass are used to eliminate dead code and to propagate integer constants forward into subscripts. In our example, if we assume that the variables KI, I, and J are no longer live upon exit of the loop, dead code elimination will rid us of them, leaving

```
DO 20 &1 = 1,100
  DO 10 &2 = 1,100
    U(3*&2-2)=U(3*&2-2)*W(2*&2+&1)
    V(3*&2-1)=V(3*&2-2)+W(2*&2+&1)
10  CONTINUE
20 CONTINUE
```

At this point, the code is completely normalized and ready for dependence testing.

5. Dependence testing

5.1. *Overview*

The objective of dependence analysis is to test every relevant pair of statements in a program at all possible levels of dependence. Thus, dependence testing is inherently expensive for at least three reasons:

(1) each of the roughly N^2 pairs of statements (for a program with N statements) must be examined for dependence,

(2) each pair must be tested once for each of the loops that surround both statements, and

(3) both of the tests for dependence are relatively expensive to perform.

Because we expected the cost of dependence testing to be high, we focused a large amount of effort on optimizing the time spent testing for dependence. The effort appears to have been well placed; PFC spends more time scanning and parsing a typical Fortran program than it spends performing dependence analysis.

The general algorithm used to implement dependence analysis is given in Figure 5. The following issues are very important in any efficient implementation of the algorithm:

(1) A method must be devised to compare each pair of statements in the program for dependence. Because of the expense of applying the layered dependence tests to a new pair of statements, PFC must avoid redundant or unnecessary comparisons. That is, it should consider a pair of statements only once, making all tests for dependences of different kinds at different layers at the same time. Additionally, it should also allow the upper bounds of all loops surrounding either of the statements to be easily found, since this knowledge is required for Banerjee's test.

(2) A method must be devised to find all the variables used and defined by a statement. Additionally, this method should provide a way for any given subscript to quickly find the terms involved in the two dependence tests.

(3) Finally both Banerjee's test and the gcd test must be carefully implemented to be as efficient as possible.

The rest of this section is partitioned to deal with each of the above issues. Section 2 describes a method for comparing each pair of statements in the program at the correct levels with no redundancy. The order of comparison generated by this method makes it easy to keep track of the upper bounds of each loop surrounding the statements. Section 3 describes the method used to store the input and output variables for each statement. Stored with the variables are the terms that are needed for Banerjee's test and the gcd test. Section 4 describes the actual implementation of

---

for each pair of statements that
    can be dependent **do**

while there are untested references to
    the array A in both statements **do**

for each level L at which the pair
    might be dependent **do**

/* the variable INDEPENDENT   */
/* remains false until the two   */
/* statements are shown to be   */
/* independent for A at this level */

INDEPENDENT ← **false**;

while not INDEPENDENT **and**
    there is an untested subscript
    position i of A **do**

if the expressions in position i of A
    in both statements are linear
then

    if gcd test shows independence **or**
    Banerjee' inequality does not hold
    then
        INDEPENDENT ← **true**
    fi
fi
od

/* Here if INDEPENDENT is true,   */
/* we have shown the statements   */
/* to be independent for A at   */
/* level L; otherwise we must   */
/* assume that a dependence   */
/* exists for A at L   */

if not INDEPENDENT
    then record the level L dependence **fi**

  od
 od
od

Figure 5. Algorithm for dependence testing.

Banerjee's test and the gcd test. Section 5 briefly describes how the parts fit together and mentions some key design decisions that influenced the entire dependence testing phase.

5.2. *Statement Comparison*

Comparing every pair of statements at all levels at which a dependence could exist is not so easy a problem as it initially appears. The brute force methods for generating comparisons are inelegant and inefficient. Additionally, maintaining the proper set of loop upper bounds can be very messy. We decided to avoid these difficulties by creating a data structure to encode the nesting of the statements in a program. This recursive data structure, DDSTMTLST, is a threaded list structure that allows quick recognition of all loops surrounding any two statements. Although DDSTMTLST is complicated, it is easy to build and it is the basis for an elegant, systematic method of comparing statements.

In DDSTMTLST every statement in a given loop is represented explicitly in a list. This list has a sublist for every nested DO statement that the loop contains. These sublists are identical in structure to the base list; that is, they are lists of statements with sublists for each nested DO statement inside them. To aid the statement comparison process, the sublists of a given list are threaded by creating a new list (a list of sublists) which holds the locations of all sublists of that list. For easy reference, a pointer to the list of sublists for a specific loop is placed in the first node of that statement list for the loop. The structure of DDSTMTLST very compactly encodes the nesting structure of the program.

Because of its recursive structure, DDSTMTLST is very easy to construct using a stack-oriented procedure. DDBLDSL is the PFC procedure that builds DDSTMTLST; it walks the AST while maintaining two lists: a list of all statements encountered at the current level and a list of all sublists (i.e. a list of pointers to all the lists of nested lists) encountered at this level. As DDBLDSL walks a statement, it adds that statement's number to the present statement list. Whenever a DO is encountered, DDBLDSL pushes the present pair of lists onto a stack and continues walking with a new, empty pair of lists. When it finds the end of a DO loop, DDBLDSL carefully pops off the last pair of lists and stores pointers to the lists just completed in the newly popped lists. While this procedure requires attention to ensure that a pointer to a list is not accidentally lost, its implementation is straightforward. The algorithm can be recursively applied at each level of nesting.

A recursive data structure such as DDSTMTLST suggests that a recursive procedure might be used for comparing statements. DDTEST, which is outlined in Figure 6, is such a procedure. Initially it is called at level 1 with DDSTMTLST as a parameter. DDTEST then moves through the statement list, calling a routine COMPARE which actually compares two statements at all levels between 1 and LEVEL. Note that DDTEST is both iterative and recursive; it iterates to move through lists and calls itself recursively to move to deeper nesting

```
procedure DDTEST (LIST, LEVEL);
    /* LIST is the list of statements        */
    /* to be compared at all nesting         */
    /* levels up to and including LEVEL       */

    /* First compare all statements in a      */
    /* nested DO loop at a deeper level       */
    for each list SUB on the
        list of sublists of LIST do
        DDTEST (SUB, LEVEL + 1)
    od;
    /* Next compare every statement on  */
    /* this list with every statement        */
    /* contained in this do loop at          */
    /* level LEVEL.                           */
    for each statement S1 in LIST do
        for each statement S2 ≥ S1 in LIST do
            /* compare does the actual          */
            /* testing at levels 1,...LEVEL    */
            COMPARE (S1, S2, LEVEL)
    od od
    /* Next compare statements in nested */
    /* loops with statements at the level.  */
    for each list L1 on the list of
            sublists for LIST do
        for each statement S1 in L1 do
            for each statement S2 in LIST do
                COMPARE (S1, S2, LEVEL)
    od od od
    /* Finally compare all statements in      */
    /* different nested loops at LEVEL       */
    for each list L1 on the list of
            sublists for LIST do
        for each S1 in L1 do
            for each list L2 ≥ L1 on the
                    list of sublists for LIST do
                for each S2 in L2 do
                    COMPARE (S1, S2, LEVEL)
    od od od od
end
```

Figure 6. Algorithm for Statement Comparison.

levels.

Although it is not immediately obvious, DDTEST is optimal in the number of statement comparisons performed. Additionally, the list structure clearly defines entries into nested regions; thus, the bounds of the current loops surrounding a pair of statements can be easily maintained with a stack. DO statements themselves are also easy to locate with DDSTMTLST, since the first statement in every list (other than the outer list) immediately follows a DO.

DDSTMTLST provides an orderly method of comparing all relevant pairs of statements within a program. Of course, this does no good unless there are quick methods of testing the pairs for dependence.

5.3. *Input and Output Lists*

If Banerjee's test and the gcd test are to be efficiently implemented, some method must be devised to quickly find the variables that a statement uses and the variables that a statement defines. Additionally, this method should include some way to locate the terms necessary to evaluate Banerjee's test and the gcd test for a given subscript. PFC handles these issues by having two lists of variables for every statement: one to hold the input variables of the statement and one to hold the output variables of the statement. The format of these lists allows both rapid determination of the common variables in two statements and the rapid location of the terms that appear in the dependence tests.

The input lists and output lists are identical both in form and in the information contained. The information contained in the lists includes:

(1) the symbol table index of the variable,

(2) the type of the variable (either SCALAR, ARRAY, or COMMON),[1]

(3) the number of dimensions of the variable (nonzero only for ARRAY types),

(4) a header for a subscript list for the variable (if it is an ARRAY),

(5) a header for the next node in the list, and

(6) a header for a list of pointers that hold the exact location of the variable in the AST.

The lists are sorted by increasing symbol table index so that variables common to two lists can be quickly found by a merge procedure. Each array reference has a header for a subscript list.

Nodes in subscript lists contain the number of the subscript, the linearity of the subscript, and a header for a coefficient list. Coefficient lists are sorted by increasing term number, and contain the coefficients of the corresponding term in the dependence tests.

Building the input output lists is a relatively simple matter. In PFC, the lists are built by DDBLDIO, a procedure which walks the AST passing down a parameter to indicate whether variables found are to be added to the input list, the output list, or to both. The lists are maintained in sorted order as the tree is walked, so that duplicates are easily detected.

The part of the list that is hardest to build is the coefficient list. The section of DDBLDIO that does this acts like a recursive descent parser: it dives into sections of AST hunting for loop induction variables, pulling out the coefficients of those it finds. The fact that all subscripts are in standardized form simplifies the task considerably.

The algorithm for COMPARE, which uses the input output lists, is given in Figure 7.

5.4. *Evaluation of Banerjee's Inequality*

The procedures executed the most often in PFC are the ones that actually evaluate Banerjee's inequality and the gcd test. Since these procedures are called once for each common variable at each common nesting level in each of N^2 pairs of statements, it is vital to PFC that these routines be efficient. Even though there is a tremendous amount of preparatory work, we still felt that the bottleneck of PFC would be the dependence testing. By being very careful in the way we evaluated the tests, we achieved a much faster running time than we expected.

In practice, the gcd test does not often determine independence. As a result, it is useful to have it terminate as rapidly as possible. Since the gcd of the terms that typically appear in subscripts becomes 1 very quickly, and since 1 will always divide $a_0 - b_0$, the gcd test terminates once the gcd becomes 1. This one optimization provides the gcd test with adequate speed.

On initial examination, Banerjee's inequality

---

[1] The COMMON type is a catchall for variables that do not fit into the mold required by the dependence tests. Declared common variables are obviously one example. Another is an array which has its diagonal written out using an implied DO on each iteration of a loop. The parts of that array used cannot be conveniently represented for dependence testing.

```
procedure COMPARE (S1, S2, LEVEL);

for I ← 1 to 3 do

case I in
begin   /* 1: true dependence of S2 on S1 */
    L1 ← output list of S1;
    L2 ← input  list of S2;
    dependence_S2_on_S1 ← TRUE;
    dependence_S1_on_S2 ← ANTI;
end;
begin   /* 2: true dependence of S1 on S2 */
    L1 ← input  list of S1;
    L2 ← output list of S2;
    dependence_S2_on_S1 ← ANTI;
    dependence_S1_on_S2 ← TRUE;
end;
begin   /* 3: Check for output dependence*/
    L1 ← output list of S1;
    L2 ← output list of S2;
    dependence_S2_on_S1 ← OUTPUT;
    dependence_S1_on_S2 ← OUTPUT;
end
esac;

    while ( not_exhausted (L1)
             & not_exhausted (L2) ) do

      if key(L1) < key(L2)
      then move_down (L1)
      else if key(L2) > key(L1)
      then move_down (L2)
      else   /* We have a match  */

          for J ← level to 1 step -1 do
          independent ← false;
          gcd (key (L1), key (L2),
              J, independent);

          if not independent then
              banerjee (key(L1), key (L2),
                      J, independent) fi;

          if not independent
            then add an edge indicating
              that S2 depends on S1 at
              level J with type
              dependence_S2_on_S1  fi;

          if not S1 = S2
            then repeat the process
                S1 depending on S2    fi
          od;

        move down L1

    fi od od  end
        Figure 7. Algorithm for COMPARE.
```

$$- b_k - \sum_{i=1}^{k-1} (a_i - b_i)^- (N_i - 1)$$

$$-(a_k^- + b_k)^+ (N_k - 2)$$

$$- \sum_{i=k+1}^{n_1} a_i^- (N_i - 1) - \sum_{i=k+1}^{n_2} b_i^+ (N_i - 1)$$

$$\leq \sum_{i=0}^{n_2} b_i - \sum_{i=0}^{n_1} a_i$$

$$\leq -b_k + \sum_{i=1}^{k-1} (a_i - b_i)^+ (N_i - 1)$$

$$+(a_k^+ - b_k)^+ (N_k - 2)$$

$$+ \sum_{i=k+1}^{n_1} a_i^+ (N_i - 1) + \sum_{i=k+1}^{n_2} b_i^- (N_i - 1)$$

appears quite complicated. The only obvious way to optimize its computation initially appears to be computing the middle term once, saving its value for future uses. However, closer examination reveals some interesting facts about the left side of the inequality. First, every term which is superscripted by a minus or a plus is nonnegative - i.e. $(a_i - b_i)^-$ has to be greater than or equal to 0 by definition of the negative part of a number. With the assumption that the upper bounds of each loop is at least 1 (except at the level at which we are testing, which must be 2), then every term that is subtracted on the left hand side of the inequality is greater than or equal to 0. Similarly, every term that is added on the right hand side is greater than or equal to 0. Thus, the inequality takes the form

$$-b_k - nonnegative\ number$$

$$\leq \sum_{i=0}^{n_2} b_i - \sum_{i=0}^{n_1} a_i$$

$$\leq -b_k + nonnegative\ number$$

As a result, at most one side of the inequality can be violated. That is, either the middle sum is less than $-b_k$, in which case only the left inequality could be false; or the middle sum is greater than $-b_k$, in which case only the right inequality could be false. If the middle sum evaluates to $-b_k$, then neither inequality can be false and we have no need to evaluate the left or right sides. This suggests a method for performing Banerjee's test:

(1)   Compute (or have available) the middle term of Banerjee's inequality.

(2)   If the middle term is less than $-b_k$, then compute the left side of the inequality. If the left side is greater than the middle term, then the statements are independent (at the level tested); otherwise we

must assume dependence.

(3) If the middle term is greater than $-b_k$, then compute the right side of the inequality. If the right side is less than the middle term, then the statements are independent (at the level tested); otherwise we must assume dependence.

(4) If the middle term equals $-b_k$, then there is no reason to compute either side of the inequality, since it cannot possibly show independence.

The above procedure has a theoretical basis in the derivation of Banerjee's inequality. The inequality is derived using the intermediate value theorem of calculus, which states that a continuous function can be 0 in a region only when its maximum over the region is greater than or equal 0 and its minimum over the region is less than or equal to 0. Only one of these conditions can be violated for a function.

The above procedure can also be very easily extended to accommodate loops whose upper bounds are symbolic. Note also that the assumptions made on the upper bounds are conservative. Since the loops are normalized, the upper bound of a loop is precisely the number of times that loop is iterated. If the assumptions made by the test are not met, then we are guaranteed that there is no dependence; hence, if the test should show dependence, it is being conservative.

Finally, note that when there is only one symbolic upper bound which has a nonzero coefficient in the case where dependence must be assumed, the *threshold* (or loop size for which that dependence is broken) can be computed from the known information. Thus, even though complete vectorization is not possible in that case, some partial vectorization may be feasible [Kenn 80].

5.5. *Overall Design*

The previous sections have presented the details of the important phases of the dependence analysis process. This section will try to piece them all together and provide insight into the major design decisions of PFC.

Probably the most notable aspect of the previous sections is the use of linked lists. Lists are used in induction variable substitution, in the algorithm that generates the statement comparisons, and as a method for storing the inputs and outputs of a statement. This extensive use of linked lists was recognized early in the design of PFC. Rather than going through the arduous task of debugging the linked list operations for every set of linked lists in PFC, we decided to implement a set of general linked

list utilities. These utilities, known as POLYLIST, are capable of creating and manipulating general linked lists. Nodes of POLYLIST lists have two programmer accessible fields: a *key* field and a *value* field. A programmer can specify any data type for these fields that he desires (hence the name POLYmorphic LIST utilities). All references to lists are in a high level notation similar to that used throughout this paper. Several examples of POLYLIST operations are given below. Their functions should be obvious from their names.

```
declare_list_type (INPUT_TYPE)
    keytype (FIXED BINARY)
    valtype (LIKE INPUT_STRUCT);

declare_list (INPUT_LIST)
    type (INPUT_TYPE)
    space(IO_SPACE);

move_to_head (INPUT_LIST);

new_head (INPUT_LIST);

move_down (INPUT_LIST);

while (not_exhausted(INPUT_LIST)) do
```

In order to provide truly polymorphic utilities, POLYLIST was written as PL/I statement macros that expand to in-line code. Thus POLYLIST not only provides data abstraction, it also executes rapidly at run time.

The concept of *extended blocks* introduced in the section on subscript normalization plays an important role in determining the sections of the program on which the dependence analysis will be called. Subscript normalization, dependence analysis, and parallel code generation are all called only on the extended blocks of a program. These are the only sections where parallel code may be generated using only data dependence; other sections require a nontrivial form of control flow analysis as well. This reduces the complexity of the analysis tremendously; the N^2 time required by DDTEST is reduced to the sum of squares of numbers smaller than N without a significant reduction in the amount of vectorization possible.

A brief outline of the entire dependence testing phase as it is presently implemented is given below:

(1) Partition the program into extended blocks.

(2) Call STDDNRM and STIVSUB to perform subscript normalization and induction variable substitution on every extended block in the program.

(3) Call DDBLDIO to build input output lists for the entire program. This is done to provide information for scalar data flow

analysis as well as for the dependence analysis.

(4) For each extended block, call DDBLDSL to build a statement list, then call DDTEST to perform the actual dependence analysis.

At this point the dependence graph exists for the extended blocks, and all the tools are ready to transform the program to parallel form.

6. Parallel Code Generation

The parallel code generation routine was outlined in Section 3. The purpose of this section is to show how the concept of layered dependence makes the generation of parallel code easier. In the process, we shall show how the topological sort and strongly-connected region finding routines are incorporated into the overall process.

Throughout the discussion in this section, we shall refer to a somewhat contrived example. The original Fortran for that example is shown in Figure 8. Its dependence graph (in which only dependences involving the numbered statements are displayed) is shown in Figure 9.

Let us track the code generation process through this example to illustrate a few points. At the top level, statements (2), (3), and (4) are involved in a large recurrence, so that code generation will be called recursively for these statements one level down. Parallel code will be generated for statement (1) after the loop for the first three.

        DO 30 I = 1, 100

            code for (2), (3), (4)
            generated at lower levels

    30 CONTINUE
    (1)   X(1:100) = Y(1:100) + 10

         DO 30 I = 1, 100
    (1)   X(I) = Y(I) + 10
         DO 20 J = 1, 100
    (2)   B(J) = A(J,N)
         DO 10 K = 1, 50
    (3)   A(J+1,K) = B(J) + C(J,K)
    10   CONTINUE
    (4)   Y(I+J) = A(J+1,N)
    20   CONTINUE
    30   CONTINUE

Figure 8. Parallel Code Generation Example.

At the next level down, the output dependences of (1), (2), and (3) on themselves, which occur because the array being assigned into does not have enough subscripts for all the surrounding loops, disappear. Also, the antidependence of (3) on (4), due to the possibility that A(J+1,K) is the same as A(J+1,N) on a successive iteration of the *outer* loop, is broken. This leaves the dependence graph shown in Figure 10. Statements (2) and (3) still form a recurrence, but code can now be generated for statement (4).

        DO 30 I = 1, 100
          DO 20 J = 1,100

            code for (2), (3)
            generated at lower levels

    20   CONTINUE
    (4)   Y(I+1:I+100) = A(2:101,N)
    30   CONTINUE
    (1)   X(1:100) = Y(1:100) + 10

The recurrence involving statements (2) and (3) will be broken at the next level down and the final code shown in Figure 11 will result. This example is pleasing because it generates vector statements at three different levels and because it illustrates, in the case of statement (2), how parallel code generation can also serve as scalar code generation. This happens when we generate code that is parallel in 0 dimensions.

There are two aspects of the code generator that are worthy of further note. First the strongly-connected region finder is a direct adaptation of Tarjan's *depth-first search* method [Tarj 72]. The time required by this

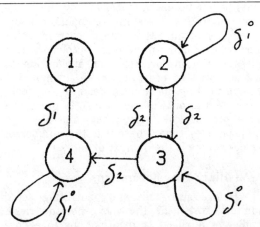

Figure 9. Dependence graph for Figure 8.

199

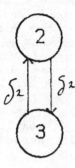

Figure 10. Dependence graph at level 2.

method is linear in the number of statements and dependence edges remaining in the graph.

Second, the statements in the graph are ordered by an adaptation of the *topological sort* [Knut 73] which computes the derived dependence relation between π-blocks on the fly. The basic idea is simple. In the first pass through the edges of the dependence graph, a distinction is made between edges within a π-block, which are ignored, and those between π-blocks, which are used to set up the dependence for topological sort and then deleted from the graph (this is fine since further processing will be at a lower level and hence *within* a region).

One wrinkle in the implementation is worthy of note. The usual linear time bound (linear in the number of vertices and edges) of topological sort had to be sacrificed for cosmetic reasons. When presented with a group of statements having no dependences among them, the version of PFC with a standard topological sort tended to rearrange those statements into random order. This unnecessary code motion causes confusion for the user attempting to read a translated program, so we eliminated it by implementing the set of nodes with no predecessors as a priority queue (heap), to produce a stable topological sort that operates in $O(n \log n + e)$ time, where n is the number of π-blocks and e is the number of edges.

7. Auxiliary Transformations

Before giving up and generating serial code for a statement, the code generator tries a number of auxiliary transformations to expose more parallelism. We will discuss several of these in this section.

```
        DO 30 I = 1, 100
          DO 20 J = 1,100
(2)         B(J) = A(J,N)
(3)         A(J+1,1:100) = B(J) + C(J,1:100)
  20      CONTINUE
(4)       Y(I+1:I+100) = A(2:101,N)
  30    CONTINUE
(1)   X(1:100) = Y(1:100) + 10
```

Figure 11. Final code for Figure 8.

7.1. *Recurrence Breaking*

A number of recurrences, particularly those based upon output dependences and antidependences, can be broken by clever renaming or the introduction of array temporaries. These transformations are described in a previous paper [Kenn 80].

In addition, a number of such recurrences are familiar patterns for which special language constructs may exist. For example, consider the following loop.

```
   S = 0.0
   DO 10 I = 1, N
     S = S + X(I)
10 CONTINUE
```

This can be easily recognized to be a sum reduction, and replaced by a call to an efficient library function.

7.2. *Loop Interchange*

Many times a recurrence at the deepest level blocks the vectorization of outer loops. Under certain conditions, loops may be interchanged to yield a new inner loop that can be vectorized. To illustrate the power of this technique, consider the standard algorithm for matrix multiplication on a scalar machine.

```
   DO 100 J = 1, 100
     DO 100 I = 1, 100
       DO 100 K = 1, 100
         C(I,J) = C(I,J) + A(I,K)*B(K,J)
100 CONTINUE
```

After loop distribution and interchange of the innermost two loops, this becomes

```
   DO 100 J = 1, 100
     DO 100 K = 1, 100
       DO 100 I = 1, 100
         C(I,J) = C(I,J) + A(I,K)*B(K,J)
100 CONTINUE
```

The parallel code generator then produces:

```
DO 100 J = 1, 100
   DO 100 K = 1, 100
      C(1:100,J) = C(1:100,J) +
                   A(1:100,K)*B(K,J)
100 CONTINUE
```

The final code can be recognized as the optimal method for matrix multiplication on a vector machine with vector registers. Since the current section of C is kept in a register until all computations involving it are done, and only then put away, a vector register machine does one vector load for every two operations -- a nice balance. The Cray-1 achieves 125 megaflops on this loop [Russ 78]. The fact that optimal vector code can be produced by a well understood transformation of the scalar code is very satisfying.

7.3. *If Conversion*

Most parallel machines have some method for conditionally executing an operation on elements of an array. This is usually accomplished by using some sort of bit mask to turn off execution of the operation in certain subscript positions. Fortran 8x provides the WHERE statement to exploit such hardware, and PFC makes an aggressive attempt to eliminate conditional transfers of control by replacing them, whenever possible, with WHERE statements.

If dependences permit, conditional assignments within loops, like the one below:

```
DO 100 I = 1, 100
   IF (A(I).GT.0) B(I) = B(I) + A(I)
100 CONTINUE
```

can be directly converted to WHERE statements:

```
WHERE (A(1:100).GT.0)
   B(1:100) = B(1:100) + A(1:100)
```

To take advantage of this possibility, PFC uses a preliminary transformation called *if conversion* which attempts to transform conditional transfers of control to conditional assignments.

```
DO 100 I = 1, 100
   IF (A(I).LT.0) GO TO 100
      B(I) = B(I) + A(I)
100 CONTINUE
```

becomes

```
DO 100 I = 1, 100
   M(I) = A(I).LT.0
   IF (.NOT.M(I)) B(I) = B(I) + A(I)
100 CONTINUE
```

which can be directly converted to vector code.

This approach is not without its complexities [AKPW 83]. The conditions controlling execution of statements tend to become complex, and require sophisticated simplification, and the handling of jumps out of loops is tricky. However, the transformation is well worth the effort, because without it, loops with conditionals might well be left in sequential form.

8. Status of the Implementation

As we pointed out in the introduction, the original implementation was based upon the Parafrase compiler developed by Kuck and others at the University of Illinois [KKLW 80, KKLP 81]. We received a version of Parafrase in December of 1978, and made a number of improvements to it including the introduction of an if conversion phase and an integer expression simplifier.

Because our improved Parafrase was too slow and used an unsuitable intermediate program form, we abandoned it in January 1981, replacing it with a front end, written at Rice, that produces abstract syntax trees as an intermediate form. We then incorporated the new standardization, dependence testing, and parallel code generation phases described here.

PFC was a great improvement over our version of Parafrase (although that program has now been substantially improved at Illinois). Particularly startling was the reduction in running time. A 300-statement Fortran program took 10 minutes of IBM 370/168 CPU time using the old translator, while PFC now takes approximately 20 seconds on the same input.

PFC currently consists of about 25,000 lines of PL/I, of which about a third are comments. This figure is a bit deceiving however, since the use of macro packages like POLYLIST effected a significant compaction of the code.

PFC is implemented under the IBM MVS operating system at Rice and under VM 370 at IBM Thomas J. Watson Research Center. We are also well along on a project to produce a companion Fortran 8x compiler.

By producing an ambitious translation of sequential Fortran to parallel Fortran at surprisingly low cost, PFC has demonstrated that a significant level of vectorization can be conveniently provided by an automatic tool. Of course in specific instances, the human programmer will always be more clever than programs like PFC. However, automatic translators may eventually free the human from much of the tedious work of converting a long program and thus permit him to concentrate his creativity on the frequently executed regions of such a program.

References

[AhHU 74] A.V. Aho, J.R. Hopcroft, and J.D. Ullman, *The Design and Analysis of Computer Algorithms*, Addison-Wesley, Reading, Massachusetts, 1974.

[AllC 72] F.E. Allen and J. Cocke, "A catalogue of optimizing transformations," *Design and Optimization of Compilers*, R. Rustin, ed., Prentice-Hall, Englewood Cliffs, New Jersey, 1972, 1-30.

[AlCK 81] F.E. Allen, J. Cocke, and K. Kennedy, "Reduction of operator strength," *Program Flow Analysis: Theory and Applications* (S.S. Muchnick and N.D. Jones, editors), Prentice-Hall, New Jersey, 1981, 79-101.

[Alle 83] J.R. Allen, "Dependence analysis for subscripted variables and its applications to program transformations," Ph.D dissertation, Department of Mathematical Sciences, Rice University, Houston, Tx. April, 1983.

[AllK 82] J.R. Allen and K. Kennedy, "PFC: a program to convert programs to parallel form," Technical Report, Department of Mathematical Sciences, Rice University, Houston, Tx. March, 1982.

[AKPW 83] J.R. Allen, K. Kennedy, C. Porterfield, and J. Warren, "Conversion of control dependence to data dependence," Proceedings of the 10'th POPL, Austin, Tx. January, 1983.

[ANSI 81] American National Standards Institute, Inc., "Proposals approved for Fortran 8x," X3J3/S6.80 (preliminary document), November 30, 1981.

[Bane 76] U. Banerjee, "Data dependence in ordinary programs," Report 76-837, Department of Computer Science, University of Illinois at Urbana-Champaign, Urbana, Illinois, November 1976.

[Burr 77] Burroughs Corporations, "Implementation of FORTRAN," Burroughs Scientific Processor brochure, 1977.

[CocK 77] J. Cocke and K. Kennedy, "An algorithm for reduction of operator strength," *Comm. ACM* 20, 11, November 1977, 850-856.

[Coha 73] W.L. Cohagen, "Vector optimization for the ASC," *Proc. Seventh Annual Princeton Conference on Information Sciences and Systems*, Dept. of Electrical Engineering, Princeton, New Jersey, 1973, 169-174.

[CoDC 74] Control Data Corporation, "Control Data STAR-100 computer system hardware reference manual," Control Data Corporation publication no. 60256000, Rev. 7, 1974.

[Cray 76] Cray Research, Inc., "Cray-1 computer system reference manual," Publication 2240004, Cray Research, Inc., Bloomington, Minnesota 1976.

[Cray 80] Cray Research, Inc., "Cray-1 computer system FORTRAN (CFT) reference manual," Publication 2240009, Cray Research, Inc., Mendota Heights, Minnesota, 1980.

[DoE 79] Department of Energy, Advanced Computing Committee Language Working Group, "FORTRAN language requirements, fourth report," draft report Department of Energy, August 1979.

[FIPS 78] Floating Point Systems, Inc., "AP-120 Programmers Reference Manual," Publication 860-7319-000, Floating Point Systems, Inc., Beaverton, Oregon, 1978.

[GibK 81] C. Gibbons, and K. Kennedy, "Simplification of functions," Rice Technical Report 476-029-10, Rice University, January 1981.

[Higb 79] L. Higbee, "Vectorization and conversion of FORTRAN programs for the Cray-1 CFT compiler," Publication 2240207, Cray Research, Inc., Mendota Heights, Minnesota, June 1979.

[HinT 72] R.G. Hintz and D.P. Tate, "Control Data STAR-100 processor design," *Compcon 72, IEEE Computer Society Conf. Proc.*, September 1972, 1-4.

[Kenn 78a] K. Kennedy, "Use-definition chains with applications," *J. Computer Languages* 3, 3, 1978, 163-179.

[Kenn 78b] K. Kennedy, "A survey of code optimization techniques," in *Le Point sur la Compilation* (M. Amirchahy and D. Neel editors), IRIA, Le Chenay, France, 1978, 115-163.

[Kenn 80] K. Kennedy, "Automatic translation of Fortran programs to vector form," Rice Technical Report 476-

029-4, Rice University, October 1980.

[Kenn 81] K. Kennedy, "A Survey of Data Flow Analysis Techniques," *Program Flow Analysis: Theory and Applications* (S.S. Muchnick and N.D. Jones, editors), Prentice-Hall, New Jersey, 1981, 1-54.

[Knut 73] D.E. Knuth, *The Art of Computer Programming, Volume 1: Fundamental Algorithms*, Addison-Wesley, Reading, Massachusetts, 1973.

[Kuck 77] D.J. Kuck, "A survey of parallel machine organization and programming," *Computing Surveys* 9, 1, March 1977, 29-59.

[Kuck 78] D.J. Kuck, *The Structure of Computers and Computations*, Volume 1, John Wiley and Sons, New York, 1978.

[KKLP 81] D.J. Kuck, R.H. Kuhn, B. Leasure, D.A. Padua, and M. Wolfe, "Compiler transformation of dependence graphs," *Conf. Record of the Eighth ACM Symposium on Principles of Programming Languages*, Williamsburg, Va., January 1981.

[KKLW 80] D.J. Kuck, R.H. Kuhn, B. Leasure, and M. Wolfe, "The structure of an advanced vectorizer for pipelined processors," *Proc. IEEE Computer Society Fourth International Computer Software and Applications Conf.*, IEEE, Chicago, October 1980.

[Leas 76] B.R. Leasure, "Compiling serial languages for parallel machines," Report-76-805, Dept. of Computer Science, University of Illinois at Urbana-Champaign, Urbana, Illinois, November 1976.

[Leve 77] J.M. Levesgue, "Applications of the Vectorizer for effective use of high-speed computers,"*High Speed Computer and Algorithm Organization* (D.J. Kuck, D.H. Lawrie, A.H. Sameh editors), Academic Press, New York, 1977, 447-449.

[Mura 71] Y. Muraoka, "Parallelism exposure and exploitation in programs," Report 71-424, Dept. of Computer Science, University of Illinois at Urbana-Champaign, Urbana, Illinois, February 1971.

[Mysz 78] M. Myszewski, "The Vectorizer System: current and proposed capabilities," Report CA-17809-1511 Massachusetts Computer Associates,

Inc., Wakefield, Massachusetts, September 1978.

[Paul 80] G. Paul, private communication, 1980.

[PauW 75] G. Paul and M.W. Wilson, "The VECTRAN language: an experimental language for vector/matrix array processing," IBM Palo Alto Scientific Center Report G320-3334, Palo Alto, California, August 1975.

[PauW 78] G. Paul and M.W. Wilson, "An Introduction to VECTRAN and its use in scientific applications programming," *Proc. LASL Workshop on Vector and Parallel Processors*, University of California Los Alamos, Scientific Laboratory, Los Alamos, New Mexico, September 1978, 176-204.

[Russ 78] R.M. Russell, "The CRAY-1 computer system," *Comm. ACM* 21, 1, January 1978, 63-72.

[Site 78] R.L. Sites, "An analysis of the Cray-1 computer," *Proc. Fifth Annual Symposium on Computer Architecture*, April 1978, 101-106.

[Tarj 72] R.E. Tarjan, "Depth first search and linear graph algorithms," *SIAM J. Computing* 1, 2, 1972, 146-160.

[Towl 76] R.A. Towle, "Control and data dependence for program transformations," Ph.D. Dissertation, Report 76-788, Dept. of Computer Science, University of Illinois at Urbana-Champaign, Urbana, Illinois, March 1976.

[Wede 75] D. Wedel, "FORTRAN for the Texas Instruments ASC system," *Sigplan Notices* 10, 3, March 1975, 119-132.

[Weth 79] C. Wetherell, "Array processing for FORTRAN," Report UCID-30175, Lawrence Livermore Laboratory, Livermore California, April 1979.

[Witt 78] W.R. Wittmayer, "Array processor provides high throughput rates," *Computer Design*, March 1978.

[Wolf 78] M.J. Wolfe, "Techniques for improving the inherent parallelism in programs," Report 78-929, Dept. of Computer Science, University of Illinois at Urbana-Champaign, Urbana, Illinois, July 1978.

Part III: Multiprocessing Supercomputers

Chapter 5: Multiprocessor Systems
Chapter 6: Research Multiprocessors
Chapter 7: Multiprocessor Design Issues

PART III
MULTIPROCESSING SUPERCOMPUTERS

Research and development of multiprocessor systems are aimed at improving throughput, reliability, flexibility, and availability. A multiprocessor contains two or more processors of approximately comparable capabilities. All processors share access to common sets of memory modules, I/O channels, and peripheral devices. Most important, the entire system must have an integrated operating system that provides interactions between the processors and their programs at various levels.

Besides the shared memories and I/O devices, each processor has its own local memory and private devices. Interprocessor communication can be achieved through the shared memories or through an interrupt network. Three chapters below (5,6,7) are devoted to multiprocessor architecture, research and design issues.

A multiprocessor hardware system is organized by an interconnection structure between the memories and the processors (and between the memories and the I/O channels, if needed). Three different interconnections have been practiced in the past: time-shared common bus, crossbar switch network, and multiport memories.

Techniques for exploiting concurrency in multiprocessors include the development of parallel language features and the detection of parallelism in user programs. Multiprocessor operating systems consist of protection schemes, system-deadlock resolution methods, interprocess communication mechanisms, and various multiple processor-scheduling strategies. Parallel algorithms for multiprocessors are also in demand, in order to explore the computing power provided.

Multiprocessor systems can be divided into two classes: the exploratory systems and the commercial multiprocessors. We consider a system to be exploratory if it is developed mainly for research purposes or for dedicated missions. Commercial multiprocessors are those systems that are available in the computer market-place. Table 2 summarizes a number of milestones in the development of multiprocessor systems for both research and industrial applications.

Improved speed is only one of the motivations for using a multiprocessor computer. Enhanced reliability and availability and the promotion of resource sharing to achieve a high performance/cost ratio are also important factors in the development of multiprocessors.

The general trend in commercial machines is that high performance is achieved with multiple highly pipelined processors. The goal is to use multiple processors that operate cooperatively to solve large user problems. Most existing commercial systems have two to four processors. Only a few systems offer 16 processors as do the Tandem and the HEP. Some research multiprocessors have more than 16 processors; for example, the Cm* consists of 50 LSI-11 processors in its system.

Similarities do exist between multiprocessors and multicomputer systems, for both are motivated by the same basic goal--the support of concurrent operations within one system. However, there exists an important distinction between them based on the extent of resource sharing and cooperation in the solution of a problem.

A multiple computer system consists of several autonomous computers that may or may not communicate with each other. An example of a multiple computer system is the IBM attached support processor system. A **multiprocessor system** is controlled by one operating system that provides interaction between the processors and their programs at the process, data set, and data element levels. An example is the Denelcor's HEP system.

There are two different architectural models for multiprocessor systems. One is a

206

Table 2.　Milestones in the development of multiprocessor systems.

Year	Multiprocessor systems and key features
1960	Burroughs D-825: 4 processors and crossbar networks
1968	CDC 7600: Dual 6600s: solid-state memory
1970	Burroughs B-6700: crossbar net, Univac 1108: 3 CPUs with multiported memories
1972	IBM 370/168 MP: 2 processors Cmmp with 16 PDP-11's crossbar connected with 16 memory modules
1976	Univac 1100/80: 4 processors, Cyber-170: 2 processors connected to a central switch
1980	Cm*: a hierarchically bus-connected systems of LS-11's IBM 308X: up-to-4 processors with high-density packaging
1984	Cray X-MP: two CPUs with shared memory and I/O subsystems Denelcor HEP: up-to-16 processors sharing up-to-128 data memory modules through a packet switched network
Planned future systems	S-1 project: 16 processors connected by crossbar switched to 16 shared memories Cray-2: 4 processors Cray-3: 16 processors ETA-10: 8 processors, each having two vector pipes

tightly coupled multiprocessor and the other is a loosely coupled multiprocessor. Tightly coupled multiprocessors communicate through a shared main memory. Hence the rate at which data can communicate from one processor to the other is on the order of the bandwidth of the memory. A small local memory or high-speed buffer (cache) may exist in each processor. A complete connectivity exists between the processors and the memory. This connectivity can be accomplished either by inserting an interconnection network between the processors and the memory or by using a multiported memory.

One of the limiting factors to the expansion of a tightly coupled system is the performance degradation due to memory contentions that occur when two or more processors attempt to access the same memory unit concurrently. The interleaved main memory is suitable for multiprocessors. The degree of conflict can be reduced by increasing the degree of interleaving. However, this must be coupled with careful data assignments to the memory modules. Another limiting factor is the restricted bandwidth due to the by processor-memory interconnection network.

Three multiprocessor systems are highlighted in the following chapters as examples of current trends in supercomputing. The multiprocessor supersystems offer another dimension of parallelism, namely multitasking, which exceeds vectorization as provided by pipelined uniprocessor systems.

As specified in Table 3, the Cray X-MP represents the latest by Cray Research in the development of vector supercomputers. Denelcor offers the first large-scale, scientific, MIMD supercomputer. The S-1 system is representative of a crossbar-switched multiprocessor as developed by a federal research agency. Both the HEP and the S-1 are meant to be tightly coupled multiprocessor systems.

Table 3. Specification of several multiprocessor supercomputers.

Features	Cray X-MP (Cray Research)	HEP-1 (Denelcor)	S-1 (Livermore Nat'l Lab.)
Number of Processors	2	1-16	16
Maximum Speed	400 Mflops	3 — 150 Mips	90 — 1500 Mflops
Uniprocessor architecture and clock rate	Similar to Cray 1 with 12 pipes and 9.5 nsec clock period	MIMD pipelining with 128 processes resident per processor	Mark II A uniprocessor: highly pipelined with separate instruction/data caches and multiple I/O ports
Interprocessor — memory connection	Multiport memory, inter-CPU communication and I/O unit.	Packet switched network of 3-ported switches	Crossbar network (16 x 16)
Main Memory	32 Mbytes (64-bit words)	128 Data Memory modules	16 memory banks with a total of 16 G bytes
Extended Memory	Solid-state Storage Device (SSD) with 3-2 M words	Mass storage subsystem with 32 I/O channels	8 I/O processors (per uniprocessor) connected to mass storage units
Possible future extension	Cray 2 with 4 processors to achieve 2 Gflops	HEP-2 with a max. speed of 1 Gflops	Presently only S-1 Mark II-A is built with ECL 100 K circuits. The 16 - processor system is yet to be completed

The Cray X-MP is a high-performance multiprocessor system with two identical CPUs that share memory and an I/O subsystem. It became available in 1983. The system can execute multiprocessor jobs and concurrent but independent uniprocessor jobs. Figure 6 shows a schematic diagram of the system organization. The CPUs can communicate with each other through the inter-CPU control unit or through the shared central memory, the shared solid-state device (SSD), and the shared input/output subsystem (IOS), which is connected to external storage devices.

The central memory is constructed with of 32 Mbytes of bipolar technology to achieve a memory cycle time of 38 nsec. There are four parallel memory access ports per processor which, when combined with the faster clock cycle time, achieve more than eight times the memory bandwidth of the Cray 1. Two of the ports are for vector fetch, one is for vector write, and one is for I/O. The memory is 32-way interleaved to support both high-speed CPU and I/O operations.

The SSD is incorporated in the system to replace discs for providing large amount of data memory. This device can be used to store large datasets that are generated and manipulated repetitively by user programs. The SSD, which is available in 256 Mbytes of storage, can also be used by the system to store system programs. Maximum burst transfer rates of 10 Gbits per second can be expected. The SSD provides a significant improvement on Cray X-MP for I/O-dominated applications.

The IOS is integrated into the system to offer control and buffering capabilities for other auxiliary storage and front-end systems. A disc cache of up to 8M words can be configured in the IOS to reduce data access time. The dual CPUs could be configured as a loosely-coupled, multiprogrammed system or as a tightly-coupled, uniprogramming system.

Each CPU is enhanced from a Cray 1 processor with additional features to permit mul-

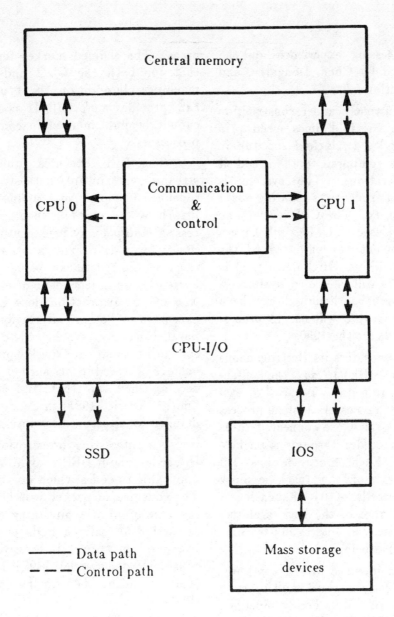

Figure 6.   Cray X-MP overall system organization. (Courtesy of Cray Research, Inc., 1983.)

tiprocessing. The basic machine cycle is 9.5 nsec. The X-MP is capable of an overall instruction issue rate of over 200 millions of instructions per second (MIPS) and can perform up to 400 Mflops on 64-bit results.

The two CPUs intercommunicate and synchronize via three clusters of shared registers. The operating system allocates the clusters to the CPU. An allocated cluster may be accessed by the CPU in either user or supervisor mode. The Cray Operating System (COS) has been designed to support concurrent independent uniprocessor jobs and multiprocessing of a single job. The Cray Fortran compiler (CFT)

allows vectorizing optimization. Front-end connections for X-MP can be the IBM/MVS, the CDC/NOS, or the NOS/BE.

The Cray X-MP guarantees chaining of linked vector operations. Compared to the Cray 1, the X-MP offers as much as a fivefold increase of the times throughput gains on a CPU combined job mix. The improvement in speed is due to two processors scheduled by the COS, a shorter clock period, a higher memory bandwidth, and guaranteed chaining.

Like the Cray 1, the X-MP is good for both short-and long-vector processing. Cray X-MP was described in Chen's article in Section 2.2. Multiprocessing experiences on the X-MP-2 are reported by Chen, Dongarra, and Hsiung (1984) in Section 5.2.

The Cray 2, currently under construction is expected to have a sixfold times speedup in scalar operations and a twelvefold speedup in vector operations as compared to the speed of the Cray 1s coperations. The system is planned to have 4 processors sharing 32M words of main memory. The CPU cycle time may be reduced to 4 nsec. The I/O will have a twentyfold improvement as compared to the current Cray 1 capability. High-density logic and memory modules will be cooled by immersion in an inert fluorcarbon liquid. It has been speculated that the Cray 3 will use 16 processors to meet the needs for the 1990s.

Denelcor, Inc., considers its Heterogeneous Element Processor (HEP) as the fifth-generation architecture today. The HEP-1 system consists of 1-16 processors (called process execution modules), which are connected to 1-128 data memory modules through a packet-switched network. Each processor has 1M words of program memory and each memory module has 128M words of 64 bits each. A functional block diagram of the HEP architecture is given in Figure 7a. Interesting features of HEP-1 are identified below.

The HEP is an intrinsic MIMD computer that can support tightly coupled multiprocessing at the process level. It is highly pipelined throughout the system, including the packet-switching network. It is the first commercially available system to use pipelining to implement multiple processes. The system allows modular growth to keep pace with growing computational demands.

It provides unlimited addressing and eliminates data dependency delays by direct internal data forwarding through the shared data memory modules. Synchronization is done by hardware. The systems use ANSI Fortran 77 with extensions. The performance of the system can increase linearly to 160 MIPS. Fifty instruction streams are allowed per processor, with a maximum of 800 user instruction streams per the entire HEP system.

The pipelined, multiple instruction stream architecture covers a wide range of application areas. The claimed market for HEP cuts into that for both the CDC and Cray Research machines. In addition, this type of architecture can provide some MIMD computations that cannot be implemented in conventional vector processors.

The HEP executes multiple instruction streams over multiple data streams in a highly pipelined fashion. An example is shown in Figure 7b, where an *add* is in progress for one process, a *multiply* may be executing for another, a *divide* for a third and a *branch* for a fourth. Because instructions being executed concurrently are independent of each other, execution of one instruction does not influence the execution of other instructions. Thus fill-in parallelism may be achieved to increase processor utilization. A single process does not achieve a speedup in such a scheme as was accomplished in the IBM 360/91 system. Smith's article (1981) in Section 5.3 contains a detailed architecture description of HEP.

An interesting observation was made by H. Jordan about HEP that MIMD parallelism is applicable to codes which do not vectorize well. The concepts of packet-switched data forwarding and of MIMD pipelining make HEP very attractive for solving PDE problems described by sparse matrices. Interested readers should consult Jordan's article (1984) in Section 5.4 for some scientific benchmark performances of HEP.

Another multiprocessor system that has potentially high performance is the S-1 project currently under development at Lawrence Livermore National Laboratory under the auspices of the U.S. Navy. The S-1 system is designed to have 16 Mark IIA uniprocessors sharing 16 memory banks through a 16x16 crossbar switch network. This is a circuit switching network, different from the buffered switching network in HEP. Each memory bank can contain as many as 2^{30} bytes of solid-state memory with a total physical address space of 16 Gbytes.

Each uniprocessor in S-1 is highly pipelined with separate program cache and data cache. Multiple I/O channels are connected to each processor. Special system instructions are developed in Mark II uniprocessors for support-

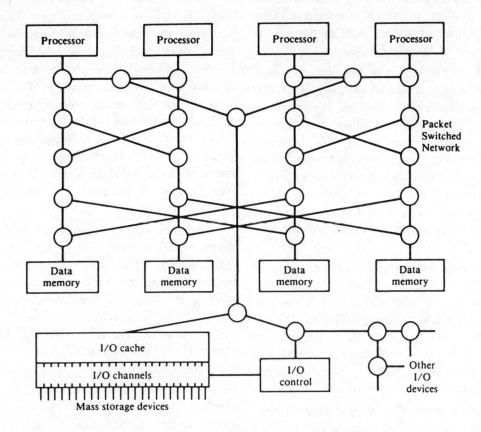

(a) The architecture of HEP with four processors.

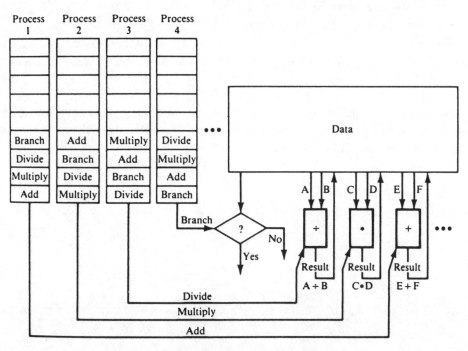

(b) MIMD processing in HEP.

Figure 7.   HEP architecture and MIMD processing. (Courtesy of Denelor, Inc., 1982.)

ing multiprocessing. This is very different from the C.mmp system, in which standard off-the-shelf PDP-11 minicomputers were used with little modification of the instruction set.

Virtual memory is another improvement of S-1 over C.mmp, as far as supporting MIMD operations is concerned. System maintenance is facilitated by connecting diagnostic processors to each uniprocessor, to the crossbar switch, and to each memory controller. The S-1 system is introduced in Widdoes article (1980) in Section 5.1. Readers may also check with the **Annual Report of the S-1 project on Architecture, Hardware, and Software** for details.

Many exploratory supercomputer systems are under development in various academic, industrial, and governmental research centers throughout the world. Carnegie-Mellon University has the C.m* project which provides a research vehicle for studying hierarchically structured processor clusters, parallel algorithms and their implementation requirements.

The construction of a large-scale multiprocessor, by the name Cedar, is under way at University of Illinois (Section 6.1). An ultra-computer prototype is presently under construction at IBM Watson Research Center in cooperation with the New York University researchers (Section 6.2).

In University of Erlangen-Nürnberg, W. Germany, the EMSY-85 multiprocessor system has been proposed for a broad spectrum of scientific applications (Section 6.3). This EMSY-85 system is evolved from the earlier EGPA system reported in Händler, et al. (1979).

The Texas Reconfigurable Array Processor (TRAC) is a research prototype machine studying a reconfigurable approach to high-speed computing (Lipovski and Tripathi, 1977). Purdue University has also several multiprocessor projects (Briggs, et al, 1982; Siegel, et al, 1981), that emphasize reconfiguration between multiple SIMD and MIMD operations. At California Institute of Technology, a group of computer scientists is developing a binary tree machine (Li and Johnson, 1983). A similar project is also in progress at the University of North Carolina at Chapel Hill.

Several design issues of multiprocessor systems are singled out by those articles included in Chapter 7. Compile-time techniques for resource management in a multiprocessing environment are introduced by Padua et al. (1980) in Section 7.1. Multicache coherence problems are addressed by Dubois and Briggs (1982) in Section 7.2.

Packet switched multistage interconnection networks are proposed by Chin and Hwang (1984) in Section 7.3. Such multipath networks are suitable for use in either control-flow multiprocessor systems or data-flow computers. The article by Stone (1977) suggests the use of network flow algorithms for multiprocessor scheduling.

For multiprocessor system control and programming issues, readers may consult the books by Enslow (1974), Satyanarayanan (1980), Wulf, Levin, and Harbison (1981), and Hwang and Briggs (1984) for detailed discussions. Parallel algorithms for multiprocessors will be treated in Part IV as will applications for supercomputers.

Chapter 5: Multiprocessor Systems

THE S-1 PROJECT:
DEVELOPING HIGH-PERFORMANCE DIGITAL COMPUTERS*

L. Curtis Widdoes, Jr. and Steven Correll

University of California, Lawrence Livermore Laboratory, Livermore, CA 94550

Abstract

Under the auspices of the U.S. Navy, we are designing and implementing a multiprocessor (the S-1) with at least ten times the computational power of the Cray-1. Our first step is to develop a general-purpose uniprocessor with a performance level comparable to the Cray-1; the multiprocessor will then be made up of 16 of these uniprocessors, sharing a main memory. The uniprocessors can be used together for large problems or separately for several smaller problems. To reduce average memory-access time, each uniprocessor has a private cache memory. We have also developed a powerful design system (SCALD) that supports extremely efficient structured design of digital logic. Using advanced compiler and verification techniques, SCALD can complete the details of a computer design starting from a high-level specification.

Introduction

Our S-1 Project has as its general goal the development of advanced digital processing technology for potential application throughout the U.S. Navy. This work involves the design and implementation of extremely high-performance general-purpose computers.

The basic goals of the S-1 Project may be divided into development-oriented and research-oriented sets.

The primary development-oriented goal is to establish methods for faster design and implementation of advanced digital processors. Our approach to this goal includes the development of a design system that supports structured computer-aided logic design and the development of automated implementation and debugging techniques.

A second development-oriented goal is to provide prototype implementations of highly cost-effective digital processors against which the Navy may measure commercial offerings. We approach this goal in three ways: by developing a durable and extensible uniprocessor instruction-set architecture (the S-1 Native Mode) that will evolve in such a manner that the developing software base is unaffected by changes in the underlying hardware, by designing a common underlying hardware structure for a class of cost-effective, high-performance S-1 Uniprocessors, and by developing a multiprocessor architecture and implementation that allows the S-1 Uniprocessors to be used in a wide variety of applications, particularly those requiring very large computing rates or high operational reliabilities.

Our primary research-oriented goal is to invent and evaluate in use the concepts and languages necessary to support practical, high-level, general-purpose digital logic design. A second goal is to provide a practical multiprocessor research environment, by implementing multiprocessor hardware with sufficient computing capability to solve real problems of interest to real users. At the same time, we intend to implement and evaluate a fundamental new multiprocessor architecture consisting of a fully-connected network of independent processors, each with a private, hardware-managed cache memory. Finally, we must invent and evaluate operating-system, language, and hardware constructs that will support the partitioning of single large problems across multiple independent processors.

The following sections divide discussion of the Project's work toward these basic goals into three categories: S-1 Multiprocessors, their constituent S-1 Uniprocessors, and the S-1 Design System that supports the design of these S-1 processors.

Multiprocessors

A multiprocessor is a network of computers that concurrently execute a number of independent instruction streams on separate data streams while closely sharing main memory. A multiprocessor design offers significant advantages over a uniprocessor design that provides an equivalent computation rate. The advantages result from the modularity inherent in a multiprocessor architecture and can be categorized as advantages of reliability, economy, and size.

The advantage of reliability has been validated by the very reliable commercial systems that handle, for example, banking transactions and computer network communications.[1] In a well-designed multiprocessor system, failure of a single module (for example, a component uniprocessor, a crossbar switch, or a memory bank) does not entail failure of the entire system. Indeed, the operating system for the S-1 Multiprocessor (called Amber) is intended to detect such module failures and automatically replace the function from the available complement of reserve modules.

Advantages of economy occur during both the design and the construction phases. The design cost per processing element is reduced asymptotically to zero as the processing element is replicated. The economy during construction is

---

*This work was performed under the auspices of the U.S. Department of Energy by Lawrence Livermore Laboratory under contract No. W-7405-ENG-48.

Reprinted from *The Digest of Papers: COMPCON S'80*, 1980, pages 282-291.

extremely important for semiconductors, since the unit replication cost of very large scale integrated-circuit chips varies nearly inversely with the replication factor, except for a small additive base cost.

Another economy is the potential reduction in the time between the design of the system and the delivery of the first operational unit. By replicating a relatively simple processing element many times and using a regular interconnection network, this time lag can be made very small; it is virtually independent of the processing power of the total system. As a result, the semiconductor technology used in a properly designed multiprocessor can be much more up to date than the technology used in a more complex processing structure. One additional economy results from the freedom of the multiprocessor designer to choose the most cost-effective uniprocessor element structure, regardless of the processing rate of the element.

Independent of these economic advantages is the advantage of size. Regardless of whether it is economical to build arbitrarily powerful uniprocessors, at some point it becomes physically impossible (with state-of-the-art technology). Multiprocessors, however, because of their modularity, can have larger processing rates. This advantage of multiprocessor structures is important because maximal computing rates will be necessary for certain applications (numerical weather prediction with its real-time constraints, for example) into the foreseeable future.

S-1 Multiprocessors

We are developing a multiprocessor that computes at an unprecedented aggregate rate on a wide variety of problems. Figure 1 is an artist's conception of the system. The S-1 Mark IIA Multiprocessor, to be implemented with second-generation S-1 Uniprocessors, each about as powerful as a Cray-1 computer, will have a computation rate

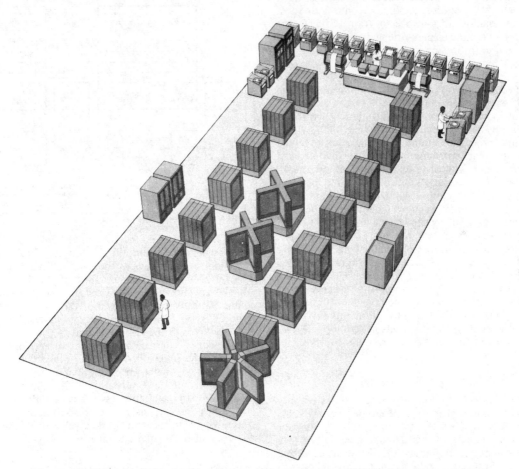

Fig. 1. The S-1 Mark IIA Multiprocessor system as it might be assembled in a computer center. The system includes 16 S-1 Mark IIA Uniprocessors (the beige and blue booklike devices arranged in two rows of 8 each along the sides of the room), 16 main memory banks (housed 4 each in the 2 blue cabinets on each side of the room near the middle of the rows of Uniprocessors), 2 Crossbar Switches (the X-shaped devices in the middle of the room) for transferring data between the Uniprocessors and the main memory, and peripheral equipment at the far end of the room, including disk drives, tape drives, printers, and a control console. The main memory shown consists of 128 million bytes but is expandable up to 16 billion bytes. The compact arrangement shown is not essential; the Uniprocessors and the memory banks may be hundreds of feet apart.

roughly ten times that of the Cray-1.* The Cray-1, in turn, has a performance two to four times greater than that of the CDC 7600 and outperforms all other existing computers in general numerical computation work.

Logical Structure

A typical S-1 Multiprocessor consists of 16 independent, identical S-1 Uniprocessors. Figure 2 shows the logical structure of the Mark IIA Multiprocessor. All 16 uniprocessors are connected to main memory through the S-1 Crossbar Switch. Each of the 16 memory banks can contain up to 1 billion bytes of semiconductor memory. Input and output are handled by peripheral processors (for example, LSI-11s); as many as eight can be attached to each S-1 Mark IIA Uniprocessor. The Synchronization Box is a shared bus connected to each member uniprocessor; one of its major functions is to transmit interrupts and small data packets from one uniprocessor to any subset of other uniprocessors in order to coordinate processing streams. Each module in an S-1 Multiprocessor is connected to a diagnostics-and-maintenance processor (an LSI-11) that allows convenient remote display-oriented maintenance and control of the multiprocessor.

All 16 S-1 Uniprocessors can execute independent instruction streams on independent data streams. Thus, all 16 uniprocessors can cooperate in the solution of a single large problem (for example, by means of a Monte Carlo-based algorithm, an increasingly popular and easily partitioned approach to physical simulation). The high-bandwidth, low-latency interprocessor communications provided by the Crossbar Switch facilitate the partitioning of physical simulation problems with little efficiency loss, but the 16 uniprocessors can also process completely independent tasks, so that each S-1 Uniprocessor might service a different set of users. Memory requests from the member uniprocessors are serviced by 16 memory banks with a aggregate maximum capacity of 16 billion nine-bit bytes. Any processor can uniformly access all of main memory through the S-1 Crossbar Switch. The programmer thus sees a huge, uniform address space, because each memory request from each uniprocessor is decoded by hardware in the Crossbar Switch and sent to the appropriate memory bank. The Crossbar Switch has a maximum peak bandwidth of more than 10 billion bits per second when all its·16 channels are transferring data simultaneously.

Cache Memory

The design of the S-1 Multiprocessor allows component uniprocessors and memory banks to be physically distributed over distances that are limited only by average bandwidth requirements (which degrade linearly with increasing cable length). To reduce the delays in accessing main memory that result from long cables, Crossbar-Switch transaction time, and relatively slow (but highly cost-effective) memory chips, each member uniprocessor contains private cache memories. These caches automatically

*Reference to a company or product name does not imply approval or recommendation of the product by the University of California or the U.S. Department of Energy to the exclusion of others that may be suitable.

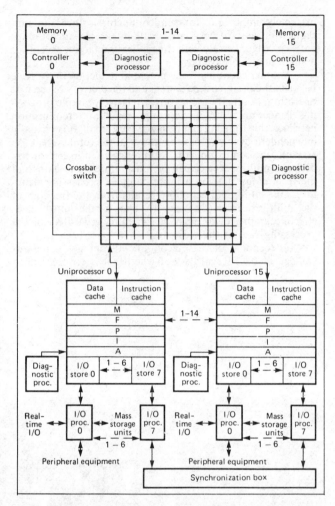

Fig. 2. The logical structure of the S-1 Mark IIA Multiprocessor, greatly simplified. Only the first and last of the 16 Uniprocessors, one of the two high-bandwidth Crossbar Switches, and the first and last of the 16 main memory banks are shown. As indicated, each of the Uniprocessors communicates with any part of the main memory through the Crossbar Switch. In the access pattern shown (dots at intersections of the Crossbar-Switch grid), each of the Uniprocessors is connected to a different memory bank. When two or more Uniprocessors request the same memory bank, the Crossbar Switch enforces queuing rules that guarantee each contender one turn in the contested memory bank before any other Uniprocessor has two. Private caches with very fast but expensive memory components within the member Uniprocessors effectively hide the combined latency of the switch and memory system.

(that is, without guidance from the programmer) retain recently referenced data and instructions in a relatively small amount of ultrahigh-performance memory, in the expectation that those data will be referenced again soon. Whenever a reference to such a retained datum or instruction is made, the information is immediately delivered directly from the cache, thus eliminating the need for a main-memory transaction. Although a similar efficiency can be realized if main memory contains a special high-speed area, such a design places on every programmer the burden of managing a variety of memory systems in order to maximize the efficiency of program execution.

The presence of caches in a multiprocessor necessarily introduces problems of cache coherence; that is, each uniprocessor must be able to read or write data in the other caches without any observable inconsistencies.[2] Without a guarantee of cache coherence, programming of certain problems in a cache-based multiprocessor would be inconceivably difficult.

The caches of the member uniprocessors of S-1 Multiprocessors are private in the sense that there are no special communication paths connecting the caches of one uniprocessor with the caches of any other uniprocessor; the cache coherence problem is therefore especially challenging. To solve it, the S-1 Multiprocessor includes a design closely related to one independently proposed in Ref. 2. A small tag is associated with each 16-word line in physical memory. This tag identifies the only member uniprocessor (if any) that has been granted permission to retain (that is, owns) the line with write access and all the processors that own the line with read access. The memory controller allows multiple processors to own a line with read access but responds with a special error flag when a request is received to grant read or write access for any line that is already owned with write access or to grant write access for any line that is already owned with read access. Any uniprocessor receiving such an access-denial response is responsible for requesting (through a simple interrupt mechanism) that other uniprocessors flush the contested line from their private caches. This procedure maintains cache coherence dynamically, and hence extremely efficiently, without requiring any effort by the programmer.

Error Detection and Correction

For reliability, all single-bit errors that occur in memory transactions are automatically corrected, and all double-bit errors are detected, regardless of whether the errors occur in the switch or in the memory system. For protection against single-point failures, the S-1 Multiprocessor allows permanent connection of multiple Crossbar Switches that can be selected electronically; the S-1 Multiprocessor can thus continue operating in the event of a single-switch failure. Furthermore, the Crossbar Switch can be configured electronically to keep a backup copy of every datum in memory, so that failure of any memory bank will not entail loss of crucial data. Each input–output peripheral processor may be connected to input–output ports on at least two uniprocessors, so failure of a single uniprocessor does not isolate any input–output device from the multiprocessor system. To make maintenance easier, each member uniprocessor, each crossbar switch, and each memory bank is connected to a diagnostic computer that can probe, report, and change the internal state of all modules that it monitors, with very high time and logic resolution.

S-1 Uniprocessors

We are developing a line of S-1 Uniprocessors to serve as the computational nodes in the S-1 Multiprocessor. The first-generation S-1 Uniprocessor (Mark I) has been implemented and evaluated in use,[3] the second-generation

(Mark IIA) machine is under way, and future generations (Mark III, Mark IV, and Mark V) have been planned in varying amounts of detail. These generations of S-1 Uniprocessors vary greatly in performance because of generation-to-generation advances in microcode, hardware structure, and implementation technology. However, all of them can conform to an identical instruction-set architecture, thereby making software transportable from uniprocessors of any earlier generation to those of any later one.

Instruction-set Architecture

The instruction-set architecture of a computer consists of those principles of its operation that a programmer without a stopwatch is capable of observing; that is, it includes no timing information. The complete hardware and microcode structure that executes an instruction-set architecture is called the implementation. The implementation of the S-1 Mark IIA Uniprocessor has been designed to allow high-speed emulation of several existing instruction-set architectures, including the DEC-10 and Univac AN/UYK-7, in addition to the S-1 instruction-set architecture (S-1 Native Mode).

It was apparent early in the S-1 Multiprocessor design that no existing instruction-set architecture was suitable to serve as the S-1 Native Mode. Because then-existing instruction-set architectures had been designed under very different technology constraints than those expected to apply to S-1 systems, they variously suffered from address-space inadequacy, insufficient operations-code space, insufficient multiprocessing-oriented features, or adverse implications for high-performance implementations.

In response to this situation, we developed the S-1 Native Mode, which is probably the most widely reviewed high-performance computer architecture ever developed. Unlike the instruction-set architectures of previous high-performance computers (for example, the CDC STAR-100 or the Cray-1), which were developed by a few designers working behind corporate proprietary screens and were then frozen, the S-1 Native Mode has been analyzed, criticized, and revised by scores of computer scientists, engineers, and application specialists in industry, academia, and Government throughout the country. It has evolved over a period of three years, during design, implementation, and operational evaluation of the S-1 Mark I Uniprocessor prototype and during design of the S-1 Mark IIA Uniprocessor.

As a consequence of this unprecedentedly extensive peer review, the S-1 Native Mode is well developed—it contains a large, consistent set of features; it is highly extensible—it can easily include new features; it is general purpose—it contains features for compiler and operating system efficiency as well as for arithmetic-intensive and real-time applications; and it is carefully tuned—it facilitates high-performance implementations of S-1 Uniprocessors and S-1 Multiprocessors.

The S-1 Native Mode allows the programmer to address uniformly, without using base registers, 2 billion nine-bit bytes of main memory, 288 times more memory than the Cray-1 (although relatively low-performance machines with large address spaces have recently appeared on the market). Indeed, it was primarily to provide for adequate address space that a 36-bit word length was adopted for the S-1 Native Mode.

Huge memories are crucial for efficient solution of large problems, such as three-dimensional physical simulations and Monte Carlo-intensive studies, which are of great current interest in a wide variety of applications that range from imcompressible fluid flow studies to acoustic ray tracing in highly stratified media. The large memory addressability of the S-1 Native Mode essentially eliminates the programming costs associated with managing multiple types of computer system storage (for example, the SCM, LCM, drum, and disk memory hierarchy of the CDC 7600, to whose efficient management major portions of the careers of some programmers have been addressed). Memory technology has advanced so far since the development of small-address-space architectures such as the CDC 7600, the DEC PDP-10, and the IBM/360 that the current production cost to the S-1 Project of a 2-billion-byte main memory using 16K-bit memory chips is less than $10 million; its long-term rate of advance is so rapid that this cost can confidently be expected to decline by almost a factor of 2 each year for the next several years.

Most software produced for S-1 systems will be written in high-level compiled languages such as the developing DOD standard language, Ada. For ease of compiler writing and for rapid, efficient execution of the compiled code, these languages require certain features in the underlying instruction-set architecture. S-1 Native Mode is compiler-oriented: it is designed to support high-level languages in general, not one high-level language in particular, and it includes the full set of operators and addressing modes necessary for a simple compiler to produce efficient code. For example, S-1 Native Mode supports expression evaluation with a unique type of 2.5-operand instruction that allows the compilation of almost all forms of arithmetic expressions without using any move instructions (instructions which simply move data from one location to another without performing logical or arithmetic operations on them).

The extent of the compiler-orientation of an instruction-set architecture can be roughly measured by counting the number of instructions necessary to represent typical high-level language programs. We have observed that the CDC 7600 requires between two and three times as many instructions to represent FORTRAN programs as does the S-1 Native Mode; the bulk of additional CDC 7600 instructions are used in addressing computations. An experiment involving seven graduate-student programmers in the Computer Science Department at the University of California, Berkeley, showed that careful hand-coding of the PDP-11 requires an average of 1.5 times as many instructions to represent a variety of high-level language programs as does the S-1 Native Mode. These and related considerations lead us to assert that no high-performance machine available today has a more compiler-oriented instruction-set architecture than the S-1 Native Mode.

The S-1 Native Mode contains unprecedentedly comprehensive floating-point semantics. Floating-point numbers can be 18, 36, or 72 bits long, using 5, 9, and 15 bits, respectively, to represent the exponent of 2, and 13, 27, and 57 bits, respectively, to represent the signed fraction. The largest format is upwards compatible with the floating-point format of the Cray-1. The 36-bit format was designed to be the workhorse for virtually all numerical applications. The 18-bit floating-point format was specially designed to support real-time signal processing at many hundred

million floating-point operations per second, but it can be highly useful in any relatively low-precision application where processing speed is at a premium (as, for example, in Monte Carlo procedures).

Compared to conventional floating-point representations, S-1 floating-point formats offer one extra bit of precision because the high-order bit of the fraction is determined from the sign and is not explicitly represented. The S-1 Native Mode also allows floating-point operations to be correctly rounded in any of several different rounding modes. For example, stable rounding minimizes expected error, and diminished-magnitude, augmented-magnitude, floor, and ceiling roundings can be used to measure the actual error developed. The S-1 Native Mode includes special floating-point symbols (not-a-number, infinities, and epsilons) which allow programs to be created and exercised that will not malfunction because of transient generation of quantities so large or small that they cannot be represented as ordinary numbers in the computer. A computer arithmetic system containing such symbols is essential for efficient use of human resources in developing and using robust computer programs.[4]

Pipelining of Instructions

Pipelining is exemplified by an automobile production line, in which a number of automobiles are in production simultaneously, each in a different stage of completion; the time between completion of construction of one automobile and the next is roughly the delay of a stage in the assembly line, rather than the time required for a single car to pass through the entire line. A stream of instructions in a pipelined computer implementation is processed in a very similar fashion.

The S-1 Native Mode was designed especially to facilitate pipelined parallelism in the fetching and decoding of instructions, the associated fetching of instruction operands, and the eventual execution of instructions. Pipelined parallelism is a conceptually simple type of parallelism that can result in extremely high computer performance levels. In general, designers of advanced instruction-set architectures for commercial computers have given little consideration to the implications of extensive pipelining, because they have developed those architectures with medium- or low-performance implementations in mind. Furthermore, pipelining has thus far been used in modern computers primarily in the execution of instructions, where it appears in the streaming of vectors of operands through pipelined arithmetic or logical operation functional units.

S-1 Uniprocessors pipeline *the preparation* and execution of instructions that specify both scalar and vector operations. Every instruction proceeds through multiple pipeline stages, including instruction preparation, operand preparation, and execution. Some stages of the pipeline, particularly those dealing with operand address arithmetic and instruction execution, necessarily have a wide variety of functions, since the pipeline must process a wide range of instructions. This variability in operation is effected through the extensive use of microcode, an architecture-defining, very low-level program that precisely specifies the operation of every pipeline stage. The variability built into the microcode-controlled pipeline facilitates high-performance emulation of other computers (for example, the Navy's Univac AN/UYK-7). The S-1 Mark I and Mark IIA Uniprocessors are the first high-performance machines to incorporate instruction-preparation pipelines fully controlled by writable microcode.

Structure and Performance

Figure 3 shows the internal logical structure of the S-1 Mark IIA Uniprocessor. The machine consists of five microengines (extremely fast, relatively special-purpose programmable controllers) operating in parallel to provide high performance. Four of the microengines form the instruction pipeline, consisting of the instruction-fetch, instruction-decode, operand-preparation, and arithmetic segments. Some segments are internally pipelined (a level of detail not shown in Fig. 3). A single microengine handles memory traffic in parallel with the operation of the instruction pipeline. A one-processor system can be configured by connecting an S-1 Mark IIA Uniprocessor directly to a memory controller; this requires neither hardware nor microcode changes.

During the design of the S-1 Mark I and Mark IIA pipelines, we made significant advances in computer technology. The Mark I introduced a new, simple branch-prediction strategy to predict the outcome of each test-and-branch operation in an instruction stream before its execution, thereby allowing subsequent instructions to be prepared without disruption. The Mark I also refined the use of dual cache memories (one for instructions, one for data) to increase total cache bandwidth. The Mark IIA allows advance computation of simple operations in early pipeline stages; this technique minimizes idling of pipeline

stages because a computation (particularly, an operand-address computation) depends on some previous result. The Mark IIA includes refined control mechanisms to coordinate the operation of multiple pipeline stages controlled by the independent programmable microengines.

The S-1 Mark IIA also employs vector operations to achieve high performance. Vector operations use multiple functional units in the pipelined arithmetic module, to achieve a peak computation rate on the S-1 Mark IIA Uniprocessor of 400 million floating-point operations per second. Any fatal error encountered during a vector operation results in a precise interrupt, so the exact location of the error can be determined by the error-handling routine; this feature is regrettably rare on existing high-performance vector processors.

Status and Plans

The S-1 Mark I was developed to be a prototype for evaluating the S-1 Native Mode and its advanced hardware and to provide the necessary computational resources for the development of the S-1 Mark IIA hardware and software. Only one S-1 Mark I has been produced; it began operating late in 1977. Constituted of 5350 ECL-10K integrated circuits, it was designed to execute floating-point arithmetic only in microcode emulation and also contained a severely reduced instruction-preparation pipeline. On a small set of floating-point-intensive scientific benchmark codes written in Pascal, the S-1 Mark I has been observed to compute between 0.3 and 0.5 times as fast as the CDC 7600, although the judicious use of hand-coded routines in crucial

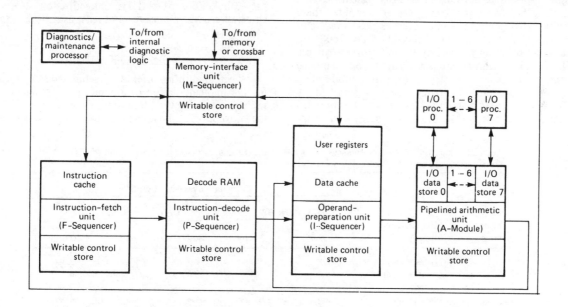

Fig. 3. The internal logical structure of the S-1 Mark IIA Uniprocessor. It consists of five distinct microengines that operate in parallel. Four of the microengines control the instruction pipeline, consisting of instruction-fetch, instruction-decode, operand-preparation, and arithmetic segments, each of which in turn is pipelined. One microengine controls memory transactions. All five microengines are controlled with writable microcode. The Uniprocessor also contains private cache memory.

inner loops on the CDC 7600 was found to increase that machine's overall performance relative to the Pascal-programmed Mark I to a speed advantage of fivefold, for our 16 000-line physical simulation code. Conversely, the maximum execution rate of the Mark I (10 million instructions per second), when combined with the powerful addressing modes and field-manipulating features of the S-1 Native Mode instruction-set architecture, permits it to execute a variety of non-floating-point-intensive codes significantly more rapidly than does the CDC 7600.

The second generation S-1 Uniprocessor, the Mark IIA, executes the same instruction set (the S-1 Native Mode) as the Mark I, but it has extensive hardware floating-point and vector operation capabilities. Its performance is expected to be comparable to that of the Cray-1 on scientific problems expressed in high-level languages such as Ada, Pascal, and FORTRAN, for just those applications in which the single-word floating-point format of the S-1 architecture is as useful as the substantially higher precision floating-point format of the Cray-1. The Cray-1 will assuredly retain primacy in high-precision, vector-intensive data processing relative to near-term S-1 Uniprocessors, since this type of computing capability cannot be justified for present or readily foreseen Navy applications, most of which stress relatively low precision, very high throughput data processing.

Table 1 shows the performance of the S-1 Mark IIA Uniprocessor compared to the CDC 7600 and the Cray-1 on several important DOE benchmark miniprograms. These miniprograms are representative of the full set used at LLL to compare the performance of advanced scientific computers; they accurately and concisely characterize the computation-intensive portions of extensive scientific code at LLL. The S-1 Mark IIA Uniprocessor computes these benchmarks at roughly the same speed as the Cray-1 and almost twice as fast as the CDC 7600. The CDC 7600 rate was measured using an optimizing compiler first available in 1974. The Cray-1 rates are based on actual performance measurements made in February, 1979, with a moderately mature optimizing and vectorizing compiler supplied by Cray Research, Inc. Although the Cray-1 executes more instructions per second than the Mark IIA, many Cray-1 instructions are expended in overhead computations. The S-1 results assume the use of 36-bit floating-point numbers, since high-precision arithmetic is often not necessary in LLL applications; however, neither the CDC 7600 nor the Cray-1 provides a low-precision floating-point format. For applications requiring high precision, the Mark IIA supports operations on the 72-bit floating-point format at roughly half the speed of operations on the 36-bit floating-point format. For low-precision applications, the Mark IIA supports operations on the 18-bit floating-point format at approximately twice the speed of operations on the 36-bit floating-point format.

The S-1 Mark IIA Uniprocessor is constituted of ECL-100K MSI circuits in performance-critical areas and ECL-10K circuits elsewhere. All Mark IIA circuits are standard, commercially available products. The transistor population of the Mark IIA's arithmetic unit alone is greater than that of the entire central processing unit of the Cray-1; gate circuit densities within this arithmetic unit are about 20 times greater than those in the Cray-1 central processing unit. The Mark IIA is in development at the present time; it is being packaged in the folded form shown in Fig. 4.

The S-1 Mark III is in an early design phase. Like the Mark I and Mark IIA Uniprocessors, the Mark III executes the S-1 Native Mode, but it is to be implemented completely in commercially available ECL-100K LSI circuits. While it will not achieve a large performance gain over the Mark IIA, it will be physically more compact because of its order-of-magnitude greater logic gate density.

We are moving as rapidly as possible toward using the technology of very large scale integrated circuits. The first generation presently planned to follow the Mark III will express the entire Mark III architecture on several VLSI chips, at a performance level at least as great as that of the Mark III.

S-1 Design System

The capabilities offered by semiconductor technology for the implementation of advanced computer designs are rapidly outpacing the capabilities developed for articulating the conception of those designs. To make best use of rapidly

Table 1. Comparison of the performances of the S-1 Mark IIA Uniprocessor, the Cray-1, and the CDC 7600. Data on Cray-1 and CDC 7600 taken from Ref. 5.

Mini-program	Miniprogram function	Computation rate, MFLOPS[a]				
		S-1 Mark IIA		Cray-1		
		Scalar[b]	Vector[c]	Scalar[d]	Vector[e]	CDC 7600
1	Hydro excerpt	9.1	59	9.3	71	5.3
2	Unrolled inner product	11	74	8.8	47	6.6
3	Inner product	8.0	65	4.4	62	4.6
5	Tridiagonal elimination	7.5	7.5	7.6	7.6	4.0
7	Equation-of-state excerpt	13	46	12.6	80	7.3

[a]MFLOPS stands for millions of floating-point operations per second.
[b]Assumes no use of vector capability.
[c]Assumes full vectorization.
[d]Obtained by turning off compiler vectorization.
[e]Obtained by turning on full compiler vectorization.

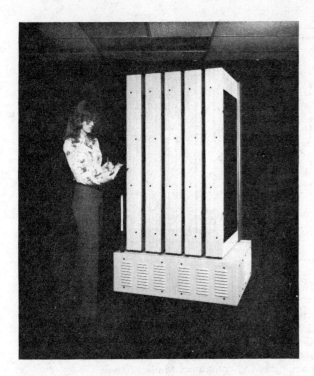

Fig. 4. The S-1 Mark IIA Uniprocessor. The package consists of identical pages. The pages unfold to expose all wire-wrap pins for maintenance. Ambient air blows up through the centers of the pages to cool the integrated circuits, which are mounted on the inside. Commercially available power supplies are mounted in the cabinet base.

improving semiconductor technology, we have developed the SCALD (Structural Computer-Aided Logic Design) System.[6]

SCALD is a graphics-based system for designing digital logic. It inputs a high-level description of a digital system and outputs magnetic tapes that are used by commercial automatic wire-wrap machines to build the hardware.

The main advantage of using SCALD is a drastic reduction in the amount of time required to design a large digital system. This reduction occurs because the designer can express his design in the same general level in which he thinks about it, freeing him from the task of actually drawing out all of the details of the logic and creating a wire list specifying its interconnection. Designs expressed in this high-level notation become much more comprehensible for all those who have to work with them—for computers, for computer designers, and for maintenance engineers. By reducing the amount of clerical work required of digital logic designers, SCALD reduces the number of designers required to execute a design project and the communication overhead per designer, thus increasing each designer's productivity and further reducing the total designer requirements of the project. Manpower savings well in excess of an order of magnitude may be realized; such savings have actually been demonstrated in practice during both the S-1 Mark I and Mark IIA design efforts.

SCALD allows designs to be recompiled rapidly when new integrated circuits become available; such circuits may simply take the place of low-level modules. Thus, a designer can quite effectively use a previous design to reduce his design time on a new project, thereby taking maximum advantage of the exponential rates of advance in component density and cost-effectiveness currently characterizing the semiconductor industry. In practice, considerable work may still be required to update a design to incorporate recent technology advances, but the required effort is likely to be much less than if the design were not expressed hierarchically.

SCALD also facilitates designing with very high accuracy, because SCALD performs design verification procedures that cannot be done by a human. Not only can SCALD verify syntactic details of the design (for example, that every gate input is connected to some output), but it can also verify that transmission lines are effectively free from signal reflections; it can certify that the logic networks defined by the designer do not contain timing errors, and it can demonstrate by simulation that the logical operation of the design is correct.

Historically, logic design has lagged far behind program design in terms of the ideals of structured design: that arbitrary modules be specified, each in terms of a few other modules, relatively independently, and that they communicate through well-defined interfaces. Logic is still typically hand-drawn by draftsmen; the specification language consists of drawings of the primitive logical elements available from integrated-circuit manufacturers and the physical connections between those logical elements. On the other hand, typical modern programming systems readily support the design of arbitrary modules (that is, routines), each in terms of a few other routines, and allow the specification of tightly structured interfaces between those routines. SCALD simply expresses these performance-proven software-engineering concepts in the world of hardware design.

SCALD consists of a set of computer programs. The Graphics Editor[7] enters drawings directly into a suitable computer, the Macro Expander compiles them, and the Router embeds them in a physical packaging system.

The Graphics Editor allows the designer to edit drawings at a graphics terminal and to print them out. The designer may create a library of shapes (macro bodies) that are generally abstractions of digital logic functions, though some may represent physical parts available from manufacturers. Each macro body is linked by name to a set of drawings, its macro definition. A macro is defined only once but may be used in the drawings any number of times. The designed system is then made up by connecting these macro bodies by lines indicating information flow. A single line in a drawing represents one or more signals (a signal vector) and may be named. Macro bodies have parameters, including parameter signal vectors. Names on signal vectors include a timing notation that allows SCALD to verify automatically (using real or estimated delays of wires and integrated circuits) that stated timing constraints will actually be satisfied by the digital logic when implemented in the specified physical package.

Figure 5 shows a sample midlevel drawing from the Mark IIA design; it represents several thousands of integrated circuits. The drawing shows the Mark IIA data cache and register file, operand queues, alignment network,

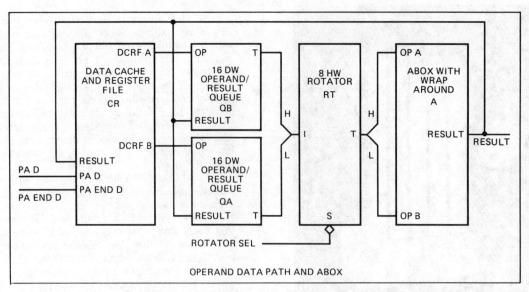

Fig. 5. A typical SCALD drawing from a middle level of the S-1 Mark IIA Uniprocessor design. This whole drawing defines a single block in a more general diagram at the next higher level. Each of the blocks in the drawing shown here is defined by a more detailed drawing at the next lower level. Thus a hierarchy is established that stretches from the most general abstraction down to the individual components of the computer. Many of these drawings can be used over and over again in the design; they are drawn once and then simply recalled by SCALD as needed. SCALD also generates a writing list, checks the design for mistakes and timing errors, and produces taped instructions for automatic wiring machines.

arithmetic module, and connections between those elements. This drawing represents the described portion of the machine accurately, in that hardware is automatically built using the drawings as a specification, but it is lacking in detail and requires definitions of its submodules for completeness.

The Macro Expander expands the design to individual integrated circuits by iteratively substituting the appropriate macro definition for each macro body in the drawings. The Macro Expander also verifies that designer-specified timing constraints are satisfied. The Macro Expander is largely technology-independent and is coded in transportable Pascal.

The Router reads an interconnection list produced by the Macro Expander and produces magnetic tapes that permit the design to be implemented by automatic and semiautomatic commercial machines. Extensive maintenance and debugging documentation is produced by the Router, which is also coded in transportable Pascal.

SCALD was used to design the S-1 Mark I and the S-1 Mark IIA. The Mark I design consisted of 211 high-level drawings (drawings used only once in the design) and 144 low-level drawings (drawings used several times). Low-level drawings form an investment in the particular technology chosen for implementation, since they have a high probability of being used again in subsequent designs. In contrast, high-level drawings represent an investment in the particular architecture being implemented and may be reused to recompile that architecture periodically into current, more cost-effective implementations. A total of two man-years was expended in the Mark I design work during an elapsed period of one calendar year.

Structured logic design consists of extending to logic design the essential power of the concepts and tools developed for simplifying the programming task; the savings in human labor expended in designing digital systems are potentially as great as those resulting from the use of compilers. Our experience has shown that SCALD has made the S-1 Mark I and Mark IIA designs more understandable, thus reducing the design efforts, enhancing design correctness, and facilitating generation of final documentation. The designs themselves serve as major portions of the final documentation because they are so readily understood; thus, the need for expensive and usually inaccurate post facto documentation has been greatly reduced. Furthermore, SCALD has increased the mutability of these designs; since macros are inherently isolated, changes in one macro definition usually require minimal changes in other parts of the design. Finally, the imposition of structure on the design and the use of computational resources in the verification task has resulted in designs of an unprecedented level of accuracy.

Summary

S-1 Project effort related to the development of high-performance computing machines is directed toward three major areas: the S-1 Multiprocessor, the S-1 Uniprocessor, and the S-1 Design System. S-1 Multiprocessors are rapidly extensible to very high powers and large memory capacities at uniprocessor cost-effectiveness levels and feature ultrareliable system performance. The S-1 Uniprocessors are general-purpose, emulation-oriented machines that are powerful and highly cost-effective and have advanced maintainability features. The S-1 Design System supports highly automated, general-purpose digital systems design and provides extensive construction and debug support of advanced computer systems.

Acknowledgments

This paper reports on work performed by the staff of the S-1 Project of the Lawrence Livermore Laboratory and the members of the software R&D teams of the Computer Science Department of Stanford University, which have operated under sub-contract to the Laboratory.

The S-1 Project has benefitted in fundamental fashions from the contributions of many people in academia, industry, and Government, and it is impossible to acknowledge our debt to even any significant fraction of them. However, it must be noted that the S-1 Multiprocessor concept is directly descended from the C.mmp Project of Carnegie-Mellon University's Computer Science Department, and we are indebted to Gordon Bell in this and many other respects. The hospitality and technical advice of Forest Baskett, Jerry Friedman, and John McCarthy of Stanford University during the Project's precarious early days was extremely valuable.

The U.S. Navy, the Project's sole sponsor, has provided enlightened and highly effective supervision in the persons of Norris Keeler, Tibor Horwath, and Joel Trimble. Edward Teller's research requirements midwifed modern scientific digital computing, and his continued keen interest in the application of computers to physical problems has profoundly impacted many related developments during the subsequent third of a century, at our Laboratory and elsewhere. His support and encouragement and that of his like-minded colleagues in our Laboratory, in the Department of Energy and Defense, and in the Congress have been crucial during the Project's inception and vital to its progress.

Notes and References

1. Such multiprocessors are described in "Tandem Non-Stop Systems," *Datapro Reports on Minicomputers*, Datapro Research Corporation, Delran, N.J. (1979), and in S. M. Ornstein *et al.*, "Pluribus—A Reliable Multiprocessor," *Proc. AFIPS 1975 Nat. Comp. Conf., Anaheim, 1975* (AFIPS Press, Montvale, N.J., 1975), vol. 44, p. 551.
2. L. M. Censier and P. A. Feautrier, "A New Solution to Coherence Problems in Multicache Systems," *IEEE Trans. Computers* C-27 (12), 1112 (1978).
3. S-1 Project Staff, *Advanced Digital Processor Technology Base Development for Navy Applications: The S-1 Project*, Lawrence Livermore Laboratory, Rept. UCID-18038 (1978).
4. J. T. Coonen, *Specifications for a Proposed Standard for Floating Point Arithmetic*, University of California, Berkeley, Electronics Research Laboratory Memorandum UCB/ERL M78/72 (1978).
5. F. McMahon, Lawrence Livermore Laboratory, private communication, October 1976.
6. SCALD is described in detail in "SCALD: Structured Computer-Aided Logic Design" and "The SCALD Physical Design Subsystem," written by T. M. McWilliams and L. C. Widdoes and published in *Proc. Ann. Design Automation Conf., 15th, Las Vegas, 1978* (IEEE, ACM, New York, 1978), p. 271.
7. D. Helliwell, *The Stanford University Drawing System*, Stanford Artificial Intelligence Laboratory, Palo Alto, California (1972).

Multiprocessing Linear Algebra Algorithms on the CRAY X-MP-2: Experiences with Small Granularity

Steve S. Chen

CRAY Research Inc.
Chippewa Falls, Wisconsin

Jack J. Dongarra†

Mathematics and Computer Science Division
Argonne National Laboratory

Christopher C. Hsiung

CRAY Research Inc.
Chippewa Falls, Wisconsin

Abstract — This paper gives a brief overview of the CRAY X-MP-2 general-purpose multiprocessor system and discusses how it can be used effectively to solve problems that have small granularity. An implementation is described for linear algebra algorithms that solve systems of linear equations when the matrix is general and when the matrix is symmetric and positive definite.

Overview of the System

'Multiprocessor' is a term that has been used for years. Our definition follows those of [8], [9], [10].

The CRAY X-MP is a follow-up to the CRAY-1S system offered by CRAY Research, Inc. The CRAY 1X-MP family is a general-purpose multiprocessor system. It inherits the basic vector functions of CRAY-1S, with major architectural improvements for each individual processor. The interprocessor communication mechanism and the provision of Solid-State Disk device (SSD) are new designs that create tremendous potential in the realm of high speed computing.

The CRAY X-MP-2 system is the first product of the CRAY X-MP family. It is a dual processor model that is housed in the identical physical chassis as that of the CRAY-1S. Each processor occupies half of the space of the original CRAY-1S. This is achieved through larger IC integration, denser packaging, and much improved cooling capacity.

The system is designed specifically to handle computation intensive and I/O intensive jobs in an efficient way. It can be used to perform simultaneous scalar and vector processing of either independent job streams or independent tasks within one job. Hardware in the X-MP enables multiple processors to be applied to a single Fortran program in a timely and coordinated manner.

All processors share a central bipolar memory (of up to 4 million words), organized in 32 interleaved memory banks. Each processor has four memory ports: two for vector fetches, one for vector store, and one for independent I/O operations. In other words, the total memory bandwidth of the two processors is up to eight times that of the CRAY-1S system. The added memory bandwidth provides a balanced architecture for memory-to-memory vector operations as typified by scientific Fortran codes.

Other features of the machine includes hardware automatic "flexible chaining" [1]. This feature allows each individual processor to have simultaneous memory fetches, arithmetic, and memory store operations in a series of related vector operations. The elimination of "chain slot time" guarantees "supervector" speed in all vector operations. It contrasts with the "fixed chaining" and unidirectional vector fetch/store of the CRAY-1S [7]. The balance between CPU speed and memory bandwidth makes the CRAY X-MP more friendly to Fortran codes. The need to resort to assembly level hand coding is drastically reduced. Other improved features of the CPU include multiple data paths and increased instruction buffer size. The machine has a faster central clock with

†Work supported in part by the Applied Mathematical Sciences Research Program (KC-04-02) of the Office of Energy Research of the U.S. Department of Energy under Contract W-31-109-Eng-38.

improved cycle time, 9.5 ns, as compared with 12.5 ns on the CRAY-1. The result is a much improved scalar and vector speed over the CRAY-1S.

In addition, a new, optional, CPU-driven Solid-State Storage Device (SSD) offers an extended central memory, an important element to buffer between fast central memory and slow disk devices. The SSD can be used as a fast-access device for large pre-stage or intermediate files generated and manipulated repetitively by user programs, or it can be used by the system for job swapping space and temporary storage of frequently used system programs.

While multiprocessing is not a new concept, the CRAY X-MP multiprocessor design is unique in many ways. It differs from most other conventional multiprocessors (See, for example, [10], [13]) in its multilevel parallelism (vectorization in the inner most loop and multiprocessing in outer loops) and its tightly coupled interprocessor communication control (sharing of registers, for example).

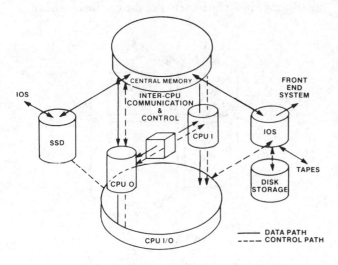

Figure 1. CRAY X-MP-2 System Organization

Additional hardware in the X-MP enables efficient and coordinated application of multiple processors to a single user program. All processors assigned to a task share a unique set of synchronization and communication registers. There are three kinds of shared registers: a set of binary semaphores, a set of index registers and a set of data registers. These registers, in cooperating with the shared central memory, allow processors to signal each other, wait for each other, and transfer data between each other. Processors can also interrupt each other through the interprocessor interrupt. These basic hardware functions provide a basic mechanism for efficient communication and synchronization between processors.

Other than hardware instructions, software support for multitasking is at the library level, where the user makes calls to ask the system for multitasking functions. Three categories of routines provide different mechanisms for parallel processing [5]. First, a task can be created to be scheduled for execution through the TSKSTART call. The calling task may wait for the termination of a created task with the TSKWAIT routine. Task is a schedulable unit that the user expects to be executed in a serial manner. It is a software entity that the programmer deals with, as the physical processor is concealed from him.

Second, tasks may need to communicate or synchronize with one another as they execute concurrently. Producing tasks may signal consuming tasks through EVPOST routine. A consuming task may wait for the signal through EVWAIT routine. As the signal is consumed, it may be reset through a EVCLEAR call.

In the third category, the LOCKON and LOCKOFF routines are used to protect the integrity of code segment or shared resources (e.g., data) among tasks.

Based on these three categories, other synchronization and communication mechanisms can be developed. Since the multitasking library employs a queueing mechanism (among others) to handle general situations, it is very flexible. Of course, the user always has the option to hand code his own synchronization routines through the use of hardware instructions.

Granularity of Tasks

A number of factors influence the performance of an algorithm in multiprocessing. These include the degree of parallelism, process synchronization overhead, load balancing, inter processor memory contention, and modifications needed to separate the parallel parts of an algorithm.

The size of the work performed in parallel, the granularity of the task, is the first critical factor in matching a parallel algorithm to an architecture which should be addressed. By granularity, we mean the amount of time the cooperating tasks execute concurrently on related codes in between synchronization points. The need to synchronize and to communicate before and after parallel work will greatly impact the overall execution time of the program. Since the processors have to wait for one another instead of doing useful computation, it is obviously better to minimize that overhead. In the situation where segments of parallel code are executing in vector mode, typically at ten to twenty times the speed of scalar mode, granularity becomes an even more important issue, since communication mechanisms are implemented in scalar mode.

Granularity is also closely related to the degree of parallelism, which is defined to be the percentage of time spent in the parallel portion of the code. Typically, a small granularity job means that parallelism occurs in an inner loop level (although not necessarily the innermost loop). In this case, even the loop setup time in outer loops will become significant without even mentioning frequent task synchronization needs.

For the CRAY X-MP family, granularity on the order of milliseconds is considered large. Many reports [1][4][5] have shown significant speedups for multitasking of large granularity problems on the CRAY X-MP-2. For example, speedups of 1.8 to 1.9 were seen when two processors were used instead of one to run a particle-in-cell code, a weather forecasting model, and a three-dimensional seismic migration code. For these problems, the multitasking library is used to implement parallel tasks. The reported successes indicate that, for large granularity codes that have high degrees of parallelism, the payoff of doing multitasking on the CRAY X-MP-2 is very significant. The use of the CRAY multitasking library to handle intertask communications proves to be very powerful. It will be interesting to see, however, how far we can push the granularity down and still get a descent speedup. As will be shown later, even when the library appears to be too coarse for small granularity tasks, the hardware capability still allows efficient handling of them. For our purposes, we would like to use matrix vector operation to test the machine behavior for small granularity tasks.

The Algorithms

Employment of automatic compilation techniques to identify parallel work [11], [12] is an approach with general applications. In linear algebra code, it may have greater pay off if we can change the algorithm to exploit structures with bigger parallel blocks.

We have chosen matrix vector operation for two reasons. First, we can easily construct the standard algorithms in linear algebra out of these types of modules. Second, matrix vector operations provides simple modules for parallel execution [2][3]. We will describe an implementation for standard LU factorization with partial pivoting for a general square matrix.

The algorithm can be described as having basically three distinct parts within a loop:

do i = 1,n
    perform the i-th matrix vector product (forms part of L)
    search for a pivot and interchange
    perform the i-th vector matrix product (forms part of U)
end

The algorithm organized storage so that the original matrix is overwritten with the factorization. The amount of work required to perform the factorization is approximately $2/3n^3$ floating point operations (here we count both additions and multiplications as operations). The factored matrix can then be used to solve systems of equations. In order to maintain stability in the algorithm,

a partial pivoting scheme is used. This helps in avoiding problems with small divisors which can cause inaccurate computations. The pivot is chosen to be the element of largest absolute value in a column. The method used is a simple variant of Crout reduction [6], but the algorithm has been expressed in terms of modules that are easy both to understand and to implement.

The algorithm described above allows for a number of alternatives for parallel implementation. That is, the available processors can be assigned to each of the three steps, allowing for multiprocessing within each. This avenue has not been investigated since the pivoting does not take as much time as the other steps. Instead, each processor will be given the task of performing one of the matrix vector operations concurrently. The algorithm can be easily modified so each matrix vector operation is independent and can proceed in parallel. The pivoting is handled by one of the two processors in a sequential fashion.

Depicted graphically, the processing of the matrix by the algorithm at the ith stage would look like the following (the matrix factors overwrite the original matrix):

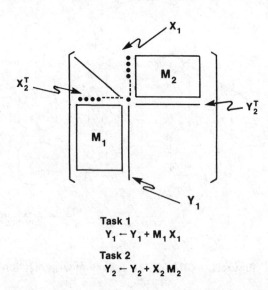

Task 1
$Y_1 \leftarrow Y_1 + M_1 X_1$

Task 2
$Y_2 \leftarrow Y_2 + X_2 M_2$

The algorithm is modified slightly to allow independent operations to be performed in parallel. The modified algorithm in no way increases the number of operations or complexity over the original algorithm. The modified algorithm just rearranges the computation within the loop to expose independent operations. The resulting modified algorithm is of the following form:

perform the 1-st matrix vector product
do i = 1,n-1
    search for a pivot and interchange
    perform the i-th vector matrix product
    perform the (i+ 1-)st matrix vector product
end
perform the n-th vector matrix product

It is now easy to see how to partition the work between

two processors: each matrix vector operation within an iteration is independent of the other. The two cooperating tasks need to synchronize $2(n-1)$ times during the course of the calculation (once before a task is started and once after). There is, however, a slight imbalance in the work of each task. At the ith step, the amount of work for each task is $O((n-i+1)i)$ and $O((n-i)i)$ operations.

To perform the synchronization between tasks, we have used task control (TSKSTART) to start a second task before the LU decomposition routine is entered. This task waits until it is directed to start up. Event control (EVPOST, EVWAIT, and EVCLEAR) is used to start and synchronize the work within the algorithm.

Table 1 describes the performance for this implementation of LU decomposition. The column labeled "Degradation from code change" reflects the loss of performance when the sequential algorithm was restructured to separate independent tasks. The numbers are obtained by running the original algorithm and the modified algorithm using no multitasking features on a single processor and taking the percentage difference. Measurements were also made of the total time spent in the parallel portion of the algorithm. As expected, small order matrices consume a greater percentage of time in non-parallel parts than do larger matrices. Even for matrices of order 50, however, over 75% of the time is used in the parallelizable portion.

We also measured the speedup of the algorithm when two processors were used. Table 2 shows the comparison between the modified (but without multitasking mechanism) one processor version and the multitasked two processor version. The column labeled "Mean granularity" is the average time spent in each of the matrix vector calls for that particular order problem. In other words, it is the average time in between synchronization calls.

The "Optimal" column is an attempt to filter out the time required to synchronize the processors and the time introduced by memory contention caused by multitasking on the two processors. These numbers were generated by running the program twice. The first run was a sequential process, using no multitasking constructs. In the second run the call to the shorter of the two parallel tasks was removed; thus, in some sense, this is the best situation (the calculation, of course, does not produce the correct results, but it provides a good measure of the overhead). The third column is the result of using the standard multitasking routines in the Multitasking (MT) library. As an alternative, there are assembly language (CAL) routines that uses hardware instruction directly. These CAL routines performs minimum synchronization function required by the code and is faster than the general purpose multitasking library routines.*

With this algorithm the work partition is well matched for two processors. The overhead in multitasking is essentially wiped out as the problem size increases and for small problems it is not a great penalty. The implementation comes very close in the limit to attaining the optimum performance.

We now focus on another algorithm for dealing with a system of equations where the matrix is symmetric and positive definite: Cholesky factorization. The algorithm can again be described in terms of a matrix vector operations, but in this case because of symmetry only half the matrix is referenced.

Table 1. Parallel Version of LU Decomposition

n	Degradation from code change	Percentage of parallel code
50	6.5%	75.1%
100	4.9%	82.0%
300	2.0%	87.5%
600	0.7%	97.0%

Table 2. Speedup of Algorithm on 2 Processors vs 1 Processor

n	Optimal	MT library calls	MT CAL calls	Mean Granularity
50	1.44	0.86	1.39	40 μsec
100	1.57	1.05	1.54	66 μsec
300	1.77	1.60	1.79	250 μsec
600	1.91	1.80	1.86	800 μsec

---

*The MT Library routines keep track of additional information on the activities of other tasks. They are better suited for larger and more tasks and are quite flexible for different programming styles. For this particular small granularity job that information is not needed, hence the CAL mechanism is more amenable. The difference in the implementation is $O(1)$ clocks for the CAL version and $O(100)$ to $O(1000)$ clocks for the multitasking library, depending on mechanism used.

As before, we can graphically describe the algorithm at the ith stage as follows:

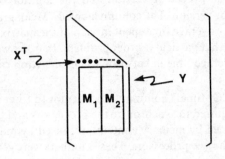

Task 1
$$Y_1 \leftarrow M_1 X$$
Task 2
$$Y_2 \leftarrow Y_2 + M_2 M_2 X$$
Then
$$Y \leftarrow Y_1 + Y_2$$

In this case, the algorithm does not divide naturally into two parts as in the previous algorithm. To distribute the work between the processors, we take the naive approach of just splitting the matrix vector operation in half, letting one processor take the left half and the other processor the right half, and then put the two parts back in a sequential part. Table 3 shows the results.

Table 3. Parallel Version of Cholesky Decomposition

n	Degradation from code change	Percentage of parallel code
50	33.1%	80.2%
100	24.2%	85.4%
300	8.0%	91.9%
600	3.5%	96.1%

As before, the percentage given here is for the modified code before multitasking mechanism is put in. The degradation in code performance is the result of the additional subroutine calls to perform the matrix vector product and the fact that one more work array has to be initialized and added to the other half in each iteration. In the following table, the modified (but without multitasking mechanism) one processor version is compared against the multitasked two processor version. Results are shown in Table 4.

As in the previous example, the improvement is substantial when two processors are used to partition the work and perform the task. For large orders, the parallel program reaches the optimal rate of speedup.

This experiment is relevant to the case when there are more than two processors. The matrix vector operation will then be split across the matrix in a similar fashion as done here. Perhaps going to a block matrix scheme to achieve the desired number of parallel tasks. We expect to observe the same trend when we can perform a similar experiment with more processors.

Note that there is a certain amount of fluctuation in between runs on the CRAY X-MP depending on background activities. The numbers we present here should be given an 1-3% tolerance.

Conclusions

The multitasking concept on the CRAY X-MP-2 has been shown to be advantageous in solving problems with relatively large granularities (that is, when there is more than one millisecond of computation that can be performed in parallel between synchronization points).

For problems with small granularity with a reasonable degree of parallelism that can be exploited, at least from the standpoint of linear algebra solvers where the granularity is in the order of microseconds, the situation can be handled just as efficiently. In general, the main sources of overhead (other than synchronization, load imbalance and code change) are memory contention and operating system service. The speedup figures of the examples presented here show that the interference from these two factors is insignificant. Our experience demonstrates that multitasking with small granularity jobs is very promising on the CRAY X-MP-2.

In the anticipation of more processors, it will be interesting to see the performance speedup for these small granularity problems through the use of more processors. As we pointed out earlier, the overhead incurred by synchronization, especially by using hardware instruction directly, is minimal in this size of problems. The deciding factor in performance will eventually be the degree of parallelism of the code.

For the LU factorization code, the degree of parallelism is about 61.1% for n=50 and 95.3% for n=600. The anticipated speedup by using four processors should be approximately 1.7 for n=50 and 3.5 for n=600.

Table 4. Speedup of Algorithm on 2 Processors vs 1 Processor

n	Optimal	MT Library calls	MT CAL calls	Mean Granularity
50	1.67	0.76	1.56	30 μsec
100	1.74	0.94	1.54	45 μsec
300	1.85	1.52	1.85	130 μsec
600	1.93	1.80	1.92	400 μsec

For the Cholesky code, the degree of parallelism is about 80.2% for n=50 and 96.4% for n=600. The anticipated speedup by using four processors should then be 2.4 for n=50 and 3.6 for n=600.

References

[1] S.C. Chen, "Large-scale and High-Speed Multi-rocessor System for Scientific Applications-CRAY-X-MP-2 Series," *NATO Advanced Research Workshop on High Speed Computation,* Nuclear Research Center, Julich, West Germany, June 1983.

[2] J.J. Dongarra and R. Hiromoto, "A Collection of Parallel Linear Equations Routines for the Denelcor HEP," *ANL/MCS-TM-15,* September 1983.

[3] J.J. Dongarra and S.C. Eisenstat, "Squeezing the Most out of an Algorithm in Cray Fortran," *ANL/MCS-TM-9,* May 1983.

[4] C.C. Hsiung and Werner Butscher, "A New Numerical Seismic 3-D Migration Model on the CRAY X-MP," *SIAM Conference on Parallel Processing and Scientific Computing,* Norfolk, VA, 1983.

[5] John L. Larson, "An Introduction to Multitasking on the CRAY X-MP-2 Multiprocessor," to appear in *IEEE Computer.*

[6] G.W. Stewart, *Introduction to Matrix Computations,* Academic Press, New York, 1973.

[7] P. M. Johnson, "An Introduction to Vector Processing," *Computer Design,* Vol. 17, No. 2, 289-97, Feb. 1978.

[8] J. L. Baer, "A Survey of Some Theoretical Aspects of Multiprocessing." *ACM Computing Surveys,* vol. 5, no. 1, March 1973, pp. 31-80.

[9] P. H. Enslow, ed., *Multiprocessors and Parallel Processing,* Wiley-Interscience, New York, 1974.

[10] P. H. Enslow, "Multiprocessor Organization." *ACM Computing Surveys,* vol. 9, no. 1, March 1977, pp. 103-129.

[11] D. A. Padua, D. J. Kuck, and D. H. Lawrie, "High-Speed Multiprocessors and Compilation Techniques." *IEEE Trans. on Comp.,* C-29, Sept. 1980, pp. 763-776.

[12] D. J. Kuck, R. H. Kuhn, D. A. Padua, B. Leasure, and M. Wolfe, "Dependence Graphs and Compiler Optimizations." *Proc. 8th ACM Symp. Principles Programming Languages,* Jan. 1981, pp. 207-218.

[13] K. Hwang and F. A. Briggs, *Computer Architecture and Parallel Processing,* McGraw-Hill, New York, 1984.

Architecture and applications of the HEP multiprocessor computer system

Burton J. Smith

Denelcor, Inc., 14221 E. 4th Avenue, Aurora, Colorado 80011

Abstract

The HEP computer system is a large scale scientific parallel computer employing shared-resource MIMD architecture. The hardware and software facilities provided by the system are described, and techniques found to be useful in programming the system are also discussed.

Introduction

The HEP computer system[1] is a large scale scientific parallel computer employing shared-resource MIMD architecture[2]. In this particular implementation, the processors are pipelined to support many concurrent processes, with each pipeline segment responsible for a different phase of instruction interpretation. Each processor has its own program memory, general purpose registers, and functional units; a number of these processors are connected to shared data memory modules by means of a very high speed pipelined packet switching network. The extensive use of pipelining in conjunction with the shared resource idea is synergistic in several useful and important ways, and results in a very flexible and effective architecture. For example, the switch used to interconnect processors and memories is modular, and is designed to allow a given system to be field-expanded. The increased memory access times that result from greater physical distances can be compensated for by using more processes in each processor because the switch is pipelined.

An overall block diagram of a typical HEP configuration is shown in Figure 1. The switch network shown has 28 nodes; it interconnects four processors, four data memory modules, an I/O cache module, an I/O control processor, and four other I/O devices. Systems of this kind can be built to include as many as 16 processors, 128 data memory modules, and 4 I/O cache modules. Each processor performs 10 million instructions per second (MIPS), and the switch bandwidth is 10 million 64 bit words per second in every network link. Data memory module bandwidth is 10 million 64 bit words per second, and each I/O cache supports sequential or random access I/O at sustained rates of 32 million bytes per second.

The remainder of this paper discusses the hardware and software architecture of the system. An overview will be given of each of the major components of the system, followed by a programmer's view of the facilities provided by these components.

Processor and data memory

A simplified diagram of the HEP processor internal organization is shown in Figure 2. The process status word (PSW) contains the program counter and other state information for a HEP process; these PSW's circulate in a control loop which includes a queue, an incrementer, and a pipelined delay. The delay is such that a particular PSW cannot circulate around the control loop any faster than data can circulate around the data loop consisting of register memory and the function units. As the program counter in a circulating PSW increments to point to successive instructions in program memory, the function units are able to complete each instruction in time to allow the next instruction for that PSW to be influenced by its effects. The control and data loops are pipelined in eight 100 nanosecond segments, so that as long as at least eight PSW's are in the control loop the processor executes 10 million instructions per second. A particular process cannot execute faster that 1.25 million instructions per second, and will execute at a lesser rate if more than eight PSW's are in the control loop.

The PSW contains a 20 bit program counter to allow for program memory configurations ranging from 32K to 1024K words. Each instruction in program memory is 64 bits long, and typically consists of an opcode and three register memory addresses. These addresses can be modified by the addition of an index value from the PSW to allow reentrant programming. The register memory consists of 2048 general purpose 64 bit registers, augmented by a 4096 location constant memory. Constant memory may only be modified by supervisor processes.

One of the function units, the scheduler function unit (SFU), is responsible for implementing load and store instructions to transmit data between register memory and data memory. When such an instruction is executed, the SFU sends a switch message packet containing a 32 bit data memory address, a return address identifying both processor and process, and 64 bits of data if a store instruction was executed. The SFU also removes the process that executed the instruction from the control loop, and does not reinsert it until a response packet is received from the switch. When that response packet arrives, the SFU writes the data portion of the response in the appropriate register if a load instruction was executed. In order to perform these functions, the SFU is equipped with a queue similar to the queue in the control loop of the processor proper, and a process migrates freely between these two queues as it initiates and completes data memory reference instructions.

The various function units of the HEP processor support the data types shown in Figure 3. The floating point formats are sign-magnitude and use a seven bit, excess 64 hexadecimal exponent. Integer formats are twos complement. The various precisions for each data type are implemented by loading and storing partial words in data memory using either the leftmost or rightmost part of the register. In addition, load instructions can specify sign extension instead of zero extension for right justified partial word load instructions.

The floating point operations implemented by the processor are floating point add, subtract, multiply, divide, and floating point compare instructions that optionally produce integer 1, floating point 1.0, or a 64 bit vector of all 1's as "true" values and zero as "false" values. Unnormalized floating point add and subtract are also implemented, as are conversion instructions between floating point and integer (the Fortran functions FLOAT, INT, and AINT). Integer functions are add, subtract, multiply, arithmetic shift, and compare instructions analogous to those for floating point. Both halves of the 128 bit twos complement product of two integers are available. Bit vector instructions include all sixteen Boolean functions, logical and circular shifts, instructions which return the numeric bit position of the leftmost "1" or "0" in a register, and instructions which set or reset a bit at a given numeric position in a register.

The control instructions available provide not only for the loading, storing and modification of the executing PSW to implement conditional branches and subroutine calls, but also for the conditional creation and termination of processes. These latter functions are performed by ordinary (unprivileged) instructions, and allow the user to control the amount of concurrency with very low overhead. A supervisor call instruction allows user processes to create supervisor processes, which in turn may execute privileged instructions to manage the user processes and perform I/O.

Cooperating parallel processes must have some way of synchronizing with each other to allow data sharing. In HEP, this facility is provided by associating an access state with each register memory and data memory location. In data memory, the access states are "full" and "empty"; a load instruction can be made to wait until the addressed location is "full" and indivisibly (i.e., without allowing an intervening reference to the location) set the location "empty". Similarly, a store instruction can wait for "empty" and then set "full" at any location in data memory. In register memory, an instruction can require that both sources be "full" and the destination "empty", and then set both sources "empty" and the destination "full". To ensure the indivisibility of this kind of operation, a third access state, "reserved", is set in the destination register location when the source data are sent to the function units, and only when the function unit stores the result is the destination set "full". No instruction can successfully execute if any of the registers it uses is "reserved".

A process failing to execute an instruction because of improper register access state is merely reinserted in the queue with an unincremented program counter so that it will reattempt the instruction on its next turn for execution. A process executing a load or store instruction that fails because of improper data memory access state is reinserted in the SFU queue and generates a new switch message on its next attempt.

One simple way to exploit the parallelism available in HEP is to run several independent programs simultaneously. To protect independent programs from each other, base and limit registers in program memory, register memory, and data memory are associated with processes. A set of processes having the same protection domain (the same base and limit register values) is called a task. HEP support up to seven user tasks and seven corresponding supervisor tasks in each processor. When a user process executes a create instruction, the new process runs in the same task as the originating process; privileged instructions exist to allow supervisors to create processes in any task or to kill all of the processes in a task.

A HEP job consists of one or more tasks, normally intended to execute on a like number of processors. The tasks making up a job have disjoint allocations in program and register memory, but an identical allocation in data memory to allow them to share data and synchronize. Supervisor calls are used by a process in one task to create a process in a different task of the same job. When a job is submitted to the system, the user specifies the maximum number of processes that will ever be active in each task; the operating system only loads the job when it can guarantee that there are enough processes available in each processor. The maximum number of user processes supported by a processor is 50, and these may be distributed in any way whatsoever among the seven (or fewer) user tasks.

Switch

The HEP switch is a synchronous, modular packet switching network consisting of an arbitrary number of nodes. Each node is connected to its neighbors (which may be processors, data memory modules, or other nodes) by three full-duplex ports. Each node receives three message packets on each of its three ports every 100 nanoseconds, and attempts to route the messages in such a way that the distance from each message to its addressed destination is reduced. To accomplish this, each node has three routing tables, one per port, which are initialized when the system is initialized. The tables are indexed by the destination address and contain the identification of the preferred port out of which the packet should be sent.

When a conflict for a port occurs, the node does not enqueue messages; instead, it routes all messages immediately to output ports. It is the responsibility of the neighbors of the node to make sure that incorrectly routed messages eventually reach their correct destinations. To help accomplish this, each message contains a priority which is initially 1 and is incremented whenever a message is routed incorrectly. In a conflict between messages of differing priority, the message with the highest priority is routed correctly. As a consequence, devices connected to the switch must immediately reinsert arriving messages not addressed to them in preference to inserting new messages.

Empty messages are just those of priority zero; zero priority messages do not increase in priority and always lose conflicts. Also, since the ports of the switch nodes and the devices connected to it are full duplex, an Eulerian circuit of the switch is guaranteed to exist. Such an Eulerian circuit traverses every port exactly once in each direction. Packets with the maximum priority of 15 are sent on such an Eulerian circuit, independent of destination address, to ensure that no conflicts between two of these messages occur. When a priority 15 message eventually reaches its addressed destination, it is recognized and removed from the switch in the normal manner. Like the routing table data, the Eulerian circuit information is loaded into each switch node when the system is initialized.

Each switch node checks the parity of the incoming messages, and also checks that the routing it performs is a permutation of the ports. If a check fails, the switch node signals the diagnostic and maintenance subsystem of the HEP that an error has occurred. The failing port or node, or a failed processor or memory for that matter, can be removed from the system just by reprogramming the routing tables to reflect the reduced configuration. To avoid splitting the system in half, the graph of the switch must be at least biconnected; that is, there must exist two disjoint paths from any node to any other. If the port connecting a processor or a memory to the switch fails in either direction, the effect is the same as if the processor or memory itself fails.

The propagation delay for a message in the switch is 50 nanoseconds for each port traversed. The pipeline rate is one message per 100 nanoseconds per port. To ensure that message routing conflicts are synchronized, the switch must be two-colorable, so that messages conflict at nodes of one color on even multiples of 50 nanoseconds and at the other color on odd multiples. Excepting this constraint, the graph of the switch is totally arbitrary. Adjacent nodes may be separated by up to four meters of connecting wire to allow a great deal of flexibility in system configuration. A HEP system may be field-expanded by adding processors, memories, and switch nodes up to the maximum allowed.

I/O facilities

The HEP High Speed I/O Subsystem (HSIOS) includes from one to four I/O cache modules, each of which serves as a buffer between the switch and 32 I/O channels. Each I/O channel can support transfer rates up to 2.5 million bytes per second. The I/O cache supports this transfer rate by all channels simultaneously, and can concurrently transfer 80 million bytes per second via its switch port for a total bandwidth of 160 million bytes per second. An I/O cache can range in size from 8 million to 128 million bytes in 8 million byte increments, so that the maximum amount of I/O cache memory implementable in a single HEP system is 512 million bytes. The reason for this large amount of memory is to allow a large page size to be used in conjunction with a large number of disks or tapes. The large page size (40 kilobytes nominal) means that mechanical delays can be made insignificant compared to data transfer times to increase channel utilization, and the large number of channels allows data to be distributed across many disks to provide high I/O bandwidth through the use of parallelism. The distribution of data is provided for by interleaving logical records among many files, one file per disk, and is accomplished not by the file system itself but by the library I/O routines that the user calls. In this way, the management of distributed data is entirely under the user's control, allowing him to exchange reliability for speed as required by his application.

The I/O channels are controlled by an I/O control processor (IOCP). The IOCP is interrupted both by the channels, when I/O operations are completed, and by arrivals of switch messages from supervisor processes running in the processors. The function of the IOCP is to schedule the I/O requests from the supervisors on the channels. To a supervisor, the IOCP-switch interface appears as a sequence of special memory locations in the data memory address space, and an I/O request is made by storing the request at one of these special locations. When the switch message arrives at the IOCP-switch interface, the IOCP services the interrupt by acquiring the message from the interface and enqueueing it internally on a queue served by the I/O channel that was requested. When the request reaches the head of the queue, it is serviced; on completion, a response message is loaded into the switch interface and sent back to the processor from which the request came. The effect seen by the supervisor process itself is extremely simple; a page I/O request was made and completed by executing a store instruction. The fact that the store instruction may have taken several milliseconds to execute has no effect on the performance of the processor if enough processes remain in the control loop.

When a file is opened, the number of cache frames allocated to the file may be specified as a parameter (the default quantity is 2). Another parameter specifies the sequential direction (forward or backward). All data transfer instructions perform sequential I/O in the specified direction, and the supervisor handling the requests attempts to "read ahead" and "write behind" the pages surrounding the current file position. To accomplish random I/O, a separate command is implemented to allow the current file position to be changed. This feature allows caching of data to proceed concurrently with user processing.

A HEP file consists of a header page and zero or more data pages. The header is kept in the I/O cache as long as the file is open, and contains either the data itself or pairs of pointers to the disk locations of the data pages and the cache frames holding those pages, if any. Since all pages are the same size, both disk and cache space allocation are performed using bit tables and are extremely fast; this is an important consideration when a large number of supervisor processes are all attempting to allocate space in parallel. To the user, a file appears to be a randomly addressable sequence of records or words, and there are no "access methods" provided by the file system itself.

When a user process executes a supervisor call to perform I/O, the supervisor process first computes the page or pages containing the data from the current file position and from the amount of data to be transferred. It then verifies that those pages are in the cache, requesting them, from the IOCP as necessary. Next, it transfers the data between the cache and the user's buffer, and changes the current file position based on the sequential direction (forward or backward). Finally, the supervisor schedules page "write behind" and "read ahead" with the IOCP as required, and returns to the user without waiting for the IOCP. If a page was never modified, it is not written on the disk by "write behind". Moreover, a reference count is maintained for each cached page and for the file as a whole to allow a file to be multiply opened by a large number of processes. A page is actually uncached only when its reference count is zero, and the file header itself is uncached when the file reference count is zero.

Fortran extensions

Two kinds of extensions were added to HEP Fortran to allow the programmer to write explicit parallel algorithms. The first class of extensions allows parallel process creation. In HEP Fortran, a CREATE statement, syntactically similar to a CALL, causes a subroutine to run in parallel with its creator. The RESUME statement, syntactically like RETURN, causes the caller of a subroutine to resume execution in parallel with the subroutine. If a subroutine was CREATEd, a RESUME has no effect, and a RETURN causes the termination of the process executing the subroutine if the subroutine was CREATEd or if it previously executed a RESUME.

The second extension allows the programmer to use the access states provided by the HEP hardware. Any variable whose name begins with the character "$" is called an asynchronous variable, and has the property that an evaluation of the variable waits until the associated location is "full" and sets it "empty" while fetching its value. An assignment to the variable waits until the variable is "empty" and then sets it "full" while storing the new value. A PURGE statement is used to unconditionally set the access state to "empty".

HEP Fortran generates fully reentrant code, and dynamically allocates registers and local variables in data memory as required by the program. For example, it is often useful to place a CREATE statement in a loop so that several parallel processes will execute identical programs on different local data. An example is shown in Figure 4; in this instance, the program creates NPROCS-1 processes all executing subroutine S, and then itself executes the subroutine S by calling it, with the result that NPROCS processes are ultimately executing S. The parameter $IP is used here to identify each process uniquely. Since parameter addresses rather that values are passed, $IP is asynchronous and is filled by the creating program and emptied within S. This prevents the creating program from changing the value of $IP until S has made a copy of it. The asynchronous variable $NP is used to record the number of processes executing S. When S is finished, $NP is decremented, and when the creating program discovers that $NP has reached zero, all NPROCS processes have completed execution of S (excepting possibly the RETURN statement).

HEP programming

The facilities provided by the HEP hardware and software are clearly well suited to pipelining as a means of parallel algorithm implementation. The access states "full" and "empty" can be viewed as a mechanism for passing messages between processes using single-word queues. It is also clear that a location can be used to implement a critical section merely by requiring processes to empty the location upon entry and fill it upon exit. Other common synchronization mechanisms can be implemented using similar techiques. Processes can be dynamically initiated and terminated to avoid busy waiting.

One frequently occurring situation in parallel programming involves the computation of recurrences of the form

$$X = X \text{ op } Y$$

where op is commutative and associative and Y does not depend on X. One example occurs in the use of $NP in Figure 4; another obvious example is vector inner product. The difficulties with merely writing

$$\$X = \$X \text{ op } Y$$

are twofold. First, all processes are competing for access to $X and interfere with each other; second, the final value of $X often must be made available to the various processes in some independent way, perhaps involving another recurrence similar to the recurrence for $NP in Figure 4.

One attractive method which avoids these difficulties requires log P locations for each of the P processes. The method simultaneously computes the final value of X and broadcasts it to the P processes in time $O(\log P)$. The idea is to implement an appropriate interconnection network (in software) that has the required computational property at each element. In this case, the property required is that the two identical element outputs be the result of applying op to the two inputs. One HEP Fortan program to accomplish this task is shown in Figure 5 with op = + and with a Staran flip network[3] interconnection.

Notice that since the function used to compute K from I is always a bijection, there is no conflict for the elements of $A by the processes. That is, only one process is attempting to fill a given location in $A and only one process is attempting to empty it. Overtaking by processes is not possible because of this fact. In addition, the same array $A can be reused immediately to perform a different function (e.g., global minimum) as long as the same network topology is used. Analogous techniques, sometimes requiring other network topologies, can be used to permute the elements of X, to sort X, to perform fast Fourier transforms, and so forth.

Another important HEP programming technique allows processes to schedule themselves. In the simplest case, a number of totally independent computational steps is to be performed that significantly exceeds the number of processes available; moreover, the execution time of the steps may be widely varying. The self-scheduling idea is to allow each process to acquire the next computational step dynamically when it finishes the previous one. In a more complex situation involving dependencies and priorities, the processes might perform a significant amount of computation in scheduling themselves, but in most cases the method is quite efficient. Figure 6 shows an example of an ordinary DO loop in which all iterations are presumed independent; Figure 7 is a parallel version of Figure 6 which uses self-scheduling. One of the most attractive benefits of self-scheduling a loop is that there is no need to worry about poor process utilization resulting from an unsatisfactory a priori schedule.

235

Conclusions

The HEP computer system represents a unique and very flexible architecture. First, its modularity is exceptional even for an MIMD computer. Second, the availability of a very natural synchronization primitive at every memory location allows the programmer a large amount of freedom in developing parallel algorithms. Finally, a mechanism is provided to allow the user to control the number of processes dynamically in order to take advantage of varying amounts of parallelism in a problem.

References

1. Smith, B.J., "A Pipelined, Shared Resource MIMD Computer,"Proceedings of the 1978 International Conference on Parallel Processing, pp. 6-8.
2. Flynn, M.J., "Some Computer Organizations and their Effectiveness, IEEE Transactions on Computers, Vol. 21, pp. 948-960 (Sept. 1972).
3. Batcher, K.E., "The Flip Network in Staran," Proceedings of the 1976 International Conference on Parallel Processing, pp. 65-71.

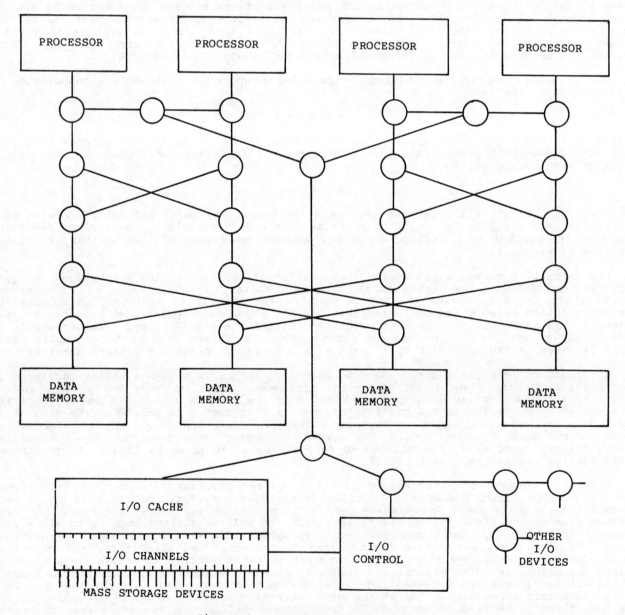

Figure 1.   A typical HEP system

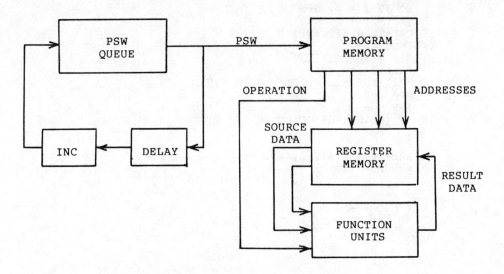

Figure 2. Simplified HEP processor

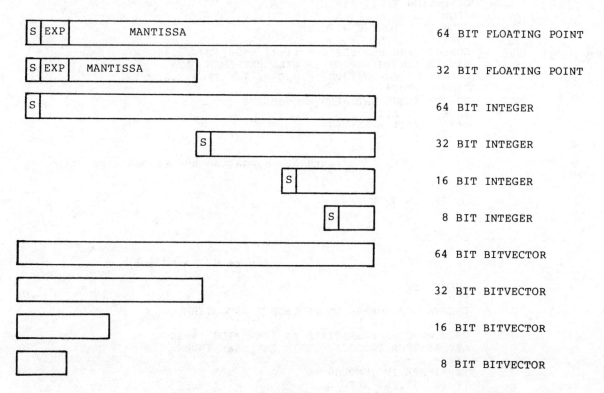

Figure 3. Data types

```
              :
        PURGE $IP, $NP
        $NP = NPROCS
        DO 10 I = 2, NPROCS
        $IP = I-1
        CREATE S($IP,$NP)
    10  CONTINUE
        $IP = NPROCS
        CALL S($IP,$NP)
C       WAIT FOR ALL PROCESSES TO FINISH
    20  N = $NP
        $NP = N
        IF (N .NE. 0) GO TO 20
              :
        SUBROUTINE S($IP,$NP)
        MYNUM = $IP
              :
        $NP = $NP-1
        RETURN
        END
              :
```

Figure 4.   HEP Fortran example

```
C       REPLACE EACH ELEMENT OF THE VECTOR X
C       BY THE SUM OF THE ELEMENTS OF X
C       USING THE INITIALLY EMPTY ARRAY $A.
C       P = 2**L PROCESSES EXECUTE THIS PROGRAM.
C       THE PROCESS IDENTIFER IS I.
        DIMENSION X(P), A(P,L)
        JPOW = 2
C       JPOW IS 2 TO THE J POWER
        DO 10 J = 1,L
C       COMPUTE THE PROCESS K = (I-1) EXOR(JPOW/2)+1
C       WITH WHICH THIS PROCESS WILL EXCHANGE DATA
        K = ((I-1)/JPOW)*JPOW + MOD (I-1 + JPOW/2,JPOW)+1
        JPOW = JPOW*2
C       NOW EXCHANGE DATA AND ACCUMULATE
        $A(K,J) = X(I)
        X(I) = X(I) + $A(I,J)
    10  CONTINUE
```

Figure 5.   Summation by network simulation

```
        DO 10 I = J, K, L
              :
    10  CONTINUE
```

Figure 6.   A DO loop

```
        PURGE $IV
        $IV = J
C       CREATE ANY NUMBER OF PROCESSES EXECUTING
    1   I = $IV
C       THIS PROCESS HAS SEIZED AN ITERATION INDEX
C       LET ANOTHER PROCESS OBTAIN THE NEXT INDEX
        $IV = I + L
C       TERMINATE IF THROUGH
        IF (I .GT. K) RETURN
              :
        GO TO 1
```

Figure 7. A self-scheduled loop

Experience with Pipelined Multiple Instruction Streams

HARRY F. JORDAN, MEMBER, IEEE

Invited Paper

Reprinted from *Proceedings of the IEEE*, Volume 72, Number 1, January 1984, pages 113-123. Copyright © 1984 by The Institute of Electrical and Electronics Engineers, Inc.

Pipelining has been used to implement efficient, high-speed vector computers. It is also an effective method for implementing multiprocessors. The Heterogeneous Element Processor (HEP) built by Denelcor Incorporated is the first commercially available computer system to use pipelining to implement multiple processes. This paper introduces the architecture and programming environment of the HFP and surveys a range of scientific applications programs for which parallel versions have been produced, tested, and analyzed on this computer. In all cases, the ideal of one instruction completion every pipeline step time is closely approached. Speed limitations in the parallel programs are more often a result of the extra code necessary to ensure synchronization than of actual synchronization lockout at execution time. The pipelined multiple instruction stream architecture is shown to cover a wide range of applications with good utilization of the parallel hardware.

INTRODUCTION

The two important influences on the speed of computing machines are the electronic speed of the underlying circuitry and the amount of parallel activity which can be accomplished. Advances in component speed have perhaps accounted for the largest speedup over the years but are beyond the scope of this paper. The increase in speed due to enhanced parallelism has been the province of computer architecture beginning with the move from serial-by-bit to parallel-by-word operation, moving through processor and I/O overlap, and now focusing on the area of concurrent data operations. Flynn [1] characterized the concurrency of data operations with respect to instruction streams by dividing architectures into four categories based on the number of instruction streams and the number of data streams. Single (SI) or multiple (MI) instruction streams may be combined with single (SD) or multiple (MD) data streams to form an architectural category. The scheme does not seem suitable for "Data Flow" machines [2] which are also outside the scope of this paper.

In this paper the categories SISD, SIMD, and MIMD will be used from the instruction set point of view without regard to whether multiple operations are carried out on separate complete processors or whether the "parallel" operations are processed by a pipeline. A machine in which a single instruction specifies operations on several data

Manuscript received June 16, 1983; revised September 19, 1983. Part of this work was performed when the author was employed as a Consultant to Denelcor Inc., Denver, CO.
The author is with the Department of Electrical and Computer Engineering, University of Colorado, Boulder, CO 80309, USA.

items is an SIMD machine. The advantage of this point of view is that pipelining then becomes an independent architectural variable which may be combined with Flynn's categories in an orthogonal manner. Data operations in the SISD case do not become parallel until pipelining is applied; the simple technique of fetch–execute overlap is one application of pipelining to SISD computers. The Illiac IV computer [3] is a nonpipelined SIMD computer for vector and matrix processing. A machine with a very similar instruction set architecture but which uses pipeline arithmetic units to support vector operations is the CRAY-1 [4], which we will call a pipelined SIMD computer.

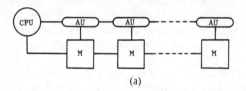

(a)

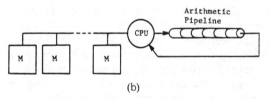

(b)

Fig. 1. SIMD architectures. (a) True SIMD or vector computer. (b) Pipelined SIMD. AU—Arithmetic Unit, CPU—Central Processing Unit, M—Memory Module.

Nonpipelined or "true" SIMD machines have the architecture shown in Fig. 1(a). This structure has been used in numerous machines of a more special purpose nature [5]–[7]. SIMD computers which have seen widespread commercial use have tended to be of the pipelined variety [4], [8]. These correspond to the general architectural configuration shown in Fig. 1(b). Of course, no commercial machine uses a single form of parallelism. Multiple pipelines are used to enhance speed and scalar arithmetic units are overlapped.

Two prototypical forms of MIMD computers or multiprocessors [9] are shown in Fig. 2(a). Although not widely available commercially, successful systems of both the shared memory form [10] and the distributed memory form

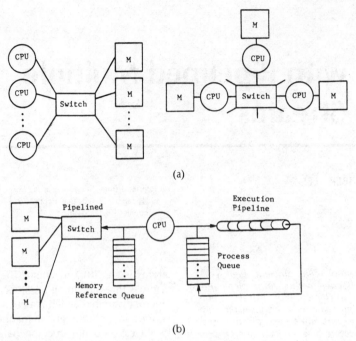

(a)

(b)

Fig. 2. MIMD architectures. (a) True MIMD or multiprocessor. (b) Pipelined MIMD. CPU—Central processing Unit, M—Memory Module.

[11] have been built. Fig. 2(b) shows the configuration of an MIMD machine in which multiple instruction streams are supported by pipelining rather than by separate complete processors. Since multiple, independent memory requests are generated by the parallel instruction streams, pipelining can also be applied effectively to the memory access path. The experience reported in this paper is based on the Denelcor HEP, a commercially available pipelined MIMD computer [12]–[14].

Applications programs for machines falling into different architectural categories require different structuring of solution algorithms for efficient operation. Put differently, given a program with a particular structure, the ways in which architectural parallelism can be applied are different. For example, programs written in a sequential programming language for a sequential machine will take full advantage of a pipelined SISD machine. To apply an SIMD machine to an already written, sequential program requires an automatic vectorizing compiler [15], [16] with a degree of success depending on program structure. MIMD machines can execute multiple sequential programs in parallel for increased throughput, but work on automatic parallelizing compilers to speed up the execution of a single, sequential program using an MIMD architecture has just begun [17].

All forms of architectural parallelism are applicable to the many large problems arising out of numerical linear algebra [18] but SIMD machines are tailored to them and can achieve extremely high performance in operations on long enough vectors. It is easy to partition the components of a vector over different instruction streams but the flexibility afforded by multiple streams is not needed and synchronization overhead may be excessive if parallelism is restricted to the level of single vector operations. Vector processing may be performed quite efficiently with respect to other work on an SISD computer as a result of predictable look ahead characteristics, but again the architecture is not specialized to it. The number of linear algebraic applications, the often large size of these problems, and the considerable

algorithm research which has taken place in this field make this type of application an important standard against which to measure performance of any parallel architecture.

In numerous applications, the opportunity for parallel data operations is evident but the operations differ from datum to datum or there is enough irregularity in the structure of the data to make SIMD processing difficult or impossible. In these applications one must either be content with pipelined SISD processing or move into the MIMD environment. Where multiple data items have irregular or conditional access patterns MIMD processing may be preferred even when vectors are involved, as in the case of sparse matrix operations. At a higher level of algorithm structure is functional parallelism, in which large modules of the program operate in parallel and share data only in specific, easily synchronized ways.

This paper will describe implementations of several algorithms in the above categories on the HEP pipelined MIMD computer. The programs are of medium to small size but all represent central parts of large scientific codes. The size of the codes allows an analysis of the efficiency of the architecture which is applicable to large code performance, but simple enough to extract information about utilization of specific parts of the architecture. Few direct comparisons with other machines of a detailed nature have been carried out and interpretation is complicated by circuit technology differences. The major thrust of this paper is to determine the extent to which the type of parallelism inherent in pipelined MIMD machines can be effectively utilized in different types of computations underlying large-scale applications.

THE HEP ARCHITECTURE

The HEP computer is an MIMD computer consisting of one or more pipelined MIMD Process Execution Modules (PEM's) which share memory. Even within a single PEM the HEP is an MIMD computer. There is no qualitative difference in the way processes are created and managed or in the way in which they communicate in a one-PEM system versus a multi-PEM system. Only the number of instructions actually executing simultaneously, about 12 per PEM, changes when more PEM's are added to a system. The applications discussed were all run on a one-PEM system so we concentrate on the architecture of a single PEM and only mention a multiple-PEM system when we discuss access to data memory. The results are thus characteristic of the pipelined MIMD architecture of Fig. 2(b).

There are several separate pipelines in a PEM but the major flavor of the architecture can be given by considering only one, the main execution pipeline. In pipelined SIMD machines the operating units are broken into small stages with data storage in each stage. Complete processing of a pair of operands involves the data passing sequentially through all stages of the pipeline. Parallelism is achieved by having different pairs of operands occupy different stages of the pipeline simultaneously. The different operand pairs are represented by different components of vectors being operated upon. In HEP, independent instructions (including operands) flow through the pipeline with an instruction being completely executed in eight steps. Independence of activity in successive stages of the pipeline is achieved not by processing independent components of vectors but by alternating instructions from independent instruction streams in the pipeline. Multiple copies of process state, including program counter, are kept for a variable number of processes—up to 128 per PEM. The hardware implements what can be viewed as extremely fine grained multiprogramming by issuing instructions from different processes successively into the pipeline. Fig. 3 contrasts

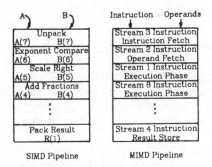

Fig. 3. SIMD versus MIMD pipelining.

pipelined SIMD processing, in which pairs of operands occupy pipeline stages, with pipelined MIMD, in which instructions accompany their operands in the pipeline. Divide instructions do not progress according to the above descriptions since floating-point divide makes use of a parallel rather than a pipelined implementation.

The previous paragraph describes the register-to-register instructions of the HEP. Those dealing with main memory (data memory) behave differently. There are four types of memory in a HEP system: program memory, register memory, constant memory, and data memory. Program memory is normally read-only and is local to a PEM. Register and constant memories are also local to a PEM and are similar in use except that constant memory may not be altered by a user process. There are 2048 registers and 4096 constants so that even if many processes run in parallel each has access to some private working storage. Data memory is shared

between PEM's and words are moved between register and data memories by means of Scheduler Function Unit (SFU) instructions.

A process is characterized by a Process Status Word (PSW) containing a program counter and index offsets into both register memory and constant memory to support the writing of reentrant code. Under the assumption that multiple processes will cooperate on a given job or task and thus share memory, memory is allocated and protected on the basis of a structure called a task. Each of up to 16 tasks is described by a Task Status Word (TSW) containing base and limit values for each memory type. The 128 possible processes are divided into a maximum of 64 user and 64 supervisor processes which must belong to tasks of corresponding types. Aside from this restriction a task may have any number of processes from zero to 64. Placing processes in different tasks serves to limit the memory which they may share. Thus independent jobs would normally be assigned to different tasks. Instruction issuing maintains a fair allocation of resources between tasks first and processes within a task second. An active process is represented by a Process Tag (PT) which points to one of the 128 possible PSW's. The main scheduler issues the next instruction corresponding to a queued PT into the execution pipeline every 100 ns. The flow of PT's is outlined in Fig. 4 which also shows the structures involved in accessing data memory.

The completion time for an SFU instruction (data memory access) is larger than for other instructions even though the pipeline step time is still 100 ns. When an SFU instruction is issued, the PT leaves the main scheduler queue and enters a queue in the SFU. When a PT comes to the head of the SFU queue a memory transaction is built and sent into the attached node of a pipelined, message-switched routing network. The transaction propagates through the switch to the appropriate memory bank and returns to the SFU with status and perhaps data. The PT is then relinked into the queue of the main scheduler. The pipelining of messages through the switch and data memory modules makes SFU instructions behave as if issued into a pipeline longer than the eight-step execution pipeline but with the same step rate. The SFU instruction scheduler and the switch routing strategy make the length of this pipeline somewhat indeterminate. It is between 20 and 30 steps in a small, moderately loaded system.

Potentially, an instruction may be completed every 100 ns. The fact that one instruction may require the result of another which is still in the pipeline is handled similarly whether the instructions are from the same or different processes. Each cell in register and data memories has a full/empty state and synchronization is performed by having an instruction wait for its operands to be full and its result empty before proceeding. The synchronizing conditions are optionally checked by the instruction-issuing mechanism and, if not fulfilled, cause the PT to be immediately requeued with the program counter of the PSW unaltered. Only registers have a third state, reserved, which is set for the result register of an instruction currently in the execution pipeline.

One other hardware mechanism illustrated in Fig. 4 is a separate, synchronous interface to a section of data memory. This "local memory" interface is pipelined with eight steps as are most other execution units. Accesses may only use the local interface if they do not involve the full/empty state of a memory location. The pipeline step time is 100 ns

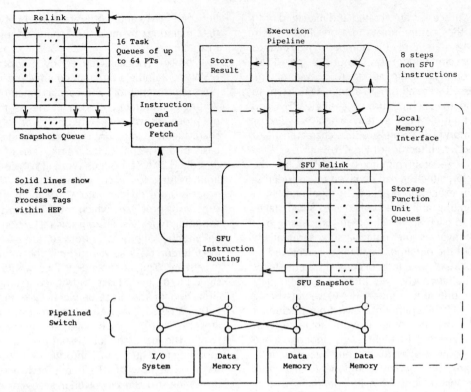

Fig. 4. The principal pipelines in HEP.

for both local and switch access to data memory. The number of steps, however, is 8 for the local interface and 20–30 for access through the switch. The existence of two memory access paths will be used below to study the influence of pipeline length on program execution time in the pipelined MIMD environment.

The Programming Model

Programming of the applications reported was done in HEP Fortran and is thus close to the machine language level. Minimal modifications were made to Fortran to give a user access to the MIMD environment of the HEP. To allow for the fact that an independent process usually requires some local variables, the process concept is tied to the Fortran subroutine. The Fortran extension is merely a second version of the CALL statement, CREATE. Control returns immediately from a CREATE statement but the created subroutine, with a unique copy of its local variables, is also executing simultaneously. The RETURN in a created subroutine has the effect of terminating the process executing the subroutine. Parameters are passed by address in both CALL and CREATE though some care must be taken in the linkage to see that changing addresses, such as array elements, are frozen at the value associated with executing the CREATE and remain static during the created subroutine's execution.

The only other major conceptual modification to Fortran allows access to the synchronizing properties of the full/empty state of memory cells. Any Fortran variable may be declared to be an "asynchronous" variable. Asynchronous variables are distinguished by names beginning with a $ symbol and may have any Fortran type. They may appear in Fortran declarative statements and adhere to implicit typing rules based on the initial letter. If such a variable appears on the right side of an assignment, wait for full, read, and set

empty semantics apply. When one appears on the left of an assignment, the semantics are wait for empty, write, and set full. To initialize the state (not the value) of asynchronous variables, a new statement:

$$\text{PURGE } a_1, a_2, \cdots, a_n$$

sets the states of $a_1, a_2, \cdots, a_n$ to empty regardless of their previous states.

A pedagogical HEP Fortran example is shown in Fig. 5. The main program and two instances of the subroutine run in parallel to compute an array of cosines of sums of pairs of angles. Note that correct operation of the program depends on the order of evaluation of the expression in statement 10. It is assumed the memory access for the leftmost occurrence of $A ($B) in the expression is executed before that for the rightmost occurrence of $A ($B). Since

```
      PROGRAM MAIN
      REAL $ANGLE1(100). $ANGLE2(100)
      REAL COSSUM(100)

      Read in the $ANGLE arrays.

      PURGE $A, $B
      CREATE TRIG($A, $ANGLE1)
      CREATE TRIG($B, $ANGLE2)
      DO 10 J = 1, 100
10    COSSUM(J) = $A*$B - $A*$B
C     COS(A1 + A2) = COS(A1)*COS(A2) - SIN(A1)*SIN(A2)


      END

      SUBROUTINE TRIG($X, $ANGLE)
      REAL $ANGLE(100)
      DO 20 I = 1, 100
      Y = $ANGLE(I)
      $X = COS(Y)
20    $X = SIN(Y)
      RETURN
      END
```

Fig. 5. A HEP Fortran example.

242

optimizing compilers do not guarantee this, the accesses should appear in two successive Fortran statements.

Effective Parallelization of Application Code

As mentioned, one way to use pipelined MIMD machines is to execute independent sequential programs simultaneously for increased throughput. If enough jobs can be held in memory at once the independence of instructions in separate streams implies maximally efficient use of the parallel hardware, with no "holes" in the pipelines resulting from synchronization delays between streams. The interesting problem, however, is to apply this type of machine to large scientific applications where turnaround time is to be minimized. We thus limit the discussion to the problem of executing one job which is partitioned over multiple instruction streams so that total execution time is minimized.

In MIMD processing there are two main ways of partitioning work across multiple instruction streams: partitioning on function and partitioning on data. Functional partitioning involves assigning different functional sections of a program to different instruction streams. These may communicate or share data in well-defined ways but are independent enough to use the parallel hardware without significant synchronization overhead. When one functional section produces results which are consumed by the next this organization is sometimes called macro-pipelining. On an SISD computer it would be characterized by coroutines. Data partitioning involves using different instruction streams to process different items of a multi-item data structure. Functional partitioning tends to introduce a limited amount of parallelism both because the number of distinct large functions is usually limited and because a single function often dominates execution time. If many smaller functions are identified, the amount of data shared is usually large enough that synchronization overhead becomes prohibitive. Hence some data partitioning must usually be applied to yield more than about ten parallel processes computing simultaneously.

An extremely simplified characterization of parallel programs is useful in indicating how to proceed in parallelizing an application. It also yields a useful empirical probe into the degree of success achieved. Let the number of parallel hardware units be P. This corresponds to P arithmetic units in an SIMD machine, a ratio of vector speed to scalar speed of P in a pipelined SIMD machine, P processors in MIMD, and P pipeline stages in a pipelined MIMD machine. Consider P as a variable and let the execution time on a machine with hardware parallelism P be $T(P)$. $P = 1$ and $T(1)$ correspond to the SISD case.

The simplest model of a parallel program is that it consists of a fraction f of operations which must be performed sequentially and a fraction $1 - f$ of operations which can be spread across P hardware units with a speedup of P, i.e., unit efficiency. The execution time for such a program on a machine with hardware parallelism P would be

$$T(P) = f \times T(1) + (1 - f) \times \frac{T(1)}{P} \qquad (1)$$

The corresponding speedup and efficiency are

$$S(P) = \frac{T(1)}{T(P)} = \frac{P}{f \times P + (1 - f)}$$

and

$$E(P) = \frac{S(P)}{P} = \frac{1}{1 + f \times (P - 1)}. \qquad (2)$$

The qualitative demands on successful parallelization come from observing that if one wants at least 50-percent efficiency of hardware utilization the fraction f of sequential code must be no larger than $1/(P - 1)$. This may be quite small if P is large so even a small amount of unparallelized code may have a significant effect on efficiency. One consequence is the importance of a good scalar processor in an SIMD machine since this serves to keep P small. Another consequence is that an environment which allows parallelizing even a small amount more code can have a significant effect on efficiency. In an MIMD machine, sequential operation arises both from single-stream execution and from synchronizations, such as critical sections, which cause all instruction streams but one to wait.

An empirical probe into the degree of parallelism in a parallel program can be obtained by assuming an execution time of the form $T(P)$, executing the program for several values of P, and determining the fraction $(1 - f)$ of parallel code by the method of least squares. This model fits a situation in which the parallel fraction of the code is done by P processes which do not change, except in the amount of work each performs, as P is varied. The model also requires hardware in which the P processes can be executed by noninterfering hardware units. This is the case in a true multiprocessor with P or more processors and is closely approximated in the pipelined MIMD hardware of a single HEP execution module provided P is no more than about five. Above $P = 5$, a simple form of single instruction stream lookahead begins to limit parallelism in HEP.

The applications programs discussed fit the required program format very well. They are composed of an arbitrary number of "self-scheduling," identical processes which result from a FORK near the beginning of the program and JOIN together near its end. The self-scheduling characterization comes from the total work being divided into a number of chores which is large relative to P. Each process obtains a chore and, when finished, determines and performs the next unassigned chore. This technique can give uneven execution time if the number of chores per process is small but is a powerful technique when the execution time of a chore is data dependent. We will thus use the probe to determine how well an application has been parallelized. It must be kept in mind that all limits to parallel execution, including such things as critical section lockout, producer–consumer delays, and multiple readers and writers synchronization delay, will all be lumped into an increase in the fraction f of sequential code.

Analysis of Applications

Results of timing and analysis of several different applications codes, ranging from a one-page subroutine through an 1800-line Fortran package for sparse linear system solution [19], will be presented. The programs are categorized into three types suggested in the Introduction. The first is the "dusty deck" Fortran program, written for a sequential processor and obscure enough in its origin or short enough in execution time that a redesign of the program is not practical. Mechanical parallelization of the program, preferably with an automatic, parallelizing compiler, is the correct approach to this type. The second type is the "vector program" which comes from the realm of numerical linear algebra and is well suited to SIMD computers. Some interesting comparisons of SIMD and MIMD performance can come from this type. The third type of program is the "nonvectorizable" program. Experience suggests that few programs are completely nonvectorizable but there is a distinct class of programs where MIMD parallelization is simpler or more natural than vectorization.

Dusty Deck Programs

An idea of the best that can be expected from the pipelined MIMD architecture can be obtained by analysis of an easily parallelized program with a simple structure. The heart of this benchmark is a numerical integration to compute the Gamma function. The integral is computed by applying Simpson's rule to sufficiently short intervals. Parallelization is done by data decomposition in which the total interval, 0 to $2 \times MM$, is divided into MM integrations over length two intervals which are done in parallel; MM is taken as 50. The length two intervals are further subdivided into MS subintervals so the amount of work to be done in one parallel chore is proportional to MS, which is on the order of 1000. Processes interact only by adding the contribution of a subinterval to a shared sum and in updating a shared loop index to get the next chore. Self-scheduling allows the number of active processes to vary without changing the program. A simple data dependency analysis would allow this parallelization to be done automatically.

The variation in execution time versus the number of parallel processes is shown in Fig. 6. The graph shows the

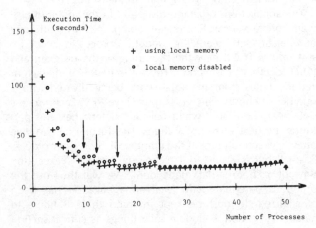

Fig. 6. Execution time for numerical integration.

execution time as a function of the number of active processes both using the local memory interface and with it disabled. The graph exhibits several features. First there is the $1/N_p$ reduction in execution time for small values of N_p as new processes make efficient use of the execution pipeline. This decrease in execution time bottoms out as the pipeline becomes full. The simple 8-step instruction pipeline is effectively extended by the effects of the SFU and the divider so that the $1/N_p$ effect does not level abruptly at $N_p = 8$. Superimposed on the above described curve is the effect of scheduling $MM = 50$ chores on N_p processes. Since all chores are the same size, the scheduling is best when N_p divides 50 evenly.

Since both local memory interface and switch are pipelined at a 100-ns step rate, the performance is expected to be similar if the pipeline is full. The switch turnaround, however, is about 2 μs as compared to 800 ns for the local interface. Thus the execution times should differ significantly for small numbers of processes where parallelism is wasted in waiting for memory turnaround but not when the number of processes is large enough to keep either pipeline full. The slowdown resulting from disabling the local memory interface is about 30 percent for small N_p and decreases to 5 percent as N_p becomes large enough to fill the pipelines. The results clearly show that a major change in pipeline length has little influence on performance when the number of processes is sufficiently large.

The data, combined with the simple structure of the program, make it possible to eliminate the scheduling effects and compute the speedup $S(N_p)$ which would be obtained in running a job consisting of N_p chores on N_p processors [14]. If N_p processes share the pipeline perfectly, i.e., a process waits only for its own instructions to complete, then $S(N_p) = N_p$. A smaller value of S indicates that, although N_p processes are queued for the pipeline, only S of them occupy actual processing stages simultaneously.

The curves of Fig. 7 indicate that when the local memory interface is being used for the majority of references, no

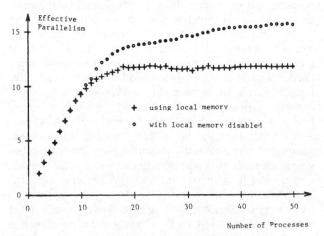

Fig. 7. Effective parallelism in numerical integration.

further benefit is obtained by using more than 18 processes. The flat asymptotic behavior indicates that there are no empty pipeline slots into which instructions from additional processes can be inserted once the asymptote is reached. These 18 processes execute as if 11.8 of them were able to run entirely in parallel. With the local memory interface disabled, all memory requests are forced through the switch, thus increasing the pipeline length so more processes are required to keep the pipeline full. Explicit interaction between processes occurs only twice for each execution of the large loop over MS so the interaction observed is almost entirely a result of hardware utilization by the processes.

One might suspect that the strictly synchronous behavior of the local memory interface would result in a very sharp knee in the local memory enabled curve of Fig. 7 at $N_p = 8$. If all memory references were local then only the divider would depart from 8-step, 100-ns per step pipelining. In fact, the store indexed (STOX) instruction cannot use the local memory interface and must go through the switch. By actual count, 25 percent of the instructions in the inner loop are STOX so a substantial amount of switch traffic exists even though all data memory is accessible via the local memory interface. Since STOX has a 2400-ns turnaround, one can estimate effective parallelism with fully loaded pipelines using the instruction count information. Three quarters of the instructions use an 8-step pipeline while one quarter share a 24-step pipe. Thus the asymptotic speedup should be the weighted average of the pipeline lengths, or 12. This compares favorably with the value of 11.8 obtained from Fig. 7. The close agreement makes it abundantly clear that when N_p is large an effective instruction completion is occurring every 100 ns. The pipelines are thus as fully utilized as is possible with the given instruction mix.

The previous example represents a best case in which the program consists of one loop such that loop body instances for different values of the index can be done completely in parallel. It has been shown [17] that data dependencies between instances of a loop body can be analyzed to extract parallelism in an MIMD environment. To obtain an idea of the degree of parallelism which can be obtained by this technique in the HEP pipelined MIMD environment, a typical sequential Fortran subroutine was parallelized by applying mechanical techniques to each of its loops and synchronizing to perform the loops in order. The program treated is a subroutine of 40 Fortran statements from the MA28 sparse matrix package of the AERE, Harwell, England [20]. The purpose of the subroutine is to sort a sparse matrix given as a list of corresponding value, row index, and column index triples so that it is stored by column.

The program consists of five disjoint loops performed sequentially, where all loops are simple except the fourth which is nested to depth two. The first loop is an initialization with independent loop body instances and is parallelized by prescheduling the work over the available processes. The second counts elements in each column using a shared vector of counts. This loop can also be prescheduled by using full/empty to synchronize each count. The probability of simultaneous access, and hence synchronization delay, on a specific count is low. The third loop is a one-step recurrence and is parallelized by an algorithm suggested by Ladner and Fisher [21]. A more thorough treatment of parallelizing general recurrences is given by Gajski [22]. The fourth loop does the actual in-place sort. The data dependencies between instances of the outer loop body are more difficult to analyze but probably within reach of an automatic parallelizer. Full/empty synchronization on the array being sorted and on the column counts suffices to allow instances of the outer loop body to be distributed over multiple processes. Since the execution time of the inner loop is data dependent, self-scheduling is more effective than prescheduling in this case. The fifth loop involves the shifting of a vector and can be parallelized by prescheduling blocks of adjacent elements over processes.

When the parallelized version of this process was executed with 20 processes, a speedup of 4.8 over the sequential version was measured for a sparse matrix with 5000 nonzeros and 400 columns. This is between the order 12 speedup which the previous example leads one to expect from completely independent loop body instances and a speedup of less than 2 which was independently measured [14] for the recurrence. This one, carefully analyzed example is typical of other mechanistic parallelizations of sequential benchmarks which have been done for HEP and suggests

that automatic parallelization of programs for a single PEM system will obtain speedups on the order of three to six.

Dense Linear Systems Programs

Work using the HEP as a test bed for MIMD algorithms to solve linear systems, both by direct methods [23] and iteratively [24], has previously been reported. Here we consider two applications which do not use new algorithms but reorganizations of sequential algorithms which are suitable to the MIMD environment. Both applications involve LU decomposition and both MIMD versions have the structure in which an arbitrary number of processes are forked at the beginning of the computation, share the work equally, and join to a single stream when the computation is complete. One application is a full matrix decomposition subroutine from the LINPACK linear algebra package [25]. The other is essentially a dense band LU decomposition arising from a partial differential equation on a rectangular grid with red–black numbering.

Both applications afford a comparison between the HEP and the CRAY-1. The CRAY-1 [4] is a pipelined SIMD computer which includes a high-speed scalar arithmetic unit in addition to the vector unit. It is implemented with high-speed Emitter Coupled Logic (ECL), has a minor cycle clock period of 12.5 ns, and uses 64-bit words. The HEP [13] pipelined MIMD machine is implemented with lower speed ECL logic, has a minor cycle clock period of 100 ns, and also uses 64-bit words. Up to 16 PEM's can be included in a HEP system but the results here are based on a single-PEM system.

The full matrix decomposition is the SGEFA subroutine from LINPACK. This program has been studied in the CRAY-1 pipelined SIMD environment by Dongarra [26]. Parallelization for HEP was straightforward and resulted in a worker subroutine executed by an arbitrary number N_p of processes. The worker subroutine computes a local maximum over $1/N_p$ of the potential pivots, synchronizes to obtain a global maximum, and reduces $1/N_p$ of the remaining rows using the pivot row determined. Although the organization of the code differs from that for the CRAY-1, the operations corresponding to different elements of a column are potentially done in parallel while operations on elements of a row are done in sequence as in the vector version. The HEP program was run with N_p going from 1 to 20 in steps of 1. The same order 100 test matrix was used as was used by Dongarra in the CRAY-1 measurements. The best execution time of 1.24 s occurred for $N_p = 17$ processes and corresponds to 0.53 MFLOPS (million floating-point operations per second). The compiler used was completely nonoptimizing and independent estimates indicate that a compiler capable of ordinary common subexpression collapse and loop invariant removal would produce HEP code which ran faster by a factor of three. Thus a better performance number to use for comparison of the architectures is probably 1.6 MFLOPS. The empirical probe into the degree of parallelization based on the execution time model of (1) indicates that 97 percent of the code is parallelized.

Dongarra obtained 14.3 MFLOPS for the fastest Fortran version of SGEFA on the CRAY-1. Assembly-code kernels for the basic vector operations gave better performance. This performance exceeds that estimated for a single PEM HEP system running a similar compiler by a factor of 9. An estimate of the fraction of the code which is vectorized is not as easy to obtain as the degree of MIMD parallelization is from the HEP measurements. Dongarra reports speedups for the order 100 test case run with two different compilers with vectorization both off and on. One gave a speedup of 5.9 while the other gave 3.3. The speedup on HEP in going from $N_p = 1$ to $N_p = 17$ processes was 6.9. It should be noted that Dongarra refers to hand-coded assembly-language programs for the CRAY-1 which perform an order of magnitude better than Fortran routines. This sort of improvement in HEP performance is not attainable by hand coding but only by adding more PEM's to the system.

The second application in this section has a more complex structure and comes from the solution of a sparse system of linear equations arising from the partial-differential equation model of an oil reservoir. The red–black numbering scheme is used on the points of a Cartesian grid to obtain a linear system with the specialized form

$$\begin{bmatrix} I & A \\ B & I \end{bmatrix}\begin{bmatrix} X_1 \\ X_2 \end{bmatrix} = \begin{bmatrix} R_1 \\ R_2 \end{bmatrix}$$

As a result of this structure it is only necessary to solve the system

$$(I - BA)X_2 = R_2 - BR_1$$

with one half as many equations and then find X_1 from $X_1 = R_1 - AX_2$. The system is strongly diagonally dominant so that pivots may be taken from the diagonal during the decomposition.

The original matrix is stored in a sparse form with each column represented by a pair of vectors, one with nonzero values and the other with corresponding row numbers. The structure of $I - BA$ is such that LU decomposition can be done with banded matrix techniques rather than those required for random sparsity. It is, however, beneficial to track the envelope of the band rather than to use a constant vector length corresponding to the maximum bandwidth. The numerical problem is thus a mixture of an easily vectorized banded dense matrix decomposition with a less vectorizable random sparse matrix multiply.

The Gauss elimination algorithm is organized somewhat differently for the SIMD and MIMD environments. The vector version [27] works down the band with a moving window on the active portion of the L matrix, simultaneously doing elimination and forward substitution so the portion of L behind the pivot may be discarded. The elimination operations are done column-wise using a single column working vector. Columns of the U matrix are put on a push-down stack as they are completed for access in reverse order during back substitution. This storage format is ideal for the back substitution, which uses the "column sweep" [28] method.

The MIMD version of the algorithm assigns different processes to different rows in the elimination so that, as in the SIMD case, the operations which are executed in parallel correspond to different rows. Since synchronization is not as precise in the MIMD algorithm, simultaneous operations do not necessarily correspond to elements of the same column. The moving window on L is retained but the working column vector is replaced by a window of working rows covering the active portion of the band. The U matrix is pushed onto the stack by row corresponding to the fact that a single process is responsible for operations corre-

sponding to a row of U during back substitution. Synchronization is tied to the availability of data using the full/empty property of memory cells in HEP rather than appearing in process control structures such as critical sections. Self-scheduling processes are used to execute a single program. Each process obtains a unit of work, or chore, performs the chore, and returns to look for more work. Four types of chores exist:

- Construct a row of the modified problem $(I - BA)X_2 = R_2 - BR_1$.
- Scale a completed pivot row and stack this row of U.
- Reduce a nonpivot row by a multiple of the pivot row.
- Do back substitution for one row of U.

Only one control structure is used for process synchronization. This is a barrier-type synchronization to prevent any process from proceeding to the back substitution until all have finished the forward phase.

Results reported here are from a data set consisting of a 515-equation system obtained from a $10 \times 10 \times 5$ reservoir model grid. The half bandwidth of $(I - BA)$ was 60 which implied good utilization of the CRAY-1 vector registers. By actual count on the SIMD version of the algorithm the number of floating-point operations was 725 030. Dr. Donald Thurnau [27] designed and ran the SIMD version on the CRAY-1 obtaining an execution time of 0.066 s. With vectorization turned off, a CRAY-1 execution time of 0.233 s was obtained. These correspond to rates of 11.0 and 3.1 MFLOPS, respectively. Comparing this factor of 3.5 speedup under vectorization with the speedups of from 3.3 to 8.4 which Dongarra obtained with vectorization turned on in timings of four LINPACK routines suggests that the sparse structure of part of this problem makes the code somewhat less vectorizable than the full-matrix LINPACK code.

The MIMD version of the algorithm was run on a single execution unit HEP with results shown in Fig. 8. The optimal number of processes was 13 giving an execution time of 2.09 s corresponding to 0.35 MFLOPS. The nonoptimizing

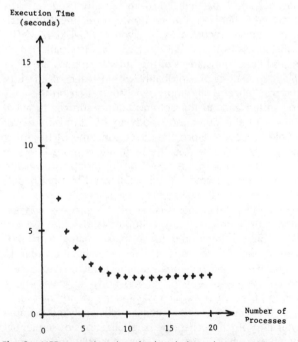

Fig. 8. HEP execution time for banded LU decomposition.

Fortran compiler was also used here. In order to get a fair estimate of results with a realistic compiler, the techniques of common subexpression collapse and loop invariant removal were applied by hand to the generated object code. This gave a 3 to 1 reduction in the number of instructions executed, corresponding to an execution time of 0.70 s or 1.04 MFLOPS. The degree of parallelization estimate from the model of (1) gives 98 percent and the speedup in going from 1 to 13 processes 6.5.

The ratio of the CRAY-1 to HEP clock speeds is 8 to 1 while the ratio of the MFLOP rate for similarly optimized code is 11 to 1. The degree of vectorization versus degree of parallelization estimates indicate that this moderatley sparse matrix-oriented code may parallelize somewhat better in the MIMD environment. The high degree of parallelization given by the empirical probe on HEP indicates that the code could be executed on a system with several execution units with very little loss in efficiency. No change in the code is required to execute it on a multiple-unit system.

Programs which Vectorize Poorly

There are many algorithms important to scientific applications which, while clearly containing operations which may be executed in parallel, do not involve vectors. Some of these algorithms can be transformed so that vector operations are introduced but the transformation may require global analysis, the transformed program may be quite obscure, and the amount of parallelism introduced may be small. In such cases, it may be better to parallelize over multiple instruction streams. Parallel algorithms for two graph-theoretic problems have been developed and tested on HEP and previously reported in the literature. They are the shortest path [29] and minimum spanning tree [30] problems. Here we focus on algorithms which were originally developed for sequential machines and which have been programmed for the MIMD environment by exploiting the opportunities for multiple process execution already present in the design.

A large number of computationally expensive scientific applications are based on the solution of large sparse systems of linear equations. The largest program for which the author has produced and analyzed an MIMD version is the MA28 package [20], [31] of Fortran subroutines for in-core LU decomposition and solution of sparse unsymmetric linear systems. The package was parallelized under the self-imposed constraints of retaining the numerical properties and user interface of the original package. Retaining the user interface had the additional effect of constraining the storage space used since all arrays with problem-dependent size are supplied by the user. Execution time statistics for the sequential version of the package [32] indicate that most of the time is spent in reduction of nonpivot rows and in the search for a pivot using the Markowitz criterion [33]. The techniques required to parallelize these sections gave good indications of both the possibilities and problems in parallelizing sparse LU decomposition.

Nonpivot row reduction can be done in parallel by multiple processes despite the nonvector logic needed to handle differing patterns of nonzeros in the pivot and nonpivot rows. However, fill-in imposes the requirement for a dynamically allocated storage scheme. MA28 uses a segmented memory approach with rows assigned to segments. In the MIMD environment such a scheme requires synchro-nized capture of free space and an eventual pause by all processes for storage compaction. While compaction itself occurs infrequently enough that it does not influence performance, the synchronization code required to allow for it represents a significant overhead. A more static allocation scheme such as paging or a hash table would be better for the MIMD environment.

To speed the sequential Markowitz search, a set of linked lists of rows and columns ordered by number of nonzeros is maintained. Assigning different rows or columns to different processes for the search incurs the overhead of synchronizing this somewhat complex shared data structure. In fact, enclosing accesses to the structure in critical sections limits potential parallelism to about six simply on the basis of the critical to noncritical code ratio. It would be worthwhile to search a few more rows or columns in parallel to reduce the complexity of shared structure.

In forward and back substitution, the MA28 package solves systems both for the original matrix and its transpose. Both solutions are equally efficient in the sequential environment but require different storage schemes for the LU factors to make parallel forward and back substitution efficient. In the substitution phase, it is fairly clear that the limited parallelism available from the hardware makes it inefficient to apply one of the highly parallel recurrence solvers [18] which increases the total number of operations significantly.

Timing data for the LU decomposition phase of the package are shown in Fig. 9 for an order 515 system with 3220 nonzeros. There is a maximum speedup of 5.5 in going from one to 15 processes and the least squares fit of (1), indicated by the solid curve in the figure, gives 86 percent as the degree of parallelization. An interesting point in interpreting the numerical results is that, because several elements may be equally good pivots according to the Markowitz criterion, different pivots may be chosen with different numbers of processes. Thus the goal of maintaining the exact numerical characteristics of the sequential algorithm is not only disturbed by effects such as the nonassociativity of floating-point operations but also by choice of the pivot sequence.

One further program deserves mention in this section on nonvectorizable algorithms. This is an adaptive quadrature originally designed by D. H. Grit and J. R. McGraw [34] based on an algorithm of Rice [35] and modified by the

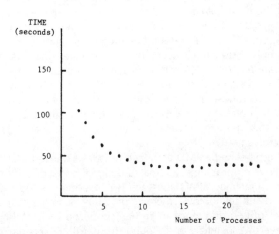

Fig. 9. Execution time for parallel sparse LU decomposition.

author to take maximum advantage both of the HEP hardware and of the Fortran runtime system. The computation is in the form of a binary tree in which an approximation and error estimate are applied to a subinterval at each node of the tree. If more accuracy is required, the subinterval is divided in two and the same algorithm is applied to each new interval. Since the number of available processes is limited it is not possible to assign every subinterval to a separate process, but a program which gives away subtrees of the computation when processes are available to do them can be designed and executed by one or many processes with the same numerical results.

A plot of execution time versus number of processes for a moderately complex integrated function has a form similar to graphs already presented. The interesting thing is the speedup. With a maximum tree depth of 14 and 5969 partitions of the original interval, the degree of parallelization is empirically estimated at 99 percent and the speedup in going from 1 to 19 processes is 11.0 when run on a HEP system having a small processor to memory switch and including single-stream lookahead. When run on this system, the "ideally" parallelizable Simpson's rule integration program previously discussed gives a maximum speedup of only about 9 because the lookahead and small switch makes the single stream execution faster by about 25 percent. The fact that the adaptive quadrature program speeds up by more than a completely parallelizable program is apparently a result of the backtracking work which must be done by a single process in handling the whole tree. The fact that multiple processes reduce this backtracking makes it beneficial to use more processes than are actually necessary to keep the MIMD pipeline full.

Conclusions

Parallel implementations of a broad range of scientific applications on the HEP pipelined MIMD computer have been presented. The fairly flat asymptotic behavior of execution time versus number of processes in all cases suggests that the pipelines in the machine are fully utilized for 20 or more processes and where the application is simple enough to determine instruction count this suggestion is borne out. A key issue in the performance of a parallel applications program is the fraction of the total processing which can be spread across parallel hardware units. An empirical probe of the degree of parallelization indicates that from 86 percent, in the case of the sparse matrix package, to 98 percent, in the case of banded LU decomposition, of the code can be executed in parallel.

Simple, automatable techniques for parallelizing existing Fortran programs for MIMD machines are possible and succeed in much the same cases as those in which automatic vectorization is successful. Distinctly better results can be obtained, however, by a global analysis of the algorithm, perhaps involving a change in the basic data structures used.

The pipelined MIMD architecture is, as expected, not as effective on problems dominated by long vector operations as is a pipelined SIMD approach but, assuming a common underlying technology, there is probably no more than a factor-of-two difference in Fortran-produced code. A high degree of parallelization is found in the MIMD versions of dense linear systems programs so that the efficiency of the SIMD architecture probably arises from hardware support for sequencing through the elements of vectors and from the highly predictable resource utilization pattern in the parallel operations.

Finally, MIMD parallelism is applicable to codes which do not vectorize well. Sparse linear systems solution is an important example of a computationally expensive application class in this category. In cases where the sequential formulation involves backtracking, a parallel implementation which reduces it may reduce the total computation performed as well as the execution time.

References

[1] M. J. Flynn, "Some computer organizations and their effectiveness," *IEEE Trans. Comput.*, vol. C-21, pp. 948–960, 1972.
[2] J. B. Dennis, "The varieties of data flow computers," in *Proc. 1st Int. Conf. on Distributed Computing Systems*, pp. 430–439, 1979.
[3] W. J. Bouknight, S. A. Denenberg, D. E. McIntyre and D. L. Slotnick, "The Illiac IV system," *Proce. IEEE*, vol. 60, pp. 369–379, 1972.
[4] R. M. Russell, "The Cray I computer system," *Comm. ACM*, vol. 21, no. 1, pp. 63–72, 1978.
[5] P. M. Flanders, D. J. Hunt, D. Parkinson, and S. F. Reddaway, "Efficient high speed computing with the distributed array processor," in *Proc. Symp. on High Speed Computer and Algorithm Organization* (University of Illinois, Urbana). New York: Academic Press, 1977.
[6] K. E. Batcher, "STARAN parallel processor system hardware," in *Proc. Nat. Computer Conf.*, pp. 405–410, 1974.
[7] ———, "Design of a massively parallel processor," *IEEE Trans. Comput.*, vol. C-29, pp. 1–9, Sept. 1980.
[8] R. Shoor, "CDC 205 runs 800 million operations/sec," *Computerworld*, pp. 1–2, June 9, 1980.
[9] M. Satyanarayanan, *MULTIPROCESSORS: A Comparative Study*. Englewood Cliffs, NJ: Prentice-Hall, 1980.
[10] W. R. Wulf, R. Levine, and H. Harbison, *Hydra/C.mmp: An Experimental Computer System*. New York: McGraw-Hill, 1980.
[11] D. Katsuki, E. S. Elsam, W. F. Mann, E. S. Roberts, J. G. Robinson, F. S. Skowronski, and E. W. Wolf, "Pluribus: An operational fault-tolerant multiprocessor," *Proc. IEEE*, vol. 66, no. 10, pp. 1146–1159, 1978.
[12] M. C. Gilliland, B. J. Smith, and W. Calvert, "HEP—A semaphore-synchronized multiprocessor with central control," in *Proc. 1976 Summer Computer Simulation Conf.* (Washington, DC), pp. 57–62, July 1976.
[13] B. J. Smith, "A pipelined, shared resource MIMD computer," in *Proc. 1978 Int. Conf. on Parallel Processing* (Bellaire, MI), pp. 6–8, Aug. 1978.
[14] H. F. Jordan, "Performance measurements on HEP–A pipelined MIMD computer," in *Proc. 10th Annu. Int. Symp. on Computer Architecture* (Stockholm, Sweden), June 1983.
[15] D. Kuck, R. Kuhn, B. Leasure, and M. Wolfe, "The structure of an advanced vectorizer for pipelined processors," in *Proc. COMPSAC 80, 4th Int. Computer Software and Applications Conf.* (Chicago, IL), pp. 709–715, Oct. 1980.
[16] J. R. Allen and K. Kennedy, "PFC: A program to convert FORTRAN to parallel form," in *Proc. IBM Int. Symp. on Parallel Processing* (Rome, NY), Mar. 1982.
[17] D. A. Padua, D. J. Kuck, and D. H. Lawrie, "High-speed multiprocessors and compilation techniques," *IEEE Trans. Comput.*, vol. C-29, no. 9, pp. 763–776, Sept. 1980.
[18] D. Heller, "A survey of parallel algorithms in numerical linear algebra," *SIAM Rev.*, vol. 20, pp. 740–777, 1977.
[19] H. F. Jordan, "Parallelizing a sparse matrix package," Computer Systems Design Group, Elec. Eng. Dep., Univ. of Colorado, Boulder, Rep. CSDG 81-1, Dec. 1981.
[20] I. S. Duff, "MA28—A set of FORTRAN subroutines for sparse unsymmetric linear equations," H. M. Stationery Office, London, England, AERE Rep. R.8730, 1977.
[21] R. E. Ladner and M. J. Fisher, "Parallel prefix computation," *J.*

ACM, vol. 27, no. 4, pp. 831–838, Oct. 1980.

[22] D. D. Gajski, "An algorithm for solving liner recurrence systems on parallel and pipelined machines," *IEEE Trans. Comput.*, vol. C-30, pp. 190–206, Mar. 1981.

[23] R. E. Lord, J. S. Kowalik, and S. P. Kumar, "Solving linear algebraic equations on a MIMD computer," in *Proc. 1980 Int. Conf. on Parallel Processing* (IEEE Computer Soc. Press), pp. 205–210, 1980.

[24] J. S. Kowalik and S. P. Kumar, "An efficient parallel block conjugate gradient method for linear equations," in *Proc. 1982 Int. Conf. on Parallel Processing* (IEEE Computer Soc. Press), pp. 47–52, 1982.

[25] J. J. Dongarra, C. B. Moler, and G. W. Stewart, *LINPACK Users' Guide*, SIAM, Philadelphia, PA, 1979.

[26] ____, "Some LINPACK timings on the CRAY-1," in *Proc. 1978 LASL Workshop on Vector and Parallel Processors*, pp. 58–75, 1978.

[27] D. H. Thurnau, Scientific Software Corp., private communications, 1982.

[28] D. J. Kuck, "A survey of parallel machine organization and programming," *ACM Comput. Surv.*, vol. 9, no. 1, pp. 29–59, Mar. 1977.

[29] N. Deo, C. Y. Pang, and R. E. Lord, "Two parallel algorithms for shortest path problems," in *Proc. 1980 Int. Conf. on Parallel Processing*, pp. 244–253, 1980.

[30] N. Deo and Y. B. Yoo, "Parallel algorithms for the minimum spanning tree problem," in *Proc. 1981 Int. Conf. on Parallel Processing*, pp. 188–189, 1981.

[31] I. S. Duff and J. K. Reid, "Some design features of a sparse matrix code," *ACM Trans. Math. Software*, vol. 5, no. 1, pp. 18–35, Mar. 1975.

[32] I. S. Duff, "Practical comparison of codes for the solution of sparse linear systems," in *Sparse Matrix Proc., 1978*, I. S. Duff and G. W. Stewart, Eds. SIAM, Philadelphia, pp. 107–134, 1979.

[33] H. M. Markowitz, "The elimination form of the inverse and its application to linear programming," *Manag. Sci.*, vol. 3, pp. 255–269, 1957.

[34] D. H. Grit and J. R. McGraw, "Programming divide and conquer on a multiprocessor," Lawerence Livermore Nat. Lab., Rep. UCRL-88710, May 1983.

[35] J. R. Rice, "Parallel algorithms for adaptive quadrature III—Convergence" *ACM Trans. Math. Software*, vol. 2, no. 1, pp. 1–30, Mar. 1976.

Chapter 6: Research Multiprocessors

CEDAR

Daniel Gajski, David Kuck, Duncan Lawrie, Ahmed Sameh
Laboratory for Advanced Supercomputers
Department of Computer Science - University of Illinois

1. Introduction and Summary

The primary goal of the Cedar project is to demonstrate that supercomputers of the future can exhibit general purpose behavior and be easy to use. The basic problems to be solved in reaching this goal are (as always) what hardware to use, what architecture to use, and what combination of software and algorithms to use in achieving the goal. The Cedar project is based on five key developments which have reached fruition in the past year and taken together offer a comprehensive solution to these problems. We will present these five key points briefly and they will be expanded in subsequent sections.

(1) **The development of VLSI components makes large memories and small, fast processors available at low cost.** Thus, highly parallel (e.g., 1024 processors) systems are not ruled out by cost or physical volume considerations as they have been in the past. Particularly important are the 32-bit one megaflop chips or chip-sets developed in the past year (by HP and TI). Thus, basic hardware building blocks will be available off-the-shelf in the next few years.

(2) Given the hardware components for a highly parallel system, accessing a parallel shared memory and moving data between memories and processors has been a traditional architectural stumbling block. Many systems have been built that have severe constraints in the memory (e.g., stride-1 access) or interconnection network (e.g., nearest neighbors only). **Based on many years of work at Illinois and elsewhere, we now have a shared memory and switch design which will provide high bandwidth over a wide range of computations and applications areas.**

(3) Compilation for parallel, pipeline, and multiprocessor systems has been another serious traditional problem. **The Parafrase project at Illinois has for more than 10 years been aimed at developing software for restructuring ordinary programs to exploit these supercomputer architectures effectively.** The success of the work has now been demonstrated by achieving high speedups on hypothetical machines as well as on most of the existing commercial supercomputers. It has also been shown that Parafrase can restructure programs to effectively exploit various levels of a memory hierarchy. An important consequence is that a compiler can be used to manage caches in a multiprocessor and thus avoid cache coherency problems.

(4) The control of a highly parallel system is another problem of long-standing concern and controversy. It is probably the most controversial of the five topics listed here, mainly because it seems to be the least amenable to rigorous analysis. From an abstract viewpoint, the traditional dataflow approach seems best because control is distributed out to the level of operations on scalar operands. In practice, it seems

This work was supported in part by the National Science Foundation under Grants No. US NSF MCS81-00512 and US NSF MCS80-01561, the US Department of Energy under Grant No. US DOE DE AC02-81ER10322, and by the Department of Computer Science at the University of Illinois at Urbana-Champaign.

that dealing with this low level of granularity has many weaknesses. **By using a hierarchy of control, we have found that dataflow principles can be used at a high level (macro-dataflow), thus avoiding some of the problems with traditional dataflow methods.** We have also demonstrated that a compiler can restructure programs written in ordinary programming languages to run well on such a system.

(5) Algorithms for systems with concurrency have been studied for a number of years. Many successes have been achieved in exploiting the array parallelism of various pipeline and parallel machines. But there have been a number of difficulties as well. It has long been realized that some of these difficulties should be surmountable using a multiprocessor because the parallelism in such a machine is not as rigid as in array-type machines. **Recent work in numerical algorithms seems to indicate great promise in exploiting multiprocessors without the penalty of high synchronization overheads which has proved fatal in some earlier studies.** Furthermore, nonnumerical algorithms have been developed at a rapidly increasing rate in the past few years. These are generally more in need of a multiprocessor than numerical algorithms, particularly in cases where the data is less well structured. Our group has been active in developing both kinds of algorithms.

To reach the goal stated in the opening paragraph, we believe that a two phase approach is necessary. The first phase is to demonstrate a working prototype system, complete with software and good algorithms. The second phase would include the participation of an industrial partner (one or more) to produce a large scale version of the prototype system called the production system. Thus, the prototype design must include details of scaling the prototype up to a larger, faster production system.

Our goal for the *prototype* is to achieve Cray-1 speeds for programs written in high level languages and automatically restructured via a preprocessing compiler. We would expect to achieve ten to twenty megaflops for a much wider class of computations than can be handled by the Cray-1 or Cyber 205. This assumes a 32-processor prototype where each processor delivers somewhat more than one megaflop.

The second phase system might use processors that deliver 10 megaflops, so a 1024 processor system should realistically deliver (through a compiler) several gigaflops by the late 1980s. Actual speeds might be higher if (as we expect) our ideas scale up to perhaps 4096 processors, if higher speed VLSI processors are available, and if better algorithms and compilers emerge to exploit the system.

An integral part of the design for the prototype and final system is to allow multiprogramming. Thus, the machine may be subdivided and used to run a number of jobs, with clusters of eight to sixteen processors, or even a single processor being used for the smallest jobs.

The remainder of this report describes how we plan to achieve these results. In Section 2, we describe the state of the art today in terms of the five points mentioned above. This provides the reader with a little more detail about why we think such a project can be successful at this time. Section 3 gives some details about what we plan to do in the next few years. Section 4 sketches the project personnel. Section 5 outlines the five year schedule of the Cedar project, and Section 6 contains a discussion of some key points of our budget.

2. State of the Art

We believe that a multiprocessor architecture with macro-dataflow control can be used to deliver low turnaround times to big users and high throughput to collections of small users. The details of our system are being designed at this time, so this report is necessarily vague on some points. Nevertheless, we believe that the system will contain a number of processor and memory clusters working from a global shared memory. In this section, we expand the five points of Section 1 in terms of our project.

2.1. Technology

In the past the supercomputer field was moving slowly, if not stagnant, because only a few large companies had the technology to build supercomputers and the financial resources to manage large design teams. Recent advances in VLSI technology have relaxed these restrictions, providing an opportunity for rapid advances in the supercomputer field.

2.1.1. Technology Availability. Presently available, off-the-shelf 64K DRAMs (with 100-200 ns access time) and floating-point arithmetic (with 2.5 MFLOPS computation rate), provide a golden opportunity for designing supercomputers in a desk top version with a small design team. However, high speed arithmetic and memory, although necessary, are not sufficient for a supercomputer implementation. In the past, most of the cost and design effort went into connecting or "glueing" these components together into a coherent entity. Today even the "glue" technology is available at low cost. A myriad of companies are offering a variety of gate arrays (with 2-8 weeks turnaround time) and design aids used to specify those gate arrays on-line. In this way, gate arrays are available to anyone with a terminal and a telephone line.

2.1.2. Design Aids. VLSI technology has brought us complexity. Many design aids like compilers, simulators, verifiers, and assemblers were developed to master complexity. Such design tools as SCALD (very successfully used in the S-1 project) which are now available commercially, can reduce the design time to only a few man years (S-1 project), and thus provide an opportunity for small university design teams to successfully build supercomputer prototypes.

2.1.3. Scalability. The other way to master complexity is by using a design methodology that generates a hierarchical and structured design. Such a design improves scalability, of which there are two types.

Architectural scalability allows for system expansion and therefore performance improvement by adding more components (processors, memories, switch modules, ...) but not adding new types of components. The cost of the system is proportional to the number of components.

Technological scalability reduces the cost of the system by denser packaging of the components which, in turn, may result in an increased performance because of shorter delay times.

The technology (silicon foundries) and the design aids (e.g., layout assemblers) are available to small design teams to achieve order of magnitude increases in performance by conversion from gate array technology to custom VLSI circuits. Furthermore, we understand structured design methodology for module interfacing and the theory of parallel memories, interconnection switches, and global control well enough to obtain another order of magnitude in performance by architectural scalability.

2.2. Memory and Interconnection

Large scale multiprocessors require access to a shared memory system and convenient interprocessor communication. Early parallel computers tended to be mesh-connected—that is, access to neighboring processors and memories was fast, but more global communication/access took proportionally more time. Vast amounts of manpower were expended devising special algorithms which could execute in this type of environment. (Pipeline processors are not immune to this problem—the performance degradation due to nonunit vector strides or irregular addressing patterns are generally recognized problems.)

In the Burroughs BSP, these problems were recognized and a memory system was designed which allowed more efficient and general access to the shared memory. Unfortunately, the techniques used in the BSP involves some expensive crossbar switch hardware [LaVo82] which it would not be feasible to use in a much larger machine (BSP had only 16 processors).

More recently, new results have shown that relatively inexpensive processor-memory communication topologies can provide similar performance to crossbar hardware [WenK76], [LaPa80], [CLYP81], [Chen81], [DiJu81a,b]. The trick is to allow each memory access to proceed independently, rather than to access data segments (e.g., array rows) in a synchronous, deterministic way. Probabilistically, the performance of these schemes is quite good. They were first used in the Burroughs FMP design [BaLu81] and have since been proposed for a number of other machines (e.g., see [GGKM82].

Basically, our idea is to use a modified shuffle exchange network which contains some redundant paths. These redundant paths provide for both fault tolerance and conflict avoidance. Studies have shown that in practice the queueing delays are quite small whether the requests are random, nonrandom, or burst mode [Chen81].

Thus, we can provide general access to shared data (and interprocessor communication) with feasible hardware. Preliminary designs indicate that we can build this type of switch containing 1,024 ports, each capable of a .5 megaword/second (32-bit) data rate, using only 512 boards each with 150 connector pads. This switch includes some fault tolerance by providing redundant data paths [AdSi82], [PaRa82], and can be further enhanced by using other fault tolerance techniques [LiLY82].

Even though these techniques are efficient, they do involve more delay than access to a processor's own memory. Our design takes advantage of higher local memory access speeds in several ways. Certain data can be cached locally without the cache coherency problem (e.g., read-only data and local variables). Furthermore, the compiler is capable of detecting cachable data and either assigning that data to an automatically cached address space, or generating code which explicitly moves data between global shared memory and local (private) memory [PaKL80].

Thus, we believe we have solved one of the biggest problems in the design of a general purpose, large scale multiprocessor's efficient access to shared memory.

2.3. Compilation

The Parafrase system will play two roles in the Cedar project. First, it is a prototype compiler and can be used to test new restructuring transformations aimed at our machine design. Secondly, it serves as a generator of performance estimates for our proposed designs. **It is very important to realize that we will have the preprocessor part of our compiler working long before we begin to build our hardware.** The system has been discussed from several points of view in [KBCD74], [KKPL81], and [KKLW80].

We currently have over 2,000 Fortran programs that we have obtained from many sources. These are used in carrying out various compiler and architecture design studies. It has always been our objective to deal first with Fortran because

    i) it is probably more difficult to restructure for supercomputers than any other high level language;

    ii) there are many standard programs available to analyze;

    iii) it will provide us with a compiler that allows access to the machine by many ordinary users (to whom we can provide many standard packages); and

    iv) it allows one to restructure "dusty decks" for a new machine.

Of course, we believe that various language extensions should be provided to users and we shall later return to some details about what these will be.

The compiler will provide the Cedar system with code that may be regarded as a dependence graph containing several types of nodes called compound functions (CFs). This macro-dataflow graph is presented to the global control unit (GCU) which oversees its execution. Some CFs are control functions executed in the GCU itself, while other nodes are computational and are passed down to clusters of processors [GaKP81].

Four important kinds of parallelism may be distinguished in the Cedar macro-dataflow code. The first is parallelism between CFs themselves. This includes executing some CFs on the GCU and some in processor clusters, as well as executing several CFs at once in different processor clusters.

The second kind of parallelism is in the loop control of the computational CFs. For example, all iterations of a loop may be executable at once and so each iteration can be assigned to a different processor. Of course, the GCU may fold a computation onto a limited number of processors and each processor will then do a number of iterations ([KuPa79], and [PaKL80]).

Third is a kind of pipelining effect achieved by moving data from global to local memories before it is needed for the computation of a CF. We can prefetch data for iteration $i+1$ while computing iteration i, for example, or we can prefetch larger blocks.

Experimental evidence shows that this approach will be effective in exploiting the local memories in clusters. This software cache management only works effectively for data that can be guaranteed (by the compiler) to be written at most once in a given phase of a computation. Otherwise, cache coherency problems can develop, and our solution to this is to force any nonsafe code to execute directly from the global shared memory. This will cause some speed decrease (by a constant factor) and should be a rather rare event in any case. The global memory has of course only one copy of the data, and hardware will ensure that the correct value is stored.

The fourth kind of parallelism will be exploited mainly for phases of computations in which there is less parallelism than processors. This involves spreading expressions across more than one processor for execution. For example, if a loop of 50 iterations could be run as 50 independent iterations, but our machine had 100 processors available, two processors could be used for each iteration. This code spreading is entirely within individual compound functions and may involve executing independent assignment statements in distinct processors or even spreading single expressions over two or more processors. Experiments to date show that spreading can be very effective in some cases but it is not a first priority technique.

2.4. Global Control

Our approach to global control of the system is quite different from existing approaches and proposals. We will explain it briefly here by comparing it to other approaches.

Machines like the BSP, Cyber 205, and Cray-1 all have vector and array instructions of some type. These instructions can access and process a lot of structured data at high speed with no synchronization delays. However, when the data becomes unstructured, difficulties develop; for example, this happens with various kinds of sparse arrays and scalar computations in general. In such cases the machines perform at very low efficiencies, dipping to 1% or less of their maximum potential. Nevertheless, for large classes of important computations, such machines are very effective.

Dataflow architecture proposals are mostly based on the idea that if one could follow the lowest level dependence arcs in a program graph via fast hardware, even the most poorly structured data could be processed rapidly. The CDC 6600 and IBM 360/91 had hardware mechanisms of this type for a few functional units. Attempts for the past ten years to scale these ideas up to supercomputer speeds have led to no implementations or prototypes with more than a few processors. Many difficulties have been encountered [GPKK82] and some of them do not seem easy to overcome. For example, dealing with large amounts of structured data has caused great difficulty here. Thus, in a sense, the dataflow proposals have problems that are complementary to those of the successful commercial supercomputers.

We believe that operations on structured data should be handled in a globally structured manner and not as a massive collection of scalar operations. This holds not only for element-by-element array operations and array reductions as in today's supercomputers, but a multiprocessor can also extend the range to certain sparse array operations. If a powerful restructuring compiler is used, even scalars entering blocks of assignment statements can be accessed in global memory as blocks of data.

Once the data has been moved to cluster memories, we attempt to process it as much as possible in a local manner. Since clusters have crossbar interconnections, no data movement constraints exist for local phases of a computation.

Thus, our approach is to structure algorithms and programs into phases (i.e., compound functions) that work on localities of the overall data structures. These localities are assigned to one or more adjacent clusters for processing. The compound functions are expected to execute for a relatively long time; we have measured this, and it is intuitively clear from the vectorization success achieved with the pipeline supercomputers. Note that our CFs can be expected to be substantially larger than the single or chained vector operations found in the pipeline supercomputers. We collect sets of operations on the same arrays and also allow IFs, reductions, etc., in the same compound function.

The dependence graph connecting these CFs is executed in the Global Control Unit (GCU) in dataflow fashion (our dependence graphs may have other arcs than dataflow arcs). The GCU can schedule and assign the CF graph to clusters using relatively sophisticated algorithms, because each CF runs for a relatively long time. This is in contrast to scheduling single arithmetic operations in traditional dataflow proposals.

2.5. Algorithms

We are fully aware that even on a general purpose multiprocessor equipped with our powerful restructuring compiler and compound functions (CFs), many sequential algorithms will not take full advantage of the parallelism offered by the machine and some will hardly be sped up at all. For this reason, we have developed a collection of numerical algorithms that are particularly suited for multiprocessors. For a given problem, we either modify the "best" sequential algorithm or create a new one so that the following criteria are satisfied:

(a) the algorithm is numerically stable,

(b) the algorithm consists of several phases, each of which consists, in turn, of two stages: (i) the execution of as many independent tasks as possible, one per processor (or cluster of processors), and (ii) the communication between the processors (or clusters) in order to update the information necessary for stage (i) of the next phase, and

(c) the time consumed in stage (ii) is much less than that consumed in stage (i), i.e., the algorithm is not communication intensive.

We have been successful in obtaining many numerical linear algebra algorithms that satisfy the above conditions, e.g., see [Same81], [GaSW82], [LaSa82], and [SaSS82]. The above studies concern solving systems of linear equations and the algebraic eigenvalue problem for applications ranging from image reconstruction and digital filters to the solution of elliptic differential equations.

We have found that, except in a few applications, multiprocessor algorithms can be designed for our proposed machine so as to achieve substantial speedup over the vector algorithms. Many algorithms for important problems do not yield vector operations in which the vectors are as long as optimal for the Cyber 205, or to a lesser extent the Cray-1.

Vector operations that are subject to control bits arising from conditional statements lead to further inefficiencies in parallel or pipeline processors, but such computations can easily be handled by the **doall** construct on our multiprocessor. Operations on sparse arrays (compactly stored using tags) can cause even more severe problems on vector machines. Most recent experiments on the "vectorization" of direct sparse system solvers on the Cray-1 [Duff82] indicate mediocre speedup over their sequential counterparts. With our global/memory switch design, random fetches cause no unusual difficulties at all.

Iterative algorithms, while more amenable to vectorization, may not achieve as high speedup on vector machines as on multiprocessors. Some examples are provided by iterative algorithms for solving elliptic difference equations [Kers81], [SaSa81], [Taft81], and [Vors82].

Other important problems that are more suitable for multiprocessors than vector or array machines include:

(1) Table lookup equation of state evaluation. Here, our hardware caching scheme will allow shared access to read-only tables from the cluster memories.

(2) The solution of elliptic and parabolic partial differential equations on irregular domains via finite element discretization. Unlike array machines, the handling of the special elements on and near the boundary on our multiprocessor will not lead to drastic deterioration in the algorithm speedup.

(3) Monte Carlo methods. For example, the Monte Carlo simulation of neutron diffusion has defied vectorization and the resulting speedup on vector machines are mediocre at best. On our multiprocessor, however, each cluster may simulate the transport process by following a sample of neutrons through the medium.

(4) Nonlinear recurrences. These are computational bottlenecks irrespective of the architecture of the machine. Recently, however, we have found in many computational codes that one is only interested in the "remote" term of the recurrence. For many such recurrences, we have been able to cast the problem as finding a single root of a nonlinear function. This we have treated by a modification of the bisection method, which we call multisectioning [KuSa72]. On a multiprocessor, with a sufficient number of the processors, the root is obtained quickly. Such an algorithm on an array or vector machine will slow down tremendously due to repeated branching. We are currently in the process of automating the procedure and including it as a feature of our restructuring compiler.

We have begun to study the applicability of Cedar to nonnumerical algorithms with some success. Many of the ideas mentioned above are applicable and we plan to continue this work.

3. Details

3.1. Introduction

In this section, we will be more specific about some of the points raised earlier. In particular, the four sections that follow discuss some details of the four areas (of the five discussed above) that we will develop under this project.

In order to integrate the discussion, we show in Fig. 3.1 an overall system diagram. More details of our preliminary view of the system are discussed in [GPVY82], [Lawr82], and [YewP82].

3.1.1. Processor Cluster. A Processor Cluster (PC) is the smallest execution unit in the Cedar machine. A chunk of program called a Compound Function can be assigned to one or more PCs.

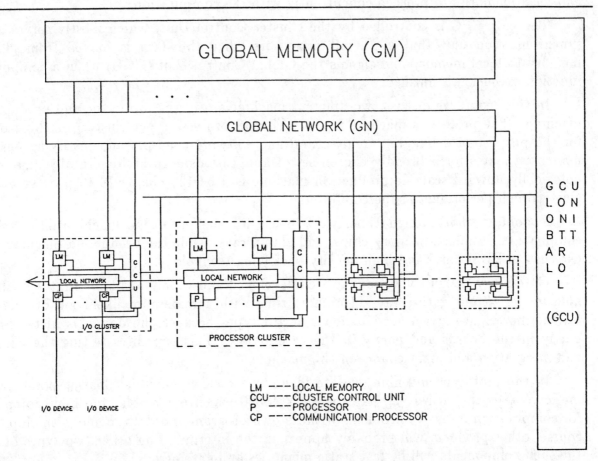

Figure 3.1 Overall system diagram.

A PC consists of n processors, n local memories, and a high speed switching network that allows each processor access to any of the local memories. Each processor can also access its own local memory directly without going through the switch. In this way, extra delay is incurred only when the data is not in its own local memory. Furthermore, each processor can directly access global memory for data that is not in local memory. Our compiler is targeted at exploiting this hierarchy of memory access speeds.

Each processor consists of a floating-point arithmetic unit, integer arithmetic unit, and Processor Control Unit (PCU), with program memory. There are no programmer accessible data registers in the processor. However, the local memory is dynamically partitionable into pseudo-vector registers of different sizes, and so it serves really as a large set of general purpose registers. There are two reasons for this type of cluster organization. Firstly, it simplifies the compiler design. Secondly, there is no need for general purpose registers since off-the-shelf floating-point arithmetic is an order of magnitude slower than medium size static memories (500 ns vs. 50 ns). Each local memory has its own global memory access unit that allows movement of data between global and local memories to proceed concurrently with the computation.

The entire PC is controlled by the Cluster Control Unit, which mostly serves as a synchronization unit that starts all processors when the data is moved from global memory to local memory and signals the Global Control Unit (GCU) when a compound function execution is finished.

In this report we discuss two different machine sizes: the prototype and production machine. The prototype machine is a 4 cluster (8 processors per cluster) machine built for the purpose of debugging architectural and software concepts and justifying performance estimates for a broadly chosen set of applications. An architecturally and technologically upward scalable production machine is a 64-128 cluster (8-16 processors per cluster) high performance supercomputer.

To obtain short design time, we will use for the prototype machine off-the-shelf components, standard memory chips, and gate arrays, while the production machine will use custom VLSI parts and high density packaging technology.

Gate array design software is so well developed and widely available that we will be able to design our gate arrays in a short time with a maximum likelihood of success. Furthermore, gate arrays lead to fewer board types because the design is hierarchical, partly in the boards and partly in the gate arrays. This expedites testing the boards, and integration and maintenance of the machine.

In the prototype machine, we are planning to use commercial floating-point arithmetic [WaMc82], [MCML82], like the TI TMS320 which is a single chip microcomputer for computation intensive problems with its own program and data memory on chip. Of course, other products will probably appear in the interim. The other two types of off-the-shelf components will be fast static memories and gate arrays.

We are planning to use the SCALD system (offered commercially by Valid Logic Systems, Inc.) to shorten our design time.

The design of the PC will proceed in four phases:

(1) Detailed functional specification;

(2) Partitioning of functional specification into board-level design with well defined interfaces between boards;

(3) Logic (Register-Transfer Level) design of each board function; and

(4) Gate array specification.

A PC will have a small number of board types (1 processor, 1 memory, 1 switch, and 2 control unit boards). Each is estimated to require one-half man year to design using the SCALD system. The manufacturing of PC boards will be contracted outside.

Communication between disks, etc., and global memory will be through a special I/O cluster. An I/O cluster is equivalent to a PC except for the processors themselves. Instead of the usual processors, the I/O cluster will have communication processors. These in turn will connect to support machines (e.g. VAX) which will provide access to disks, terminals, etc.

3.1.2. Global Memory Switch.
Our ability to provide fast access to a global, shared memory for several thousand processors is a direct result of recent work on shuffle-exchange networks. Early work in this area concentrated on SIMD performance of these networks, but more recent work has shown that they deliver excellent performance in a multiprocessor environment as well.

Our network is based on an extension of the omega network [Lawr75] and is similar in concept to the omega network designed for the Burroughs FMP machine [Burr79]. That network was nominally 1024x1024, and was a circuit switching network where the data path at each node was 11 bits wide. They estimated that the minimum time required to set up a connection would be 120 ns.

Our initial design differs in several respects from the FMP design. It is based on the use of 8x8 switches located on 150 pin boards, rather than 2x2 switches. Data paths are six bits wide, and we assume 2.5 ns/gate delay time. Taking into account expected delays due to conflicts, time multiplexing of 120-bit packets, memory access, and return transmission, we estimate an expected delay time of less than 2 μs/1024 words between processor and memory. For a 1024 processor machine, this would be done on 512 boards, or about one-half board per processor. (Using the same techniques we can design networks to provide average global memory access in as little as 500 ns, but these designs would require as many as 8 boards per processor.)

An example of one of these networks connecting 16 processors to 8 memories is shown in Fig. 3.2. This example uses 4x4 switches, but illustrates the principles we will use in constructing the 1024 port global network. We have discovered ways to add redundancy in larger networks that allow us to use this redundancy both for conflict avoidance and fault tolerance [Padm83]. Notice that unlike the omega network, this network allows more than one path between any processor port and any output port. This path redundancy provides both fault tolerance and conflict avoidance. Thus, from every switch (except the last) there are at least two valid paths. If either of these is either blocked by another message or by a failure, a connection can still be made via an alternate path. (A total blockage can exist if *all* alternate paths are blocked by conflicts

Processors   <------- **Global Switch** ------->   **Memories**

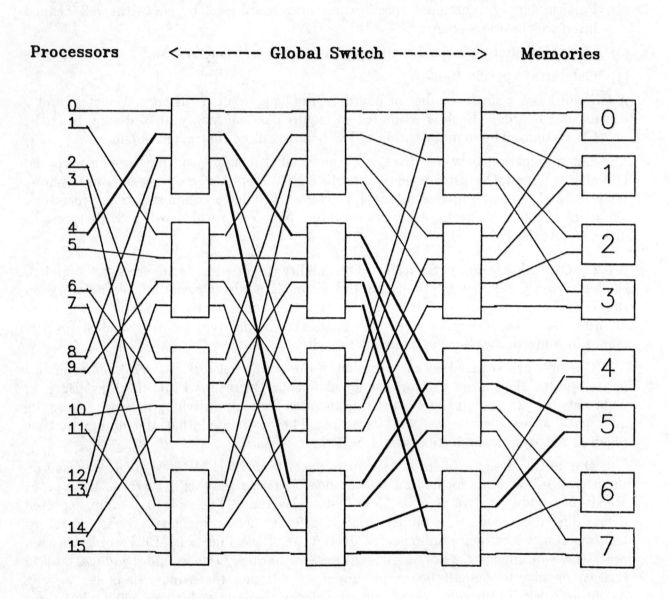

Figure 3.2 Example of a global network connecting 16 processors
with eight memories. Notice the redundant paths from processor
4 to memory 5.

with other messages and/or faults. However, analytic and simulation results indicate that the probability of conflicts is significantly lower with the redundant paths than without them, and that the probability of there being enough faults to block a message is so small that the mean time between fault-blocked-messages is on the order of one year even for the production machine.) The control logic which allows this conflict/fault aviodance is distributed throughout the network and is not very different from the classical omega control algorithm.

We will refine these designs to achieve a good balance between board count, fault tolerance and performance, and will build a prototype network using a combination of MSI/LSI and gate array packages. The prototype network would be identical to the larger network in all ways except size (the prototype would employ the same 8x8 modules but the total network would have only 64 ports).

3.1.3. Memory System

The overall memory system has a great deal of structure to it, but the user need not concern himself with anything but the global shared memory. However, the fast local memories present in the design can be used to mask the approximately 2 μs access time to global memory. Each cluster of eight processors contains eight local memories (16K of 50 ns access each). A given processor can access its own local memory module directly, or any local memory in its cluster through the cluster network.

User transparent access to these local memories will be provided in several ways. First, program code can be moved from global to local memories in large blocks by the cluster and global control units. Time required for these transfers will be masked by computation. Second, the optimizing compiler will generate code to cause movement of blocks of certain data between global and local memory. Third, automatic caching hardware (using the local memories) will be available for certain data where the compiler cannot determine *a priori* the details of the access patterns but where freedom from cache coherency problems can be certified.

All levels of memory include operand level synchronization facilities (similar to the full/empty bit of the Denelcor HEP), and the global shared memory includes the (programmer) option of virtual memory.

Figure 3.3 shows a programmers view of the memory system. Both the cluster and local memories include cache space (which is physically implemented in the local 16K memories) for global memory accesses. This cache is different from most cache memory schemes in that not all global memory accesses are cached–only those predetermined by the programmer or compiler. In this way we avoid the cache consistancy problems which plague most multiprocessor cache designs. Thus only read-only data (or data that is determined by the compiler to be read-only during a short phase of a program) or data that is only written by a single processor (private data) is cached.

Thus a user need only be concerned with a single uniform globally shared memory, and he could quickly design a program to execute from this memory. When he is satisfied with his results, he can use the optimizing compiler to improve his performance by making better use of the entire memory hierarchy and by utilizing more parallelism.

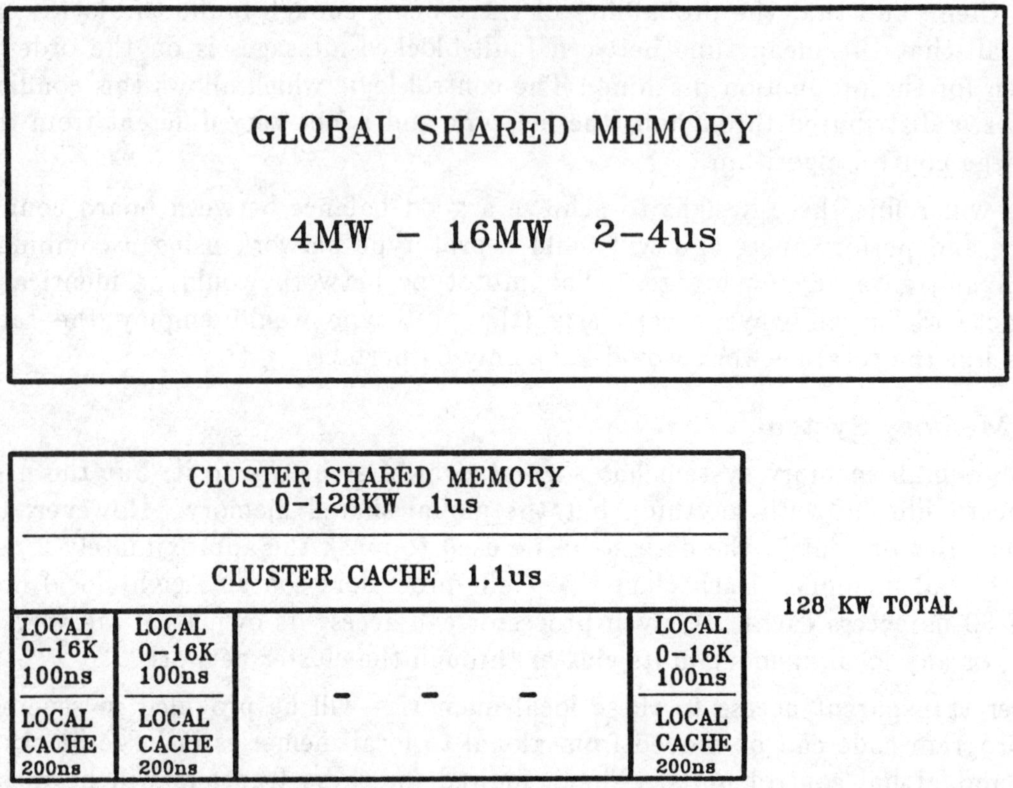

```
┌─────────────────────────────────────────────────────┐
│                                                       │
│                                                       │
│              GLOBAL SHARED MEMORY                     │
│                                                       │
│                                                       │
│            4MW  -  16MW    2-4us                      │
│                                                       │
│                                                       │
│                                                       │
└─────────────────────────────────────────────────────┘
```

```
┌───────────────────────────────────────────────────┐
│              CLUSTER SHARED MEMORY                  │
│                 0-128KW   1us                       │
├───────────────────────────────────────────────────┤
│              CLUSTER CACHE   1.1us                  │
├───────┬───────┬──────────────────────┬─────────────┤
│ LOCAL │ LOCAL │                      │ LOCAL       │
│ 0-16K │ 0-16K │                      │ 0-16K       │
│ 100ns │ 100ns │      -  -  -         │ 100ns       │
├───────┼───────┤                      ├─────────────┤
│ LOCAL │ LOCAL │                      │ LOCAL       │
│ CACHE │ CACHE │                      │ CACHE       │
│ 200ns │ 200ns │                      │ 200ns       │
└───────┴───────┴──────────────────────┴─────────────┘
```

128 KW TOTAL

Figure 3.3 Programmers view of the memory system.

3.1.4. Global Control Unit.

The execution of a program is limited by the parallelism exhibited by the control mechanism. In a von Neumann machine, the parallelism is limited by a serial control mechanism in which each statement is executed separately in the order specified by the program.

The execution speed can be increased by using parallel control flow or dataflow mechanisms [TrBH82]. Each of these mechanisms tries to execute all independent operations in parallel, where the operation is a typical arithmetic operation (e.g., addition, multiplication, etc.) or control operation (e.g., decision). However, the number of resources (e.g., operational units) in the machine is limited and sometimes not all independent operations can be executed in parallel. Therefore, the resources must be allocated and deallocated in the order specified by the computation. The price paid for parallelism is in the form of extra time or hardware needed to allocate operational units to instructions and keeping track of the execution order, the process we call scheduling. Proposed dataflow architectures are very inefficient on regular structures because of this fine granularity of their operations. When data is structured (vectors, matrices, records), the control and dataflow is very regular and predictable and there is no need to pay high overhead for scheduling.

In our system, we adapt to the granularity of the data structure. We treat large structures (arrays) as one object. We reduce scheduling overhead by combining together as many scalar operations as possible, and executing them as one object[Corn81]. In our machine, each Processor Cluster (PC) can be considered as an execution unit of a macro-dataflow machine. Each PC executes a chunk of the original program called a compound function (CF).

From the GCU point of view, a program is a directed graph called a flow graph. The nodes of this graph are compound functions and the arcs define the execution order for the compound functions of a program. The graph may have cycles.

The nodes in our graph can be divided into two groups: Computational (CPF) and Control (CTF). All CTFs are executed in the GCU, and all the CPFs are done by clusters. All CPFs have one predecessor and one successor. CTFs are used to specify multiple control paths, conditional or unconditional.

The compound function graph is executed by the GCU. Each node requires two different types of action:

(1) Computation of the original part of the program specified in the CF which may be done by the GCU itself or allocated to PCs. The latter case is for CPFs, and it requires their scheduling and preparation. The CTFs either do not have this part at all, or perform computation related to control.

(2) Graph update after the executable part of a node is done (if it had one). Successors of each node are updated and checked for readiness. The updating consists of recording that the predecessor node was executed. A node is ready when all its predecessors in the graph are done. When a node is finished, the predecessor information is reinitialized for the next execution of the node (if it is a cycle, for instance). An example of the Parafrase output is shown in Fig. 3.4. On the left hand side of Fig. 3.4 are the CPF numbers and their scope. The dependence graph is generated using those CPFs. From the dependence graph, we generate the flow graph (Fig. 3.5) which drives our GCU. The flow graph is generated by insertion of CTFs which simplify the software and hardware of the GCU. The CTFs in Fig. 3.5 are SIGNAL, WAIT, MERGE, SELECT, DO and DOEND.

The second problem of dataflow architectures is storage allocation, deallocation and movement of data, resulting in slow data access. In our machine, data is stored permanently in global memory and it can be shared there by all PCs. The data is moved into the assigned PC before the execution of a CF and later stored back to global memory. In this way the movement of data is minimized while the order and locality of data is preserved. **Thus, the macro-dataflow architecture combines the control mechanism of dataflow architectures and storage management of the von Neumann machine.** At this moment we are studying the completeness and efficiency of different sets of CFs. We will spend the next year in analyzing a number of benchmark programs with respect to the selected set of CFs.

```
CF number
 2    +--        DO 16 i = 1, N
      !             "
      !             "
      !             "
      !      8    WK1 = EK - Z(i)
      !          T6 = EK + Z(i)
      !          WKM1 = -T6
 4    !          S1 = ABS(WK1)
      !          SM = ABS(WKM1)
      !          WK = WK1/A(i,j)
      !          WKM = WKM1/A(i,j)
      !          SELECTORS = KP1(i).GT.N
 5    !          IF (SELECTORS) GOTO 15
      !+--       DOALL 9 j = 1, N - i
      !*            T7(j) = WKM * A(i,i+j)
 7    !*            T8(j) = Z(i+j) + T7(j)
      !*            R2(j) = ABS(T8(j))
      !+--    9    CONTINUE
      !+--       DO 11 j = 1, N - i
 9    !!            SM = SM + R2(j)
      !+--   11    CONTINUE
      !+--       DOALL 12 j = 1, N - i
      !*            T9(j) = WK * A(i,i+j)
 8    !*            Z(i+j) = Z(i+j) + T9(j)
      !*            R1(j) = ABS(Z(i+j))
      !+--   12    CONTINUE
      !          T3 = 0E0
      !+--       DO 13 j = 1, N - i
10    !!            T3 = T3 + R1(j)
      !+--   13    CONTINUE
      !          T10 = T3 + S1
12    !          SELECTOR6 = T10.GE.SM
13    !          IF (SELECTOR6) GOTO 15
14    !          T = WKM - WK
      !          WK = WKM
      !+--       DOALL 14 j = 1, N - i
15    !*            T11(j) = T * A(i,i+j)
      !*            Z(i+j) = Z(i+j) + T11(j)
      !+--   14    CONTINUE
18    !      15  Z(i) = WK
19    +--   16  CONTINUE
```

Figure 3.4 Program from LINPAK.

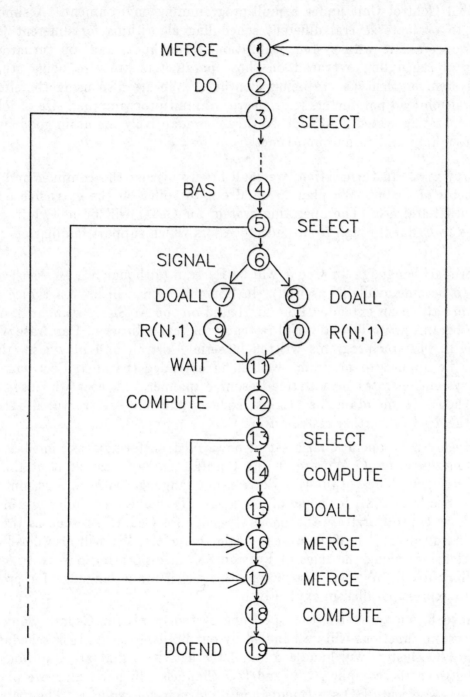

Figure 3.5 Macro-dataflow dependence graph.

In order to increase the system utilization and throughput, multiprogramming seems to be an essential system feature. We are studying different scheduling schemes in the Global Control Unit under a multiprogramming environment. A simulator has been built to evaluate several different scheduling algorithms for different job mixes. The main concerns are with system utilization, throughput, and job turnaround time. The effects of scheduling overhead on those parameters are also being studied, and potential system bottlenecks are being identified. We are also using the simulator to study several job load parameters (e.g., degree of multiprogramming, size of job, etc.) to design the operating system and GCU so they can adaptively maintain good system utilization, throughput and turnaround time.

3.1.5. Software. In this section, we shall briefly discuss the compiler and operating system aspects of Cedar. We plan to build our compiler on the extensive background we have with Parafrase. The operating system for Cedar will be new, but we plan to allow access to Cedar through front-end processors which support familiar operating systems.

The primary language for Cedar will be Fortran (although we expect several other languages to become available as well). In Fortran, users will have a choice of writing programs directly in an extended Fortran (based on the ANSI 8X standard), or of using their old programs as is. The powerful restructuring capabilities of Parafrase will usually be brought to bear on programs written in serial Fortran and may also (though not necessarily) be applied to programs written in extended (parallel) Fortran. Since the Parafrase system operates in a source-to-source manner, the user who used Parafrase can then choose to maintain his original code or the new, restructured version (thus obviating the need for further restructuring.)

We already have operational a set of powerful transformations aimed at multiprocessor systems in general. We are tuning Parafrase now to target it at the emerging Cedar architecture. The output is a Fortran-like language with various multiprocessor extensions. See [KPSW81] for some of our ideas. To make a compiler, we must attach a back end system to Parafrase that generates code for Cedar. As soon as the details of the Cedar hardware are clarified, we can begin this effort. We will also develop a set of Fortran extensions along the lines of Fortran 8X, incorporating our own ideas as well (e.g., see [KPSW81]). We will also accept this as an input language for programmers who wish to express parallelism explicitly.

We have begun to sketch the operating system goals for Cedar. Some standard operating system functions will be handled by our hardware, e.g., task scheduling in the GCU. The I/O clusters will handle some of the activities that are traditionally at the interface between the compiler, OS, and I/O channels. In particular, we plan to have the I/O clusters execute I/O statements and do format conversions. They will also handle page faults between the global memory and disk system. We also plan to attach front end processors to the I/O clusters.

A front end processor will provide various user services. We would expect it to be a network node in any installation and in the Department of Computer Science at the University of Illinois we will attach it to a VAX/Ethernet network within the department. The point is that users should be able to access the system through an interface with which they are familiar and happy (VMS, UNIX, NOS, or whatever). Thus, a user would submit a job through a front end processor which communicates it to an I/O cluster, which in turn can initiate I/O directly or begin execution through the GCU. Results will be returned through the I/O cluster to the front end processor for output, graphics display, etc. In this way, we hope to make the architectural details of the Cedar system as invisible to the user as possible.

3.1.6. Algorithms

Numerical algorithms for solving important problems in nuclear reactor safety studies, obtaining energy by controlled fusion, atmospheric modeling, and hydrodynamic simulation, just to name a few, have taxed the capabilities of existing computers to the limit. The availability of vector machines such as the Cray and Cyber 205 resulted in some speedup for many of the classical algorithms used to treat the above problems. Such speedups, however, have not been substantial for many applications. This is especially true for algorithms such as the particle-in-cell scheme for fusion studies and Monte-Carlo simulations in transport problems. Here speedups afforded by vector machines have been at best mediocre—a factor of 2 or 3 over sequential time. It is for such major applications that we wish to demonstrate the power of a multiprocessor. Some preparations are necessary, however, before we tackle such tasks. We have been laying the foundation by developing some basic multiprocessor algorithms that are counterparts of well developed and well understood sequential algorithms.

(a) Direct linear system solvers for dense and banded cases.

(b) Iterative methods for solving large, sparse, and structured positive definite linear systems that arise from the finite element and finite difference discretization of linear elliptic and parabolic partial differential equations.

(c) Direct methods for solving less structured, sparse, nonsymmetric systems of equations that arise from circuit and electric power network simulation.

Some work has been done by our group in the past 10 years that should make this task easier. (E. g., see the recent overview in [Same83].) Essentially we have completed multiprocessor counterparts to two mathematical software packages, Linpack [Dong79] and Eispack [Smit74 and Garb77] for handling direct linear solvers for dense and banded systems as well as the linear least squares problem, and the algebraic eigenvalue problem (dense and banded), respectively. We plan to produce similar versions for Fishpack [AdSS78] and Itpack [GrKY79] for handling largely positive definite elliptic difference equations. In producing these packages, we use the Parafrase system to produce most of the multiprocessor routines. For those achieving low speedups with Parafrase, the algorithms are altered or completely changed to suit the architecture of the machine. In either case the numerical stability of the resulting multiprocessor algorithms will be tested using our software package that is linked to Parafrase (e.g., see [LaSa80] and [Past81].) We expect that some algorithms in these packages, whether designed by hand or restructured by Parafrase, will have to be redesigned based on simulation results.

After these supporting packages become available for our multiprocessor, we shall concentrate on the following problems:

1. Iterative multiprocessor algorithms for solving symmetric indefinite and nonsymmetric linear systems arising from finite difference and finite element discretization of elliptic and parabolic partial differential equations. The effort will start with Chebyshev methods [Mant77 and Mant78], and those due to Lanczos [Saad81 and Saad82]

2. Solving the Helmholtz problem on irregular domains. We plan to compare our multiprocessor conformal mapping techniques [KaSa83] with the well developed capacitance matrix method [PrWi76 and OLWi79].

3. The large sparse linear least squares problems that arise from (i) the linearized geodetical network adjustment [GoPl80], and (ii) the image reconstruction problem [AnHu77 and Herm78]. In both cases a practical problem may contain over 10^6 equations in 10^4 unknowns. Variations of the Lanczos algorithm [PaSa82], and projection methods [Tana71 and BjEb79] will be investigated for suitability on the Cedar machine.

4. The particle-in-cell method used in fluid dynamics [Harl64], and the Monte-Carlo method for neutron transport [Davi63] and penetration and diffusion of fast charged particles [Berg63].

3.2. Ultimate Goal

Our ultimate goal is a multigigaflop machine by the early 1990s. The system would deliver high performance over a wide applications range and would be multiprogrammable for a number of small jobs. This is what we refer to as the second phase of our project.

After four years, we plan to be in a position to demonstrate a working system and to deliver register-transfer level diagrams together with timing diagrams to an industrial partner. We will have exposed our design to industrial scrutiny much earlier via our advisory panel (see Section 4). The panel will serve to make our design one that could be fabricated by industry and it should cause interest in some companies directly.

As was pointed out earlier, **we plan to execute a design that will be architecturally scalable and technologically scalable.** Our work will include studies that demonstrate architectural scalability, via simulation and experimentation on the prototype system. The industrial partner will, of course, have to invest some time and money in the technological scaling of the system (e.g., by VLSI redesign of the processors). Custom VLSI would give a cost and size reduction as well for production systems.

Notice that if a processor of 5-10 megaflops were used in a 1024-2048 processor system, peak performance in the 10 gigaflops range is possible. We believe that by using a powerful restructuring compiler, efficiencies of higher than 25% can be attained over a wide range of applications. **In particular, we believe that such a multiprocessor can achieve two to eight gigaflops over a much wider range of applications than is possible by extending the pipelined architectures that are successful today.**

An important advantage of our multiprocessor design is that it is conveniently partitionable for VLSI, compared with the conventional pipeline processors. This should lead to cost advantages as well as fabrication advantages. Notice that a 10 megaflops VLSI processor might need a clock period of 15-25 ns, far slower than the current highest speed pipeline clocks (which are attempting to go below 5 ns).

If our prototype project is successfully carried out as planned, it would seem very likely that one or more industrial partners would be interested in building a multigigaflops system. Important factors here are that a working compiler and a number of application codes will be developed in parallel with the prototype, and these could be moved (more or less intact) to a production system.

REFERENCES

[AdSi82]   G. B. Adams and H. J. Siegel, "A Multistage Network with an Additional Stage for Fault Tolerance," *Proc. of the 15th Hawaii Int'l. Conf. on Systems Sciences,* Jan. 1982.

[AdSS78]   J. Adams, P. Swartztrauber, and R. Sweat, "FISHPACK: Efficient Fortran Subprograms for the Solution of Seperable Elliptic Partial Differential Equations, Version 3," National Center for Atmospheric Research, Boulder Colorado, 1978.

[AnHu77]   H. C. Andrews and R. R. Hunt, *Digital Image Restoration,* Prentice Hall, 1977.

[BaLu81]   G. H. Barnes and S. T. Lundstrom, "Design and Validation of a Connection Network for Many-Processor Multiprocessor Systems," *IEEE Computer,* Vol. 14, No. 12, pp. 31-41, Dec. 1981.

[Berg63]   M. Berger, "Monte-Carlo Calculations of the Penetration and Diffusion of Fast Charged Particles," *Methods in Computational Physics, 1,* Academic Press, pp. 135-213, 1963.

[BjEl79]   A. Bjorck and T. Elfving, "Accelerated Projection Methods for Computing Pseudoinverse Solutions of Systems of Linear Equations," *BIT 19,* pp. 145-163, 1979.

[Burr79]   Burroughs Corporation, "Numerical Aerodynamic Simulation Facility Feasibility Study," Mar. 1979.

[Chen81]   P-Y Chen, "Multiprocessor Systems: Interconnection Networks, Memory Hierarchy, Modeling and Simulations," Ph.D. thesis, Univ. of Ill. at Urb.-Champ., Dept. of Comput. Sci. Rpt. No. 82-1083, Jan. 1982.

[CLYP81]   P-Y. Chen, D. H. Lawrie, P-C. Yew, and D. A. Padua, "Interconnection Networks Using Shuffles," *IEEE Computer,* Vol. 14, No. 12, pp. 55-64, Dec. 1981.

[Corn81]   Cornish, M., "Lecture Notes in Dataflow Computer Architecture,/*(rq MIT, 1981.

[Davi63]   D. Davis, "Critical Size Calculations for Newton Systems by the Monte-Carlo Method," *Methods in Computational Physics, 1,* Academic Press, pp. 67-88, 1963.

[DiJu81a]   D. M. Dias and J. R. Jump, "Analysis and Simulation of Buffered Delta Networks," *IEEE Trans. on Computers,* Vol. C-30, No. 4, pp. 273-282, April 1981.

[DiJu81b]   D. M. Dias and J. R. Jump, "Packet Switching Interconnection Networks for Modular Systems," *IEEE Computer,* Vol. 14, No. 12, pp. 43-53, Dec. 1981.

[Dong79]   J. J. Dongarra, *et. al., Linpack User's Guide,* SIAM, 1979.

[Duff82]   I. Duff, "The Solution of Sparse Linear Equations on Vector Computers," SIAM 30th Anniversary Mtg., Stanford, CA, July 1982.

[GaKP81]   D. D. Gajski, D. J. Kuck, and D. A. Padua, "Dependence Driven Computation," *Proc. of the COMPCON 81 Spring Computer Conf., San Francisco, CA,* pp. 168-172, Feb. 1981.

[Garb77]   B. S. Garbow, *et. al., Matrix Eigensystem Routines—EISPACK Guide Extension,* Lecture Notes in Computer Science, 51, Springer—Verlag, 1977.

[GaSW82]   D. D. Gajski, A. H. Sameh, and J. A. Wisniewski, "Iterative Algorithms for Tridiagonal Matrices on a WSI-Multiprocessor," *Proc. of the 1982 Int'l. Conf. on Parallel Processing,* Batcher, Meilander, & Potter (eds.), pp. 82-89, IEEE Computer Society Press, Aug. 1982.

[GGKM82]   A. Gottlieb, R. Grishman, C. P. Kruskal, K. P. McAuliffe, L. Rudolf, and M. Snir, "The NYU Ultracomputer—Designing a MIMD Shared-Memory Parallel Processor," *Proc. of the Ninth Annual Symp. on Computer Architecture,* pp. 27-42, April 1982.

[GoPl80]   G. H. Golub and R. J. Plemmons, "Large Scale Geodetic Least Squares Adjustment by Dissection and Orthogonal Decomposition," *Linear Algebra and Its Applications, 38,* pp. 3-28, 1980.

[GPKK82]   D. D. Gajski, D. A. Padua, D. J. Kuck, and R. H. Kuhn, "A Second Opinion on Dataflow Machines and Languages," Invited paper, Special Dataflow Issue, *IEEE Computer,* Vol. 15, No. 2, pp. 58-69, Feb. 1982.

[GPVY82]   D. D. Gajski, J-K. Peir, A. Veidenbaum, and P-C. Yew, "Preliminary Specification of the P-Machine," Cedar document no. 2, Univ. of Ill. at Urb.-Champ., Dept. of Comput. Sci., Aug. 1982.

[GrKY79]   R. Grimes, D. Kincaid, and D. Young, "ITPACK 2.0 User's Guide," Center for Numerical Analysis, The University ofTexas at Austin, 1979.

[Harl64]   "The Particle-in-cell Computine Method for Fluid Dynamics," *Methods in Computational Physics, 3,* Academic Press, pp. 319-343, 1964.

[Herm78]   G. T. Herman, "The Use of Sparse Matrices for Image Reconstruction from Projections," in *Sparse Matrix Proceedings,* I Duff and G. W. Stewart, eds., pp. 176-196, 1978.

[KaSa83]   E. Kamjina and A. Sameh, "Numerical Conformal Mapping Methods on Multiprocessors," in preparation, 1983.

[KBCD74] D. Kuck, P. Budnik, S-C. Chen, E. Davis, Jr., J. Han, P. Kraska, D. Lawrie, Y. Muraoka, R. Strebendt, and R. Towle, "Measurements of Parallelism in Ordinary FORTRAN Programs," *IEEE Computer,* Vol. 7, No. 1, pp. 37-46, Jan. 1974.

[Kers81] D. Kershaw, "The Solution of Single Linear Tridiagonal Systems and Vectorization of the ICCG Algorithm on the Cray-1," Lawrence Livermore Lab., Tech. Rpt. UCID-19085, June 1981.

[KKLW80] D. J. Kuck, R. H. Kuhn, B. Leasure, and M. Wolfe, "The Structure of an Advanced Vectorizer for Pipelined Processors," *Proc. of COMPSAC 80, The 4th Int'l. Computer Software and Applications Conf.,* Chicago, IL, pp. 709-715, Oct. 1980.

[KKPL81] D. J. Kuck, R. H. Kuhn, D. A. Padua, B. Leasure, and M. Wolfe, "Dependence Graphs and Compiler Optimizations," *Proc. of the 8th ACM Symp. on Principles of Programming Languages (POPL),* Williamsburg, VA, pp. 207-218, Jan. 1981.

[KPSW81] D. Kuck, D. Padua, A. Sameh, and M. Wolfe, "Languages and High-Performance Computations," Invited paper, *Proc. of the IFIP Working Conf. on The Relationship Between Numerical Computation and Programming Languages,* Boulder, CO, Aug. 1981 (North-Holland).

[KuPa79] D. J. Kuck and D. A. Padua, "High-Speed Multiprocessors and Their Compilers," *Proc. of the 1979 Int'l. Conf. on Parallel Processing,*

[KuSa72] D. Kuck and A. Sameh, "Parallel Computation of Eigenvalues of Real Matrices," in *Information Processing 71* Vol. II, pp. 1266-1272, North-Holland Publishing Co., Amsterdam-London, 1972.

[LaPa80] D. H. Lawrie and D. A. Padua, "Analysis of Message Switching with Shuffle-Exchanges in Multiprocessors," *Proc. of the Workshop on Interconnection Networks for Parallel and Distributed Processing,* W. Lafayette, IN, H. J. Siegel (ed.), pp. 116-123, April 1980.

[LaSa80] J. Larson and A. Sameh, "Automatic Roundoff Error Analysis—A Relative Error Approach," *Computing,* 24, pp. 275-279, 1980.

[LaSa82] D. Lawrie and A. Sameh, "The Complexity of the Computation and Communication of a Parallel Banded System Solver," submitted for publication, 1983.

[LaVo80] D. Lawrie and C. Vora, "The Prime Memory System for Array Access," *Proc. of the 1980 Int'l. Conf. on Parallel Processing,* Harbor Springs, MI, pp. 81-90, Aug. 1980.

[Lawr75] D. H. Lawrie, "Access and Alignment of Data in an Array Processor," *IEEE Trans. on Computers,* Vol. C-24, No. 12, pp. 1145-1155, Dec. 1975.

[Lawr82] D. Lawrie, "Memory Access Mechanisms in Cedar," Cedar document no. 1, Univ. of Ill. at Urb.-Champ., Dept. of Comput. Sci., Sept. 1982.

[LiLY82] J. E. Lilienkamp, D. H. Lawrie, and P-C. Yew, "A Fault Tolerant Interconnection Network Using Error Correcting Codes," *Proc. of the 1982 Int'l. Conf. on Parallel Processing,* Bellaire, MI, pp. 123-125, Aug. 1982.

[Mant77]   T. A. Manteuffel, "Tchebychev Iteration for Nonsymmetric Linear Systems," *Numer. Math.* 28, pp. 307-327, 1977.

[Mant78]   T. A. Manteuffel, "Adaptive Procedure for Estimating Parameters for the Nonsymmetric Tchebychev Iteration," *Numer. Math.* 31, pp. 183-208, 1978.

[MCML82] K. McDonough, E. Candel, S. Magar, and A. Leigh, "Microcomputer with 32-bit Arithmetic Does High-Precision Number Crunching," *Electronics,* pp. 105-110, Feb. 1982.

[OLWi79]   D. O'Leary and O. Widlund, "Capacitance Matrix Methods for the Helmholtz Equation on General Three-dimensional Regions," *Math. Comp. 33,* pp. 849-880, 1979.

[Padm83]   K. Padmanabhan, PhD Thesis, University of Illinois, inpreparation, 1983.

[PaKL80]   D. A. Padua, D. J. Kuck, and D. H. Lawrie, "High-Speed Multiprocessors and Compilation Techniques," *IEEE Trans. on Computers,* Vol. C-29, No. 9, pp. 763-776, Sept. 1980.

[PaRa82]   D. S. Parker and C. S. Raghavendra, "The Gamma Network: A Multiprocessor Interconnection Network with Redundant Paths," *Proc. of the 9th Annual Symp. on Computer Architecture,* pp. 73-80, April 1982.

[PaSa82]   C. Paige and M. Saunders, "LSQR—An Algorithm for Sparse Linear Equations and Sparse Least Squares," *ACM TOMS 8,* pp. 43-71, 1982.

[Past81]   M. Pasternak, "A Comparison of Parallel and Sequential Linear System Solvers," M.S. Thesis, Department of Computer Science, University of Illinois at Urbana-Champaign, 1981.

[PrWi76]   W. Proskurowski and O. Widlund, "On the Numerical Solution of Helmholtz's Equation by the Capacitance Matrix Method," *Math. Comp. 30,* pp. 433-468, 1976.

[Saad81]   Y. Saad, "Krylov Subspace Methods for Solving Large Unsymmetric Linear Systems," *Math. Comp. 37,* pp. 105-126, 1981.

[Saad82]   Y. Saad, "The Lanczos Biorthogonalization Algorithm and other Oblique Projection Methods for Solving Large Unsymmetric Systems," *SIAM J. on Numerical Analysis, 19,* pp. 485-506, 1982.

[Same81]   A. Sameh, "Parallel Algorithms in Numerical Linear Algebra," *Proc. of the CREST Conf. on Design of Numerical Algorithms for Parallel Processing,* Univ. of Bergamo, Bergamo, Italy, June 1981 (Academic Press).

[Same83]   A. Sameh, "An Overview of Parallel Algorithms in Numerical Linear Algebra," *First International Colloquium on Vector and Parallel Computing in Scientific Applications,* Paris, March 1983.

[SaSa81]   Y. Saad and A. Sameh, "Iterative Methods for the Solution of Elliptic Difference Equations on Multiprocessors," Invited paper, *Proc. of CONPAR 81, Conf. on Analyzing Problem-Classes and Programming for Parallel Computing,* Nurnberg, F. R. Germany, pp. 395-413, June 1981 (Springer-Verlag).

[SaSS82]   Y. Saad, A. Sameh, and P. Saylor, "Parallel Iterative Methods for Elliptic Difference Equations," to be submitted, 1982.

[Smit74]   B. T. Smith, *et. al., Matrix Eigensystem Routines—EISPACK Guide,* Lecture Notes in Computer Science, 6, Springer—Verlag, 1974.

[Taft81]   C. K. Taft, Jr., "Preconditioning Strategies for Solving Elliptic Difference Equations on a Multiprocessor," Univ. of Ill. at Urb.-Champ., Dept. of Comput. Sci, 1982.

[Tana71]   K. Tanabe, "Projection Methods for Solving a Singular System of Linear Equations and Its Applications," pp. 203-214, 1971.

[TrBH82]   P. C. Treleaven, D. R. Brownbridge, and R. P. Hopkins, "Data-Driven and Demand-Driven Computer Architectures," *Comput. Surveys,* Vol. 14, No. 1, pp. 93-143, Mar. 1982.

[Vors82]   H. A. van der Vorst, "A Vectorizable Variant of Some ICCG Methods," *SIAM Journ. Scientific and Statistical Computing,* Vol. 3, No. 3, pp. 350-356, Sept. 1982.

[WaMc82]   F. Ware and W. McAllister, "C-MOS Chip Set Streamlines Floating-Point Processing," *Electronics,* pp. 149-152, Feb. 10, 1982.

[WenK76]   K-Y Wen, "Interprocessor Connections—Capabilities, Exploitation, and Effectiveness," Univ. of Ill. at Urb.-Champ., Dept. of Comput. Sci. Rpt. No. 76-830, Oct. 1976.

[YewP82]   P-C. Yew, "Simulators and Machine-Design Related Problems," Cedar document no. 4, Univ. of Ill. at Urb.-Champ., Dept. of Comput. Sci., Aug. 1982.

The NYU Ultracomputer—Designing an MIMD Shared Memory Parallel Computer

ALLAN GOTTLIEB, RALPH GRISHMAN, CLYDE P. KRUSKAL, KEVIN P. MCAULIFFE, LARRY RUDOLPH, AND MARC SNIR

Abstract—We present the design for the NYU Ultracomputer, a shared-memory MIMD parallel machine composed of thousands of autonomous processing elements. This machine uses an enhanced message switching network with the geometry of an Omega-network to approximate the ideal behavior of Schwartz's paracomputer model of computation and to implement efficiently the important fetch-and-add synchronization primitive. We outline the hardware that would be required to build a 4096 processor system using 1990's technology. We also discuss system software issues, and present analytic studies of the network performance. Finally, we include a sample of our effort to implement and simulate parallel variants of important scientific programs.

Index Terms—Computer architecture, fetch-and-add, MIMD, multiprocessor, Omega-network, parallel computer, parallel processing, shared memory, systolic queues, VLSI.

Manuscript received January 13, 1982; revised June 28, 1982. This work was supported in part by the National Science Foundation under Grant NSF-MCS79-07804, and by the Applied Mathematical Sciences Program of the Department of Energy under Grant DE-AC02-76ER03077.

A. Gottlieb, R. Grishman, K. P. McAuliffe, and M. Snir are with the Courant Institute of Mathematical Sciences, New York University, New York, NY 10012.

C. P. Kruskal is with the Department of Computer Science, University of Illinois, Urbana, IL 61801.

L. Rudolph was with the Department of Computer Science, University of Toronto, Toronto, Ont., Canada. He is now with the Department of Computer Science, Carnegie-Mellon University, Pittsburgh, PA 15213.

I. INTRODUCTION

WITHIN a few years advanced VLSI (very large scale integration) technology will produce a fast single-chip processor including high-speed floating-point arithmetic. This leads one to contemplate the level of computing power that would be attained if thousands of such processors cooperated effectively on the solution of large-scale computational problems.

The NYU "Ultracomputer" group has been studying how such ensembles can be constructed for effective use and has produced a tentative design that includes some novel hardware and software components. The design may be broadly classified as a general purpose MIMD machine accessing a central shared memory via a message switching network with the geometry of an Omega-network. (For related designs see [3], [37], [38], [42], and [44].)

The major thrust of this paper is to outline and justify, in some detail, the proposed hardware and present the analytic and simulation results upon which parts of the design are based. We also discuss system software issues and describe some of our ongoing efforts to produce parallel versions of important scientific programs (but the reader should see [13] and [18] respectively for a more detailed treatment of these last two topics). Section II of the present report reviews the idealized computation model upon which our design is based; Section III presents the machine design; Section IV analyzes network performance; Section V highlights a parallel scientific program; and Section VI summarizes our results.

II. Machine Model

In this section we first review the paracomputer model, upon which our machine design is based, and the fetch-and-add operation, which we use for interprocessor synchronization. After illustrating the power of this model, we examine some alternative models and justify our selection. Although the paracomputer model to be described is not physically realizable, we shall see in Section III that close approximations can be built.

A. Paracomputers

An idealized parallel processor, dubbed a "paracomputer" by Schwartz [36] and classified as a WRAM by Borodin and Hopcroft [2], consists of autonomous processing elements (PE's) sharing a central memory. The model permits every PE to read or write a shared memory cell in one cycle. In particular, simultaneous reads and writes directed at the same memory cell are effected in a single cycle.

We augment the paracomputer model with the "fetch-and-add" operation (described below) and make precise the effect of simultaneous access to the shared memory. To accomplish the latter we define the *serialization principle:* The effect of simultaneous actions by the PE's is as if the actions occurred in some (unspecified) serial order. For example, consider the effect of one load and two stores simultaneously directed at the same memory cell. The cell will come to contain some one of the quantities written into it. The load will return either the original value or one of the stored values, possibly different from the value the cell comes to contain. Note that simultaneous memory updates are in fact accomplished in one cycle; the serialization principle speaks only of the effect of simultaneous actions and not of their implementation.

We stress that paracomputers must be regarded as idealized computational models since physical limitations, such as restricted fan-in, prevent their realization. In the next section we review the technique whereby a connection network may be used to construct a parallel processor closely approximating our enhanced paracomputer.

B. The Fetch-and-Add Operation

We now introduce a simple yet very effective interprocessor synchronization operation, called fetch-and-add, which permits highly concurrent execution of operating system primitives and applications programs. The format of this operation is F&A(V, e), where V is an integer variable and e is an integer expression. This indivisible operation is defined to return the (old) value of V and to replace V by the sum $V + e$. Moreover, fetch-and-add must satisfy the serialization principle stated above: If V is a shared variable and many fetch-and-add operations simultaneously address V, the effect of these operations is

exactly what it would be if they occurred in some (unspecified) serial order, i.e., V is modified by the appropriate total increment and each operation yields the intermediate value of V corresponding to its position in this order. The following example illustrates the semantics of fetch-and-add: Assuming V is a shared variable, if PEi executes

$$ANS_i \leftarrow F\&A(V, e_i),$$

and if PE$_j$ simultaneously executes

$$ANS_j \leftarrow F\&A(V, e_j),$$

and if V is not simultaneously updated by yet another processor, then either

$$
\begin{array}{ccc}
ANS_i \leftarrow V & & ANS_i \leftarrow V + e_j \\
& \text{or} & \\
ANS_j \leftarrow V + e_i & & ANS_j \leftarrow V
\end{array}
$$

and, in either case, the value of V becomes $V + e_i + e_j$.

For another example consider several PE's concurrently applying fetch-and-add, with an increment of 1, to a shared array index. Each PE obtains an index to a distinct array element (although one does not know beforehand which element will be assigned to which PE). Furthermore, the shared index receives the appropriate total increment.

Section III presents a hardware design that realizes fetch-and-add without significantly increasing the time required to access shared memory and that realizes simultaneous fetch-and-adds updating the same variable in a particularly efficient manner.

C. The Power of Fetch-and-Add

Since in a parallel processor the relative cost of serial bottlenecks rises with the number of PE's, users of future ultra-large-scale machines will be anxious to avoid the use of critical (and hence necessarily serial) code sections, even if these sections are small enough to be entirely acceptable in current practice.

If the fetch-and-add operation is available, we can perform many important algorithms in a completely parallel manner, i.e., without using any critical sections. For example Gottlieb et al. [13][1] present a completely parallel solution to the readers-writers problem[2] and a highly concurrent queue management technique that can be used to implement a totally decentralized operating system scheduler. (The queue management technique is reprinted in the Appendix of the present paper.) We are unaware of any other completely parallel solutions to these problems.[3] To illustrate the nonserial behavior of these algorithms, we note that given a single queue that is

---

[1] As explained in [12], the replace-add primitive defined in [13] and used in several of our earlier reports is essentially equivalent to the fetch-and-add primitive used in the present paper.

[2] Since writers are inherently serial, the solution cannot strictly speaking be considered completely parallel. However, the only critical section used is required by the problem specification. In particular, during periods when no writers are active, no serial code is executed.

[3] Reed and Kanodia [31] give a completely parallel solution to those readers-writers problems for which it suffices to detect, rather than prevent, the concurrent execution of multiple reader tasks with a single writer task. (After detecting such an occurrence, the reader tasks are "undone" and "redone").

neither empty nor full, the concurrent execution of thousands of inserts and thousands of deletes can all be accomplished in the time required for just one such operation. Other highly parallel fetch-and-add-based algorithms appear in [18], [24], [25], and [33].

D. Generalizing Fetch-and-Add

One can define a more general fetch-and-ϕ operation that fetches the value in V and replaces it with $\phi(V, e)$. Of course defining $\phi(a, b) = a + b$ gives fetch-and-add. If ϕ is both associative and commutative, the final value in V after the completion of concurrent fetch-and-ϕ's is independent of the serialization order chosen.

We now show that two important coordination primitives, swap and test-and-set, may also be obtained as special cases of fetch-and-ϕ. (It must be noted, however, that the fetch-and-add operation has proved to be a sufficient coordination primitive for all the highly concurrent algorithms developed to date.) We use the brackets { and } to group statements that must be executed indivisibly and define test-and-set to be a value-returning procedure operating on a shared Boolean variable.

$$\text{TestAndSet}(V)$$
$$\{\text{Temp} \leftarrow V$$
$$V \leftarrow \text{TRUE}\}$$
$$\text{RETURN Temp.}$$

The swap operation is defined as exchanging the values of a local variable L (which specifies a processor register or stack location) and a variable V stored in central memory

$$\text{Swap}(L, V)$$
$$\{\text{Temp} \leftarrow L$$
$$L \leftarrow V$$
$$V \leftarrow \text{Temp}\}$$

It is easy to see that

TestAndSet(V) is equivalent to Fetch&OR(V, TRUE).

Similarly, a swap operation can be effected by using the projection operator π_2, where $\pi_2(a, b) = b$; i.e.,

Swap(L, V) is equivalent to $L \leftarrow$ Fetch&$\pi_2(V, L)$.

We conclude this discussion of fetch-and-ϕ by showing that this operation may be used as the sole primitive for accessing central memory. Specifically, we show how to obtain the familiar load and store operations as degenerate cases of fetch-and-ϕ. To load the local variable L from a variable V stored in central memory one simply executes

$$L \leftarrow \text{Fetch}\&\pi_1(V, *)$$

where $\pi_1(a, b) = a$ and the value of $*$ is immaterial (and thus need not be transmitted). Similarly, to store the value of L into V one executes

$$* \leftarrow \text{Fetch}\&\pi_2(V, L)$$

where the $*$ indicates that the value returned is not used (and thus again need not be transmitted).

E. Alternate Machine Models

In this subsection we discuss several other heavily researched models of parallel processors and explain our choice of a large-scale MIMD shared memory machine.

One line of study pioneered by Kung (see, e.g., [27]), focuses on the great economic and speed advantages obtainable by designing parallel algorithms that conform well to the restrictions imposed by VLSI technology, in particular algorithms and architectures that lay out well in two dimensions. These "systolic" processor designs are already having a significant impact on signal processing, an impact that will doubtless increase dramatically over the next several years. However, for computations having complex control and data flow, the systolic architecture is less well suited. We do expect that VLSI systolic systems will be used for those subcomponents of our machine having regular control and data flow; the design of one such component, an enhanced systolic queue, is presented in Section III-D.

The current generation of supercomputers may be roughly classified as SIMD shared memory machines by considering their vector pipelines to be multiple processors each executing the same instruction [41]. Effective use of such machines is only attained by algorithms consisting primarily of vector operations. Although it is far from trivial to "vectorize" algorithms, such a program has been successfully undertaken at many supercomputer sites. Once again, however, some problems (especially those with many data dependent decisions) appear to resist effective vectorization. Rodrigue, Giroux, and Pratt [32] of Lawrence Livermore National Laboratory write:

Vector and array processors were designed with the idea of solving fluid-type problems efficiently. In general these machines do not lend themselves well to particle tracking calculations. For a scientific laboratory such as LLNL, the computer should be able to handle both forms of calculation, but it remains to be seen whether this goal will ever be achieved.

This goal is achieved by rejecting SIMD machines in favor of the MIMD paracomputer model, which our simulation studies have shown to be effective for both fluid-type [34] and particle tracking calculations [19].

Yet a third alternative model, specifically architectures derived from very general abstract "dataflow" models of parallel computation, have been pursued by other researchers (see the February 1982 Special Issue of *Computer* and the references contained therein). Recent work in this area has stressed the advantages of a purely applicative, side-effect-free programming language for the description of parallel computation. Although such dataflow machines have been discussed for several years, no completely satisfactory physical design has yet emerged. Without commenting on the relative merits of applicative programming, we note that Gottlieb and Schwartz [14] show how a dataflow language may be executed with maximal parallelism on our machine (see also [17]).

The final model we consider is a message passing alternative to shared memory. Except for very small systems, it is not

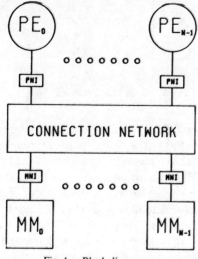

Fig. 1. Block diagram.

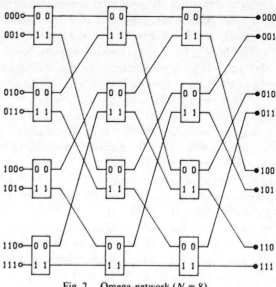

Fig. 2. Omega-network ($N = 8$).

possible to have every PE directly connected to every other PE. Thus it may be necessary to route messages via intermediate PE's. In the original ultracomputer design of Schwartz [36] the programmer specified the routing explicitly. By tailoring algorithms to the particular interconnection geometry, one can obtain very high performance. However, we found such a machine to be significantly more difficult to program than one in which the entire memory is available to each PE (see [8], [10], [11], and [35]). If the geometry is hidden from the programmer by having the individual PE's perform the necessary routing, a more loosely coupled machine results. In recent years such machines have been much studied for distributed computing applications. Although message passing architectures are indeed quite attractive for distributed computing, we believe that for the applications we have emphasized, thousands of processors cooperating to solve a single large-scale scientific problem, the more tightly coupled model featuring high speed concurrent access to shared memory is more effective.

III. Machine Design

In this section we present the design of the NYU Ultracomputer, a machine that appears to the user as a paracomputer, and we justify our design decisions. As indicated above, no machine can provide the single-cycle access to shared memory postulated in the paracomputer model; our design approximates a paracomputer by using a message switching network with the geometry of the Omega-network of Lawrie [29][4] to connect $N = 2^D$ autonomous PE's to a central shared memory composed of N memory modules (MM's). Thus, the direct single cycle access to shared memory characteristic of paracomputers is replaced by an indirect access via a multicycle connection network. Each PE is attached to the network via a processor network interface (PNI) and each MM is attached via a memory network interface (MNI). Fig. 1 gives a block diagram of the machine.

After reviewing routing in the network, we show that an analogous network composed of enhanced switches provides

[4] Note that this network has the same topology as the rectangular SW banyan network of Goke and Lipovsky [7].

efficient support for concurrent fetch-and-add operations. We then examine our choice of network and local memory. To conclude this section we present a detailed design for the switches and describe the PE's, MM's, and network interfaces. As will be shown both the PE's and MM's are relatively standard components; the novelty of the design lies in the network and in particular in the constituent switches and interfaces.

A. Network Design

For machines with thousands of PE's the communication network is likely to be the dominant component with respect to both cost and performance. The design to be presented achieves the following objectives.

i) Bandwidth linear in N, the number of PE's.

ii) Latency, i.e., memory access time, logarithmic in N.

iii) Only $O(N \log N)$ identical components.

iv) Routing decisions local to each switch; thus routing is not a serial bottleneck and is efficient for short messages.

v) Concurrent access by multiple PE's to the same memory cell suffers no performance penalty; thus interprocessor coordination is not serialized. We are unaware of any significantly different design that also attains these goals.

1) *Routing in an Omega-Network:* The manner in which an Omega-network can be used to implement memory loads and stores is well known and is based on the existence of a (unique) path connecting each PE-MM pair. To describe the routing algorithm we use the notation in Fig. 2: both the PE's and the MM's are numbered using D-bit identifiers whose values range from 0 to $N - 1$; the binary representation of each identifier x is denoted $x_D \cdots x_1$; upper ports on switches are numbered 0 and lower ports 1; messages from PE's to MM's traverse the switches from left to right; and returning messages traverse the switches from right to left. A message is transmitted from $PE(p_D \cdots p_1)$ to $MM(m_D \cdots m_1)$ by using output port m_j when leaving the stage j switch. Similarly, to travel from $MM(m_D \cdots m_1)$ to $PE(p_D \cdots p_1)$ a message uses output port p_j at a stage j switch.

The routing algorithm just presented generalizes immediately to a D-stage network composed of k-input-k-output switches (instead of the 2×2 switches used above) connecting k^D PE's to k^D MM's: The ports of a switch are numbered 0 to $k - 1$ and the identifiers are written in base k. Although the remainder of this section deals exclusively with 2×2 switches, all the results generalize to larger switches, which are considered in Section IV.

2) Omega-Network Enhancements: To prevent the network from becoming a bottleneck for machines comprising large numbers of PE's, an important design goal has been to attain a bandwidth proportional to the number of PE's. This has been achieved by a combination of three factors (see Section IV for an analysis of network bandwidth).

i) The network is pipelined, i.e., the delay between messages equals the switch cycle time not the network transit time. (Since the latter grows logarithmically, nonpipelined networks can have bandwidth at most $O(N/\log N)$.)

ii) The network is message switched, i.e., the switch settings are not maintained while a reply is awaited. (The alternative, circuit switching, is incompatible with pipelining.)

iii) A queue is associated with each switch to enable concurrent processing of requests for the same port. (The alternative adopted by Burroughs [3] of killing one of the two conflicting requests also limits bandwidth to $O(N/\log N)$, see [26].)

Since we propose using a message switching network, it may appear that both the destination and return addresses must be transmitted with each message. We need, however, transmit only one D bit address, an amalgam of the origin and destination: When a message first enters the network, its origin is determined by the input port, so only the destination address is needed. Switches at the jth stage route messages based on memory address bit m_j and then replace this bit with the PE number bit p_j, which equals the number of the input port on which the message arrived. Thus, when the message reaches its destination, the return address is available.

When concurrent loads and stores are directed at the same memory location and meet at a switch, they can be combined without introducing any delay by using the following procedure (see [13] and [21]).

i) Load-Load: Forward one of the two (identical) loads and satisfy each by returning the value obtained from memory.

ii) Load-Store: Forward the store and return its value to satisfy the load.

iii) Store-Store: Forward either store and ignore the other.

Combining requests reduces communication traffic and thus decreases the lengths of the queues mentioned above, leading to lower network latency (i.e., reduced memory access time). Since combined requests can themselves be combined, the network satisfies the key property that any number of concurrent memory references to the same location can be satisfied in the time required for just one central memory access. It is this property, when extended to include fetch-and-add operations as indicated below, that permits the bottleneck-free implementation of many coordination protocols.

3) Implementing Fetch-and-Add: By including adders in

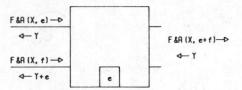

Fig. 3. Combining Fetch-and-Adds.

the MNI's, the fetch-and-add operation can be easily implemented: When $F\&A(X, e)$ is transmitted through the network and reaches the MNI associated with the MM containing X, the value of X and the transmitted e are brought to the MNI adder, the sum is stored in X, and the old value of X is returned through the network to the requesting PE. Since fetch-and-add is our sole synchronization primitive (and is also a key ingredient in many algorithms), concurrent fetch-and-add operations will often be directed at the same location. Thus, as indicated above, it is crucial in a design supporting large numbers of processors not to serialize this activity.

Enhanced switches permit the network to combine fetch-and-adds with the same efficiency as it combines loads and stores: When two fetch-and-adds referencing the same shared variable, say $F\&A(X, e)$ and $F\&A(X, f)$, meet at a switch, the switch forms the sum $e + f$, transmits the combined request $F\&A(X, e + f)$, and stores the value e in its local memory (see Fig. 3). When the value Y is returned to the switch in response to $F\&A(X, e + f)$, the switch transmits Y to satisfy the original request $F\&A(X, e)$ and transmits $Y + e$ to satisfy the original request $F\&A(X, f)$.

Assuming that the combined request was not further combined with yet another request, we would have $Y = X$; thus the values returned by the switch are X and $X + e$, thereby effecting the serialization order "$F\&A(X, e)$ followed immediately by $F\&A(X, f)$." The memory location X is also properly incremented, becoming $X + e + f$. If other fetch-and-add operations updating X are encountered, the combined requests are themselves combined, and the associativity of addition guarantees that the procedure gives a result consistent with the serialization principle.

Although the preceding description assumed that the requests to be combined arrive at a switch simultaneously, the actual design can also merge an incoming request with requests already queued for output to the next stage (see Section III-D).

To combine a fetch-and-add operation with another reference to the same memory location we proceed as follows.

i) Fetch&Add-Fetch&Add: As described above, a combined request is transmitted and the result is used to satisfy both fetch-and-adds.

ii) Fetch&Add-Load: Treat Load(X) as Fetch&Add(X, 0).

iii) Fetch&Add(X, e)-Store(X, f): Transmit Store($e + f$) and satisfy the fetch-and-add by returning f.

Finally, we note that a straightforward generalization of the above design yields a network implementing the fetch-and-ϕ primitive for any associative operator ϕ [12].

4) Other Considerations: We now turn our attention to other issues concerning the proposed network design.

Since the introduction of queues in each switch leads to stochastic delays and the network is pipelined, it is possible for memory references from a given PE to distinct MM's to be satisfied in an order different from the order in which they were issued. This reordering can violate the serialization principle specified in our model (see [28]). A simple-minded solution to this problem is not to pipeline requests to read-write shared variables; however, this approach is overly conservative since most such request can be safely pipelined.

Since the analyses thus far obtained require the introduction of simplifying assumptions (see Section IV), and we are unable to perform faithful simulations of full 4096 PE networks, we cannot confidently predict the expected network latency. Our preliminary analyses and partial simulations have yielded encouraging results.

A potential serial bottleneck is the memory module itself. If every PE simultaneously requests a distinct word from the same MM, these N requests are serviced one at a time. However, introducing a hashing function when translating virtual addresses to physical addresses, assures that unfavorable situations occur with probability approaching zero as N increases. On average, the most requests directed at a single MM is (asymptotically) only log N/log log N [44]. Furthermore, the probability that all MM's receive less than log N requests (asymptotically) exceeds $1 - 1/P(N)$ for any polynomial P.

The hardware complexity due to the decision to adopt a queued message switching network introduces significant processing at each stage. Although the internal cycle time of the switches may be important for today's technology, we expect that by the end of the decade any on-chip delay will be dominated by the chip-to-chip transmission delays. (Since the switch bandwidth will be pin limited, the added internal complexity will not increase the component count.)

B. Local Memory

The negative impact of the large network latency can be partially mitigated by providing each PE with a local memory in which private variables reside and into which read-only shared data (in particular, program text) may be copied. Storing shared read-write data in the local memory of multiple PE's must, in general, be prohibited: the resulting memory incoherence would otherwise lead to violations of the serialization principle. We shall show in Section III-D that in certain special cases, this restriction may be relaxed.

One common design for parallel machines is to implement a separately addressable local memory at each PE, imposing upon compilers and loaders the onus of managing the two level store. The alternative approach, which we intend to implement, is the one conventionally used on uniprocessors: The local memory is implemented as a cache. Experience with uniprocessor systems shows that a large cache can capture up to 95 percent of the references to cacheable variables, effectively shifting the burden of managing a two level store from the software to the hardware (see [20]).

C. The Switches

We now detail an individual network switch, which is essentially a 2 × 2 bidirectional routing device transmitting a message from its input ports to the appropriate output port on the opposite side. The PE side sends and receives messages to and from the PE's via input ports, called FromPEi, where i = 0, 1, and output ports, called ToPEi. Similarly, the MM side communicates with the MM's via ports FromMMi and ToMMi. (Note that in our figures the To and From ports are coalesced into bidirectional ports.)

As indicated above, we associate a queue with each output port. The head entry is transmitted when the switch at the adjacent stage is ready to receive it (the message might be delayed if the queue this message is due to enter is already full).

To describe the process whereby requests are combined in a switch, we view a request as consisting of several components: function indicator (i.e., load, store, or fetch-and-add), address, and data. The address itself consists of the amalgamation of part of the PE number and part of the MM number, and the internal address within the specified MM. For ease of exposition, we consider only combining homogeneous requests (i.e., requests with like function fields); it is not hard to extend the design to permit combining heterogeneous requests. For each request, R-new, that enters a ToMM queue[5], we search the requests already in this queue using as key the function, MM number, and internal address from R-new.[6] If no request matches R-new, then no combining is possible and R-new simply remains the tail entry of the output queue. Otherwise, let R-old denote the message in the ToMM queue that matches R-new. Then, to effect the serialization R-old followed immediately by R-new, the switch performs the following actions: The addresses of R-new and R-old are placed into a Wait Buffer (to await the return of R-old from memory) and R-new is deleted from the ToMM queue. If the request is a store then the datum of R-old (in the ToMM queue) is replaced by the datum of R-new. If the request is a fetch-and-add then the datum of R-old is replaced by the sum of the two data. In addition, for fetch-and-adds, the datum of R-old is sent to the wait buffer. Thus, each entry sent to the wait buffer consists of the address of R-old (the entry key); the address of R-new; and, in the case of a combined fetch-and-add, a datum. (Note that stores and fetch-and-adds can both be implemented by using an ALU that receives the data of R-old and R-new and returns either the sum of the two numbers or just R-new.)

Before presenting the actions that occur when a request returns to a switch from a MM, we make two remarks. First, we will use two Wait Buffers (one associated with each ToMM queue) since access to a single wait buffer would be rate limiting. Second, the key of each entry is the Wait Buffer uniquely identifies the message for which it is waiting since the PNI is to prohibit a PE from having more than one outstanding reference to the same memory location.

After arriving at a FromMM port, a returning request, R-ret, is both routed to the appropriate ToPE queue and used to search associatively the relevant wait buffer. If a match

---

[5] Although we use the term queue, entries within the middle of the queue may also be accessed.

[6] The design of the ToMM queue, permitting this search and subsequent actions to be performed with minimal delay, is detailed in Section III-C1.

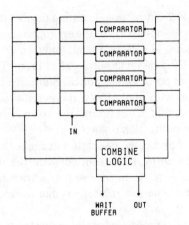

Fig. 4. Systolic ToMM queue.

occurs, the entry found, R-wait, is removed from the buffer and its function indicator, PE and MM numbers, and address are routed to the appropriate ToPE queue. If the request was a load, the data field is taken from R-ret; if a fetch-and-add, the R-wait data field is added to the R-ret data field.

To summarize the necessary hardware, we note that in addition to adders, registers, and routing logic, each switch requires two instances of each of the following memory units. For each unit we have indicated the operations it must support.

i) ToMM-queue: Entries are inserted and deleted in a queue-like fashion, associative searches may be performed, and matched entries may be updated.

ii) ToPE-queue: Entries may be inserted and deleted in a queue-like fashion.

iii) Wait-buffer: Entries may be inserted and associative searches may be performed with matched entries removed.

Note that it is possible for more than two requests to be combined at a switch. However, the structure of the switch is simplified if it supports only combinations of pairs since a request returning from memory could then match at most one request in the wait buffer, eliminating the need for contention logic. Another advantage of not supporting multiple combinations within one switch is that it permits the pipelined implementation of the ToMM queue described below.

The switch can be partitioned into two essentially independent components, each implementing a unidirectional switch. The communication between the two components is restricted to the information pertaining to combined messages, that is, the information sent from the ToMM queues to the wait buffers. Since requests are combined relatively infrequently, the link between the two components can have a small bandwidth. We are currently investigating other possible partitions for a switch while noting that its increased functionality hinders a bit-slice implementation.

1) *The ToMM Queue:* As illustrated in Fig. 4 our ToMM queue is an enhancement of the VLSI systolic queue of Guibas and Liang [15]. We first describe the queue-like behavior of this structure and then explain how the necessary searching is accomplished.

Items added to the queue enter the middle column, check the adjacent slot in the right column, and move into this slot if it is empty. If the slot is full, the item moves up one position

in the middle column and the process is repeated. (Should the item reach the top of the middle column and still be unable to shift right, the queue is declared full.) Meanwhile, items in the right column shift down, exiting the queue at the bottom.

Before giving the enhancements needed for searching, we make four observations: the entries proceed in a FIFO order; as long as the queue is not empty and the switch in the next stage can receive an item, one item exits the queue at each cycle; as long as the queue is not full a new item can be entered at each cycle[7]; items are not delayed if the queue is empty and the next switch can receive them.

The queue is enhanced by adding comparison logic between adjacent slots in the right two columns, permitting a new entry moving up the middle column to be matched successively against all the previous entries as they move down the right column.[8] If a match is found, the matched entry moves (from the middle column) to the left column, called the "match column." Entries in the match column shift down at the same rate as entries on the right column of the queue. A pair of requests to be combined will therefore exit their respective columns at the same time and will thus enter the combining unit simultaneously.

Note that it is possible to reduce the width of the ToMM queue by having each request split into several successive entries. If requests are transmitted between switches as a series of successive packets, a ToMM queue with a width matching the size of these packets would avoid the assembly and disassembly of messages, resulting in a complete pipelining of the message processing. The smaller size of comparators and adders may also result in faster logic. A detailed description of the VLSI switch logic appears in [40].

D. The Network Interfaces

The PNI (processor-network interface) performs four functions: virtual to physical address translation, assembly/disassembly of memory requests, enforcement of the network pipeline policy, and cache management. The MNI (memory-network interface) is much simpler, performing only request assembly/disassembly and the additions operation necessary to support fetch-and-add. Since the MNI operations as well as the first two PNI functions are straightforward, we discuss only pipelining policy and cache management.

Before detailing these two functions, we note two restrictions on pipelining memory request (i.e., issuing a request before the previous one is acknowledged). As indicated above, pipelining requests indiscriminately can violate the serialization principle (Section III-A4), and furthermore, pipelining requests to the same memory location is not supported by our current switch design (Section III-C).

Since accessing central memory involves traversing a mul-

---

[7] The number of cycles intervening between successive insertions must, however, be even (zero included).

[8] Actually, an item is matched against half of the entries moving down the right column. Since we packetize messages (see below) we can arrange for each item to be matched against its corresponding item in each request moving down the right column (this is particularly easy if each message consists of an even number of packets). If, however, an entire request is contained in one packet, then one needs either twice as many comparators or two cycles for each motion.

tistage network, effective cache management is very important. To reduce network traffic a write-back update policy was chosen: writes to the cache are not written through to central memory; instead, when a cache miss occurs and eviction is necessary, updated words within the evicted block are written to central memory. Note that cache generated traffic can always be pipelined.

In addition to the usual operations described above, which are invisible to the PE, our cache provides two functions, release and flush, that must be specifically requested and can be performed on a segment level or for the entire cache. We now show that judicious use of release and flush further reduces network traffic.

The release command marks a cache entry as available without performing a central memory update. This enables a task to free cache space allocated to virtual addresses that will no longer be referenced. For example, private variables declared within a begin-end block can be released at block exit. Thus, the release operation reduces network traffic by lowering the quantity of data written back to central memory during a task switch. Moreover, if (prior to a task switch) another virtual address maps to a released cache address, no central memory update is necessary.

Release also facilitates caching shared read-write data during periods of read-only access: if a set of tasks sharing read-write data can guarantee that during a period of time no updates will occur, then the data is eligible for caching for the duration of this period. Subsequently, the data must be released and marked uncacheable to insure that no task uses stale data.

The flush facility, which enables the PE to force a write-back of cached values, is needed for task switching since a blocked task may be rescheduled on a different PE. To illustrate another use of flush and release, consider a variable V that is declared in task T and is shared with T's subtasks. Prior to spawning these subtasks, T may treat V as private (and thus eligible to be cached and pipelined) providing that V is flushed, released, and marked shared immediately before the subtasks are spawned. The flush updates main memory, the release insures that the parent task will not use stale data, and marking V shared enables T's subtasks to reference V. Once the subtasks have completed, T may again consider V as private and eligible for caching. Coherence is maintained since V is cached only during periods of exclusive use by one task.

To increase performance one may define a combined flush-and-release command that can be implemented using only a single scan through the cache directory.

E. The Processors and Memory Modules

The MM's are standard components consisting of off the shelf memory chips. The PE's, however, need to be a (slightly) custom design since we require the fetch-and-add operation. Moreover, to utilize fully the high bandwidth connection network, a PE must continue execution of the instruction stream immediately after issuing a request to fetch a value from central memory. The target register would be marked "locked" until the requested value is returned from memory; an attempt to use a locked register would suspend execution.

Note that this policy is currently supported on large scale computers and is becoming available on one chip processors [30]. Software designed for such processors would attempt to prefetch data sufficiently early to permit uninterrupted execution and a cache designed for such processors would not lock up despite outstanding cache misses (see [23] for one such design).

If the latency remains an impediment to performance, we would hardware-multiprogram the PE's as in the CHOPP design [42] and the Denelcor HEP machine [4]. Note that k-fold multiprogramming is equivalent to using k times as many PE's—each having relative performance $1/k$. Since, to attain a given efficiency, such a configuration requires problems of larger size, we view multiprogramming as a last resort.

Although we have not given sufficient attention to I/O, we note that I/O processors can be substituted for arbitrary PE's in the system. More generally, since the design does not require homogeneous PE's, a variety of special purpose processors (e.g., FFT chips, matrix multipliers, voice generators, etc.) can be attached to the network.

F. Machine Packaging

We conservatively estimate that a machine built in 1990 would require four chips for each PE-PNI pair, nine chips for each MM-MNI pair (assuming a 1 Mbyte MM built out of 1 Mbit chips), and two chips for each 4-input-4-output switch (which replaces four of the 2×2 switches described above). Thus, a 4096 processor machine would require roughly 65 000 chips, not counting the I/O interfaces. Note that the chip count is still dominated, as in present day machines, by the memory chips, and that only 19 percent of the chips are used for the network. Nevertheless, most of the machine volume will be occupied by the network, and its assembly will be the dominant system cost due to the nonlocal wiring required.

It is possible to partition an N input, N output Omega network built from 2×2 switches into $\sqrt{N}$ "input modules" and $\sqrt{N}$ "output modules." An input module consists of $\sqrt{N}$ network inputs and the $\sqrt{N} \, (\lg N)/4$ switches that can be accessed from these inputs in the first $(\lg N)/2$ stages of the network.[9] An output module consists of $\sqrt{N}$ network outputs and the $\sqrt{N} \, (\lg N)/4$ switches that can be accessed from these outputs in the last half of the network. Moreover, as noted by Wise [45], it is possible to arrange the switches of each module so that, between any two successive stages, all lines have the same length (Fig. 5). Finally, if the input boards are stacked vertically on one rack, the output boards are stacked vertically on another rack, and the two racks are stacked one atop another, such that the boards on one rack are orthogonal to the boards on the other rack, then all off board lines will run nearly vertically between the two sets of boards as illustrated in Fig. 6. The same strategy can be used for networks built of $k \times k$ switches. (Figs. 5 and 6 are reprinted with permission from [45].)

We propose using this layout for a 4K processor machine

---

[9] We use lg for the base 2 logarithm.

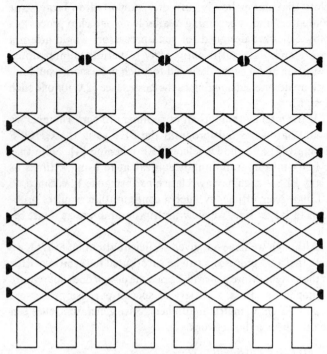

Fig. 5. Layout of network on boards.

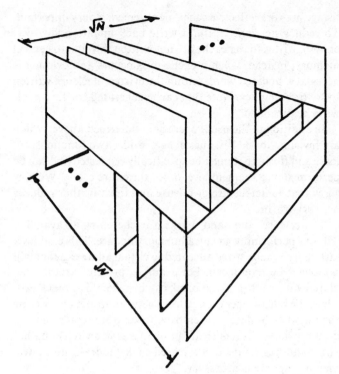

Fig. 6. Packaging of network boards.

constructed from the chips described at the beginning of this section. This machine would include two types of boards: "PE boards" that contain the PE's, the PNI's, and the first half of the network stages and "MM boards" that contain the MM's, the MNI's, and the last half of the network stages. Using the chip counts given above, a 4K PE machine built from two chip 4×4 switches would need 64 PE boards and 64 MM boards, with each PE board containing 352 chips and each MM board containing 672 chips. Since the PE chips will be near the free edge of the PE board and the MM chips will be near the free edge of the MM board, I/O interfaces can be connected along these edges. Bianchini and Bianchini [1] have considered machines built from single chip 2×2 switches. Their analysis shows that an air cooled 4096 PE ultracomputer can easily be packaged into a $5 \times 5 \times 10$ ft enclosure.

IV. COMMUNICATION NETWORK PERFORMANCE

Since the overall ultracomputer performance is critically dependent on the communication network and this network is likely to be the most expensive component of the completed machine, it is essential to evaluate the network performance carefully so as to choose a favorable configuration.

A. Performance Analysis

Although each switch in the network requires a significant amount of logic, it appears feasible to implement a 2×2 switch on one chip using today's technology. Further, we believe it will be feasible in 1990 technology to implement 4×4 or even 8×8 switches on one chip. It seems, however, that the main restriction on the switch performance will be the rate at which information can be fed into and carried from the chip, rather than the rate at which that information can be processed within the chip. The basic hardware constraint will therefore be the number of bits that can be carried on or off the chip in one unit of time (one cycle).

Suppose that 400 bits can be transferred on or off the chip in one cycle (which we estimate, for 1990 technology, to be on the order of 25 ns). If each message transmitted through the network consists of approximately 100 bits (64 bits of data), then a 2×2 switch needs two cycles for the transfer of the 800 bits involved in the relaying of two messages in each direction. It is, however, possible to pipeline the transmission of each message, so that the delay at each switch is only one cycle if the queues are empty.

The chip bandwidth constraint does not determine a unique design for the network. It is possible to replace 2×2 switches by $k \times k$ switches, time multiplexing each line by a factor of $k/2$. It is also possible to use several copies of the same network, thereby reducing the effective load on each one of them and enhancing network reliability. We present performance analyses of various networks in order to indicate the tradeoffs involved.

A particular configuration is characterized by the values of the following three parameters.

i) k—the size of the switch. Recall that a $k \times k$ switch requires $4k$ lines.

ii) m—the time multiplexing factor, i.e., the number of switch cycles required to input a message. (To simplify the analysis we assume that all the messages have the same length.)

iii) d—the number of copies of the network that are used.

The chip bandwidth limits the k/m ratio, which we may thus take to be independent of the network configuration. Note that for any k a network with n inputs and n outputs can be built from $(n \lg n)/(k \lg k)$ $k \times k$ switches and a proportional number of wires. Since our network contains a large number of identical switches, the network's cost is essentially proportional to the number of switches and independent of their complexity. Thus the cost of a configuration is $d(n \lg n)/(k \lg k)$ (we are neglecting the small cost of interfacing the d copies of the network).

In order to obtain a tractible mathematical model of the network we have made the following simplifying assumptions.

1) Requests are not combined.
2) Requests have the same length.
3) Queues are of infinite size.
4) Requests are generated at each PE by independent, identically distributed, time-invariant random processes.
5) MM's are equally likely to be referenced.

Let p be the average number of messages entered into the network by each PE per network cycle. If the queues at each switch are large enough ("infinite queues") then the average switch delay is approximately

$$1 + \frac{m^2 p(1 - 1/k)}{2(1 - mp)}$$

cycles (see [26]; similar results can be found in [16] and [6]). The average network traversal time (in one direction) T equals the number of stages times the switch delay plus the setting time for the pipe, i.e.,

$$T = \frac{\lg n}{\lg k}\left(1 + \frac{m^2 p(1 - 1/k)}{2(1 - mp)}\right) + m - 1.$$

Let us note the following facts.

1) The network has a capacity of $1/m$ messages per cycle per PE. That is each PE cannot enter messages at a rate higher than one per m cycles, and conversely the network can accommodate any traffic below this threshold. Thus, the global bandwidth of the network is indeed proportional to the number of PE's connected to it.

2) The initial 1 in the expression for the switch delay corresponds to the time required for a message to be transmitted through a switch without being queued (the switch service time). The second term corresponds to the average queueing delay. This term decreases to zero when the traffic intensity p decreases to zero and increases to infinity when traffic intensity p increases to the $1/m$ threshold. The surprising feature of this formula is the m^2 factor, which is explained by noting that the queueing delay for a switch with a multiplexing factor of m is roughly the same as the queueing delay for a switch with a multiplexing factor of one, a cycle m times longer, and m times as much traffic per cycle.

We now use these formulas to compare the performance of different configurations. Let us assume that using $k \times k$ switches the time multiplexing factor m equals k. Using d copies of the network reduces the effective load on each copy by a factor of d. Thus the average transit time for a network consisting of d Omega-networks composed of $k \times k$ switches is

$$T = \frac{\lg n}{\lg k}\left(1 + \frac{k(k-1)p}{2(d - kp)}\right) + k - 1$$

cycles, where p is, as before, the average number of messages sent to the network by each PE per cycle. As expected, delays decrease when d increases. The dependency on k is more subtle. Increasing k decreases the number of stages in the network, but increases the pipelining factor, and therefore increases the queueing delays and the pipe setting delay.

We have plotted in Fig. 7 the graphs of T as a function of the traffic intensity, p, for different values of k and d. We see that for reasonable traffic intensities a duplicated network composed of 4×4 switches yields the best performance (but see the next paragraph for a preliminary evaluation for networks consisting of two-chip switches). A network with 8×8 switches and $d = 6$ also yields an acceptable performance, at approximately the same cost as the previous network. Since the bandwidth of the first network is $d/k = 0.5$ and the bandwidth of the second is 0.75, we see that for a given traffic level the second network is less heavily loaded and thus should provide better performance for traffic with high variance. Of course a final determination of an optimal configuration requires more accurate assessments of the technological constraints and the traffic distribution. The pipelining delays incurred for large multiplexing factors, the complexity of large switches, and the heretofore ignored cost and performance penalty incurred with interfacing many network copies, will probably make the use of switches larger than 8×8 impractical for a 4K PE parallel machine.

The previous discussion assumed a one chip implementation of each switch. By using the two chip implementation described at the end of Section III-C, one can nearly double the bandwidth of each switch while doubling the chip count. As delays are highly sensitive to the multiplexing factor m, this implementation would yield a better performance than that obtained by taking two copies of a network built of one chip switches. (It would also have the extra advantage of decreasing the gate count on each chip.) Thus, the ultimate choice may well be one network built of 4×4 switches, each switch consisting of two chips.

We now return to the five assumptions listed above. The first two assumptions, that all messages are of equal (maximal) length and traverse the entire network, are clearly conservative. In practice, messages that do not carry data (load requests and store acknowledgements) would be shorter, and merged messages do not each traverse the entire network.

Simulations have shown that queues of modest size (≤ 8) give essentially the same performance as infinite queues.

Although the requests generated by PE's cooperating on a single problem are not independent, the presence of a large number of PE's and a number of different problems will tend to smooth the data. On the other hand, even in a large system the pattern of requests by a single PE will be time dependent and further analytic and simulation studies are needed to determine the effect of this deviation from our assumed model.

Finally, by applying a hashing function when translating from virtual to physical addresses, the system can ensure that each MM is equally likely to be referenced.

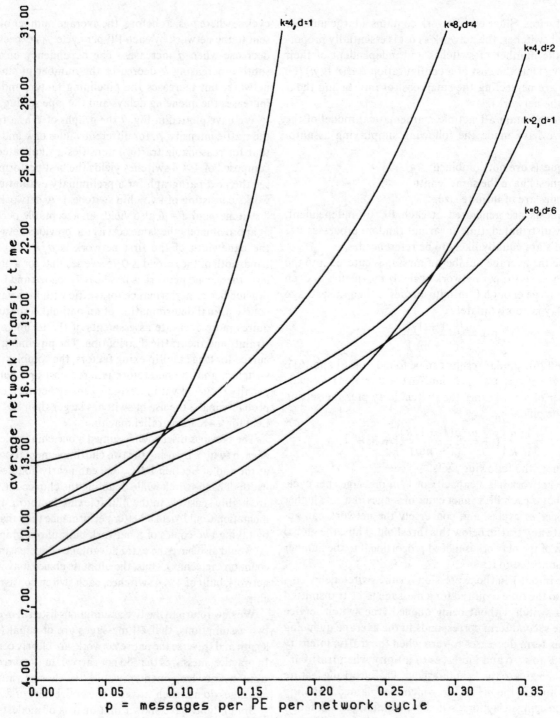

Fig. 7. Transit times for different configurations.

B. Network Simulations

Our discussion of the possible configurations for the communication network still lacks two essential ingredients: an assessment of the traffic intensity we expect to encounter in practical applications, and an assessment of the impact of the network delay on the overall performance.

We routinely run parallel scientific programs under a paracomputer simulator (see [9]) to measure the speedup obtained by parallelism and to judge the difficulty involved in creating parallel programs (see Section V). A recent modifi-

cation allows us to simulate an approximation to the proposed network design rather than an ideal paracomputer: Since an accurate simulation would be very expensive, we used instead a multistage queueing system model with stochastic service time at each stage (see [39]), parameterized to correspond to a network with six stages of 4×4 switches, connecting 4096 PE's to 4096 MM's. A message was modeled as one packet if it did not contain data and as three packets otherwise. Each queue was limited to fifteen packets and both the PE instruction time and the MM access time were assumed to equal twice

286

TABLE I
NETWORK TRAFFIC AND PERFORMANCE

	avg. CM access time	idle cycles	idle cycles per CM load	memory ref. per instr.	shared ref. per instr.
1	8.94	37 percent	5.3	0.21	0.08
2	8.83	39 percent	4.5	0.19	0.08
3	8.81	22 percent	4.9	0.25	0.05
4	8.85	19 percent	3.5	0.24	0.06

the network cycle time. Thus the minimum central memory access time, which consists of the MM access time plus twice the minimum network transit time, equals eight times the PE instruction time.

We have monitored the amount of network traffic generated by several scientific programs under the pessimistic assumption that no shared data is cached and the optimistic assumption that all references to program text and private data are satisfied by the cache. The programs studied were as follows.

i) A parallel version of part of a NASA weather program (solving a two dimensional PDE), with 16 PE's.

ii) The same program, with 48 PE's.

iii) The TRED2 program described in Section V, with 16 PE's.

iv) A multigrid Poisson PDE solver, with 16 PE's.

Table I summarizes simulations of these four programs. The time unit is the PE instruction time. In these simulations the number of requests to central memory (CM) are comfortably below the maximal number that the network can support and indeed the average access time is close to the minimum. (Since each PE was a CDC 6600-type CPU, most instructions involved register-to-register transfers.) Specifically, only one instruction every five cycles for the first two programs (and one every four for the last two) generated a data memory reference.[10] Moreover only one data memory reference out of 2.6 in the first two programs, and one reference out of five for the last two programs were for shared data. We note that the last two programs were designed to minimize the number of accesses to shared data. As a result the number of idle cycles was significantly higher for the first two programs. Since the code generated by the CDC compiler often prefetched operands from memory, the average number of idle cycles per load from central memory was significantly lower than the central memory access time.

We conclude that were these studies repeated on actual hardware the traffic intensity would be low (p <.04), and prefetching would mitigate the problem of large memory latency. The first conclusion, however, must be strongly qualified. The simulator we used is much less sensitive to fluctuations in the network traffic than an actual network would be. Moreover, we have ignored both cache generated traffic and the effect of operating system programs.

V. SIMULATIONS AND SCIENTIFIC PROGRAMMING

As indicated above we use an instruction level paracomputer simulator to study parallel variants of scientific programs.

[10] Since for the first two programs, the PE's were idle (waiting for a memory reference to be satisfied) approximately 40 of the time, five cycles corresponds to approximately three instructions.

Applications already studied include radiation transport, incompressible fluid flow within an elastic boundary, atmospheric modeling, and Monte Carlo simulation of fluid structure. Current efforts include both extending the simulator to model the connection network more faithfully and running programs under a parallel operating system scheduler.

The goals of our paracomputer simulation studies are, first, to develop methodologies for writing and debugging parallel programs and second, to predict the efficiency that future large scale parallel systems can attain. As an example of the approach taken, and of the results thus far obtained, we report on experiments with a parallelized variant of the program TRED2 (taken from Argonne's EISPACK library), which uses Householder's method to reduce a real symmetric matrix to tridiagonal form (see [22] for details).

An analysis of the parallel variant of this program shows that the time required to reduce an $N \times N$ matrix using P processors is well approximated by

$$T(P, N) = aN + dN^3/P + W(P, N)$$

where the first term represents "overhead" instructions that must be executed by all PE's (e.g., loop initializations), the second term represents work that is divided among the PE's, and $W(P, N)$, the waiting time, is of order $\max(N, \sqrt{P})$. We determined the constants experimentally by simulating TRED2 for several (P, N) pairs and measuring both the total time T and the waiting time W. (Subsequent runs with other (P, N) pairs have always yielded results within one percent of the predicted value.) Table II summarizes our experimental results and supplies predictions for problems and machines too large to simulate (these values appear with an asterisk). In examining this table, recall that the efficiency of a parallel computation is defined as

$$E(P, N) = T(1, N)/(P * T(P, N)).$$

Although we consider these measured efficiencies encouraging, we note that system performance can probably be improved even more by sharing PE's among multiple tasks. (Currently the simulated PE's perform no useful work while waiting.) If we make the optimistic assumption that all the waiting time can be recovered, the efficiencies rise to the values given in Table III.

VI. CONCLUSION

Until now the goal of building high performance machines has been achieved at the price of increasingly complex hardware structures, and ever more exotic technology. It is our belief that the NYU Ultracomputer approach offers a simpler alternative, which is better suited to advanced VLSI technology: high performance is obtained by assembling large quantities of identical computing components in a particularly effective manner. The 4096 PE Ultracomputer that we envision has roughly the same component count as found in today's large machines. The number of different component types, however, is much smaller, each component being a sophisticated one chip VLSI system. Such machines would be three orders of magnitude faster and would have a main storage

TABLE II
MEASURED AND PROJECTED EFFICIENCIES

N \ PE	Reduction of Matrices to Tridiagonal Form				
	16	64	256	1024	4096
16	62 percent	26 percent	7 percent	1 percent*	0 percent*
32	87 percent	60 percent	25 percent	6 percent*	1 percent*
64	96 percent	86 percent	59 percent	27 percent*	7 percent*
128	99 percent*	96 percent*	86 percent*	59 percent*	24 percent*
256	100 percent*	99 percent*	96 percent*	86 percent*	58 percent*
512	100 percent*	100 percent*	99 percent*	96 percent*	85 percent*
1024	100 percent*	100 percent*	100 percent*	99 percent*	96 percent*

TABLE III
PROJECTED EFFICIENCIES

N \ PE	Reduction of Matrices to Tridiagonal Form				
	16	64	256 (without waiting time)	1024	4096
16	71 percent	37 percent	12 percent	3 percent	0 percent
32	90 percent	69 percent	35 percent	12 percent	3 percent
64	97 percent	90 percent	68 percent	35 percent	12 percent
128	99 percent	97 percent	90 percent	68 percent	35 percent
256	100 percent	99 percent	97 percent	90 percent	68 percent
512	100 percent	100 percent	99 percent	97 percent	90 percent
1024	100 percent	100 percent	100 percent	99 percent	97 percent

three orders of magnitude larger than present day machines.

Our simulations indicate that the NYU Ultracomputer would be an extremely powerful computing engine for large numerical applications. The low coordination overhead and the large memory enable us to use efficiently the high degree of parallelism available. The usefulness of these machines is not restricted to numerical computations: they are true general-purpose computers. Finally, our limited programming experience, on an instruction level simulator, indicates that the manual translation of serial codes into parallel Ultracomputer codes is a relatively straightforward task.

To demonstrate further the feasibility of the hardware and software design we intend to construct a 64 PE prototype, which will use commercial microprocessors and memories together with custom-built VLSI components for the network.

APPENDIX

Management of Highly Parallel Queues

Since queues are a central data structure for many algorithms, a concurrent queue access method can be an important tool for constructing parallel programs. In analyzing one of their parallel shortest path algorithms, Deo et al. [5] dramatize the need for this tool.

> However, regardless of the number of processors used, we expect that algorithm PPDM has a constant upper bound on its speedup, because every processor demands private use of the Q.

Refuting this pessimistic conclusion, we show in this appendix that, although at first glance the important problem of queue management may appear to require use of at least a few inherently serial operations, a queue can be shared among processors without using any code that could create serial bottlenecks. The procedures to be shown maintain the basic first-in first-out property of a queue, whose proper formulation in the assumed environment of large numbers of simultaneous insertions and deletions is as follows: if insertion of a data item p is completed before insertion of another data item q is started, then it must not be possible for a deletion yielding q to complete before a deletion yielding p has started.

In the algorithm below we represent a queue of length Size by a public circular array Q[0: Size-1] with public variables I and D pointing to the locations of the next items to be inserted and deleted (these correspond to the rear and front of the queue respectively). Initially $I = D = 0$ (corresponding to an empty queue).

We maintain two additional counters, $\#Ql$ and $\#Qu$, which hold lower and upper bounds respectively for the number of items in the queue, and which never differ by more than the number of active insertions and deletions. Initially $\#Ql = \#Qu = 0$, indicating no activity and an empty queue. The parameters QueueOverflow and QueueUnderflow appearing in the program shown below are flags denoting the exceptional conditions that occur when a processor attempts to insert into a full queue or delete from an empty queue. (Since a queue is considered full when $\#Qu \geq$ Size and since deletions do not decrement $\#Qu$ until after they have removed their data, a full queue may actually have cells that could be used by another insertion.) The actions appropriate for the Queue Overflow and QueueUnderflow conditions are application dependent: One possibility is simply to retry an offending insert or delete; another possibility is to proceed to some other task.

Critical section-free Insert and Delete programs are given below. The insert operation proceeds as follows: First a test-increment-retest (TIR) sequence is used to guarantee the existence of space for the insertion, and to increment the upper bound $\#Qu$. If the TIR fails, a QueueOverflow occurs. If it succeeds, the expression Mod(Fetch&Add(I, 1), Size) gives the appropriate location for the insertion, and the insert procedure waits its turn to overwrite this cell (see [13]). Finally, the lower bound $\#Ql$ is incremented. The delete operation is performed in a symmetrical fashion; the deletion of data can be viewed as the insertion of vacant space.

```
Procedure Insert (Data, Q, QueueOverflow)
        If TIR (#Qu, 1, Size) Then {
                MyI ← Mod(Fetch&Add(I, 1), Size)
                Wait turn at MyI
                Q[MyI] ← Data
                Fetch&Add(#Ql, 1)
                QueueOverflow ← False }
        Else QueueOverflow ← True
End Procedure
Procedure Delete (Data, Q, QueueUnderflow)
        If TDR (# Ql, 1) Then {
                MyD ← Mod(Fetch&Add(D, 1), Size)
                Wait turn at MyD
                Data ← Q[MyD]
                Fetch&Add(#Qu, −1)
                QueueUnderflow ← False }
        Else QueueUnderflow ← True
End Procedure

Boolean Procedure TIR (S, Delta, Bound)
        If S + Delta ≤ Bound Then
                If Fetch&Add(S, Delta) ≤ Bound Then
                        TIR ← true
                Else { Fetch&Add(S, −Delta)
                        TIR ← false }
        Else      TIR ← False

End Procedure
Boolean Procedure TDR (S, Delta)
        If S − Delta ≥ 0 Then
                If Fetch&Add(S, −Delta) ≥ 0 Then
                        TDR ← True
                Else { Fetch&Add(S, Delta)
                        TDR ← false }
        Else      TDR ← False

End Procedure
```

Although the initial test in both TIR and TDR may appear to be redundant, a closer inspection shows that their removal permits unacceptable race conditions. This point is also expanded in Gottlieb *et al.* [13] where other fetch-and-add based software primitives are presented as well.

It is important to note that when a queue is neither full nor empty our program allows many insertions and many deletions to proceed completely in parallel with no serial code executed. This should be contrasted with current parallel queue algorithms, which use small critical sections to update the insert and delete pointers.

References

[1] R. Bianchini and R. Bianchini, Jr., "Wireability of the NYU Ultracomputer," Courant Institute, NYU, NY, Ultracomputer Note 43, 1982.

[2] A. Borodin and J. E. Hopcroft, "Routing, merging, and sorting on parallel models of computation," in *Proc. 14th Annu. Ass. Comput. Mach. Symp. Theory Computing*, 1982, pp. 338–344.

[3] Burroughs Corp., "Numerical aerodynamic simulation facility feasibility study," NAS2-9897, Mar. 1979.

[4] Denelcor Corp., "Heterogeneous element processor principles of operation," Denver, CO, Pub. 9 000 001, 1981.

[5] N. Deo, C. Y. Pang, and R. E. Lord, "Two parallel algorithms for shortest path problems," in *Int. Conf. Parallel Processing*, 1980, pp. 244–253.

[6] D. Dias and J. R. Jump, "Analysis and simulation of buffered delta networks," *IEEE Trans. Comput.*, vol. C-30, pp. 273–282, 1981.

[7] L. R. Goke and G. J. Lipovsky, "Banyan networks for partitioning multiprocessor systems," in *Proc. 1st Annu. Symp. Comput. Arch.*, 1973, pp. 21–28.

[8] A. Gottlieb, "PLUS—A PL/I based Ultracomputer simulator I," Courant Institute, NYU, NY, Ultracomputer Note 10, 1980.

[9] ——, "WASHCLOTH—The logical successor to soapsuds," Courant Institute, NYU, NY, Ultracomputer Note 12, 1980.

[10] ——, "PLUS—A PL/I based Ultracomputer simulator II," Courant Institute, NYU, NY, Ultracomputer Note 14, 1980.

[11] A. Gottlieb and C. P. Kruskal, "MULT—A multitasking Ultracomputer language with timing, I & II," Courant Institute, NYU, NY, Ultracomputer Note 15, 1980.

[12] ——, "Coordinating parallel processors: A partial unification," *Comput. Arch. News*, pp. 16–24, Oct. 1981.

[13] A. Gottlieb, B. Lubachevsky, and L. Rudolph, "Basic techniques for the efficient coordination of very large numbers of cooperating sequential processors," *ACM TOPLAS*, Jan. 1983.

[14] A. Gottlieb and J. T. Schwartz, "Networks and algorithms for very large scale parallel computations," *Computer*, vol. 15, pp. 27–36, Jan. 1982.

[15] L. J. Guibas and F. M. Liang, "Systolic stacks, queues, and counters," in *Proc. Conf. Advanced Research VLSI*, Jan. 1982.

[16] R. G. Jacobsen and D. P. Misunas, "Analysis of structures for packet communications," in *Proc. Int. Conf. Parallel Processing*, 1977.

[17] S. D. Johnson, "Connection networks for output-driven list multiprocessing," Dept. Comput. Sci., Indiana Univ., Indiana, PA, Tech. Rep. 114, 1981.

[18] M. Kalos, "Scientific calculations on the Ultracomputer," Courant Institute, NYU, NY, Ultracomputer Note 30, 1981.

[19] M. Kalos, G. Leshem, and B. D. Lubachevsky, "Molecular simulations of equilibrium properties," Courant Institute, NYU, NY, Ultracomputer Note 27, 1981.

[20] K. R. Kaplan and R. V. Winder, "Cache-based computer systems," *Computer*, vol. 6, pp. 30–36, 1973.

[21] D. Klappholz, private communication, 1981.

[22] D. Korn, "Timing analysis for scientific codes run under WASHCLOTH simulation," Courant Institute, NYU, NY, Ultracomputer Note 24, 1981.

[23] D. Kroft, "Lockup-free instruction fetch/prefetch cache organization," in *Proc. 8th Annu. Symp. Comput. Arch.*, 1981, pp. 81–88.

[24] C. P. Kruskal, "Upper and lower bounds on the performance of parallel algorithms," Ph.D. dissertation, Courant Institute, NYU, NY, 1981.

[25] ——, "Replace-add based paracomputer algorithms," in *Proc. Int. Conf. Parallel Processing*, 1982.

[26] C. P. Kruskal and M. Snir, "Some results on multistage interconnection networks for multiprocessors," Courant Institute, NYU, NY, Ultracomputer Note 41, 1982; also in *Proc. Princeton Conf. Inform. Sci. Syst.*, 1982.

[27] H. T. Kung, "The structure of parallel algorithms," in *Advances in Computers*, vol. 19, M. C. Yovits Ed. New York: Academic, 1980, 65–112.

[28] L. Lamport, "How to make a multiprocessor computer that correctly executes multiprocess programs," *IEEE Trans. Comput.*, vol. C-28, pp. 690–691, 1979.

[29] D. Lawrie, "Access and alignment of data in an array processor," *IEEE Trans. Comput.*, vol. C-24, pp. 1145–1155, 1975.

[30] G. Radin, "The 801 minicomputer," in *Symp. Architectural Support Programming Languages and Operating Systems*, 1982, pp. 39–47.

[31] D. P. Reed and R. K. Kanodia, "Synchronization with eventcounts and sequencers," *Commun. Ass. Comput. Mach.*, vol. 22, pp. 115-123, 1979.

[32] G. Rodrigue, E. D. Giroux, and M. Pratt, "Perspectives on large-scale scientific computing," *Computer*, vol. 13, pp. 65-80, Oct. 1980.

[33] L. S. Rudolph, "Software structures for ultraparallel computing," Ph.D. dissertation, Courant Institute, NYU, NY, 1981.

[34] N. Rushfield, "Atmospheric computations on highly parallel MIMD computers," Courant Institute, NYU, NY, Ultracomputer Note 22, 1981.

[35] J. T. Schwartz, "Preliminary thoughts on Ultracomputer programming style," Courant Institute, NYU, NY, Ultracomputer Note 3, 1979.

[36] J. T. Schwartz, "Ultracomputers," *ACM TOPLAS*, pp. 484-521, 1980.

[37] H. J. Siegel and R. J. McMillen, "Using the augmented data manipulator in PASM," *Computer*, vol. 14, pp. 25-34, 1981.

[38] B. J. Smith, "A pipelined shared resource MIMD computer," in *Proc. Int. Conf. Parallel Processing*, 1978, pp. 6-8.

[39] M. Snir, "NETSIM—Network Simulator for the Ultracomputer," Courant Institute, NYU, NY, Ultracomputer Note 28, 1981.

[40] M. Snir and J. Solworth, "The ultraswitch—A VLSI network node for parallel processing," Courant Institute, NYU, NY, Ultracomputer Note 39, 1982.

[41] H. S. Stone, "Parallel computers," in *Introduction to Computer Architecture*, H. S. Stone, Ed. Chicago, IL: SRA, 1980, pp. 318-347.

[42] H. Sullivan, T. Bashkow, and D. Klappholz, "A large scale homogeneous, fully distributed parallel machine," in *Proc. 4th Annu. Symp. Comput. Arch.*, 1977, pp. 105-124.

[43] R. J. Swan, S. H. Fuller, and D. P. Siewiorek, "Cm*—A modular, multi-microprocessor," in *Proc. AFIPS Conf.*, vol. 46, 1977, pp. 637-644.

[44] D. S. Wise, "Compact layout of Banyan/FFT networks," in *Proc. CMU Conf. VLSI Systems and Computations*, Kung, Sproull, and Steele, Eds. Rockville, MD: Computer Science Press, 1981, pp. 186-195.

[45] G. H. Gonnet, "Expected length of the longest probe sequence in hash code searching," *J. Ass. Comput. Mach.*, pp. 289-304, Apr. 1981.

Ralph Grishman was born in New York, NY, on January 6, 1948. He received the A.B. and Ph.D. degrees in physics from Columbia University, New York, in 1968 and 1973, respectively.

Since 1973 he has been on the faculty at New York University, NY, where he is currently an Associate Professor in the Department of Computer Science. His main research area is computational linguistics, but he also has a long-standing interest in computer system design and construction. Before becoming involved with the Ultracomputer group, he designed a medium-scale scientific computer which is now in production use at New York University.

Dr. Grishman is a member of the Association for Computational Linguistics and the Association for Computing Machinery.

Clyde P. Kruskal was born on May 25, 1954. He received the A.B. degree in mathematics and computer science from Brandeis University, Waltham, MA, in 1976, and the M.S. and Ph.D. degrees in computer sciences from New York University in 1978 and 1981, respectively.

Currently, he is a Visiting Research Assistant Professor in the Department of Computer Science, University of Illinois, Urbana. His research interests include the analysis of sequential and parallel algorithms, and the design of parallel computers.

Kevin P. McAuliffe was born in Newark, NJ on March 16, 1956. He received the B.A. and M.S. degrees in computer science from New York University, NY, in 1978 and 1980 respectively.

He is currently pursuing the Ph.D. degree in computer science at New York University, where he also lectures in the Department of Computer Science. His current interests are computer architecture and operating systems.

Larry Rudolph received the B.S. degree from Queens College, City University of New York, NY, in 1976 and the M.S. and Ph.D. degrees from the Courant Institute, New York University, New York, in 1978 and 1981, respectively.

He spent the 1981-82 academic year as a Postdoctorial Fellow in the Department of Computer Science, University of Toronto, Ont., Canada. Currently, he is a Research Associate at Carnegie-Mellon University, Pittsburgh, PA. His research interests include parallel/distributed computing, robust parallel approximation schemes, and computational geometry.

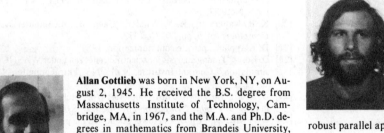

Allan Gottlieb was born in New York, NY, on August 2, 1945. He received the B.S. degree from Massachusetts Institute of Technology, Cambridge, MA, in 1967, and the M.A. and Ph.D. degrees in mathematics from Brandeis University, Waltham, MA, in 1968 and 1973, respectively.

During 1971-1972 he was an Acting Instructor at the University of California, Santa Cruz, and during 1972-1973 he was an Instructor at the State College of Massachusetts, North Adams. From 1973-1979 he was with York College, City University of New York, first as an Assistant Professor and then as an Associate Professor. Since 1979 he has been working on the NYU Ultracomputer project at the Courant Institute, NYU, where he is now a Research Associate Professor. His academic interests include parallel processors and parallel algorithms, algorithmic analysis, operating systems, differential topology, and computer chess.

Dr. Gottlieb is a member of the Association for Computing Machinery, the American Mathematical Society, the New York Academy of Sciences, and the Society of Sigma Xi, and is an affiliate member of the IEEE Computer Society.

Marc Snir was born in Paris, France, on October 10, 1948. He received the B.Sc. degree and the Ph.D. degree in mathematics from the Hebrew University of Jerusalem, Israel, in 1972 and 1979, respectively.

In 1979 he was Research Fellow in the Department of Computer Science, University of Edinburgh, Scotland. Since 1980 he has been an Assistant Professor in the Department of Computer Science, New York University, where he is actively involved in the Ultracomputer project. His research interests include parallel processing, interconnection networks, complexity of parallel algorithms, inductive logic, and VLSI design.

EMSY85 - The Erlangen Multi-Processor System for a
Broad Spectrum of Applications.

G. Fritsch, W. Kleinoeder, C.U. Linster and J. Volkert

Institute of Computer Science (IMMD)
University of Erlangen - Nuremberg
Federal Republic of Germany

ABSTRACT

A new Erlangen multiprocessor system, EMSY85, will consist of a grid-like array of microprocessors operating asynchronously, each of which is coupled via memory with a limited number of its neighbors. We intend to demonstrate that for a broad spectrum of applications the system's performance can grow nearly in proportion to the number of processors in the array. The operating system is based on UNIX*. A programming environment for parallel programs makes the system attractive to the users. Many design decisions have been based on the results of an existing pilot project.

1. Introduction and Motivation

Numerous attempts have been made in the past few years to increase computing power by means of multiprocessor systems with various architectures. Two such systems have been implemented in Erlangen, SYMPOS [12,15], which is a symmetrical system, and EGPA** [5], which is hierarchical.

The experience gained with applications on these two projects led scientists at the Computer Science Department (IMMD) of the University of Erlangen - Nuremberg to conceive EMSY85, which will be implemented in the next few years. EMSY85 consists of a grid-like array of microprocessors operating asynchronously, each of which is coupled via memory with a limited number of its neighbors. Because of the large number of processors, a symmetrical system (each processor has access to each memory modul) is unrealistic [6]. On the other hand because of the many computation-intensive user applications with a matrix structure, a processor field with a grid structure was chosen. Above this array there is a hierarchy of processors, whose job it is to supervise the array and to transport data between

processors that happen not to be neighbors. The higher-level processors can also perform tasks other than supervision. Thus EMSY85 is also well suited for tree-like user applications. In addition, results from the pilot project EGPA lead us to believe that many user applications with a subtask structure that is neither grid-like nor tree-like can easily be mapped onto, and computed efficiently on EMSY85.

Therefore the project's main goal is to show that for a broad spectrum of applications, system performance can indeed grow nearly in proportion to the number of processors in the array. We are thus planning to test a large number of algorithms from such fields as physics, chemistry, operations research and image-processing, many of which have already shown large speedups on the pilot project. In order to make the system attractive to potential users, the complexity of programs written for the system must not be essentially greater than that of programs written for a monoprocessor. Not only must the system's higher-level language contain constructs for asynchronous programming, there must be a programming environment capable of supporting the development of

---

* UNIX is a Trademark of Bell Laboratories.
** EGPA was supported by the Federal Ministry for Research and Development, F.R.Germany

Reprinted from *The Proceedings of the 1983 International Conference on Parallel Processing*, 1983, pages 325-330. Copyright © 1983 by The Institute of Electrical and Electronics Engineers, Inc.

parallel software.

The paper describes five aspects of the EMSY85 project: the hardware, the operating system, the programming environment, measurement and performance aspects and applications.

2. The EMSY85 - Architecture

The Erlangen multiprocessor system EMSY85 will consist of identical Processor-Memory Modules (PMMs). Each PMM will consist, in turn, of an iAPX 286/287 microprocessor and a one-half megabyte multiport memory. The PMMs are arranged hierarchically in four levels (A,B,C,D) as shown in Fig. 1.

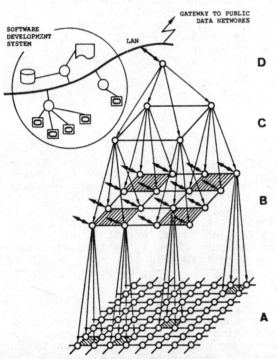

Fig. 1: EMSY 85 - Hardware-Structure: Four hierarchical levels A, B, C, D. Some of the elementary pyramids are highlighted.

○ Processor - Memory - Module (PMM) of EMSY 85
── symmetric multiport-memory connection between neighboring PMMs
→ asymmetric multiport-memory connection between PMMs of different hierarchical level
↔ I/O communication to elementary pyramid, supported by I/O processor

At the topmost level there is only a single PMM, for which there will be several standby processors to increase the system's reliability. At each lower level, each PMM is connected to exactly four neighbors at the same level, i.e. each processor has access to the memories of its neighboring PMMs. Thus at each level the hardware has a grid structure.

In addition to the horizontal accesses, each PMM, except of course the very lowest, has access to four PMMs at the next lower level. The vertical connections are equipped to broadcast data downward to all four of the lower PMMs simultaneously, say, to transmit code segments. On the other hand, though the lower PMMs do not have memory-access to those at higher levels, they are able to interrupt their supervising PMM. These substructures, consisting of four processors and their supervisor, are called elementary pyramids c.f. Figure 2.

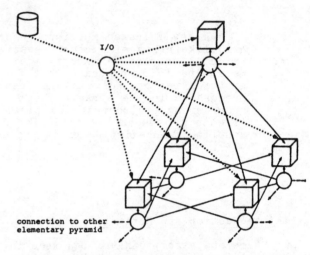

○ Processor - ⬜ Memory - Module (PMM)

Fig. 2: EMSY 85 - Elementary pyramid

Several of them are highlighted in Figure 1. Each elementary pyramid has an I/O processor with the corresponding I/O devices, for the most part, Winchester disks. The I/O processor, which has access to all of its elementary pyramid memories, is controlled by the supervising PMM.

The overall arrangement of EMSY85's PMMs is, as the preceding discussion suggests, pyramidal. The topmost PMM is connected to a network containing several software-development processors on which the operating system and applications are in development.

An EMSY85 pyramid can, of course, be extended downward arbitrarily, by adding new levels. Such an extension increases significantly the computing power of the system.

For many kinds of computations, the main computing load will be carried by the lowest level, leaving the higher levels underutilized. For such applications it would be reasonable to taper the pyramid so that each lower level in an elementary pyramid has nine, or even sixteen, rather than merely four PMMs.

Experience with the pilot project, EGPA, which was built using five powerful miniprocessors, has shown however that excessive tapering can lead to bottlenecks at the higher levels that restrict the system's overall performance. EMSY85 will therefore have two manually switchable configurations, one more strongly tapered than the other:

Lowest level PPMs: 8 x 8   9 x 9

Element. pyramid PPMs: 4 + 1   9 + 1

Number of levels   4   3

Total PPMs: 64+16+4+1 = 85   81+9+1 = 91

3. EMOS - the EMSY85 Operating System

The operating system, which is based on UNIX will be structured in a hierarchy analogous to the hardware. The operating system consists of more or less autonomous subsystems, one per processor. Each of the subsystems has a common kernel, but the subsystems on the lowest level are rudimentary and increase in power toward the top of the pyramid.

The opinion, often found in the literature, that UNIX is unsuited to multiprocessor systems can no longer be maintained without qualification. The multiprocessor project "SYMPOS - An Operating System for Homogeneous Multiprocessor Systems" has shown that UNIX can be modified with relatively little effort and essentially without changing its structure. The effort for such a modification depends on the complexity and homogeneity of the hardware, the desired user-friendlyness, and the planned spectrum of applications. In addition, the question is relevant whether the user should have the possibility of implementing genuinely concurrent processes, or merely quasi-concurrent processes. Considering all of these parameters, we estimate a total effort of 4 to 16 man-years.

In order to avoid the phenomenon of processor-thrashing in memory-coupled multiprocessor systems, we adopted and expanded on an idea that found limited application in the CMU multiprocessor projects [8]. The problem consists of relieving the bottleneck involved in common memory-access; the solution consists of maximizing the amount of code and data for local functions loaded into local memory. The procedure leads to an

operating system that consists of a number of local subsystems based on a common kernel. This approach was implemented so successfully in SYMPOS that it will be adopted for EMSY85. Subsystems of varying power for the different hardware levels are easily provided since the system is partitioned into modules that can be freely combined to form a complete system.

In spite of the fact that EMSY85 is not a symmetrical system, similar problems arise since every memory is equipped with seven ports, independently of the size of the elementary pyramid. In view of the number of accessing processors, measures similar to those in SYMPOS will certainly be necessary to prevent bottlenecks.

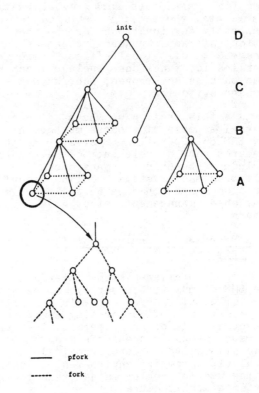

Fig. 3: EMSY 85 - Process-Structure

UNIX insiders will note the congruence between the hardware structure and UNIX's process structure. It is thus fairly easy to extend the original process-management to a distributed system. We shall use the **fork** function (spawn a process) as an example.

In the local environment, i.e. on a single processor, **fork** functions as

293

usual. There is in addition a distributed version, **pfork** whose effect is analogous to its local cousin. The difference is merely that for a **pfork** process a new hardware environment is initialized. The two processors involved must process a common physical memory space; in case more than one generation level is involved the memory spaces may be disjunct. The hardware to which a **pfork** process is assigned can be influenced by parameters such as access to non-local data segments, processor assignment, and so forth.

Figure 3 shows a typical process structure resulting from multiple **pfork** and **fork** operations. The process identifiers consist of a triple identifying hardware level, processor number, and local process identifier.

In addition to the multiprocessor-specific analogues **fork, wait, exit, alarm**, etc. there will be a number of completely new functions for the coordination of asynchronous processes and management of global files. The new coordination functions include mechanisms such as semaphores, lock/unlock and message switching.

In this section we have discussed several aspects of process management in the EMSY85 Operating System. Further research areas relevant to the project include resource management in multiprocessor-systems, online reconfiguration after hardware failures and adaptable management strategies, among others.

4. A Programming Environment for Parallel Programs

The operating-system interface in the EMSY85 multiprocessor system permits the implementation of a user's algorithm as a system of cooperating concurrent processes. In order to permit the use of such a multiprocessor system by non-specialists, tools are provided in a parallel programming environment oriented to the user's problem rather than to the system's architecture.

Of course it would be ideal if the task could be distributed automatically to the various processors. The user could then program his application as if it were a sequential process. Current experience with the EGPA system leaves us skeptical about the success of completely automatic analysis of sequential into parallel algorithms.

The parallel programming environment therefore assumes the following model: an application consists of sequential subtasks and a description of their interdependencies, either concurrent or sequential. The individual subtasks are formulated in a powerful higher-level programming language (C, because of the use of UNIX). There is a programming package that permits easy formulation of the required synchronization by means of such calls as

"execute subtask x on processor y"

"wait for the termination of subtask x on processor y"

The programming package implicitly includes the generation of the requisite system of processes, handles the individual calls necessary for process communication (e.g. using messages), and initiates the subtasks on their respective processors. This approach has been successfully tested in the pilot project [13].

Another approach that is much easier to use and which has proved efficient as well, has been borrowed from data-flow theory. The theory that applies to elementary operations such as "+" or "*" yields an elegant generalization to subtasks, viewed as complex operations, which we call macro data-flow. The synchronization dependencies between subtasks can be expressed in analogous fashion. In the EGPA pilot project we have shown that these tools are especially attractive for applications whose asynchronous structure is extremely complex [10].

5. Measurement and Performance Evaluation

The measurement and evaluation subproject of EMSY85 is intended to support the users in optimizing performance, whether they be implementing the operating system, the programming environment, or applications. Since the simultaneous operation of nearly one hundred processors is beyond human comprehension without some kind of visual support, there is a software-measurement system applicable to all levels of the system, whose measurement points can be selected arbitrarily. A trace of the selected events is recorded along with timing information.

Then a direct evaluation of this information is made possible by an online visual-display package. Not only can the system's current status be displayed, the trace data can be used to display the flow of events in slow-motion.

Since the measurement points are

chosen using the programming environment, the data can be displayed in the
user's notation, i.e. with his symbolic
names, rather than as hexadecimal
numbers.

It would, of course, involve excessive implementation effort to attempt to
find an "optimal" version among several
candidate implementations by measuring
their performance. However a modeling
and evaluation procedure for complex
tasks based on stochastic analysis of
the measurement data permits a choice
among interesting variants [9]. The
task model used to implement this subsystem is based, as are the
environment's other programming-support
tools, on the data-flow approach.

A survey of research on hardware
and software measurement as well as performance evaluation in the EGPA pilot
project, which constituted the planing
basis for the measurement and evaluation
software in EMSY85, can be found in [3].

6. Applications

EMSY85 will be capable of implementing a broad spectrum of applications. Among them will be tasks that
require intensive computation, e.g.
problems from physics, operations
research and pattern-recognition.

Such problems can often be reduced,
either directly or via discretization,
to problems in linear algebra. An
important research area is the discovery
of appropriate asynchronous algorithms,
especially for the solution of large
systems of linear equations with either
sparse matrices ($10^{**}6$ unknowns), e.g.
finite elements or systems of differential equations, or dense ($10^{**}3$ to $10^{**}4$
unknowns). These problems are not difficult to implement on EMSY85 because of
the close match between the structure of
the tasks and the system's array. For
other classes of tasks, the match is not
as felicitous. For such problems, strategies must be developed for mapping the
problem onto EMSY85's hardware structure. Not all applications algorithms
can be adapted without modification, and
must in fact sometimes be re-developed
from scratch. Such problematic tasks,
e.g. from pattern-recognition, nonlinear programming (say for technical
installations), simulation of complicated systems (telephone networks, multiprocessors, VLSI circuits), and so
forth, are also to be investigated.
These will require research in the
decomposition of tasks, the adapting of
asynchronous algorithms, and the design
and implementation of parallel programs.
The computing demands of several of

these tasks, especially those from
pattern-recognition, comprise both high
computation speed and high data-transfer
rates.

By means of these applications, we
intend to show that, for problems of
sufficient size, the system's performance improves nearly linearly in the
number of array-processors (level A).
Considering the breadth of the applications areas, EMSY85 will have thus proven itself to be a multi-purpose system.

As a result of experience with the
pilot-project EGPA (Erlangen General-
Purpose Array), we are convinced that we
shall indeed be able to demonstrate the
expected improvement. EGPA's hardware
structure corresponds to a single elementary pyramid in EMSY85, consisting of
four array PMMs and one supervisory PMM.
Thus the limiting speed-up for an algorithm run on EGPA (versus a monoprocessor) is four-to-one.

We list below a number of applications actually tested on EGPA along with
their speed-up factors.

Subject:	Speed up:
Linear algebra [7]:	
-Matrix inversion	
(200 x 200 dense)	
Gauss-Jordan	3.8
column-substitution	ca. 4.0
-Matrix multiplication	3.7
(200 x 200)	
-Solving of linear equations	
Gauss-Seidel	ca. 4.0
Differential equations [2]:	
-Relaxation	ca. 3.5
Image processing and graphics:	
-Topographical representation [10]	3.6
-Illumination of the topo-	
graphical model	2.4
-Line following	ca. 2.9
(vectorizing of a grey-level	
matrix)	
-Distance transformation	ca. 3.0 - 3.3
[4]	
Non linear programming [1]:	
-Search for minima of a multi-	
dimensional object function	
given by an algebraic term	ca. 3.2
Graph theory:	
-network flow with neighborhood	3.5
support (each idle processor	
helps one of its neighbors)	
Text formating [14]:	2.6

These encouraging results, which span a
broad spectrum of applications, were an

essential factor in the design of EMSY85. On the basis of theoretical investigations, speedups proportional to the number of processors at the lowest level can be expected on systems of the same type.

7. Conclusions

The University's Institute of Computer Science is working hand in hand with an industrial partner, Siemens' Corporate Laboratories for Information Technology in Munich. The cooperation is in the design, development and production of the hardware, as well as in the development and testing of parallel algorithms for computation-intensive applications such as the simulation of complex systems.

The EMSY85 project employs about fifty scientists at the University from the following academic chairs in the Computer Science Department: Computer Architecture, Performance Evaluation, Operating Systems, Programming Languages and Pattern Recognition. The German Federal Ministry for Research and Development is supporting EMSY85.

8. Acknowledgements

The authors gratefully acknowledge the contributions of all members of the Erlangen Group to this paper. They also would like to thank Mrs. L. Lange for drawing the figures.

References

1. Fritch,G., H. Mueller
   "Parallelization of a Minnimization Problem for Multiprocessor Systems"
   CONPAR'81, Lecture Notes in Computer Sience No.11,453-463,Springer Verlag Berlin-Heidelberg-New York 1981

2. Fromm, H.J.
   "Multiprozessor-Rechneranlagen: Programmstrukturen, Maschinenstrukturen und Zuordnungsprobleme"
   Arbeitsberichte des IMMD, Univ. Erlangen-Nuernberg, Band 15, Nr.5 '82

3. Fromm, H.J., U. Herksen, U. Herzog, K.H. John, R. Klar and W. Kleinoeder
   "Experiences with Performance, Measurement and Modeling of a Processor Array"
   IEEE Transactions on Computers, vol. C-32, no. 1, Jan. 1983

3. Goessmann, M., J. Volkert und H. Zischler
   "Image Proc. and Graphics on EGPA"
   EGPA-Int. Paper(to be published)

5. Haendler, W., F. Hofmann, H.J. Schneider
   "A General Purpose Array with a Broad Spectrum of Applications"
   Computer Architecture, Workshop of the G. I. Erlangen/R.F.Germany, May 1975

6. Haendler,W.
   "Aspects of Parallelism in Computer Architecture"
   Parallel Computers - Parallel Mathematics Feilmeier, M. (ed)
   North Holland Publishing Company, Amsterdam, 1977

7. Henning, W., M Vajtersic and J. Volkert
   "Matrix Inversion Algorithm for the Parallel Computer EGPA"
   EGPA-Int. Paper(to be published)

8. Jones, A.K. and P. Schwarz
   "Experience Using Multiprocessor Systems - A Status Report"
   Computing Surveys, Vol.12, No.2, June 1980

9. Kleinoeder, W.
   "Stochastische Bewertung von Aufgabenstrukuren fuer hierarch. Mehrrechnersysteme"
   Arbeitsberichte des IMMD Univ. Erlangen-Nuernberg Band 15 Nr.11 '82

10. Kneissl, F.
    "Realisierung von Datenflussmech. auf hierachische Mehrrechnersysteme"
    Arbeitsberichte des IMMD Univ. Erlangen-Nuernberg, Band 15 Nr.12 '82

11. Kneissl, F.
    "Macro Data Flow on EGPA Config."
    EGPA-Int. Paper(to be published)

12. Linster, C.U.
    "SYMPOS/UNIX - Ein Betriebssystem fuer homogene Polyprozessorsysteme"
    Arbeitsberichte des IMMD Univ. Erlangen-Nuernberg, Band 14 Nr.3 '81

13. Rathke, M.
    "Benutzung der Parallel-Schnittstelle des EGPA-Rechners"
    EGPA-Int. Dokumentation

14. Rathke, M.
    "SAP: Ein optimistischer Algorithmus fuer die parall. Textverarbeitung"
    EGPA-Int. Paper(to be published)

15. Wurm, F.X.
    "Auftragssystem fuer eine Multiprozessoranlage"
    Arbeitsberichte des IMMD, Univ. Erlangen-Nuernberg, Band 13 Nr.7 '80

Chapter 7: Multiprocessor Design Issues

Reprinted from *IEEE Transactions on Computers*, Volume C-29, Number 9, September 1980, pages 763-776. Copyright © 1980 by The Institute of Electrical and Electronics Engineers, Inc.

High-Speed Multiprocessors and Compilation Techniques

DAVID A. PADUA, DAVID J. KUCK, MEMBER, IEEE, AND DUNCAN H. LAWRIE, MEMBER, IEEE

Abstract—The purpose of this paper is to present some ideas on multiprocessor design and on automatic translation of sequential programs into parallel programs for multiprocessors. With respect to machine design, two subjects are discussed. First, a multiprocessor allowing parallelism at a very low level is sketched and then, a brief discussion on the interconnection network is presented.

In the automatic translation section, a few techniques are briefly described and illustrated by many examples Finally, the conclusion of the paper mentions some of the advantages multiprocessors have over pipelined and array computers for computation-bound programs.

Index Terms—Automatic translation, compilers, high-speed multiprocessors, interconnection networks, multiprocessors, parallel processing, pipelining, vectorizers.

Manuscript received August 1, 1979; revised April 4, 1980. This work was supported in part by the National Science Foundation under Grants US NSF MCS77-27910 and MCS76-81686, and the Lawrence Livermore Laboratory, Livermore, CA under Contract US DOE SBC UCAL 5498609.

The authors are with the Department of Computer Science, University of Illinois at Urbana-Champaign, Urbana, IL 61801.

I. MULTIPROCESSORS

IN this paper multiprocessors are defined as computer systems with more than one independent control unit. Multiprocessors can be used to obtain either high-throughput, by means of multiprogramming, or low-turnaround time, by executing programs in parallel. Our main concern in this paper will be with turnaround time. Specifically, emphasis will be given to the fast parallel execution of computation-bound programs.

It is appropriate, first, to mention that our motivation is to allow the fast execution of a larger class of programs than can be handled on pipelined or parallel array machines. We have developed algorithms [2], [8], [10], [11], [15], [23] that are very effective for speeding up Fortran-like programs for array machine computation; some early results were reported in [9]. Even though very good vectorization results can now be obtained for most Fortran programs, some programs lead to difficulties. Although a detailed description is beyond the scope of this paper, our PARAFRASE program analyzer can automatically characterize a number of these difficulties. In order to motivate this paper, we will outline some of these difficulties now.

The algorithms described in Section II of this paper can be useful for a wide class of machines that are capable of executing a number of scalar operations simultaneously. Section I-A sketches one such example, but the Denelcor HEP [21] is another example, as are data flow-type proposals. We call these MES machines for multiple execution of scalar operations. This is in distinction to the various parallel and pipelined array machines which we denote as SEA (single execution of array operations) or MEA (multiple execution of array operations) machines. For further discussion of single and multiple instruction and execution sequence machines, see [8].

Specifically, our goal is to show how certain programs that are not amenable to SEA processing or efficient MEA processing can be substantially speeded up and executed efficiently on MES systems that are properly designed. We assume that a number of preliminary transformations have been performed on a standard serial Fortran-like program and that a high quality dependence graph has been constructed [2], [8]. At this point a program consists of blocks that are one of three types: blocks of scalar assignment statements, scalar conditional blocks, and Π-blocks (Π-blocks are defined in Section II-A.; for now, consider them as some sort of elementary entity) arising from loops (we will ignore I/O statements).

The multiprocessor we define can process a block of scalar assignment statements or a scalar conditional block in a cluster of processors; our system has a number of clusters so that independent blocks can be handled simultaneously. Most of the time spent in most programs arises from loops, so that the Π-blocks arising from loops are of the most concern, as we shall see in Section II.

A Π-block may access data arrays using a *linear access* method (e.g., with subscripting as a linear function of index variables) or using a *nonlinear access* method (e.g., with subscripted subscripts or pointers). Each of these data access methods can be used with any of three types of Π-blocks which contain: array operations, linear recurrences, or nonlinear recurrences. By an *array* operation, we mean a statement that operates on one or more arrays in an element-by-element way to produce a resulting array (e.g., matrix addition). A simple *linear recurrence* is defined as an assignment statement whose

right-hand side is a linear combination of the left-hand side variable, e.g.,

$$x_i = a_i * x_{i-1} + b_i * x_{i-2} + c_i$$

whereas the right-hand side is a nonlinear combination in the *nonlinear recurrence* case, e.g.,

$$x_i = a_i * x_{i-1} * x_{i-2} + b_i * x_{i-2}/x_{i-3} + c_i.$$

These ideas can be extended to multiple statement Π-blocks.

Let us consider linear access computations for each of these types of Π-blocks. In array operations, SEA and MES machines are equally effective, but when modified by a number of conditional statements (see Example 4 in Section II-A) the SEA machine may be forced to operate on very sparse arrays. The MES machine has no such problem since each iteration can follow a separate path through the loop, maintaining high efficiency. Linear recurrences may be handled quickly and efficiently on either type of system using various high-speed recurrence algorithms [2], [8]. Nonlinear recurrences (nonlinearizable ones) must be executed serially on array machines, however, in cases where they appear (or may be transformed to appear) in a loop containing many Π-blocks, the MES pipelining technique described in Section II-B usually leads to high speedup with high efficiency. Speedup and efficiency results are summarized in Section II-C.

Now, consider nonlinear access computations. For each type of Π-block, the above discussion of linear access computations can be repeated, except that data access and alignment now may become a severe problem. For example, in the simple case of an array operation we may have to add two arrays, each of which is indexed by a different just-computed array (the subscripted subscript problem). Whereas conflict-free array access and alignment has been studied in detail for SEA machines in the linear access case (see Section I-B), and random access to parallel memories has been widely studied, and high-expected bandwidths have been demonstrated, data alignment in this case has been little studied. In Section I-B, we present and analyze a new network for global random data alignment. This network may be useful for all three kinds of Π-blocks in the case of nonlinear access to data.

In Section I-A, the sketch of a multiprocessor is given. This multiprocessor, called a high-speed multiprocessor, allows the successful exploitation of parallelism at a very low level. In Section I-B, the design of the processor-memory interconnection network is discussed. Later, in Section II, techniques for the automatic translation of sequential programs into parallel programs for multiprocessors are presented, and finally Section III mentions a few of the advantages that multiprocessors have over pipelined and array computers for computation-bound programs.

A. A High-Speed Multiprocessor

The high-speed multiprocessor sketched next offers some improvement over current machines for a number of algorithms and programs.

First, we describe a processor cluster (PC) that can behave

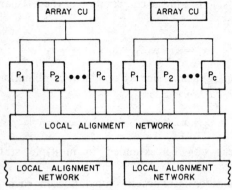

Fig. 1.   Two processor clusters.

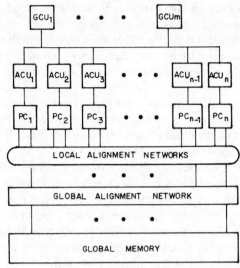

Fig. 2.   A high-speed multiprocessor.

as an SIASEA (single instruction, array; single execution, array) machine or as an MISMES (multiple instruction, scalar; multiple execution, scalar) machine. Each processor in the cluster is a fairly traditional machine, with a scalar control unit and processor, together with a local memory. Thus, each processor may carry out an independent computation. The processor capabilities can be chosen to meet the intended application areas, but the use of LSI processors is clearly attractive (e.g., 32-bit floating-point microprocessors). The cluster size is also a design variable, but from the viewpoints of both technology and applications effectiveness, 8 to 16 processors per cluster seem appropriate.

Fig. 1 shows two such processor clusters (containing c processors each) interconnected via a set of local alignment networks (LAN's). These alignment networks can be used to communicate within one cluster (each can use half of the LAN independently) or adjacent clusters can intercommunicate through the shared LAN. Each cluster also has an array control unit that accepts an array instruction set and drives all c processors in lock-step fashion.

The alignment networks can be used to communicate data between processors and memories. They may also be used, simultaneously, to send status bits between processors. One important feature of each processor control unit is that the execution of each instruction is conditional on a set of status bits. These can be set by other processors in the cluster (or outside the cluster). Thus, a set of computations running in a PC can be made dependent at the instruction level. For example, data computed in processor 1 can be stored in a local memory, processor 1 can set an appropriate bit in processor 2, and processor 2 can fetch the result of processor 1 to proceed with its computation. This technique makes very tight coupling possible. For example, if each processor is computing one iteration of a loop and there are data dependencies from one statement to the next between iterations, these can be quickly satisfied. As another example, a PC could evaluate an arithmetic expression tree quickly by appropriate alignments (see [22]).

Next, consider a collection of PC's to form a complete system. Fig. 2 shows a collection of n PC's plus a set of global control units (GCU's), a global alignment network (GAN), and a global memory (slower levels in the memory hierarchy are ignored here). The GCU's allow a collection of PC's to work together either in an array or scalar fashion. Thus, the entire system could be partitioned to handle several jobs at

once, but the key point is that any job may be handled in either an SEA, MEA, or MES mode. Program memory is associated with each control unit.

B. The Global Alignment Network (GAN)

The GAN will serve two purposes. One is the synchronous transfer of program and data from the global memory to the local memories. For example, a vector may be transferred in such a way that each element of the vector goes to a different local memory. Another example is the broadcasting of a program segment to several local memories as is required for the **forall** scheme described in Section II-B1).

The synchronous function of the GAN will be accomplished by one or more synchronous interconnection networks like those described in [14], [13], [20], and [25]. These synchronous networks will be controlled by the GCU's.

A second purpose of the GAN is the asynchronous transfer of data between global and local memories. The need for this arises because the different processors may request or produce data in an unstructured fashion. When this is the case, requests to the asynchronous components of the GAN will be issued by each processor. Asynchronous interconnection networks have been studied less than the synchronous ones. One of the few possibilities explored is the use of the *omega network* [14] as an asynchronous network. This was proposed for the Burroughs' NASF computer [3]. The behavior of this network has been analyzed by stochastic methods in [16]. A second possibility for asynchronous networks is described in the remainder of this section.

The network to be described is similar to the one presented by Lang in [13]. The one-stage shuffle-exchange network contains $N = 2^n$ locations; in each one of these locations a register will be placed. These registers are connected to the input of a shuffle network which, in turn, is connected to $N/2$ exchange elements (Fig. 3). The exchange elements are two-input–two-output switches with two possible settings: straight and exchange (Fig. 4). The outputs of the exchange elements are connected back to the registers, as shown in Fig. 3. We conceive the network as carrying messages between locations

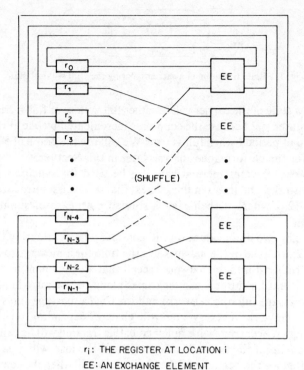

r_i : THE REGISTER AT LOCATION i

EE : AN EXCHANGE ELEMENT

Fig. 3.   The one-stage shuffle-exchange network.

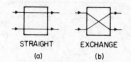

STRAIGHT   EXCHANGE

(a)   (b)

Fig. 4.   The two settings of the exchange elements.

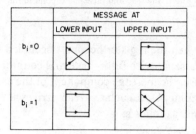

Fig. 5.   How the exchange elements are set.

(registers). Processors and global memory modules will have access to the registers and will be the producers and consumers of the messages. These messages will be in one of the following four categories:

1) data going from a processor to a global memory module for storage,

2) an address going from a processor to a global memory module,

3) data going from a global memory module to a processor, and

4) an acknowledgment going from a global memory module to a processor. This is to inform the processor that the data sent out by the processor was received by the global memory module.

To describe the behavior of the network, let us assume by now that only one message, say $\underline{M}$, is going to traverse the network. Let us also assume that the message originates at location $\underline{L}_0$ and is destined for location $\underline{L}_d$. The source of the message (i.e., either a processor or a global memory module with access to the register at $\underline{L}_0$) will place the message $\underline{M}$ into the register at $\underline{L}_0$; $\underline{M}$ will be augmented with the value $\underline{L}_d$ in binary (an n-bit word). This n-bit word will be called _destination tag_ henceforth, and will be used to route $\underline{M}$ through the network.

The network will work by *periods;* as we will see shortly, it takes n periods for a message to reach its destination. During each period, the message and the destination tag will go through an exchange element and will be latched into a register that could be different than the register where they were at the beginning of the period.

It remains to discuss how the exchange elements are set. Let us say that the destination tag is $b_1 b_2 \cdots b_n$, where the b_i's are bits and b_1 is the most significant. During the ith period, bit

b_i will be used to set the exchange element; the setting is done in base to the value of b_i and depending on the input to the exchange element to which the register containing the message is connected. Fig. 5 describes the way the exchange elements are set. The previous method is called destination tag method and was introduced in [14] where it is also explained why it works.

If we now assume that several messages are traversing the network at the same time, the situation becomes more complex. In this network, all registers are latched simultaneously, and by the time the registers are latched all exchange elements are set according to the rules defined for the network. In general, these rules cannot be as straightforward as the ones shown in Fig. 5 because *conflicts* could arise. A conflict will occur when both input registers of an exchange element have messages, and the destination tags of these messages are such that one requires straight setting and the other one the exchange setting. These conflicts are of paramount importance in the design and analysis of the network, as we will see shortly.

It will be assumed that two messages simultaneously in the network may have the same destination tag, and that the messages can be placed in the network during any period. Clearly, under these assumptions conflicts will arise. A possible approach to solve conflicts is described next.

For purposes of explanation, let us say that at any time all registers are occupied by elements we will call *carriers*. A carrier is defined as the four-tuple ⟨full, counter, destination-tag, message⟩. The destination-tag and message components have the meanings described above. The full component has a logical value; if false, the carrier does not contain a message, and therefore the last three components of the carrier are meaningless. If full is true, a message is contained in the carrier.

The counter component is a value between 1 and $n + 1$. When counter = $n + 1$ (and full = true), then message is at its final destination. When counter = i (and, again, full = true) where $1 \leq i \leq n$, then the ith bit of destination-tag will be used to set the exchange elements as explained later.

Let us say that from a given location, $\underline{L}_0$, a component $\underline{C}$ (either a processor or a memory module) desires to send a message $\underline{M}$ to location $\underline{L}_d$. First, $\underline{C}$ will wait until the beginning

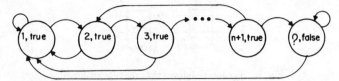

Fig. 6. State transition graph of a carrier. (The number corresponds to the value of counter, and true and false correspond to the value of full.)

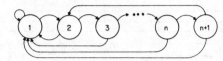

Fig. 7. State transition of a carrier ignoring the "full = false" state.

of a period when the register becomes occupied by a carrier with full = false, or with full = true and counter = $n + 1$; in this latter case, the message component of the carrier is read before proceeding. Once such a carrier arrives at L_0, C will set its components as follows.

full = true
counter = 1
destination-tag = L_d
message = M.

The carrier will then continue traversing the network. Thus, during the current period the exchange element will be set using the first bit of the destination tag. We can say that a period is divided into two halves; during the first half the contents of the registers are read and/or updated; during the second half the exchange elements are set and the registers latched to obtain new values.

As long as there are no conflicts, the counter will be incremented by one at the end of each period. If no conflicts arise for n periods, the carrier will be at the final destination of the message. Conflicts will clearly occur only if both carriers at the input of an exchange element have their full components equal to true.

When a conflict happens, the exchange element will select one of the two carriers on its inputs and reject the other; the setting of the exchange element will be done according to the selected carrier. At the beginning of the next period, the counter of the selected carrier will be incremented by one. The rejected carrier will go through the exchange element towards a wrong location, and its counter will be reset to 1; thus, the rejected carrier will start traversing the network as if it had just been introduced. A carrier with full = true will retain the values of full, destination-tag, and message until counter becomes $n + 1$; then either destination-tag and message are replaced by new values or full is set to false.

We will consider two ways by which an exchange element may select a carrier when a conflict arises.

a) Select a carrier at random.

b) Select the carrier with the largest value of counter; and, in the case of a tie, select a carrier at random.

If we define the state of a carrier by its full and counter components, then the graph of transition between the different states is the one shown in Fig. 6. In this Fig., the transitions departing from the state full = true, counter = $n + 1$ deserve some explanation; the other transitions should be self-explanatory. Let us consider two consecutive periods, $i - 1$ and i. If the carrier is in the state full = true, counter = $n + 1$ immediately after the end of period $i - 1$, then during the first half of period i, either full is set to false or counter is set to 1, as explained above. Immediately after the end of period i, the

new state of the carrier will be either full = false or full = true, counter = 2 because the counter is incremented by one at the end of period i when full = true. We will use the graph of Fig. 6 for the performance analysis later in this Section.

The previous method can also be used for synchronous networks, and it was in this context that it was first introduced in [24] where its behavior is studied by means of simulation.

The two main values we will consider when evaluating the performance of the network are the time for a message to be introduced into the network (recall that a component has to wait until a suitable carrier comes along before introducing a message into the network) and the time a message stays in the network. These values will change, depending on the fraction of carriers with full = true; this fraction will be called the *load* of the network. As we will see, the load will greatly influence the behavior of the network. It will, then, be convenient to guarantee that the load is at most a certain value ℓ. This can be achieved by having several one stage shuffle-exchange networks, connecting a subset of the processors to each one of them, and forcing each processor to have only one message per network at a given time. (This is why the acknowledgment from memory to processor is required.) We now proceed with the analysis of the behavior of the network.

We will make the assumption of the independent reference model, namely, that the destination of a message is location L_d with probability $1/N$ for $1 \le L_d \le N$. Let us first study the average time, measured in network periods, that a message will remain in the network. To this end, we will use the state transition of a carrier (Fig. 6); however, when a carrier is in the state "full = false," no message is being transported by it and we must ignore this state. Therefore, we will use the state transition diagram of Fig. 7.

Let Q_i^j be the probability that a carrier will go from the state "counter = i" to the state "counter = j." As stated before, there are two strategies for the setting of the exchange element. In the first strategy, one carrier is selected at random. Let us assume that the load is ℓ. Then, from the assumption that the addresses are generated at random, it can be concluded that the probability of a conflict arising for a carrier in the "full = true" state is

$$P(\text{conflict}) = \frac{\ell}{2}.$$

This is because a conflict will arise if the carrier at the other exchange element input is in the "full = true" state (the factor ℓ comes from this), and the destination-tag bits of both carriers coincide ($\frac{1}{2}$ because the addresses are random). Now, because the exchange elements are set at random when a conflict arises, the probability that the carrier will have its counter component reset to 1 is

302

$$P(\text{reset}) = \tfrac{1}{2} P(\text{conflict}) = \frac{\ell}{4}.$$

From these considerations, the following values for Q_i^j are obtained.

$$Q_i^j = \begin{cases} \dfrac{\ell}{4} & j = 1 \\[2mm] \left(1 - \dfrac{\ell}{4}\right) & j = i+1,\, i = 1, 2, \cdots, n \\[2mm] \left(1 - \dfrac{\ell}{4}\right) & i = n+1,\, j = 2 \\[2mm] 0 & \text{otherwise} \end{cases}$$

If we say that P_i is the steady-state probability of a carrier being in the state "counter $= i$," then a simple calculation shows that

$$P_i = \begin{cases} \dfrac{\ell}{4} & i = 1 \\[3mm] \left(1 - \dfrac{\ell}{4}\right)^{i-1}\left(\dfrac{\ell}{4} + P_{n+1}\right) & 2 \le i \le n+1. \end{cases}$$

From this we conclude that

$$P_{n+1} = \frac{\ell}{4} \frac{(1 - \ell/4)^n}{1 - (1 - \ell/4)^n}.$$

Therefore, the expected number of periods a message will stay in the network, given this strategy, will be (recall $N = 2^n$):

$$\text{ET}_{\text{random}}(N) = \frac{1}{P_{n+1}} = \frac{4}{\ell}\left(N^{-\log_2(1 - \frac{\ell}{4})} - 1\right).$$

The function $\text{ET}_{\text{random}}(\cdot)$ is plotted in Fig. 8 for $\ell = 1, \tfrac{1}{2}$, and $\tfrac{1}{4}$, and $4 \le \log_2 N \le 20$.

The second strategy is in selecting the carrier whose counter component is larger, and when there is a tie, making a random choice. In this case, and with the same notation as before, we have

$$Q_i^j =$$

$$\begin{cases} \dfrac{\ell}{2}\left[1 - \dfrac{P_1 + P_{n+1}}{2}\right], & \begin{array}{l} j = 1,\, i = 1 \\ \text{or } j = 1,\, i = n+1 \end{array} \\[3mm] 1 - \dfrac{\ell}{2}\left[1 - \dfrac{P_1 + P_{n+1}}{2}\right], & \begin{array}{l} j = 2,\, i = 1 \\ \text{or } j = 2,\, i = n+1 \end{array} \\[3mm] \dfrac{\ell}{2}\left[1 - \displaystyle\sum_{j=1}^{i-1} P_j - P_{n+1} - \dfrac{P_i}{2}\right], & j = 1,\, i = 2, \cdots, n \\[3mm] 1 - \dfrac{\ell}{2}\left[1 - \displaystyle\sum_{j=1}^{i-1} P_j - P_{n+1} - \dfrac{P_i}{2}\right], & j = i+1,\, i = 2, \cdots, n \\[3mm] 0, & \text{otherwise.} \end{cases}$$

In this case, we were not able to find a closed form expression for the average number of periods a message will stay in the network $[\text{ET}_{\text{priority}}(N)]$. However, this value can be quickly obtained by numerical methods. The function $\text{ET}_{\text{priority}}(\cdot)$ is plotted in Fig. 9 for $\ell = 1, \tfrac{1}{2}$, and $\tfrac{1}{4}$, and $4 \le \log_2 N \le 20$.

The processors and the global memory modules will have

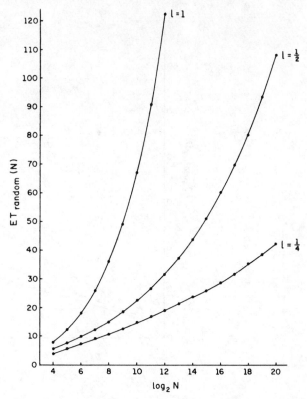

Fig. 8. Graph of $\text{ET}_{\text{random}}$.

to wait until a carrier with full = false appears before introducing a message into the network. The average waiting time for such an event is

$$(1 - \ell) \sum i\ell^i = \ell^2, \qquad \text{if } \ell < 1.$$

Since it has been assumed that a processor has at most one message in any one-stage shuffle-exchange network, no queues of messages will be formed between the processor and the network. However, queues are possible between a global memory module and the interconnection network.

The length of these queues will be small if ℓ is small enough. For example, if the cycle and access time of a memory module is equal to two periods of the network, the load ℓ is less than $\tfrac{1}{2}$, and we assume that the memory module will always place a message every 2 periods into the same queue; then we will show that a message arriving at the queue will, on the average, find $\ell^2/(1 - 2\ell)$ messages in front of it.

In the interval between successive arrivals (two periods in this case), only one element will be removed from the queue with probability $2(1 - \ell)$, two elements with probability ℓ^2, and none with probability $(1 - \ell)^2$. Thus, if we consider the number of elements in the queue just before an arrival as determining the state of the system, we will have the following transition matrix, where the first row and column correspond to state 0, the second row and the second column to state 1, etc.

$1 - \ell^2$	ℓ^2	0	0	0	$\cdots$
$(1 - \ell)^2$	$2\ell(1 - \ell)$	ℓ^2	0	0	$\cdots$
0	$(1 - \ell)^2$	$2\ell(1 - \ell)$	ℓ^2	0	$\cdots$
0	0	$(1 - \ell)^2$	$2\ell(1 - \ell)$	ℓ^2	$\cdots$
$\vdots$	$\vdots$	$\vdots$	$\vdots$		

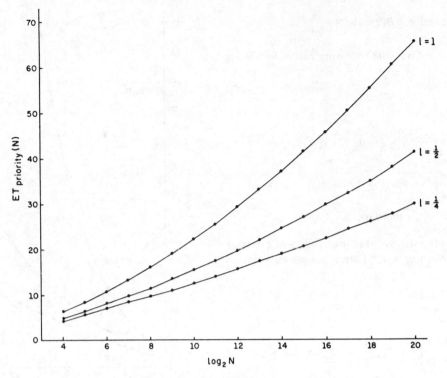

Fig. 9. Graph of ET_priority.

Let us say that P_i is the steady-state probability of our memory-queue system being in state i; then it is easy to see from the transition matrix that

$$P_i = \left[\left(\frac{\ell}{1-\ell}\right)^2\right]^i P_0, \qquad i = 0, 1, \cdots,$$

and, therefore,

$$P_0 \sum_{i=0}^{\infty} \left[\left(\frac{\ell}{1-\ell}\right)^2\right]^i = 1 \text{ or } P_0 = \frac{1-2\ell}{1-\ell^2}.$$

The average number of elements in the queue just before an arrival is then

$$P_0 \sum_{i=0}^{\infty} i \left[\left(\frac{\ell}{1-\ell}\right)^2\right]^i = \frac{\ell^2}{1-2\ell},$$

as we indicated above. This last value is fairly small, less than one, if $\ell \leq 1/3$. If the memory cycle time is larger than two periods, it is clear that the average length of the queue will be even smaller. We can, therefore, conclude that if it is assumed that the memory cycle time is larger than or equal to 2 network periods and $\ell \leq 1/3$, the average queue length will not produce any significant delays.

A final comment; if the global memory is used for synchronization, the previously described network could cause difficulties in the sense described by Lamport in [12]. To avoid these difficulties processors should not be allowed to issue a fetch or a store before all previous fetches and stores are completed.

II. COMPILER TECHNIQUES

This section deals with the automatic translation of sequential programs into parallel programs for multiprocessors. One reason for doing automatic translation is to attain program portability. Most of the programs in existence are sequential programs; their conversion into parallel programs for multiprocessors will be facilitated by an automatic translator. Also, the conversion of programs between different parallel machines (pipeline, array, multifunction, multiprocessor, etc.) could profit from automatic translation. For example, a sequential version of the program could be used to generate different parallel programs. (Techniques to translate sequential programs into parallel programs for pipeline or array machines are discussed elsewhere; see, for example, [9], [10], and [15].)

The benefit that could be obtained from portability is potentially high. In [18], Rice reports that the conversion of a numerical program from a sequential machine to another costs roughly 15 percent of the original program cost. We do not have data on the cost of conversion from sequential to parallel programs, but we believe that it is bound to be much higher than 15 percent.

There are other reasons for the importance of automatic translation. The techniques and their development improve our understanding of the parallel processing problem from both the software and machine design points of view. Also, the same facilities used for automatic translation can be used to gather data for machine design.

The rest of this section is organized into two parts. Section II-A. introduces the basic concepts needed to explain the translation algorithms. Many of these concepts are similar to those presented in [8, sect. 2.4]; they are presented here for completeness and to define the notation. Then, Section II-B. discusses algorithms that are useful for translation for multiprocessors in general. A discussion of translation algorithms specific to the architecture described above will be presented in a future paper.

A. Basic Concepts

The basic concepts to be presented now deal with relationships between statements. Only four types of statements, **goto, if,** assignment, and **for** will be considered. Extensions of this work to include other types of statements are possible; however, the four statements above suffice to express most of the concepts required for automatic translation. Thus, I/O statements can be replaced by assignment statements, and procedure calls can be replaced by the body of the procedure in the absence of recursion, or, in some cases, by an iterative construct if recursion is present [19]. Statements can be classified as simple and compound. Assignment and **goto** are simple statements. The **for** statements (this includes all the statements in its body) and the **if** statements (including all the statements in the **then** and **else** parts) are compound. Henceforth, the word statement will stand for simple or compound statement.

The algorithms discussed in Section II-B. require information on the interaction of the statements in the source program. This information will be mainly provided by the relationship of *dependence* defined below. Since the algorithms in Section II-B. deal only with **for** loops and with forward-flow sequences of statements, dependence will be defined only in these two contexts. A *forward-flow sequence of statements* is defined as a sequence of statements such that all branches in it are to statements appearing later in the sequence.

In the definition of dependence the concept of *simple variable* will be used. A simple variable is a variable having no components. Array variables, record variables, etc. are assumed to have simple variables as their components.

Definition 1: Given two statements $\underline{S}$ and $\underline{T}$ in a forward-flow sequence of statements, such that $\underline{S}$ precedes $\underline{T}$ in the sequence

a) $\underline{T}$ is *data dependent* on $\underline{S}$ iff there exists a simple variable $\underline{v}$ such that $\underline{S}$ assigns a value to $\underline{v}$ and $\underline{T}$ fetches the value of $\underline{v}$.

b) $\underline{T}$ is *antidependent* on $\underline{S}$ iff there exists a simple variable $\underline{v}$ such that $\underline{T}$ assigns a value to $\underline{v}$ and $\underline{S}$ fetches the value of $\underline{v}$.

c) $\underline{T}$ is *output dependent* on $\underline{S}$ iff there exists a simple variable $\underline{v}$ such that both $\underline{T}$ and $\underline{S}$ assign values to $\underline{v}$.

Henceforth, the dependence relations will be represented by a directed acyclic graph (DAG) where the nodes represent statements, and the arcs dependence; this DAG will be called *dependence graph.* In the dependence graph there will be a type of arc for each type of dependence; those corresponding to the dependences defined above are shown in Figs. 10(a)–(c).

Example 1: The sequence of statements

$\underline{S}$: $A := B + C$;

$\underline{T}$: $D := A + E$;

$\underline{U}$: $A := A + D$;

$\underline{V}$: **if** $x < 0$ **then** $F := D + 1$; **end if**;

$\underline{W}$: **if** $x > 0$ **then** $G := F + A$; **end if**;

Fig. 10. Graphical representation of dependence. T is (a) data dependent, (b) antidependent, (c) output dependent, or (d) control dependent on S.

Fig. 11. Dependence graph for Example 1.

has the dependence graph shown in Fig. 11. Notice that there is no dependence between $\underline{V}$ and $\underline{W}$ because only one of them will have its **then** part executed. ∎

To define dependence for statements inside **for** loops one additional concept will be required. Given a multiply-nested **for** loop of the form

$$\textbf{for } i1 = 1 \textbf{ to } n1 \textbf{ do}$$

$$\textbf{for } i2 = 1 \textbf{ to } n2 \textbf{ do}$$

$$\cdot$$
$$\cdot$$

$$\textbf{for } ik = 1 \textbf{ to } nk \textbf{ do}$$

$$\cdot$$

$$\textbf{end};$$

$$\cdot$$

$$\textbf{end};$$

$$\textbf{end}$$

and a statement $\underline{S}$ inside it, $\underline{S}_{\ell 1, \ell 2, \ldots, \ell k}$, called an *instance* of $\underline{S}$, will stand for $\underline{S}$ when $i1 = \ell 1, i2 = \ell 2, \cdots$, and $ik = \ell k$. An instance $\underline{S}_{\ell 1, \ell 2, \ldots, \ell k}$ of a statement $\underline{S}$ is said to precede another instance $\underline{T}_{m1, m2, \ldots, mk}$ of a statement T iff $\underline{S}_{\ell 1, \ell 2, \ldots, \ell k}$ is executed before $\underline{T}_{m1, m2, \ldots, mk}$.

Definition 2: Given two, not necessarily distinct, statements $\underline{S}$ and $\underline{T}$ both inside the same **for** loop, and one instance of each, respectively, $\underline{S}_{\ell 1, \ell 2, \ldots, \ell k}$ and $\underline{T}_{m1, m2, \ldots, mk}$, such that $\underline{S}_{\ell 1, \ell 2, \ldots, \ell k}$ precedes $\underline{T}_{m1, m2, \ldots, mk}$:

a) $\underline{T}_{m1, m2, \ldots, mk}$ is *data dependent* on $\underline{S}_{\ell 1, \ell 2, \ldots, \ell k}$ iff there exist a simple variable $\underline{v}$ such that $\underline{S}_{\ell 1, \ell 2, \ldots, \ell k}$ assigns a value to $\underline{v}$ and $\underline{T}_{m1, m2, \ldots, mk}$ fetches the value of $\underline{v}$.

b) $\underline{T}_{m1, m2, \ldots, mk}$ is *antidependent* on $\underline{S}_{\ell 1, \ell 2, \ldots, \ell k}$ iff there exists a simple variable $\underline{v}$ such that $\underline{T}_{m1, m2, \ldots, mk}$ assigns a value to $\underline{v}$ and $\underline{S}_{\ell 1, \ell 2, \ldots, \ell k}$ fetches the value of $\underline{v}$.

c) $\underline{T}_{m1, m2, \ldots, mk}$ is *output dependent* on $\underline{S}_{\ell 1, \ell 2, \ldots, \ell k}$ iff there exists a simple variable $\underline{v}$ such that both

Fig. 12.   Dependence graph for Example 2.

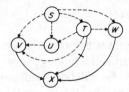

Fig. 13.   Dependence graph for Example 5.

$T_{m1,m2, \ldots, mk}$ and $\underline{S}_{\ell 1, \ell 2, \ldots, \ell k}$ assign values to v.

Definition 3: A statement $\underline{T}$ is *data dependent, antidependent,* or *output dependent* on statement $\underline{S}$ ($\underline{T}$ and $\underline{S}$ not necessarily distinct and both inside the same **for** loop) iff there exist instances $\underline{S}_{\ell 1, \ell 2, \ldots, \ell k}$ of $\underline{S}$ and $\underline{T}_{m1,m2, \ldots, mk}$ of $\underline{T}$ such that $\underline{T}_{m1,m2, \ldots, mk}$ is, respectively, data dependent, antidependent, or output dependent on $\underline{S}_{\ell 1, \ell 2, \ldots, \ell k}$.

Example 2: Given the loop

for i = 1 **to** m **do**

    for j = 1 **to** n **do**

        $\underline{S}$: $A(i, j)$: = $A(i - 1, j) + C(j) + C(j - 1)$;

        $\underline{T}$: $C(j)$: = $D(j) + A(i, j)$;

    end;

end;

the statements $\underline{S}$ and $\underline{T}$ have the dependence graph shown in Fig. 12.   ∎

There is one more type of dependence called *control dependence.* This dependence relation is obtained by manipulating **if** statements. The translator will transform **if** statements before the dependence relations are computed following two steps. First, the translator creates an assignment statement where the Boolean expression of the **if** statement is assigned to a Boolean variable, say b. Then all statements whose execution is controlled by the **if** statement will be followed by either **when** b or by **when not** b depending on whether they are executed when the Boolean expression is true or when it is false.

Example 3: The sequence of statements

    A: = $B + 1$;

    if A < 5 **then** C: = $A + 1$; **goto** 5;

        else D: = $A + 1$; **goto** 7;

    end if;

    5: E: = $A + 1$;

    7: F: = $A + 1$;

will become

    A: = $B + 1$;

    b: = A < 5;

    C: = $A + 1$ **when** b;

    D: = $A + 1$ **when not** b;

    E: = $A + 1$ **when** b;

    F: = $A + 1$;   ∎

When more than one **if** statement controls the execution of a statement, it becomes necessary to expand the previous idea, allowing Boolean expressions after the **when.**

Example 4: The sequence of statements

    if A < 5 **then goto** 5; **end if;**

    if B < 7 **then if** C < 5 **then** D: = 1; **end if;**

                    goto 5;

              else goto 6;

    end if;

    5: E: = 1;

    6: B: = $E + D$;

will be replaced by

    $\underline{S}$: $b1$: = A < 5;

    $\underline{T}$: $b2$: = B < **when not** $b1$;

    $\underline{U}$: $b3$: = C < 5 **when not** $b1$ **and** $b2$;

    $\underline{V}$: D: = 1 **when not** $b1$ **and** $b2$ **and** $b3$;

    $\underline{W}$: E: = 1 **when** $b1$ **or** $b2$;

    $\underline{X}$: B: = $E + D$;   ∎

The statements whose execution is controlled by an **if** statement are said to be *control dependent* on the assignment statement created by the compiler for that **if** statement. Control dependence is represented graphically as shown in Fig. 10(d).

Example 5: The dependence graph for the transformed segment in Example 4 is shown in Fig. 13.   ∎

Control dependence is really a form of data dependence. However, in some architectures the Boolean variables created by manipulating the **if** statements are handled differently from the other data. For that reason, control dependence is considered different from data dependence. However, for most multiprocessors this distinction is not necessary. Practical methods for computing the dependence relations can be found in [10], [23], and [2].

A final comment on dependences. It is convenient to have as few dependence relations as possible; this will often increase the parallelism the translator can exploit. One way to decrease the number of dependences is by using data flow languages [5] which do not allow antidependences or output dependences. For more conventional languages, the translator can eliminate antidependences and output dependences by techniques such as *renaming* and *scalar expansion* illustrated in the next two examples.

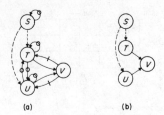

Fig. 14. Dependence graph for Example 7.

Fig. 15. Dependence graph for Example 8.

Example 6: The sequence of statements of Example 1 can be changed by replacing $\underline{U}$ by statement

$$\underline{U'}: AA: = A + D;$$

and statement $\underline{W}$ by

$$\underline{W'}: \text{ if } x < 0 \text{ then } G: = F + AA; \text{ end if;}$$

These changes will remove the antidependence and the output dependence arcs in Fig. 11. The method used in this example is called *renaming.* ∎

Example 7: The loop

for $i = 1$ **to** n **do**

   if $A(i) < 0$ **then** $X: = B(i);$

         else $X: = C(i);$

   end if;

   $D(i): = X + 1;$

end;

will be transformed into

for $i = 1$ **to** n **do**

   $\underline{S}: b: = A(i) < 0;$

   $\underline{T}: X: = B(i) \text{ when } b;$

   $\underline{U}: X: = C(i) \text{ when not } b;$

   $\underline{V}: D(i): = X + 1;$

end;

with the dependence graph shown in Fig. 14(a). If, in the previous **for** loop, all occurrences of b are replaced by $b(i)$, and all occurrences of X by $X(i)$ then the dependence graph in Fig. 14(b) will result. The method used in this example is called *scalar expansion.* ∎

Many times it is convenient to attach additional information to the dependence relations. Assume a (possibly multiply nested) **for** loop and two, not necessarily distinct, statements $\underline{S}$ and $\underline{T}$ inside it. Assume also that $\underline{T}$ is data dependent on $\underline{S}$. Associated with this data dependence relation will be a set of k-tuples (where k is the degree of nesting of the loop containing S and T) called *distance vectors.* A k-tuple $\langle m_1, \cdots, m_k \rangle$ will belong to the set of distance vectors associated with the data dependence of $\underline{T}$ on $\underline{S}$ if there exist instances $\underline{T}_{i1,i2, \ldots, ik}$ and $\underline{S}_{j1,j2, \ldots, jk}$ such that the first is data dependent on the second and

$$\langle m_1, \cdots, m_k \rangle = \langle i1 - j1, \cdots, ik - jk \rangle.$$

The same type of information will be associated with antidependences and output dependences. Graphically, distance vector sets will be written next to the dependence arc.

Example 8: The dependence graph of the statements in the loop

for $i = 1$ **to** n **do**

   for $j = 1$ **to** m **do**

   $\underline{S}: A(i, j): = A(i - 1, j + 1) + A(i - 1, j);$

   $\underline{T}: B(i, j): = B(i - 1, j - 1) + A(i, j - 1);$

   end;

end;

is shown in Fig. 15, where $\{\langle 1, -1 \rangle, \langle 1, 0 \rangle\}, \{\langle 0, 1 \rangle\}$, and $\{\langle 1, 1 \rangle\}$ are the distance vector sets. ∎

To conclude this section, the concept of Π-*block* and one of its uses will be presented. Given a (possibly multiply nested) **for** loop and the dependence graph of the statements in its body, a Π-block is defined as the set of statements corresponding to a strongly connected component [1] of the dependence graph.

Example 9: The dependence graph of the statements inside the loop

for $i = 1$ **to** n **do**

   $\underline{S}: A(i): = B(i - 1) + 1;$

   $\underline{T}: C(i): = A(i) + D(i - 1);$

   $\underline{U}: B(i): = A(i) + 1;$

   $\underline{V}: D(i): = C(i) + 1;$

   $\underline{W}: E(i): = D(i) + F(i - 1);$

   $\underline{X}: F(i): = D(i) - F(i - 1);$

end;

is given in Fig. 16. The Π-blocks in this case are $\{\underline{S}, \underline{U}\}, \{\underline{T}, \underline{V}\}, \{\underline{W}\}$, and $\{\underline{X}\}$. ∎

The concept of dependence is extended to Π-blocks by saying that a Π-block Π_1 is data dependent, antidependent, or output dependent on another Π-block Π_2 iff there exist two statements, $\underline{T} \in \Pi_1$, and $\underline{S} \in \Pi_2$ such that $\underline{T}$ is, respectively, data dependent, antidependent, or output dependent on $\underline{S}$.

One of the main uses of the concept of Π-block is *loop distribution.* Given a **for** loop and the Π-blocks of statements in its body, loop distribution consists of creating a **for** loop from each Π-block. The header of each **for** loop will be identical to the header of the original **for** loop.

Example 10: The loop in Example 9 will have the following form after distribution:

Fig. 16. Dependence graph for Example 9.

```
for i = 1 to n do
  S:   A(i): = B(i − 1) + 1;
  U:   B(i): = A(i) + 1;
end;
  for i = 1 to n do
  T:   C(i): = A(i) + D(i − 1);
  V:   D(i): = C(i) + 1;
end;
  for i = 1 to n do
  W:   E(i): = B(i) + F(i − 1);
end;
  for i = 1 to n do
  X:   F(i): = D(i) − F(i − 1);
end;                               ■
```

B. Basic Transformations

This section discusses three types of transformations that the translator can apply to extract parallelism from sequential programs. The first two deal with **for** loops and the third with forward-flow sequences of statements.

1) forall transformations: The first transformation to be discussed will convert each iteration of a **for** loop into a *process* [7]. A **for** loop transformed in this way will be called a **forall** loop. The easiest case for this transformation will be when there are no cycles in the dependence graph of the loop body, and all distance vectors are zero. Given these convenient conditions the body of the original **for** loop will become the body of the **forall** loop without the need for any changes.

Example 11: The distance vectors corresponding to the dependence graph in Fig. 14(b) are all zero. Therefore, the loop of Example 7 can be transformed into

```
forall i = 1 to n do
  S:   b(i): = A(i) < 0;
  T:   X(i): = B(i) when b(i);
  U:   X(i): = C(i) when not b(i);
  V:   D(i): = X(i) + 1;
end;
```

Using n processors, the previous **forall** loop can be executed in about three units of time (assuming unit execution time per statement, and neglecting the execution time of T if $b(i)$ is false, and of U otherwise). The sequential execution time of the same loop is about $3n$ units of time.   ■

Clearly, not all loops will be this simple. In general, to guarantee correctness, synchronization between the resulting processes will be required. Henceforth, it will be assumed that the machine code will take care of the synchronization. This

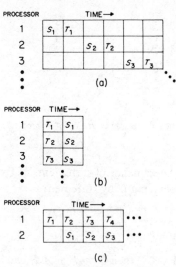

Fig. 17. Time lines for Examples 12 and 15. (a) **forall** without reordering. (b) **forall** with reordering. (c) Pipelining.

can be done by using synchronization instructions similar to the well known P and V operators, by using a few tag bits next to each memory cell as is done in the HEP computer of Denelcor [21], by using the status bits mentioned in Section I-A., or by a combination of them. In the examples that follow, the synchronization will not be stated explicitly; however, from the dependences it will be clear where synchronization must be done.

When there are no cycles in the dependence graph but the distance vectors are not all zero, the body of the loop must be reordered in such a way that all dependence graph arcs go forward; this is accomplished by doing topological sorting on the dependence graph. This reordering will help speedup.

Example 12: If the loop

```
for i = 1 to n do
  S:   A(i): = B(i − 1) + 2;
  T:   B(i): = C(i) + 1;
end;
```

is executed as **forall** without reordering the statements, then its parallel execution time will be the same as the sequential execution time. The time lines for this case are shown in Fig. 17(a). Maximum parallelism is obtained by interchanging S and T, as can be seen in Fig. 17(b).   ■

When cycles are present the procedure will be very similar to the one depicted above. To reorganize the body of the loop, first all statements belonging to the same Π-block are brought together, and then the Π-blocks are topologically sorted.

Example 13: The loop of Example 9 will be transformed into

```
forall i = 1 to n do
  S:   A(i): = B(i − 1) + 1;
  U:   B(i): = A(i) + 1;
  T:   C(i): = A(i) + D(i − 1);
  V:   D(i): = C(i) + 1;
  X:   F(i): = D(i) − F(i − 1);
  W:   E(i): = D(i) + F(i − 1);
end;
```

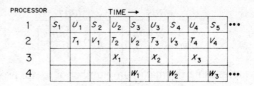

Processor										
				TIME →						
1	S_1	U_1	T_1	V_1	X_1	W_1				
2			S_2	U_2	T_2	V_2	X_2	W_2		
3					S_3	U_3	T_3	V_3	X_3	W_3
⋮										

Fig. 18. Time lines for Example 13.

Processor										
				TIME →						
1	S_1	U_1	S_2	U_2	S_3	U_3	S_4	U_4	S_5	⋯
2	T_1	V_1	T_2	V_2	T_3	V_3	T_4	V_4		
3			X_1		X_2		X_3			
4				W_1		W_2		W_3		⋯

Fig. 20. Time lines for Example 16.

Processor												
					TIME →							
1	S_1	$T_{1,1}$	$T_{1,2}$	$T_{1,3}$	$T_{1,4}$	⋯	$T_{1,n-1}$	$T_{1,n}$			
2	S_2		$T_{2,1}$	$T_{2,2}$	$T_{2,3}$	⋯	$T_{2,n-2}$	$T_{2,n-1}$	$T_{2,n}$		
3	S_3			$T_{3,1}$	$T_{3,2}$	⋯	$T_{3,n-3}$	$T_{3,n-2}$	$T_{3,n-1}$	$T_{3,n}$	
⋮											

Fig. 19. Time lines for Example 14.

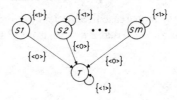

Fig. 21. Dependence graph for Example 17.

The time lines for the execution of this **forall** when n processors are used are shown in Fig. 18. Assuming unit execution time for all statements, the **forall** will take about $2n + 4$ time units to execute; this is roughly $\frac{1}{3}$ the execution time of the original **for** loop. ∎

One interesting observation about the **forall** scheme is that the *wavefront method* [11] arises naturally. This is illustrated in the next example.

Example 14: The loop

> **for** $i = 1$ **to** n **do**
> $\underline{S:}$ $C(i): = A(i) + D(i) + 1;$
>
>   **for** $j = 1$ **to** n **do**
> $\underline{T:}$ $B(i, j): = C(i) + B(i - 1, j) + B(i, j - 1);$
>   **end**;
> **end**;

when transformed into a **forall** will execute as shown in the time lines of Fig. 19. The execution of statement $\underline{T}$ is the same as if the wavefront method had been applied. ∎

2) Pipelining: The second transformation to be discussed, called pipelining, consists simply of distributing a **for** loop and making a process out of each resulting **for** loop; synchronization operators are inserted to guarantee correctness. As will be seen, in some cases **forall** gives better speedup and in other cases pipelining gives better speedup.

Example 15: If the loop of Example 12 is transformed by the pipelining method the time lines of Fig. 17(c) will result. The execution time in this case will be $n + 1$ time units which could be much larger than the 2 time units taken by the **forall** method. ∎

Example 16: Consider the loop of Example 9. If the pipelining transformation is applied to it, and four processors are used, the time lines shown in Fig. 20 will result at execution time. The execution time is, in this case, $2n + 3$ which is fairly close to the result of $2n + 4$ obtained in Example 13. ∎

Example 17: Assume the loop

> **for** $i: = 1$ **to** n **do**
> $\underline{S1}; \underline{S2}; \cdots; \underline{Sm}; \underline{T}$
> **end**;

and the dependence graph of Fig. 21. Assuming unit execution time per statement, the pipelining execution time is

$$T^{\text{pip}} = n + 1;$$

whereas the **forall** execution time is

$$T^{\text{forall}} = n + m.$$

For large m and small n, pipelining will be much faster than **forall**. ∎

Sometimes, when inner **for** loops are present, unrolling them will increase the number of processes that may be used to execute the **for** loop by the pipelining method, and this may decrease the execution time.

3) Speedup and Efficiency of **forall** *and Pipelining:* Let T_Q be the execution time of a construct when Q processors are used (in particular T_1 is the sequential execution time). The speedup S_Q and the efficiency E_Q, given that Q processors are used, are defined as follows:

$$S_Q = \frac{T_1}{T_Q},$$

and

$$E_Q = \frac{T_1}{QT_Q}.$$

Consider a **for** loop with n iterations and m Π-blocks. First, assume that all Π-blocks require the same execution time per iteration, say τ. Let δ be the maximum difference between the completion times of the computations in all processors, and P be the number of processors used. In the **forall** case $\delta_{\max} = (P - 1)\tau$ occurs when for at least one Π-block, successive iterations cannot be overlapped, while in the pipelining case $\delta_{\max} = (P - 1)\tau$ when each Π-block has a dependence arc to the succeeding Π-block and no two Π-blocks can have their executions overlapped. Thus, we have for both the **forall** and pipelining schemes

$$T_P \leq \delta_{\max} + \left\lceil \frac{nm\tau}{P} \right\rceil < P\tau + \left\lceil \frac{nm\tau}{P} \right\rceil$$

and

$$S_P \geq \frac{nm\tau}{\delta_{\max} + \left\lceil \frac{nm\tau}{P} \right\rceil} > \frac{nm\tau}{P\tau + \left\lceil \frac{nm\tau}{P} \right\rceil}.$$

Furthermore, using the maximum number of useful processors we have

$$S_P \geq \frac{nm}{n+m} \qquad \begin{cases} P = n \text{ for } \textbf{forall} \\ P = m \text{ for } \textbf{pipelining} \end{cases}$$

Now, let us try to increase the efficiency without decreasing the speedup. First, notice that if $n = m$, using $P = n$ processors we have

$$S_n > \frac{n}{2}$$

and

$$E_n > \frac{1}{2}$$

for either **forall** or pipelining.

When $n \neq m$, efficiency could in general be very low. However, if $\delta = \delta_{\max}$, when using the maximum number of useful processors for either pipelining or **forall,** maximum speed can be achieved by using just $P = \min(m, n)$ processors. Then, for both the **forall** and pipelining schemes

$$E_P > \frac{nm\tau}{\min(m, n)(n+m)\tau} \geq \frac{1}{2}.$$

The quantity $P = \min(m, n)$ is obtained by allowing the execution of more than one iteration in the same processor for the **forall** case, and of more than one Π-block in the same processor for the pipelining case.

Consider now the **forall** scheme with, possibly, different execution times for different Π-blocks and constant execution time for the different iterations of the same Π-block. Let σ be the execution time of one iteration of the **for** loop. If, as often happens in practice, when the **forall** is executed in n processors, successive iterations always differ in their completion times by τ units of time (with the earlier iteration finishing before the later iterations), then we have

$$T_p = \sigma + (n-1)\tau,$$

and

$$P = \min\left(\left\lceil \frac{\sigma}{\tau} \right\rceil, n\right)$$

processors will suffice to execute the forall at maximum speed. The efficiency will now be

$$E_p = \frac{n\sigma}{P(\sigma + (n-1)\tau)} > \frac{1}{2}$$

and the speedup

$$S_p > \frac{1}{\frac{1}{n} + \frac{\tau}{\sigma}} \left(\approx \frac{\sigma}{\tau} \text{ for large } n \right).$$

For pipelining, efficiency can be enhanced in two ways. First, by having one processor execute more than one process

(the Π-blocks), as discussed above. The second method is called *clustering*. This is done by partially distributing the sequential **for** loop; that is, by creating a **for** loop for a subset, or cluster, of Π-blocks instead of having that done for each individual Π-block. Thus, in Example 10, W and X could be in the same **for** loop. This will allow the pipelining of Example 16 to require three instead of four processors. In this case the time lines in Fig. 20 will have to be modified, and processor 3 will execute $\underline{X}$ and $\underline{W}$ ($\underline{W}_i$ will occupy the empty slot after $\underline{X}_i$).

Clustering is NP-complete in the strong sense. This can be shown by a straightforward argument using 3-partition [6, p. 96]. However, simple heuristics seem to work well in many cases.

4) Speading: The last method to be mentioned here consists of taking a forward-flow sequence of statements and creating several processes to exploit parallelism. Such problems are studied under the heading of scheduling theory [4]. Since the use of these methods in automatic translation for multiprocessors has been widely studied (see, for example, [17]), they will not be discussed here. The only remark worth making at this point is that spreading can be used on top of pipelining or **forall** to decrease the execution time.

III. CONCLUSION

We are presently augmenting the PARAFRASE analyzer and vectorizer with the algorithms of Section II. This will allow us to compile Fortran programs for hypothetical MES machines as well as SEA and MEA machines. We then will be able to characterize an MES machine in more detail. However, we believe that an MES approach will be effective in several areas where array machines (parallel or pipeline) are weak. These include the following:

1) **for** loops with a high degree of branching.

While most such loops can be easily vectorized, they can lead to inefficient array machine computation because of the resulting short vectors. If each processor can follow an independent path through the loop, however, high efficiency is possible.

2) **for** loops with nonlinear recurrences.

Nonlinear recurrences that cannot be linearized or vectorized at all, if contained in a loop with a large number of statements, can be easily speeded up by pipelining across a high-speed multiprocessor.

3) **for** loops that are executed repeatedly with widely varying loop limits.

Each processor can execute a loop with its own limit. Upon finishing such an execution, any processor can be restarted with another limit (or even another loop), thus providing dynamic scheduling of a set of loops. In parallel machines with lock-step synchronization, inefficiencies arise when certain processors drop out of the computation. In all array machines, such computation can lead to short vectors that are inefficient.

4) **for** loops containing arrays with subscripted subscripts.

Random stores and fetches can cause conflicts in most parallel memories and alignment networks. If addresses are uniformly distributed across the memory unit, high-effective bandwidth can still be achieved. Data alignment has been a serious unresolved problem, but the network of Section I-B should be very useful in this case.

It is certain that some overhead due to synchronization will be incurred in a high-speed multiprocessor. As it is tightly coupled, however, we believe that this can be made rather small. Nevertheless, for computations that can be effectively vectorized, an array control unit is provided because it offers a number of advantages.

REFERENCES

[1] A. V. Aho, J. E. Hopcroft, and J. D. Ullman, *The Design and Analysis of Computer Algorithms.* Reading, MA: Addison-Wesley, 1974.

[2] U. Banerjee, S.-C. Chen, D. J. Kuck, and R. A. Towle, "Time and parallel processor bounds for Fortran-like loops," *IEEE Trans. Comput.,* vol. C-28, pp. 660–670, Sept. 1979.

[3] Burroughs Corporation, "Numerical Aerodynamic Simulation Facility Feasibility Study," Mar. 1979.

[4] E. G. Coffman, Ed., *Computer and Job-Shop Scheduling Theory.* New York: Wiley, 1976.

[5] J. B. Dennis, "First version of a data flow procedure language," in *Programming Symp. Proc., Colloque sur la Programmation,* B. Robinet, Ed., *Lecture Notes in Computer Science,* Vol. 19. New York: Springer-Verlag, 1974, pp. 362–376.

[6] M. R. Garey and D. S. Johnson, *Computers and Intractability.* San Francisco: Freeman, 1979.

[7] J. J. Horning and B. Randell, "Process Structuring," *Comput. Surveys,* vol. 5, pp. 5–30, Mar. 1973.

[8] D. J. Kuck, *The Structure of Computers and Computations,* vol. 1. New York: Wiley, 1978.

[9] D. J. Kuck, P. Budnik, S-C. Chen, E. Davis, Jr., J. R. Han, P. Kraska, D. Lawrie, Y. Muraoka, R. Strebendt, and R. Towle, "Measurements of parallelism in ordinary Fortran programs," *IEEE Trans. Comput.,* vol. C-23, pp. 37–46, Jan. 1974.

[10] D. J. Kuck, Y. Muraoka, and S.-C. Chen, "On the number of operations simultaneously executable in Fortran-like programs and their resulting speed-up," *IEEE Trans. Comput.,* vol. C-21, pp. 1293–1310, Dec. 1972.

[11] R. H. Kuhn, "Optimization and interconnection complexity for parallel processors, single-stage networks, and decision trees," Ph.D. dissertation, Dep. Comput. Sci., Univ. of Illinois, Urbana-Champaign, Rep. 80-1009, 1980.

[12] L. Lamport, "How to make a multiprocessor computer that correctly executes multiprocess programs," *IEEE Trans. Comput.,* vol. C-28, pp. 690–691, Sept. 1979.

[13] T. Lang, "Interconnections between processors and memory modules using the shuffle-exchange network," *IEEE Trans. Comput.,* pp. 496–503, May 1976.

[14] D. H. Lawrie, "Access and alignment of data in an array processor," *IEEE Trans. Comput.,* vol. C-24, pp. 1145–1155, Dec. 1975.

[15] B. R. Leasure, "Compiling serial languages for parallel machines," M.S. thesis, Dept. Comput. Sci., Univ. of Illinois, Urbana-Champaign, Rep. 76-805, Nov. 1976.

[16] J. H. Patel, "Processor-memory interconnections for multiprocessors," in *Proc. 6th Annu. Symp. Comput. Architecture,* Apr. 1979, pp. 168–177.

[17] C. V. Ramamoorthy, K. M. Chandy, and M. J. Gonzalez, Jr., "Optimal scheduling strategies in a multiprocessor system," *IEEE Trans. Comput.,* vol. C-21, pp. 137–146, Feb. 1972.

[18] J. R. Rice, "Software for numerical computation," in *Research Directions in Software Technology,* P. Wegner, Ed. Cambridge, MA: Mass. Inst. Technol., 1979, pp. 688–708.

[19] J. S. Rohle, "Converting a class of recursive procedures into nonrecursive," *Software Practice and Experience,* vol. 7, pp. 231–238, Apr. 1977.

[20] H. J. Siegel, "The theory underlying the partitioning of permutation network," *IEEE Trans. Comput.,* this issue, pp. 791–801.

[21] B. J. Smith, "A pipelined, shared resource MIMD computer," in *Proc. the 1978 Int. Conf. Parallel Processing,* pp. 6–8, Aug. 1978.

[22] L. A. Swanson, "Simulation of a tree processor," M.S. thesis, Dept. Comput. Sci., Univ. of Illinois, Urbana-Champaign, Rep. 72-503, Jan. 1972.

[23] R. Towle, "Control and data dependence for program transformations," Ph.D., dissertation, Dep. Comput. Sci., Univ. of Illinois, Urbana-Champaign, Rep. 76-788, Mar. 1976.

[24] K. Y. Wen, "Interprocessor connections—Capabilities, exploitation and effectiveness," Ph.D. dissertation, Dep. Comput. Sci., Univ. of Illinois, Urbana-Champaign, Rep. 76-830, Mar. 1976

[25] P.-C. Yew and D. H. Lawrie, "An easily controlled network for frequently used permutations," in *Proc. Workshop on Interconnection Networks Parallel Distributed Processing,* H. J. Siegel, Ed., pp. 72–73, Apr. 1980.

David A. Padua was born in Caracas, Venezuela in 1949. He received the Licenciate degree from the Universidad Central de Venezuela in 1973, and the Ph.D. degree in computer science in 1979 from the University of Illinois at Urbana-Champaign.

He is currently Visiting Assistant Professor at the University of Illinois at Urbana-Champaign.

David J. Kuck (S'59–M'69) was born in Muskegon, MI on October 3, 1937. He received the B.S.E.E. degree from the University of Michigan, Ann Arbor, in 1959, and the M.S. and Ph.D. degrees from Northwestern University, Evanston, IL, in 1960 and 1963, respectively.

From 1963 to 1965, he was a Ford Postdoctoral Fellow and Assistant Professor of Electrical Engineering at the Massachusetts Institute of Technology, Cambridge. In 1965 he joined the Department of Computer Science, University of Illinois, Urbana, where he is now a Professor. Currently, his research interests are in the coherent design of hardware and software systems. This includes the development of the PARAFRASE system, a program transformation facility for array and multiprocessor machines. His recent computer systems research has included theoretical studies of upper bounds on computation time, empirical analysis of real programs and the design of high-performance processing, switching, and memory systems for classes of computation ranging from numerical to nonnumerical. The latter work includes the study of interactive text processing and database systems, from the point of view of both the computer and the user.

Dr. Kuck has served as an Editor for a number of professional journals, including the IEEE TRANSACTIONS ON COMPUTERS, and is presently an area editor of the *Journal of the Association for Computing Machinery.* Among his publications are *The Structure of Computers and Computations,* vol. I. He has consulted with many computer manufacturers and users and is the founder and president of Kuck and Associates, Inc., an architecture and optimizing compiler company.

Duncan H. Lawrie (S'66–M'76) is currently an Associate Professor of Computer Science at the University of Illinois at Urbana-Champaign. He has been active in the area of parallel computation and other very large computation systems since 1966, when he worked on the Illiac IV computer. Since then, he has contributed to the design of several other machines, including most recently, the Burroughs Scientific Processor. He specializes in research and consulting in the area of design, construction, and the use of very large computing systems.

Dr. Lawrie has served as a referee for the IEEE TRANSACTIONS ON COMPUTERS, as well as several national conferences. He has been Program Co-Chairman for the Symposium on High-Speed Computer and Algorithm Organization, Program Co-Chairman for the 9th International Conference on Parallel Processing, and was a member of the Program Committee for the Workshop on Interconnection Networks. He is a member of Tau Beta Pi, Eta Kappa Nu, Sigma Xi, the Association for Computing Machinery, and the American Association of University Professors.

Effects of Cache Coherency in Multiprocessors

MICHEL DUBOIS, MEMBER, IEEE, AND FAYÉ A. BRIGGS, MEMBER, IEEE

Reprinted from *IEEE Transactions on Computers*, Volume C-31, Number 11, November 1982, pages 1083-1099. Copyright © 1982 by The Institute of Electrical and Electronics Engineers, Inc.

Abstract—In many commercial multiprocessor systems, each processor accesses the memory through a private cache. One problem that could limit the extensibility of the system and its performance is the enforcement of cache coherence. A mechanism must exist which prevents the existence of several different copies of the same data block in different private caches. In this paper, we present an in-depth analysis of the effects of cache coherency in multiprocessors. A novel analytical model for the program behavior of a multitasked system is introduced. The model includes the behavior of each process and the interactions between processes with regard to the sharing of data blocks. An approximation is developed to derive the main effects of the cache coherency contributing to degradations in system performance.

Index Terms—Cache, cache coherence, multicache consistency, multiprocessors, performance evaluation.

I. INTRODUCTION

CACHES have proved to be highly effective in increasing the throughput of small and large uniprocessor systems [7], [3], [15], [2]. This success has prompted their use in commercial [13] and scientific [17] tightly coupled multiprocessor systems. Many issues related to caches are common to both uniprocessor and multiprocessor systems. An overview of these issues is presented in [10], and the reader is assumed to be familiar with them in the following discussion. There are two basic configurations of caches in multiprocessors: the shared cache or the private cache. A *shared* cache is referenced by all the processors, as shown in Fig. 1(a). It is usually a high-speed buffer for a fixed section of memory (i.e., one or several modules). A *private* cache is dedicated to one single processor but buffers blocks from several main memory sections. A system with private caches is depicted in Fig. 1(b). Cache organization, block size, cache size, and replacement algorithms are not restricted by any of the configurations. Generally, a set-associative cache with LRU replacement policy within each set is adopted.

The cache coherence problem affects the system design at various levels. Inconsistencies may occur between cache and memory and also between different caches. The side effects on I/O processing caused by data inconsistencies between the caches and the main memory are usually resolved by con-necting the I/O devices to the processors, with some slight degradations. Each I/O processor and its associated CPU compete for the cache. Moreover, cache space is also occupied by I/O processing. Since a shared cache contains blocks that cannot be present in any other cache, the coherence problem between cache and memory is the only potential problem for shared caches. In a system with private caches, coherence problems also exist between the different caches. Therefore, private cache systems are more complex to design than shared cache systems. However, the private cache concept has the potential for high performance. Each reference to a shared cache must traverse an interconnection network. Thus the performance of the shared cache is limited by the delay in the switching network and the contention between concurrent requests to the same cache module. A private cache is next to the processor; hence, most references can be completed at the cache speed, if the hit ratio is high enough. Consequently, higher throughputs are expected from private cache systems. The performance of the system with shared caches has been investigated in [18]. Another type of shared cache has been proposed in [1]. In this scheme, the cache modules are next to the processors and may experience high traffic and contention problems. The study proposed to use a so-called "common/cache pended transactions bus" to reduce the potential problems. In [9], we have described a hybrid system with both shared and private caches. Many commercial multiprocessor systems, such as IBM 370/168 MP, IBM 3081, and UNIVAC 1100/80 MP are systems with private caches [13].

In this paper, we consider only the system with private caches, and study the effects of the cache coherency on the system performance. For analytical tractability we restrict this study to fully associative caches.

II. CACHE COHERENCE SOLUTIONS

The enforcement of multicache consistency has a detrimental impact on system performance. It has two causes. The first, and most obvious, is the result of data sharing between processes participating in a multitasked algorithm, or between independent operating system processes running on different processors. A second and somewhat subtle cause is the migration of processes. Assume, for example, that process A executes on processor 1, then is allowed to migrate to processor 2 and finally migrates back to processor 1. If the cache is not swept on a context switch, then some stale data could still be present in the cache of processor 1 when process A is scheduled on processor 1 for the second time.

To solve the coherence problem, static solutions have been

Manuscript received January 4, 1982; revised June 28, 1982. This work was supported by the National Science Foundation under Contract ECS 80-16580. Revision of this paper was made while F. A. Briggs was with the IBM Thomas J. Watson Research Center.

M. Dubois is with Thomson-CSF/LCR Domaine de Corbeville, B.P.10, 91401, Orsay, France.

F. A. Briggs is with the Department of Electrical Engineering, Rice University, Houston, TX 77251.

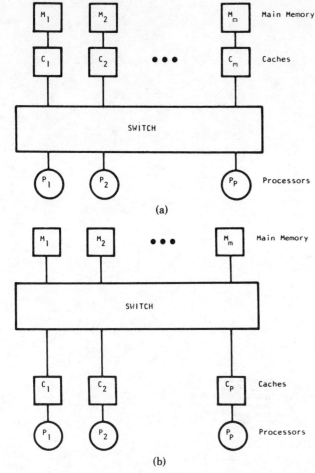

Fig. 1. Multiprocessor system. (a) With shared cache. (b) With private cache.

proposed. Namely, pages in shared memory are tagged at compile time as *cacheable* or *noncacheable*. All pages containing shared writable data must be noncacheable. References to noncacheable data are sent directly to the main memory. If the degree of sharing is large, the resulting performance degradation may be important, since the memory is typically 5–10 times slower than the cache. Moreover, the static solution is not applicable to systems in which processes can migrate, unless the cacheable blocks of a migrating process are invalidated selectively in the cache. The dynamic approach to solving the cache coherence problem is usually to connect each pair of caches through a high-speed link. The write-through policy is used, and on each write all the other caches are signaled in parallel with the memory update. When a cache controller receives a signal, it must service it by searching the cache content for the received block address. If present, the cache block-frame is invalidated. If w_t is the probability of a write for each processor and there are P processors in the system, the average number of signals received per processor reference is $(P - 1) w_t$. This number can become quite large as P increases beyond 2 or 4. Note also that the total number of one-way links between the caches is $P(P - 1)$. A simple approach would be to tie the caches on a bus or on several buses. But the traffic on these buses would be such that the response time would be unacceptable. Note that to ensure

correctness of execution, a processor which sends a message must wait for an acknowledge signal from all other processors before it can complete a write operation. Proposals to improve this scheme involve filtering most of the write signals by recording information about the status of each memory block in a *global table* (GT). The global table can be interrogated by any processor. To limit the accesses to the global table, local flags are also distributed among the cache directories. Depending on the status of the local flags and the type of request, the processor is allowed to proceed or has to consult the global table.

The philosophy behind the cache coherence check is that an arbitrary number of caches can have a copy of a block, provided that all the copies are identical. They are identical if the processor associated with each of the caches has not attempted to modify its copy since the copy was brought in its cache. We refer to such a copy as a *read-only* copy (RO). To be able to modify a block copy in its cache, a processor must own the block copy with read and write access right. We refer to such a copy as a *read-write* copy (RW). Only one processor can, at any time, own a read-write copy of a block.

To enforce the cache consistency rule, global as well as local information is constantly updated by the cache and memory controllers. When a processor k loads a data block i on a read miss, the processor obtains a read-only copy of the block in its cache. This information is recorded in the global table and in the cache directory (by resetting a local RW flag in the cache directory). As long as the copy of block i remains present in the cache, processor k can read it without any consistency check. If processor k wants to write into its copy of block i, it must make sure that all other copies of block i in other caches are invalidated. To do this, the global table is consulted. It should indicate the processor caches that own a copy of block i. The global table is updated to record the fact that processor k owns block i with read-write access right. Finally, the local RW flag is set to indicate that the block is modified.

In this implementation, a block copy in a cache is invalidated whenever the cache receives a signal from some other processor trying to write into it. Moreover, a cache owning a read-write copy may receive a signal from a remote cache controller requesting to own a read-only copy. In this case, the read-write copy becomes read-only. The high level flowcharts of Fig. 2 describe the mechanisms enforcing the cache coherence checks on read [Fig. 2(a)] and write [Fig. 2(b)] operations when a write-back write policy is adopted for the cache. There are three main sources of performance degradations in the algorithms of Fig. 2(a) and (b). These sources are

1) degradation of the average hit ratio, due to block invalidation;

2) traffic between caches to enforce the coherence rules;

3) accesses to the global table.

Consider a block i present in the cache. If the coherency is disabled, the next time block i is referenced—if ever—a miss occurs only if block i has been replaced. When the coherence is enforced, there are more chances that the next reference to block i will result in a miss, since block i may be invalidated before it is replaced. The net effect is a degradation of the hit ratio, in direct relation to the invalidation traffic intensity

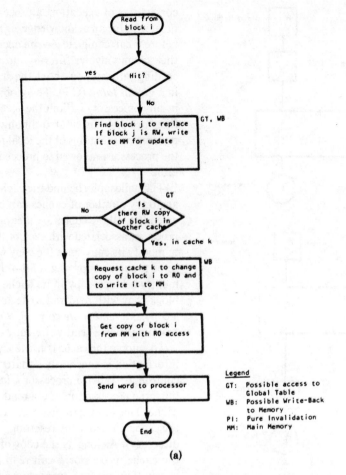

(a)

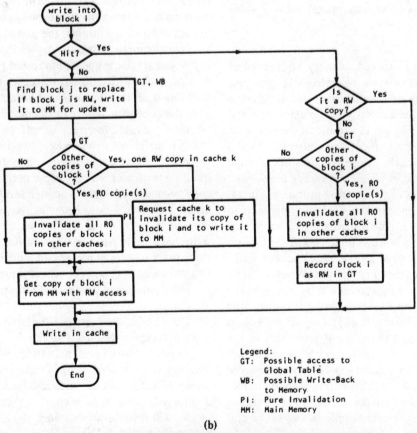

(b)

Fig. 2. Flowcharts describing actions to maintain cache consistency.
(a) Read operation. (b) Write operation.

314

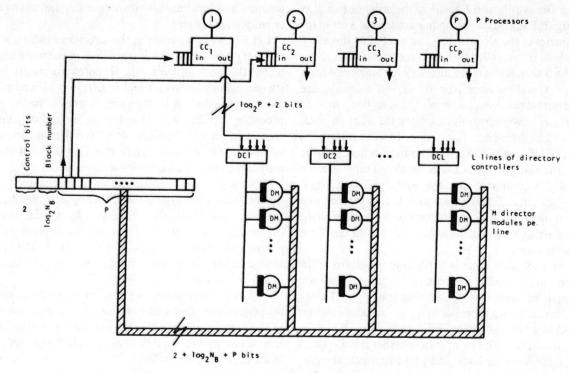

Fig. 3. An example implementation of a distributed global table to enforce cache consistency.

between caches.

The degradations caused by the traffic between caches come from the overhead incurred by processors requesting to own data block copies and by processors receiving an injunction to modify the status of one block in their caches. When a processor requests ownership of a copy of a block of data, there are two cases in which it may have to wait. The first case occurs when the request is for an RW copy and at least one other processor owns an RO copy. The other case occurs when the request is for a copy when some other processor owns an RW copy. The waiting period is longer in the latter case, since one write-back to memory has to be completed before the processor can read the requested block. Received signals necessitate invalidation and updates of RW flags in the cache and also result in an increase of the write backs to memory. This effect increases the traffic between the processor and the memory. A write-back is completed "in the background" if a buffer is provided ("flagged register swap") or "on line," otherwise ("flagged swap") [10]. In the implementation shown in Fig. 2(a) and (b), main memory is used as the means of communication between the processors. Another implementation consists in exchanging block copies on a dedicated interprocessor communication system, as a high-speed bus. This is referred to as a cache-to-cache transfer. Such a transfer retains the status of the block at the destination cache. In this case, a given block copy is written back to memory only when it is RW and is replaced. We consider only the first implementation in our analysis. The model developed in this paper could be utilized to analyze the second implementation.

The accesses to the global table result in conflicts. Some of this traffic can be reduced by reducing the time spent in the global table in the case of a hit when requesting a write on an

RO copy. This can be accomplished by incorporating an *exclusive* bit for each block-frame in the cache so that when the bit is set, it indicates that it is the only cache that contains an RO copy of the block [19]. In this case, the cache does not have to access the global table to determine whether there are other RO copies that would have to be invalidated before the write is completed. However, the global table would still be consulted to update the state of the copy of the block. The introduction of the exclusive bit neither affects the degradations in the hit ratio nor the increase in write-backs to memory.

The degradations are implementation dependent. Tang has proposed to replicate all the cache directories in the global table [16]. This implementation is expensive, because it requires associative addressing. Moreover, interrogations of the table must be accomplished by searching all the directory copies in parallel, which reduces the concurrency in accessing the global table. In [6], a different organization was proposed, in which more concurrency is possible. For each block in main memory there is an entry in the directory. Each entry contains P "presence" flags and one "modified" flag. The modified flag is set if some processor owns an RW copy of the block: in this case, the copy in main memory is stale. For block i, presence flag k is raised if and only if processor cache k has a copy of block i. These presence flags limit the number of caches having a copy of the block. The modified flag, when it is reset, permits read-only accesses. In these implementations there is a cooperation between the cache controllers and the memory controller in the processing of invalidation signals.

The organization of the cache coherence mechanism given in [16] and [6] can be distributed. To improve the concurrency in the coherence mechanism, the organization of the global table may be a two-dimensional array of directory modules as in an L-M memory [4], with L small, of the order of 1 or 2, as shown in Fig. 3. Each directory module consists of a set of interleaved entries of the global table, and a set of M directory modules, which is controlled by a directory controller, share the same bus. The modules of the directory are numbered from 0 to $L \cdot M - 1$, and the lines, from 0 to $L - 1$. Modules are interleaved across the lines, i.e., module j is on line $j \mod L$. Entries are interleaved across the modules: if i is the physical address of a block (this address is obtained by discarding the $\log_2 B$ least significant bits of a word address, where B is the block size), the entry for block i is in the global table module $i \mod (L \cdot M)$. As a consequence, the least significant $\log_2 L$ bits of the block physical address are used to find the line, and the next least significant $\log_2 M$ bits point to the module on the line. The remaining most significant bits are the address of the entry in the module.

Each cache controller submits requests to the global table. The requests are ultimately processed by the appropriate module controller, identified by decoding the physical block address. A request from a processor to the global table contains ($\log_2 P + 2$) bits partitioned into three fields: $\log_2 P$ bits for the processor number, 1 bit to indicate whether it is a request for ownership or for write-back, and 1 bit to indicate the type of ownership, i.e., RO or RW. Each entry in the directory module has $P + 1$ bits: P presence bits and one modified bit [6]. Of course, a processor which has initiated a request must wait until completion of the request. Accesses to the global table are made for each miss and for the write hits on RO copies. In the case of a miss, two successive requests may be submitted: one for recording the removal of the replaced block and one for getting access to the missing block. Possible accesses to the global table are indicated in Fig. 2. Each directory module can be microcoded to decode the processor request, read the entry and translate it into a new entry for the block requested (i.e., a new set of presence flags and a new modified flag). Depending on the nature of the request and the status of the flags in the entry, the module controller may act in two ways. If no signal has to be sent to other processors, then the flags are updated to reflect the newly granted request in a read-modify-write cycle, and the processor is signaled to resume computation. If local flags have to be updated and if block copies have to be invalidated, the processor has to wait. The module controller then puts a request on the invalidation signal bus (IS bus). This bus, as shown in Fig. 3, permits the sending of signals to all the concerned cache controllers in parallel. These signals are buffered so as to release the bus as quickly as possible. Since all the modules have access to the IS bus, conflicts occur. The module controller holds the request on the IS bus until the request is stored in the cache controller buffers. This results in the blocking of other requests to the module. Another cause of blocking is the waiting time when a processor owning an RW of a block has to write the block back to memory before the request can be granted. Only the module is blocked in this case. The IS bus may be released. A request to the IS bus by a module contains $\log_2 N_B$ bits to indicate the block's physical address, and P bits which determine the cache controller(s) to which the request applies. Two additional control bits indicate the type of signal (write to memory and invalidate, write to memory and change to RO, or simply invalidate).

Let $E[i, *]$ be an entry in the directory module, where i is the entry address, which is contained in the most significant bits of the block address. $E[i, j]$ represents the jth bit of the ith entry. For j between 1 and P, $E[i, j] = 1$ if and only if the block corresponding to the entry is present in the cache of processor j. If $E[i, P + 1] = 1$, then one and only one cache contains a copy of the block, which is different from the copy in memory (RW copy). If $E[i, P + 1] = 0$, either there is no copy of the block in a cache or the copies are all RO. We denote by PN the processor number initiating the request, by RF the bit designating the type of ownership request, and by WB the bit indicating whether the request is for a write-back or for ownership of a copy. The flowchart for a directory module controller is shown in Fig. 4. In this flowchart, DR is the data register of the module and SB represents a combinational logic function Oring the first P bits of DR.

The model we develop in the following section captures all the performance degradations except for the access contentions to the global table and the blocking of a processor resulting from its request for an RW copy when RO copies of the same block exist in other caches.

III. Workload Model for a Multiprocessor with Private Caches

A workload model for MIMD systems is, in general, much more complex than for uniprocessor systems. It must include a description of each stream as well as a specification of the interactions between streams. Good parsimonious models are thus particularly difficult to develop. The problem of validation is compounded by the fact that traces of multitasked MIMD programs are difficult to obtain. The cooperation between processors requires special instructions and mechanisms not present in multiple SISD systems (e.g., user level synchronization mechanisms). Few compilers exist that can produce object codes to run on multitasked systems. Moreover, the reference strings may be different from one run to the other, depending on the timing of events in the system. Algorithms running in MIMD mode may be either synchronized or asynchronous [11]. In particular, asynchronous algorithms may have random traces for different runs of the same programs. In this regard, the stochastic modeling approach in studying MIMD processes is all the more appropriate.

In this section, we propose a simple analytical model of program behavior to analyze the effects of the cache coherence problem on the performance of multiprocessors with private caches. We assume first that the MIMD algorithm is decomposed into P processes, each running on one processor. The P processes are stochastically homogeneous, i.e., their traces are realizations of the same stochastic process. When the cache block size is fixed, the reference string corresponding to each realization of a process trace is the merging of two streams: one for private and read-only shared block (referred to as P-block) references and the other for writable shared block (referred to as S-block) references. The notion of sharing for writable data set should be made more precise. A block is an S-block

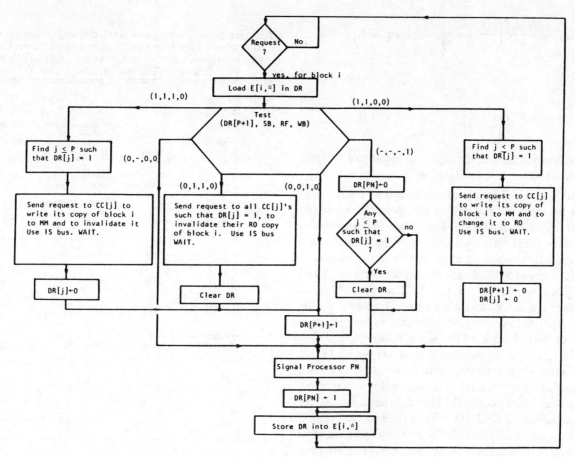

Fig. 4. Flowchart of the action of a directory module controller.

if it was referenced at least once in a cache and caused another cache to invalidate or change the status of the copy of that block in its cache. We refer to the request to invalidate or change the status of a copy of a shared block in another cache as *cross-interrogate*. Thus, the set of S-blocks are the set of cross-interrogated blocks in a run of the program trace.

With probability q_s, the next reference is for an S-block, and with probability $(1 - q_s)$, it is for a P-block. References to P-blocks do not affect cache coherence. However, they contribute to the accesses to the global table for miss references and also for hit references involving a write on an RO copy. Also, they do not create invalidation traffic, nor do they degrade the hit ratio of the other caches. For the references to P-data, any model could be chosen. However, in the examples we ran, the model for the P-block reference stream is a least recently used stack model (LRUSM) with coefficients derived from the linear paging model [8], [14], [12]. Besides analytical tractability, this model has the advantage that by modifying one parameter, the locality of the references to P-blocks is tuned at will. The references to S-blocks are drawn as in the independent reference model (IRM) [14]. The cache is managed as a fully associative cache with LRU replacement. The overall program behavior is observed in Fig. 5. There are N_p P-blocks and N_s S-blocks. The P-block references are characterized by a stack distance probability distribution a_i, such that

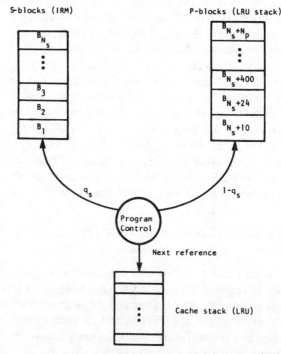

Fig. 5. Model of program behavior, with S-blocks accessed with fixed probability distribution and P-blocks references with LRU stack model. *Note:* Arbitrarily, S-blocks are numbers from 1 to N_s and P-blocks from $N_s + 1$ to $N_s + N_p$.

317

$$a_i = \frac{G(N_p)}{b}\left(\frac{1}{i-1} - \frac{1}{i}\right), \qquad \text{for } i \neq 1$$

and

$$a_i = G(N_p)\left(1 - \frac{1}{b}\right), \qquad \text{for } i = 1 \text{ [14]}.$$

The coefficient b reflects the degree of locality of P-block references. $G(N_p)$ is a normalization factor such that $\sum_{i=1} a_i = 1$. The P-data and S-data characterizations permit us to obtain the hit ratio as a function of the cache size when the coherence mechanism is disabled. The P-data characterization is not required if the hit ratio curve can be obtained from a program trace for the given multiprocessor configuration.

The references to S-blocks are made according to a fixed probability distribution p_i, $i = 1, \cdots, N_s$. The probability that a reference to a given S-block i is a write reference is w_i, for $i = 1, \cdots, N_s$. Therefore, the probability that a given reference is to read an S-block i is $q_s p_i (1 - w_i)$. Similarly, the probability that a reference is a write on S-block i is $q_s p_i w_i$. In this model, the effects of process migration on the cache coherence are neglected. This approximation is tantamount to neglecting transients after a context switch. The idea that S-blocks are accessed according to the IRM reflects the fact that shared writable data are usually in different memory locations than P-blocks and that accesses to them exhibit less locality than accesses to P-blocks. As for the models of program behavior for uniprocesses, the model in Fig. 5 may describe a process behavior during a phase of a program [8]. Phases are separated by abrupt transitions during which the parameters of the model may change. The model developed here assumes recurring events. In reality, a block may be written into and never referenced thereafter. The model implies, however, that a block is always eventually referenced again.

In practice, the workload parameters for a P-way multiprocessor can be obtained by running the program trace for the P-way workload and identifying the separate streams. From a run of the trace, we can obtain for each processor, the parameters q_s, p_i distribution and w_i probabilities for the cross-interrogated blocks in addition to the hit ratio curve as a function of the cache size. For a symmetric and homogeneous multiprocessor, the parameters for one processor can be used in the analytical model developed in this paper.

IV. Degradations Due to the Cache Coherence Check

Since the model is recurrent, we can consider two successive accesses to a given S-block i in any one processor. We will refer to these accesses as the *previous* and the *next* accesses. According to the model, the previous and the next accesses are separated by a geometrically distributed number of references with mean $(1/p_i q_s) - 1$.

There are two types of S-block i that may reside in the cache after a previous reference. In the first case, the previous reference terminates with an RO copy of S-block i in the cache.

TABLE I
POSSIBLE EVENTS AND ASSOCIATED OVERHEAD BETWEEN TWO
SUCCESSIVE REFERENCES TO S-BLOCK i IN A GIVEN CACHE
(A) WITH ENABLED CACHE COHERENCE CHECK (B) WITH
DISABLED CACHE COHERENCE CHECK

(A)				
Case	Previous Reference	Event	Overhead	Next Reference
$E_{s1,i}$	RO	I	invalidate block	not present
$E_{s2,i}$	RO	R	None	not present
$E_{s3,i}$	RO	None	None	present (RO)
$E_{p1,i}$	RW	I	invalidate block write back block	not present
$E_{p2,i}$	RW	R	write back block	not present
$E_{p3,i}$	RW	None	None	present (RW)
$E_{p4,i}$	RW	S then I	switch to RO write back block and invalidate block	not present
$E_{p5,i}$	RW	S then R	switch to RO write back block	not present
$E_{p6,i}$	RW	S	switch to RO write back block	present

(B)			
Previous Reference	Event	Overhead	Next reference
RO	None	None	present (RO)
RO	R	None	not present
RW	None	None	present (RW)
RW	R	write back block	not present

At the time of the next reference to it, the RO copy may not be present in the cache for two reasons: either it has been chosen for replacement, or it has been invalidated following a write request to S-block i from another processor. Both cases result in a miss at the next reference. The invalidation of an RO copy does not require any block transfer to memory. A hit at the next access occurs only if S-block i has not been replaced and if no other processor has attempted to write into S-block i since the previous reference.

In the other case, the previous reference terminates with an RW copy of S-block i in the cache. The possible events that occur (with respect to S-block i) before the next reference to it are more numerous than for an RO copy. A miss on S-block i occurs at the next reference either because the block copy was replaced or because it was invalidated after another processor attempted to write into it. Before an RW copy is replaced, invalidated or referenced again, the RW copy may have been changed to RO, if another processor has obtained an RO copy since the last reference to it. Table I(A) summarizes the various events that can occur on a given S-block i in between two references to it when the cache coherence mechanism is enabled. I, R and S represent "invalidate," "replace," or "switch from RW to RO," respectively. Table I(B) shows the case in which the coherence mechanism is disabled. To evaluate the effect of the cache coherence check, both cases must be studied.

A. Cache with Disabled Coherence Check

To evaluate the effect of the cache coherence check, we first examine the system without cache coherence enforcement,

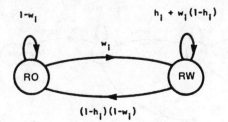

Fig. 6. Markov graph of reference pattern to S-block i with disabled cache coherence mechanism.

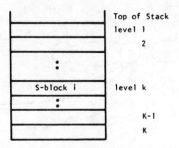

Fig. 7. Snapshot of the LRU stack cache.

which can be observed by running one of the processes on a uniprocessor. We assume that the curve of the hit ratio as a function of the cache size is known for a given block size. This curve can be obtained by simulation from a trace or by analytical methods. Let $h(K)$ denote this function, with K as the cache size. The determination of $h(K)$ is a classical problem and will not be addressed here. The hypotheses of the program behavior were stated in Section III.

We first evaluate the probability of a write-back on each S-block i. In the following, we designate by h_i the probability that a reference to S-block i results in a hit (i.e., S-block i is present in the cache at the time of a reference to it). The Markov graph of Fig. 6 describes the reference pattern to S-block i. An S-block i can assume one of two states, RO and RW. State transitions occur right after a reference to S-block i. Let us denote these instances by $t_{k,i}^+$, where $t_{k,i}$ is the time of the kth reference to S-block i. At time $t_{k,i}^+$ (for any k), S-block i is in state RW if it was not replaced in the cache since the latest write to it *or* if the kth reference to it was a write. In this case, the "modified bit" is raised in the cache for S-block i, at time $t_{k,i}^+$. At time $t_{k,i}^+$, for any k, block i is in state RO in all other cases, i.e., the cases when block i has been replaced since the latest write to it *and* the kth reference is a read; the "modified bit" for block i is then reset at time $t_{k,i}^+$. The steady-state probability that S-block i is written back between two references to it is

$$w_{bi} = P_{RW,i} \cdot (1 - h_i), \qquad (1)$$

where $P_{RW,i}$ is the long term probability that the state of S-block i is RW at time $t_{k,i}^+$, and $(1 - h_i)$ is the probability that S-block i is replaced at the next reference to it.

Solving the Markov chain of Fig. 6 yields

$$P_{RW,i} = \frac{w_i}{w_i + (1 - w_i)(1 - h_i)},$$

so that

$$w_{bi} = \frac{w_i(1 - h_i)}{w_i + (1 - w_i)(1 - h_i)}. \qquad (2)$$

In between two successive references, S-block i may be replaced. For an S-block i in state RO, a write-back is not required when the block is being replaced, because it has not been modified. If the previous reference was in state RW, the block is not present at the next reference to it in the cache, with a probability $(1 - h_i)$.

The parameters $(1 - h_i)$ for $i = 1, \cdots, N_s$ in (2) depend on the program behavior. Because a uniprocessor system is as-

sumed, the physical timing of events is irrelevant to the hit ratio estimation. The only useful timing consideration is the *virtual time* [14]. The virtual time measures the number of references the processor has made since the beginning of the program execution. Determining $(1 - h_i)$ is a very complex problem, even with the simplified model hypotheses. A solution is possible under the following approximation. To understand the approximation, the reader is referred to Fig. 7 in which a snapshot of the cache's LRU stack is displayed at any virtual time. In this configuration of the stack, S-block i is at level k. The approximation assumes that the probability that the next reference is for a block contained in any level higher than k, given that the referenced block is not S-block i, is simple $h(k - 1)$, and is independent of the previous references. Similarly, the probability that the next reference is at a level lower than or equal to k, given that S-block i is not referenced, is $[1 - h(k - 1)]$. In summary, the probabilities that the next reference in the stack configuration of Fig. 7 is for S-block i, or for another block at a level higher than k, or for another block at a level lower than k, are $q_s p_i$ or $(1 - q_s p_i) h(k - 1)$ or $(1 - q_s p_i)[1 - h(k - 1)]$, respectively. In this approximation, the probability of accessing the cache stack at a given level is independent of previous references. Thus, we call this approximation the *"instantaneous hit ratio"* approximation. The hypothesis of instantaneous hit ratios leads to a first order Markov behavior for the position of an S-block in the LRU stack. The factor $(1 - h_i)$ is estimated for any S-block i from the following theorem.

Theorem: Given the model of Section III for program behavior and the instantaneous hit ratio approximation, the probability that an S-block i is *not present* in a cache of size K at the time of reference is given by

$$1 - h_i = \prod_{k=0}^{K-1} \frac{1}{1 + \dfrac{q_s p_i}{(1 - q_s p_i)[1 - h(k)]}}.$$

Proof: The instantaneous hit ratio approximation results in the simple Markov graph description of Fig. 8(a), in which the state is the position of S-block i in the LRU stack. At virtual time 0, when the Markov process is started, S-block i is in position (or state) 1. We thus examine the stack just after a reference to S-block i. Whenever S-block i is referenced (with probability $q_s p_i$), the next state is state 1. Whenever a block is referenced at a level lower than the level k of S-block i [with probability $(1 - q_s p_i)(1 - h(k - 1))$], S-block i is moved to level $k + 1$. With probability $(1 - q_s p_i)h(k - 1)$, a

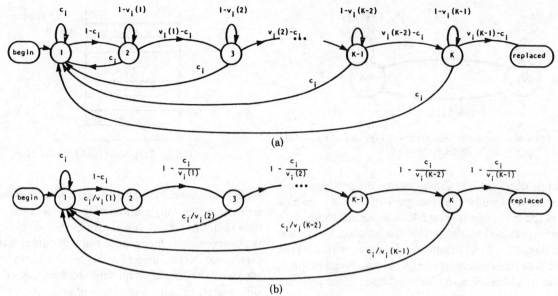

Fig. 8. Markov graph description of S-block i behavior, with disabled cache coherence mechanism, where $c_i = q_s p_i$ and $v_i = 1 - h(k)(1 - c_i)$. (a) State corresponding to position of S-block i in stack. (b) State embedded at time of state transition.

block at a level higher than k is referenced, and thus S-block i's position does not change. The probability that S-block i is replaced before the next reference is equal to the probability that the Markov process of Fig. 8(a), started in state 1, is absorbed in the state "Replaced" before it visits state 1 again. To evaluate this probability, a simplified Markov process embedded at the time of state transitions is shown in Fig. 8(b). The transition probabilities for each state i, $i > 1$, of the simplified graph are now conditional on the fact that the next state is always different from the present state. The probability that the process starting in state 1 reaches the state "replaced" before another visit to state 1 is

$$1 - h_i = \prod_{k=0}^{K-1} \frac{[1 - h(k)](1 - q_s p_i)}{1 - h(k)(1 - q_s p_i)} , \qquad (3)$$

which proves the theorem.

A combination of (2) and (3) yields the probability of a write back of any S-blocks i for arbitrary probability distributions of S-block accesses and write, and hit ratio curves.

B. Cache with Enabled Coherence Check

When the cache coherence enforcement mechanism is enabled, signals are received from other processors' caches. The problem of incorporating these external signals in the model above is very complex, because, contrary to the single processor case, it requires keeping track of the physical timing of each discrete event occurring in the P processors. Since this complexity is probably not tractable, it is desirable to develop an approximation. Let us refer to the processor or its cache under study as the *local* processor or cache; otherwise it is the *remote* processor or cache. The basic assumption is that, between two successive references of the local processor, each of the remote processors complete one and only one reference. This hypothesis is not verified in practice. However, it is adequate,

TABLE II
POSSIBLE MODIFICATIONS OF THE STATE OF S-BLOCK i BETWEEN TWO SUCCESSIVE REFERENCES IN THE CACHE, WHERE $P_{wi} = (1 - q_s p_i w_i)^{P-1}$ AND $P_{si} = (1 - q_s p_i)^{P-1}$

State of S-block i at previous reference	Changes of the state of S-block i between the two references	Probability
Not present	Not present	1
Present, RO	Present, RO	P_{wi}
	Invalidated	$1 - P_{wi}$
Present, RW	Present, RW	P_{si}
	Present, RO	$P_{wi} - P_{si}$
	Present, RO, then invalidated	$(1 - P_{wi}) - w_i(1 - P_{si})$
	Simply invalidated	$w_i(1 - P_{si})$

because the processors are assumed to be homogeneous. This approximation is made *only* to evaluate the mean intercache traffic and hit ratio degradations. It is not made to study the overall system performance. Synchronization at every reference would indeed be a very gross approximation in this context. We can introduce the concept of virtual time, as in single processor systems [14]. To each processor is associated a virtual clock which is incremented whenever a reference is made to the cache. The approximation assumes that the physical times corresponding to a given virtual time are of the same order in all the processors.

Given this hypothesis, we can assume that, between two references in the local cache, any one of the remote processors accesses S-block i with probability $q_s p_i$ and writes into S-block i with probability $q_s p_i w_i$. As a result, the state of a block may change between two successive references to the cache. The possible state changes for a given S-block i are given in Table II. Below we derive the probability of occurrence of each state change.

Lemma 1: If the previous reference in the local cache ended with an RO or RW copy of S-block i, then the state of the copy is unchanged at the next reference with probability, $P_{wi} = (1 - q_s p_i w_i)^{P-1}$ or $P_{si} = (1 - q_s p_i)^{P-1}$ respectively.

Proof: The RO or RW copy is unchanged if none of the $P - 1$ remote processors attempts to write into or reference S-block i respectively before the next reference. The results follow easily. □

From Lemma 1, the probability that S-block i is invalidated before the next reference can then be obtained, since this is the probability that at least one of the $P - 1$ remote processors attempts to write into S-block i. This probability is $1 - P_{wi}$ and is independent of the previous state of S-block i. Also, the probability of at least one reference from the remote processors is $1 - P_{si}$.

Lemma 2: If the previous reference in the local cache ended with an RW copy of S-block i, then the state of the copy is changed to RO before the next reference with probability $P_{wi} - P_{si}$.

Proof: This is the probability that all references from the $P - 1$ remote processors were reads. The probability of at least one reference from the $P - 1$ remote processors is $1 - P_{si}$ from Lemma 1. The probability that at least one of the references from the $P - 1$ remote processors was a write is $1 - P_{wi}$. Hence the probability that all references from the remote processors were reads is $(1 - P_{si}) - (1 - P_{wi}) = P_{wi} - P_{si}$. □

Lemma 3: If the previous reference in the local cache ended with an RW copy of S-block i, then the copy is first changed to RO, then invalidated before the next reference with probability $(1 - P_{wi}) - w_i(1 - P_{si})$.

Proof: The copy is first changed to RO then invalidated if several references are made from the remote processors with the first one being a read and at least another one being a write. The probability of at least one write is $1 - P_{wi}$. The probability that the first reference from a remote processor to reach the local cache is a write is $w_i(1 - P_{si})$, since $1 - P_{si}$ is the probability of at least one remote reference and w_i is the probability that the first one is a write. Hence the result follows. □

A summary of these probabilities corresponding to the associated state changes is tabulated in Table II. These probabilities will be used to determine the hit radio degradations in the next subsection.

1) Degradations in the Average Hit Ratio: To estimate the effect of the cache coherence check on the hit ratio, we compute the individual miss ratios $(1 - h_i)$ of (3) under invalidations. Invalidations are the only events affecting the hit ratio. The Markov graph is depicted in Fig. 9(a) and the transition probabilities for the events are obtained from Table II. It is more complex than the Markov graph of Fig. 8(a) because of the added possibility of an invalidation. This Markov graph can be solved by successive reductions, as indicated in Fig. 9(b) and (c), where $Q = 1 - P_{wi}(1 - q_s p_i)$. The probability of absorption in the state "replaced" is the probability of replacement and is equal to

$$P_{R,i} = \prod_{k=0}^{K-1} \frac{[1 - h^*(k)](1 - Q)}{1 - h^*(k)(1 - Q)}$$
$$= \prod_{k=0}^{K-1} \frac{[1 - h^*(k)] P_{wi}(1 - q_s p_i)}{1 - h^*(k) P_{wi}(1 - q_s p_i)}. \quad (4)$$

(The asterisk on h indicates the hit ratio when the cache coherence check is enabled.) If the block was referenced or invalidated before replacement, the probability that it was referenced is $(P_{wi} q_s p_i)/[1 - P_{wi}(1 - q_s p_i)]$. Similarly, the probability that it was invalidated is $(1 - P_{wi})/[1 - P_{wi}(1 - q_s p_i)]$.

The probability of invalidation is thus

$$P_{I,i} = \frac{1 - P_{wi}}{1 - P_{wi}(1 - q_s p_i)}(1 - P_{R,i}) \quad (5)$$

and the probability of a reference while the block copy is still present in the cache is

$$h_1^* = q_s p_i \cdot P_{wi}(1 - P_{r,i})/[1 - p_{wi}(1 - q_s p_i)]$$
$$= (q_s p_i \cdot P_{wi} \cdot P_{I,i})/(1 - P_{wi}). \quad (6)$$

From (3) and (4), the effect of invalidations on the hit ratio can be evaluated as follows.

As was mentioned in Section II, the deterioration of the hit ratio comes mainly from the increased probability of misses on S-blocks. The probabilities of a miss on a given S-block i are $q_s p_i(1 - h_i^*)$ if the coherence is enforced, and $q_s p_i(1 - h_i)$ if it is not.

Thus, we have

$$1 - h^*(K) = 1 - h(K) + \sum_{i=1}^{N_s} q_s p_i[(1 - h_i^*) - (1 - h_i)]$$

or

$$h^*(K) = h(K) - q_s \sum_{i=1}^{N_s} p_i(h_i - h_i^*). \quad (7)$$

Fig. 10 displays the hit ratio curves as a function of the cache size. These curves were verified with simulation to check the instantaneous hit ratio approximation and the approximation of (7). In all the results we show in this paper, the distribution p_i, of the accesses to S-blocks is a uniform distribution ($p_i = 1/N_s$), and w_i is also a constant, independent of i. Values of $w_i = 0.1$ and $N_p = 1024$ are also adopted throughout. When the probability q_s is 0.01, the effect on the hit ratio is negligible. For a high degree of sharing ($q_s = 0.1$), the hit ratio may deteriorate considerably, even for $P = 16$ (up to 10 percent). The curves are different for $N_s = 64$ or $N_s = 16$, but the overall effect is similar.

In practice, the hit ratio degradation may not be as severe as shown for a large number of processors and a high degree of sharing since a block which is invalidated in the local cache may never be referenced again in the cache. Invalidating such a block increases the instantaneous cache size by one. The effect of this phenomenon on the hit ratio is difficult to analyze.

Note that $h_i^* \leq h_i$ because of the invalidations. Also, the hit ratio degradation, $h(K) - h^*(K)$, has q_s as an upper bound. This bound may be achieved when the cache is so large that $h_i \simeq 1$ and the invalidation traffic is so intense that $h_i^* \simeq 0$. This bound is visible in Fig. 10. In practice, h_i^* can be replaced by h_i in (4)-(6) in order to estimate h^* from (7).

2) Increase in Write-Backs and Traffic Between Caches:

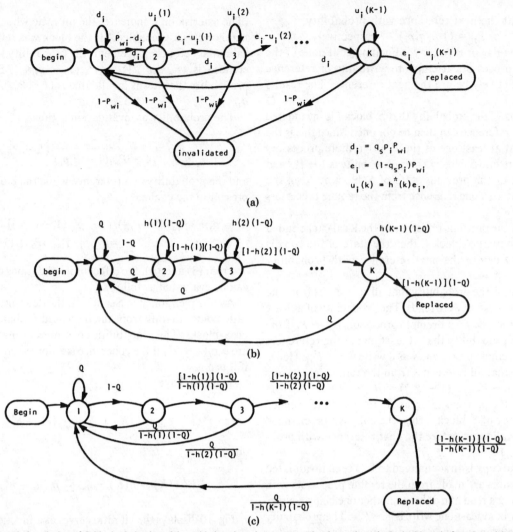

Fig. 9. Markov graph description of S-block i behavior with enabled cache coherences mechanism, where h^* is the hit ratio function with enabled coherence mechanism and $Q = 1 - P_{wi}(1 - q_s p_i)$. (a) State corresponding to position of S-block i in stack. (b) Result of lumping states 1 and "invalidated" from (a). (c) Result of embedding states of (b) at the times of state transitions.

From (5), the total invalidation traffic reaching the cache is thus estimated as

$$T_I = q_s \sum_{i=1}^{N_s} p_i P_{I,i} \leq q_s. \tag{8}$$

All components of this invalidation traffic do not result in the same overhead. In Table I(A), we have indicated the possible changes in the state of a given S-block i between two successive references to it, and the corresponding overhead. Estimating the probability of each of these transitions is the goal of the following analysis.

We designate by $P^*_{RO,i}$ and $P^*_{RW,i}$ the probabilities that the copy of S-block i is RO and RW respectively, immediately after a reference to S-block i has been completed when the cache coherence mechanism is enabled. Let $P(E_{s1,i})$, $P(E_{s2,i})$ and $P(E_{s3,i})$ designate the probabilities that events $E_{s1,i}$, $E_{s2,i}$ and $E_{s3,i}$ [Table I(A)] occur, respectively, on an RO copy between two successive references to it. These probabilities were computed above, because the probabilities of occurrence of a replacement or invalidation are independent of the state of the copy. Namely,

$$P(E_{s1,i}) = P_{I,i} \qquad [\text{see } (5)]$$
$$P(E_{s2,i}) = P_{R,i} \qquad [\text{see } (4)]$$
$$P(E_{s3,i}) = h^*_i \qquad [\text{see } (6)].$$

[Note that to compute these probabilities we can use the new hit ratio $h^*(K)$, computed from (7).]

Six different events can occur when the copy of S-block i is RW after the previous reference to it. From the definition of each event [Table I(A)], we can readily obtain the following relationships:

$$P(E_{p1,i}) + P(E_{p4,i}) = P_{I,i}$$
$$P(E_{p2,i}) + P(E_{p5,i}) = P_{R,i}$$
$$P(E_{p3,1}) + P(E_{p6,i}) = h^*_i. \tag{9}$$

During each virtual time unit, one of four events can occur with respect to an RW copy of S-block i (see Table II). Fig. 11 depicts the resulting Markov graph for an RW copy. If we lump the first three events together, we obtain again the simplified Markov graph of Fig. 9(b), with $Q = 1 - P_{si}(1 - q_s p_i)$.

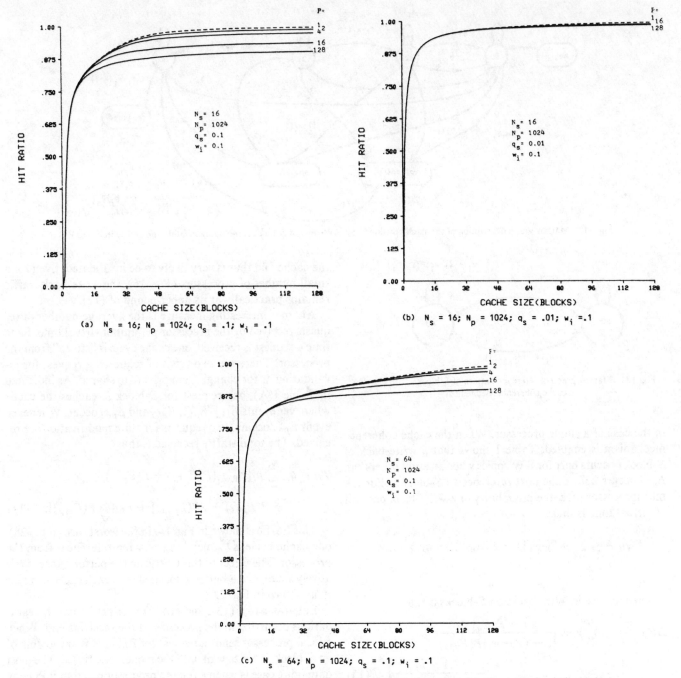

Fig. 10. Hit ratio versus cache size. The dotted curve is for the case when the cache coherence mechanism is disabled.

From this graph, $P(E_{p2,i})$ is readily estimated, as $P_{R,i}$ was in (4), i.e.,

$$P(E_{p2,i}) = \prod_{k=0}^{K-1} \frac{[1 - h^*(k)]P_{si}(1 - q_s p_i)}{1 - h^*(k)P_{si}(1 - q_s p_i)}.$$

Then,

$$P(E_{p1,i}) = \frac{w_i(1 - P_{si})}{1 - P_{si}(1 - q_s p_i)}[1 - P(E_{p2,i})]$$

and

$$P(E_{p3,i}) = \frac{P_{si} \cdot q_s p_i}{1 - P_{si}(1 - q_s p_i)}[1 - P(E_{p2,i})]. \quad (10)$$

Equations (9) and (10) can be solved to find all the proba-

bilities. The probabilities $P^*_{RO,i}$ and $P^*_{RW,i}$ are derived from Fig. 12 as $P_{RO,i}$ and $P_{RW,i}$ were from Fig. 6. The stationary solution to the Markov graph is

$$P^*_{RW,i} = \frac{w_i}{1 - (1 - w_i)P(E_{p3,i})} \text{ and } P^*_{RO,i} = 1 - P^*_{RW,i}.$$

(11)

Equations (4)–(6) and (9)–(11) permit us to estimate most of the performance degradations due to the cache coherence mechanism. The increase in the number of write-backs is found as follows. By (2) and (3), the probability of a write-back on S-blocks per unit of virtual time is estimated as $q_s \sum_{i=1}^{N_s} p_i w_{bi}$,

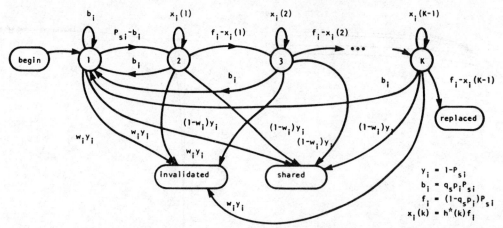

Fig. 11. Markov graph description of the stack position of an RW copy of S-block i, including invalidation and switches to RO.

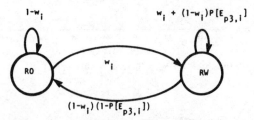

Fig. 12. Markov graph of reference pattern of S-block i with enabled cache coherence mechanism.

in the case of a single processor. When the cache coherence mechanism is enabled, Table I shows that a write-back of S-block i occurs only for RW copies when an event other than $E_{p3,i}$ occurs before the next reference to S-block i. For the multiprocessor case, the probability of a write-back per unit of virtual time is thus

$$P_{WB} = q_s \sum_{i=1}^{N_s} p_i P_{RW,i}^* [1 - P(E_{p3,i})] \le q_s \sum_{i=1}^{N_s} p_i w_i .$$

(12)

The increase in write-backs on S-blocks is thus

$$\Delta P_{WB} = q_s \sum_{i=1}^{N_s} p_i w_i \left[\frac{1 - P(E_{p3,i})}{1 - (1 - w_i) P(E_{p3,i})} - \frac{1 - h_i}{1 - (1 - w_i) h_i} \right].$$

(13)

The probability of a write-back on P-blocks is also modified slightly because of the hit ratio degradation. This effect cannot be evaluated because we do not model the write references to P-blocks. If this modification is small, (13) gives the increase in traffic between the memory and the processor due to cache coherence. This increased traffic is particularly detrimental if the write-backs are not buffered. In Fig. 13, our results for P_{WB}, the probability of writing back an S-block per unit of virtual time, are shown in the case of $q_s = 0.1$. When there is no invalidation ($P = 1$), the probability of a write-back goes to 0 as the cache size increases. This is due to the fact that the hit ratio tends to one, and thus replacement is infrequent. With invalidations, however, the increase of the cache size and of the hit ratio has the effect that an S-block remains longer in

the cache and thus is very likely to be invalidated. Even for a small number of processors ($P = 16$), the write-back traffic remains practically at its upper bound of (12).

Another interesting measure is the average number of requests received by the processor per unit of virtual time. Each time a request is received, one cache cycle is "stolen" from the processor. There are two types of requests: a request for invalidation or for change from private to shared. As indicated in Table I(A), one request for S-block i reaches the cache whenever events $E_{s1,i}$, $E_{p1,i}$, $E_{p5,i}$ and $E_{p6,i}$ occur. Whenever event $E_{p4,i}$ occurs, two requests for state modification are received. The total traffic received is thus

$$T_R = q_s \sum_{i=1}^{N_s} p_i [P_{RW,i}^* [P(E_{p1,i}) + P(E_{p5,i}) + P(E_{p6,i}) + 2P(E_{p4,i})] + P_{RO,i}^* \cdot P(E_{s1,i})]. \quad (14)$$

This traffic is shown in Fig. 14. In the worst case ($P = 128$), one cache cycle is "stolen" in every ten references from the processor. The effect of this traffic on the performance is relatively small, and a buffer associated with each cache can ease it, as shown in Fig. 3.

Equations (8), (13), and (14) are for performance degradations occurring in the processor at the receiving end. When a local processor sends a request for RO or RW ownership of an S-block, it has to wait until the request is satisfied. The most damaging case is when a remote processor owns an RW copy of the block. In this case, the block copy has to be invalidated in remote cache and has to be written back to memory before the local processor can fetch it. For this type of request, there is one unique sender and one unique receiver. By symmetry, the probability that one processor receives a request for an RW copy must be equal to the probability that it sends one. Note that such a request for an S-block i is received in case of events $E_{p1,i}$, $E_{p4,i}$, $E_{p5,i}$, and $E_{p6,i}$. Thus,

$$T_{S,RW} = q_s \sum_{i=1}^{N_s} p_i P_{RW,i}^* [P(E_{p1,i}) + P(E_{p4,i}) + P(E_{p5,i}) + P(E_{p6,i})] \le q_s \sum_{i=1}^{N_s} p_i P_{RW,i}^* [1 - P(E_{p3,i})]$$

$$\le q_s \sum_{i=1}^{N_s} p_i w_i . \quad (15)$$

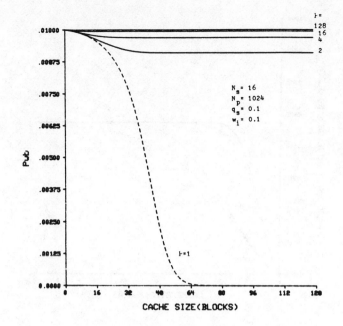

(a) $N_s = 16$; $N_p = 1024$; $q_s = .1$; $w_i = .1$

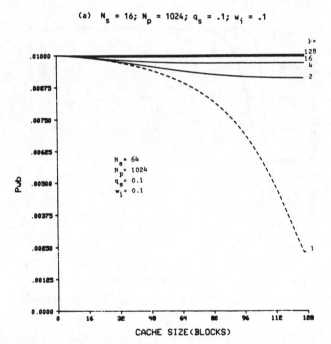

(b) $N_s = 64$; $N_p = 1024$; $q_s = .1$; $w_i = .1$

Fig. 13. Probability of a write-back per processor reference. The dotted curve is for the case with disabled cache coherence mechanism.

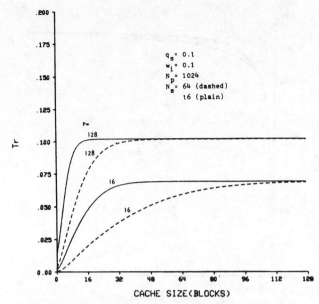

Fig. 14. Probability of receiving a signal from a remote cache per processor reference.

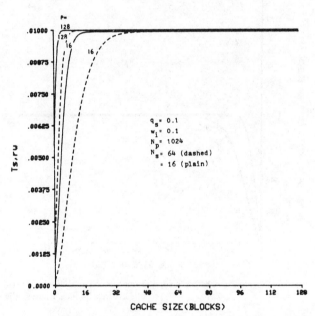

Fig. 15. Blocking probability per processor reference when requesting a block with an RW copy in a remote cache.

This traffic is shown in Fig. 15. The probability that, for a given reference, the processor has to wait for a block transfer from another processor to the memory quickly reaches 0.01. This contribution can thus be quite large when the sharing of data between processes is intense.

Similarly, the total traffic for invalidation of an RO copy in remote caches or change of state from RO to RW in a local cache is

$$T_{S,\mathrm{RO}} = q_s \sum_{i=1}^{N_s} p_i P_{\mathrm{RO},i}^* \, P(E_{s1,i}). \qquad (16)$$

The graph for this traffic is not shown. Equations (15) and (16) are required to estimate the effective degradation of a processor's performance due to multicache consistency.

V. COMPARISON WITH SIMULATION RESULTS

The first approximation made in this paper was to assume that each processor makes one and only one reference between two consecutive references of the processor under study. This assumption permitted the definition of a virtual time, unique for all processors. Simulation of the whole multiprocessor system would be required in order to take into account the effect of the exact physical timing of events in the cache. It was not attempted, and thus, the first approximation is still to be

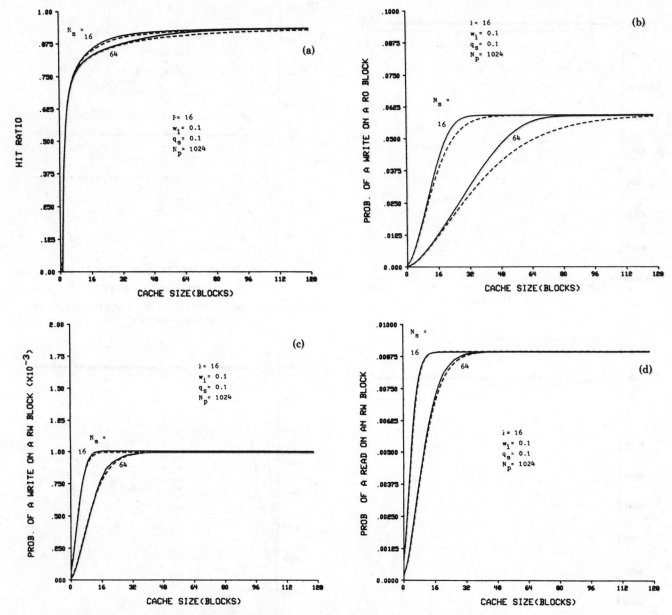

Fig. 16.   Comparison between simulations and the analytical approximation for $P = 16$, $w_i = 0.1$, $q_s = 0.1$, $p_s = 1/N_s$, $N_p = 1024$. The simulation results are in solid lines whereas the model approximations are in dotted lines.

verified. Within the context of this first assumption, the second approximation—the instantaneous hit ratio approximation—is easier to evaluate. The definition of the virtual time permits the simulation of the behavior of one cache in isolation. We have developed a methodology through which the hit ratio and the various components of the traffic between caches can be estimated in one simulation run, for all cache sizes, under invalidations caused by the cache coherency. The following simulation results are displayed in Fig. 16 in solid lines: the hit ratio [Fig. 16(a)], the probabilities that another processor requests an RW copy of an RO block [Fig. 16(b)] or of an RW block [Fig. 16(c)] in the cache, and the probability that another processor requests an RO copy of an RW block in the cache [Fig. 16(d)]. The simulations were run for $P = 16$, $N_p = 1024$, $q_s = 0.1$, $w_i = 0.1$, and $p_i = \dfrac{1}{N_s}$, for all i. The total number of cache references generated was 10^5 for each cache

size. The theoretical approximations appear as dotted lines in Fig. 16. The approximation is good, especially for the hit ratio. The hit ratio is the most reliable estimate, because more than 90 000 hits occur during each simulation run. The theoretical estimate for the probability of a write from another processor on an RO block in the cache is good for $N_s = 16$, but slightly less for $N_s = 64$ (about 5000 such events occur in the simulation). The other two simulation results are somewhat less reliable with 100 events for the case in Fig. 16(c) and 900 events for the case in Fig. 16(d). They still compare very well with the curves obtained analytically, lending confidence to the analysis and to the robustness of the model.

VI. EFFECT ON PROCESSOR'S PERFORMANCE

The overall effect of the enforcement of multicache consistency on the performance is to degrade the throughput of each processor participating in the multiprocessing environment. The degradation can be expressed as a fraction of the processor's performance in uniprocessor (UP) mode—that is, when the cache coherence mechanism is disabled. Of course, this degradation is a function of the system workload, the architectural configuration and the implementation of the coherence checking mechanism.

In the UP mode, the main degradation is due to cache misses. Hence if d_m is the average delay (in cache cycles) observed in fetching the missed block, the penalty is $T_{UP} = d_m \cdot (1 - h(K))$, where $1 - h(K)$ is the miss ratio in UP mode. When the coherence mechanism is enabled [multiprocessing (MP) mode], three types of penalties may be experienced by each reference to the local cache. The first is the miss penalty. Each miss, which occurs with a probability of $1 - h^*(K)$, encounters an average delay of d_m^* cycles to fetch the missed block. Note $d_m^* \geq d_m$, since $1 - h^*(K) > 1 - h(K)$, the traffic to main memory may be higher, resulting in more memory conflicts. The second penalty is that due to a wait for invalidations of RO blocks in remote caches or a change of state from RO to RW in a local cache. The probability of this occurring is $T_{S,RO}$ from (16). The average wait time, $d_{I,RO}$ cycles, experienced for this penalty is a function of the implementation of the coherence mechanism and the invalidation traffic. The third penalty is that due to invalidation of an RW block or a change of state from RW to RO in a remote cache. The probability of this occurring is $T_{S,RW}$ from (15). The average delay can be denoted by $d_{I,RW} \geq 2d_m^*$, since two block transfers are required each time this penalty occurs.

Hence the average delay encountered by a reference to the cache in MP mode is

$$T_{MP} = d_m^* (1 - h^*(K)) + d_{I,RO} T_{S,RO} + d_{I,RW} T_{S,RW}$$
$$(17)$$

From T_{UP} and T_{MP} the fractional degradation in a processor's throughput due to the enforcement of multicache consistency can be estimated. It is obvious that the effect of different MP workloads on the degradation can be studied by the model developed in this paper.

VII. Conclusion

In this paper, we have studied the effects of the cache coherency on the hit ratio of a cache and on the traffic between the caches. An analytical model for multitasked program behavior has been introduced. This analytical model includes the sharing of blocks between processors. Locality properties of P-blocks and S-blocks are reflected by a different model for each. To obtain a tractable solution, it is assumed that between two references of a given processor, any other processor makes one and only one reference. This assumption is only made for the study of coherency and, in this context, is reasonable. Simulations are possible at this level of abstraction. We have, however, derived approximate analytical formulas for the effects of coherency. These derivations are based on the instantaneous hit ratio approximation. Simulations have shown that such an approximation was very good.

In general, for processes with a low degree of sharing ($q_s =$

0.01), the effects of coherency are very low, even with a large number of processors. When the degree of sharing is large ($q_s = 0.1$), the main degradations are in the hit ratio and in the blocking time resulting from accesses to blocks owned by other processors with RW right.

The model does not evaluate the effects of contention for the global table. To limit these contentions, we have organized the global table in an $L \cdot M$ configuration. The effects of access conflicts can be studied through other models [4].

The cache coherency in multiprocessors is a very interesting and very complex problem to analyze. Measurements on a real system are practically excluded. Simulation of a multiprocessor system based on P individual traces is very expensive and complex, as well as very difficult to verify. Analytical models are an attractive alternative. Once the model has been developed, the gathering of results is easy and inexpensive. Predictions of the performance degradations due to coherency are possible within the limitation of a reasonable set of approximations. For example, the model for the effects of coherency could be included in a global model of a cache-based multiprocessor, like the one derived in [5], and could contribute to the understanding of the cost-performance tradeoffs in such systems. In interpreting these models, one should keep in mind that they are based on a set of hypotheses regarding the program behavior. Up to now, no real attempt has been made to model the behavior of cooperating processes in a multitasked system. Much work remains to be done in the development and validation of these multiprocessor program models. In this respect, our approach breaks new ground in the field of modeling. It has the advantage of being both tractable and reasonable.

Acknowledgment

The authors express their gratitude to S. Kazemi for his help in developing the simulation programs to lend confidence to the analytical models. We are also grateful to Dr. P. L. Rosenfeld, Dr. L. Liu, Dr. K. So, and Dr. J. M. Knight at the IBM Thomas J. Watson Research Center for their comments on this paper. Finally, we are indebted to the editors and referees for their many helpful suggestions.

References

[1] T. K. Abdel-Hamid and S. E. Madnick, "A study of the multicache-consistency problem in multi-processor computer systems," Cen. Inform. Res., M.I.T., Tech. Rep. 16, Sept. 1981.
[2] M. Badel and J. Leroudier, "Performance evaluation of a cache memory for a minicomputer," presented at the 4th Int. Symp. Modelling and Performance Evaluation Comput. Syst., 1979.
[3] J. D. Bell et al., "An investigation of alternative cache organizations," IEEE Trans. Comput., vol. C-23, Apr. 1974.
[4] F. A. Briggs and E. S. Davidson, "Organization of semiconductor memories for parallel pipelined processors," IEEE Trans. Comput., vol. C-26, Feb. 1977.
[5] F. A. Briggs and M. Dubois, "Performance of cache-based multiprocessors," presented at the ACM Conf. Measurement Modeling Comput. Syst., Sept. 1981.
[6] L. M. Censier and P. Feautrier, "A new solution to coherence problems in multicache systems," IEEE Trans. Comput., vol. C-27, Dec. 1978.
[7] C. J. Conti, "Concepts for buffer storage," IEEE Comput. Group News, vol. 2, Mar. 1969.

[8] P. Denning, "Working sets past and present," *IEEE Trans. Software Eng.*, vol. SE-6, Jan. 1980.

[9] M. Dubois and F. A. Briggs, "Efficient interprocessor communication for MIMD multiprocessor systems," in *Proc. 8th Int. Symp. Comput. Architecture*, May 1981.

[10] K. R. Kaplan and R. O. Winder, "Cache-based computer systems," *IEEE Computer*, vol. 6, Mar. 1973.

[11] H. T. Kung, "The structure of parallel algorithms," in *Advances in Computers*, vol. 19, M. C. Youits, Ed.   New York: Academic, 1980, pp. 65-112.

[12] J. H. Saltzer, "A simple linear model of demand paging performance," *Commun. Ass. Comput. Mach.*, vol. 17, Apr. 1974.

[13] M. Satyanarayanan, "Commercial multiprocessing systems," *IEEE Computer*, May 1980.

[14] J. R. Spirn, *Program Behavior: Models and Measurements.*   New York: Elsevier, 1977.

[15] W. D. Strecker, "Cache memories for PDP-11 family computers," in *Proc. 3rd Annu. Symp. Comput. Architecture*, Jan. 1976.

[16] C. K. Tang, "Cache system design in the tightly coupled multiprocessor system," in *Proc. AFIPS*, 1976.

[17] L. C. Widdoes, "The S-1 project: Development of high performance digital computers," in *Dig. Paper, COMPCON '80*, IEEE Comput. Soc., San Francisco, CA, Feb. 1980.

[18] C. Yeh, "Shared cache organization for multiple-stream computer systems," Univ. Illinois, Urbana-Champaign, Tech. Rep. R-904, CSL, Jan. 1981.

[19] W. C. Yen and K. S. Fu, "Memory organization and synchronization mechanism of multiprocessing computer systems," School Elec. Eng., Purdue Univ., West Lafayette, IN, Tech. Rep., TR-EE 81-34, Oct. 1981.

Michel Dubois (S'79-M'81) was born in Charleroi, Belgium, in 1953. He received the Ingénieur Civil Electricien degree from the Faculté Polytechnique de Mons, Belgium, the M.S. degree from the University of Minnesota, Minneapolis, in 1978, and the Ph.D. degree from Purdue University, West Lafayette, IN, in 1982, all in electrical engineering.

During his studies in the U.S., he was funded by grants from the Faculté Polytechnique de Mons and by research and teaching positions. He is now with the Central Research Laboratory, Thomson-CSF, Domaine de Corbeville, France, where he designs architectures for very large scale integration. His main interests are in computer architecture and digital image processing.

Fayé A. Briggs (M'77), for a photograph and biography, see p. 982 of the October 1982 issue of this TRANSACTIONS.

PACKET SWITCHING NETWORKS FOR MULTIPROCESSORS AND DATAFLOW COMPUTERS

Chi-Yuan Chin, Member, IEEE, and **Kai Hwang**, Senior Member, IEEE

Abstract - Most packet switched multistage networks have been proposed to use a unique path between any source and destination. We propose to add a few extra stages to create multiple paths between any source and destination. Connection principles of such Multipath networks for packet switching are presented. Performance of such networks is analyzed for possible use in multiprocessor systems or in dataflow computers.

The major improvement of the proposed networks lies in significantly reduced packet wait delays in buffers, especially under heavy traffic conditions. The tradeoffs between reduced network delays and increased hardware cost are studied. Optimal design criteria and systematic procedures are provided for developing multipath packet switching networks.

Keywords - Multistage interconnection network, buffered 2-by-2 switches, packet switching, inter-processor-memory networks, arbitration network, distribution network, dataflow computers, multiprocessor systems.

1. INTRODUCTION

Multistage Interconnection Networks (MINs), constructed by buffered 2-by-2 switches, can be applied for packet switching in a multiprocessor computer system. As illustrated in Fig. 1, the buffered network provides interconnections (address mapping) among processors and memory modules in a multiprocessor system [29-32]. With minor modification, they can be also used for resource arbitration or token distribution in a dataflow computer [3, 22-25].

Many packet switching MINs have been proposed in recent years. Tripathi and Lipovski [1] modified the one-sided Banyan networks into a bidirectional packet switching network. Hopper and Wheeler [2] introduced a class of binary routing networks for packet switching. Dennis, et al [3] suggested packet switching networks for a data flow computer prototype. They used a recursive construction method to create tree, rectangular, and triangular networks. Dias and Jump [4,5] proposed a class of buffered delta networks for packet switching. Three switching strategies for designing packet switching cells are also studied in Kumar and Jump [6, 40].

In all the above approaches to designing packet switched MINs, a unique path exists between any source and destination. When the packet traffic becomes heavy, the waiting queue length in some switching cells of a unique-path MIN may become too long to be acceptable. Thus, we propose multiple-path networks to balance the traffic load in the network. A multiple-path packet switching network has been developed in the HEP multiprocessor [7, 8] using 3-ported switching cells.

C.Y. Chin is with General Electric Company, Corporate Research and Development, Schenectady, New York 12345. K. Hwang is with the School of Electrical Engineering, Purdue University, W. Lafayette, Indiana 47907. This research was supported in part by NSF under grant ECS-80-16580. A preliminary version of the work, under the title "Connection Principles for Multipath Packet Switching Networks", has been presented in the *11th Annual Int'l Symposium on Computer Architecture*, Ann Arbor, Mich., June 5-7, 1984. This paper has been accepted for publication in the IEEE Trans. Computers, special issue on *Parallel Processing*, November 1984.

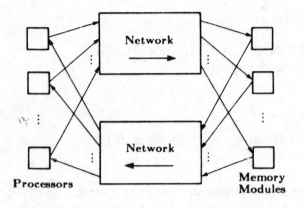

(a) Inter-processor-memory networks

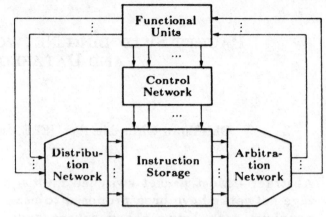

(b) Networks in a static dataflow computer

Figure 1. Application of packet switching networks in multiprocessors and in dataflow computers

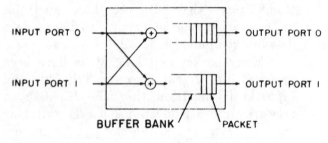

(a) Buffered 2-by-2 switching cells

Interstage connections

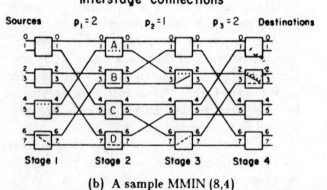

(b) A sample MMIN (8,4)

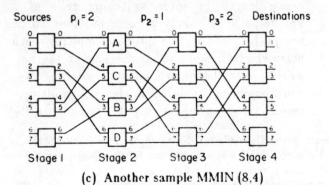

(c) Another sample MMIN (8,4)

Figure 2. A multipath multistage interconnection networks with 8 nodes and 4 stages

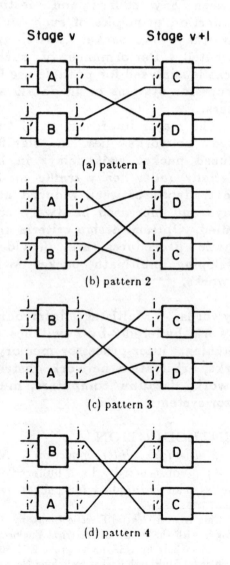

(a) pattern 1

(b) pattern 2

(c) pattern 3

(d) pattern 4

Figure 3. Basic link patterns for constructing the k-connections between stages.

Our proposed network differs from the HEP network in basic building blocks and in network topologies. Other related studies on multistage networks, that can be modified for packet switching, are listed in references [9, 11-13, 15-21, 34-39].

In this paper, we propose a new class of *Multipath, Multistage Interconnection Network* (MMIN) for packet switching communications. The proposed networks are structured with buffered 2-by-2 switching cells. Multiple connection paths are created between any (source, destination) pair by adding extra stages to the MIN networks. At each switching cell, there are two kinds of delay in passing a packet to the next stage. The *wait delay* is caused by a packet waiting in the cell buffer before it can be transmitted. The *transmit delay* is the time actually needed for transmitting a packet to the next stage. The transmit delay for a fixed length packet is a constant between stages. The wait delay is a random variable with a nonnegative value.

The sum of transmit delay and wait delay at a switching cell is called the *cell delay*. The sum of all cell delays in the successive stages from the source to the destination is called the *network delay*. We consider "average" network delays instead of "worse-case" delays in the performance analysis of packet switching networks. The average delays should reflect the network performance more closely for mixed workload under moderate and heavy traffic conditions. When the network is underutilized with light traffic, the wait delays in buffers should be small in either unique-path or multipath networks.

In a multipath network, packets can be distributed to multiple paths. Therefore, the average wait delay in each switching cell is much shorter than that in a unique-path MIN. However, packets are routed with more transmit delays in a multipath network, due to the added extra stages. When the packet load is light, the transmit delays dominate the network delay, and a multipath network will perform slightly worse than an MIN. When the packet load becomes heavier, the network delay is entirely decided by the wait delays.

The network performance is thus improved with less network delays.

This paper presents basic connection principles of multipath networks for packet switching. For a network with n nodes, the number of required stages is proved to be in the range $[\log_2 n + 1, 2\log_2 n - 1]$. For practical purposes, we consider MMIN(2^m,h) with n nodes and h stages such that $n = 2^m$ and $h > m$ for some integer $m = \log_2 n$ throughout the paper.

In Section 2, we introduce bijection mappings for generating the interstage connection patterns. In Section 3, useful connection properties of MMINs are presented. Switching cell delays and optimal packet distribution strategies among multiple paths are discussed in Section 4. Optimal design criteria for multipath networks are presented in Section 5. The performance of multipath networks will be compared with that of unique-path networks for packet switching in either multiprocessor or dataflow computers. The comparison emphasizes heavy traffic conditions, in which the network tends to become the performance bottleneck in any large modular systems [5, 29].

2. INTERSTAGE CONNECTIONS

The proposed network is unidirectional and constructed by 2-by-2 switching cells with buffers as modeled in Fig. 2a. A decision must be made for each packet arriving at each input port to be switched into one of the two output buffer banks, waiting for transmission to the next stage. The upper and lower input/output ports of each switching cell are labeled *port 0* and *port 1*, respectively. Several implementations of such switching cells were suggested in Kumar, Dias and Jump [6] and in Chin and Hwang [39]. We assume sufficiently large buffer banks in each switching cell, so that overflow will not occur. In fact, four or five buffers in each buffer bank will be sufficient for practical network designs [5].

Connection Patterns

Each stage in an MMIN(n,h) consists of $n/2$ switching cells as exemplified in Fig. 2b for an MMIN(8,4). The input/output ports at each intermediate stage are identified by integers $0, 1, 2, ..., 2^m - 1$. All port numbers are binary coded. Source and destination ports are denoted by capitals, such as $I = (i_{m-1}, ..., i_1, i_0)_2$. A (source, destination) pair will be denoted by (I,J). Port numbers at each intermediate stage are denoted by lower case letters such as $i = (i_{m-1}, ..., i_1, i_0)_2$.

Two ports i and j are called *neighbors*, if $\lfloor i/2 \rfloor = \lfloor j/2 \rfloor$. At each stage, the ports can be numbered subject to the following constraints:

(1) Two numbers assigned to the ports of the same switching cell must be neighbors. The smaller number is always assigned to the upper port.

(2) The two input ports and two output ports of any switching cell must be assigned the same numbers at the upper and lower positions accordingly.

Note that the ports at each stage are not necessary to be sequentially labeled from the top as in Fig. 2b. Permuted orders are allowed such as the order at the stage 2 in Fig. 2c. For an MMIN(n, h), there are $(n/2)!$ different labeling methods at each stage.

The k-connection

Adjacent stages are interconnected by a bijection mapping. There are $h-1$ *interstage connections* in an MMIN(n,h) network. The network in Fig. 2b has three interstage connections. Let p_j be the connection pattern between stage j and stage $j+1$ for $1 \leq j \leq h-1$. For any port $i = (i_{m-1} ... i_k ... i_1 i_0)_2$, we define the *k-th conjugate* of port i as $i(k) = (i_{m-1} ... i_{k+1} i_0 i_{k-1} ... i_1 i_k)_2$, for $0 \leq k \leq m-1$. In other words, $i(k)$ is obtained from i by switching bits i_k and i_0. Denote the *link* connecting output port x at stage v to input port y at stage $v+1$ as (x,y) for $1 \leq v \leq h-1$. We formally specify *interstage patterns* by the following mappings:

A *k-connection* for $k \in \{1, 2, ..., m-1\}$ is a bijection, defined by mapping the port $i = (i_{m-1} \cdots i_k \cdots i_1 i_0)_2$ to its k-th conjugate $i(k) = (i_{m-1} \cdots i_0 \cdots i_1 i_k)_2$ for all $i \in \{0, 1, ..., 2^m-1\}$.

Since there are $(n/2)!$ different port-labeling methods at each stage, each k-connection can assume $[(n/2)!]^2/(n/4)!$ different topological patterns. In Fig. 2, two *2-connection* patterns for $n = 8$ are shown at the first and the third interstage connections. The output port $4 = (100)_2$ is connected to the input port $1 = (001)_2$, and the output port $5 = (101)_2$ is linked to the input port 5. More precisely, the k-connection is constructed with four basic 4-by-4 "butterfly" patterns, as shown in Fig. 3. For examples, each k-connection in Fig. 2 is constructed by two butterfly patterns shown in Fig. 3a.

The two MMIN(8,4) networks in Fig. 2 are constructed with two 2-connections and one 1-connection. We choose the interstage pattern $p_i = k$, if a k-connection is used to achieve the interstage links between stage i and $i+1$. The topology of an MMIN(n,h) network is specified by a *connection sequence* of $h-1$ interstage patterns $(p_1, p_2, p_3, ..., p_{h-1})$, for $1 \leq p_i \leq m-1$. Two examples of MMIN(8,5) are given in Fig. 4 corresponding to connection sequence $(2, 1, 1, 2)$ in Fig. 4a and to connection sequence $(2, 1, 2, 1)$ in Fig. 4b.

Basically, a connection sequence is formed such that each $k \in \{1, 2, ..., m-1\}$ appears at least once in the sequence. This property is necessary to ensure that there is a fixed number of paths between any (I,J) pair. For examples, the connection sequence $(1, 1, 1, 1)$ for an MMIN(8,5) will provide either no path or 8 paths between any (I,J) pair. This poor selection of a connection sequence generates essentially two isolated MMIN(4,5). The constraints on legitimate connection sequences will become more apparent, after we present the packet switching methods.

Since $h-1 > m-1$ in an MMIN(2^m, h), some connection patterns must be repeated in the sequence. It is the repeated patterns that can generate multiple paths. If $h = m$, the

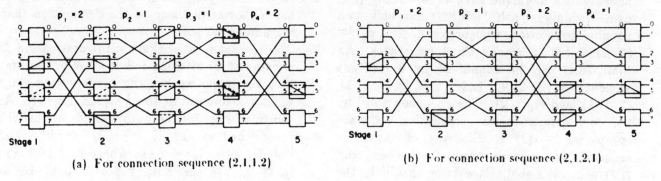

(a) For connection sequence (2,1,1,2)

(b) For connection sequence (2,1,2,1)

Figure 4.   Two MMIN(8,5) designs with respect to two different connection sequences

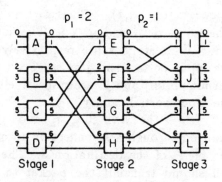

(a) For connection sequence (2,1)

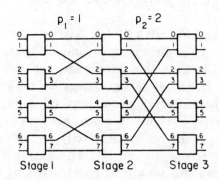

(b) For connection sequence (1,2)

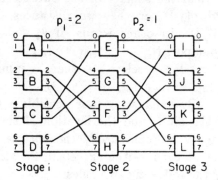

(c)   A Delta network obtained from (a) by port relabeling

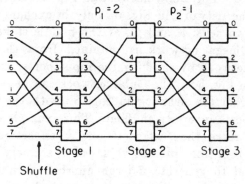

(d)   An Omega network obtained from (c) by shuffling input ports

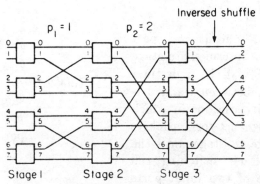

(e)   A cube network obtained from (b) with inversely shuffled output ports

Figure 5. Various multistage networks with n=8 nodes and h=3 stages

network has a unique path between any (I,J) pair. A unique-path MIN(8,3) has only two possible connection sequences, i.e. $(p_1, p_2) = (1, 2)$ or $(2, 1)$, among the three stages. An MMIN(8,4) can be connected by 6 different sequences: $(2, 1, 2)$, $(1, 1, 2)$, $(1, 2, 1)$, $(2, 2, 1)$, $(2, 1, 1)$, and $(1, 2, 2)$. The one, shown in Fig. 2b, corresponds to the connection sequence $(p_1, p_2, p_3) = (2, 1, 2)$. Any of these six sequences can provide two paths between any (I,J) pair. We shall show later that only the sequences $(2, 1, 2)$ and $(1, 2, 1)$ will result in a minimum average network delay.

Relations with Other MINs

It is shown by examples that, by using the k-connection mappings, we can generate the Delta networks, Omega networks, and the Cube networks via a port relabeling method. Figure 5 shows various networks, MIN(8,3), that can be constructed by using the k-connection, for $k \epsilon \{1, 2\}$. Figure 5a and 5b shows two networks, constructed by using our k-connection sequences $(2, 1)$ and $(1, 2)$, respectively.

The Delta network in Fig. 5c differs from the network in Fig. 5a only in exchanging the two cells, F and G, at the middle stage. The Omega network is obtained from the Delta network by shuffling the input ports, as shown in Fig. 5d. The Cube network can be obtained from the network in Fig. 5b with the output ports inversely shuffled. This example demonstrates the fact that our k-connection mappings (for different values of k) are very powerful to generate a large number of multistage networks with simple port relabeling and input/output shuffling.

Packet Switching Method

Consider an output port $i = (i_{m-1}i_{m-2} \cdots i_1i_0)_2$ at an intermediate stage v. Let $J = (\ell_{m-1}\ell_{m-2} \cdots \ell_1\ell_0)_2$ be a destination. The *distance*, $d(i,J)$, between i and J is equal to the number of bit positions in which they differ. In a multistage network, packets are transmitted from stage to stage until the destination is reached. Each switching cell transmits a packet to one of two input ports

at the next stage such that the selected port has a shorter distance to the destination than the unselected port.

Consider a packet with destination J arriving at a switching cell at stage v. Assume that the interstage pattern p_v, following stage v, is a k-connection for $k \epsilon \{1,2,...,m-1\}$. As shown in Fig. 3a, the output ports of this cell could be as $i = (i_{m-1} \cdots i_k \cdots i_1 0)_2$ and $i' = (i_{m-1} \cdots i_k \cdots i_1 1)_2$, where $i' = i+1$ and $i_k = 0$. Or the output ports could be as another two $j = (j_{m-1} \cdots j_k \cdots j_1 0)_2 = (i_{m-1} \cdots \bar{i}_k \cdots i_1 0)_2$ and $j' = (j_{m-1} \cdots j_k \cdots j_1 1)_2 = (i_{m-1} \cdots \bar{i}_k \cdots i_1 1)_2$, where $j' = j+1$ and $j_k = 1$. The output ports i and i' at stage v are respectively linked to the input ports i and j at stage $v+1$, and the output ports j and j' are respectively linked to the input ports i' and j'.

Only the k-th bit, i_k and j_k, can be changed through a k-connection to match with the bit ℓ_k of the destination J. The switching cell should transmit the packet to the input port whose k-th bit coincides with ℓ_k in order to yield the shorter of the two distances $d(i,J)$ and $d(j,J)$, or the two distances $d(i',J)$ and $d(i',J)$. In other words, if $\ell_k = 0$, select the input port $(i_{m-1} \cdots i_{k+1} 0 i_{k-1} \cdots i_1 i_0)_2$. If $\ell_k = 1$, select the input port $(i_{m-1} \cdots i_{k+1} 1 i_{k-1} \cdots i_1 i_0)_2$.

By exhausting four possible combinations of the bit ℓ_k and the location of the packet at stage v, we can specify the port selection process at each switching cell in an MMIN $(2^m,h)$ by the following two rules:

Rule 1. For any stage v, $1 \leq v < h$, which is followed by an interstage pattern $p_v = k$, the packet should be switched to the upper port, if $\ell_k = 0$, and to the lower port, if $\ell_k = 1$.

Rule 2. At the last stage h, the packet should be switched to the upper port, if $\ell_0 = 0$, and to the lower port, if $\ell_0 = 1$.

The above switching method can be applied to any packet at any cell, no matter at which input port the packet arrives. A packet must be transmitted to match the k-th bit of the next input port with the k-th bit of the destination through a k-connection pattern. Since all k-connection patterns for $k \in \{1,2,...,m-1\}$ must appear in the connection sequence of an $MMIN(2^m,h)$, all m bits (except the least significant bit) in the source code I should match with the destination J in h-1 successive stages.

When the packet finally arrives at the last stage, all bits of the source code (except the least significant bit) have been converted to match with the corresponding bits of the destination. Rule 2 is then applied at the last stage to converge to the destination. Note that packet switching at an intermediate stage is determined exclusively by checking one bit of the destination number, which is governed by the connection pattern following the stage.

3. SWITCHING PROPERTIES

To route a packet from source I to destination J in a network, there exists a sequence of links forming a *path* for (I,J). All the intermediate output port labels (either 0 for upper port or 1 for lower port) contained in the path are concatenated to form a binary number $(s_1s_2 ...s_h)_2$, called the *path code*. Each path code can uniquely determines a path from I to J. For examples, the code $(0101)_2$ determines the solid-line path in Fig. 2b, from source I=6 to destination J=3.

The path code is exclusively determined by its destination number and by the connection sequence. Packets from different sources to the same destination must use the same collection of path codes. In Fig. 2, the code for the dot-line path from source 4 to destination 3 is $(0101)_2$, which is also the path code for the solid-line path for destination 3. Thus the same path code can be used to route packets from different sources to the same destination.

The Path Book and Implications

Since m < h, there must be repeated patterns in the connection sequence. If there are more than one "k-connection" pattern for some k in a sequence, a packet for (I,J) has at least two opportunities to adjust the k-th bit in I to match with the destination J. However, the packet must be transmitted via the output port j_k at the stage followed by the last k-connection, in order to ensure that the k-th bit of any port on the remaining path matches with the k-th bit of J.

In an $MMIN(2^m,h)$ with connection sequence $(p_1,p_2,...,p_{h-1})$, the bit s_v in a path code $(s_1s_2 \cdots s_v \cdots s_h)_2$ must equal j_k in the destination code $J = (j_{m-1} \cdots j_k \cdots j_1j_0)_2$, if the v-th interstage pattern $p_v = k$ and the remaining patterns following stage $v+1$ are different from this k-connection. Furthermore, the last bit s_h in a path code should be equal to j_0. Those bits in a path code that can not be changed are called *constant bits*. The remaining bits in a path code are called *variable bits*; each can be either 0 or 1. We define a *path book* $(t_1t_2 \cdots t_h)_2$ as a collection of path codes $(s_1s_2 \cdots s_h)_2$ such that $t_i = s_i$, if s_i is a constant bit; and $t_i = d$, if t_i is a variable bit, for any $1 \leq i \leq h$, where d means a "don't care" condition.

A path book contains all possible path codes leading to a common destination. All path codes can be generated by assigning constant 0 or 1 to the variable bits in a path book. For examples, to reach destination 3 in Fig. 2b, two path codes $(0101)_2$ and $(1101)_2$ are generated from the path book $(d101)_2$.

The positions of constant bits in any path book are fixed for a given network. There are m-1 possible values, 1,2,...,m−1, for the k-connection patterns in an $MMIN(2^m,h)$. Thus, there are m constant bits and h-m variable bits in any path book. Each variable bit implies two possible fanout paths. If bit t_v of the corresponding path book $(t_1t_2 \cdots t_h)_2$ is a variable bit, the switching cells at stage v are called *fanout cells,* and the stage v is called a *fanout stage.* We present below several interesting switching properties which are useful to the design and optimization of multistage networks.

Property 1. The path book is unique for each fixed destination. Each path book consists of 2^{h-m} path codes for an MMIN(2^m, h).

Proof: Since packets from different sources to the same destination must have the same constant bits in their path codes, the path book is thus unique for each destination. There are h-m variable bits in each path book. This implies that each path will pass through h-m fanout cells. Since each fanout cell branches to two paths, there are 2^{h-m} paths specified in the path book.

$$\text{Q.E.D.}$$

Property 2. In an MMIN(2^m,h) with a connection sequence $(p_1, p_2, ..., p_{h-1})$, there exists a path from source $I = (i_{m-1} \cdots i_1 i_0)_2$ to output port $j = (j_{m-1} \cdots j_1 j_0)_2$ at stage v, if there exists at least one k-connection between stage 1 and stage v for any $k \in \{ x \mid i_x \neq j_x \text{ for } 1 \leq x \leq m\text{-}1\}$.

Proof: Since bit i_k of source number I for any $k \in \{1, 2, ..., m\text{-}1\}$ can be adjusted before stage v to match with bit j_k of port j, the source I must have at least one path leading to port j at stage v.

$$\text{Q.E.D.}$$

Thus, if h > m, we have an MMIN(2^m,h) network. If h = m, the network degenerates to be a unique-path network. By Property 1, there are $2^2 = 4$ paths between any source and destination in the MMIN(8,5) shown in Fig. 4. Property 2 implies that there exists a path between source I and output port j at stage v, if the number I can be adjusted from stage 1 to stage v to match with the number j. For examples, in Fig. 2b, source $6 = (110)_2$ can reach port $3 = (011)_2$ at stage 2, since the interstage pattern $p_1 = 2$. However, the port $5 = (101)_2$ at stage 2 can not be reached by source 6, since there is no 1-connection before stage 2. The ports which can be reached by one of the paths from I to J are called the *reachable ports* for the (I,J) pair.

The sequence of output port labels (either 0 or 1) from a source I to a port j at stage v is called a *subpath code*. A *subpath book* can be similarly defined. There are also variable bits and constant bits in a subpath book for each intermediate port. Even if a subpath is a prefix of a path, a variable bit in the path book may become a constant bit in the subpath book. Similar to a path book, the subpath book for each intermediate port can be also uniquely specified. As an example, the subpath book from either source 4 or 6 to port 2 at stage 3 consists of only one path $(010)_2$ in Fig. 2b.

Let $\alpha_k(v)$ be the number of times that a given k-connection appears in a connection sequence up to stage v. Let $\beta_k(v) = \alpha_k(v)-1$, if $\alpha_k(v) \neq 0$, and $\beta_k(v) = 0$, if $\alpha_k(v) = 0$. Thus, $\gamma = \sum_{k=1}^{m-1} \beta_k(v)$ is the total number of variable bits in a subpath book to stage v. Since there are γ variable bits in the subpath book, there are 2^γ subpaths from source I to port j. Let ω be the number of fanout stages after stage v. Then each subpath at stage v will be fanned out into 2^ω paths. In total, there are $2^{\gamma+\omega}$ paths from source I to port j. The following property is observed:

Property 3. Consider an output port j at stage v. Let γ be the number of variable bits in a subpath book leading to port j. Let ω be the number of fanout stages after stage v. If port j can be reached from a source I, then there are exactly $2^{\gamma+\omega}$ paths from source I to port j.

In Fig. 4a, the MMIN(8,5) has two 1-connection patterns before stage 4. Thus, $\gamma = 1$, $\omega = 0$, and the subpath book from source 3 to port 5 at stage 4 is $(0d01)_2$. There are $v - \gamma = 3$ constant bits and $\gamma = 1$ variable bit in the subpath book. Note that $\gamma = 0$ for the output ports at the first three stages. There is one fanout stage after stage 1 ($\omega = 1$). Therefore, there are $2^{\gamma+\omega} = 2$ paths for each (I,j) at stage 1. Property 3 shows that the path books can be effectively used to enumerate the multiple paths.

Port Sharing among Multiple Paths

Paths for different (I,J) pairs may share some switch ports at intermediate stages. The port sharing property is characterized below:

Property 4. If two paths, for (I_1,J_1) and (I_2,J_2) share a port **s** at stage v (as shown in Fig. 6), then there are exactly $2^{\gamma+\omega}$ paths from I_1 to J_1 and $2^{\gamma+\omega}$ paths from I_2 to J_2 sharing the same port **s**, where γ is the number of variable bits in the subpath book leading to port **s**, and ω is the number of the fanout stages after the stage v.

Proof: By Property 3, the number of paths leading to port **s** is $2^{\gamma+\omega}$ for either source I_1 or source I_2. Thus the $2^{\gamma+\omega}$ paths from I_1 to J_1 must join the $2^{\gamma+\omega}$ paths from I_2 to J_2 at port **s** due to the uniqueness of the subpath book.

Q.E.D.

Theorem 1. Let $q = \gamma+\omega$, be the sum of variable bits in a subpath book leading to stage v and fanout stages after stage v. If the path books for (I_1,J_1) and (I_2,J_2) share a port **s** at certain stage v, then there are exactly 2^{h-m-q} ports being shared at stage v, each of which has 2^q paths sharing the port.

Proof: Denote path books for (I_1, J_1) and (I_2, J_2) as $(x_1 \cdots x_v \cdots x_h)_2$ and $(y_1 \cdots y_v \cdots y_h)_2$, respectively. The prefix $x_1 \cdots x_v$ must be the same as the prefix $y_1 \cdots y_v$, due to the port sharing at stage v. The number of paths covered by the variable bits is 2^{h-m} up to stage v. By Properties 1 and 3, there are $2^{h-m}/2^q = 2^{h-m-q}$ ports at stage v to accommodate 2^{h-m} paths for each (I,J) pair. Since subpath codes from different sources to the same reachable port must be identical, the proof is thus complete by Property 4.

Q.E.D.

In Fig. 4a, the values of h-m and q for stage 4 in the MMIN(8,5) are 2 and 1, respectively. Thus, for $(I,J) = (3,5)$, there are $2^{h-m-q} = 2$ ports at stage 4, i.e. port 1 and port 5, each of which is shared by $2^q = 2$ paths as shown in Fig. 4a. All paths for the (3,5) pair and the (5,4) pair share ports 0, 2, 4, and 6 at stage 3, and share ports 1 and 5 at stage 4. Ports 1 and 5 at stage 4 are shared by all paths for all (I,J) pairs, where $0 \leq I \leq 7$ and $4 \leq J \leq 5$. No paths for other (I,J) pairs can share the two ports.

Thus, associated with a stage v in an MMIN(2^m, h), all (I,J) pairs can be divided into $w = 2^m/2^{h-m-q} = 2^{2m-h+q}$ groups. All pairs in the same group must share the same set of ports. Furthermore, all paths for all pairs in the same group share 2^{h-m-q} ports at stage v. This port sharing property will be used to optimize packet distributions for minimizing cell delays in the network.

4. NETWORK DESIGN CRITERIA

The procedures to design an MMIN(2^m, h) are to select a connection sequence (p_1, p_2, ..., p_{h-1}) such that equal number of paths exist between any (I,J) pair. Thus, each *k*-connection for k ϵ {1, 2, ..., m-1} must appear at least once in the sequence. For an MMIN(8,5), any of the 14 sequences in Table 1 satisfies the above design requirements. However, only four of these sequences (two were shown in Fig. 4.) will result in a minimum average network delay. Since the network delay is severely affected by the packet distribution, we need to find an optimal packet distribution method.

Optimal Packet Distribution

The intent of using an MMIN is to distribute the packets among multiple paths so that wait delays in intermediate buffers can be shortened. Given the packet arrival rate for any (I,J) pair, a packet distribution method is *optimal*, if the packets are transmitted through the network with a minimum average network delay.

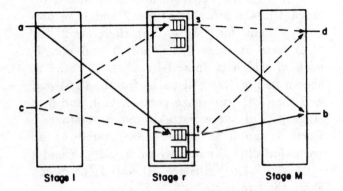

Figure 6.   Port sharing by multiple paths in an MMIN.

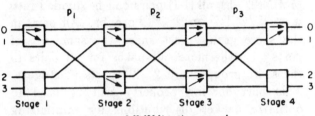

(a) An MMIN(4,4) network

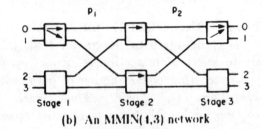

(b) An MMIN(4,3) network

Figure 7.   Two network configurations for illustrating stage limitation.

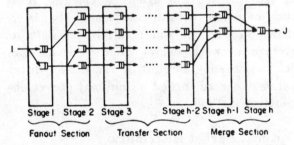

(a) An optimal design with a port degree of 4h-7

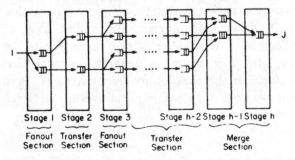

(b) An arbitrary design with a port degree of 4h-9

Figure 8   Various types of stages in a multipath and multistage network.

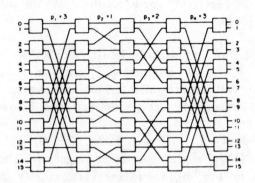

(a)   An MMIN   (16,5)   with   connection sequence (3,1,2,3)

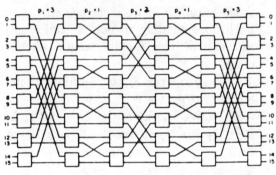

(b) An   MMIN   (16,6)   with   connection sequence (3,1,2,1,3)

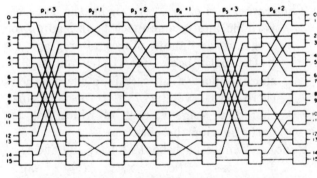

(c) An   MMIN   (16,7)   with   connection sequence (3,1,2,1,3,2)

Figure 9.   Three optimally designed MMIN (16,h)'s for h=5,6, and 7.

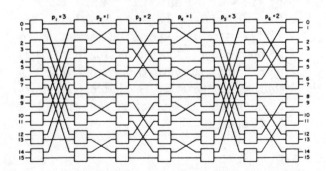

Figure 10.   An arbitrarily designed MMIN(16,7) with connection sequence (3,1,3,1,2,2).

338

Table 1. Connection sequences for MMIN(8,5)

(1,1,1,2)	(1,1,2,1)	
(1,2,1,1)	(2,1,1,1)	* Optimal
(1,1,2,2)	(1,2,1,2)*	sequences
(1,2,2,1)*	(2,1,1,2)*	
(2,1,2,1)*	(2,2,1,1)	
(2,2,2,1)	(2,2,1,2)	
(2,1,2,2)	(1,2,2,2)	

Lemma 1. For a given (I, J) pair in an MMIN(2^m, h), uniformly distributing packets to all reachable output ports at each intermediate stage **v** will result in a minimum average cell delay per packet.

Proof: Let q be defined as in Theorem 1. There are 2^{2m-h+q} independent groups of (I,J) pairs at stage v. Consider a group with all shared ports labeled from 1 to u $= 2^{h-m-q}$. Let R_g be the packet arrival rate for output port g, where $1 \leq g \leq u$. Let $R = \sum_{g=1}^{u} R_g$ be the packet arrival rate for the particular group. By Kleinrock's independence assumption [33], each output port g can be modeled as an M/M/1 queue with a packet arrival rate R_g and a service capacity C at each output port. Let 1/L be the average packet length in bits per packet. Thus the average cell delay D(v) for the particular group at stage v equals

$$D(v) = \frac{1}{R} \sum_{g=1}^{u} \frac{R_g}{C \cdot L - R_g}$$

We need to find the optimal distribution of $\{R_g\}$ in minimizing D(v). Solving the following derivative

$$\frac{\partial D(v)}{\partial R_g} = \frac{C \cdot L}{R \cdot (C \cdot L - R_g)^2} - \frac{C \cdot L}{R \cdot (C \cdot L - R_u)^2}$$

$$= 0$$

for any $g \in \{1,2,...,u\}$, we obtain a uniform distribution: $R_1 = R_2 = \cdots =$

$R_u = R/u$. This implies that uniformly distributing packets for each (I, J) pair can result in a minimum delay.

Q.E.D.

Lemma 1 reveals the optimal packet distribution for a single stage. The method for optimally distributing packets in consecutive stages is described below:

Theorem 2. Among all the packets for each (I,J) pair, equally distributing the packets at each fanout cell to two output ports will result in a minimum average network delay per packet.

Proof: By the properties of k-connections, distributing packets for each (I,J) pair equally to two output ports at each fanout cell will result in a uniform packet distribution among all reachable output ports at each stage. By Lemma 1, packets will be transmitted with minimum average cell delays in all stages. Thus, the distribution method will result in a minimum average network delay.

Q.E.D.

Using the above packet distribution method, the packet load can be balanced in the network, as exemplified below. Let r_1 and r_2 be the packet generation rates for the pairs (3,5) and (5,4) in Fig. 3a, respectively. The rates for other (I,J) pairs are assumed to be zero. Thus, at stage 1, the output ports 2, 3, 4, and 5 are loaded with rates $r_1/2$, $r_1/2$, $r_2/2$, and $r_2/2$, respectively. At stage 3, the packet load will be further balanced. The output ports 0, 2, 4, and 6 are loaded with equal packet rate $(r_1 + r_2)/4$. Once the packet load is balanced among the multiple paths, a shorter average cell delay will be resulted. Thus, the shorter wait delay in an MMIN is due to two factors, i.e. load balancing and multiple paths.

Limitation on Stages

A multipath network is *optimally designed,* if packets can be transmitted with a minimum average network delay. Of course, the packet distribution scheme described in

Theorem 2 must be employed. By Property 1, adding every extra stages will double the number of paths for an (I,J) pair. Some of the paths may share the same output port at certain stages due to Property 4. In other words, the added paths may not necessarily provide more reachable output ports. Thus, the network delay can not be reduced indefinitely by adding an excessive number of stages.

An example is shown in Fig. 7 to clarify this phenomenon. Without loss of generality, we focus on the paths for the (0,0) pair. There are 4 paths from source 0 to destination 0 in Fig. 7a. The situation for packets entering stage 3 is the same as for packets entering stage 2 of Fig. 7b. Each port shares 50% of the packets from source 0 to destination 0. The cell delays at stage 2 of the MMIN(4,3) and at stage 3 of the MMIN(4,4) are equal. Although the MMIN(4,4) has more paths, it did not shorten the wait delays. It even prolongs the packet transmit delay due to the use of one extra stage. In fact, including stage 2 and interstage connection p_2 in the MMIN(4,4) did not help reduce the network delay. We show next how to avoid unnecessary stages in a multipath network.

Lemma 2. If there are three identical interstage patterns, $p_a = p_b = p_c = k$ for some k and $1 \le a < b < c \le h-1$, in the connection sequence of an MMIN(n, h), then the middle interstage pattern p_b and its prior stage b can be deleted to shorten the average network delay.

Proof: Consider a path book $(x_1x_2 \cdots x_a \cdots x_b \cdots x_c \cdots x_h)_2$ for an MMIN(n, h). The x_a and x_b must be variable bits. Now construct an MMIN(n, h-1) by deleting stage b and p_b from the h-stage network. The new network has h-2 interstage connections. The connection pattern p_v of MMIN(n, h-1) equals that of p_v in MMIN(n, h) for $1 \le v < b$, and equals that of p_{v+1} in MMIN(n, h) for $b \le v < h$. Thus, the new path book is encoded as $(y_1y_2 \cdots y_a \cdots y_b \cdots y_{c-1} \cdots y_{h-1})_2$, where

$$y_v = \begin{cases} x_v, & \text{for } 1 \le v < b; \\ x_{v+1}, & \text{for } b \le v < h. \end{cases}$$

At stage b+1 in the MMIN(n, h), the k-th bit of the reachable output ports have value either 0 or 1, regardless of the existence of p_b. In other words, if the paths in the path book $(x_1x_2 \cdots x_a \cdots x_b \cdots x_c \cdots x_h)_2$ visit port j at stage b+1 in the MMIN(n, h), the new path book $(y_1y_2 \cdots y_a \cdots y_b \cdots y_{c-1} \cdots y_{h-1})_2$ also has paths passing through port j at stage b in the MMIN(n, h-1). Since the first b-1 stages and the last h-b stages for both networks have identical connection patterns, by Theorem 2, the average cell delay $D_1(u)$ at stage u of the h-stage network equals the delay $D_2(v)$ at stage v of the (h-1)-stage network, where $v = u$, if $1 \le v < b$, and $v = u+1$, if $b \le v < h$, i.e.

$$D_2(v) = \begin{cases} D_1(v), & \text{for } 1 \le v < b; \\ D_1(v+1), & \text{for } b \le v < h. \end{cases}$$

Thus, we have proved that

$$D_1 = \sum_{u=1}^{h} D_1(u) > \sum_{v=1}^{h-1} D_2(v) = D_2$$

where D_1 and D_2 are the average network delays for the two cases. Thus the stage b and the interstage pattern p_b in the MMIN(n, h) can be deleted.

Q.E.D.

Lemma 2 indicates that having the stage b and the interstage pattern p_b will not increase more reachable ports for any (I,J) pair at stage b + 1. Thus, stage b and connection pattern p_b can be deleted for a better network *performance and cost* ratio. We thus conclude that any interstage pattern should not repeat itself more than twice in an optimally designed multipath network.

Theorem 3. The number of required stages, h, in an optimally designed network $MMIN(n, h)$ must be confined in the following range:

$$\log_2 n + 1 \leq h \leq 2 \log_2 n - 1 \quad (1)$$

Proof: The lower bound is automatic by definition of an $MMIN(n, h)$. Since there are only $\log_2 n - 1$ possible interstage patterns, the upper bound is obtained immediately from Lemma 2. Increasing the stages beyond $2 \log_2 n - 1$ will not further improve the network performance. Instead, it will cause longer delays and higher hardware cost due to added redundancy.

Q.E.D.

5. NETWORK OPTIMIZATION

By Theorem 3, there are at most two interstage patterns having the same *k*-connection for some *k* in any optimally designed network. For every *k*-connection pattern that appears twice, the stage before the first *k*-connection fans out each path into two, whereas the stage after the second one merges two paths into one path. By Property 1, there are 2^{h-m} paths being fanned out. It requires $h-m$ stages to fan out a single path to 2^{h-m} paths as shown in Fig. 8a. These stages are called *fanout stages*. Similarly, we needs the same number of stages to merge 2^{h-m} paths into one destination. These stages are called *merge stages*. The remaining stages of the network are *transfer stages*.

Optimal Networks

By Theorem 1, at an intermediate stage v of $MMIN(2^m, h)$, the number of the reachable output ports for any (I,J) pair is a constant, i.e. 2^{h-m-q}. Thus, the total number of ports that can be reached for any (I,J) pair in h stages is also a constant. This constant is called the *port degree*, which is the single most important topological property of a network. For examples, the port degree for the network in Fig. 8a is $2 + 4(h-3) + 2 + 1 = 4h - 7$. By changing the interstage connection patterns, the port degree of an $MMIN(2^m, h)$ will be

different. As an example, the port degree of the network in Fig. 8b is $2 + 2 + 4(h-4) + 2 + 1 = 4h - 9$. An upper bound on the port degree of a multipath network is obtained below.

Theorem 4. In any $MMIN(2^m, h)$ network, the port degree is upper bounded by

$$B(2^m, h) = (2m - h + 3) \cdot 2^{h-m} - 3 \quad (2)$$

Proof: To achieve the highest port degree, the paths are required to fanout at the earlier stages as possible. Each stage at the transfer section must have 2^{h-m} reachable ports. There are $h - 2(h - m) = 2m - h$ transfer stages. The upper bound on the port degree equals the summation of three factors: $\sum_{i=1}^{h-m} 2^{i-1} + \sum_{i=1}^{h-m} 2^{i-1} + (h - 2(h - m)) \cdot 2^{h-m} = (2m - h + 3) \cdot 2^{h-m} - 3$.

Q.E.D.

By Theorem 4, we need to fan out the paths in a network as early as possible and to merge them as late as possible in order to have more reachable output ports at transfer stages in achieving the maximum port degree. An $MMIN(n, h)$ with a maximum port degree $B(n,h)$ is to be proved as an optimal network.

Theorem 5. An $MMIN(n, h)$ is optimally designed, if the port degree of the network is equal to the upper bound $B(n,h)$ obtained in Eq. (2).

Proof: Consider an $MMIN(n, h)$ network A, which is designed to achieve the upper bound of the port degree, as exemplified in Fig. 8a. Let another $MMIN(n, h)$ network B be constructed from A by mixing transfer stages into fanout and/or merge sections as exemplified in Fig. 8b. The number of reachable ports for an (I,J) pair in any transfer stage mixed into other sections of network B (e.g. stage 2 in Fig. 8b) must be fewer than that in any transfer stage of network A. There are more pair groups in these mixed transfer stages. By Theorem 2, the packet arrival rates at the mixed transfer stages in network B should be less uniformly distributed than that of any transfer stage in network A. By Lemma 1, network A must always have lower average network delay than network B.

Q.E.D.

Optimal Design Procedures

A systematic method is given below for designing an optimal MMIN(n, h) with an optimal *connection sequence* $(p_1, p_2, ..., p_{h-1})$. Two sequential steps are required to generate such an optimal sequence. Note that m = $\log_2 n$ is used in all specifications and Lemma 2 must be satisfied.

Step 1: Pick any permutation $\phi = (\phi(1), \phi(2), ..., \phi(m-1))$ over the set S = {1, 2, ..., m-1}. Assign $(p_{h-m+1}, p_{h-m+2}, ..., p_{h-1}) = (\phi(1), \phi(2), ..., \phi(m-1))$ as the suffix connection sequence among the last m stages.

Step 2: Pick another permutation $\theta = (\theta(p_m), \theta(p_{m+1}), ..., \theta(p_{h-2}), \theta(p_{h-1}))$ over the set T = {$p_m, p_{m+1}, ..., p_{h-2}, p_{h-1}$} obtained in Step 1. Assign $(p_1, p_2, ..., p_{h-m-1}, p_{h-m}) = (\theta(p_m), \theta(p_{m+1}), ..., \theta(p_{h-2}), \theta(p_{h-1}))$ as the prefix connection sequence among the first h-m+1 stages.

Step 1 ensures the inclusion of all *k*-connection patterns where $k \epsilon$ {1, 2, ..., m-1} in the network. Thus from any source, packets can reach any destination. Step 2 replicates the last h-m interstage patterns in the first h-m+1 stages. Therefore, the first h-m stages of the network form a fanout section, and the last h-m stages form a merge section. By Theorem 4, the port degree of such an MMIN(2^m, h) equals the upper bound B(2^m,h). Thus, the network is optimally designed with a minimum network delay as proved in Theorem 5.

There are (m-1)! and (h-m)! possible choices for the permutations ϕ and θ, respectively. Thus, there are in total (m-1)!·(h-m)!

different connection sequences which will result in optimal MMIN (2^m, h) designs. Note that in general the set T $\subseteq$ S. When T = S, the permutation ϕ and θ may and may not be the same. When T $\subset$ S, the ϕ and θ are definitely different. Figure 4 shows two connection sequences {p_1, p_2, p_3, p_4} for designing an optimal MMIN(8, 5).

The network MMIN(8,5) in Fig. 4a is used to illustrate the above design procedures. We first pick a permutation $\phi = (\phi(1), \phi(2)) = (1, 2)$ over the set S = {1, 2}, and assign the suffix sequence $(p_3, p_4) = (\phi(1), \phi(2)) = (1, 2)$ as shown in Fig. 4a. Then we pick another permutation $\theta = (\theta(p_3), \theta(p_4)) = (2, 1)$ over the set T = {p_3, p_4} = {1, 2} and obtain the prefix sequence $(p_1, p_2) = (\theta(p_3), \theta(p_4)) = (2, 1)$. In Fig. 4, both network designs (with connection sequences (2, 1, 1, 2) and (2, 1, 2, 1)) are optimal with the same port degree, i.e. 2+4+4+2+1 = 13, which equals the upper bound B(8,5). As shown in Table 1, there are two more connection sequences, i.e. (1, 2, 1, 2) and (1, 2, 2, 1), which are optimal.

Figure 9 shows three optimal designs, MMIN(16, 5), MMIN(16, 6), and MMIN(16, 7), for a network with 16 nodes. The port degrees of these three networks are B(16,5) = 9, B(16,6) = 17, and B(16,7) = 29, respectively. The MMIN(16, 7) network can be designed from 36 optimal connection sequences out of 540 possible connection sequences, which will guarantee 8 paths for each (I,J) pair. Figure 10 shows an arbitrarily designed MMIN(16, 7) with the connection sequence (3, 1, 3, 1, 2, 2). The port degree of this network is 17 which is lower than the upper bound B(16,7) = 29. Thus this network is not optimally designed and should have longer network delays as compared with the optimal network in Fig. 9c.

6. PERFORMANCE ANALYSIS

Adding extra stages increases the path multiplicity between every (I,J) pair. Packets are thus distributed among multiple paths, which leads to the significantly reduced wait delays at successive stages. On the other hand, the extra stages add to extra circuit transmit delays in the network. The tradeoffs between these two contradictory objectives are analyzed below.

Let t_i be the packet arrival rate at port i, for $i \epsilon \{0, 1, ..., n-1\}$, at stage v. At the steady state, the *stage arrival rate* $T = \sum_{i=0}^{n-1} t_i$ becomes a constant from stage to stage. Let $R = T/n$ be the *mean arrival rate*, averaged over n ports at stage v. Due to our initial assumption, saturation will not take place in the buffer banks. The queue length at each output port can be considered infinite. Let $1/L$ be the average packet length in bits per packet. With Kleinrock's independence assumptions [33], we model each port as an M/M/1 queue with a service rate C which equals the physical transmit rate of the port.

Derived from Theorem 1, We divide all (I,J) pairs at a stage v into $w = 2^{2m-h+q}$ groups. Each group has 2^{h-m-q} reachable ports. Packets for any (I,J) pair are distributed uniformly to all reachable output ports. Thus, ports belonging to the same group s will have the same packet arrival rate, r_s, for $s \epsilon \{1, 2, ..., w\}$. The average *port delay* at each port of group s is thus equal to $(C \cdot L - r_s)^{-1}$. Note that the average value, $\frac{1}{w} \sum_{s=1}^{w} r_s$, must be equal to $R = T/n$. Let $G(w) = \{ (r_1, r_2, ..., r_w) \mid 0 \leq r_s \leq C$ for $1 \leq s \leq w$, and $\frac{1}{w} \sum_{s=1}^{w} r_s = R \}$ be a set of all possible combinations of port arrival rates in w groups. Thus, the average cell delay, $S(w|x)$, for a given rate combination $x \epsilon G(w)$ is calculated by

$$S(w|x) = \frac{1}{w \cdot R} \sum_{s=1}^{w} \frac{r_s}{C \cdot L - r_s}$$

The probability $f(x)$ for any combination $x \epsilon G(w)$ is assumed uniformly distributed. After considering all possible rate combinations, the *average cell delay*, $Z(w)$, at a stage with group w is calculated by

$$Z(w) = \sum_{x \epsilon G(w)} S(w|x) \cdot f(x)$$

$$= \frac{1}{w \cdot R} \sum_{x \epsilon G(w)} \sum_{s=1}^{w} \frac{r_s}{C \cdot L - r_s} \cdot f(x) \qquad (3)$$

In an optimal MMIN(2^m, h), the *average cell delay*, D_v, at stage v is obtained by substituting the group number into Eq. (3), i.e.

$$D(v) = \begin{cases} Z(2^{m-v}) & \text{for } 1 \leq v \leq h-m \\ & \text{(fanout section)} \\ Z(2^{2m-h}) & \text{for } h-m < v \leq m \\ & \text{(transfer section)} \\ Z(2^{m+v-h}) & \text{for } m < v \leq h \\ & \text{(merge section)} \end{cases}$$

Thus, the *average network delay*, $M_{n,h}$, of an optimal MMIN(n, h) can be evaluated by

$$M_{n,h} = \sum_{v=1}^{h} D_v$$

$$= Z(2^m) + 2 \sum_{v=1}^{h-m} Z(2^{m-v})$$

$$+ (2m-h-1) \cdot Z(2^{2m-h}) \qquad (4)$$

In a unique-path MIN(2^m, m), there are always 2^m groups of (I,J) pairs at each stage. The average network delay, U, is thus equal to

$$U = \sum_{v=1}^{m} m \cdot Z(2^m) \qquad (5)$$

We normalize the average cell delay with respect to the service delay, $1/(C \cdot L)$, at each output port. The normalized delay can be obtained by setting $C \cdot L = 1$, and confining r_s in the range $0 \leq r_s \leq 1$.

To exhaust all possible rate combinations in G(w), the time required to compute Z(w) will be in the order of 10^6, 10^{12}, and 10^{24}, ..., summations for w = 2, 4, and 8, ..., respectively; if 0.001 is selected as the sampling scale for the packet rates. Thus, the summation and averaging method is computationally impractical to evaluate Z(w) for any $w \geq 4$. Thus, we have to computer Z(w) by random sampling.

Figure 11 compares the network delays $M_{n,h}$ and U with respect to the number of stages in a network with size n = 64. The average delay of the multipath network is significantly reduced, especially under heavy traffic conditions. When the traffic is light, the delay performance of the proposed networks deteriorates slightly. The improvement is obtained by distributing packets to multiple paths using load balancing. This figure also demonstrates that adding a few extra stages is sufficient to achieve a significantly reduced network delay for practical network sizes.

Figure 12 shows the *improvement* of average network delays, $(U - M_{n,h})$, of various multipath networks from the unique-path networks in various sizes, under heavy traffic condition. The performance of the multipath network can be enhanced by increasing both the network size and the number of extra stages.

The network delays depends on the connection sequence and port degree. However, all optimal networks with the same size should perform equally. The difference between optimally and arbitrarily designed networks is analyzed below using the sample networks in Figs. 7, 9, and 10.

The average network delay for the MMIN(4,4) in Fig. 7a is

$$M_{4,4} = 2\,Z(2) + Z(1) + Z(4) \qquad (6)$$

The average network delay for the MMIN(4,3) in Fig. 7b equals

$$M_{4,3} = 2\,Z(2) + Z(4) \qquad (7)$$

Figure 13 compares $M_{4,3}$ from $M_{4,4}$ on the same plot. The MMIN(4,4) always performs worse than the MMIN(4,3). The extra stage in MMIN(4,4) did not improve the performance. Instead, it caused longer delays. This result confirms the upper bound, $2\log_2 n - 1$, on the number of stages in a multipath network.

The network MMIN(16,7) in Fig. 9c is optimal; whereas the network in Fig. 10 is arbitrarily designed. The average network delay $M^o_{16,7}$ for the optimal network in Fig. 9c equals

$$M^o_{16,7} = 2\,Z(8) + 2\,Z(4) + 2\,Z(2)$$
$$+ Z(16) \qquad (8)$$

The average network delay $M^a_{16,7}$ for the arbitrarily designed network in Fig. 10 equals

$$M^a_{16,7} = 4\,Z(8) + 2\,Z(4) + Z(16) \qquad (9)$$

Figure 14 plots both network delays, which verify the superiority of the optimal design sequence.

7. CONCLUSIONS

A new class of multipath, multistage, interconnection networks has been introduced for packet switched communications in a multiprocessor system or in a dataflow computer. The packet traffic loads are balanced among multiple paths, so that the wait delay in network buffers can be minimized. With the increase of a few stages, the hardware cost of the proposed MMIN networks will have the same complexity, $O(n \log n)$, as in a unique-path MIN, where n is the network size. The concept of k-connection introduced in this paper provides a generalized approach to the specification and implementation of such multipath networks.

In fact, many connection patterns, such as perfect shuffle, cube connections, and Banyan connections, can be established using the proposed k-connection principles. The optimum design criteria for packet switching networks are useful for developing multiprocessor systems or data flow computers, both of which demand pipelined, packet switching with distributed control. With multiple paths, the network bottleneck in a large modular computer system can be greatly alleviated. The overall system performance of the multiprocessor can thus be greatly enhanced.

Another approach to reducing the buffered delays in packet switching networks is to use priority queues (instead of FIFO queues) in crossbar switches as suggested in the companion paper [39]. One can also combine the multipath approach with the priority approach to developing prioritized, multipath, MINs for packet switching. Fault tolerance capability

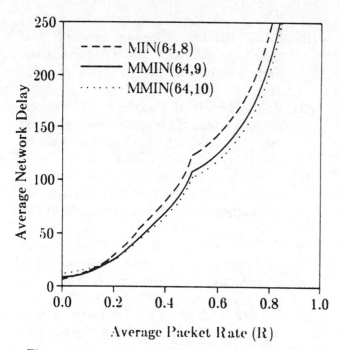

Figure 11. Performance of single-path and multipath networks with n=64 nodes

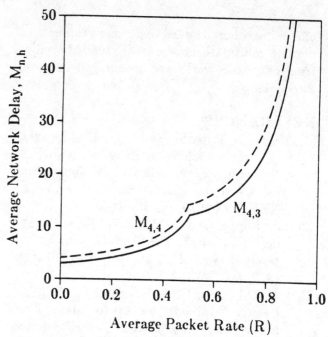

Figure 13. Performance comparison between two networks: MMIN(4,3) and MMIN(4,4).

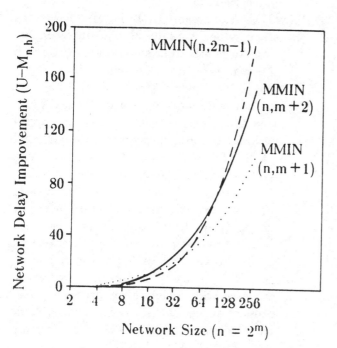

Figure 12. Delay improvement of multipath networks over single-path networks

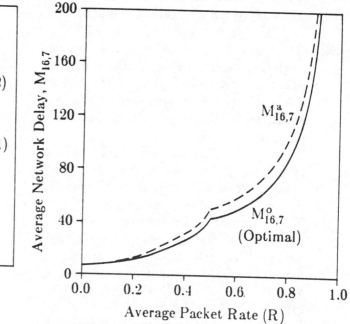

Figure 14. Delay performances of an optimal network and a nonoptimal network for MMIN(16,7).

offers another interesting motivation to develop multipath networks. Extended studies from our basic works are encouraged in these directions.

REFERENCES

[1] A. R. Tripathi and G. J. Lipovski, "Packet switching in Banyan networks," *Proceeding of the 6-th Annual Symposium on Computer Architecture*, New York, NY., April 1979, pp. 160-167.

[2] A. Hopper and D. Wheeler, "Binary routing networks," *IEEE Transactions on Computers*, Vol. C-28, No. 10, October 1979, pp. 699-703.

[3] J. B. Dennis, G. A. Boughton, and C. K. Leung, "Building blocks for data flow prototypes," *Symposium on Computer Architecture*, May 1980, pp. 193-200.

[4] D. M. Dias and J. R. Jump, "Analysis and simulation of buffered delta network," *IEEE Transactions on Computers*, Vol. C-30, No. 4, April 1981, pp.273-282.

[5] D. M. Dias and J. R. Jump, "Packet switching interconnection networks for modular systems," *IEEE Computer*, Vol. 14, No. 12, December 1981, pp. 43-53.

[6] M. Kumar, D. M. Dias, and J. R. Jump, "Switching strategies in a class of packet switching networks," *The 10th Annual International Symposium on Computer Architecture*, Vol. 11, No. 3, June 13-17, 1983, pp. 284-300.

[7] B. J. Smith, "Architecture and application of the HEP multiprocessor computer system," *Real Time Signal Processing IV*, Proceedings of SPIE, August 1981.

[8] H. F. Jordan, "Performance measurements on HEP - a pipelined MIMD computer," *The 10th Annual International Symposium on Computer Architecture*, Vol. 11, No. 3, June 13-17, 1983, pp. 207-212.

[9] J. H. Patel, "Performance of processor-memory interconnections for multiprocessors," *IEEE Transactions on Computers*, Vol. C-20, No. 10, October 1981, pp. 771-780.

[10] K. E. Batcher, "Sorting networks and their applications," *Spring Joint Computer Conference*, Vol. 32, 1968, pp. 307-314.

[11] P. Y. Chen, D. H. Lawrie, P. C. Yew, and D. A. Padua, "Interconnection networks using shuffles," *IEEE Computer*, Vol. 14, No. 12, Dec. 1981, pp. 55-64.

[12] H. Stone, "Parallel processing with the perfect shuffle," *IEEE Transactions on Computers*, Vol. C-20, No. 2, February 1971, pp. 153-161.

[13] C. Wu and T. Feng, "The reverse-exchange interconnection network," *IEEE Transactions on Computers*, Vol. C-29, No. 9, September 1980, pp. 801-811.

[14] V. Benes, *Mathematical Theory of Connecting Networks*, Academic Press, N.Y., 1965.

[15] C. D. Thompson, "Generalized connection networks for parallel processor interconnection," *IEEE Transactions on Computers*, Vol. C-27, No. 12, December 1978, pp. 1119-1125.

[16] G. B. Adams and H. J. Siegel, "The extra stage cube: a fault-tolerant interconnection network for supersystems," *IEEE Transactions on Computers*, Vol. C-31, No. 5, May 1982, PP. 443-454.

[17] E. Horowitz and A. Zorat, "The binary tree as an interconnection network: applications to multiprocessor systems and VLSI," *IEEE Transactions on Computers*, Vol. C-30, No. 4, April 1981, pp. 247-253.

[18] S. B. Wu and M. T. Liu, "A cluster structure as an interconnection network for large multimicrocomputer systems," *IEEE Transactions on Computers*, Vol. C-30, No. 4, April 1981, pp. 254-265.

[19] D. P. Agrawal, "Graph theoretical analysis and design of multistage interconnection networks," *IEEE Transactions on Computers*, Vol. C-32, No. 7, July 1983, pp. 637-648.

[20] D. K. Pradhon and K. L. Kodandapani, "A uniform representation of single and multiple interconnection networks used in SIMD machines," *IEEE Transactions on Computers*, Vol. C-29, No. 9, September

1980, pp. 777-790.

[21] T. Y. Feng, "A survey of interconnection networks," *IEEE Computer,* December 1981, pp. 12-30.

[22] D. D. Gajski, D. J. Kuck, and Padua, "Dependence driven computations," *Proceedings of Compcon,* February 1981, pp. 168-172.

[23] J. Gurd and I. Watson, "Data driven system for high-speed parallel computing," *Computer Design,* Parts I & II, June-July 1980.

[24] Arvind, V. Kathail, and K. Pingali, "A dataflow architecture with tagged tokens," *Technique Memo 174,* Laboratory for Computer Science, MIT, September 1980.

[25] K. P. Gostelow and R. E. Thomas, "Performance of a simulated dataflow computer," *IEEE Transactions on Computers,* October 1980, pp. 905-919.

[26] S. P. Su, "Pipelining and dataflow techniques for designing supercomputers," *Ph.D. Thesis,* School of Electrical Engineering, Purdue University, December 1982.

[27] Arvind and R. A. Iannucci, "A critique of multiprocessing von Neumann style," *Proceedings on Computer Architecture,* June 13-17, 1983, pp. 426-436.

[28] P. C. Treleaven, D. R. Brownbridge, and R. P. Hopkins, "Data-driven and demand-driven computer architecture," *ACM Computing Surveys,* March 1982, pp. 93-144.

[29] K. Hwang and F. A. Briggs, *Computer Architecture and Parallel Processing,* McGraw-Hill Book Co., New York, Chaps. 7 and 10, March 1984.

[30] L. C. Widdos, Jr., "The S-1 project: Developing high-performance digital computers," *Digest of papers: Compcon,* Spring 1980, pp. 282-291.

[31] D. Gajski, D. Kuck, D. Lawrie, and A. Sameh, "Cedar- A large scale multiprocessor," *Proceedings of the 1983 International Conference Parallel Processing,* 1983, pp. 524-529.

[32] A. K. Jones and P. Schwarz, "Experience using multiprocessing systems - A status report," *ACM Computing Surveys,* June 1980, pp. 121-178.

[33] L. Kleinrock, *Communication Networks: Stochastic Message Flow and Delay.* New York: McGraw-Hill, 1964.

[34] L. N. Bhuyan and D. P. Agrawal, "Design and performance of generalized interconnection networks," *IEEE Transactions on Computers,* Vol. C-32, No. 12, December 1983, pp. 1081-1090.

[35] C. P. Kruskal and M. Snir, "The performance of multistage interconnection networks for multiprocessors," *IEEE Transactions on Computers,* Vol. C-32, No. 12, December 1983, pp. 1091-1098.

[36] K. Padmanabhan and D. H. Lawrie, "A class of redundant path multistage interconnection networks," *IEEE Transactions on Computers,* Vol. C-32, No. 12, December 1983, pp. 1099-1108.

[37] E. Opper and M. Malek, "Resource allocation for a class of problem structures in multistage interconnection network-based system," *Proceedings of the 3rd Int'l Conference on Distributed Computing Systems,* October 1982, pp. 106-113.

[38] Y. A. Oruc and M. Y. Oruc, "Equivalence Relations Among Interconnection Networks," *Journal of Parallel and Distributed Computing,* Vol. 1, No. 2, Dec. 1984.

[39] C. Y. Chin and K. Hwang, "Priority queueing analysis of packet switching networks," *Proceedings of Int'l Conference on Parallel Processing,* August 1984.

[40] M. Kumar and J. R. Jump, "Performance enhancement in buffered delta networks using crossbar switches and multiple links," *Journal of Parallel and Distributed Computing,* Vol. 1, No. 1, August 1984.

Multiprocessor Scheduling with the Aid of Network Flow Algorithms

HAROLD S. STONE, MEMBER, IEEE

Abstract—In a distributed computing system a modular program must have its modules assigned among the processors so as to avoid excessive interprocessor communication while taking advantage of specific efficiencies of some processors in executing some program modules. In this paper we show that this program module assignment problem can be solved efficiently by making use of the well-known Ford-Fulkerson algorithm for finding maximum flows in commodity networks as modified by Edmonds and Karp, Dinic, and Karzanov. A solution to the two-processor problem is given, and extensions to three and *n*-processors are considered with partial results given without a complete efficient solution.

Index Terms—Computer networks, cutsets, distributed computers, Ford–Fulkerson algorithm, load balancing, maximum flows.

I. INTRODUCTION

DISTRIBUTED processing has been a subject of recent interest due to the availability of computer networks such as the Advanced Research Projects Agency Network (ARPANET), and to the availability of microprocessors for use in inexpensive distributed computers. Fuller and Siewiorek [8] characterize distributed computer systems in terms of a coupling parameter such that array computers and multiprocessors are tightly coupled, and computers linked through ARPANET are loosely coupled. In loosely coupled systems the cost of interprocessor communication is sufficiently high to discourage the execution of a single program distributed across several computers in the network. Nevertheless, this has been considered for ARPANET by Thomas and Henderson [17], Kahn [12], and Thomas [16].

In this paper we focus on the type of distributed system that Fuller and Siewiorek treat as systems with intermediate coupling. A primary example of this type of system is the multiprocessor interface message processor for ARPANET designed by Bolt, Beranek, and Newman (Heart *et al.* [10]). Two-processor distributed systems are widely used in the form of a powerful central processor connected to a terminal-oriented satellite processor. Van Dam [18] and Foley *et al.* [7] describe two-processor systems in which program modules may float from processor to processor at load time or during the execution of a program. The ability to reassign program modules to different processors in a distributed system is essential to make the best use of system resources as programs change from one computation phase to another or as system load changes.

Manuscript received November 7, 1975; revised July 9, 1976. This work was supported in part by the National Science Foundation under Grant DCR 74-20025.

The author is with the Department of Electrical and Computer Engineering, University of Massachusetts, Amherst, MA 01002.

In this paper we treat the problem of assigning program modules to processors in a distributed system. There are two kinds of costs that must be considered in such an assignment. In order to reduce the cost of interprocessor communication, the program modules in a working set should be coresident in a single processor during execution of that working set. To reduce the computational cost of a program, program modules should be assigned to processors on which they run fastest. The two kinds of assignments can be incompatible. The problem is to find an assignment of program modules to processors that minimizes the collective costs due to interprocessor communication and to computation. We show how to make such an assignment efficiently by using methods of Ford and Fulkerson [6], Dinic [3], Edmonds and Karp [4], and Karzanov [13] that have been developed for maximizing flows in commodity networks. The two-processor assignment problem can be stated as a commodity flow problem with suitable modifications. We show how to construct a graph for the *n*-processor problem for which a minimal cost cut is a minimal cost partition of the graph into *n* disjoint subgraphs. We give partial results for finding the minimal cost cut but, unfortunately, an efficient solution has not yet been obtained.

In Section II of this paper we discuss the computer model in more detail. Section III reviews the essential aspects of commodity flow problems. The main results of this paper appear in Section IV, in which we show how to solve the two-processor problem, and in Section V, in which we consider the *n*-processor problem. A brief summary with an enumeration of several questions for future research appears in the final section.

II. THE MULTIPROCESSOR MODEL

We use a model of a multiprocessor based on the multiprocessor system at Brown University [18], [15]. In this model, each processor is an independent computer with full memory, control, and arithmetic capability. Two or more processors are connected through a data link or high-speed bus to create a multiprocessor system. The processors need not be identical; in fact, the system cited above has a System/360 computer linked to a microprogrammable minicomputer. This much of the description of the model fits many systems. The distinguishing feature of the multiprocessor under discussion is the manner in which a program executes. In essence, each program in this model is a serial program, for which execution can shift dynamically from processor to processor. The two processors may both be multiprogrammed, and may execute concurrently on different programs, but may not execute concurrently on the same program.

A program is partitioned into functional modules some of

Reprinted from *IEEE Transactions on Software Engineering*, Volume SE-3, Number 1, January 1977, pages 85-94. Copyright © 1977 by The Institute of Electrical and Electronics Engineers, Inc.

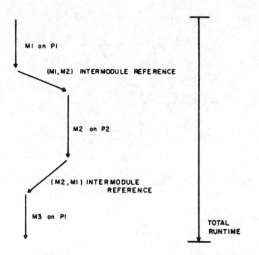

Fig. 1. Module $M1$ calls module $M2$ on a distributed computer system.

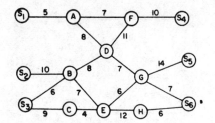

Fig. 2. Commodity flow network.

which are assigned to particular processors, the remainder of which are permitted to "float" from processor to processor during program execution. Some modules have a fixed assignment because these modules depend on facilitites within their assigned processor. The facilities might be high-speed arithmetic capability, access to a particular data base, the need for a large high-speed memory, access to a specific peripheral device, or the need for any other facility that might be associated with some processor and not with every processor.

When program execution begins, the floating modules are given temporary assignments to processors, assignments that reflect the best guess as to where they should reside for maximum computation speed. As execution progresses, the floating modules are free to be reassigned so as to improve execution speed and to reflect the changing activity of the program. Here we presume that interprocessor communication incurs relatively high overhead, whereas computations that make no calls to other processors incur zero additional overhead. Fig. 1 shows the sequence of events that occur when module $M1$ on processor $P1$ calls module $M2$ on processor $P2$. The program state shifts from processor $P1$ to processor $P2$, and returns to processor $P1$ when module $M2$ returns control to $M1$. Instead of transferring state to $P2$, it may be better to colocate $M1$ and $M2$ on the same computer. The choice depends on the number of calls between $M1$ and $M2$, and on the relationship of $M2$ and $M1$ to other modules.

The advantage of this type of approach over other forms of multiprocessing is that it takes advantage of program locality. When activity within a program is within one locality, in ideal circumstances all the activity can be forced to reside within one processor, thereby eliminating conflicts due to excessive use of shared resources. The locality need not be known beforehand, because program modules tend to float to processors in which their activity is highest. Another type of multiprocessor is exemplified by C.mmp (Wulf and Bell [19]) in which up to 16 minicomputers and 16 memories are linked together through a crossbar. The coupling among processors in this system is very tight because potentially every memory fetch accesses memory through the crossbar. Conflicts are potentially high because two or more processors may attempt to access the same memory module simultaneously for an extended period of time.

In the present model, we eliminate the costly crossbar, the degradation on every memory access due to delays through the crossbar, and the potential for conflicts on every memory access to further degrade memory access. If this model is more effective than the crossbar architecture of C.mmp, it is because the costly interprocessor calls incurred in practice occur rarely due to the ability to assign program working sets to a single processor. Whether or not this is the case has not been settled. The question of the relative effectiveness of this architecture and the crossbar architecture has barely been investigated at this writing. The memory assignment algorithm described in the following sections indicates that it is possible to control a distributed computer of the type under study here reasonably efficiently, thereby opening the door to further and deeper studies of this idea.

III. MAXIMUM NETWORK FLOWS AND MINIMUM CUTSETS

In this section we review the commodity flow problem for which Ford and Fulkerson formulated a widely used algorithm [6]. The algorithm is reasonably fast in practice, but the original formulation of the algorithm is subject to rather inefficient behavior in pathological cases. Edmonds and Karp [4] have suggested several different modifications to the Ford-Fulkerson algorithm so as to eliminate many of the inefficiencies, at least for the pathological examples, and to obtain improved worst-case bounds on the complexity of the algorithm. Dinic [3] and Karzanov [13] have derived other ways to increase speed.

In this section we shall describe the problem solved by the Ford-Fulkerson algorithm as modified by Edmonds and Karp, but we shall refer the reader to the literature for descriptions of the various implementations of the algorithm. The important idea is that we can treat an algorithm for the solution of the maximum flow problem as a "black box" to solve the module assignment problem. We need not know exactly what algorithm is contained in the black box, provided that we know the implementation is computationally efficient for our purposes.

The maximum flow problem is a problem involving a commodity network graph. Fig. 2 shows the graph of such a network.

The nodes labeled S_1, S_2, and S_3 are source nodes, and the nodes labeled S_4, S_5, and S_6 are sink nodes. Between these subsets of nodes lie several interior nodes with the entire collection of nodes linked by weighted branches. Source nodes represent production centers, each theoretically capable

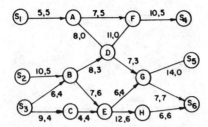

Fig. 3. Flow in a commodity flow network.

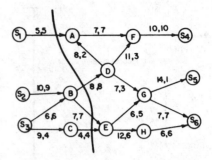

Fig. 4. Maximum flow and minimum cut in a commodity flow network.

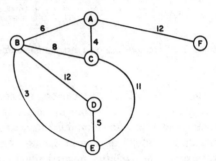

Fig. 5. Intermodule-connection graph.

of producing an infinite amount of a specific commodity. Sink nodes represent demand centers, each of which can absorb an infinite amount of the commodity. The branches represent commodity transport linkages, with the weight of a branch indicating the capacity of the corresponding link.

A *commodity flow* in this network is represented by weighted directed arrows along the branches of the network, with the weight of the arrow indicating the amount of the flow on that branch, and the direction of the arrow indicating the direction of the commodity flow. Fig. 3 shows a commodity flow for the graph in Fig. 2. Each arrow in Fig. 3 carries a pair of numbers, the first of which is the capacity of that branch and the second of which is the actual flow on that branch. A *feasible* commodity flow in this network is a commodity flow originating from the source nodes and ending at the sink nodes such that: 1) at each intermediate node, the sum of the flows into the node is equal to the sum of the flows out of the node; 2) at each sink node the net flow into the nodes is nonnegative, and at each source node the net flow directed out of the node is nonnegative; and 3) the net flow in any branch in the network does not exceed the capacity of that branch. Note that the flow in Fig. 3 is a feasible flow according to this definition. The three constraints in this definition guarantee that interior nodes are neither sources nor sinks, that source nodes and sink nodes are indeed sources and sinks, respectively, and that each branch is capable of supporting the portion of the flow assigned to it.

The *value* of a commodity flow is the sum of the net flows out of the source nodes of the network. Because the net flow into the network must equal the net flow out of the network, the value of a commodity flow is equal to the sum of net flows into the sink nodes. The value of the flow in Fig. 3 is 18. A *maximum flow* is a feasible flow whose value is maximum among all feasible flows. Fig. 4 shows a maximum flow for the network in Fig. 2.

The maximum flow in Fig. 4 is related to a cutset of the network. A *cutset* of a commodity network is a set of edges which when removed disconnects the source nodes from the sink nodes. No proper subset of a cutset is a cutset. Note that branches (S_1, A), (B, E), (B, D), and (C, E) form a cutset of the graph in Fig. 4. The *weight* of a cutset is equal to the sum of the capacities of the branches in the cutset. The weight of the above cutset is 24, which is equal to the value of the maximum flow. This is not a coincidence, because central to the Ford-Fulkerson algorithm is the following theorem.

Max-flow, Min-cut Theorem (Ford and Fulkerson [6]): The value of a maximum flow in a commodity network is equal to the weight of a minimum weight cutset of that network.

The proof of this theorem and a good tutorial description of algorithms for finding a maximum flow and minimum weight cutset appear in Ford and Fulkerson [6]. A very clear treatment of both the Ford-Fulkerson algorithm and the Edmonds-Karp modifications appear in Even [5]. At this point we note that the commodity flow problem as described can be solved in a time bounded from above by the fifth power of the number of nodes in the graph. All of the variations of the maximum flow algorithm of interest compute both a maximum flow in the graph and find a minimum weight cutset. We shall make use of this fact in solving the module assignment problem because each possible assignment corresponds to a cutset of a commodity graph, and the optimum assignment corresponds to a minimum weight cutset.

IV. THE SOLUTION TO THE TWO-PROCESSOR ASSIGNMENT PROBLEM

In this section we show how the maximum-flow algorithm finds an optimal partition of a modular program that runs on a two-processor system. In the following section we show how this algorithm generalizes to systems with three or more processors.

To use the maximum flow algorithm we develop a graphical model of a modular program. Fig. 5 shows a typical example in which each node of the graph represents a module and the branches of the graph represent intermodule linkages. The modules should be viewed as program segments which either contain executable instructions plus local data or contain global data accessible to other segments. The weights on the

TABLE I

Module	P_1 Run Time	P_2 Run Time
A	5	10
B	2	∞
C	4	4
D	6	3
E	5	2
F	∞	4

branches indicate the cost of intermodule references when the modules are assigned to different computers. We assume that the cost of an intermodule reference is zero when the reference is made between two modules assigned to the same computer.

The cost function used to compute the branch weights may vary depending on the nature of the system. Initially we choose to minimize the absolute running time of a program, without permitting dynamic reassignments. We modify the constraints later. The weight of a branch under this assumption is the total time charged to the intermodule references represented by the branch. Thus if k references between two modules occur during the running of a program and each reference takes t seconds when the modules are assigned to different computers, then the weight of the branch representing these references is kt.

The graph in Fig. 5 captures the notion of the costs for crossing boundaries between processors. This is only part of the assignment problem. We must also consider the relative running time of a module on different processors. One processor may have a fast floating-point unit, or a faster memory than another processor, and this may bias the assignment of modules. Table I gives the cost of running the modules of the program in Fig. 5 on each of two processors. The symbol ∞ in the table indicates an infinite cost, which is an artifice to indicate that the module cannot be assigned to the processor. Since our objective in this part of the discussion is to minimize the total absolute running time of a program, the costs indicated in Table I give the total running time of each module on each processor.

In this model of a distributed computing system, there is no parallelism or multitasking of module execution within a program. Thus the total running time of a program consists of the total running time of the modules on their assigned processors as given in Table I plus the cost of intermodule references between modules assigned to different processors. Note that an optimum assignment must take into consideration both the intermodule reference costs and the costs of running the modules themselves. For the running example, if we assume that B must be assigned to P_1, and F must be assigned to P_2, then the optimum way of minimizing the intermodule costs alone is to view B and F as source and sink, respectively, of a commodity-flow network. The minimum cut is the minimum intermodule cost cut, and this assigns B, C, D, and E to P_1, and A and F to P_2. On the other

hand, an optimum way to minimize only the running time of the individual modules is to assign A, B, and C to P_1 and D, E, and F to P_2. But neither of these assignments minimize the total running time.

To minimize the total running time, we modify the module interconnection graph so that each cutset in the modified graph corresponds in a one-to-one fashion to a module assignment and the weight of the cutset is the total cost for that assignment. With this modification, we can solve a maximum flow problem on the modified graph. The minimum weight cutset obtained from this solution determines the module assignment, and this module assignment is optimal in terms of total cost.

We modify the module interconnection graph as follows.

1) Add nodes labeled S_1 and S_2 that represent processors P_1 and P_2, respectively. S_1 is the unique source node and S_2 is the unique sink node.

2) For each node other than S_1 and S_2, add a branch from that node to each of S_1 and S_2. The weight of the branch to S_1 carries the cost of executing the corresponding module on P_2, and the weight of the branch to S_2 carries the cost of executing the module on P_1. (The reversal of the subscripts is intentional.)

The modified graph is a commodity flow network of the general type exemplified by the graph in Fig. 2. Each cutset of the commodity flow graph partitions the nodes of the graph into two disjoint subsets, with S_1 and S_2 in distinct subsets. We associate a module assignment with each cutset such that if the cutset partitions a node into the subset containing S_1, then the corresponding module is assigned to processor P_1. Thus the cut shown in Fig. 6 corresponds to the assignment of A, B, and C to P_1 and D, E, and F to P_2.

With this association of cutsets to module assignments it is not difficult to see that module assignments and cutsets of the commodity flow graph are in one-to-one correspondence. (The one-to-one correspondence depends on the fact that each interior node is connected directly to a source and sink, for otherwise, a module assignment might correspond to a subset of edges that properly contains a cutset.) The following theorem enables us to use a maximum flow algorithm to find a minimum cost assignment.

Theorem: The weight of a cutset of the modified graph is equal to the cost of the corresponding module assignment.

Proof: A module assignment incurs two types of costs. One cost is from intermodule references from processor to processor. The other cost incurred is the cost of running each module on a specific processor. The cutset corresponding to a module assignment contains two types of branches. One type of branch represents the cost of intermodule references for modules in different processors, and a particular assignment. All costs due to such references contribute to the weight of the corresponding cutset, and no other intermodule references contribute to the weight of the cutset.

The second type of branch in a cutset is a branch from an internal node to a source or sink node. If an assignment places a module in processor P_1, then the branch between that node and S_2 is in the cutset, and this contributes a cost equal to the cost of running that module on P_1, because the

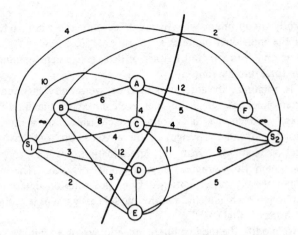

Fig. 6. Modified module-interconnection graph and a cut that determines a module assignment.

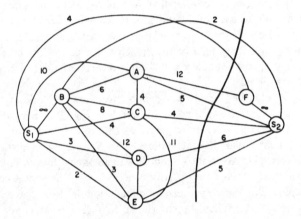

Fig. 7. Minimum cost cut.

branch to S_2 carries the P_1 running time cost. Similarly, the cost of assigning a module to P_2 is reflected by adding the cost of running that module on P_2 to the weight of the cutset.

Thus the weight of a cutset accounts for all costs due to its corresponding assignment, and no other costs contribute to the weight. This proves the theorem.

The theorem indicates that an optimal assignment can be found by running a maximum flow algorithm on the modified graph. A maximum flow algorithm applied to the graph shown in Fig. 6 produces the minimum weight cutset shown in Fig. 7. The corresponding module assignment is different from the assignment that minimizes the cost of intermodule references and the assignment that minimizes the individual running time costs, and its total cost is lower than the total cost of either of the two other assignments.

At this point the basic essentials for treating the module assignment problem as a maximum flow problem are clear. There remain a number of details concerning the practical implementation of the algorithm that merit discussion.

The running example indicates how to select an optimum *static* assignment that minimizes total running time. We mentioned earlier that it makes sense to change assignments dynamically to take advantage of local behavior of programs and the relatively infrequent changes in program locality. To

solve the dynamic assignment problem we essentially have to solve a maximum flow problem at each point in time during which the working set of a program changes. Fortunately, the dynamic problem is no harder than the static one, except for the need to solve several maximum flow problems instead of a single one. The only additional difficulty in dynamic assignments is detecting a change in the working set of a program. Since a control program must intervene to perform intermodule transfers across processor boundaries, it should monitor such transfers, and use changes in the rate and nature of such transfers as a signal that the working set has changed. Thus we can reasonably expect to solve the dynamic assignment problem if it is possible to solve a static assignment problem for each working set.

The major difficulty in solving a static assignment problem is obtaining the requisite data for driving the maximum flow algorithm. It is not usually practical to force the user to supply these data, nor is it completely acceptable to use compiler generated estimates. Some of the data can be gathered during program execution. The cost of each invocation of a module on a particular processor can be measured by a control program, and it usually measures this anyway as part of the system accounting. However, we need to know the cost of running a module on each processor to compute an optimal assignment, and we certainly cannot ship a module to every other processor in a system for a time trial to determine its relative running time.

A reasonable approximation is to assume that the running time of a module on processor P_1 is a fixed constant times the running time of that module on processor P_2 where the constant is determined in advance as a measure of the relative power of the processors without taking into consideration the precise nature of the program to be executed. Under these assumptions if we can gather data about intermodule references, we can obtain sufficient data to drive the maximum flow algorithm. If after making one or more assignments a module is executed on different computers, sufficient additional information can be obtained to refine initial estimates of relative processor performance. The refined data should be used in determining new assignments as the data are collected.

How do we collect data concerning intermodule references? Here the collection of data follows a similar philosophy as for running time measurements. Initially an analysis of the static program should reveal where the intermodule references exist, and these in turn can be assumed to be of equal weight to determine an initial assignment. We assume that we automatically measure the intermodule references across processor boundaries because all such references require control program assistance. In measuring these references we obtain new data that refine the original estimates. If as a result of the refinement of these data we reassign modules, then we obtain new data about intermodule links that further refine the data, which in turn permit a more accurate appraisal of a minimum cost assignment.

At this writing the control methodology described here has been implemented by J. Michel and R. Burns on the system described by Stabler [15] and van Dam [18]. That system gathers the requisite statistics in real time in a suitable form

Fig. 8. Module-interconnection graph.

TABLE II

Module	P_1 Time	P_2 Time	P_3 Time
A	4	-	-
B	-	6	-
C	-	-	7
D	10	7	5
E	4	7	3

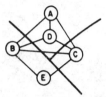

Fig. 9. Cut representing a module assignment to three processors.

for input to the algorithm. It is too early to say how effective the statistics gathering and automatic reassignment processes are in performing load balancing, but it is safe to say that the ability to gather suitable statistics automatically has been demonstrated.

In closing this section we take up one last subject, that of considering objective functions other than total running time. There are many suitable cost functions one may wish to use. For example, instead of absolute time, one may choose to minimize dollars expended. For this objective function, the intermodule reference costs are measured in dollars per transfer, and the running time costs of each module are measured in dollars for computation time on each processor, taking into account the relative processor speeds and the relative costs per computation on each processor. Many other useful objective functions can be met by choosing the cost function appropriately. We should also point out that generalizations of the maximum flow algorithm are applicable to module assignment problems under more complex cost measures. The most notable maximum flow problem generalization is the selection of a maximum flow with minimum cost. For this problem each flow is associated with both a flow value and a cost. The algorithm selects among several possible maximum flows to return the one of minimum cost. The equivalent problem for the module assignment problem is to find an assignment that achieves fastest computation time and incurs the least dollar cost of all such assignments.

The fact that the two-processor assignment problem is mapped into a commodity flow problem for solution suggests that the flow maximized in the commodity flow problem corresponds to some physical entity flowing between the two-processors in the two-processor assignment problem. There is no such correspondence, however, since the maximal flow value corresponds to time in a two-processor assignment, and not to information flow.

V. EXTENSION TO THREE OR MORE PROCESSORS

In this section we show how the module assignments to three or more processors can be accomplished by using the principles described in the previous section. We first obtain a suitable generalization of the notion of cutset. Then we describe a procedure to construct a modified graph of a program such that its cutsets are in one-to-one correspondence with the multiprocessor cutsets, and the value of each cutset is equal to the cost of the corresponding assignment. Finally we consider how to solve the generalized multiprocessor flow problem, and obtain partial results but no efficient solution.

Let us take as a running example the three-processor program shown in Fig. 8 with the running times for each pro-

cessor given in Table II. Since we have to assign the nodes to three rather than to two processors, we need to generalize the notion of cutset. Let us designate the source and sink nodes of a commodity network to be distinguished nodes, and we say they are distinguished of type *source* or type *sink*. For the n-processor problem we shall have n types of distinguished nodes. This leads naturally to the following definition.

Definition: A *cutset* in a commodity flow graph with n types of nodes is a subset of edges that partitions the nodes of the graph into n disjoint subsets, each of which contains all of the distinguished nodes of a single type plus a possibly empty collection of interior nodes. No proper subset of a cutset is also a cutset.

A cutset for the network of Fig. 8 appears in Fig. 9. We shall deal with networks in which there is a single distinguished node of each type, and this node represents the processor to which the interior nodes associated with it are assigned.

Proceeding as before we modify the intermodule reference graph of a program to incorporate the relative running time costs of each module on each processor. Again we add a branch from each interior node to each distinguished node as in the two-processor case. The weight on each such branch is computed by a formula explained below and exemplified in Fig. 10. The weights are selected so that, as in the two-processor case, the value of a cutset is equal to total running time.

For simplicity Fig. 10 does not show the branches from nodes A, B, and C to nodes to which they are not assigned. Suppose that module D runs in time T_i on processor P_i, $i = 1, 2, 3$. Then the branch from node D to distinguished node S_1 carries the weight $(T_2 + T_3 - T_1)/2$, and likewise the branches to nodes S_2 and S_3 carry the weights $(T_1 + T_3 - T_2)/2$, and $(T_1 + T_2 - T_3)/2$, respectively. Under this weight assignment, if D is assigned to processor P_1, the arcs to S_2 and S_3 are cut, and their weights total to T_1, the running time of D on P_1.

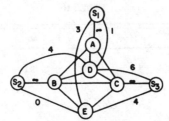

Fig. 10. Modified module-interconnection graph for a three-processor assignment.

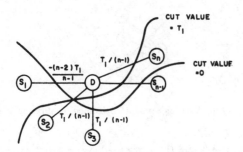

Fig. 11. Two possible assignments of module D in an n-processor system.

This idea generalizes naturally to n-processors. The running time of D on P_1 contributes to the weight of the branches from D to every distinguished node S_i, $i = 1, 2, \cdots, n$. Its contribution to the branch to S_1 is $-(n-2)T_1/(n-1)$. Its contribution to the branch to S_i, $i \neq 1$, is $T_1/(n-1)$. If D is assigned to S_1, then $n-1$ branches are cut, each of which contributes $T_1/(n-1)$ to the cutset, giving a net contribution of T_1. If D is assigned to S_i, $i \neq 1$, then $n-2$ branches contribute $T_1/(n-1)$ to the cutset weight and the branch to S_1 contributes $-(n-2)T_1/(n-1)$ for a net contribution of zero. This is shown graphically in Fig. 11. Consequently, under the graph modification scheme described here, we obtain the desired property that the weight of a cutset is equal to the cost of the corresponding module assignment.

One problem with this scheme is that some individual edges of the graph may have a negative capacity, and this cannot be treated by maximum flow algorithms. This problem can easily be overcome, however. Suppose that among the branches added to node D is an arc with negative weight $-W$, and this is the most negative of the weights of the branches added to node D. Then increase the weights of all branches added to D by the amount $W + 1$, and we claim that no branch has negative weight after this change. Moreover, every cut that isolates D from a distinguished node breaks precisely $(n-1)$ of the branches added to D, contributing a value to the cutset of $(n-1)(W+1)$ plus the run time of D on the processor corresponding to the cut. The term $(n-1)(W+1)$ is a constant independent of the assignment so that an assignment that minimizes the cutset weight in the present graph is an assignment that finds a minimum time solution of the original problem.

At this point we come to the question of finding a minimum cutset in an n-processor graph. The solution can be found

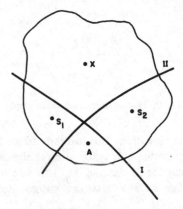

Fig. 12. Two cutsets in a graph.

by exhaustive enumeration but the computational complexity of such an approach is quite unattractive. It seems natural that the n-processor problem can be reduced to several two-processor flow problems, and can be attacked efficiently in this way. In the remainder of this section we show that a two-processor flow can give information about the minimal cut in an n-processor graph, but we are unable to produce a complete efficient algorithm.

Specifically, consider what happens when we run a two-processor flow from S_1 to the subset $\{S_i: 2 \leqslant i \leqslant n\}$, where the nodes in the subset are all sink nodes for the flow. This two-processor flow produces a cutset that associates some nodes with S_1, and the remainder of the nodes in the graph to the subset of $n-1$ distinguished nodes. Does this flow give any information about the minimum cut in the n-processor graph? Indeed it does, as is shown by the following theorem. The proof technique is similar to the proof technique used by Gomory and Hu [9] and Hu [11].

Theorem: Let node A be associated with distinguished node S_1 by a two-processor flow algorithm. Then A is associated with S_1 in a minimum cost partition of the n-processor graph.

Proof: Without loss of generality, suppose that A is associated with S_1 by the two-processor flow algorithm, and that it must be associated with S_2 in a minimum cost partition. We prove the theorem by showing that A can be moved from S_2 to S_1 in the minimum cost partition without altering the cost of the partition. Fig. 12 shows the cutset I that associates A with S_1 when the two-processor flow is run, and the cutset II that associates A with S_2 in the minimum cost partition. These cutsets cross each other, thus dividing the graph into four disjoint regions. Let us denote the four regions as S_1, S_2, A, and X according to the nodes appearing in these regions in Fig. 12. (Region X may be empty, but this will not upset the proof.) Let $c(U, V)$ denote the sum of the weights of all branches between two regions U and V.

Since II is a minimal cut the value of II does not exceed the value of a cut that fails to include A with S_2. Thus,

$$c(S_2, X) + c(S_2, S_1) + c(A, X) + c(A, S_1) \leqslant c(S_2, X)$$
$$+ c(S_2, S_1) + c(S_2, A). \qquad (1)$$

From this we find that $c(A, S_1) \leqslant c(S_2, A) - c(A, X)$, and since all costs are nonnegative we may add $2c(A, X)$ to the right-hand side of the inequality and obtain

$$c(A, S_1) \leqslant c(S_2, A) + c(A, X). \qquad (2)$$

By hypothesis the algorithm associates node A with S_1, with a cost for cut I equal to $c(S_1, X) + c(S_1, S_2) + c(A, X) + c(S_2, A)$. However, if cut I veers slightly to exclude node A, and otherwise remains the same, the cost of the new cut is $c(S_1, X) + c(S_1, S_2) + c(A, S_1)$. Since I is a minimal cost cut, we must have

$$c(A, S_1) \geqslant c(S_2, A) + c(A, X). \qquad (3)$$

From (2) and (3) we find that the inequality in (3) can be changed to equality. Since (3) holds with equality, by substituting (3) into (1) we find $2c(A, X) \leqslant 0$, which must hold with equality since all costs are nonnegative. Then (1) holds with equality. Thus cut II can be altered to exclude node A from S_2's subset and include A with S_1's subset without changing the cost of partition. This proves the theorem.

The previous theorem suggests that a two-processor algorithm may be used several times to find a minimum n-processor cutset. There are some difficulties in extending the theorem, however, that have left the n-processor problem still unsolved. Among the difficulties are the following.

1) The theorem states that a node associated with a distinguished node by a two-processor flow belongs with that node in the minimum n-processor cutset. Unfortunately, it is easy to construct examples in which a node that belongs with a particular distinguished node in a minimum n-processor cutset fails to be associated with that node by a two-processor flow.

2) Suppose a two-processor flow is run that results in the assignment of one or more nodes to a particular distinguished node. Let these nodes and the corresponding distinguished node be removed from the graph, and run a new two-processor flow from some other distinguished node S_i to all of the other distinguished nodes. In the cut found by this algorithm the nodes associated with S_i need not be associated with S_i in a minimum cost n-processor partition. In other words, the theorem does not apply when graph reduction is performed.

We conjecture that at most n^2 two-processor flows are necessary to find the minimum cost partition for n-processor problems, since there are only $n(n-1)/2$ different flows from one distinguished node to another distinguished node. These flows should somehow contain all the information required to find a minimal cost n-processor partition. It is possible that only n two-processor flows are required to solve the problem since Gomory and Hu [9] have shown that there are only $n-1$ independent two-terminal flows in an n-terminal network. This problem remains open at present.

VI. Summary and Conclusions

The two algorithms presented here provide for the assignment of program modules to two processors to minimize the cost of a computation on a distributed computer system. The algorithm uses a maximum flow algorithm as a subroutine so the complexity of the module assignment is dependent upon the implementation of the maximum flow algorithm used. Fortunately, the maximum flow algorithm is generally effi-

cient and there are various modifications of the algorithm that take advantage of special characteristics of the module to obtain increased efficiency (see Dinic [3], Karzanov [13]). To obtain truly optimal assignments, the costs for intermodule transfers and relative running times have to be known. However, if good estimates are available, these can be used to obtain near-optimal assignments that are satisfactory in a pragmatic sense.

One may choose to use the assignment algorithm in a static sense, that is, to find one assignment that holds for the lifetime of a program, and incurs least cost. We believe it is more reasonable to reassign modules dynamically during a computation at the points where working sets change. Each dynamic assignment then is chosen to be optimal for a given working set. Dynamic identification of working sets and the identification of times at which a working set changes is still a subject of much controversy with proposals favoring particular schemes [2] or disfavoring those schemes [14]. Progress in this area will in turn lead to progress in the ability to make dynamic module assignments in a distributed processor system.

The model presented here is highly simplified and idealized, but it is useful in real systems. Foley et al. [7] can use our algorithms in place of their backtracking algorithms to do module reassignment in their distributed computer systems. We suspect that the maximum flow approach is more efficient than backtracking because worst-case performance of backtracking has a much greater complexity than maximum flow algorithm complexity. However, the actual performance of their algorithm may be quite different from worst-case performance, and could have a small average complexity, perhaps lower than the average complexity of maximum flow algorithms. No data on actual running times appears in Foley's report, so there is no information on which to base estimates of relative running times.

There are a number of open problems related to the research reported here. We mention just a few of them here.

1) If the minimum cost module assignment is not unique, then what additional criteria are useful in selecting the most desirable minimum cost assignment? Given such criteria, this form of the problem can be solved by using efficient algorithms to find a maximum flow of minimal cost. Such algorithms are described by Ford and Fulkerson [6] and Edmonds and Karp [4].

2) If a program is divided into tasks that can execute simultaneously under various precedence constraints, how can modules be assigned so as to minimize the cost of computation? This differs from the multiprocessor scheduling problem studied by Coffman and Graham [1] and by others in that there is no cost incurred in that model for interprocessor references.

3) If the various processors in distributed computer systems are each multiprogrammed, and queue lengths become excessive at individual processors, how might modules be reassigned to minimize costs of computation over several programs?

4) Given that a module reassignment incurs a processor-to-processor communi:ation cost, how might the cost of

reassigning a module be factored into the module assignment problem?

Since distributed computer systems are still in early stages of development it is not clear which one of the research questions listed here will emerge to become important questions to solve for distributed computer systems as they come of age. The implementation of the methodology described here on the system at Brown University suggests that automatic load balancing among different processors can be done. We hope that the present and future research will show not only the possibility of load balancing but that it can be done efficiently and that load balancing is an efficient method for tapping the power of a distributed computer system.

ACKNOWLEDGMENT

The author is deeply indebted to Professor Andries van Dam for providing the inspiration and motivation for the research, and to J. Michel and R. Burns for implementing the ideas described here on the ICOPS system at Brown University. Discussions with Professor W. Kohler, S. Bokhari, and P. Jones provided additional stimulation that contributed to the research.

REFERENCES

[1] E. G. Coffman, Jr., and R. L. Graham, "Optimal scheduling for two-processor systems," *Acta Informatica*, vol. 1, pp. 200–213, 1972.
[2] P. J. Denning, "Properties of the working set mode," *Commun. Ass. Comput. Mach.*, vol. 11, pp. 323–333, May 1968.
[3] E. A. Dinic, "Algorithm for solution of a problem of maximum flow in a network with power estimation," *Soviet Math. Doklady*, vol. 11, no. 5, pp. 1277–1280, 1970.
[4] J. Edmonds and R. M. Karp, "Theoretical improvements in algorithm efficiency for network flow problems," *J. Ass. Comput. Mach.*, vol. 19, pp. 248–264, Apr. 1972.
[5] S. Even, *Algorithmic Combinatorics*. New York: Macmillan, 1973.
[6] L. R. Ford, Jr., and D. R. Fulkerson, *Flows in Networks*. Princeton, NJ: Princeton Univ. Press, 1962.
[7] J. D. Foley *et al.*, "Graphics system modeling," Rome Air Development Center, Final Rep. Contract F30602-73-C-0249, Rep. RADC-TR-211, Aug. 1974.
[8] S. H. Fuller and D. P. Siewiorek, "Some observations on semiconductor technology and the architecture of large digital modules," *Computer*, vol. 6, pp. 14–21, Oct. 1973.
[9] R. E. Gomory and T. C. Hu, "Multiterminal network flows," *J. SIAM*, vol. 9, pp. 551–570, Dec. 1961.
[10] F. E. Heart *et al.*, "A new minicomputer/multiprocessor for the ARPA network," in *Proc. 1973 Nat. Comput. Conf.*, *AFIPS Conf. Proc.*, vol. 42. Montvale, NJ: AFIPS Press, 1973.
[11] T. C. Hu, *Integer Programming and Network Flows*. Reading, MA: Addison-Wesley, 1970.
[12] R. E. Kahn, "Resource-sharing computer communications networks," *Proc. IEEE*, vol. 60, pp. 1397–1407, Nov. 1972.
[13] A. V. Karzanov, "Determining the maximal flow in a network by the method of preflows," *Soviet Math. Doklady*, vol. 15 no. 2, pp. 434–437, 1974.
[14] B. G. Prieve, "Using page residency to select the working set parameter," *Commun. Ass. Comput. Mach.*, vol. 16, pp. 619–620, Oct. 1973.
[15] G. M. Stabler, "A system for interconnected processing," Ph.D. dissertation, Brown Univ., Providence, RI, Oct. 1974.
[16] R. H. Thomas, "A resource sharing executive for the ARPANET," in *Proc. 1973 Nat. Comput. Conf.*, *AFIPS Conf. Proc.*, vol. 42. Montvale, NJ: AFIPS Press, 1973.
[17] R. H. Thomas and D. Henderson, "McRoss—A multi-computer programming system," in *Proc. 1972 Spring Joint Comput. Conf.*, *AFIPS Conf. Proc.*, vol. 40. Montvale, NJ: AFIPS Press, 1972.
[18] A. van Dam, "Computer graphics and its applications," Final Report, NSF Grant GJ-28401X, Brown University, May 1974.
[19] W. A. Wulf and C. G. Bell, "C.mmp—A multi-miniprocessor," in *Proc. 1972 Fall Joint Comput. Conf.*, *AFIPS Conf. Proc.*, vol. 41, Part II. Montvale, NJ: AFIPS Press, 1972, pp. 765–777.

**Harold S. Stone** (S'61–M'63) received the B.S. degree from Princeton University, Princeton, NJ, in 1960 and the M.S. and Ph.D. degrees from the University of California, Berkeley, in 1961 and 1963, respectively.

While at the University of California he was a National Science Foundation Fellow and Research Assistant in the Digital Computer Laboratory. From 1963 until 1968 he was with Stanford Research Institute, and from 1968 until 1974 he was Associate Professor of Electrical and Computer Science at Stanford University. He is currently Professor of Electrical and Computer Engineering at the University of Massachusetts, Amherst. He has recently been engaged in research in parallel computation, computer architecture, and advanced memory system organization. In the past he has performed research in several areas including combinatorial algorithms, operating systems, and switching theory. He has authored over thirty technical publications, and is an author, coauthor, or editor of five text books in computer science. He has also been a Visiting Lecturer at the University of Chile, the Technical University of Berlin, and the University of Sao Paulo, and has held a NASA Research Fellowship at NASA Ames Research Center.

Dr. Stone is a member of Sigma Xi and Phi Beta Kappa. He has served as Technical Editor of *Computer Magazine*, and as a member of the Governing Board of the IEEE Computer Society.

Part IV: Algorithms and Applications

Chapter 8: Parallel Algorithms
Chapter 9: Supercomputer Applications

PART IV
ALGORITHMS AND APPLICATIONS

Recent developments in parallel algorithms for vector machines and multiprocessor systems are presented in Chapter 8. Sameh's article (1983) presents numerical algorithms for solving two important problems on multiprocessors. The first problem concerns solving large-scale banded positive definite linear systems such as those frequently required for finite-element analysis. The second problem is related to solving the large, sparse, eigenvalue problems of the form $A \cdot x = \lambda \cdot B \cdot x$ where A and B are symmetric and sparse and B is positive and definite.

The paper (Section 8.2) by Thompson (1983) provides a comprehensive analysis of the area-time complexity of 13 sorting networks, which can be implemented on VLSI chips. Many of these VLSI sorters enjoy a high degree of parallelism.

The paper (Section 8.3) by Dekel, Nassimi, and Sahni (1981) proposes several efficient algorithms for matrix multiplication on cube-connected and perfect-shuffle computers. It is also shown that many graph problems can be solved efficiently by the use of matrix multiplication algorithms.

The article (Section 8.4) by Rice (1983) identifies 12 sources of very large least-square problems such are encountered with the use of supercomputers for geodetic surveys, Tomography, photogrammetry, molecular structure analysis, terrestrial gravity field study force methods in structure analysis, and soluti partial differential equations. Experts' opinions are expressed in this report on the effectiveness of using supercomputers for solving computationally intensive problems.

Chapter 9 is devoted to scientific/engineering applications of supercomputers. The development of supercomputers is driven by the demands of these applications. An excellent treatment of the applications of supercomputers in the United States has been

given in Fernbach's revised article in Section 9.1. Rodrique and his associates have provided some insights on large-scale scientific computations in Section 9.2. Various application issues have been also addressed in the books by Hockney and Jesshope (1981), Rodrigue (1982), Evans (1982), and Hwang and Briggs (1984).

In January 1984, a special issue on **Supercomputers - Their Impact on Science and Technology** appeared in *IEEE Proceedings*. This special issue, edited by George Paul of IBM, contains several interesting articles on digital scene simulation (Demos, Brown and Weenberg 1984), supercomputer support for magnetic fusion energy research (Section 9.3), and supercomputing for aerodynamics applications (Peterson 1984) (Section 9.4),

The special issue also presents other articles for studies of molecular dynamics (Bowler and Pawley 1984), for finite element analysis (Gloudeman 1984), for petroleum reservoir modeling (Nolen and Stanat 1984), for VLSI circuit design (Fichtner et al. 1984), and for solving PDE problems in aerodynamics. We briefly categorize these important applications of supercomputers into four major areas as summarized in Table 4.

Predicative scientific modeling is done through extensive simulation experiments on high-performance computers. Often, large-scale numerical computations need to be performed on a tremendous volume of data arrays, in order to achieve the desired accuracy and turnaround time for weather forecasting, climate predication, oceanographic studies, astrophysical explanations, world economics of modeling, government census, and biological system simulations. The demand for speed has never been satisfied with the use of present-day computers in scientific simulations.

In structural analysis, finite-element analysis requires the use supercomputers to

358

Table 4. Important applications of modern supercomputers.

Objectives: Representative Applications
Predicative Modeling and Simulations: • Numerical Weather Forecasting   • Oceanography and Astrophysics   • Socioeconomics and Government Use   • Biological System Simulation
Engineering Design and Automation: • Finite-Element Structural Analysis   • Computational Aerodynamics   • Artificial Intelligence and Expert Systems   • CAD/CAM/CAD/OA   • Remote Sensing Applications
Energy Resources Exploration: • Seismic Exploration   • Oil Field (Reservoir) Modeling   • Plasma Fusion Energy Research   • Nuclear Reactor Safety

Medical, Military, and Basic Research:
 • Computer-Assisted Tomography
 • Genetic Engineering
 • Weapons Research and Effects
 • Strategic Computing
 • Basic Research (Quantum Mechanics,
    VLSI Circuit Analysis,
    Polymer Chemistry, etc.)

solve large systems of algebraic equations. Computational aerodynamics offers an economic alternative for designing of advanced aircraft without building an expensive wind tunnel (Ballhaus 1984).

Supercomputers are in demand for the advancement of artificial intelligence and design automation, which include signal/image processing, pattern and speech recognition, computer vision and scene analysis, logical inference for developing knowledge database and expert systems, CAD/CAM for industrial automation, intelligent robotics, remote sensing for earth-resource surveys, etc.

Supercomputers have important applications for discoveing oil and gas and managing of their recovery, developing a workable plasma-related fusion energy applications; and for ensuring nuclear reactor safety. The use of computer technology for energy results in lower production costs and higher safety measures.

Seismic signal processing and oil-field reservoir modeling both demand the use of supercomputers to provide accuracy and to save processing time. Magnetic fusion research programs are being aided by vector supercomputers at the Lawrence Livermore National Laboratory and at Princeton's Plasma Physics Laboratory (Fuss and Tull 1984).

The potential for fusion energy has become greater as a result of the Tokamak experiments being supported by computational simulation programs. The U.S. *National Magnetic Fusion Energy Computer Center* is currently using two Cray 1 and one CDC 7600 to aid the controlled plasma experiments. Nuclear reactor design and safety control can be aided also by real-time computer simulations.

Supercomputers are also in demand in modern medical diagnosis, such as in developing fast computer-assisted tomographic scanners in generating three-dimensional and stop-action pictures of a human heart. Genetic engineers demand fast computers for studying molecular biology, for artificial synthesis of protein, and for gel matching in estimating the mutation rate of the human species.

Weapons research agencies have used most of the available supercomputers in the design of multiwarhead missiles, in the study of atomic weapon effects, in intelligence gathering, antiballistic programs, cartographic surveys, robotics warfare, etc.

Basic research in almost every scientific area demands the use of supercomputers. Just to name a few, computational physicists and chemists study quantum mechanics, fluid dynamics, molecular dynamics, and crystal growth using supercomputers.

Semiconductor manufacturers use supercomputers to aid the analysis and synthesis of VLSI circuits. Vectorized SPICE code is now being developed to enhance electronic circuit analysis.

Breakthroughs in many of these scientific applications depend on the availability of reliable computing systems, capable of suggesting new theories, interpreting experiments, modelling real processes, and providing accurate calculations within reasonable time.

Chapter 8: Parallel Algorithms

On Two Numerical Algorithms for Multiprocessors *

A. Sameh
Department of Computer Science
University of Illinois at Urbana-Champaign

1. Introduction

In this paper we present multiprocessor algorithms for solving two important problems. The first problem concerns solving large banded positive definite linear systems such as those that arise from the numerical solution of two-point boundary value problems via the finite-element method. The second problem is that of approximating few of the smallest (or largest) eigenvalues and the corresponding eigenvectors of large sparse generalized eigenvalue problems $Az = \lambda Bz$, where A and B are symmetric and sparse with B being positive definite.

Both algorithms are designed so as to minimize interprocessor communication, hence reducing synchronization penalties. Each algorithm consists of several stages with the most time-consuming stages consisting of independent tasks (one task per processor) that can be performed with no interprocessor communication.

Higher speedup may be achieved in each algorithm if each of these independent tasks can be performed on a tightly coupled cluster of processors. These clusters are, in turn, interconnected via a global switch.

2. Block-tridiagonal systems

Block tridiagonal linear systems of equations arise in many applications in engineering and mathematical physics. In many important situations these systems are symmetric positive definite. Let the system under consideration be given by

$$Az = f , \qquad (2.1)$$

where $A = [B_{j-1}^T, A_j, B_j]$ is of order $n = \gamma m$, $\gamma \gg 1$, and B_j, A_j are each of order m. Further, we assume that the system (2.1) arises from the numerical treatment of a boundary-value problem via the finite element method. In other words A and f may be generated whenever needed. We wish to solve this system on a multiprocessor consisting of p processors, where we assume that $q = n/p$ is an integer. If the system (2.1) is partitioned into p block-rows, then the i-th of which, $1 \leq i \leq p$, is of the form

$$[(O, E_i), T_i, (G_i, O)] , \qquad (2.2)$$

or

---

* This work is supported in part by the National Science Foundation under grant US NSF MCS 81-17010.

$$
\begin{array}{cccccc}
B_{\alpha-1}^T & A_\alpha & B_\alpha & & 0 & \\
0 & B_\alpha^T & A_{\alpha+1} & B_{\alpha+1} & & 0 \\
\cdot & & \cdot & & \cdot & \\
0 & & & B_{i\nu-1} & A_{i\nu} & B_{i\nu}
\end{array}
$$

where $\alpha = (i-1)\nu+1$, with ν being the integer q/m. Note that $B_0 = B_\gamma = 0$. The algorithm we propose here, see [SaKu78] and [LaSa83], consists of the following stages.

Stage 1:

Each processor $1 \le i \le p$, generates the $m \times m$ matrices A_k and B_{k-1}, $k = (i-1)\nu+1, \ldots, i\nu$ as well as the corresponding part of the right-hand side f_i.

Stage 2:

Using the Cholesky factorization of each matrix T_i, solve in each processor i the linear systems

$$
T_i U_i = E_i, \; T_i V_i = G_i, \quad T_i g_i = f_i \tag{2.3}
$$

at a cost of $O(m^2 n/p)$ arithmetic operations. Now we have the linear system

$$
Cx = g
$$

where C is a block-tridiagonal matrix of the form

$$
C = [(O, U_i), I_q, (V_i, O)] . \tag{2.4}
$$

Stage 3:

Solve the independent system which consists of the $(p-1)$ pairs of the m equations above and m equations below each partitioning line in (2.4). We denote this banded system of order $2m(p-1)$ by

$$
Wy = h , \tag{2.5}
$$

where W is of the form

$$
\begin{array}{cccccc}
I & P_1 & 0 & O & & \\
Q_2 & I & 0 & R_2 & & \\
S_3 & 0 & I & P_3 & 0 & 0 \\
& & Q_4 & I & 0 & R_4 \\
& & S_5 & 0 & I & P_5 \\
& & & & Q_6 & I
\end{array}
\;\ddots
$$

$$
\begin{array}{cccc}
I & P_{k-3} & 0 & 0 \\
Q_{k-2} & I & 0 & R_{k-2} \\
S_{k-1} & 0 & I & P_{k-1} \\
& & Q_k & I
\end{array}
$$

$$(2.6)$$

in which $k = 2(p-1)$. Note that the first m rows of (2.5) are contained in processor 1, processor i, $2 \leq i \leq p-1$, contains rows $(2i-3)m+1$, $(2i-3)m+2$,..., $(2i-1)m$, and the last m rows are contained in processor p.

The cost of solving this reduced system depends on how these processors are interconnected:

(1) If these processors are linearly connected, then the system (2.5) is solved sequentially. The matrix P_1 and the corresponding part of the right-hand side h_1 are transmitted from processor 1 to processor 2 where the first block in (2.6) is reduced to the upper triangular form using Gaussian elimination without pivoting. This is possible since it can be shown that all the eigenvalues of W are positive. Once P_3 and the corresponding part of the right-hand side are updated, they are transmitted to processor 3,... and so on. Finally, (2.6) is reduced to the upper triangular form

$$
\begin{array}{cccc}
I & P_1 & 0 & \\
 & H_2 & 0 & R_2 \\
 & & I & \hat{P}_3 & 0 \\
 & & & H_4 & 0 & R_4 \\
 & & & & I & \hat{P}_5 \\
 & & & & & H_6
\end{array}
\tag{2.7}
$$

$$
\begin{array}{ccc}
0 & & \\
0 & R_{k-2} & \\
I & \hat{P}_{k-1} & \\
 & H_k &
\end{array}
$$

where each H_j is upper triangular. This system may be solved sequentially by transmitting data in the opposite direction, from processor p towards processor 1. The solution vector y yields $2m(p-1)$ components of x, the solution of (2.1), in positions $jq-m+1$,..., $jq+m-1$, $jq+m$ for $j = 1, 2,..., p-1$. The cost of this option is $O(m^3 p)$ time steps.

(2) On the other extreme, if these p processors have access to a global memory via a reasonably powerful interconnection network with a broadcasting facility, then the reduced system (2.6) may be solved at a lower cost using the following algorithm.

(a) Solve in each processor i, $1 \leq i \leq p-1$, the linear systems

$$
\begin{vmatrix} I_m & P_{2i-1} \\ Q_{2i} & I_m \end{vmatrix} \begin{vmatrix} Y_{2i-1}^{(1)} & Z_{2i-1}^{(1)} & h_{2i-1}^{(1)} \\ Y_{2i}^{(1)} & Z_{2i}^{(1)} & h_{2i}^{(1)} \end{vmatrix} = \begin{vmatrix} S_{2i-1} & 0 & h_{2i-1} \\ 0 & R_{2i} & h_{2i} \end{vmatrix},
\tag{2.8}
$$

where $h^T = (h_1^T, h_2^T, \ldots, h_{2(p-1)}^T)$ is the right-hand side in (2.5), and P_j, Q_j are as given in (2.6). For $p = 9$, the system is now of the form,

$$
\begin{array}{|cccc|cc}
\hline
I & 0 & 0 & Z_1^{(1)} & & \\
0 & I & 0 & Z_2^{(1)} & & \\
Y_3^{(1)} & 0 & I & 0 & 0 & Z_3^{(1)} \\
Y_4^{(1)} & 0 & 0 & I & 0 & Z_4^{(1)} \\
\hline
& & Y_5^{(4)} & 0 & I & 0 \\
& & Y_6^{(1)} & 0 & 0 & I \\
\end{array}
$$

$$
\begin{array}{cc|cccc}
I & 0 & 0 & Z_{11}^{(1)} & & \\
0 & I & 0 & Z_{12}^{(1)} & & \\
\hline
Y_{13}^{(1)} & 0 & I & 0 & 0 & Z_{13}^{(1)} \\
Y_{14}^{(1)} & 0 & 0 & I & 0 & Z_{14}^{(1)} \\
& & Y_{15}^{(1)} & 0 & I & 0 \\
& & Y_{16}^{(1)} & 0 & 0 & I \\
\end{array}
$$

Figure 1

(b) For the sake of illustration let $p-1 = 2^\theta$. Now, for $j = 2, 3, \dots, \theta$ we perform the following steps:

(i) In each processor i, $1 \le i \le 2^{\theta-j+1}$, solve the linear systems

$$
\begin{vmatrix} I_m & Z_{\sigma(i)}^{(j-1)} \\ Y_{3+\sigma(i)} & I_m \end{vmatrix} \begin{vmatrix} Y_{\sigma(i)}^{(j)} & Z_{\sigma(i)}^{(j)} & h_{\sigma(i)}^{(j)} \\ Y_{3+\sigma(i)}^{(j)} & Z_{3+\sigma(i)}^{(j)} & h_{3+\sigma(i)}^{(j)} \end{vmatrix} =
$$

$$
\begin{vmatrix} Y_{\sigma(i)}^{(j-1)} & 0 & h_{\sigma(i)}^{(j-1)} \\ 0 & Z_{3+\sigma(i)}^{(j-1)} & h_{3+\sigma(i)}^{(j-1)} \end{vmatrix} , \tag{2.9}
$$

where $\sigma(i) = (2i-1)2^{(j-1)} - 1$, $Y_l^{(j)} = 0$ for $l < 1 + 2^{(j-1)}$, and $Z_l^{(j)} = 0$ for $l > 2^{(\theta+1)} - 2^{(j-1)}$.

(ii) Retrieve the rest of the $m \times m$ matrices $Y_\nu^{(j)}$ and $Z_\nu^{(j)}$ as well as the updated portions of the right-hand sides $h_\nu^{(j)}$. For $i = 1, 2, \dots, 2^{\theta-j+1}$, obtain

$$
Z_{\nu(i)}^{(j)} = - Z_{\nu(i)}^{(j-1)} Z_{3+\sigma(i)}^{(j)} , \tag{2.10a}
$$

$$
Y_{\nu(i)}^{(j)} = Y_{\nu(i)}^{(j-1)} - Z_{\nu(i)}^{(j-1)} Y_{3+\sigma(i)}^{(j)} , \tag{2.10b}
$$

$$
h_{\nu(i)}^{(j)} = h_{\nu(i)}^{(j-1)} - Z_{\nu(i)}^{(j-1)} h_{3+\sigma(i)}^{(j)} , \tag{2.10c}
$$

where $\nu(i) = (i-1)2^j + 1, \dots, (2i-1)2^{j-1}$ with $\nu(i) \ne \sigma(i)$, and

$$
Z_{\eta(i)}^{(j)} = Z_{\eta(i)}^{(j-1)} - Y_{\eta(i)}^{(j-1)} Z_{\sigma(i)}^{(j)} , \tag{2.11a}
$$

$$Y_{\eta(i)}^{(j)} = - Y_{\eta(i)}^{(j-1)} \, Y_{\sigma(i)}^{(j)} \,, \tag{2.11b}$$

$$h_{\eta(i)}^{(j)} = h_{\eta(i)}^{(j-1)} - Y_{\eta(i)}^{(j-1)} \, h_{\sigma(i)}^{(j)} \,, \tag{2.11c}$$

where $\eta(i) = \nu(i) + 2^{j-1}$ with $\eta(i) \neq 3 + \sigma(i)$. Y_l, Z_l, and h_l, in equations (2.10) and (2.11), are evaluated using one processor for each matrix multiplication.

Figure 2 shows the form of the matrix of coefficients of the reduced system for $j = 3$, for the case where $p = 9$.

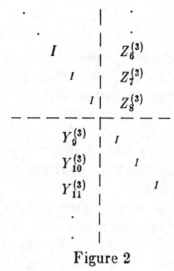

Figure 2

(c) Solve the linear system

$$\begin{vmatrix} I_m & Z_{p-2}^{(\theta)} \\ Y_{p+1}^{(\theta)} & I_m \end{vmatrix} \begin{vmatrix} h_{p-2}^{(\theta+1)} \\ h_{p+1}^{(\theta+1)} \end{vmatrix} = \begin{vmatrix} h_{p-2}^{(\theta)} \\ h_{p+1}^{(\theta)} \end{vmatrix} \tag{2.12}$$

in one processor, where $y_{p-2} = h_{p-2}^{(\theta+1)}$ and $y_{p+1} = h_{p+1}^{(\theta+1)}$ and retrieve the rest of the solution of (2.5):

$$y_i = h_i^{(\theta+1)} = h_i^{(\theta)} - Z_i^{(\theta)} h_{p+1}^{(\theta+1)} \,, \quad 1 \le i \le p-3 \,, \quad i = p-1 \,,$$
$$y_i = h_i^{(\theta+1)} = h_i^{(\theta)} - Y_i^{(\theta)} h_{p-2}^{(\theta+1)} \,, \quad i = p \,, \quad p+2 \le i \le 2p-2 \,, \tag{2.13}$$

using as many processors as possible, one processor for each matrix-vector multiplication.

The bottleneck in this algorithm is clear from (2.10), (2.11), and (2.13); several matrices are to be multiplied by the same matrix or vector. Consider, for example, the case of obtaining $Z_\nu^{(3)}$ for $p = 9$. From (2.10a) and (2.11a) we see that $Z_1^{(2)}$, $Z_2^{(2)}$, and $Z_4^{(2)}$ are to be multiplied by $Z_6^{(3)}$, while $Y_6^{(2)}$, $Y_7^{(2)}$, and $Y_8^{(2)}$ are to be multiplied by $Z_3^{(3)}$. Assigning one processor to each matrix multiplication and assuming that m is not too small, it is possible to overlap the time consumed by broadcasting by that of the arithmetic. If the two $m \times m$ matrices to be multiplied are $A = [a_1, a_2, \ldots, a_m]$ and $B = [b_1, b_2, \ldots, b_m]$

where $b_j^T = (\beta_{1j}, \ldots, \beta_{mj})$, then the j-th column of the product $C = AB = [c_1, c_2, \ldots, c_m]$ is given by $c_j = Ab_j = \sum_{i=1}^{m} \beta_{ij} a_i$. Hence, each broadcast of β_{ij} correspond to approximately $2m$ arithmetic operations. Consequently the cost of this option is $O(m^3 \log_2 p)$ time steps.

Stage 4:

Once the solution of (2.5) is obtained, the remaining components of solution of (2.1) are obtained via perfect parallelism. In each processor $1 \leq i \leq p$ the remaining q-$2m$ components of the subvector z_i, of order q, are retrieved using the fact that

$$z_i = g_i - U_i y_{2i-3} - V_i y_{2i} .$$

This stage consumes, therefore, $O(mn/p)$ time steps.

The total cost of this algorithm clearly depends on the relationship between m, n, and p, as well as the architecture of the machine.

I. If the number of processors p is much smaller than n, the above algorithm consumes time proportional to $m^2 n/p$. Further, provided that the matrix of coefficients of (2.1) can be generated in the p processors, the processors need only be connected linearly. The algorithm achieves maximum speedup when p is proportional to $\sqrt{n/m}$.

II. If p is proportional to n/m, then provided that these p processors are tightly coupled via an interconnection network allowing broadcasts, option 2 of stage 3 becomes viable leading to an algorithm for solving (2.1) in time proportional to $m^3 \log_2 n$. This scheme may be regarded, in this case, as an alternative to block-cyclic reduction [Hell76].

Finally, we would like to point out that the systems (2.3) may be solved using the preconditioned conjugate gradient algorithm, [MeVo77] and [CoGO76]. This can be more economical especially if $q = n/p$ is large and the matrices T_i in (2.3), $1 \leq i \leq p$, are sparse within the band. The cost of the algorithm can be further reduced if we have $p = O(\sqrt{n/m})$ clusters of processors with each cluster consisting of $(2m+1)$ processors. Each processor handling one system of (2.3) using the sequential conjugate gradient algorithm with a preconditioning strategy.

3. The sparse generalized eigenvalue problem

The problem of computing a few of the smallest (or largest) eigenvalues and eigenvectors of the large, sparse, generalized eigenvalue problem

$$Az = \lambda Bz , \tag{3.1}$$

where A and B are symmetric matrices of large order n, with B being positive definite, arise in many important applications [BaWi73], [Grub78], and [Fisc82]. We present a new method: "trace minimization", [SaWi82] and [Gole82], which is suitable for multiprocessors for handling this problem. This method is competitive with the Lanczos algorithm, [Parl80], for solving (3.1), especially when the matrices A and B are so large and sparse with a sparsity pattern such that the Cholesky factor of either matrix has to be contained in auxiliary storage.

The main idea behind our algorithm, [SaWi82], depends on the following observation:

Let $\mathbf{Y}$ be the set of all $n \times p$, $p < n$, matrices Y for which $Y^T BY = I_p$. Then

$$\min_{Y \epsilon \mathbf{Y}} tr(Y^T AY) = \sum_{i=1}^{p} \lambda_i , \tag{3.2}$$

where $tr(A) = \sum_{i=1}^{n} \alpha_{ii}$ denotes the trace of A, and $\lambda_1 \leq \lambda_2 \leq \cdots \leq \lambda_p < \lambda_{p+1} \leq \cdots \leq \lambda_n$ are the eigenvalues of (A, B).

Let Y_k be an $n \times p$ matrix approximating the p eigenvectors corresponding to the smallest p eigenvalues of (3.1), i.e.

$$Y_k^T AY_k = \sum_k = diag(\sigma_1^{(k)}, \ldots, \sigma_p^{(k)}) , \tag{3.3a}$$

and

$$Y_k^T BY_k = I_p . \tag{3.3b}$$

Now, choose an $n \times p$ correction matrix Δ_k and a $p \times p$ scaling matrix S_k to construct the new iterate

$$Y_{k+1} = (Y_k - \Delta_k)S_k \tag{3.4}$$

so that

$$Y_{k+1}^T AY_{k+1} = \Sigma_{k+1} = diag(\sigma_1^{(k+1)}, \ldots, \sigma_p^{(k+1)}) , \tag{3.5a}$$

$$Y_{k+1}^T BY_{k+1} = I_p , \tag{3.5b}$$

and

$$tr(Y_{k+1}^T AY_{k+1}) < tr(Y_k^T AY_k) . \tag{3.5c}$$

The most time-consuming part of this algorithm is the choice of Δ_k which ensures that (3.5c) holds. Several choices are possible, we present here the one resulting from the following constrained optimization problem

$$\begin{aligned} &minimize \; tr(Y_k - \Delta_k)^T A(Y_k - \Delta_k) \\ &subject \; Y_k^T B\Delta_k = 0 . \end{aligned} \tag{3.6}$$

Without loss of generality we assume that A is positive definite, for if A is indefinite, (3.1) is replaced by

$$(A - \eta B)x = (\lambda - \eta)Bx ,$$

where η is chosen so that $(A - \eta B)$ is positive definite, i.e., $\eta < \lambda_1 < 0$. For a positive definite A then, (3.6) is reduced to the p problems:

$$\text{minimize } (y_j^{(k)} - d_j^{(k)})^T A (y_j^{(k)} - d_j^{(k)})$$

$$\text{subject } Y_k^T B d_j^{(k)} = 0, \quad \text{for } 1 \leq j \leq p, \tag{3.7}$$

where $y_j^{(k)} = Y_k e_j$ and $d_j^{(k)} = \Delta_k e_j$, in which e_j is the j-th column of I_n. Let the orthogonal factorization of BY_k be given by $Q_k R_k$, where Q_k is an $n \times p$ matrix with orthonormal columns and R_k an upper triangular matrix of order p. Also, let $\tilde{Q}_k$ be an $n \times (n-p)$ matrix with orthonormal columns such that $[Q_k, \tilde{Q}_k]$ is an orthogonal matrix. Now, the problems in (3.7) are equivalent to solving the p independent positive definite linear systems

$$(\tilde{Q}_k^T A \tilde{Q}_k) g_j^{(k)} = \tilde{Q}_k^T A y_j^{(k)}, \quad i \leq j \leq p, \tag{3.8}$$

where $d_j^{(k)} = \tilde{Q}_k g_j^{(k)}$.

Dropping all sub- and superscripts from (3.8), and using the conjugate gradient algorithm starting with the initial iterate for g to be zero, we can obtain estimates for $(y-d)$ directly. The C.G. scheme for (3.8) is therefore given by:

(i) <u>initialization</u>

$$z_0 = y,$$

$$r_0 = (I-P)Az_0, \quad \text{where } P = (I-QQ^T),$$

and

$$p_0 = r_0$$

(ii) <u>for $i = 0, 1, 2,...$</u>

$$z_{i+1} = z_i - \alpha_i p_i,$$

$$\alpha_i = r_i^T r_i / p_i^T A p_i,$$

$$r_{i+1} = r_i - \alpha_i (I-P) A p_i, \tag{3.9}$$

$$p_{i+1} = r_{i+1} + \beta_i p_i,$$

$$\beta_i = r_{i+1}^T r_{i+1} / r_i^T r_i.$$

The C.G. algorithm is terminated once a measure of the error in z_i falls below the corresponding measure of the error in the eigenvector y. It can be shown [SaWi82] that for the j-th system the C.G. iteration (3.9) may be terminated after m steps when

$$\alpha_m \| r_m \|_2^2 \leq (\sigma_j / \sigma_{p+1})^2 (\alpha_0 \| r_0 \|_2^2), \tag{3.10}$$

where σ_i is the current estimate of λ_i.

This globally convergent algorithm may be summarized as follows:

Stage 1 (Initialization)

Choose an $n \times s$ matrix Y such that Y is of rank s. Here s is slightly more than p, the number of desired eigen pairs. Usually $s \geq p+1$.

368

Stage 2 (B-orthonormalization)

Obtain $\hat{Y}$ in the space spanned by Y such that $\hat{Y}^T B \hat{Y} = I_s$. This is done via a generalization of the Gram-Schmidt process [Luen69].

Stage 3 (Forming a section)

Obtain the spectral decomposition $\hat{Y}^T A \hat{Y} = U \Sigma U^T$. Now, $\tilde{Y} = \hat{Y} U$ yields the section

$$\tilde{Y}^T A \tilde{Y} = \Sigma \text{ ,and } \tilde{Y}^T B \tilde{Y} = I_s \text{ .}$$

Here, $\Sigma = diag(\sigma_1, \sigma_2, \ldots, \sigma_s)$.

Stage 4 (Convergence)

Accept $(\sigma_j, \tilde{y}_j)$ as an eigen pair if $\max_{1 \leq j \leq p} ||A\tilde{y}_j - \sigma_j B\tilde{y}_j||_1$ is below a specified tolerance.

Stage 5 (Factorization)

Obtain the orthogonal factorization $B\tilde{Y} = QR$.

Stage 6 (Updating)

Solve the s independent positive definite systems in (3.8) using the C.G. algorithm. The j-th C.G. process is terminated when the stopping criterion (3.10) is satisfied. The s resulting solution vectors form the columns of the new matrix Y; go to stage 2.

This trace minimization technique, which has a linear rate of convergence, can be improved tremendously if it is applied to the s eigenvalue problems

$$(A - \nu_j B)z_j = (\lambda_j - \nu_j)Bz_j \text{ , } \quad 1 \leq j \leq s \text{ .}$$

Here, ν_j is a suitable shift chosen from the Ritz values σ_j, $1 \leq j \leq s$, obtained in stage 3. In this case, stages 1 through 5 remain unchanged. In stage 6, however, we solve the s linear systems in (3.8), via the C.G. process, with the matrix A in the j-th system replaced by $(A - \nu_j B)$. An appropriate strategy for choosing these shifts is necessary to maintain global convergence and to ultimately achieve cubic convergence, see section 3 in [SaWi82]. If we shift the j-th problem by the Ritz value σ_j too late, we needlessly take several passes of stages 1-6 at the slower linear rate of convergence when a cubic rate of convergence is possible. On the other hand, if we shift the j-th problem by σ_j too soon, global convergence is lost; this is heralded by a nondescent step in the C.G. process in stage 5.

The algorithm is suitable for multiprocessors. Let us assume that we have a ring of s linearly connected processors with each having enough local memory to contain few vectors each of order n. Further, we assume that each processor can simultaneously perform an arithmetic operation, receive a floating-point number from an immediate neighbor, and send a previously computed number to the other immediate neighbor.

Making the crucial, and not unreasonable, assumption that the elements of A and B can be generated whenever needed, the most time-consuming part of the algorithm (stage 6) is performed with perfect speedup. Stages 2 to 5, however, require interprocessor communication.

The spectral decomposition, in stage 3, of $\hat{Y}^T A \hat{Y}$ is handled via the one-sided Jacobi method, [Luk80], which is suitable for implementation on our linearly connected set of processors, [Same82]. Also, an organization of the orthogonal factorization of $B\tilde{Y}$ on the above ring is given in [Same82]. A related algorithm, that of the Gram-Schmidt B-orthogonalization of the columns of Y, stage 2, i.e., the factorization $Y = \hat{Y}R$ where $\hat{Y}^T B \hat{Y} = I_s$ with $R = [\rho_{ij}]$ being an upper triangular matrix of order s, is given by:

$$Y = [y_1^{(1)}, \ldots, y_s^{(1)}] \,,$$

For $i = 1, 2, \ldots, s$

$$\rho_{ii} = (y_i^{(i)^T} B y_i^{(i)})^{1/2}$$

$$\hat{y}_i = y_i^{(i)}/\rho_{ii}$$

For $j = i+1, \ldots, s$

$$\rho_{ij} = \hat{y}_i^T B y_j^{(i)}$$

$$y_j^{(i+1)} = y_j^{(i)} - \rho_{ij}\hat{y}_i$$

The above Gram-Schmidt scheme is performed by pipelining across the processors of our ring and is completed in $O(sn)$ time steps plus the time required for s multiplications of an n-vector by the matrix B.

Different algorithm organizations of stages 2, 3, 5 and 6 are necessary for higher speedup if we have a CEDAR-like architecture [GKLS83] consisting of s clusters, and where the matrices A and B are contained in the global memory.

The choice algorithm for solving (3.1) on a sequential machine is that due to Lanczos [Parl80]. In each step of the Lanczos algorithm we need to solve accurately a system of linear equations of the form $Bu = h$. This high accuracy is necessary to assure that the Lanczos vectors in steps $j-1$, j, and $j+1$ are B-orthonormal. Further, linear independence among the Lanczos vectors, until convergence to the extreme eigenvalues of (3.1), should be maintained in order to avoid spurious eigenvalues and to minimize the number of the Lanczos steps. This is achieved either by selective orthogonalization [Parl80] or periodic reorthogonalization [Grca81]. Both strategies may require auxiliary storage for large problems leading to an I/O bound algorithm on multiprocessors. While a comprehensive comparison between the trace minimization and the Lanczos algorithms must await actual experiments on multiprocessors of different architectures, we suspect that our trace minimization scheme is to be preferred for multiprocessors with limited interconnection networks and for exceedingly large problems.

References

[BaWi73]   K. Bathe and E. Wilson, Solution methods for eigenvalue problems in structural mechanics, *Intl. J. Num. Meth. Eng. 6*, 213-226.

[CoGO76]   P. Concus, G. Golub, D. O'Leary, A generalized conjugate gradient method for the numerical solution of elliptic partial differential equations, in *Proc. Sparse Matrix Computation,* ed. J. Bunch and D. Rose, Academic Press, 1976.

[Fisc82]   C. Fischer, Approximate solution of Schrodinger's equation for atoms, in *Numerical Integration of Differential Equations and Large Linear Systems,* ed. J. Hinze, *Lecture Notes in Mathematics 968,* Springer-Verlag, 1982, 71-81.

[GKLS83]   D. Gajski, D. Kuck, D. Lawrie, A. Sameh, Plan for the construction of a large scale muiltiprocessor, Department of Computer Science (Cedar Doc. No. 3), University of Illinois at Urbana-Champaign, February 1983.

[Gole82]   A. Golebiewski, Variational pseudo-gradient method for determination of m first eigenstates of a large real symmetric matrix, in *Numerical Integration of Differential Equations and Large Linear Systems,* J. Hinze, ed., *Lecture Notes in Mathematics 968,* Springer-Verlag, 1982, 370-383.

[Grca81]   J. Grcar, Analysis of the Lanczos algorithm and of the approximation problem in Richardson's method, Ph.D. thesis, Department of Computer Science, University of Illinois at Urbana-Champaign, 1981.

[Grub78]   A. Gruber, Finite hybrid elements to compute the ideal magnetohydrodynamic spectrum of an axisymmetric plasma, *J. Comp. Physics 26,* 1978, 379-389.

[Hell76]   D. Heller, Some aspects of the cyclic reduction algorithm for block tridiagonal linear systems, *SIAM J. Num. Anal. 13,* 1976, 484-496.

[LaSa83]   D. Lawrie and A. Sameh, The computation and communication complexity of a parallel banded system solver, submitted for publication, 1983.

[Luen69]   D. Luenberger, *Optimization by Vector Space Methods,* J. Wiley, 1969.

[Luk80]   F. Luk, Computing the singular-value decomposition on the Illiac IV, *ACM Trans. Math. Software 6,* 1980, 524-539.

[MeVo77]   J. Meijerink and H. van der Vorst, An iterative solution method for linear systems of which the coefficients matrix is a symmetric M-matrix, *Math. Comp. 31,* 1977, 148-162.

[Parl80]   B. Parlett, *The Symmetric Eigenvalue Problem*, Prentice-Hall, 1980.

[SaKu78]   A. Sameh and D. Kuck, On stable parallel linear system solvers, *J. ACM 25*, 1978, 81-91.

[Same82]   A. Sameh, Solving the linear least squares problem on a linear array of processors, *Proc. Purdue Workshop on Algorithmically Specialized Computer Organization*, W. Lafayette, Indiana, September 1982, Academic Press (to appear).

[SaWi82]   A. Sameh and J. Wisniewski, A trace minimization algorithm for the generalized eigenvalue problem, *SIAM J. Num. Anal. 19*, 1982, 1243-1259.

The VLSI Complexity of Sorting

CLARK D. THOMPSON

Reprinted from *IEEE Transactions on Computers*, Volume C-32, Number 12, December 1983, pages 1171-1184. Copyright © 1983 by The Institute of Electrical and Electronics Engineers, Inc.

Abstract—The area–time complexity of sorting is analyzed under an updated model of VLSI computation. The new model makes a distinction between "processing" circuits and "memory" circuits; the latter are less important since they are denser and consume less power. Other adjustments to the model make it possible to compare pipelined and nonpipelined designs.

Using the new model, this paper briefly describes thirteen different designs for VLSI sorters. (None of these sorters is new, but few have been laid out or analyzed in a VLSI model.) The thirteen sorting circuits are used to document the existence of an area * time^2 tradeoff for the sorting problem. The smallest circuit is only large enough to store a few elements at a time; it is, of course, rather slow at sorting. The largest design solves an N-element sorting problem in only $O(\lg N)$ clock cycles. The area * time^2 performance figure for all but three of the designs is close to the theoretical minimum value $\Omega(N^2 \lg N)$.

Index Terms—Area-time complexity, bitonic sort, bubble sort, heapsort, mesh-connected computers, parallel algorithms, shuffle-exchange network, sorting, VLSI, VLSI sorter.

I. INTRODUCTION

SORTING has attracted a great deal of attention over the past few decades of computer science research. It is easy to see why: sorting is a theoretically interesting problem with a great deal of practical significance. As many as a quarter of the world's computing cycles were once devoted to sorting [19, p. 3]. This is probably no longer the case, given the large number of microprocessors running dedicated control tasks. Nonetheless, sorting and other information-shuffling techniques are of great importance in the rapidly growing database industry.

The sorting problem can be defined as the rearrangement of N input values so that they are in ascending order. This paper examines the complexity of the sorting problem, assuming it is to be solved on a VLSI chip. Much is already known about sorting on other types of computational structures [19, pp. 1–388], and much of this knowledge is applicable to VLSI sorting. However, VLSI is a novel computing medium in at least one respect: the size of a circuit is determined as much by its intergate wiring as by its gates themselves. This technological novelty makes it appropriate to reevaluate sorting circuits and algorithms in the context of a "VLSI model of computation."

Using a VLSI model, it is possible to demonstrate the existence of an area * time^2 tradeoff for sorting circuits. A preliminary study of this tradeoff is contained in the author's

Manuscript received March 15, 1982; revised June 10, 1982. This work was supported by the National Science Foundation under Grant ECS-81-10684.

The author is with the Computer Science Division, University of California, Berkeley, CA 94720.

Ph.D. dissertation [42], in which two sorting circuits were analyzed. This paper analyzes eleven additional designs under an updated model of VLSI computation. The updated model has the advantage of allowing fair comparisons between pipelined and nonpipelined designs.

None of the sorting circuits in this paper is new, since all are based on commonly known serial algorithms. All have been proposed before for hardware implementation. However, this is the first time that most of these circuits have been analyzed for their area and time complexity in a VLSI implementation. Ten of the sorters will be seen to have an area * time^2 performance in the range $O(N^2 \lg^2 N)$ to $O(N^2 \lg^5 N)$. Since it is impossible for any design to have an area * time^2 product of less than $\Omega(N^2 \lg N)$ [44], these designs are area- and time-optimal to within logarithmic factors.[1]

A number of different models for VLSI have been proposed in the past few years [5], [7], [16], [25], [37], [42], [43], [46]. They differ chiefly in their treatment of chip I/O, placing various restrictions on the way in which a chip accesses its input. Typically, each input value must enter the chip at only one place [42] or at only one time and place [5]. Savage [36] has characterized these as the "unilocal" and "semelective" assumptions, respectively.

The model of this paper builds on its predecessors, removing as many restrictions on chip I/O as possible. Following Kedem and Zorat [16], the unilocal assumption could be relaxed by allowing a chip to access each input value from k different I/O memories. Kedem's proof suggests that clever use of such "multilocal" inputs could improve a chip's area * time^2 performance by a factor of k^2. Unfortunately, there seem to be neither interesting sorting circuits that take advantage of multilocal data, nor examples of naturally occurring multilocal inputs. Thus, the new model retains the unilocal assumption.

The semelective assumption is much less justifiable than the unilocal assumption. It is perfectly feasible to design a chip that makes multiple accesses to problem inputs, outputs, and intermediate results contained in off-chip memory. In a break from previous practice in theoretical VLSI models, the area of this off-chip memory is not included in the total area of a chip. This serves to clarify the area * time^2 tradeoff for sorting circuits; memory area seems to be involved in a (lg area) * time tradeoff, at least for circuits with fixed I/O bandwidth and small amounts of memory [13]. Leaving memory area out of the new model permits the analysis of sublinear size circuits.

---

[1] Knuth's notation for the base-two logarithm $\lg \triangleq \log_2$ is used throughout this paper. See [20] for standard definitions of order notation for lower ($\Omega(\ )$), exact ($\Theta(\ )$), and upper ($O(\ )$) bounds.

It also makes the model's area measure more sensitive to the power consumption of a circuit, since memory cells have a low duty cycle and generally consume much less power per unit area than do "processing" circuits.

Other authors have used nonsemelective models, although none has elaborated quite so much on the idea. Lipton and Sedgewick [25] point out that the "standard" AT^2 lower bound proofs do not depend on semelective assumptions. Hong [14] defines a nonsemelective model of VLSI with a space-time behavior which is polynomially equivalent to that of eleven other models of computation. His equivalence proofs depend upon the fact that VLSI wiring rules can cause at most a quadratic increase in the size of a zero-width-wire circuit. Unfortunately, Hong's transformation does not necessarily generate optimal VLSI circuits from optimal zero-width-wire circuits, since a quadratic factor cannot be ignored when "easy" functions like sorting are being studied.

Lipton and Sedgewick [25] point out another form of I/O restriction, one that is not removed in this paper's model. In most situations it is natural to restrict one's attention to circuits which produce their outputs at fixed locations. For example, the most significant bit of the largest output value in a "where-oblivious" circuit might be constrained to appear at I/O port 1, regardless of the problem inputs.

Adoption of the where-oblivious restriction begs an important theoretical question: what does "sorting" mean? Is it determining the rank order of the inputs? Is it permuting the inputs into sorted order, given their ranks? Or does it involve both ranking and permuting? The where-oblivious restriction adopted above implies an affirmative answer to the last question.

From a practical point of view, a sorting circuit should be required to rank and permute its inputs. It is possible to conceive of uses for circuits that can only rank or can only permute, but most applications require both. For example, consider the problem of removing the duplicate records that are frequently produced by projection operations on a relational database. The duplicates can be detected and purged in a straightforward fashion once the records are permuted into rank order (on any remaining key), thereby saving space and time in later database operations.

A historical argument can also be made in favor of requiring a "sorting" circuit to rank and permute its data. The original meaning of "sorting" is "separating or arranging according to class or kind" [19, p. 1], a process that would seem to involve both classification and movement. Thus, for practical and historical reasons, the interesting study of "ranking circuits" is left to other papers and other authors. Only (ranking and permuting) = "sorting" circuits are studied here.

The catalog of I/O restrictions is not yet complete. In both Vuillemin's [46] and Thompson's [43] models of pipelined VLSI computation, analogous inputs and outputs for different problems must be accessed through identical I/O ports. For example, input 1 of problem 2 must enter the chip at the same place as input 1 of problem 1. While this seems to be a natural assumption for a pipelined chip, it leads to a number of misleading conclusions about the optimality of highly concurrent designs. For instance, the highly parallelized bubble sort design

of Section III-L is nearly area $*$ time^2 optimal under the old models, but it is significantly suboptimal under the model of this paper.

When the restriction on pipelined chip inputs is removed, it becomes impossible to prove an $\Omega(N^2 \lg N)$ lower bound on area $*$ time^2 performance until the definitions of area and time are adjusted.

In the new model, the area performance A of a design is its "area per problem," equal to its total processing area $A_{processing}$ divided by its degree of concurrency c. Thus, it does not matter how many copies of a chip are being considered as a single design: doubling the number of chips doubles both its concurrency and its total area, leaving its area performance invariant. The old definition of area performance was the total area of a design (including its "memory area") with no correction factor for its concurrency.

The time performance of a design can be measured in a number of ways. Vuillemin [46] concentrates on the data rate D (or I/O bandwidth), a measure of a circuit's throughput. While this is an important parameter, a circuit's data rate is not a very useful definition of time performance under this paper's unrestricted I/O model. A design consisting of two identical sorting chips would have twice the data rate of either of its chips considered separately. As with the area measure discussed above, it would be possible to "normalize" a circuit's data rate by dividing by its concurrency. The resulting measure defies easy interpretation; fortunately, a better measure is available.

Vuillemin [46] also considers the period T_p between successive presentations of complete sets of problem inputs. This measure is closely related to a circuit's data rate D, for it is numerically equal to the problem size (in bits) divided by D. As such, it suffers from similar difficulties of interpretation when inputs are not assumed to form a single stream.

The time measure adopted here is the delay T_d between the presentation of one set of problem inputs and the production of the outputs from that problem. This measure is obviously unaffected by replication: two sorting chips have the same delay as one. In defense of the delay measure, it can be argued that a design's delay is a more fundamental limitation than its data rate or period. As indicated above, the latter measures can always be improved by replicating the design and splitting its I/O stream. Also note that an upper bound result on T_d implies an upper bound result on T_p. That is, a circuit's period need be no larger than its delay, since idle time serves no useful purpose in this paper's model of computation.

As Vuillemin [46] notes, any lower bound on circuit area in terms of its period T_p or data rate D immediately implies a similar bound in terms of its delay T_d. By this reasoning, T_p is the stronger time measure for lower bounds, just as T_d is the stronger time measure for upper bounds. Vuillemin's $AT_p^2 = \Omega(N^2)$ lower bound on the complexity of sorting N numbers thus implies an analogous result for the T_d metric. His proof must also be adapted to this paper's metric of area performance and to its less-restricted model of I/O behavior. However, one can do better than an $AT_d^2 = \Omega(N^2)$ result. Vuillemin's "transitivity" argument for sorting is somewhat weak in the sense that it only measures the complexity of permuting the least significant bit of each input word. By considering $\epsilon \lg N$ of the least significant bits, it is possible to show that $AT_p^2 = \Omega(N^2 \lg N)$ for the problem of sorting N words of $(1 + \epsilon)\lg N$ bits each [44].

There is reason to believe that an even stronger lower bound is obtainable. An $AT_d^2 = \Omega(N^2 \lg^2 N)$ result has been shown for a slightly more restricted model of I/O, in which all the bits of each input value must be read through the same I/O port [42]. (In the present model, bit 0 of an input could be read on the other side of the chip from bit 1 of that input.) It is difficult to imagine how a circuit could take advantage of such a "nonlocalized" I/O pattern and thus subvert the $\Omega(N^2 \lg^2 N)$ lower bound. Indeed, all of the circuits presented in this paper access the bits of each input value in a localized fashion, and thus none do better than $AT_d^2 = O(N^2 \lg^2 N)$.

This paper is organized in the following fashion: Section II discusses the new VLSI model of computation, then defines it precisely; Section III sketches thirteen different designs for VLSI sorters and analyzes the area–time performance of each; Section IV compares the performances of each of the designs, with some discussion of the "constant factors" ignored by the asymptotic model; and Section V concludes the paper with a list of some of the open issues in VLSI complexity theory.

In an attempt to keep the paper to a reasonable length, the constructions of Section III are described as briefly as possible. Readers wishing to "fill in the details" will have to follow the references, where applicable, and then exercise their own ingenuity. This is a regrettable situation, but an inevitable one since there is no accepted "high-level design language" for VLSI.

II. MODEL OF VLSI COMPUTATION

In all theoretical models of VLSI, circuits are made of two basic components: wires and gates. A gate is a localized set of transistors, or other switching elements, which perform a simple logical function. For example, a gate may be a "j-k flip-flop" or a "three input NAND." Wires serve to carry signals from the output of one gate to the input of another.

Two parameters of a VLSI circuit are of vital importance, its size and its speed. Since VLSI is essentially two-dimensional, the size of a circuit is best expressed in terms of its area. Sufficient area must be provided in a circuit layout for each gate and each wire. Gates are not allowed to overlap each other at all, and only two (or perhaps three) wires can pass over the same point.

A convenient unit of area is the square of the minimum separation between parallel wires. In the terminology of [26], this paper's unit of area is equal to $(4 \lambda)^2$, where λ is a constant determined by the processing technology. Each unit of area thus contains one, two, or three overlapping wires; or else it contains a fraction of a gate. The actual size of this area unit becomes smaller as technology improves. In 1978, it was typically $150~\mu m^2 = 1.5 \times 10^{-6}$ cm^2; eventually, it may be as small as $0.4~\mu m^2$ [26, p. 35].

The speed of a synchronous VLSI circuit can be measured by the number of clock pulses it takes to complete its computation. Once again, the actual size of this time unit is a technological variable. In 1978, a typical MOS clock period was 30–50 ns; and this may decrease to as little as 2–4 ns [26]. For the superconducting technology of Josephson junctions, a clock period of 1–3 ns is achievable today, using a process for which the area unit is 25 μm^2 [17].

The speed of a VLSI circuit may be adversely affected by the presence of a very long wires, unless special measures are taken. In many VLSI processes, a minimum-sized transistor cannot send a signal from one end of the chip to the other in one clock period. To accomplish such unit-delay cross-chip communication, and to achieve large fanouts, special "driver" circuits are employed. These drivers amplify the current of the signal; $O(\lg k)$ stages of amplification are required to drive a length-k wire [26, p. 14] or to drive k inputs. The use of $O(\lg k)$-stage drivers is reflected in the VLSI model's loading rules, as formalized in Assumption 1f). Under these rules, each stage of a driver has twice as many unit-area gates as the preceding one. The gates are wired in parallel, so each stage has twice the current sourcing (or sinking) capability of its predecessor. Furthermore, the stages are individually clocked. Thus, the driver behaves like an $O(\lg k)$-bit shift register with unit bandwidth and unit-power input requirements. Every wire, even the longest one, had a throughput of one bit per time unit; however, a length-k wire has $T_d = O(\lg k)$ delay. As argued in [43], the area of the long-wire driver circuits can be ignored (up to constant factors), as long as there is room to lay out the wires they drive.

Assumption 1f (the "logarithmic delay assumption") is used here because it leads to realistic circuit designs and time bounds, as well as to an interesting theoretical question. As it turns out, the time bounds obtained for VLSI sorting under this assumption are rarely different from the ones that would be obtained under a "unit-delay" assumption (in which each gate is able to transmit its output all the way across the circuit, in one clock period). The only exceptions might be the highly parallelized versions of the long-wire networks discussed in Sections III-J and III-K. Driver delays will exceed single-bit comparison delays in these networks unless one is able to lay them out with the smallest possible maximum wire-lengths. This is an attractive open problem, at least for the N-vertex shuffle-exchange network of Section III-J: can it be embedded with a maximum wire length of only $O(N/\lg^2 N)$?

From a practical standpoint, it may be argued that the logarithmic delay assumption is either too severe or too lenient, depending on the technology. The former is currently the case in the I^{2}L and Josephson junction processes [11], [17]. As of now, both are really unit-delay technologies. Minimum-sized gates can drive wires the entire length of a chip without significantly increasing logic delay. However, the results of this paper still apply if the drivers are omitted from the circuit constructions of Section III.

It seems unlikely that the logarithmic delay assumption will ever be too lenient on synchronous MOS circuits. Seitz [38] projects a signal transmission velocity of $(1$ cm$)/(3$ ns$)$ in a fully developed MOS technology. This means that a cross-chip communication will only take a few clock periods, even if the "chip" is as large as a present-day "wafer." In other words, the time performance of the fully developed MOS technology is only slightly overestimated by the logarithmic delay assumption. The true delay would best be modeled as logarithmic plus a small constant. Modeling delay as a linear function of distance, as suggested by Chazelle and Monier [7], would greatly exaggerate the importance of delay in the determination of the speed of such circuits.

If circuits ever become much faster or much larger than envisioned today, the logarithmic delay assumption should be modified. As a case in point, consider the Josephson junction circuit assemblies currently built by IBM. They are 10 cm on a side, and they run on a 1-3 ns clock [17]. The wires in these circuits are superconductors, but, of course, they cannot transmit information at a velocity greater than (a fraction of) the speed of light. Right now, the clock frequency and circuit dimensions are just small enough to allow a signal to propagate from one side of the circuit to the other in one clock period. Any increase in either speed or size would make this impossible. The computational limitations of such enhanced (and hypothetical) technologies could be analyzed under Chazelle and Monier's linear delay assumption.

Thus far in the discussion, only "standard features" have been introduced to the VLSI model. The interested reader is referred to [42] for more details on the practical significance of the model, and to [37] for an excellent introduction to the theoretical aspects of VLSI modeling.

As noted in the introduction, a major distinction between the model of this paper and most previous VLSI models is the way in which it treats "I/O memory." Here, only a nominal area charge is made for the memory used to store problem inputs and outputs, even if this memory is also used for the storage of intermediate results.

In the new model, each input and output bit is assigned a place in a k-bit "I/O memory" attached to one or more "I/O ports." Two types of access to the I/O memory are distinguished. If the bits are accessed in a fixed order, the I/O memory is organized as a shift register and accessed in $O(1)$ time per bit. If the access pattern is more complex, a random access memory (RAM) is used. Such a memory has an access delay of $O(\lg k)$ [26, p. 321]. The random access time covers both the internal delays of the memory circuit as well as the time it takes the I/O port to transmit (serially) $O(\lg k)$ address bits to the RAM.

This paper's serial I/O interfaces may seem a bit artificial, since typical RAM's are accessed with word-parallel address and data lines. More careful consideration reveals that any such word-parallel RAM interface could be simulated with several serial interfaces at no cost in asymptotic area and time.

Allowing more than one I/O port to connect to a single I/O memory makes it easy to model the use of multiport memory chips. Their usage must be restricted, however, to remove the (theoretical) temptation to use multiport memories and printed-circuit board wiring as a means of avoiding on-chip wiring. (Note that a two-port memory provides a communication channel between its two I/O ports, eliminating any need for an on-chip wire between them.) The restriction is that all I/O ports connecting to a single memory must be physically adjacent to each other in the chip layout. This avoids any possibility of "rat's-nest" wiring to the memory chips, making the model essentially unilocal rather than multilocal [36] in its I/O assumptions.

The model makes a few assumptions as possible about the actual location of the I/O memory circuitry, even though this can have a large effect on system timing. If the memory is placed on a different chip from the processing circuitry, its access time is considerably increased. Fortunately, this will not always invalidate the model's timing assumptions. The $O(\lg k)$ delay of a k-bit RAM will dominate the delay of an off-chip driver, if k is large enough. Alternatively, if k is small, it should be relatively easy to locate the RAM on the processor chip. As for off-chip "shift register" I/O memories, there should be no particular difficulty in implementing these in such a way that one input or output event can happen every $O(1)$ time units.

As indicated above, time charges for off-chip I/O are problematical and may be underestimated in the current model. Area charges for I/O are also troublesome. Here, I/O ports are assumed to have $O(1)$ area even though they are obviously much larger than a unit-area wire crossing or an $O(1)$ area gate. It is also assumed that a design can have an unlimited number of I/O ports. In reality, chips are limited to one or two hundred pins, and each pin should be considered a major expense (in terms of manufacturing, reliability, and circuit board wiring costs). An attempt is made in Section IV to use more realistic estimates of I/O costs when evaluating the constructions in Section III.

The complete model of VLSI computation is summarized below.

Assumption 1—Embedding:

a) A VLSI circuit consists of wires and nodes embedded in the Euclidean plane. In graph-theoretic terms, wires are hyperedges joining two or more nodes. These hyperedges are embedded as a tree of (two-ended, straight-line) wire segments and arbitrarily positioned "fan-out points."

b) Wire segments have unit width; the length of a wire is the total length of all its wire segments.

c) At most two wires may cross over each other at any point in the plane.

d) A node occupies $O(1)$ area. Thus, a node has at most $O(1)$ input wires and $O(1)$ output wires. (In general, a node can implement any Boolean function that is computable by a constant number of TTL gates. Hence, an "and gate" or a "j-k flip-flop" is represented by a single node: see Assumption 4.)

e) Wires may not cross over nodes, nor can nodes cross over nodes.

f) Unboundedly long wires and large fan-outs are permissible under the following loading rule. A length-k wire may serve as the input wire for n nodes only if it is the output wire for at least $c_w k + c_g n$ nodes. (In electrical terms, the output nodes work in parallel as current sources or sinks for the capacitive load represented by a wire. The "loading constants" c_w, c_g are always less than one—otherwise it would be impossible to connect two nodes together—but their precise values are technology-dependent.)

Assumption 2—Problem Definition:

a) A chip has degree of concurrency c if it solves c problem instances simultaneously.

b) Each of the N input variables in a problem instance takes on one of M different values with equal likelihood.

c) $M = N^{1+\epsilon}$, for some fixed $\epsilon > 0$. Furthermore, a nearly nonredundant code is used, so that each input and output value is represented as a word with $\approx(1 + \epsilon)(\lg N) = \Theta(\lg N)$ bits. (This assumption makes it possible to express area and time bounds in terms of N alone. It also seems to be required in the proof of a strong lower bound on the area $*$ time^2 complexity of the sorting problem [44].)

d) The output values of a problem instance are a permutation of its input values into increasing order.

Assumption 3—Timing:

a) Wires have unit bandwidth. They carry a one-bit "signal" in each unit of time.

b) Nodes have $O(1)$ delay. (This assumption, while realistic, is theoretically redundant in view of Assumption 3a).)

Assumption 4—Transmission Functions:

a) A transmission function is associated with each node, defining how its outputs and internal state react to the signals on its input wires. More precisely, the "state" of a node is a bit-vector that is updated every time unit according to some fixed function of the signals on its input wires. Similarly, the signals appearing on the output wires of a node are some fixed function of its current state. (With this definition, a node is seen to have the functionality of a finite state automaton of the Moore variety.)

b) If outputs from two or more nodes are connected to the same wire, their output signals must never disagree. To ensure this, the nodes must have identical transmission functions and be connected to the same input wires. (A weaker version of this assumption allows "or-tying" of output wires [44].)

c) Nodes fall into three classes: logic nodes, I/O ports, and I/O memories. I/O memories are further classified as either "RAM-type" or "shift-register-type" memories.

d) I/O memories may not be connected directly to logic nodes.

e) Logic nodes and I/O ports are limited to $O(1)$ bits of state.

f) A $(k_1 \times k_2)$-bit I/O memory contains $k_1 k_2 + \lg k_1 k_2$ bits of state. An "address register" is formed of $\lg k_1 k_2$ bits of state. The other $k_1 k_2$ bits in the state vector are "data."

g) Each problem input bit is assigned to a fixed (i.e., problem-independent) position in some I/O memory's data area. Problem inputs are initially available only at these positions. At the beginning of a computation, all other state bits are initialized to fixed, problem-independent values.

h) Each problem output bit is assigned to a fixed position in an I/O memory. At the completion of a computation, the memory data corresponding to the output bits must have the values defined in Assumption 2. (Note that Assumptions 4a), 4b), 4g), and 4h) make the model deterministic, whereoblivious [25], and unilocal [36].)

i) I/O ports connected to RAM-type $(k_1 \times k_2)$-bit memories can run a memory cycle every $O(k_2 + \lg k_1)$ time units. (These memory cycles are allocated on a first-come, first-serve basis among the $O(1)$ ports connected to a single memory.) During the first $\lg k_1$ time units of a cycle, the port receives a bit-serial "word address" on an input wire. The next input signal is interpreted as a read/write indicator. If a write cycle is indicated, the following k_2 input signals are written into the address word in the memory. Alternatively, during the last k_2 time units of a read cycle, the value of the addressed

word appears in bit-serial format on the I/O port's output wire.

j) I/O ports connected to shift-register-type $(k_1 \times k_2)$-bit memories can run a memory cycle every $O(k_2)$ time units. As in the case of a RAM-type memory, cycle requests are served in a FIFO basis. During the first (third, fifth, etc.) time unit of a cycle, the value of the currently addressed data bit is available on the port's output wire. During even-numbered time units of a cycle, the signal appearing on the port's input wire is written into the addressed data bit, and the memory's address register is incremented mod $k_1 k_2$.

Assumption 5—Area, Time Performance:

a) The total processing area $A_{processing}$ of a chip is the number of unit squares in the smallest enclosing rectangle.

b) The area performance A of a chip is its total area divided by its degree of concurrency c.

c) The total time T_{total} is the average number of time units that elapse between the beginning and end of a computation on c problem instances.

d) The time performance T_d of a chip is the average (over all problem instances) of the number of time units between the first and last memory cycles accessing the data in a particular problem instance.

e) The period T_p of a chip is equal to T_{total} divided by c. Note that $T_p \leq T_d \leq T_{total}$, since a chip with $T_p > T_d$ must be "wasting time" between successive problem instances, and thus could be redesigned to have $T_p = T_d$. Also note that if $c = 1$, then $T_p = T_d = T_{total}$.

f) The I/O bandwidth of a sorting chip is the (average) total number of bits read or written into its I/O memories, divided by T_{total}.

III. CIRCUIT CONSTRUCTIONS

This section presents thirteen constructions for sorting chips. Each will be briefly described in its own subsection. First, however, we present a few useful building blocks.

A serial comparison-exchange module (a "comparator") can be built of $O(1)$ gates [27] in $A = O(1)$ area. It has two bit-serial data inputs, A and B, and two bit-serial data outputs, $\max(A, B)$ and $\min(A, B)$. These inputs and outputs are serialized in a binary code, most-significant bit first.

In some applications, two control lines are added to the comparison-exchange module. The four control states are 1) unconditionally "pass-through" the two inputs; 2) unconditionally "swap" the two inputs; 3) send the larger of its two inputs to output 1; 4) send the smaller of its two inputs to output 1. These more complex modules can still fit in $O(1)$ area and produce two output bits every $O(1)$ time units.

Comparison-exchange modules may be pipelined, as illustrated in Fig. 1 for the case of seven-bit words. Pairs of input values enter the module from the top, and move downwards through the array at the rate of one row per time unit. In each row, the circular element performs a comparison-exchange operation on one bit of the inputs; the square elements pass their inputs through unchanged. Information about the "direction" of the comparison-exchange for each pair of input values travels diagonally through the array, from one circle to the next.

A pipelined comparison-exchange module for $O(\lg N)$-bit

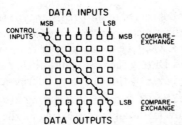

Fig. 1.   A pipelined comparison-exchange module.

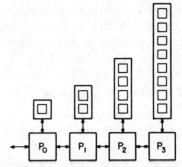

Fig. 2.   The (lg N)-processor heapsort for $N = 16$.

words can do a complete comparison-exchange operation every $T_p = O(1)$ time units with a delay of $T_d = O(\lg N)$ time units. The total area of the comparator as drawn is $O(\lg^2 N)$, and its concurrency is lg N, giving it an area performance of $A = O(\lg N)$. In most applications the square boxes can be deleted, since the input and output data are already "staggered." This reduces $A_{\text{processing}}$ to $O(\lg N)$, giving the pipelined comparator an area performance of $A = O(1)$. Note that this is identical to the area performance of the nonpipelined comparator.

A third building block is the programmed control unit (PCU). A PCU is used to generate a large number of control signals from a very small area. In the constructions below, entire sorting algorithms are encoded into $O(1)$ PCU instructions. Each instruction is $O(\lg N)$ bits long, and executes in $T_d = O(\lg N)$ time units. The instruction set includes branches, arithmetic operations (shifts, adds, and negations), tests, and register-register moves. A PCU has $O(1)$ different registers. One of these registers is connected to the control lines of a comparison-exchange module. Another register is used to generate address and control signals for any I/O ports in the vicinity.

In the constructions below, the term "bit-serial processor" is used to denote the combination of a PCU, $O(1)$ I/O ports, and a bit-serial comparison-exchange module. Each processor can fit into an $O(1)$-by-$O(\lg N)$ unit rectangle, and can perform one comparison-exchange operation every $T_p = T_d = O(\lg N)$ time units.

"Word-parallel processors" are used to augment the performance of some of the designs. A word-parallel processor is constructed from a PCU, a pipelined comparison-exchange module, and $O(\lg N)$ I/O ports connected to shift-register memories. (There seems to be no reason to use a parallel processor with a random-access memory, since the delay of a serial processor matches the delay of an $O(N)$-word RAM.)

A word-parallel processor can perform one comparison-exchange operation every $T_p = O(1)$ time units, for its inputs are easily "staggered" in the manner required by its pipelined comparison-exchange module. Finally, a word-parallel processor fits into an $O(1)$-by-$O(\lg N)$ units rectangle. It thus occupies the same area as does a serial processor, to within constant factors.

Now we are ready to examine sorting circuits for VLSI. The designs are presented in order of increasing parallelism.

A. Uniprocessor Heapsort

This is the smallest sorter imaginable. It has one bit-serial processor running a standard heapsort algorithm [19, pp. 145-149] on N words of data. Each comparison-exchange and each "random" access to the input data takes $O(\lg N)$ time,

so a complete heapsort takes $T_d = T_p = O(N \lg^2 N)$ units of time. The area performance of this design is $A = O(\lg N)$.

Other fast sorting algorithms, such as mergesort or quicksort, could be used in a uniprocessor design. However, none would yield a better AT_d^2 performance, since all require $O(N \lg N)$ random accesses to the processor's I/O memory.

B. (lg N)-Processor Heapsort

Heapsort can be parallelized on a linear array of lg N bit-serial processors, one for each level of the heap [2], [40] (see Fig. 2). The heap operations are pipelined; during an insertion (or deletion) a data element moves down (or up) the heap by one level every $O(\lg N)$ time units. The processor at the top of the heap stores one data element, the smallest value that has been encountered. The kth processor ($0 \le k < \lg N$) handles 2^k elements, storing them in a ($2^k \times \lg N$)-bit RAM. Total sorting time is $T_d = T_p = O(N \lg N)$, and the area is $A = O(\lg^2 N)$.

C. $(1 + \lg N)$-Processor Mergesort

The mergesort algorithm, like the heapsort, fits quite nicely on about lg N processors [45]. Two variable-length FIFO queues are associated with each processor; processor P_k ($0 \le k \le \lg N$) has two 2^k-word queues attached to its output lines.

Referring to Fig. 3, processor $P_k (k > 0)$ merges sorted lists of length 2^{k-1} into sorted lists of length 2^k. It does this by placing the smaller of the elements at the head of its two input queues onto the tail of one of its output queues. Once an entire output list of 2^k elements is complete, the processor starts filling its other output queue. This process repeats as long as inputs are presented to the chip.

Processor P_o is a special case. It merely "splits" its input stream into two, placing alternate elements onto its left-hand and right-hand output queues. These elements should be considered sorted lists of length 1, since they are "merged" into sorted lists of length 2 by processor P_1.

To achieve maximal performance, it is tempting to use pipelined, word-parallel processors. Unfortunately, it seems to be impossible to use these efficiently. There is no way to decide which data elements should next be entered into the pipeline until the previous comparison is complete and the appropriate queue is popped. Thus bit-serial processors are used in this paper's mergesort design.

The FIFO queues between processors are most easily built of RAM memory. A 2^k-word RAM's $O(k)$ access time is fast

378

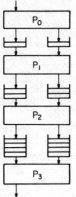

Fig. 3. The $(1 + \lg N)$-processor mergesort for $N = 8$.

enough to keep up with a bit-serial processor working on $O(\lg N)$-bit words, since $k \leq \lg N$. (Alternatively, as pointed out by an ingenious referee, each variable-length 2^k-word FIFO could be implemented with two 2^k-word shift registers. Processor P_{i+1} can empty one of the shift registers while P_i fills up the other one. Even though it requires twice as much memory, the referee's idea is advantageous if shift register memory cells are much smaller or cheaper than RAM memory cells. The idea does, however, have a constant factor disadvantage in time since it introduces an additional $O(2^i)$ delay between P_i's output stream and P_{i+1}'s input stream.)

The time performance of the mergesorter is limited by the data rate of its individual processors. It takes $T_d = O(N \lg N)$ time units for all the input elements to clear the first processor, and another $O(N \lg N)$ time units for the elements to percolate through the $O(N)$ words of internal FIFO storage. Total time for a sort is thus $T_d = O(N \lg N)$. The area of the design is $A = O(\lg^2 N)$, since each of the $1 + \lg N$ processors fits into an $O(\lg N)$ area rectangle.

D. $(\lg N)$-Processor Bitonic Sort

Superficially, this design is very similar to the previous two in that it uses $O(\lg N)$ processors with geometrically varying memory sizes. In this case, processor $P_k(0 \leq k < \lg N)$ has an auxiliary $(N/2^{k+1})$-word fixed-length FIFO queue, as illustrated in Fig. 4. (If the feedback path from $P_{\lg N-1}$ to P_0 were deleted, Fig. 4 would be identical to the "cascade" design for pipelined FFT computation [9].)

The processors execute a bitonic sorting algorithm [19, p. 237]. For the purposes of this paper, the bitonic sort algorithm can be described as $\lg N$ "global iterations." Each global iteration consists of $\log N$ "distance-$(N/2^{k+1})$ operations" on the N input values, in the following order: a distance-$N/2$ operation, a distance-$N/4$ operation, ..., a distance-2 operation, and finally a distance-1 operation. As indicated by the repeated use of the index k, processor P_k is responsible for performing all distance-$(N/2^{k+1})$ operations. With this in mind, a global iteration is seen to be one complete pass of the data around the ring of processors in Fig. 4.

The "distances" in the "operations" refer to the natural indexing of data values within the bitonic sorter. Initially, input x_i enters processor P_0 just before input x_{i+1}. Using its $N/2$-word FIFO queue, P_0 is able to compare input $x_{N/2+i}$ with input x_i, and to exchange these values (if necessary) before

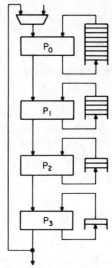

Fig. 4. The $(\lg N)$-processor bitonic sorter for $N = 16$.

passing a naturally indexed sequence $(x'_0, x'_1, \cdots)$ to processor P_1. In other words, processor P_k does compare-exchange operations on data values whose indexes differ only in the kth most significant bit. These index pairs are of the form $(i, N/2^{k+1} + i)$.

Finally, the "direction" of each processor's comparison-exchange operations is not fixed during the course of the bitonic sort algorithm. Sometimes x_i and $x_{N/2^{k+1}+i}$ should be interchanged if $x_i > x_{N/2^{k+1}+i}$, sometimes they should be interchanged if $x_i < x_{N/2^{k+1}+i}$, and sometimes they need not be interchanged under any circumstances (this last is a "no-op" distance-$(N/2^{k+1})$ operation). These three possibilities are reflected in three patterns of data flow through individual processors. When it uses pattern number 1, processor P_k performs a "no-op" by placing the elements it receives from processor P_{k-1} onto the back of its FIFO queue, and sending the elements that come off the front of its queue to processor P_{k+1}. In pattern number 2, processor P_k does a comparison-exchange on the element at the front of its queue and the element it receives from processor P_{k-1}, sending the smaller of the two to processor P_{k+1} and placing the larger on the back of its queue. Pattern number 3 is the same as pattern number 2, except that the larger of the two elements is sent to the next processor and the smaller is placed on the back of the queue. The complete bitonic sort algorithm is summarized in Fig. 5.

Interpreting the algorithm of Fig. 5, processor P_k executes pattern number 1 on the first $(\lg N - k - 1)N$ elements it encounters. This corresponds to $(\lg N - k - 1)$ "global" iterations of the outermost loop in Fig. 5. Processor P_k becomes active in its reordering of the data stream only during the last $k + 1$ global iterations. It alternately fills its queue with new elements (executing $N/2^{k+1}$ instances of pattern number 1) and performs comparison-exchanges of the queue data with the incoming data (executing $N/2^{k+1}$ instances of pattern number 2 or 3).

The conditional expressions of statements 7 and 8 may be implemented with three counters (for g, i, and j) in each processor. The DIV and MOD operations merely select one bit of these counters to control the pattern of data flow. Thus, the bitonic sort can be performed on $\lg N$ bit-serial processors of $O(\lg N)$ area, for a total area of $A = O(\lg^2 N)$. It takes $T_p =$

```
1.   FOR g ← 0 TO lg N - 1 DO
2.     FOR j ← 0 TO 2^t-1 DO
3.       FOR i ← 0 TO N/2^{t+1}-1 DO    /* Fill up FIFO with new data */
4.         {execute pattern 1};
5.       OD;
6.       FOR i ← 0 TO N/2^{t+1}-1 DO  /* Perform comparison-exchanges as necessary */
7.         IF g < lg N - k - 1 THEN {execute pattern 1}
8.         ELSEIF ((j DIV (2^{t+i+1}/N)) MOD 2) = 0 THEN {execute pattern 2}
9.         ELSE {execute pattern 3} FI;
10.      OD;
11.    OD;
12.  OD.
```

Fig. 5.   The bitonic sort algorithm executed by processor P_k of Fig. 4.

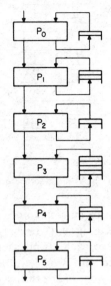

Fig. 6.   The $(1/2)(\lg N)(1 + \lg N)$-processor bitonic sorter for $N = 8$.

$O(\lg N)$ time for a data element to pass through a bit-serial processor, so that each "global iteration" takes $O(N \lg N)$ times. Total time for a bitonic sort on bit-serial processors is thus $T_d = O(N \lg^2 N)$.

The area * time^2 performance of the design may be improved by using word-parallel processors. Now each global iteration requires only $O(N)$ time, if $O(\lg N)$ communication lines are provided between processors. Total time is $T_d = O(N \lg N)$; total area is still $A = O(\lg^2 N)$. Note that this parallelized design requires $O(\lg^2 N)$ I/O ports, in order to provide sufficient memory bandwidth to the FIFO queues. Also, portions of the control algorithm will have to be hard-wired, so that the three counters described above can be incremented in $O(1)$ time.

It is interesting that the lg N processor heapsorter has exactly the same area and time performance as the lg N processor bitonic sorter, even though the heapsorter does not use parallelized comparators. The heapsort algorithm requires each of the lg N processors to make "random accesses" to their local memory. The extra time taken by these slower accesses is exactly balanced by the greater number of comparison-exchange operations required by the bitonic sorting algorithm.

(Chung, Luccio, and Wong have also proposed a lg N-processor bitonic sort for a magnetic bubble memory system [8]. Their algorithm has an inferior time performance to the one described above, since only one of their processors is active at any time.)

E. $O(\lg^2 N)$-Processor Bitonic Sort

This design "unrolls" the lg N-processor bitonic sort, so that each processor is responsible for only one distance-$N/2^{k+1}$ operation. Since about half of the lg$^2 N$ operations of the bitonic sort algorithm are no-ops, only about $(1/2) \lg^2 N$ processors are required in this version of the algorithm; see Fig. 6. Each processor fits in an $O(1)$-by-$O(\lg N)$ unit rectangle, so the entire design occupies $O(\lg^3 N)$ area.

A surprisingly large amount of time and FIFO storage area is saved by eliminating the no-ops when "unrolling" the bitonic sort on lg N processors. Since a distance-$N/2^{k+1}$ operation is implemented with $N/2^{k+1}$ words of FIFO storage, and since all but $k + 1$ of the distance-$(N/2^{k+1})$ operations are no-ops, the total storage is $\Sigma(k + 1)(N/2^{k+1})$, or a little less than $2N$ words. The problem solution time is proportional to the length

of this pipeline, or $T_d = O(N)$ if word-parallel processors are used. The area performance is half of its total area, $A = O(\lg^3 N)$, because the pipeline stores two problems at a time.

The AT_d^2 performance of this design is a factor of lg N better than that of the previous design. To understand this phenomenon, it is helpful to compare the performance of one $O(\lg^2 N)$-processor bitonic sorter with that of a collection of lg N identical (lg N)-processor bitonic sorters. Both have the same amount of total area, and both solve lg N sorting problems in $T_{\text{total}} = O(N \lg N)$ time (if word-parallel processors are used). Due to the elimination of the no-ops, however, the $O(\lg^2 N)$-processor implementation solves each sorting problem with logarithmically less delay.

F. $\sqrt{N \lg N}$-Processor Bitonic Sort

Chung, Luccio, and Wong have recently proposed implementing a bitonic sort on $\sqrt{N \lg N}$ processors in a linear array [8]. Here, each processor has $\sqrt{N/\lg N}$ words of shift register storage. It can run a serial bubble sort algorithm on its local store in $T_d = O(N/\lg N)$ time, if it uses word-parallel processors. Working together, the entire array performs an N-element sort in $T_d = O(N)$ and $A = O(\sqrt{N \lg^3 N})$. The total area increases to $A = O(N \lg N)$ if the shift registers are made of logic nodes rather than I/O memories, in order to decrease the circuit's unreasonably large I/O bandwidth.

According to the model of this paper, this approach is highly nonoptimal in an AT_d^2 sense. It is no faster, but much larger, than the $O(\lg^2 N)$-processor bitonic sorting design.

G. $(N/2)$-Comparable Bubble Sort

As noted by a number of researchers, the bubble sorting algorithm can be fully parallelized on a linear array of $N/2$ bit-serial (or pipelined) comparison-exchange modules [3], [6], [8], [12], [15], [24], [28], [29]. Each module performs the following simple computation: Of the two data elements it receives from its left- and right-hand neighbors, it sends the smaller to the left and the larger to the right. The array can be initialized in parallel with zeros, then serially loaded with N data elements through the leftmost module. If it is then "flushed out" by loading maximal elements through the leftmost module, the N data elements will emerge from the leftmost module in $O(N)$ comparison times.

The area of the $N/2$-comparator bubble sorter is $A = O(N \lg N)$, since each comparator occupies $O(\lg N)$ area. When bit-serial modules are used, each comparison takes $O(\lg N)$ time, so $T_d = O(N \lg N)$. Word-parallel modules improve the bubble-sorter's delay to $T_d = O(N)$. Even so, its AT_d^2 performance remains dismal. According to the $AT_d^2 = \Omega(N^2 \lg N)$ lower bound, a sorter with $O(N \lg N)$ processing area should sort in about $T_d = O(\sqrt{N})$ time.

There are at least three other ways of sorting N numbers on $O(N)$ processors with similar area-time performance figures. Heapsort can be run on a balanced binary tree of N bit-serial processors [26, pp. 297-299]. This tree structure can also be used to perform the broadcast operations required in recently proposed implementations of enumeration sort [49] and radix sort [10], [47] on N processors. If built from bit-serial processors, these designs would have $A = O(N \lg N)$, $T_d = O(N \lg N)$. It might be possible to use pipelined comparators and word-parallel communication lines efficiently in these designs, although it is not obvious how this can be done. In any event, the AT_d^2 performance of these designs is intrinsically cubic (instead of quadratic) in N, making them highly nonoptimal for large sorting problems.

H. N-Processor Bitonic Sort on Mesh

The bitonic sort can be adapted to run very efficiently on N bit-serial processors connected in a square mesh [31], [42]. Word-parallel connections are used in the mesh in order to speed up the movement of data over long distances.

The operation of this algorithm is rather complicated and will not be explained here. It is sufficient to know that the $O(N \lg^2 N)$ comparison-exchanges in the bitonic sort require a total of $O(\lg^3 N)$ of the N processors' time. However, it can take as much as $O(\sqrt{N})$ time to rearrange the data among the processors in preparation for the next comparison-exchange step. Fortunately, only a few of the comparison-exchange operations take this amount of time, so that the total time to sort N elements is only $T_d = O(\sqrt{N})$.

To achieve the time bound asserted above, it is necessary to move words of data from one processor to the next in $O(1)$ time. This is a little difficult to arrange, since the wires between neighboring processors are $O(\lg N)$ units long. According to the model's loading rules [see Assumption 1f)], $T_d = O(\lg\lg N)$ time is required to amplify a signal for a wire of this length. Once a signal has been applied, it can be received, gated, and retransmitted in $T_d = O(1)$ time by $O(\lg N)$ identical, unit-sized nodes working in concert.

The total area of the design is $A = O(N \lg^2 N)$. Note that the N processors take up only $O(N \lg N)$ area. The word-parallel data paths (and their high-power drivers) require more room than the processors themselves, in the asymptotic limit.

(Batcher's odd-even sorting algorithm [21] or a merge sort algorithm [41] may have constant factor advantages for some N. Aside from these constant factors, both algorithms can be implemented on the mesh with the same AT_d^2 performance as that derived above for Batcher's bitonic sort.)

I. N-Processor Bitonic Sort on Shuffle-Exchange Net

Stone notes that the bitonic sort is easily adapted to run on N bit-serial processors interconnected in the shuffle-exchange pattern [39]. If bit-serial interconnections are used, the $O(N \lg^2 N)$ comparison-exchanges in the bitonic sort take a total of $T_d = O(\lg^3 N)$ time.

Given that this design sorts so quickly, it should not be surprising that it cannot be laid out in a small amount of area. Indeed, it is possible to prove that the smallest layout for the shuffle-exchange graph occupies $\Omega(N^2/\lg^2 N)$ area [42]. An embedding of this size has been recently obtained [18], [23]. This embedding can be "stretched" in the vertical direction in $O(\lg N)$ places to make room for N bit-serial processors, each occupying an $O(1)$-by-$O(\lg N)$ rectangle. The modified embedding has area $A = O(N^2/\lg^2 N)$, and its longest wires are of length $O(N/\lg N)$.

The AT_d^2 performance of this design is a little suboptimal. One might attempt to improve it by adding parallelism to the interprocessor communication lines. If, for example, k wires were laid down for every edge in the shuffle-exchange graph, the resulting network could conceivably sort k times faster. Unfortunately, network area would increase by a factor of k^2, leaving the AT_d^2 performance figure unchanged.

(To achieve the factor of k speedup alluded to in the previous paragraph, the processors would have to be fitted with parallel comparison-exchange modules. More significantly, the size of each processor would have to be increased, so that it could drive its output wires with only $O(\lg N)/d$ delay. Thus, it seems that the maximum-possible speedup factor of $k = \Theta(\lg N)$ would be very difficult to achieve in a layout $\Theta(\lg N)$ times as large: there would only be $O(N)$ area available for each of the N processors; each of the $\Theta(\lg N)$ gates in each processor could be implemented with at most $O(N/\lg N)$ unit-sized nodes; the longest wires in a Leighton-style layout would have length $O(N)$; the long-wire driver delay would be $O(\lg\lg N)$; the time per comparison-exchange would be dominated by these long-wire delays; and the resulting circuit would sort in $T_d = O(\lg^2 N \lg\lg N)$ instead of $O(\lg^2 N)$. The problem with this construction is that no one knows how—or whether it is possible—to lay out the N-node shuffle-exchange graph using edges of length at most $O(N/\lg^2 N)$ [23].)

J. N-Processor Bitonic Sort on the PCCC

Preparata and Vuillemin [33] have shown that their "cube-connected cycles" (CCC) interconnection pattern can run the bitonic sort algorithm as efficiently as the shuffle-exchange pattern; $A = O(N^2/\lg^2 N)$ and $T_d = O(\lg^3 N)$. Their network has the advantage of having a simple, asymptotically optimal, layout; the asymptotically optimal layout for the shuffle-exchange graph is much less uniform. On the other hand, the bitonic sort algorithm for the CCC is somewhat more complicated than the bitonic sort on the shuffle-exchange.

Quite recently, the CCC design has been improved to achieve AT_d^2 optimality over a wide range of areas and times. The new construction is called the "pleated cube-connected cycles" (PCCC) [4]. The idea behind the construction is to provide more "short" wires for the shorter-distance operations of the bitonic sort algorithm (see Section III-D). The less-frequent long-distance operations are performed more slowly over fewer "long" wires. As the average wire length of a PCCC increases, its area increases but its sorting time decreases. The result is a family of networks whose areas range from $A = O(N \lg N)$ to $A = O(N^2/\lg^4 N)$. Each network sorts in AT_d^2-optimal time: from $T_d = O(\sqrt{N \lg N})$ to $T_d = O(\lg^3 N)$.

The times quoted for the PCCC are for bit-serial implementations. Conceivably, parallel PCCC networks could be devised to run a bitonic sort in $A = O(N^2/\lg^2 N)$ and $T_d = O(\lg^2 N)$. Any such construction would be complicated by the problem of wire delays that was encountered in the attempt in Section III-I to speed up the shuffle-exchange network.

(Another approach to improving the CCC's performance is suggested by Reif and Valiant [34]. They have devised a probabilistic algorithm that would run in $T_d = O(\lg^2 N)$ time on the $A = O(N^2/\lg^2 N)$ CCC, if each processor had access to a random number generator. It would be interesting to know if this time performance is achievable by a deterministic algorithm, in keeping with this paper's model of computation.)

K. $(N \lg^2 N)$-Comparator Bitonic Sort

Batcher's bitonic sorting network [19, p. 237] can be laid out explicitly on a VLSI chip. Each of the $(1/2)(\lg^2 N + \lg N)$ parallel comparison-exchange operations is implemented by a row of $N/2$ bit-serial comparison-exchange modules. The bit-serial interconnections between the rows of comparators require more room than the comparators themselves, at least asymptotically. The wiring in front of the comparators doing a "distance-$(N/2^{k+1})$ operation" takes up an $O(N/2^{k+1})$ by $O(N)$ area of the chip. (As in Section III-D, $0 \le k < \lg N$.) The total area occupied by the network is thus $\Sigma(k + 1) \cdot (N^2/2^{k+1}) = O(N^2)$, since there are $k + 1$ distance-$(N/2^{k+1})$ comparison-exchange operations.

The total delay through the network is $T_d = \Theta(\lg^3 N)$, for each of the $\Theta(\lg^2 N)$ rows adds $\Theta(\lg N)$ delay. Since there are no feedback paths, the network is easily pipelined with a concurrency of $\Theta(\lg^2 N)$. The area performance is the total area divided by the concurrency $A = O(N^2/\lg^2 N)$.

An improvement can be made to the construction outlined above, leading to a better AT_d^2 performance. There is no need for multiple stages of amplification at the outputs of the bit-serial comparators if the comparators themselves are "scaled up" to match the length of their output wires. One such comparator for a distance-$(N/2^{k+1})$ operation occupies $O(N/2^{k+1})$ area. (An $O(\lg N)$-stage driver is needed at the output of each distance-(1) comparator to amplify its signal for the following scaled-up comparator.) The total area is still $O(N^2)$: the comparators now take up space asymptotically equal to that of the long-wire drivers in the original construction.

Sorting delay is decreased since bits travel from one row of comparators to the next in $T_d = O(1)$ time. The improved network has total delay $T_d = O(\lg^2 N)$, concurrency $O(\lg N)$, and area performance $A = O(N^2/\lg N)$.

Pratt has pointed out that shellsort [19, p. 84] can be implemented on either $(\lg^2 N)$ or $(N \lg^2 N)$ processors with the same AT_d^2 performance as the bitonic sort.

As this article was going to press, an $O(N \lg N)$-comparator, $O(\lg N)$-depth sorting network was reported [1]. Implemented in a fully parallel fashion, it could be built of $O(\lg N)$ rows of $N/2$ comparators each. The connections between the rows are "expander graphs" with an average wire length of $\Theta(N)$. Total area is $O(N^2 \lg N)$. Sorting delay need only be $T_d = O(\lg N)$ if each comparator is "scaled-up" by a factor of N. Thus, $AT_d^2 = O(N^2 \lg^3 N)$, an asymptotic improvement over the $O(N \lg^2 N)$-comparator bitonic sorter. This asymptotic improvement is nonetheless a constant-factor disaster, for there are an astronomically large number of rows in the currently proposed "$O(\lg N)$-depth" construction.

L. N^2-Comparator Bubble Sort

A final attempt can be made to optimize the bubble sort for VLSI, providing a different comparison-exchange module for each of the N^2 comparisons in a bubble sort on N elements [19, p. 224]. The resulting network is not very impressive. If built from bit-serial comparators, it occupies $O(N^2)$ area. Total delay through the network is $T_d = O(N)$, and $N/\lg N$ problem instances will fit in it at any given time. Its area performance is its total area divided by its concurrency, $A = O(N \lg N)$. Note that the same time performance can be obtained in a small fraction of this area with the $\lg^2 N$-processor bitonic sorting design.

When built of pipelined comparison-exchange modules, the N^2-processor bubble sorter occupies a total of $N^2 \lg^2 N$ area. Its concurrency increases to about $N \lg N$, giving it the same area performance as before, $A = O(N \lg N)$. Strangely enough, its time performance worsens, becoming $T_d = O(N \lg N)$. The reason for this anomalous behavior is that the bit-serial implementation is already fully pipelined.

M. (N^2)-Processor Rank Sort

Consider a square array of N^2 processors, interconnected in the following peculiar way. The N processors in each row are the leaves of a balanced binary tree; the internal vertices of the "row trees" provide bit-serial communication paths between the root of the tree and its N "leaf" processors. Similarly, a "column tree" provides connections between the N processors in each column of the array. Each processor is thus a leaf vertex in two orthogonal trees.

This network has been called by various names, including the "orthogonal tree network" [32] and the "mesh of trees" [22], [23]. Fig. 7 illustrates it for the case $N = 4$.

A brute-force sorting algorithm can be implemented on this network, as pointed out by the authors cited above. (Muller and Preparata [30] describe this algorithm without reference to the natural shape of the orthogonal tree network.) Each of the N inputs to a sorting problem can be presented to one of the root vertices of a row tree. The inputs are then broadcast

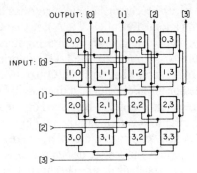

OUTPUT: [0] [1] [2] [3]

INPUT: [0] >

[1] >

[2] >

[3] >

Fig. 7. The orthogonal tree network for $N = 4$.

TABLE I
AREA-TIME BOUNDS FOR THE SORTING PROBLEM

Design	Area Perf. (A)	Time Perf. (T_d)	AT_d^2
Lower bound	-		$\Omega(N^2 \lg N)$
1. Uniprocessor (s.)	$\lg N$	$N \lg^2 N$	$N^2 \lg^5 N$
2. $\lg N$ - proc. heapsort (s.)	$\lg^2 N$	$N \lg N$	$N^2 \lg^4 N$
3. $\lg N$ - proc. mergesort (s.)	$\lg^2 N$	$N \lg N$	$N^2 \lg^4 N$
4. $\lg N$ - proc. bitonic (p.)	$\lg^2 N$	$N \lg N$	$N^2 \lg^4 N$
5. $\lg^2 N$ - proc. bitonic (p.)	$\lg^3 N$	N	$N^2 \lg^3 N$
6. $\sqrt{N \lg N}$ - proc. bitonic (p.)	$N \lg N$	N	$N^3 \lg N$
7. $N/2$ - comp. bubble (p.)	$N \lg N$	N	$N^4 \lg N$
8. N - proc. bitonic, mesh (s.)	$N \lg^2 N$	$\sqrt{N}$	$N^2 \lg^2 N$
9. N - proc. bitonic, S-E (s.)	$N^2/\lg^2 N$	$\lg^3 N$	$N^2 \lg^4 N$
10. N - proc. bitonic, PCCC (s.)	$N^2 \lg^2 N / T_d^2$	$\lg^3 N \le T_d \le \sqrt{N \lg N}$	$N^2 \lg^2 N$
11. $N \lg^2 N$ - comp. bitonic (p.)	$N^2/\lg N$	$\lg^2 N$	$N^2 \lg^3 N$
12. N^2 - comp. bubble (s.)	$N \lg N$	N	$N^4 \lg N$
13. N^2 - proc. rank sort (s.)	$N^2 \lg^2 N$	$\lg N$	$N^2 \lg^4 N$

to the leaves of the tree, so that each processor in a row has a copy of that row's input. Next, the column trees come into play: the jth leaf processor of the jth column tree sends a copy of its input to its root. This value is "broadcast" downwards through the column trees, so that processor (i, j) now contains copies of two input values, $input[i]$ and $input[j]$.

The next step in the sorting algorithm is to compute the ranks of the inputs. The ith row tree evaluates the rank of input i by "summing" the results of comparing $input[i]$ with $input[j]$. To be more specific, processor (i, j) compares its two input values, sending a "1" up through its row tree if $input[i] > input[j]$ or if $((input[i] = input[j])$ and $(i > j))$. These values are summed by the row trees. A moment's reflection should convince the reader that the sum of the values in row i is the rank of $input[i]$, with ties being broken by the $i > j$ calculation. The root of each row tree will have a different integer from the range of possible ranks, $[0, N - 1]$.

The input ranks are next broadcast to the leaf vertices of the row trees. Finally, processor (i, j) sends up ("selects") the value of $input[i]$ through its column tree if $rank[i] = j$. The sorted values are now available at the roots of the column trees.

It is a straightforward exercise to verify that the internal vertices can perform the broadcast, summation, and selection operations in a bit-serial fashion with $O(1)$ bits of storage and $O(1)$ logic devices.

It remains to establish the area and time complexity of this sorting procedure. Since broadcast, summation, and selection operations are performed on trees with N leaves, the best

possible time performance is $T_d = O(\lg N)$. Also, as proved in [23], the minimum possible area for the orthogonal tree network is $O(N^2 \lg^2 N)$. These performance figures are in fact achievable, but only with careful design.

Observe that in Fig. 7 the wires connecting vertices in the row and column trees are not all of the same length. The closer one gets to the root, the longer the wires; the wires double in length from one level of the tree to the next. Thus, each logic device in an internal vertex on level k should be built of $O((N \lg N)/2^k)$ unit-sized nodes, enabling the vertex to drive its $O((N \lg N)/2^k)$-length wires at unit delay, as required. Since there are $O(1)$ logic devices in an internal vertex, and since there are 2^k vertices at level k, each level fits into the $O(1)$-by-$O(N \lg N)$ rectangle available to it in the "obvious" $O(N^2 \lg^2 N)$-area layout suggested by Fig. 7.

IV. COMPARISON OF THE DESIGNS

The area and time performance of the thirteen sorting circuits is summarized in Table I below. For easy reference, the designs are numbered from 1 to 13 in correspondence with Sections III-A–III-M in which they are discussed. The "s" or "p" in the design's name indicates whether it is implemented with serial or pipelined comparators. The "area performance" column gives each design's processing area divided by its concurrency, in accordance with the definition in Section II. This metric is an indication of the power consumed per sorting problem. A design's "time performance," as formally defined in Section II, can be characterized as the elapsed time between the first input to the circuit and the last output from the chip for each sorting problem.

Table I shows that nearly all the designs considered in this paper are within a factor of $O(\lg^k N)$ of being optimal in an AT_d^2 sense. The sole exceptions are the bubble sorters and the $\sqrt{N \lg N}$-processor bitonic sorter.

Table II contains additional information about the sorters. (The PCCC design appears twice in this table, on lines 10a and 10b, in its slowest and fastest forms. Intermediate figures are possible: see Section III-J.) The first entry for each design shows its concurrency, defined as the number of sorting problems that should be solved simultaneously to achieve the maximum possible area performance. The second and third entries indicate the total "processing" and "memory" area required in a system containing that design. (One bit of RAM or shift-register memory occupies one unit of area.) The final entry is the design's processor-memory bandwidth in bits/(unit time). This entry is also equal to the number of I/O ports required on the design's "processing" chip, since all the designs keep all their ports busy essentially all the time.

Thus far in the paper, A_{memory} and I/O bandwidth have not been considered explicitly. Furthermore, $A_{processing}$ has largely ignored in deference to the theoretically "correct" area performance measure $A = A_{processing}/c$. From a systems perspective, however, the measures of Table II are more important than those of Table I. A design will occupy circuit board area proportional to $A_{processing} + A_{memory}$, and its "processing"

TABLE II
OTHER PERFORMANCE MEASURES

Design	Concurrency	$A_{processing}$	A_{memory}	I/O B.W.
1. Uniprocessor	1	$\lg N$	$N \lg N$	1
2. $\lg N$ - proc. heapsort	1	$\lg^2 N$	$N \lg N$	$\lg N$
3. $\lg N$ - proc. mergesort	1	$\lg^2 N$	$N \lg N$	$\lg N$
4. $\lg N$ - proc. bitonic	1	$\lg^2 N$	$N \lg N$	$\lg^2 N$
5. $\lg^2 N$ - proc. bitonic	2	$\lg^3 N$	$N \lg N$	$\lg^3 N$
6. $\sqrt{N \lg N}$ - proc. bitonic	1	$N \lg N$	$N \lg N$	$\lg N$
7. $N/2$ - proc. bubble	1	$N \lg N$	$N \lg N$	$\lg N$
8. N - proc. bitonic, mesh	1	$N \lg^2 N$	$N \lg N$	$\sqrt{N} \lg N$
9. N - proc. bitonic, S-E	1	$N^2/\lg^2 N$	$N \lg N$	$N/\lg^2 N$
10a. N - proc. bitonic, PCCC	1	$N \lg N$	$N \lg N$	$\sqrt{N} \lg N$
10b. N - proc. bitonic, PCCC	1	$N^2/\lg^4 N$	$N \lg N$	$N/\lg^2 N$
11. $N \lg^2 N$ - proc. bitonic	$\lg N$	N^2	$N \lg^2 N$	N
12. N^2 - proc. bubble	$N/\lg N$	N^2	N^2	N
13. N^2 - proc. rank sort	1	$N^2 \lg^2 N$	$N \lg N$	N

portion will have to have enough pins to support its I/O bandwidth.

Of course, a sorting circuit should not be selected just because it is asymptotically optimal. A digital engineer is interested only in actual speeds and sizes. Although the model of computation of this paper is not exact enough to permit such analyses, some statements can be made about the relative sizes and speeds of the designs.

The smallest design is clearly the $O(\lg N)$ area uniprocessor. Somewhat surprisingly, this design is nearly AT_d^2 optimal if it is programmed to use any of the $O(N \lg N)$-step serial algorithms.

If more sorting speed is desired, the $(\lg N)$-processor heapsort design becomes attractive. It requires almost exactly $\lg N$ times as much area as the uniprocessor design, since the processors and programs for the two designs are very similar. The design has the smallest possible delay of any sorter that receives its inputs in a single bit-serial stream, since the first output is available immediately after the last input has been received. (The $N/2$-processor bubble sorter is the only other design considered in this paper that has this property. All others introduce at least an $O(\lg N)$ delay between the last input time and the first output time.)

A major drawback of $(\lg N)$-processor heapsorter is that it requires $\lg N$ independently addressable memories, one for each processor. The total memory-processor bandwidth increases proportionately (see Table II) to $\lg N$ bits per time unit.

The $(\lg N)$-processor bitonic design has been the same area and time performance as the $(\lg N)$-processor heapsort design. The former has the advantage of a slightly simpler control algorithm, and it uses the simpler shift-register type of I/O memory; the latter uses a more efficient sorting algorithm and hence less memory bandwidth.

The $(\lg^2 N)$-processor bitonic sorter is smaller than either of the $(\lg N)$ processor designs, for moderately sized N. Its control algorithm is extremely simple, so that a "processor" is not much more than a comparison-exchange module. Its major drawback is that it makes continuous use of $(1/2) * (\lg N) * (\lg N + 1)$ word-parallel shift-register memories, of various sizes.

The $(\sqrt{N \lg N})$-processor bitonic sorter has been entered in Table II with a total area of $O(N \lg N)$, so that there is room on the chip for all of its temporary storage registers. Otherwise, it would require $\sqrt{N \lg N}$ separate I/O memories. It has the same speed and a somewhat better I/O bandwidth than the $(\lg^2 N)$-processor bitonic sorter just discussed. However, the latter's shift registers could also be placed on the same chip as its processing circuitry, equalizing the I/O bandwidth for the two designs. When "constant factors" are taken into consideration, the $(\sqrt{N \lg N})$-processor design is clearly much larger than the $(\lg^2 N)$-processor design, because it has more processors and a much more complicated control algorithm.

The $(N/2)$-processor bubble sorter has a couple of significant advantages that are not revealed in either Table I or Table II. Its comparators need very little in the way of control hardware, so that at least for small N, it occupies less area than any of the preceding designs. Also, it can be used as a "self-sorting memory," performing insertions and deletions on-line. (The uniprocessor and the $(\lg N)$-processor heapsorter can also be used in this fashion.) However, for even moderately sized N, the bubble sorter's horrible AT_d^2 performance becomes noticeable. For example, when $N = 256$, the $(\lg^2 N)$-processor bitonic sorter's 36 comparators and 491 words of storage probably occupy less room than the 128 comparators in a bubble sorter. Nonetheless, the bubble sorter always maintains about a 2:1 delay advantage over the $(\lg^2 N)$-processor bitonic sorter, when similar comparators are used.

The N-processor mesh-type bitonic sorter is the first design to solve a sorting problem in sublinear time. Unfortunately, it occupies a lot of area. Each of its processors must run a complicated sorting algorithm, reshuffling the data among themselves after every comparison-exchange operation. Its I/O bandwidth must also be large, since it solves sorting problems so rapidly. However, constant factor improvements may be made to its area and bandwidth figures by reprogramming the processors so that each handles several data elements at a time. Also, large area and bandwidth are not always significant problems: in an existing mesh-connected multiprocessor, the N processors are already in place and the I/O data may be produced and consumed by local application routines.

The next three designs in Tables I and II are variants on a fully parallelized bitonic sort. The shuffle-exchange sorter has a slight area advantage over the CCC or PCCC sorter because of its simpler control algorithm. However, the CCC and PCCC are somewhat more regular interconnection patterns, so that they may be easier to wire up in practice. Both designs are smaller in total asymptotic area than the $(N \lg^2 N)$-processor bitonic sorter, which solves $\lg N$ problems at a time. Nonetheless, the control structure of this last design is so simple that, as a rough guess, it takes less area than the others for all $N < 2^{20}$. (Of course, if a shuffle-exchange or PCCC processor has already been built, the additional area cost for programming the sorting algorithm is very small.)

There seems to be little to recommend the N^2-processor bubble sorter. It has the same I/O bandwidth, a bit more total area, and a much worse time performance than the $(N \lg^2 N)$-processor bitonic sorter.

Finally, the N^2-processor rank sorter can be characterized as being larger but not all that much faster than the N- and (N lg N)-processor bitonic sorters. Its chief interest is theoretical: it sorts in a minimal number, $O(\lg N)$, of gate delays. No other sorting circuit of equivalent time performance could possibly beat its area performance by more than a logarithmic factor or two, considering the theoretical limit of $AT_d^2 = \Omega(N^2 \lg)$. However, it remains an open question whether it is possible to build a $T = O(\lg N)$ sorter that occupies even a little less area.

V. Closing Remarks

At the time of this writing, there are a number of important open questions in VLSI complexity theory. A simply stated but seemingly perplexing problem is to find out how much area can be saved when additional "layers" of wiring are made available by technological advances. It is known that a k-level embedding can be no smaller than $1/k^2$ of the area of a two-level embedding [42, pp. 36–38], but it is not known whether this bound is achievable. (Some results on k-level embedding have been obtained recently [35].)

A second problem is to derive matching upper and lower bounds for the area $*$ time^2 complexity of the sorting problem. The best upper bound is $AT_d^2 = O(N^2 \lg^2 N)$, achieved by the N-processor bitonic sort on a mesh and by the PCCC. As discussed in Section I, the best lower bound is $AT_p^2 = \Omega(N^2 \lg N)$ [44], which leaves a gap of $O(\lg N)$. The gap can be closed by adding the assumption that all lg N bits of each input value are read in through a single I/O port [42]. (The current model allows the bits of each input value to be read in through different ports.) It seems probable that the $AT_p^2 = \Omega(N^2 \lg^2 N)$ result for word-oriented, "localized" I/O can be extended to handle the less restrictive model of this paper. On the other hand, it is conceivable that such a bound is impossible because of the existence of some yet-to-be-discovered sorting circuit with an AT_d^2 performance better than that of the bitonic sort on the mesh or PCCC.

A third problem is to evaluate separately the VLSI complexity of the "ranking" and "permutation" subproblems of the sorting problem, as discussed in Section I. Current lower bounds for the sorting problem can be viewed as arguments about the data flow required in a permuter; they seem to say little about the problem of ranking the data. Lower bounds on ranking would presumably be more subtle and give more insight into how "control information" must flow in a sorting circuit.

Another set of problems is opened up by the fact that the area $*$ time^2 bounds are affected greatly by nondeterministic, stochastic, or probabilistic assumptions in the model. My intuition is that the VLSI complexity of sorting is not sensitive to such assumptions, but it would be nice to be sure of this. Counterintuitive results have already been proved: equality testing is very easy if the answer need only be "probably" correct [25], [48].

A final and very important problem in VLSI theory is the development of a stable model. Currently there are almost as many models as papers. If this trend continues, results in the area will become difficult to report and describe. However, it is far from settled whether wire delays should be treated as being linear or logarithmic in wire length, and the costs of off-chip communication remain unknown.

Acknowledgment

Referee 1's detailed and thought-provoking report is gratefully acknowledged.

References

[1] M. Ajtai, J. Komlós, and E. Szemerédi, "An $O(n \log n)$ sorting network," in *Proc. 15th Annu. ACM Symp. Theory Comput.*, Apr. 1983, pp. 1–9.
[2] P. K. Armstrong, U.S. Patent 4 131 947, Dec. 26, 1978.
[3] P. K. Armstrong and M. Rem, "A serial sorting machine," *Comput. Elect. Eng.*, Pergamon, vol. 9, Mar. 1982.
[4] G. Bilardi, M. Pracchi, and F. P. Preparata, "A critique of network speed in VLSI models of computation," *IEEE J. Solid-State Circuits*, vol. SC-17, pp. 696–702, Aug. 1982.
[5] R. Brent and H. T. Kung, "The area-time complexity of binary multiplication," *J. Ass. Comput. Mach.*, vol. 28, pp. 521–534, July 1981.
[6] T. C. Chan, K. P. Eswaren, V. Y. Lum, and C. Tung, "Simplified odd-even sort using multiple shift-register loops," *Int. J. Comput. Inform. Sci.*, vol. 7, pp. 295–314, Sept. 1978.
[7] B. Chazelle and L. Monier, "Towards more realistic models of computation for VLSI," in *Proc. 11th Annu. ACM Symp. Theory Comput.*, Apr. 1979, pp. 209–213.
[8] K.-M. Chung, F. Luccio, and C. K. Wong, "On the complexity of sorting in magnetic bubble memory systems," *IEEE Trans. Comput.*, vol. C-29, pp. 553–562, July 1980.
[9] A. Despain, "Very fast Fourier transform algorithms for hardware implementation," *IEEE Trans. Comput.*, vol. C-28, pp. 333–341, May 1979.
[10] Y. Dohi, A. Suzuki, and N. Matsui, "Hardware sorter and its application to data base machine," in *Proc. 9th Annu. Symp. Comput. Arch.* (*ACM SIGARCH Newsletter*), vol. 10, Apr. 1982, pp. 218–225.
[11] S. A. Evans, "Scaling I^2L for VLSI," *IEEE J. Solid-State Circuits*, vol. SC-14, pp. 318–326, Apr. 1979.
[12] L. J. Guibas and F. M. Liang, "Systolic stacks, queues, and counters," in *Proc. 1982 Conf. Advanced Res. VLSI*, Massachusetts Inst. Technol., Cambridge, Jan. 1982, pp. 155–164.
[13] J.-W. Hong and H. T. Kung, "I/O complexity: The red-blue pebble game," in *Proc. 13th Annu. ACM Symp. Theory Comput.*, May 1981, pp. 326–333.
[14] J.-W. Hong, "On similarity and duality of computation," Peking Munic. Computing Center, Peking, People's Repub. China, 1981, unpublished.
[15] G. Kedem, "A first in, first out and a priority queue," Dep. Comput. Sci., Univ. Rochester, Rochester, NY, Tech. Rep. 90, Mar. 1981.
[16] Z. M. Kedem and A. Zorat, "Replication of inputs may save computational resources in VLSI," in *Proc. 22nd Symp. Found. Comput. Sci.*, IEEE Comput. Soc., Oct. 1981.
[17] M. B. Ketchen, "AC powered Josephson miniature system," in *Proc. 1980 Int. Conf. Circuits Comput.*, IEEE Comput. Soc., Oct. 1980, pp. 874–877.
[18] D. Kleitman, F. T. Leighton, M. Lepley, and G. L. Miller, "New layouts for the shuffle-exchange graph," in *Proc. 13th Annu. ACM Symp. Theory Comput.*, May 1981, pp. 334–341.
[19] D. E. Knuth, *The Art of Computer Programming, Vol. 3: Sorting and Searching.* Reading, MA: Addison-Wesley, 1973.
[20] ——, "Bit omicron and big omega and big theta," *SIGACT News*, vol. 8, pp. 18–24, Apr.–June 1976.
[21] M. Kumar and D. S. Hirschberg, "An efficient implementation of Batcher's odd-even merge algorithm and its application in parallel sorting schemes," *IEEE Trans. Comput.*, vol. C-32, pp. 254–264, Mar. 1983.
[22] F. T. Leighton, "New lower bound techniques for VLSI," in *Proc. 22nd Symp. Found. Comput. Sci.*, IEEE Comput. Soc., Oct. 1981.
[23] ——, "Layouts for the shuffle-exchange graph and lower bound techniques for VLSI," Ph.D. dissertation MIT/LCS/TR-724, M.I.T. Lab. for Comput. Sci., Massachusetts Inst. Technol., Cambridge, June 1982.
[24] C. E. Leiserson, "Area-efficient VLSI computation," Ph.D. dissertation CMU-CS-82-108, Comput. Sci. Dep., Carnegie-Mellon Univ., Pittsburgh, PA, Oct. 1981.

[25] R. J. Lipton and R. Sedgewick, "Lower bounds for VLSI," in *Proc. 13th Annu. ACM Symp. Theory Comput.*, May 1981, pp. 300–307.

[26] C. Mead and L. Conway, *Introduction to VLSI Systems.* Reading, MA: Addison-Wesley, 1980.

[27] H. P. Moravec, "Fully interconnecting multiple computers with pipelined sorting nets," *IEEE Trans. Comput.*, vol. C-28, pp. 795–798, Oct. 1979.

[28] A. Mukhopadhyay and T. Ichikawa, "An *n*-step parallel sorting machine," Dep. Comput. Sci., Univ. Iowa, Iowa City, Tech. Rep. 72-03, 1972.

[29] A. Mukhopadhyay, "WEAVESORT—A new sorting algorithm for VLSI," Univ. Central Florida, Orlando, Tech. Rep. 53-81, 1981.

[30] D. E. Muller and F. P. Preparata, "Bounds to complexities of networks for sorting and for switching," *J. Ass. Comput. Mach.*, vol. 22, pp. 195–201, Apr. 1975.

[31] D. Nassimi and S. Sahni, "Bitonic sort on a mesh-connected parallel computer," *IEEE Trans. Comput.*, vol. C-28, pp. 2–7, Jan. 1979.

[32] D. Nath, S. N. Maheshwari, and P. C. P. Bhatt, "Efficient VLSI networks for parallel processing based on orthogonal trees," Dep. Elec. Eng., Indian Inst. Technol., New Delhi, India, 1981, unpublished.

[33] F. Preparata and J. Vuillemin, "The cube-connected cycles: A versatile network for parallel computation," in *Proc. 20th Annu. Symp. Found. Comput. Sci.*, IEEE Comput. Soc., Oct. 1979, pp. 140–147.

[34] J. H. Reif and L. G. Valiant, "A logarithmic time sort for linear size networks," in *Proc. 15th Annu. ACM Symp. Theory Comput.*, Apr. 1983, pp. 10–17.

[35] A. L. Rosenberg, "Three-dimensional VLSI, I: A case study," in *Proc. CMU Conf. VLSI,"* Comput. Sci. Press, Oct. 1981, pp. 69–79.

[36] J. Savage, "Planar circuit complexity and the performance of VLSI algorithms," in *VLSI Systems and Computations*, H. T. Kung, B. Sproull, and G. Steele, Eds. Woodland Hills, CA: Comput. Sci. Press, Oct. 1981.

[37] ——, "Area-time tradeoffs for matrix multiplication and related problems in VLSI models," *J. Comput. Syst. Sci.*, vol. 22, pp. 230–242, Apr. 1981.

[38] C. L. Seitz, "Self-timed VLSI systems," in *Proc. Caltech Conf VLSI*, Dep. Comput. Sci., California Inst. Technol., Pasadena, Jan. 1979, pp. 345–356.

[39] H. Stone, "Parallel processing with the perfect shuffle," *IEEE Trans. Comput.*, vol. C-20, pp. 153–161, Feb. 1971.

[40] Y. Tanaka, Y. Nozaka, and A. Masuyama, "Pipeline searching and sorting modules as components of data flow database computer," in *Proc. Int. Fed. Inform. Processing*, Oct. 1980, pp. 427–432.

[41] C. D. Thompson and H. T. Kung, "Sorting on a mesh-connected parallel computer," *Commun. Ass. Comput. Mach.*, vol. 20, pp. 263–271, Apr. 1977.

[42] C. D. Thompson, "A complexity theory for VLSI," Ph. D. dissertation CMU-CS-80-140, Comput. Sci. Dep., Carnegie-Mellon Univ., Pittsburgh, PA, Aug. 1980.

[43] ——, "Fourier transforms in VLSI," *IEEE Trans. Comput.*, vol. C-32, pp. 1047–1057, Nov. 1983.

[44] C. D. Thompson and D. Angluin, "On AT^2 lower bounds for sorting," unpublished manuscript, May 1983.

[45] S. Todd, "Algorithm and hardware for a merge sort using multiple processors," *IBM J. Res. Develop.*, vol. 22, pp. 509–517, Sept. 1978.

[46] J. Vuillemin, "A combinational limit to the computing power of VLSI circuits," *IEEE Trans. Comput.*, vol. C-32, pp. 294–300, Mar. 1983.

[47] L. E. Winslow and Y.-C. Chow, "Parallel sorting machines: Their speed and efficiency," in *Proc. AFIPS 1981 Nat. Comput. Conf.*, Fall 1981, pp. 163–165.

[48] A. C. Yao, "Some complexity questions related to distributive computing," in *Proc. 11th Annu. ACM Symp. Theory Comput.*, May 1979, pp. 209–213.

[49] H. Yasuura, N. Takagi, and S. Yajima, "The parallel enumeration sorting scheme for VLSI," Dep. Inform. Sci., Kyoto University, Kyoto, Japan, Yajima Lab. Res. Rep. ER-81-03, Apr. 1982.

SIAM J. COMPUT.
Vol. 10, No. 4, November 1981

© 1981 Society for Industrial and Applied Mathematics
0097-5397 81 1004-0001 $01.00 0

PARALLEL MATRIX AND GRAPH ALGORITHMS*

ELIEZER DEKEL[†], DAVID NASSIMI[‡] AND SARTAJ SAHNI[†]

Abstract. Matrix multiplication algorithms for cube connected and perfect shuffle computers are presented. It is shown that in both these models two $n \times n$ matrices can be multiplied in $O(n/m + \log m)$ time when n^2m, $1 \le m \le n$, processing elements (PEs) are available. When only m^2, $1 \le m \le n$, PEs are available. two $n \times n$ matrices can be multiplied in $O(n^2/m + m(n/m)^{2.61})$ time. It is shown that many graph problems can be solved efficiently using the matrix multiplication algorithms.

Key words. cube connected computer, perfect shuffle computer, parallel algorithm, matrix multiplication, graph algorithm, complexity

1. Introduction. This paper is concerned with the development of general purpose matrix multiplication and graph algorithms for single instruction stream, multiple data stream (SIMD) parallel computers (see Flynn [10] for a classification of computer models). All SIMD computers have the following characteristics:

(1) They consist of p processing elements (PEs). The PEs are indexed $0, 1, \cdots, p - 1$ and an individual PE may be referenced as in PE (i). Each PE is capable of performing the standard arithmetic and logical operations. In addition, each PE knows its index.

(2) Each PE has some local memory.

(3) The PEs are synchronized and operate under the control of a single instruction stream.

(4) An enable/disable mask can be used to select a subset of the PEs that are to perform an instruction. Only the enabled PEs will perform the instruction. The remaining PEs will be idle. All enabled PEs execute the same instruction. The set of enabled PEs can change from instruction to instruction.

While several SIMD models have been proposed and studied, in this paper we wish to make a distinction between the shared memory model (SMM) and the remaining models, all of which employ an interconnection network and use no shared memory. In the shared memory model, there is a common memory available to each PE. Data may be transmitted from PE (i) to PE (j) by simply having PE (i) write the data into the common memory and then letting PE (j) read it. Thus, in this model it takes only $\theta(1)$ time for one PE to communicate with another PE. Two PEs are not permitted to write into the same word of common memory simultaneously. The PEs may or may not be allowed to simultaneously read the same word of common memory. If the former is the case, then we shall say that read conflicts are permitted.

Most algorithmic studies of parallel computation have been based on the SMM [2], [4], [8], [9], [14], [15], [20], [21], [27]. This model is, however, not very realistic as it assumes that the p PEs can access any p words of memory (1 word per PE) in the same time slot. In practice, however, the memory will be divided into blocks so that no two PEs can simultaneously access words in the same block. If two or more PEs wish to access words in the same memory block, then the requests will get queued. Each PE will be served in a different time slot. Thus, in the worst case $O(p)$ time could be spent

---

* Received by the editors May 24, 1979, and in revised form October 10, 1980. This research was supported in part by the National Science Foundation under grant MCS 78-15455.

† Department of Computer Science, University of Minnesota, Minneapolis, Minnesota 55455.

‡ Department of Electrical Engineering and Computer Science, Northwestern University, Evanston. Illinois 60201.

transferring data to the p PEs. All the papers cited earlier ignore this and take the time for a simultaneous memory access by all PEs to be $O(1)$.

SIMD computers with restricted interconnection networks appear to be more realistic. In fact, the ILLIAC IV is an example of such a machine. There are several other such machines that are currently being fabricated. The largest of these is the massive parallel processor (MPP) designed by K. Batcher. It has $p = 16K$. A block diagram of a SIMD computer with an interconnection network is given in Fig. 1.1. Observe that there is no shared memory in this model. Hence, PEs can communicate among themselves only via the interconnection network.

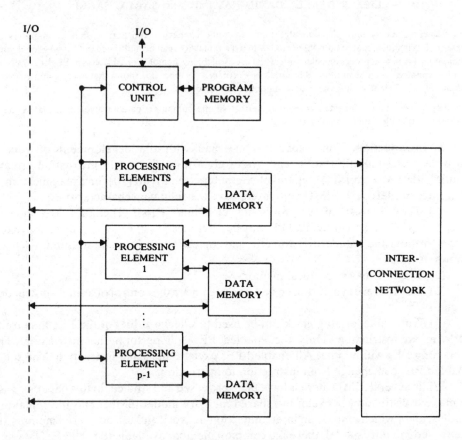

FIG. 1.1. *Block diagram of an* SIMD *computer.*

While several interconnection networks have been proposed (see [29]), we shall consider only three interconnection networks in this paper. These are: mesh, cube, and perfect shuffle. The corresponding computer models are described below. Fig. 1.2 shows the resulting interconnection pattern.

(i) *Mesh connected computer* (MCC). In this model the PEs may be thought of as logically arranged as in a k-dimensional array $A(n_{k-1}, n_{k-2}, \cdots, n_0)$, where n_i is the size of the ith dimension and $p = n_{k-1} * n_{k-2} * \cdots * n_0$. The PE at location $A(i_{k-1}, \cdots, i_0)$ is connected to the PEs at locations $A(i_{k-1}, \cdots, i_j \pm 1, \cdots, i_0)$, $0 \le j < k$, provided they exist. Data may be transmitted from one PE to another only via this interconnection pattern. The interconnection scheme for a 16 PE MCC with $k = 2$ is given in Fig. 1.2(a).

(ii) *Cube connected computer* (CCC). Assume that $p = 2^q$ and let $i_{q-1} \cdots i_0$ be the binary representation of i for $i \in [0, p-1]$. Let $i^{(b)}$ be the number whose binary representation is $i_{q-1} \cdots i_{b+1} \bar{i}_b i_{b-1} \cdots i_0$, where $\bar{i}_b$ is the complement of i_b and $0 \le b < q$. In the cube model, PE (i) is connected to PE $(i^{(b)})$, $0 \le b < q$. As in the mesh model, data can be transmitted from one PE to another only via the interconnection pattern. Fig. 1.2(b) shows an 8 PE CCC configuration.

(iii) *Perfect shuffle computer* (PSC). Let p, q, i and $i^{(b)}$ be as in the cube model. Let $i_{q-1} \cdots i_0$ be the binary representation of i. Define SHUFFLE (i) and UNSHUFFLE (i) to, respectively, be the integers with binary representation $i_{q-2} i_{q-3} \cdots i_0 i_{q-1}$ and $i_0 i_{q-1} \cdots i_1$. In the perfect shuffle model, PE (i) is connected to PE $(i^{(0)})$, PE (SHUFFLE (i)) and PE (UNSHUFFLE (i)). These three connections are, respectively, called *exchange*, *shuffle*, and *unshuffle*. Once again, data transmission from one PE to another is possible only via the connection scheme. An 8 PE PSC configuration is shown in Fig. 1.2(c).

It should be noted that the MCC model requires $2k$ connections per PE, the CCC model requires $\log p$ (all logarithms in this paper are base 2) and the PSC model requires only three connections per PE. The SMM requires a large (and impractical) amount of PE to memory connections to permit simultaneous memory access by several PEs. It should also be emphasized that in any time instance, only one unit of data (say one word) can be transmitted along an interconnection line. All lines can be busy in the same time instance, however.

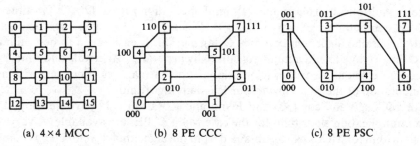

(a) 4×4 MCC   (b) 8 PE CCC   (c) 8 PE PSC

Fig. 1.2. *Boxes represent PEs.*

Each of the four models (including the SMM) described above has received much attention in the literature. Agerwala and Lint [2], Arjomandi [3], Csanky [8], Eckstein [9] and Hirschberg [14] have developed algorithms for certain matrix and graph problems using a SMM. Hirschberg [15], Muller and Preparata [20] and Preparata [27] have considered the sorting problem for the SMM. The evaluation of polynomials on the SMM has been studied by Munro and Paterson [21], while arithmetic expression evaluation has been considered by Brent [4] and others. Efficient algorithms to sort and perform data permutations on an MCC can be found in Thompson and Kung [32], Nassimi and Sahni [22], [23] and Thompson [31]. Thompson's algorithms [31] can also be used to perform permutations on a CCC and a PSC. Lang [18], Lang and Stone [19] and Stone [30] show how certain permutations may be performed using shuffles and exchanges. Nassimi and Sahni [25] develop fast sorting and permutation algorithms for a CCC and a PSC.

Gentleman [13] and Abelson [1] have studied the inherent complexity of parallel matrix computations. Gentleman [13], for example, has shown that at least $0.35N$ routing steps are needed to compute the product of two $N \times N$ matrices on an MCC. Also, $O(\log N)$ routes are needed to do this on a CCC or PSC.

In this paper, we are primarily concerned with the problem of multiplying two $n \times n$ matrices. The matrix multiplication problem is a very important and fundamental computational problem. The reason for this is that many other problems are best solved using matrix multiplication. In the case of parallel computations even some problems that are normally not solved using matrix multiplication turn out to be efficiently solved using matrix multiplication (or a variation of matrix multiplication). Some examples of problems in this category are:

   (a) Find the shortest distance between all pairs of vertices in a graph. This problem is traditionally solved using a dynamic programming algorithm [16].
   (b) Transitive closure. This is traditionally also solved using dynamic programming [16].

(c) Radius, diameter and centers of a graph.

(d) Breadth-first spanning tree. This is traditionally found using a breadth-first search.

(e) Topological sort. This is normally done using a special graph traversal [16]. etc.

These and other graph problems that are efficiently solved using matrix multiplication are described in greater detail in § 4. In almost all of the cases considered in § 4, the application of matrix multiplication is quite straightforward. Nonetheless, we describe how matrix multiplication (or a variation) may be used in each case. This serves to highlight the difference in the thought pattern needed to arrive at an efficient parallel algorithm versus an efficient single processor algorithm.

The matrix multiplication problem for SMMs and MCCs has been extensively studied. Savage [28] presents an $O(\log n)$ algorithm to multiply two $n \times n$ matrices on a SMM with $n^3/\log n$ PEs. The problem may be easily solved in $O(n)$ time when only n^2 PEs are available. Both these algorithms are obtained from the classical $O(n^3)$ matrix multiplication algorithm. Chandra [6] has obtained an $O(\log n)$ implementation of Strassen's multiplication algorithm. His implementation runs in $O(n^{\log 7}/p)$ time on a p PE SMM computer when $p \leqq n^{\log 7}/\log n$. When $p = n^{\log 7}/\log n$, the complexity of Chandra's parallel algorithm becomes $O(\log n)$. This is easily seen to be optimal as it takes $O(\log n)$ time to add n numbers optimally in parallel. Agerwala and Lint [2] have obtained an efficient algorithm to multiply Boolean matrices. Their algorithm is an implementation of the well-known four Russians algorithm.

For MCCs, Van Scoy [33] and Flynn and Kosaraju [11] have developed $O(n)$ matrix multiplication algorithms for the case when n^2 PEs are available. A very simple $O(n)$ algorithm for MCCs can be obtained from the algorithm developed by Cannon [5] for 2 dimensional MCCs with wraparound. A two dimensional MCC with wraparound is an MCC as defined here with the following additional PE connections:

(i) Let PE (i, j) denote the PE in position (i, j) of the $n \times n$ PE array. PE $(i, 0)$ is connected to PE $(i, n-1)$, $0 \leqq i < n$.

(ii) PE $(0, j)$ is connected to PE $(n-1, j)$, $0 \leqq j < n$.

Cannon's algorithm can be easily adapted to run in $O(n)$ time on an $n \times n$ MCC without wraparound.

We begin, in § 2, by developing the matrix multiplication algorithms for CCCs. First, algorithms are presented for the case of n^3 and n^2 PEs. The algorithm for the case of $n^2 m$ PEs, $1 \leqq m \leqq n$ is then obtained by combining together the algorithms for the cases of n^3 and n^2 PEs. The resulting algorithm is of complexity $O(n/m + \log m)$. Note that when $m = n/\log n$, $n^3/\log n$ PEs are used and the complexity is $O(\log n)$. When $m = 1$, n^2 PEs are used and the complexity is $O(n)$. Next, we discuss how two $n \times n$ matrices may be multiplied in $O(n^3/m^2)$ time when m^2 PEs, $1 \leqq m \leqq n$, are available. This complexity is easily lowered to $O(n^2/m + m(n/m)^{2.61})$ if Pan's [26] algorithm is used in place of the classical matrix multiplication algorithm. In § 3, these results are extended to obtain PSC algorithms of the same complexity. Also, in § 3, we present an interesting algorithm to compute $(A * B)^T$ on an n^3 PE PSC. This algorithm is faster than the corresponding PSC algorithm to compute $A * B$.

As mentioned earlier, the matrix multiplication algorithms obtained can be used to obtain efficient algorithms for several graph problems. These are discussed in § 4.

2. Cube connected computer. In presenting our algorithms, we shall make use of the following conventions and notation.

(i) "←" will be used to denote an assignment requiring data movement between PEs that are directly connected. ":=" will be used to denote an assignment in which all variables in the left- and right-hand side of ":=" are local to the same PE or to the control unit.

(ii) We shall use i_r to denote bit r in the binary representation of i. Thus the binary representation of i is $i_{u-1}i_{u-2} \cdots i_0$ for some u. $i^{(b)}$ will denote the number with binary representation $i_{u-1}i_{u-2} \cdots i_{b+1}\bar{i}_b i_{b-1} \cdots i_0$, where $\bar{i}_b = 1 - i_b$.

(iii) PE (k) will denote the PE with index k. Similarly, $A(k), B(k), C(k)$, etc., will denote memory locations or registers in PE (k).

(iv) PEs may be enabled by providing a selectivity function. This function can be placed after any statement. Operations are performed only on enabled PEs. For example, the statement

$$A(i) := B(i) + C(i), \qquad (i_2 = 0)$$

has the selectivity function $(i_2 = 0)$. As a result, the addition and assignment is carried out only in PEs whose index i has bit 2 equal to 0. The statement

$$A(i^{(b)}) \leftarrow B(i), \qquad (i_0 = 1)$$

specifies a data route. Data from the B register of PEs with index i and $i_0 = 1$ is routed to the A register of corresponding PEs with bit b equal to $1 - i_b$.

(v) The complexity of an algorithm is the sum of the PE time needed and the communication time (i.e., the time needed to route data from PE to PE). A *unit-route* is a data transmission from a PE to another PE to which it is directly connected. In a unit-route all PEs can transmit one word of data each to one of the PEs to which they are directly connected.

2.1. CCCs with n^3 PEs. Consider a CCC with $n^3 = 2^{3q}$ PEs. Conceptually, these PEs may be regarded as arranged in an $n \times n \times n$ array pattern. If we assume, that the PEs are indexed in row major order, the PE, PE (i, j, k) in position (i, j, k) of this array has index $in^2 + jn + k$ (note that array indices are in the range $[0, n-1]$). Hence, if $r_{3q-1} \cdots r_0$ is the binary representation of the PE position (i, j, k) then $i = r_{3q-1} \cdots r_{2q}$, $j = r_{2q-1} \cdots r_q$ and $k = r_{q-1} \cdots r_0$. Using $A(i, j, k)$, $B(i, j, k)$ and $C(i, j, k)$ to represent memory locations in PE (i, j, k), we can describe the initial condition for matrix multiplication as

$$\left. \begin{array}{l} A(0, j, k) = a_{jk} \\ B(0, j, k) = b_{jk} \end{array} \right\}, \qquad 0 \leq j < n, \quad 0 \leq k < n.$$

a_{jk} and b_{jk} are the elements of the two matrices to be multiplied. The desired final configuration is

$$C(0, j, k) = c_{jk}, \qquad 0 \leq j < n, \quad 0 \leq k < n,$$

where

(2.1)
$$c_{jk} = \sum_{l=0}^{n-1} a_{jl} b_{lk}.$$

Our algorithm computes the product matrix C by directly making use of (2.1). The algorithm has three distinct phases. In the first, elements of A and B are distributed over the n^3 PEs so that we have $A(l, j, k) = a_{jl}$ and $B(l, j, k) = b_{lk}$. In the second phase the products $C(l, j, k) = A(l, j, k) * B(l, j, k) = a_{jl} b_{lk}$ are computed. Finally, in the third phase the sums $\sum_{l=0}^{n-1} C(l, j, k)$ are computed. The details are spelled out in procedure CCM1 (Algorithm 2.1). In this procedure all PE references are by PE index (recall that the index of PE (i, j, k) is $in^2 + jn + k$). Lines 1–10 implement phase 1. The loop of lines 1 to 4 copies the data initially in PE $(0, j, k)$ to the PEs, PE (i, j, k), $1 \leq i < n$ (recall that bits $3q - 1, \cdots, 2q$ of a PE index yield the i value). Following this loop, we have

$$\left. \begin{array}{l} A(i, j, k) = a_{jk} \\ B(i, j, k) = b_{jk} \end{array} \right\}, \qquad 0 \leq i < n.$$

Note that $A(i, j, i) = a_{ji}$. In lines 5 to 7, $A(i, j, i)$ is replicated over $A(i, j, k)$, $0 \leq k < n$ with the result that $A(i, j, k) = a_{ji}$, $0 \leq k < n$. The loop of lines 8–10 replicates $B(i, i, k) = b_{ik}$ over $B(i, j, k)$, $0 \leq j < n$. In line 11, the product $C(i, j, k) = A(i, j, k) * B(i, j, k) = a_{ji} b_{ik}$ is computed in PE (i, j, k), $0 \leq i < n$, $0 \leq j < n$ and $0 \leq k < n$. Finally, the loop of lines 12–14 computes the sum

391

$$C(0, j, k) = \sum_{i=0}^{n-1} C(i, j, k) = \sum_{i=0}^{n-1} a_{ji} b_{ik} = c_{jk}.$$

The analysis of CCM1 is quite straightforward. The processor communication time in each of the last three **for** loops is that for q unit-routes. The first **for** loop requires $2q$ unit-routes. Hence, the total communication time is that for $5q = O(\log n)$ unit-routes. The PE time is clearly seen to be $O(\log n)$.

ALGORITHM 2.1.

```
line    procedure CCM1 (A, B, C) //CCC multiplication algorithm using n³ PEs//
1           for l := 3q - 1 down to 2q do
2               A(j^(l)) ← A(j), (j_l = 0)
3               B(j^(l)) ← B(j), (j_l = 0)
4           end
5           for l := q - 1 down to 0 do //replicate A(i, j, i) into A(i, j, *)//
6               A(j^(l)) ← A(j), (j_l = j_{2q+l})
7           end
8           for l := 2q - 1 down to q do //replicate B(i, i, k) into B(i, *, k)//
9               B(j^(l)) ← B(j), (j_l = j_{q+l})
10          end
11          C(j) := A(j) * B(j)
12          for l := 2q to 3q - 1 do //add terms//
13              C(j) ← C(j) + C(j^(l))
14          end
15      end CCM1
```

2.2. CCCs with n^2 PEs. Two $n \times n$ matrices can be multiplied in $O(n)$ time on a CCC with n^2 PEs. It is instructive to first look at Cannon's algorithm [5] for MCCs with wraparound. This algorithm is given as procedure MCCMULT (Algorithm 2.2). $A(i, j)$, $B(i, j)$ and $C(i, j)$ refer to memory locations (or registers) A, B and C in PE (i, j), $0 \le i < n$ and $0 \le j < n$. Initially, $A(i, j) = a_{ij}$ and $B(i, j) = b_{ij}$. The algorithm consists of two identifiable phases. In phase 1 the A and B values are aligned so that the product $A(i, j) * B(i, j)$ gives one of the n terms in the sum for c_{ij} (recall that $c_{ij} = \sum_{k=0}^{n-1} a_{ik} b_{kj}$). Lines 1–4 produce the desired alignment. The elements in the ith row of A are shifted left circularly i times while the elements in the jth column of B are shifted up circularly j times. The net result is that, following this loop, $A(i, j) = a_{i,(j+i) \bmod n}$ and $B(i, j) = b_{(i+j) \bmod n, j}$. Note that $A(i, j) * B(i, j)$ is a valid product pair for $c(i, j)$.

In the second phase the A values in each row are shifted left circularly one position and B values in each column are shifted up circularly one position. This shift retains compatibility in A and B. The A and B values in each PE are multiplied to get a new term of C. Repeating this shift-multiply operation $n - 1$ times, all the terms in c_{ij} can be generated and added to obtain the product matrix (see lines 6–10 of Algorithm 2.2). The total communication time is that for $4(n - 1)$ unit-routes. The overall algorithm complexity is $O(n)$.

ALGORITHM 2.2.

```
line    procedure MCCMULT (A, B, C)
1           for l := 1 to n - 1 do //align A and B//
2               A(i, j) ← A(i, (j + 1) mod n), (i ≥ l)
3               B(i, j) ← B((i + 1) mod n, j), (j ≥ l)
4           end
5           C(i, j) := A(i, j) * B(i, j) //initialize C//
6           for l := 1 to n - 1 do
7               A(i, j) ← A(i, (j + 1) mod n)
8               B(i, j) ← B((i + 1) mod n, j)
9               C(i, j) := C(i, j) + A(i, j) * B(i, j)
10          end
11      end MCCMULT
```

Cannon's algorithm is easily adapted to run in $O(n)$ time on an $n \times n$ MCC without wraparound. The left circular shifts of rows of A and the upward circular shifts of columns of B are easily simulated. First, we reverse and shift right the first half of each row of A to obtain

$$A'(i, j) = A(i, n - 1 - j), \qquad \frac{n}{2} \leqq j \leqq n - 1, \quad 0 \leqq i \leqq n - 1.$$

Next, the first half of each column of B is reversed and shifted down to yield

$$B'(i, j) = B(n - 1 - i, j), \qquad \frac{n}{2} \leqq i \leqq n - 1, \quad 0 \leqq j \leqq n - 1.$$

Each of these reversal-shift operations can be accomplished using $3n/2 - 2$ unit-routes (see Nassimi and Sahni [23] for details).

Now, a left circular shift of A is accomplished by the following instructions:

$$T(i, n/2) := A(i, n/2),$$

$$A(i, j) \leftarrow A(i, j + 1), \qquad 0 \leqq j \leqq n - 2,$$

$$A(i, n - 1) := A'(i, n - 1),$$

$$A'(i, j) \leftarrow A'(i, j - 1), \qquad n/2 + 1 \leqq j \leqq n - 1,$$

$$A'(i, n/2) := T(i, n/2).$$

An upward circular shift of the columns of B can be obtained similarly. Since each shift takes two unit-routes, MCCMULT can be run in $8(n - 1) + 2 * (3n/2 - 2) = 11n - 12$ unit-routes on an MCC with no wraparound.

Our CCC multiplication algorithm has the same two phases as does Cannon's. However, the initial alignment and later shifting pattern are substantially different. We assume that $n^2 = 2^{2q}$ PEs are available. Conceptually, these PEs may be viewed as in an $n \times n$ array (see Fig. 2.1). Once again, we shall use two different notations to refer to the jth PE. PE index is hardware determined. $A(j)$, $B(j)$, $C(j)$ will refer to memory locations or registers in PE (j). In the $n \times n$ array, we assume that the index of the PE in position (i, j) is the same as the row-major index of the position. Thus if PE (k) is at position (i, j) of the array then $k = in + j$. So, we can, without confusion, refer to the PE in position (i, j) as PE (i, j). Similarly, we can use the notation $A(i, j)$, $B(i, j)$ and $C(i, j)$. Our, algorithm, however, will only use the notation $A(j)$, $B(j)$, $C(j)$.

j \ i	0	1	2	3
0	0 0000	1 0001	2 0010	3 0011
1	4 0100	5 0101	6 0110	7 0111
2	8 1000	9 1001	10 1010	11 1011
3	12 1100	13 1101	14 1110	15 1111

FIG. 2.1. *Array view of a 16 PE CCC. Each square represents a PE. The number in a square is the PE index (both decimal and binary representations are provided).*

Procedure CCM2 (Algorithm 2.3) is a formal statement of our multiplication algorithm. It is assumed that A and B have been initialized so that $A(i, j) = a_{ij}$ and $B(i, j) = b_{ij}$, $0 \leqq i < n$, $0 \leqq j < n$. The algorithm computes $C(i, j) = c_{ij} = \sum_{k=0}^{n-1} a_{ik} b_{kj}$, $0 \leqq i < n$, $0 \leqq j < n$. Lines 1–5 obtain the initial alignment. Lines 6–13 form the product matrix by repeated shift-multiply-add steps. The loop of lines 1–5 results in the following configuration (Lemma 2.1):

$$A(i, t) = a_{i, i \oplus t},$$

(2.2)

$$B(i, t) = b_{i \oplus t, t}.$$

$i \oplus t$ denotes an *exclusive or* of the binary representations of i and t. Hence, the initial product of line 6 computes $C(i, t) = a_{i, i \oplus t} * b_{i \oplus t, t}$, which is one of the terms in the sum for c_{it} (see (2.1)). FUNC (line 8) is a function that controls the shifting of A and B values. It returns a bit index in the range $[0, q - 1]$ (recall that $n = 2^q$). Note that the q least significant bits in a PE index (using the one-dimensional indexing scheme) determines the column index for the two-dimensional indexing scheme while the q most significant bits determine the row index. Keeping this in mind, we easily see that line 10 moves the elements in A along rows while line 11 moves elements of B along columns. Thus in line 12 we always have $A(i, t) = a_{i,p}$ and $B(i, t) = b_{r,t}$ for some p and r. Lemma 2.2 shows that $r = p$ always so that we get a valid pairing in $A(i, t)$ and $B(i, t)$. From the construction of FUNC (yet to be specified) it will follow that no a or b value can show up in the same PE more than once.

Algorithm 2.3.

```
line   procedure CCM2 (A, B, C)
             //multiply two n × n matrices on a CCC with n² PEs//
             //obtain initial alignment//
  1        for l := 0 to q − 1 do
  2            k := q + l
  3            A(j) ← A(j^(l)), (j_k = 1)
  4            B(j) ← B(j^(k)), (j_l = 1)
  5        end
  6        C(j) := A(j) * B(j)
  7        for k := 1 to n − 1 do //shift-multiply//
  8            l := FUNC (k) //get a bit index l ∈ {0, 1, ⋯, q − 1}//
  9            m := q + l
 10            A(j) ← A(j^(l))
 11            B(j) ← B(j^(m))
 12            C(j) := C(j) + A(j) * B(j)
 13        end
 14    end CCM2
```

Hence, each time the product $A(j) * B(j)$ is computed in line 12, a new term of (2.1) is formed. This implies that when the loop of lines 7–13 terminates, the product matrix will have been computed.

LEMMA 2.1. *When the loop of lines 1–5 of CCM2 terminates, (2.2) correctly represents the values for $A(i, t)$ and $B(i, t)$, $0 \leq i < n, 0 \leq t < n$.*

Proof. Using the two-dimensional notation, lines 3–4 of CCM2 may be written as

$$A(i, t) \leftarrow A(i, t^{(l)}), (i_l = 1),$$

$$B(i, t) \leftarrow B(i^{(l)}, t), (t_l = 1).$$

From this, the correctness of (2.2) is easily established. □

LEMMA 2.2. *Whenever line 12 of CCM2 is reached, $A(i, t) = a_{ir}$ and $B(i, t) = b_{rt}$ for some r (note that $j = in + t$), $0 \leq i < n$ and $0 \leq t < n$.*

Proof. Let $A^k(j) = A^k(i, t)$ be the value of $A(j)(= A(i, t))$ when line 12 is reached on iteration k of the loop of lines 7–13. Let l_k be the value assigned to l (line 8) in this iteration. From line 10 it follows that $A^k(j) = A^{k-1}(j^{(l_k)}), k \geq 1$. From Lemma 2.1, we know that $A^0(j) = A^0(i, t) = a_{i,t'}$ where $t' = i \oplus t$. Consequently, $A^k(i, t) = a_{i,r}$ where $r = t' \oplus z^{l_k, \cdots, l_1}$ and $z^{l_k, \cdots, l_1}$ is obtained from 0 by successively complementing bits l_k, $l_{k-1}, \cdots, l_1$ in the binary representation of 0 (recall that the specification of FUNC requires that $0 \leq \text{FUNC} (\ ) < q$). The same argument shows that $B^k(i, t) = b_{s,t}$ where

$s = t' \oplus z^{l_k, \cdots, l_1}$ ($B^k(\ )$ is defined analogous to $A^k(\ )$). Therefore, $r = s$ for all k, $k \geq 1$. □

We now proceed to specify FUNC. We are looking for a function that will generate a sequence of $n - 1$ integers in the range $[0, q - 1]$ such that, by successively complementing along each bit in this sequence, all elements of a row will pass through each PE in that row (and so by adding q to each element in the sequence we can get every element in a column to go through each PE in that column). In other words, in terms of the notation of Lemma 2.2, we want the sequence of integers

$$\{z^{l_1}, z^{l_2, l_1}, \cdots, z^{l_{n-1}, \cdots, l_1}\}$$

to be some permutation of $\{1, 2, \cdots, n - 1\}$. It is very easy to arrive at a suitable FUNC if we think recursively. Divide a row into two halves. All PEs in the left half have bit $q - 1 = 0$ while those in the right half have bit $q - 1 = 1$. If we have a bit sequence S_{q-2} that can be used when the number of PEs in a row is 2^{q-1} then this sequence will cause all elements in each half of a 2^q PE row to go through each PE in that half. By complementing on bit $q - 1$ we can exchange halves and then reuse S_{q-2} to make each element go through the PEs it has not already gone through. So, we obtain

$$S_{q-1} = S_{q-2}, q - 1, S_{q-2} \quad \text{and} \quad S_0 = 0.$$

When $q = 4$, the sequence to use is

$$S_3 = S_2, 3, S_2$$
$$= S_1, 2, S_1, 3, S_1, 2, S_1$$
$$= S_0, 1, S_0, 2, S_0, 1, S_0, 3, S_0, 1, S_0, 2, S_0, 1, S_0$$
$$= 0, 1, 0, 2, 0, 1, 0, 3, 0, 1, 0, 2, 0, 1, 0.$$

(a) Initial

row \ column	00	01	10	11	
00	00	01	02	03	A
	00	01	02	03	B
01	10	11	12	13	A
	10	11	12	13	B
10	20	21	22	23	A
	20	21	22	23	B
11	30	31	32	33	A
	30	31	32	33	B

(b) After lines 1–5

	00	01	10	11
00	00	01	02	03
	00	11	22	33
01	11	10	13	12
	10	01	32	23
10	22	23	20	21
	20	31	02	13
11	33	32	31	30
	30	21	12	03

(c) $k = 1, l = 0$

01	00	03	02
10	01	32	23
10	11	12	13
00	11	22	33
23	22	21	20
30	21	12	03
32	33	30	31
20	31	02	13

(d) $k = 2, l = 1$

03	02	01	00
30	21	12	03
12	13	10	11
20	31	02	13
21	20	23	22
10	01	32	23
30	31	32	33
00	11	22	33

(e) $k = 3, l = 0$

02	03	00	01
20	31	02	13
13	12	11	10
30	21	12	03
20	21	22	23
00	11	22	33
31	30	33	32
10	01	32	23

FIG. 2.2. *Data movement in CCM2 when $n = 4$.*

Observe that the recursion sequence results in a gray code and is similar to that used in the towers-of-Hanoi problem. It should be easy to see how FUNC may be incorporated into CCM2, inline, using only $O(q) = O(\log n)$ control unit memory. The time needed to generate the entire sequence is $O(n)$.

As far as the complexity of CCM2 is concerned, exactly $2(q + n - 1)$ unit-routes are needed. Both the PE and communication times are $O(n)$.

Example 2.1. We illustrate the working of procedure CCM2 when $n = 4$. Fig. 2.2 shows the data movement caused by CCM2. Fig. 2.2(a) gives the initial configuration. The square in row i and column j denotes PE $(i, j) =$ PE $(4i + j)$. The first entry in each PE is its A value and the second is its B value. The example matrices have $a_{ij} = b_{ij} = ij$. For convenience, we have labeled the columns and rows by their index in binary. Figure 2.2(b) gives the $A(i, j)$ and $B(i, j)$ values following the initial alignment. As can be seen, $A(i, j) = ii \oplus j$ and $B(i, j) = i \oplus jj$ (note that by $ii \oplus j$ we mean a number with first digit i and second digit $i \oplus j$). In the shift loop (lines 7–13) the sequence of l values is 0, 1, 0. Figures 2.2(c), (d) and (e) show the new A and B values following lines 11 and 12 for each of the three iterations of the shift loop. As is evident, for each PE (i, j) the four $A(i, j)$, $B(i, j)$ pairings in Figs. 2.2(b) to 2.2(e) yield a distinct term in sum for c_{ij} (see (2.1)). □

2.3. CCCs with n^2m, $1 \leqq m \leqq n$ PEs. By combining together algorithms CCM1 and CCM2 one can obtain an efficient parallel multiplication algorithm for CCCs with n^2m, $1 \leqq m \leqq n$, PEs. We shall assume that n and m are powers of 2. So, m divides n. The matrices, A and B, to be multiplied, can each be partitioned into m^2 $n/m \times n/m$ equal sized submatrices A_{ij} and B_{ij}, $0 \leqq i < m$ and $0 \leqq j < m$ (see Fig. 2.3). The product matrix C may be similarly partitioned. It is easy to see that C_{ij} is given by:

$$(2.3) \qquad C_{ij} = \sum_{k=0}^{m-1} A_{ik}B_{kj}, \qquad 0 \leqq i < m, \quad 0 \leqq j < m.$$

A_{00}	A_{01}	A_{02}	A_{03}
A_{10}	A_{11}	A_{12}	A_{13}
A_{20}	A_{21}	A_{22}	A_{23}
A_{30}	A_{31}	A_{32}	A_{33}

FIG. 2.3. *Partitioning of A into 16 submatrices.*

The partitioned matrices may be viewed as an $m \times m$ matrix with each element being an $n/m \times n/m$ matrix. The n^2m PEs in the CCC may be viewed as forming an $m \times n \times n$ array PE (i, j, k), $0 \leqq i < m$, $0 \leqq j < n$ and $0 \leqq k < n$. For each fixed i, the PEs in this array form an $n \times n$ array which can be partitioned into m^2 $n/m \times n/m$ arrays $PE_{i,j,k}$, $0 \leqq j < m$, $0 \leqq k < m$. The initial configuration for matrix multiplication is given by $A_{0,j,k} = A_{jk}$ and $B_{0,j,k} = B_{jk}$, $0 \leqq j < m$, $0 \leqq k < m$. $A_{0,j,k}$ and $B_{0,j,k}$ denote the A and B registers of the PE partition $PE_{0,j,k}$. A and B can be multiplied using (2.3), CCM1 and CCM2. First, the partitioned submatrices of A and B are replicated as in lines 1 to 10 of CCM1 to obtain $A_{i,j,k} = A_{ji}$ and $B_{i,j,k} = B_{ik}$, $0 \leqq i < m$, $0 \leqq j < m$ and $0 \leqq k < m$. This replication requires only $O(\log m)$ time. The product of line 11 of CCM1 is now a product of two $n/m \times n/m$ matrices A_{ji} and B_{ik}. The number of PEs available to carry out each product $A_{ji} * B_{ik}$ is n^2/m^2 (i.e., the PE partition $PE_{i,j,k}$). So, CCM2 can be used to implement line 11 of CCM1 in $O(n/m)$ time. Finally the addition loop of lines 12 to 14 (which perform the summation of (2.3)) is easily implemented in $O(\log m)$ time. The resulting algorithm is procedure CCM3. The correspondence between CCM3 and the two earlier algorithms is easily seen. Lines 1–10 of CCM3 correspond to lines 1–10 of CCM1, lines 11–23 of CCM3 correspond to lines 1–13 of CCM2, and lines 24–26 of CCM3 correspond to lines 12–14 of CCM1. CCM3 requires $O(n/m + \log m)$ unit-routes and PE time. One readily sees that when $m = 1$, CCM3 works exactly like CCM2 and when $m = n$, CCM3 makes the same data moves as does CCM1. An interesting special case is when $m = n/\log n$. Now, only $n^3/\log n$ PEs are available and the complexity of CCM3 is still $O(\log n)$.

ALGORITHM 2.4.

procedure CCM3 (A, B, C, n, m) //multiply two $n \times n$ matrices on a CCC with $n^2 m$ PEs//

```
0      q := log n; h := log m
1      for l := 2q + h - 1 down to 2q do //copy A, B//
2          A(j^{(l)}) ← A(j), (j_l = 0)
3          B(j^{(l)}) ← B(j), (j_l = 0)
4      end
5      for l := q - 1 down to q - h do //copy A submatrices//
6          A(j^{(l)}) ← A(j), (j_l = j_{q+h-l})
7      end
8      for l := 2q - 1 down to 2q - h do //copy B submatrices//
9          B(j^{(l)}) ← B(j), (j_l = j_{h+l})
10     end
```

//Now multiply two $n/m \times n/m$ matrices in each $1 \times n/m \times n/m$ PE partition//

```
11     for l := q - h - 1 down to 0 do //Initial alignment//
12         k := q + l
13         A(j^{(l)}) ← A(j), (j_k = 1)
14         B(j^{(k)}) ← B(j), (j_l = 1)
15     end
16     C(j) := A(j) * B(j)
17     for k := 1 to n/m - 1 do //shift-multiply-add//
18         l := FUNC (k) //get a bit index l ∈ {0, 1, ⋯ , q - h - 1}//
19         r := q + l
20         A(j) ← A(j^{(l)})
21         B(j) ← B(j^{(r)})
22         C(j) := C(j) + A(j) * B(j)
23     end
```

//Final add//

```
24     for l := 2q + h - 1 down to 2q do
25         C(j) ← C(j) + C(j^{(l)})
26     end
   end CCM3
```

2.4. CCCs with m^2 PEs, $1 \leq m \leq n$. The partitioning strategy of § 2.3 can also be used when only m^2, $1 \leq m \leq n$ PEs are available. In this case A and B are partitioned into A_{ij} and B_{ij}, $0 \leq i < m$ and $0 \leq j < m$ as before. The PEs are viewed as forming an $m \times m$ array PE_{ij}, $0 \leq i < m$ and $0 \leq j < m$. Initially, PE_{ij} contains the n^2/m^2 elements of A_{ij} as well as the n^2/m^2 elements of B_{ij}. The matrix product can be formed proceeding essentially as in procedure CCM2 with n and q respectively replaced by n/m and $\log (n/m)$. The routes of lines 3, 4, 10 and 11 of CCM2 now involve n^2/m^2 elements each and the product of line 6 (or 12) is a product of two $n/m \times n/m$ matrices. This product takes $O(n^3/m^3)$ time using the classical matrix multiplication algorithm. If Pan's [26] matrix multiplication algorithm is used then line 6 takes $O((n/m)^\beta)$ time where $\beta \approx 2.61$. Hence the overall complexity of CCM2 when adapted to the case of m^2 PEs is

$$O\left(\frac{n^2}{m} + m\left(\frac{n}{m}\right)^\beta\right) = O\left(\frac{n^2}{m} + \frac{n^{2.61}}{m^{1.61}}\right).$$

The interesting special case of n PEs falls into the case just discussed when $m = \sqrt{n}$ (provided of course n is a perfect square). Actually, for the case of n PEs there exists a very straightforward $O(n^2)$ algorithm for matrix multiplication. The algorithm uses the classical matrix multiplication algorithm and starts with column i of A and B in PE (i). We leave it to the reader to fill in the details of this algorithm.

3. Perfect shuffle computer.

3.1. PSC with n^3 PEs. An $O(\log n)$ multiplication algorithm for an $n^3 = 2^{3q}$ PSC can be arrived at by simulating the routes in procedure CCM1 using the technique used by Nassimi and Sahni [25]. The resulting algorithm will require 13 log n unit-routes. A slightly faster algorithm (i.e., 10 log n unit-routes) can be obtained for PSCs. We shall use the same three-dimensional view of PEs and the same initial configuration as was used in § 2.1. The following unit-route statements will be used:

(i) $A(j^{(0)}) \leftarrow A(j) \cdots$ routing along the EXCHANGE connection.

(ii) $A(\text{SHUFFLE }(j)) \leftarrow A(j) \cdots$ routing along the SHUFFLE connection.

(iii) $A(\text{UNSHUFFLE }(j)) \leftarrow A(j) \cdots$ routing along the UNSHUFFLE connection.

The basic steps in the PSC multiplication algorithm are the same as those used in CCM1. Their implementation is somewhat different. Procedure PSCM1 multiplies two $n \times n$ matrices on a PSC with n^3 PEs. It uses only 10 log n routes. The algorithm is self explanatory and we shall not explain it further. The initial configuration is $A(0, i, t) = a_{i,t}$ and $B(0, i, t) = b_{i,t}$.

ALGORITHM 3.1.

line	procedure PSCM1 (A, B, C) //PSC multiplication algorithm, n^3 PEs//
1	for $b := 0$ to $q - 1$ do //copy A, B//
2	$\quad A(\text{SHUFFLE }(i)) \leftarrow A(i)$
3	$\quad B(\text{SHUFFLE }(i)) \leftarrow B(i)$
4	$\quad A(j^{(0)}) \leftarrow A(j), (j_0 = 0)$
5	$\quad B(j^{(0)}) \leftarrow B(j), (j_0 = 0)$
6	end //now we have $A(i, t, p) = a_{i,t}$ and $B(i, t, p) = b_{i,t}$//
7	for $b := 0$ to $q - 1$ do
8	$\quad A(\text{SHUFFLE }(i)) \leftarrow A(i)$
9	end //now we have $A(i, t, p) = a_{p,i}$ and $B(i, t, p) = b_{i,t}$//
10	$\quad C(j) := A(j) * B(j)$ //now $C(i, t, p) = a_{p,i} * b_{i,t}$//
11	for $b := 0$ to $q - 1$ do
12	$\quad C(\text{SHUFFLE }(i)) \leftarrow C(i)$
13	$\quad C(j) \leftarrow C(j) + C(j^{(0)})$
14	end //now $C(t, p, i) = c_{p,t}, 0 \leq i < n$// //In particular, $C(t, p, t) = c_{p,t}$//
15	for $b := 0$ to $q - 1$ do
16	$\quad C(\text{SHUFFLE})(i)) \leftarrow C(i)$
17	$\quad C(j^{(0)}) \leftarrow C(j), (j_0 = j_q = 1)$
18	end //now $C(p, t, 0) = c_{p,t}$//
19	for $b := 0$ to $q - 1$ do
20	$\quad C(\text{UNSHUFFLE }(i)) \leftarrow C(i)$
21	end //now $C(0, p, t) = c_{p,t}$//
22	end PSCM1

It is important to note that PSCM1 uses only twice as many unit-routes as does CCM1. Recall that each PE in a PSC is connected to only 3 PEs while in a CCC each PE is connected to log n other PEs.

We now momentarily deviate from the matrix multiplication problem and consider the related problem of computing $C = (A * B)^T$ (i.e., the transpose of the product). Surprisingly, we can compute $(A * B)^T$ using fewer unit-routes (only 8 log n) than used by PSCM1 to compute $A * B$. The algorithm to compute $(A * B)^T$ can be obtained from PSCM1 by replacing lines 15–21 by the following code:

```
for b := 0 to q - 1 do
    C(UNSHUFFLE (i)) ← C(i)
end
```

3.2. PSCs with n^2m, $1 \leq m \leq n$ PEs. Procedure CCM3 can be adapted to run on an n^2m PE PSC in time $O(n/m + \log n)$, $1 \leq m \leq n$. Lines 0–16 and 24–26 are easily implemented using $O(q+h) = O(\log n)$ shuffles, unshuffles, and exchanges (see the simulation method described in [25]). A straightforward adaptation of lines 17 to 23 would require $O(n/m \log n)$ unit-routes as the data routing of lines 20 and 21 would require $O(\log n)$ shuffles and unshuffles, and one exchange each time. A faster implementation of lines 17 to 23 can, however, be obtained. This requires us to rearrange the As and Bs so that bits l and r (lines 20 and 21 of CCM3) are adjacent. Define $\beta(j)$ to be the following permutation of the binary bits $j_{2q+h-1}, \cdots, j_0$ in the representation of any PE index j:

$$\beta(j) = \beta(j_{2q+h-1} \cdots j_0)$$

$$= j_{2q+h-1} \cdots j_{2q-h} j_{q-1} \cdots j_{q-h} j_{2q-h-1} j_{q-h-1} j_{2q-h-2} j_{q-h-2} \cdots j_q j_0.$$

Observe that line 20 of CCM3 exchanges A values only along bits $q-h-1, \cdots, 0$ while line 21 exchanges B values only along bits $2q-h-1, \cdots, q$. If preceding the loop of lines 17 to 23, A and B are permuted according to β, then lines 20 and 21 can be replaced by

$$A(j^{(2l)}) \leftarrow A(j),$$

$$B(j^{(2l+1)}) \leftarrow B(j).$$

When the loop of lines 17 to 23 terminates, the C values will have to be permuted according to β^{-1} to get back the configuration currently obtained by CCM3. So, an equivalent code for lines 17 to 23 is

```
17.1'    A(β(j)) ← A(j)
17.2'    B(β(j)) ← B(j)
18'      for k := 1 to n/m − 1 do
19'          l := FUNC (k)
20'          A(j^(2l)) ← A(j)
21'          B(j^(2l+1)) ← B(j)
22'          C(j) := C(j) + A(j) * B(j)
23'      end
23.1'    C(j) ← C(β(j))
```

Define the initial *state* of any register to be 0. If a shuffle is performed on a register its state becomes $q-1$. At this time bit $q-1$ is in position 0 (a shuffle transforms from $j_{q-1} \cdots j_0$ to $j_{q-2} \cdots j_0 j_{q-1}$). Another shuffle changes the state to $q-2$. The state $q-1$ can be restored now by an unshuffle. Let POSITION $(\langle A, B, C \rangle, i, j)$ be a PSC algorithm that sets registers A, B, and C in state j if they were originally in state i. Clearly, this can be done using $\min \{|i-j|, 2q+h-|i-j|\}$ shuffles or unshuffles. Lines 17.1' to 23.1' are now simulated on a PSC by the following code:

```
17    A(β(j)) ← A(j)
18    B(β(j)) ← B(j)
19    STATE := 0
20    for k := 1 to n/m − 1 do //shift-multiply-add//
21        l := FUNC (k)
22        call POSITION (⟨A, B, C⟩, STATE, 2l)
23        A(i^(0)) ← A(i) //simulate 20'//
24        A(UNSHUFFLE (i)) ← A(i)
          B(UNSHUFFLE (i)) ← B(i)
          C(UNSHUFFLE (i)) ← C(i) //state becomes 2l + 1//
25        B(i^(0)) ← B(i) //simulate 21'//
26        C(j) := C(j) + A(j) * B(j)
27        STATE := 2l + 1
28    end
29    call POSITION (C, STATE, 0)
30    C(j) ← C(β(j))
```

399

It is easy to see that lines 17 to 30 above will have the same effect on a PSC as will lines 17.1′–23.1′ on a CCC. We now examine the complexity of lines 17 to 30. The permutations β and β^{-1} used in lines 17, 18, and 30 fall in the class of bit-permute-complement (BPC) permutations considered by Nassimi and Sahni [24]. All BPC permutations on an n^2m PE PSC can be performed in $O(\log n^2m) = O(\log n)$ time for $1 \leq m \leq n$. In the loop of lines 20 to 28 only line 22 takes more than $O(1)$ time. So, let's concentrate on this line. The sequence of bit indices generated by FUNC has the property

$$S_{t-1} = S_{t-2}, t-1, S_{t-2}.$$

Since S_{t-2} ends in 0, when $l = t-1$ in the loop, STATE = 0. Hence, the number of unshuffles, needed by the call to POSITION from line 22 is $2(t-1)$ (this assumes that A, B, and C can be routed in one step). On the next iteration $l = 0$ and STATE = $2(t-1)+1 = 2t-1$. So, $2t-1$ shuffles are needed at line 22. Let $R(t-1)$ be the total number of shuffles and unshuffles needed in all calls to POSITION from line 22. From the preceding discussion we obtain the recurrence

$$R(t-1) = \begin{cases} 2R(t-2)+4t-3, & t > 1, \\ 0, & t = 1. \end{cases}$$

We may solve for R using one of the standard methods to solve recurrence equations. The solution to our recurrence equation is $R(t-1) = q*2^{t-1} - 4(t-1) - 9 = O(2^t)$. Since, in our case, $t = q-h$, the time spent in the loop of lines 20–28 is $O(2^{q-h}) = O(n/m)$. Hence, the overall complexity of the resulting PSC algorithm is $O(n/m + \log n)$.

By choosing a slightly different function for FUNC, the number of shuffles and unshuffles needed by line 22 can be reduced by a factor of almost 2. This new FUNC generates the sequence given by

$$S_0 = 0,$$

$$S_1 = 1, 0, 1 \quad \text{(instead of 0, 1, 0),}$$

$$S_{t-1} = S_{t-2}, t-1, S_{t-2}, \quad t > 2.$$

3.3. PSCs with m^2, $1 \leq m \leq n$ PEs. From the discussions of §§ 2.4 and 3.2 it should be clear how to obtain a PSC algorithm of complexity $O(n^2/m + m(n/m)^{2.61})$ for the case when m^2 PEs are available, $1 \leq m \leq n$.

4. Applications to graph problems. Efficient parallel algorithms for several graph problems may be obtained using the matrix multiplication algorithms of §§ 2 and 3. We discuss some of these in the following subsections. Analyses are provided only for the case of n^3 PEs. It holds for $n^3/\log n$ PEs too if CCM3 is used. The following discussion assumes we are dealing with n vertex graphs. Central to many of these applications is the repeated squares method of computing the transitive closure of an $n \times n$ boolean matrix (i.e., $A^* = (A+I)^n = (((A+I)^2)^2 \cdots)^2)$. Since this requires $\log n$ matrix multiplications, transitive closures may be determined in $O(\log^2 n)$ time on n^3 PE PSCs and CCCs.

4.1. All-pairs shortest-paths. The all-pairs shortest-path matrix A is an $n \times n$ matrix such that $A(i, j)$ is the length of a shortest path from i to j in a weighted n-vertex graph. Let $A^k(i, j)$ denote the length of a shortest path from i to j going through at most k intermediate vertices. Clearly, $A(i, j) = A^n(i, j)$. Let $A^0(i, j)$ be the length of the edge $\langle i, j \rangle$ if $\langle i, j \rangle$ is in the graph. Let $A^0(i, j)$ be $+\infty$ if $\langle i, j \rangle$ is not in the graph and 0 if $i = j$. It should be easy to see that

$$A^k(i, j) = \min_l \{A^{k/2}(i, l) + A^{k/2}(l, j)\}.$$

Hence, A^n may be computed from A^0 by computing $A^2, A^4, A^8, \cdots, A^n$. A^k may be computed from $A^{k/2}$ using the matrix multiplication algorithm with $+$ substituted for $*$ and min substituted for $+$. The complexity of the resulting algorithm is $O(\log^2 n)$ on an n^3 PE PSC or CCC.

4.2. Radius, diameter and centers. The radius, diameter and centers of a graph may be trivially computed in $O(\log n)$ time (on an n^3 PE PSC or CCC) from the all-pairs shortest-path matrix (which itself requires $O(\log^2 n)$ to compute).

4.3. Median and median length. Let $d(i, j)$ be the length of a shortest path from i to j. Let $h(i)$ be the weight of vertex i. Vertex v is a *weighted median* [12] of the graph iff

$$\sum_{j=1}^{n} h(j)d(v, j) \leqq \sum_{j=1}^{n} h(j)d(k, j), \qquad 1 \leqq k \leqq n.$$

When $h(j) = 1$, $1 \leqq j \leqq n$, vertex v is simply a *median* of the graph. $\sum_{j=1}^{n} h(j)d(v, j)$ is called the *weighted median length* of the graph. For any graph these quantities can be easily computed once the shortest-path matrix A has been determined. The sum $\sum_{1}^{n} h(j)d(k, j) = \sum_{1}^{n} h(j)A(k, j)$ can be computed for all k in $O(\log n)$ time on an n^3 PE PSC and CCC. The minimum of these can also be found in this much time.

4.4. Shortest-path, breadth-first, minimum depth and least median spanning trees. A shortest-path spanning tree with root v is a spanning tree of the given graph. Its root is vertex v and the distance from v to each vertex j equals $d(v, j)$. ($d(v, j)$ is the shortest distance from v to j in the graph.) Let $R(i, j)$ be a vertex index such that $R(i, j) = 0$ or $A(i, R(i, j)) + A(R(i, j), j) = A(i, j)$. $R(i, j) = 0$ iff the shortest i to j path has no intermediate vertices. Otherwise $R(i, j)$ gives a vertex that is halfway along the i to j path (i.e., if there are p intermediate vertices then $R(i, j)$ is either the $\lfloor p/2 \rfloor$th or $\lceil p/2 \rceil$th vertex). Clearly, $R(i, j)$ can be computed in $O(\log^2 n)$ time along with the computation of $A(i, j)$. A shortest-path spanning tree rooted at v may be obtained from $R(i, j)$ in $O(\log^2 n)$ time. If $R(v, j) = 0$ then j is a child of v and we may set PARENT $(j) = v$. If $R(i, j) = k$ then j is a descendent of k and we need to examine $R(k, j)$. $R(k, j)$ can be routed to PE (i, j) in $O(\log n)$ time. If $R(k, j) = 0$ then set PARENT $(j) = k$. Otherwise j is a descendent of $R(k, j)$. Since $R(i, j)$ is midway from i to j and $R(k, j)$ midway from $R(i, j)$ to j, etc., we will have to follow down at most $\log n$ R values before discovering the parent of j. Hence, all nodes will know their parents in the spanning tree in $O(\log^2 n)$ time plus the $O(\log^2 n)$ time needed to compute R initially.

A breadth-first spanning tree can be obtained in the same way as above by starting with $A^0(i, j) = 1$ if (i, j) is an edge in the graph, $A^0(i, j) = \infty$ if (i, j) not in the graph and $A^0(i, j) = 0$ if $i = j$. Note that $A(v, j)$ is the depth (less one) of node j in the breadth-first spanning tree with root v. Hence, the depth $D(v)$ of the spanning tree rooted at vertex v is $\max_j \{A(v, j)\} + 1$. A minimum depth spanning tree may be obtained in $O(\log^2 n)$ time by first computing A as for a breadth-first spanning tree, then computing $D(j)$ for all j (this takes only $O(\log n)$ time). Next, $\min (D(j))$ is computed (again only $O(\log n)$ time is needed). The j value with minimum $D(j)$ is the root of the minimum depth spanning tree. Now find the breadth-first spanning tree with root j. A shortest median spanning tree may be found similarly.

4.5. Max gain. Let G be a directed acyclic graph. Let $w(i, j) \geqq 0$ be the weight of edge $\langle i, j \rangle$ (assume $w(i, j) = 0$ if $\langle i, j \rangle$ not in G). The gain on an i, j path is the product of the edge weights on that path. W is the max gain matrix iff $W(i, j)$ is the maximum gain for every pair i, j. Clearly, this matrix may be computed in $O(\log^2 n)$ time using an approach similar to that used for the all-pairs shortest-path matrix.

4.6. Topological sort and critical paths. These problems are described in [16]. Given an acyclic directed graph $G = (V, E)$, we are required to list the vertices in topological order. This can be done in $O(\log^2 n)$ time using matrix multiplication. Let $A^0(i, j) = 1$ if $\langle i, j \rangle \in E(G)$, $A^0(i, j) = -\infty$ if $\langle i, j \rangle \notin E(G)$ and $A^0(i, i) = 0$ if $0 \leqq i \leqq n - 1$.

401

Use the all pairs shortest path algorithm to compute the lengths of the longest paths. This requires using max in place of the min used on the all-pairs shortest-path algorithm. Set $A(0, i) = 0$ for all i with the property that $A(t, i) \le 0$, $0 \le r < n$. Note that now $A(0, i) = 0$ for exactly those vertices in G that have no predecessors. Also note that $A(i, i) > 0$ for i iff G has a directed cycle. This is not possible as G is acyclic. Let $i_1, i_2, \cdots, i_k$ be the values of i for which $A(0, i) = 0$. For each j for which $A(0, j) \ne 0$, compute $A(0, j) = \max_{1 \le p \le k} \{A(i_p, j)\}$. This can clearly be done in $O(\log n)$ time on both an n^3 PE PSC and CCC. $A(0, j)$ gives the length of the longest path from any node with no predecessors to node j. Now sort the pairs $[A(0, j), j]$, $0 \le j < n$ into non-decreasing order of $A(0, j)$. This can be done in $O(\log n)$ time on an n^3 PSC or CCC using the algorithm of [25]. If the pair $[A(0, j), j]$ ends up in PE $(0, k)$ then vertex j is the kth vertex in the topological order. The correctness of this statement is easily verified.

The strategy just described can also be used to determine early and late start times for tasks in an activity on edge network (see [16]). In such a network each edge represents an activity and has a length associated with it. The early start time for any activity $\langle i, j \rangle$ is the length of the longest path in the given directed acyclic graph from the start vertex, 0, to vertex i. The early start times can easily be found in $O(\log^2 n)$ time using the first part of the above strategy. Once the early start times are known, the earliest time the project can be finished is known. From this the latest start times (i.e., the time by which an activity must start so that the project length doesn't increase) can be computed in another $O(\log^2 n)$ steps. With both the early and late start times known the critical activities and critical paths are readily obtainable.

From the discussions of the preceding six subsections it should be clear that, as far as parallel computing is concerned, matrix multiplication is a very central problem. Several graph problems may be efficiently solved by a very straightforward application of matrix multiplication. In the examples we have given, the parallel way to solve a graph problem is quite different from the methods used in the best known sequential algorithms. This difference doesn't always show up. For example, the algorithm of [7] for the bottleneck (or maximum flow matrix) problem directly translates into an $O(\log^2 n)$ parallel algorithm. Similarly the algorithms obtained in [17] for the shortest cycle problem and the problem of determining if a graph has a triangle directly translate to $O(\log^2 n)$ and $O(\log n)$ matrix multiplication based parallel algorithms. Several other graph problems can be trivially solved in $O(\log^2 n)$ time on a parallel machine using matrix multiplication. We shall refrain from listing these here.

REFERENCES

[1] H. ABELSON, *Lower bounds on information transfer in distributed computations*, Proc. 19th IEEE Symposium on Foundations of Computer Science, 1978, pp. 151–158.

[2] T. AGERWALA AND B. LINT, *Communication in parallel algorithms for Boolean matrix multiplication*, Proc. 1978 IEEE Int. Conference on Parallel Processing, 1978, pp. 146–153.

[3] E. ARJOMANDI, *A study of parallelism in graph theory*, Ph.D. thesis, Dept. of Computer Science, University of Toronto, December 1975.

[4] R. P. BRENT, *The parallel evaluation of general arithmetic expressions*, J. Assoc. Comput. Mach., 21 (1974), pp. 201–206.

[5] L. E. CANNON, *A cellular computer to implement the Kalman filter algorithm*, Ph.D. thesis, Montana State University, 1969.

[6] A. CHANDRA, *Maximal parallelism in matrix multiplication*, IBM Tech. Rept. R C 6193, Sept. 1976.

[7] I-NGO CHEN, *A new parallel algorithm for network flow problems*, Proc. 1974 Sagamore Computer Conference, 1974, pp. 306–307.

[8] L. CSANSKY, *Fast parallel matrix inversion algorithms*, Proc. 6th IEEE Symposium on Foundations of Computer Science, October, 1975, pp. 11–12.

[9] D. ECKSTEIN, *Parallel graph processing using depth-first search and breadth-first search*, Ph.D. thesis, University of Iowa, 1977.

[10] M. J. FLYNN, *Very high speed computing systems*, Proc. IEEE, 54 (1966), pp. 1901–1909.

[11] M. FLYNN AND R. KOSARAJU, *Processes and their interactions*, Kybernetics, 5 (1976), pp. 159–163.

[12] H. FRANK AND I. T. FRISCH, *Communication, Transmission and Transportation Networks*, Addison-Wesley, Reading, MA, 1971.

[13] W. M. Gentleman, *Some complexity results for matrix computations on parallel processors*, J. Assoc. Comput. Mach., 25 (1978), pp. 112–115.

[14] D. S. Hirschberg, *Parallel algorithms for the transitive closure and the connected component problems*, Proc. 8th ACM Symposium on Theory of Computing, May, 1976, pp. 55–57.

[15] D. S. Hirschberg, *Fast parallel sorting algorithms*, Comm. A.C.M., 21 (1978), pp. 657–661.

[16] E. Horowitz and S. Sahni, *Fundamentals of Data Structures*, Computer Science Press, Potomac, MD, 1976.

[17] A. Itai and M. Rodeh, *Finding a minimum circuit in a graph*, this Journal, 7 (1978), pp. 413–423.

[18] T. Lang, *Interconnections between processors and memory modules using the shuffle-exchange network*, IEEE Trans. Comput., C-25 (1976), pp. 496–503.

[19] T. Lang and H. Stone, *A shuffle exchange network with simplified control*, Ibid., C-25, (1976), pp. 55–65.

[20] D. E. Muller and F. P. Preparata, *Bounds to complexities of networks for sorting and for switching*, J. Assoc. Comput. Mach., 22 (1975), pp. 195–201.

[21] I. Munro and M. Paterson, *Optimal algorithms for parallel polynomial evaluation*, JCSS, 7 (1973), pp. 189–198.

[22] D. Nassimi and S. Sahni, *Bitonic sort on a mesh-connected parallel computer*, IEEE Trans. Comput., C-28, (1979), pp. 2–7.

[23] ———, *An optimal routing algorithm for mesh-connected parallel computers*, J. Assoc. Comput. Mach., 27 (1980), pp. 6–29.

[24] ———, *A self routing Benes network and parallel permutation algorithms*, IEEE Trans. Comput., to appear.

[25] ———, *Parallel permutation and sorting algorithms and a new generalized connection network*, J. Assoc. Comput. Mach., to appear.

[26] V. Ya. Pan, *New methods for the acceleration of matrix multiplications*, Proc. 20th IEEE Symposium on Foundations of Computer Science, 1979, pp. 28–38.

[27] F. P. Preparata, *New parallel-sorting schemes*, IEEE Trans. Comput., C-27 (1978), pp. 669–673.

[28] C. Savage, *Parallel algorithms for graph theoretic problems*, Ph.D. thesis, University of Illinois, Urbana, August 1978.

[29] H. Siegal, *A model of SIMD machines and a comparison of various interconnection networks*, IEEE Trans. Comput., C-28 (1979), pp. 907–917.

[30] H. Stone, *Parallel processing with the perfect shuffle*, Ibid., C-20 (1971), pp. 153–161.

[31] C. D. Thompson, *Generalized connection networks for parallel processor interconnection*, IEEE Trans. Comput., C-27 (1978), pp. 1119–1125.

[32] C. D. Thompson and H. T. Kung, *Sorting on a mesh-connected parallel computer*, Comm. A.C.M., 20 (1977), pp. 263–271.

[33] F. Van Scoy, *Parallel algorithms in cellular spaces*, Ph.D. dissertation, University of Virginia, 1976.

VERY LARGE LEAST SQUARES PROBLEMS AND SUPERCOMPUTERS

John R. Rice
Department of Computer Science
Purdue University
West Lafayette, Indiana 47907

1. SUMMARY AND PRINCIPAL CONCLUSIONS

This paper comes from a workshop held at Purdue University and reflects the participants views as filtered by the author. The principal participants are listed at the end.

The goals of the workshop were: (a) to provide an interchange between different groups working on very large least squares problems, (b) to provide an interchange between computer scientists involved with supercomputer systems and scientists using supercomputers and (c) to assess the state of the art in solving very large least squares problems. This workshop is one of a series held by the Purdue Center for Parallel and Vector Computing and supported by the Army Research Office, the National Science Foundation and the Office of Naval Research. The number of participants was kept small so as to allow for discussions in depth and complete expressions of views.

Twelve sources of very large least squares problems were identified (see Section 2), the ones principally involved in the discussions were

> Geodetic surveys
> Photogrammetry
> Molecular structures
> Gravity field of the earth
> Partial differential equations

A brief review of the current methods used in these problems is given in Section 3.

There were extensive discussions of issues of both a general nature and specific to the very large least squares problem. These issues involved the least squares problems, methods for their solution, the use of supercomputers and future developments. These are detailed in Section 4, the principal conclusions are summarized below. This paper summarizes lengthy discussions and reflects their general tenor; no participant is likely to agree in detail with all statements made here.

A. *Problems.* There are several important least squares problems that require supercomputer power. There is substantial similarity in the structure of the problems from different areas; the matrices possess a block structure (sometimes at two levels) which reflects a "local connection" nature in the underlying physical problem.

B. *Methods.* Most of the standard least squares methods are being used somewhere. There is a definite need for a comprehensive software package for least squares that includes sparse matrix facilities.

C. *Computations*. Programming effort is more often a bottleneck than computer time, but neither are likely to be dominant, (the most common dominant effort is to get the data). The preprocessing, postprocessing and general inefficiency in using masses of data on several devices is an important bottleneck. Current pipeline machines and attached processors sacrifice portability and clarity to high efficiency.

D. *Future*. The most promising area for algorithm improvement is in the handling of sparsity. There are important least squares problems that require much more resources (including computer power) than are currently available. Supercomputer architectures are not going to stabilize, so it is important that high level, somewhat architecture independent languages (even a clean Fortran extension) can be used by scientists. Reasonable portability is essential for many reasons, including the success of "national resource" supercomputer centers. *A very critical need is to make supercomputers easier to use.*

2. VERY LARGE LEAST SQUARES PROBLEMS

We first describe the very large least squares problems that were considered. References are given for more information about most of the problems; there were a few of them about which very little was known first hand.

A. **The Geodetic Survey Problem.** The existing geographical survey points are not completely consistent because of errors in the measurements. A classical procedure has been to adjust the measurements to obtain a best least squares fit to the nonlinear relationships that must hold. The National Geodetic Survey (NGS) currently has a program under way to adjust the measurements for the entire North American continent. This computation will involve about 540 thousand variables and 6.5 million relationships. The adjustment of the geodetic measurements for the entire earth is planned for the future.

See [Golub and Plemmons, 1980, Plemmons, 1979] for details of this problem. Its main features are:

(i)   A natural multilevel block structure. Data and computations are usually organized by, say, counties, then by states, then by countries.

(ii) Highly variable accuracy in data. Some survey data is over 50 years old and much less accurate than recent data.

(iii) Very good approximate solutions available for iteration on the nonlinearities.

(iv) Data is expensive to obtain; the least squares computation costs are a moderate part of the whole process.

B. **The Photogrammetry Problem.** When one takes a series of aerial photographs, one neither knows the locations on the photographs nor the locations of the cameras. One identifies some points on the photographs whose ground locations are known precisely (these are often marked on the ground so they show up clearly in the photos). Overlapping photos are taken showing these points several times; this information is combined with knowledge of the camera properties to create a model of the camera locations. The parameters are then determined as a least squares solution of this nonlinear model. The camera parameters and the ground point parameters are obtained in a simultaneous solution. In large systems a block elimination scheme is often employed so that a reduced system of only camera parameters is solved first, followed by a "back solution" for the others. The total number of unknown parameters (6 per camera, 3 per ground point) can number in the hundreds for a modest system, and in the thousands for a large system.

Similar computations occur in the precise measurement of the position and shape of large structures such as radio telescopes.

The main features of this problem are:

(i) There is a natural block structure within the least squares normal equations' coefficient matrix. Each photograph and each ground point contribute such a block. Non-zero off-diagonal terms are limited to a band which arises from the "local connection" nature (similar to the geodetic problem) of the photographs and ground point.

(ii) Raw data is collected in two places: (a) obtaining the photographs, and (b) measuring the point locations on the photographs. Obtaining the data is an expensive process, however individual point measurements may be repeated or added relatively inexpensively. The least squares computation is the other major step in producing the final results.

C. **The Molecular Structures Problem.** The linear least squares problem is in the inner loop of a complex process depicted by the following (simplified) steps.

1. Collect Data
   Grow single crystals of a pure macromolecular substance of sufficient size
   Obtain x-ray diffraction patterns
   Preprocess pictures and use symmetry to enhance data quality

2. Determine approximate molecular structure
   Uses various chemical and physical procedures plus considerable analysis of data

3. Create nonlinear least squares problem
   Include basic covalent process of atomic interactions
   Include 10 to 15 types of "restraints" which incorporate various chemical and molecular facts.

4. Iterate
   Linearize problem by Newton's method
   Discard "most" terms in the Jacobian matrix J
   Solve $J*\Delta x = b$ for the Newton step as a linear least squares problem

5. Reconstruct Computed Molecule
   The numbers are postprocessed to produce a visual model

6. Evaluate Computed Molecule
   The computed models and observed electron densities are compared visually. If they agree to within the uncertainty of the nonlinear least squares, the model is accepted
   Otherwise:

identify water and other solvent structures
reorient certain submolecules
add or delete atoms or submolecules
add restraints on the structure
go back to step 3

There are three positional variables for each atom in the molecule; a simple molecule has a few hundred atoms, a complex one (e.g. a small virus) has a few million. Current work involves molecules with several tens of thousands of atoms. This least squares problem is thus embedded in a large, complex scientific project. The linear least squares problem in the inner loop may take 10-30 minutes on a Class VI computer and the nonlinear iteration requires solving many of these. Even so, this is not necessarily the dominant part of the computation. There may be a stack several feet high of X-ray films with thousands of information spots on each; runs to preprocess this data can require over many hours or a day even on a Class VI computer. See [Hendrickson and Konnert, 1980] for more details on the overall problem and [Blumdell and Johnson, 1976] for more details on the mathematical model and least squares problem.

This problem may be interpreted as 2 1/2 dimensional, the molecule is like a long sausage that winds around itself. Most of the terms in the model refer to local relationships (positions or angles) along the molecule. With an appropriate numbering of the atoms, these relationships produces a "local connection" nature in the least squares problem. All of the important local connection terms in J are near the main diagonal and the others are negligible. However, where the sausage folds over itself, there are non-local (in the numbering system) effects. The folding is not random, one of the major unsolved problems in molecular structures is how and why these giant molecules fold. These non-local terms are in the "restraints" and are a crucial part of determining the structure; they produce "randomly" scattered small blocks away from the main diagonal of J.

The main features of this problem are:

(i)   There are several large scale computational steps involved.

(ii) The least squares problem has a local-connection structure modified by a relatively small number of other terms.

(iii) The blocks in the matrix J are small (3 by 3 to 20 by 20 or so).

(iv) There is only a very rough initial approximation for the nonlinear problem, it probably has terms missing (at least in the beginning) so the least squares residuals are not "small".

(v)   The outer loop involves someone visually comparing electron density maps with the current model, usually using a computer graphics system. This is the most time consuming aspect of the work.

D. **Gravity Field of the Earth**. There is a standard model of gravity using spherical harmonics which is derived from viewing the earth as a homogeneous ellipsoidal planet. As more accuracy is desired, one adds more terms to compensate for the nonhomogeneous mass distribution and the actual shape of the earth. NASA has a mission GRM (Geopotential Research Mission) to collect a massive amount of near earth data to be used to determine many thousands of terms in the expansion in spherical harmonics. This will be a standard least squares fitting problem, it is not a sparse matrix problem because the spherical harmonics do not have any "local support" behavior.

An alternative (not part of NASA's plan) is to use a piecewise polynomial representation of the gravity field. The idea behind this is that the detailed effects of irregular shapes and masses are not well modeled by spherical harmonics and one is going to obtain the usual slow convergence properties of polynomial and trigonometric approximations will lead to a least squares problem with quite regular sparsity structure. For more details on this problem see [NASA,1982], [Moore et al,1982].

The main features of this problem are:

(i)   A massive amount of data, very expensive to collect.

(ii) Very regular and uniform structure in the data, the problem and the underlying models.

(iii) The classical model leads to a full matrix least squares problem.

(iv) The possible piecewise polynomial model leads to a sparse least squares problem with a very regular structure. The blocks in the matrix are relatively small, about 10 by 10.

E. **The Least Squares Method for Partial Differential Equations** (PDEs). There is a classical least squares (finite element) method for solving PDEs that is rarely used in practice. It is closely related to other widely used methods (e.g. collocation and Galerkin) and the probable reason for its "neglect" is that people feel that it offers no apparent advantage over the more standard methods. See [Rice, 1983] for a discussion of this method.

This method would be used primarily with piecewise polynomial basis functions which would lead to least squares problem with a regular block sparsity structure, similar to that which appears in the more standard PDE methods. The number of unknowns can easily reach 1 million for three dimensional PDEs, there would be a small number (1 to 10) of equations per unknown.

The principal features of this problem are:

(i)   There is very little data, the equations are generated mathematically.

(ii) There is a very regular block sparsity structure to the problem. The blocks are small to moderate in size (4 by 4 to 50 by 50).

(iii) The number of equations can be very large, there are applications where one solves a large sequence of very similar problems.

F. **Tomography.** This is a specialized application where one reconstructs an object by taking X-ray cross sections. It is similar to data fitting in that one has a fixed number of data from a continuum; it differs from data fitting in that one observes various linear functionals (e.g. integrals) from the continuum rather than actual values. See [Herman, 1976, 1978 and 1980] for more information.

The principal characteristics of these problems are:

(1)   The systems of equalities and inequalities are huge, order about a million.

(2)   The sparsity is somewhat haphazard, less than 1 per cent of the matrix elements are non-zero.

(3)   The principal computational tool is the row-action method, see [Censor, 1981].

G. Force Method in Structural Analysis.

There are two principal methods of matrix structural analysis, the displacement (or stiffness) method and the force (or flexibility) method. The force method has certain advantages for multiple redesign problems or non-linear elastic analysis because it allows the solution of modified problems, by least squares computations, without restarting the total computation from the beginning. This can result in significant savings for large scale problems. See [Kaneko, Lawo and Thierauf, 1982] and [Kaneko and Plemmons, 1984] for details.

The main features of this problem are:

i.   The force method consists of two stages. Stage 1 involves the computation of a basis matrix B for the null space of the equilibrium matrix E for the structure and stage 2 involves the solution of a certain least squares problem with B serving as the observation matrix. B can be dense even though E is sparse, depending upon the method for computing B.

ii.   There is very little data. The elements of E are generated mathematically and B is computed from E.

iii. Engineering substructuring methods can lead to a block angular form for the least squares matrix B, similar in form to those of the observation matrices in the Geodetic and Photogrammetry problems.

H. Very Long Base Line Problem.
The object is to measure astronomical distances by using interferometer methods with base lines that are thousands of miles (using geographically separated radio telescopes) or millions of miles (using observations taken at different points on the earth's orbit around the sun). There are enormous quantities of data that are relatively inaccurate.

I. Digital Terrain Modeling.
The digital terrain modeling problem is a combination of the photogrammetry problem discussed earlier and the surface fitting problem discussed next. The terrain information is obtained by photogrammetry and then a mathematical model is obtained by another least squares fit. In some application the modeling can be done locally which decouples the latter least squares problem and makes it simply a large sequence of independent, small least squares problems.

J. Surface Fitting.
One has a physical surface where many positions are known. The surface is modeled by piecewise polynomials of modest degree (1 to 3) joined with some smoothness (continuity, perhaps less, perhaps one or two continuous derivatives). The model has parameters which are determined by a least squares fit to the observed data.

The size of these problems commonly varies from rather small, say a few dozen parameters, up to fairly large, perhaps a thousand parameters. One can, of course, visualize almost arbitrarily large problems, especially if one goes to three dimension problems. The matrices involved have the block structure expected from a "local basis" model of the surface. See [Schumaker, 1978].

The principal characteristics of these problems are:

(i)   Usually modest to moderate in size, that is 50 to 1000 unknowns and 2 to 5 observations per unknown.

(ii) A fairly regular block structure in the matrices with modest sized blocks, say 4 by 4 to 16 by 16.

K. Cluster Analysis and Pattern Matching. Some pattern recognition algorithms are essentially least squares problems (usually nonlinear). One usually has a modest sample of values and a very flexible model with a relatively small number of parameters; a few hundred values and 5 to 50 parameters are common. As we become more adept at these problems, we can expect the size of the problem to grow very substantially.

The principal characteristics of these problems are:

(i) Modest to moderate in size, but potentially quite large.

(ii) Considerable variation in structure as widely different models may be used. Many models probably give full matrices.

3. METHODS AND MATRIX STRUCTURES

The linear least squares problem is formulated mathematically with an n by m matrix $A = (a_{ij})$, unknowns x_i, $i = 1$ to m and data b_j, $j = 1$ to n. One wishes to solve $Ax = b$, but $n > m$ so this system is generally inconsistent. Thus one determines the least squares solution x so that

$$\sum_{j=1}^{n} \left(\sum_{i=1}^{m} a_{ij} x_i - b_j \right)^2 = ||Ax - b||_2^2 = \text{minimum}$$

In the discussion that follows, we assume that $n > m$ and m is large. See [Lawson and Hanson, 1974], [Rice, 1981] for more information.

A. The Normal Equations. A simple analysis shows that the least squares solution x satisfies the linear system

$$A^T A x = A^T b$$

which is an m by m system with a symmetric and (normally) positive definite coefficient matrix $A^T A$. The total work for this solution method is, including forming $A^T A$, $m^2 n/2 + m^3/6$ multiplications. The main advantage of this approach is simplicity, the disadvantages are (i) the computation might be less stable numerically and (ii) any sparsity structure in A is usually destroyed.

B. The Residual Equations. Let $r_j = \sum_{i=1}^{m} a_{ij} x_i - b_j$ be the residual of the j-th equation. Then a simple analysis shows that x and r solve the system

$$\begin{pmatrix} I & A \\ A^T & 0 \end{pmatrix} \begin{pmatrix} r \\ x \end{pmatrix} = \begin{pmatrix} b \\ 0 \end{pmatrix}$$

This system is larger than the normal equations, $(n+m)$ by $(n+m)$, but retains the sparsity of A. This system is indefinite.

C. Orthogonalization. One may apply an orthogonal matrix Q to $Ax = b$ to obtain

410

$$Q \, A\mathbf{x} = Q\mathbf{b}$$

and determine Q so that $QA = R$ is "upper triangular". That is

$$R = \begin{bmatrix} T \\ 0 \end{bmatrix}$$

where T is square and upper triangular. One then solves $T\mathbf{x} = \mathbf{b}\cdot$ where $\mathbf{b}\cdot$ is the first n elements of $Q\mathbf{b}$. The elementary reflections or elementary rotation matrices are usually recommended to construct Q. See [Lawson and Hanson, 1978] or [Rice, 1981] for more details. The total work for this solution method is $m^2n - m^3/6$. The main advantages of this method are numerical stability and the potential of using any sparity that A might have, the disadvantage is that it is twice as much work as the normal equations (assuming that m^2n dominates m^3, as it usually does).

D. Iteration, Splitting and Conjugate Gradient Methods. Since the normal equations are symmetric and positive definite, most standard iteration methods are applicable. The convergence of such methods can often be accelerated by splitting the problem. Consider a linear system $C\mathbf{x} = \mathbf{d}$ written in the form

$$M\mathbf{x} = N\mathbf{x} + \mathbf{d}$$

Thus C is split into $M - N$ and the idea is to choose M so that $M\mathbf{z} = \mathbf{f}$ is easy to solve and M^{-1} is a good (reasonable?) approximation to C^{-1}. Various iterations can then be defined to use M in a useful way, the simplest is the iteration

$$M\mathbf{x}^{(k+1)} = N\mathbf{x}^{(k)} + \mathbf{d}$$

Choosing M as diag(C) gives the Jacobi method, choosing M as the lower triangular part of C gives Gauss-Seidel.

A particularly effective iteration is the conjugate gradient method where one takes

$$M\mathbf{z}^{(k)} = (\mathbf{d} - C\mathbf{x}^{(k)}) = \text{residual at } k\text{-th iteration}$$
$$\mathbf{x}^{(k+1)} = \mathbf{x}^{(k-1)} + w_{k+1}(\alpha_k \mathbf{z}^{(k)} + \mathbf{x}^{(k)} - \mathbf{x}^{(k-1)})$$

The parameters w_{k+1} and α_k are determined by separate computations, see [Concus, Golub and O'Leary, 1976] for further details.

Iteration with splitting (and the conjugate gradient method in particular) are attractive for the residual equations form of the problem, because the sparsity of A is completely preserved. Even though the residual form involves a much larger matrix than the normal form, it might require much less storage in a computation if the sparsity of A is exploited.

4. DISCUSSION: ISSUES AND RESPONSES

A set of issues was prepared before the workshop and they received extensive discussion. Issues as originally presented are listed along with a summary of the discussions.

PROBLEMS

A. *Do the problems from different areas have similarities?*

There is a surprising amount of similarity. The matrix A can almost always be put in the following form (sometimes called the dual block angular form):

$$\begin{pmatrix} A_1 & & & & & B_1 \\ & A_1 & & & & B_2 \\ & & A_3 & & & B_3 \\ & & & \cdot & & \cdot \\ & & & & \cdot & \cdot \\ & & & & A_k & B_k \\ & & & & & D \end{pmatrix}$$

This reflects a "local connection" structure in the underlying physical problem (the spherical harmonics expansion of gravity is one exception). There is a wide variation in the number and size of the blocks. Some problems have large block with k modest in size (10-100) while others have much smaller blocks but many more of them. A number of the problems have two levels of sparsity structure. That is, the blocks A_i and/or B_i are themselves large sparse matrices, usually with this same general pattern of sparsity. There might be some difference in the sparsity patterns between the two levels. The molecular structures problem has this structure with a relatively small number of other blocks scattered through the matrix.

B. *What is the scientific significance of these problems?*

Some of these problems are integral parts of large national scientific programs (e.g. geodetic survey, very long base line and gravity model). Others are ubiquitous in some important areas (e.g. PDE computations, digital terrain modeling, structural analysis, photogrammetry). Still others are integral parts of the developing frontiers of significant scientific research programs (e.g. molecular structures, tomography, pattern analysis).

C. *Are there very large least squares problems of potential interest that have not yet been seriously attempted?*

Three problems were mentioned: PDE computations, geological structure (the analog of the gravity problem, but below the surface of the earth) and cell biology (the natural long range extension of the molecular structures problem).

METHODS

D. *What methods are thought to be the most suitable for these problems?*

There is no clear "winner" yet. The exploitation of sparsity is not yet thoroughly explored; different patterns of sparsity give the advantage to different methods. The normal equations and conjugate gradient (applied to the residual equations) are the most widely used. A drawback of the conjugate gradient method is the difficulty in simultaneously obtaining variance and covariance information.

The impact of vector computers will be substantial but, again, no clear pattern has yet emerged. These calculations deal primarily with very long, very sparse vectors. Substructuring is naturally applicable to these problems for the multiprocessor computers. Again, the algorithmic questions are mostly open.

E. *Is it practical to use the same methods - or same algorithms - or same software - in different applications areas?*

There are definite similarities in the problems from different application areas; this implies that similar methods are applicable. There is not enough generally used software to give as real experience in applying the same software in different applications areas. However, limited experience plus informed conjecture suggests that some software can be used widely. Well designed software could be modified or parameterized to give good efficiency in a variety of applications.

F. *How much exchange of know-how is there between scientists in different application areas? between numerical analysts or computer scientists and scientists?*

There is some exchange of know-how, but it is not systematic nor uniform. The amount of isolation among groups interested in essentially the same problem seems to be typical of science in general.

COMPUTATIONS

G. *Is the vectorization of the linear algebra the major step in adapting methods to current supercomputers?*

There is definitely much more to be done than to vectorize the linear algebra (although this must be done also). The principal task is to reorganize the algorithms so as to exploit the natural sparsity in the problems and yet also exploit the vector processing power of the supercomputers. Experiences were reported where it was as difficult to overcome "non-numerical" bottlenecks (like I/O or page thrashing) as to make the arithmetic run fast. The opinion was expressed that obtaining efficient, well organized software is a bigger hurdle than devising vector algorithms or reorganizing algorithms to be vectorizable.

Current supercomputers were strongly criticized for inadequate Fortran support. To obtain good performance on Cyber 205 or Cray 1 requires a lot of detailed idiosyncratic changes in the codes which renders them totally useless for any other computer. The view was expressed that many people do not want to invest years in codes that cannot be used by their colleagues and which become useless once a newer machine is acquired.

H. *Is least squares computation the major part of the total computations?*

The least squares computation is almost always in the "inner loop" of the computations and thus a significant computational expense. However, it is rarely the dominant part of the computation. Input/output, data processing, preprocessing and postprocessing are also significant computations and some applications also involve significant numerical computations of other types (e.g. nonlinear systems of equations).

I. *What is the nature of the difficulty in getting the data for very large least squares computations?*

There are a couple of areas (PDEs and quantum mechanics) where obtaining the data is a minor part of the problem. For most applications, this is a major part of the problem and for some (e.g. geodetic survey, molecular structures determination, and gravity field analysis) the cost of obtaining the data completely dominates the computational (and programming) costs.

J. *How does programming supercomputers for very large least squares computations compare with programming ordinary machines?*

A high level of general dissatisfaction was expressed for programming the current Class VI machines. They were described as "a pain"; the resulting software is totally non-transportable and generally obscure. The attached array processors are no better. This is not inherently the nature of supercomputers; one participant had considerable experience with the TI-ASC machine and felt it was much more "usable" than his current experience with the Cyber 205.

K. *Is computer time a major bottleneck in getting results for these problems?*

Yes, but it is not dominant in most cases. The preprocessing and postprocessing of results tends to require a lot of human attention and involve delays of various kinds (e.g. getting files from one machine to another, getting output plotted, making tapes, etc.). These activities slow down the whole process much more than the few hours that one is waiting for the "scientific computations" to be done. One sometimes has to wait many hours (or even days) to obtain adequate amounts of computer time.

L. *Is programming effort a major bottleneck in getting results for these problems?*

Yes. It is sometimes more of a bottleneck than computer time, but still usually not the dominant factor. There is often considerable difficulty in finding people who have the desired knowledge of supercomputers, programming and the application area.

THE FUTURE

M. *What are the prospects for being able to solve the very large least squares problems at the frontiers of science? Do we need much faster computers - or much faster algorithms - or both?*

The prospects are good. Both faster computers and faster algorithms are needed; neither one obviously dominates the other. It is just as important to have better user interfaces, better languages and supporting tools as it is to have faster computers and algorithms.

N. *Is it more important to make the computer faster or easier to use?*

The question is misleading; the critical task is to make the very fast computers easy to use.

O. *What would be the scientific impact of much greater computational powers in these areas.*

It would do a lot of good (no specific list of impact areas was generated). Perhaps the greatest impact would come from the ability to do conceptually straight forward things better. A great deal of effort is now required to solve a lot of problems that have little technical difficulty or novelty; this is taking away from the time available for problems that require a lot of thought.

P. *What are the prospects of discovering significantly better supercomputer algorithms for least squares?*

They seem good for two reasons. First, one can see that it is possible to devise better ways of handling sparsity, data and memory space. Second, history tells us that it is unwise to believe that better methods will not appear.

WRAP-UP OBSERVATIONS

Q. There is a strong need for a flexible package (or several packages) of sparse least squares routines

R. Supercomputer hardware is not going to stabilize. People cannot rewrite and tailor massive codes for each new architecture (never mind variances on a theme) that appears. Thus scientists must keep programs expressed at high levels and processors for these languages must be developed for each new architecture.

S. The concept of a set of "national resource" supercomputer access sites is not viable without reasonable transportability of working programs among the supercomputers.

5. WORKSHOP PARTICIPANTS

The principal participants in the workshop are listed below with their relevant field of expertise and affiliation.

James Bethel (photogrammetry)	Purdue University
Iquacio Fita (molecular structures)	Purdue University
Dennis Gannon (supercomputers)	Purdue University
Gene Golub (numerical linear algebra)	Stanford University
Wayne Hendrickson (molecular structures)	Naval Research Laboratory
Greg Kramer (applications programmer)	Purdue University
Charles Lawson (numerical linear algebra)	Jet Propulsion Laboratory
Robert Plemmons (matrix computation, geodesy)	North Carolina State

John Rice (supercomputers)   Purdue University
Michael Rossmann (molecular structures) Purdue University
Ahmed Sameh (supercomputers)   University of Illinois

6. REFERENCES

Abad-Zapatero, C., Abdel-Meguid, S.S., Johnson, J.E., Leslie, W.A.G., Rayment, I., Rossmann, M.G., Suck, D. and Tsukihara, T., *Structure of southern bean mosaic virus at 2.8: A resolution*, Nature (London), 286, (1980), pp. 33-39.

Blundell, T.L. and Johnson, L.N., *Protein Crystallography*, Academic Press, New York and London, (1976).

Brandt, A., McCormick, S. and Ruge, J., *Algebraic multigrid for automatic multigrid solution with applications to geodetic computations*, to appear.

Bjorck, A., *Iterative refinement of linear least squares solutions I*, BIT 7, (1967), pp. 257-278.

Bjorck, A., *Methods for sparse linear least squares problems*, In: Sparse Matrix Computations, (J.R. Bunch and D.J. Rose, eds.), Academic Press, New York, pp. 177-194.

Buehner, M., Ford, G.C., Moras, D., Olsen, K.W., and Rossmann, M.G., *Three-dimensional structure of D-glyderaldehyde-3-phosphate dehydrogenase*, J. Mol. Biol. 90, (1974), pp. 25-49.

Censor, Y., *Row-action methods for huge sparse systems and their applications*, SIAM Review 23, (1981), pp. 444-466.

Concus, P. Golub, G.H. and O'Leary, D.P., *A generalized conjugate gradient method for the numerical solution of elliptic partial differential equations*, In: Sparse Matrix Computation, (J.R. Bunch and D.J. Rose, eds.), Academic Press, N.Y., (1976).

deBoor, C. and Rice, J., *Extremal polynomials with applications to Richardson iteration for indefinite system*, SIAM J. Sci. Stat. Comput. 3, (1982), pp. 47-57.

George, J. and Heath M., *The solution of sparse least squares problems using Givens rotations*, Linear Algebra App. 34, (1980), pp. 69-83.

George, J., Heath, M. and Plemmons, R., *Solution of large-scale sparse least squares problems using auxiliary storage*, SIAM J. Sci. Stat. Comput. 2, (1981), pp. 416-429.

George, J., Golub, G.H., Heath, M. and Plemmons, R., *Least squares adjustment of large-scale geodetic networks by orthogonal decomposition*, to appear.

Golub, G., *Numerical methods for solving linear least-squares problems*, Numer.

Math. 7, (1965), pp. 206-216.

Golub, G. and Plemmons, R., *Large scale geodetic least squares adjustments by dissection and orthogonal decomposition*, Linear Algebra and Appl. 34, (1980), pp. 3-28.

Golub, G. and Reinsch, C., *Singular value decomposition and least squares solutions*, Numer. Math. 14, (1970), pp. 403-420.

Golub, G. and Wilkinson, J., *Note on the iterative refinement of least squares solutions*, Numer. Math. 9, (1966), pp. 139-148.

Heath, M., Plemmons, R. and Ward, R., *Sparse orthogonalization schemes for structural optimization using the force method*, to appear.

Hendrickson, W.A., *A procedure for representing arbitrary phase probability distributions in a simplified form*, Acta Cryst. B27, (1971), pp. 1472-1473.

Hendrickson, W.A., *Radiation damage in protein crystallography*, J. Mol. Biol. 106, (1976), pp. 889-893.

Hendrickson, W.A., *Transformations to optimize the supercompposition of similar structures*, Acta Cryst. A35, (1979), pp. 158-163.

Hendrickson, W.A., Klippenstein, G.L. and Ward, K.B. *Tertiary structure of myohemerythrin at low resolution*, Proc. Natl. Acad. Sci. USA 72, (1975), pp. 2160-2164.

Hendrickson, W.A. and Konnert, J.H., *Stereochemically restrained crystallographic least-squares refinement of macromolecular structures*, In: Biomolecular Structure Conformation, Function and Evolution (R. Srinivasan, ed.) Pergamon, Oxford, 1, (1981), pp. 43-57.

Hendrickson, W.A. and Konnert, J.H., *A restrained parameter thermal factor refinement procedure*, Acta Cryst. A36, (1980), pp. 344-350.

Hendrickson, W.A. and Konnert, J.H., *Incorporation of stereochemical information into crystallographic refinement*, In: Computing in Crystallography (R. Diamond, S. Rameseshan and K. Venkatesan, eds.) Indian Academy of Sciences, Bangalore, (1980), pp. 1301-1323.

Hendrickson, W.A. and Ward, K.B., *Pseudosymmetry in the structure of myohemerythrin*, J. Biol. Chem. 252, (1977), pp. 3012-3018.

Herman, G.T., *An introduction to some basic mathematical concepts on computed tomography*, In: Roentgen-Video-Techniques for Dynamic Studies of Structure and Function of the Heart and Circulation (P. Heintzen, ed.), Georg Thieme Publishers, Stuttgart, Germany, (1978).

Herman, G.T., *Image reconstruction from projections: The fundamentals of computerized tomography*, Academic Press, New York, (1980).

Herman, G.T. and Lent, A., *A computer implementation of a Bayesian analysis of image reconstruction*, Info. and Control 31, (1976), pp. 363-384.

Hume, D., Litsey, J. and Plemmons, R., *Software for ordering large sparse least squares prior to Givens reduction*, Proc. 1981 Army Numer. Anal. Computers Conf., ARO Rpt. 81-3, (1981), pp. 267-282.

Kaneko, I. and Plemmons, R., *Minimum norms solution to linear elastic problems*, Inter. J. Numer. Meth. Engin., to appear.

Lawson, C.L., *Sparse matrix methods based on orthogonality and conjugacy*, JPL TM 33-616, (1973).

Lawson, C.L., *Solving large dense least squares problems using two levels of storage*, JPL internal report CM 366-466, (1979).

Lawson, C.L. and Hanson, R.J., *Solving least squares problems*, Prentice-Hall, (1974).

Lawson, C.L. and Ekelund, J.E., *An out-of-core least squares program*, JPL internal report CM 366-435, (1977).

Lawson, C.L., Hanson, R.J., Kincard, D.R. and Krogh, F.T., *Basic linear algebra subprograms for fortran usage*, ACM Trans. Math. Software, 5, (1979), pp. 308-323.

Moore, J., Smith, D., Keating, T. and Langel, R., *Geopotential research mission (GRM)*, Goddard Space Flight Center, Greenbelt, MD, (1982).

Murthy, M.R.N., Reid, T.J., III, Sicignanco, A., Tanaka, N. and Rossmann, M.G., *Structure of beef liver catalase*, J. Mol. Biol. 152, (1981), pp. 465-499.

NASA, NASA Geodynamics Program, Annual Report 1981, NASA Tech. Memo. 85126, (1982).

Pagano, M., Golub, G. and Luk, F., *A large sparse least squares problem in photogrammetry*, In: Proc. Computer Science and Statistics; Twelfth Annual Symposium on the Interface, Waterloo, Canada, (1979), pp. 26-28.

Paige, C. and Saunders, M., *LSQR: An algorithm for sparse linear equations and sparse least squares*, ACM Trans. Math. Software 8, (1982), pp. 43-71.

Rice, J.R., *Matrix computations and mathematical software*, McGraw-Hill, (1981).

Rice, J.R., *Numerical methods, software and analysis*, McGraw-Hill, (1983).

Rossmann, M.G., Abad-Zapatero, C., Murthy, M.R.N., Liljas, L., Jones, T.A. and Strandberg, B., *Structural comparisons of some small spherical plant viruses*, J. Mol. Biol., 165, (1983), pp. 711-736.

Rossman, M.G., Abad-Zapatero, C., Hermodson, M.A. and Erickson, J.W., *Subunit interactions in southern bean mosaic virus*, J. Mol. Biol. 166, (1983), pp. 37-83.

Saad, Y., *Iterative solution of indefinite symmetric linear systems by methods using orthogonal polynomials over two disjoint intervals*, SIAM J. Num. Analys. 20, (1983), pp. 784-811.

Sameh, A., *Solving the linear least squares problem on a linear array of processors*, In: Purdue Workshop on Algorithmically Specialized Computer Organizations, (Gannon, Seigel and Snyder, eds.) Academic Press, (1984).

Schumaker, L.L., *Fitting surfaces to scattered data*, In: Approximation Theory III (Lorentz et al., eds.), Academic Press, (1970), pp. 203-268.

Chapter 9: Supercomputer Applications

Applications of Supercomputers in the U.S.—Today and Tomorrow

Sidney Fernbach

The era of the modern supercomputer began when it was realized that sequential computers were reaching their limits because of the finite speed of light. The first generation of such supercomputers saw the construction of the Burroughs Illiac IV, the Control Data Corporation STAR 100, and the Texas Instrument Advanced Scientific Computer (ASC). All of these became available in the early '70's for productive work. Although successful in establishing directions for the future, each was declared to be a failure. Illiac IV was the first large scale realization of the SOLOMON parallel processing concept proposed by Slotnick many years earlier. It was installed at the Ames Research Center, a NASA facility in Mountain View, CA, in 1972. It consisted of 64 processing elements (p.e.'s) operating in lock-step fashion with operands in each independent, small memory, carrying out instructions issued out of a single control unit. The machine was applied to the solution of the Navier-Stokes equations arising in Aerodynamics problems. When the large 500 megabit, one-gigabit/sec disk was used as main memory and the small high speed memory in each p.e. as a buffer memory, the machine was able to fulfill the performance envisioned for it in the aerodynamics field. Because of it's delay in delivery—hampered by reliability problems encountered in pushing state-of-the-art hardware technology, and because of the lack of appropriate software the machine was not very successful in achieving its full mission. It was finally turned off in 1981. STAR 100 and ASC each used pipelining technology to achieve high speed. When a highly vectorized job was performed, these machines were very capable.

Both fared poorly in scalar performance. The world was not quite ready to vectorize everything. These machines saw productive use however, for a number of years in fluid flow, meteorologic and seismic problems.

Control Data built four STAR 100's, two went to the Lawrence Livermore National Laboratory (LLNL), one to NASA/Langley, and the fourth to the CDC Data Services Center. At LLNL the major use of the systems was for hydrodynamics. Initially gains of only two (over a 7600) or so were obtained, but by optimization techniques, it was possible to get almost complete vectorization and boost performance levels up to four or even five times the 7600. It was estimated that an additional factor of two would be achieved, if it were possible to use 32 (rather than 64) bit arithmetic. This was not given a serious try, however. The NASA/Langley machine was used for computational fluid dynamics; namely, solving the Navier-Stokes equations, among other things.

The biggest user on the CDC Data Center machine eventually turned out to be an oil company with a petroleum reservoir modeling problem. (This is now running on the Cyber 205.)

Texas Instruments installed it's first complete ASC in Holland to be used in its petroleum industry activities. It was later moved back to Texas where it and several others were dedicated to seismic work. Texas Instruments built seven systems, one for environmental research at the Geophysics Fluid Dynamics Laboratory (GFDL) in Princeton, New Jersey, a research facility of the U.S. National Oceanographic and Atmospheric Administration; one for the U.S. Naval Research Laboratory (NRL) in Washington, D.C.; one for the Ballistic Missile Defense site at Huntsville, Alabama; and the others for internal use.

The largest was that for GFDL, a four pipe machine. It has been used very extensively for research in general circulation models. Only recently has it been superseded by a CYBER 205.

Besides these concepts, other architectures for high speed computations have been proposed and executed. The Goodyear Aerospace Corporation STARAN is one such system. A number of bit oriented parallel processors are now in actual use. It has been suggested that the concept be extended to byte or word oriented processors to make the system more useful in large scale problems such as weather forecasting. This was never done. Goodyear, however, has built a follow-on machine to be used for image processing by NASA. This is the Massively Parallel Processor (MPP), currently in use at NASA/Goddard.

Another case is that of PEPE. Bell Telephone Laboratory, in the U.S., designed a system for use in Ballistic Missile Defense. This concept was later taken over by Systems Development Corporation who had a prototype built by Burroughs. It also is operating, but no great effort has been made to extend its capabilities into the more generalized scientific application areas for which supercomputers are being built.

As can be seen, most attempts to gain performance involve putting a number of CPU's together, or by adding special purpose, functional boxes to the system, or by performing a large number of partial operations simul-

Revised from *The Proceedings of the Symposium on Supercomputer Architecture*, Tokyo, Japan, October 1981.

taneously on a large number of operands in a single or multi-pipe arrangement. Most multiprocessors to date have consisted of but two or at-most four processors, used primarily in a multi-programmed fashion rather than in a multiprocessor fashion. A few companies have integrated array processors into their high performance CPU's.

The second generation of supercomputers began in 1972 when Seymour Cray, who had designed the 6600/7600 for Control Data Corporation left that company and founded Cray Research, Incorporated (CRI) where he designed a vector machine. The Cray-1 seemed like a speeded-up 7600 with the addition of vector capabilities. At the time of this writing, over 70 have been sold worldwide. Table I shows the current distribution of supercomputers worldwide by area of application. Most of these are Cray systems.

Table I. Current Worldwide Distribution of Supercomputers by Application (1984)

NUCLEAR ENERGY (WEAPONS, REACTORS)	17
ENVIRONMENT	10
DEFENSE	10
SERVICE BUREAUS	8
UNIVERSITIES	11
RESEARCH	8
PETROLEUM	13
AEROSPACE	10
AUTOMOTIVE	3
ELECTRONICS	2
INDUSTRIAL	3
ANIMATION	1

Control Data, as a result of its learning experiences with STAR has enhanced the STAR concept. The CDC Cyber 205 adds a high performance scalar unit to the modernized vector processor to improve performance where complete vectorization is not possible. This is a machine completely rebuilt in LSI. Some twenty (20) of these have been installed, several for commercial use (in weather, petroleum, government, and university), and several for service bureau use.

The only current computer architectural concept in competition with vector processing is multiprocessing. In this case a number of essentially stand-alone CPU's may share a common memory and work jointly with each other on a single problem. Less research has been carried out on the application of multiprocessing than of vector processing and hence there is no strong inclination for industry to pursue this architectural concept at this time. Denelcor and CDC have built multiprocessors, but these are not in widespread use as yet. Many U.S. universities are also assembling multiprocessors for research purposes. The next five years will tell us how much this design can enhance vector processing alone.

The idea of vector processing is rather old (in the

lifetime of digital computers). In the 50's, before computers were even a decade old, special purpose vector-like function boxes (array processors) were being added to general purpose digital computers, to assist in seismic work. Such devices are now in widespread proliferation throughout the world. Now that 3-D problems are being considered in many applications, however, the large vector processors may overtake and supplant the AP's for such computations because of their greater cost-effectiveness.

Those companies with systems in production or on the drawing boards are as shown in Table II.

Table II. Companies or Facilities Planning or Building Supercomputers

MULTIPROCESSORS	VECTORPROCESSORS
Denelcor/HEP 1, HEP2	Cray/CRAY-1, CRAY X-MP, CRAY-2
LLNL/S-1	CDC/CYBER/205
CDC/CYBER Plus	ETA Systems/GF 10
	Hitachi S 810/10, 20
	Fujitsu VP 100, 200
	NEC SX 1, 2

LARGE SCALE COMPUTERS WITH INTEGRATED ARRAY PROCESSORS
Univac/1100+AP
Trilogy
Hitachi/280+AP
NEC/ACOS 1000

It has been shown on numerous occasions that total performance is a strong function of how well vectorized a particular code might be. Figure 1 shows the performance as a function of a percentage vectorization. In some machines, performance is also a strong function of how long a vector is. It is important, therefore, to structure problems meant for current supercomputers to best fit the machine. This structuring may necessarily affect the way in which the mathematical representation of the problem is set up, the discretization of the problem, and the coding. Compilers are being designed that will automatically vectorize, where vectors can be recognized. The state-of-the art is such, however, that the gains made from automatic vectorization are not yet as great as they may be in the future.

When Univac I was designed, it was intended for statistical work in the analysis of the 1950 U.S. Census. The early machines that were delivered saw service in the U.S. Army Map Service, U.S. Air Force Logistics, Atomic Energy Commission Nuclear Research, U.S. Navy Inventory, Railroad Company car movements, and many other areas. It wasn't long before computers and computer types started to proliferate. They were put into operation to handle relatively simple tasks such as airplane reservations as well as the most difficult research problems such as long range weather forecasting. At first the governments (the U.S. in particular) were the biggest consumers. As such they were also instrumental in making some hardware/software design decisions. This soon began to change. The banking, insurance, and airline industries turned to computing in a big way. Within a decade, computers became very pervasive in industry.

After the rapid performance gains in the early years of computing, there was a slowdown. A great break in computer performance improvement for the scientific world came in the late 60's with the introduction of the CDC 6600 and later the 7600. More parallelism as well as the use of higher speed components in these machines led to a gain of a factor of 25 by the end of the decade. The early CDC supercomputers were used in nuclear and environmental research. Today they are in more widespread use. A distribution of the past generation of supercomputers is shown in the column marked Class IV in Table III. It includes IBM 370/195's as well as CDC 7600's. Not only Control Data's early supercomputers, but also large systems of other manufacturer's were being put to use in many industrial areas. The IBM 370/168 performance wise is in the same ballpark as the CDC 6600. Not counting similar machines such as those manufactured by Fujitsu or Hitachi, there are at least 2000 370/168-like machines installed in the U.S. alone today. Evidently, the *need* for large scale computing has grown enormously during the past 30 years. Today's large computers would have been considered supercomputers 10-20 years ago. Today's supercomputers will be considered state-of-the-art standard equipment 10-20 years from now.

Large scale computer systems in the past have been used in government (57%), industry (35%), and education

(8%). In government, the applications have been primarily to nuclear reactor and weapons research, environment, space, nuclear and plasma physics, and defense. In industry, the applications have been primarily in banking, automotive and aircraft design, petroleum and nuclear areas.

Thus far, the use of the current supercomputers is for similar applications, but the mix is different. As in previous eras, the government becomes the first major buyer, then industry comes in when the systems have been well checked out. Neither the banking industry nor the insurance industry have yet become involved with the supercomputers of today. On the other hand, the petroleum industry has shown much more aggressiveness in using supercomputers than ever before and now automobile manufacturers and electronics companies are getting involved as well. The mix thus far is 51% in government and 36% in industry. (Table III, Class VI.)

Over 90 systems of the class VI supercomputers have already been installed and many more are being considered. Some of these are or will be in service bureaus where they are being tried out for new applications. The areas in which these supercomputers are expected to serve a long and useful life are environment, energy, aerodynamics, petroleum, electronics, and general research.

There seems to be an interesting phenomena taking place. There was a period of time in the mid-seventies when supercomputers were neither being manufactured nor sold. With the successful appearance of the CRAY-1, the market for supercomputers began a steep rise. Despite the fact that the overwhelming number of computers installed in the U.S. lie in the size category costing less

Table III. Percentage Distribution of Supercomputers (Class IV, VI)

	CLASS IV*	CLASS VI#
GOVERNMENT	57	51
ENVIRONMENT	7	10
AEROSPACE	2	7
RESEARCH	10	8
WEAPONS	10	16
OTHER MILITARY	28	11
INDUSTRY	35	36
REACTOR	5	2
AEROSPACE (inc. Airlines)	13	3
ELECTRONICS	0	2
AUTOMOTIVE	0	3
PETROLEUM	5	14
SERVICE	5	8
MISC.	6	4
UNIVERSITY	8	12

* CDC 7600 CLASS & IBM 370/195
# CDC CYBER 205, CRAY 1, FUJITSU VP 100, HITACHI S 810/20

than $500,000, and only a few are of the size category costing more than $1.5 million, the growth rate is greatest for those under $50,000 and those over $500,000.

Environment—Meteorology

In the U.S., the National Center for Atmospheric Research (NCAR), the Geophysics Fluid Dynamics Laboratory, NASA's Goddard Laboratory for Atmospheric Science, the Naval Fleet Numeric Oceanographic Center, and the National Weather Bureau, already have supercomputers installed, or on order, to carry out their research programs as well as their forecasting work.

From the earliest days of computing, the application to weather prediction was considered an ideal problem. von Neumann, among others, gave early consideration to the prospect of solving the general circulation model equations with the computer.

In these studies, we specify the dynamic and basic physical laws and hope that the model will come up with the right answers. The major applications in this field are those of turbulence and global atmospheric simulation. These are involved in weather prediction as well as in climate studies.

Besides the fluid dynamics equations, these problems now involve other physical phenomena such as evaporation and condensation of water, solar heating, infra-red cooling, and surface frictional drag.

If cloud physics is considered, there is the additional requirement of having drop size and charge spectra. When all these things are put together, even today's supercomputers cannot cope with the problems.

Current turbulence models operate in either two-D or three-D (dimensions), climate models in 3-D, cloud models in 3-D, plus two droplet sizes. There is a need for additional variables and for finer resolution, but these cannot be readily accommodated unless the performance of the computer can be upped by a significant factor, much greater than two.

The methods generally used in attacking the problems were based on finite differences. More and more, however, spectral representation in terms of the coefficients of a chosen set of basis functions is being used. In global atmospheric problems surface harmonics are used as the basis functions. These provide a representation which avoids coordinate singularities at the poles (They are invariant under a rotation). Integration procedures in spectral transform methods involve a transform at each time step—between the spectral and grid domains. The amount of arithmetic involved for a given resolution between the grid-point and spectral transform models is not significant. The latter used the Fast Fourier Transform.

Today we find the meteorologists among the heaviest users of the very large scale computers for research as well as for the daily weather forecasting chores.

Environment—Oceanography

The field of oceanography has been somewhat neglected insofar as large scale computing is concerned. Only recently has there been a significant movement in the U.S. civilian sector for a supercomputer to be used in the advancement of physical oceanography. The U.S. Navy has had a supercomputer in its Fleet Numerical Oceanographic Center for sometime now. There is no doubt that the role of the ocean in climate, fishery management, weather prediction, and management of ocean resources is highly important. Coupling of the atmosphere and the ocean is of considerable importance in models to improve medium range weather forecasts as well as short term climate forecasts. This coupling is poorly understood because of lack of observation and analysis of the nonlinear processes involved. The ability of the ocean to store and transfer heat and to exchange it with the atmosphere, however, is significant.

The problems in oceanography are similar to those of the atmosphere. Space variability, however, exists on a smaller scale and time variability on a larger scale. Time steps may be measured in hours, time period duration in years, and space scale in tens of kilometers as opposed to seconds, days, and kilometers respectively, in the atmospheric problem.

Several types of general circulation models are contemplated, one being an eddy resolving model, the other, one in which currents and density structures are time averaged. To do a complete simulation of the Pacific Ocean with adequate resolution (1° grid) for 50 years (adequate time for formation of surface and intermediate waters) would take 1000 hours on a Class VI computer. The National Center for Atmospheric Research (NCAR) has recently added to its supercomputer capability to provide computer time for problems in oceanography.

Energy—Nuclear Reactors

In the energy field, large scale computing has been the work horse for getting its work done from the beginning of the computer era. Nuclear reactors were born almost simultaneously with the computer. Without the computer neither reactors nor nuclear weapons would have been built and advanced through the stages as we now perceive them.

Now that nuclear reactor safety has become so critical, it is fortunate that the class VI computer is available because the problems have become so large.

Many reactor design codes depend on finite-difference, steady state, multi-group neutron diffusion theory calculations. Much of the CPU time is spent in iterations. The performance gains in going from the last generation of "conventional" machines to the new supercomputer has been a factor of 2 to 3 for realistic problems.

One of the favorite techniques in use for solving problems such as radiation or particle transport is the Monte

Carlo method. This is primarily useful if the physical phenomena or the geometrics involved are too complex to describe by equations (which they are in many of the nuclear reactor or weapons designs). The precision that can be obtained can be quite good especially if a very large number of particles are followed. As the number of particles becomes increasingly large, the average result approximates the expected mean. The Monte Carlo codes consist mostly of a collection of random decision points with simple arithmetic in-between.

Because a Monte Carlo solution can cost ten times as much as a diffusion solution in a given problem, speed of performance is essential. Even though Monte Carlo problems seem to be scalar in nature, vectorization techniques are being devised for today's supercomputers that provide major gains in processing such codes.

The other major direction supercomputers are or will be taking is that of multiprocessing. Since the particles being followed in the Monte Carlo techniques are usually independent of each other, a multiprocessor system may be used very effectively for this type of problem.

Energy—Nuclear Weapons

In the weapons laboratories, there is a great reliance on the techniques worked out for solving shock hydrodynamics problems. Both Lagrangian (mesh moves with fluid) and Eulerian (fluid moves through mesh) methods (or a combination of both) are used. Meshes are quite large because of unique or complex geometries. The numbers of variables that need to be computed at each mesh point can also become large. A standard mesh is usually readily vectorizable on these supercomputers. The equations are based on conservation of mass, momentum, and energy. They are 3-D and time dependent. In some applications involving transport, other details such as direction and frequency are needed.

Often the 3-D problem is reduced to 2-D by considering axial symmetry. This, of course, cuts the problem running time significantly.

Energy—Inertial Fusion

A still "hot" research program in the search for alternate sources of energy is that of inertial confinement. The idea is based on getting energy from the nuclear fusion process initiated by compressing a small amount of DT fuel with some driver, like a laser beam. The compression process applied to a tiny pellet containing the fuel should ignite thermonuclearly and burn the DT mixture, thereby releasing a number of energetic neutrons. In this process, the scientist must calculate the detailed mechanism of laser light absorption, energy transport, hydrodynamics implosion, and thermonuclear burn over a range of six orders of magnitude of density and temperature.

This type of problem is both extremely non-linear and non-local. It strains even the most powerful supercomputer.

In one example, there were only 5000 lines of FORTRAN in the code, but the running time per problem was 50-100 hrs. In the case referred to here, the PIC (particle-in-cell) method was used for simulating the laser light absorption. The electron transport portion was handled by multi-group diffusion. The PIC method solves the equations of motion of the charged particles in the presence of a self-consistent electromagnetic field determined from Maxwell's equations. Most of the computer time is spent in advancing the particle positions and velocities. The field equations are easily vectorizable as are two-thirds of the arithmetic operation in the particle advance. In a vector computer, however, two-thirds of the total time is spent in the remaining one-third of the calculation interpolating between particle and grid.

Energy—Magnetic Fusion

In 1974 a study was initiated by an organization, which has now become part of the U.S. Department of Energy, to determine the computing needs of the plasma physicists and engineers involved in the magnetic fusion research program.

By 1981 a Class VI system acquired in 1979 was saturated and a second class VI machine was installed. The potential for magnetic fusion to provide the means to achieve an alternate source of energy has come closer to reality. This came about as a result of the close cooperative effort of the experimental program with the theoretical computational program.

Numerical techniques evolved to study plasmas are basically of two types: one of following microscopic, electromagnetic field and particle distribution functions for studying turbulence, growth and saturation of strong plasma instabilities; the other of studying fluids for macroscopic and long-time description of the plasma.

Aerodynamics

One of the engineering sciences where the large scale computer has made significant contributions is that of aerodynamics. Now the addition of super-computers, has whetted the appetite of aerodynamicists even more and they have been setting up the requirements for another generation of supercomputers, a 1000 Megaflop machine. The NASA-Ames Research Center in California through its NAS programs is hoping to have such a system installed before the end of this decade. In the meantime, the Ames Research Center already has a major Class VI computer in operation and is intending to acquire two more in 1984.

The use of the supercomputers for the aerodynamicist is such that it will allow him to complement the wind tunnel testing—which will probably not be eliminated. It will provide for better coupling between theory and experiment, thus leading to better interpretation and understanding of flow phenomena.

Current codes are limited to those problems not dominated by viscous effects. Applications to complex real situations characteristic of complete aircraft design are not yet possible.

Petroleum

In petroleum, the major use of computers in the past has been for seismic exploration. From the 1950's on, array processors were developed as special adjuncts to main frames to allow for faster computing in this important activity. Even today most seismic applications involve large scale computers to which array processors have been added. The seismic data processing problem is actually signal processing. An analog signal digitized on tape is fed into a computer, where the signal is recovered and interpreted.

The growing importance of reservoir modeling, however, has made it clear that even more powerful systems are needed. The supercomputer fulfills this requirement while at the same time allowing for effective replacement of the large computer with its array processor.

The reservoir problem is one in which finite difference methods are used in solving large scale 3-D representations of an oil field. Using core samples, known geologic information, producing well output, a model is constructed which is used to project forward into time the expected performance of the oil field. The model is tested out on the past experience with the reservoir.

Electronics

Electronics engineers have been able to accomplish much of their basic work using minicomputers. Now, however, computer design as well as chip design have become so complex that large computers are being used to simulate circuits, architectural designs, and software. As time goes on, the growing complexity will require larger and larger systems. The engineer can no longer do without the computer-aided-design (CAD) techniques being developed to make for realistic turn around-time in complex designs. The supercomputer is already being used by the semiconductor industry and computer manufacturer for these purposes.

General Research — Chemistry

The chemists in the U.S. have long recognized the need for large scale computers. They were among the first to put their large quantum chemistry jobs on the early university computers. Large scale problems that chemists have to solve are those in:

1. Quantum Mechanics
   Variational solutions are utilized to solve the Schroedinger Equation. This will continue to be applied to more complex molecules.

2. Statistical Mechanics
   Molecular dynamics as well as Monte Carlo techniques have been used to determine properties of molecular fluids such as water. Successful work has been done in gas models, but more complex systems need to be tackled.

3. Polymer Chemistry
   Huge molecules in a solvent as well as their entanglement with each other in concentrated solutions need to be simulated in a realistic manner.

4. Crystallography
   These studies have been going on for a long time now, but the structure of even more complex proteins is yet to be determined.

General Research—Medicine/Bioengineering Genetics

In medicine, the large computer has been used rather sparingly until now. With the great advances in genetic engineering, however, there is a growing need for large scale computations to simulate biological systems. Techniques being used are similar to the ones developed by the chemists.

General Research—Physics

In the early years of computing, the U.S. physics community was very heavily involved, particularly with respect to applications for analyzing particle tracks generated in devices such as bubble chambers or spark chambers. There were other uses such as modeling of the nucleus in the nuclear physics field. A recent National Science Foundation (NSF) study resulted in a recommendation that a supercomputer be acquired for nationwide physics research.

The applications mentioned were many. For example, in quantum field theory there is a need to carry out integrals of 6th or 8th order; the algebra for quark theory is very complex and requires symbolic manipulation by using programs such as MACSYMA; in statistical mechanics, molecular dynamics or Monte Carlo techniques must be used to tackle complex liquid systems.

The structure of matter in the condensed state needs much work. Perfect and imperfect solids, disordered and amorphous materials, liquid metals and alloys, surfaces, interfaces, artificial as well as exotic materials must be studied.

The Solid State Sciences Committee also reported the need for electronic structure determination of complex bulk solids, polymers and biomaterials. Only with the advent of linearized, augmented plane-wave methods did realistic self-consistent calculations of electronic levels of thin metal films become possible. Even a modest system strained the resources of most computers. Now, with supercomputers one can tackle even more complex problems, for example, the sticking of atoms on surfaces,

426

absorption and disassociation of the molecules subsequent motion and reaction of the atoms on the surface.

In nuclear physics, the shell model and other models of the nucleus have become much more complex; high energy scattering, heavy ion collisions and a few body (3-5) reactions all could use large computer systems.

Professor Kenneth Wilson (Cornell University) received the 1982 Nobel Prize in Physics for his work in lattice gauge theory. Continuing efforts in this study will require a many fold increase in performance of current supercomputers.

General Research—Astrophysics

Much recent work has been done in astrophysics on large scale computers by those who have had access to national laboratory supercomputer facilities. For other astrophysicists, the needs for their participation in research in the exciting problems of Stellar evolution do exist. The dynamic range of study is very extreme, from billions of years to milliseconds. Involved are the areas of magneto-hydrodynamics, radiative transport, atomic physics, transition from order to chaos.

The physics of supernovae is also at the forefront of investigation. Here again large scale computing is essential to cope with the complexities of shock hydrodynamics, nuclear physics and general relativity.

One example of a problem that was of interest concerned itself with the dynamics of galaxies. Three-dimensional n-body integrations were run in this study. A large number of particles (10^5) move self-consistently under Newtonian forces. Graphic methods were used for the output because this was the only way one could study the results. The pictures of the results derived were not only complex but also of an unexpected nature. This work was performed on an array processor (Illiac IV).

General Research—Economics

The social sciences have not yet obtained their fair share of supercomputer capability. Some of their problems are very large, but the support money for research is not as great as it is in the physical or biological sciences. A great deal of econometrics has been going to computers. For example, models of the world economy, of supply and use of basic minerals, and of the utilization of the world's energy resources have been developed. Recently Control Data Corporation awarded a large grant to a research institute headed by Wassily Leontief, who received a Nobel Prize for his work in economic science. Personnel in his institute are using a CDC 205 in continuing his work in input-output theory and methodology.

What then is the future of the supercomputer of today? We have been using vector processors. By the end of 1984, there should be over 100 of them on order or installed. Approximately one-third of them will be in private industry, in service bureaus, or being used for seismic exploration; another third will be used in energy and defense, and the remainder will be used in education, environment, space, etc. This is a substantial number and will be the base from which vector processing could grow much greater. There is no doubt that the needs in defense and energy are significant and will continue to require even greater capability. It is expected that the industrial use will grow most rapidly. The petroleum/seismic needs are very great. Vector processing is a natural for that segment of industry. The aircraft and automotive design industries as well as the electronics industry will adapt supercomputers to their use fairly rapidly. Weather forecasting after 20 or more years of digital computing experiences is barely making it. The definition of the problem keeps pace with computer manufacturers ability to provide additional computer power. New concepts in vector processing will allow for important advances in the area. In energy development (apart from the seismic exploration for fossil fuel), there are tremendous tasks ahead, particularly in the design and use of laser or magnetic fusion devices, as well as in solving the problems that arise in making fission devices safe and reliable. Many vector machines are already being used here, and many more will be needed before the new energy sources become realities.

Medical needs will see the eventual sharing of vector resources. A natural set of problems for vector machines is the general business activities encountered in industry and government alike. Persons engaged in these areas of activity are as yet too unsophisticated to make use of such systems. It may take another generation to overcome the reluctance of businessmen/women to learn the intricacies of computing, let alone vector computing.

With all the work going on in attacking the multiprocessor hardware problems, it seems reasonable to assume that a number of systems, hopefully general purpose will be in operation by 1985. We shall learn then all the difficulties we must go through to use such systems effectively. Clearly by 1990, there will be numerous machines we now call supercomputers to be used in all types of applications. The multiprocessors themselves should be very useful wherever single processors were used, but where the single processor has run out of steam.

For the more sophisticated scientific research problem the best solution, in my view will be the pipelined multiprocessor—a system with relatively few processors but with each capable of streaming data through at clock speed.

Whether or not more exotic components than those derived from silicon will make their way into supercomputers, it is hard to predict at this time. No doubt parts of a machine may appear with such components, but it is hardly likely that an entire architectural system will be cooled to Josephson Junction (JJ) temperatures, in the near future, for example. As a matter of fact, IBM has recently greatly reduced its research in JJ technology. If silicon is to be replaced, the most likely successor will probably be gallium arsenide.

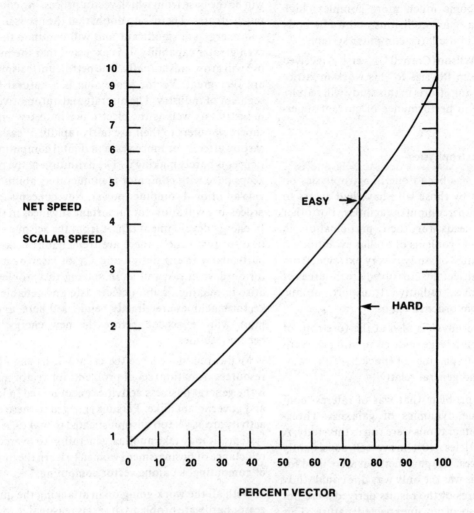

NET SPEED
─────────
SCALAR SPEED

PERCENT VECTOR

EASY

HARD

Figure 1.   Difficulty in Attaining High Net Speed with Vector — Scalar Performance Mismatch (10:1)

An in-depth study of the computational environment at
Lawrence Livermore National Laboratory provides insights
into the types of systems needed for detailed numeric modeling.

LARGE-SCALE SCIENTIFIC COMPUTATION

Garry Rodrigue, E. Dick Giroux, and Michael Pratt
Lawrence Livermore National Laboratory

At large scientific laboratories the computer has emerged, in the past two decades, as one of the most heavily used scientific tools. Detailed numerical simulations of physical processes substitute for actual experiments and predict the effects of known or extrapolated characteristics of matter and energy. Using simulations has several advantages:

- Computer simulations are far cheaper than experiments.
- Computer versatility means that a wider range of problems can be analyzed.
- The computer gives an understanding of physical problems that cannot be obtained from experiments alone.

Increased use of computer simulation has not, of course, eliminated the need for laboratory experiments. Rather, numerical models must be constantly improved to agree with experimental results.

The strong interaction among experiment, theory, and computation is shown in Figure 1. Typically, a prototype experiment is performed and the numerical models are refined until the computations are accurate. The interaction can, however, be more complicated: theoretical science develops mathematical models that computational science solves numerically; the numerical results may then suggest new theories. Experimental science provides data for computational science, and computational science can

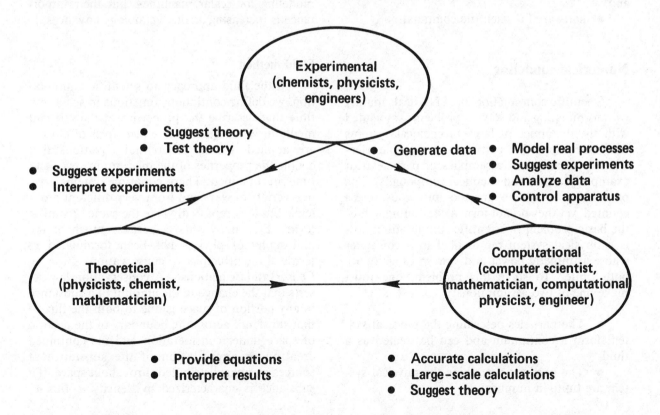

Figure 1. Schematic representation of the interaction among experiment, theory, and computation.

EHO219-6/84/0000/0429$01.00 © 1980 IEEE

model processes that are hard to approach in the laboratory (particle fusion, for example).

Theoretical and experimental scientists ("users" in our parlance) use large production codes (computer programs). The computational scientist's responsibility is to provide the best possible codes—those that yield accurate results with minimal user effort—by applying advanced technologies in numerical modeling, hardware engineering, and software mechanics.

In this article, we describe the numerical modeling, hardware, and software used at Lawrence Livermore National Laboratory, the history of computation at LLNL, and future needs as we perceive them. We discuss these aspects of computer technology in terms of LLNL, the computational environment the authors are most familiar with. We assume that computer needs here are typical of other large scientific laboratories where the major computational efforts concern the dynamics of large mechanical systems. An examination of these needs gives insights into the required nature of systems for large scientific computation. The discussion is divided into three parts:

- numerical modeling,
- hardware for large-scale computation, and,
- software for scientific computation.

Numerical modeling

Scientific computation at LLNL deals mainly with formulating and solving problems associated with the dynamics of large mechanical systems that are composed of particles (for example, electrons or photons) or assemblies of particles (for example, plasmas and chemical compounds). The particles in a system are too numerous to be counted, yet they do not form a continuum. Thus, the basic problem in scientific computation: how is a physical system represented in a computer whose arithmetic power and storage capacity are both finite? To solve this problem, one must make one of two assumptions:

- The particles describing the physical system form a continuum and can be treated as a fluid.
- The particles describing the physical system are finite in number.

With the fluid method, integral or differential equations are derived by applying the laws of Newtonian mechanics. Problems arise when we try to solve these integro-differential equations in the computer. With the finite particle method, mathematical models describing particle interactions are formulated; solution of these models yields the dynamics of the finite particle system. Here, computational problems arise in the techniques used to compute particle behavior.

In either case, the complexity of the mathematical models is limited, at least in part, by the ability of the computer to solve them. Other factors to consider include accuracy of the solutions, computer hardware demands, and computational time.

Models suitable for the new "parallel" computers differ radically from models developed for traditional "scalar" machines. (Scalar computers can process no more than three data elements per instructions. Parallel machines, on the other hand, can handle several computational activities simultaneously.) An effective computational model for a parallel computer must include information on non-interactive and weakly interactive behavior of system parts. Such considerations are not important in computational modeling for scalar machines, but their importance is increasing as the technology advances.

Fluid method

In the fluid approach to scientific computation, we define continuous functions in space and time that describe the properties of the relevant medium. When quantitative principles of physics are applied, partial differential equations that couple the properties of the medium in space and time are obtained. These equation systems arise in a variety of ways and from very different problems, but they repeatedly take the same or similar forms. Essentially, this is because much of the philosophy of physics has been formulated in terms of the principles of conservation.

Conservation equations. A conservation law asserts that the change in the amount of a substance in any portion of space is due to both the flux of that substance across the boundary of the portion of space under consideration and the continued creation or annihilation of the substance at sources or sinks distributed throughout space. If a substance is characterized by density u, flux F, rate of generation or annihilation S, and the portion under consideration R, then the conservative law can be stated as

$$\int_R u \Big|_s^t = - \int_s^t \int_R \text{div}\,(F) + \int_s^t \int_R S$$

where $s =$ start time, $t =$ termination time, and div (F) is the divergence of F in space. If s tends to t and R shrinks to a point, the differential conservation law becomes

$$\frac{\partial u}{\partial t} = -\text{div}\,(F) + S.$$

Fluid dynamics equation can be derived from the laws of conservation of mass (ρ), momentum (M), and energy (E). The properties of the fluids under study determine the particular mathematical form of the flux (F) and source (S). Assume that there are no sources or sinks (that is, $S = 0$) and that the fluid is not viscous. Then the equations of fluid dynamics are

mass:

$$\frac{\partial \rho}{\partial t} = - \left[\frac{\partial(\rho v_1)}{\partial x} + \frac{\partial(\rho v_2)}{\partial y} + \frac{\partial(\rho v_3)}{\partial z} \right]$$

momentum:

$$\frac{\partial(\rho v_1)}{\partial t} = - \left[\frac{\partial(\rho v_1^2)}{\partial x} + \frac{\partial}{\partial y}(\rho v_1 v_2) + \frac{\partial}{\partial z}(\rho v_1 v_3) \right] - \frac{\partial \rho}{\partial x}$$

$$\frac{\partial(\rho v_2)}{\partial t} = - \left[\frac{\partial}{\partial x}(\rho v_1 v_2) + \frac{\partial}{\partial y}(\rho v_2^2) + \frac{\partial}{\partial z}(\rho v_2 v_3) \right] - \frac{\partial \rho}{\partial y}$$

$$\frac{\partial(\rho v_3)}{\partial t} = - \left[\frac{\partial}{\partial x}(\rho v_1 v_3) + \frac{\partial}{\partial y}(\rho v_2 v_3) + \frac{\partial}{\partial z}(\rho v_3^2) \right] - \frac{\partial \rho}{\partial z}$$

energy:

$$\frac{\partial(\rho E)}{\partial t} = -\rho \left[\frac{\partial v_1}{\partial x} + \frac{\partial v_2}{\partial y} + \frac{\partial v_3}{\partial z} \right]$$

$$\left[\frac{\partial(\rho E v_1)}{\partial x} + \frac{\partial(\rho E v_2)}{\partial y} + \frac{\partial(\rho E v_3)}{\partial z} \right]$$

where $x, y,$ and $z =$ Cartesian coordinates; $\rho = \rho(x,y,z,t) =$ density; and

$$\left. \begin{aligned} v_1 &= v_1(x,y,z,t) \\ v_2 &= v_2(x,y,z,t) \\ v_3 &= v_3(x,y,z,t) \end{aligned} \right\} = \text{fluid velocity;}$$

$E = E(x,y,z,t) =$ internal energy; and

$p = p(E,\rho) =$ pressure.

The last relation for pressure—the equation of state—means that there are five equations in five unknowns; ρ, v_1, v_2, v_3 and E. Typically, the equation of state can be calculated independently of the fluid equations. The fluid equations are nonlinear, and except in special cases, their explicit solutions are not known and little understood.

Finite differences. Because computer arithmetic is both finite and discrete, fluid equations can be formulated only in discrete form. Differencing is the most widely used means of doing so, although the finite element method is also becoming popular. Differencing, in a sense, is a reverse process of the fluid method in that one moves from the continuous to the finite. Here, the computer begins to constrain the physical problem. The continuum of the spatial domain (R) is replaced by a mesh or lattice of points when the differencing approximations to the equations are set up. For each point, there are associated approximations to the unknown variables in the fluid equations and characteristic properties of the medium, such as temperature and pressure. The number of points in the mesh depends on the desired resolution of the computational approximations. For a three-dimensional region, the number of points to be stored is often inordinately large, and the problem can become memory-bound rapidly. Therefore, some sort of symmetry is imposed on the physical problem to eliminate one or two coordinates from the mathematical problem. That is, the region of interest becomes one- or two-dimensional.

In a two-dimensional mesh,

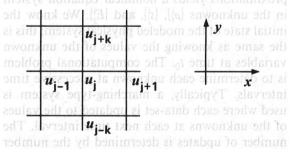

partial derivative terms are approximated by finite differences, e.g.,

$$\frac{\partial f}{\partial x}(u_j,t) \simeq \frac{f(u_{j+1},t) - f(u_{j-1},t)}{2(u_{j+1} - u_{j-1})}$$

$$= \frac{f^t_{j+1} - f^t_{j-1}}{2(u_{j+1} - u_{j-1})}$$

$$\frac{\partial f}{\partial y}(u_j,t) \simeq \frac{f(u_{j+k},t) - f(u_{j-k},t)}{2(u_{j+1} - u_{j-k})}$$

$$= \frac{f^t_{j+k} - f^t_{j-k}}{2(u_{j+k} - u_{j-k})}$$

The quantities $\{f^t_j\}$ can be any one of the unknowns in the fluid equations (density and velocity) and the value of each unknown is computed at each instance of time (t). Like a space derivative, a series of time intervals is defined

and the time derivative replaced by a difference scheme, e.g.,

$$\frac{\partial f(u_j,t_i)}{\partial t} \simeq \frac{f(u_j,t_{i+1}) - f(u_j,t_i)}{\Delta t_{i+1}}$$

$$= \frac{f^{i+1}_j - f^i_j}{\Delta t_{i+1}}$$

Time evolution. Replacing the derivatives in the fluid conservation equations with difference approximations yields a nonlinear equation system in the unknowns $\{\rho^i_r\}$, $\{s^i_j\}$, and $\{E^i_j\}$. We know the initial state of the modeled physical system; this is the same as knowing the values of the unknown variables at time t_0. The computational problem is to determine each unknown at successive time intervals. Typically, a marching-type system is used where each data-set is updated to the values of the unknowns at each next time interval. The number of updates is determined by the number of time-steps. Only one update is necessary if t_{end} is known — we take the single time-step $\Delta t = t_{end} - t_0$. However, if t_{end} is known or if the

physical system is quite active, it is necessary to "sneak up" on the termination time with as many as 10,000 interceding time-steps. The computational goal is to update as rapidly as possible, take the minimum number of intermittent time-steps, and get accurate answers.

The quest for this goal over the past 20 years has resulted in the development of extraordinarily sophisticated mathematical techniques and computational hardware. Whether the new mathematical techniques prompted the development of new hardware or vice versa cannot be stated: the evolution of each phase is difficult to follow, let alone understand.

The updating procedure dictates the particular time interval size Δt necessary for the desired accuracy. Computational difficulty depends on the complexity of the problem. For example, consider volatile chemical reactions, where interfaces in the region of active fluid necessitate elaborate difference approximations. Ideally, one would want to compute a data value $f^{t+\Delta t}_j$ using the minimal information from the precomputed $\{f^t_j\}$. However, just how much information is needed — from only a few values in $\{f^t_j\}$ to all the values in $\{f^t_j\}$ and some values in $\{f^{t+\Delta t}_j\}$ — is dictated by the complexity of the physical problem. When several physical variables are coupled and values of one variable set are needed to compute variables of other variable sets, the situation becomes even more complicated. The $\{f^{t+\Delta t}_j\}$ can be calculated with an explicit mathematical formula (this is called an explicit update) or by solving a complicated system of nonlinear equations (implicit update).

As a general rule, the accuracy required in an update is directly proportional to the difficulty of the actual computation, which is in turn proportional to the complexity of the system of equations to be solved. The real difficulty is in solving linear systems of equations, or of inverting matrices. The matrices involved range from simple tridiagonal systems, which can be solved by first and second order recursion relations, to large nonsymmetric, non-sparse systems, which must be solved by elaborate iterative methods. The numerical algorithms used for up-dating, whether they involve matrices or not, depend on the sophistication of the computer used in features such as vector capability (the rapid processing of many successive data elements as a single instruction is executed), arithmetic precision, memory size, and input/output capabilities.

Computational overhead, physical. Before updating can begin, equations of state must be calculated. These calculations evaluate intrinsic properties of the fluid, such as pressure and temperature, as the physical entities of density, momentum, and energy change in time, thus forming the physical parameters of the fluid equations. Equation-of-state quantities, since they do not have explicit mathematical expressions, are represented by polynomial approximations to experimentally generated data. An illustration: let D be a two-dimensional region on which a mesh of points $\{u_i, v_j\}$ has been defined. Then an equation of state $\Lambda(u,v)$ is given by

$$\Lambda(u,v) = \sum_{k=1}^{3} \sum_{m=1}^{3} C(i,j,k,m)u^{k-1}v^{m-1}$$

where $u_{i-1} \leq u < u_i$ and $v_{j-1} \leq v < v_j$. Hence, associated with each point (u_i, v_j) are the nine values $C(i,j,k,m)$ that are stored in large equation-of-state tables. To evaluate $\Lambda(u,v)$, we must locate the point (u,v) in the mesh and read the set of coefficients for the table. This defines the so-called table look-up problem in scientific computation. Often, however, u and Λ are given, and the problem is to determine v so that $\Lambda = \Lambda(u,v)$ where $\Lambda(u,v)$ is given by the polynominal approximation above. This is an "inverse" table look-up.
Computational overhead, mathematical. The coefficients of the difference formulas must be evaluated before data can be updated. These overhead calculations depend on the coordinate system used to describe the governing fluid equations.

In scientific calculations, there are two types of coordinate systems, Eulerian and Lagrangian. In an Eulerian representation, the dependent variables (velocity, density, and energy) are considered functions of space and time. Once a set of spatial mesh points, r_i, z_j is defined on the region of interest (R), the set remains fixed and the fluid moves past these points. The computed values of the velocity, density, and energy can be envisioned as a sampling these fluid properties as the fluid moves by the mesh points in time.

In the Lagrangian representation, an entirely different approach is taken. One labels a given differential mass of fluid by its position, say r_0, at time t_0, and then solves for both the position of this unit of mass as well as for velocity and energy as functions of time. That is, microscopic portions of the fluid are followed, and changes in energy, pressure, and velocity are calculated.

Computationally, a mesh of points r_i, z_j is defined on the original region (R) and these points are allowed to move with the fluid. That is, the mesh moves with time, as shown in Figure 2.

Mathematically, neither representation completely characterizes fluid dynamics, but there are computational advantages and disadvantages to each. Lagrangian calculations are simpler than Eulerian because the Lagrangian mesh is frozen in the fluid. Since the mesh points move with the fluid, they automatically keep track of fluid boundaries and material interfaces; these boundaries and interfaces are a problem with Eulerian meshes. Since the Lagrangian mesh is fixed, each mesh point represents the same amount of mass, and the density resolution is invariant with time. Thus, Lagrangian calculations are more accurate.

On the other hand, Lagrangian methods fail badly for fluid flows that are not smooth. When the flow fields depart from essential smoothness, the mesh becomes uneven and irregular, eventually leading to inaccuracy. As the flows become turbulent and the mesh is distorted, the calculation breaks down altogether. A severely restricted computational Δt results from mesh distortion; more data updates must be taken to cover the same period of time.

Finite-particle method

The underlying assumption in the fluid method is that the physical particles in the mechanical system form a continuum. The other method assumes that the number of particles is countable. In the finite-particle method, the computer monitors the kinematics and physical properties of each particle as it interacts with the other particles in the system. When particles collide, new particles with different physical properties are created. (For example, when a neutron collides with a nucleus of a fissile substance, fission can occur and several additional neutrons appear.) The trajectories and properties of each new particle are determined probabilistically (thus, the computer tracking techniques are called Monte Carlo methods) and are characterized by reaction cross-sections. The cross-sectional information depends heavily on details of the collision itself, such as the incidence particle, energy transmitted, trajectory angle, and isotope generation. This information is typically contained in large tables in the memory; these tables are accessed when a collision occurs.

The path of a particle can be illustrated by a tree (see Figure 3), where each branch represents

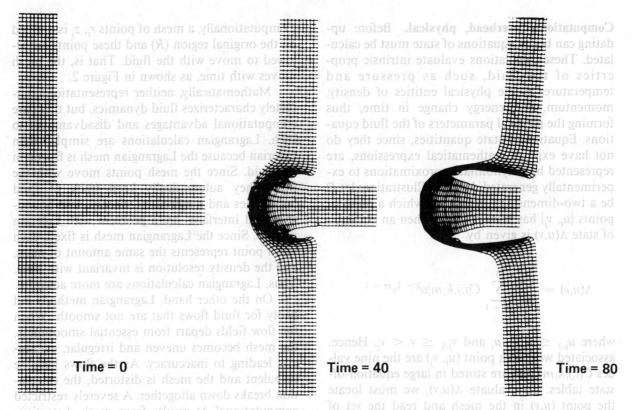

Time = 0 **Time = 40** **Time = 80**

Figure 2. Configuration plots of a tungsten cylinder impacting a steel plate. Note that the mesh moves with time.

the creation of particles. Generally speaking, the tree may extend indefinitely, as long as sufficient energy is available in the particle. In practice, however, the tree is computed only for a finite number of branches. It is usually obvious from the condition of the problem where to end the

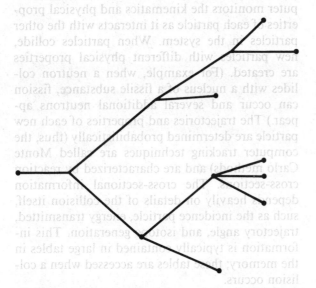

Figure 3. A tree illustrates the path of a particle; each branch represents the creation of a particle.

tree; this point is called the census time. A tree is constructed for each particle. With a set of trees, physical characteristics are determined at census time, e.g., the number of particles of various types at a specified instant of time, the energy distribution, and the energy involved. The computational procedure for developing the tree is typically as follows: move along any one branch, performing the processing and remembering all the branching (the particle "history" calculations). At the end of that branch, move backward one branch and eliminate that branch. Then move along any recorded branch. If no branchings are recorded for this point, return yet another branch backward. The computation on this tree ends for this time interval when all of the tree has been eliminated. All of the trees are processed in this manner, then census time calculations are performed.

Monte Carlo techniques pose a difficult problem for computer designers. The methods require enormous amounts of memory for cross-sectional data and particle histories as well as fast computer registers, since a number of decisions must be made. Vector and array processors were designed with the idea of solving fluid-type problems efficiently. In general, these machines do not lend themselves well to particle-tracking calculations.

For a scientific laboratory such as LLNL, the computer should be able to handle both forms of calculations, but it remains to be seen whether this goal will ever be achieved.

Illustrative hardware for large scientific computation

As highlighted in the preceding section, large scientific computation is usually dominated by solution of dynamical equations describing physical systems.

The LLNL Computer Center (LCC) serves the calculational needs of some 2000 scientists and engineers. A network, called Octopus, includes major and support computers, storage media, input/output devices, and local terminals. All Octopus facilities are bound together in a web of computing resources. With the terminals in their offices and laboratories, users can access the entire network. Major equipment is located in two adjacent buildings with the users' terminals within a half-mile radius of the central facilities.

Users' needs vary. There are thousands of codes; some are little used and small, others are components of large (20,000 to 200,000 lines of source program) code systems that are heavily used in physical simulations. The computer center provides timeshared services around the clock. Nights and weekends are biased toward production code runs (supervised by computer operators), while week days are biased toward timeshared use of the computer for code development, short code runs, critical production runs, and servicing large production problems.

The computational facility must provide sufficient computational ability so that a scientist can either finish a calculation during a single production period or run the problem until it crashes and requires human attention. The calculational load at LLNL is such that a production code problem can ordinarily be allocated no more than two hours per night or six hours per weekend. Scientists running large problems use the daytime timesharing facilities to analyze and—if necessary—correct the previous night's production run, and to formulate new problems.

The following is a description of current LLNL computer center hardware, divided into four functional areas: major computers, the network, storage media, and input/output equipment. A brief history of LLNL mainframe acquisitions and their characteristics precedes a discussion of LLNL future hardware needs in the same four areas.

Current major computers

The major computers in the LLNL computer network are referred to as "worker" computers because they do the bulk of the scientific calculations. Currently, there are eight worker computers in the Livermore Computer Center network: one Cray Research, Inc., X-MP/24 computer, four Cray-1 computers, and three Control Data Corporation Model 7600 computers. (In addition to this network, the National Magnetic Fusion Energy Computer Center is also located at the laboratory. It has two Cray-1's and one CDC 7600; in 1985 it will install a Cray-2 computer.) The X-MP/24 is the most recently installed unit at the LCC. A similar but much more powerful version of this is expected to be announced soon, and the X-MP/24 may be upgraded. Later some of the older computers will be released.

A brief description of the most interesting characteristic of each of these computers follows.
CDC 7600. The CDC 7600 has a 12-word instruction stack that support sequential processing. There are 24 operating registers, some 18-bit (for addressing) and some 60-bit (full word size). The computer clock period is 27.5 nanoseconds per cycle. The arithmetic processor uses ones-complement arithmetic.

The machine has 65,536 words (60 bits per word) of small core memory (SCM). This memory has a 27.5 nanosecond-per-word maximum transfer rate. In addition, the machine has 512,000 words (60 bit) of 1760-nanosecond read/write-time large core memory (LCM). Both memories have parity checking.

The instruction stack can hold up to 48 instructions (many instructions require only 15 bits). A calculational module, which loops only within the stack and requires no additional instructions to be fetched to the stack from memory, can operate at a very high rate.

The number of bits in the 18-bit address registers is insufficient to access all addresses in the 512,000-word extended memory; thus the software must perform address arithmetic in the 60-bit registers to access LCM. The machine instruction set includes a "block copy" instruction that can be used to quickly move up to 1023 adjacent words of data between SCM and LCM at a 27.5 nanosecond-per-word transfer rate. The highest calculation rate is obtained by utilizing the block copy instruction and instruction stack.

Cray-1. There are two models of the Cray-1 at LLNL, the 1a and the improved model 1s, two of each. The Cray-1 does both sequential (scalar) and array (vector) operations. The Model 1a units have 1,048,576 (1M) words of bipolar memory while the 1s machines utilize a newer chip technology to provide 2M-word memories. The 1s units also provide more efficient access to memory for the input and output of data from and to auxiliary storage devices. The memory has single-error correction and double-error detection (SECDED). The memory cycle time is 50 nanoseconds.

The basic machine cycle (clock period) is 12.5 nanoseconds. Floating-point calculations use sign-magnitude arithmetic. There are 16 primary scalar registers and 128 intermediate scalar registers. There are eight vector registers of 64 words each and the machine word length is 64 bit.

The intermediate registers transfer data at a rate of one word per clock period for the vector registers and one word every two clock periods for the scalar registers.

Vector operations are done by fetching data from main memory to the vector registers, performing vector calculations using the data, and then returning the results to memory. Elements can be fetched from, or stored to, memory with any increment between successive element addresses.

Long vectors (over 64 elements) must be done by implementing software to sequence through 64-element groups.

The vector start-up time for various operations ranges from six to 11 clock periods. Once a vector operation has been initiated, a result is produced each period. However functional units can be "chained"—that is, an element result from one operation can be utilized by another operation (providing that the subsequent operation uses a different functional unit) so that vector operations overlap. As a result of this chaining capability, many subsequent operations are virtually "free." For example, a 64-element vector add followed by a 64-element vector multiply will be done in 79 clock periods (six clocks for the add start-up, seven clocks for the multiply start-up, and 64 clocks for the element processing), 64 fewer clocks than without chaining. This does not include the time necessary to load the vector registers from main memory, nor to store the results into memory. A vector load from memory may be chained with a subsequent functional unit calculation.

The machine instruction set lacks a divide operation, including instead a "reciprocal" operation that produces results of insufficient accuracy. Accurate division requires a four-instruction sequence (a reciprocal and three multiplication instructions).

Cray X-MP/24. The X-MP/24 is the first commercially available large-scale multiprocessor computer. There are two separately programmable CPU's which share a four-million-word (64 bit per word) bipolar memory. Each processor's architecture is similar to that of the Cray-1s but is faster and includes additional hardware features which augment the vector processing speed through more overlapping of the vector processes. The basic cycle time is 9.5 nanoseconds. Each processor has a typical throughput capability of from 1.25 to 2.5 times that of the Cray-1s.

The two CPU's may be utilized to calculate completely independent job streams, or may be coordinated to run in parallel on separate but related portions of a single numerical model. Hardware-provided semaphores which can be set and tested by the two processing units allow the programmer to coordinate the two portions of the calculations through repeated starting and stopping of processes and joining of results. There is speculation that a four-processor version of the X-MP will announced by Cray Research, Inc., and it is likely that the X-MP/24 would be upgraded to that version. This upgrade would require more memory (perhaps 8M words) because of the demands of the two additional processors. The upgrade may also include the addition of a solid-state disk (SSD).

Comments. Each of the computers utilizes a number of peripheral processors (computers) for transferring data to and from the primary memory and peripheral devices.

Note that the Star 100 streamed data directly between memory and the vector pipelines, while the Cray-1 uses intermediate storage (the vector registers) in the calculational process.

There is a tremendous contrast in the physical size of the Star-100 computers (see Table 1) and the Cray-1's which followed them at LLNL. The central processing unit and memory of the 1970 machine used over 1000 square feet of floor space. The CPU of the Cray-1 (first model produced in 1977) is housed in a cylinder about six feet high and six feet in diameter (the machine uses a 3/4 arc of the cylinder, with an open core diameter of about three feet). The X-MP/24 is

Table 1. Large-scale scientific computers at Lawrence Livermore National Laboratory.

	Number of mach.	Year first acquired	Year last unit released	Memory size in K words	Bits per word	Multiply time, μs	Comments
Remington Rand Univac 1	1	1952	1959	1	48	2150	Vacuum-tube processor. Acoustic delay line memory. Decimal arithmetic. No floating-point arithmetic. Steel magnetic tape.
IBM 701	2	1953	1957	2	36	456	No floating-point arithmetic. Electrostatic memory.
IBM 704	4	1956	1961	8–32	36	204	Magnetic core memory. Tube CPU.
IBM 709	2	1958	1963	32	36	204	Same as 704, but separate I/O processor.
IBM 7090	3	1961	1970	32	36	24	Transistorized.
IBM 7094	2	1963	1972	32	36	10	— —
Remington Rand LARC	1	1960	1968	30	48	12	Decimal arithmetic.
IBM 7030 Stretch	1	1962	1970	96	64	2	Had SECDED memory.
CDC 1604	1	1962	1963	32	48	36	— —
CDC 3600	2	1963	1969	32	48	6.4	— —
CDC 6600	4	1964	— —	132	60	1	First timesharing computer. Has relocation registers.
CDC 7600	5	1969	— —	500	60	0.1375	Has two memories.
CDC Star 100	2	1970	1980	1000	64	0.040	Vector processor.
Cray-1a	4	1979	— —	1000	64	0.0125	Vector processor. Bipolar, SECDED memory.
Cray-1s	2	1981	— —	2000	64	0.0125	— —
Cray X-MP/24	1	1984	— —	4000	64	0.0095	Two processors.

only slightly larger than the Cray-1, in spite of its much greater power.

With programs that are reasonably well suited to the machine, the CDC 7600 performs at a rate of from 3 to 5 megaflops (million floating point arithmetic operations per second) and the Cray-1s at 20 to 50 megaflops. Each processor of the X-MP/24 has a typical performance rate of from 30 to 100 megaflops (the total calculation rate of the machine is twice this).

Current network

Octopus, the main computer network at LLNL, interconnects the work computers, storage devices, message concentrators, and I/O devices.

Most system users have in their offices or laboratories a keyboard/printer terminal or a keyboard/soft copy terminal and a video display unit. Over 1500 keyboard terminals are interconnected through the central network. Used by scientists for limited input/output, text editing, etc., the terminals monitor and control jobs on the worker computers. Currently, 60 remote-job-entry terminals, consisting of a card reader and a non-impact printer, are conveniently accessible to most users.

The network utilizes many mini- and midicomputers for routing data sets and controlling support processes such as storage and I/O devices.

Figure 4 shows a greatly simplified schematic of the network. The Cray-1 computers are indicated by the "C"-shaped configurations, and the CDC 7600's as the large "U" shapes. The squares are the midicomputers and minicomputers. The two minis shown in the lower right-hand corner of the schematic are used to monitor and control user access to data in the system through verification of a user-entered "combination" number. The mini shown in the upper left is used to access direct input digital data from experiments. The heavy line connecting all the units represents a high-speed data transmission system known locally as "Octobus."

The network is modular, so malfunctioning components can be worked on, replaced, or added, without taking the entire system down. This property allows a new worker computer to

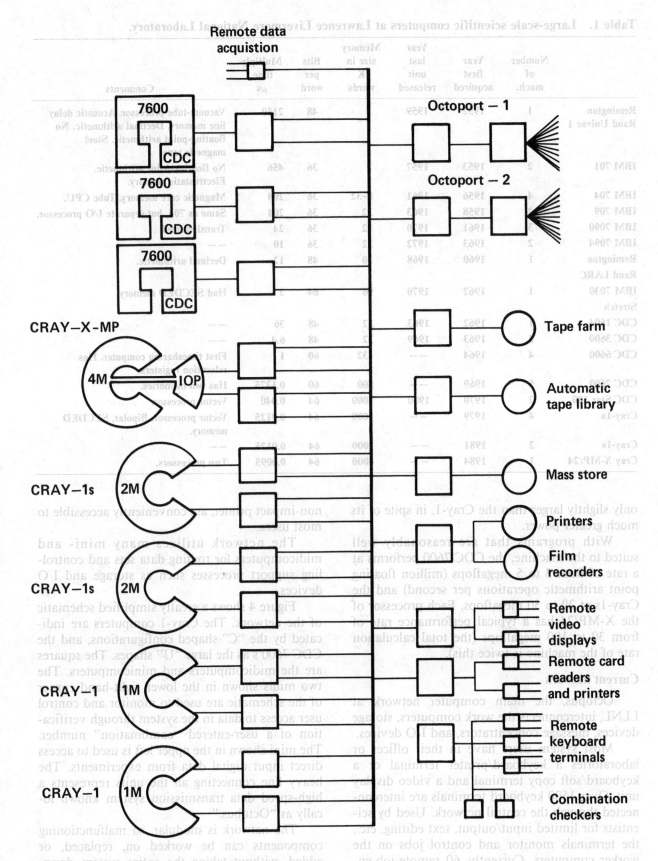

Figure 4. Schematic representation of the Octopus network. The largest figures represent worker computers, the squares the midi- and minicomputers.

be installed with nearly immediate access to support facilities. The Octobus high-speed data transmission device is manufactured by Network Systems Corporation (Hyperchannel). Addressed data packets are carried along a common bus and "picked off" by an addressee interface. A single interface serves each Octobus resource. All components of the system are thus connected, thereby greatly simplifying the network and providing greater system component flexibility. High-speed multiport devices (Octoports) are attached to Octobus to service equipment that requires high data speeds.

An interesting use of small processors in conjunction with the network is to, in effect, replace a remote keyboard terminal with a microprocessor or minicomputer and use it to monitor and control the worker computers, transport files, etc. Some users can request, for example, that a mini telephone them at home and inform them—currently through an audio code—of machine failures, job failures, etc.

Current storage

In addition to the primary memory of each worker computer, each main unit has captive secondary disk storage units which support ongoing scientific calculations and timesharing activities.

Each CDC 7600 accesses six CDC Model 819 disks, each with a capacity of 5×10^9 bits, and has eight CDC 844 disk drives, each with a capacity of 7.1×10^8 bits. The Cray machines have secondary storage consisting of 12 Cray DD29 disks, each with a capacity of 1×10^{10} bits.

In the network (and accessible to it for data file storage) is a CDC 28500 mass storage device, a California Computer Corporation ATL (Automatic Tape Library) and many tape units for handling 1/2-inch wide magnetic tape (mostly 9 track). Numerous disks are used as staging memory, invisible to the user. The ATL provides automated access to 2000 online high-density (6250 bits per inch) tapes. Each tape has a storage capacity of 10^9 bits.

The mass store has magnetic tape cartridges as the storage medium. Mechanical arms transfer the cartridges between storage racks and read/write stations. The capacity of the LLNL unit is 10^{12} bits. It does not offer a shelving capability.

Current input and output

The LLNL computer facility has a relatively light input load but an extremely heavy output load since the mathematical models that use most of the computer time produce great amounts of text and graphical output. This can be contrasted with some other scientific installations that do data reductions of experimental results and, therefore, have large amounts of input but relatively small output.

Data input to the network is mainly via terminals, punched cards, and magnetic tape (cassette and reel).

The office terminals (keyboard/printer and video) provide timesharing and interactive I/O capabilities.

The remote-job-entry terminals each have a Documentation Incorporated Model M300 card reader and a Verstatec Corporation Matrix Model 1200A 600-line-per minute non-impact printer. The card reading capability is now little used.

Two Honeywell electrostatic-paper page printers with an output capacity of 15,000 lines per minute are currently producing about three million pages per month.

Five Informational International Incorporated FR-80 film recorders record text and plot data on 105-mm (microfiche), 35-mm, and 16-mm photographic film. Presently, the recorders are producing about nine million pages per month, mostly microfiche.

A recent addition to output capacity is two IBM 3800 Laser Printers, each of which produces 16,000 lines per minute of high-quality printed material using laser technology. These will replace the Honeywell printers which are obsolete.

A Dicomed Corporation D48 color recorder, which produces colored, varied-intensity, and fine-resolution 16-mm and 35-mm output, permits interactive manipulation of the video image before recording. In addition to other uses, it processes result data from computer simulations into motion pictures of the modeled event.

One minicomputer in the network is used for data input directly from experiments.

History of LLNL's major computers

The computer center acquired its first major computer in 1952, the first year that LLNL (then known as the University of California Radiation Laboratory at Livermore) was in operation. The performance of that computer, a Remington Rand Univac 1, suffers in any comparison with a modern minicomputer system. Since that time, 37 major computers of 15 different models have been acquired. The latest acquisition is the Cray-1.

From the earliest machine to the Cráy X-MP, the computing power of a major computer has increased by a factor of 250,000 to 500,000 or more. It has been calculated that the Livermore Computer Center will now do as much calculation in less than 2 minutes as the Univac 1 could do in a year. The computing center, utilizing several machines, nearly doubled its computer power each year through 1964 and every four years since 1964.

The Octopus network was inaugurated in 1964 in conjunction with the installation of a CDC 6600 computer, the first LLNL-acquired computer suitable for timesharing. Before that, daytime users operated the computer "hands on," and operators ran individual jobs during off hours.

Table 1 lists LLNL's machines by type, number, year of installation, last year of service, primary memory size in units of 1000 words, word size in bits, and characteristic multiply times, along with some general comments. The multiply times are given only to indicate calculational speed; a more thorough picture would require many qualifying comments.

The first two machines, the Univac 1 and the IBM 701, did not do floating-point arithmetic. An interesting fact is that the electrostatic memory of the IBM 701 was so subject to failure that passing a hand over the surface of a storage tube caused it to lose data.

Note that the X-MP's floating-point multiply (vector multiply) is 226,000 times faster than the Univac's fixed-point multiply.

Future hardware needs

In general, it is anticipated that the demands for computational services at LLNL will result in continued growth of the Octopus network. The development of more sophisticated calculational techniques—and the availability of mainframe computers capable of utilizing them—is one reason for growth. As sufficiently powerful mainframes are developed known—but currently unexploited—calculation techniques will also come into use.

As the physical systems being modeled become increasingly complex, more detailed modeling is needed. Currently, most modeling is two-dimensional, but greater use of three-dimensional modeling—tremendously more demanding of computer resources—is expected in the future.

In recent years, LLNL's scope of activities has broadened to encompass many additional energy-related research tasks. This trend will continue, with a consequent additional demand for computational services.

Future worker computers. Economic factors are such that LLNL will meet its mainframe calculational needs through the acquisition of more powerful computers, rather than through the proliferation of current models or the acquisition of many less-powerful computers. The demands for computer housing, network connections, operation personnel, etc., preclude using more than five to seven mainframes. High-performance computers provide "more bang per buck" than lesser units in a large, scientific environment.

Through the sixties, designers of new sequential machines obtained large increases in calculational rates by using advanced circuit technologies, faster primary memories, overlapping instruction execution, etc. Vector and parallel machines developed as the result of efforts to push performance beyond the capabilities of sequential processors.

The speed at which electricity is conducted has become a limiting factor in increasing calculational speeds. Partly because of this, machines are becoming smaller as their performance increases. (No wire in the Cray-1's CPU is longer than three feet.) Decreased machine size concentrates component-generated heat and increases circuit cooling problems. The Cray-1 uses direct contact of copper circuit boards with freon-cooled aluminum frame members. Four 20-ton refrigerant units cool the machine. A wag has suggested that the supercomputer of the future will be about the size of the head of a pin and will operate at a white-hot temperature.

Over the years, the rate of increase in sequential calculational rates has been decreasing, while a large rate increase has been realized through the application of vector and parallel architectures. The Cray X-MP's use scalar, vector, parallel, multiprocessor (separate instruction stream) technologies. Machines of the future may utilize data flow or other emerging technologies.

Some comments about high-performance machine design:

(1) The logic concerned with calculational control and memory management constitutes a large and important part of most scientific applications codes. The instruction set of a machine must include data manipulation operations that do these tasks at a rate compatible with the execution rate of the arithmetic operations.

440

(2) The size of primary memory and the execution rates of the processor should be closely related. A slow processor cannot economically use a large memory, nor can a fast processor be adequately utilized by a small memory.

(3) Vector machines that require long vectors for efficient operation (i.e., a long vector start-up time) need relatively larger memories than scalar or short vector (short start-up time) machines. This is because programs using long vectors require that a large portion of the memory be allocated for storing intermediate result vectors.

(4) Long vector machines are well suited to doing explicit calculations but are not as well suited to doing implicit calculations.

(5) A vector machine must have scalar calculational rates in balance with the vector rates. With a poor scalar-to-vector balance, virtually all calculations must be vectorized to achieve acceptable rates. Complete vectorization is not obtainable because some algorithms cannot be vectorized and economic considerations preclude vectorization of all parts of a code or all codes used on a machine.

Table 2 illustrates how important it is that a machine have a reasonable scalar-to-vector calculation rate balance. It shows the running-time result of various degrees of vectorization on a machine whose vector processor rates are 25 times greater than the scalar processor rate. It shows, for example, that a program that is 75 percent vectorized (in terms of operations performed) will take 7 times longer to run than if it were fully vectorized.

The calculational algorithms in use on current and past machines were chosen partially because of their compatability with the machine architectures. The development of machines with very large and fast primary memories and very fast "gather scatter" processors will allow users to exploit the advantages of Monte Carlo calculation methods.

Table 2. Scalar-to-vector ratio of 1 to 25.

Percent of scalar operation	Percent of vector operation	Run time
0	100	4
10	90	13.6
25	75	28
50	50	52
75	25	76
90	10	90.4
100	0	100

The future network. The decreasing cost and increasing capability of mini- and microcomputers permits their use for many local tasks, thus taking some of the burden from the mainframes. The terminal computers communicate with the central network resources through data-file transportation and by message transmission. Some LLNL groups plan to use local processing for tasks other than those previously mentioned, including running application programs. The daytime would be devoted mainly to interactive uses and the off-hours to the running of application programs.

Large application codes are actually groups of codes that run in conjunction with each other. In addition to the "physics" module, there are programs for tasks such as creating a new problem data base from input data, producing text or plot output from the data base, altering the data base to make problem adjustments, and converting from other data bases. It has been suggested that associated processors used in conjunction with the mainframes do the auxiliary functions so that the worker computers could be devoted entirely to physics processing. However, for the most of the large physics codes at LLNL, this is impractical. The auxiliary tasks are in themselves large programs that require powerful processors, and the attributes that make a worker computer do physics calculations well are quite similar to those needed for auxiliary processing. LAN's (local area networks) are now being used at LLNL, and others are being designed, including a lab-wide network to link virtually all computer resources.

Future storage. Which technology will provide the very large and fast storage system needed by LLNL is uncertain. No currently available product can provide the speed, size, and archival capabilities demanded.

Machines of the near future will have SSD's (solid state disks) of more than 100,000,000 words, which will provide nearly instantaneous access to large amounts of data while they are running.

Future output. As the power of LLNL's worker computers continues to grow, the amount of output will grow correspondingly. Much of the long-term storage capacity is used to retain problem data base files. These files contain much of the data that has previously been edited and plotted to hard copy or film output. An interactive, fast, reliable retrieval-conversion-display system would allow users to forego much of the hard copy processing. There would be a need for locally accessible hard copy processing facilities for printing and plotting selected output.

As machines have grown in calculating power, it has become increasingly difficult for users to monitor the calculation because of the huge amount of data involved. On occasion, computer-generated motion pictures have been used to advantage, lending additional insights into the physical processes being investigated. However, the processing time and expense have been such that movies are rarely used for immediate problem analysis. It is expected that faster, specialized equipment will permit the regular use of movies as an output means.

A recently developed diagnostic capability allows a scientist, the user of some of the simulation model codes, to have automatically put onto videotape the results of a code run as the problem progresses in time. Data is sent to a microcomputer as the problem runs, and a movie is produced for subsequent viewing. For example, a videotape can be made at night when the problem is run, and then viewed the next morning.

The increasing interest in three-dimensional calculations demands the development of better tools for analyzing these problems. Thus far, using two-dimensional projections, etc., has been helpful but not entirely satisfactory; scientists need to examine internal variables, flow patterns, etc., to "see" inside three-dimensional models. The huge amount of data involved requires very fast, inexpensive processors. Perhaps new hardware can be developed to provide the necessary capability.

Software for scientific computation

Computers are somewhat unique among the tools of the scientist's trade—proper hardware is only part of the tool; software is also required. Operating systems, compilers, assemblers, loaders, utility routines, and other service modules are needed to support the simulation programs, called codes at LLNL.

Early applications systems

The earliest scientific applications codes were characterized by severe limitations on size, speed, and output, at least by today's standards. As likely as not, the scientists involved in those early codes were closer to the hardware and to each step in the problem solution process than they are today. They may even have performed their own programming in machine code, prepared their own input, run their own programs, or collected their own output. Turnaround time was a function of

when the user could schedule a time slot on the machine. There was only one program, the "number cruncher" itself, with a front end that accepted input and some output coding to send problem dumps and listings to some output medium. Input was probably on punched cards, and output was most likely long lists of numbers produced on a mechanical printer. Any graphs that were needed were drawn by hand from these listings. Physical models tended to be crude and one-dimensional.

As the machines became larger and faster, the models were made more sophisticated and more of the work was automated. Also, the people working on these problems began to specialize: scientists became code developers or code users; applications programmers began to assume the tasks of translating the physical models into computer instructions and writing the programs which performed the automated support functions; system programmers began to produce tools such as assemblers, compilers, operating systems, and subroutine libraries. Computer graphics routines were developed to aid in handling the large amounts of data being generated. Higher-level programming languages such as Fortran were developed to increase programmer productivity.

The users could no longer run their own jobs in a hands-on mode because of the computer time that was wasted in changing from one job (and user) to the next. Control programs that accepted jobs off-line via a medium such as tape were written to eliminate this time wastage. Thus, batch operating systems were born, and batch turnaround time was—and still is—measured in hours or days, depending on the type of queue and priority system.

A great leap forward in productivity occurred at LLNL in 1964 with the implementation of the first interactive timesharing operating system on the CDC 6600. Turn-around time was suddenly reduced to a matter of minutes or seconds. Interactive computer graphics via a television monitor display system also arrived in 1964. By the late sixties a large number of support programs whose only purpose was to feed and analyze output from the number crunchers had come into being. The scientific applications code had become a code system.

Present applications systems

Large-scale scientific applications codes account for the existence of a computational facility at LLNL in its present form, but they by no means account for all of that computations that are actually performed there. In fact, much of the work load would not look out of place at any scientifically based computer center. The major feature of the LLNL computational facility dictated by the large applications code system is the presence of the latest in supercomputers.

A major applications code at LLNL is actually an integrated system of modules in which any program may be run by either human beings at terminals or by other programs. The programs that communicate with each other do so by exchanging small packets of information called messages, or by sharing access to data bases residing on disk or in memory. Many applications code systems at LLNL are distributive: each of the modules may run on one or more of the worker computers. Figure 5 is a simplified diagram of the major modules that might go together to make up

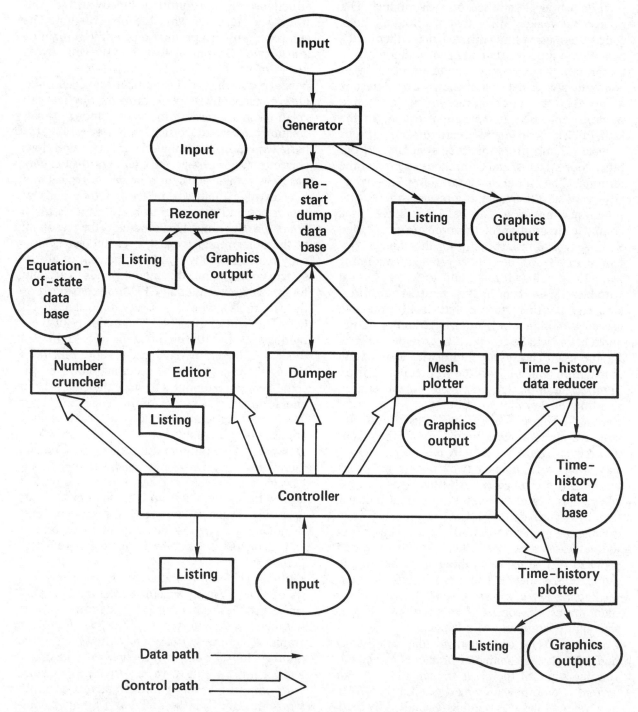

Figure 5. Major modules of a generic scientific applications code system.

443

a generic scientific applications code system. The flow of data is represented on the diagram by arrows. The flow of messages which represents control of one program by another is represented by broad arrows. Not shown are the many smaller service modules which would also belong to the system.

Before examining the software engineering implications involved in such a system, we shall provide a brief description of each module. The point of view taken will be that of a fluid methods code system using finite differencing. Other methods require different, but analogous, modules.

Generator. The generator module accepts input and generates a data base known as the restart dump. The generator is run in an interactive mode by the user, and the input can be in the form of disk files containing card images, portions of restart dumps from this code system and from other code systems, and commands entered at the terminal. The output, or restart dump (procedurally every start is treated as a restart—there is no initial start-up), is a data base that serves as a complete description of the problem at a given time. A typical restart dump for this kind of system at LLNL will describe a problem containing from 2000 to 40,000 zones and 10 to 50 physical variables (mass, coordinates, temperature, pressure, etc.) per zone, making up a disk file that can exceed a million words in size. Graphics output and a listing will be generated to provide feedback for the user. The restart dump will also contain instructions meant for the controller, editor, dumper, mesh plotter, time-history data reducer, and time-history plotter modules.

Rezoner. The rezoner module is used in an interactive mode to clean up or modify the restart dump data base. For example, this may be necessary when a Lagrangian two-dimensional mesh has been run through enough time steps that the zoning has begun to scramble from turbulence, thereby decreasing the size of the time steps and causing the problem to "slow down." Thus, input to the rezoner can be either a badly distorted problem or one to which the user wishes to add more zones or detail. The user will display intermediate results on a video display device, and the final output will consist of, in addition to the restart dump, graphics and a listing.

Controller. The controller module coordinates and controls the running of problems by actually running some of the other modules in the code system. Communication between the controller and the modules it is running is handled by sending messages back and forth via the operating sys-

tem. Input to the controller can be in a number of forms. The user can run his own job by conversing with the controller via a terminal, or the user can set up an instruction sheet and have the job run during off-hours by a computer operator.

Instructions to the controller regarding frequency of restart dumps, edits, mesh plots, and entries to the time-history data base are placed in the restart dump by the generator. Additional instructions can be submitted directly to the controller via a terminal while the job is running. The controller will also produce a print file containing a history of the run so that the user will have a record of what happened.

Number cruncher. The number-cruncher module is concerned with performing the physical calculations in a series of time steps. Among the calculations involved are such things as solving the basic equations, handling boundary conditions correctly, and accessing the equation-of-state data base via a table look-up scheme. A typical run may involve hundreds to tens of thousands of time steps and may take from 10 minutes to 10 hours of CPU time. This module is the reason all of the other modules exist, even though it typically represents only five to 30 percent of all the system coding. Since this module tends to account for 80 to 90 percent of all CPU time consumed by the system as a whole, it is very important that it be as efficient as possible. The majority of these modules at LLNL run in a memory-contained mode, i.e., the entire data base is kept in memory during the run. It may be necessary, however, for some very large modules to stage the data base to and from disk in blocks during each time step. These modules tend to be very slow because they are usually I/O bound.

Dumper. The dumper module writes restart dumps to long-term storage media at specific intervals during a run. These restart dumps protect against losing an entire run because of machine or operating system failure. They also serve as links to other code systems or as input to generators and rezoners, and can be input to postrun data processors.

Editor. The editor module produces printed edits of a problem at specified intervals during a run. Since these edits consist of page after page of numbers, they are generally not as useful as graphical output. Occasionally, however, some numbers must be accurate to three or more digits, and for this the edit serves a purpose. Also, since edits comprise a very complete picture of problem status, they can be useful as a problem spotting and debugging tool.

Mesh plotter. The mesh-plotter module generates pictures of the problem at specified intervals. The entire problem may be plotted by drawing all of the mesh lines, or perhaps only those lines separating different materials will be drawn. Velocity arrows may be drawn at each intersection point to indicate the direction and magnitude of movement within the mesh. Isoplots of quantities like pressure or temperature may be overlaid on mesh plots. Blowups may be made of specific areas within the problem. Plots made at fairly close intervals may be strung together on sprocketed film to produce a motion picture of the run. All of these pictures are extremely important in reducing the billions of calculations to a form that can be readily comprehended by the user.

Time-history data-base reducer and plotter. The time-history data-reducer module extracts data from the problem at specified intervals, placing it in a time-history data base on a long-term storage medium. Usually, a few thousand data points are saved at several hundred time points, producing a time-history data base of a half a million to a million data points. Immediately after the run, the time-history module plots these data points against time, e.g., pressure vs time for a specified zone or collection of zones. The module also produces an edit of this data base. Data bases from a number of runs can be collected together by various code systems, and results can be compared by the user in an interactive mode. In this way, results from various production code systems, running what may be essentially the same problem, can be compared. Time-history data bases can also serve as input to other code systems.

Software engineering considerations

As can be seen from the preceding simplified description, the software engineering requirements for LLNL's applications code systems cover a very broad spectrum. In size alone, such systems typically consist of from 100,000 to 200,000 lines of source files, which means that they are worked on by teams of applications computer scientists. The tasks involved include vector programming, data base manipulation, dynamic memory allocation, job control logic, graphics input and output, printed output, and interactive computer operator and user interfaces. In a real LLNL applications code system, there may be anywhere from 10 to 50 separate code modules which must run on different mainframes such as the CDC 7600, Cray-1a or -1s, and Cray X-MP. The languages used include a local dialect of Fortran and various assembly languages. In addition, a heavy reliance is placed on utilizing other products of LLNL systems computer scientists, and the capabilities provided by the Octopus network through the worker-computer operating system have become an indispensable element of the set of tools.

A brief discussion of the various attributes required in large LLNL applications code systems follows. It should be noted that, although they are discussed separately, maximizing any one attribute almost always affects one or more of the other attributes. Thus, as is true in every area of computer science, a major portion of the applications computer scientist's responsibility is to make decisions concerning these trade-offs.

Efficiency

Users want to run the largest possible problems in the shortest possible time with as much calculational accuracy as possible. Since achieving any one of these goals usually has a negative effect on the other two, trade-offs are necessary. If the problem data base takes up too much memory, less room is available for simulation coding and vice versa. If the simulation coding is too extensive, the problems will probably run too slow. If the problem data base does not fit in memory, but must be staged in from disk, the problem will almost certainly be I/O bound and run too slow. And so on.

Among the techniques that have been developed to allow maximum efficient use of the supercomputer are the following:

(1) Vector programming. This technique, which should really be called array processing, is a complex area of study and practice. It includes, depending on the particular supercomputer involved, such techniques as parallel processing, pipeline processing, and operation scheduling. On the CDC 7600, for example, it is possible to write the equivalent of a DO LOOP in such a manner that it fits in the instruction stack, thereby increasing speed by a factor of up to 2.7 over regulation (optimized) Fortran. This technique is exploited by an LLNL subroutine library named, appropriately enough, STACKLIB. Similar techniques are used to speed up specific algorithms by using assembly language subroutines on the Cray machines. Coding techniques such as these are, of course, machine-dependent and are, therefore, used only in the most time-critical modules of a code system.

(2) Dynamic memory allocation. In order to squeeze the largest possible problem into memory, array allocations may be set at run time instead of compile time. This allows different size problems to be run, with widely varying types of data base allocations, at no penalty in wasted memory. For example, one problem may have very large alpha arrays and another very large beta arrays, or the array sizes may change during the course of a problem. In these circumstances, setting array allocation at compile time involves trade-offs that waste memory at least some of the time for some of the problems. Language extensions allowing dynamic memory allocations are available in modern Fortran compilers, but this coding technique involves a lot of extra programming effort. A subroutine library, MMLIB, was developed by LLNL applications computer scientists to manage a heap memory allocation scheme.

(3) Data-base tools. To assist in working with the large data bases required by these code systems, a collection of tools has been developed by LLNL applications computer scientists. A file format, ACF, and I/O library, ACFLIB, allow the accessing of data by symbolic name rather than absolute location. In this way applications code system modules are shielded from the details and made relatively immune to the effects of change. For example, if a particular piece of data, ranging from a floating-point scalar number to a three-dimensional array to a text string, is to be read from a disk file, the following procedure is implemented using ACFLIB and MMLIB subroutines: the file is opened; the presence of the data is verified and its attributes (e.g., data type, dimensionality, length, etc.) are determined; memory is allocated to hold the data; and the data is read into the memory provided. Note that the actual location of the data in the file was known only by ACFLIB. In addition, interactive data-base tools, such as editors, plotters, and machine-to-machine translators have been implemented on top of ACFLIB. Thus, for example, restart dumps from different applications code systmes can be edited by one shared tool.

Although much work was been done in the area of developing compilers, automatic vectorizers, and other software to vectorize and dynamically allocate memory automatically, much of the actual speed-up is still obtained by the direct labor of the code-development scientist, mathematician, and computer scientist. To illustrate current capabilities encountered at LLNL, a typical code system runs in the neighborhood of one to 100+ megaflops with a problem completion time ranging anywhere from 15 minutes to four hours and beyond. It is important to remember that increases in these capabilities put an increasing amount of stress on output data-reduction techniques and capacities.

Reliability

As far as the users are concerned, if they do not receive their output, the problem did not run, no matter how much CPU time and other resources were consumed. In addition, if there are bugs in the computational model, the user may waste a considerable amount of effort before they are discovered. These considerations mandate the use of all available software engineering techniques for minimizing errors and producing reliable software. For example, a code system with many users may have 25 or more test problems that will be run and verified before a new version of the system is released for production use. Another reliability improvement tool involves producing a run log for each production problem which contains a record of everything that happened during the run (e.g., operator commands, the time and cycle of restart dumps, timing statistics showing where the CPU, I/O, and system time are being used, and of course, a record of all errors, fatal and nonfatal, together with diagnostic snapshots detailing the cause of the problem).

Maintainability

Some of these code systems have been in existence for a decade or more on three or more generations of hardware, and they have been written in multiple languages. Given the size, complexity, and lifetime involved, it is imperative that all available techniques be utilized to ensure the maintainability of these systems. The applications computer scientist must keep current in such areas as structured design, top-down design, bottom-up design, configuration control, "go to-less" programming, and so on. As an additional payoff, of course, techniques that enhance the maintainability of a code system also enhance its reliability.

Documentation

The documentation of a production code system is very important, and its presence—or absence—will affect the system's reliability and maintainability. One somewhat unusual feature of LLNL code systems is that they never go through the normal design, development, testing, and delivery stages, i.e., they are never completed in the usual sense. Research on and development of these systems is an ongoing process. Since the applications computer scientist is in such close contact with the code system users, the documentation tends to be considerably more informal than it might be in a more structured environment.

Portability

The portability attribute has two facets. The first and most commonly thought of is the transportation of software between one installation and another. This usually involves considerations such as writing a program in standard Fortran, avoiding hardware-dependent problem formulations, and developing in-house operating systems and subroutine libraries that provide an invariant interface to various mainframes. The second portability facet is the transportation of software from one type or generation of supercomputer to another type or to the next generation of supercomputer to another type or to the next generation. This usually involves considerations such as using locally developed Fortran extensions and machine-dependent problem formulations in order to make the most effective use of each supercomputer. Since these two facets are in conflict, if both of them are required for a code system, some compromises are in order. The details of these compromises are a function of the code system requirements. For example, many of the large code systems are never transported outside of LLNL, and the portability techniques used in these cases involve making the time-critical modules relatively machine-dependent in nature and constructing the remaining modules in a relatively machine-independent, but not installation-independent, manner.

Human engineering

The code system is usually conversing with either a user or a computer operator. Thus it is important that the man/machine interface be well engineered to avoid confusion and loss of time and that user documentation be produced and made available in a timely manner.

Tools

To need these requirements the following tools have been developed at LLNL.

Octopus network. As described previously, the Octopus network provides an extremely powerful set of tools to applications computer scientists and physical scientists. It is safe to say that LLNL could not accomplish its mission without this network and the services it provides.

Operating systems. All of the operating systems currently in use at LLNL on the CDC 7600, Cray 1a or Cray 1s, and Cray X-MP were developed—wholly or in part—and are maintained by LLNL systems computer scientists. This local control is very important for providing apt and timely responses to users' needs. The subroutine library BASELIB has been developed at LLNL to assist in making requests of any of the operating systems in a relatively machine-independent manner. This is an important aid in developing machine-independent code system modules.

Assemblers, compilers, loaders, and debuggers. All of these tools are produced and supported by LLNL systems personnel, again to ensure the timeliness and aptness of response to user's needs. Of particular importance is an extended version of Fortran produced at LLNL called LRLTRAN. It contains such things as vector and dynamic memory allocation extensions, a macro capability, bit/byte manipulation capability, and an in-line assembly language capability. It also produces a symbol table for each subroutine which serves as input to a symbolic interactive debugger. In addition, extensive use is made of vendor-supplied assemblers and compilers.

Subroutine libraries. In addition to BASELIB, LLNL systems computer scientists provide the applications computer scientists with such tools as graphics libraries and Fortran I/O libraries. The applications people themselves develop and share more special-purpose libraries such as ACFLIB, MMLIB, special-purpose graphics libraries, and the previously mentioned STACKLIB. Many of the big code systems make use of 10 or more subroutine libraries.

Utility routines. This category includes such things as interactive text editors, file transport routines, disk-to-tape and tape-to-disk routines, interactive file editors, and other file management tools. There are currently over 50 of these utility routines at LLNL. Making use of any of the Octopus network capabilities almost invariably involves the running of one or more of these utility routines, either by a human being or by another program.

Looking to the future

If infancy, adolescence, and finally, maturity, can be regarded as developmental stages of software, it is reasonable to argue that within the last decade LLNL's systems have progressed through adolescence and are approaching maturity. The signs are there: the slowing down of phenomenal, almost exponential, growth in the speed and size of supercomputers and the increasing maturity and complexity of the code systems residing on the giant number-crunchers.

Future increases in productivity will be achieved by continuing increases in software and hardware complexity and sophistication. We at LLNL see promise in two areas: multitasking and distributed computing.

Multitasking

We define multitasking as one program making use of two or more CPU's having access to a common memory. It is commonly accepted by those in the supercomputer field that future increases in computational speed will come largely via this route. Our first experience with multitasking at LLNL will be with the Cray X-MP/24, which has two CPU's and four million words of memory. This machine will allow us to gain experience with the concurrency problems inherent in multitasking, including re-entrant subroutine libraries and locking down critical data regions.

Distributed processing

Another potentially profitable field for improvement lies in increasing the distributive nature of these code systems. Instead of manipulating source files on the same interactive mainframe used to crunch numbers, such tasks as text editing, compilation, and loading could be accomplished on a support processor located in the scientist's office. These support processors might take the form of intelligent scientific workstations containg 16- or 32-bit miniprocessors linked together into local area networks that can be linked via high bandwidth lines to the supercomputers. Perhaps tasks such as mesh generation and manipulation or the running of small code-development problems could be performed locally. For decades most output has been processed offline to avoid tying up mainframe resources, and any applications-system function not requiring supercomputer-scale resources is a logical candidate for future diversion to some sort of support processor. As these functions are distributed over various types of processors, the role of software in integrating and coordinating them will beome increasingly important.

NLTSS

A new operating system, called NLTSS (for Network or New Livermore Time Sharing System), is being developed at LLNL to replace the present timesharing system, LTSS (also developed at LLNL and in use at a number of supercomputer sites), which is now almost twenty years old. NLTSS is a distributed network operating system built within the LINCS (Livermore Interactive Network Communication Structure) architecture to specifically address distributed computing. It is also amenable to addressing multitasking.

Output

Increases in number-crunching capability and capacity will require that more attention be paid to the processing and displaying of results. If we were suddenly—and miraculously—supplied with a supercomputer that ran 100 times faster than our current machines and ran problems 100 times larger than current ones, we would not be able to cope with the flood of output. In particular, techniques in three-dimensional graphics need to be improved to make them more effective and efficient. Movies of each problem run, delivered within hours of the termination of the run, would be very helpful to the users. The capability is there in hardware and software, but the users cannot afford the cost in resources to make use of it. At present it can cost more supercomputer time to make a movie of a run than it cost to make the calculation.

Software engineering

We can see from the above that successful applications computer scientists will continue to exploit and integrate the efforts of systems programmers and other applications programmers. Improvements will be needed in all areas of the emerging discipline of software engineering, including structured design and programming, software validation and testing, configuration control, modularity, documentation, and training.

Summary

Computing installations designed for large scientific computation must serve a whole spectrum of needs, but is is also clear that a key requirement is for hardware and software which is optimized for solving partial differential equations and other equations describing physical systems. These computational tasks have been of central importance in the design of supercomputers and continue to be a driving force for future developments.

The magnitude of many of the problems examined at LLNL and other scientific laboratories is such that they will tax the capability of any computing system produced in the near future.

Acknowledgment

This work was performed under the auspices of the U.S. Department of Energy at Lawrence Livermore National Laboratory under contract No. W-7405-Eng-48.

Selected bibliography

1. J. A. Baker, E. Franceschini, and D. L. Wentz, Jr., *Proceedings of the AESOP-SCIE Symposium on Advanced Computing*, CONF-781061, LLNL, Livermore, Calif., Oct. 1978.
2. D. Braddy, J. Kohn, and L. Stringer, *ACFLIB User's Manual*, LCSD-451, LLNL, Livermore, Calif., March 1982.
3. F. P. Brooks, Jr., *The Mythical Man-Month*, Addison-Wesley, Reading, Mass., 1975.
4. R. Cooper, *User Manual for MMLIB—A General-Purpose Memory Manager*, LCSD-416, LLNL, Livermore, Calif., September 1983.
5. W. P. Crowley, *Numerical Methods in Fluid Dynamics*, UCRL-51824, LLNL, Livermore, Calif., May 1975.
6. O. J. Dahl, E. W. Dikstra, and C. A. R. Hoare, *Structured Programming*, Academic Press, London, 1972.
7. F. W. Dorr, "The CRAY-1 at Los Alamos," *Datamation*, Vol. 24, No. 10, Oct. 1978, pp. 113-120.
8. P. J. Du Bois, *NLTSS Overview*, UCID-20035, LLNL, Livermore, Calif., November 1983.
9. J. G. Fletcher and R. W. Watson, *An Overview of LINCS Architecture*, UCID-19294, LLNL, Livermore, Calif., November 1982.
10. W. D. Gardner, "Los Alamos—Cradle of Computing," *Datamation*, Vol. 24, No. 8, Aug. 1978, pp. 78-80.
11. E. D. Giroux, *Implementation of a Large Mathematical Model on the STAR-100 Computer*, UCRL-52277, LLNL, Livermore, Calif., May 1977.
12. E. D. Giroux, *Vectorizing and Machine-Spanning Techniques,* UCRL-89740, LLNL, Livermore, Calif., Sept., 1983.
13. C. P. Hendrickson, "When You Wish Upon a STAR," *Digest of Papers, COMPCON 77 Spring*, Feb. 28-Mar. 3, 1977, pp 4-7.
14. H. Katzan, Jr., *Computer Systems Organization and Programming*, Science Research Associates, Chicago, 1976.
15. D. E. Knuth, *Fundamental Algorithms, The Art of Computer Programming*, Vol. 1, Addison-Wesley, Reading, Mass., 1968.
16. D. E. Knuth, *Seminumerical Algorithms, The Art of Computer Programming*, Vol. 2, Addison-Wesley, Reading, Mass., 1969.
17. D. E. Knuth, *Sorting and Searching, The Art of Computer Programming*, Vol. 3, Addison-Wesley, Reading, Mass., 1973.
18. N. R. Lincoln, "Supercomputer Development—The Pleasure and the Pain," *Digest of Papers, COMPCON 77 Spring*, Feb. 28-Mar. 3, 1977, pp. 21-25.
19. J. T. Martin, R. G. Zwakenberg, and S. V. Solbeck, *Livermore Time-Sharing System, Part III, Chapter 207: LRLTRAN Language Used with the CHAT and STAR Compilers*, 4th ed., LLNL, Livermore, Calif., Dec. 1974.
20. F. H. McMahon, L. J. Sloan, and G. A. Long, *STACKLIB—A Vector Function Library of Optimum Stack-Loops for the CDC-7600*, UCID-30083, LLNL, Livermore, Calif., 1972.
21. G. J. Meyers, *Software Reliability: Principles and Practices*, Wiley-Interscience, New York, 1976.
22. W. Noh, *Numerical Methods in Hydrodynamic Calculations*, UCRL-52112, LLNL, Livermore, Calif., June 1976.
23. D. Potter, *Computational Physics*, John Wiley, New York, 1973.
24. M. Pratt, *Requirements for Migration of NSSD Code Systems from LTSS to NLTSS*, UCID-30198, LLNL, Livermore, Calif., February 1984.
25. R. Richtmeyer and K. Morton, *Different Methods for Initial-Value Problems*, Interscience, New York, 1967.
26. G. Strang and G. Fu, *Analysis of the Finite Element Method*, Prentice-Hall, Englewood Cliffs, N.J., 1973.
27. G. M. Weinberg, *The Psychology of Computer Programming*, Van Nostrum Reinhold, New York, 1971.

 **Garry Rodrigue** is a research scientist in the Computer Research group of Lawrence Livermore National Laboratory in Livermore, California. He is currently engaged in research on advanced high-speed parallel computers. Previously a member of the mathematics faculty at Kent State University, he has also worked on the computational staffs of RCA and the Naval Weapons Research Laboratory. Rodrigue holds a BA and a PhD in mathematics from the University of Southern California.

 **E. Dick Giroux** is a computer scientist at Lawrence Livermore National Laboratory. Currently he is the leader of a group of computer scientists engaged in designing and implementing physical simulation mathematical models to run on large-scale computers. Since joining the laboratory in 1956, he has worked with virtually all of the supercomputers of each era, including most recently the Cray-1 and Cray X-MP/24. Giroux has authored a number of papers, articles, and reports regarding mathematical modeling on large-scale computers. He holds a BS degree from Montana State University.

 **Michael Pratt** is a computer scientist and group leader in the Computation Department of the Lawrence Livermore National Laboratory. In addition to his work on the software engineering of large-scale applications code systems, he has worked in the area of information storage, retrieval, and analysis for biomedical applications. He received a BS in physics from the University of California, Berkeley, in 1960 and an MS in mathematics from California State University at Hayward in 1969.

Centralized Supercomputer Support for Magnetic Fusion Energy Research

DIETER FUSS AND CAROL G. TULL

Reprinted from *Proceedings of the IEEE*, Volume 72, Number 1, January 1984, pages 32-41. Copyright © 1984 by The Institute of Electrical and Electronics Engineers, Inc.

Invited Paper

High-speed computers with large memories are vital to magnetic fusion energy research. Magnetohydrodynamic (MHD), transport, equilibrium, Vlasov, particle, and Fokker–Planck codes that model plasma behavior play an important role in designing experimental hardware and interpreting the resulting data, as well as in advancing plasma theory itself. The size, architecture, and software of supercomputers to run these codes are often the crucial constraints on the benefits such computational modeling can provide. Hence, vector computers such as the CRAY-1 offer a valuable research resource.

To meet the computational needs of the fusion program, the National Magnetic Fusion Energy Computer Center (NMFECC) was established in 1974 at the Lawrence Livermore National Laboratory. Supercomputers at the central computing facility are linked to smaller computer centers at each of the major fusion laboratories by a satellite communication network. In addition to providing large-scale computing, the NMFECC environment stimulates collaboration and the sharing of computer codes and data among the many fusion researchers in a cost-effective manner.

I. Introduction

From the beginning of magnetic fusion research in the 1950's, high-speed digital computers have been a vital tool in this effort. The staggering problem of reproducing starlike conditions in the laboratory is solvable only because large computers have been able to use mathematical "models" to simulate these conditions. This has been especially true for our attempts to analyze and predict the complex behavior of plasmas that—while trapped inside intense

Manuscript received May 23, 1983; revised August 5, 1983. This work was performed under the auspices of the U.S. Department of Energy under Contract W-7405-ENG-48. This document was prepared as an account of work sponsored by an agency of the United States Government. Neither the United States Government nor the University of California nor any of their employees, makes any warranty, express or implied, or assumes any legal liability or responsibility for the accuracy, completeness, or usefulness of any information, apparatus, product, or process disclosed, or represents that its use would not infringe privately owned rights. Reference herein to any specific commercial products, process, or service by trade name, trademark, manufacturer, or otherwise, does not necessarily constitute or imply its endorsement, recommendation, or favoring by the United States Government or the University of California. The views and opinions of authors expressed herein do not necessarily state or reflect those of the United States Government thereof, and shall not be used for advertising or product endorsement purposes.

The authors are with the Lawrence Livermore National Laboratory, National Magnetic Fusion Energy Computer Center, Livermore, CA 94550, USA.

magnetic fields—interact with neutral particles and sources of electromagnetic energy. In the 10 years since computer modeling became a reliable complement to laboratory experiment, the demand for computer power from fusion-plasma researchers jumped twenty-fold. Now, complex codes that model plasmas in as many as three dimensions predict plasma behavior with remarkable success. These calculations generate an enormous demand for computing power.

Over the past decade, computational physics activities within magnetic fusion energy (MFE) have produced dramatic transformations in the way magnetic fusion research is carried out. On the theoretical physics side, this is characterized by the emphasis on applied physics aspects of the program and in particular by the attempts to interpret each new theoretical concept in terms of its direct experimental implications. On the experimental side, computational studies not only provide a concrete foundation for the interpretation of experimental data, but also enable the exploration necessary for the optimal design of new machines and the investigation of additional phenomena. In general, computational physics programs have increased our knowledge of the effects of the most important physical parameters in present-day experiments, have enabled us to select more optimal parameters for the design of new experiments, and, above all, have increased our understanding of plasma physics behavior.

In the future, as the fusion program moves on to large, complex, experimental systems with burning plasmas, computational studies will provide critical input for guiding system design, predicting system performance, and discovering and solving unanticipated problems. Supercomputers are expected to play a particularly cost-effective role in these activities. They will be used to simulate the characteristics of plasma confinement experiments and fusion power reactors. Eventually they can be expected to model whole systems before actual construction.

The National Magnetic Fusion Energy Computer Center (NMFECC) was established by the U.S. Department of Energy in 1974 at the Lawrence Livermore National Laboratory. Physicists working in the numerical simulation of plasmas recognized in the early 1970's that large-scale computing would be necessary for the continued progress of fusion research. It was evident that the most effective way to provide the capability would be to build a centralized computer center equipped with a nationwide network to bring the computing power to magnetic fusion researchers wherever they were.

The NMFECC began with a borrowed CDC 6600 in 1974, which was replaced with the Center's own CDC 7600 in 1975. In 1978 and 1981 the Center acquired CRAY-1 computers, which are among the most powerful, general-purpose scientific computers available. The network became operational in 1976 with five major fusion research sites and has since expanded to 23 sites. The Center now serves over 2000 magnetic fusion researchers across the nation (including users not directly connected to the network), enabling them to share information, codes, data, manpower, and computer resources.

II. The Role of Computer Simulation in Magnetic Fusion Research

A. Five Kinds of Plasma Models

Magnetic fusion theory focuses on the behavior of a plasma as it interacts with magnetic fields. Plasma phenomena are diverse and complex: they occur over enormous spatial and temporal ranges, and a complete description of a plasma would necessarily involve the solution of complex fluid, particle, and kinetic equations. Because such equations are not amenable to analytical solutions, plasma theorists must resort to computer simulations and advanced computational techniques.

The behavior of a high-temperature plasma confined by a magnetic field is simulated by a variety of numerical models. Short time-scale models give detailed knowledge of the plasma on a microscopic scale, while other, longer time-scale models compute macroscopic properties of the plasma dynamics. Plasma models fall into one of five different categories:

1. time-dependent macroscopic fluid (magnetohydrodynamic (MHD) or transport) codes,
2. time-independent macroscopic (equilibrium) codes,
3. Vlasov and particle codes,
4. Fokker–Planck codes,
5. hybrid codes.

A natural time division separates the codes used to simulate the time-dependent fluid behavior of plasmas. MHD phenomena occur on the fastest time scale, and transport phenomena occur on a slower time scale.

Hybrid codes combine two or more basic models, and thus two or more computational techniques. For example, plasma simulations that combine fluid and particle models can describe the physics more completely and more efficiently than would be possible with a pure model of either type.

B. MHD Codes

Magnetohydrodynamics is the study of how a conducting fluid (here, a plasma of ions and electrons) behaves in a complex magnetic field. MHD codes are typically used to investigate the time-dependent behavior of plasma instabilities. The main question to be answered is whether or not a particular MHD mode will be unstable, and if so, how fast it will grow and whether it will saturate before spoiling the plasma confinement.

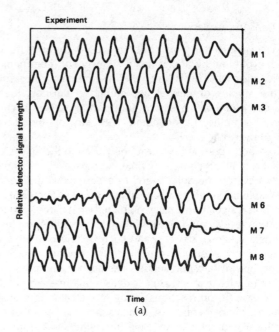

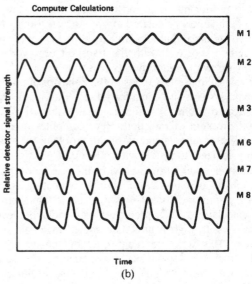

Fig. 1. Relative signal strength at six detectors (a) in an experimental fusion device and (b) as calculated for the same plasma conditions using resistive magnetohydrodynamic (MHD) codes on a supercomputer.

Perhaps the most successful area in plasma physics research in the last several years has been the analysis of the nonlinear evolution of ideal and resistive MHD modes with three-dimensional codes. These codes have played a key role in guiding the theory in the understanding of magnetic island development, which is essential in determining the regimes in parameter space where the confined plasma will be stable. Even more important than the design studies is the validity of the codes in interpreting experimental results where previously the results were not at all understood. This is illustrated in the excellent agreement seen in Fig. 1, which compares experimental results from the plasma diagnostics in a large experimental device and the results of the computer calculations. This is only one of several examples where resistive MHD codes have provided decided breakthroughs in both the interpretation of experiments and the understanding of the theory.

C. Transport Codes

Macroscopic transport codes are used to simulate the time evolution of a plasma in a magnetic confinement device over most of its lifetime. These models are essential in the studies of neutral and impurity transport in the plasma confinement region. Transport processes such as these determine the economic feasibility of one reactor design over others.

Transport codes are now routinely used in the analysis of data from all on-going experimental devices. These codes have proven to be quite useful in experimental design and the exploration of new operating regimes. For example, transport calculations have predicted that large impurity radiation levels could cause hollow temperature profiles in planned Tokamak devices, and such hollow profiles were subsequently observed experimentally. Another successful application of transport models has been to the physics of higher density plasmas. Higher density plasmas are needed to increase fusion reactions, while at the same time maintaining confinement. Here studies have shown that the nonlinear evolution of resistive instabilities is a dominant effect in producing enhanced transport. That is, the transport coefficients calculated from the resistive MHD-saturated mode amplitudes and used in transport analysis have agreed very well with the transport observed in the experiments with higher density plasmas.

The role of impurity species in the behavior of plasmas in Tokamak systems is complicated by the need to add sophisticated atomic physics calculations to the already difficult problem of transport. Here computer models are essential to an understanding of the problem; for example, partially ionized tungsten with 50 bound electrons has a complicated level structure with thousands of possible transitions. Compared with simple estimates, computer models predict radiation levels that are 60 times stronger. Such calculations have predicted high radiation levels in Tokamaks with high-Z limiters made of materials such as tungsten. This was later confirmed by the experimental results from two Tokamaks. Subsequently, the tungsten limiters were replaced by low-Z limiters, resulting in reduced radiation losses and higher central temperatures in the plasma.

D. Equilibrium Codes

Time-independent macroscopic codes calculate the equilibrium condition that balances the internal plasma pressure with the total magnetic field pressure. Once an external magnetic field configuration is determined for plasma equilibrium, the stability of the configuration is studied with sophisticated energy minimization models.

Equilibrium codes have been an extremely valuable and cost-saving tool in the experimental design and control of Tokamak plasmas. Several experiments have studied the shape of a plasma in a cross section of a toroidal device to determine the optimal configuration for confinement. Plasma shaping is controlled by sets of external conducting coils. Nonlinear equilibrium codes are used to determine the coil positions and current variations needed for optimal confinement. In a recent toroidal experiment [1], hundreds of thousands of dollars were saved in power supplies and control circuitry as a result of an equilibrium calculation that showed how an optimal configuration can be pro-

duced by combining three types of external coils into one set. In addition, the computed coil design resulted in much more flexibility in the shaping of the magnetic fields for stability studies. An operational benefit of the new design is that the coil current requirements are only 50 percent of that needed for the original design.

E. Particle Codes

Particle codes are fundamental in that they compute in detail the motion of particles under the influence of their self-consistent electric and magnetic fields, as well as any externally imposed fields. These codes give phase-space distribution functions, fluctuation as well as wave spectra, and orbits of individual particles. They are ideal for providing detailed information on the growth and saturation of strong microinstabilities and the effects of turbulence.

Ohmic heating alone is insufficient to attain ignition in a magnetically confined plasma. Consequently, auxiliary heating techniques are being actively sought, with the most promising being neutral beam heating and heating by radio frequency (RF) waves. An important step in the design of a neutral beam system is an analysis of the injector optics. Ion beam optics are modeled using the Maxwell-Vlasov equations in two or three space dimensions. Effects of various electrode configurations, accelerating potentials, apertures, and other parameters are studied. Discoveries from this modeling have already led to a 30-percent increase in the injection efficiency in current toroidal devices and a savings of more than 1 million dollars in beam lines. The three-dimensional code used in this analysis requires several hours on the CRAY-1 to study one configuration.

F. Fokker–Planck Codes

Fokker–Planck models are kinetic descriptions of a plasma in which the collision term in the Boltzmann transport equation has been approximated by the high-temperature, low-density Fokker–Planck collision operator. This model is used where a detailed knowledge of the distribution function of one or more of the plasma species is required. Fokker–Planck simulations have become essential in many studies including the simulation of particle losses in open-ended fusion systems (magnetic mirrors), the heating of plasmas by energetic neutral beams, and the thermalization of alpha particles in deuterium-tritium plasmas.

The important role of computing in neutral-beam injection experiments has been recognized for more than a decade. Multispecies Fokker–Planck calculations of the expected power enhancement in mirror machines have played a driving role in the conceptual development of the mirror program. As a result, a developed computational base was available to Tokamak researchers when the first Tokamak neutral-beam tests were proposed in the early 1970's. Models for neutral-beam heating in Tokamaks have advanced to such an extent that direct comparison with experiment is now possible.

G. Engineering Applications

Engineering activities in the magnetic fusion program have increased substantially, because of the successes achieved in proof-of-principle plasma physics experiments over the last decade. A complete reactor analysis involves a wide range of engineering calculations including the following:

1. neutron and radiation analysis,
2. thermomechanical analysis and design,
3. electrical engineering,
4. coil-shaping and magnetic-field analyses,
5. plasma engineering,
6. chemical engineering,
7. tritium handling,
8. safety and environmental studies.

Engineering and reactor-design calculations are highly desirable from an economic point of view. The costs of the largest engineering analyses (e.g., two- and three-dimensional finite-element models and neutron/radiation transport models) represent a minor fraction of the costs of materials and reactor fabrication. Extensive computational efforts involving several of these models were necessary in the conceptual and design planning for the two reactor-size devices currently under construction and will continue as future reactors are designed.

Reference [1] reviews the goals and achievements of computer modeling in supporting both the theoretical and experimental fusion programs.

III. The Role of The National Magnetic Fusion Energy Computer Center

The foregoing discussion of five kinds of plasma models and the typical problems suited to each shows the primary need of fusion researchers for large-memory, high-speed mainframes. Closely related secondary needs include extensive and economical storage for data and results, easy access by a geographically dispersed research community, the convenience of both interactive and batch processing, and software utilities designed to promote productivity, as well as collaboration among researchers. The NMFECC provides hardware and software to meet these needs in the most cost-effective way.

Supercomputer resources (a CDC 7600 and two CRAY-1's) reside at one national center, along with file storage and communications devices. A network of microwave (satellite) links and dedicated data lines ties these central computers to others whose size and location reflect local research priorities and demand. This network approach allows research projects to be sited anywhere in the United States without regard to local constraints, and it therefore greatly increases the flexibility of the fusion program.

A. Large-Machine Central Resources

The CDC 7600, which was once the main scientific computer in the network, performs calculations in a scalar mode. The CDC 7600 processes the same types of jobs as the CRAY's, although its speed is slower and its memory is smaller. Its capability, however, is far from insignificant—it can perform up to 20 million mathematical operations per second. With 65 000 words of semiconductor memory and 512 000 words of magnetic core memory, it easily qualifies as a major computational resource.

The CRAY-1, acquired in 1978, and the CRAY-1S, acquired in 1981, are vector computers. That is, whenever possible, they perform calculations in a vector processing mode rather

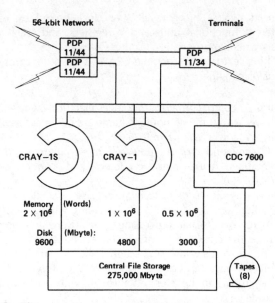

Fig. 2. Three major computers and their shared file storage devices at the National Magnetic Fusion Energy Computer Center (NMFECC).

than in scalar mode. The scalar speeds on the CRAY's are typically twice as fast as on the CDC 7600. For vectorizable calculations, speeds three to five times faster than the CDC 7600 are common. These three computers offer both interactive and batch processing of large-scale scientific jobs. Fig. 2 shows the main hardware and associated communication connections at NMFECC.

The CRAY's especially suit the needs of fusion researchers because their design focuses on simulating complex physical processes such as magnetohydrodynamics. Independent benchmark studies have shown the CRAY-1 can support 138 million floating-point operations per second (MFLOPS) for sustained periods on specific applications [2]. Even higher rates—up to 250 MFLOPS—can occur in short bursts.

Such comparatively high performance results from the CRAY-1 internal architecture. Each functional unit is designed to carry out many calculations in discrete steps, with each step producing partial results used in subsequent steps.

The CRAY-1 has 12 functional units, organized in four groups: address, scalar, vector, and floating-point. Each functional unit is pipelined into single clock segments. All of the functional units can operate concurrently so that, in addition to the benefits of pipelining (each functional unit can be driven at a rate of 1 result per clock period), one also has parallelism across the units.

The functional units take input operands from and store result operands only to A, S, and V registers. There are eight 24-bit address (A) registers, eight 64-bit scalar (S) registers, and eight 64-element vector (V) registers. This large amount of register storage is crucial to the CRAY-1's architecture. Chaining could not take place if vector register space were not available for the storage of final or intermediate results. The chaining technique takes advantage of the parallel operation of functional units by using the result stream of one vector register simultaneously as an input operand set for another operation in a different functional unit, thus avoiding intermediate memory references. In the more general case, parallel operations on vectors allow the generation of two or more results per clock period by using different functional units and V registers, and scalar registers where appropriate, as sources of operands.

Other features enhance the CRAY-1's scientific computational capabilities:

- It is so compact that the distances electrical signals must travel within the computer's frame are minimal, resulting in a 12.5-ns clock period.
- Its semiconductor memory (up to 4 million words) is equipped with logic to detect and correct errors (SECDED).
- It has 64-bit words to facilitate precise calculations.
- Vector start-up is very small. Deciding when to choose vector over scalar processing is relatively unimportant since the crossover point is between 4 and 10 elements.
- The CRAY-1's addressing scheme allows complete flexibility. Arrays can be accessed by column, row, or diagonal; they can be stepped through with any constant stride.
- The Fortran compiler, CFT, automatically detects loops that can take advantage of the hardware vector instructions.
- The disk storage subsystem consists of four Cray Research, Inc. disk control units, each of which controls four disk storage units. Each storage unit holds 76.854 billion bits of data.

The other important architectural characteristics of the CRAY-1 hardware are described in detail in [2].

B. Efficient Data and Code Storage

A central file management system (FILEM) provides reliable file storage and retrieval. This system, which is accessible both interactively and by batch jobs, is used to store any file for more than 24 h. Files can be stored permanently or temporarily, and they may be grouped under directories. This means that users need not juggle tapes or—even worse—decks of punched cards. FILEM is sufficiently flexible that files can be completely private—or shared files can be created to make it easier for groups to work together. The CDC 7600 performs virtually all of the tasks associated with FILEM file custodianship.

FILEM currently has three levels of storage: staging disks, a mass storage device, and a tape library, as shown in Fig. 3. The CDC 7600 allows files to migrate to and from each level, depending on how frequently the file is referenced.

The first level of storage, the staging disk system, consists of Memorex disks. This system's capacity is 38 billion bits—in other words, 4.8 billion characters—with an average access time of 35 ms. Files referenced as frequently as once a week are likely to be on disk.

A CDC 38500 MASS (Multi-Access Storage Subnetwork) is the Center's second level of long-term storage. This automated tape cartridge store–retrieve system holds 500 billion bits—62 billion characters. The MASS store backs up files on the staging disks. Its pneumatic robot locates the proper tape cartridge and sends it to a station where it is automatically mounted and read. This process takes about 20 s. Files referenced about once a month are likely to be stored in the MASS storage device.

The Braegan Automated Tape Library (CalComp 7110) is the Center's slowest, but most economical, storage device.

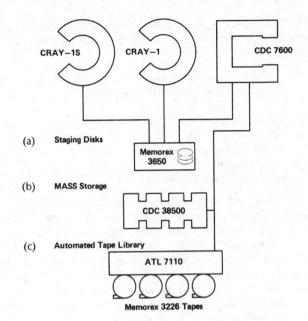

Fig. 3. Three levels of file storage at NMFECC, including (a) Rapid-access staging disks. File life is 1 week and access time is 35 ms. (b) Medium-speed MASS storage cartridges. File life is 12 weeks and access time is 10 s. (c) Slow-speed automatic tape library. File life is infinite and access time is 2 min.

It is also the Center's largest: The device can hold 2 trillion bits (360 billion characters) on 2000 tapes. A robot that runs on a track through a tape vault picks up and delivers requested tapes to one of four high-density tape drives. It may take 2 to 5 min to access a file, depending on its location on the tape. Files referenced as infrequently as once a year are stored in the automated tape library.

C. Flexible Communications Network

The NMFECC network is a general-purpose network designed to provide users with reliable input/output of text and graphics data. The network enables any terminal to log-on to any host computer.

The network interconnects:

- all computers at the Center, including its large mainframes, its User Service Center (USC), and its User Service Station;
- Remote USC's that support local computing, experimental data acquisition, printers, and terminals;
- Remote User Service Stations (RUSS's) that support printers and terminals;
- the Advanced Research Projects Agency Network (ARPANET) via the User Service Center at the NMFECC;
- dial-up terminals via TYMNET and commercial telephone lines.

The major trunks of the network are 56 000-bit/s satellite links. The branches off the trunk are 4800- or 9600-bit/s leased telephone lines. The NMFECC monitors and maintains the communications subnetwork, which controls the flow of messages between the computers. (Fig. 4 shows the configuration of the microwave links and land lines.)

The NMFECC network was planned to allow distributed, rapid service as well as effective use of the main computers. Accordingly, local computing and output capability is

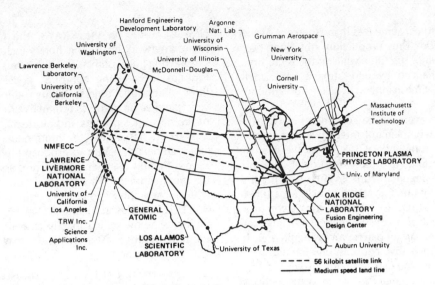

Fig. 4. NMFECC's communications network (1983) that connects widely dispersed users to the mainframes in California using 56-kbit microwave links or dedicated telephone lines.

provided at "secondary" USC's, which are physically located at national laboratories, major universities, and a few private corporations—the places where the population of MFE researchers is concentrated.

Each USC houses a DECSystem-10 KL computer, which is connected to the NMFECC network (so that the USC can function as a remote output and job-entry station) and to a local network (to acquire experimental data from fusion experiments). Each USC also functions as a terminal concentrator that links local, directly controlled, and dial-up terminals to other computers on the NMFECC network. Each USC can handle text editing, compilations, and graphics display, as well as run smaller programs that do not require the power of the mainframe computers at Livermore. Several sites have chosen to base their operation on VAX-series computers. These systems fill the same roles as USC's but are somewhat less powerful.

Sites that do not need the complete capabilities offered by a USC typically are connected to the network via a RUSS, which is a terminal concentrator and printer with a link to the network. An "economy model," the mini-RUSS is also available. The mini-RUSS economizes on the printer in its system and on the number of terminal lines it supports.

Dial-up capability gives isolated users direct access to the main computers and to all other network hosts. Hard-copy output for remote users is printed in Livermore and delivered by U. S. mail or by contract carriers.

D. Software to Enhance User Productivity

Good software can improve research productivity. Accordingly, NMFECC offers a broad spectrum of specialized software. Staff consultants and specialists are also available for direct personal assistance to all users.

The NMFECC approach to software is based on the principle that the cost of people power is continually increasing while the cost of computer power is rapidly decreasing. Assuming a (conservative) salary plus overhead figure of 50 000 dollars per year per user, the 2000 NMFECC users represent a cost of 100 million dollars per year. Everything should be done to maximize the productivity of these users. This leads to a dual policy of:

1. Minimizing the costs of application-code conversion, reprogramming, and retraining for a new computer. This means that the center must provide the same (upward compatible) user interface to the system, utilities, and libraries on each new supercomputer at the center.

2. Providing timesharing on the supercomputers for debugging, for immediate display of output, and for interrogation of runs during execution.

Interactive Operating System: The system used on the CRAY mainframes is CTSS, which was developed by NMFECC computer scientists from a time-sharing system that has been evolving for 20 years at Lawrence Livermore National Laboratory. CTSS is a fully interactive system that lends itself to rapid code development. All user services, from text editing and symbolic/dynamic debugging to batch processing and displaying of graphic and alphanumeric output, execute on the same system.

CTSS offers many desirable features [3]:

- one program can start and run another,
- programs can exchange messages with one another,
- program size can expand and contract after the program begins to run,
- asynchronous, word-addressable, random-access disk I/O is available,
- excellent system recovery eliminates the need for restart dumps,
- with minor changes, a code developed and debugged in time-sharing mode can run in batch-processing mode or vice versa,
- a code can send its graphics output to various media, including film or online graphic terminals,
- CTSS can serve hundreds of terminals and jobs simultaneously. A user can run as many as five jobs under the control of one terminal, and can submit jobs to several batch streams.

Timesharing and Batch Alternatives: Timesharing on a supercomputer frequently raises questions about CPU utilization. Statistics on the two NMFECC CRAY-1's show that CTSS delivers 90–95 percent of the CPU to user codes over a 24-h period. These statistics also show that 90 percent of the jobs run on the NMFECC CRAY-1's take less than 1 s to complete execution and consume less than 2 percent of the CPU over a 24-h period. Thus production jobs (long-running jobs) get almost all of the CPU, while at the same time user efficiency is enhanced by dedicating a very small portion of the CPU to timesharing activities (short-running jobs).

Sophisticated yet convenient batch processing is still available, however, to complement interactive computing. The batch system that runs under CTSS allows the user to submit and check the status of a job—or to delete the job even if it has already begun to run. BATCH, which runs programs either in background or at night, includes a timer feature for delayed start-up. The BATCH subsystem provides administrative controls to ensure that each major user division receives its fair share of batch processing time each week. With these administrative controls, division administrators can reorder the job queues in their jurisdictions.

Support for the User Community: To read instructions for NMFECC software, users can consult online the full text of over 200 pieces of documentation, equivalent to over 16 000 pages of help information. DOCUMENT, a flexible and friendly interface program, directs users to answers in this large database [4].

DOCUMENT is human-engineered: it accepts concise commands from experienced users, yet also offers step-by-step tutorial conversation for newcomers. Alphabetical, subject, and revision-date catalogs are available online. All documents are divided into section by topic, each with its own keyword. A user can display any section at a terminal simply by typing the keyword desired. DOCUMENT supplements this online viewing with on-demand printing. A user can easily send any document to one of several output devices: local printer, high-speed central printer, or microfiche film recorders.

A utility called LIBRIS manages a database of abstracts describing user-created physics, engineering, mathematical, and computer science codes. Other users can search these abstracts automatically or interactively to find codes pertinent to a given research problem. Authors submitting abstracts to LIBRIS also make their source codes available to the NMFECC community through FILEM.

To provide maximum interactivity for screen editing, graphics, and menu-driven utilities, routines have been developed that combine the responsiveness of personal computers with the storage capacity and calculating power of NMFECC's CRAY-1's. With the "distributed editor," for example, the personal computer displays a "window" into the file, interprets commands from the user, and updates the display while forwarding the changes to the CRAY-1. The CRAY-1 supplies information to the personal computer on request, updates the file, and performs global searches and replacements.

News items and mail can be electronically generated and distributed to the NMFECC user community by all of its members. Users can post online news notices either at a local site or for everyone on the system. Letters and notes can be keyed in on the system, then sent to any one user or to a distribution list. Any recipient, when notified that the message has arrived, can choose to print or display, then save or delete that message. Because mail delivery can be deferred to a given date, electronic mail is useful for announcing meetings and for scheduling.

A general-purpose graphics software library serves NMFECC users on the CRAY's, the CDC 7600, and the remote network hosts. This library includes simple routines for drawing lines, points, and characters, as well as complex routines for drawing contours, grids, shaded areas, and three-dimensional objects. Utility routines allow the user to view pictures on graphics terminals or to print them on any of the network's printers and plotters.

NMFECC has access to Information International FR80 film recorders designed to produce high-quality images on 35-mm film (in black and white or color), 16-mm film, and 105-mm microfiche. This system produces vectors and characters for graphic computer output microfilm (COM). NMFECC also has a Dicomed D48 film recorder that will soon provide the same capabilities as the FR80's and will, in addition, produce raster gray-scale images of equal quality.

IV. COMPUTATIONAL LIMITS AND THE NEED TO OPTIMIZE ALGORITHMS

A. Limits of Existing Computers

Despite the extremely important role simulation models have assumed in magnetic fusion research, they are severely limited by the capacity and capability of the current generation of supercomputers. For example, the most general resistive MHD problems currently being solved involve the solution of eight simultaneous, nonlinear, partial differential equations in three dimensions. This is a formidable task on any existing computer system today. Furthermore, in order to make the analysis tractable one must make many approximations, including reductions in dimensionality, linearization, and restrictions to a particular geometry. MHD models are seriously constrained by these limitations and further progress in this area will be slow until they are removed.

To make three-dimensional MHD codes applicable to geometries such as stellarators and to simultaneously include enough details to ensure a complete description of the important physics effects will require a computer with approximately 10 times the CPU speed of the CRAY-1 to keep the execution times within tens of hours. Furthermore, a ten-fold increase in memory size is needed to allow realistic representation of three-dimensional calculations.

Particle simulation codes have grown from simple one-dimensional electrostatic models (in which the self-consistent electric field is computed, but the magnetic field is either absent or constant in time) to three-dimensional electromagnetic models. Despite their sophistication, simultaneous resolution of very fast and very slow time scales is still limited. Implicit and orbit-averaging methods improve the situation somewhat, but routine three-dimensional simulation with realistic parameters is simply not practical with present supercomputers. Furthermore, with the increase of grid resolution allowed by improved computers and methodology, the scope of particle simulations has grown to encompass nonlocal effects and more realistic geometries. This further adds to the complexity of codes and leads to renewed demand for more powerful computers.

At present, large-scale simulations in two- and three-dimensions are mainly limited by the size of the memory of the CRAY-1. With necessary diagnostics this restricts electromagnetic particle codes to grids on the order of 128 × 32 or 64×64 in two dimensions and to $32 \times 16 \times 8$ for three-dimensional particle codes. The advent of computers with memory sizes in the range of 30 to 60 million words will allow grid sizes of 512×128 in electromagnetic codes.

Recent progress with hybrid models is impressive but computationally expensive. For example, two-dimensional meshes of size 128×128 with 20 particles per cell lead to 2-million-word memory requirements. Progress on three-dimensional codes, while an absolute necessity for the design of future experiments and eventual fusion reactors, requires more computer power than is currently available.

Many other significantly important computer simulations [1] are being delayed while waiting for the advent of the next generation of supercomputers. In the meantime, researchers are using algorithm optimization to gain as much speed and resource savings as possible from existing supercomputers.

B. The Need for Optimization

Algorithm optimization for the CRAY-1 is imperative because of the high demand for computer resources. Numerical methods from nearly all areas of numerical analysis are used in applications codes on the MFE network. For example, they include finite-difference methods, finite-element methods, eigenvalue-extraction and root-finding techniques, linear matrix systems, discrete–ordinate algorithms, Monte Carlo methods, numerical integration, function approximation, and function evaluation. The optimization of these solvers in practice proceeds as follows. First, the sequence of steps in an algorithm is examined for recursiveness and replaced with an equivalent set of vectorizable operations when possible. Next, the inner loops in the Fortran coding may need modifications and rearrangement to take advantage of the automatic vectorization of the CRAY Fortran (CFT) compiler. Finally, some analysts perform very sophisticated and detailed timing analysis for the most time-consuming applications codes and algorithms to locate sections of the coding where further optimization with machine coding is warranted.

Most applications codes do achieve better than scalar speeds on the CRAY-1 because portions of the calculations will vectorize. The exceptions to this are calculations that are either recursive or random in nature. For example, two of the most important types of calculations that are not readily vectorizable because of randomness are Monte Carlo transport and particle gathering for field calculations in electromagnetic particle simulations.

C. Automatic Vectorization with CFT

The CFT compiler has an automatic vectorization feature, which greatly facilitates the use of the vector hardware. More specifically, the compiler is designed to examine first all loops or the inner loops within a nested set to determine if the operation sequence is vectorizable. The next level of the compiler optimization algorithm is the scheduling of instructions within either a scalar or vector block. Whenever possible this does allow for chaining of operations in a vector block and efficient use of registers in scalar blocks. Some rearrangement of the Fortran coding statements is also usually necessary in order to take full advantage of compiler vectorization. Guidelines for Fortran coding changes that allow for more vectorization are discussed in

detail in [7]. Timing studies comparing the costs of numerical solvers with and without compiler optimization are presented in two of the next examples of algorithm optimization. In these examples, the analyst selected one of the following compiler options: CFT with ON = V or CFT with OFF = V. In the first case the compiler vectorization is enabled, whereas in the second case all vector processing is inhibited. Thus this is a good measure of the practical improvements realized from vector parallel processing.

D. Vectorization: The ICCG Case

The evolution of the ICCG algorithm [6], [5] for solving two-dimensional partial differential equations using a 9-point differencing scheme is an interesting demonstration of algorithm modification for vectorized processing. The ICCG algorithm is an iterative technique for solving sparse systems of linear equations of the form $Mx = y$, where M is nonsingular and, in this case, it is in a block tridiagonal form. The ICCG method consists of finding an approximate Cholesky decomposition for M and then applying the conjugate gradient algorithm. With the exception of the Cholesky decomposition, ICCG is trivially vectorizable on the CRAY-1.

In the first version of the ICCG algorithm, the approximation for the Cholesky decomposition consisted of forcing the factored matrices to match the sparsity pattern of the original M matrix by setting elements to zero and adding an error matrix, which contained all terms set to zero in the factored matrix. Although this method saves considerable time and storage, it is still not vectorizable. The search for a vectorizable Cholesky approximate led to the research in vectorizing tridiagonal solvers. The steps in the standard form of a tridiagonal solver are recursive. However, cyclic reduction, an alternate form for solving tridiagonal systems, is vectorizable. The method for integrating this into ICCG is to first perform a cyclic reduction on an exact decomposition of the block matrix and then to use the previously developed approximation by forcing a tridiagonal sparsity pattern on the elementary matrices. This vectorized version of ICCG applied to several types of physics problems has resulted in calculational savings of a factor of 3 to 5 over the original scheme [6].

E. Fokker–Planck Equations

The multispecies Fokker–Planck equations are nonlinear, second-order, time-dependent partial differential equations. Reference [8] describes the analytical reformulation of these equations using symmetry conditions and polynomial expansion into a form tractable for numerical solution. The finite difference solution then consists of two separate parts: the calculation of a set of coefficient functions and the time advancement of the Fokker–Planck operator. The set of coefficient functions consists of very complicated expressions and must be evaluated at every grid point in the velocity space mesh. Since these calculations represent a major portion of the total calculation time it is essential to accomplish as much vectorization as possible. The time integration is performed either using a splitting or an alternating direction implicit (ADI) scheme. The task of optimizing these calculations [8] involved a relatively quick rearrangement of the loops in the Fortran coding and the allocation of some additional storage arrays so that both of

Table 1 Timing Comparisons for the Fokker–Planck Equation

Mesh Size	Calculation	Timing Improvement $\dfrac{\text{CFT (ON = V)}}{\text{CFT (OFF = V)}}$
32 × 13	Time Advance	3.17
	Coefficients	2.76
	Both Calculations	2.86
46 × 19	Time Advance	3.63
	Coefficients	2.97
	Both Calculations	3.15
64 × 46	Time Advance	4.40
	Coefficients	3.37
	Both Calculations	3.65

Table 2 Timing Comparisons for Three Finite-Element Routines Coded in Both Fortran and Assembly Language

Coding	Routine 1 Time (ns)	Routine 1 Time/CAL Time	Routine 2 Time (ns)	Routine 2 Time/CAL Time	Routine 3 Time (ns)	Routine 3 Time/CAL Time
Vector Length *n* = 1:						
CAL	800.0	1.00	3000.0	1.00	600.0	1.00
CFT (ON = V)	220.0	2.75	9000.0	3.00	1400.0	2.33
CFT (OFF = V)	2100.0	2.63	4000.0	1.33	1300.0	2.17
COMPASS	2300.0	2.88	2000.0	0.67	1000.0	1.67
Vector Length *n* = 8:						
CAL	362.5	1.00	375.0	1.00	175.0	1.00
CFT (ON = V)	937.5	2.59	1125.0	3.00	337.5	1.93
CFT (OFF = V)	850.0	2.34	1000.0	2.67	662.5	3.79
COMPASS	1012.5	2.79	1000.0	2.67	1050.0	6.00
Vector Length *n* = 64:						
CAL	70.3	1.00	109.4	1.00	56.3	1.00
CFT (ON = V)	167.2	2.38	203.2	1.86	75.0	1.33
CFT (OFF = V)	576.6	8.20	734.4	6.71	531.3	9.44
COMPASS	446.9	6.36	562.5	5.14	478.1	8.50
Vector Length *n* = 1000:						
CAL	30.7	1.00	57.0	1.00	46.6	1.00
CFT (ON = V)	69.8	2.27	97.0	1.70	49.2	1.06
CFT (OFF = V)	540.0	17.59	666.0	11.68	513.7	11.02
COMPASS	365.3	11.90	442.0	7.75	386.4	8.29

the expensive calculations were fully vectorized. Table I shows that the vectorized CFT coding achieves an average speed increase of from 2.86 to 3.65 over the scalar CFT speeds.

F. Finite-Element Approximations

As another example of algorithm optimization, consider a finite-element approximation to the matrix equations arising in continuum and fluid mechanics. These approximations yield large sparse matrix systems, although the sparsity pattern in this case is not, in general, a tridiagonal pattern. The direct solution of these equations consists of a triangular decomposition of the matrix followed by a forward-and-backward substitution step. A variable band, active column algorithm [9] is one direct solution method that is most adaptable to parallel processing. Table II is a timing comparison for three vectorizable routines in the algorithm to illustrate the advantages of both automatic vectorization and chaining. This is an example in which there is a significant speed gain over the automatically vectorized coding from the compiler when the routines are coded in machine language (CAL). There are two reasons for this. First, the

machine language coding can take advantage of reorganizing the instruction sequence to avoid cycle losses due to memory conflicts as well as attempting to overlap the calculations with memory fetches and stores. In addition, sophisticated coding in machine language can result in more vector chaining. The average speed gain of the CAL coding over the CFT coding with vectorized inner loops is about 2.1.

Table II also illustrates the effect of the vector start-up time for short vectors. For short vector lengths (*n* = 1 and *n* = 8) the CFT with ON = V is actually slower than CFT with OFF = V using the scalar hardware. However, once the sets of vector registers become fully utilized (*n* greater than or equal to 64) the start-up times become insignificant and the vector functional unit speeds become the dominant factor. Interestingly enough, in some cases, the CDC 7600 COMPASS is still faster than the scalar CRAY speeds.

G. Compiler Algorithm Development

The two previous examples demonstrate the importance of compiler algorithm development. In both cases, these timing studies were run sometime before the most recent algorithms were added to the CFT compiler. Throughout the years since the first CRAY-1 was installed the compiler has continually been improved. The latest algorithm change, which should be available at the NMFECC in the next few months, is a new scheduling algorithm for scalar instructions. This modification may well remove the speed crossover observed in the preceding example between the COMPASS timings and the CFT with OFF = V timing. However, compiler and other system software design issues such as this one have arisen in many other situations. For example, timing analyses have been performed for several applications codes as well as for algorithms, to compare the CFT compiler with another compiler developed for the CRAY-1. Results show that the performance characteristics can be quite different depending on both the compiler algorithms and the nature of the calculation in the application code.

V. FUTURE TRENDS IN HIGH-SPEED COMPUTING

Supercomputers with much faster processing speeds and much larger memories are needed now to meet the demand for more realistic modeling of plasma physics and fusion reactors. Both the United States and Japan have active development programs to produce the next generation of supercomputers. The new architectures being proposed in these efforts all include memory sizes at least as large as 512 million bytes and increased CPU speeds primarily achieved by providing more parallelism (either through more vector pipes, more functional units, or more CPU's).

Multiprocessor systems appear to offer the best hope for large increases in computer power. Machines with small numbers of processors (2 to 4) are currently available commercially, and machines with more processors (8 to 32) are likely to be available between 1985 and 1990. The task of NMFECC will be to develop software approaches that will efficiently support increasing numbers of processors within the coming years. As a reference point, it has taken over five years to develop software to efficiently support and utilize vector technology. Multiprocessor support and utilization is expected to be significantly more difficult.

Processors are most efficiently utilized when the cost of applying them to a user code is small relative to the time spent there. Speedups obtained when this is true will approach the number of processors. From a systems point of view, assignment of the available processors on a program-by-program basis to obtain higher overall throughput represents the best guess in the absence of other information of how to most efficiently utilize the processors. The modifications to the CTSS operating system necessary to support a multiprocessor on this basis are few and there are no other changes necessary to the vast body of underlying software.

With a small number of processors, a job load consistently greater than or equal to the number of processors, and a scheduling strategy biased towards throughput, the opportunity to apply more than one processor to a program will be small. This opportunity will occur primarily with full or almost full memory jobs. However, we expect that the number of processors relative to the memory size will be increasing in the future so that the ability to apply multiple processors to a single program will become increasingly important. The changes necessary to the support software and to the application codes to do this are substantial.

From the point of view of numerical algorithm design and development, it is fortunate that the efforts to parallel process with vector functional units should extend quite naturally over to a multiprocessor environment. That is, where now a parallel sequence of calculations is processed by a single set of functional units, in the future this sequence of operations may be split into n parts and scheduled for the n processors, each having a full set of functional units. Similarly, multiple vector loops extending over several code blocks as well as scalar operations can be scheduled for the multiprocessors.

In conclusion, the NMFECC has a dual responsibility to its users: to operate and maintain the computational facilities that currently exist, while planning to procure and install machines of the future with significantly improved memory size and execution speed.

Fortunately, computers are becoming cheaper to own and operate as their computing power increases. This historical trend implies that codes designed to set up MFE experiments and to predict their behavior will become more economical—even though these codes currently strain NMFECC's computational resources.

REFERENCES

[1] J. Killeen, "Magnetic fusion energy and computers," U. S. Department of Energy, Washington, DC, Rep. DOE/ER-0159, 1983.

[2] R. M. Russell, "The CRAY-1 computer system," *Comm. ACM*, vol. 21, no. 1, pp. 63–72, Jan. 1978.

[3] K. W. Fong, "The National MFE Computer Center CRAY time sharing system," Lawrence Livermore Nat. Lab., Livermore, CA, Rep. UCRL-88569, 1983.

[4] T. R. Girill and C. H. Luk, "DOCUMENT: An interactive online solution to four documentation problems," *Comm. ACM*, vol. 26, no. 5, pp. 328–337, May 1983.

[5] D. S. Kershaw, "The incomplete Cholesky-conjugate gradient method for the iterative solution of systems of linear equations," *J. Comp. Phys.*, vol. 26, pp. 43–65, Jan. 1978.

[6] A. Friedman and D. Kershaw, "Vectorized incomplete Cholesky conjugate gradient (ICCG) package for the CRAY-1 computer," in *Laser Program Annual Report* UCRL-500021-81, Lawrence Livermore Nat. Lab., Livermore, CA, 1982.

[7] P. J. Sydow, *CRAY Computer Systems Technical Note—Optimization Guide*. Mendota Heights, MN: Cray Res. Inc., 1982, SN-0220.

[8] M. G. McCoy, A. A. Mirin, and J. Killeen, "A vectorized Fokker–Planck package for the CRAY-1," Lawrence Livermore Nat. Lab., Livermore, CA, Rep. UCRL-83206, 1979.

[9] R. L. Taylor, E. L. Wilson, and S. J. Sackett, "Direct solution of equations by frontal and variable band active columns methods," in *Proc. Europe U. S. Workshop on Nonlinear Finite Element Analysis in Structural Mechanics* (Ruhr-Universität, Bochum, Germany, July 28–31, 1980), pp. 527–552.

Impact of Computers on Aerodynamics Research and Development

VICTOR L. PETERSON

Invited Paper

Factors motivating the development of computational aerodynamics as a discipline are traced back to the limitations of the tools available to the aerodynamicist before the development of digital computers. Governing equations in exact and approximate forms are discussed together with approaches to their numerical solution. Example results obtained from the successively refined forms of the equations are presented and discussed, both in the context of levels of computer power required and the degree of the effect that their solution has on aerodynamic research and development. Factors pacing advances in computational aerodynamics are identified, including the amount of computational power required to take the next major step in the discipline. Finally, the Numerical Aerodynamic Simulation (NAS) Program—with its 1987 target of achieving a sustained computational rate of 1 billion floating-point operations per second operating on a memory of 240 million words—is briefly discussed in terms of its projected effect on the future of computational aerodynamics.

INTRODUCTION

Computers are playing an increasingly important role in aeronautical research and development. A contributing factor is the profound effect that computers are having on aerodynamics, a technical discipline important to the design of all aerospace vehicles. Computational aerodynamics, although spawned less than 20 years ago and severely limited by currently available computational power, is already emerging as an important aerodynamic design tool. Indeed, the discipline has been used in the design of aircraft that are flying today.

The objective of computational aerodynamics is to simulate aerodynamic flows, using high-speed digital computers to solve numerically approximating sets of the fluid dynamic equations. The discipline is actually a composite of four fields of study: aerodynamics, fluid physics, mathematics, and computer science. Obviously, aerodynamics is involved since the goal is to determine the motion of gases and their effects on bodies moving through them. Fluid physics comes into play in the course of modeling turbulent momentum and heat-transport terms in the full governing equations. Mathematics is drawn upon in the course of developing efficient algorithms for solving the equations with numerical methods. Finally, computer science contributes to the development of new languages and compilers to permit more efficient coding of the equations for solution on computers having various architectures.

Manuscript received May 25, 1983.
The author is with NASA Ames Research Center, Moffett Field, CA 94035, USA.

There are both economic and technical reasons for accelerating the development of computational aerodynamics. It is well known that the cost of conducting the experiments required to provide the empirical database for new aeronautical vehicles is increasing rapidly with time. Two factors account for this increase: 1) the cost of performing wind-tunnel and flight experiments is rising rapidly as the cost of labor and energy goes up; and 2) more importantly, the actual amount of experimentation required is increasing almost exponentially with each new generation of increasingly refined vehicles. Also well known is the fact that the performance of new aerospace vehicles often is compromised because of the inability of test facilities to simulate all aspects of the full-scale vehicle flight environment. On the other hand, the equations governing fluid flows are well known, numerical methods for solving them are being continuously improved, and the cost of performing calculations is decreasing with time.

The objectives of this paper are to review some of the milestones in the historical development of aerodynamics, to discuss the governing equations and approaches to their solution, to provide examples of advances made possible by computers, to discuss factors pacing future advances, to identify future computer requirements, and to outline the approach being taken by NASA to meet the requirements.

HISTORICAL PERSPECTIVE

Sir Isaac Newton published the law governing friction in a viscous fluid in 1726, and Claude Louis M. H. Navier, together with Sir George G. Stokes, later generalized the laws governing the motion of viscous fluids in the form of a system of mathematical equations that were published in 1823 and 1845. Even so, it was after the Wright brothers historic flight in 1903 before aerodynamic theory began to yield useful formulas relating lift and drag to the shape and attitude of a geometric body. Prandtl, in 1918, gave modern wing theory a practical mathematical form but even then results were strictly valid only for very-low-speed or incompressible flows. It was not until 1925, when Ackeret published the first two-dimensional theory for lift and drag at supersonic speeds, that effects of air compressibility on aerodynamic shapes could be calculated. Additional theories for supersonic aerodynamics were published in the late 1930's and early 1940's but it was after World War II before the transonic flow regime began to yield to systematic theoretical treatment. Well over 100 years since Navier and Stokes derived the underlying governing equations of viscous fluid flows, it is still not possible to calculate viscous flows about generalized three-dimensional aircraft shapes in a completely rigorous way. How then, have we managed to conquer the principles of flight and refine them to their present state?

Long before the theoreticians applied the laws of physics to the derivation of formulas for the aerodynamic behavior of heavier-than-air craft, experimentalists were hard at work trying to uncover the secrets of flight. The drawings and notes of Leonardo da Vinci are excellent examples of such studies conducted in the fifteenth and sixteenth centuries A.D. The first wind tunnel, designed in 1871 by Francis Herbert Wenham, was used to make systematic measurements of air resistance. Before that time, experiments mostly involved the observation of bodies moving in a fluid rather than observations of bodies held at rest in a moving fluid, even though Newton nearly 200 years before had clearly stated that forces acting between a solid body and a fluid are the same whether the body moves with a certain uniform velocity through the fluid originally at rest or the fluid moves with the same velocity against the body at rest. Although the Wright brothers carried out nearly 1000 gliding flights before the historic powered flight in 1903, they also conducted over 50 h of wind-tunnel tests and developed the ability to utilize the results of model experiments for their full-scale design. The value of measurements made on small models tested in wind tunnels of limited size to the problem of designing a much larger full-sized aircraft was increased immensely when Osborne Reynolds in 1883 began to search for the prevailing law of similarity in fluid mechanics. He found that if the ratio between inertial and viscous forces remains unchanged then flow patterns will remain similar; thus it was possible to relate results obtained on small-scale models tested in wind-tunnel environments to the behavior of full-scale aircraft in free-flight. Later, it was found that Mach number, the ratio of flight speed to sound speed, involved another law of similarity that must be obeyed to obtain realistic results when compressibility effects are important. A more complete summary of the early development of aerodynamics can be found in [1].

The importance of wind tunnels to the aerodynamicist grew along with the degree of sophistication of aerospace vehicles. Accordingly, large complexes of elaborate test facilities have continued to evolve over the years, although only a handful of major new facilities has been constructed in the past 20 years. In fact, the wind tunnels have and are being used as analog computing devices to integrate the now well-known partial differential equations of fluid dynamics. Digital computers now are beginning to complement the wind tunnels in aerodynamic research and development and even to serve as an attractive alternative to wind tunnels in some limited cases. What are the factors that are driving aerodynamicists to computers at an exponentially accelerating rate even though the magnificent achievements in aeronautics continue to be made largely on the basis of experiment?

Several factors contribute to the compelling motivation for developing and applying computational aerodynamics methodology. First, the physics of fluid flows can be represented by mathematical equations, and computers have become sufficiently large to solve approximating sets of these equations numerically in a practical amount of time

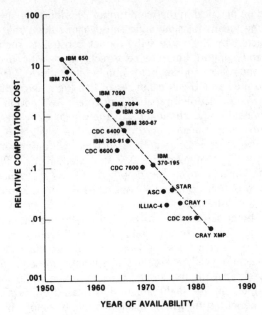

Fig. 1. Relative cost trend for numerically simulating a given flow with a given algorithm on large computers.

and at reasonable cost. Second, wind-tunnel costs and computational costs appear to be changing in importantly different ways. For example, increased complexity and broadened performance envelopes of aircraft have increased the number of wind-tunnel hours expended in the development of a new aircraft by a factor of about 1000 over the past 80 years. Concurrently, the cost per hour of testing also has increased by about a factor of nearly 1000. Thus wind-tunnel testing costs have escalated nearly a millionfold over this period of time. On the other hand, the cost of numerically simulating a given flow with a given algorithm is shown by the data in Fig. 1 to have decreased by a factor of about 1000 in just 25 years. Third, all wind tunnels have some or all of the fundamental limitations: for example, model size (Reynolds number), temperature, wall interference, model support interference, unrealistic aeroelastic model distortions under load, stream nonuniformity (turbulence level), and test gas (of concern for flight in atmospheres of other planets). Finally, both commercial and military aircraft designs and design processes have become extremely sophisticated and internationally competitive so that every conceivable promising opportunity for improving design tools must be thoroughly explored.

The goals of computational aerodynamics and the potential benefits to be derived from pursuing them are severalfold. The first goal is to provide a rapid and inexpensive means for simulating fluid flows. The aim is to develop tools for use in aircraft design that will complement the wind tunnel by providing some of the needed data more quickly and at lower cost. The second goal is to provide a more powerful combination of theory and experiment than is now available. The idea here is to be able to numerically simulate aerodynamic experiments conducted in test facilities and thereby provide the means for improved interpretation and understanding of observed phenomena. The third goal is to make possible an enhanced understanding of the influence of design variables on aircraft performance. This will follow from being able to explore far more combinations of the design variables on the computer than would be practical in the wind tunnel. The fourth goal is to have the means for simulating aerodynamic flows that are unaffected by the usual wind-tunnel constraints such as wall and support interference effects, aeroelastic distortions, and Mach- and Reynolds-number limitations. In addition to providing direct estimates of free-flight aerodynamics, the computational capability, of course, will permit the determination and elimination of the effects of wind-tunnel constraints on measured data. The last goal, and perhaps the most important, is associated with optimizing aerodynamic configurations. Powerful mathematical theories of optimization can be combined with the aerodynamic codes to permit optimum shapes to be developed subject to given constraints.

The potential benefits to be derived from a numerical simulation capability are quite obvious. Significantly improved preliminary designs will result from being able to search economically a large design space for the configuration best satisfying the desired mission profile while simulating the true free-flight situation. Increased efficiency of wind-tunnel testing will be made possible by being able to reduce the number of configurations that must be tested. If the most promising configurations are first identified computationally, the testing program can be aimed at verifying and refining a smaller number of candidate aerodynamic shapes. Clearly, this will help to make better use of the scarce and costly high-Reynolds-number test facilities. Together, all of the factors discussed lead to the conclusion that computational aerodynamics will permit new aerospace vehicles to be designed in shorter periods of time and with greater assurance of meeting performance specifications.

The serious development of computational aerodynamics as a discipline has been under way for only about 15 years. Over this short period of time the discipline has grown from relative obscurity to become the very centerpiece of this country's aeronautical research and development efforts. Today, the two basic tools used for aerodynamic design are wind tunnels and computers. Although wind tunnels are still the principal source of flow simulations for aircraft design, the relative roles of the two tools are expected to change in the years to come.

EQUATIONS, APPROXIMATIONS, AND SOLUTION APPROACHES

Although later found to be an approximation to the more basic nonlinear Boltzmann equation governing molecular transport, the equations governing the motion of viscous fluids, which Navier and Stokes derived well over 100 years ago, are definitely suitable for the practical purposes of aircraft design. These equations are written in a highly compact vector form below.

$$\text{Mass:} \quad \frac{\partial p}{\partial t} + \text{div}\,(\rho V) = 0$$

$$\text{Momentum:} \quad \rho \frac{DV}{Dt} = \text{div}\,\sigma_{ik}$$

$$\text{Energy:} \quad \rho \frac{D(e + V^2/2)}{Dt} = \text{div}\,(\sigma_{ik}V) - \text{div}\,q$$

$$\text{State:} \quad e = e(p, \rho)$$

where

$$\frac{D(\ )}{Dt} = \frac{\partial(\ )}{\partial t} + (V \cdot \text{grad})(\ ) = \text{material derivative}$$

$$\sigma_{ik} = -p\delta_{ik} + \tau_{ik} \qquad = \text{fluid stress tensor}$$

$$\tau_{ik} = 2\mu\epsilon_{ik} + \lambda\,\text{div}\,V\delta_{ik} \qquad = \text{viscous stress tensor}$$

$$\epsilon_{ik} = (1/2)\left(\frac{\partial u_i}{\partial x_k} + \frac{\partial u_k}{\partial x_i}\right) \qquad = \text{rate of deformation tensor}$$

$$q = -k\,\text{grad}\,T \qquad = \text{heat flux vector}$$

and

e	internal energy
k	thermal conductivity
p	pressure
T	temperature
u_i, u_j, u_k	velocity components
V	fluid velocity vector
x_i, x_j, x_k	coordinate directions
δ_{ik}	Kronecker delta
λ	bulk viscosity coefficient
μ	shear viscosity coefficient
ρ	fluid density.

Although somewhat innocuous in appearance, their solution is marked by insidious pitfalls. Apart from being strongly coupled partial differential equations containing over 60 partial derivative terms when expanded in terms of Cartesian coordinates, they contain the physics governing all scales of turbulence of which between four and five decades of scales are of practical importance, depending on the Reynolds number. Boundary conditions associated with complex aircraft shapes further complicate their treatment.

It is not possible to obtain closed-form solutions to these full equations for situations of interest in aircraft design. Even with the level of computational power available today, the complete equations cannot, within practical constraints, be solved numerically in their full form, except in highly simplified situations. Therefore, various degrees of approximation have been evoked over the years to obtain useful results. The four major levels of approximation to the full equations that stand out in order of their evolution and complexity are discussed in [2] and are summarized in Table 1.

Long before the advent of electronic digital computers, mathematicians and aerodynamicists devised methods for solving the linearized equations governing inviscid flows that are everywhere either subsonic or moderately supersonic. This was possible because only three partial derivative terms are retained in the equations. The first solutions for two-dimensional airfoils were obtained in about 1930 and for three-dimensional wings in about 1940. With the development during the 1960's of computers of the IBM-360 and CDC-6600 class, it became practical to compute inviscid flows about somewhat idealized, complete aircraft configurations. This level of approximation (level I) is still heavily used today but because the equations neglect all viscous terms, as well as inviscid nonlinear terms, such calculations provide only a minor complement to wind-tunnel simulations in the overall design process. For many years, it has been customary to increase the value of this level of approximation by making corrections for viscous effects based on the so-called boundary-layer theory. This approach works reasonably well when flows do not en-

Table 1 Major Levels of Approximation to the Navier–Stokes Equations and the Time Period for Initiation of Major Efforts to Treat them Computationally

Approximation Level	Capability	Initiation Time Period	
		Research	Applications
I Linearized Inviscid	Subsonic/Supersonic •Pressure distributions •Vortex and wave drag	1950's	1960's
II Nonlinear Inviscid	Above Plus •Transonic •Hypersonic	1960's	1970's
III Re-Averaged Navier–Stokes Model Turbulence	Above Plus •Total drag •Separated flow •Stall/buffet/flutter	1970's	1980's
IV Large Eddy Simulation Model Subgrid Scale Turbulence	Above Plus •Turbulence structure •Aerodynamic noise	1970's	1990's
Exact Full Navier–Stokes Equations	Above Plus •Laminar/turbulent transition •Dissipation	Increasing intensity of research 1970's →	

counter severe adverse pressure gradients and remain everywhere attached to surfaces over which they pass.

The advent of the computer brought the next level (level II) of approximation into the realm of practical usefulness. By including the nonlinear terms in the equations, it is possible to treat flows at all Mach numbers, including transonic and hypersonic, although viscous terms are still neglected. Hand-calculated solutions for the transonic flow over a nonlifting airfoil were reported in 1948 [3] and over a lifting airfoil with detached bow wave at transonic speeds in 1954 [4]. However, the first transonic solutions for a practical lifting airfoil with embedded shock wave required the use of a computer and did not appear in the literature until 1970 [5]. This latter achievement can be interpreted as the turning point in computational aerodynamics, for it marks the beginning of a series of advances that would not have been possible without computers.

Level III of approximation is now in the stages of vigorous development. This level of approximation does not neglect any of the terms in the Navier–Stokes equations. The basic equations are averaged over a time interval that is long relative to turbulent eddy fluctuations, yet small relative to macroscopic flow changes. Such a process introduces new terms representing the time-averaged transport of momentum and energy which must be modeled using empirical information. Computers are required to work with this level of approximation but the potential advantages are enormous. Realistic simulations of separated flows, of unsteady flows, such as buffeting, and of total drag should be possible as the ability to model the turbulence terms matures. Combined with computer optimization methods, these simulations should make it possible to develop aerodynamically optimum designs. Landmark advances of the last decade include the investigation of shock-wave interaction with a laminar boundary layer in 1971 [6], the treatment of high-Reynolds-number transonic airfoil flows in 1974 [7], and the first three-dimensional laminar flow over an in-

clined body of revolution in 1974 [8]. Relatively large amounts of computer time are required using the level III approximation. Although two-dimensional flows can be computed in a matter of minutes on state-of-the-art Class VI computers with current numerical methods, the routine computation of three-dimensional flows is not yet practical: they require about 100 times more calculations than two-dimensional flows.

Level IV of approximation involves the direct numerical simulation of turbulent eddies over a range of scales sufficiently broad to capture the transport of nearly all momentum and energy. Only the small eddies that dissipate energy, transport little energy or momentum, tend toward isotropy and are nearly "universal" in character are modeled. Under such conditions, the computed results involve essentially no empiricism. This level of approximation is being used today on a limited basis to research the physics of turbulence at a level of detail not possible through experiment. Computer times for simulations of very basic flows, such as those in channels, range up to 80 h on current supercomputers. Ultimately, this work should provide information that will lead to improved methods for modeling turbulence in the level III approximation, as well as to unlock secrets of the generation of aerodynamic noise and the manipulation of friction drag. A comprehensive review of the so-called process of "large-eddy simulation" is given in [9].

Considerable effort is being expended to develop numerical methods for solving the governing equations, particularly for the II, III, and IV levels of approximation. Approaches based on finite-difference algorithms are the most popular, although work with the level I approximation is largely based on paneling methods and that for the level IV approximation frequently involves consideration of spectral methods.

Finite-difference methods involve the use of a computational mesh engulfing the aerodynamic configuration and

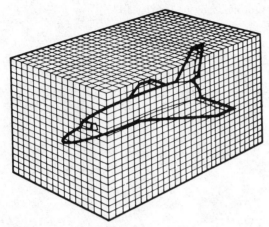

Fig. 2. Idealized representation of a computational mesh surrounding an aircraft configuration.

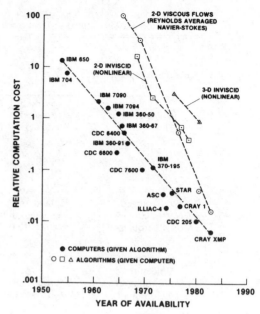

Fig. 3. Comparison of numerical simulation cost trend resulting from improvements in algorithms with that owing to improvements in computers.

extending far enough in all directions to where outer boundary conditions can be expressed in terms of known quantities. An idealized representation of a computational mesh is shown in Fig. 2. In actual practice, most meshes being used today are highly complicated nets that conform to geometric contours and involve stretching and clustering designed to tailor grid spacings commensurate with the physical detail that must be captured to provide an accurate solution. The concept is to solve the governing equations for all of the flow variables for the parcels of fluid within each little volume formed by the grid. Obviously, if computers had unlimited speeds and memories, the grid could be refined to the point of resolving all scales of motion without approximation.

Numerical methods are being tailored to take advantage of advanced computer architectures involving vector and concurrent processing. One such method is the implicit approximate-factorization scheme of [10]. Using a coordinate transformation to map the grid into a rectangular computational volume with boundary conditions on the exterior face permits the approximate-factorization method to be written

$$A_x A_y A_z Q^{n+1} = B_{xyz} Q^n$$

where Q is the vector of flow variables; n refers to the time step or iteration step; A_x, A_y, and A_z are block-tridiagonal matrices relating the flow variables along grid coordinates x, y, and z; and B_{xyz} is the matrix relating variables calculated from the previous time level. The solution is advanced at each time level by calculating $R = B_{xyz} Q^n$ and then successively performing matrix inversions along each x, y, and z grid line to obtain, respectively,

$$S_1 = A_x^{-1} R, \quad S_2 = A_y^{-1} S_1, \quad \text{and} \quad Q^{n+1} = A_z^{-1} S_2.$$

Since the Q^n data are known at all grid points, the first operation exhibits volume parallelism; that is, there are no data precedence requirements that prevent the simultaneous execution at all points within the computational volume. Furthermore, all interior point calculations are identical and form volume vectors. The boundary condition data are also known and they form plane vectors. The matrix inversion sweeps along the coordinate directions and can proceed simultaneously along all grid points in planes normal to the sweep direction. Thus one sees plane

parallelism applied in a serial fashion as the calculations proceed from plane to plane. Numerous other methods are described in the literature.

The thrust of the work in algorithm development is aimed at increasing the degree of vectorization, economy of calculation at each time step, numerical stability, accuracy, and ease of memory management. A considerable amount of attention is also being directed to developing mathematical representations of complex aircraft geometries and automated computational grid generators. Advancements in algorithm development are keeping pace with advancements being made in computer speed. This is illustrated by the results shown in Fig. 3 where reductions in the cost of doing a computation owing to improvements in both computers and algorithms are compared. Improvements in computers have reduced the cost of doing a computation with a given algorithm by a factor of almost 100 in a period of 15 years. Improvements in algorithms have reduced the cost of doing a computation with a given computer by almost a thousandfold over the same period of time. These advancements compound to result in an astounding overall increase in cost effectiveness of nearly 10^5.

EXAMPLES OF ADVANCES

In aerodynamics, the linearized equations for inviscid flows were the first to be coded for solution on digital computers. Computers were used to replace laborious hand calculations associated with obtaining results from closed-form solutions for varieties of flow conditions and simple configurations. Later, in the 1960's, methods for treating shapes with more complex boundary conditions were developed. These are termed "panel methods" inasmuch as complete aircraft geometries are modeled by a large number of contiguous surface panels. Because the equations are linear, the complete solution can be built up by using the principle of superposition and accounting for the influence on all other panels of flows satisfying the boundary condi-

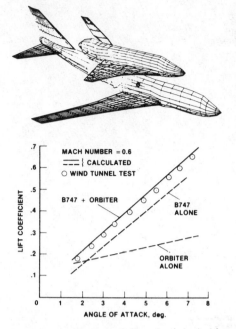

Fig. 4. Example application of linearized inviscid panel method to Space Shuttle Orbiter mounted on a B-747.

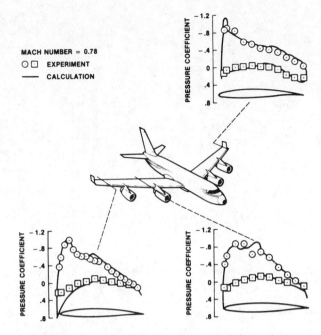

Fig. 5. Example application of nonlinear inviscid equations to simulate flow about modified Boeing KC-135 airplane.

tions on each individual panel. The panel methods have reached a high degree of sophistication and they still are used in aircraft design in situations in which the flow is everywhere either subsonic or moderately supersonic.

An example of results using the linearized inviscid panel method is illustrated in Fig. 4 for the Shuttle Orbiter mounted on top of the Boeing 747 carrier aircraft. These results [11] show that accurate determinations of the lift characteristics for the combined configuration and for each vehicle during separation of the Orbiter from the carrier can be obtained by using about 1000 panels. Configuration orientations selected from the computational design phase were tested in a wind tunnel to validate results.

For many years, both civilian and military aircraft have operated for extended periods of time in the transonic flow regime, which cannot be treated accurately with the linearized equations. Therefore, once computers became sufficiently large and widely available, finite-difference methods for treating the nonlinear inviscid equations began to receive serious attention. One of the first solutions for a three-dimensional wing was obtained in 1972; it took 18 h of computation on an IBM-360 model 67. Improvements in computers and algorithms have reduced the time required to treat these simpler configurations to less than 1 min on today's Class VI machines.

A number of successful design applications have been made for transport aircraft, business jets, missiles, and projectiles using the nonlinear inviscid equations. Results of one such application, shown in Fig. 5, involved computing the flow about the wing, fuselage, pylon, nacelle, and winglet of a modified KC-135 aircraft configuration. This calculation was done by Boppe and Stern in 1980 [12] and it required about 15 min on a CDC-7600 machine. Chordwise pressure coefficients C_p at three selected wing stations are displayed along with measurements. Results for other parts of the configuration compare equally favorably with the calculations.

Results computed using the inviscid equations, particularly when corrected for viscous effects by using the boundary-layer equations, are quite satisfactory for aerodynamically clean configurations operating at or near cruise conditions. However, many of the more crucial design situations are difficult, if not impossible, to treat without accounting for the nearly inviscid outer flows and the viscous inner flows in a fully coupled fashion. Examples of these are inlet, engine, and exhaust flows; airframe–propulsion system integration; stall and buffet; vortex-enhanced lift; maneuvering loads; and performance near performance boundaries. These design problems are also very difficult to treat experimentally in wind-tunnel tests.

The Reynolds-averaged form of the Navier–Stokes equations (level III) is suitable for treating the problems that are dominated by viscous effects. Therefore, they are receiving increasing attention now that Class VI computers are becoming widely available. Most of the applications to date have been for two-dimensional problems although some pioneering work has been done on simple three-dimensional objects.

Results of an early attempts to calculate the buffet boundary over a range of transonic Mach numbers for a lifting airfoil are shown in Fig. 6 [13]. In addition to giving a good estimate of the buffet boundary, the calculations also provide detailed information about the physics of the flow. For example, the boundary is nearly level at Mach numbers below about 0.7, because the flow is separating and reattaching near the leading edge of the airfoil at high angle of attack. On the other hand, the boundary slopes become steep at the higher Mach numbers owing to shock-wave-induced flow separation near the trailing edge at lower angles of attack. Other information, such as the time-dependent magnitude of the buffeting force, is also determined by the calculation.

Results from [14] of a three-dimensional calculation of the laminar flow about a body of revolution composed of a

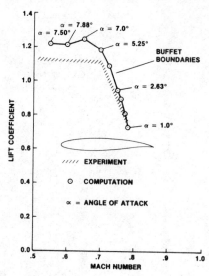

Fig. 6. Example application of Reynolds-averaged Navier–Stokes equations to simulate turbulent-flow buffet boundaries for a lifting supercritical airfoil.

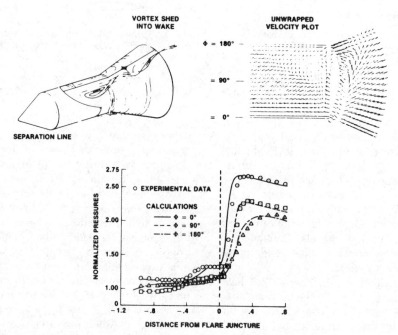

Fig. 7. Example of numerically simulated supersonic laminar flow about an inclined body of revolution: Mach number = 2.8, angle of attack = 4°.

cone, cylinder, and flare are presented in Fig. 7, wherein calculated pressure distributions are shown to agree well with measurements. A study of flow–velocity vectors near the surface of the body clearly shows the region of flow separation in the vicinity of the flare.

Results from [15] for a more complex situation involving the turbulent supersonic flow over an axisymmetric conical afterbody containing a centered propulsive exhaust flow are presented in Fig. 8. Computed density contours in the vicinity of the boattail region and exhaust plume show excellent qualitative agreement, with features of the flow made visible by the use of Schlieren photography in the experimental investigation reported for the same flow conditions in [16]. Calculations such as these provide extensive additional information about the flows that is difficult if not impossible to obtain from experiments.

Larger computers will be required before the Reynolds-averaged Navier–Stokes equations are used routinely in design applications. Steady two-dimensional flows can be calculated in a matter of minutes, but time-dependent two-dimensional and steady three-dimensional flows about simple objects still require from 1 to 20 h to compute on Class VI machines. Nevertheless, it is now possible to develop this technology so that when larger computers do become available, the methods and the turbulence models necessary for treating a wide range of important problems should be available.

Research on the highest level of approximation to the Navier–Stokes equations (level IV) involving the direct numerical simulation of the most important scales of turbulence is beginning to produce information on the physics of turbulence that was heretofore inaccessible. An experiment

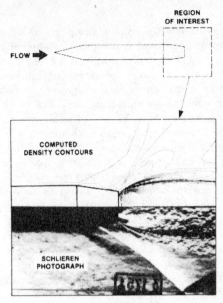

Fig. 8. Example of numerically simulated turbulent flow over an axisymmetric conical afterbody containing a centered propulsive jet: stream Mach number = 2, jet Mach number = 2.5, jet static pressure—9 times free-stream static pressure.

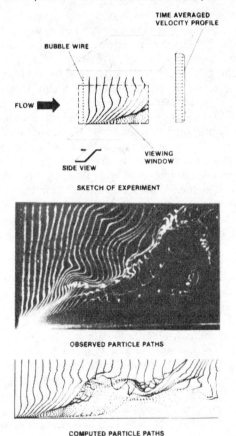

Fig. 9. Particle paths in low-speed channel flow made visible experimentally by photographing intermittently released hydrogen bubbles and computationally by tagging fluid elements in a direct numerical simulation.

in which particle paths in a turbulent flow on a channel wall were traced by observing time histories of hydrogen bubbles generated by pulsed heating of a wire [17] was duplicated numerically [18]. Comparisons of these calculated and measured results are reproduced in Fig. 9. The

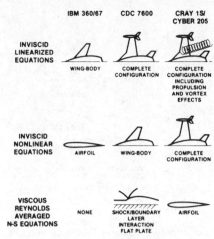

Fig. 10. Pictorial representation of the effect that increasing computer power has had on applications of computational aerodynamics.

velocity profile of the steady mean flow as it would appear either from measurements or from calculations, using the Reynolds-averaged form of the equations (level III approximation) is sketched for reference. It is striking to note that a steady turbulent flow when observed in this detail, displays large irregularly shaped and time-dependent flow structures. Furthermore, there is an obvious correlation between the measured and calculated particle paths. More importantly, the calculations provide additional information about the flow, such as magnitudes of Reynolds stresses, pressure–strain relationships, and the other flow variables at every mesh point in space and increment in time.

Class VI computers are large enough to do a limited amount of this type of research on the simplest of flows but application of this technology to even a symmetric airfoil is not yet feasible.

The effect that increasing computer power has had on computational aerodynamics in a practical engineering sense is displayed pictorially in Fig. 10. Presently, available machines are adequate for treating relatively complex configurations with the inviscid flow equations. Of course, the type of information derived from the computations is limited (e.g., no effects of flow separation). The viscous flow equations, being more complex and requiring fine computational meshes, demand substantially greater computational power to solve. Thus the types of problems that can be solved with a given computer are necessarily less complex. In effect, a designer has to make the choice between treating simple configurations with complex physics and treating complex configurations with simple physics. It is obvious, though, that in both the inviscid- and viscous-flow situations each new generation of computers has resulted in corresponding advances in the value of computational aerodynamics as a design tool. The discipline will begin to mature when both complex configurations and complex physics can be treated together in a practical amount of computer time.

Another way to conceptualize the effect that a new generation of computers has on the frontiers in both research and applications is illustrated in Fig. 11. First, it is noted that at any point in time, problems being treated in a research environment are more complex than those being treated in an applications environment. The introduction of a new computer very quickly stimulates research by permit-

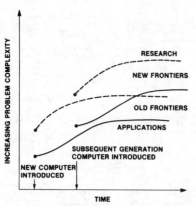

Fig. 11. Effect of increasing computer power on frontiers in research and applications.

ting even higher degrees of problem complexity to be considered. In a few years, the major benefits achievable with the new computer are derived and the state of the art approaches a new asymptote. Meanwhile, the level of capability in the applications environment also begins to rise toward a new asymptote but only after a delay that is due both to the time required to change software and the time required for the more advanced machines to become available to the general users. The process repeats itself with the introduction of each new generation of computers. It is also observed that a new capability developed in a research mode on one computer often ends up being applied on the next generation machine. Ideally, users would like to have access to the next generation of computers just before advances start to become limited by the power of the current generation.

FACTORS PACING ADVANCES IN COMPUTATIONAL AERODYNAMICS

It is clear from the preceding discussion that available computer power is limiting the size and complexity of problems that can be addressed with computational aerodynamics. Apart from this most important factor, which is discussed in the next section, there are several other key factors pacing the development of computational aerodynamics. Probably in order of descending importance, these are turbulence modeling, grid and geometry definition, solution-algorithm development, management of large databases, and management acceptance of results. Each of these factors will be discussed briefly.

The Reynolds-averaged Navier–Stokes equations are expected to form the backbone of applications codes for many years to come. Though they embody the effects of all terms in the full governing equations, those that govern turbulence are modeled with empirical information in order to avoid the problem of computationally resolving the many orders of magnitude of turbulence scales. The models depend on constants which until recently could only be obtained through physical experiments. It is relatively easy to find a set of constants that will apply to one type of fluid flow but it is difficult to develop a single model that will apply universally to all types of flows. Current models are generally adequate for problems involving only small regions of flow separation but improvements are needed to handle more general situations.

For at least three reasons, the prospects of developing improved turbulence models are much brighter than they were in the past. First, major advances are being made in the development of fluid-flow diagnostic equipment. A good example is the laser velocimeter which provides the means for nonintrusively measuring individual components of mean and fluctuating velocities of small elements of a moving fluid. Second, computers and numerical methods are now efficient enough to permit the viscous-flow equations to be solved routinely, at least for simple geometries. This allows many models to be tested over wide ranges of flow conditions in a reasonable period of time. Finally, turbulence now can be investigated computationally for a few simple flows by direct numerical simulation. These solutions are providing information on the physics of turbulence that cannot be obtained through experiments. Working hand-in-hand, the computational fluid dynamicist and the fluid physicist should be able to advance the understanding of turbulence at a much faster rate than was heretofore possible.

The task of representing geometries and surrounding computational grids increases in complexity along with the treatment of more elaborate configurations and refined flow physics. Problems with grid definition stem mainly from the fact that computer speed and memory are limited. Elaborate methods are required to minimize the number of grid nodes while retaining sufficiently close spacing to capture the correct solution to the equations. Mesh points must be suitably clustered in regions of high flow gradients but can be more widely distributed in regions of low gradients. The situation is further complicated by the fact that locations of high flow gradients are not usually known *a priori*; they can move around as solutions evolve and, of course, they can be unsteady even in a fully developed flow. The more sophisticated grids that are solution adaptive must be redefined after every iteration in the solution. This imposes the requirement that the grid-generation scheme be numerical in nature and computationally efficient. Although there has been great progress in the development of numerical methods for generating grids, there is no universally accepted method for discretizing three-dimensional flow fields. Furthermore, suitable criteria for determining optimum grids do not yet exist.

Enormous amounts of data are associated with the solutions for flows about three-dimensional configurations, and the problem of managing these data gets larger along with the computers. Current computers disgorge a few million words of data for each problem solved and this number will rise to tens and perhaps hundreds of millions with the next generation. Graphics devices to display results are keeping pace, but the procedures for managing result files need attention. Production of full-color, three-dimensional movies of output files can itself require noticeable computer time on a Class VI machine but probably an insignificant amount compared with that invested in the original problem solution. The problem lies in managing the data-flow display and storage without requiring an unreasonable amount of the user's time. Local workstations with graphics devices, high-speed communication lines, and the associated software are required to solve this problem.

Experience shows that many managers of aircraft design groups are suspicious of results obtained by computation. Many of them moved out of research activities before

Table 2 Perspective on the Use of Computers for Computational Aerodynamics

	Computer Requirements	
	Practical Engineering Computations	Research Computation (Code Development)
Computer Class	(~ 10 min CPU Time)	(hrs CPU Time)
IBM 360/67 CDC 6600	2D inviscid nonlinear 3D inviscid linearized	3D inviscid nonlinear
CDC 7600	3D inviscid nonlinear	2D Reynolds-averaged Navier–Stokes
ILLIAC-IV CRAY-1S CYBER 205	2D Reynolds-averaged Navier–Stokes	3D Reynolds-averaged Navier–Stokes
35 × CRAY-1S	3D Reynolds-averaged Navier–Stokes	large eddy simulation

computers were large enough to do scientific and engineering work in the aeronautical disciplines that could not be done as well or better either with closed-form theory, rules of thumb, or experimentation. There is no question that results of computation still need to be treated with some degree of suspicion, but there are many examples of situations in which computed results have been proved superior, more quickly obtained, and less costly than information obtained with more conventional approaches. Forward-looking management is required to permit the computer to assume an increasing role in the aeronautical design process. This problem will solve itself with the passage of time.

FUTURE COMPUTER REQUIREMENTS

Available computational power is limiting the discipline of computational aerodynamics. Governing equations are known and are trustworthy; numerical solution procedures are available and important problems remain to be solved.

A perspective of the amount of computational power that is required can be obtained by reviewing the historical use of computers for computational aerodynamics. Some pertinent data are given in Table 2. Experience has shown that computational methods are not routinely used in the aerodynamic design environment unless the time required to obtain a simulation is of the order of 10 to 15 min. Short computation times are required to make it practical to sort through many possible configurations early in the design cycle when aerodynamic factors can have the largest effect on the shape of a new aircraft. Simpler forms of the aerodynamic equations, such as the two-dimensional inviscid nonlinear or the three-dimensional inviscid linear, can be solved in 10 min or less on machines of the IBM-360 model 67 or CDC-6600 class. When machines of this class were first made available to the research community they were used to pioneer solution methods for the more sophisticated three-dimensional inviscid nonlinear equations. Then, as more powerful machines of the CDC-7600 class became available, it became possible for industry designers to routinely use the two-dimensional inviscid nonlinear methods while the researchers moved on to develop methods for solving the next higher level of approximation to the governing equations. Current Class VI computers are adequate to solve routinely the two-dimensional Reynolds-averaged Navier–Stokes equations and to research extensions to three dimensions but they fall far short of making the three-dimensional viscous-flow simula-

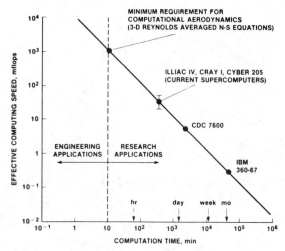

Fig. 12. Relationship between the time required to solve the three-dimensional Reynolds-averaged Navier–Stokes equations and the speed of performing arithmetic operations: 1985 algorithms, 10^7 grid points.

tions practical for design work. A much more powerful machine is required before the next major step can be taken in computational aerodynamics.

The relationship between the time required to compute a flow with the three-dimensional Reynolds-averaged Navier–Stokes equations using 10^7 grid points and the speed of a computer is shown in Fig. 12. These results show that a computer must perform at least 1 billion floating-point operations per second on a sustained basis in order to complete the simulation in 10 min. This minimum required speed is based on the use of improved algorithms projected to be available in 1985. It is interesting to note that the solution of the same problem would take about a month on an IBM-360 model 67, a day on a CDC-7600, and several hours on a Class VI machine. Existing computers clearly are not adequate. Implicit in these results is the assumption that data-transfer speeds to and from memory are fast enough to keep pace with the processing units.

The other aspect of computational power that must be considered is memory. About 30 words of memory are required for each grid point used in Reynolds-averaged Navier–Stokes simulations. Thus a calculation involving 10 million grid points would require high-speed access to about 300 million words. Routine solution of problems of this size obviously will require major advances in the meth-

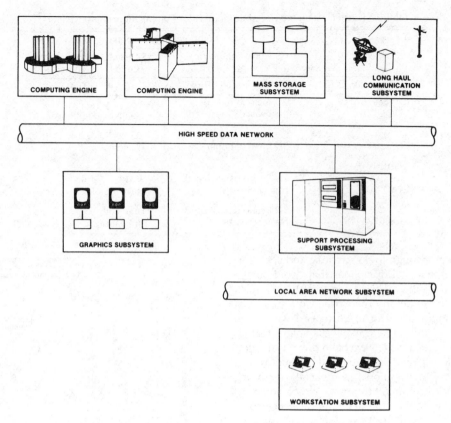

Fig. 13. Schematic of fully developed NAS processing system network.

ods and equipment for displaying results in a form suitable for analysis.

A computer having a high-speed memory ranging in size from 200 to 300 million words and a sustained computational rate of at least 1 billion floating-point operations per second will provide the capability required to advance computational aerodynamics to the level of being a major alternative to wind-tunnel testing in the early stages of vehicle design and a major complement to wind tunnels in the later stages of design refinement. In addition, it would provide the tool required to research applications of direct numerical simulation of turbulent eddies, the highest level of approximation to the complete Navier–Stokes equations.

APPROACH TO MEETING THE REQUIREMENTS

Prospects for having the computational power required to take the next major step in computational aerodynamics before the end of this decade appear very bright. This optimism is based, in part, on results of over 8 years of focused studies initially undertaken by NASA in 1975 and leading to the current Numerical Aerodynamic Simulation (NAS) Program. The overall objectives of the NAS Program are twofold: 1) to act as the pathfinder in advanced, large-scale computer system capability through systematic incorporation of state-of-the-art improvements in computer hardware and software and 2) to provide a national computational capability available to NASA, DOD, other government agencies, industry, and universities, as a necessary element in insuring continuing leadership in computational aerodynamics and related disciplines.

The initial goal of the activity, originally called the Com-

putational Aerodynamic Design Facility Project, was to develop a system having a sustained computational speed of 1 billion floating-point operations per second, a working memory of 40 million words, and an archival storage of at least 10 billion words. Over the years of these studies, requirements were refined to reflect advances being made both in the discipline of computational aerodynamics and in the development of large-scale scientific computers. The current plan of the NAS Program calls for a systematic and evolutionary development of a computational system using commercially available equipment. The principal goals now are to provide the sustained processing rate of 1 billion floating-point operations per second, a high-speed working memory of 240 million words, and an on-line mass storage system of 800 billion bytes by 1987 with an intermediate operational performance capability in 1985. Beyond 1987, the goal is to continue to expand the computational capability as succeeding generations of high-speed computers become available. A diagram of the fully developed NAS processing system network as now envisioned is shown in Fig. 13.

The projected 1987 performance envelope of the NAS system operating on the Reynolds-averaged Navier–Stokes equations along with that for several other computers is presented in Fig. 14. Speed and memory requirements for simulating steady flows about representative airfoils, wings, and aircraft at Reynolds numbers ranging from 10^6 to 10^8 are shown for comparison. Also shown are requirements for calculating flows about several other components of aircraft. All of the requirements are based on solving the Reynolds-averaged Navier–Stokes equations in 15 min of processing time with algorithms expected to be available in 1985.

AC   AIRCRAFT
W   WING
HR   HELICOPTER ROTOR
CB   COMPRESSOR BLADE,
      OR TURBINE BLADE
IB   INCLINED BODY

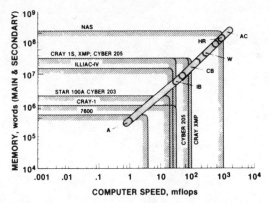

Fig. 14. Computer speed and memory requirements compared with large computer capabilities: Reynolds-averaged Navier–Stokes equations, 1985 algorithms, 15-min runs.

CONCLUDING REMARKS

Principles of aerodynamics led to the first successful powered flight of a heavier-than-air craft at the beginning of this century. Over the intervening years, a blend of theory and experiment has resulted in evolutionary refinements to aircraft technologies. The advent of the computer marked the beginning of a revolutionary period of accelerating advances in the understanding of fluid dynamic flows. The aerodynamicist is no longer limited to working only with the extremely approximate forms of the governing equations that are amenable to solution by hand. Successively more complex approximations to the full governing equations are being solved as computational power increases, and each new level of capability changes the relative roles of wind tunnels and computers.

The next major step in computational aerodynamics requires a computer having a sustained computational rate of 1 billion floating-point operations per second and a memory capacity of at least 240 million words. With this level of capability, computers will serve both as major complements to wind tunnels in the aeronautical design process and as powerful tools for advanced fluid dynamics research. The goal of NASA's Numerical Aerodynamic Simulation Program is to reach this level of computational capability in 1987. Beyond that, about three more orders of magnitude of improvement are required before the discipline of computational aerodynamics can fully mature.

A pathway to the future has been charted. Given the expected levels of emphasis, computers will continue to play an increasingly important role in aeronautical research and development, and the remaining barriers to solving the full Navier–Stokes equations will be broken.

REFERENCES

[1] T. von Karman, *Aerodynamics*. New York: McGraw-Hill, 1963.

[2] D. R. Chapman, "Computational aerodynamics development and outlook," AIAA Paper 79-0129, Jan. 1979.

[3] H. Emmons, "Flow of a compressible fluid past a symmetrical airfoil in a wind tunnel and in free air," NACA Tech. Note TN-1746, 1948.

[4] W. G. Vincenti and C. B. Wagoner, "Theoretical study of the transonic lift of a double-wedge profile with detached bow wave," NACA Rep. 1180, 1954.

[5] R. Magnus and H. Yoshihara, "Inviscid transonic flow over airfoils," *AIAA J.*, vol. 8, no. 12, pp. 2157–2162, Dec. 1970.

[6] R. W. MacCormack, "Numerical solutions of the interaction of a shock wave with a laminar boundary layer," in *Lecture Notes in Physics*, vol. 8. New York: Springer-Verlag, 1971, pp. 151–163.

[7] G. S. Deiwert, "Numerical simulation of high Reynolds number transonic flow," AIAA Paper 74-603, June 1974.

[8] C. P. Li, "A numerical study of laminar flow separation on blunt flared cones at angle of attack," AIAA Paper 74-585, June 1974.

[9] J. H. Ferziger, "Large eddy numerical simulations of turbulent flows," *AIAA J.*, vol. 15, no. 9, pp. 1261–1267, Sept. 1977.

[10] R. M. Beam and R. F. Warming, "An implicit factored scheme for the compressible Navier–Stokes equations," *AIAA J.*, vol. 16, no. 4, pp. 393–402, Apr. 1978.

[11] A. L. de Costa, "Application of computational aerodynamic methods to the design and analysis of transport aircraft," ICAS Paper, presented at the Eleventh Congress of the International Council of the Aeronautical Sciences, Lisbon, Portugal, Sept. 10–16, 1978.

[12] C. W. Boppe and M. A. Stern, "Simulated transonic flows for aircraft with nacelles, pylons and winglets," AIAA Paper 80-0130, Jan. 1980.

[13] L. L. Levy and H. E. Bailey, "Computation of airfoil buffet boundaries," *AIAA J.*, vol. 19, no. 11, pp. 1488–1490, Nov. 1981.

[14] C. M. Hung, "Numerical solution of supersonic laminar flow over an inclined body of revolution," *AIAA J.*, vol. 18, no. 8, pp. 921–928, Aug. 1980.

[15] G. S. Deiwert, "A computational investigation of supersonic axisymmetric flow over boattails containing a centered propulsive jet," AIAA Paper 83-0462, Jan. 1983.

[16] J. Agrell and R. A. White, "An experimental investigation of supersonic axisymmetric flow over boattails containing a centered propulsive jet," FFA Tech. Note AU-913, 1974.

[17] H. T. Kim, S. J. Kline, and W. C. Reynolds, "The production of turbulence near a smooth wall in a turbulent boundary layer," *J. Fluid Mech.*, vol. 50, pt. 1, pp. 133–160, 1971.

[18] P. Moin and J. Kim, "Numerical investigation of turbulent channel flow," *J. Fluid Mech.*, vol. 118, pp. 341–377, 1982.

Part V: Future Trends in Supercomputers

Chapter 10: Dataflow Computers
Chapter 11: VLSI Computing Systems
Chapter 12: Future Perspectives

PART V
FUTURE TRENDS IN SUPERCOMPUTERS

Assessed below are future perspectives of supercomputers and their impact on science and technology. Computer scientists have been constantly searching for new approaches to designing high-performance machines. Dataflow and VLSI offer two mutually supportive approaches toward the design of future supercomputers.

Reviewed below are the requirements of data-driven computations, functional programming languages, and various dataflow system architectures which have been challenged in recent years.

In VLSI computing, several papers are included to show the topological structures of processor arrays for large-scale numeric computations and for symbolic manipulations. Techniques for directly mapping parallel algorithms into silicon chips are in great demand. This necessitates the use of VLSI/CAD tools and supercomputers for large-scale circuit analysis.

Data-driven computations offer an alternative approach to improving computer performance in large-scale, scientific/engineering calculations. Readers can find background information on dataflow computers from the articles in Chapter 9. The dataflow approach intends to deviate from the inherently sequential processing in conventional von Neumann machines.

Instead of using shared memory cells among multiple processors, the dataflow machine simply forwards data tokens (operands and results) directly among instructions. The execution of an instruction is driven entirely by the availability of its required operands. In other words, the execution sequence should be constrained only by data dependency. There is no need to create an artificial ordering in user programs. Even the program counter is unnecessary in sequencing the instructions for execution in a dataflow system.

In contrast, the von Neumann sequential computers are known as control-flow machines. Asynchronous computations are performed in a dataflow computer with distributed control mechanisms. The dataflow computing is purely functional and free from side effects. It has the advantages of having localized effects without having far-reaching data dependencies. Usually, the single-assignment rule is applied in functional programming. Iterative computations can be unfolded into parallel computations. The dataflow functional programming lacks history sensitivity in procedure calls.

Research on dataflow computers was initiated with the analysis of dataflow program graphs and the development of functional programming languages. Since then, dataflow languages have been proposed including the Irvine dataflow (ID) language, and the value algorithmic language (VAL), to mention just two among several single-assignment languages.

There are a dozen dataflow research prototype machines being developed worldwide. The Dennis machine at MIT (Section 10.1) is a static dataflow multiprocessor system using VAL. The Arvind machine at MIT is a dynamic dataflow system using ID and tagged tokens (Arvind 1980) (Section 10.4).

There are other dynamic systems, such as the Manchester machine (Gurd and Watson 1980) developed in England and the Eddy system (Takahashi and Amamiya 1983) (also Section 10.3) developed in Japan. The first operational data-driven machine (DDM) was developed by Davis (1975).

In France, a dataflow multiprocessor system, LAU, was constructed with 32 bit-slice microprocessors. The LAU system is based on a single-assignment language (Syre et al. 1980).

Most of the dataflow projects emphasize run-time simultaneity at the instruction level. The performance of such fine-granularity dataflow computers could be very poor, unless one could overcome the difficulty of a high system overhead when detecting the parallelism and scheduling the available resources (Gajki et al. 1982, also in Section 10.2).

The computation granularity can be raised to high-level dataflow computing at the compound function or procedure levels, in order to overcome the high overhead problem. Furthermore, one can consider that variable resolution dataflow computations are conducted at multiple levels of computing granularity (Hwang and Su 1983; Gaudiot 1982).

This variable resolution approach demands much more in the developing efficient schemes for program partitioning, time and space complexity estimations, and dynamic adaptive resource management. The development of dataflow supercomputers is still in its infancy. With the advent of VLSI technology, functional programming languages, and high demands made for current computations, we can expect the dataflow approach to have a major role in the future.

In addition to university research efforts, there are three huge R&D programs in microelectronics and supercomputing that have been launched in the United States in recent years. The Microelectronics and Computer Technology Corp. (MCC) was established at Austin, Texas, by 12 major U.S. corporations as a nonprofit, joint venture to develop long-range research on the new generation of computers.

The Semiconductor Research Corp. (SRC) is another joint venture by 13 U.S. chip manufacturers and computer companies. The SRC, headquartered at Research Triangle Park in North Carolina, does not perform its own research; instead, it acts as the sponsoring agency overseeing research at various academic installations.

The Pentagon's Defense Advanced Research Projects Agency (DARPA) recently announced its Strategic Computing (SC) project (DARPA 1983) to push for advanced supercomputing and artificial intelligence technologies. DARPA's computer director, Robert Kahn, said: "We want some architectures that

are good for building semantic memories, memories that can hold knowledge. Other kinds of systems are good for logic processing. We want architectures that can do very rapid signal processing and structures that can handle very large amounts of data in communications."

This SC project, once completed, will significantly advance a broad base of machine intelligence technology to increase the nations security and economic strength. Potential military applications include autonomous systems, pilot's associate, and battle management.

In Japan, a national project is under way to develop a 10-Gflops computer system. This nine-year project is to be completed in 1989. Major applications of national interest to Japan include meteorology, nuclear energy, and aerodynamics, to mention a few. This project involves research and development activities in new architectures and new device technologies, and the construction and evaluation of the final system.

As regards of architecture, typical codes in the major applications fields have been collected for the analysis of parallel structure of the frequently used algorithms. Particular attention has been paid to nuclear energy software, because of the variety of algorithms involved therein. In the area of new device technologies in Japan, material and process techniques for the Josephson junction device, the high-electron-mobility transistor (HEMT) device, and the gallium arsenide (GaAs) device have been the main challenges in Japan (Kashiwagi and Miura 1983; and Stone 1984).

The rapid advent of very-large-scale integrated (VLSI) technology has created a new architectural horizon in the direct implementation of parallel algorithms in hardware. The new high-resolution lithographic technique has made possible the fabrication of 10^5 transistors in a negative channel, metal oxide semiconductor (NMOS) chip. It has been projected that by the late 1980s it will be possible to fabricate VLSI chips that contain more than 10^7 individual transistors. One such chip may be capable of more functions than one of today's large minicomputers.

The use of VLSI technology in designing high-performance multiprocessors and pipelined computing devices is currently under intensive investigation in both industrial and university environments. The multiprocessors are expected to be regularly interconnected. Pipelining makes it possible to overlap I/O devices with internal computations.

Pipelined multiprocessing is a distinct feature of most of the proposed VLSI computing structures that have been proposed in the literature. Most described VLSI arithmetic devices are for vector and matrix computations. Both globally structured arrays and modular computing networks have been suggested for signal and image processing (Hwang and Su, 1983).

Four articles are selected to provide the readers with some guidelines regarding the VLSI computing systems being developed. The article in Section 11.1 introduces a family of reconfigurable processor arrays that can implement a number of computing algorithms (Snyder 1982).

The concept of systolic arrays (H. T. Kung and Leiserson 1978) is extended to wave-front array processors in the article by S. Y. Kung (Section 11.2). Hwang and Cheng (1982) have developed a class of partitioned matrix algorithms that can be applied to develop VLSI matrix arithmetic processors (Section 11.3).

The recent article by Kung and Lam (1984) addresses the fault-tolerance issue in systolic arrays for yield enhancement in wafer scale integration (WSI) implementation. A two-level pipelined method is introduced in this paper for systolic array designs.

The three papers in Chapter 12 present different viewpoints on the future of supercomputers. The article by Treleaven and Lima (1984) assesses the relative merits of logic, dataflow, and control-flow computers. An overview to the development of the fifth-generation computers in Japan is provided by Moto-oka (1983) in Section 12.2.

The final article (Section 12.3) presents some very inspiring thoughts from Professor Lotfi Zadeh of University of California at Berkeley on scientific approaches to cope with the imprecision or fuzziness of the real world. This is of utmost importance to probe certain (AI) problems.

Zadeh considers supercomputers playing important roles in three areas: **numerical analysis, large databases,** and **knowledge engineering.** So far, supercomputers have been applied primarily to numerical analyses. The Japanese fifth-generation project is toward the development of AI-oriented supercomputers. Fuzzy sets and fuzzy logic offer initial steps to bring the computing model closer to human reasoning and eventually the use of supercomputers for knowledge engineering and intelligence applications.

Chapter 10: Dataflow Computers

*Programmability with increased performance? New strategies to
attain this goal include two approaches to data flow architecture:
data flow multiprocessors and the cell block architecture.*

Data Flow Supercomputers

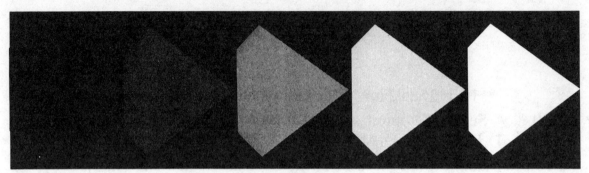

Jack B. Dennis
MIT Laboratory for Computer Science

The architects of supercomputers must meet three challenges if the next generation of machines is to find productive large-scale application to the important problems of computational physics. First, they must achieve high performance at acceptable cost. Instruction execution rates of a billion floating-point operations each second are in demand, whereas current architectures require intricate programming to attain a fraction of their potential, at best around one tenth of the goal. Brute force approaches to increase the speed of conventional architectures have reached their limit and fail to take advantage of the major recent advances in semiconductor device technology. Second, they must exploit the potential of LSI technology. Novel architectures are needed which use large numbers but only a few different types of parts, each with a high logic-to-pin ratio. In a supercomputer, most of these parts must be productive most of the time; hence the need to exploit concurrency of computation on a massive scale. Third, it must be possible to program supercomputers to exploit their performance potential. This has proven to be an enormous problem, even in the case of computations for which reasonably straightforward Fortran programs exist. Thus present supercomputer architectures have exacerbated rather than resolved the software crisis.

It appears that the objectives of improving programmability and increasing performance are in conflict, and new approaches are necessary. However, any major departure from conventional architectures based on sequential program execution requires that the whole process of program design, structure, and compilation be redone along new lines. One architecture under consideration is a multiprocessor machine made of hundreds of intercommunicating microcomputer processing elements. This architecture has attracted wide interest, but has many drawbacks; even if the processing elements had full float-ing-point capability and ran at a million instructions per second, at least one thousand would be required to attain a billion instructions per second performance. For such a number of processing elements there is no known way of permitting access to a shared memory without severe performance degradation. Similarly, no known way of arranging conventional microprocessors for synchronization or message passing allows efficient operation while exploiting fine grain parallelism in an application. And finally, there is no programming language or methodology that supports mapping application codes onto such a multiprocessor in a way that achieves high performance.

Language-based computer design can ensure the programmability of a radical architecture. In a language-based design the computer is a hardware interpreter for a specific base language, and programs to be run on the system must be expressed in this language.[1] Because future supercomputers must support massive concurrency to achieve a significant increase in performance, a base language for supercomputers must allow expression of concurrency of program execution on a large scale. Since conventional languages such as Fortran are based on a global state model of computer operation, these languages are unsuitable for the next generation of supercomputers and will eventually be abandoned for large-scale scientific computation. At present, functional or applicative programming languages and data flow models of computation are the only known foundation appropriate for a supercomputer base language. Two programming languages have been designed recently in response to the need for an applicative programming language suitable for scientific numerical computation: ID, developed at Irvine,[2] and Val, designed at MIT.[3,4]

Data flow architectures offer a possible solution to the problem of efficiently exploiting concurrency of computation on a large scale, and they are compatible with

EHO219-6/84/0000/0480$01.00 ©1980 IEEE

COMPUTER

modern concepts of program structure. Therefore, they should not suffer so much from the difficulties of programming that have hampered other approaches to highly parallel computation.

The data flow concept is a fundamentally different way of looking at instruction execution in machine-level programs—an alternative to sequential instruction execution. In a data flow computer, an instruction is ready for execution when its operands have arrived. There is no concept of control flow, and data flow computers do not have program location counters. A consequence of data-activated instruction execution is that many instructions of a data flow program may be available for execution at once. Thus, highly concurrent computation is a natural consequence of the data flow concept.

The idea of data-driven computation is old,[5,6] but only in recent years have architectural schemes with attractive anticipated performance and the capability of supporting a general level of user language been developed. Work on data-driven concepts of program structure and on the design of practical data-driven computers is now in progress in at least a dozen laboratories in the US and Europe. Several processors with data-driven instruction execution have been built, and more hardware projects are being planned. Most of this work on architectural concepts for data flow computation is based on a program representation known as data flow program graphs[7] which evolved from work of Rodriguez,[8] Adams,[9] and Karp and Miller.[10] In fact, data flow computers are a form of language-based architecture in which program graphs are the base language. As shown in Figure 1, data flow program graphs serve as a formally specified interface between system architecture on one hand and user programming language on the other. The architect's task is to define and realize a computer system that faithfully implements the formal behavior of program graphs; the language implementer's task is to translate source language programs into their equivalent as program graphs.

The techniques used to translate source language programs into data flow graphs[11] are similar to the methods used in conventional optimizing compilers to analyze the paths of data dependency in source programs. High-level programming languages for data flow computation should be designed so it is easy for the translator to identify data dependence and generate program graphs that expose parallelism. The primary sources of difficulty are unrestricted transfer of control and the "side effects" resulting from assignment to a global variable or input arguments of a procedure. Removal of these sources of difficulty not only makes concurrency easy to identify, it also improves program structure. Programs are more modular, and are easier to understand and verify. The implications of data flow for language designers are discussed by Ackerman.[12]

This article presents two architectures from the variety of schemes devised to support computations expressed as data flow graphs. First we explain data flow graphs by examples, and show how they are represented as collections of activity templates. Next we describe the basic instruction-handling mechanism used in most current projects to build prototype data flow systems. Then we develop the two contrasting architectures and discuss the reasons for their differences—in particular the different approaches to communicating information between parts of a data flow machine.

Data flow programs

A data flow program graph is made up of actors connected by arcs. One kind of actor is the operator shown in Figure 2, drawn as a circle with a function symbol written inside—in this case +, indicating addition. An operator also has input arcs and output arcs which carry tokens bearing values. The arcs define paths over which values from one actor are conveyed by tokens to other actors. Tokens are placed on and removed from the arcs of a program graph according to firing rules, which are illustrated for an operator in Figure 3. To be enabled, tokens must be present on each input arc, and there must be no token on any output arc of the actor. Any enabled actor may be fired. In the case of an operator, this means removing one token from each input arc, applying the specified function to the values carried by those tokens, and placing tokens labeled with the result value on the output arcs.

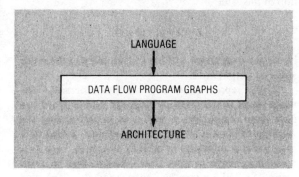

Figure 1. Program graphs as a base language.

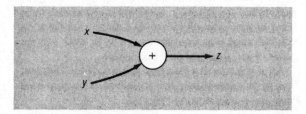

Figure 2. Data flow actor.

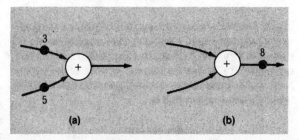

Figure 3. Firing rule: (a) before; (b) after.

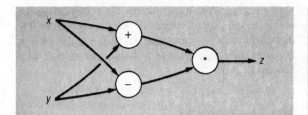

Figure 4. Interconnection of operators.

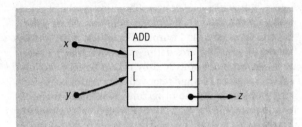

Figure 5. An activity template.

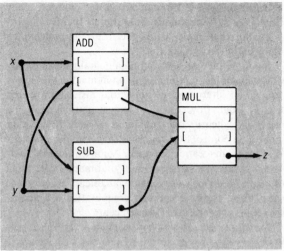

Figure 6. Configuration of activity templates for the program graph of Figure 4.

Operators may be connected as shown in Figure 4 to form program graphs. Here, presenting tokens bearing values for x and y at the two inputs will enable computation of the value

$$z = (x + y) * (x - y)$$

by the program graph, placing a token carrying the result value on output arc z.

Another representation for data flow programs—one much closer to the machine language used in prototype data flow computers—is useful in understanding the working of these machines. In this scheme, a data flow program is a collection of activity templates, each corresponding to one or more actors of a data flow program graph. An activity template corresponding to the plus operator (Figure 2) is shown in Figure 5. There are four fields: an operation code specifying the operation to be performed; two receivers, which are places waiting to be filled in with operand values; and destination fields (in this case one), which specify what is to be done with the result of the operation on the operands.

An instruction of a data flow program is the fixed portion of an activity template. It consists of the operation code and the destinations; that is,

instruction:

< opcode, destinations >

Figure 6 shows how activity templates are joined to represent a program graph, specifically the composition of operators in Figure 4. Each destination field specifies a target receiver by giving the address of some activity template and an input integer specifying which receiver of the template is the target; that is,

destination:

< address, input >

Program structures for conditionals and iteration are illustrated in Figures 7 and 8. These use two new data flow actors, switch and merge, which control the routing of data values. The switch actor sends a data input to its T or F output to match a true or false boolean control input. The merge actor forwards a data value from its T or F input according to its boolean input value. The conditional program graph and implementation in Figure 7 represent computation of

$$y: = (IF\ x > 3\ THEN\ x + 2\ ELSE\ x - 1) * 4$$

and the program graph and implementation in Figure 8 represent the iterative computation

$$WHILE\ x > 0\ DO = x - 3$$

Execution of a machine program consisting of activity templates is viewed as follows. The contents of a template activated by the presence of an operand value in each receiver take the form

operation packet:

< opcode, operands, destinations >

Such a packet specifies one result packet of the form

result packet:

< value, destination >

for each destination field of the template. Generation of a result packet, in turn, causes the value to be placed in the receiver designated by its destination field.

Note that this view of data flow computation does not explicitly honor the rule of program graphs that tokens must be absent from the output arcs of an actor for it to fire. Yet there are situations where it is attractive to use a program graph in pipelined fashion, as illustrated in Figure 9a. Here, one computation by the graph has produced the value 6 on arc z while a new computation represented

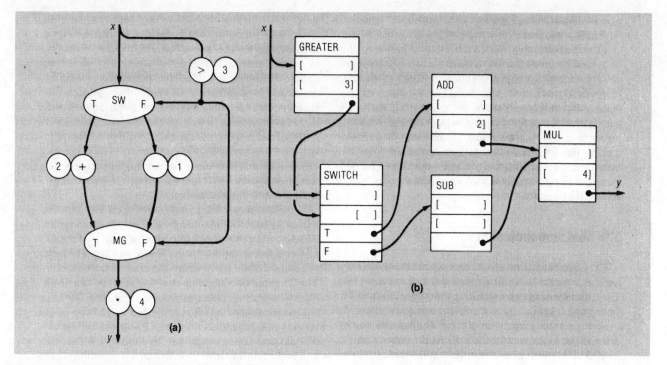

Figure 7. A conditional schema (a) and its implementation (b).

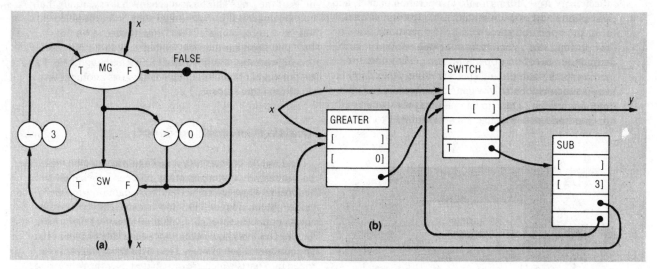

Figure 8. An iterative schema (a) and its implementation (b).

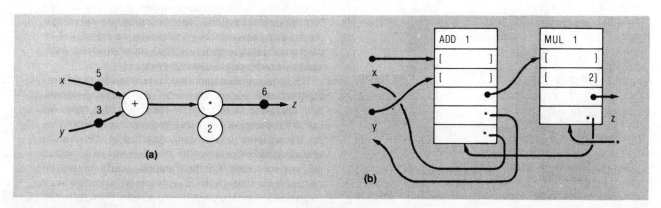

Figure 9. Pipelining in a data flow program (a) and its implementation (b).

by input values 5 and 3 on arcs x and y is ready to begin. To faithfully implement this computation, the add instruction must not be reactivated until its previous result has been used by the multiply instruction. This constraint is enforced through use of acknowledge signals generated by specially marked designations ($*$) in an activity template. Acknowledge signals, in general, are sent to the templates that supply operand values to the activity template in question (Figure 9b). The enabling rule now requires that all receivers contain values, and the required number of acknowledge signals have been received. This number (if nonzero) is written adjacent to the opcode of an activity template.

The basic mechanism

The basic instruction execution mechanism used in several current data flow projects is illustrated in Figure 10. The data flow program describing the computation to be performed is held as a collection of activity templates in the activity store. Each activity template has a unique address which is entered in the instruction queue unit (a FIFO buffer store) when the instruction is ready for execution. The fetch unit takes an instruction address from the instruction queue and reads the activity template from the activity store, forms it into an operation packet, and passes it on to the operation unit. The operation unit performs the operation specified by the operation code on the operand values, generating one result packet for each destination field of the operation packet. The update unit receives result packets and enters the values they carry into operand fields of activity templates as specified by their destination fields. The update unit also tests whether all operand and acknowledge packets required to activate the destination instruction have been received and, if so, enters the instruction address in the instruction queue. During program execution, the number of entries in the instruction queue measures the degree of concurrency present in the program. The basic mechanism of Figure 10 can exploit this potential to a limited but significant degree: once the fetch unit has sent an operation packet off to the operation unit, it may immediately read another entry from the instruction queue without waiting for the instruction previously fetched to be completely processed. Thus a continuous stream of operation packets may flow from the fetch unit to the operation unit so long as the instruction queue is not empty.

This mechanism is aptly called a circular pipeline—activity controlled by the flow of information packets traverses the ring of units leftwise. A number of packets may be flowing simultaneously in different parts of the ring on behalf of different instructions in concurrent execution. Thus the ring operates as a pipeline system with all of its units actively processing packets at once. The degree of concurrency possible is limited by the number of units on the ring and the degree of pipelining within each unit. Additional concurrency may be exploited by splitting any unit in the ring into several units which can be allocated to concurrent activities. Ultimately, the level of concurrency is limited by the capacity of the data paths connecting the units of the ring. This basic mechanism is essentially that implemented in a prototype data flow processing element built by a group at the Texas Instruments Company.[13] The same mechanism, elaborated to handle data flow procedures, was described earlier by Rumbaugh,[14] and a new project at Manchester University uses another variation of the same scheme.[15]

The data flow multiprocessor

The level of concurrency exploited may be increased enormously by connecting many processing elements of the form we have described to form a data flow multiprocessor system. Figure 11a shows many processing elements connected through a communication system, and Figure 11b shows how each processing element relates to the communication system. The data flow program is divided into parts which are distributed over the processing elements. The activity stores of the processing elements collectively realize a single large address space, so the address field of a destination may select uniquely any activity template in the system. Each processing element sends a result packet through the communication network if its destination address specifies a nonlocal activity template, and to its own update unit otherwise.

The communication network is responsible for delivering each result packet received to the processing element that holds the target activity template. This network, called a routing network, transmits each packet arriving at an input port to the output specified by information contained in the packet. The requirements of a routing network for a data flow multiprocessor differ in two important ways from those of a processor/memory switch for a conventional multiprocessor system. First, information flow in a routing network is in one direction—an im-

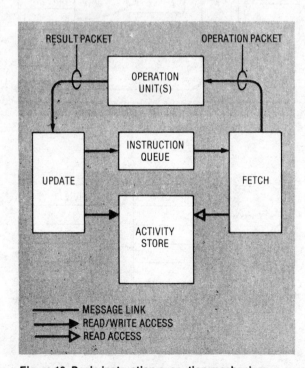

Figure 10. Basic instruction execution mechanism.

COMPUTER

mediate reply from the target unit to the originating unit is not required. Second, since each processing element holds many enabled instructions ready for processing, some delay can be tolerated in transmission of result packets without slowing down the overall rate of computation.

The crossbar switch in conventional multiprocessor systems meets requirements for immediate response and small delay by providing for signal paths from any input to any output. These paths are established on request and maintained until a reply completes a processor/memory transaction. This arrangement is needlessly expensive for a data flow multiprocessor, and a number of alternative network structures have been proposed. The ring form of communication network is used in many computer networks, and has been used by Texas Instruments to couple four processing elements in their prototype data flow computer. The drawback of the ring is that delay grows linearly with size, and there is a fixed bound on capacity.

Several groups have proposed tree-structured networks for communicating among processing elements.[16,17,18] Here, the drawback is that traffic density at the root node may be unacceptably high. Advantages of the tree are that the worst case distance between leaves grows only as $\log_2 N$ (for a binary tree), and many pairs of nodes are connected by short paths.

The packet routing network shown in Figure 12 is a structure currently attracting much attention. A routing network with N input and N output ports may be assembled from $(N/2) \log_2(N)$ units, each of which is a 2×2 router. A 2×2 router receives packets at two input ports and transmits each received packet at one of its output ports according to an address bit contained in the packet. Packets are handled first come, first served, and both output ports may be active concurrently. Delay through an $N \times N$ network increases as $\log_2 N$, and capacity rises nearly linearly with N. This form of routing network is described in Leung[19] and Tripathi and Lipovski.[20] Several related structures have been analyzed for capacity and delay.[21]

The cell block architecture

In a data flow multiprocessor (Figure 11), we noted the problem of partitioning the instructions of a program among the processing elements to concentrate communication among instructions held in the same processing element. This is advantageous because the time to transport a result packet to a nonlocal processor through the routing network will be longer (perhaps much longer) than the time to forward a result locally.

At MIT, an architecture has been proposed in response to an opposing view: each instruction is equally accessible to result packets generated by any other instruction, regardless of where they reside in the machine.[22,23] The structure of this machine is shown in Figure 13. The heart of this architecture is a large set of instruction cells, each of which holds one activity template of a data flow program. Result packets arrive at instruction cells from the distribution network. Each instruction cell sends an operation packet to the arbitration network when all operands and signals have been received. The function of the

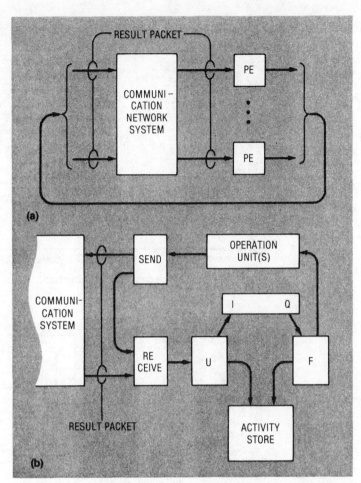

Figure 11. Data flow multiprocessor: (a) connection of many processing elements through a communication system; (b) relationship of each PE to the communication system.

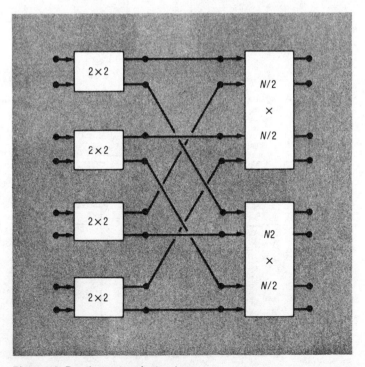

Figure 12. Routing network structure.

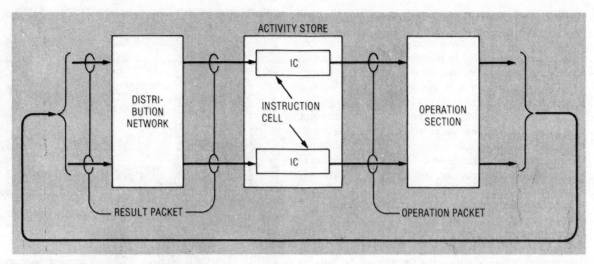

Figure 13. Genesis of the cell block architecture.

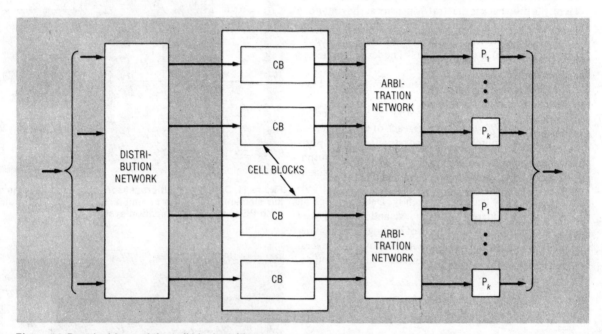

Figure 14. Practical form of the cell block architecture.

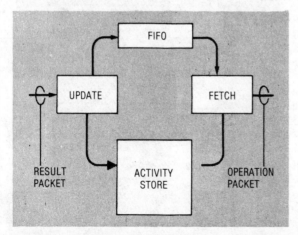

Figure 15. Cell block implementation.

operation section is to execute instructions and to forward result packets to target instructions by way of the distribution network.

The design in Figure 13 is impractical if the instruction cells are fabricated as individual physical units, since the number of devices and interconnections would be enormous. A more attractive structure is obtained if the instruction cells are grouped into blocks and each block realized as a single device. Such an instruction cell block has a single input port for result packets and a single output port for operation packets. Thus one cell block unit replaces many instruction cells and the associated portion of the distribution network. Moreover, a byte-serial format for result and operation packets further reduces the number of interconnections between cell blocks and other units.

The resulting structure is shown in Figure 14. Here, several cell blocks are served by a shared group of functional units $P_i, \ldots, P_k$. The arbitration network in each section of the machine passes each operation packet to the appropriate functional unit according to its opcode. The number of functional unit types in such a machine is likely to be small (four, for example), or just one universal functional unit type might be provided, in which case the arbitration network becomes trivial.

The relationship between the cell block architecture and the basic mechanism described earlier becomes clear when one considers how a cell block unit would be constructed. As shown in Figure 15, a cell block would include storage for activity templates, a buffer store for addresses of enabled instructions, and control units to receive result packets and transmit operation packets. These control units are functionally equivalent to the fetch and update units of the basic mechanism. The cell block differs from the basic data flow processing element in that the cell block contains no functional units, and there is no shortcut for result packets destined for successor instructions held in the same cell block.

Discussion and conclusions

In the cell block architecture, communication of a result packet from one instruction to its successor is equally easy (or equally difficult, depending on your point of view) regardless of how the two instructions are placed within the entire activity store of the machine. Thus the programmer need not be concerned that his program might run slowly due to an unfortunate distribution of instructions in the activity store address space. In fact, a random allocation of instructions may prove to be adequate.

In the data flow multiprocessor, communication between two instructions is much quicker if these instructions are allocated to the same processing element. Thus a program may run much faster if its instructions are clustered to minimize communication traffic between clusters and each cluster is allocated to one processing element. Since it will be handling significantly less packet traffic, the communication network of the data flow multiprocessor will be simpler and less expensive than the distribution network in the cell block architecture. Whether the cost reduction justifies the additional programming effort is a matter of debate, contingent on the area of application, the technology of fabrication, and the time frame under consideration.

Although the routing networks in the two forms of data flow processor have a much more favorable growth of logic complexity ($N \log N$) with increasing size than the switching networks of conventional multiprocessor systems, their growth is still more than linear. Moreover, in all suggested physical structures for $N \times N$ routing networks, the complexity as measured by total wire length grows as $O(N^2)$. This fact shows that interconnection complexity still places limits on the size of practical multiunit systems which support universal intercommunication. If we need still larger systems, it appears we must settle for arrangements of units that only support communication with immediate neighbors.

The advantage data flow architectures have over other approaches to high-performance computation is that the scheduling and synchronization of concurrent activities are built in at the hardware level, enabling each instruction execution to be treated as an independent concurrent action. This allows efficient fine grain parallelism, which is precluded when the synchronization and scheduling functions are realized in software or microcode. Furthermore, there are well-defined rules for translating high-level programs into data flow machine code.

What are the prospects for data flow supercomputers? Machines based on either of the two architectures presented in this paper could be built today. A machine having up to 512 processing elements or cell blocks seems feasible. For example, a 4×4 router for packets, each sent as a series of 8-bit bytes, could be fabricated as a 100-pin LSI device, and fewer than one thousand of these devices could interconnect 512 processing elements or cell blocks. If each processing unit could operate at two million instructions per second, the goal of a billion instructions per second would be achieved.

Yet there are problems to be solved and issues to be addressed. It is difficult to see how data flow computers could support programs written in Fortran without restrictions on and careful tailoring of the code. Study is just beginning on applicative languages like Val and ID.[24,25] These promise solutions to the problems of mapping high-level programs into machine-level programs that effectively utilize machine resources, but much remains to be done. Creative research is needed to handle data structures in a manner consistent with principles of data flow computation. These are among the problems under study in our data flow project at MIT. ■

Acknowledgment

This paper is based on research supported by the Lawrence Livermore National Laboratory of the University of California under contract 8545403.

References

1. J.B. Dennis, "On the Design and Specification of a Common Base Language," *Proc. Symp. Computers and Automata,* Polytechnic Press, Polytechnic Institute of Brooklyn, Apr. 1971, pp. 47-74.

2. Arvind, K.P. Gostelow, and W. Plouffe, *An Asynchronous Programming Language and Computing Machine,* Dept. of Information and Computer Science, University of California, Irvine, Technical Report 114a, Dec. 1978, 97 pp.

3. W.B. Ackerman and J.B. Dennis, *VAL: A Value Oriented Algorithmic Language, Preliminary Reference Manual,* Laboratory for Computer Science, MIT, Technical Report TR-218, June 1979, 80 pp.

4. J.R. McGraw, *Data Flow Computing: The VAL Language,* submitted for publication.

5. R.R. Seeber and A.B. Lindquist, "Associative Logic for Highly Parallel Systems," *AFIPS Conf. Proc,* 1963, pp. 489-493.

6. R.M. Shapiro, H. Saint, and D.L. Presberg, *Representation of Algorithms as Cyclic Partial Orderings,* Applied Data Research, Wakefield, Mass., Report CA-7112-2711, Dec. 1971.

7. J.B. Dennis, "First Version of a Data Flow Procedure Language," *Lecture Notes in Computer Sci.,* Vol. 19, Springer-Verlag, 1974, pp. 362-376.

8. J.E. Rodriguez, *A Graph Model for Parallel Computation,* Laboratory for Computer Science, MIT, Technical Report TR-64, Sept. 1969, 120 pp.

9. D.A. Adams, *A Computation Model With Data Flow Sequencing,* Computer Science Dept., School of Humanities and Sciences, Stanford University, Technical Report CS 117, Dec. 1968, 130 pp.

10. R.M. Karp and R.E. Miller, "Properties of a Model for Parallel Computations: Determinacy, Termination, Queueing," *SIAM J. Applied Math.,* Vol. 14, Nov. 1966, pp. 1390-1411.

11. J.D. Brock and L.B. Montz, "Translation and Optimization of Data Flow Programs," *Proc. 1979 Int'l Conf. on Parallel Processing,* Bellaire, Mich., Aug. 1979, pp. 46-54.

12. W.B. Ackerman, "Data Flow Languages," *AFIPS Conf. Proc.,* Vol. 48, 1979 NCC, New York, June 1979, pp. 1087-1095.

13. M. Cornish, private communication, Texas Instruments Corp., Austin, Tex.

14. J.E. Rumbaugh, "A Data Flow Multiprocessor," *IEEE Trans. Computers,* Vol. C-26, No. 2, Feb. 1977, pp. 138-146.

15. I. Watson and J. Gurd, "A Prototype Data Flow Computer With Token Labelling," *AFIPS Conf. Proc.,* 1979 NCC, New York, June 1979, pp. 623-628.

16. A. Davis, "A Data Flow Evaluation System Based on the Concept of Recursive Locality," *AFIPS Conf. Proc.,* Vol. 48, 1979 NCC, New York, June 1979, pp. 1079-1086.

17. A. Despain and D. Patterson, "X-Tree: A Tree Structured Multi-Processor Computer Architecture," *Proc. Fifth Annual Symp. Computer Architecture,* Apr. 1978, pp. 144-150.

18. R.M. Keller, G. Lindstrom, and S.S. Patil, "A Loosely-Coupled Applicative Multi-processing System," *AFIPS Conf. Proc.,* 1979 NCC, New York, June 1979, pp. 613-622.

19. C. Leung, *On a Design Methodology for Packet Communication Architectures Based on a Hardware Design Language,* submitted for publication.

20. A.R. Tripathi and G.J. Lopovski, "Packet Switching in Banyan Networks," *Proc. Sixth Annual Symp. Computer Architecture,* Apr. 1979, pp. 160-167.

21. G.A. Boughton, *Routing Networks in Packet Communication Architectures,* MS Thesis, Dept. of Electrical Engineering and Computer Science, MIT, June 1978, 93 pp.

22. J.B. Dennis and D.P. Misunas, "A Preliminary Architecture for a Basic Data-Flow Processor," *Proc. Second Annual Symp. Computer Architecture,* Houston, Tex., Jan. 1975, pp. 126-132.

23. J.B. Dennis, C.K.C. Leung, and D.P. Misunas, *A Highly Parallel Processor Using a Data Flow Machine Language,* Laboratory for Computer Science, MIT, CSG Memo 134-1, June 1979, 33 pp.

24. Arvind and R.E. Bryant, "Design Considerations for a Partial Differential Equation Machine," *Proc. Computer Information Exchange Meeting,* Livermore, Calif., Sept. 1979, pp. 94-102.

25. L. Montz, *Safety and Optimization Transformation for Data Flow Programs,* MS Thesis, MIT, Dept. of Electrical Engineering and Computer Science, Feb. 1980, 77 pp.

Jack B. Dennis, professor of electrical engineering and computer science at MIT, leads the Computation Structures Group of MIT's Laboratory for Computer Science, which is developing language-based computer system architectures that exploit high levels of concurrency through use of data flow principles. Associated with the laboratory since its inception in 1963 as Project MAC, Dennis assisted in the specification of advanced computer hardware for timesharing and was responsible for the development of one of the earliest timeshared computer installations.

Dennis received his DSc degree in electrical engineering from MIT in 1958. He is a member of Eta Kappa Nu, Tau Beta Pi, and Sigma Xi, and is a fellow of the IEEE.

*Due to their simplicity and strong appeal to intuition,
data flow techniques attract a great deal of attention.
Other alternatives, however, offer more hope for the future.*

A Second Opinion
on Data Flow Machines
and Languages

D. D. Gajski, D. A. Padua, and D. J. Kuck
University of Illinois

R. H. Kuhn
Northwestern University

Reprinted from *Computer*, February 1982, pages 58-70. Copyright © 1982 by
The Institute of Electrical and Electronics Engineers, Inc.

Simultaneity is a key to high-speed computation.
Assuming hardware components of a given speed, it is the
only remaining consideration in achieving raw speed.
Simultaneity can be shackled by dependences, however,
and years of hardware and software work have been
devoted to understanding the types of dependences and
how they can be obeyed or removed from a computation.

Dependence types. There are three types of dependence[1]: data, control, and resource. The first two arise in
programs and the third in machines. Therefore, exact
definitions depend on the type of language and machine
under consideration, although many nearly universal dependences exist.

We will discuss three types of *data dependence*[1] (see
Kuck et al.[2] for a fourth type): flow dependence, output
dependence, and antidependence. *Flow dependence* exists from the computation to the use of a variable. *Output
dependence* exists between two subsequent computations
of the same variable. *Antidependence* exists from the use
of a variable to its next computation. These three types
ensure that the intended values are, in fact, used in a computation.

Control dependence types vary from language to language. For example, loop dependences exist from a loop
header to each statement inside the loop, conditional
dependences exist from an IF to its THEN and ELSE
parts, and GOTO dependences exist from a GOTO to its
destination.

Resource dependences arise when programs are compiled for and executed on a particular machine. For example, the existence of an adder and a multiplier that can be

sequenced simultaneously by the control unit allows these
two (but no more) arithmetic operations to be executed at
once. A four-way interleaved memory allows simultaneous access to four words, but no more. A single program
counter, a single arithmetic unit, and a single memory led
to the so-called von Neumann machine, and these resource dependences were reflected in the definition of
Fortran and other high-level programming languages.

Dependence observation. Given a problem to solve on
some machine, it is useful to observe dependences at five
points in the selection, preparation, and execution of an
algorithm. These are in (1) algorithm choice, (2) programming, (3) compiling, (4) instruction processing (control
unit), and (5) instruction execution (processor, memory,
interconnection).

A given algorithm has certain built-in data dependences. For example, in certain iterative computations,
an iterate must be computed before it can be used. However, other algorithms that solve the same problem might
have less sequential dependence. For example, many
highly concurrent algorithms to solve linear recurrences
are known,[1] and the use of any of these relaxes the sequentiality between iterations.

Once an algorithm has been selected, the programming
language and programming style used to express the
algorithm can introduce additional dependences, as well
as encode its inherent dependences. For example, a complex expression could be computed once, then stored, and
subsequently used in several other expressions. This introduces flow dependences. Usually, programmers are
not concerned with the number or type of dependences

they introduce. Some languages or styles prevent or try to avoid certain types of dependences in programs. For example, the single-assignment approach advocated in data flow languages avoids output and antidependences.

Compilers can remove and/or introduce dependences. For example, a block of assignment statements in any language can easily be compiled into a form that obeys the single-assignment rule. In fact, all three types of data dependences can be removed automatically to produce a completely independent set of assignment statements[2]; statement substitution is used to remove flow dependences. On the other hand, two array variables must not have a dependence, but a compiler that examines only array names and not subscripts will introduce a spurious dependence. For example, if $1 \leq I \leq n$, there is no dependence between $A[2I]$ and $A[2I-1]$. This will be missed if the check is only for the array name A.

Consider the instruction processing carried out by a control unit. Assumptions about data, control, and resource dependence are always built into the hardware of a control unit. For example, the traditional von Neumann machine assumes that machine instructions are processed one at a time, with some simultaneity possible in multiple address instruction formats. Multifunction machines such as the CDC 6600 have look-ahead control units that examine two or more instructions and check dependences at runtime. If data and control dependences in the instruction stream allow and resources are available, the control unit can sequence several instructions at once.

More recent machines (e.g., the CDC Cyber 205 and the Burroughs BSP) have machine instructions that can express array operations such as vector add or recurrence operations such as inner product. If the compiler recognizes such an operation (because it is, for example, programmed sequentially or expressed in a vector extension to a sequential language), it can generate a single machine instruction that carries it out by using a fast, highly parallel algorithm. In parallel or pipeline machines, the control unit must access chunks of the operands, process them, and store chunks of the result until the operation is finished. In the case of recurrence operations, the control unit must carry out a sequence of steps. These might correspond to a complex dependence graph in which simultaneity was maximized when the machine was designed. For example, a vectorized inner product could be a vector multiply followed by a summation tree. Thus, an entire small loop from a sequential program has all of its dependences mapped onto the control-unit hardware for fast runtime sequencing.

The line between instruction processing and instruction execution is somewhat blurred across various types of computers. In machines with array instruction sets, the control unit knows, by virtue of the way in which its array instructions were implemented, exactly how to sequence its memory, processor, and interconnection network parts to carry out an operation. In other types of machines, the control unit decodes instructions, processes addresses, and decides that an instruction can be issued. The individual steps, however, are not executed until all of the dependences of the instructions are satisfied. This principle is used in the Scoreboard of the CDC 6600,[3] the Tomasulo algorithm of the IBM 360/91,[4]

and in current data flow proposals. The point is that the processor, memory, and interconnection networks themselves can ensure satisfaction of all dependences. For example, if there is a great deal of randomness in a program arising, perhaps, from conditional statements or irregular subscripts, the intuitive notion is that little can be preplanned and that execution time-dependence handling is, in fact, necessary for fast computation.

Article overview. In this article we undertake two tasks. The first is to sketch the principles and practices of data flow computation and to point out a number of shortcomings of this approach to high-speed computation. The second is to sketch an alternative that leads to high-speed computation through higher-level use of dependence graphs.

The data flow approach and our alternative are roughly characterized in Figure 1. The data flow approach usually begins with a special programming language, which researchers hope can be easily compiled into a dependence graph. (Ordinary languages can also be used.) The problem then becomes one of efficiently mapping this onto a machine that has decentralized control hardware. Often, this machine is capable of exploiting substantially less parallelism than exists in the program because it lacks the hardware to cause the dependence graph constraints to be followed as quickly as possible at runtime. That is, queues of partially completed computations are relied upon to keep the machine busy, and the queue lengths absorb some of the parallelism of the program.

Our approach can begin with either a data flow language or an ordinary programming language. A program is first put into a standard form (normalized). Next, a dependence graph is generated by, for example, analysis of array subscripts. Then some arcs are removed by program transformation, and some nodes and arcs are abstracted* because they represent high-level constructs for

---

*Abstraction here refers to the process of reducing a subgraph to a higher-level node.

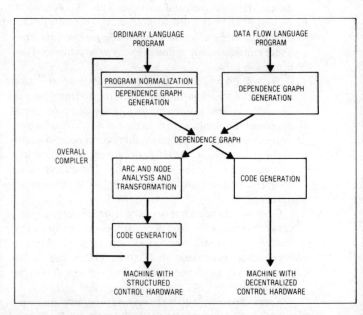

Figure 1. Comparison of methods.

which special algorithms (instructions) can be used. Finally, code generation produces high-level machine instructions that contain much of the dependence structure of the original program, but transformed for high-speed evaluation. The machine that executes the generated code can have a degree of simultaneity that is matched to the program and still execute it efficiently, because most dependence testing need not be done at runtime. However, this approach relies on compilation techniques more powerful than those usually assumed by data flow people.

Other sections of this article investigate the principles of data flow architecture and proposed data flow languages.

Data flow principles

In contrast to the sequential, one-instruction-at-a-time, memory cell semantics of the von Neumann model, the data flow model of computation is based on two principles:

(1) *Asynchrony.* All operations executed when and only when the required operands are available.

(2) *Functionality.* All operations are functions; that is, there are no side effects.

The first denotes an execution mechanism in which data values pass through data flow graphs as tokens and an operation is triggered whenever all input tokens are present at a node in the graph. The second principle implies that any two enabled operations can be executed in either order or concurrently.

Dynamic parallelism. Even when there is data dependence between operations of the same iteration of a loop, there is nothing to stop further iterations from proceeding, even though one iteration is not totally completed. This causes tokens to accumulate on certain arcs of the data flow graph. It is then no longer possible to declare a node executable by the presence of any two tokens on its input, as they might belong to totally different parts of the computation. There are five possible solutions to this problem:

(1) *The use of a re-entrant graph is prohibited.* That is, each stage of the iteration must be described by a separate graph. This solution obviously requires large amounts of program storage. It also requires dynamic code generation if the loop's iteration depth is only known at runtime. Both of these deficiencies can result in significant overhead in practical systems.

(2) *The use of a re-entrant graph is allowed, but an iteration is not allowed to start before the previous one has finished.* This approach does not allow for parallelism between iterations and requires extra instructions or hardware to test the completion of an iteration. It is used in the LAU system.[5]

(3) *The use of a data flow graph is limited by allowing only one token to reside on each arc of the graph at any time.* This is accomplished by allowing an operation to be executable only when all its input tokens are present and no tokens exist on its output arc. This approach, which implies sequential but pipelined use of the data flow

graph, allows exploitation of more parallelism than do the previous two solutions. Pipelining is implemented through the use of acknowledge signals, which are returned to the nodes in the graph that generated those values by the nodes that consumed the values.[6,7] These acknowledge signals approximately double the number of arcs in the corresponding data flow graph, and therefore double the traffic through the data flow machine.

(4) *The tokens are assumed to carry their index and iteration level as a label.* This label is usually called *color*. A node is executable only if all input tokens have the same color. The labeling method permits the use of pure static code and enables maximum use of any parallelism that exists in the problem specification. This is clearly at the cost of the extra information that must be carried by each token and the extra nodes (instructions) for labeling and delabeling.[8,9] The penalty of this approach is obviously extra time for calculating labels, or extra hardware (silicon area) if calculation is concurrent.

(5) *The tokens are queued on arcs in order of their arrival.* This solution can deliver as much parallelism as the labeling approach, but requires large queues, which are very costly.

To compare the performance of data flow machines that use these five approaches, consider the program in Figure 2a. Assume that division takes three time units, multiplication two, and addition one. The hypothetical data flow machine has four processing units, each capable of executing any operation. We idealize the machine by assuming that memory and interconnection delays are zero.

Our example program dictates a certain order of execution, which is determined by the simplified data flow program in Figure 2b. Obviously, the critical path is $a_1, b_1, c_1, c_2, \ldots, c_8$, which results in a lower bound on execution of 13 time units.

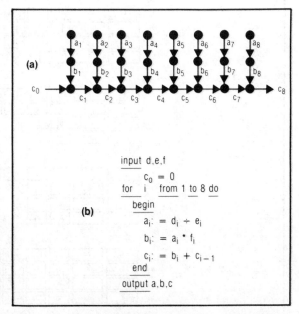

```
input d,e,f
        c_0 = 0
for  i   from 1 to 8 do
     begin
        a_i: = d_i ÷ e_i
        b_i: = a_i * f_i
        c_i: = b_i + c_i-1
     end
output a,b,c
```

Figure 2. A nonsense example: (a) program; (b) simplified data flow graph.

COMPUTER

Since there is one division, one multiplication, and one addition in each iteration of the loop, it will take $6 \times 8 = 48$ time units (Figure 3a) to execute the complete loop when using the one-iteration-at-a-time strategy described in approach (2), above. This is basically a sequential execution, and one processor would suffice. In practice, the computation is distributed over all four processors, but the utilization of processors remains at $12/48 = 0.25$.

The one-token-per-arc strategy (3) practically turns into pipelining of the block of assignment statements inside the loop, as shown in Figure 3b. Execution time is determined by the longest operation (division) in the loop. Thus, $3 \times 8 + 3 = 27$ time units are necessary, with utilization at $12/27 = 0.44$. Approaches (1), (4), and (5) are similar. They achieve the best performance and utilization, as shown in Figure 3c. They need only 14 time units, with utilization equal to $12/14 = 0.86$. However, a random-scheduling strategy (followed in many data flow architecture proposals) can result in less than optimal execution, as shown in Figure 3d, where 18 time units were needed to finish the computation. The detection of possible critical paths and scheduling along these paths is a problem that none of the proposed data flow machines have solved.

For comparison, a possible execution on a vector machine with a vectorizing compiler is shown in Figure 3e. A mediocre vectorizing compiler would detect that the first and second statements in the loop can be vectorized. The execution time is 18 and the utilization $12/18 = 0.66$. A good vectorizing compiler would detect the recurrence in the third statement, substitute a different algorithm, and lower the execution time to 14 with a utilization of one, as shown in Figure 3f. Note that recurrences arise frequently in ordinary programs.[10]

It is obvious from this simple example that the sequential machine offers the worst performance and the data flow machine with labeled tokens the best. Pipelined and vector machines are somewhere between those extremes, although the vector machine with a good optimizing compiler was competitive with the data flow machine in our example. Remember, however, that our models are gross oversimplifications of real machines. Since there are no hard facts on performance of data flow machines, it remains to be seen whether the overhead in token labeling, data storage, and instruction communication will lower their theoretical upper bound on performance.

Performance under a low degree of parallelism. The data flow graph can be considered the machine language of a data flow machine. Each node of the graph represents an instruction, and the arcs pointing from each node can be thought of as the addresses of instructions receiving the

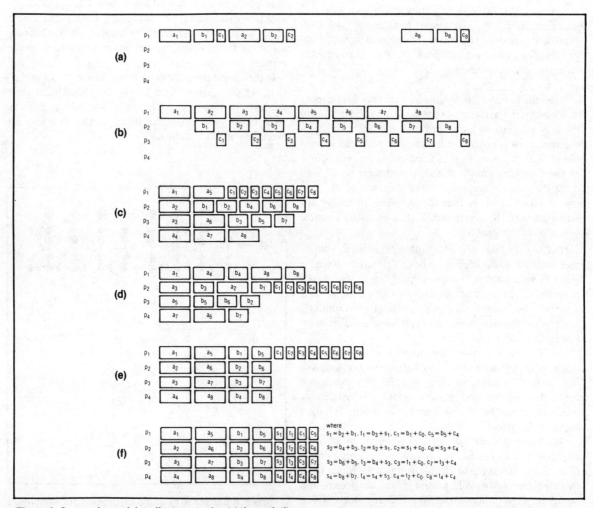

Figure 3. Comparison of data flow strategies (a) through (f).

result. Roughly speaking, a data flow machine consists of four components: an instruction memory that contains all instructions in the data flow graph, a set of processing units that perform the operations specified by each instruction, an arbitration network that carries instruction packets to appropriate processing units, and a distribution network that carries the result packets back to the instruction memory. Obviously, the instruction memory can be partitioned into several modules, to match the bandwidth of the processing units and communication networks. We assume also that one unit of time is needed to pass through each of the four components of our data flow model.

In contrast to the data flow model, the von Neumann model consists of a central processing unit and a memory. The central processing unit has a general-purpose register file and an arithmetic-logic unit. Each register-to-register operation takes one unit of time, as do fetch and store from memory.

To crudely compare the performance and the program size of these two models, we considered several programs that, like the one given by Arvind, Kathail, and Pingali,[11] integrate function f from a to b over n intervals of size h by the trapezoidal rule. We concluded that the data flow model apparently requires more instructions than the von Neumann model. This code inefficiency stems from two principles of the data flow model:

(1) *Distributed control.* Each datum (or path in the graph) is controlled individually. There are several separate SWITCH instructions (at least one for each variable assignment inside the body of a loop) that correspond to one BRANCH instruction in the von Neumann model. Similarly, several independent MERGE instructions substitute for one JUMP instruction.

(2) *No explicit storage.* Since only values are passed from one instruction to the other, values that do not change during the computation from one iteration to the other must circulate in one way or another through the system.

These redundancies lower the expected performance when the degree of parallelism (the number of operations executable in parallel) is equal to or greater than the ideal rate (the maximum possible number of operations executed concurrently).

In terms of raw speed on small programs, the von Neumann model requires less time. This performance advantage is the consequence of two things:

(1) *Instruction pipelining.* In von Neumann computers, the fetch, decode address generation, and execution phases of an instruction are allowed to overlap. Thus, each instruction averages only one time unit in a reasonably sequential code. On the other hand, the data flow model does not allow pipelining on the critical path. That is, each instruction must complete before the new one—which uses the result from the previous one—can start.

(2) *Local storage.* A data flow machine is basically a memory-to-memory machine, since there is no concept of storage. It usually helps to keep all the input parameters to a subroutine in high-speed, general-purpose registers, as in our examples. This lack of locality severely degrades the performance of the data flow machines on programs with a low degree of parallelism.

One might argue that although the data flow processor is slower in raw speed, it is faster overall because it contains many overlapped processing units operating in parallel. Still, the degree of parallelism must be taken into account. In a crude approximation appropriate to this case, the data flow machine can be thought of as a long pipeline. To keep the pipeline saturated, the degree of parallelism must be larger than the number of stages in the pipeline. Under low parallelism, the pipeline is not saturated for a long period of time and serious degradation of performance occurs. For comparison, Cray-1 computers have functional unit pipelines with five to eight stages in which register fetches are included. Data flow machines have pipelines many times longer. They include functional units, communication networks, and instruction memory. Therefore, we can expect them to perform poorly under low parallelism. If features for parallelism exploitation such as token labeling and array management are added, the performance under low parallelism becomes even worse.

Data flow machines require a parallelism of several hundred independent instructions to saturate the pipeline. Arvind et al.[11] have computed, for example, that for a data flow machine with 100-microsecond interprocessor communication time and 64 processing units, each of which performs a floating-point operation in 10 microseconds, the degree of parallelism to keep the machine saturated is 640. To date, the only programs with such a high degree of parallelism are computationally intensive numerical calculations that operate on large arrays of data. Unfortunately, data flow machines do not handle arrays of data very efficiently because of their emphasis on fine-grain, operation-level concurrency.

Structures storage. If tokens are allowed to carry vectors, arrays, and other structures in general, the result is a large transmission and storage overhead. This is particularly the case when operators modify only a small part (possibly only one element) of the whole structure. For this reason, Dennis[6] suggested that all structures be represented by a finite, acyclic, directed graph having one or more root nodes arranged so that each node can be reached over some directed path from some root node (that is, a forest of trees with possibly common nodes).

Arrays are stored as trees, with array elements at the leaves. For example, an array $A = [a_{i,j}]$, $1 \leq i,j \leq 3$ can be stored as a ternary tree. Obviously, trees of any order can be used for storing arrays.

According to the functionality principle of the data flow model, a data structure must be free of any side-effects. An easy way to accomplish this is to forbid any sharing or overlapping of structures. Since every structure would have its own private area of memory, there would be no side effects. However, this is prohibitively expensive since it requires each structure to be completely copied whenever its value is duplicated. The solution proposed by Dennis is to share the structures whenever possible and use the reference count technique. Each node of a structure has a reference count, which is the total number of pointers to that node from other nodes and tokens in the data flow program. For example, if a copy B of the array A is created, the pointer for B points to the same root node as the pointer for A (Figure 4a).

When an APPEND operator is used, it is necessary to copy all nodes with a reference count greater than one, as well as their successors, on the directed path from the root to the selected node. For example, if an array B' is obtained from B by setting $a_{23} = 0$, the structure in Figure 4b will be generated. Similarly, B'' can be obtained from B' by setting $a_{33} = 0$ (Figure 4c). The above two operations, setting $a_{23} = 0$ and $a_{33} = 0$, are completely independent of each other but cannot be executed concurrently; by the asynchrony principle of the data flow model, concurrent execution could result in two different structures, B' and B''' (Figure 4d), from which it is very difficult to obtain B''.

Here we see that a simple operation, such as setting a row or a column in a matrix to zero, requires sequential execution, which in turn significantly degrades performance for large structures. The performance degradation can come from two independent mechanisms used in this scheme. The first mechanism uses the reference count to share data. Therefore, there will be many unnecessary accesses to the memory in order to change the reference count without using data. This occurs for all operations that create or destroy pointers. For example, when a SWITCH operator destroys a token, the count must be decreased. The second mechanism uses tree structures to store arrays. If the order of the tree is small, large arrays will be stored as trees of considerable depth and therefore many memory references will be needed to access an array element. On the other hand, there is an unnecessary data transmission and wasted space due to excessively large memory blocks when the order is large.

To avoid the excessive storage demand and slow access time due to the functional semantics of the data structure operations, Arvind and Thomas[12] proposed I-structures, array-like data structures whose storage is allocated before expressions to produce them are invoked. Since an I-structure construction is not strictly ordered (to improve parallelism), it is possible that part of a program might attempt to read an element before that element's creation. Therefore, a presence bit is associated with every element, and an attempt to read an empty location causes deferral of the read operation. Unfortunately, when the element is finally created all deferred reads must be executed. Checking for those deferred reads on every write slows down the access of I-structures in comparison with the simple von Neumann model and a language based on it, in which the programmer has some control over storage.

Basically, two observations can be made:

(1) Instead of sending data in only one direction—from place of creation to place of consumption—a request (address in the von Neumann model) must be sent in one direction, with the I-structure value (data) returning in the other direction. This unnecessarily increases traffic through the system.

(2) Since memory is allocated before it is used, the problem of optimally distributing I-structures over many processors to minimize traffic through the networks has been introduced. This problem, well known as the *memory contention problem*, has plagued designers of vector machines and multiprocessors for years.

In summary, the proposed I-structures, although expected to solve data storage and access problems more efficiently, are a small step back toward the von Neumann model.

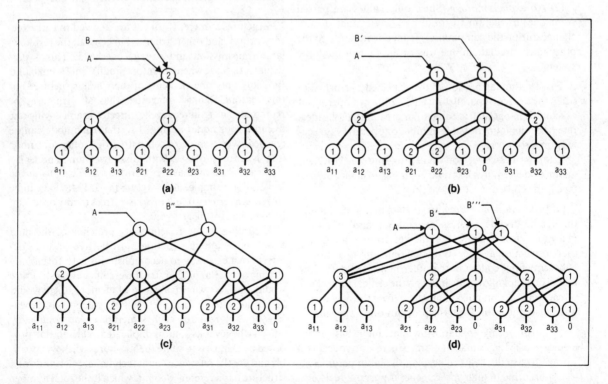

Figure 4. Storage scheme for a 3 × 3 array.

Data flow languages

The success of any computer, data flow or otherwise, depends on the quality of its programming languages. Data flow machines demand high-level languages, since graphs, their machine language, are not an appropriate programming medium; they are error-prone and hard to manipulate.

Three high-level language classes have been considered by data flow researchers. The first is the *imperative* class. For instance, the Texas Instruments group considered the use of a modified ASC Fortran compiler for their data flow machine.[13] Compiler techniques for the translation of imperative high-level languages into data flow graphic languages have also been studied at Iowa State University.[14] The second is the *functional* class. By functional languages, we mean those resembling pure Lisp, which is based on Church's lambda calculus, and Backus' FP, which is based on Curry's combinatory logic. This second class is now being studied in a data flow context at the University of Utah.[15]

The third class—our focus here—consists of the so-called *data flow languages,* which are designed with data flow machines in mind. The most notable examples are Id,[9,12] LAU,[5] and Val.[16] The syntax of these languages is essentially that of imperative languages. For example, all data flow languages include IF and LOOP statements. On the other hand, their semantics are basically that of functional languages.

Below, focus on the two characteristics that set data flow languages apart: the functional semantics of the language and the implicit expression of parallelism. Data flow languages have many other characteristics, which are not unique. For example, the freedom from side effects and the locality of effects have been mentioned as being of paramount importance,[17] and we agree. However, some imperative languages possess these characteristics.

Functional semantics. A consequence of this first characteristic is that in data flow languages variables stand for values and not for memory locations. Imperative languages like Fortran, PL/I, and Pascal allow programmers to be aware of and have some control over the primary memory allocation for both programs and data. Thus, in PL/I we can classify variables as static or dynamic, and memory can be explicitly requested and freed.

In data flow and functional languages, on the other hand, programmers deal only with values. These languages do not allow the explicit control of memory allocation, relying instead on mechanisms like garbage collection to keep memory utilization at a reasonable level.

Functional semantics offers parallel processing the advantage of a simplified translation process. Thus, data flow languages are free of side effects. This makes it possible to translate subroutines separately, without unnecessarily constraining parallelism. Again, freedom from side effects is not unique to data flow languages; imperative languages can also be side-effect free.

Another welcome consequence of functional semantics is the single assignment rule.[18] Thanks to this rule,

parallelism is less constrained by anti dependences and output dependences than it is in conventional imperative languages. Consider, for example, the following Fortran program:

$$
\begin{array}{ll}
1 & A = D + 1 \\
2 & B = A + 1 \\
3 & A = 0.
\end{array}
$$

It is easy to see that statement 3 cannot be executed until statement 2 fetches $A;$ that is, statement 3 is antidependent on statement 2. In a data flow language, the use of A in statement 3 is not valid; a different variable must be used in place of A to allow execution of statements 1 and 2 to be concurrent with statement 3.

On the other hand, a compiler can very easily rid imperative language programs of antidependences and output dependences by using the simple transformation techniques of renaming and expansion. Renaming, as its name indicates, changes variable names to avoid antidependences and output dependences. This transformation would replace A in statement 3 with some other variable. To understand expansion, consider the following Fortran loop:

$$
\begin{array}{lll}
\text{DO} & 10 & I = 1, N \\
& X = A(I) + 1 & \\
10 & B(I) = X**2 &
\end{array}
$$

The different iterations of this loop cannot be executed in parallel, since there is only one memory location corresponding to X and because N locations would be needed for all iterations to proceed in parallel. After expansion, the scalar variable X would be replaced by a vector of N elements, and the occurrences of X would be replaced by $X(I)$. This would allow parallelism, at the expense of using more memory. We have found these techniques, as implemented in the Parafrase system,[2] to be successful almost all the time.

Some data flow researchers have been unaware of this fact. This has led them to believe that functional semantics makes a big difference in terms of efficient parallel object code, but this does not seem to be true.

Consider the following quotation from Arvind.[19]

A straightforward Fortran program would do this in the following way.

```
C   X IS AN ARRAY OF N + 2 ELEMENTS
C   X(1) AND X(N + 2) REMAIN CONSTANT
    N1   = N + 1
    DO   20 K  = 1, KMAX
    DO   10 I  = 2, N1
    Y(I) = (X(I - 1) + (X(I) + X(I + 1))/3
10  CONTINUE
    DO   15 I  = 2, N1
    X(I)  = Y(I)
15  CONTINUE
20  CONTINUE                              (1)
```

A compiler can easily generate good code for a multiple processor machine from the above program. Even if a programmer is clever, and avoids copying array Y into X by switching back and forth between X and Y, a vectorizing compiler will be able to deal with it effectively. However, if array X is large, and a programmer decides to avoid using another array Y altogether, the following program may result:

COMPUTER

```
      N1  =  N + 1
      DO  20 K  = 1, KMAX
      T1  =  X(1)
      T2  =  X(2)
      DO   10 I  = 2, N1
      X(I) = , (T1 + T2 + X(I + 1))/3.
      T1  =  T2
      T2  =  X(I + 1)
   10 CONTINUE
   20 CONTINUE                              (2)
```

It would be extremely difficult for a compiler to detect a transformation in which all the elements of array X are relaxed simultaneously.

When the last Fortran program is transformed by Parafrase, the simple expansion technique leads to the following program. It can be effectively executed in parallel (loops 2, 3, and 4 are detected by Parafrase as vector operations).

```
      N1  =  N + 1
      DO  1    I  = 1, KMAX
          T1(I)  =  X(1)
          T2(I)  =  X(2)
          DO  2  J  = 1, N1
   2          T2(J + 1)  =  X(J + 2)
          DO  3  J  = 1, N1
   3          T1(J + 1)  =  T2(J)
          DO  4  J  = 1, N1
              X(J + 1)  =  (T1(J) + T2(J) + X(J + 2))/3
   4 CONTINUE
```

The functional semantics might have advantages besides those related to parallel processing. For example, data flow languages might help produce programs that are easier to verify and understand than those in imperative languages. But so far, no scientific evidence has been produced to either confirm or deny such advantages.

Our main objection to functional semantics is that it denies the programmer direct control of memory allocation. Thus, the success of data flow languages depends on how efficiently garbage collection can be implemented and on the specific compiler algorithms used to control memory allocation.

Implicit parallelism. The second characteristic is that parallelism is often implicit in data flow languages. Thus, a data flow language compiler must compute the flow dependences and use them to generate parallel machine code. Implicit parallelism is a worthy goal; it can save the programmer tedious, error-prone tasks. However, we would like to make some observations on compiler techniques and on the need for explicit parallelism.

Compiler techniques. The algorithms used by a data flow compiler determine how much implicit parallelism can be exploited. Therefore, implicit parallelism and compilers must be discussed together. The data flow literature discusses two compiler techniques: flow dependence computation and loop unraveling.[9] These techniques must be developed further if data flow compilers are to successfully exploit implicit parallelism.

Flow dependence is computed by using variable names only. It is very important, however, to look at subscripts, as well. Consider, for example, the Fortran program in Figure 5a. A compiler that ignores the subscripts will not detect the parallelism in this program. Furthermore, the application of loop unraveling when the target machine is a data flow multiprocessor requires some study. Now consider the Fortran program in Figure 5b. If the different iterations of the inner loop are distributed across the data flow processors, a speed-up on the order of N could be obtained. However, if the distribution is done on the basis of the outer loop, and M is much smaller than the number of processors, the speed-up will be substantially smaller.

There are other important techniques that are not discussed in the data flow literature. These include techniques for handling memory allocation and deallocation for code and data (see "functional semantics," above) and techniques that define the storage layout of arrays when the target machine is a multiprocessor.

Explicit vs. implicit parallelism. Implicit parallelism is not sufficient for a powerful programming language, for at least two reasons. The first is the spurious flow dependences mentioned above, and the second is the need to express in summary form the parallel evaluation of recurrences.

Spurious flow dependences are due to the limitations of the compiler. Some can be removed by improving the compiler algorithms; others might be impossible to remove. The discussion of Figure 5a, above, provides an example of how to remove limitations by improving the compiler algorithm. An example in which the limitations cannot be removed is shown in Figure 5c. The Fortran program in this figure is the same as the one in Figure 5a, except that 1 is replaced by $W(K)$. Since $W(K)$ is not known at compile time, it is not possible to determine how or even if this program can be executed in parallel.

Parallel execution is possible in cases like the program in Figure 5c, but only through explicit parallelism. The programmer might know that $W(K)$ is always less than some small value and therefore know that the wavefront algorithm[20] can be applied successfully. In the LAU language and in Val, the programmer could handle this by using the FORALL construct or the EXPAND constructs. However, it is not possible to handle this problem in Id, which has no form of explicit parallelism.

```
(a)    DO  11  I = 1, N
           DO  11  J = 1, N
               A(I,J) = A(I-1,J) + A(I,J-1)

(b)    DO  12  I = 1, M
           DO  12  J = 1, N
               A(I,J) = A(I-1,J) + 1

(c)    DO  13  I = 1, N
           DO  13  J = 1, N
               A(I,J) = A(I-W(K),J) + A(I,J-W(K))
```

Figure 5. Fortran programs: (a) requiring subscript analysis for parallelism detection; (b) with inner loop parallel and outer loop sequential; (c) with parallelism that cannot be detected by a compiler.

It should be clear from the previous example that data flow languages need better ways to express general forms of parallelism. It is not clear what those constructs must be, and it is not clear that these constructs can be nicely incorporated in a data flow language.

Only the designers of Val have recognized the need to express recurrences. However, they provide only reduction-type recurrences such as sums and minimums. Other types of recurrences arise often enough to require their inclusion in a parallel programming language.[10] Examples include general arithmetic recurrences and boolean recurrences originating from IF statements inside loops.

Comments. It has been claimed that data flow languages have some advantages over imperative languages for parallel processing and programming in general. Functional semantics, however, is not a real advantage, since well-known compiler techniques applied to a good imperative language allow equal exploitation of parallelism. Also, implicit parallelism requires translation techniques as complicated as those used to extract parallelism from imperative languages. In fact, most of the techniques used in Parafrase[2,21] to translate Fortran programs into parallel programs can be used without change in data flow compilers.

Certainly, data flow languages have nice features, such as freedom from side effects, which are very advantageous for the compiler writer and programmer. However, these do not justify the effort required for the introduction of a totally new class of programming languages. Clearly, imperative languages with these characteristics can be designed.

The immensity of introducing a new language class becomes clear when we consider all the work required before data flow languages stand a chance of becoming common tools. This work must start with syntax; data flow languages are verbose. This verbosity might be a consequence of the syntactic similarity between data flow and imperative languages. The language designers, striving to make the semantic difference clear, introduced unnecessary keywords like NEW in Id, and cumbersome expressions like $Y[I:X(I)]$ in Val to denote an array Y with the Ith element replaced by $X(I)$.

Work is also necessary in the area of explicit parallelism. Data flow languages need constructs to specify parallelism in a general form and to specify general forms of recurrences. Finally, the functional semantics could be a source of difficulty, since it implies that memory allocation is not a concern of the programmer.

Conclusion

In all high-speed computer systems, it is important to achieve two goals:

(1) the discovery of as much potential simultaneity as possible in the computations to be performed; and

(2) the delivery at runtime of as much of the potential simultaneity as possible.

We have discussed various aspects of these points and argued that data flow researchers have done little to further our understanding of the first. It would appear that their contributions have been more concentrated on the second point, but there are a number of shortcomings in data flow ideas in this regard. It is possible to design much better machines than those available today—supersystems, in fact—but by following a bottom-up approach, the data flow people have made it difficult to reach their goal. Data flow notions are quite appealing at the scalar level, but array, recurrence, and other high-level operations become difficult to manage.

In pursuit of the first goal, data flow researchers have introduced the concept of value instead of location into high-level languages. In principle, this was a praiseworthy move. From the compiler point of view, however, there is little improvement over imperative languages. Explicit parallelism and nontrivial compiler techniques are still needed, mostly because of array variables. I-structures represent an attempt to free data flow languages from these two concerns.[12] They essentially allow the flow dependences between array element operations to be automatically satisfied at runtime. It is unlikely, however, that such a mechanism will efficiently solve many of the problems associated with flow dependence between arrays.

We question whether programming language design, as practiced by data flow researchers, is germane to the task of high-speed computer design. We are not prepared to make a pronouncement on programming languages for parallel processing; both applicative and imperative languages have advantages and drawbacks. We do, however, have some questions. First, are data flow languages marketable? To date, the high-speed computer market has been dominated by conservatism and software compatibility. Can data flow languages, as currently proposed, overcome this conservatism? Second, will data flow languages enhance programmer productivity? (The emphasis in imperative programming language design has also been toward increasing programmer productivity.) Although data flow researchers have made some claims to this effect, they remain, to our knowledge, unsubstantiated.

An alternative approach. A much better approach to successful high-speed machine design begins by acknowledging that the programming interface to a high-speed machine requires more latitude than is allowed by current data flow architectures. The following alternative incorporates that latitude. We define *compound functions* with the following properties:

• They represent computational tasks for which good speed-up can be achieved (in most cases) by using multiple processors.

• The compound operations that implement them allow simple control of a substantial amount of hardware in parallel.

• Fast compiler algorithms for deriving them from programs can be written in ordinary sequential programming languages.

Six such compound functions are discussed in Gajski et al.[22]: array operations, linear recurrences, FORALL loops, pipeline loops, blocks of assignment statements, and compound conditional expressions.

We can view a program as a dependence graph connecting compound function nodes. A function dispatch unit must schedule the execution of the compound function nodes. Since the times required by the nodes can be determined at runtime, the function dispatch unit might be considered a data flow machine. We call this a *dependence-driven computation* because several types of data and control dependence are used in determining the execution sequence.

As we return to the second goal of high-speed computer systems—the delivery of simultaneity at runtime—our criticisms of data flow processing should be put in perspective. High-speed computer architecture, in general, has many flaws and weaknesses: Pipeline processors often suffer from long start-up times, and parallel or multiprocessors can waste processor cycles because of mismatches between machine size and problem size. It is very difficult to design a multipurpose machine that is well-matched to a wide range of computations.

The scope of the problem is such that an appeal to engineering intuition should be made at this point. Such an appeal yields three observations:

(1) Dependences should be attacked on all fronts, subject to system design constraints.

(2) Designers should be guided by previously successful designs, when such designs are consistent with the overall constraints.

(3) Deterministic analysis and system operation should be favored over probabilistic analysis and system operation.

With regard to point 1, some data flow researchers have ignored explicit parallelism, and most have considered compiling techniques only superficially. With regard to point 2, data flow researchers often claim that an entirely new approach to high-speed computation is needed. The frequent occurrence of such constructs as array and recurrence operations, however, justifies the exploitation of well-known designs for conflict-free memory access and centrally synchronized global instructions. Adherence to point 3 can guarantee rather than maximize the likelihood of good system performance. In regard to all these aspects, data flow researchers tend not to exploit the global regularity in the problem because the focus is on a small granularity.

Summary of arguments. The following is a brief summary of the arguments against the data flow approach with respect to the principal architectural components in a high-speed computer system.

First, consider main memory array access, which is by far the biggest bandwidth load in many computations. Well-known methods can achieve conflict-free array access[23]; they have been demonstrated in the Burroughs BSP.[24] While data flow people claim to be trying to eliminate the von Neumann bottleneck[25] between CPU and memory, they have created several new bottlenecks of their own. Array access conflicts arise due to asynchrony, shared data cannot be accessed in parallel, unnecessary memory accesses can arise, and tree-like storage of arrays can lead to multiple accesses per array element. Furthermore, data flow programs tend to waste memory space for programs and arrays.

In the area of interconnection networks, data flow machines with nontrivial parallelism (only four-processor machines have been built) will have the same types of problems found in other architectures. No interesting new results in this area have come from data flow researchers; the problem remains an important one.

With respect to processing speeds, data flow architectures seem to inherently deliver less than maximum speed-ups. Control unit pipelining and instruction look-ahead cannot be exploited to the degree they are in other architectures. Furthermore, since data paths contain very long pipelines, data flow machines suffer from the same long pipeline-filling problems as other pipelined processors, and one must settle for less than maximum speed-up. Thus, the performance is weak for programs with low parallelism.

Several practical aspects of data flow machines are worrisome. To date, no one has proposed a way to handle input/output operations, although they seem to be solvable, and debugging data flow programs could be difficult. We have already remarked on the questionable marketability of a data flow processor. As far as we know, there is no difference between the ability to implement a highly parallel data flow processor (with its global arbitration and distribution networks) using present VLSI technology, and the ability to implement a more conventional machine. Finally, there has been no discussion of the diagnosability and maintainability of data flow machines. These could be difficult areas for machines without program counters or deterministic behavior.

We have tried to level pointed criticism directly at data flow principles or at least at a majority of data flow systems. Our task was complicated by several factors. The design of a computing system from language to machine covers a lot of ground, and some researchers gloss over some aspects of the problem. Several groups have independently interpreted data flow principles with different design goals, and these goals are not always spelled out. Finally, a paper design is rarely as good as a practical implementation. Hence, we have had a difficult time discerning exactly what the data flow principles are.

Although we have attempted to point out weaknesses, we should add that data flow does have a good deal of potential. In small-scale parallel systems, data flow principles have been successfully demonstrated. When simultaneity is low, irregular, and runtime-dependent, data flow might be the architecture of choice. In very large-scale parallel systems, data flow principles still show some potential for high-level control. When several compound functions are to be executed in parallel, data flow offers some software engineering benefits, such as elimination of side effects.

It is in medium-scale parallel systems that data flow has little chance of success. Pipelined, parallel, and multiprocessor systems are all effective in this range. For data flow processing to become established here, its inherent inefficiencies must be overcome.

Most data flow researchers are engaged at too low a level of abstraction in dealing with dependence graphs and their relations to machines. They have placed much importance on language design issues that are not always inherently tied to their architecture. While they sometimes imply a radically new approach to high-speed computation, they are plagued by its standard problems. ∎

Acknowledgment

We are in debt to Arvind, who provided help in many ways during the writing of this article. Furthermore, we want to acknowledge Burton J. Smith and the anonymous referees whose constructive comments greatly improved the article. Finally, we thank Vivian Alsip for the high-quality job of typing and retyping the manuscript.

This work was supported in part by the National Science Foundation under Grants US NSF MCS76-81686 and MCS80-01561 and the US Department of Energy under Grant US DOE DE-AC02-81ER10822.

References

1. D. J. Kuck, *The Structure of Computers and Computations,* Vol. I, John Wiley & Sons, New York, 1978.

2. D. J. Kuck, R. H. Kuhn, D. A. Padua, B. Leasure, and M. Wolfe, "Dependence Graphs and Compiler Optimizations," *Proc. 8th ACM Symp Principles Programming Languages,* Jan. 1981, pp. 207-218.

3. J. E. Thornton, *Design of a Computer, The Control Data 6600,* Scott, Foresman and Co., Glenview, Ill., 1970.

4. R. M. Tomasulo, "An Efficient Algorithm for Exploiting Multiple Arithmetic Units," *IBM J. Research and Development,* Vol. 11, No. 1, Jan. 1967, pp. 25-33.

5. D. Conte, N. Hifdi, and J. C. Syre, "The Data Driven LAU Multiprocessor System: Results and Perspectives," *Proc. IFIP Congress,* 1980.

6. J. B. Dennis, "First Version of a Data Flow Procedure Language," *Lecture Notes in Computer Science,* Vol. 19, Springer-Verlag, 1974, pp. 362-376.

7. J. B. Dennis, "Data Flow Supercomputers," *Computer,* Vol. 13, No. 11, Nov. 1980, pp. 48-56.

8. I. Watson and J. Gurd, "A Practical Data Flow Computer," *Computer,* this issue.

9. Arvind, K. P. Gostelow, and W. E. Plouffe, *An Asynchronous Programming Language and Computing Machine,* Dept. of Information and Computer Science Report TR 114a, University of California, Irvine, Dec. 1978.

10. D. J. Kuck, "Parallel Processing of Ordinary Programs," in *Advances in Computers,* Vol. 15, M. Rubinoff and M. C. Yovits, eds., Academic Press, New York, 1976, pp. 119-179.

11. Arvind, V. Kathail, and K. Pingali, *A Data Flow Architecture with Tagged Tokens,* Laboratory for Computer Science, Technical Memo 174, MIT, Cambridge, Mass., Sept. 1980.

12. Arvind and R. H. Thomas, *I-Structures: An Efficient Data Type for Functional Languages,* Laboratory for Computer Science, Technical Memo 178, MIT, Cambridge, Mass., Sept. 1980.

13. J. C. Jensen, "Basic Program Representation in the Texas Instruments Data Flow Test Bed Compiler," unpublished memo, Texas Instruments, Inc., Jan. 1980.

14. S. J. Allan and A. E. Oldehoeft, "A Flow Analysis Procedure for the Translation of High Level Languages to a Data Flow Language", *Proc. Int'l Conf. Parallel Processing,* Aug. 1979, pp. 26-34.

15. R. M. Keller, B. Jayaraman, D. Rose, and G. Lindstrom, *FGL Programmer's Guide,* Dept. of Computer Science AMPS Technical Memo 1, University of Utah, Salt Lake City, Utah, July 1980.

16. W. B. Ackerman and J. B. Dennis, *VAL—A Value-Oriented Algorithmic Language, Preliminary Reference Manual,* Laboratory for Computer Science Technical Report 218, MIT, Cambridge, Mass., June 1979.

17. W. B. Ackerman, "Data Flow Languages," *Computer,* this issue.

18. L. G. Tesler and H. J. Enea, "A Language Design for Concurrent Processes," *AFIPS Conf. Proc.,* Vol. 32, 1968 SJCC, pp. 403-408.

19. Arvind, "Decomposing a Program for Multiple Processor Systems," *Proc. Int'l Conf. Parallel Processing,* Aug. 1980, pp. 7-16.

20. R. H. Kuhn, *Optimization and Interconnection Complexity for: Parallel Processors, Single-Stage Networks, and Decision Trees,* PhD thesis, Dept. of Computer Science Report 80-1009, University of Illinois, Urbana-Champaign, Ill., Feb. 1980.

21. D. A. Padua, D. J. Kuck, and D. H. Lawrie, "High-Speed Multiprocessors and Compilation Techniques," *IEEE Trans. Computers,* Vol. C-29, No. 9, Sept. 1980, pp. 763-776.

22. D. D. Gajski, D. J. Kuck, and D. A. Padua, "Dependence Driven Computation," *Proc. Compcon Spring,* Feb. 1981, pp. 168-172.

23. P. P. Budnik and D. J. Kuck, "The Organization and Use of Parallel Memories," *IEEE Trans. Computers,* Vol. C-20, No. 12, Dec. 1971, pp. 1566-1569.

24. D. Lawrie and C. Vora, "The Prime Memory System for Array Access," submitted for publication, 1980.

25. J. Backus, "Can Programming be Liberated from the von Neumann Style? A Functional Style and Its Algebra of Programs," *Comm. ACM,* Vol. 21, No. 8, Aug. 1978, pp. 613-641.

Daniel D. Gajski is an associate professor in the Department of Computer Science at the University of Illinois, Urbana-Champaign. Before joining the university in 1978, he had 10 years of industrial experience in digital circuits, switching systems, supercomputer design, and VLSI structures. His research interests are in computer system design, algorithm design for supercomputers, hardware and silicon compilers, and design automation. He received the Dipl. Ing. and MS degrees in electrical engineering from the University of Zagreb, Yugoslavia, and the PhD in computer and information sciences from the University of Pennsylvania.

David A. Padua is Professor Agregado at the Universidad Simón Bolívar in Venezuela. From 1979 to 1981, he was a visiting assistant professor at the University of Illinois.

He received the degree of Licenciado en Computación from the Universidad Central de Venezuela in 1973 and a PhD in computer science from the University of Illinois in 1979.

David J. Kuck is a professor in the Department of Computer Science at the University of Illinois, Urbana-Champaign. He joined the department in 1965. Currently, his research interests are in the coherent design of hardware and software systems. This includes the development of the Parafrase system, a program transformation facility for array and multiprocessor machines.

Kuck has served as an editor for a number of professional journals; among his publications is *The Structure of Computers and Computations, Vol. 1.* He has also consulted with many computer manufacturers and users and is the founder and president of Kuck and Associates, Inc., an architecture and optimizing compiler company.

Kuck received the BSEE degree from the University of Michigan, Ann Arbor, in 1959, and the MS and PhD degrees from Northwestern University in 1960 and 1963.

Robert H. Kuhn is an assistant professor at Northwestern University in the Department of Electrical Engineering and Computer Science. His interests are in machine organization and VLSI design. He is currently on the editorial board of *Computer* and is a member of the ACM and IEEE.

Kuhn obtained his PhD in computer science at the University of Illinois in 1980 and received a master's degree in computer science from the University of Connecticut in 1976. At Illinois, he worked with D. J. Kuck on vectorizing compilers for pipelined machines and parallel computer organization.

A DATA FLOW PROCESSOR ARRAY SYSTEM : DESIGN AND ANALYSIS

Naohisa TAKAHASHI and Makoto AMAMIYA

Musashino Electrical Communication Laboratory
Nippon Telegraph and Telephone Public Corporation
3-9-11 Midoricho Musashino-shi Tokyo 180 Japan

Abstract

This paper presents the architecture of a
highly parallel processor array system which
executes programs by means of a data driven control
mechanism. The data driven control mechanism makes
it easy to construct an MIMD (multiple instruction
stream and multiple data stream) system, since it
unifies inter-processor data transfer and
intra-processor execution control. The design
philosophy of the data flow processor array system
presented in this paper is to achieve high
performance by adapting a system structure to
operational characteristics of application
programs, and also to attain flexibility through
executing instructions based on a data driven
mechanism.

The operational characteristics of the
proposed system are analyzed using a probability
model of the system behavior. Comparing the
analytical results with the simulation results
through an experimental hardware system, the
results of the analysis clarify the principal
effectiveness of the proposed system. This system
can achieve high operation rates and is neither
sensitive to inter-processor communication delay
nor sensitive to system load imbalance.

1. Introduction

There is an urgent need for a super-high speed
computer (e.g. one to ten Giga FLOPS) to calculate
large-scale scientific problems, such as
aerodynamics, plasma physics and other problems
[1,2]. It is necessary to develop highly parallel
machines like processor array systems.

In conventional processor array systems, such
as ILLIAC IV [3], it is difficult to obtain high
performance for various types of problems. The
main reason is the control mechanism gap between
inter-PE (processing element) data transfer control
and intra-PE execution control. That is, the
inter-PE data transfer and inter-PE synchronization

are controlled based on the data driven concept,
while intra-PE execution is controlled by a
pre-defined sequential (imperative) program.

The data flow machine, on the other hand, is
expected to solve such problems, since it can
exploit parallelism among instructions without any
explicit synchronization control [4,8,9,10].

This paper provides an alternative approach to
construct a data flow machine, a data flow
processor array system, whose major application
domain is large-scale scientific calculations. The
data flow processor array system presented in this
paper is designed to achieve high performance by
adapting a system structure to operational
characteristics of application programs, while
attaining flexibility through executing
instructions based on a data driven control
mechanism.

The operational characteristics of the
proposed system are analyzed using a probability
model of the system behavior. Then, the analytical
results are compared with the simulation results
through an experimental hardware system. These
analysis and simulation results clarify the
principal effectiveness of the data flow processor
array architecture.

2. Basic design

2.1 Design philosophy

The basic structure of the data flow processor
array system is a two dimensional processor array.
The data flow concept is adopted in execution
control of each PE so as to implement a highly
parallel MIMD system. The reason why the data flow
concept is adopted for execution control in each PE
is that the data flow control makes it possible to
unify inter-PE data transfer and intra-PE execution
control. The array structure for inter-PE
connections reduces network cost, which is a
serious problem in data flow machine architecture.

In the following, problems in the conventional
parallel processor architecture are discussed from
the viewpoint of performance and flexibility, both
of which are important factors in parallel
processing system design.

(1) SIMD machines and pipeline machines
In an SIMD machine, such as ILLIAC IV [3], and
a pipeline processor, such as CRAY I [6],
conceptually, the same operations are applied to a
large amount of data in parallel. If the parallel
execution part is explicitly described using

do-loop-like ~~statement~~ in Fortran or its extended
version, the compiler can detect it and generate
efficient machine codes. Only a few types of
parallelism, however, can be described and detected
automatically by compiler. Furthermore, it is
difficult to write such a program as simplified
operations to be applied to multiple data.

(2) Conventional MIMD machines

Conventional MIMD machines are computer
complex consisting of many von Neumann type
sequential processors. Their programs are written
in languages which can support the asynchronous
multi-process control description. In the MIMD
machine, therefore, parallel execution is described
in terms of asynchronous processes. As such
languages are designed in a general framework, the
MIMD machine can execute a larger number of
different types of parallel programs. However, it
is difficult to achieve high performance in
parallel computations, due to the overhead in
process synchronization. So that, it is necessary
to make each process body larger in order to reduce
the process switching overhead. As a result, it is
difficult to obtain a high degree of parallelism,
because of the sequential execution in each
process.

(3) Data flow machines in general framework

One of the good points in data flow machines
is that programmers need not pay attention to the
physical structure of the machine or to the
mechanism for detecting the parallel execution
part, since the machine can exploit parallelism
maximally according to the data dependency
structure of the given program. Several efforts
are taken so as to realize this merit in the
machine organization [8,9,14]. It is especially
important to reduce its network cost, data
communication overhead, and resource allocation and
scheduling overhead, when the data flow machine is
designed as a special purpose high performance
machine.

These design factors are considered from the
viewpoint of trade-off between system performance
and programming ease. In large scale scientific
calculations, the overhead in conventional MIMD
machines and general purpose dataflow machines is
serious. On the other hand, SIMD machines are not
appropriate for programming ease and flexibility.

The philosophy in designing the data flow
processor array system is as follows.

(1) Array or mesh structure, in which parallel
structure is inherent, is the underlying common
structure in scientific calculations. Therefore,
it is natural to construct the machine by
connecting each PE in an array structure, in the
sense of reducing both the network cost and
inter-PE communication overhead. Furthermore, data
identification mechanism, such as token labeling,
which is inevitable in data flow machines, is
simplified by using static resource allocation.
Static resource allocation means that the parallel
program body which computes each mesh point is
allocated statically to the predefined PE.

(2) By using the data driven controls mechanism in
each PE, it is possible to unify the control of
execution within a parallel body, inter parallel
body communication and synchronization, and dynamic

resource (number cruncher) allocation to each
parallel body. As multiprocess control may be
simplified by the use of the data driven control
concept, all of the controls stated above are
realized by the enabled instruction firing control.
The overhead involved in process management in
conventional MIMD machines is absorbed in primitive
hardware mechanism. Furthermore, due to the
pipelined processing among hardware modules within
a PE, inter-PE data communication control is
overlapped with the calculations in number
crunchers,

2.2 Logical representation of data flow program
(1) Language hierarchy
Application programs are written in high-level
language Valid-N. They are compiled into
intermediate codes represented in an abstract data
flow graph, as shown in Figs. 1 and 2.
Intermediate codes are then transformed into
machine codes, which are represented in primitive
data flow graph. Features for each representation
level are as follows.

(a) High-level functional language Valid-N [5,10]
Valid-N is a numerical version of Valid, which
is a functional language for data flow machines.
The basic design philosophy is that Valid semantics
imposes a functional programming concept, while its
syntax offers programmers the conventions to write
programs in Algol style. Further description for
Valid is found in paper [10].

```
-- multiplication of two complex numbers
c_multiply : function (a,b,c,d)
             return(real,real,real,real)
= {x=a*c-b*d;
   y=a*d+b*c;
   abs=sqrt(x**2+y**2;
   arg=arctan(y/x);
   return(x,y,abs,arg)}
```

Fig. 1. A Valid program example

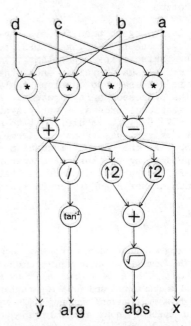

Fig. 2. An abstract data flow graph example.

502

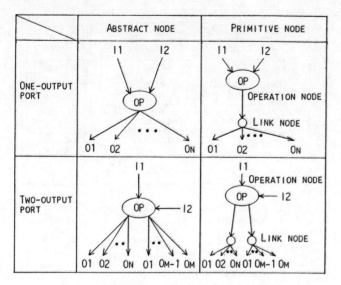

Fig. 3. Abstract and primitive nodes.

(b) Abstract data flow graph

Abstract data flow graphs consist of abstract nodes and arcs. Abstract nodes represent operations and arcs define the data dependency between two abstract nodes. Abstract nodes have at most two input ports and at most two output ports. In case of two output ports, only one of them is selected according to the input value (switch nodes). An arbitrary number of arcs can be connected to an output port.

(c) Primitive data flow graph

Each node in abstract data flow graphs is divided into two types of primitive nodes, an operation-node and a link-node, as shown in Fig. 3. A link node makes it possible to transfer an output value to multiple nodes with no extra copy instructions, while an operation node has only one destination name.

Operation-node and link-node are defined as follows.

```
operation-node
    == label:<operation-name,
        attribute-of-operand1
        [,attribute-of-operand2],
        link-node1 [,link-node2]>
link-node
    == label:<destination-1,..., destination-m>
destination-i
    == <operation-node, input-port-number>
```

Here, the paired symbol [and] means that the enclosed part may be omitted. If an operation-node is a one-operand type, attribute-of-operand2 is omitted. If the operation is branching control, link-node1 is selected as true case destination and link-node2 is selected as false case destination. Link-node2 is omitted, in all of the operations, except for branching control operations. Attribute-of-operand specifies whether the operand data is invariant or variant. When it is invariant, the operand data are used in common among many execution environment. Loop invariant data, for example, are used in all phases of a loop body. Such invariant data are held in the operand memory during the loop execution, while variant data disappear once they are used to execute operation nodes. This loop invariant control reduces the execution time [7]. Link-node

destinations are specified by operation-node name and an input port number which tells whether the operand is 1st operand or 2nd operand of the operation node.

(2) Data identification and coloring mechanism

All data have a "color", which represents their execution environment so as to allow more than one token to be travelling on an arc. In order to realize highly distributed control mechanism, it is important to decentralize the coloring control. It is also necessary to mechanize the coloring control so as to extract maximal parallelism to the extent that resources allow.

This system uses mixed strategy with static coloring and dynamic coloring. In static coloring, execution environments are predefined and a unique color is assigned to each of them. In dynamic coloring, colors are assigned to each environment dynamically. An execution environment is represented by a (color) name which has the following structure.

```
Execution environment name
    == <parallel-body-name, loop-count,
        instantiation-name>
```

The coloring mechanisms for each field of the execution environment name are as follows.

(a) Parallel body name

An m dimensional array index (I1, I2; ... ,Im), written in a high-level language is translated into one dimensional logical index LI, which represents a parallel body name. A parallel body is created for each of the logical array elements. Before execution, logical parallel bodies are allocated to the PEs according to several mapping strategies. For example, parallel body LI is allocated to the PE i of i = LI mod N (N is the number of PEs). The PE name (PEname) and physical parallel body name (pbn), which identify an allocated PE and array element within the PE, are given by a function "map",

$$(PEname, \ pbn) \ = \ map(D,LI).$$

Here, D consists of a mapping specification code and array-size.

(b) Loop count

Loop counts make it possible to execute several loop phases concurrently and to reduce the number of synchronizing operations. Such a loop computation mechanism is shown in Fig. 4. If the loop count field has n bits, then $2^{**}n$ loop bodies may be executed in parallel.

The Lin operator located in the loop body entrance is a gate operator which passes an initial value only when all data in the loop body have flowed out. In case of the nested loop, initial values for an inner loop are serialized by means of signal S0 and S. The signal S0, which is sent from the entrance of the outer loop, makes it possible to pass the first initial value. The signal S, which is generated at the end of the inner loop, makes it possible to pass the other initial values sequentially. Loop count is initialized to zero when the initial value is flowed into the loop body, then incremented (with Lup operation) every time the new iteration phase is activated until loop count overflow occurs (in modulo $2^{**}n$). When loop count overflow has occured, all output data for Lup operations are synchronized using and-gates. The Lout operator located in the loop

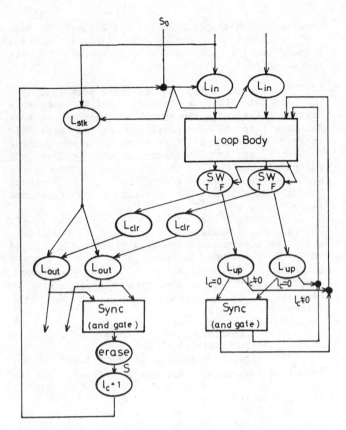

Fig. 4. Loop computation mechanism.

body exit replaces loop count with that for the outer environment, which the Lstk operator has extracted upon the entry of this loop and transmitted to the Lout operator.

(c) Instantiation name

Instantiation-name field identifies each activated function. Instantiation names are predetermined at compile time (i.e. statically) based on the caller-callee function relationship analysis. This static instantiation name assignment strategy imposes a constraint on the function call flexibility, e.g. a general recursive call is prohibited. This constraint, however, causes no problem in the application domain in this system .

2.3 Processing element structure

Each PE is a circular pipeline, consisting of Instruction memory section, Operand memory section, Operation section and Communication section, as shown in Fig. 5. Each section operates as follows.

(1) Instruction memory section

Instruction memory stores operation-nodes. On the arrival of each operand packet, the instruction memory controller fetches its operation-node from the instruction memory, and sends both the fetched instruction and operand data to the Operand memory section.

(2) Operand memory section

Operand memory stores operand data for two-operand type instructions. If the arrived operand is an operand for a two-operand type operation, the operand memory controller searches

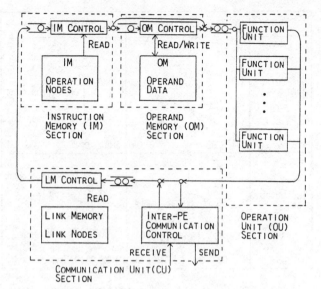

Fig. 5. Data flow processing element structure.

for its paired operand associatively. When the paired operand is found, an instruction packet is constructed and sent to the Operation section. When no paired operand is found, the arrived operand data is stored in the operand memory with a key attached.

The environment name and operation-node name are used as a key for associative search, except for the operation-node with loop-invariant, in which the loop-count field in environment name is not used as the key because the invariant data is used in common among all loop phase executions. If the arrived operand data is an operand of the one-operand operation, the instruction packet is directly constructed.

(3) Operation section

Operation section, which consists of several function units including number crunchers, executes several instruction packets in parallel. The execution results (result packets) are sent to the Communication section.

(4) Communication section

Communication section consists of Link memory and Inter-PE communication controller. Inter-PE communication controller sends result packets to Link memory or to other PEs according to the calculated destination. Communication controller also receives result packets from other PEs and transmits them to Link memory of its own PE. Link memory stores link-nodes. The link memory controller constructs operand packets. The same number of operand packets as that for the destined operation nodes, which is specified in the Link memory, are copied and sent to the instruction memory.

Result packets, operand packets and instruction packets have the following structure.
Result packet
    == <control-information,
        execution-environment-name,
        link-node-name, value>
Operand packet
    == <control-information,
        execution-environment-name,
        operation-node-name, value>

Instruction packet
     == <execution-environment-name,
          operation-name,
          link-node-name, value1 [, value2]>
Here, control-information designates a system
control packet, which means system operations such
as loading programs and erasing data.

3. Performance Evaluation

The operational characteristics of the
proposed system are analyzed using a probability
model of the system behavior. Then, the analytical
results are compared with the simulation results
through an experimental hardware system[11,15].

3.1 Performance analysis based on a probability model
(1) Analysis model
In the following analysis, a set of
operations, which have no data dependencies and are
executable in parallel, is called a step. Each
step is counted according to the execution order.
The number of operations in step i is called the
degree of parallelism in step i and is represented
by Pi.

In order to simplify the analysis, the
following characteristics are assumed for data flow
programs in a PE.
(P-1) The probability density function $g(Pi)$ for
the parameter Pi, which is assumed to be 2-Erlang
distribution with average P, is given as follows.
$$g(Pi) = \begin{cases} (2/P) * Pi * \exp(-2*Pi/P) & (Pi > 0) \\ 0 & (Pi < 0) \end{cases} \quad (3-1)$$
(P-2) The number of two-operand operations, $N2i$,
and one-operand operations, $N1i$, in step i are
given as $N2i=U2*Pi$ and $N1i=(1-U2)*Pi$ for all i by
defining the ratio of two operand operations to one
operand operations, $U2$.
(P-3) The operations in step (i+1) are executed
after the operations in step i.

PE behaviors are assumed to be as follows.
(M-1) The amount of time to execute an operation
does not depend on the kind of the operations and
is $Tf0$ clocks.
(M-2) Every PE has f function units, and each
function unit can execute all kinds of operations.
Operation section takes Tf ($Tf = Tf0/f$) clocks, in
average, to execute one operation.
(M-3) Every PE consists of S pipeline stages, and
each pipeline stage takes $T1$ clocks except for
function units.
(M-4) All queue lengths are infinite, and there is
no blocking influence.

(2) Operation rates for function units : ρ
Average operation rates for function units in
step i, ρ_i, are calculated for the case of $Pi>S$ and
$Pi<S$, respectively, as follows.

Case (i) $Pi > S$
Since there is no idle stage in the circular
pipeline and operand packets arrive at the Operand
Memory continuously, Pi instruction packets are
generated and executed during $(2*N2i + N1i)*T1$
clocks. Therefore, an average operation rate
during this period is given as follows.
$$\rho_i = Pi * Tf / ((2*N2i + N1i)*T1)$$
$$= Tf/((1+U2)*T1) \quad (3-2)$$

Case (ii) $Pi < S$
Since Pi operations are executed during $S*T1$
clocks, the average operation rate is given as
follows.
$$\rho_i = Pi * Tf / (S * T1) \quad (3-3)$$

Combining Eqs. (3-2) and (3-3), an average
operation rate during the entire execution is given
as follows.
$$\rho = \{1/(1+U2)* \int_{S}^{\infty} g(Pi)dPi + 1/S* \int_{0}^{S} Pi*g(Pi)dPi\}*Tf/T1 \quad (3-4)$$
Integrating two terms in Eq. (3-4) gives the
following formula.
$$\rho = \{1/(1+U2) - P/S\}*(1+2S/P)*\exp(-2S/P) + P/S - 2S/P*\exp(-2S/P) \quad (3-5)$$

(3) Loop invariant data control effects
The loop-invariant data control effects,
described in Section 2.2, are discussed from the
viewpoint of the average operation rate calculated
above.

By storing loop-invariant data in the Operand
Memory during loop execution, system performance
can be enhanced for the following reasons.
(a) Since two-operand operations with a
loop-invariant can be handled just as one-operand
operations, instruction packets are directly
constructed.
(b) Two control operations, SW and Lup, can be
removed for a loop-invariant data.
For the case of very large P, the enhancement
effects can be given as follows, from formula
(3-5).

$$E = \frac{\{\text{Average operation rate, with loop-invariant}\}}{\{\text{Average operation rate, without loop-invariant}\}}$$
$$= 1 / (1 - 3*U'*U2/(1+U2)) \quad (3-6)$$

Here, U' is the ratio of operations with
loop-invariant to two-operand operations.

(4) Sensitivities
Two indices, sensitivity to communication
delay and sensitivity to load changes, are defined
to represent the multi-processor system
characteristics. Those are calculated using
average operation rates of function units as
follows.

(a) Sensitivity to communication delay
Communication sensitivity (CS) specifies the
processing speed sensitivity to a change in the
inter-PE communication delay in the system. It is
given as follows.

$$CS = \frac{\left| \frac{d}{dt}\left\{\frac{1}{\text{response time when } T=t}\right\}\right|}{\frac{1}{\{\text{response time when } T=0\}}} \quad (3-7)$$

Here T is the inter-PE communication delay
time.

In order to simplify the analysis, it is
assumed that the number of pipeline stages is
increased by $t/T1$, when inter-PE communication
delay is t. By substituting $(S+t/T1)$ for S in
formula (3-5) and differentiating it with respect
to t, the following formula is given from formula

(3-7).

$$CS = |1/\beta(S)\{(1+X*(1-1/(1+U2)) + 2/X*(1+1/X))$$
$$* \exp(-X)-2/X/X\}*P/2| \qquad (3-8)$$
where, $X = 2*(S+t/T1)/P$.

(b) Sensitivity to load changes

In multi-processor systems, the system load amount and the resource allocation strategy have an effect on the system performance. If system loads can not be equally allocated to each of the PEs, the system performance will degrade. For example, the system response time is determined by the response time for the most heavily loaded PE. On the other hand, if the function units in the system are held in one processor and execute any operation, system loads will be equally allocated to each of the function units. If the total number of function units in the system is constant, the response time depends on the number of function units in one PE.

Load sensitivity (LS) is defined as sensitivity between the processing speed and the change in the total load amount in the system. LS is given as follows using the number of function units within a PE, f, and system loads, L.

$$LS = \left|\frac{d}{dL}\left(\frac{1}{T(f,L)}\right)\right|/\left(\frac{1}{T(F,L)}\right) \qquad (3-9)$$

Here, F is the total number of function units in a system and T(f,L) is a response time.

It is difficult to estimate T(F,L) in general. However, when the parallelism degree is very high and inter-PE data dependency does not affect T(F,L), formula (3-9) is converted into

$$LS = \frac{Lm(F,L)}{F}\left|\frac{d}{dL}\left(\frac{f}{Lm(f,L)}\right)\right| \qquad (3-10)$$

Here, Lm(f,L) is the largest load amount allocated to a PE.

3.2 Experimental System

The experimental system (Eddy : Experimental system for data driven processor array [11,15]) has been developed to confirm the feasibility of the data flow processor array system, i.e. the feasibility of functional language, programming scheme for highly parallel execution, and its performance.

The Eddy hardware consists of 4 X 4 PEs and two broadcast control units (BCUs), as shown in Fig. 6. Each PE is composed of two microprocessors (Z8001). It is connected directly with eight neighboring PEs. The BCU can load/unload programs and data to/from all PEs, or all PEs in column or row, at the same time.

The software system implemented on each PE simulates the circular pipeline data flow control of the PE in detail, using logical simulation clocks. It generates statistical data, such as operation rates of the function units and average queue length.

3.3 Case study
(1) Average operation rates of function units

Average operation rates are calculated from formula (3-5) and are compared with the simulation by Eddy[15]. In experiments on Eddy, the following parameters are used :

Problem size = from 4x4 to 24x24 mesh points
Number of PEs = 4x4
Number of circular pipeline stages = 17
Number of function units per PE = 4
Execution time for a function unit = 5 or 10 clocks
Execution time for other stages = 1 clock

These parameter values correspond to S=17, Tf=1.25 or 2.5, and T1=1, in the analytical model.

Two kinds of programs were written in intermediate codes which represent abstract data flow graph and were translated into object codes for simulation experiments. The structures of those programs give the following parameters for performance estimation.

Parameters U2 and P are set to 0.381 and 2.333*m/2, respectively, from the program structure for solving a partial differential equation by Red-black S.O.R. method[15], whose program written in Valid is shown in Fig. 8. Parameter m is the number of mesh points allocated to a PE. The average operation rate curve calculated from formula (3-5) is shown in Fig. 9. Simulation results are also plotted in the figure.

For a matrix multiplication program[15] shown in Fig. 10, which is also written in Valid, parameters U2 and P are set to 0.538 and 3.25*m,

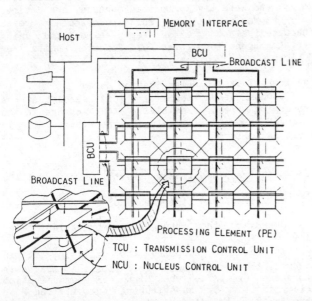

Fig. 6. Experimental system Eddy organization.

Fig. 7. Eddy hardware system.

```
for (k,x) : (1..kmax,x0) do
  {new x = for each i in (1..n), j in (1..n) do
        newx[i,j] = if mod(i+j,2)=1
                    then x[i,j]
                         -w*(a[i,j]*x[i+1,j]
                            +b[i,j]*x[i,j+1]
                            +c[i,j]*x[i-1,j]
                            +d[i,j]*x[i,j+1]
                            +e[i,j]*x[i,j]
                            -q[i,j])/e[i,j]
                    else x[i,j]
                         -w*(a[i,j]*newx[i+1,j]
                            +b[i,j]*newx[i,j+1]
                            +c[i,j]*newx[i-1,j]
                            +d[i,j]*newx[i,j+1]
                            +e[i,j]*newx[i,j]
                            -q[i,j])/e[i,j]
        return array(newx)}
```

Fig. 8. Red-black S.O.R. program

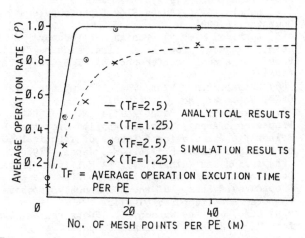

Fig. 9. Average operation rates of function units.
(red-black S.O.R. program)

```
for each i in (1..M1), j in (1..M1) do
  c[i,j] = for (k,sum) : (1..M1) do
           {new sum = sum+a[i,k]*b[k,j]}
return array(c)
```

Fig. 10. Matrix multiplication program

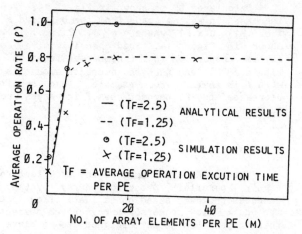

Fig. 11. Average operation rates of function units.
(matrix multiplication)

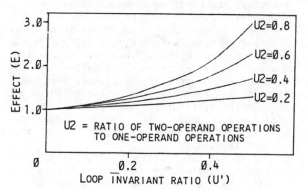

Fig. 12. Loop invariant control effects.

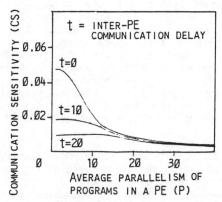

Fig. 13. Communication sensitivity curves.

respectively. Parameter m is the number of array elements in a PE. The average operation rate curve and the simulation results are shown in Fig. 11.

From Figs. 9 and 11, it can be said that the proposed system exploits sufficient parallelism in the practical importance region. It can be also said that the average operation rate is approximated with formula (3-5) and that the results of the following analysis, which are calculated from formula (3-5), are ensured.

(2) Loop-invariant control effects

The relationship between U' and E calculated from Eq. (3-6) is shown in Fig. 12, in which U2 varies from 0.2 to 0.8 and U' varies from 0 to 0.5. From the figure, it can be seen that the response time is reduced by loop-invariant control.

(3) Sensitivities
(a) Communication sensitivity

Using the same values as were used in experiments on Eddy, parameters S and T1 are 17 and 1, respectively. The relationships between the average parallelism within a PE and the communication sensitivity at each of the communication delay times, which are calculated from Eq. (3-8) for a typical U' value, are shown in Fig. 13. As shown in Fig. 13, communication sensitivity becomes very small when average

parallelism becomes large. In this system, it can be concluded that the inter-PE communication delay problem is not serious for programs which have large parallelism.

(b) Load sensitivity

In the case of mesh problems, in which each of the mesh points requires the same amount of load, the following formula is given from formula (3-10).

$$LS = \frac{M1^2}{F} \left| \frac{f}{(\lceil (M1+1)/P1 \rceil)^2} - \frac{f}{(\lceil M1/P1 \rceil)^2} \right| \qquad (3\text{-}11)$$

Here, mesh size is M1 x M1, total number of function units is F1 x F1, and number of PEs is P1 x P1.

Calculated LS is shown in Fig. 14, for the increase in system loads from the balanced state (i.e. M1 = c x F1, where c = 1, 2, ...). As shown in Fig. 14, load sensitivities are in inverse proportion to f (number of function units within a PE), and that the decrease amount is large when f is small. For example, load sensitivity decreases by 25 percent when f increases from one to four.

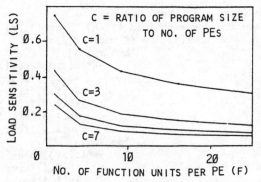

Fig. 14. Load sensitivity curves.

4. Conclusion

This paper has presented the architecture of a highly parallel processor array system which executes programs based on a data flow control. The data flow processor array system presented in this paper has been designed to achieve high performance by adapting the system structure to the operational characteristics of application programs, and also to attain flexibility through executing instructions by means of a data driven mechanism.

The operational characteristics of the proposed system were analyzed using a probability model of the system behavior. Comparing the analysis data with the simulation results for simple programs through experimental system Eddy, it can be said that the proposed system exploits parallelism inherent in the application programs efficiently and is neither sensitive to inter-processor communication delay nor sensitive to load imbalance.

Although the principal effectiveness of the proposed architecture was shown, much more work remains to be done for a practical system development. Analysis and simulation are continuing for much more complicated programs. A hardware system for the data flow processing element described in this paper is now under development [12]. It will clarify the performance of each part of the processing element and will provide simulation parameters for Eddy. Network architecture operational characteristics for the data flow processor array system are also being studied analytically by using a probability model [13]. The results of these studies will confirm the feasibility of the proposed system.

Acknowledgements

The authors wish to express their gratitude for guidance and encouragement received from Dr. N. Kuroyanagi, director of the Research Division at Musashino Electrical Communication Laboratory, and Mr. K. Yamashita, director of the first research section. They also wish to thank the members of the architecture research group in the first research section for fruitful discussions.

References

[1] Bright, L.G., "The Numerical Aerodynamics Simulation, An Overview," Proc. of 1977 CAM-I, (1979).

[2] Bailey, F.R., "Computational Limits on Scientific Applications," COMPCON 78 Spring Conference, (1978).

[3] Bouknight et al., "The Illiac IV system," Proc. IEEE, 60, (1972).

[4] Dennis, J.B., "Data Flow Supercomputers," IEEE Computer, (1980).

[5] Amamiya, M., "A Design Philosophy of High Level Language for Data Flow Machine "Valid"," Proc. of annual conference of I.E.C.E., Japan, (1981).

[6] Russel, R.M., "The CRAY-1 Computer System," CACM, Vol. 21, No. 1, (1978).

[7] Takahashi, N. and Amamiya, M., "A Data Flow Processor Array System Applied to the Large Scientific Calculation," Papers of Technical Group on Electric Computer, I.E.C.E., Japan, (1980).

[8] Arvind and Kathail, V., "A Multiple Processor Dataflow Machine that Supports Generalized Procedures," Proc. of the 8th Annual Symposium on Computer Architecture, (1981).

[9] Gurd, J. and Watson, I., "Data Driven System for High Speed Computing," Computer Design, (July 1980).

[10] Amamiya, M., Hasegawa, R. and Mikami, H., "List processing with a Data Flow Machine," to appear in Lecture Notes in Computer Science, RIMS Symposia on Software Science and Engineering, Kyoto, Springer-Verlag.

[11] Takahashi, N., Yoshida, M., Onai, R. and Amamiya, M., "An Experimental System for Data Driven Processor Array," Proc. of annual conference of Japan Information Processing Society, (June 1981).

[12] Yoshida, M., Takahashi, N. and Amamiya, M., "An Execution Controller for a Data Driven Processor Array System," ibid., (Oct. 1981).

[13] Naruse, T. and Amamiya, M., "Performance Evaluation on Communication Network of a Processor Array System," ibid., (Oct. 1981).

[14] Amamiya, M., Hasegawa, R., Nakamura, O., and Mikami, H., "A list-processing-oriented data flow machine architecture," Proc. of the 1982 National Computer Conference, AFIPS, (1982).

[15] Amamiya, M., Takahashi, N., Naruse, T. and Yoshida, M., "A Data Flow Processor Array for Solving Partial Differential Equations," Proc. Int. Symp. on Applied Mathematics and Information Science, Kyoto University (March 1982).

A Critique of Multiprocessing von Neumann Style

Arvind

Robert A. Iannucci

Laboratory for Computer Science
Massachusetts Institute of Technology
545 Technology Square
Cambridge, Massachusetts 02139

Abstract

In recent years, there have been many attempts to construct multiple-processor computer systems. The majority of these systems are based on von Neumann style uniprocessors. To exploit the parallelism in algorithms, any high performance multiprocessor system must, however, address two very basic issues - the ability to tolerate long latencies for memory requests and the ability to achieve unconstrained, yet synchronized, access to shared data. In this paper, we define these two problems, and examine the ways in which they are addressed by some of the current and past von Neumann multiprocessor projects. We then proceed to hypothesize that the problems *cannot* be solved in a von Neumann context. We offer the data flow model as one possible alternative, and we describe our research in this area.

Key words and phrases: caches, cache coherence, data flow, multiported memories, multiprocessors, packet communication, von Neumann architecture

1. Fundamental Issues in Multiprocessor Architectures

In the early days of computing, the issue of constructing a multiple-processor computing system was viewed as little more than an interesting intellectual exercise; after all, it seemed clear that machines could be made to operate faster simply by increasing the speed of the underlying technology. Given this view, it seemed that the style of machine organization for potential multiprocessing was not of overriding importance. The von Neumann organization, because of its sequential nature, was conceptually simple and easy to realize. Hence, it is not at all surprising that an entire community (and industry) was born with a built-in bias towards sequential computing. While understandable, this tacit assumption about machine organization has inherent limits which, form our present vantage point, sit just beyond the horizon.

Attention has been focused in the recent past on constructing multiprocessor systems [19, 20, 21, 22, 23, 11] - attention derived from a desire for more performance, greater fault tolerance, the ability to exploit the rather curious economics of a single-chip computer, or whatever. What has *not* been done sufficiently is a re-evaluation of the assumptions that led us to where we are now. This is painfully clear when one observes that von Neumann style uniprocessors still form the building block for the majority of multiprocessor projects or proposals. Many variations on the von Neumann theme have been explored (*e.g.*, pipelining, multiple functional units, vector instructions), but not much has been done with the sequential control required for instruction execution. There are good reasons to believe that this re-evaluation is overdue.

In this paper, we will use the term *multiprocessor* to refer to a computing system that exploits parallelism in programs through replication of resources. Although we will examine some special purpose machines, our primary interest here is in *general purpose parallel computers*, *i.e.*, computers that can exploit parallelism, when present, in any algorithm. Further, we are interested in the property of *scalability* - that the system can be made incrementally more powerful by adding incrementally more hardware resources (and without reprogramming). The basic building blocks of a multiprocessor are

- **Processing elements:** These perform arithmetic and logical operations, and are provided with an interface to communication and memory elements;

- ›**Communication elements:** These are used to construct an interconnection network. The resulting network has a number of *ports*, each with a bounded *bandwidth*. The purpose of the network is to interconnect various processing elements with each other and/or with memory elements; and

- **Memory elements:** Collectively, these provide the repository for program and data storage. Processing elements can, either directly or indirectly, access the data in the various memory elements via the network.

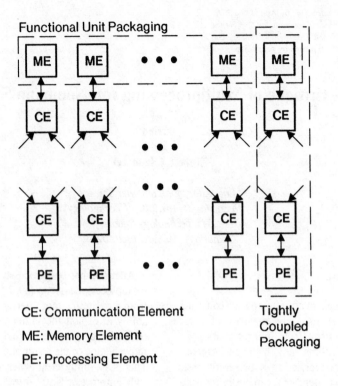

Functional Unit Packaging

CE: Communication Element

ME: Memory Element

PE: Processing Element

Tightly
Coupled
Packaging

Figure 1-1: An Abstract Multiprocessor

Scaling of the multiprocessor involves incremental additions to all of the above. Modularity, an important design characteristic, allows scaling without redesign, *i.e.*, modules are constructed for each of the above, and an arbitrarily large machine (within the physical limits of packaging) is built by simply plugging these together. See Figure 1-1.

Note that we have said nothing about the programmer's view of the system (*e.g.*, explicit *vs.* implicit specification of parallelism and communication), the programming methodology, the network topology, packaging, etc. For our purposes here, we are concerned with the shared memory multiprocessor model, and we will consider tightly coupled memory/processor pairs which use a message passing methodology as shared memory machines. An equivalence between the shared memory model and the message passing model based on storage for messages, timing, and synchronization can be established.

1.1. The Issues

Let us review for a moment some of the issues which seem fundamental, at least from an engineering point of view, in the construction of any multiprocessor - von Neumann or not.

Issue 1: Ability to Tolerate Memory Latency

Latency is the time between issuing a memory request and getting a response. As the number of ports in the network increases, it stands to reason that the average latency of a memory request will have to increase if only due to the switching time in the network. Given the rate at which a processing

element can issue memory requests and the bandwidth of each memory element (bits per second per port), it is clear that at some point, the memory units, on the average, will not be able to respond to each processor request without causing the processor to idle.

The key observation, then, is that it is absolutely necessary that each processor be able to issue multiple memory requests in succession without intervening memory responses. It is also quite reasonable to assume that, because of contention, the memory responses may arrive out of order unless some constraints are placed on the memories and network interconnections. The problem is unsolvable for a truly scalable multiprocessor unless some assumptions about program behavior are made. The kind of assumptions we have in mind are that the distribution of memory references with respect to the distance from the issuing processor does not get worse as the number of processors and memory elements increases.

Traditional ways of circumventing the latency problem attempt to exploit spatial locality. Instruction prefetching is the most successful technique; the inherent sequentiality of the von Neumann machine assures some measure of locality. Exploiting spatial locality in data references is more difficult. General register architectures subscribe to the notion that the user will somehow know what data will be referenced most frequently; however, it is well known that optimal register usage essentially amounts to solving the coloring problem on large graphs [16], and is very difficult to achieve.

A dynamic scheme for exploiting locality is the (demand)

cache for main memory. This scheme is difficult to apply in a multiprocessor context due to the cache coherence problem. Censier and Feautrier [7] define the problem as follows: *"A memory scheme is coherent if the value returned on a LOAD instruction is always the value given by the latest STORE instruction with the same address."* In a multiprocessor context, it is easy to see that this may lead to difficulties. Suppose we have a two-processor system tightly coupled through a single main memory. Each processor has its own cache, to which it has exclusive access. Suppose further that two tasks are running, one on each processor; and we know that the tasks are designed to communicate through one or more shared memory cells. In the absence of caches, this scheme can be made to work. However, if it so happens that the shared address is present in both caches, the individual processors can read and write the address and *never* see any changes caused by the other processor. Using a store-through design instead of a store-in design does not completely solve the problem either. What is logically required is a mechanism which, upon the occurrence of a write to location x, invalidates all other cached copies of location x wherever they may occur, and guarantees that subsequent LOADs will get the most recent (cached) value. This can incur significant overhead and complexity.

Several approximate solutions for keeping cache coherence exist, but all such schemes inevitably introduce overhead and/or decrease parallelism (*e.g.*, due to lockout of page-sized areas of memory). Schemes have been proposed to explicitly interlock writing or to bypass the cache (and flush it if necessary) on a write; in either case, the complexity goes up and the performance goes down rapidly as the machine is scaled.

Another attempt at tolerating memory request latency is by performing context switching at a very low level (analogous to task switching when an I/O request is made in a multiprogrammed operating system). Thus, while one computation waits for the memory to respond, the processor resumes another, parallel computation. Of course, the scheme works only if the context switching itself does not generate any memory references. This is done by duplicating programmer-visible registers (*i.e.*, the processor state). The problem here is again the increase in processor complexity as the machine is scaled.

Uniprocessors such as the Xerox Alto [24], the Xerox Dorado [15], and the Symbolics 3600 have used the technique of microcode-level context switching to allow sharing of the CPU resource by the I/O device adapters. This is very different than the type of context switching needed in multiprocessors. While both schemes rely on replication of hardware registers and other state information, the uniprocessor application requires only a fixed number of disjoint contexts - established by the number of I/O adapters plus the emulator itself. In the multiprocessor case, it will be necessary to have an unbounded number of tasks to achieve scalability. To illustrate this, consider the problem of expanding such a system. As memory elements are added, the depth of the communication network will grow. Hence, the number of low-level contexts to be maintained will also have to increase to match the increase in memory latency time.

Issue 2: Ability to Share Data without Constraining Parallelism

A much more troublesome issue is that of sharing data between two or more processes while maintaining proper synchronization. One manifestation of this is the *write-write race* two processes attempt to write data into the same location. The meaningfulness of this is not at all clear, and the problem can be properly avoided by some software convention, perhaps assisted by some run-time checking. Functional languages avoid this problem totally because *updating* the value of a variable has no meaning in such languages.

The real problem, however, is not a pathological case like the write-write race: it is the real problem of the *read-before-write* race. To illustrate this problem, consider two routines running on two different processors, both accessing a two-dimensional array of numbers. One routine is creating the elements, in order, and writing them into the array. The other routine is waiting to read the elements. One possible way of avoiding a read-before-write race would be to allow the *entire* array to be written prior to allowing the consumer routine to begin processing. By this simpleminded transfer of control, there is no synchronization problem, but neither is there any chance for parallelism. On a single processor, the computation cannot be made faster by overlapping the production and consumption of a data structure, and this sort of scheme works well. It defeats the purpose of multiprocessing, however.

A more common scheme is to synchronize on a per-row or per-column basis of the array (as appropriate); this incurs more overhead, but constrains parallelism less. The extreme approach would be to synchronize the two routines on a per-element basis. It should be obvious that doing so is impractical with current methods and requires fundamental changes at the hardware level.

This example oversimplifies the real situation - consider the case where the elements are not produced in a regular (*i.e.*, row order or column order) way, or the case of a nonuniform data structure. The question remains: is it necessary to sacrifice parallelism for proper synchronization of reads-before-writes? We will show in section 2 that synchronization can be achieved with no loss of parallelism.

1.2. A Survey of von Neumann Multiprocessors

We examine a few of the planned or existing von Neumann machines that are described in the literature. Each one fails to satisfy at least one of the above two basic issues. We have ignored commercially-available 2 or 4 processor systems because, to the best of our knowledge, such systems have not been used in a manner in which processors cooperate on solving one problem. The main motivation for such systems has been higher performance in a multiprogrammed environment, and even in that limited area the performance of these systems has been far from impressive.

In our discussions, one figure of merit that is used in evaluating multiprocessor systems is ALU utilization/idle time. This assumption orients our discussion toward favoring machines designed for solving problems which can be expressed in numerical terms. Another important class of computation is the *symbolic* type in which the ALU utilization metric is less useful. One multiprocessor in this category is the Connection Machine. While it does not fit our model, we examine it in some detail because it is an interesting second-generation SIMD architecture.

1.2.1. C.mmp

C.mmp was a tightly-coupled multiprocessor built on a base of PDP-11 minicomputers connected into a single global memory through a high-speed crossbar switch [23]. The processors ran asynchronously, and could use local memory without interfering with the global memory. The switch speed was comparable to the speed of a local memory reference, but the cost of building a larger switch which maintains the same performance level grows at least quadratically. This reliance on technology doesn't solve the memory latency problem; it merely circumvents it. However, the investigators were clear on the point that the machine was exploratory in nature, and felt that scalability was only a secondary goal.

Interprocessor communication was facilitated by the shared memory and a cross-processor interrupt scheme. Synchronization was performed at several levels due to the recognized need to keep the overhead of this operation very low. High-level semaphores were maintained by Hydra on data objects to properly handle synchronized sharing. It is clear that the performance cost of this relative to, say, an ALU operation is rather high unless some potential parallelism is traded away.

The original design called a local cache for each processor, but only one processor in the machine was ever fitted with one (and it was never used by Hydra). The reason is, quite simply, the cache coherence problem.

1.2.2. Cm*

Cm* differed from its predecessor in several ways; notably, that the machine used a kind of hierarchical network to interconnect a number of microprocessors, each with its own memory [20, 21]. One might have guessed that this physical locality when combined with spatial locality in programs and data would have resulted in less communication overhead; the idea was intuitively appealing. This hope manifested itself in the design of the communication strategy - any processor making a nonlocal memory reference would idle until the reference was completed. Because of the hierarchical structure, this meant that greater interprocessor distances translated into longer memory reference times and decreased processor utilization.

Packet switching instead of circuit switching was used in the communication network (another difference from C.mmp) to avoid processor deadlock. Kmap, the communications controller, was actually a context-switching processor which could tolerate the long-latency remote memory references. Unfortunately, the processors (LSI-11s) could not perform similar low-level context switches during a remote reference. It would be interesting to speculate on the behavior of Cm* if micro-tasking processors had been used.

In fact, Cm* demonstrated quite clearly the importance of Issue 1; the effect of processor idle time put an upper limit on the number of processors that could cooperate on even highly parallel programs (*e.g.*, chaotic relaxation) [9]. As far as Issue 2 was concerned, synchronization was based on a message system, but the underlying mechanism was the shared-memory, lockable segment.

1.2.3. The NYU Ultracomputer

Another shared memory multiprocessor is the NYU Ultracomputer [11]. Their solution to the synchronization problem is the atomic FETCH-AND-ADD instruction (sometimes called REPLACE-ADD). The instruction format is FETCH-AND-ADD(*address, value*), and works as follows: suppose two processors, i and j, simultaneously execute FETCH-AND-ADD instructions with arguments (A, v_i) and (A, v_j) respectively. After one instruction cycle, the contents of A will become $(A) + v_i + v_j$. Processors i and j will receive, respectively, either (A) and $(A) + v_i$, or $(A) + v_j$ and (A) as results. Indeterminacy is a direct consequence of the race to update memory cell A. The implementation of FETCH-AND-ADD calls for a synchronous packet communication network which connects n processors to an n-port memory. If two packets collide, say FETCH-AND-ADD(A, x) and FETCH-AND-ADD(A, y), the switch extracts the values x and y, forms a new packet (FETCH-AND-ADD($A, x + y$)), forwards it to the memory, and stores the value of x temporarily. When the memory returns the old value of location A, the switch returns two values ((A) and $(A) + x$). Hence, one memory reference may involve as many as $\log_2 n$ additions, and implies substantial hardware complexity.

The issue of processor latency has not been specifically addressed, and there are serious questions in our minds as to whether such a network ($t_{switch} \ll t_{memory}$) is realizable. We also do not understand the implications of basing a whole programming model on such an instruction as FETCH-AND-ADD.

1.2.4. VLIW Architectures - ELI-512 and the Polycyclic Processor

Another approach which seems to be coming into vogue these days is the horizontally-microprogrammed processor in which a smart compiler (or a patient and talented human) is able to fold many parallel operations into a single machine cycle. Examples of this are the ELI-512 [10], the ESL Polycyclic processor [17], the AP-120B [8], and numerous programmable signal processing machines.

While these machines are able to resolve run-time sharing conflicts (by moving them to compile time) and are usually able to plan memory references and control transfers in advance of the need (*e.g.*, the delayed jump), these machines suffer from their special-purpose nature. Except in the simplest of cases, compilers require "hints" from the programmer or, in some cases, rely on luck in doing the code generation. Clearly, these machines are not suited at all to real-time multiuser multiprogramming, interrupt handling, or anything which relies on the ability to efficiently switch contexts.

We believe that this technique is effective in its currently--

realized context - special purpose computation with small scale (4 to 8) parallelism, but the technique is not sufficiently general as to allow significant scaling up.

1.2.5. SIMD Revisited: the Connection Machine

Recently, there have been proposals to revive and to improve upon SIMD architectures (*e.g.*, Illiac IV [6]). The Connection Machine [13] proposal can be viewed in this context although it is intended for an entirely different class of problems than Illiac IV. It generalizes the communications scheme of Illiac IV, but still uses a single instruction stream with each processor having the capability of not participating in an instruction.

Illiac IV had 64 fairly powerful processors connected in an 8×8 rectangular, end-around grid topology. Each processor could directly access only its local memory (2K words). Using communication registers (one per processor) data could be shifted in one step to any of the four neighboring processors. Thus, in seven steps, a processor could access data from any other processor. However, because a single instruction controlled all processors, every processor had to wait even if one processor needed data from nonlocal memory. Also, if one processor wanted to transmit (shift) data to the processor to its east and another to its west, two machine instructions had to be executed. The need for such communication was poorly understood at that time, and Illiac IV executed a very small subset of scientific problems efficiently.

The Connection Machine proposal envisions a million processors, each consisting of 12 32-bit registers, some flag bits, and one 1-bit ALU. The processors[1] are connected in an Illiac IV-like grid with similar restrictions. However, groups of 64 processors are also connected by a 14 dimensional hypercube - there are 2^{14} groups. The bit-serial communication through the hypercube links is packet oriented; each processor can transmit or receive a message to/from any other processor. In the absence of conflicts, a message will reach its destination in at most 14 steps; but, because of conflicts, some messages will take significantly more steps than the required minimum number. A global flag is raised when all processors are done communicating, and only then can the next instruction begin.

It is clear that the speed of one bit ALU operations is irrelevant because it will be insignificant in comparison with the communication time - a processor will spend almost all (90%?, 99%?) of its time communicating. This machine, because of its single instruction sequence nature, also does not fit the model of the multiprocessor presented in this paper. Our model implicitly assumes that the goal of a general purpose parallel machine is to execute ALU operations (*e.g.*, addition, multiplication, comparison) as efficiently as possible by overlapping ALU operations with communications. However, for the class of applications in which communication predominates computation, our framework and metrics are not applicable. Many such situations occur in applied artificial intelligence

programs where more time is spent exploring the connectivity of a large graph rather than computing with the information found at the nodes of the graph. The relevance of Issue 1 for the Connection Machine is not clear, and Issue 2 does not arise in a SIMD architecture.

2. Proposed Solutions: Data Flow Architectures

In this section we present a memory structure which allows efficient synchronization at the atomic level, and we also present an architecture which offers the ultimate in flexibility in issuing overlapped memory requests.

2.1. I-Structure Storage

If we associate with each memory cell in a machine special flags (called *presence* bits) which indicate the memory cell's status - written or unwritten - we have the ability to solve the read-before-write race problem as follows: assume that a memory module has just received a request to read a particular memory location and to forward the contents to instruction x. The memory module interrogates the presence bits associated with that location. If the bits indicate that the cell has already been written into, the contents are retrieved and forwarded to instruction x. If the bits indicate that the location is empty, the memory module puts the read request aside, and marks the empty location to indicate that a read request is outstanding.[2]

Now, when a write request for that location arrives at some time in the future, the memory module notices the pending read request, and forwards the newly-arrived datum to instruction x (as well as writing it into memory and setting the presence bits accordingly). Note that the memory module must maintain a list of deferred read requests (see Figure 2-1) as there may be more than one *read* of a particular address before the corresponding *write*. We call this type of memory *I-Structure Storage*. The issues involved with building such a memory, and the design for an I-Structure memory controller are discussed extensively in [12].

This mechanism, when coupled with a processor which is able to issue multiple, overlapped memory requests and which can tolerate out-of-order responses, allows the uncoupling of memory latency from the performance of a multiprocessor. The penalty of such a scheme in terms of the demands placed on memory elements is not excessive. A read operation is as efficient as in a traditional memory. Write operations take twice as long, however, due to the prefetching of presence bits. Many different implementation strategies are possible which can largely eliminate this penalty.

---

[1] It is probably better to view these processors as cells of a "smart" memory.

[2] The idea of associating a status bit with each memory cell is not new - the Denelcor HEP multiprocessor [18] uses this idea to synchronize cooperating parallel processes which share registers and/or memory cells. Unsatisfiable requests result in a busy-waiting condition - *i.e.*, there is no such thing as a *deferred read* list.

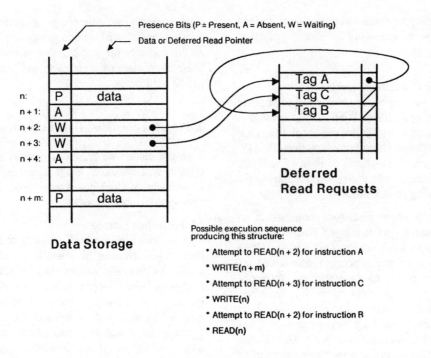

Presence Bits (P = Present, A = Absent, W = Waiting)

Data or Deferred Read Pointer

n:	P	data
n + 1:	A	
n + 2:	W	●
n + 3:	W	●
n + 4:	A	
n + m:	P	data

Data Storage

Tag A	●
Tag C	
Tag B	

Deferred Read Requests

Possible execution sequence producing this structure:

* Attempt to READ(n + 2) for instruction A
* WRITE(n + m)
* Attempt to READ(n + 3) for instruction C
* WRITE(n)
* Attempt to READ(n + 2) for instruction B
* READ(n)

Figure 2-1: I-Structure Storage

2.2. Data Flow Processing Element

When one desires to build a machine capable of issuing multiple memory requests and of tolerating long latencies, the most troublesome aspect of von Neumann architecture is the built-in sequentiality (*viz.*, the program counter). By eliminating the notion of control flow for program sequencing, we can circumvent this problem directly. One alternative to sequential control flow is *data flow*, where the execution of instructions is triggered solely by the availability of the operands. In order to explain the operation of a data flow processor, we must digress for a moment to discuss program and data representation.

2.2.1. Program Representation

Data flow compilers translate high-level programs into directed graphs; vertices in the graph correspond to machine instructions, and edges correspond to the data dependencies which exist between the instructions.

The implication is, quite simply, that instructions which depend on other instructions should be sequenced accordingly; but where no dependence (edge) exists, instructions can be executed in parallel. A simple example of this graphical translation is shown in Figure 2-2, compiled from the following ID program which integrates a function f from a to b over n intervals of size h by the trapezoidal rule:

$$\text{(initial } s \leftarrow (f(a)+f(b))/2;$$
$$x \leftarrow a+h$$
$$\textbf{for } i \textbf{ from } 1 \textbf{ to } n\text{-}1 \textbf{ do}$$
$$\textbf{new } x \leftarrow x+h;$$
$$\textbf{new } s \leftarrow s+f(x)$$
$$\textbf{return } s)*h$$

The graph shown is somewhat stylized; the box marked f represents the subgraph necessary for invoking function f (which is, itself, a graph). Instructions D, D^{-1}, L, and L^{-1} are included to provide proper entry, iteration, and exit by manipulating context-identifying information (discussed in the next section). The remainder of the operators are arithmetic, relational, and conditional instructions whose function should be self-evident. The graph generated by the compiler is reentrant.

2.2.2. Data Representation

It is the processor's task to propagate data values through this graph, triggering instructions when the operands are available. Data values are carried on logical entities called *tokens*; a token contains not only a data value but also the name of the instruction to which it belongs. Conceptually, tokens move about on the vertices of the graph. Instructions are enabled for execution when tokens are present on all input vertices. Upon execution, the instruction absorbs the input tokens, and produces an output token for the next instruction in the graph. A program is said to *terminate* when no enabled instructions are left.

Our execution model allows more than one token to be present on an arc; and, therefore, the next-instruction label also contains some dynamic, or context-sensitive information. In their full generality, these next-instruction labels or *activity names* contain four parts:

- **u:** The *context* field, which uniquely identifies the context in which a code block is invoked. The context itself is specified by an activity name, thus making the definition recursive.

514

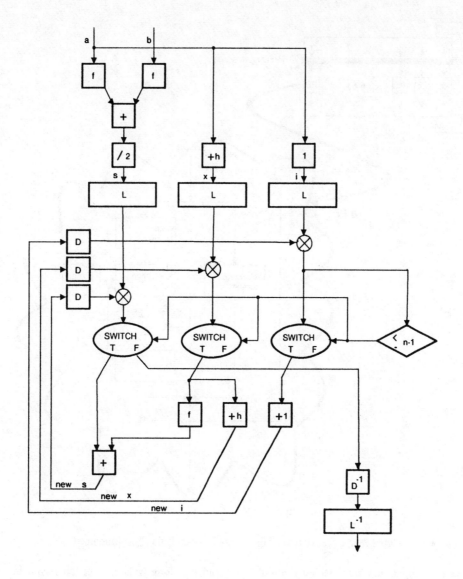

Figure 2-2: Compilation of the Loop Expression for the Trapezoidal Rule

- c: The *code block* name. Each procedure and each loop has a unique code block name.

- s: The *statement* (instruction) number within the code block.

- i: The *initiation* number, which identifies the loop iteration in which this activity occurs. This field is 1 if the activity occurs outside a loop.

Activity names, then, define an unbounded namespace. Names in this space are mapped dynamically into a finite namespace. The activity name plus some mapping information uniquely define the runtime *tag* and processing element (PE) number.

Since instructions may have more than one input operand, we also include two more pieces of information on each token: the

total number of operands required by its target instruction (called *nt* - number of tokens), and an index value (called the *port*) which specifies the operand number associated with this token. Tokens of this type are called *normal* tokens, abbreviated as $d=0$.[3] A more complete discussion of formats is given in [3]. The complete token, then, looks like this:

$$\langle d=0, PE, tag, nt, port, data \rangle$$

2.2.3. Structure of the Processing Element

Figure 2-3 is a block diagram of an abstract data flow machine and its processing element. Assume that the program to be executed has been compiled into a directed graph, and an encoding of this graph is stored in the *program memory*. As

---

[3]The reason for this notation has been lost in historical obscurity.

515

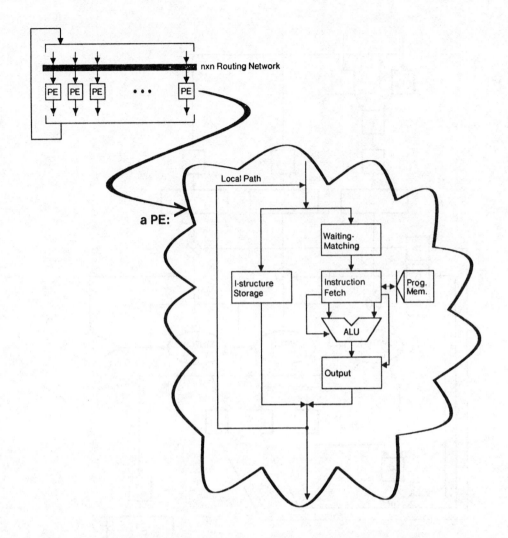

Figure 2-3: Organization of the Tagged-Token Data Flow Machine

tokens arrive at the machine's input, they are classified according to type. The d=0 tokens (above) which require partners (nt≥2) are routed to the the *waiting - matching* section.

Since each token carries the name of its target instruction, we can match up related tokens (*e.g.*, the two input operands for an addition) by comparing the tags that they carry. This is the function of the waiting - matching section. When a match is found, the pair is passed on to the *instruction fetch* unit. When a match is expected but not found, the token remains in the waiting - matching unit's associative memory until its partner arrives. The instruction fetch unit also directly receives d=0 tokens which require no partners (nt=1).

The instruction fetch unit looks up the operation code and other information associated with the token-carried names, and passes this enabled instruction on to the *ALU*. At this point, no other information is needed to carry out the operation save that which is in this enabled instruction packet.

The ALU output represents a datum which is ready to move off to its target instruction; but first, it has to be put in a token. We build this output token by computing a new tag, using the old tag along with information stored in the instruction itself. The *output* section handles these operations.

The output section also computes the PE number for the new token. A routing translation table turns this PE number into a network routing address. See Figure 2-4 for a more detailed view of the PE.

Other paths through the processing element provide for the cases where an incoming token is destined for the I-Structure Storage (d=1), or is destined for the PE Controller (d=2).

2.2.4. References to Data Structures

Conceptually, in a data flow graph, even a data structure is represented by a single token which is replicated on encountering a fork. The two most common operations on data structures are SELECT (to select a specific element of a data structure) and APPEND (to generate a new data structure which differs from the input structure in one selected position). In any reasonable implementation, however, data structures reside in some storage (I-structure storage in our machine), and tokens carry only pointers to the structure. Thus, a SELECT operation

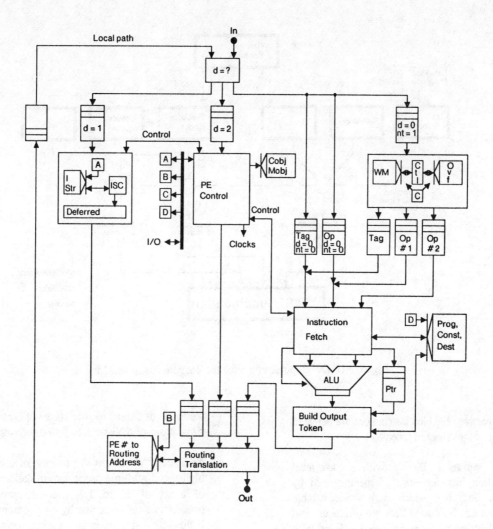

Figure 2-4: Data Flow Processing Element

becomes a FETCH instruction while an APPEND operation becomes a STORE instruction.[4]

Now, to understand how I-structure storage references are processed consider an enabled FETCH instruction in the data flow graph. This instruction will be sent the ALU for processing. The ALU constructs a special token (d=1) which contains the address of the I-structure element to be read, the name of the PE on which this element resides, the FETCH opcode, and the name (tag and PE number) of the instruction which is to receive the result of the FETCH. The token is then forwarded to the proper I-structure controller, and the ALU proceeds to process the next enabled instruction.

This token makes its way through the network and is routed to the I-structure controller on the appropriate PE. The actual FETCH is performed as described previously, possibly after being

deferred. When the FETCH operation is complete, a new token is formed to forward the fetched datum to the target instruction.

STORE operations are similar - a STORE instruction in the graph is executed, causing a data value and an address to be built into a d=1 token. The new token is forwarded to the appropriate PE which completes the operation by writing the data value, checking for and processing any deferred read requests, and setting the presence bits.

2.3. Review of the Issues

As we have seen, data flow provides a means whereby a processing element can issue many simultaneous memory requests, can tolerate long latencies (given that the program being executed is sufficiently parallel), and can deal with responses that arrive out of order. The mechanisms which make this work are

- **Tagged tokens:** By having each datum carry context-identifying information with it, no time-ordering ambiguities can arise.

---

[4]There is a minor complication in that some APPENDS can cause a new copy of a data structure to be created. This is not germane to the main discussion here; the interested reader may refer to [5].

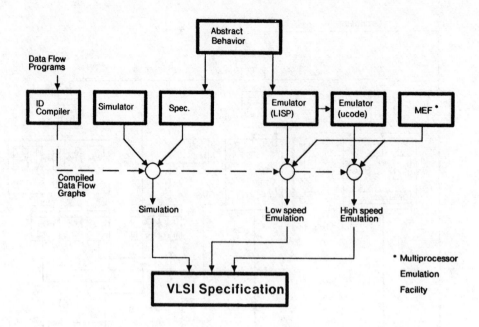

Figure 3-1: Development Plan for the Tagged-Token Machine

- **Associative pairing:** Enabled instructions are detected by matching of these tagged tokens.

- **I-structure storage:** By providing low-level synchronization bits per word of memory and by enforcing a discipline which defers unsatisfiable requests, data can be shared between producers and consumers with no performance overhead and with no loss of parallelism.

Many other issues are involved with the design of a tagged token data flow machine, and many other benefits accrue. The interested reader is directed to the literature [2, 5, 4, 1].

3. Construction of a Testbed

Many people find data flow an interesting and exciting research direction for a number of reasons. We feel that, because data flow addresses the fundamental problems that have haunted von Neumann multiprocessors, it offers a fresh perspective and the hope that we will be able to exploit the thousand-fold parallelism "grail" after which so many have sought.

In our group, we are currently pursuing a two-pronged attack on the problem of constructing a practical prototype machine which embodies these principles (refer to Figure 3-1):

- **Simulation:** We have built a detailed simulation model of the tagged-token machine which interprets graphs produced by our compiler for the Irvine Dataflow (ID) language. The model accounts for communication as well as processing *simulated* time. We are installing an IBM 4341 MG2 processor which

we will dedicate to the task of running these simulations of realistic data flow programs.

- **Emulation:** We are in the process of constructing a high-speed multiple processor emulation facility out of a set of 32 to 128 user-microprogrammable processors interconnected by a programmable, high-bandwidth, fault-tolerant packet communication network [14]. This emulator will also interpret the graphs generated by our compiler, but at much higher speeds. What is lost is the detailed internal timings of the abstract data flow machine; but what is gained is the ability to run very large application programs to learn about the behavior of programs in a multiple processor data flow environment.

The key element to building the emulation facility is the packet communication network module, one of which is integrated with each microprogrammable processor. The network topology will be a seven dimensional hypercube with each connection implemented as a 4 megabyte per second bit-serial link. This topology was chosen for its flexibility. Each switch module also includes a routing table which allows the experimenter to specify any *emulated* topology which can be mapped onto the hypercube. The hardware has the capability of exploiting the redundancy in the hypercube network for message routing and for fault tolerance. Table-based routing also allows the facility to be statically partitioned into two or more smaller emulation machines.

The idea of closely associating a switch module and a microprogrammable processor allows much of the low-level maintenance and fault recovery logic to reside in microcode. The hardware provides the essential fault-detection mechanisms, and is flexible enough to allow for simple error recovery under the control of a microcode task.

It is our belief that this microcodable emulation facility will provide enough flexibility to actually study the effects of the two issues raised in this paper.

References

1. Arvind, and K. P. Gostelow. The U-Interpreter. *Computer* (February 1982).

2. Arvind, K. P. Gostelow, and W. Plouffe. An Asynchronous Programming Language and Computing Machine. Tech. Rep. 114a, Department of Information and Computer Science, University of California, Irvine, California, December, 1978.

3. Arvind, and R. A. Iannucci. Instruction Set Definition for a Tagged-Token Data Flow Machine. Memo 212, Computation Structures Group, Laboratory for Computer Science, MIT, Cambridge, Mass., December, 1981. revised February, 1983

4. Arvind, and V. Kathail. A Multiple Processor Dataflow Machine That Supports Generalized Procedures. The 8th Annual Symposium on Computer Architecture, May, 1981, pp. 291-302.

5. Arvind, and R. E. Thomas. I-Structures: An Efficient Data Type for Functional Languages. Tech. Rep. TM-178, Laboratory for Computer Science, MIT, Cambridge, Mass., September, 1980.

6. Bouknight, W. J., S. A. Denenberg, D. E. Mcintyre, J. M. Randall, A. H. Sameh, and D. L. Slotnick. The ILLIAC IV System. *Proc. of the IEEE 60*, 4 (April 1972).

7. Censier, L. M., and P. Feautrier. A New Solution to the Coherence Problems in Multicache Systems. *IEEE Transactions on Computers C-27*, 12 (December 1978), 1112-1118.

8. Charlesworth, A. E. An Approach to Scientific Array Processing: the Architectural Design of the AP-120B/FPS-164 Family. *Computer 14*, 9 (September 1981), 18-27.

9. Deminet, J. Experience with Multiprocessor Algorithms. *IEEE Transactions on Computers C-31*, 4 (April 1982), 278-288.

10. Fisher, J. A. Very Long Instruction Word Architectures and the ELI-512. Tech. Rep. 253, Yale University, Department of Computer Science, December, 1982.

11. Gottlieb, A., R. Grishman, C. P. Kruskal, K. P. McAuliffe, L. Rudolph, and M. Snir. The NYU Ultracomputer - Designing an MIMD Shared Memory Parallel Computer. *IEEE Transactions on Computers C-32*, 2 (February 1983), 175-189.

12. Heller, S. K. An I-Structure Memory Controller. Master Th., Dept. of Electrical Engineering and Computer Science, MIT, Cambridge, Mass., June, 1983.

13. Hillis, W. D. The Connection Machine: Computer Architectue for the New Wave. Tech. Rep. 646, Artificial Intelligence Laboratory, MIT, Cambridge, Mass., September, 1981.

14. Iannucci, R. A. Packet Communication Switch for a Multiprocessor Computer Architecture Emulation Facility. Memo 220, Computation Structures Group, Laboratory for Computer Science, MIT, Cambridge, Mass., October, 1982.

15. Lampson, B. W., and K. A. Pier. A Processor for a High-Performance Personal Computer. Xerox Palo Alto Research Center, January, 1981.

16. Radin, G. The 801 Minicomputer. Proceedings of the Symposium on Architectural Support for Programming Languages and Operating Systems, March, 1982. Same as Computer Architecture News 10,2 and SIGPLAN Notices 17,4

17. Rau, B., D. Glaeser, and E. Greenwalt. Architectural Support for the Efficient Generation of Code for Horizontal Architectures. Proceedings of the Symposium on Architectural Support for Programming Languages and Operating Systems, March, 1982. Same as Computer Architecture News 10,2 and SIGPLAN Notices 17,4

18. Smith, B. J. A Pipelined, Shared Resource MIMD Computer. Proceedings of the 1978 International Conference on Parallel Processing, 1978, pp. 6-8.

19. Sullivan, H., and T. R. Bashkow. A Large Scale, Homogenous, Parallel Machine. The Fourth Annual Symposium on Computer Architecture, March, 1977.

20. Swan, R. J., S. H. Fuller, and D. P. Siewiorek. Cm* - A Modular Multiprocessor. Proceedings of the National Computer Conference, 1977.

21. Swan, R. J., A. Bechtolsheim, K-W. Lai, and and J. Ousterhout. The Implementation of the Cm* Multi-microprocessor. Proceedings of the National Computer Conference, 1977.

22. Widdoes, L. The S-1 Project: Developing High-Performance Digital Computers. COMPCON Spring '80, February, 1980, pp. 282-291.

23. Wulf, W. A., R. Levin, and S. P. Harbison. *Hydra/C.mmp: An Experimental Computer System.* McGraw-Hill, 1981.

24. *ALTO: A Personal Computer System - Hardware Manual.* Xerox Palo Alto Research Center, Palo Alto, California, 94304, 1979.

Chapter 11: VLSI Computing Systems

11.1: Introduction to the Configurable Highly Parallel Computer by
L. Snyder

11.2: On Supercomputing with Systolic/Wavefront Array Processors by
S. Y. Kung

11.3: Partitioned Matrix Algorithms for VLSI Arithmetic Systems by
K. Hwang and Y.-H. Cheng

11.4: Wafer-Scale Integration and Two-Level Pipelined Implementations
of Systolic Arrays by H.T. Kung and M.S. Lam

Reprinted from *Computer*, January 1982, pages 47-56. Copyright © 1982 by
The Institute of Electrical and Electronics Engineers, Inc.

*Architectures for this computer family are built around
a lattice of programmable switches and data paths that allows arbitrary
connection patterns — an approach that preserves locality.*

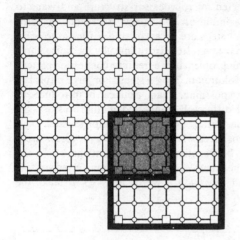

Introduction to the Configurable, Highly Parallel Computer

Lawrence Snyder, Purdue University

polymorphism, *n.*(1): capability of assuming
different forms; capability of wide variation.
Webster's Third International Dictionary

When von Neumann computers were still new and exciting, scientists noted in popular accounts that unlike mechanical devices, computers are polymorphic—their function can be radically changed simply by changing programs. Polymorphism *is* fundamental, but this familiar and obvious fact receives little mention any more, even though it underlies important advances such as time-sharing and programmable microcode. Now, however, as we are confronted with the potential for highly parallel computers made possible by very-large-scale integrated circuit technology, we may ask: What is the role of polymorphism in parallel computation? To answer this question, we must review the characteristics of parallel processing and the benefits and limitations of VLSI technology.

Algorithmically specialized processors

Perhaps the most important characteristic of VLSI circuit technology is that the manufacturing processes use photolithography to create copies of a circuit.[1] Fabrication by photolithography (or the newer X-ray lithography) requires a fixed number of steps to produce a circuit, independent of the circuit's complexity. It costs no more to make copies of a chip containing a NAND gate than to make copies of a chip containing a microprocessor, although yields will likely be higher for the former and wire bonding costs higher for the latter. Because preparing and debugging the lithographic masks is expensive,

the technology favors parallel processing techniques that employ many copies of the same circuit, even if it is complex.

Uniformity is the source of leverage in VLSI, and recognition of this caused a flurry of research during the past five years that resulted in a number of proposals for devices we may call *algorithmically specialized processors*. By focusing on computationally intensive problems and carefully dissecting algorithms for them, researchers have developed algorithmically specialized processors with several important characteristics:

- Construction is based on a few easily tessellated processing elements.
- Locality is exploited; that is, data movement is often limited to adjacent processing elements.
- Pipelining is used to achieve high processor utilization.

Examples of algorithmically specialized processors include designs for LU decomposition,[2,3] the main step in solving systems of linear equations; the solution of linear recurrences[2]; tree processors,[4-6] used in searching, sorting, and expression evaluation; dynamic programming,[7] a general problem-solving technique with numerous applications; join processing,[8] for data base querying; and many others.

Algorithmically specialized processing components must be joined together to solve a large, computationally intensive problem. This composition step is crucial, since whole problems tend to be multiphased and these components tend to be specialized to an algorithm used in only one phase. For example, to solve a system of linear equations ($Ax=b$), one might use a processor component to form the LU decomposition of the matrix A ($A=LU$) and then use a linear recurrence solver component to perform the substitution phases ($Ly=b$ and $Ux=y$). As

EHO219-6/84/0000/0521$01.00 © 1982 IEEE

another example, queries in data-base query languages are formed by composing operations such as "search" and "join."

If the component processors are implemented on chips, one way to compose them is to wire them together. This solution is inflexible because the components are dedicated to a particular problem and cannot be used for another problem. Another compositional scheme is to join the processors to a bus as "peripherals." This is more flexible since a processor can be used in different phases, but the bus becomes a bottleneck and time is wasted in interphase data movement.

Still another approach is to replace the dedicated processing elements with more general microprocessors and simply program the algorithmically specialized processing function. This solution is much more flexible because different components can use the same devices by changing programs, provided the interconnection pattern is the same. The bus bottleneck is eliminated. There is a loss in performance with this polymorphism, however, since cir-

cuit implementation of the primitive actions is replaced by the slower process of instruction execution.

But the main problem with this approach is that algorithmically specialized processors often use different interconnection structures (Figure 1). There is no guarantee that the consecutive phases of the computation can be done efficiently in place. For example, if we have an $n \times n$ mesh-connected microprocessor structure and want to find the maximum of n^2 elements stored one per processor, $2n - 1$ steps are necessary and sufficient to solve the problem. But a faster algorithmically specialized processor for this problem uses a tree interconnection pattern to find the solution in $2 \log n$ steps. For large n this is a benefit worth pursuing. Again, a bus can be introduced to link several differently connected multiprocessors, including mesh- and tree-connected multiprocessors. Data could be transferred when a change in the processor structure would be beneficial. But the bottleneck is quite serious; in the example, data has to be transferred at a rate proportional to $n^2/\log n$ words per step to make the

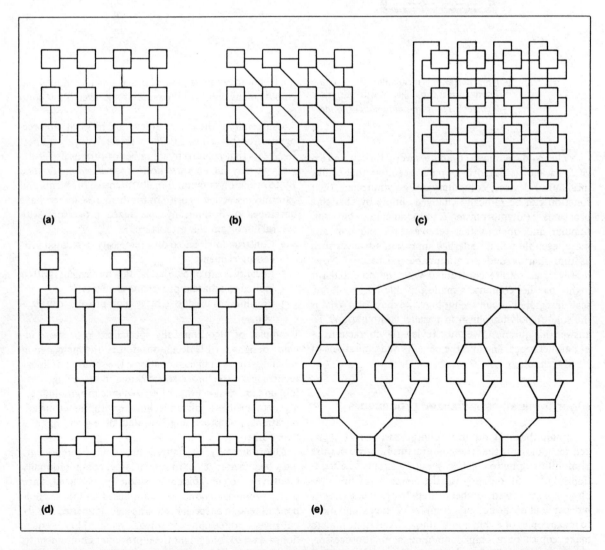

Figure 1. Interconnection patterns for algorithmically specialized processors: (a) mesh, used for dynamic programming[7]; (b) hexagonally connected mesh used for LU decomposition[2]; (c) torus used for transitive closure[7]; (d) binary tree used for sorting[4]; (e) double tree used for searching.[5]

COMPUTER

transfer worthwhile. What we need is a more polymorphic multiprocessor that does not compromise the benefits of VLSI technology.

The configurable, highly parallel, or CHiP computer is a multiprocessor architecture that provides a programmable interconnection structure integrated with the processing elements. Its objective is to provide the flexibility needed to compose general solutions while retaining the benefits of uniformity and locality that the algorithmically specialized processors exploit.

The CHiP architecture overview

The CHiP computer is a family of architectures each constructed from three components: a collection of homogeneous microprocessors, a switch lattice, and a controller. The switch lattice is the most important component and the main source of differences among family members. It is a regular structure formed from programmable switches connected by data paths. The microprocessors (hereafter called processing elements, or PEs) are not directly connected to each other, but rather are connected at regular intervals to the switch lattice. Figure 2 shows three examples of switch lattices. Generally, the layout will be square, although other geometries are possible. The perimeter switches are connected to external storage devices. A production CHiP computer might have from 2^8 to 2^{16} PEs. (With current technology only a few PEs and switches can be placed on a single chip. As improvements in fabrication technology permit higher device densities, a single chip will be able to host a larger

region of the switch lattice. Moreover, as discussed below, the CHiP architecture is quite suitable for "wafer-level" fabrication.)

Each switch in the lattice contains local memory capable of storing several configuration settings. A configuration setting enables the switch to establish a direct, static connection between two or more of its incident data paths. (This is circuit switching rather than packet switching.) For example, we achieve a mesh interconnection pattern of the PEs for the lattice in Figure 2a by assigning north-south configuration settings to alternate switches in odd-numbered rows and east-west settings to switches in the odd-numbered columns. Figure 3 illustrates the configuration; Figure 4 gives the configuration settings of a binary tree.

The controller is responsible for loading the switch memory. (This task is performed via a separate intercon-

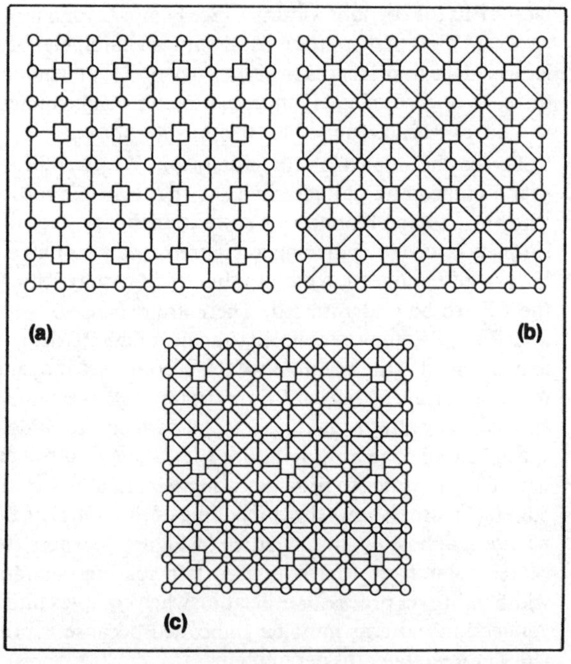

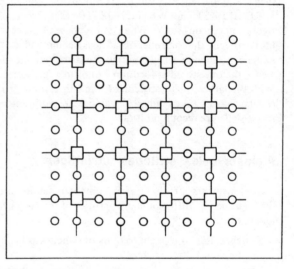

Figure 3. The switch lattice of Figure 2a configured into a mesh pattern.

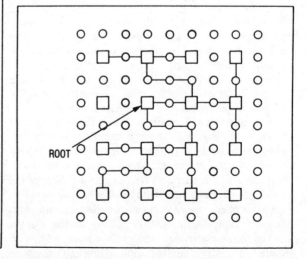

Figure 4. The switch lattice of Figure 2a configured into a binary tree.

Figure 2. Three switch lattice structures. Circles represent switches; squares represent PEs.

nection "skeleton.") The switch memory is loaded preparatory to processing and is performed in parallel with the PE program memory loading. Typically, program and switch settings for several phases can be loaded together. The chief requirement is that the local configuration settings for each phase's interconnection pattern be assigned to the same memory location in all switches. For example, in each switch, location 1 might be used to store the local configuration to implement a mesh pattern; location 2 might store the local configuration for the tree interconnection pattern, etc.

CHiP processing begins with the controller broadcasting a command to all switches to invoke a particular configuration setting. For example, suppose it is the setting stored at location 1 that implements a mesh pattern. With the entire structure interconnected into a mesh, the individual PEs synchronously execute the instructions stored in their local memory. PEs need not know to whom they are connected; they simply execute instructions such as READ EAST, and WRITE NORTHWEST. The configuration remains static. When a new phase of processing is to begin, the controller broadcasts a command to all switches to invoke a new configuration setting, for instance the one stored at location 2 implementing a tree. With the lattice thus restructured, the PEs resume processing, having taken only a single logical step in interphase structure reconfiguration.

A closer look at switches and lattices

The members of the CHiP computer family are distinguished by different characteristics of the switches and lattices.

Switches. It is convenient to think of switches as being defined by several parameters:

m—the number of wires entering a switch on one data path or data path width,
d—the degree or number of incident data paths,
c—the number of configuration settings that can be stored in a switch.

The value of m reflects the balance struck between parallel and serial data transmission. This balance will be influenced by several considerations, one of which is the limited number of pins on the package containing the chips of the CHiP lattice. Specifically, if a chip hosts a square region of the lattice containing n PEs, then the number of pins required is proportional to $m\sqrt{n}$.

The value of d will usually be 4, as in Figure 2a, or 8, as in Figure 2c. Figure 2b shows a mixed strategy that exploits the tendency of switches to be used in two different roles. Switches at the intersection of the vertical and horizontal switch corridors tend to perform most of the routing, while those interposed between two adjacent PEs act more like extended PE ports for selecting data paths from the "corridor buses." Specializing the degree of the switch to these activities reduces the number of bits required to specify a configuration setting and thus saves area.

The value of c is influenced by the number of configurations that may be needed for a multiphase computa-

tion and the number of bits required per setting. The latter number depends on the degree and the crossover capability of the switch.

Crossover capability is a property of switches and refers to the number of distinct data path groups that a switch can simultaneously connect. We speak of data path groups rather than data path pairs because fanout is permitted at a switch, allowing it to connect more than a pair of data paths. Crossover capability is specified by an integer g in the range 1 to $d/2$. Thus 1 indicates no crossover and $d/2$ is the maximum number of distinct paths intersecting at a degree d switch. Like the three parameters mentioned above, the crossover capability g is fixed at fabrication time.

The number of bits of storage needed for a switch is a modest dgc. This provides a bit for each direction of each crossover group of each configuration setting. This value can be reduced by providing for the loading of switch settings while the CHiP processor is executing. This quality, called asynchronous loading, permits a smaller value of c by taking advantage of two facts: algorithms often use configurations that differ in only a few places, and configurations often remain in effect long enough to prepare for future settings.

Lattices. From Figure 2 it is clear that lattices can differ in several ways. The PE degree, like the switch degree, is the number of incident data paths. Most algorithms of interest use PEs of degree eight or less. Larger degrees are probably not necessary since they can be achieved either by multiplexing data paths or by logically coupling processing elements (e.g., two degree-four PEs could be coupled to form a degree-six PE where one serves only as a buffer). The latter method leads to some loss in PE utilization, however.

We can call the number of switches that separate two adjacent PEs the corridor width, w. (See Figure 2c for a $w=2$ lattice.) This is perhaps the most significant parameter of a lattice, since it influences the efficiency of PE utilization, the convenience of interconnection pattern embeddings, and the overhead required for the polymorphism.

To see the impact of corridor width, let us embrace graph embedding parlance and say that a switch lattice "hosts" a PE interconnection pattern. In theory, even the simplest lattice (like the one in Figure 2a) can host an arbitrary interconnection pattern, but to do so may require the PEs to be underutilized. There are two reasons for this: First, PEs may be coupled to achieve high PE degree, as mentioned at the beginning of this section. Second, and more important, adjacent PEs in the (logical) guest interconnection pattern may have to be assigned to widely spaced PEs in the hosting lattice (i.e., separated by unused PEs) in order to provide enough data paths for the edges. (Figure 5 shows the embedding of the complete bipartite graph, $K_{4,4}$, in the lattice of Figure 2c where the center column of PEs is unused.) Increasing corridor width improves processor utilization when complex interconnection patterns must be embedded because it provides more data paths per unit area.

How wide should corridors be? It depends on which interconnection patterns are likely to be hosted and how economically necessary it is to maximize PE utilization.

For most of the algorithmically specialized processors developed for VLSI implementation, a corridor width of two suffices to achieve optimal or near optimal PE utilization. However, to be sure of hosting all planar interconnection patterns of n nodes with reasonably complete processor utilization, a width proportional to log n suffices and may in fact be necessary.[9] To host patterns such as the shuffle-exchange graph efficiently will require even wider corridors; on the average w must be at least proportional to $n/\log n$.[10]

Selecting a corridor width is difficult, especially if it is a nonconstant width. The benefit, in some cases, is higher PE utilization; the cost is a loss of some locality (in all cases), more area overhead, and increased problems with pin limitations. Preliminary evidence indicates that $w \leq 4$ provides a reasonable cost/benefit trade-off, but further experimentation and analysis are required.[11]

Embedding an interconnection pattern

In addition to the conventional polymorphism derived from PE programming, we have provided for a second variety in the programmable switches. This requires interconnection pattern programming, i.e., specification of a global interconnection pattern. When viewed in a programming language context, the source program is a global interconnection pattern that a compiler translates into an object code of individual switch settings suitable for loading into the switches by the CHiP controller. Our concern here, however, is limited to one particular interconnection pattern: the complete binary tree. This example will illustrate the differences between embedding into the plane and embedding into the CHiP lattice.

The complete binary tree has $2^p - 1$ PEs, one at each node. One possible layout of this structure in the CHiP lattice is a direct translation of the hyper-H strategy[1] illustrated in Figure 1d. Figure 6 illustrates this embedding into the lattice of Figure 2a, and it is clear that many (asymptotically one half) of the PEs are unused in this naive approach. The problem is that although the hyper-H is an excellent embedding on plain silicon where the placement of PEs and data paths is arbitrary, CHiP lattice embeddings must conform to the prespecified PE and data path sites. As we shall see, this constraint is not onerous.

To illustrate an optimal embedding in terms of maximizing the use of PEs, let's assume that we have an $n \times n$ CHiP lattice where $n = 2^k$ for some integer k. This gives 2^{2k} PEs, so a binary tree of depth $2k$ fits with only one unused PE, since it has $2^{2k} - 1$ nodes. We'll call this unused PE a "spare."

We proceed inductively by pairing two embedded subtrees to form a new tree one level higher. For the basis of the induction it is convenient to use a three-node binary tree embedded with one spare in a 2×2 portion of the lattice. Pairing square subtree embeddings produces rectangles with sides in ratio 2:1. Pairing these rectangles yields squares again. In general, we pair two subtrees, each with $2^{2k} - 1$ nodes and a spare, to produce a new $2^{2k+1} - 1$ node tree in which one of the subtree spares becomes the root of the new tree and the other spare

becomes the spare of the new tree. The challenge is to place the spares at the proper sites for the next step in the induction.

If we adopt the strategy of the hyper-H embedding and locate the root at the center of the tree, it makes sense to place a spare at the middle of one side. Then, when this

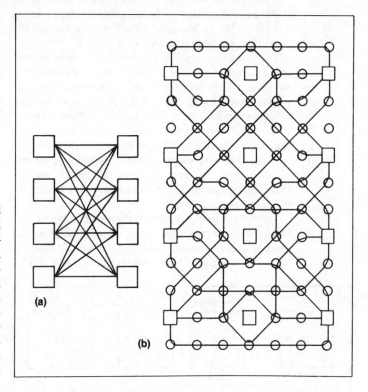

Figure 5. Graph $K_{4,4}$ shown in (a) is embedded into the lattice of Figure 2c using a switch with crossover value $g = 2$.

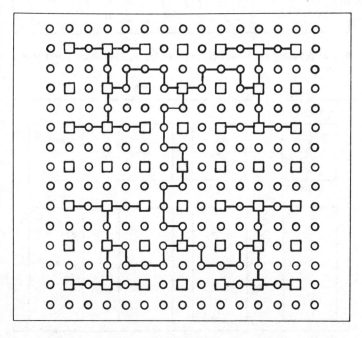

Figure 6. The hyper-H tree (Figure 1d) directly embedded into the switch lattice of Figure 2a; the switches are not shown.

tree is paired to form the next larger tree, there is a spare at the interface ready to become the new root. This will be in the center of the new tree as we intend. (Of course, since the sides always have an even number of PEs, "middle" here means adjacent to the midpoint of one side.) But we cannot pair two trees with their spares in the middle of one side because this would leave us with either a buried spare that is difficult to use when forming the next larger tree, or a spare on the perimeter at a site inappropriate for the embedding of the next larger tree (Figure 7).

The solution is to pair one subtree with a spare located at the middle of one side with a subtree whose spare is at the corner. The spare in the middle becomes the root of the new tree, and the corner spare can be located (using reflection) to become either a middle spare or a corner spare of the new tree, depending on which is needed for the next inductive step. Thus, at each step in the induction we must use—and we can create—two types of embeddings: middles and corners (Figure 8). Notice that the basis tree, embedded in a 2×2 portion of the lattice, actually serves as both types.

Trees, of course, are planar; that is, they can be embedded in the plane without crossovers. But following the preceding algorithm with the lattice in Figure 2a makes it appear as though crossovers are required, at least during the early stages of the embedding. It is possible, using basis elements of fifteen-node trees embedded in 4×4 square regions of the lattice, to achieve a completely planar embedding. A solution[12] is shown in Figure 9.

Solving a system of linear equations

In order to illustrate how the CHiP processor can be used to compose algorithms, we pose the problem of solving a system of linear equations, i.e., to solve $Ax = b$ for an $n \times n$ coefficient matrix A of bandwidth p and n vector b. We shall use two algorithmically specialized processors due to H. T. Kung and C. E. Leiserson as described in Mead and Conway.[1] The first is an LU-decomposition systolic array processor that factors A into lower and upper triangular matrices L and U.

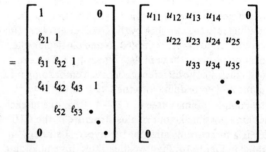

The second systolic processor solves a lower triangular linear system $Ly = b$ where L is the output from the decomposition step. (We call this the LTS solver.) The final result vector x can be found by solving $Ux = y$ where U is the upper triangular matrix from the first step and y is the vector output of the second step. By rewriting U as a lower triangular system, we can use another instance of the LTS solver. Our approach will be to compose these pieces into a harmonious process to solve the entire problem.

The first problem we must solve is the embedding of the Kung-Leiserson systolic processors. These algorithmically specialized processors are defined for $n \times n$ arrays of bandwidth p. (Figure 10 shows the LU-decompositon processor for a $p = 7$ system. Figure 11 shows a suitable lower triangular system solver processor.) Since the LU-decomposition processor is hexagonally connected, it will be convenient to embed the processors into the lattice shown in Figure 2b. The obvious strategy is to connect the processors in such a way that the lower triangular output L of the decomposition step connects directly to the input of the lower triangular system solver. It is also obvious that these embeddings should be placed at the perimeter of the CHiP lattice so that matrix A and vector b can be

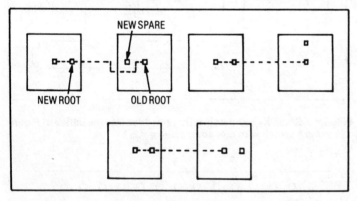

Figure 7. Paring subtrees using spares located at the midpoint of one side.

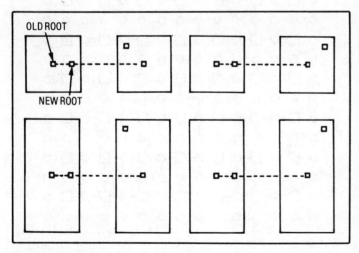

Figure 8. The formation of middle and corner embeddings using a middle and corner pair.

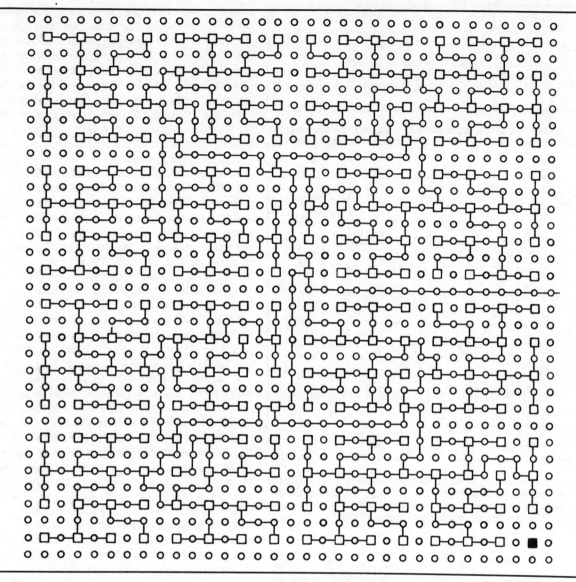

Figure 9. Planar embedding of a 255-node complete binary tree into the lattice of Figure 2a.

received from external storage. Figure 12 shows such an embedding where the PE labelings correspond to those given in Figures 10 and 11.

Several simple transformations have been employed to accomplish the embedding. The most noticeable is that the hexagonal structure has been slightly deformed to accommodate the rectangular CHiP lattice, and the LU-decomposition processor has been rotated clockwise 120 degrees. The constant inputs (0's and -1) that appear on the perimeter of the systolic array have been suppressed, since they can be generated internally to the PEs. The output wires carrying the L matrix result have been assigned to one of the available ports and routed to the inputs of the LTS solver. Finally, to embed the double channel between PEs of the LTS solver, we have routed data diagonally out of the north-east port into the south-east port. Notice that since the diagonal elements of L are all 1, they are not explicitly produced.

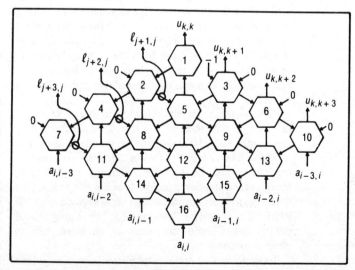

Figure 10. The Kung-Leiserson systolic array for LU-decomposition. Labelings indicate data paths. For timings, see Mead and Conway.[1]

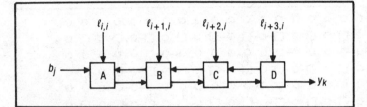

Figure 11. The Kung-Leiserson systolic LTS solver. Labelings indicate data paths for elements of L and b. For timings, see Mead and Conway.

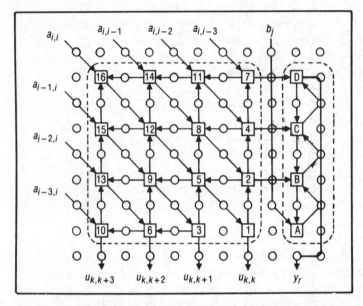

Figure 12. The embedding of the LU-decomposition processor and the LTS solver in the lattice of Figure 2b. Although the data paths are bidirectional, we have used arrows to emphasize the direction of data movement. PE labelings correspond to Figures 10 and 11.

The next problem is the rewriting of U as a lower triangular system suitable for input into another embedded LTS solver. We must wait until U has been entirely produced before performing this operation. So, rather than writing the elements of U to external storage as they are produced, we thread them through the lattice (assuming there is sufficient space to store them all). We also thread the y vector output from the LTS process along with U. Then, in the second phase of our algorithm, we can process the elements through another embedded LTS solver.

Perhaps the most elegant way to thread U and y through the lattice is to use the Aleliunas-Rosenberg graph embedding.[13] The scheme has the advantage of not requiring a large bundle of wires along the perimeter of the lattice when the threads double back. (Figure 13 illustrates the embedding required for doubling back.) As the U and y values are produced, they are passed from PE to PE. (They could be "concentrated" by storing several per PE.) When U and y are completely produced, the first phase is finished.

Between the first and second phases we make a minor reconfiguration. This reconfiguration would not have been necessary had the phase 1 configuration been

somewhat more clever, but as an example it would have been more confusing. The second configuration embeds the LTS solver into the fourth row of processors (Figure 14). The inputs to this group of processors come from reversing the flow direction of the threaded values from phase 1. Notice that this flow reversal has the effect of renumbering the matrix U in the lower triangular form appropriate for the LTS solver. The appropriate values of the y vector are also available at the proper locations. The outputs from the second phase emanate from the western port of processor$_{4,1}$. These are the values solving $Ax = b$.

To summarize, the system of linear equations $Ax = b$ is solved in two phases on the CHiP processor. In phase 1 an embedded LU-decomposition processor takes A as input and produces matrices L and U as output. The L output is immediately input to an LTS solver that also takes b as input and solves $Ly = b$. The vector y and the matrix U are threaded through the lattice. Phase 1 completes when A has been decomposed. In phase 2 another embedded LTS solver takes the threaded output from phase 1, by reversing its flow, and solves $Ux = y$.

Phase 2 makes scant use of parallelism; it runs in the same time as phase 1, and the data are already in the CHiP processor. The interphase reconfiguration is not essential, but there are algorithms to solve the phase 2 problem that employ configurability to make effective use of parallelism.[14] A complete development of the approach is not possible here, but the essential idea set forth by Chen, Kuck, and Sameh[15] is straightforward: A transformation on U enables us to decompose the matrix into blocks $B_1, \ldots, B_k$ whose product yields the result. Because the product operation is associative, the whole product can be formed by taking pairwise products in parallel, then pairwise products of the results, etc. By reconfiguring the threaded portion of the lattice using one of several rather complicated interconnection patterns that either implicitly or explicitly embed a tree, we can perform these pairwise products in parallel. The result is a faster parallel algorithm made possible by configurability.

Characteristics of our approach

The algorithmically specialized processors translate *mutatis mutandis* into programs for the CHiP computer. Thus, we have a ready supply of algorithms that can effectively use the parallel processor. Of course, all of these algorithms use one interconnection structure, and it is possible that improved algorithms might be found that exploit the availability of multiple interconnection structures.

Configurability provides both interphase and intraphase flexibility. This distinction, though not clearcut, tends to correlate with the use of pipelining. If a problem is solved by a sequence of phases where each completes before the next begins, we tend to use regular configurations that change at the completion of a phase (interphase). The whole lattice is in a mesh or tree pattern. For a series of pipelined algorithms that can be coupled together, we tend to form regions of the lattice dedicated to each algorithm with data paths interconnecting the regions. We refer to this as intraphase configurability

COMPUTER

because within one phase we interconnect several regular structures. Clearly, we need not change configurations to exploit the advantage of configurability.

Both types of configurability are useful in adapting to changes on problem size. For example, two separate small problems might operate concurrently on different regions of the CHiP processor using entirely different interconnection schemes. One pattern could change while the other remains fixed, by loading switches of the fixed region with two copies of the same configuration setting. Pipelined processors, whose size is usually a function of the input width, can be tailored to the right size at loading time.

Another consequence of configurability is its high fault tolerance. If an error is detected in a processor, data path, or switch, we can simply route around the offending device. For convenience, we might choose to leave other processors unused to square-up the lattice when it is important to have matching dimensions.

Perhaps the most intriguing consequence of configurability's fault tolerance is the possibility of wafer-level fabrication. That is, instead of dicing a wafer and discarding the faulty processor chips, we can leave a VLSI wafer whole and simply route around the unusable processors. (We could use the dicing corridors for data paths and switches.) For example, if a wafer contains 100 processor chips and yield characteristics indicate that roughly one third are faulty, then a wafer is acceptable if we can find an 8×8 sublattice that is functional. The mapping of the switches to host the 8×8 in the 100 could be done on the wafer by specially designed circuitry. Although the number of pins required for the wafer would be large, their number is proportional to the perimeter rather than the area. This actually reduces the total number of wires bonded.

By integrating programmable switches with the processing elements, the CHiP computer achieves a polymorphism of interconnection structure that also preserves locality. This enables us to compose algorithms that exploit different interconnection patterns. In addition to responding to problems of different sizes and characteristics, the flexibility of integrated switches provides substantial fault tolerance and permits wafer-level fabrication. ∎

References

1. Carver Mead and Lynn Conway, *Introduction to VLSI Systems,* Addison-Wesley, Reading, Mass., 1980.

2. H. T. Kung and C. E. Leiserson, "Systolic Arrays (for VLSI)," Technical Report CS-79-103, Carnegie-Mellon University, Pittsburg, Pa., Apr. 1979.

3. D. B. Gannon, "On Pipelining a Mesh-Connected Multiprocessor for Finite Element Problems by Nested Dissection," *Proc. Int'l Conf. Parallel Processing,* 1980, pp. 197-204.

4. Sally Browning, "The Tree Machine: A Highly Concurrent Programming Environment," PhD thesis, California Institute of Technology, Jan. 1980.

5. Jon L. Bentley and H. T. Kung, "A Tree Machine for Searching Problems," *Proc. Int'l Conf. Parallel Processing,* 1979, pp. 257-266.

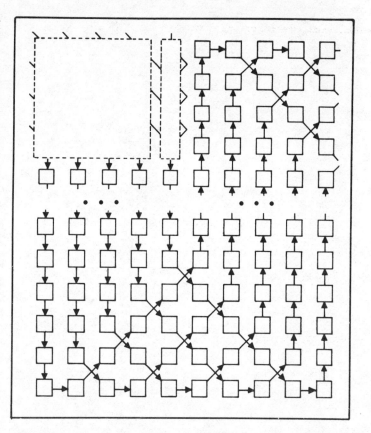

Figure 13. The Aleliunas-Rosenberg embedding of the threads doubling back. The arrows indicate the direction of flow of the *U* and *y* values.

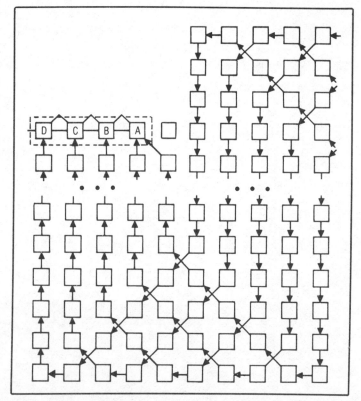

Figure 14. The simple phase 2 embedding.

On Supercomputing with Systolic/Wavefront Array Processors

SUN-YUAN KUNG, SENIOR MEMBER, IEEE

Invited Paper

Reprinted from *Proceedings of the IEEE*, Volume 72, Number 7, July 1984.
Copyright © 1984 by The Institute of Electrical and Electronics Engineers, Inc.

In many scientific and signal processing applications, there are increasing demands for large-volume and/or high-speed computations which call for not only high-speed computing hardware, but also for novel approaches in computer architecture and software techniques in future supercomputers. Tremendous progress has been made on several promising parallel architectures for scientific computations, including a variety of digital filters, fast Fourier transform (FFT) processors, data-flow processors, systolic arrays, and wavefront arrays. This paper describes these computing networks in terms of signal-flow graphs (SFG) or data-flow graphs (DFG), and proposes a methodology of converting SFG computing networks into synchronous systolic arrays or data-driven wavefront arrays. Both one- and two-dimensional arrays are discussed theoretically, as well as with illustrative examples. A wavefront-oriented programming language, which describes the (parallel) data flow in systolic/wavefront-type arrays, is presented. The structural property of parallel recursive algorithms points to the feasibility of a Hierarchical Iterative Flow-Graph Design (HIFD) of VLSI Array Processors. The proposed array processor architectures, we believe, will have significant impact on the development of future supercomputers.

I. INTRODUCTION

The increasing demands for high-performance signal processing and scientific computations indicate the need for tremendous computing capability, in terms of both volume and speed. The availability of low-cost, high-density, fast processing/memory devices will presage a major breakthrough in future supercomputer designs, especially in the design of highly concurrent processors.

Current parallel computers can be characterized into three structural classes: vector processors, multiprocessor systems, and array processors [13]. The first two classes belong to the general-purpose computer domain. The development of these systems requires a complicated design of control units and optimized schemes for allocation of machine resources. The third class, however, belongs to the domain of special-purpose computers. The design of such systems requires a broad knowledge of the relationship between parallel-computing algorithms and optimal-computing hardware and software structures.

It is this last class that we shall focus upon, since it offers a promising solution to meet real-time processing requirements. Especially, locally interconnected computing networks, such as systolic and wavefront arrays, are well suited to efficiently implement a major class of signal processing algorithms due to their massive parallelism and regular data flow [15], [17]. Such architectures promise real-time solutions to a large variety of advanced computational tasks.

This paper first discusses some important design considerations for massively parallel VLSI array processors and the algorithmic background of these array processors. This will lead to a systematic software/hardware design approach. Specifically, we discuss the methodology of imposing systolic architectures and/or data-flow computing onto signal-flow graph computing networks. The concept of computational wavefronts, which leads to systolic-type and wavefront-type architectures, is reviewed. A wavefront programming language is proposed to broaden the applications of the wavefront/systolic type arrays.

A. Architectural Considerations in Array Processor Design

There are many important issues in designing array processor systems, such as processor interconnection, system clocking, and modularity [19].

Interconnection in massively parallel array processors is the most critical issue of the system design, since communication is very expensive in terms of area, power, and time consumption [26]. Therefore, communication has to be restricted to *localized interconnections*. To avoid global interconnections, local and regular data movements are strongly preferred. This is the most salient characteristic of systolic and wavefront arrays.

The clocking scheme is also a very critical issue. In the globally synchronous scheme, there is a global clock network which distributes the clock signal over the entire array. For very large systems, the clock skew incurred in global clock distribution is a nontrivial factor, causing unnecessary slowdown in the clock rate [18], [10]. Under this circumstance, the self-timed scheme is more preferable.

Large design of layout costs suggest using repetitive modular structures, i.e., a few different types of simple (and often standard) cells. Thus we have to identify the primitives that can be implemented efficiently and optimally realize the potential of new device technologies.

Programmable processor modules (as opposed to dedicated modules) are favored due to cost-effectiveness considerations. The high cost of designing such modules may be amortized over a broader applicational domain. Indeed, a major portion of scientific computations can be reduced to a basic set of matrix operations and other related algo-

Manuscript received February 9, 1984; revised March 5, 1984. This research was supported in part by the Office of Naval Research under Contracts N00014-81-K-0191 and N00014-83-C-0377 and by the National Science Foundation under Grant ECS-82-12479.

The author is with the Department of Electrical Engineering, University of Southern California, Los Angeles, CA 90089, USA.

rithms. These should be exploited in order to simplify the hardware module.

B. Mapping Parallel Algorithms onto Locally Interconnected Computing Networks

There are quite a few software packages for scientific computation and image/signal processing algorithms available today. For example, LINPAK [9] and EISPAK [29] are popular packages for many scientific computations, especially those using various types of matrix operations (such as). However, the execution time of these algorithms, running on conventional computers, is often too slow for real-time applications. Fortunately, VLSI and other new techniques have made high-speed parallel processing economical and feasible. When mapping these algorithms onto parallel processors, typical questions often raised are: "How to fully utilize the inherent concurrency in these algorithms?" "How are these algorithms best implemented in hardware?" "What kind of array processor(s) should one turn to for a specific application?"

After examining most of the algorithms collected in the aforementioned packages, some prominent traits surface, such as localized operations, intensive computation, and matrix operands. The common features of these algorithms should be exploited to facilitate the design of array processors for signal processing applications.

An array processor is composed of an array of processor elements (PE) with direct (static) or indirect (dynamic) interconnections, including linear, orthogonal, hexagonal, tree, perfect-shuffle, or other types of structures. The most critical issue is communication, i.e., moving data between PE's in a large-scale interconnection network.

Correspondingly, a communication-oriented analysis on parallel algorithms will be most useful for mapping algorithms onto the arrays. To conform with the constraints imposed by VLSI, this paper will emphasize a special class of algorithms, i.e., *recursive* and *locally dependent* algorithms.[1]

For proper communication in an interconnected computing network, each PE in the array should know

a) **where** to send (or fetch) data, and
b) **when** to send (or fetch) data.

When mapping a locally recursive algorithm onto a computing network, it allows a simple solution to the question "a) **where** to send the data?" because the data movements can be confined to nearest neighbor PE's. Therefore, locally interconnected computing networks will suffice to execute the algorithm with high performance.

The conventional approach to the second question "b) **when** to send the data?" is to use a globally synchronous scheme, where the timing is controlled by a sequence of "beats" [30]. A prominent example is the systolic array [16], [15] However, locality can have two meanings in array processor designs: localized data transactions and/or localized timing scheme (i.e., using self-timed, data-driven control). In fact, the class of locally recursive algorithms permits both locality features; these should be exploited in the

architectural designs. An example for such a design is the wavefront array [17].

II. Signal-Flow Graph (SFG) Computing Networks

The most useful graphical representation for scientific and signal processing computations is the signal-flow graph (SFG). While the graphical representations are most popularly used for signal processing flow diagrams, such as FFT and digital filters, etc., the SFG representations in fact cover a broad domain of applications, including linear and nonlinear, time-varying and time-invariant, and multidimensional systems. For convenience, this paper will treat only time-invariant SFG systems.[2]

Notations: In general, a **node** is often denoted by a circle representing an arithmetic or logic function *performed with zero delay*, such as multiply, add, etc. (cf. Fig. 1(a)). An **edge**, on the other hand, denotes either a function

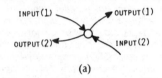

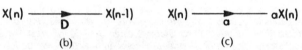

Fig. 1. Examples of SFG graphical denotations. (a) An operation node with (two) inputs and (two) outputs. (b) An edge as a delay operator. (c) An edge as a multiplier.

or a delay. Unless otherwise specified, for a large class of signal processing SFGs, the following conventions are adopted for convenience. When an edge is labeled with a capital letter D (or D', $2D'$, etc.), it represents a time-delay operator with delay time D (or D', $2D'$, etc.) (see Fig. 1(a)). On the other hand, if an edge is labeled with a lower case letter, such as a, a_i, b_i, it represents a multiplication by a constant a, a_i, b_i (see Fig. 1(b)).

When the concept of the SFG was originally conceived, there was little consideration given to the locality preferences in parallel-computing network design. Hence this paper addresses the issue of systematic approaches of mapping SFGs into locally interconnected parallel-array processors.

There are two major classes of SFGs: those with *local interconnections*, and those with *global interconnections*. A typical example of a global SFG is one representing the FFT algorithm. The principle of the (decimation-in-time) FFT is based on successively decomposing the data, say $\{x(i)\}$, into *even* and *odd* parts. This partitioning scheme will result in global communication between PEs. More precisely, the FFT recursions can be written as (using the "in-place" computing scheme [27])

---

[1] In a recursive algorithm, all processors do nearly identical tasks and each processor repeats a fixed set of tasks on sequentially available data.

[2] This incurs no loss of generality, since any internal time-varying parameters can be equivalently represented by an (external) input signal.

$$x^{(m+1)}(p) = x^{(m)}(p) + w_N^r x^{(m)}(q)$$

$$x^{(m+1)}(q) = x^{(m)}(p) - w_N^r x^{(m)}(q)$$

with p, q, r varying from stage to stage. The "distance" of the global communication involved will be proportional to $|p - q|$. An SFG for the (decimation-in-time) FFT, with space and time indices properly labeled, is shown in Fig. 2. Note

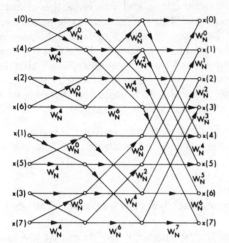

Fig. 2. A signal-flow graph (SFG) for the decimation-in-time FFT algorithm.

that in the last stage the maximum distance is $|p - q| = N/2$ (see [27]). For example, the maximum distance will be 512 units for a 1024-point FFT. Thus the FFT algorithm is a *global one*, since the recursion involves globally separated indices. Therefore, FFT computing structures will call for spatially global interconnections, and cannot be easily mapped onto systolic or wavefront arrays.

In contrast to the FFT algorithm, most other recursive signal processing algorithms are *local*, i.e., the spatial separations between nodes are within a certain limit. Therefore, the corresponding SFGs are "localizable." For examples, the SFGs for FIR and IIR filters can be easily implemented with spatially local SFGs. Generally, an IIR (infinite impulse response) filter is defined by the difference equation

$$y(k) = \sum_{m=1}^{N} x(k - m)b(m) + \sum_{m=1}^{N} y(k - m)a(m). \quad (1)$$

(Note that FIR filtering, linear convolution, and transversal filterings are simply special cases when $a(m) = 0$.)

A popular SFG[3] [27] for (1) is shown in Fig. 3.

We note that this SFG has spatially local interconnections. But it is not *temporally local*, since according to the SFG, propagating a datum "X" from, say, the left-most node to the right-most node uses "zero" time. More precisely, the SFG imposes the requirement that the datum "X" has to be **broadcast** to all the nodes on the upper path. This is certainly undesirable from a systolic design perspective

---

[3]For this section, a node (circle) commonly denotes addition when there are multiple outputs and single input to the node. It denotes a branching node if there is one input and multiple outputs.

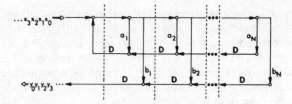

Fig. 3. Direct form design of ARMA (IIR) filter. The SFG is spatially localized but *not temporally localized*.

(and unrealistic for a circuit implementation). This will be the focus point of the next section.

III. SYSTOLIZATION OF SFG COMPUTING NETWORKS

A. Systolic Array

Systolic processors [16], [15] are a new class of "pipelined" array architectures. According to Kung and Leiserson [16], "A systolic system is a network of processors which rhythmically compute and pass data through the system." For example, it is shown in [16] that some basic "inner product" PEs ($Y \leftarrow Y + A*B$) can be *locally* connected together to perform digital filtering, matrix multiplication, and other related operations. The systolic array features the important properties of modularity, regularity, local interconnection, a high degree of pipelining, and highly synchronized multiprocessing. The data movements in a systolic array are often described in terms of the "snapshots" of the activities [16].

There are no formal or coherent definitions of the systolic array in literature. In order to have a formal treatment of the subject, however, we shall adopt the following definition:

1) Definition: Systolic Array: A systolic array is a computing network possessing the following features:

a) *Synchrony:* The data are rhythmically computed (timed by a global clock) and passed through the network.

b) *Regularity (i.e., Modularity and Local Interconnections):* The array should consist of modular processing units with regular and (spatially) local interconnections. Moreover, the computing network may be extended indefinitely.

c) *Temporal Locality:* There will be at least one unit-time delay allotted so that signal transactions from one node to the next can be completed.

d) *Pipelinability (i.e., O(M) Execution-Time Speed-Up):* A good measure for the efficiency of the array is the following

$$\text{Speed-Up Factor} = \frac{\text{Processing Time in a Single Processor}}{\text{Processing Time in the Array Processor}}$$

A systolic array should exhibit a *linear-rate pipelinability*, i.e., it should achieve an $O(M)$ speed-up, in terms of processing rates, where M is the number of processor elements (PEs).

We note that a *regular* SFG, such as the canonic SFG for ARMA filters, is already very close to a systolic array. The major difference being that most SFGs are not given in temporally localized form. Therefore, it is important to be able to convert them into localized ones. The topic of imposing temporal locality into a computing network has been a focus point of several researchers, including a series of publications by Fettweis [31], Leiserson [22]–[24], etc., and, more recently, the works reported in [20], [25], [14], [2]. The main advantage of the (cut-set) scheme proposed here (largely based on [20]) lies in its simplicity to use and its straightforward proof. Our proof is based on a graph-theoretical result—the *colored arc lemma*, which will be discussed momentarily.

2) Systolic Array for ARMA (IIR) Filter: Before discussing the general procedure, let us first take a look at an example. The canonic SFG for an ARMA Filter in Fig. 3 can be easily converted into a local-type one. Our first step in Fig. 4(a) is to rescale the time unit by setting $D = 2D'$. After shifting one of the two delays from the upper edges to the corresponding lower edges, a modified design can be derived as in Fig. 4(a).

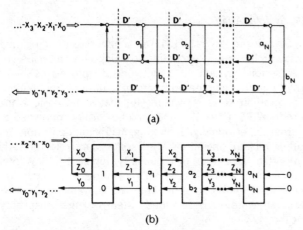

(a)

(b)

Fig. 4. (a) A modified SFG for an ARMA filter—a systolized version. (b) A systolic array for an ARMA (IIR) filter.

To verify that Fig. 4(a) yields the same transfer function as Fig. 3, one can simply check that the transfer function remains the same [20]. A more general proof will be discussed in a moment.

Let us now demonstrate how the modified form can be trivially converted into a systolic design. To do this, the operation time for one multiplication, one addition, and data transfer are merged with the uni-time delay D'. Therefore, the delay D', the multiplier, and the adder in each single section (defined by means of dashed lines) in Fig. 4(a) are all merged into an "inner product" processor. This leads to an overall systolic array configuration for IIR filter as shown in Fig. 4(b).

Now we are ready to discuss a general systematic procedure for converting SFGs into systolic arrays. First, we need a procedure to convert an SFG into a temporally localized SFG, which contains only nonzero-delay edges between modular sections.

Definition: Cut-Set:
  A *cut-set* in an SFG is a minimal set of edges which partitions the SFG into two parts.

B. A Cut-Set (Temporal) Localization Procedure

The localization procedure is based on two simple rules:

Rule (i) Time-Scaling: All delays D may be scaled, i.e., $D \rightarrow \alpha D'$, by a single positive integer α. Correspondingly,

the input and output rates also have to be scaled by a factor α (with respect to the new time unit D') (see Fig. 4(a)).

Rule (ii) Delay-Transfer: Given any cut-set of the SFG, we can group the edges of the cut-set into *inbound edges* and *outbound edges*, depending upon the directions assigned to the edges. Rule (ii) allows advancing k (D') time units on all the outbound edges and delaying k time units on the inbound edges, and *vice versa*. It is clear that, for a (time-invariant) SFG, the general system behavior is not affected because the effects of lags and advances cancel each other in the overall timing. Note that the input–input and input–output timing relationships will also remain exactly the same only if they are located on the same side. Otherwise, they should be adjusted[4] by a lag of $+k$ time units or an advance of $-k$ time units.

We shall refer to these two basic rules as the (cut-set) *localization rules.* Based on these rules, we assert the following:

Theorem:
All computable[5] SFG's are temporally localizable.

Proof of the Theorem: We claim that the localization Rules (i) and (ii) can be used to "localize" any (targeted) zero-delay edge, i.e., to convert it into a nonzero-delay edge. This is done by choosing a "good" cut-set and apply the rules upon it. A good cut-set including the "target edge" should not include any "bad edges," i.e., those zero-delay edges in the opposite direction of the target edge. This means that the cut-set will include only i) the target edge, ii) nonzero delay edges going in either direction, and iii) zero-delay edges going in the same direction. Then, according to Rule (ii), the nonzero delays of the opposite-direction edges can "give" one or more spare delays to the target edge (in order to localize it). If there are no spare delays to give away, simply scale all delays in the SFG according to Rule (i) to create enough delays for the transfer needed.

Therefore, the only thing left to prove is that such a "good" cut-set always exists. For this, we refer to Fig. 5., in which we have kept only all of the zero-delay *successor edges* and the zero-delay *predecessor edges* connected to the target edge, and removed all the other edges from the graph. In other words, Fig. 5 depicts the bad edges which should not be included in the cut-set. As shown by the dashed lines in Fig. 5, there must be "openings" between these two sets of bad edges—otherwise, some set of zero-delay edges would form a zero-delay loop, and the SFG would not be computable. Obviously, any cut-set "cutting" through the openings is a "good" cut-set, thus the existence proof is completed. (The author was later advised by a colleague that the existence proof discussed above is in fact a result known as the *colored arc lemma* in graph theory.) It is clear that repeatedly applying the localization Rule (ii) (and (i), if necessary) on the cut-sets will eventually lead to a temporally localized SFG.

---

[4]If there is more than one cut-set involved, and if the input and output are separated by more than one cut-set, then such adjustment factors should be accumulated.

[5]An SFG is meaningful only when it is computable, i.e., there exists no zero-delay loop in SFG.

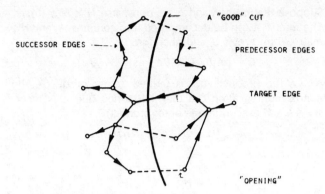

Fig. 5. "Openings" between bad edges ensure the existence of a "good" cut-set. This may be used as a clue for selecting a "good" cut-set.

C. Systolization Procedure

As we have claimed earlier, a regular SFG is *almost* equivalent to a systolic array and can be easily systolized. The systolization procedure, essentially based on the cut-set localization rules, is outlined below:

1) *Selection of Basic Operation Modules:* The choice may not be unique. In general, the finer the granularity of the basic modules, the more efficient (in speed) a systolic array will be. (A comparison of two possible lattice modules for a systolic array will be discussed in the next subsection.)

2) *Applying Localization Rules:* If the given SFG is regular, i.e., modular and spatially local, then regular cut-sets can be selected and the above rules can be used to derive a regular and temporally localized SFG.[6]

3) *Combination of Delay and Operation Modules:* To convert such an SFG into a systolic form, we need only to successfully introduce a delay into each of the operation modules, such as $A + B*C$. Combine the delay with the module operation to form a basic systolic element. All the extra delays will be modeled as pure delays without operations.

4) *Verification of the Arrays:* An SFG representation for linear, time-invariant systems is directly verifiable by the Z-transform technique. The correctness of the transformation to a systolic design is also guaranteed by the cut-set rules. Therefore, there is no need to display snapshots for the verification purpose. Nevertheless, one may find snapshots a simple and useful tool for a better appreciation of the movement of data.

IV. EXAMPLES OF THE SYSTOLIZATION PROCEDURE

In this section, we shall apply the systolization procedure to some one- and two-dimensional SFGs.

A. Systolic Lattice Filters

For the one-dimensional case, a very interesting example is the systolic implementation of a digital lattice filter, which should have many important applications to speech and seismic signal processing. For this example, let us now

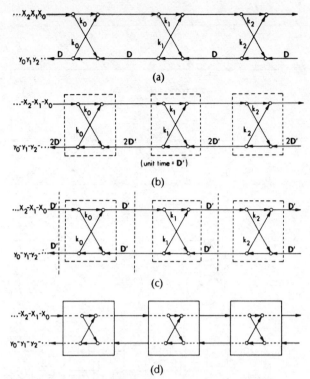

Fig. 6. (a) An SFG for AR lattice filters. (b) Time-rescaled SFG for AR lattice filters (type A). (c) "Localized" SFG for AR lattice filters (type A). (d) Systolic array for AR lattice filters (type-A).

apply the transformation rules to the SFG for an autoregressive (AR) lattice filter, as shown in Fig. 6(a). There are two possible choices of basic operation modules for the lattice array: (A) a lattice operation module,[7] and (B) a multiply/add (AM) basic module. Note that in each lattice operation there are two MA operations—implying that the lattice operation uses twice the time of MA.

1) *Lattice Systolic Array (Type-A):* By localization Rule (i), we first double each delay, i.e., $D \rightarrow 2D'$ as shown in Fig. 6(b). Apply (uniformly) the cuts to the SFG and subtract one delay from each of the left-bound edges and, correspondingly, add one delay to each of the right-bound edges in the cut-sets. This yields Fig. 6(c). Finally, by combining the delays with the lattice module, we have the final systolic structure, as in Fig. 6(d). Note that, because of the time-scaling, the input sequence $\{x(i)\}$ will be interleaved with "blanks" to match the adjusted delays. It is clear that $\alpha = 2$ and the array can yield an $M/2$ execution-time speedup.

2) *Lattice Systolic Array (Type-B):* By the localization Rule (i), we first triple each delay; i.e., $D \rightarrow 3D'$. (The resultant SFG is the same as what is shown in Fig. 6(b), but substituting $2D'$ by $3D'$.) Apply uniform cut-sets to the SFG as shown in Fig. 7(a). Subtract two delays from each left-bound edge, and, correspondingly, add two delays to every right-bound edge in the cut-sets. This yields Fig. 7(a). Now let us use a cut-set partitioning the upper edges from the lower edges as shown in Fig. 7(b). Transfer one delay from the down-going edges to the up-going ones. The result is depicted in Fig. 7(b). Finally, by combining the delays with

---

[6]In order to preserve the modular structure of the SFG (a basic feature of systolic design), the cut-set localization should be applied uniformly across the network. Otherwise, the resultant array may not be systolic.

[7]That is, the lattice operation is now treated as a single module—a desirable choice of CORDIC implementation.

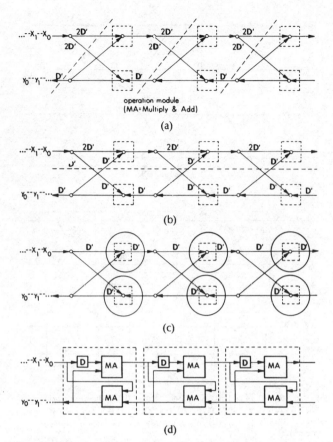

(a)

(b)

(c)

(d)

Fig. 7. (a) Time-rescaled SFG (and cut-sets) for AR lattice filters (type-B). (b) Partially localized SFG—first step. (c) "Localized" SFG—all operations are ready to merge with the corresponding uni-time delays D'. (d) Systolic array for AR lattice filters (type-B) with the small squares denoting pure delays.

the Multiply–Add Module (cf. Fig. 7(c)), a systolic structure is obtained as shown in Fig. 7(d). Note that because of time scaling the input sequence $\{x(i)\}$ will be interleaved with two "blanks" to match the adjusted rates. It is clear that the array can achieve a $2M/3$ execution-time speedup.[8] In terms of speed, this systolic design is superior to the Type-A design.

B. Two-Dimensional Systolic Arrays

The systolization procedures can be applied to two-dimensional networks. Although the descriptions of two-dimensional activities are often cumbersome; fortunately, the SFG representations of two-dimensional algorithms (especially, the (temporally) nonlocalized version) are often much easier to comprehend. With the procedures discussed in the previous section, the conversion of a two-dimensional SFG to a systolic array is straightforward.

A typical example used for illustrating a two-dimensional array operation is matrix multiplication. Let

$$A = [a_{ij}] \qquad B = [b_{ij}]$$

and

$$C = A \times B.$$

[8]Note that since the upper and lower MA modules in each PE are never simultaneously active, only one MA hardware module suffices to serve both functional needs.

Suppose that both A and B are nonsparse $N \times N$ matrices. The matrix A can be decomposed into columns A_i and the matrix B into rows B_j and, therefore,

$$C = [A_1 B_1 + A_2 B_2 + \cdots + A_N B_N]$$

where the product $A_i B_i$ is termed "outer product." The matrix multiplication can then be carried out in N recursions (each executing one outer product)

$$c_{i,j}^{(k)} = c_{i,j}^{(k-1)} + a_i^{(k)} b_j^{(k)} \qquad (2)$$

$$a_i^{(k)} = a_{ik}$$

$$b_j^{(k)} = b_{kj}$$

for $k = 1, 2, \cdots, N$ and there will be N sets of wavefronts involved.

1) Systolizing an SFG for Matrix Multiplication: The simplest matrix multiplication array design is one letting columns A_i and rows B_i be broadcast instantly along the square array as shown in Fig. 8(a). All outer products will then be sequentially summed via a loop with single delay. This design is not suitable for VLSI circuit design since it needs to use global communication. However, there is a rapidly growing interest in the developments of optical array processors, [12], [3]. From an optical interconnection perspective this SFG may be directly implementable.

If local interconnection is preferred, the proposed procedure in Section III can again be used to systolize the SFG. Let us apply Rule (ii) to the cut-sets shown in Fig. 8(a). The systolized SFG will have one delay assigned to each edge and thus represent a localized network. According to Rule (ii), the inputs from different columns of B and rows of A will have to be adjusted by a certain number of delays before arriving at the array. By counting the cut-sets involved in Fig. 8(a), it is clear that the first column of B needs no extra delay, the second column needs one delay, the third needs two (i.e., attributing to the two cut-sets separating the third column input and the adjacent top-row processor), etc. Therefore, the B matrix will be skewed as shown in Fig. 8(c). A similar arrangement can be applied to A.

2) Multiplication of a Banded Matrix and a Full Matrix: Let us look at a slightly different, but commonly encountered, type of matrix multiplication problem. This involves a banded-matrix A, $N \times N$, with bandwidth P, and a rectangular matrix B, $N \times Q$. This situation arises in many application domains, such as DFT and time-varying (multichannel) linear filtering, etc. In most applications, $N \gg P$ and $N \gg Q$, and this makes the use of $N \times N$ arrays for computing $C = A \times B$ very uneconomical.

Fig. 9(a) shows that, with slight modification to the SFG in Fig. 8(a), the same speedup performance can be achieved with only a $P \times Q$ rectangular array (as opposed to an $N \times Q$ array). Now, the left memory module will store the matrix A along the band-direction (see Fig. 9(a)) and the upper module will store B the same as before.

Note that the major modification to the array is that, between the recursions of outer products, there should be an upward shift of the partial sums. This is because the input matrix A is loaded in a skewed fashion. The final result (C) will also be outputted from the I/O ports of the top-row PEs.

Applying the systolization procedure leads to the data array as depicted in Fig. 9(b).

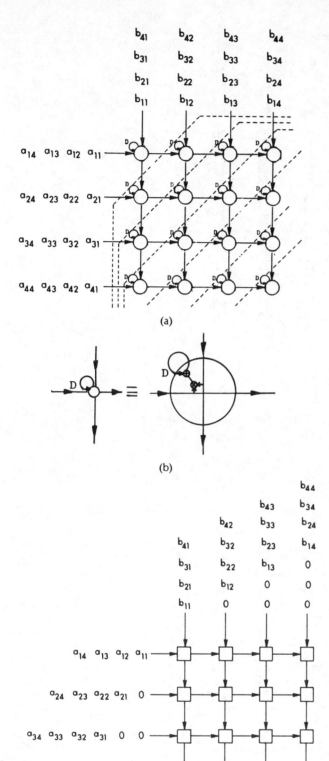

(a)

(b)

(c)

Fig. 8. (a) An SFG for matrix multiplication. (b) The detailed diagram of the processing nodes. (c) A systolic array for matrix multiplication.

3) Multiplication of Two Banded Matrices: Another interesting case is the situation when both A and B are banded matrices, with bandwidths P and Q, respectively. Let us assume that $N \gg P$ and $N \gg Q$, where P and Q are bandwidths for A and B, respectively. Then it is possible to

achieve full parallelism with only a $P \times Q$ rectangular array (as opposed to an $N \times N$ array).

Now, the left- and upper memory modules will store the matrices A and B (respectively) along the band direction (see Fig. 10(a)). The delayed feedback edge (with partial sum of the outer products) will be along the diagonal direction (to the N–W direction). This is because both A and B are stored in the skewed version of Fig. 10(a). Applying the systolization procedure to the cut-sets as shown in Fig. 10(a) will call for a triple scaling of $D \to 3D'$. (This is because each north–west-bound delay edge is "cut" twice.) The procedure leads to an array configuration depicted in Fig. 10(b), which is topologically equivalent to the two-dimensional hexagonal array proposed in [16], [15]. Similarly to what happens in the hexagonal array, the output data (of the matrix C) are also pumped from the both sides.

4) Systolizing an SFG for LU Decomposition: In LU decomposition, a given matrix C is decomposed into

$$C = A \times B$$

where A is a lower- and B an upper-triangular matrix. The recursions involved are

$$C_{ij}^{(k)} = C_{ij}^{(k-1)} - a_i^{(k)} * b_j^{(k)} \qquad (3)$$

where

$$a_i^{(k)} = \frac{1}{c_{kk}^{(k)}} C_{i,k}^{(k-1)}$$

$$b_j^{(k)} = C_{k,j}^{k-1}$$

for $k = 1, 2, \cdots, N;\ k \leqslant i \leqslant N$
$$k \leqslant j \leqslant N.$$

The SFG representation for the above iterations is shown in Fig. 11. Note that it bears a great similarity to the SFG for multiplication of two banded matrices. Therefore, by almost the same systolization procedure as shown in Fig. 10, a systolic array for LU decomposition can be obtained. The resultant configuration of the array (not shown here) is very similar to Fig. 10(b).

C. Linear-Rate Pipelinability

Although the above systolization procedure is essentially complete, it is useful to find out how well the operations of an algorithm can be pipelined through the array (i.e. the pipelinability). The answer is rather straightforward:

We assert that the array has a linear-rate pipelinability *if and only if* α remains constant with respect to M, where M is the number of processor elements (PEs). It is clear that if the total time-scaling factor is α (i.e., $D = \alpha D'$), then the data input rate is slowed down by α. Consequently, in average only one of α PEs can be active. This implies that the full processing rate speedup M reduces to $\alpha^{-1}M$. If α remains constant with respect to M, then the array is pipelinable with a linear-rate speedup.

For most practical computational models the scaling factor α is 1, 2, or 3. For example: in the ARMA and lattice (type-A) systolic arrays, $\alpha = 2$, and in the lattice (type-B) array, $\alpha = 3$, regardless of how large M is. The same is true for most two-dimensional graphs, e.g., the SFGs for matrix multiplications, and LU decomposition, etc. However, there are examples of SFGs that, when localized, lead to nonconstant α. The arrays then cannot exhibit $O(M)$ execution-time speedups.

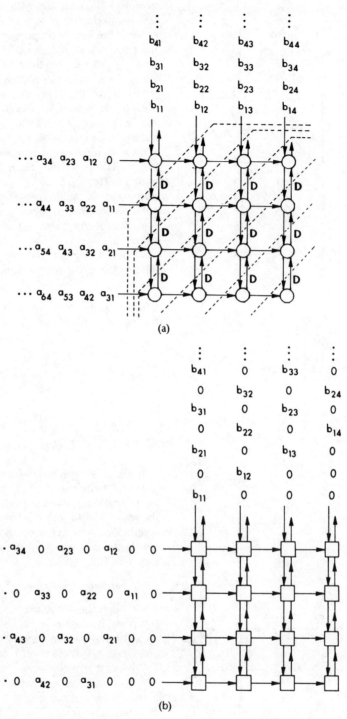

Fig. 9. (a) An SFG for matrix multiplication with one banded matrix. (b) Systolic array for matrix multiplication with one banded matrix.

1) An Example of Nonpipelinable SFGs: As an example of a regular but nonpipelinable SFG, let us look at the SFG shown in Fig. 12(a), which is originally due to Dewilde [8], [14]. Note that there exist no simple, uniform cuts with which to proceed the conversion. In fact, applying the localization rules with nonuniform cut-sets as shown in Fig. 12(a) (where the numbers in parentheses indicate the order of the cut-sets to apply the localization rules) will lead to a temporally localized array as depicted in Fig. 12(b). Note that the final time-scaling factor α turns out to be linearly proportional to M. This means that the speed

performance of the "parallel" array processor is basically no different from a sequential computer, because no efficient pipelining is possible. Therefore, the array is said to be nonsystolic.

D. Improving Processing Speed and Utilization Efficiency

1) Multirate Systolic Array—Improving Processing Speed [20]: Note that due to the recaling of time units, the input data $\{x_i\}$ have to be interleaved with "blank" data (see Figs. 4, 6, 7), and the throughput rate becomes $(\alpha T)^{-1}$. This

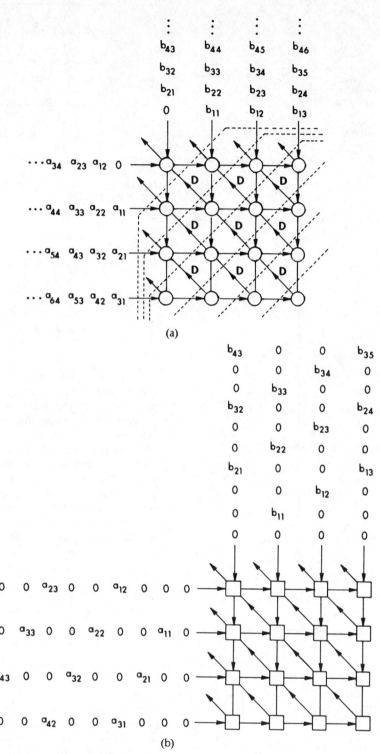

Fig. 10. (a) An SFG for multiplication of two banded matrices. (b) Systolic array for multiplication of two banded matrices.

rate is slower than that of the direct form design ($1.0T^{-1}$), because the data-transfer operation ($X \rightarrow X'$) alone consumes the same time as a multiply-and-add operation, an unnecessary delay. There are two solutions to this problem: one is to use a multirate systolic array and the other is to use a wavefront array based on asynchronous data-driven computing.

A multirate systolic array is a generalized systolic array, allowing different operations to consume different time

units. As we have mentioned earlier, the finer the granularity in defining the basic module, the better the efficiency. For maximal efficiency, the granularity has to go all the way down to the bit level for a data-transfer operation, while the arithmetic operation may remain at the word level. For the ARMA filter design example, we can assign Δ as the time unit for a data transfer and T for a multiply-and-add. Consequently, in the circuit representation in Fig. 4(a), we replace D' on the feedforward path (for X) by Δ, and D' on

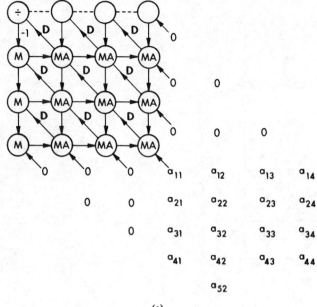

$$
\begin{array}{cccccccc}
 & & & a_{11} & a_{12} & a_{13} & a_{14} \\
0 & 0 & 0 & a_{21} & a_{22} & a_{23} & a_{24} \\
 & 0 & a_{31} & a_{32} & a_{33} & a_{34} \\
 & & a_{41} & a_{42} & a_{43} & a_{44} \\
 & & & a_{52}
\end{array}
$$

(a)

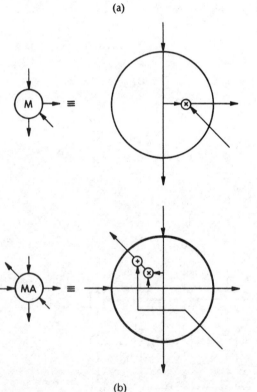

(b)

Fig. 11. (a) An SFG for LU decomposition. (b) The detailed diagram of the processing nodes.

the feedback paths (for Y and Z) by Δ. This means that the X data are pumped to the right with a delay of Δ, while the data Y and Z are transferred (to the left) with a (much longer) delay T. These modifications lead to a multirate systolic array as shown in Fig. 13. Since the original basic delay interval (D) is now replaced by $\Delta + T$; therefore, the input/output sequences $\{x_0, x_1, x_2, \cdots, \}$ and $\{y_0, y_1, y_2, \cdots, \}$ have to be pumped in and out by an interval $(T + \Delta)$, and attain a throughput rate of $1/(T + \Delta)$. In fact, a multirate systolic array is equivalent to a synchronized version of the wavefront array discussed in the next section.

2) Sharing Operation Modules—Improving Utilization Ef-

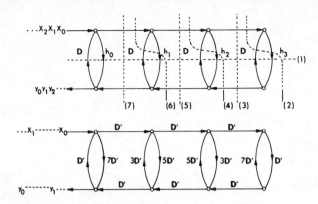

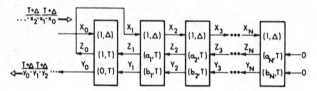

Fig. 12. (a) A nonsystolizable SFG example. (b) Localized but nonpipelinable SFG.

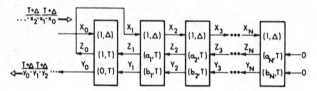

Fig. 13. A multirate systolic array for ARMA (IIR) filter.

ficiency: It is possible to improve the processor utilization rate by as much as α times, where α is the time-scaling factor used in the localization process. The scheme is straightforward, noting that the interval between data will have to be α units apart, and therefore only one of α consecutive processor modules will be active at any instant. Therefore, a group of α consecutive PEs can *share a common arithmetic unit* without compromising the throughput rates. Now let us use an example for a better illustration. Note that, according to the snapshots for the lattice systolic array (B) as depicted in Fig. 14, *only one upper MA module is active* in every three PEs at any time instant, and the same is true for the lower MA module. Therefore, as shown in Fig. 14, the three PEs can be combined into a (macro)PE and share the two common MA modules (one upper and one lower). A special-purpose ring register (with *period* = α) can be designed to handle the resource scheduling.

V. Data-Flow Principle and Wavefront Array [17]

One problem associated with the systolic is that the data movements are controlled by global timing-reference "beats." In order to synchronize the activities in a systolic array, extra delays are often used to ensure correct timing. However, the price of this is an unnecessary slowdown in throughput rates. More critically, the burden of having to synchronize the entire computing network will eventually become intolerable for very- (or ultra-) large-scale arrays. The solution to the problem is to substitute the need for correct "timing" by correct "sequencing," as is used in data-flow computers and wavefront arrays. This leads to a completely different way of tackling the question "b) **when** to send data?" as posed in Section I-B. This time the answer lies in a data-driven, self-timed approach.

A. Data-Flow Multiprocessor

A data-flow multiprocessor [7] is an asynchronous, data-driven multiprocessor which runs programs expressed in

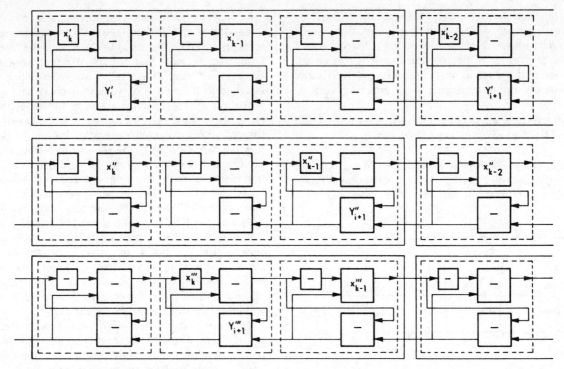

Fig. 14. Snapshots and time sharing of three PEs within a (macro)PE. (a) Snapshot at $t = i$. (b) Snapshot at $t = i + 1$. (c) Snapshot at $t = i + 2$.

data-flow graph form. Since the execution of its instructions is "data-driven," i.e., the triggering of instructions depends only upon the availability of operands and resources required, unrelated, instructions can be executed concurrently without interference. The principal advantages of data-flow multiprocessors over conventional multiprocessors are simple representation of concurrent activity, relative independence of individual PEs, greater use of pipelining, and reduced use of centralized control and global memory. However, for a general-purpose data-flow multiprocessor, the interconnection and memory conflict problems remain very critical. Such problems can be eliminated if the concepts of *modularity* and *locality* are imposed onto data-flow multiprocessors. This idea is the key motivation leading to concept of Wavefront Arrays.

B. Wavefront Arrays

Definition: Wavefront Array: A Wavefront Array is a computing network possessing the following features:

1) *Self-Timed, Data-Driven Computation:* No global clock is needed, since network is self-timed.

2) *Modularity and Local Interconnection:* Basically the same as in a systolic array. However, the wavefront array can be extended indefinitely without having to deal with the global synchronization problem.

3) *O(M) Speedup and Pipelinability:* (Similar to the systolic array.)

Note that the major difference distinguishing a wavefront array from a systolic array is the data-driven property. Consequently, the temporal locality condition (see 3 in the definition of Systolic Array) is no longer needed, since there is no explicit timing reference in the wavefront arrays. By relaxing the strict timing requirement, there are many advantages gained, such as speed and programming simplicity.

C. Incorporating Data-Flow Computing into Computing Networks

Our main goal here is to demonstrate that *all SFG computing networks can be converted into data-driven computing models.* Therefore, by properly incorporating the data-flow feature, every regular and modular SFG can be converted into a wavefront array.

In a self-timed system, the exact timing reference is ignored; instead, the central issue is sequencing. *Getting a data token in a self-timed system is equivalent to incrementing the clock by one time-unit in a synchronous system.* Therefore, the delay operators D will be replaced by self-timed delays, i.e., handshaked "separator" registers.[9] In other words, the conversion of an SFG into a data-driven system involves substituting the delay D with implicit or explicit separators, and replacing the global clock by data handshaking. This process incorporates the data-flow principle into SFG's or systolic arrays.

Theorem: (Equivalence Transformation between SFG's and DFG's)

The computation of any SFG can be equivalently executed by a self-timed, data-driven machine with a data-flow graph (DFG) identical to the SFG, apart from substituting every time-delay operator D (controlled by a global clock) in the SFG with a *separator* ($\lozenge$) that is locally controlled by handshaking.

Proof: What needs to be verified is that the global timing in the SFG can be (comfortably) replaced by the corresponding sequencing of the data tokens in the DFG.

---

[9] A handshaked separator is a device, symbolized by a diamond $\lozenge$, which prevents any incoming data from directly passing through *until* the handshaking flag signals a "pass."

Note that the transfer of the data tokens is now "timed" by the processing node. This ensures that the relative "time" between data tokens received at the node is the same as it was in the SFG, as far as that individual node is concerned. By mathematical induction, this can be extended to show the correctness of the sequencing in the entire network.

For convenience, we shall term this trivial transformation the *SFG/DFG Equivalence Transformation*.

Example: Linear Phase Filter Design: As an example, let us now apply the rules to the SFG for a very popular linear phase filter, as shown in Fig. 15(a).[10] By the SFG/DFG

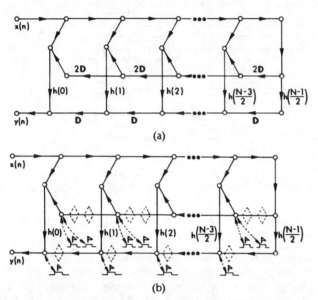

Fig. 15. (a) SFG for linear-phase filters. (b) Data-driven model (delta-flow graph) for the linear-phase filter.

equivalence transformation, the data-flow graph is derived as in Fig. 15(b). Now note that there are two separators inserted into every middle-level edge with handshaking (symbolized by "flags") to the branching node immediately succeeding them. In other words, the transfers occurring in the two separators are synchronized. In order to ensure the correct sequencing of data, the W data should propagate twice as slowly as the Y data do. Note that the separators play the role of ensuring such a correct sequencing.

Initial States: The general principle is that, all the separators are assigned initial values (regarded as data token), which are the same as those assigned to the delay registers in the corresponding SFG. We note that the initial state assignment under the SFG/DFG transformation is straightforward. This simplicity compares very favorably with the initial state reassignments in the systolization rule, where (because of the retiming involved in the systolization procedure) such reassignments may sometimes become rather complicated.

[10]Linear phase filters are very often used in one- and two-dimensional convolutions. They have two key features: one, that they have a symmetrical impulse response function, i.e., $h(n) = h(N - 1 - n)$, and two, they do not add phase distortion to the signal. Fig. 15(a) shows an SFG which takes advantage of the symmetry property, and reduces the amount of multiplier hardware by one half.

For a detailed illustration on the relationship between the initial states and the correctness of sequencing of data transfers in DFGs, let us again look into the linear phase filter example. Note that one initial zero is assigned to the separator of each Y-data edge; and two initial zeros are assigned to the two separators in each W-data edge. The "0" of the Y-data separator, when requested by the Y-summing node, will be passed to meet the V data arriving from the upper node. When the operation is done, a "data-used" flag will then be sent to the separator, clearing the way for sending the next Y data from the right-hand PE. The situation is similar for the W summing node, but only one "0" is "used" and the W data are still one separator away from meeting the "X" data in the summing node. It will have to wait until the Y data and the second "0" meet in the lower summing node. This explains why the propagation of W is slower than Y. (This is just what is needed to ensure a correct sequencing of data transfers.) Note also that there will be handshaking circuits needed for the nodes in the upper branches. Since there are no associated delays, there will be no initial data-tokens for the nodes.

1) Converting SFG's into Wavefront Arrays: The SFG/DFG equivalence transformation helps establish a theoretical footing for the wavefront array as well as provide more insights towards the programming techniques. The transformation implies that all regular SFGs can be easily converted into wavefront arrays, making modularly designed wavefront processing elements very attractive to use. Furthermore, because there is no concept of (global) time in a self-timed system, temporal locality is no longer an issue of concern. Therefore, the procedure of converting an SFG into a wavefront array is simpler than that of systolizing an SFG.

Another important feature is that data-flow graphs often provide useful clues for programming the data-driven wavefront arrays. An exemplificative program for the wavefront processing for linear phase filters, written in MDFL—Matrix Data Flow Language, will be discussed later.

VI. Wavefront Arrays and Computational Wavefronts

For further illustration, let us apply the SFG/DFG equivalence transformation to several one- and two-dimensional computing networks, e.g., ARMA and lattice filters, matrix multiplication, LU decomposition, etc.

A. One-Dimensional Wavefront Arrays

1) Wavefront Array for ARMA (IIR) Filter: Following the conversion strategy, an asynchronous wavefront model is derived as shown in Fig. 16. Therefore, at each node in Fig. 16, the operation is executed when and only when the required operands (data tokens) are available. An immediate advantage of this model is that a data transfer operation $(X \rightarrow X')$ uses only negligible time, Δ, compared with the time needed for an arithmetic operation. More precisely, the throughput rate achieved by the wavefront array is approximately $1.0(T + \Delta)^{-1}$, i.e., almost twice that of the pure systolic array in Fig. 4(b).

It is important to note that the pipelining in a wavefront array is different from the traditional idea of pipelining. Under the wavefront notion, $X^{(k)}$ is initiated at the leading PE ($n = 0$), and then propagated rightward across the processor array, activating the MA operations in all of the data-driven PEs. The updated data $\{ Y_{n+1}^{(k)}, Z_{n+1}^{(k)} \}$ in the sum-

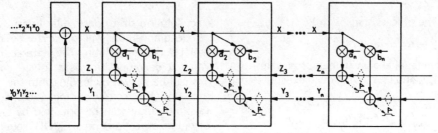

Fig. 16. Wavefront array for ARMA (IIR) filter. (Asynchronous, data-driven model, i.e., operations take place only on availability of appropriate data.)

ming nodes are fed back leftward, ready for the next wavefront. In this case, a reflection of the wave plays an interesting role. For convenience, we shall call such reflection a "ripple" wave. As illustrated in Fig. 17, a ripple from the kth wavefront in the $(n + 1)$th PE will be needed (and expected) by the $(k + 1)$th wavefront in the nth PE.

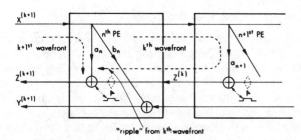

Fig. 17. A "ripple" wave from $(n + 1)$th PE to nth PE.

2) Wavefront Array for Lattice Filter: In general, the data-driven model is not only faster (with maximized pipelining) but also has a simpler (self-timed) design, since a global timing reference is no longer required. For example, the (data-driven) wavefront model for the AR lattice as shown in Fig. 18 (compatible with the sytolic array Type-B) is considerably simpler than its systolic counterpart. Due to the data-driven nature of a wavefront array, it is guaranteed that the operation on the X data will have to wait until the Y data operation is done and the result transferred to the upper MA module. Therefore, the appropriate delays naturally fall into place, yielding the correct sequencing of the data. In contrast, in the (Type-B) systolic structure, the two kinds of signals, X (right-bound) and Y (left-bound), are propagating at different speeds, as shown in the snapshots in Fig. 14. Therefore, the (pure) systolic version is more complex than the wavefront solution, due to the timing of the complicated "ripple" effect.

B. Pipelining of Two-Dimensional Computational Wavefronts

From an algorithmic analysis perspective, the notion of computational wavefronts offers a very simple way to ap-

preciate the wavefront computing. The separators are the handshaking device ensuring that the computational wavefronts are orderly following, instead of overtaking, their previous fronts.[11] We shall illustrate the wavefront concept and the related architecture and language designs with the matrix multiplication example. The computational wavefront for the first recursion in matrix multiplication will now be examined.

The application of conversion rules to the (original) SFG is fairly straightforward. Basically, imposing handshaking upon all cut-sets will ensure correct sequencing. To see that this is true, a general configuration of computational wavefronts traveling down a processor array is illustrated in Fig. 19.

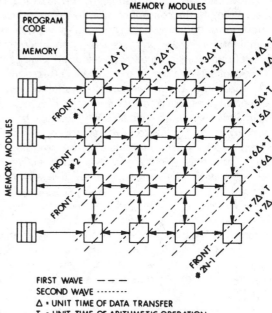

Fig. 19. Propagation of two-dimensional computational wavefronts.

Suppose that the registers of all the processing elements (PEs) are initially set to zero

$$C_{ij}^{(0)} = 0, \qquad \text{for all } (i, j)$$

the entries of A are stored in the memory modules on the left (in columns), and those of B in the memory modules

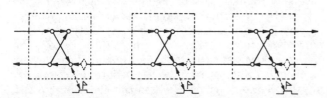

Fig. 18. Wavefront array for lattice filter.

---

[11]In fact, applying the data-flow concept along uniform cuts will lead to a self-timed, regular, and locally interconnected array—a wavefront array. As a matter of fact, the "wavefronts" will correspond to the cuts.

543

on the top (in rows). The process starts with PE (1,1):

$$C_{11}^{(1)} = C_{11}^{(0)} + a_{11} * b_{11}$$

is computed. The computational activity then propagates to the neighboring PEs (1, 2) and (2,1), which will executive in parallel

$$C_{12}^{(1)} = C_{12}^{(0)} + a_{11} * b_{12}$$

and

$$C_{21}^{(1)} = C_{21}^{(0)} + a_{21} * b_{11}.$$

The next front of activity will be at PEs (3,1), (2,2), and (1,3), thus creating a computational wavefront traveling down the processor array. It may be noted that wave propagation implies localized data flow. Once the wavefront sweeps through all the cells, the first recursion is over (see Fig. 19).

As the first wave propagates, we can execute an identical second recursion in parallel by pipelining a second wavefront immediately after the first one. For example, the (i,j) processor will execute

$$C_{ij}^{(2)} = c_{ij}^{(1)} + a_{i2} * b_{2j}$$

and so on.

1) Why the Name "Wavefront Array"?: The principle of wavefront processing is to successively pipeline the computational wavefronts as fast as resource and data availability allow, according to the concept of data-flow computing. As a justification for the name "wavefront array," we note that the computational wavefronts are similar to electromagnetic wavefronts (they both obey Huygens' principle) since each processor acts as a secondary source and is responsible for the propagation of the wavefront. In addition, wave-propagation implies localized data flow as well as localized control (handshaking). The pipelining is feasible because the wavefronts of two successive recursions will never intersect (Huygens' wavefront principle), thus avoiding any contention problems. (From the hardware perspective, the desired "separation" between two consecutive wavefronts is reaffirmed by the "separators" with proper handshaking.)

In other words, it is possible to have wavefront propagating in several different fashions. In the extreme case of nonuniform clocking, the wavefronts are actually crooked. However, what is important is that the order of task sequencing must be correctly followed. The correctness of the sequencing of the tasks is ensured by the wavefront principle [17].

2) Wavefront Array for LU Decomposition: By tracing backwards through the iterations in (3), we note that

$$C = c_{ij}^{(0)} = \sum_{k=1}^{N} a_i^{(k)} b_j^{(k)} = AB \quad (4)$$

where $A = \{a_{mn}\} = \{a_m^{(n)}\}$, and $B = \{b_{mn}\} = \{b_n^{(m)}\}$ are the outputs of the array.

In comparison with (2) and (4), (3) is basically a reversal of the matrix multiplication recursions. Therefore, its wavefront processing should be similar to what is shown in Fig. 19. In fact, by converting the SFG as shown in Fig. 11 into a DFG, such a wavefront array can be directly obtained.

3) Least Square Error Solution and SVD: In many applications, we will be faced with solving a least square solution of an overdetermined linear system, as opposed to an exact solution of a nonsingular linear system. In this case, QR decomposition will prove to be much more useful than LU decomposition. The natural topology associated with QR decomposition is a square interconnect pattern. This can be shown by looking into the mathematical iterations and the corresponding SFGs. Similar systolic and wavefront arrays can be obtained by carrying out the systolization procedure or SFG/DFG equivalence transform. The details (omitted here) will be published in a later report.

The eigenvalue and SVD (singular value decomposition) problems are considerably more complicated. However, in [11], [21], it is shown that the notion of computational wavefronts can be employed to track down the activities in a square or linear array for computing eigenvalues or singular values.

VII. Wavefront Array Software/Hardware (WASH)

A. Programming Array Processors

The actual implementation of systolic or wavefront arrays can be either dedicated or programmable processors. Programmable arrays are preferred, due to the high cost of hardware implementation and the increasing varieties of application demands. Therefore, it is equally important to develop a complete set of software packages for most wavefront/systolic-type processing. For that, a formal algorithmic notation and programming language will be indispensable.

General guidelines for algorithmic notations for array processors are problem orientation, executability, and semantic simplicity. More importantly, an adequate language criteria must take into account the characteristics and the constraints of the arrays. Examples for appropriate array processing notations, which incorporate the language criteria for systolic/wavefront array processors, are CRYSTAL, [4] data space notation, [5] and the wavefront language (MDFL) [17].

B. Wavefront Language and Software Development

The effectiveness of programming in a processor array is directly related to the algorithm analysis technique. Our description of parallel algorithms hinges upon the notion of a computational wavefront. This leads to a special-purpose, wavefront-oriented language, termed Matrix Data Flow Language (MDFL) [17]. This denotation is in many ways very similar to the data space notation, which is based on the notion of applicative state transition systems described in [1], [5]. Among other commonalities shared by the two notations is, in particular, that they are both based on the data-flow principle [6].

The wavefront language is tailored towards the description of computational wavefronts and the corresponding data flow for the class of algorithms which exhibit the recursion and locality properties. Rather than requiring a program for each processor in the array, MDFL allows the programmer to address an entire front of processors. The wavefront idea can facilitate the description of parallel and pipelined algorithms and drastically reduce the complexity of parallel programming. To translate the global MDFL notation into microinstructions for the PEs, a preprocessor is needed. For a wavefront array, the design of such a preprocessor is relatively easy, since we do not have to consider the timing problems associated with a synchronous systolic array.

As an example, let us now take a look at the computation of

$$C = A \times B.$$

The matrix multiplication can be carried out in N (outer product) recursions (see (1)). A general configuration of computational wavefronts traveling down a processor array is illustrated in Fig. 19. An example of an MDFL program for the corresponding array processing of the matrix multiplication is given in Fig. 20. (For the time being, please ignore the bracketed instructions.)

```
BEGIN
SET COUNT N;
REPEAT;
   WHILE WAVEFRONT IN ARRAY DO
      BEGIN
         {[FETCH C, DOWN;]}
         FETCH A, LEFT;
         FETCH B, UP;
         FLOW A, RIGHT;
         FLOW B, DOWN;
            (* NOW FORM C: = C + A × B)
         MULT A, B, D;
         ADD C, D, C;
         {[FLOW C, UP;]}
      END;
   DECREMENT COUNT;
UNTIL TERMINATED;
ENDPROGRAM.
```

Fig. 20. An MDFL program for matrix multiplication.

Note that, initially matrix A is stored (row by row) in the left Memory Module (MM). Matrix B is in the top MM and is stored column by column. The final result will be in the C registers of the PEs. This example illustrates the typical simplicity of the MDFL programming language.

1) Flexibilities with the Wavefront Programming: To demonstrate the flexibility of wavefront-type programmability, let us look at the multiplication of a banded-matrix A, $N \times N$, with bandwidth P, and a rectangular matrix B, $N \times Q$. Only a slight modification to the program in Fig. 20 is needed. First, the data storage in the memory modules will be the same as in Fig. 16(a). The major modification on the wavefront propagation is that, between the recursions of outer products, there should be an upward shift of the partial sums. (This is because the input matrix A is loaded in a skewed fashion.) Therefore, the program (see Fig. 20) remains almost the same, except for the two added bracketed instructions to shift partial sums upward.

Another major flexibility offered by the wavefront programming technique is that software reconfigurability can be used to map a linear or bilinear array onto a square array hardware. Therefore, a (hardwired) square array may be used for purpose of linear (or bilinear) wavefront array processing.

2) An Example on Linear Phase Filtering: In order to demonstrate the simplicity of programming based on the DFG representation, an MDFL program implementing the DFG for the linear phase filter (cf. Fig. 15(b)) is shown in

```
BEGIN
REPEAT;
   WHILE WAVEFRONT IN ARRAY DO
      BEGIN
         FETCH X, LEFT;
         FLOW X, RIGHT;
         TRANSFER W2 TO W1;
         FLOW W1, LEFT;
         FETCH W2, RIGHT;
         (! NOW COMPUTE V: = (W1 + X) + × H(K))
         ADD W1, X, U;
         MULT U, H(K), V;
         FETCH Y, RIGHT;
         (! NOW COMPUTE Y: = Y + V)
         ADD Y, V, Y;
         FLOW Y, LEFT;
      END;
   DECREMENT COUNT;
UNTIL TERMINATED;
ENDPROGRAM.
```

Fig. 21. An MDFL program for linear-phase filter.

Fig. 21.[12] The simple mapping between the DFG and the programming codes suggests a potentially significant impact of the SFG/DFG equivalence transformation to both the hardware and software developments of array processors.

The power and flexibility of the wavefront array and MDFL programming are best demonstrated by the broad range of the applicational algorithms suitable for the wavefront array [17]. Such algorithms can be roughly classified into three groups:

1) Basic Matrix Operations: such as a) Matrix Multiplication, b) Banded-Matrix Multiplication, c) Matrix–Vector Multiplication, d) LU Decomposition, e) LU Decomposition with Localized Pivoting, f) Givens Algorithm, g) Back Substitution, h) Null Space Solution, i) Matrix Inversion, j) Eigenvalue Decomposition, and k) Singular Value Decomposition.

2) Special Signal Processing Algorithms: a) Toeplitz System Solver, b) One- and Two-Dimensional Linear Convolution, c) Circular Convolution, d) ARMA and AR Recursive Filtering, e) Linear Phase Filtering, f) Lattice Filtering, g) DFT, and h) Two-Dimensional Correlation (image matching).

3) Other Algorithms: PDE (partial difference equation) solution.

Note that, if the communication constraint is relaxed, our technique for converting an SFG for a given application into a wavefront array will also work with other global-type algorithms, such as the FFT algorithm, the Householder transformation, the Kalman filter network, or other non-regularly interconnected arrays. The only additional requirement lies in routing the physical connections between PEs.

It is worth noting that the cut-set rules can be potentially very useful for designing fault-tolerant arrays. For systolic arrays without feedback, it has been shown in [32], [33] that a retiming along cut-sets allows a great degree of fault tolerance. The discussion in Section III-B should offer a theoretical basis for improving fault-tolerance of arrays with feedback via the cut-set retiming procedure. More interest-

---

[12]Note that the separators in the DFG are implemented simply by adding three lines of (internal register–transfer) code to the program, as opposed to adding a separate buffer register external to the PE.

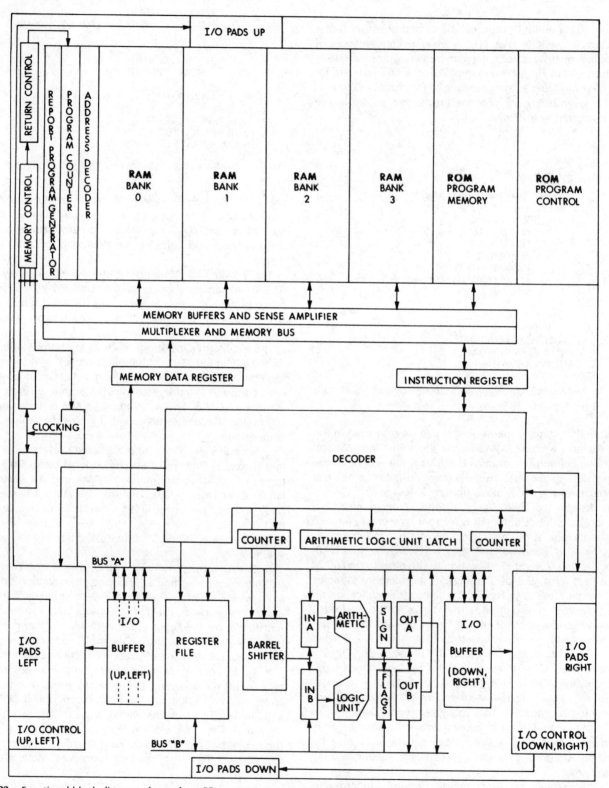

Fig. 22. Functional block diagram of wavefront PE.

546

ingly, with a slight modification, the self-timed feature of wavefront arrays offers a way of achieving the same fault-tolerance efficiency without any need of retiming.

In summary, in the first phase of the software development project, we 1) define the application/ algorithm domain, 2) develop a language tailored to the application, and 3) design a (language-based) wavefront architecture. In order to maximize the application algorithm domain (with minimal hardware overhead), the next phase is to develop a complete software library of all algorithms suitable for systolic/wavefront-type parallel processing. This software library, combined with design automation tools such as silicon compilers, will facilitate the construction of future VLSI systems design. The success of the project will demand joint and cohesive efforts from all related disciplines. For this end, we welcome any suggestions from interested readers and colleagues.

C. Hardware Design

In this subsection we will give an overview of the architecture of a PE, to be used as a basic module in a programmable array processor. A typical example will be the design of a PE to be used in a wavefront array. The basic wavefront array is either a square array of $N \times N$ PEs, a linear array of $1 \times N$ PEs, or a bilinear array of $2 \times N$ PEs. The PEs are orthogonally connected and are identical. The hardware of the PE is designed to support the features of the Matrix Data Flow Language (MDFL) introduced previously. Given the current state of the process technology, with a minimum feature size of 2 μm or less, we estimate the area of the chip taken by a PE to be 6 $\times$ 6 mm^2.

1) Architectural Outline: The PE that we have designed is a special-purpose microprocessor. The functional block diagram of the PE is shown in Fig. 22. The main functional blocks are datapath, program memory, I/O control units, and instruction decoder.

Our design objective is to limit the complexity of the datapath, preferring a regular and easy layout design. We have adopted a 32-bit-wide datapath for fixed-point computations. Moreover, the ALU in the PE is designed to support the operations that are of major importance for signal processing applications, such as multiplication and rotation. To speed up the throughput of the PE, we used a two-level pipelining scheme.

The PE can simultaneously perform data transfers in four directions. The transfer of data is controlled by an I/O controller, one for each of the four directions, which handles the two-way handshaking functions.

2) Instruction Set: The instruction set of the PE was selected to optimize the performance of the wavefront array as a whole. To reduce the complexity of the control unit, in a manner similar to that used in the RISC design [28], we wanted each instruction to take exactly one clock cycle. This implies that complex instructions should be decomposed into sequences of simpler (primitive) instructions. An example is the multiplication instruction, which is decomposed into three instructions: one for initializing the processor registers with the correct data, one that does the main multiplication step, and the last one which transfers the result back to the register file. The instruction set is divided into arithmetic instructions, register transfer instructions, conditional and unconditional jump instructions, and program loading instructions.

3) Design Specification and Verification: The PE described in this section is currently being specified and verified using the ISPS language. The ISPS language allows not only the specification of the design of a single PE, but also the simulation of an entire wavefront array. More importantly, it facilitates the verification of the correctness and suitability of the architecture of the PE before designing the lower (logic, circuit, layout) levels of the PE. It will also be an important tool for the development of the host interface, the memory units, etc.

VIII. CONCLUSIONS

The rapid advance in VLSI device technology and design techniques have encouraged the development of massively parallel-array processors. We have stressed the importance of modularity, communication, and system clocking in the design of VLSI arrays. For signal processing applications, a large number of algorithms possess the properties of recursiveness and locality. These properties naturally led to the systolic and wavefront arrays.

The two types of arrays share the important common feature of using a large number of modular and locally interconnected processors for massive pipelined and parallel processing. However, in several key aspects, the wavefront array is noticeably distinctive from the systolic array: First, it uses data-driven computing and thus gets around the burden of having to synchronize a (potentially ultra-) large-scale array. [18] Second, it maximizes the pipelining efficiency and offers a speed achievable only by multirate systolic arrays. Third, the data-flow principle allows a simpler language design facilitating a formal description of the activities. Finally, it can easily cope with the variations of communication delays in dynamically interconnected systems, such as reconfigurable waferscale integration designs.

In conclusion, we have shown that both the systolic and data-flow principles will play a major role in future supercomputing, especially for number crunching problems. Most computing networks described in signal-flow graphs (SFGs) can be systematically converted into systolic or wavefront arrays, following the procedures proposed. This should encourage more practitioners to develop advanced hardware and software for massively parallel-array processors. The impacts of the novel architectures upon future supercomputer designs cannot be overestimated.

ACKNOWLEDGMENT

The author wishes to thank his colleagues in the VLSI signal processing group at the University of Southern California, for their very valuable contributions to the Wavefront Array Software/Hardware (WASH) Project. He is also grateful to Dr. H. Lev-Ari of the Stanford University for many useful comments which were incorporated into this final draft.

REFERENCES

[1] J. Backus, "Can programming be liberated from the von Neumann style? A functional style and its algebra of programs," *Commun. ACM*, vol. 21 pp. 613–641, 1978.
[2] C. Caraiscos and B. Liu, "From digital filter flow-graphs to systolic arrays, " submitted to *IEEE Trans. Acoust., Speech, Signal Processing*, 1984.

[3] H. J. Caulfield, W. T. Rhodes, M. J. Foster, and S. Horvitz, "Optical implementation of systolic array processing," *Opt. Commun.*, vol. 40, pp. 86–90, Dec. 1981.

[4] M. Chen and C. Mead, "Concurrent algorithms as space-time recursion equations," to appear in *VLSI and Modern Signal Processing*, S. Y. Kung *et al.*, Eds., Englewood Cliffs, NJ: Prentice Hall.

[5] A. B. Cremers and T. N. Hibbard, "The semantic definition of programming languages in terms of their data spaces," *Informatik-Fachberichte*, vol. 1, pp. 1–11 (Berlin, Springer-Verlag), 1976.

[6] A. B. Cremers and S. Y. Kung, "On programming VLSI concurrent array processors," in *Proc. IEEE Workshop on Languages for Automation* (Chicago, IL, 1983), pp. 205–210; also in *INTEGRATIONS* (The VLSI Journal), vol. 2, no. 1, Mar. 1984.

[7] J. B. Dennis, "Data flow supercomputers," *IEEE Computer*, vol. 13, pp. 48–56, Nov. 1980.

[8] P. Dewilde, personal communication, 1983.

[9] J. J. Dongarra *et al.*, *LINPACK USER'S GUIDE.* Philadelphia, PA: SIAM PUB., 1979.

[10] M. Franklin and D. Wann, "Asynchronous and clocked control structures for VLSI based interconnection networks," presented at the 9th Annual Symp. on Computer Architecture, Apr. 1982, Austin, TX.

[11] R. J. Gal-Ezer, "The wavefront array processor," Ph.D. dissertation, Dept. of Electrical Engineering, University of Southern California, Dec. 1982.

[12] J. W. Goodman, F. Leonberger, S. Y. Kung, and R. Athale, "Optical interconnections for VLSI systems," this issue, pp. 850–866; also prepared as an ARO Palantir Meeting Report.

[13] K. Hwang and F. Briggs, *Computer Architectures and Parallel Processing.* New York: McGraw-Hill, 1984.

[14] J. V. Jagadish, T. Kailath, G. G. Mathews, and J. A. Newkirk, "On pipelining systolic arrays," presented at the 17th Asilomar Conf. on Circuits, Systems, and Computers, Pacific Grove, CA, Nov. 1983, also "On hardware description from block diagrams," in *Proc. IEEE ICASSP* (San Diego, CA, Mar. 1984).

[15] H. T. Kung, "Why systolic architectures," *IEEE Computer*, vol. 15, no. 1, Jan. 1982.

[16] H. T. Kung and C. E. Leiserson, "Systolic arrays (for VLSI)," in *Proc. Sparse Matrix Symp.* (SIAM), pp. 256–282, 1978.

[17] S. Y. Kung, K. S. Arun, R. J. Gal-Ezer, and D. V. Bhaskar Rao, "Wavefront array processor: Language, architecture, and applications," *IEEE Trans. Comput.* (Special Issue on Parallel and Distributed Computers), vol. C-31, no. 11, pp. 1054–1066, Nov. 1982.

[18] S. Y. Kung and R. J. Gal-Ezer, "Synchronous vs. asynchronous computation in VLSI array processors," in *Proc. SPIE Conf.* (Arlington, VA), 1982.

[19] S. Y. Kung and J. Annevelink, "VLSI design for massively parallel signal processors," *Microprocessors and Microsystems* (Special Issue on Signal Processing Devices), vol. 7, no. 4, pp. 461–468, Dec. 1983.

[20] S. Y. Kung, "From transversal filter to VLSI wavefront array," in *Proc. Int. Conf. on VLSI 1983*, IFIP (Trondheim, Norway), 1983.

[21] S. Y. Kung and R. J. Gal-Ezer, "Eigenvalue, singular value and least square solvers via the wavefront array processor," in *Algorithmically Specialized Computer Organizations*, L. Snyder *et al.*, Eds. New York: Academic Press, 1983.

[22] C. E. Leiserson, "Area-efficient VLSI computation," Ph.D. dissertation, Carnegie-Mellon University, Pittsburgh, PA, Oct. 1981.

[23] C. E. Leiserson, F. M. Rose, and J. B. Saxe, "Optimizing synchronous circuitry by retiming," in *Proc. Caltech VLSI Conf.* (Pasadena, CA), 1983.

[24] C. E. Leiserson and J. B. Saxe, "Optimizing synchronous systems," *J. VLSI Comput. Syst.*, vol. 1, no. 1, pp. 41–67, 1983.

[25] H. Lev-Ari, "Modular computing networks: A new methodology for analysis and design of parallel algorithms/architectures," Tech. Memo ISI-29, Integrated Systems Inc., Palo Alto, Ca., 1983.

[26] C. Mead and L. Conway, *Introduction to VLSI Systems.* Reading, MA: Addison-Wesley, 1980.

[27] A. Oppenheim and R. Schafer, *Digital Signal Processing.* Englewood Cliffs, NJ: Prentice-Hall, 1975.

[28] D. A. Patterson and C. H. Sequin, "A VLSI RISC," *IEEE Computer*, vol. 14, Sept. 1981.

[29] B. T. Smith *et al.*, *Matrix Eigensystem Routines, EISPACK Guide*, vol. 6 of *Lecture Notes in Computer Science*, 2nd ed. New York: Springer-Verlag, 1976.

[30] J. D. Ullman, *Computational Aspects of VLSI.* Rockville, MD: Computer Science Press, 1984.

[31] A. Fettweis, "Realizability of digital filter networks," *AEU* (Electronics and Communication), vol. 30, pp. 90–96, 1976.

[32] H. T. Kung and M. S. Lam, "Fault-tolerant VLSI systolic arrays and two-level pipelining," in *Proc. SPIE Symp.*, vol. 431, pp. 143–158, Aug. 1983.

[33] ____, "Fault-tolerance and two-level pipelining in VLSI systolic arrays," in *Proc. Conf. on Advanced Research in VLSI* (MIT, Cambridge, MA, Jan. 1984), pp. 74–83.

Partitioned Matrix Algorithms for VLSI Arithmetic Systems

KAI HWANG, SENIOR MEMBER, IEEE, AND YENG-HENG CHENG

Reprinted from *IEEE Transactions on Computers*, Volume C-31, Number 12, December 1982, pages 1215-1224. Copyright © 1982 by The Institute of Electrical and Electronics Engineers, Inc.

Abstract—A new class of partitioned matrix algorithms is developed for possible VLSI implementation of large-scale matrix solvers. Fast matrix solvers are highly demanded in signal/image processing and in many real-time and scientific applications. Only a few functional types of VLSI arithmetic chips are needed for submatrix computations after partitioning. This partitioned approach is not restricted by problem sizes and thus can be applied to solve arbitrarily large linear systems of equations in an iterative fashion. The following four matrix computations are shown systematically partitionable into submatrix operations, which are feasible for direct VLSI implementation.

- *L-U* decomposition of a dense matrix.
- Inversion of a triangular matrix.
- Multiplication of two compatible matrices.
- Solving a triangular system of equations.

Let n be the order of a linear system and m be feasible VLSI chip size such that $n \gg m$ in practice. Our partitioned matrix algorithms require $O(n)$ or $O(n^2/m)$ computation times (as opposed to $O(n^3)$ time required in a serial computer) using, respectively, $O(n^2/m^2)$ or $O(n/m)$ VLSI arithmetic chips of size $O(m^2)$. The partitioned triangular system solver requires $O(n)$ time with $O(n/m)$ VLSI chips of size $O(m)$. Architectural design tradeoffs, application requirements, and performance assessment of the proposed VLSI matrix computing structures are also provided.

Index Terms—Computer architecture, computer arithmetic, linear system of equations, matrix computations, numerical analysis, parallel processing, real-time applications, very large scale integration (VLSI).

I. INTRODUCTION

LARGE-SCALE matrix computations are needed in solving high-order *linear system of equations* (LSE), $A \cdot x = b$, in many important scientific and engineering application areas. So far, SIMD array processors or pipelined vector supercomputers have been used to solve large LSE's by predeveloped software packages [3], [6], [14], [16]. Fast matrix algorithms for solving LSE's have been suggested by Crout [1], Kant and Kimura [9], Sameh and Kuck [15] and by many other researchers. The recent advent in *very large scale integration* (VLSI) microelectronic technology has created a new architectural horizon to implement large-scale vector/matrix computations directly in hardware. In this paper, we develop a class of "partitioned" matrix algorithms for possible VLSI implementation of fast matrix solvers.

It has been projected by Mead and Conway [11] that by the late 1980's it will be possible to fabricate 10^7 or 10^8 transistors on a monolithic chip. VLSI computing structures have been suggested by Kung and Leiserson [10], Preparata and Vuillemin [13], Hwang and Cheng [5], and Nash *et al.* [12]. A VLSI computing device contains not only a large number of processing cells but also a large number of interconnection paths throughout the integrated chip. The length and organization of these communication paths set a lower bound on the chip area and time delays required for system operations. Systolic VLSI arrays [10] were proposed with a global structure that must be limited in their array sizes due to bounded chip area and I/O packaging constraints.

Based on the state-of-the-art of electronic packaging technologies, we can only expect VLSI arithmetic devices for regularly structured functions with limited I/O terminals. A modular approach to fabricate VLSI devices is amenable from the viewpoints of feasibility and applicability. We choose a matrix partitioning approach to overcome these technological constraints in constructing large-scale matrix solvers. Our "partitioned" algorithms are for modular VLSI implementation of the following four classes of matrix computations:

- *L-U* decomposition by a new variant of Gaussian elimination.
- Normal inversion of a nonsingular triangular matrix.
- Multiplication of two compatible matrices.
- Solving a triangular system of equations by back substitution.

We reserve the parameter, n, for the *order* of a given dense matrix A, and the parameter, m, as the size of available VLSI arithmetic chips, where the *ratio* $k = n/m$ is an integer. We shall use boldface italic capital letters, $A, L, U, V, \cdots$, to denote $n \times n$ matrices; italic capitals, A_{ij}, L_{ij}, for $m \times m$ submatrices; boldface italic lower case letters, $x, b, d, \cdots$, as n-element column vectors; and italic lower case letters, $a_{ij}, x_i, \cdots$, as matrix entries or vector components. All analytical results on hardware complexity and system performance are expressed in terms of these parameters n, m, and k under the assumption $n \gg m$, which holds for practical applications. The proposed VLSI matrix solvers can be applied in digital signal processing, structural analysis, seismic exploitation, fluid dynamics, image processing, pattern recognition, computer-assisted tomography, numeric weather forecasting, artificial intelligence, and various real-time applications [6], [7].

Manuscript received February 17, 1981; revised December 1, 1981 and July 7, 1982. This work was supported by the National Science Foundation under Grants MCS-78-18906 and ECS-80-16580.

K. Hwang is with the School of Electrical Engineering, Purdue University, West Lafayette, IN 47907.

Y.-H. Cheng is with the Department of Computer Engineering and Science, Tsing-Hua University, Beijing, China.

II. VLSI Matrix Computations

For *L-U* decomposition by Gaussian elimination, we consider only nonsingular LSE's in which all the principal minor submatrices of $A = (a_{ij})$ are nonsingular. This provides a necessary and sufficient condition to produce a unique lower triangular matrix $L = (l_{ij})$ with $l_{11} = l_{22} = \cdots = l_{nn} = 1$, and a unique upper triangular matrix $U = (u_{ij})$ such that $L \cdot U = A$. In Crout's reduction method [1], the matrix $A = L \cdot U$ is decomposed according to the following computations for $i = 1, 2, \cdots, n$.

$$\begin{cases} u_{ik} = a_{ik} - \sum_{j=1}^{i-1} l_{ij} u_{jk} \text{ for } k = i, i+1, \cdots, n. \\ l_{ki} = \left[a_{ki} - \sum_{j=1}^{i-1} l_{kj} \cdot u_{ji} \right] / u_{ii} \text{ for } k = i, i+2, \cdots, n. \quad (1) \\ \text{provided } l_{ii} = 1 \text{ for } i = 1, 2, \cdots, n. \end{cases}$$

Crout's method does not require to interchange columns and, thus, eliminates the recording of intermediate results. Instead of dealing with one row or one column at a time, we have modified Crout's method to a new variant of Gaussian elimination by processing rows/columns of $m \times m$ submatrices in parallel. This submatrix approach leads to the partitioned *L-U* decomposition algorithm to be described in Section III.

After the *L-U* decomposition, one can transform the original system $A \cdot x = b$ to $L \cdot U \cdot x = b$ and then to an equivalent triangular system characterized by $U \cdot x = L^{-1} \cdot b = d$. With this triangularized system, one can compute the solution vector x by $x = U^{-1} \cdot d$. The inverse matrices U^{-1} and L^{-1} always exist, because U and L are both nonsingular. We denote the inverse matrix $U^{-1} = V = (v_{ij})$, which is again a triangular matrix with entries calculated by

$$\begin{cases} v_{kk} = 1/u_{kk} \text{ for } k = 1, 2, \cdots, n \\ v_{ij} = - \left(\sum_{k=i+1}^{j} u_{ik} \cdot v_{kj} \right) / u_{ii} \text{ for all } j > i. \quad (2) \end{cases}$$

In Section IV, we shall partition the above computations to enable block generation of v_{ij} entries.

In fact, the (d_j) elements in vector d can be generated automatically by applying partitioned *L-U* decomposition of an $n \times (n + 1)$ matrix obtained by adding the b vector as the $(n + 1)$th column in matrix A, that is $a_{i,n+1} = b_i$ for $i = 1, 2, \cdots, n$. The solution vector x is computed by *back substitution*. This sequence of computations can be also done in subvectors to be described in Section IV.

$$\begin{cases} x_n = d_n/u_{nn} \\ x_i = \left[d_i - \sum_{j=i+1}^{n} u_{ij} \cdot x_j \right] / u_{ii} \quad (3) \\ \text{for } i = n-1, n-2, \cdots, 2, 1 \end{cases}$$

III. Primitive VLSI Matrix Chips

Four primitive types of VLSI arithmetic chip types are functionally introduced in Fig. 1 and Fig. 2. These VLSI chips will be used as building blocks in implementing the partitioned matrix algorithms. These chip types are used to perform $m \times$ m submatrix or m-element subvector computations. Each chip is constructed with a cellular array of multipliers, dividers, and interface latches for pipelined operations [4], [10], [12]. Detailed schematic logic designs of these primitive VLSI chips can be found in reference [5], [7]. Only their functional specifications are given here.

The *D*-type chips are for *L-U decomposition* of each intermediate $m \times m$ submatrix, $\hat{A}_{rr} = L_{rr} \cdot U_{rr}$, along the principal diagonal of A ($\hat{A}_{rr}$ will be defined shortly). The *I*-type chips are for the inversion of triangular $m \times m$ submatrices L_{rr} and U_{rr}. The input/output arithmetic specifications of *D*-type and *I*-type chips are shown in Fig. 1. Both chip types have a fixed delay of $2m$ time units, where one time unit equals the time required to perform one *multiply-add* operation, $a \times b + c = d$, or one *divide* operation, $a/b = c$, by one step processor in the cellular processor array [5], [7], [10].

The *M*-type is the predominant chip type to be used in the construction of various matrix solvers. Accumulative *chain matrix multiplications* are performed by an *M*-type chip as specified in Fig. 2. The number, r, of pairs of $m \times m$ matrices to be multiplied and added is determined by the external input sequence. Therefore, the time delay of *M*-type chips is equal to $r \cdot m + 1$. The *V*-type chips are deduced from *M*-type chips. *V*-type performs the *accumulative submatrix-vector multiplications*. The delay of *V*-type chip is also measured as $r \cdot m + 1$. Because each *D*-type, *I*-type or *M*-type VLSI chip contains an array of $m \times m$ step processors [5], [7], [10], we consider their interior chip complexity as $O(m^2)$. Each *V*-type chip contains a pipeline of m step processors and thus has an interior chip complexity of $O(m)$. The time delays of *D*-type and *I*-type chips have order $O(m)$ and those for *M*-type and *V*-type chips are $O(m \cdot r)$, depending also on the number r of input pairs.

IV. Partitioned *L-U* Decomposition

A systolic array of n^2 step processors can perform the *L-U* decomposition in $4n$ time units [10]. However, such a systolic array in a single chip may require $4n \times w$ input/output terminals, where w is the length of matrix elements. For large n (say $n \geq 1000$) with typical operand length $w = 32$ bits, it is rather impractical to fabricate an $n \times n$ systolic array in a monolithic chip with over $4n \times w = 128\,000$ I/O terminals. Our partitioned approach will circumvent this problem by using $m \times m$ VLSI array modules, where m is much smaller than n in at least two orders of magnitude. Of course, I/O port sharing and time-division multiplexing are often used to satisfy the IC packaging constraints, even for small m [4].

Our partitioning method to perform triangular decomposition is illustrated in Fig. 3. The given matrix $A = (a_{ij})$ is partitioned into k^2 submatrices of order $m \times m$ each. The submatrix computation sequence is also marked. This method is equivalent to Crout's method, when $m = 1$. However, we assume $m \geq 2$ in general. This sequence of submatrix computations can be best illustrated by partitioning an example matrix A of order $n = 6$ using size $m = 2$ VLSI chips. Here the ratio $k = n/m = 6/2 = 3$ (Fig. 4). In total, $k \times (k + 1) = 3 \times 4 = 12$ submatrices in L and U are to be generated for $L \cdot U = A$.

At step 1, we perform *L-U* decomposition of submatrix A_{11} using a *D*-type chip to generate two triangular submatrices L_{11}

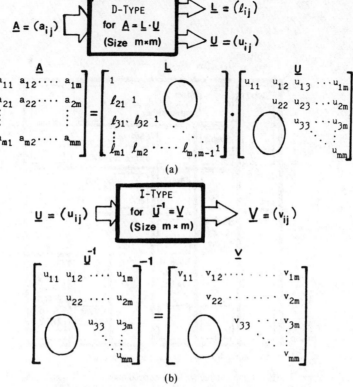

(a)

(b)

Fig. 1. Functional specification of D-type and I-type VLSI arithmetic chips. (a) D-type chip for L-U decomposition of submatrix. (b) I-type chip for submatrix inversion.

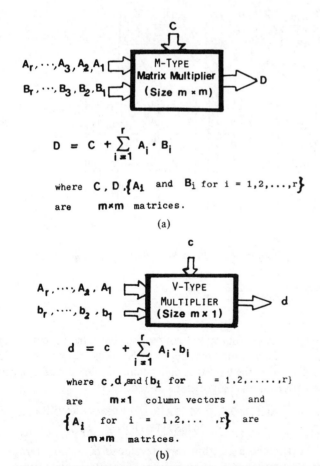

$$D = C + \sum_{i=1}^{r} A_i \cdot B_i$$

where C, D, $\{A_i$ and B_i for $i = 1, 2, \ldots, r\}$ are $m \times m$ matrices.

(a)

$$d = c + \sum_{i=1}^{r} A_i \cdot b_i$$

where c, d, and $\{b_i$ for $i = 1, 2, \ldots, r\}$ are $m \times 1$ column vectors, and $\{A_i$ for $i = 1, 2, \ldots, r\}$ are $m \times m$ matrices.

(b)

Fig. 2. Functional specification of M-type and V-type VLSI arithmetic chips. (a) M-type chip for matrix multiplication. (b) V-type chip for matrix-vector multiplication.

and U_{11}, such that $A_{11} = L_{11} \cdot U_{11}$. Two I-type VLSI chips are then used to compute the inverse submatrices L_{11}^{-1} and U_{11}^{-1} at step 2. The following matrix multiplications are then performed by $2(k - 1)$ M-type chips in parallel..

$$\begin{cases} L_{p1} = A_{p1} \cdot U_{11}^{-1} & \text{for } p = 2, 3, \cdots, k \\ U_{1q} = L_{11}^{-1} \cdot A_{1q} & \text{for } q = 2, 3, \cdots, k \end{cases} \quad (4)$$

For the example 6×6 matrix, submatrices L_{21}, L_{31}, U_{12} and U_{13} are generated at step 2 as shown in Fig. 4.

In subsequent steps, we need to generate the following intermediate submatrices using M-type chips.

$$\hat{A}_{pq} = A_{pq} - \sum_{s=1}^{r-1} L_{ps} \cdot U_{sq} \quad (5)$$

for $p, q = 2, 3, \cdots, k$.

Local L-U decompositions are then performed on $\hat{A}_{rr}$ at successsive odd-numbered steps as shown in Fig. 2.

$$L_{rr} \cdot U_{rr} = \hat{A}_{rr} \quad \text{for } r = 2, 3, \cdots, k \quad (6)$$

The remaining off-diagonal submatrices L_{pr} and U_{rq} are computed by inverting the diagonal submatrices U_{rr} and L_{rr}, and then multiplying them by intermediate submatrices $\hat{A}_{pr}$ and $\hat{A}_{rq}$ at successive even-numbered steps. For $r = 2, 3, \cdots$, k, we need to compute

$$\begin{cases} L_{pr} = \hat{A}_{pr} \cdot U_{rr}^{-1} & \text{for } p = r + 1, \cdots, k \\ U_{rq} = L_{rr}^{-1} \cdot \hat{A}_{rq} & \text{for } q = r + 1, \cdots, k \end{cases} \quad (7)$$

For the example 6×6 matrix in Fig. 4, the intermediate matrix $\hat{A}_{22}$ is computed at step 3. By performing $L_{22} \cdot U_{22} = \hat{A}_{22}$, we obtain two triangular submatrices L_{22} and U_{22}. In-

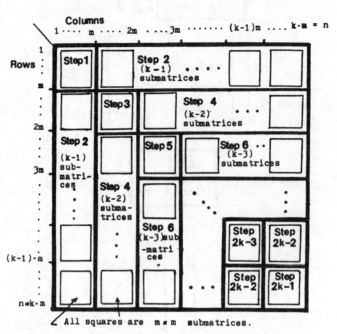

$$k = n/m$$

Columns

$1 \cdots m \cdots 2m \cdots 3m \cdots (k-1)m \cdots k \cdot m = n$

Rows

Step 1 | Step 2 $(k-1) \cdots$ submatrices

Step 3 | Step 4 $(k-2)$ submatrices

Step 2 $(k-1)$ sub-matrices | Step 5 | Step 6 $\cdots$ $(k-3)$ submatrices

Step 4 $(k-2)$ submatrices

Step 6 $(k-3)$sub-matrices | Step $2k-3$ | Step $2k-2$

Step $2k-2$ | Step $2k-1$

$n = k \cdot m$

All squares are $m \times m$ submatrices.

Fig. 3. Partitioning sequence for L-U decomposition of a nonsingular $n \times n$ matrix with $m \times m$ submatrices in $2k - 1$ steps, where $k = n/m$.

$$A = \begin{bmatrix} a_{11} & a_{12} & a_{13} & a_{14} & a_{15} & a_{16} \\ a_{21} & a_{22} & a_{23} & a_{24} & a_{25} & a_{26} \\ a_{31} & a_{32} & a_{33} & a_{34} & a_{35} & a_{36} \\ a_{41} & a_{42} & a_{43} & a_{44} & a_{45} & a_{46} \\ a_{51} & a_{52} & a_{53} & a_{54} & a_{55} & a_{56} \\ a_{61} & a_{62} & a_{63} & a_{64} & a_{65} & a_{66} \end{bmatrix} = \begin{bmatrix} A_{11} & A_{12} & A_{13} \\ A_{21} & A_{22} & A_{23} \\ A_{31} & A_{32} & A_{33} \end{bmatrix} = \begin{bmatrix} L_{11} & 0 & 0 \\ L_{21} & L_{22} & 0 \\ L_{31} & L_{32} & L_{33} \end{bmatrix} \cdot \begin{bmatrix} U_{11} & U_{12} & U_{13} \\ 0 & U_{22} & U_{23} \\ 0 & 0 & U_{33} \end{bmatrix} = L \cdot U$$

Steps

Step 1. $A_{11} = L_{11} \cdot U_{11}$

Step 2. $L_{21} = A_{21} \cdot U_{11}^{-1}$; $L_{31} = A_{31} \cdot U_{11}^{-1}$

$U_{12} = L_{11}^{-1} \cdot A_{12}$; $U_{13} = L_{11}^{-1} \cdot A_{13}$

Step 3. $\hat{A}_{22} = A_{22} - L_{21} \cdot U_{12} = L_{22} \cdot U_{22}$

$\hat{A}_{23} = A_{23} - L_{21} \cdot U_{13}$; $\hat{A}_{32} = A_{32} - L_{31} \cdot U_{12}$

Step 4. $U_{23} = L_{22}^{-1} \cdot \hat{A}_{23}$; $L_{32} = \hat{A}_{32} \cdot U_{22}^{-1}$

Step 5. $\hat{A}_{33} = A_{33} - (L_{31} \cdot U_{13} + L_{32} \cdot U_{23}) = L_{33} \cdot U_{33}$

$$L \cdot U = \begin{bmatrix} 1 & 0 & 0 & 0 & 0 & 0 \\ l_{21} & 1 & 0 & 0 & 0 & 0 \\ l_{31} & l_{32} & 1 & 0 & 0 & 0 \\ l_{41} & l_{42} & l_{43} & 1 & 0 & 0 \\ l_{51} & l_{52} & l_{53} & l_{54} & 1 & 0 \\ l_{61} & l_{62} & l_{63} & l_{64} & l_{65} & 1 \end{bmatrix} \cdot \begin{bmatrix} u_{11} & u_{12} & u_{13} & u_{14} & u_{15} & u_{16} \\ 0 & u_{22} & u_{23} & u_{24} & u_{25} & u_{26} \\ 0 & 0 & u_{33} & u_{34} & u_{35} & u_{36} \\ 0 & 0 & 0 & u_{44} & u_{45} & u_{46} \\ 0 & 0 & 0 & 0 & u_{55} & u_{56} \\ 0 & 0 & 0 & 0 & 0 & u_{66} \end{bmatrix}$$

Fig. 4. Partitioned L-U decomposition of an example matrix of order $n = 6$ with 2×2 ($m = 2$) VLSI chips in $2k - 1 = 2 \cdot 3 - 1 = 5$ steps.

verting these submatrices and then multiplying them to $\hat{A}_{23}$ and $\hat{A}_{32}$, we obtain additional submatrices $U_{23} = L_{22}^{-1} \cdot \hat{A}_{23}$ and $L_{32} = \hat{A}_{32} \cdot U_{22}^{-1}$ at step 4. Intermediate submatrix $\hat{A}_{33} = A_{33} - (L_{31} \cdot U_{13} + L_{32} \cdot U_{23})$ is calculated at step 5. Performing L-U decomposition on $\hat{A}_{33}$, we obtain the last two submatrices L_{33} and U_{33} at step 5.

The above iterative procedures are summarized in *Algorithm 1* for partitioned L-U decomposition of any nonsingular dense matrix A of order n. Submatrix computations are specified in groups in (4), (5) and (7). Each group can be computed in parallel within each step by multiple VLSI chips.

Submatrix computations can be also computed in sequential order, if only limited number of VLSI chips are available. We shall analyze the hardware chip counts and speed performance of various matrix algorithms in Section V.

V. PARTITIONED MATRIX INVERSION AND BACK SUBSTITUTION

Partitioned algorithms are developed below for iterative inversion of an $n \times n$ nonsingular triangular matrix using I-type and M-type VLSI chips. For clarity, we demonstrate the partitioning method by finding the inverse of an example

552

Algorithm 1 (Partitioned *L-U* Decomposition)

Inputs: An $n \times n$ dense matrix $A = (a_{ij})$ partitioned into k^2 $m \times m$ submatrices A_{ij} for $i, j = 1, 2, \cdots, k$, where $n = k \cdot m$.

Outputs: $k \cdot (k + 1)$ submatrices L_{pq} for $q \le p = 1, 2, \cdots, k$ and U_{rs} for $s \ge r = 1, 2, \cdots, k$, each of order $m \times m$.

Procedures:

1) Decompose A_{11} into L_{11} and U_{11} such that $L_{11} \cdot U_{11} = A_{11}$.

2) Compute inverse matrices L_{11}^{-1} and U_{11}^{-1}, compute $L_{p1} = A_{p1} \cdot U_{11}^{-1}$. $U_{1p} = L_{11}^{-1} \cdot A_{1p}$ for $p = 2, 3, \cdots, k$.

3) For $q \leftarrow 2$ to $(k - 1)$ step 1 do

   compute $\hat{A}_{qq} = A_{qq} - \sum_{s=1}^{q-1} L_{qs} \cdot U_{sq}$;

   decompose $\hat{A}_{qq} = L_{qq} \cdot U_{qq}$;

   compute the matrices L_{qq}^{-1} and U_{qq}^{-1}.

   For $p \leftarrow (q + 1)$ to k step 1 do

   compute $\hat{A}_{pq} = A_{pq} - \sum_{s=1}^{r-1} L_{ps} \cdot U_{sq}$

   and $\hat{A}_{qp} = A_{qp} - \sum_{s=1}^{r-1} L_{qs} \cdot U_{sp}$ for $r = \min(p,q)$;

   compute $L_{pq} = \hat{A}_{pq} \cdot U_{qq}^{-1}$; $U_{qp} = L_{qq}^{-1} \cdot \hat{A}_{qp}$.
   Repeat
   Repeat

4) Compute $\hat{A}_{kk} = A_{kk} - \sum_{s=1}^{k-1} L_{ks} \cdot U_{sk}$;

   decompose $\hat{A}_{kk} = L_{kk} \cdot U_{kk}$.

Step 1 : $\quad v_{11} \approx u_{11}^{-1}$; $\quad v_{22} = u_{22}^{-1}$; $\quad v_{33} = u_{33}^{-1}$

Step 2 : $\quad v_{12} = -v_{11} \cdot (u_{12} \cdot v_{22})$; $\quad v_{23} = -v_{22} \cdot (u_{23} \cdot v_{33})$

Step 3 : $\quad v_{13} = -v_{11} \cdot (u_{12} \cdot v_{23} + u_{13} \cdot v_{33})$

Fig. 5. Partitioned matrix inversion of an example matrix of order $n = 6$ with $m = 2$ submatrix chips in $k = n/m = 6/2 = 3$ steps.

6×6 upper triangular matrix, $U = (u_{ij})$ with 2×2 array modules (for $n = 6$ and $m = 2$). The inverse matrix $V = (v_{ij}) = U^{-1}$ is partitioned into $k^2 = 9$ submatrices as shown in Fig. 5.

First, we perform the inversions of all diagonal submatrices to generate $V_{pp} = U_{pp}^{-1}$ for $p = 1, 2, \cdots, k$. Such inversions are always possible due to the nonsingularity of matrix U. It follows that $k - 1$ submatrices in the first off-diagonal are computed at step 2. For the example system in Fig. 5, we have to compute V_{12} and V_{23} at step 2, and V_{13} at step 3. These re-

Algorithm 2 (Partitioned Matrix Inversion)

Inputs: $m \times m$ submatrices U_{pq} of matrix $U = (u_{ij})$ for all $q \ge p = 1, 2, \cdots, k$.

Outputs: $k \cdot (k + 1)/2$ submatrices V_{pq} of the inverse matrix $V = U^{-1}$ for all $q \ge p = 1, 2, \cdots, k$, each of order $m \times m$.

Procedures:

1) For $p \leftarrow 1$ to k step 1 do

$$V_{pp} = U_{pp}^{-1}$$

   Repeat

2) For $q \leftarrow 1$ to $(k - 1)$ step 1 do
   For $p \leftarrow 1$ to $k - q$ step 1 do

$$W_{p,p+q} = \sum_{r=1}^{q} U_{p,p+r} \cdot V_{p+r,p+q}; \tag{8}$$

$$V_{p,p+q} = -V_{pp} \cdot W_{p,p+q}.$$

   Repeat
   Repeat

Algorithm 3 (Partitioned Matrix Multiplication)

Inputs: $m \times m$ submatrices A_{pr} and B_{rq} of the matrix $A = (a_{ij})$ and matrix $B = (b_{ij})$, where $p, q, r = 1, 2, \cdots, k$.

Outputs: $m \times m$ submatrices C_{pq} of the resulting product matrix $C = (c_{ij})$, where $p, q = 1, 2, \cdots, k$.

Procedures:

For $p \leftarrow 1$ to k step 1 do

   For $q \leftarrow 1$ to k step 1 do

$$C_{pq} = \sum_{r=1}^{k} A_{pr} \cdot B_{rq} \tag{9}$$

   Repeat
   Repeat

cursive steps for generating the inverse matrix $V = U^{-1}$ are summarized in *Algorithm 2*. The computations in (8) can be also performed by *M*-type chips. Because of the two-level looping, this algorithm require the same orders of chip count and speed complexity as those for *Algorithm 1*.

Partitioned multiplication of two large $n \times n$ matrices, say $A \cdot B = C$, is rather straightforward. We include it here for completeness. Basically, each $m \times m$ submatrix C_{pq} of matrix C is obtained by performing the cumulative multiplications specified in (9) using exclusively *M*-type chips. Partitioned matrix multiplication is specified in *Algorithm 3*.

Back substitution for solving $U \cdot x = d$ was specified in (3). The method can be partitioned into sections of m-element subvectors. Fig. 6 presents the partitioned solution of $U \cdot x = d$ with known $U = (u_{ij})$ and $d = (d_1, d_2, \cdots, d_6)^T$. Subvectors $[x_5, x_6]^T$, $[x_3, x_4]^T$ and $[x_1, x_2]^T$ are computed sequentially with back substitution. In general, $k = n/m$ steps are needed in the back substitution. Matrix U is partitioned into $k \times (k + 1)/2$ submatrices of order $m \times m$. The solution vector x is divided into k subvectors and so is the transformed vector d. *Algorithm 4* summarizes the partitioned back-substitution operations. The computations of d_p in (10) are carried out by *V*-type chips. Boundary conditions $U_{p,k+1} = O$ and $x_{k+1} = O$ were assumed.

VI. VLSI ARCHITECTURES AND PERFORMANCE ANALYSIS

VLSI chip requirements and speed complexity of partitioned matrix algorithms are analyzed in this section. We consider two architectural configurations for the proposed VLSI matrix algorithms. In a *strictly parallel configuration*, all submatrix operations at each step are performed in parallel by multiple VLSI chips, and thus results in a minimum time delay per each

$$
\begin{bmatrix}
u_{11} & u_{12} & u_{13} & u_{14} & u_{15} & u_{16} \\
0 & u_{22} & u_{23} & u_{24} & u_{25} & u_{26} \\
 & & u_{33} & u_{34} & u_{35} & u_{36} \\
 & & 0 & u_{44} & u_{45} & u_{46} \\
 & & & & u_{55} & u_{56} \\
 & & & & 0 & u_{66}
\end{bmatrix}
\cdot
\begin{bmatrix}
x_1 \\ x_2 \\ x_3 \\ x_4 \\ x_5 \\ x_6
\end{bmatrix}
=
\begin{bmatrix}
d_1 \\ d_2 \\ d_3 \\ d_4 \\ d_5 \\ d_6
\end{bmatrix}
$$

$$
\begin{bmatrix} x_5 \\ x_6 \end{bmatrix}
=
\begin{bmatrix} u_{55} & u_{56} \\ 0 & u_{66} \end{bmatrix}^{-1}
\cdot
\begin{bmatrix} d_5 \\ d_6 \end{bmatrix}
\qquad \underline{(\text{Step 1})}
$$

$$
\underset{(\text{Step 2})}{\begin{bmatrix} x_3 \\ x_4 \end{bmatrix}}
=
\begin{bmatrix} u_{33} & u_{34} \\ 0 & u_{44} \end{bmatrix}^{-1}
\cdot
\left(
\begin{bmatrix} d_3 \\ d_4 \end{bmatrix}
-
\begin{bmatrix} u_{35} & u_{36} \\ u_{45} & u_{46} \end{bmatrix}
\cdot
\begin{bmatrix} x_5 \\ x_6 \end{bmatrix}
\right)
$$

$$
\begin{bmatrix} x_1 \\ x_2 \end{bmatrix}
=
\begin{bmatrix} u_{11} & u_{12} \\ 0 & u_{22} \end{bmatrix}^{-1}
\cdot
\left\{
\begin{bmatrix} d_1 \\ d_2 \end{bmatrix}
-
\left(
\begin{bmatrix} u_{13} & u_{14} \\ u_{23} & u_{24} \end{bmatrix}
\cdot
\begin{bmatrix} x_3 \\ x_4 \end{bmatrix}
\right.
\right.
$$

$$
\underset{(\text{Step 3})}{}
\left.
\left.
+
\begin{bmatrix} u_{15} & u_{16} \\ u_{25} & u_{26} \end{bmatrix}
\cdot
\begin{bmatrix} x_1 \\ x_2 \end{bmatrix}
\right)
\right\}
$$

Fig. 6. Partitioned VLSI triangular system solver based on subvector back substitution.

Algorithm 4 (Partitioned Triangular System Solver)

Inputs: $m \times m$ submatrices U_{pq} of U for $q \geq p = 1, 2, \cdots, k$. The coefficient subvectors d_p for $p = 1, 2, \cdots, k$, each having m consecutive elements of the vector d.

Outputs: The subvector x_p of the solution vector $x = [x_1, x_2, \cdots, x_n]^T$, where $x_p = [x_{(p-1)m+1}, x_{(p-1)m+2}, \cdots, x_{pm}]^T$ for $p = 1, 2, \cdots, k$.

Procedures:

For $p \leftarrow k$ to 1 in step (-1) Compute

$$U_{pp}^{-1} \text{ from } U_{pp};$$

$$\hat{d}_p = d_p - \sum_{q=p+1}^{k} U_{pq} \cdot x_q; \qquad (10)$$

$$x_p = U_{pp}^{-1} \cdot \hat{d}_p.$$

Repeat

step. The total time delay among all steps is also minimized by overlapping some step operations. In a *serial-parallel configuration*, the number of available VLSI chips in each step is upper bounded. Thus, some parallel-executable operations may have to be executed sequentially. Of course, serial-parallel operations will result in longer time delays due to limited hardware.

To implement *Algorithm 1* in hardware, we need to use one *D*-type two *I*-type, and a large number of *M*-type VLSI chips. The number of needed *M*-type chips depends on the chosen architectural configuration. In Table I, we traced the step-by-step operations of *Algorithm 1* with a minimum-delay analysis. We have structured the algorithm for minimum data dependency in successive steps. In other words, some adjacent computation steps are overlapped in a lookahead fashion. Maximal concurrencies are achieved by parallelism within

each step and overlapping between successive steps. The total time delay of *Algorithm 1* implemented in strictly parallel mode is equal to

$$T = 6n + 2n/m - 4m - 2 \doteq O(n), \text{ if } n \gg m \gg 1 \quad (11)$$

For large n, *M*-type chips predominate the chip requirement of *Algorithm 1*. We plot in Fig. 7 the actual chip count in successive steps, $3q$ for $q = 2, 3, \cdots, k - 1$, of *Algorithm 1*. The chip requirement increases steadily until the looping index $q = 13$. The effect of resource sharing between adjacent steps becomes apparent for $q \geq 13$. The peak of each curve corresponds to the minimum number, M, of *M*-type chips required to achieve the minimum delay T in (11). This number has been estimated algebraically to be

$$M \doteq n^2/(11m^2) \text{ for } n \gg m \gg 1 \quad (12)$$

From (11) and (12), we conclude that the partitioned *L-U* decomposition (*Algorithm 1*) can be realized with $O(n^2/m^2)$ VLSI chips with interior chip complexity $O(m^2)$.

Using a uniprocessor, $O(n^3)$ time steps are needed to perform the *L-U* decomposition. It is interesting to note that the triple product of the *chip count* $O(n^2/m^2)$, the *compute time* $O(n)$, and the chip size $O(m^2)$ yields the uniprocessor compute time $O(n^3)$; that is

$$O(n^2/m^2) \cdot O(n) \cdot O(m^2) = O(n^3) \quad (13)$$

This property is called *conservation law* between available hardware *chips* and achievable *speed*.

TABLE I
TIME AND HARDWARE COMPLEXITIES OF THE PARTITIONED
L-U DECOMPOSITION (ALGORITHM 1)

Step	Submatrix Computations	Time Complexity		VLSI Chip Count		
		Start Time	Delay	D-Type	I-Type	M-Type
1	$A_{11} = L_{11} \cdot U_{11}$	0	$2m$	1		
2	$L_{11}^{-1},\ U_{11}^{-1}$	$2m$	$2m$		2	
	$L_{p1} = A_{p1} \cdot U_{11}^{-1}$ $U_{1p} = L_{11}^{-1} \cdot A_{1p}$	$4m$ (for p=2,3,...,k)	$m+1$			$2(k-1)$
3_2 (q=2)	$\hat{A}_{22}$	$5m+1$	$m+1$			1
	$\hat{A}_{22} = L_{22} \cdot U_{22}$	$6m+2$	$2m$	1		
	$L_{22}^{-1},\ U_{22}^{-1}$	$8m+2$	$2m$		2	
	$\hat{A}_{p2}, \hat{A}_{2p}$	$9m+1$ (for p=3,4,...,k)	$m+1$			$2(k-2)$
	$L_{p2},\ U_{2p}$	$10m+2$ (for p=3,4,...,k)	$m+1$			
	$\vdots$	$\vdots$	$\vdots$			$\vdots$
3_{k-1} (q=k-1)	$\hat{A}_{k-1,k-1}$	$(5m+2)(k-2)-1$	$(k-2)m+1$			1
	$L_{k-1,k-1};\ U_{k-1,k-1}$	$(6m+2)(k-2)$	$2m$	1		
	$L_{k-1,k-1}^{-1};\ U_{k-1,k-1}^{-1}$	$(6m+2)(k-2)+2m$	$2m$		2	
	$\hat{A}_{k,k-1};\ \hat{A}_{k-1,k}$	$(5m+2)\cdot(k-2)+(4m-1)$	$(k-2)m+1$			
	$L_{k,k-1};\ U_{k-1,k}$	$(6m+2)(k-2)+4m$	$m+1$			$2 \cdot 1$
4	$\hat{A}_{kk}$	$(5m+2)(k-1)-1$	$(k-1)m+1$			1
	$\hat{A}_{kk} = L_{kk} \cdot U_{kk}$	$(6m+2)(k-1)$	$2m$	1		
Total Compute Time		$T = 6n + \dfrac{2n}{m} - (4m+2) \doteq O(n)$ for $n \gg m \gg 1$				
Total VLSI Chip Count		$M \doteq O(n^2/m^2)$ for $n \gg m \gg 1$		1	2	$\dfrac{1}{11}(n/m)^2$

Note: q is the looping index used in Algorithm 1 and k = n/m.

The chip count, $O(n^2/m^2)$, is too high to be of practical value, because of the fact that $n \gg m$. Therefore, we have to bound the chip count with a linear order, $O(n/m)$, in a serial-parallel implementation of the partitioned matrix algorithms. One can use $2n/m - 1$ M-type chips to implement a serial-parallel architecture for *Algorithm 1*. Using $O(n/m)$ chips yields the following prolonged time delay for *Algorithm 1*.

$$T' = n^2/m - n/2 + 2n/m + 17m$$
$$- 2 \doteq O(n^2/m) \text{ for } n \gg m \gg 1 \quad (14)$$

The conservation law is again preserved in this serial-parallel architecture. In this case, we observe that

$$O(n/m) \cdot O(n^2/m) \cdot O(m^2) = O(n^3) \quad (15)$$

Similar analyses can be made to estimate the chip counts and time delays for *Algorithm 2* and *Algorithm 3*. As shown in Table II, both VLSI matrix algorithms can be implemented by $O(n^2/m^2)$ VLSI chips with $O(n)$ time delays for the strictly parallel architecture; and by $O(n/m)$ chips with $O(n^2/m)$ times for the serial-parallel configuration. Only I-type and M-type chips are needed in *Algorithm 2*. *Algorithm 3* requires to use only M-type chips. To solve a triangular LSE's

(*Algorithm 4*), one I-type chip and $n/2m$ V-type chips are needed. The total time delay is $O(n)$. Only $O(n/m)$ VLSI chips are used in *Algorithm 4*. Only the strictly parallel architecture is suggested for constructing the VLSI triangular system solver. Again we have preserved the conservation law. In this case, we observe that

$$O(n/m) \cdot O(n) \cdot O(m) = O(n^2) \quad (16)$$

where $O(n^2)$ is the compute time of using a uniprocessor to solve a triangular system. VLSI matrix arithmetic pipelines have been designed by Hwang and Su [7] based on the serial-parallel architecture.

It is obvious that tradeoffs exist between the chip counts and time delays of all partitioned matrix algorithms. The tradeoffs in implementing *Algorithm 1* are plotted in Fig. 8. The time delay is a monotonic decreasing function of the chip count. When the chip count exceeds the upper bound M [see (12)], the minimum time delay is achieved as shown by the flat portion of the curves in Fig. 8. By presetting a speed requirement, one can use these curves to decide the minimum number of VLSI chips needed to achieve the desired speed performance. On the other hand, one can predict the speed performance under prespecified hardware allowance. This tradeoff study

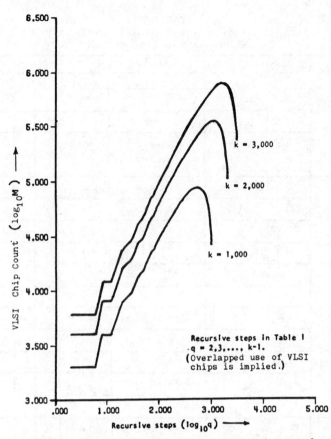

Fig. 7. VLSI chip requirements in successive computation steps of
Algorithm 1.

TABLE II
VLSI CHIP REQUIREMENTS AND SPEED PERFORMANCES OF
VARIOUS PARTITIONED MATRIX ALGORITHMS

VLSI Architecture and Complexity / Matrix Algorithm	Strictly Parallel System Architecture with Minimum Time Delays		Serial-Parallel System Architecture with Bounded Chip Count	
	VLSI Chip Count and Types	Total Compute Time	VLSI Chip Count and Types	Total Compute Time
Algorithm 1 for L-U Decomposition	$O\left(n^2/m^2\right)$ D, I, M*	$O(n)$	$O(n/m)$ D, I, M*	$O\left(n^2/m\right)$
Algorithm 2 for Inversion of Triangular Matrix	$O\left(n^2/m^2\right)$ I, M*	$O(n)$	$O(n/m)$ I, M*	$O\left(n^2/m\right)$
Algorithm 3 for Matrix Multiplication	$O\left(n^2/m^2\right)$ M*	$O(n)$	$O(n/m)$ M*	$O\left(n^2/m\right)$
Algorithm 4 for Solving Triangular LSEs	$O(n/m)$ I, V*	$O(n)$	Note: All measures are based on the assumption n>>m>>1, where n is the matrix order and m is the VLSI chip size.	

* Dominating Chip Type to be used.

556

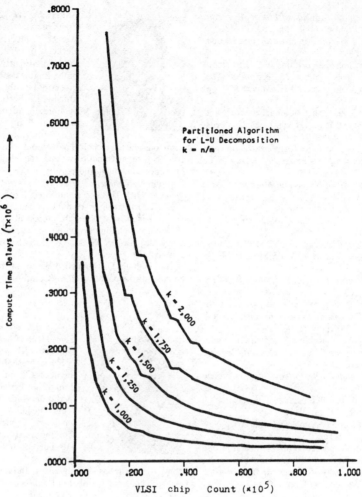

Fig. 8. Compute time delays of Algorithm 1 versus available numbers of VLSI submatrix chips.

VII. Conclusions

We have modified the Gaussian elimination procedure through a block partitioning approach. Our partitioned VLSI matrix algorithms can be implemented with $O(n^2/m^2)$ chips in linear time $O(n)$, or with $O(n/m)$ chips in quadratic time $O(n^2/m)$. In either case, we have achieved a significant speedup over the $O(n^3)$ compute time of a serial uniprocessor. M-type chips are the major type of VLSI chips to be used in implementing matrix solvers. In systolic arrays, the chip complexity is of order $O(n^2)$. In our modular approach, it has been reduced to $O(m^2)$. For $n \gg m$, this implies higher feasibility based on the projected VLSI chip and packaging technologies.

Design tradeoffs of VLSI architectures have to satisfy the conservation law between operating speed and total chip counts. Our partitioned approach offers better extensibility, maintainability, and flexibility to digital system designers. Optimized design must consider high performance/cost ratio. The proposed partitioning matrix algorithms are also suitable for software implementation. The tradeoffs between hardware and software approaches should be an interesting research topic.

Toward the eventual realization of fast VLSI matrix solvers with standard VLSI chips, there are still many practical problems yet to be solved; such as computer-aided layout of VLSI circuits, operand buffering within chips, I/O port sharing and multiplexing, packaging and reliability issues, etc. We firmly believe that partitioning is a logical and feasible approach to designing large-scale matrix manipulation machines. Modulation through algorithmic partitioning is much better off than through unstructured physical circuit partitioning, as far as the systemization of VLSI computing architecture is concerned.

References

[1] P. D. Crout, "A short method for evaluating determinants and solving systems of linear equations with real or complex coefficients," in *Proc. American Inst. Elec. Eng.*, vol. 40, 1941, pp. 1235–1240.
[2] D. K. Faddeev and V. N. Faddeeva, *Computational Methods of Linear Algebra*, translated by R. C. Williams from Russian. San Francisco, CA: Freeman, 1963, pp. 140–163.

[3] G. Forsythe and C. B. Moler, *Computer Solution of Linear Algebraic Systems.* Englewood Cliffs, NJ: Prentice-Hall, 1967, pp. 27-48.

[4] K. Hwang, *Computer Arithmetic: Principle, Architecture and Design.* New York: Wiley, 1979, ch. 6 and 8.

[5] K. Hwang and Y. H. Cheng, "Partitioned algorithms and VLSI structures for large-scale matrix computations," in *Proc. IEEE Comput. Soc. 5th Symp. Comput. Arithmetic*, Ann Arbor, MI, May 1981, pp. 220-230.

[6] K. Hwang, S. P. Su, and L. M. Ni, "Vector computer architecture and processing techniques," in *Advances in Computers*, vol. 20, M. C. Yovits, Ed. New York: Academic, 1981, pp. 115-197.

[7] K. Hwang and S. P. Su, "VLSI architectures for feature extraction and pattern classification," *J. Comput. Graphics Image Processing*, to be published.

[8] E. Isaacson and H. B. Keller, *Analysis of Numerical Methods.* New York: Wiley, 1966, pp. 29-52.

[9] R. M. Kant and T. Kimura, "Decentralized parallel algorithms for matrix computations," in *Proc. 5th Annu. Symp. Comput. Arch.*, Palo Alto, CA, Apr. 1978, pp. 96-100.

[10] T. H. Kung and C. E. Leiserson, "Systolic arrays (for VLSI)," in *Sparse Matrix Proc.*, Duff et al., Eds., Soc. Ind. App. Math., PA, 1979, pp. 256-282.

[11] C. Mead and L. Conway, *Introduction To VLSI Systems.* Reading, MA: Addison-Wesley, 1980, pp. 263-332.

[12] J. G. Nash, S. Hansen and G. R. Nudd, "VLSI processor array for matrix manipulation," in *VLSI Systems and Computations*, Kung et al., Eds., Computer Science Press, 1981, pp. 367-378.

[13] F. P. Preparata and T. Vuillemin, "Optimal integrated circuit implementation of triangular matrix inversion," in *Proc. Int. Conf. Parallel Processing*, Aug. 1980, pp. 211-216.

[14] J. R. Rice, *Matrix Computations and Mathematical Software.* New York: McGraw-Hill, 1981, pp. 45-51.

[15] A. Sameh and D. Kuch, "On stable parallel linear system solvers," *J. Ass. Comput. Mach.*, vol. 25, pp. 81-91, Jan. 1978.

[16] J. R. Stoer and R. Bulirsh, *Introduction to Numerical Analysis.* New York: Springer-Verlag, 1980, pp. 159-168.

[17] J. R. Westlake, *A Handbook for Numerical Matrix Inversion and Solution of Linear Equations.* New York: Wiley, 1968.

[18] D. M. Young and R. T. Gregory, *A Survey of Numerical Mathematics*, vol. 2. Reading, MA: Addison-Wesley, 1973, pp. 779-834.

Kai Hwang (M'72-SM'81) received the Ph.D. degree in electrical engineering and computer science from the University of California at Berkeley in 1972.

He is presently an Associate Professor of Computer Engineering at the School of Electrical Engineering, Purdue University, West Lafayette, IN. During 1981-1982, he visited Academia Sinica (Chinese Academy of Sciences) and National Taiwan University as a Visiting Professor in Computer and Information Engineering. He has published numerous journal technical papers and book chapters in the areas of computer architecture, arithmetic systems, sequential machines, file structures, performance modeling, and parallel processing. He is the author of the book *Computer Arithmetic: Principles, Architecture and Design* (New York: Wiley, 1979). He also coauthored the book *Computer Architecture and Parallel Processing*, to be published in the McGraw-Hill Computer Science Series. His current research interest lies mainly in advanced computer architecture, including array/pipeline vector computers, multiprocessor and computer networks, VLSI computing structures, dataflow and supercomputer applications.

Dr. Hwang a Distinguished Visitor of the IEEE Computer Society and a member of the Association for Computing Machinery.

Yeng-Heng Cheng graduated from Tsing-Hua University, Beijing, China, in 1957.

He is presently on the faculty of the Department of Computer Engineering and Science at Tsing-Hua University, where he has participated in the development of several minicomputer systems. During 1979-1981, he visited Purdue University as a Visiting Researcher in the area of Computer Architecture and Parallel Processing. His current teaching/research interests include performance evaluation, multiple mini/micro computers, database management, and local area computer networks.

Mr. Cheng is a member of the Electronics Society in China.

Wafer-Scale Integration and Two-Level Pipelined Implementations
of Systolic Arrays

H. T. Kung and Monica S. Lam

Department of Computer Science
Carnegie-Mellon University
Pittsburgh, Pennsylvania 15213

February 1984

This paper is to appear in *Journal of Parallel and Distributed Processing*, Vol. 1, No. 1, 1984.

A preliminary version appears in *Proceedings of the MIT Conference on Advanced Research in VLSI*, January 1984, pp. 74-83.

This research was supported in part by the Office of Naval Research under Contracts N00014-76-C-0370, NR 044-422 and N00014-80-C-0236, NR 048-659, and in part by the Defense Advanced Research Projects Agency (DoD), ARPA Order No. 3597, monitored by the Air Force Avionics Laboratory under Contract F33615-81-K-1539.

Abstract

This paper addresses two important issues in systolic array designs. How do we provide fault-tolerance in systolic arrays for yield enhancement in wafer-scale integration implementations? And, how do we design efficient systolic arrays with two levels of pipelining? The first level refers to the pipelined organization of the array at the cellular level, and the second refers to the pipelined functional units inside the cells.

The fault-tolerant scheme we propose replaces defective cells with clocked delays. This has the distinct characteristic that data can flow through the array with faulty cells at the original clock speed. We will show that both the defective cells under this fault-tolerant scheme and the second level pipeline-stages can simply be modeled as additional delays in the data paths of "generic" systolic designs. We introduce the mathematical notion of a *cut* to solve the problem of how to allow for these extra delays while preserving the correctness of the original systolic array designs.

The results obtained by applying the techniques described in this paper are encouraging. When applied to systolic arrays without feedback cycles, the arrays can tolerate large numbers of failures (with the addition of very little hardware) while maintaining the original throughput. Furthermore, all of the pipeline stages in the cells can be kept fully utilized through the addition of a small number of delay registers. However, adding delays to systolic arrays with cycles typically induces a significant decrease in throughput. In response to this, we have derived a new class of systolic algorithms in which the data cycle around a ring of processing cells. The *systolic ring* architecture has the property that its performance degrades gracefully as cells fail. Using our cut theory and ring architectures for arrays with feedback, we have effective fault-tolerant and two-level pipelining schemes for most systolic arrays.

As a side-effect of developing the ring architecture approach we have derived several new systolic algorithms. These algorithms generally require only one-third to one-half of the number of cells used in previous designs to achieve the same throughput. The new systolic algorithms include ones for LU-decomposition, QR-decomposition and the solution of triangular linear systems.

1. Introduction

In recent years many systolic algorithms have been designed and several prototypes of systolic array processors have been constructed[1, 2, 3, 4]. Major efforts are currently devoted to building systolic arrays for large, real-life applications. In this paper, we will consider two implementation techniques for building high-performance systolic arrays: wafer-scale integration (WSI) and fabrication using pipelined components.

Fabrication flaws on a wafer are inevitable. It is necessary for a WSI circuit to be "fault-tolerant" so that wafers with defective components can still be used. A common approach is to include redundant circuitry in the design and avoid defects by programming the interconnection of the constituent elements. In particular, the laser-programming technology has been applied successfully to program the redundant circuitry in VLSI RAMs as a yield enhancement measure[5]. The MIT Lincoln Laboratory[6] has also been experimenting on the use of laser-programmable links to build wafer-scale processor arrays.

Systolic arrays are well-suited to the application of wafer-scale integration. They consist of large numbers of small and identical (thus interchangeable) cells and their regular and localized interconnection greatly simplify the problem of routing around defective cells. On the other hand, systolic architectures guarantee full exploitation of their constituent cells to achieve maximum parallelism. The more cells an array has, the more powerful it is. Wafer-scale integration has the potential to provide a very cost-effective and reliable way of implementing high-performance systolic systems.

Before WSI systolic arrays can become a reality, we must solve the problem of how to construct fault-tolerant arrays. After the cells are tested (by wafer-probing, for example), how do we route around the defects to build a functional array? (See Figure 1-1 (a)). This paper describes a "*systolic*" approach which provides fault-tolerance at a very low cost and admits of a graceful degradation in performance as the number of defects increases.

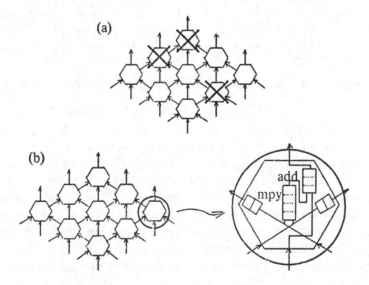

Figure 1-1: Two problems addressed in the paper: (a) fault-tolerance
for arrays with faulty cells and (b) two-level pipelining

The use of pipelined components for implementing cells of systolic arrays is especially attractive for applications requiring floating-point operations. Commercially available floating-point multiplier and adder chips can deliver up to 5 MFLOPs per device. To achieve such high throughput, they typically have three or more pipeline stages[7]. These components, when used to implement systolic cells, form a *second level of pipelining*[8], the first being the pipelined organization of systolic arrays at the cellular level. While this additional level of

---

561

pipelining can increase the system throughput, it considerably complicates the design of systolic array algorithms. Our solution to this problem is to devise a methodology to transform existing systolic designs which assume single-stage cells to arrays consisting of pipelined cells.

We will show that both the "fault-tolerance" and the "two-level pipelining" problems can be solved by the same mathematical reasoning and techniques. Our results imply that once a "generic" systolic algorithm is designed, other versions of the algorithm (for execution on arrays with failed cells, or for implementation using different pipelined processing units) can be systematically derived. The techniques of this paper can also be applied to other computation structures, such as FFT processor arrays.

In the next section we will introduce our approach to the problems, using as an example the simplest type of systolic arrays—uni-directional linear arrays. As we will see, systolic arrays without feedback admit of a much simpler solution and they will be discussed in section 3. In section 4, we will propose a new architecture, the "systolic ring", which can be used in place of many systolic arrays with feedback cycles and are much more amenable to fault-tolerant measures. Section 5 includes a summary and some concluding remarks.

2. Fault-Tolerance and Two-Level Pipelining for Uni-directional Linear Arrays

Figure 2-1 depicts a systolic array[9] for the convolution computation with four weights $w_1, \ldots, w_4$. In this array the data flow only in *one* direction, that is, both x_i and y_i move from left to right (with x_i going through an additional "delay register" following each cell). This is an example of a systolic array without feedback cycles—an array where none of the values in any data stream depends on the preceding values in the same stream. (For an example of an array with feedback cycles, see Figure 4-1 (a)).

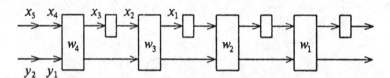

Figure 2-1: Uni-directional linear systolic array for convolution

Depicted in 2-2 (a) is an example of a 5-cell array with one faulty element. The defective cell in the middle is replaced with two "bypass" registers (drawn in dotted lines)—one for the x-data stream and one for the y-data stream. It can easily be shown that this array correctly solves the same problem as the array of Figure 2-1. For example, y_1 picks up $w_4 \cdot x_4$, $w_3 \cdot x_3$ and $w_2 \cdot x_2$ at the first, second and fourth cell respectively. The degradation in performance due to the defect is slight. The maximum convolution computed by this array in one pass can have only 4 rather than 5 weights, and the latency of the solution is increased by one cycle. However, the computational throughput, often the most important factor in performance, remains the same at one output per cell cycle. Figure 2-2 (b) depicts the cell specification for this fault-tolerant scheme, using reconfigurable links. Note that the input/output register in a systolic cell can be used as a bypass register in case the cell fails. Therefore no extra registers are needed to implement this fault-tolerant scheme.

A basic assumption of this paper is that the probability of the interconnection links and registers failing is very small and thus negligible. This is reasonable because these components are typically much simpler and smaller than the cells themselves. Furthermore, they can be implemented conservatively and/or with high redundancy to increase the yield.

In the proposed scheme data move through all the cells. At failed cells, data items are simply delayed with bypass registers for one cycle, and no computation is performed (Figure 2-3 (a)). We call fault-tolerant schemes of this type *systolic* in view of the fact that data travel *systolically* in a defective array from cell to cell, at the original clock speed.

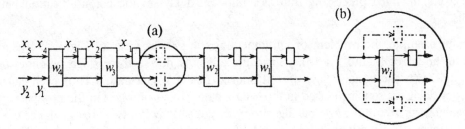

Figure 2-2: (a) Defective cell replaced with registers and (b) cell specification

For uni-directional linear arrays, the systolic fault-tolerant scheme proposed here has the advantages that it utilizes *all* the live cells and maintains the throughput rate of a flawless array (Figure 2-3 (a)). As illustrated in Figure 2-3 (b), other fault-tolerant schemes previously proposed in the literature either suffer from low utilization of live cells[10, 11, 12, 13], or reduced throughput due to a slower system clock required by the fact that the communication between logically adjacent cells can now span a large number of failures[14, 15, 16, 17]. Moreover, as will be shown in the next section, our systolic fault-tolerant technique can be generalized to two-dimensional arrays.

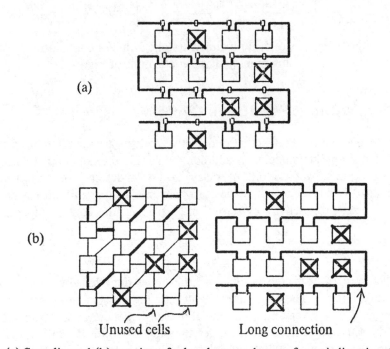

Figure 2-3: (a) Systolic and (b) previous fault-tolerant schemes for uni-directional linear arrays

We now examine more carefully the idea behind our fault-tolerant scheme for the linear array of Figure 2-2. Because of the unit delay introduced by the bypass registers, all the cells after the failed one receive data items one cycle later than they normally would. Since both the x- and y-data streams are delayed by the same amount, the relative alignment between the two data streams remains unchanged. Thus, all the cells after the third one receive the same data and perform the same function, with a one-cycle delay, as would the cell preceding it in a normal array. For this reason, an n-cell, uni-directional, linear array with k defective cells will perform the same computation as a perfect array of $n - k$ cells.

The above reasoning also implies that the correctness of a uni-directional linear array is preserved, if the *same* delay of any length of time is introduced uniformly to *all* the data streams between two adjacent cells. This result is directly applicable to the implementation of two-level pipelined arrays. We can interpret the stages in a given pipelined processing unit as additional delays in the communication between a pair of adjacent cells.

Consider, for example, the problem of implementing the systolic array of Figure 2-1 using the pipelined multiplier and adder of Figure 1-1 (b). Since the adder is now a three-stage pipeline unit instead of a single-stage unit, two additional delays are introduced in the y-data path. Thus each cell requires a total number of four delay registers be placed in the x-data path—one is implicit in the original cell definition, the second is the delay register in the original algorithm design, and the last two are to balance the two new delays in the y-data stream. The resulting two-level pipelined array is depicted in Figure 2-4. This design has been proposed previously[8], but it is reproduced here as a special example of a general theory.

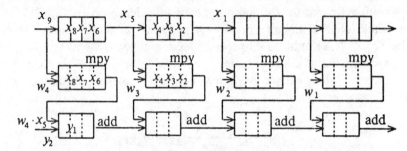

Figure 2-4: Two-level pipelined systolic array for convolution, using pipelined arithmetic units of Figure 1-1 (b)

3. Systolic Arrays without Feedback Cycles

From the previous section we see that both the defective cells in a fault-tolerant array and the pipeline-stages in systolic cells can simply be modeled as additional delays in the data paths. Thus by solving the one problem of how, if possible, to allow for additional delays in systolic designs, we can transform generic systolic designs to fault-tolerant or two-level pipelined designs. A general theory of adding and removing register delays to a system has been proposed by Leiserson and Saxe[18] in the context of optimizing synchronous systems.

3.1. The *Cut Theorem*

We model a systolic array as a directed graph, with the nodes denoting the combinational logic and the edges the communication links[19]. The edges are weighted by the number of registers on the links. We say that two designs are *equivalent* if, given an initial state of one design, there exists for the other design an initial state such that (with the same input from the host, i.e., the outside world) the two designs produce the same output values (although possibly with a constant delay). In other words, as far as the host is concerned, the designs are interchangeable provided the possible differences in the timing of the output are taken into account.

We define a *cut* to be a set of edges that "partitions" the nodes in a graph into two disjoint sets, the *source set* and the *destination set*, with the property that these edges are the only ones connecting nodes in the two sets and are all directed from the source to the destination set.

We say that a systolic design is a "delayed" system of another design if the former differs from the latter by having additional delays on some of the communication links. Thus the graph representations of the two designs are the same except for the weights on the edges that correspond to the communication links with additional delays.

> **Theorem 1:** (*Cut Theorem*) For any design, adding the same delay to all the edges in a cut and to those pointing from the host to the destination set of the cut will result in an equivalent design.

Proof: Let S be the original design partitioned by a cut into sets A and B, the source and the destination set respectively. Let S' be the same as S (with its corresponding sets A' and B'), with the difference that d delays are now added onto the edges in the cut. We will show that by properly initializing S' (at t_0), the output values from A and A' will be identical and that the output values from B are the same as those from B', but lagging behind by d clock cycles.

We define the initial state of A' to be identical to the state of A at time t_0. Since none of the edges in the cut feed into A', directly or indirectly, nodes in A' behave exactly the same way as the corresponding ones in A and thus produce the same outputs.

Let $r_1(e'), \ldots, r_d(e')$ be the delay registers on any edge in the cut, e', with $r_1(e')$ being closest to the source node and $r_d(e')$ closest to the destination node. First, we assign the initial state of B' to be identical to the state of B at time $t_0 - d$. We then initialize the registers $r_1(e'), \ldots, r_d(e')$ with the values of the data on the corresponding edge in S at time $t_0 - 1, t_0 - 2, \ldots, t_0 - d$, respectively. In this way, the input data received by the nodes in set B' from time t_0 to $t_0 + d - 1$ is identical to those received by B from $t_0 - d$ to $t_0 - 1$ and so the configuration of B' at $t_0 + d$ and that of B at t_0 are identical. Since the outputs from A' are the same as those from A, all the inputs arriving at B' starting from time $t_0 + d$ are the same as those arriving at B, except that they lag behind by d cycles due to the additional delay registers. Therefore the nodes in B' will behave the same way as the corresponding ones in B with a d cycle delay. $\square$

We say that a delayed system S' is *derivable* from S if there exists a set of cuts $C_1, C_2, \ldots, C_n$ with their cut delays $d_1, d_2, \ldots, d_n$, such that

$$\forall \, e' \in S' \text{ , number of additional delays on } e' = \sum_{\{i \, | \, e' \in C_i\}} d_i.$$

Since equivalence is associative, the cut theorem implies that if a "delayed" design is derivable from the original design then the two designs are equivalent.

Since a cut partitions the nodes of a graph into two sets with data flowing uni-directionally between them, it cannot cross any feedback cycle. On the other hand, for any given edge not in a feedback cycle, we can always construct a cut set that contains it. Therefore any number of delays on the data paths in a graph without feedback can always be incorporated if we have the option of inserting other delays into the system.

3.2. Linear Arrays Without Feedback

We will now apply the above results to the examples we discussed previously. As depicted in Figure 3-1 (a), the edges between any two adjacent cells of a uni-directional linear array form a cut. Hence by the cut theorem, we can see immediately that both the defective array of Figure 2-2 (a) and the two-level pipelined array of Figure 2-4 are equivalent to the original array of Figure 2-1. Figure 3-1 (b) depicts a less obvious cut, consisting entirely of all the output edges from the multipliers. This implies that the convolution array will function correctly regardless of the number of pipeline stages present in the multipliers (provided the number is the same for all the multipliers in the array). For instance, if all the four-stage multipliers in Figure 2-4 were replaced with ten-stage multipliers, the resulting systolic convolution array would still be correct.

3.3. Two-Level Pipelining for Two-Dimensional Systolic Arrays

It is just as simple to apply the cut theorem to two-level pipelined arrays of two dimensions. Let us consider the example of a hexagonal systolic array that can perform band matrix multiplication[20] (Figure 3-2 (a)). Two results follow directly from the cut theorem:

1. The edges under each dashed line in Figure 3-2 (a) define a cut. All vertical edges, each representing an adder's output (Figure 3-2 (b)), intersect two dashed lines while all the other edges intersect only one. Thus by the cut theorem, if the number of pipeline stages in all the adders is

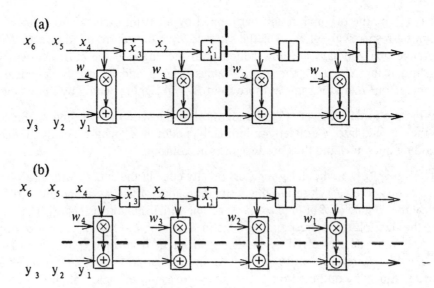

Figure 3-1: Two types of cuts for a uni-directional linear systolic array for convolution

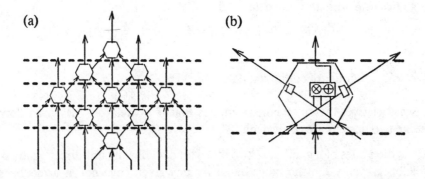

Figure 3-2: (a) Hexagonal systolic array without feedback loops and (b) original cell definition

increased by $2k$, then for each cell, k delays must be added to the other data paths. Figure 1-1 (b) depicts the case when $k=1$.

2. Consider the output edges of all the multipliers in the array. Like those in the uni-directional linear convolution array (Figure 3-1 (b)), these edges define a cut since none of the outputs from the adders are fed back into the multipliers. By the cut theorem, we conclude that these systolic cells can be implemented using pipelined multipliers of any number of stages without any further modification, provided the number of stages is the same for all the multipliers.

3.4. Two-Level Pipelining for the FFT Processor Arrays

The cut theorem can be applied to two-level pipelined designs for any processor arrays without cycles. We consider here as an example, the well known processor array for computing fast Fourier transforms (FFTs). For an n-point FFT, the array has $\log_2 n$ stages of $n/2$ processors for performing butterfly operations. The data are shuffled between any two consecutive stages according to a certain pattern[21, 22]. Figure 3-3 depicts the so-called constant geometry version of the FFT algorithm (for $n=16$), that allows the same pattern of data shuffling to be used for all stages. In the figure the processors for butterfly operations are represented by circles, and the number h by an edge indicates that the result associated with the edge must be multiplied by ω^h, where ω is a primitive n-th root of unity.

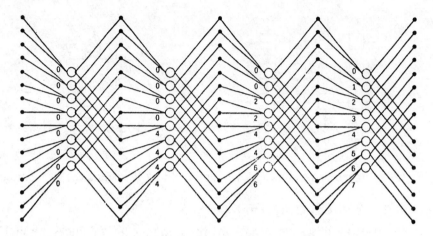

Figure 3-3: Constant geometry version of the FFT algorithm

A butterfly operation,

$$(a_{real} + ja_{imag}) \pm (b_{real} + jb_{imag}) \cdot (w_{real} + jw_{imag})$$
$$= [a_{real} \pm (b_{real} \cdot w_{real} - b_{imag} \cdot w_{imag})] + j[a_{imag} \pm (b_{real} \cdot w_{imag} + b_{imag} \cdot w_{real})],$$

involves four real multiplications and six real additions. Figure 3-4 (a) depicts a straightforward processor implementation for the butterfly operation using four multipliers and six adders. The time that the processor takes to perform a butterfly operation is the total delay of one multiplier and two adders.

To increase the throughput for calculating butterfly operations, we implement the processors with pipelined multipliers and adders. Suppose that these functional units each have five pipeline stages, as in the case of some recent floating-point chips[7]. By the cut theorem, the pipeline delays on the b_{real} and b_{imag} data paths have to be balanced by the same number of delays on the a_{real} and a_{imag} input lines. The two-level pipelined design of the processor is shown in Figure 3-4 (b).

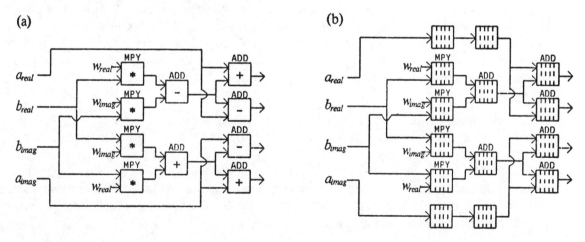

Figure 3-4: (a) Processor for the butterfly operation, and (b) corresponding two-level pipelined processor

3.5. Systolic Fault-Tolerant Schemes for Two-Dimensional Arrays

Let us consider as an example the rectangular array of Figure 3-5 (a) where the data move forwards and downwards. Among many other applications, this array can perform matrix multiplication with either an operand or the partial result matrix stored in the array during the computation. We will first discuss the constraints that a correct implementation must satisfy and then we will study several redundancy schemes.

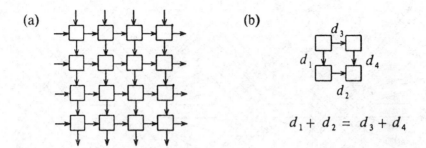

$$(a) \qquad\qquad (b)$$

$$d_1 + d_2 = d_3 + d_4$$

Figure 3-5: (a) Rectangular systolic array without feedback loops and (b) local correctness criterion

3.5.1. The Local Correctness Criterion

By exploiting the regularity in systolic arrays, the following theorem reduces the problem of establishing equivalence between two designs to smaller problems which can be solved using only "local information".

Theorem 2: Let S be a mesh-connected systolic design without feedback and S' be a "delayed" version. S' is equivalent to S if for each square of adjacent cells in the grid, the number of delays on each of the two paths joining the two diagonally-opposite corners is the same.

Proof: Let V_i and E_i be the nodes and (vertical) edges in the ith column in grid S'. We form two subgraphs G_1' and G_2', such that G_1' contains all the nodes and edges to the left of the ith column and G_2' contains all those to the right, and in addition, they each contain V_i and E_i. We will first show that graph S' is derivable from S if subgraphs G_1' and G_2' are derivable from the corresponding subgraphs in S, G_1 and G_2, respectively.

Let C be a cut in subgraph G_1'. If C does not intersect E_i, all the nodes in V_i must belong to the destination set of the cut. Since there are no direct links between any nodes in the source set and the nodes in $S' - G_1'$, C is also a cut in S'. By the same token, any cut in subgraph G_2' that does not contain any edges in E_i is a cut in S'.

It is obvious that a cut can have at most one edge in E_i. Suppose the cuts C_1 in G_1' and C_2 in G_2' both contain the same edge e in E_i. For both subgraphs, all the nodes in V_i that are above e belong to the source set, and those below belong to the destination set. We observe that $C_1 \cup C_2$ partitions the nodes of S' also into a source set and a destination set, with the former being the union of the source sets in the two subgraphs and the latter the union of destination sets. Therefore, $C_1 \cup C_2$ is a cut in S'.

Without loss of generality, let the delay associated with all the cuts be 1. (A cut with d delays is equivalent to d identical cuts, each with 1 delay.) If G_1' and G_2' are derivable from G_1 and G_2 respectively, then for each edge $e \in E_i$ with $d(e)$ delays, there exist exactly $d(e)$ cuts containing e in each of the two subgraphs. Therefore all the cuts containing edges in E_i in the two subgraphs can be paired up to form cuts in S'. We have already shown that the cuts in the subgraph that do not contain any edges in E_i are also cuts in S'. Therefore if G_1' and G_2' are derivable from G_1 and G_2 respectively, then S' is also derivable from S.

The above result implies that we can cut up the grid S' into vertical strips and show that S' is equivalent to S by proving the equivalence of each of the strips. By applying the same argument on the horizontal links, we can further subdivide the strips into squares, each containing only four cells. The equivalence problem is now reduced to solving the equivalence for each of the squares. An edge from each of the two paths that connect the two diagonally-opposite corners constitute a cut. Therefore if the number of delays on each of the two paths of a square is the same, then the

568

square is derivable from its counterpart in S. If this condition holds for each square, then S' is derivable from, and thus equivalent to S. □

The criterion for correctness as derived from this theorem is represented graphically in Figure 3-5 (b).

This theorem can be generalized to any array where we can find paths that partition the graph representing the array into disjoint subgraphs. For example, in the case of a hexagonal array without feedback cycles (Figure 3-2 (a)), the constraints for equivalence are simply reduced to the local criterion that for each unit triangle of three adjacent cells, the number of delays on each of the two paths connecting two of the corners of the triangle has to be the same.

3.5.2. Redundancy Schemes

The utilization of live cells for the rectangular systolic array of Figure 3-5 (a) depends on the availability of two hardware resources: delay registers in the live cells and the channel width. The results of Section 3.1 imply that if sufficient delay registers are available in the cells, the "systolic" approach can fully utilize all the live cells without any penalty to the throughput rate of the system. In general, a lower utilization can be expected with a smaller number of delay registers. The other factor that might decrease the utilization is the channel width. If there are not sufficient tracks in the channels, we might not be able to implement the interconnection desired.

We have conducted several experiments to study the tradeoff between the utilization of live cells and the required hardware resources. We implemented four heuristic programs modeling different redundancy schemes. We ran Monte Carlo simulations on three different array sizes and cell failure rates ranging from 5% to 65%. The distribution of defects is assumed to be identical for all the cell locations on the wafer. The different schemes are described in the following and their examples are illustrated in Figure 3-6.

1. *No additional hardware.* Because of the limitation in routing, we resort to a simple scheme where for each defective cell, we skip either the row or the column that contains the cell. The criterion of correctness is trivially satisfied. A greedy algorithm is used here; the row or column containing the most failures is eliminated first.

2. *No delay register and unlimited channel width.* In this scheme, all the cells in the final array are chosen so that the links only point in the forward or downward direction. This guarantees that the number of delays on each link is equal to the manhattan distance between the two end points of the link, and thus the local correctness criterion is satisfied for each unit square of the array. Our basic strategy is to build the array row by row, picking as the next cell the one that satisfies the criterion and excludes the least number of live cells from being used. A simple maze-runner is also implemented to determine the number of tracks required for interconnection.

3. *One delay register per data path and unlimited channel width.* The additional delay increases the flexibility in the assignment scheme, but it also complicates the algorithm of the program. We modified the program in scheme 2 such that if necessary, a delay register may be added to the new edges being created and to the old edges that are in the same row or column as the new ones, provided, of course, they do not have delay registers on them already.

4. *Unlimited delay registers and unlimited channel width.* How many delay registers are necessary to achieve 100% utilization? The scheme we chose requires delay registers be placed *only* on the *logically* vertical connections and none on the horizontal ones. The n live cells are partitioned into horizontal strips, each containing $\sqrt{n}$ cells. The cells in each strip are connected to form the rows and then connected to the corresponding cells in their neighboring rows. Delays are then assigned only to the logically vertical connections to satisfy the correctness criterion.

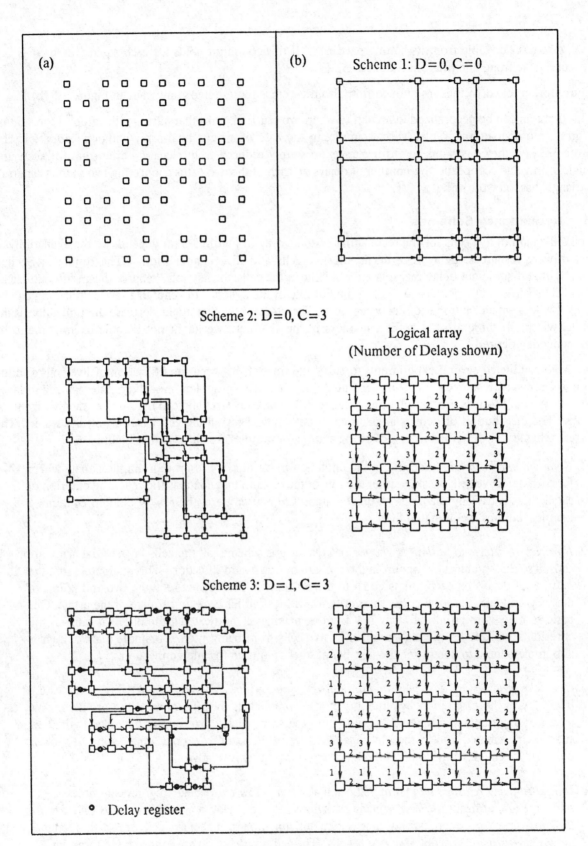

Figure 3·6: (a) Live cells (72 out of 100 cells) and
(b) array configurations under different redundancy schemes
(D represents number of delay registers and C the redundant tracks in channel)

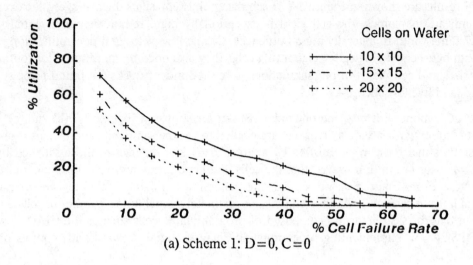

(a) Scheme 1: D=0, C=0

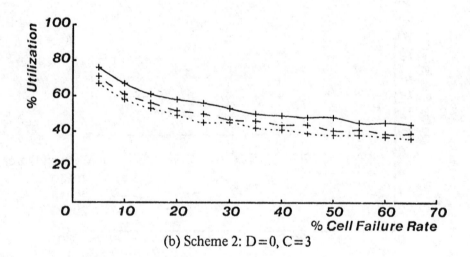

(b) Scheme 2: D=0, C=3

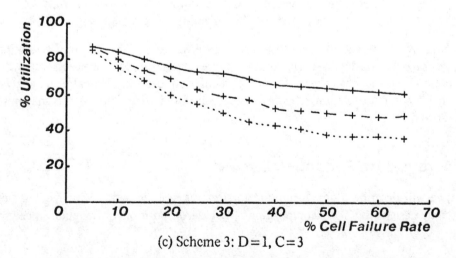

(c) Scheme 3: D=1, C=3

Figure 3-7: Utilization under different redundancy schemes
(D represents number of delay registers and C the redundant tracks in channel)

The empirical results are shown in Figure 3-7. Each data point represents the average value over 100 trials. These results indicate that unless the cell yield is exceptionally high, redundancy is essential (see Figure 3-7 (a)). The channel width is generally not a bottleneck. While low yields and poor utilization increase the length of the path between two logically neighboring cells, they also open up more space for routing. For the range of array sizes and cell yields in our simulations, three redundant tracks are found to be sufficient for schemes 2 and 3, and five for scheme 4.

The expected utilizations with zero and one delay register are shown in Figures 3-7 (b) and (c). The larger the array size, the more hardware delay registers are needed to get the same utilization. This is obvious since the set of constraints that have to be satisfied by a larger array is a superset of those satisfied by a smaller array. We have to bear in mind, however, that the cells in a larger array are typically smaller and thus have lower failure rates. From Figure 3-8, we see that the maximum number of delay registers required on the logically vertical links to achieve 100% utilization is approximately equal to the number of cells on a side of a wafer. We note that for systolic arrays composed of programmable cells such as the CMU Programmable Systolic Chip (PSC)[23, 24], implementing programmable delay is straightforward and requires no extra circuitry.

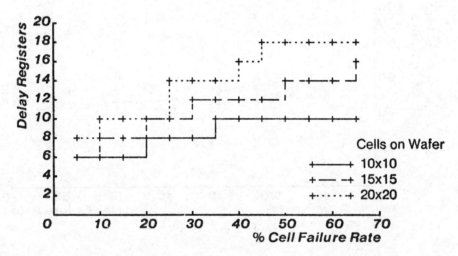

Figure 3-8: Maximum number of delays required by 98% of the trials to achieve 100% utilization using scheme 4

These experiments give us a general idea of the expected efficiency of the different redundancy schemes using the systolic approach. In-depth studies using a more precise model are necessary to determine the optimal or near-optimal redundancy scheme for any particular application. Probabilistic analyses[16, 17] have been performed for other fault-tolerant schemes where utilization is limited by the maximum length of interconnection allowed

4. Systolic Arrays with Feedback Cycles

In this section we will describe a new technique for treating systolic arrays with feedback cycles. Such arrays include systolic designs for LU-decomposition[25], QR-decomposition[26], triangular linear systems[25] and recursive filtering[27].

4.1. Computation of Simple Recurrences—An Example of Cyclic Systolic Arrays

To illustrate the basic ideas, we consider the computation of the following simple recurrence of size $n-1$:

given: the initial values $\{y_0, y_{-1}, \ldots, y_{-n+2}\}$

compute: the output sequence $\{y_1, y_2, \ldots\}$ as defined by

$$y_i = \sum_{j=1}^{n-1} y_{i-j}$$

Although summation is used here, the computation structure presented below generalizes to any associative operator. An n-cell systolic array with feedback cycles[27] is capable of performing this simple recurrence computation of size up to $n-1$. Depicted in Figure 4-1 (a) is such an array where $n=6$. The partial sums, y_4', y_5', y_6', move down the array from left to right picking up the completed sums that are moving in the opposite direction, y_1, y_2, y_3. The computation of each sum is completed when it reaches the end of the array. Note that this is a 2-slow[19] system, in the sense that only half its cells are active at all time.

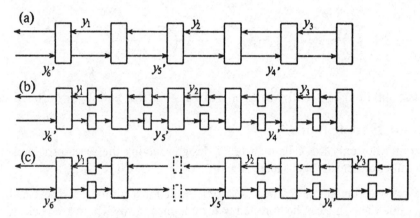

Figure 4-1: Linear array with feedback: (a) original array, (b) reduced throughput and (c) single failure

A naive attempt at achieving fault-tolerance involves slowing the system down even further. In the array of Figure 4-1 (b) data pass through an extra register per cell. This is a 4-slow system, performing the same computation as the 2-slow version, but at half its throughput. Suppose that the third cell from the left were to fail. The original function of the array could be preserved by simply allowing cells 2 and 4 to communicate through a bypass register (as illustrated in Figure 4-1 (c)). A drawback of this approach is that the performance of the array degrades rapidly with respect to the number of consecutive failed cells that need to be tolerated. Note that systolic arrays with feedback cycles are initially 2- or 3-slow in general, and in order to tolerate k consecutive failures, the throughput must be further decreased by a factor of $k+1$.

The recurrence of size $n-1$ computed by an n-cell bi-directional linear array (illustrated in Figure 4-1 (a)) can also be implemented on an $n/2$-cell ring with uni-directional data flow (as in Figure 4-2 (a)). The systolic ring works as follows. The $n/2$ most recently computed results are stored in each of the $n/2$ cells, while the next $n/2$ partial sums travel around the ring to meet these stored values. Every two cycles, a sum is completed and a new computation begins. For example at time 0 in Figure 4-2 (a), y_4' is ready to pick up its last term y_3 while y_6' is ready for its first term y_1. The final value of y_4 then travels to cell "a" to replace y_1. At time 2, y_5' and y_7' will pick up their last and first terms respectively. Like the bi-directional systolic array of Figure 4-1 (a), this systolic ring has a computational rate of one output every two cycles. However, all its cells are active at any time, therefore only half as many cells are needed.

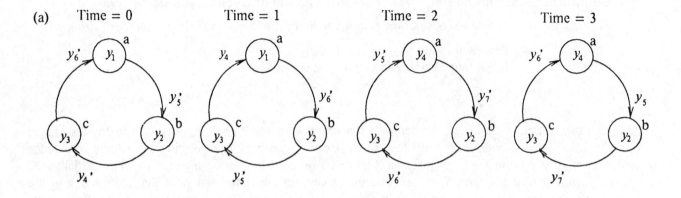

(a)   Time = 0   Time = 1   Time = 2   Time = 3

(b)   Time = 3

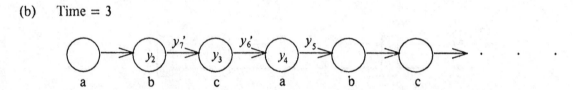

Figure 4-2: (a) Four consecutive snapshots of a systolic ring and (b) its unrolled structure

4.2. Fault-Tolerant Systolic Rings

Systolic rings require not only less cells than other designs solving the same problems, they also degrade gracefully as the number of defective cells increases.

Each cell in the systolic ring computes with a stored result for a period of $2n$ cycles before the result is replaced by a new value. The ring can be unrolled to form a linear array where each cell stores only one result in its whole lifetime, as shown in Figure 4-2 (b). This transformation reduces the ring structure to one without feedback, and thus allows us to analyze its fault-tolerant behavior using the results of the preceding section.

Figure 4-3 (a) shows an example of a 4-cell systolic ring with one defect and Figure 4-3 (b) shows its unrolled version. A defect in the ring of m cells translates to a defect in every block of m cells in the linear array. Recall that in an array without feedback, the bypass registers corresponding to the defects will cause a delay in the action of the cells but not the functionality of the array. It is therefore the case that the defective ring computes the recurrence correctly. However, due to the delay through the defective cell, the $m-1$ live cells produce results at a reduced rate of $m-1$ outputs every $2m-1$ $(=2[m-1]+1)$ cycles.

Although a defective systolic ring solves problems at a slower rate than a flawless ring with the same number of live cells, it can solve larger problems. The additional delay through the defective cell means that the live cells have an extra clock cycle before they have to store a new result. This cycle can be effectively used to compute with one more recurrence term. Figure 4-3 (a) shows the ring of $m-1$ live cells solving a maximum size problem with $2m-2$ $(=[2(m-1)-1]+1)$ recurrence terms. The following theorem summarizes the result of this section.

> **Theorem 3:** A perfect ring of size m can solve recurrences of sizes up to $2m-1$ at a throughput rate of $1/2$. If k cells fail, it can solve problems of sizes up to $2m-k-1$ at a throughput rate of $(m-k)/(2m-k)$. In other words, the reduction in throughput due to the k failures is only $k/(2m-k)$ of the original.

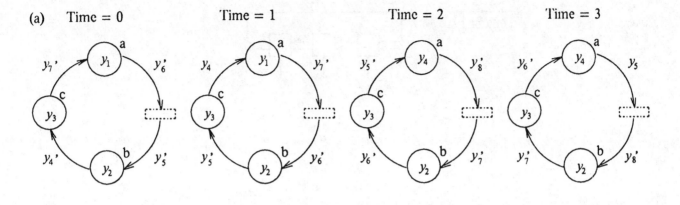

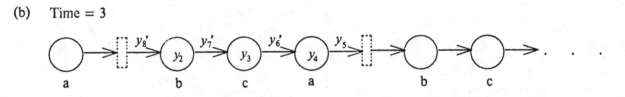

Figure 4-3: (a) Four consecutive snapshots of a systolic ring with one failure and (b) its unrolled structure

4.3. Two-Level Pipelining for Systolic Rings

By going through a similar argument as above for the two-level pipelined array, we can obtain the following result:

> **Theorem 4:** A systolic ring of m p-stage pipelined cells can solve recurrences of sizes up to $(p+1)m-1$ at a throughput rate of $1/(p+1)$. If k of the m cells fail, this ring can solve problems up to size $(p+1)m-pk-1$ at a throughput rate of $(m-k)/[(p+1)m-pk]$. In other words, the reduction in throughput is only $k/[(p+1)m-pk]$ of the original.

4.4. Other Examples of Systolic Ring Architectures

We have shown in the previous section that the ring structure is suitable for solving simple recurrences where each result is dependent on a fixed number of previous results. This characterizes many of the problems solved by systolic arrays with feedback. We will describe some of the examples in this section.

4.4.1. Solution of Triangular Linear Systems

Let $A=(a_{ij})$ be a nonsingular $n \times n$ band, lower triangular matrix with bandwidth q. Suppose that A and an n-vector $b=(b_1,\ldots,b_n)^T$ are given. The problem is to solve $Ax=b$ for $x=(x_1,\ldots,x_n)^T$. This can be viewed as a recurrence problem of size $q-1$. A ring of $q/2$ cells is sufficient to solve the problem at a throughput of one result every two cycles. As a comparison, the previous bi-directional linear systolic array[25] has the same throughput, but it uses twice as many cells. The ring is also more robust—with k failures in a ring of m cells, the throughput is only reduced from $1/2$ to $(m-k)/(2m-k)$.

Figures 4-4 and 4-5 illustrate the data flow pattern of a perfect 3-cell ring and a 4-cell ring with one failure, respectively, when solving a triangular linear system with bandwidth $q=6$. While this problem size is the largest the former ring can handle in one pass, the latter one can solve linear systems with bandwidth up to $q=7$. As a result, the cells in the defective ring of Figure 4-5 are idle one-seventh of the time. In the figure, a cell is assumed to be idle for one cycle if the input has a "don't care" value, denoted by "×".

The final step in the computation of each result (x_i) involves a subtraction (from b_i) and a division (by a_{ii}).

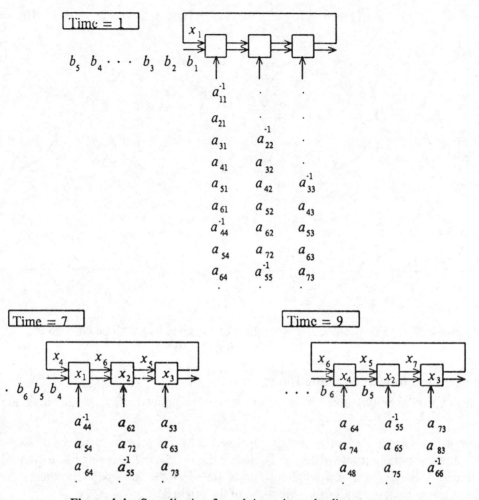

Figure 4-4: Systolic ring for solving triangular linear systems

This needs to be performed by every cell. To avoid having to provide each cell with a division capability and an external data path, we precompute the reciprocals of the diagonals outside the ring and send the additional input (b_i) to the cells via a systolic path.

The layout of a ring of processors is very straightforward, as shown in Figure 4-6. Similar to uni-directional linear arrays, defects on a ring can simply be bypassed via the cells' input/output registers.

4.4.2. Triangularization of a Band Matrix

The usefulness of the systolic ring approach is not limited to linear array solutions—Figure 4-7 (a) depicts a two-dimensional ring structure for triangularizing a band matrix A, with bandwidth $w=6$ and $q=3$ sub-diagonals. This ring structure can perform the QR-decomposition, an important computation for linear least squares approximation, and it can also solve linear systems using the stable computation technique of neighbor pivoting[28].

Each ring in the structure of Figure 4-7 eliminates a subdiagonal, with the bottommost ring handling the bottommost subdiagonal. The operations of a ring are illustrated by Figure 4-7 (b). The parameters needed for performing the elimination (e.g. Givens rotations for QR-decomposition) pass around the ring after they are generated. Suppose p_i is the parameter generated by the element eliminated in row i and the element above it. If the data input a_{ij} is not on the subdiagonal to be eliminated, it is updated on the arrival of p_i. It stays in the cell for one cycle to compute with p_{i+1} and then moves on to the next ring. If a_{ij} is to be

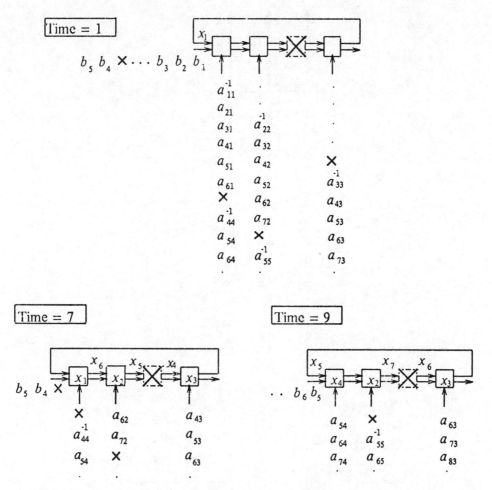

Figure 4-5: A single failure in a systolic ring for solving triangular linear systems

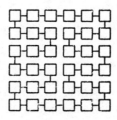

Figure 4-6: Layout of a Systolic Ring

eliminated, it is computed with the stored value, $a_{i-1,j}$, to get p_i, which is then passed down the ring. The output of each ring is the result obtained by eliminating the last subdiagonal of the input array. The uppermost ring outputs the entries of the triangular matrix that we want to compute. Note that corresponding to the elimination of each subdiagonal, a new super-diagonal is created. In the systolic ring, the new elements for this super-diagonal take the place previously occupied by the elements of the eliminated subdiagonal.

Unlike the data values circulating the rings in the previous examples, the p_i are computed before they are passed around. However, they have the same property that they are produced every two cycles and need to meet with $w-1$ input values before they can be discarded. Therefore, from our previous analysis, q rings of

(a)

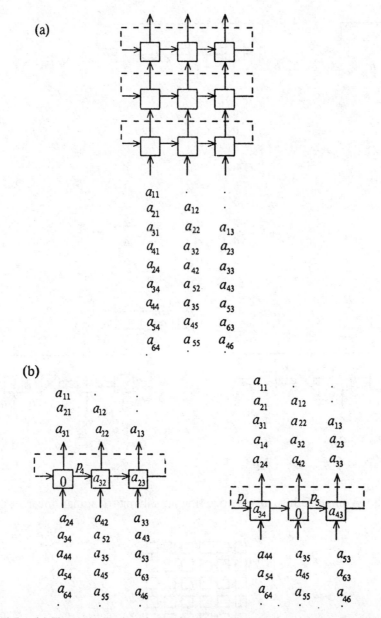

Figure 4-7: (a) Two-dimensional systolic ring structure for matrix triangularization and (b) two snapshots of the bottommost ring

$w/2$ cells each are required for triangularizing a band matrix with bandwidth w and q subdiagonals. This architecture requires about half the amount of hardware and achieves the same throughput of a previous solution of QR-decomposition[26]. An efficient layout of this ring architecture is shown in Figure 4-8 (a). Every two consecutive rows correspond to one ring.

The analysis of the fault-tolerant behavior of this ring structure is very similar to the one-dimensional ring. A system with n rings can be unrolled to form a mesh-connected acyclic array with n cells on one side and an "unbounded" number on the other. The throughput rate is reduced from $1/2$ to $n/(2n+k)$ if k defects are tolerated in each of the n rings in the final array. Also, by applying theorem 2, we can simplify the correctness constraints on the final configuration to get a local criterion that has to be satisfied by each unit square in the logical grid. This criterion is depicted in Figure 4-8 (b).

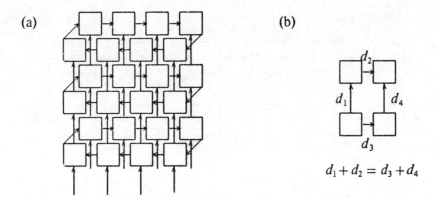

$d_1 + d_2 = d_3 + d_4$

Figure 4-8: (a) Layout of the two-dimensional ring structure for matrix triangularization, and (b) the local correctness criterion

4.4.3. LU-Decomposition of a Band Matrix

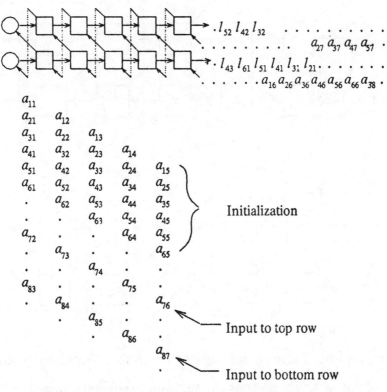

Figure 4-9: Systolic ring architecture for LU-decomposition

Figure 4-9 depicts a two-dimensional systolic ring architecture for the LU-decomposition of a band matrix, $A = LU$. For a given matrix A with bandwidth $2q-1$ we need to use $q/3$ rows of cells, with q cells in each row. The $q/3$ most recently computed rows of u_{ij}'s are stored in the cells as they are generated, while the l_{ij}'s are passed down the rows. Figure 4-10 shows the snapshots of this structure at various stages in the computation. By viewing this structure as an array of rings, its performance can be analyzed using the result of Theorem 4 with parameter $p=2$. The throughput of this array is the same as the previous design[25] which uses, however, three times as many cells.

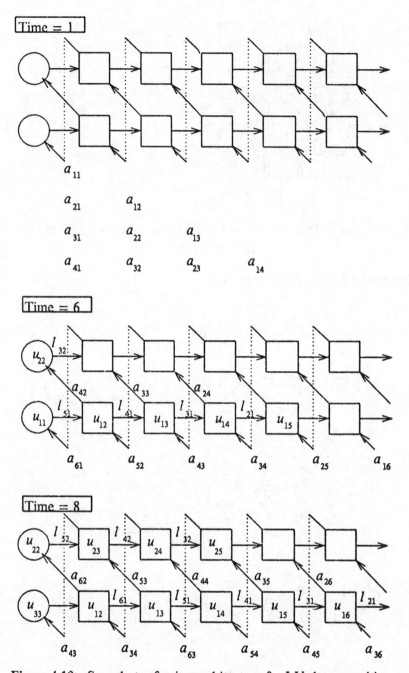

Figure 4-10: Snapshots of a ring architecture for LU-decomposition

This two-dimensional ring architecture admits of a surprisingly efficient layout. See Figure 4-11 (b). The numbers on the cells indicate the original row the cells are in. This layout can be obtained by the following method. Starting with the original architecture (Figure 4-11 (a)), we first bring the top and bottom rows together and get a cylindrical structure. We then expand the space between each row by one cell's length, so that if we flatten out the cylinder, the consecutive rows in the "front" and "back" surfaces will be interleaved. But before we flatten out the cylinder, we first "twist" it by one cell's length in the direction that shortens the inter-row links.

By going through the analysis of the unrolled structure, we get the following results. If k faults are bypassed in the communication links in each of the column of connections in Figure 4-11 (b), then the throughput is

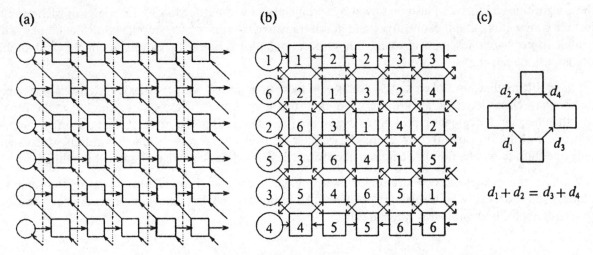

Figure 4-11: (a) Two-dimensional ring architecture for LU-decomposition,
(b) its layout and (c) the local correctness criterion

reduced from $1/3$ to $n/(3n+k)$ where n is the number of rows in the final array. Also, the local criterion that has to be satisfied by each group of four cells is illustrated in Figure 4-11 (c).

4.5. General Remarks on Systolic Rings

The systolic ring architecture has some disadvantages over other systolic architectures, but they are compensated for by its superior fault-tolerance performance. One of the possible disadvantages is that we need to provide an additional data path to unload the values during the computation, as the computed results are continuously stored in the ring. This is, however, not the case for the triangularization schemes of section 4.4.2.

In many of the conventional cyclic algorithms, only one or a few boundary cells may require special processing capability and extra input/output bandwidth. However, with some ring architectures, every cell is required to assume the role of a boundary cell. Algorithm-dependent methods can sometimes be used to alleviate the problem of having to provide each cell with special functionality. For instance, in the previous example of solving triangular linear systems, instead of providing each cell with the capability to divide, we precompute the reciprocals of the diagonals.

5. Summary and Concluding Remarks

The fault-tolerant approach proposed in this paper is tailored to systolic arrays. By using the additional information about systolic data flows we are able to design schemes that are usually more effective than other schemes designed for general processor arrays. Our systolic fault-tolerant scheme has the characteristic that the maximum interconnection length is not increased. This eliminates a source of inefficiency, such as increased system cycle time or driver area, common to most other approaches.

For uni-directional linear arrays, our systolic fault-tolerant technique achieves 100% utilization of live cells, without extra registers nor interconnection links. For two-dimensional arrays without feedback cycles, the utilization of live cells on a wafer increases with the number of redundant channels and delay registers available in the cells. The number of delay registers needed to achieve the same utilization also increases with the cell failure rate and the size of the original array on the wafer. Our empirical studies indicate for a wafer with $n \times n$ cells, approximately n delay registers per cell are needed to achieve 100% utilization.

Although many systolic algorithms with feedback have been proposed, some of the same problems to which these algorithms address can also be solved by systolic arrays without feedback. Examples of such problems include convolution, graph connectivity and graph transitive closure[9, 29, 30]. Acyclic implementations usually exhibit more favorable characteristics with respect to fault-tolerance, two-level pipelining, and problem decomposition in general.

For problems that have been solved exclusively by systolic arrays with feedback cycles, this paper introduces a new class of systolic algorithms based on a ring architecture. These systolic rings have the property that the throughput degrades gracefully as the number of failed cells in the rings increases. Furthermore, as a byproduct of the ring architecture approach, we have derived several new systolic algorithms which require only one-third to one-half of the cells used in previous designs while achieving the same throughput.

We have shown that the two-level pipelining problem in systolic arrays can be solved by the same techniques used to solve the fault-tolerance problem. An important task left for the future is the development of software to solve both problems automatically.

References

1. Evans, R. A., et al., "A CMOS Implementation of a Systolic Multi-Bit Convolver Chip," *VLSI '83*, Anceau, F. and Aas, E. J., eds., North-Holland, August 1983, pp. 227-235.

2. Kung, H. T., "On the Implementation and Use of Systolic Array Processors," *Proceedings of International Conference on Computer Design: VLSI in Computers*, IEEE, November 1983, pp. 370-373.

3. Symanski, J. J., "NOSC Systolic Processor Testbed," Tech. report NOSC TD 588, Naval Ocean Systems Center, June 1983.

4. Yen, D. W. L. and Kulkarni, A. V., "Systolic Processing and an Implementation for Signal and Image Processing," *IEEE Transactions on Computers*, Vol. C-31, No. 10, October 1982, pp. 1000-1009.

5. Smith, R. T., et al., "Laser Programmable Redundancy and Yield Improvement in a 64K DRAM," *IEEE Journal of Solid-State Circuits*, Vol. SC-16, No. 5, October 1981.

6. Lincoln Laboratory, "Semiannual Technical Summary: Restructurable VLSI Program," Tech. report ESD-TR-81-153, MIT Lincoln Lab, March 1981.

7. Woo, et al., "ALU, Multiplier Chips Zip through IEEE Floating-Point Operations," *Electronics*, Vol. 56, No. 10, May 19 1983, pp. 121-126.

8. Kung, H. T., Ruane, L. M., and Yen, D. W. L., "Two-Level Pipelined Systolic Array for Multidimensional Convolution," *Image and Vision Computing*, Vol. 1, No. 1, February 1983, pp. 30-36. An improved version appears as a CMU Computer Science Department technical report, November 1982

9. Kung, H. T., "Why Systolic Architectures?," *Computer Magazine*, Vol. 15, No. 1, January 1982, pp. 37-46.

10. Aubusson, R. C. and Catt, I., "Wafer Scale Integration—A Fault Tolerant Procedure," *IEEE Journal of Solid-State Circuits*, Vol. SC-13, No. 3, June 1978, pp. 339-344.

11. Fussel, D. and Varman, P., "Fault-Tolerant Wafer-Scale Architectures for VLSI," *Proceedings of the 9th International Symposium on Computer Architecture*, April 1982, pp. 190-198.

12. Koren, I., "A Reconfigurable and Fault-Tolerant VLSI Multiprocessor Array," *The 8th Annual Symposium on Computer Architecture*, IEEE & ACM, May 1981, pp. 442.

13. Manning, F. B., "An Approach to Highly Integrated, Computer-Maintained Cellular Arrays," *IEEE Transactions on Computers*, Vol. C-26, No. 6, June 1977, pp. 536-552.

14. Rosenberg, A. L., "On Designing Fault-Tolerant Arrays of Processors," Tech. report CS-1982-14, Duke University, 1982.

15. Rosenberg, A. L., "The Diogenes Approach to Testable Fault-Tolerant Networks of Processors," Tech. report CS-1982-6, Duke University, 1982.

16. Leighton, F. T. and Leiserson, C. E., "Wafer-Scale Integration of Systolic Arrays," *Proceedings of 23rd Annual Symposium on Foundations of Computer Science*, IEEE, October 1982, pp. 279-311.

17. Greene, J. W. and El Gamal, A., "Configuration of VLSI Arrays in the Presence of Defects," Tech. report, Information Systems Lab, Stanford University, May 1983.

18. Leiserson, C. E. and Saxe, J. B., "Optimizing Synchronous Systems," *Journal of VLSI and Computer Systems*, Vol. 1, No. 1, 1983, pp. 41-68.

19. Leiserson, C. E., *Area-Efficient VLSI Computation*, PhD dissertation, Carnegie-Mellon University, 1981. The thesis is published by the MIT Press, Cambridge, Massachusetts, 1983.

20. Weiser, U. and Davis, A., "A Wavefront Notation Tool for VLSI Array Design," *VLSI Systems and Computations*, Kung, H.T., Sproull, R.F., and Steele, G.L., Jr., eds., Computer Science Press, Inc., Computer Science Department, Carnegie-Mellon University, October 1981, pp. 226-234.

21. Rabiner, L. R. and Gold, B., *Theory and Application of Digital Signal Processing*, Prentice-Hall, Englewood Cliffs, New Jersey, 1975.

22. Stone, H. S., "Parallel Processing with the Perfect Shuffle," *IEEE Trans. Computers*, Vol. C-20, February 1971, pp. 153-161.

23. Fisher, A. L., Kung, H. T., Monier, L. M. and Dohi, Y., "Architecture of the PSC: A Programmable Systolic Chip," *Proceedings of the 10th Annual International Symposium on Computer Architecture*, June 1983, pp. 48-53.

24. Fisher, A. L., Kung, H. T., Monier, L. M., Walker, H. and Dohi, Y., "Design of the PSC: A Programmable Systolic Chip," *Proceedings of the Third Caltech Conference on Very Large Scale Integration*, Bryant, R., ed., Computer Science Press, Inc., California Institute of Technology, March 1983, pp. 287-302.

25. Kung, H. T. and Leiserson, C. E., "Systolic Arrays (for VLSI)," *Sparse Matrix Proceedings 1978*, Duff, I. S. and Stewart, G. W., eds., Society for Industrial and Applied Mathematics, 1979, pp. 256-282. A slightly different version appears in *Introduction to VLSI Systems* by C. A. Mead and L. A. Conway, Addison-Wesley, 1980, Section 8.3, pp. 37-46.

26. Heller, D. E. and Ipsen, I. C. F., "Systolic Networks for Orthogonal Equivalence Transformations and Their Applications," *Proceedings of Conference on Advanced Research in VLSI*, Massachusetts Institute of Technology, Cambridge, Massachusetts, January 1982, pp. 113-122.

27. Kung, H. T., "Let's Design Algorithms for VLSI Systems," *Proceedings of Conference on Very Large Scale Integration: Architecture, Design, Fabrication*, California Institute of Technology, January 1979, pp. 65-90. Also available as a CMU Computer Science Department technical report, September 1979.

28. Gentleman, W. M. and Kung, H. T., "Matrix Triangularization by Systolic Arrays," *Proceedings of SPIE Symposium, Vol. 298, Real-Time Signal Processing IV*, Society of Photo-Optical Instrumentation Engineers, August 1981, pp. 19-26.

29. Guibas, L. J., Kung, H. T. and Thompson, C. D., "Direct VLSI Implementation of Combinatorial Algorithms," *Proceedings of Conference on Very Large Scale Integration: Architecture, Design, Fabrication,* California Institute of Technology, January 1979, pp. 509-525.

30. Tchuente, M. and Melkemi, L., "Systolic Arrays for Connectivity Problems and Triangularization for Band Matrices," Tech. report R.R. No. 366, IMAG, Institut National Polytechnique de Grenoble, March 1983.

Chapter 12: Future Perspectives

Reprinted from *Computer*, March 1984, pages 47-56. Copyright © 1984 by The Institute of Electrical and Electronics Engineers, Inc.

The current prediction is that fifth-generation computers will be logic machines departing from traditional computer design, but decentralized control flow architectures seem more suitable for the 1990's.

SPECIAL FEATURE

Future Computers: Logic, Data Flow, . . ., Control Flow?

Philip C. Treleaven, University of Reading
Isabel Gouveia Lima, University of Newcastle upon Tyne

Since the International Conference in Tokyo in October 1981 when Japan launched its National Fifth-Generation project,[1,2] there has been a growing acceptance in the computer science community that the von Neumann computer will become less and less important. As computing moves from a sequential, centralized world to a parallel, decentralized world in which a large number of systems must work together, a new generation of general-purpose computers will be required. The nature of both data and processing tasks is changing. We are handling vast quantities of nonnumeric data, such as sentences, symbols, speech, graphics, and images, and processing is becoming less concerned with scientific calculation and more with artificial intelligence applications. If we really look closely at "new" developments in handling these evolving needs, we see that the von Neumann architecture of 30 years ago has remained largely unchanged; it is the software systems that have been extended repeatedly to cope with increasingly sophisticated applications.

Both technologically and socially we are ready for the future generation of computers. Important and highly relevant areas of computing research are on the threshold of major advances,[3] including

- *Artificial intelligence,* which include methodologies to express "knowledge" and to infer from knowledge, and human-oriented I/O in natural languages, speech, and pictures.
- *Software engineering,* which includes new higher level programming languages and computational

models and programming environments building on systems such as Unix.
- *Computer architecture,* which includes distributed architectures supporting computer networks, parallel architectures giving high-speed computers for numerical calculations, and VLSI architectures to make full use of the potential of VLSI technology.
- *VLSI technology,* which includes VLSI CAD systems (that is, new methods for semiautomatic design of logic circuits) and new devices such as those using gallium arsenide and Josephson junctions.

Another reflection of our changing needs is the expansion of computing from primarily scientific application in the 1950's to commercial and industrial application in the 1960's and 1970's, and to consumer use in the 1980's and 1990's. As a result, fifth-generation computers will form the cornerstone of "intelligent" consumer electronics such as sophisticated televisions, video recorders, and learning aids.[4,5]

We can safely say that there is a definite trend toward general-purpose decentralized computing, but what form the future computer will take is not as clear. Researchers in a number of areas are attempting to identify potential architectures, and any one of the following are likely candidates: (1) fifth-generation computers, (2) supercomputers, (3) VLSI processor architectures, and (4) integrated communications and computers. Each offers unique advantages—and disadvantages—in terms of its application to future computing needs.

After examining each of these potential candidates for the future computer, we will attempt to determine the "ideal" choice or combination of choices that will allow us both computational control and system flexibility.

This article is based on "The New Generation of Computer Architecture" presented at the 10th International Symposium on Computer Architecture, 1983.

Candidates for the future computer

Fifth-generation computers. Fifth-generation computers are knowledge information processing systems designed to support knowledge-based expert systems.[6] Expert systems, in turn, embody modules of organized knowledge about specific areas of human expertise. They also support sophisticated problem-solving and inference functions, providing users with a source of intelligent advice on some specialized topic. Future expert systems will also provide human-oriented I/O in the form of natural languages, speech, and picture images. For example, an expert system for medical diagnosis could operate in a way analogous to the way a physician, a surgeon, and a patient interact and use their knowledge to make a diagnosis.

Symbol manipulation. In expert systems, "knowledge" is often represented in terms of IF-THEN rules of the form[7]

```
IF  condition__1 and
    condition__2 and
         .
         .
         .
    condition__n

THEN  implication (with significance)
```

If all conditions are true, then the implication is true, with an associated local significance factor. While a set of rules is searched, an overall significance factor is maintained, and when this significance becomes unacceptably low, the search is abandoned and a new set of rules is searched.

As observed by Japanese researchers,[1] this structure of expert systems is most closely matched by the structure of logic programming (its computational model). In a logic programming language such as Prolog, statements are relations of a restricted form called "clauses," and the execution of such a program is a suitably controlled logical deduction from the clauses forming the program. The following logic program for a family tree consists of four clauses:[8,9]

```
father(bill, john).
father(john, tom).

grandfather(X, Z) :- father(X, Y), mother(Y, Z).
grandfather(X, Z) :- father(X, Y), father(Y, Z).
```

The first two clauses define that Bill is the father of John, and John is the father of Tom. The second two clauses use the variables X, Y, and Z to express the rule that X is the grandfather of Z, if X is the father of Y and Y is either the mother or father of Z. Such a program can be asked a range of questions—from "Is John the father of Tom?" [father(john, tom)?] to "Is there any A who is the grandfather of any C?" [grandfather(A, C)?].

The possible operation of a computer based on logic is illustrated in the following using the family tree program. Execution of, for example, "grandfather(bill, R)?" will match with each "grandfather( )" clause:

```
grandfather(X = bill, Z = R) :- father(bill, Y), mother(Y,R).
grandfather(X = bill, Z = R) :- father(bill, Y), father(Y, R).
```

Both clauses will attempt in parallel to satisfy their goals, a concept called OR-parallelism. The first clause will fail, being unable to satisfy the "mother( )" goal from the program. The second clause has two goals "father( ), father( )", which it attempts to solve in parallel, a concept called AND-parallelism. The latter concept involves pattern matching and substitution to satisfy both the individual goals:

```
grandfather(X = bill, Z = R)
  :- father(bill, Y), father(Y, R).
  :- father(bill, Y = john), father(Y = bill, R = john).
```

and the overall consistency:

```
  :- father(bill, Y = john), father(Y = john, R = tom).
```

Organization. A possible fifth-generation computer organization is a highly microprogrammed (control-flow-based) Prolog machine[10,11] analogous to current Lisp machines. Although we can expect a number of such designs in the near future, Prolog machines are not true logic machines, just as Lisp machines are not considered reduction machines. In the Japanese 5-G project, however, fifth-generation computers are viewed as comprising three specialized component machines[1] linked by a common logic machine language and architecture (Figure 1).

Future potential. Fifth-generation computers form the basis of what is called intelligent consumer electronics. Further growth of this type of computer is motivated by the fact that these electronics will be *the* major money-earning industry in the 1990's.

Supercomputers. Supercomputers are aimed at large-scale numerical calculations and attempt to achieve a high performance by exploiting parallelism. They may be envisaged as parallel "mainframe" computers, replacing the Cray 1, built from identical, powerful processors whose instruction execution is based on a concurrent alternative to the traditional sequential control flow architecture. For supercomputers, data flow is a major theme of research. In a data flow computer, instruction execution is data driven; the availability of input operands triggers the execution of the instruction that consumes the inputs. The most important properties of data flow are that instructions pass their results directly to all the consuming instructions and that an instruction is executed when it has received all its inputs—properties that influence the general-purpose nature of data flow.

Data flow computers are most naturally programmed in a very high level form called single-assignment languages. Single-assignment languages are based on a rule stating that a variable may appear on the left-hand side of only one statement in a program fragment. Thus, data dependencies in a program can be easily detected and statements can be specified in any order. The following procedure in ID[12] illustrates single-assignment programming:

Procedure for inner-product $\Sigma\ a_i * b_i$

```
procedure inner-product (a, b, n)
    initial s <- 0
    for i from 1 to n do
        new s <- s + (a[i] * b[i])
    returns s)
```

In this procedure two arrays *a* and *b*, both of length *n*, are taken as input and inner-product *s* is returned. These statements have the following interpretation:

$$s_0 <- 0$$

$$s_1 <- s_0 + (a[1] * b[1])$$
$$s_2 <- s_1 + (a[2] * b[2])$$
$$. . .$$
$$s_n <- s_{n-1} + (a[n] * b[n])$$
$$\text{return } s_n$$

and hence obey the single-assignment rule. Since execution is driven by the availability of data, all multiplications can execute in parallel, after which the tree of partial results will be summed to produce the result s_n.

Figure 2 shows the possible operation of a computer based on data flow in the context of the inner-product example. In the figure, each data flow instruction consists of an operator; two input operands, which are either literals or required data tokens; and a reference such as $i1/2$ defining a consumer instruction and argument position for the result data token. Data tokens are used to pass data from one instruction to another and to cause the execution of instructions. An instruction is enabled for execution when all its input arguments are available, that is, when all its data tokens have arrived. The operator then consumes the data tokens, performs the required operation, and using the embedded reference stores a copy of the result data token into the consumer instruction(s).

Organization. Data flow computers are usually based on a packet communication machine organization, consisting of a circular instruction execution pipeline of resources in which processors, communications, and memories are interspersed with "pools of work" (Figure 3).[13]

In this organization an executing program is viewed as a number of independent information packets, all of which are conceptually active, that split and merge. For a parallel computer, packet communication is a very simple strategy for allocating packets of work to resources. Each packet to be processed is placed with similar packets in one of the pools of work. When a resource becomes idle, it takes a packet from its input pool, processes it and places a modified packet in an output pool, returning them to the idle state. A number of data flow machines, based on packet communication, are already operational.[13]

Future potential. Supercomputers form the basis for large-scale numerical calculations, such as those in energy and weather forecasting. Their development is motivated by demands for higher performance numerical processing, which remain largely unsatisfied.

VLSI processor architectures. Processor architectures to exploit VLSI are aimed at defining a new VLSI generation of components to succeed the conventional microprocessor. Microprocessors containing over 100,000 transistors are starting to become commonplace. However, attempting to make larger scale single processors in VLSI scaled to submicron dimensions becomes self-defeating, due to communication problems and the escalating costs of designing and testing such complex processors. One obvious solution (stimulated by the VLSI design philosophy of Mead and Conway[14]) is

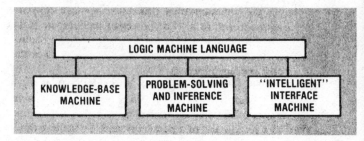

Figure 1. Fifth-generation computer organization. The first block is analogous to filestore plus databases, the second to a CPU, and the third to I/O devices.

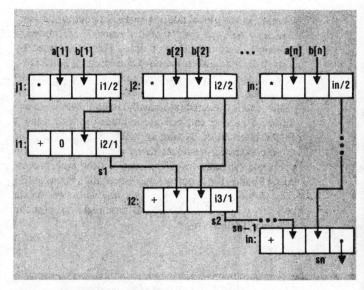

Figure 2. Data flow program for "inner-product."

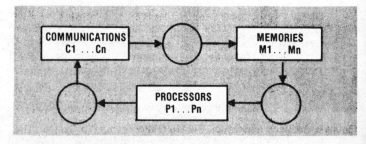

Figure 3. Packet communication computer.

588

miniature microcomputers that can be replicated like memory cells and operate as a multiprocessor architecture.[15] For a semiconductor manufacturer to specify a new VLSI generation of components it is necessary to specify a system architecture defining communication and co-operation between both general-purpose and special-purpose microcomputers. The fundamental problem to be solved is how to orchestrate a single computation so that it can be distributed across the ensemble of processors.[16] Two elegant VLSI system architectures (the former special-purpose and the latter general-purpose) are Kung's programmable systolic chip,[17] and Inmos's transputer[18] and Occam programming language[19] based on communicating processes. A more conventional approach to a VLSI processor architecture is illustrated by the reduced instruction set multi-microcomputer system developed at the University of Newcastle upon Tyne (see Figure 4).[20]

Organization. The central idea in RIMMS is that each primitive microcomputer should be able to operate alone or as a component of a parallel system. To achieve this, each microcomputer's memory provides storage for a program fragment (process), and forms part of a global (two-level) address space. The 16-bit address consists of the high eight bits to define a specific microcomputer/process, and the low eight bits to define a subsidiary memory location. Thus, a process can access any location in the global address space. In addition, a location may be used for "shared memory" or "message passing" communication of data. This is achieved by four, interchangeable, memory operations (Figure 5).

Although any location in the global address space may be accessed, a process is always executed by its local processor and is executed (atomically) to completion. In addition, a process can activate another process, using a FORK instruction, as long as its processor is idle. (This atomic execution removes many of the sychronization problems typically found in control flow multiprocessors.) Finally, the processor implementation[20] has a simple, 16-bit von Neumann data path, with two visible registers (C-program counter, D-base register), plus the two-level address space.

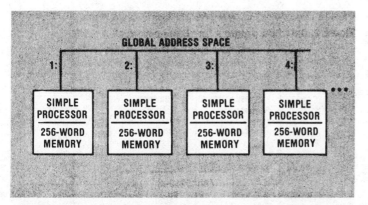

Figure 4. Reduced Instruction Set Multi-Microcomputer System. The 16-bit address space in RIMMS allots eight bits to define the specific microcomputer/process and eight bits for the word in memory.

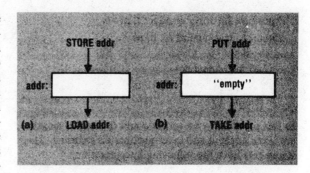

Figure 5. RIMMS four, interchangeable memory operations in shared memory (a) and message passing (b). STORE and LOAD have traditional (shared memory) semantics, while PUT may only overwrite "empty" and TAKE may only remove a nonempty value, thus supporting message passing.

Future potential. VLSI processor architectures form the basis of general-purpose and special-purpose micros for exploiting VLSI. Their development is motivated by the desire to identify the new VLSI generation of microelectronic components.

Integrated communications and computers. Integrated data communications and computers represent the fusion of wide-area computer networks, local-area computer networks, and parallel computer architectures to form a fully integrated computer-communications network. Data communications and computers, specifically computer networks and parallel computers, have developed independently from each other, with advances in both technologies being sustained by the rapid development of semiconductor devices. However, full integration of the decentralized systems shown in Figure 6 has long been advocated.[21] To achieve this integration, all component computers must conform to a common decentralized system architecture—allowing them to be programmed to cooperate in information communication and program execution (see Figure 6).

In these decentralized systems the most important related issues are communications and addressing of information, rather than parallelism and instruction execution. Thus, the systems are usually based on control flow architectures enhanced with operating system concepts. One example is the Newcastle Connection distributed Unix system,[22] a novel software subsystem added to a set of standard Unix systems,[23] interconnecting them as a distributed system. The resulting distributed system (which could employ a variety of wide and local area networks) is functionally indistinguishable at both the "Shell" command language level and at the system call level, from a conventional, centralized Unix system.

Organization. The system's success stems from its hierarchical information and naming structure (for directories, files, devices, and commands). Here, the structures of each Unix system are joined together as a single structure, in which each Unix system behaves as a directory. The result is that each user, on each Unix system, can inspect any directory, read or write any file, use any device, or execute any command, regardless of its location within the overall structure (see Figure 7).

Future potential. Integrated communications and computers represent the merging of wide-area networks, local-area networks, and parallel computer architectures. Work in this area is motivated by the infrastructure of the so-called information society.

Evaluating the candidates

Fifth-generation computers, supercomputers, VLSI processor architectures, and integrated communications and computers provide us with four complementary views of future computing, yielding a composite image of the future computer system as highly decentralized at all levels with computers linked together in an integrated computer-communications network (Figure 8). Computers of the future will support a range of applications from the numerical calculations of supercomputers to the symbol manipulation of fifth-generation computers. Thus, programming languages will range from traditional procedural ones, to very high level languages such as Prolog. Machine organizations will support concurrency, possibly using data-driven and demand-driven techniques. Implementations will use the latest general-purpose and special-purpose VLSI technology.

This overview of future computers seems quite reasonable, but to identify the underlying computational concepts of future general-purpose, decentralized computers, we must further investigate the various choices of architecture and languages.

There are five basic categories of computer architecture (top of Figure 9), from "low level" architectures such as control flow that specify exactly *how* a computation is to be executed to high-level architectures such as logic that merely specify *what* is required. Associated with each architecture is a corresponding category of programming languages. In a control-flow computer, explicit flow(s) cause the execution of instructions. In a procedural language (Basic, Fortran), the basic concepts are a global memory of cells, assignment as the basic action, and (sequential) control structures for the statement execution.

The next category is data flow computers and single-assignment languages. In a data flow computer,[13] input operands trigger the instruction, which consumes the inputs. In a single-assignment language (ID, Lucid, Val, Valid), data "flow" from one statement to another, execution of statements is data-driven, and identifiers obey the single-assignment rule.[24] In the next category, reduction computers and applicative languages,[13] the requirement for a result triggers the execution of the instruction that will generate the value. In applicative languages (Pure Lisp, SASL, FP), application functions are applied to structures, and all structures are expressions in the mathematical sense. Next are actor computers and object-oriented languages. In an actor computer,[25] the arrival of a message for an instruction causes the instruction to execute. In an object-oriented language (Small-

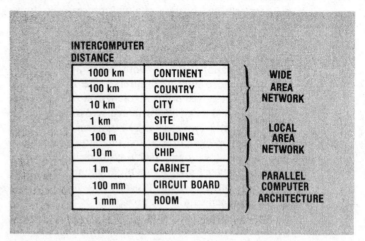

Figure 6. Spectrum of decentralized systems. All these systems must conform to a decentralized architecture before full system integration is possible.

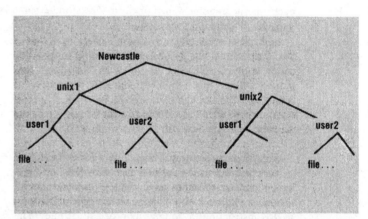

Figure 7. The Newcastle Connection of Unixes—a decentralized system. In this configuration, a user can access any file regardless of its location. For example, user1 can copy a file (file 1) belonging to user2 on machine unix2 simply by typing "cp file1 /../unix2/user2/file2," where "cp" means copy, "/" means a path name starts at the root directory, and ".." indicates the parent directory.

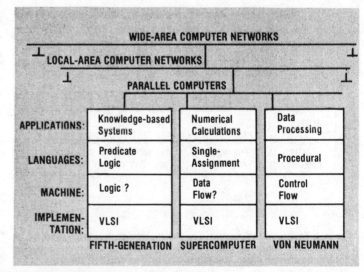

Figure 8. Future computer system architecture.

talk), objects are viewed as active and may contain state, and objects communicate by sending messages.

Last are logic computers and predicate logic languages. In a logic computer,[10] an instruction is executed when it matches a target pattern, and parallelism or backtracking is used to execute alternatives to the instruction. In a predicate logic language (Prolog), statements are relations of a restricted form, and execution is a suitably controlled logical deduction from the statements.[9]

A critical part of evaluating what goes into the "perfect" future computer is determining the component architectures and languages. Two computational issues are important here: decentralized computation—how to organize and program a network of heterogeneous computers—and general-purpose computation—how to efficiently support a class of algorithms.

Decentralized computation. For this type of computation, essential architectural characteristics are system structuring of components, cooperation of components, extensibility of structure, diversity of components, and diversity of programming styles.

Such a decentralized architecture, analogous to that of the international telephone network, would support the cooperation of dissimilar hardware and software components. Since this architecture should be capable of spanning different types of computers (logic, control flow), decentralized computation must be considered the supreme research topic for future computers.

General-purpose computation. Our main concern here is to determine which architecture—low-level or high-level—lends itself more to a general-purpose system. Moreover, we must also wonder whether the massive investment in traditional control flow can realistically be discarded in favor of, say, logic. A low-level model, such as control flow, specifies exactly *how* an algorithm is to be executed and is advantageous because of the flexibility of mechanisms and control over execution. A high-level model, such as logic, merely specifies *what* algorithm is to be executed but has powerful abstraction mechanisms and "safe" programs. In short, what we are comparing is similar to the efficiency (but hazards) of assembly languages and the power (but constraints) of high-level languages. High-level computer models, while particularly attractive in their ability to help manage software complexity, have not been widely successful because of the broad spectrum of applications for general-purpose computers.

Clearly, then, a surface look at the pluses and minuses of low- and high-level architectures doesn't help us. Further examination of the underlying computational concepts, however, does reveal some interesting relationships.

Basically, computer architectures share two fundamental mechanisms.[13] The *data mechanism* defines the way a particular argument is communicated (and shared) by a number of instructions. It has two subgroups:

- shared memory, in which a single copy of the argument is communicated via a shared memory accessible to all instructions, and
- message passing, in which a unique copy of the argument is communicated via a message from the source to the destination instruction.

The second fundamental mechanism is the *control mechanism,* which defines how one instruction causes the execution of one or more others. This mechanism has four subgroups:

- control-driven, in which an instruction is executed when it is selected by flow(s) of control;
- data-driven, in which an instruction is executed when some combination of its arguments are available;

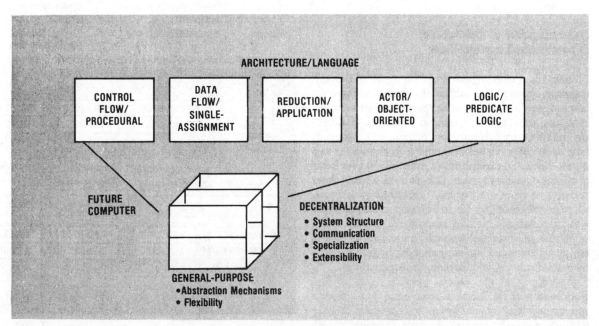

Figure 9. Relationship of data and control mechanisms and categories of computers.

- demand-driven, in which an instruction is executed when the result it produces is needed by another, already active instruction; and
- pattern-driven, in which an instruction is executed when some enabling pattern (or condition) is matched.

We believe that Figure 10 best illustrates the relations among the categories of computers and data and control mechanisms. As the figure shows, in each category of computer, data mechanisms and control mechanisms are largely incompatible sets of alternative concepts. (For example, control flow has shared memory and is control driven, whereas data flow has message passing and is data driven.) Hence each category, although universal in the sense of a Turing machine, has specific advantages and disadvantages for computation, related to its choice of mechanisms.

In making the final choice of computer then, we must consider one last thing. Categories of computers supporting message-passing data mechanisms inevitably include a subsidiary mechanism for shared memory. In addition, categories of computers supporting data-, demand-, and pattern-driven control mechanisms frequently have a subsidiary control-driven mechanism arguably to alleviate computational problems.[26]

Thus for representing computation, shared memory seems the most important data mechanism and control driven execution seems the most basic control mechanism. Using these mechanisms it is relatively easy to implement and support the other mechanisms. Control flow would seem, therefore, to embody the most fundamental computational concepts. The challenge then becomes to introduce into control flow the other data and control mechanisms, to make control flow even more general-purpose. We conclude, therefore, that future computers should and will be based on decentralized control flow architectures.

The computer of the future: decentralized control flow

Table 1 is a comparison of the principles of the von Neumann computer and those of decentralized control flow architecture. As the table shows, decentralized architecture provides the minimum principles of decentralized hardware and software components but extends them so that they can be configured to work together as a system. In fact, decentralization principles are the basis of current operating systems such as Unix. Clearly these operating systems are "virtual" decentralized systems, whose principles reflect the environment in which people wish to program. Our task therefore is to isolate and refine this decentralized control flow model so that it may be incorporated into programming languages, computer architectures, and machine implementations.

Illustrations of the various possible levels of implementation of the decentralized control flow architecture are provided by the Newcastle Connection and the RIMMS discussed earlier. A more "idealized" implementation may be possible with the Recursive Machine proposed by Bob Barton and Wayne Wilner.[25]

Structure. So what will the future computer look like? In general, as Figure 11 shows, it will have a hierarchical structure composed of a network of computers, each of which may in turn be a computer system. The figure also

	DATA MECHANISMS	
	SHARED MEMORY	MESSAGE PASSING
CONTROL DRIVEN	CONTROL FLOW (VON NEUMANN)	CONTROL FLOW (COMMUNICATING PROCESSES)
DATA DRIVEN		DATA FLOW
DEMAND DRIVEN	REDUCTION (STRING)	REDUCTION (GRAPH)
PATTERN DRIVEN	LOGIC	ACTOR

(left label: CONTROL MECHANISMS)

Figure 10. Relationship of data and control mechanisms and categories of computers.

**Table 1.
Comparison of von Neumann and decentralized architectures.**

ATTRIBUTE	VON NEUMANN	DECENTRALIZED
Computer	Single processor and memory	Network of computers behaving as processor and memory
Memory	Vector of fixed-size memory cells	Nested organization of variable-size memory cells (like file structure of operating system)
Addressing	One-level cell address space	Contextual address space of cells (like international telephone network)
Programming	Low-level machine language (instruction consists of primitive operator and operands)	High-level machine language (as in Lisp, in which instructions may be recursively defined)
Execution	Sequential control flow	Parallel, decentralized control flow (as with Unix commands)

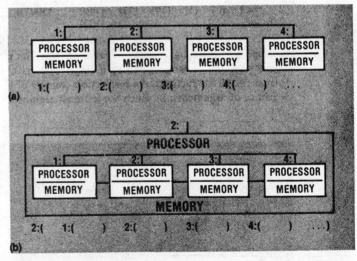

Figure 11. Structure of a decentralized control flow computer network (a) and single system (b). The tops of both (a) and (b) depict the hardware and the bottoms depict software.

shows a direct correspondence (at the higher levels) between the physical system structure and the logical information structure. This relationship is particularly important for programming, since each computer system in the hierarchy may be programmed as a single computer and accessed using its address (by other computers) as if it were a single memory cell.

Memory. Memory in the computer consists of a nested organization of variable-size memory cells. Such a memory could be implemented by traditional Lisp cells; however, delimited strings[25,27] seem a more ideal implementation. When information is represented as nested delimited strings, a delimited string is considered a variable-size memory cell. A delimited string consists of two alphabets of characters, namely delimiting characters left bracket "(" and right bracket ")", and data characters binary 0 and 1. Thus an array of the numbers 0 to 9 is encoded as

((0) (1) (10) (11) (100) . . . (1001))

A memory cell may have any of five systemwide operations—LOAD, STORE, PUT, TAKE, EXECUTE—performed on its contents, as illustrated in Figure 12. LOAD, STORE, and EXECUTE operations have traditional shared memory semantics. PUT and TAKE support message passing and "poll" a memory cell; PUT may store only into an empty cell and TAKE removes a nonempty value. An empty memory cell is represented by "( )". These operations, therefore, support both forms of communication of data found in computing.

Addressing. Addressing of information is based on a contextual address space, in which each memory cell is considered a context and a related cell is identified by a selector. An address is a sequence of selectors specifying a path from the point of reference in the structure to the target memory cell. For instance, to access the whole of the array just discussed from elsewhere in the surrounding context, its selector, say 2, is used; whereas to access a subsidiary number (100) the address 2/5 is used:

```
2:   ( 1:(0) 2:(1) 3:(10) 4:(11) 5:(100) . . . (1001))
2   = (   (0)   (1)   (10)   (11)   (100) . . . (1001))
2/5 =                               (100)
```

Programming. Program representation is based on a high-level machine language using a single (recursive) format for all instructions. An instruction consists of a sequence of arguments, in which the leftmost argument defines the operation. An operation may be a simple operator such as +

(operator arg1 arg2 arg3 arg4 . . .)

or the address of a procedure for a call

(address arg1 arg2 arg3 arg4 . . .)

The types of arguments supported by instructions are closely tied to the data and control mechanisms supported by the computer. For example the "union" or argument types found in control flow, data flow, and reduction are

- *literal,* such as (+ 2 . . .), found in every computer;
- *unknown,* such as (+ ( ) . . .), used by data flow as a "place-holder" for dynamically generated values; delays evaluation until the value is available for the instruction;
- *address,* such as (+ a . . .), a reference used by control flow instructions to load or store a value;
- *procedure call,* such as (p . . .), a reference used by reduction to cause the evaluation of the addressed operand; and
- *expression,* such as (. . .(+ 2 a). . .), used by reduction to nest instructions.

Program execution is implicitly control-driven, with parallelism being specified by special control operators. For instance, based on Unix commands, instructions could be separated by infix controls defining sequential (instruction;instruction), parallel (instruction & instruction), and pipelined instruction | instruction) execution of the two adjacent instructions. Elementary data- and demand-driven styles of execution may also be supported. Data-driven execution is supported by using the empty memory cell ( ) to delay execution until the argument is available. Demand-driven execution is supported by the built-in procedure call just described.

Various developments at the University of Newcastle upon Tyne are based on variants of the decentralized control flow architecture: the Newcastle Connection distributed Unix system[22] and the RIMMS[20] mentioned previously; the interactive Basix programming language;[28] and the Lego multi-microcomputer system.[27] The Basix language combines features of programming languages like Basic and Lisp with features normally found only in operating systems (Unix Shell). For example, Basix has a single notion of object that serves the roles of variables, messages, programs, files, and directories. The Lego computer involves the implementation of a VLSI processor from a network of miniature microcomputers that cooperate in the concurrent execution of a program. It implements delimited strings and contextual addressing.

There is a growing belief in the computer science community that by 1990 the traditional von Neumann computer will be superseded by a new decentralized computer architecture. Various categories of computers (data flow, reduction, actor, logic) are being promoted as the von Neumann successor, but the most prominent is logic for fifth-generation computers. The drawback to using these novel computers, however, is that they are largely unproven and represent a "revolutionary" solution—

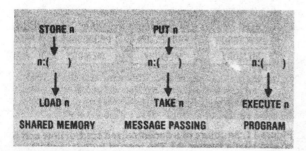

Figure 12. Memory cell operations.

one that discards the massive investment in traditional control flow computing.

We feel that a "decentralized" computer architecture encompassing fifth-generation computers, supercomputers, and even von Neumann computers is a more promising way to achieve many of the very ambitious goals characterizing Japan's fifth-generation project. In addition, we feel all these computers will be based on control flow (although the future importance of knowledge-based systems or even of logic programming languages is not discounted.) Thus, we propose an "evolutionary" approach involving decentralized control flow architecture, which we base on the following assumptions:

- The communication and cooperation of heterogeneous processors (and processes) will be the most important task in the 1990's.
- Recursive structuring of computer systems is essential for decentralized processing whether involving mainframe computers or miniature microcomputers.
- Control flow is the most primitive and fundamental form of computation.
- Future computers will evolve from conventional von Neumann computers.

Thus, highly parallel and decentralized computer systems will, and should, supplant the traditional von Neumann computer only if they can match the latter's generality and flexibility, as exemplified by the large variety of both conventional and very novel programming languages and styles that it supports with reasonable effectiveness. The important aspect of the von Neumann model that gives this flexibility is that it is a control flow model allowing the programmer (or compiler/interpreter) direct control over the low-level operation of the target machine when this is necessary. The key to the future generation of computers would seem to be some extended form of control flow that overcomes its deficiencies for decentralized concurrent systems, but retains its flexibility and generality.

Moreover, while extrapolation of trends in academic computing research concludes that future computers will be parallel logic machines, extrapolation of industrial trends reveals a totally different picture, namely decentralized control flow systems. ∎

Acknowledgments

Numerous people have contributed to the ideas presented here. We thank members of Japan's fifth-generation project, Tohru Moto-oka and Shunichi Uchida, for their explanations. We also thank Allen Newell of Carnegie-Mellon University and our colleagues in the Computer Architecture Group at the University of Newcastle for helping us to present our ideas. Finally, we thank the Distributed Computing Systems Panel of the UK Science and Engineering Research Council for funding and encouraging future computing research in the United Kingdom.

References

1. T. Moto-oka et al., "Challenge for Knowledge Information Processing Systems (Preliminary Report on Fifth-Generation Computer Systems)," *Proc. Int'l Conf. Fifth-Generation Computer Systems,* North-Holland, Amsterdam, 1982.

2. P. C. Treleaven and I. Gouveia Lima, "Japan's Fifth-Generaton Computer Systems," *Computer,* Vol. 15, No. 8, Aug. 1982, pp. 79-88.

3. S. Uchida, *Towards a New Generation Computer Architecture,* Institute for New Generation Computer Technology, tech. report TR/A-100, Tokyo, Jul. 1982.

4. E. A. Feigenbaum and P. McCorduck, *The Fifth-Generation,* Addison-Wesley, Reading, Mass., 1983.

5. J. J. Servan-Schreiber, *The World Challenge,* Collins, London, 1981.

6. E. A. Feigenbaum, "Knowledge Engineering: The Applied Side of Artificial Intelligence," Computer Science Dept., Stanford University, memo HPP-80-21, 1980.

7. R. O. Duda and J. G. Gaschnig, "Knowledge-Based Expert Systems Come of Age," *Byte,* Vol. 6, No. 9, Sept. 1981, pp. 238-281.

8. R. Ferguson "PROLOG: A Step Toward the Ultimate Computer Language," *Byte,* Vol. 6, No. 11, Nov. 1981, pp. 384-399.

9. R. Kowalski, "Logic for Problem Solving," Elsevier North-Holland, Amsterdam, 1979.

10. S. Uchida et al., *The Personal Sequential Inference Machine,* Institute for New Generation Computer Technology, tech. report TM-002, Tokyo, Nov. 1982.

11. D. H. Warren, *Logic Programming and Compiler Writing,* Dept. of Artificial Intelligence, University of Edinburgh, research report 44, Sept. 1977.

12. Arvind and K. P. Gostelow, "The U-Interpreter," *Computer,* Vol. 15, No. 2, Feb. 1982, pp. 42-49.

13. P. C. Treleaven et al., "Data-Driven and Demand-Driven Computer Architecture," *ACM Computing Surveys,* Vol. 14, No. 1, Mar. 1982, pp. 93-143.

14. C. A. Mead and L. A. Conway, *Introduction to VLSI Systems,* Addison-Wesley, Reading, Mass., 1980.

15. P. C. Treleaven, "VLSI Processor Architectures," *Computer,* Vol. 15, No. 6, June 1982, pp. 33-45.

16. C. Seitz, "Ensemble Architectures for VLSI—A Survey and Taxonomy," *Proc. Conf. Advanced Research in VLSI,* P. Penfield, ed., MIT Press, Cambridge, Mass., Jan. 1982, pp. 33-45.

17. A. L. Fisher et al., "Architecture of the PSC: A Programmable Systolic Chip," *Proc. 10th Int'l Symp. Computer Architecture,* June 1983, pp. 48-53.

18. I. Barron et al., "Transputer Does 5 or more MIPS Even When Not Used in Parallel," *Electronics,* Vol. 56, No. 23, Nov. 1983, pp. 109-115.

19. R. Taylor and P. Wilson, "OCCAM Process-Oriented Language Meets Demands of Distributed Processing," *Electronics,* Vol. 55, No. 23, Nov. 1982, pp. 89-95.

20. L. Foti et al., "Reduced Instruction Set Multi-Microcomputer System (RIMMS)," Computing Laboratory, University of Newcastle upon Tyne, internal report, Aug. 1983.

21. K. Kobayashi, "Computer, Communications and Man: The Integration of Computer and Communications with Man as an Axis," *Computer Networks,* Vol. 5, No. 4, Jul. 1981, pp. 237-250.

22. D. Brownbridge et al., "The Newcastle Connection, or UNIXes of the World Unite!," *Software—Practice and Experience,* Vol. 12, No. 12, Dec. 1982, pp. 1147-1162.

23. D. M. Richie and K. Thompson, "The UNIX Time-Sharing System," *Comm. ACM,* Vol. 17, No. 7, Jul. 1974, pp. 365-375.

24. W. B. Ackerman, "Data Flow Languages," *Computer,* Vol. 15, No. 2, Feb. 1982, pp. 15-25.

25. W. T. Wilner, *Recursive Machines,* Xerox Palo Alto Center, Palo Alto, Calif., internal report, 1980.

26. Arvind and R. A. Iannucci, "A Critique of Multiprocessing von Neumann Style," *Proc. 10th Int'l Symp. Computer Architecture,* June 1983, pp. 426-436.

27. P. C. Treleaven and R. P. Hopkins, "A Recursive Computer Architecture for VLSI," *Proc. Ninth Int'l Symp. Computer Architecture,* Apr. 1982, pp. 229-238.

28. I. Gouveia Lima et al., "Decentralized Control Flow Programming," *Proc. IFIP World Computer Congress,* Sept. 1983, pp. 487-492

Philip C. Treleaven is a senior research fellow in the Department of Computer Science at the University of Reading, England. His previous employment includes serving as research associate in the Computing Laboratory at the University of Newcastle upon Tyne, where he led the Computer Architecture Group, and work with International Computers, Ltd. Treleaven's research interests include decentralized computer architectures, new forms of programming languages, fault-tolerant computing, and VLSI. He holds a BTech from Brunel University, England, and an MSc and PhD in computer science from Manchester University, England, where he initiated data flow research. He is a member of the ACM, the IEEE and the British Computer Society. Treleaven has been an invited speaker at a number of conferences including the 1981 International Conference on Fifth-Generation Computer Systems in Tokyo.

Isabel Gouveia Lima is a research associate in the Computing Laboratory at the University of Newcastle upon Tyne, England, where she works in the Computer Architecture Group. Her research interests include new forms of programming languages, machine translation systems, and commercial applications of decentralized computers. From 1973 to 1980, she was employed as a business systems analyst by Banrisul Processamento de Dados ltda., the data processing firm of the Banco do Estado do Rio Grande do Sul, SA, in Brazil. In 1978, she was awarded a scholarship at the Eindhoven University of Technology in Holland. Gouveia Lima holds a BA in communications and a degree of licentiate in English teaching, both from the Universidade Federal do Rio Grande do Sul, Brazil. She is a member of the ACM and of the specialist group on expert systems of the British Computer Society.

Questions about this article can be directed to Isabel Gouveia Lima, Computing Laboratory, University of Newcastle upon Tyne, Newcastle upon Tyne, England NE1 7RU.

OVERVIEW TO THE FIFTH GENERATION COMPUTER SYSTEM PROJECT

Department of Electrical Engineering,
The University of Tokyo, Tokyo, Japan

SUMMARY

Computers which have high performances for non-numeric data
processing should be developed in order to satisfy and expand new applications which will become predominant fields in information processing of
the 1990s.

Knowledge information processing forming the main part of applied
artificial intelligence is expected to be one of the important fields in 1990s
information processing and the dedicated computers for this have been
selected as the main theme of the national project of the Fifth Generation
computers.

The key technologies for the Fifth Generation Computer System
(FGCS) seem to be VLSI architecture, parallel processing such as data
flow control, logic programming, knowledge base based on relational
database, and applied artificial intelligence and pattern processing.

Inference machines and relational algebra machines are typical of the
core processors which constitute FGCS.

INTRODUCTION

The Fifth Generation computers are defined as the computers which
will be used predominantly in 1990s. Supercomputers will be used in
scientific and engineering calculations and simulations. Database
machines and present mainframe computers will be networked in order to
organise worldwide information systems. Many microcomputers will be
used as system elements in various social systems. However, many computer industries are already earnestly developing these computers for
future use.

Non-numeric data processing, including symbol processing and applied
artificial intelligence will play more important roles than at present in
the future information processing field. Non-numeric data such as sentences, speeches, graphs, and images will be used in tremendous volume
compared to numerical data. Computers are expected to deal with non-
numeric data mainly in future applications. However, present computers
have much less capability in non-numeric data processing than in numeric
data processing.

SOCIAL DEMANDS

The objective of this project is to realise new computer systems to
meet the anticipated requirements of the 1990s. Roles that FGCSs are
expected to play include the following:

1 To enhance productivity in low-productivity areas among non-
   standardised operations in the tertiary industries.
2 To overcome constraints on resources and energy by minimising
   energy consumption and control for optimisation of energy conversion efficiencies.
3 To realise medical, educational, and other support systems for solving

ever more complex, multifaceted, social problems including, but not
limited to, transition to an elderly society.
4 To contribute to international society and to help internationalisa-
   tion of Japanese society through international cooperation, machine
   translation, and in other ways.

Computer application fields will be extremely diversified in the 1990s,
and modes of utilisation will be widened to encompass everything from
giant information networks with worldwide connections to system components. Everybody will be using computers in daily life without thinking
anything of it. For this objective, an environment will have to be created
in which a man and a computer find it easy to communicate freely using
multiple information media, such as speech, text, and graphs.

TECHNICAL BACKGROUND

The changes from one generation to the next in computer technology have so far been made to accommodate changes in device technology. Such hindsight tells us, then, that there have been no major
changes in the basic design philosophy and utilisation objectives of computers.

With Fifth Generation computers, however, the expected generational
change is more like a 'generic change' which involves not only a change in
device technology, to VLSIs, but also simultaneous changes in design
philosophy and in fields of application.

The design philosophy behind conventional von Neumann computers
was based on using a minimum of hardware to configure systems of
maximum simplicity, capable of efficient processing using adequate
software, because in von Neumann's day hardware was expensive, bulky,
short-lived, and consumed a lot of power. From this viewpoint, the
stored-program, sequentially-controlled systems were superior and high
speeds and large capacities were pursued for economic reasons, resulting
in the emergence of today's giant computers.

The key factors leading to the necessity for rethinking the conventional computer design philosophy just described include the following:

1 Device speeds are approaching the limit imposed by the speed of
   light.
2 The emergence of VLSI reduces hardware costs substantially, and an
   environment permitting the use of as much hardware as is required
   will shortly be feasible.
3 To take advantage of the effect of VLSI mass production, it will be
   necessary to pursue parallel processing.
4 Current computers have extremely poor performance in basic functions for processing speeches, texts, graphs, images and other nonnumerical data, and for artificial intelligence type processing such as
   inference, association, and learning.

Computers, as the name implies, were designed as machines to perform numerical computations. Computer applications have, however,
expanded without major changes in design philosophy, into such fields as
control systems, processing of multiple information media, database
management systems, and artificial intelligence systems. However, for
computers to be employed at numerous application levels in the 1990s,
they must evolve from machines centred around numerical computations

to machines that can assess the meaning of information and understand the problems to be solved. For this evolution, in the immediate future, the following will be required:
1 Realisation of basic mechanisms for inference, association, and learning in hardware, making them the core functions of the Fifth Generation computers.
2 Preparation of basic artificial intelligence software in order to fully utilise the above functions.
3 Advantageous use of pattern recognition and artificial intelligence research achievements, in order to realise man/machine interfaces that are natural to man.
4 Realisation of support systems for resolving the 'software crisis' and enhancing software production.

In order to solve the problems faced by current computer technologies, achievements in related technologies such as VLSI technology, software engineering, and artificial intelligence research will have to be integrated, and the interim achievements of this project will be fed back to these technologies so that they can continue to advance.

RESEARCH AND DEVELOPMENT TARGETS

Knowledge information processing systems (KIPS) will be investigated in the Japanese national project.[1][2] They will be based on innovative theories and technologies, and hence capable of accommodating such functions as intelligent conversation functions and inference functions employing knowledge bases that will be required in the 1990s. The functions of FGCSs may be roughly classified as follows:
1 Problem-solving and inference.
2 Knowledge-base management.
3 Intelligent interface.

These functions will be realised by making individual software and hardware systems correspond. A conceptual image of the system is shown in Figure 1. In this diagram, the modelling (software) system is the project's ultimate target for software development, and the machine (hardware) system the ultimate target for hardware development. The upper half of the modelling system circle corresponds to the problem-solving and inference functions, the lower half to the knowledge-base management function. The portion that overlaps the human system circle on the left corresponds to the intelligent interface function. The diagram also illustrates that the intelligent interface function relies heavily on the two former groups of functions. This diagram shows how the emphasis in computer systems will have shifted decisively towards the human system by significant enhancement of the logic level of the hardware system and by the positioning of the modelling system between the hardware and man.

The interface between the software and hardware systems will be the kernel language. The entire software system will be realised in the kernel language, and the hardware system will directly execute the kernel language.

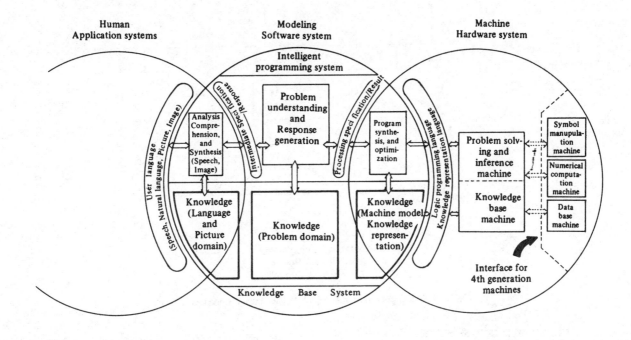

Fig. 1. Conceptual diagram of a Fifth Generation Computer System as viewed from the standpoint of programming

THE PROBLEM-SOLVING AND INFERENCE SYSTEM

Research into the problem-solving and inference mechanism will concentrate on the problem solving and inference functions, the ultimate goal being a cooperative problem-solving system. In such a system, a single problem will be solved by two or more problem-solving systems cooperating with each other.

It will be necessary to develop high performance inference machines capable of serving as core processors that use rules and assertions to process knowledge information. Existing artificial intelligence technology has been developed to be based primarily on LISP. However, it seems more appropriate to employ a Prolog-like logic programming language as the interface between software and hardware due to the following considerations: the introduction of VLSI technology made possible the implementation of high level functions in hardware; in order to perform parallel processing, it will be necessary to adopt new languages suitable for parallel processing; such languages will have to have a strong affinity with relational data models.

The Fifth Generation Kernel Language (FGKL) has been defined as a language which will determine the interface between the hardware and software of Fifth Generation computers.

The maximum capability of the inference machine is from 100 MLIPS to 1 GLIPS. The inference executing speed, 1 LIPS (logical inference per second), denotes one syllogistic inference operation per second. One inference operation, executed by a current computer is believed to require 100 to 1000 steps; thus, 1 LIPS corresponds to 100 to 1000 instr/sec. The current generation machines are rates at 10^4 to 10^5 LIPS.

To realise such performance capabilities, the essential research and development will concentrate not only on speeding up the basic devices, but also on high-level parallel architectures to support the symbol processing that is the key to inference. A hardware architecture suited to the new parallel inferences based on the data-flow control mechanism will be researched and developed.

As an example of proposed architectures in a parallel inference engine, the parallel processor investigated at the Univ. of Tokyo, which is able to execute Prolog-like language directly, is shown in Figure 2. The main components of this inference engine consist of numerous unify processors with definition memories and numerous memory modules with activity controllers. They are connected through switching networks. In addition, there are a system manager which enables communication with external devices and unify processors by serving as an interface and an activity manager which supervises the activity controllers.

The target scale for the hardware encompasses ultimately about 1000 processing elements, and the requisite VLSI manufacturing technology for such hardware will be researched and developed.

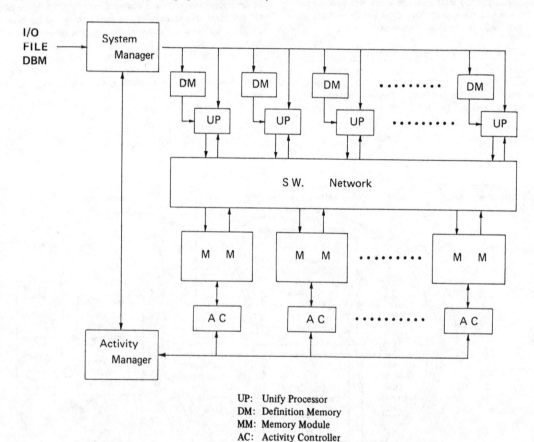

UP: Unify Processor
DM: Definition Memory
MM: Memory Module
AC: Activity Controller

Fig. 2. System Organization of Parallel Inference Engine at the Univ. of Tokyo

THE KNOWLEDGE-BASE SYSTEMS

The intention of software for the knowledge-base management function will be to establish knowledge information processing technology, where the targets will be development of knowledge representation systems, knowledge-base design and maintenance support systems, large-scale knowledge-base systems, knowledge acquisition experimental systems, and distributed knowledge management systems. These systems will then be integrated into a cooperative problem-solving system. One particularly important aim will be semi-automated knowledge acquisition, that is, systems will be equipped with a certain level of learning functions.

For the knowledge-base management function, relational database interfaces and consistency testing functions will have to be realised in the kernel language.

Research into and development of the knowledge-base machine will aim at developing a hardware mechanism that fulfils the demands for knowledge representation systems and large-scale knowledge-base systems, and is capable of efficiently supporting storage, retrieval, and renewal of a large volume of knowledge data. This mechanism will ultimately be integrated in the prototype FGCS.

Regarding the target knowledge-base management function in research into and development of the knowledge-base machine, the aim in performance capabilities based on a database machine with a 100 to 1000 Gbyte capacity, will be to retrieve the knowledge bases required for answering a question within a few seconds.

To realise such performance capabilities, a parallel architecture, capable of speedily supporting the symbol processing function intended

598

to handle a large capacity data management function and knowledge data, will be indispensable. Research and development will be conducted for a parallel processing hardware architecture intended for parallel processing of new knowledge bases, and which is based on a relational database machine that includes a high-performance hierarchical memory system, and a mechanism for parallel relational operations and knowledge operations.

The knowledge base system is expected to be implemented on a relational database machine which has some knowledge base facilities in the Fifth Generation Computer System, because the relational data model has a strong affinity with logic programming. Relational calculus has a close relation with the first order predicate logic. Relational algebra has the same ability as relational calculus in the description of a query. These are reasons for considering a relational algebra machine as the prime candidate for a knowledge base machine.

The relational algebra machine GRACE is being investigated at the Univ. of Tokyo. GRACE adopts a relational algebra processing algorithm based on hash and sort, and can join in $O((N+M)/n)$ time where n is the number of processors and N and M are the cardinalities of two joined relations. GRACE is a typical example of proposed arthitectures of knowledge base machines in the FGCS Project.

The clustering feature of the hash operation can reduce the load of join processing. The simple join algorithm takes time proportional to the product of two relations' cardinalities. However, if two relations are clustered on the join attribute, that is, the tuples are grouped into disjoint buckets based on the hashed value of the join attribute, there is no joining between tuples from buckets of different ids (hashed value of the join attribute). The duplicate elimination task in projection also used to be a big burden in relational data base systems. The above approach can be applied to projection operations quite as well as to join operations.

Another technique utilizing hash is the "Joinability Filter" which can be found in CAFS and LEECH[3].

The two approaches discussed above are mutually independent, so

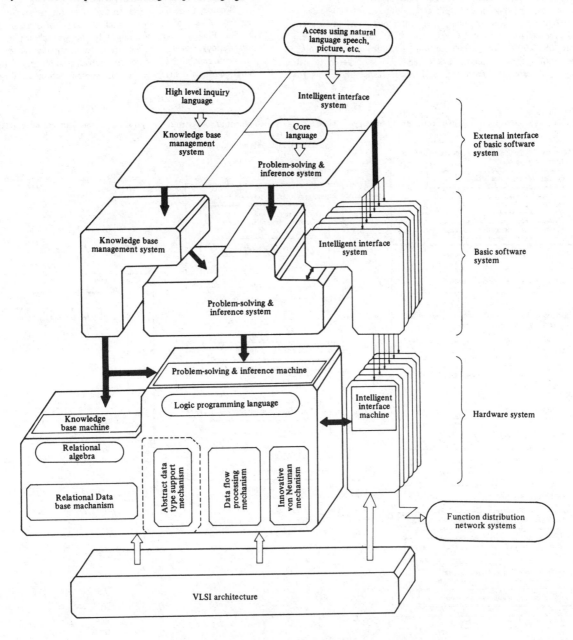

Fig. 3. Basic configuration of the Fifth Generation Computer Systems

that both joinability filter processing which decreases the candidate tuples and clustered processing can be integrated together.

The great reduction of processing load for join and projection operations was realised via the hash based relational algebra processing method.

THE INTELLIGENT INTERFACE SYSTEM

The intelligent interface function will have to be capable of handling man/machine communication in natural languages, speeches, graphs, and images so that information can be exchanged in a way natural to a man. As natural language processing provides the basis for translation, English and other languages are to be included as well as Japanese in the objects for processing. Ultimately, the system will cover a basic vocabulary (excluding technical terms) of up to 10,000 words and up to 2,000 grammatical rules, with a 99% accuracy in syntactic analysis. The fewer the grammatical rules, the higher the system capabilities.

On speech processing, speech input and output systems will be developed. The object of speech inputs will be continuous speech in Japanese standard pronunciation by multiple speakers, and the aims here will be a vocabulary of 50,000 words, a 95% recognition rate for individual works, and recognition and processing three times the real time of speech, though this may vary somewhat depending on hardware capabilities. As for

processing of graphs and picture images, the target system to be developed will be capable of structurally storing roughly 10,000 pieces of graph and image information and utilising them for knowledge information processing.

Meanwhile, there will also be research into and development of dedicated hardware processors and high-performance interface equipment for efficiently executing processing of speech, graph, and image data. Furthermore, methods for exchanging information that are natural to man, through parallel utilisation of such multiple media data, will have to be established.

BASIC CONFIGURATION OF THE FGCS

The software and hardware systems that realise the three functions mentioned above will be coupled to form a general-purpose machine. Its conceptual structure is shown in Figure 3.

Because, in actual use, a variety of performance capabilities will be required of each of the three functions, the configuration will have to be flexible enough to provide not only the general-purpose machine, but also various system configurations to accommodate the various performance capabilities required by individual applications, that is, specific function-intensive machines in which some functions are enhanced.

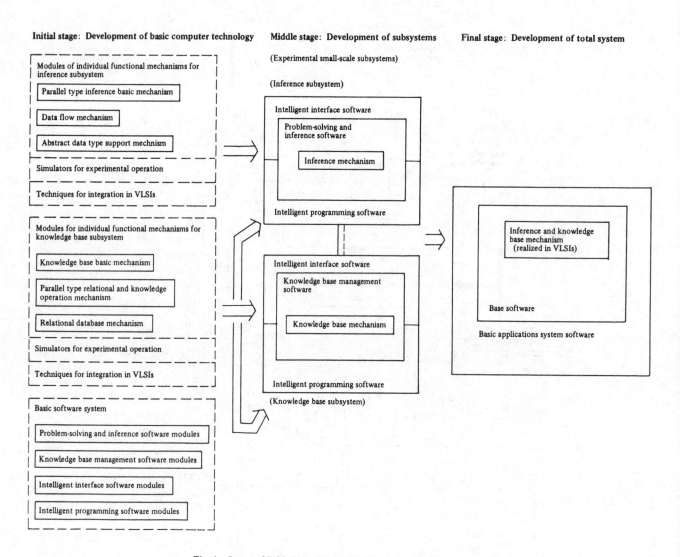

Fig. 4. Stages of Fifth Generation computer research and development

600

These machines will have the Fifth Generation computer kernel language as their common machine language, and they will be interconnected in networks to form a distributed processing system.

BASIC APPLICATION SYSTEMS IN FGCS

Several basic application systems will be developed with the intention of demonstrating the usefulness of the FGCS and the system evaluation. These are machine translation systems, consultation systems, intelligent programming systems and an intelligent VLSI-CAD system.

CONCLUSION

The research and development targets of the FGCS are such core functions of knowledge information processing as problem-solving and inference systems and knowledge-base systems that cannot be handled within the framework of conventional computer systems.

There is no precedent for this innovative and large-scale research and development anywhere in the world. We will therefore be obliged to move toward the target systems through a lengthy process of trial and error, producing many original ideas along the way.

Since the establishment under this project of the basic computer techniques that will be required in the 1990s is vital, plans will have to encompass as wide an extension of basic techniques as possible. Taking these aspects into consideration, the research and development period set for this project is 10 years, divided, as shown in Figure 4, into an initial stage (three years), a middle stage (four years), and final stage (three years).

As a research and development project involving advanced technologies from many fields, as well as from the viewpoint of its being an international contribution by Japan, the Fifth Generation Computer Project should be promoted through some form of international cooperation. Various formats are conceivable for such international cooperation buy, based on experience gained during the past four years of basic technological development, the research and development work will be served best by extremely close interrelations among the various development themes. Thus a form of cooperation that comes readily to mind is for interested governments or enterprises to promote original research and development at their own expenses, periodically exchanging achievements to the mutual benefit of all involved.

The Japanese national project of FGCS started in April, 1982 and is expected to run for 10 years. The initial step is the preliminary three-year stage in which the project is dealt with by the Institute of New Generation Computer Technology (ICOT).

REFERENCES

(1) T. Moto-oka (Ed.), Fifth Generation Computer Systems, North Holland, 1982.
(2) P.C. Treleaven, I. G. Lime, Japan's Fifth Generation Computer systems, IEEE Computer, Vol. 15, No. 8, Aug. 1982, 79-88.
(3) D. R. McGregar et al., High Performance Hardware for Database System, Systems for Large Data Bases, North-Holland, 1976, 103-116.

"Coping with the Imprecision of the Real World" by L.A. Zadeh from *Communications of the ACM*, Volume 27, Number 4, April 1984, pages 304-311. Copyright 1984 by The Association for Computing Machinery, Inc., reprinted by permission.

COPING WITH THE IMPRECISION OF THE REAL WORLD

An Interview with Lotfi A. Zadeh

The tools researchers use to probe certain AI problems, says this Berkeley professor, are sometimes too precise to deal with the "fuzziness" of the real world.

Q. Professor Zadeh, in this interview today, you agreed to talk mainly about the limits of traditional logic in dealing with many of the problems in the field of artificial intelligence (AI) and your approach toward helping to overcome those difficulties. Before getting into those issues, though, could you first give our readers a brief overview of what you see as the major areas for computer applications in the years ahead?

ZADEH. In the years ahead, there will be three major areas of computer applications. One, in the traditional vein, is the use of computers for purposes of numerical analysis. Numerical analysis will be very important in a number of fields—particularly in scientific computations and simulation of large-scale systems.

For such purposes, there will be a need for larger and larger computers. This is especially true for applications in meteorology, in nuclear physics, in modeling of large-scale economic systems, in the solution of partial differential equations, and in the simulation of complex phenomena like turbulence, fluid flow, etc.

Area number two will be concerned with masses of data—large databases. This is the sort of thing that is playing and will be playing an important role in banking, insurance, records processing, information retrieval, etc. What will be important in these areas is not so much number-crunching capabilities as the capability to store massive amounts of data and to access whatever data are needed rapidly and at a reasonably low cost.

Furthermore, in these areas, computer networking, of course, will be playing an essential role. For you will have to have access not just to a single database but to a collection of interconnected databases. In response to this need, we will see many advances in computer networking during the next several years.

The third major area for computer applications is what has come to be known as *knowledge engineering*. This area has received considerable publicity during the past few years, particularly since the Japanese have highlighted it as an area of prime concern. This is a rapidly growing field in terms of importance and breadth of applications.

Knowledge engineering is one of the major areas of AI. And within knowledge engineering, a field of primary importance is that of expert systems. True, there may be exaggerated expectations of what expert systems can accomplish at this juncture, but as Jules Verne observed at the turn of the century, scientific progress is driven by exaggerated expectations.

So we have these three major areas for computer applications in the years ahead. All will be *growing* in importance. But knowledge engineering, I think, will be growing in importance more rapidly than the other two, because it is the youngest and, in a sense, the most pervasive of the three.

In saying that knowledge engineering is going to become very important, I don't want to imply that the other two will become less important. They will become more important also. But in relative terms, knowledge engineering will certainly be much more important than it is today.

Now, what I'm going to say will relate to this third area, rather than the first two.

Q. Do you see supercomputers playing an important role only in the area of numerical analysis?

ZADEH. Supercomputers pertain to all three areas: *numerical analysis*, *large databases*, and *knowledge engineering*. But they apply primarily to the first area: numerical analysis. There is at this point some controversy as to how the available research funds should be distributed between the efforts to build supercomputers and to build machines that will be AI oriented.

These are somewhat distinct efforts. The Japanese are pushing both of them. And in the United States, the emphasis on AI-oriented types of computers is just beginning to become strong, largely as a reaction to the Japanese effort. As you may know, Edward Feigenbaum of Stanford University is a leading advocate of the establishment of a U.S. National Center for Computer Technology as a rallying point for the U.S. effort.

Q. **I'm not perfectly clear on the distinction between a supercomputer and an AI-oriented device, which I believe is sometimes referred to as a fifth generation computer. Could you clarify?**

ZADEH. Fifth generation has become somewhat of a misnomer. Basically, the Fifth Generation Project is perhaps the most publicized of the several ambitious research programs undertaken by the Japanese. Another one of those programs is called the Supercomputer Project.

The Fifth Generation Project is not hardware oriented. Rather it is intended to exploit the advances in hardware that might be achieved under the other projects in the overall program.

For supercomputers, the emphasis is on large-scale computations relating to scientific and technological applications. For AI-oriented computers, on the other hand, the emphasis is shifted away from "data" to "knowledge."

What matters in the case of these AI-oriented computers is their ability *to infer* from the information resident in a large knowledge base—especially when this information is imprecise, incomplete, or not totally reliable.

We can expect that advances in the design of supercomputers—on both the hardware and the software levels—will have a significant impact on the architecture of AI-oriented machines.

Of course, the supercomputer is not a unique concept. It can take a variety of forms. Parallel processing may play a major role in AI-oriented applications—especially in pattern recognition, natural language processing, and inference from large knowledge bases. Whether this will actually happen within the next decade is a matter of conjecture.

During the past 20 years, parallel processing has been a highly promising area for research. Yet what could actually be accomplished with parallel processing has always lagged behind expectations. At this juncture, however, it's possible that important breakthroughs may be around the corner.

But there are many problems in AI that will not be helped to an appreciable extent by the availability of supercomputers, whether they will be von Neumann-type supercomputers or some other kind. The reason why this is so is because the limitation is not so much computing power, but our lack of understanding of some of the processes required to perform even simple cognitive tasks.

Lotfi A. Zadeh, a professor of electrical engineering and computer science, has been a member of the faculty at the University of California at Berkeley since 1959. Born in the Soviet Union of Iranian parents, Zadeh came to the U.S. in 1944 and studied at MIT and Columbia, from which he got his Ph.D. in 1949. After serving on the Columbia faculty during the 1950s, Zadeh went to Berkeley. Dissatisfied with the use of very precise mathematics to describe the sometimes highly imprecise real world, Zadeh, during the 1960s, developed the theory of fuzzy sets. In recent years, his controversial ideas on "fuzzy thinking" have begun to win a following in some quarters of the world.

Q. **You say that there are many problems that won't be solved by the availability of supercomputers. Could you give an example of such a problem?**

ZADEH. Let me start with a problem basic to most other problems: the problem of summarization. Now, when I talk about summarization, I am not talking about summarizing a short stereotypical story. That capability we have, thanks to Roger Schank, his associates at Yale University, and others within the AI community.

But what we have no understanding of, whatsoever, is how to summarize a nonstereotypical story that is not a short story.

Q. **Could you give an example of a stereotypical story?**

ZADEH. An example would be accounts of automobile accidents. They tend to be stereotypical. In other words, in the story there is an indication of what kind of accident it was, when it occurred, where it occurred, whether there were injuries, etc.

Q. **I see. It has a predetermined structure?**

ZADEH. Yes. When I say stereotypical, I mean it has a predetermined structure. So if you have a predetermined structure, then you can understand the story and you can summarize it.

Now, the reason why summarization is so difficult—it is far more difficult than machine translation from one language to another language—is because summarization requires understanding. And the ability of a computer to summarize a short, stereotypical story would be a little bit like the ability of a person who sees a story of that kind in the newspaper and doesn't understand completely the language in which the story is written. Nonetheless, he can discern a few words here and there and, on that basis, summarize the story. Many people could do that if they have some minimal competence in the language in which the story is written. But that minimal competence is completely inadequate when it comes to summarizing something that is not stereotypical and not short.

Q. **You said that it is very difficult and often impossible at present to write a program to summarize a story. So why is that an important point?**

ZADEH. The ability to summarize is an acid test of the ability to understand, which in turn is a test of intelligence and competence. Suppose I asked a person not familiar with mathematics to summarize a paper in a mathematical journal. It would be impossible for him to summarize it, because he doesn't understand what that paper is about, what the results are, what the significance is, and so forth.

So in a situation like that, it wouldn't help us to have a supercomputer. It wouldn't help us to have all the supercomputers in the world put together. That's not where the problem lies.

Q. **Professor Zadeh, could you give me a few other examples of problems that will still defy solution even with major advances in supercomputer design?**

ZADEH. Take the problem of identification of ethnic origin. Humans can do that. You can look at a person and say, "Gee, he looks Irish," or whatever. Now, it would be impossible at this point to write a program that would look at somebody's picture and identify the ethnic origin of that person. I don't want to say that it's impossible period. I'm merely saying that at this moment it's impossible.

Another problem is estimation of age. Assume that you look at somebody, and you say, "Well, this person must be around 35." Again, we cannot write a program that would enable a computer to do it at this point. And we can't put our finger on subtle differences, like the difference between a person who is 20 years old and somebody who is 10.

Q. **Why is that? Why is it impossible to write a program to estimate a person's age from an analysis of physical features?**

ZADEH. Because we don't understand too well how we arrive at assessments of that kind. In other words, in order to write a program, we have to have an understanding of how we do it. The limitation in problems of this kind is that we cannot articulate the rules that we employ subconsciously to make that kind of an assessment.

Of course, you know, there are certain things that might not be so difficult. It's not so difficult to differentiate between a person who is 70 years old and a person who is, for instance, 5 years old. But I'm talking about kinds of problems in the estimation of age that are not as trivial as that. And we know that you cannot base it entirely on wrinkles or color of hair. It's the totality of these things put together that enable us to make an assessment.

Still another problem of that same type is the problem of the identification of a musical tune. People can identify a tune if they hear just a few bars. They generally can guess who the composer is, even though they may never have heard this piece before. In other words, there's something about the way the music composed by a particular composer sounds that makes it possible

for us to say, "Well, this is Mozart," even though we may never have heard that piece before.

Again, if somebody asked how you guessed that it was Mozart, you would not be able to put down on paper the criteria that you have employed.

Q. **You're saying that this process of recognizing that a short burst of music is from Mozart, Beethoven, or someone else is something going on unconsciously or intuitively?**

ZADEH. It's something that we can do without being able to articulate the rules. In other words, the decisional algorithms that we employ for this purpose are opaque rather than transparent.

The problems that I mentioned—ethnic origin identification, age estimation, composer identification, or tune recognition—all of these are problems in pattern recognition. Many of these problems are far from solution at this point. And they present right now a stumbling block to such applications as speech recognition for connected speech.

Q. **What is the point of all these examples? What is the lesson here?**

ZADEH. What I have said so far is intended merely to give the reasons for my feeling that the availability of supercomputers will not help us much in solving problems of that kind. This is the issue that I was really addressing myself to.

But at this point, all I'm trying to say is that the supercomputer effort and the AI-oriented type of computer effort to develop machines that can perform nontrivial cognitive tasks are not quite the same. There is some interaction between them, but they are qualitatively different.

Let us return now to area number three, *knowledge engineering.* What I have to say here will be at considerable variance with the widely held positions within the AI community.

AI, as we know it today, is based on two-valued logic—that is, the classical Aristotelian logic. And it is generally assumed that all you need as a foundation of AI is first-order logic.

Q. **You say that AI today is based on two-valued logic. Is that a yes-or-no kind of logic?**

ZADEH. Yes, that's right. It's a yes-or-no kind of logic. Actually, two-valued logic encompasses a variety of logical systems, all of which share the basic assumption that truth is two-valued. One of these logical systems is what is called first-order logic. And so the assumption that many people make is that first-order logic, perhaps with some modifications, is sufficient.

Q. **Does a simple example come to mind of first-order logic?**

ZADEH. Well, suppose you say, "All men are mortal. Socrates is a man. Therefore Socrates is mortal." This would be a very simple example of reasoning in first-order logic.

Briefly, within the AI community at this point, there are two camps. One camp, the conservative camp, takes the position that AI, and more generally knowledge engineering, should be based on logic, and in particular on first-order logic. One of the main proponents of this view is John McCarthy of Stanford University. Other prominent proponents include Nils Nilsson of SRI, Wolfgang Bibel of the University of Munich, Robert Kowalski of London, and Alain Colmerauer of Marseilles, France.

Now the other camp takes the position that logic is of limited or no relevance to AI. They believe that first-order logic is too limited to be able to deal effectively with the complexity of human cognitive processes. Instead of systematic, logical methods, this second camp relies on the use of ad hoc techniques and heuristic procedures. The prime exponents of this position are Roger Schank of Yale University and, more recently and less emphatically, Marvin Minsky of MIT.

Q. How does your position, Professor Zadeh, differ from those in the two AI camps you mentioned—the conservatives who believe in first-order logic and the other camp that believes logic has only limited relevance?

ZADEH. The position that I take—and this is really what differentiates me from most of the people in AI—is that we need logic in AI. But the kind of logic we need is not *first-order logic*, but *fuzzy logic*—that is, the logic that underlies inexact or approximate reasoning.

I feel this way because most of human reasoning—almost all of human reasoning—is imprecise. Much of it is what might be called common sense reasoning. And first-order logic is much too precise and much too confining to serve as a good model for common sense reasoning.

The reason why humans can do many things that present-day computers cannot do well or perhaps even at all is because existing computers employ two-valued logic.

To put it another way, the inability of today's computers to solve some of those problems I mentioned earlier is not that we don't have enough computing capacity. Rather, the computers we have today—in terms of both hardware and software—are not oriented toward the processing of fuzzy knowledge and common sense reasoning. This is where the problem lies in my view.

Q. Doesn't that view—the idea that computers don't mimic human thought processes very well—imply that there is something sacred about the way human beings think? Isn't it possible that the way humans think about things is not very good and that it might be possible to conceive an artificial way of thinking that is superior?

ZADEH. Of course, one could take the position, as some workers in AI do, that it is not essential to mimic the human mind in the design of AI systems. One argument is that when we design an aircraft, so goes one of the arguments, we don't design it like a bird. But somehow this plane-design analogy doesn't seem to pertain to the design of AI systems. For when we actually attempt to build AI systems that can perform humanlike cognitive tasks we invariably seem to come back to the human model. The human model is a pretty good one—better than many people thought.

Q. Could you elaborate a bit more on just what fuzzy logic is?

ZADEH. Let me do that. I will explain the main differences between fuzzy logic and classical two-valued logic. In classical two-valued systems, all classes are assumed to have sharply defined boundaries. So either an object is a member of a class or it is not a member of a class.

Now, this is okay if you are talking about something like mortal or not mortal, dead or alive, male or female, and so forth. These are examples of classes that have sharp boundaries.

But most classes in the real world do not have sharp boundaries. For example, if you consider characteristics or properties like tall, intelligent, tired, sick, and so forth, all of these characteristics lack sharp boundaries. Classical two-valued logic is not designed to deal with properties that are a matter of degree. This is the first point.

Now, there is, of course, a generalization of two-valued logic. And these generalized logical systems are called multivalued logics. So in multivalued logical systems, a property can be possessed to a degree.

Q. I'm not perfectly clear here. Consider the word "tall." Are you saying "tall" can take on multiple values?

ZADEH. Yes, tallness becomes a matter of degree, as does intelligence, tiredness, and so forth. Usually you have degrees between zero and one. So you can say, for example, that a person is tall to the degree 0.9. These degrees are grades of membership that may be interpreted as truth values.

In classical logic, there are just two truth values: true/false (or one and zero). In multivalued logical systems, there are more than two truth values. There may be a finite or even an infinite number of truth values, that is, an infinite number of degrees to which a property may be possessed.

In a three-valued system, for instance, something can be true, false, or on the boundary. Or you can have systems in which one has a continuum of truth values from zero to one.

Q. Who first developed multivalued logic?

ZADEH. The person best known in that connection is a Polish mathematician by the name of J. Lukasiewicz. He first developed the concept of multivalued logic during the 1920s.

Q. Could you give an example or two of a situation that requires multivalued logic?

ZADEH. Well, you would need a multivalued system

605

to be able to say something like "John is tall." For tall is a property that requires an infinity of truth values to describe it. So something as simple as "John is tall" would require multivalued logic—unless you arbitrarily establish a threshold by saying "somebody over 6 feet tall is tall, and those who are less than 6 feet tall are not tall." In other words, unless you artificially introduce some sort of a threshold like that, you will need multivalued logic.

But even though these multivalued logical systems have been available for some time, they have not been used to any significant extent in linguistics, in psychology, and in other fields where human cognition plays an important role.

Q. Why hasn't multivalued logic been used?
ZADEH. The reason such systems haven't been used is that multivalued logic doesn't go far enough. And this is where *fuzzy logic* enters the picture.

What differentiates fuzzy logic from multivalued logic is that in fuzzy logic you can deal with fuzzy quantifiers, like "most," "few," "many," and "several."

Fuzzy quantifiers have something to do with enumeration, that is, with counting. But they are fuzzy because they don't give you the count exactly, but fuzzily. For instance, you say "many" or "most."

In multi-valued logic you have only two quantifiers, "all" and "some," whereas in fuzzy logic you have all the fuzzy quantifiers. This is one of the important differences.

Q. Now are those the only fuzzy quantifiers?
ZADEH. Well, the ones that I mentioned are merely examples. In reality, there is an infinite number of fuzzy quantifiers. For example, you can say "not very many," "quite a few," "many more than 10," "a large number," "many," "few," or "very many." There is an infinite number of ways in which you can describe in an approximate fashion a count of objects.

Q. Besides the fuzzy quantifiers, what else distinguishes fuzzy logic from multivalued logic?
ZADEH. Another key difference is that in fuzzy logic *truth* itself is allowed to be fuzzy. So it is okay to say that something is "quite true." You can say "it's more or less true." You can also use fuzzy probability like "not very likely," "almost impossible," or "rarely." In this way, fuzzy logic provides a system that is sufficiently flexible and expressive to serve as a natural framework for the semantics of natural languages.

Furthermore, it can serve as a basis for reasoning with common sense knowledge, for pattern recognition, decision analysis, and other application areas in which the underlying information is imprecise. Within the restricted framework of two-valued and even multivalued systems, these problem areas have proved to be difficult to deal with systematically.

The crux of the problem, really, is the excessively wide gap between the precision of classical logic and the imprecision of the real world.

Q. Does fuzzy logic, then, provide a good match with the imprecise real world?
ZADEH. I don't wish to imply that fuzzy logic is in any sense an ultimate system. I do believe, however, that it is far better suited for dealing with real-world problems than the traditional logical systems.

Q. At this juncture, Professor Zadeh, could you encapsulate what you feel is your most important point so far?
ZADEH. Yes. It is that the limitation in knowledge engineering is not the unavailability of supercomputers. But it is the fact that computers—both their hardware and software—are based on a kind of logic that is not a good model for human reasoning.

Ultimately, the problem lies at the hardware level. For computers are basically digital devices: they deal with discrete bits of information. Fuzzy information, on the other hand, is not discrete. With fuzzy information, one thing merges into another.

Now an important point is this: even though present-day computers are based on two-valued logic, they can be programmed to process fuzzy information using fuzzy logic. But doing this does not represent an efficient use of the computational capabilities of present-day computers.

Q. You're saying there are problems with both the hardware and the software of existing computer systems, but that you can overcome them so that traditional computers can still handle fuzzy information?
ZADEH. Yes, you can overcome the hardware limitations of current computers with software. But doing that involves an inefficient use of computers.

The ability of the human mind to reason in fuzzy terms is actually a great advantage. Even though a tremendous amount of information is presented to the human senses in a given situation—an amount that would choke a typical computer—somehow the human mind has the ability to discard most of this information and to concentrate only on the information that is task relevant. This ability of the human mind to deal only with the information that is task relevant is connected with its ability to process fuzzy information. By concentrating only on the task-relevant information, the amount of information the brain has to deal with is reduced to a manageable level.

Q. So you can work with traditional computers, but they are inefficient because they are fundamentally incompatible with fuzzy information. What kind of computer could you use then?
ZADEH. At some point, we may be able to conceive computers that are radically different from existing computers in that the operations they perform are rooted in fuzzy rather than two-valued logic. In other words, they may need a different kind of hardware.

There has been talk about "chemical," "biological," or "molecular" computers.

Some imaginative thinkers are talking about computers of that kind, but we don't have them yet.

Q. What is a molecular computer?
ZADEH. It's difficult to say. But if you compare the way the human brain works with the way a modern computer works, I think that you will find there are some fundamental differences. The human brain, in a way that we don't understand too well at present, uses fuzzy logic.

So the hardware—if you may call it that—of the human brain is the kind of hardware that is effective for manipulating imprecise information. When one uses the term molecular computer, or biological computer or chemical computer, what one has in mind is something that approximates the way in which the human brain processes information. And therein lies a fundamental challenge: how to develop a better understanding of how the human brain processes this fuzzy information so effectively.

Q. How much is presently understood about how the brain processes information?
ZADEH. Scientists know a lot about the functioning of the brain at the neuron level. But how does the activity at that level aggregate into thinking processes? Trying to understand the brain at the neuron level is like trying to understand the functioning of a telephone system in a large city by examining the wiring of a telephone set. We can understand something on the microlevel but are unable to integrate that into an understanding of functioning on higher levels.

Q. I don't completely understand your reasons for writing off traditional computers. Maybe people haven't tried hard enough or long enough, as yet, to make them work for certain AI applications?
ZADEH. In fact, I'm not writing off traditional computers in regard to their ability to process fuzzy information. Rather, my position is that we do not have a good understanding at this point as to how to use them efficiently for handling fuzzy information.

In fact, I believe that there will be a growing number of applications of fuzzy logic in a wide variety of fields using present-day computers. But, ultimately, to achieve a higher level of efficiency, it may be necessary to employ computers that are specially designed for dealing with fuzzy information.

To give one example, speech recognition is a problem far from a satisfactory solution. We do have speech recognition systems with limited capability to understand speech. But all of these systems do not scale up. That is, they can not be merely modified and improved in an evolutionary way until they come close to the human ability to understand speech. So it's obvious that what is needed is an altogether different approach.

Q. I'm not perfectly clear when you say these systems won't scale up. Could you expand on that point?
ZADEH. Yes. In some situations we have a system

that has a limited capability. But we see clearly how, by improving that system, we can raise its level of performance to a point where it can compete with humans in terms of certain abilities.

Now, within AI, this is generally not the case. That is, many AI systems do not scale up: They reach very quickly the limit of their ability. In other words, you cannot push them beyond that point.

Q. Could you give an example of a system that does not scale up?
ZADEH. A good example, to go back to what I said previously, are the programs that can summarize. These programs reach the limit of their ability very quickly—in terms of the length of the story they can summarize or in terms of the degree to which the story is nonstereotypical. And you cannot go beyond those limits without radically altering the approaches used.

Another example. Before we had integrated circuits, we depended on vacuum tubes in the design of our computers, and you could push the capabilities of those early computers only up to a point. We had to come up with something new, the concept of an integrated circuit, and eventually very large-scale integration (VLSI). Those breakthroughs greatly increased our capability to compute, to store, and more generally, to process information.

That was a situation that called for something radically different. And it wasn't a matter of evolution—but of revolution.

And so I think that we are faced with a somewhat similar situation in the case of computers that can perform high-level cognitive tasks. That is, we cannot hope to be able to solve the problems of the kind I mentioned earlier, in particular the problem of summarization, through evolutionary improvements in present computer hardware or software.

Q. In other words, some of the more difficult problems in AI won't be solved by innovations in supercomputer architecture—innovations like parallel processing?
ZADEH. That's right, such innovations aren't going to help much.

But there is more to this fuzzy logic than simply the enhancement of the ability of computers to solve various problems—to perform nontrivial cognitive tasks. Accepting fuzzy logic will also call for a certain fundamental shift in attitudes, particularly in theoretical computer science. At this point theoretical computer science is mathematical in spirit, in the sense that it is oriented toward the discovery and proof of results that can be stated as theorems.

Unfortunately, there is an incompatibility between precision and complexity. As the complexity of a system increases, our ability to make precise and yet nontrivial assertions about its behavior diminishes. For example, it is very difficult to prove a theorem about the behavior of an economic system that is of relevance to real-world economics.

607

What I anticipate in the future is a growing recognition of the necessity to find an accommodation with the pervasive imprecision of the real world. This change is needed to be able to make assertions that are not just nontrivial theorems, but something of relevance to practice. In computer science today, people use two-valued logic to establish certain results. But such results are often limited in their relevance to the real world—because they are excessively precise. In other words, we have to accord acceptance to assertions that do not adhere to high standards of precision.

This accommodation with imprecision will require the use of fuzzy logic. Gradually and perhaps rather slowly, there will be a growing acceptance of fuzzy logic as a conceptual framework for computer science.

Now, it is a little bit more difficult to articulate this particular position than some of the earlier things that I said. For this gets into issues that relate not just to computer science but, more generally, to science itself. Science at this point is based on two-valued logic. So what I'm talking about is a significant shift in attitude, not just in computer science, but more generally in scientific thinking.

At this point there is a long-standing and deep-seated tradition of according respectability to what is mathematical and precise. We may have to retreat from this tradition in order to be able to say something useful about complex systems and in particular about systems in which human reasoning plays an important role.

Q. Okay, then, there have been instances in the past where scientists have been too preoccupied with mathematics and precision and, as a result, have failed to come up with useful results. Does an example come to mind?
ZADEH. Yes. Take economics. Time and again, it has been demonstrated that what actually happens in the realm of economics is very different from what the experts predicted. These experts might be using large-scale econometric models, sophisticated mathematics, large-scale computers, and the like. Despite all that, the forecasts turn out to be wrong—very wrong.

Why? Two reasons. One is that economic systems are very complex. Second, and more important, human psychology plays an essential role in the behavior of such systems. And this complexity, together with human reasoning, makes the classical mathematical approaches, based on two-valued logic, ineffective.

So, again, to approximate the way humans can sort through large masses of data and arrive at some sort of a qualitative conclusion, it might be necessary to use fuzzy logic.

Q. Has fuzzy logic been able to solve some of the difficult problems in AI you mentioned earlier? Or is it still just a promise?
ZADEH. These problems are intrinsically complex, and fuzzy logic by itself does not provide a solution to them. Rather, it merely enhances our ability to do so without guaranteeing success. It's a little like finding a

cure for cancer. You may develop a technique that may help in finding a cure but it doesn't guarantee a cure will be found.

Fuzzy logic, then, is a necessary but not sufficient condition to finding solutions to these problems. It is a tool that enhances our ability to deal with problems that are too complex and too ill-defined to be susceptible to solution by conventional means. It will be an ingredient of the tools that will eventually be used to solve these problems.

Q. Have you made any headway in persuading people that they needn't always be superprecise, that in fact such an approach may be an inappropriate approach for attacking certain types of problems?
ZADEH. It will be a slow process. It's not very easy to change some of the basic attitudes people have been educated with, like the attitude that we must be very precise and that we have to try to come up with results that can be stated as theorems. It's difficult to change these attitudes.

Let me draw an analogy with the way people dress. Classical logic is like a person who comes to a party dressed in a black suit, a white, starched shirt, a black tie, shiny shoes, and so forth. And fuzzy logic is a little bit like a person dressed informally, in jeans, tee shirt, and sneakers. In the past, this informal dress wouldn't have been acceptable. Today, it's the other way around. Somebody who comes dressed to a party in the way I described earlier would be considered funny.

Changes in attitude may take place not only in dress but also in science, music, art, and many other fields. And, in science, there may be an increasing willingness to realize that excessively high degree of formalism, rigor, and precision is counterproductive.

Freedom of expression in science could exhibit itself as a movement away from two-valued logic and toward fuzzy logic. Fuzzy logic is much more general and it gives you much more flexibility.

Q. How long will it take for traditional scientific attitudes about precision to change and fuzzy logic to take hold?
ZADEH. Well, I think it will take something on the order of perhaps a couple of decades. Fuzzy logic is making inroads, but it is not something that has coalesced into a broad movement. In other words, there are pockets. These pockets exist in various fields, and of course, there are some people who view these pockets with suspicion and hostility—just as some people who are conservative look with suspicion on those who dress informally.

The difficulty of persuading people has to do also with the question of where does respectability lie. Traditionally, respectability went along with being more mathematical, more precise and more quantitative. And these attitudes go back to Lord Kelvin who said that it's not really a science if it's not quantitative.

But fuzzy logic now challenges that. There are many things that cannot be expressed in numbers, for exam-

608

ple, probabilities that have to be expressed as "very likely," or "unlikely." Such linguistic probabilities may be viewed as fuzzy characterizations of conventional numeric probabilities.

And so in that sense fuzzy logic represents a retreat. It represents a retreat from standards of precision that are unrealistic.

There are many parallels to that sort of thing in the history of human thought, where people didn't realize that the objectives they set were unrealizable.

Q. Does an example or two come to mind of a situation where scientists had to retreat from standards of precision that were not attainable?
ZADEH. Well, a good example of that sort of thing is statistical mechanics. People in the beginning of the nineteenth century were firm believers in the possibility of using the mechanics that were developed at that time by people like Lagrange and applying those mechanics to the solution of all sorts of problems involving the motion of bodies. But then they encountered the "two-body," "three-body," and "n-body" problems, and it became clear that they could not push this too far. That's where the groundwork was laid for statistical mechanics.

So statistical mechanics represented a retreat, a retreat in the sense that you say, "Well, I cannot say something precisely, but I'll say it statistically."

Now, the same thing happened in the case of the solution of differential equations. Today we freely accept numerical solutions. It is hard to realize that the idea of a numerical solution was not acceptable even as recently as perhaps 30–40 years ago.

Q. The rise of numerical analysis, then, constituted a retreat. Was it more of a brute force approach rather than an elegant, logical approach to the solution of differential equations?
ZADEH. Effectively, yes. People were simply not willing to say that, if you use the computer to come up with a numerical solution, you have really done something worthwhile. Somehow we tend to forget that things that are acceptable today were not acceptable 20 to 30 years ago.

Q. I can remember reading books on science of a few decades ago that always spelled science with a capital S.
ZADEH. Yes. It's that kind of veneration or worship I'm talking about. I sometimes use a word that offends people who take the more traditional view, and that word is *fetishism*—fetishism of precision and rigor in the context of classical logic.

There is also what might be referred to as "the curse of respectability in science." In trying to be respectable, scientists deny themselves the use of more flexible logical systems in which truth is a matter of degree.

Q. Is there anything that could be done to get certain people to stop worshiping precision?

ZADEH. I think it has to be a natural process. But because of the current emphasis on AI, and in particular on expert systems, there is a rapidly growing interest in inexact reasoning and processing of knowledge that is imprecise, incomplete, or not totally reliable. And it is in this connection that it will become more and more widely recognized that classical logical systems are inadequate for dealing with uncertainty and that something like fuzzy logic is needed for that purpose.

Q. Since you first developed the concept of fuzzy logic in the 1960s, Professor Zadeh, has there been much of a growth in interest? Have others picked up the banner?
ZADEH. Between then and now, somewhere between 3,000 and 4,000 papers have been written worldwide on fuzzy sets and their applications. And there are two regular journals: *Fuzzy Sets and Systems*, in English, and *Fuzzy Mathematics*, in Chinese. In addition, a quarterly entitled *Bulletin on Fuzzy Sets and their Applications* is published in France. The countries where most activity is taking place at this point are the Soviet Union, China, Japan, France, Great Britain, West Germany, East Germany, Poland, Italy, Spain and India. There has been less activity in the United States.

There is growing acceptance, but there is also considerable skepticism and in some instances hostility. At this point the largest number of researchers working on fuzzy sets is in China.

There appears to be more sympathy for other than two-valued systems in oriental countries, perhaps because their logic is not like Western, Cartesian logic. There is a greater acceptance of truth that is neither perfect truth nor perfect falsehood. This is particularly characteristic of Hindu, Chinese, and Japanese cultures.

Q. Professor Zadeh, that's the end of our questions. We on the editorial staff of *Communications* thank you warmly for giving our readers some of your views.
ZADEH. It was my pleasure.

RECOMMENDED READING
- Dubois and Prade. *Fuzzy Sets and Systems: Theory and Applications.* Academic Press, New York, 1980. This is a good, broad introduction to the subject.
- *Fuzzy Information and Decision Processes.* Elsevier North-Holland, New York, 1982. This is a recent volume of edited papers dealing with both theory and applications.
- *Fuzzy Sets and Possibility Theory.* Pergamon Press, New York, 1982. This is also a recent volume of edited papers dealing with both theory and applications.
- *Fuzzy Reasoning and Its Applications.* Academic Press, New York, 1981. A volume of edited papers.
- *Fuzzy Sets.* Plenum Press, New York, 1980.
- There are three periodicals devoted to fuzzy sets: *Fuzzy Sets and Systems*, Elsevier North-Holland, New York; *Bulletin on Fuzzy Sets and Their Application*, published in Toulouse, France; and *Fuzzy Mathematics* (in Chinese), published in Wuhan, China.

References

Ackerman, W. B. and Dennis, J. B. (1979). "VAL-A Value-Oriented Algorithmic Language," TR-218, Lab. for Computer Science, M.I.T., June.

Ackland, B., Weste, N., and Burr, D. J. (1981). "An Integrated Multiprocessing Array for Time Warp Pattern Matching," Proc. of 8th Ann. Symp. on Computer Architecture, pp. 197-216.

Adams, G. B. and Siegel, H. J. (1982). "The Extra Stage Cube: A Fault-Tolerant Interconnection Network for Supersystems," IEEE Trans. Computers, Vol. C-31, May, pp. 443-454.

Adams, L. (1983). "An M-Step Preconditioned Conjugate Gradient Method for Parallel Computation," Proc. of Int'l. Conf. on Parallel Processing, pp. 36-43.

Agerwala, T. (1977). "Some Extended Semaphore Primitives," Acta Informatica 8, Springer-Verlag.

Agrawal, D. P. (1982). "Graph Theoretical Analysis and Design of Multistage Interconnection Networks," IEEE Trans. Computers, Vol. C-32, July, pp. 637-648.

Agrawal, D. P. and Jain, R. (1982). "A Pipelined Pseudoparallel System Architecture for Real-Time Dynamic Scene Analysis," IEEE Trans. Computers, Vol. C-31, pp. 952-962.

Ahmed, H. M., Delosme, J.-M., and Morf, M. (1982). "Highly Concurrent Computing Structures for Matrix Arithmetic and Signal Processing," IEEE Computer, Vol. 15, No. 1, pp. 65-86.

Ajmone, M. et al. (1983). "Modeling Bus Contention and Memory Interference in a Multiprocessing System," IEEE Trans. Computers, C-32, pp. 60-72.

Alexander, P. (1983). "Array Processors in Medical Imaging," Computer, Vol. 16, No. 6, pp. 17-31.

Algiere, J. L. and Hwang, K. (1983). "Sparse Matrix Techniques for Circuit Analysis on the Cyber 205," TR-EE 83-40, Purdue University, West Lafayette, Indiana, October.

Allen, J. R. and Kennedy, K. (1984). "PFC: A Program to Convert FORTRAN to Parallel Form," in Supercomputers: Design and Applications (K. Hwang, ed.), IEEE Computer Society Press, August.

Amano, H., Yoshida, T., and Aiso, H. (1983). "(SM)²: Sparse Matrix Solving Machine," Proc. of 10th Ann. Symp. on Computer Architecture, pp. 213-221.

Amdahl, G. M., Blaauw, G. A., and Brooks, F. J., Jr. (1964). "Architecture of The IBM System/360," IBM Journal of Research and Development, Vol. 8, No. 2, pp. 87-101.

Anderson, D. W., Earle, J.G., Goldschmidt, R.E., and Powers, D.M. (1967). "The IBM System/360 Model 91: Floating-Point Execution Unit," IBM Journal of Research and Development, January, pp. 34-53.

Anderson, D. W., Sparacio, F. A., and Tomasulo, R. M. (1967). "The IBM System/360 Model 91: Machine Philosophy and Instruction Handling," IBM Journal of Research and Development, Vol. 11, No. 1, pp. 8-24.

Anderson, J. P., Hoffman, S. A., Shifman, J., and Williams, R. J. (1962). "D825-A Multiple Computer System for Command and Control," Proc. AFIPS Fall Joint Computer Conf., Vol. 22, pp. 86-96.

Andrews, G. J. and McGraw, J. R. (1976). "Language Features for Parallel Processing and Resource Control," Proc. of the Conf. on Design and Implementation of Programming Languages, Ithaca, New York, October.

Andrews, G. R. (1981). "Parallel Programs: Proofs, Principles and Practice," Comm. of the ACM, Vol. 24, No. 3, pp. 140-146.

Arden, B. W. and Ginosar, R. (1982). "MP/C: A Multimicroprocessor/Computer Architecture," IEEE Trans. Computers, C-31, pp. 455-473.

Arnold, C. N. (1982). "Performance Evaluation of Three Automatic Vectorizer Packages," Proc. of Int'l. Conf. on Parallel Processing, pp. 235-242.

Arnold, C. N. (1983). "Vector Optimization on the CYBER 205," Proc. of Int'l. Conf. on Parallel Processing, pp. 530-536.

CH0219-6/84/0000/0611$01.00 © 1984 IEEE

References

Ackerman, W. B. and Dennis, J. B. (1979). "VAL-A Value-Oriented Algorithmic Language," *TR-218*, Lab. for Computer Science, M.I.T., June.

Ackland, B., Weste, N., and Burr, D. J. (1981). "An Integrated Multiprocessing Array for Time Warp Pattern Matching," *Proc. of 8th Ann. Symp. on Computer Architecture*, pp. 197-216.

Adams, G. B. and Siegel, H. J. (1982). "The Extra Stage Cube: A Fault-Tolerant Interconnection Network for Supersystems," *IEEE Trans. Computers*, Vol. C-31, May, pp. 443-454.

Adams, L. (1983). "An M-Step Preconditioned Conjugate Gradient Method for Parallel Computation," *Proc. of Int'l. Conf. on Parallel Processing*, pp. 36-43.

Agerwala, T. (1977). "Some Extended Semaphore Primitives," *Acta Informatica 8*, Springer Verlag.

Agrawal, D. P. (1982). "Graph Theoretical Analysis and Design of Multistage Interconnection Networks," *IEEE Trans. Computers*, Vol. C-32, July, pp. 637-648.

Agrawal, D. P. and Jain, R. (1982). "A Pipelined Pseudoparallel System Architecture for Real-Time Dynamic Scene Analysis," *IEEE Trans. Computers*, Vol. C-31, pp. 952-962.

Ahmed, H. M., Delosme, J.-M., and Morf, M. (1982). "Highly Concurrent Computing Structures for Matrix Arithmetic and Signal Processing," *IEEE Computer*, Vol. 15, No. 1, pp. 65-86.

Ajmone, M. et al. (1983). "Modeling Bus Contention and Memory Interference in a Multiprocessing System," *IEEE Trans. Computers*, C-32, pp. 60-72.

Alexander, P. (1983). "Array Processors in Medical Imaging," *Computer*, Vol. 16, No. 6, pp. 17-31.

Algiere, J. L. and Hwang, K. (1983). "Sparse Matrix Techniques for Circuit Analysis on the Cyber 205," *TR-EE 83-40*, Purdue University, West Lafayette, Indiana, October.

Allen, J. R. and Kennedy, K. (1984). "PFC: A Program to Convert FORTRAN to Parallel Form," in *Supercomputers: Design and Applications*, (K. Hwang, ed.), *IEEE Computer Society Press*, August.

Amano, H., Yoshida, T., and Aiso, H. (1983). "(SM)²: Sparse Matrix Solving Machine," *Proc. of 10th Ann. Symp. on Computer Architecture*, pp. 213-221.

Amdahl, G. M., Blaauw, G. A., and Boorks, F. J., Jr. (1964). "Architecture of The IBM System/360," *IBM Journal of Research and Development*, Vol. 8, No. 2, pp. 87-101.

Anderson, D. W., Earle, J.G., Goldschmidt, R.E., and Powers, D.M. (1967). "The IBM System/360 Model 91: Floating-Point Execution Unit," *IBM Journal of Research and Development*, January, pp. 34-53.

Anderson, D. W., Sparacio, F. A., and Tomasulo, R. M. (1967). "The IBM System/360 Model 91: Machine Philosophy and Instruction Handling," *IBM Journal of Research and Development*, Vol. 11, No. 1, pp. 8-24.

Anderson, J. P., Hoffman, S. A., Shifman, J., and Williams, R. J. (1962). "D825-A Multiple Computer System for Command and Control," *Proc. AFIPS Fall Joint Computer Conf.*, Vol. 22, pp. 86-96.

Andrews, G. J. and McGraw, J. R. (1976). "Language Features for Parallel Processing and Resource Control," *Proc. of the Conf. on Design and Implementation of Programming Languages*, Ithaca, New York, October.

Andrews, G. R. (1981). "Parallel Programs: Proofs, Principles and Practice," *Comm. of the ACM*, Vol. 24, No. 3, pp. 140-146.

Arden, B. W. and Ginosar, R. (1982). "MP/C: A Multimicroprocessor/ Computer Architecture," /Computer Architecture," *IEEE Trans. Computers*, C-31, pp. 455-473.

Arnold, C. N. (1982). "Performance Evaluation of Three Automatic Vectorizer Packages," *Proc. of Int'l. Conf. on Parallel Processing*, pp. 235-242.

Arnold, C. N. (1983). "Vector Optimization on the CYBER 205," *Proc. of Int'l. Conf. on Parallel Processing*, pp. 530-536.

Arnold, C. P., Parr, M. I., and Bewe, M. B. (1983). "An Efficient Parallel Algorithm for the Solution of Large Sparse Linear Matrix Equations," *IEEE Trans. Computers,* Vol. C-32, pp. 265-272.

Arnold, J. S., Casey, D. P., and McKinstry, R. H. (1974). "Design of Tightly-Coupled Multiprocessing Programming," *IBM Systems Journal,* No. 1.

Arnold, R. G., Berg, R. O., and Thomas, J. W. (1982). "A Modular Approach to Real-Time Supersystems," *IEEE Trans. Computers,* C-31, pp. 385-398.

Arvind and Brock, J. D. (1984). "Resource Managers in Functional Programming," *Journal of Parallel and Distributed Computing,* Vol. 1, No. 1, August.

Arvind and Iannucci, R. A. (1983). "A Critique of Multiprocessing von Neumann Style," *Proc. of 10th Ann. Symp. Computer Architecture,* June, pp. 426-436.

Arvind, Gostelow, K. P., and Plouffe, W. (1978). "An Asynchronous Programming Language and Computing Machine," *TR-114a,* Department of Information and Computer Science, University of California, Irvine, December

Arvind and Gostelow, K. P. (1982). "The U Interpreter," *IEEE Computer,* Vol. 15, No. 2, pp. 42-50, February

Arvind, Kathail, V., and Pingali, K. (1980). "A Data Flow Architecture with Tagged Tokens," *Technical Memo 174,* Laboratory for Computer Science, MIT, September.

Association of Computing Machinery (1980). "Special Issue on Computer Architecture," *Comm. of the ACM,* Vol. 21, No. 1, January.

Awerbuch, B. and Shiloach, Y. (1983). "New Connectivity and MSF Algorithms for Ultracomputer and PRAM," *Proc. of Int'l. Conf. on Parallel Processing,* pp. 175-179.

Baba, T. et al. (1983). "Hierarchical Micro-Architectures of a Two-Level Microprogrammed Multiprocessor Computer," *Proc. of Int'l Conf. on Parallel Processing,* pp. 478-485.

Baccelli, F. and Fleury. T. (1982). "On Parsing Arithmetic Expressions in a Multiprocessing Environment," *Acta Informatica,* Vol. 17, pp. 287-310.

Backus, J. (1978). "Can Programming be Liberated from the von Neumann Style? A Functional Style and its Algebra of Programs," *Comm. of the ACM,* Vol. 21, No. 8, August, pp. 613-641.

Baer, J. L. (1980). *Computer Systems Architectures,* Computer Science Press., Rockville, Maryland.

Baer, J. L. and Ellis, C. (1977). "Model, Design, and Evaluation of a Compiler for a Parallel Processing Environment," *IEEE Trans. on Soft. Eng., SE-3,* November, pp. 394-405.

Bahandarkar, D. P. (1975). "Analysis of Memory Interference in Multiprocessors," *IEEE Trans. Computers, C-24,* September, pp. 897-908.

Bain, W. L., Jr. and Ahuja, S. R. (1981). "Performance Analysis of High-Speed Digital Buses for Multiprocessing Systems," *Proc. 8th Ann. Symp. on Computer Architecture,* May, pp. 107-131.

Ballhaus, W. F. (1984). "Supercomputing in Aerodynamics," in *Frontier in Supercomputing,* University of California Press.

Banerjee, U., Gajski, D., and Kuck, D. (1983). "Accessing Sparse Arrays in Parallel Memories," *J. of VLSI .....and Computer Systems,* Vol. 1, No. 1, pp. 69-99.

Barke, D. F. (ed.) (1980). *Very Large Scale Integration (VLSI): Fundamentals and Applications,* Springer-Verlag, New York.

Barlow, R. H., Evans, D. J., and Shanehchi, J. (1982). "Comparative Study of the Exploitation of Different Levels of Parallelism on Different Parallel Architectures," *Proc. of Int'l. Conf. on Parallel Processing,* pp. 34-40.

Barnes, G. H., Brown, R.M., Kato, M., Kuck, D.J., Slotnick, D.L., and Stokes, R.A. (1968). "The ILLIAC IV Computer," *IEEE Trans. Computers,* August, pp. 746-757.

Barnwell, T. P., III and Hodges, C. J. M. (1982). "Optimal Implementation of Signal Flow Graphs on Synchronous Multiprocessors," *Proc. of Int'l. Conf. on Parallel Processing,* pp. 90-95.

Baskett, F. and Keller, T. W. (1977). "An Evaluation of the CRAY-1 Computer," In *High Speed Computer and Algorithm Organization* edited by D. J. Kuck, *et al.*) Academic Press, New York, pp. 71-84.

Batcher, K. E. (1976). "The Flip Network in STARAN," *Int'l. Conf. Parallel Processing*, August, pp. 65-71.

Batcher, K. E. (1977). "The Multi-dimensional Access Memory in STARAN," *IEEE Trans. Computers*, pp. 174-177.

Batcher, K. E. (1980). "Design of a Massively Parallel Processor," *IEEE Trans. Computers*, Vol. C-29, September, pp. 836-840.

Batcher, K. E. (1982). "Bit-serial Parallel Processing Systems," *IEEE Trans. Computers*, C-31, pp. 377-384.

Baudet, G. M. (1978). "Asynchronous Iterative Methods for Multiprocessors," *Journal of the ACM*, Vol. 25, No. 2, pp. 226-244, April.

Beijing Review (1984). "Galaxy Supercomputer," *Beijing Review*, Vol. 27, Peking, China, January, p. 8.

Bell, C. G., Mudge, J. C., and McNamara, J. (1978). *Computer Engineering: A DEC View of Hardware Systems Design*, Digital Press, Bedford, Massachusettes.

Bell, J., Casasent, D., and Bell, C. G. (1974). "An Investigation of Alternative Cache Organizations," *IEEE Trans. Computers*, C-23, April, pp. 346-351.

Benes, V. E. (1965). *Mathematical Theory of Connecting Networks and Telephone Traffic*, Academic Press, New York.

Bensoussan, A., Clingen, C. T., and Daley, R. C. (1972). "The MULTICS Virtual Memory: Concepts and Design," *CACM 15*, May, pp. 308-315.

Berger, P., Brouaye, P., and Syre, J. C. (1982). "A Mesh Coloring Method for Efficient MIMD Processing in Finite Element Problems," *Proc. of Int'l. Conf. on Parallel Processing*, pp. 41-46.

Bernstein, A. J. (1966). "Analysis of Programs for Parallel Processing," *IEEE Trans. Elec. Computers*, E-15, October, pp. 746-757.

Berra, P. B. and Oliver, E. (1979). "The Role of Associative Array Processors in Database Machine Architecture," *IEEE Computer*, March, pp. 53-61.

Bhandarkar, D. P. (1975). "Analysis of Memory Interference in Multiprocessors," *IEEE Trans. on Computers*, C-24, Sept. 897-908.

Bhandarkar, D. P. (1977). "Some Performance Issues in Multiprocessor System Design," *IEEE Trans. Computers*, Vol. C-26, No. 5, pp. 506-511, May.

Bhuyan, L. N. (1984). "On the Performance of Loosely Coupled Multiprocessors," *Proc. of the 11th Annual Int'l Symp. on Computer Architecture*, Ann Arbor, Michigan, June 5-7, pp. 256-262.

Bhuyan, L. N. and Lee, C. W. (1983). "An Interference Analysis of Interconnection Networks," *Proc. of Int'l. Conf. on Parallel Processing*, pp. 2-9.

Bic, L. (1984a). "Data-Driven Logic: A Basic Model," *Proc. of the Int'l Workshop on High-Level Computer Architecture*, May, pp. 1.20-1.25.

Bic, L. (1984b). "Execution of Logic Programs on a Dataflow Architecture," *Proc. of the 11th Annual Int'l Symp. on Computer Architecture*, Ann Arbor, Michigan, June 5-7, pp. 290-296.

Bisiani, R., Mauersberg, H., and Reddy, R. (1983). "Task-Oriented Architecture," *Proc. of IEEE*, Vol. 71, No. 7, pp. 885-898.

Bode, A. and Händler, W. (1980, 1982). *Rechnerarchitektur: Grundlagen und Verfahren*, Springer-Verlag, Berlin (Volumes 1 and 2).

Bonuccelli, M. A. et al. (1983). "A VLSI Area Machine for Relational Data Bases," *Proc. of 10-th Ann. Symp. on Computer Architecture*, pp. 67-75.

Borgeson, B. R., Hanson, M. L., and Hartley, P. A. (1978). "The Evolution of the Sperry Univac 1100 Series: A History, Analysis, and Projection," *Communication of the ACM*, Vol. 21, No. 1, January, pp. 25-43.

Borodin, A., Gathen, J. V., and Hopcroft, J. (1982). "Fast Parallel Matrix and GCD Computations," *Information and Control*, Vol. 52, No. 3, pp. 241-256.

Bose, P. and Davidson, E. S. (1984). "Design of Instruction Set Architectures for Support of High-Level Languages," *Proc. of the 11th Annual Int'l Symp. on Computer Architecture*, Ann Arbor, Michigan, June 5-7, pp. 198-207.

Bouknight, W. J., Denenberg, S. A., McIntyre, D. E., Randall, J. M., Sameh, A. H., and Slotnick, D. L. (1972). "The Illiac IV System," *Proc. IEEE*, Vol. 60, No 4, April, pp. 369-388.

Bovet, D. P. and Vanneschi, M. (1976). "Models and Evaluation of Pipeline Systems," In *Computer Architectures and Networks*, (Gelenbe and Mahl, eds.), North Holland, pp. 99-111.

Bowler, K. C. and Pawley, G. S. (1984). "Molecular Dynamics and Monte Carlo Simulations in Solid-State and Elementary Particle Physics," *Proc. Of IEEE*, Jauary, pp. 42-55.

Brengle, T. A., Cohen, B. I., and Stewart, M. E. (1983). "Simulating Field-Reversed Magnetic-Mirror Fusion Devices," *Computer*, Vol. 16, No. 6, pp. 44-50.

Brent, R. (1974). "The Parallel Evaluation of General Arithmetic Expressions," *Journal of the ACM*, Vol. 21, No. 2, pp. 201-206, April.

Brent, R. P. and Goldschlager, L. M. (1982). "Some Area-Time Tradeoffs for VLSI," *SIAM J. Computers*, Vol. 11, pp. 737-747.

Brent, R. P. and Kung, H. T. (1982). "A Regular Layout for Parallel Adders," *IEEE Trans. Computers*, C-31, pp. 260-264.

Briggs, F. A. and Davidson, E. S. (1977). "Organization of Semiconductor Memories for Parallel-Pipelined Processors, *IEEE Trans. Computers*, February pp. 162-169.

Briggs, F. A. and Dubois, M. (1983). "Effectiveness of Private Caches in Multiprocessor Systems with Parallel-Pipelined Memories," *IEEE Trans. Computers*, Vol. C-32, No. 1, January, pp. 48-59.

Briggs, F. A., Dubois, M., and Hwang, K. (1981). "Throughput Analysis and Configuration Design of a Shared-Resource Multiprocessors Systems: PUMPS," *Proc. The 8th Ann. Symp. Computer Architecture*, IEEE Computer Society, May, pp. 67-80.

Briggs, F. A., Fu, K. S., Hwang, K., and Wah, B. W. (1982). "PUMPS Architecture for Pattern Analysis and Image Database Management," *IEEE Trans. Computers*, Vol. C-31, No. 10, October, pp. 969-982.

Brinch Hansen, P. (1975). "The Programming Language Concurrent Pascal," *IEEE Trans. of Software Engineering*, SE-1, 6 199-207, June.

Brock, J. D. and Montz, L. B. (1979). "Translation and Optimization of Data Flow Programs," *Proc. of the 1979 Int'l Conf. on Parallel Processing*, August, 46-54.

Brode, B. (1981). "Precompilation of Fortran Programs to Facilitate Array Processing," *IEEE Computer*, Vol. 14, No. 9, pp. 46-51.

Bronson, E. C. and Siegel, L. J. (1982). "A Parallel Architecture for Acoustic Processing in Speech Understanding," *Proc. of Int'l. Conf. on Parallel Processing*, pp. 307-312.

Browning, S. A. (1980). "The Tree Machine: A Highly Concurrent Computing Environment," *Ph.D. Thesis*, Dept. of Computer Science, California Institute of Technology, Pasadena, California.

Bucher, I. Y. (1983). "The Computational Speed of Supercomputers," In *Performance Evaluation Review: Proc. ACM Sigmetrics Conf. on Measurement and Modeling of Computer Systems*, pp. 151-165, August.

Bucholz, W. (1962). *Planning a Computer System: Project Stretch*, McGraw-Hill, New York, New York.

Bucy, R. S. et al. (1983). "Nonlinear Filtering and Array Computation," *Computer*, Vol. 16, No. 6, pp. 51-61.

Budnik, P. P., and Kuck, D. J. (1971). "The Organization and Use of Parallel Memories," *IEEE Trans. Computers*, Vol. 20, pp. 1566-1569, December.

Buehrer, R. E. et al. (1982). "The ETH-Multiprocessor EMPRESS: A Dynamically Configurable MIMD System," *IEEE Trans. Computers*, C-31, pp. 1035-1044.

Burkley, J. T. (1982). "MPP VLSI Multiprocessor Integrated Circuit Design," In *Proc. of Int'l. Conf. on Parallel Processing*, pp. 268-270.

Burkowski, F. J. (1984). "A Vector and Array Multiprocessor Extension of the Sylvan Architecture," *Proc. of the 11th Annual Int'l Symp. on Computer Architecture,* Ann Arbor, Michigan, June 5-7, pp. 4-11.

Burnett, G. J. and Coffman, E. G. (1970). "A Study of Interleaved Memory Systems," *Proc. Spring Joint Computer Conf., AFIPS,* SJCC, Vol. 36, pp. 467-474.

Burroughs Co. (1977). "BSP: Implementation of FORTRAN," *Document No. 61391,* November, (18 pages).

Buzbee, B. L. et al. (1983). "Supercomputing Value and Trends," unpublished slide presentation, July, Los Alamos National Laboratory, Computing Division, Los Alamos, New Mexico.

Buzen, J. P. (1975). "I/O Subsystem Architecture," *Proc. IEEE, 63,* June, pp. 871-879.

Carlson, W. W. and Hwang, K. (1984). "On Structural Data Accessing in Dataflow Computers," *Proc. of the First Int'l. Conf. on Computers and Applications,* Beijing, China, June 20-24.

Case, R. P. and Padegs, A. (1978). "Architecture of the IBM System 370," *Comm. of the ACM,* Vol. 21, No. 1, pp. 73-96, January.

Castan, M. and Organick, E. I. (1982). "u3L: An HLL-RISC Processor for Parallel Execution of FP-Language Programs," *Proc. of 9th Ann. Symp. on Computer Architecture,* pp. 238-247.

Censier, L. M., and Feautrier, P. (1978). "A New Solution to Coherence Problems in Multicache Systems," *IEEE Trans. Computers,* C-27, December, pp. 1112-1118.

Cezzer, R. and Klappholz, D. (1983). "Process Management Overhead in a Speedup-Oriented MIMD System," *Proc. of Int'l. Conf. on Parallel Processing,* pp. 395-403.

Chamberlin, D. D. (1971). "Parallel Implementation of a Single Assignment Language," *Ph.D. Thesis,* Stanford University, January.

Chamberlin, D. D., Fuller, S. H., and Liu, L. Y. (1973). "An Analysis of Page Allocation Strategies for Multiprogramming Systems with Virtual Memory," *IBM Journal of Research and Development* p. 17.

Chandy, K. M. (1975). "Models for the Recognition and Scheduling of Parallel Tasks on Multiprocessor Systems," *Bulletin of the Operations Research Society of America,* Vol. 23, Suppl. 1, p. B-117, Spring.

Chang, D., Kuck, D. J., and Lawrie, D. H. (1977). "On the Effective Bandwidth of Parallel Memories," *IEEE Trans. Computers,* Vol. C-26, No. 5, pp. 480-490, May.

Charlesworth, A. E. (1981). "An Approach to Scientific Array Processing: The Architectural Design of the AP-120B/FPS-164 Family," *IEEE Computer,* December, pp. 12-30.

Chen, C. L. (1984). "Error-Correcting Codes for Semiconductor Memories," *Proc. of the 11th Annual Int'l Symp. on Computer Architecture,* Ann Arbor, Michigan, June 5-7, pp. 245-247.

Chen, N. F. and Liu, C. L. (1974). "On a Class of Scheduling Algorithms for Multiprocessor Computing Systems," *Proc. of the Conf. on Parallel Processing,* Raquette Lake, New York, August.

Chen, S. C. (1983). "Large-Scale and High-Speed Multiprocessor System for Scientific Applications," In *Proc. of NATO Advanced Res. Workshop on High-Speed Computing,* (Kawalick, ed.), West Germany, June.

Chen, S. C., Dongarra, J., and Hsiung, C. C. (1984). "Multiprocessing for Linear Algebra Algorithms on the Cray X-MP-2: Experience with Small Granularity," *Journal of Parallel and Distributed Computing,* Vol. 1, No. 1, August.

Chen, T. C. (1980). "Overlap and Pipeline Processing," in *Introduction to Computer Architecture,* Chap. 9, (Stone, ed.), Science Research Associates, Inc., Chicago, pp. 427-486.

Chern, M. Y. and Murata, T. (1983). "A Fast Algorithm for Concurrent LU Decomposition and Matrix Inversion," *Proc. of Int'l. Conf. on Parallel Processing,* pp. 79-86.

Chiang, Y. P. and Fu, K. S. (1983). "Matching Parallel Algorithm and Architecture," *Proc. of Int'l. Conf. on Parallel Processing,* pp. 374-380.

Chin, C. Y. (1984). "Packet Switching Networks and Routing Algorithms," *Ph.D. Thesis*, School of Electrical Engineering, Purdue University, W. Lafayette, Indiana, May.

Chin, C. Y. and Hwang, K. (1984a). "Multipath Packet Switching Networks for Multiprocessors and Dataflow Computers," *IEEE Trans. Computers*, accepted to appear.

Chin, C. Y. and Hwang, K. (1984b). "Connection Principles for Multipath Packet Switching Networks," *Proc. of the 11th Annual Int'l Symp. on Computer Architecture*," Ann Arbor, Michigan, June 5-7, pp. 99-109.

Chin, F. Y., Lam, J., and Chen I-N. (1982). "Efficient Parallel Algorithms for Some Graph Problems," *Comm. of the ACM*, Vol. 25, pp. 659-665.

Chow, C. K. (1974). "On Optimatization of Storage Hierarchies," *IBM Journal of Research and Development*, May, pp. 194-203.

Chow, Y. C. and Kohler, W. H. (1979). "Models for Dynamic Load Balancing in a Heterogeneous Multiple Processor System," *IEEE Trans. Computers*, May, pp. 354-361.

Chu, K. H. and Fu, K. S. (1982). "VLSI Architectures for High-Speed Recognition of Context-Free Languages and Finite State Languages," *Proc. of 9th Ann. Symp. on Computer Architecture*, pp. 43-49.

Chu, Y. and Abrams, M. (1981). "Programming Languages and Direct-Execution Computer Architecture," *IEEE Computer*, Vol. 14, July, pp. 22-40.

Chu, Y. and Abrams, M. (1984). "An Ada Concurrency Instruction Set," *Proc. of the Int'l Workshop on High-Level Computer Architecture*, Los Angeles, California, May, pp. 7.1-7.9.

Coffman, E. G., Jr., Elphick, M. J., and Shoshani, A. (1971). "System Deadlocks," *ACM Computing Surveys*, Vol. 3, pp. 67-78.

Coffman, E. G., ed. (1976). *Computer and Job-Shop Scheduling Theory*, John Wiley, New York.

Cohen, E. and Jefferson, D. (1975). "Protection in the Hydra Operating System," *Proc. of the 5th Symp. on Operating System Principles*, November, pp. 141-160.

Cohen, T. (1978). "Structured Flowcharts for Multiprocessing," *Computer Languages*, Vol. 13, No. 4, pp. 209-226.

Cohler, E. U. and Storer, J. E. (1981). "Functionally Parallel Architecture for Array Processors, *IEEE Computer*, Vol. 14, No. 9, pp. 41-44.

Connors, W. D., Florkowski, J. H., and Patton, S. K. (1979). "The IBM 3033: An Inside Look," *Datamation*, May, pp. 198-218.

Conrad, V. and Wallach (1977). "Iterative Solution of Linear Equations on a Parallel Processor System," *IEEE Trans. Computers*, September, pp. 838-847.

Conti, C. J. (1969), "Concepts for Buffer Storage," *Computer Group News*, March, pp. 9-13.

Control Data Corp., (1979a). *CDC Cyber 200 Fortran Language 1.4 Reference Manual*, Pub. No. 60456040.

Control Data Corp., (1979b). *CPC Cyber 200 Operating System 1.4 Reference Manual*, Pub. No. 60457000, Vol. 1 of 2.

Control Data Corp. (1980). *CDC Cyber 200/Model 205 Technical Description*, November.

Conway, M. (1963). "A Multiprocessor System Design," *Proc. AFIPS Fall Joint Comput. Conf.*, Spartan Books, New York, pp. 139-146.

Cooper, R. G. (1977). "The Distributed Pipeline," *IEEE Trans. Computers*, November pp. 1123-1132.

Cordennier, V. (1975). "A Two Dimension Pipelined Processor for Communication in a Parallel System, In *Proc. 1975 Sagamore Computers Conf. on Parallel Processing*, pp. 115-121.

Crane, B. A., Gilmartin, M. J., Huttenhoff, J. H., Rus, P. T., and Shively, R. R. (1972). "PEPE Computer Architecture," *IEEE Compcon*, pp. 57-60.

Cray Research, Inc., (1977). *CRAY-1 Computer System Hardware Reference Manual*, Bloomington, Minnesota, Pub. No. 2240004.

Cray Research, Inc. (1978). *CRAY-1 Computer System Preliminary CRAY FORTRAN (CFT) Reference Manual*, Bloomington, Minnesota, Pub. No. 2240009.

Cray Research Inc. (1979). *Cray-1 Fortran (CFT) Reference Manual*, Pub. No. 2240009, December.

Crustafson, R. N. and Sparacio, F. J. (1982). "IBM 3081 Processor Unit: Design Considerations and Design Process," *IBM Journal of Research and Development*, Vol. 26, No. 1, January, pp. 12-21.

Culik, K., Graska, J., and Salomaa, A. (1983). "Systolic Automata for VLSI on Balanced Trees," *Acta Informatica*,

Danielsson, P. E. and Levialdi, S. (1981). "Computer Architectures for Pictorial Information Systems," *IEEE Computer*, Vol. 14, No. 11, pp. 53-67.

DARPA (1983). "Strategic Computing: New-Generation Computing Technology," Defense Advanced Research Projects Agency, Arlington, Virginia, October.

Dasgupta, S. and Clafsson, M. (1982). "Towards a Family of Languages for the Design and Implementation of Machine Architectures," *Proc. of 9th Ann. Symp. on Computer Architecture*, pp. 158-170.

Datawest Corp. (1979). "Real Time Series of Microprogrammable Array Transform Processors," Prod. Bulletin Series B.

Davidson, E. S. (1971). "The Design and Control of Pipelined Function Generators," *Proc. 1971 Int'l. IEEE Conf. on Systems, Networks, and Computers*, Oaxtepec, Mexico, January, pp. 19-21.

Davis, A. L. (1975). "The Architecture and System Methodology of DDM1: A Recursively-Structured Data Driven Machine," *Proc. of 5th Symp. on Computer Architecture*, pp. 210-215.

Davis, A. L. and Keller, R. M. (1982). "Data Flow Program Graphs," *IEEE Computer*, Vol. 15, No. 2, pp. 26-40.

Davis, C. G. and Couch, R. L. (1980). "Ballistic Missile Defense: A Supercomputer Challenge," *IEEE Computer*, November pp. 37-46.

Dekel, E., Nassimi, D., and Sahni, S. H. (1981). "Parallel Matrix and Graph Algorithms," *SIAM J. Computers*, Vol. 10, pp. 657-675.

Deminet, J. (1982). "Experience with Multiprocessor Algorithms," *IEEE Trans. Computers*, C-31 (4), pp. 278-288, April.

Demos, G., Brown, M. D., and Weinberg, R. A. (1984). "Digital Scene Simulation: The Synergy of Computer Technology and Human Creativity," *Proc. of IEEE*, January, pp. 22-31.

Denelcor, Inc. (1981). "Heterogeneous Element Processor: Principles of Operation," April.

Denning, P. J. (1978). "Operating Systems Principles for Data Flow Networks," *IEEE Computer Magazine*, July, pp. 86-96.

Denning, P. J. (1980). "Working Sets Past and Present," *IEEE Trans. Software Eng.*, Vol. SE-6, No. 1, January

Denning, P. J. and Swartz, S. C. (1972). "Properties of the Working Set Model," *Communications of the ACM*, 15.

Dennis, J. B. (1980). "Data Flow Supercomputers," *IEEE Computer Magazine*, November, pp. 48-56.

Dennis, J. B., Leung, C. K., and Misunas, D. P. (1979). "A Highly Parallel Processor Using a Data Flow Machine Language," *CSG Memo 134-1*, Lab for Computer Science, M.I.T., June.

Dennis, J. B., Boughton, G. A., and Leung, C. K. (1980). "Building Blocks for Data Flow Prototypes," *Symp. on Computer Architecture*, May, pp. 193-200.

Dennis, J. and Gao, R. (1983). "Maximum Pipelining of Array Operations on Static Dataflow Machine," *Proc. of 1983 Int'l. Conf. on Parallel Processing*, August, pp. 23-26.

Dennis, J. B., and Weng, K. (1977). "Application of dataflow computation to the weather problem," in *High Speed Computer and Algorithm Organization*, edited by D. J. Kuck, et al., Academic Press, New York, pp. 143-157.

Department of Defense, U.S. (1982). *Reference Manual for the Ada Programming Language*, Washington, D.C., July.

Despain, A. M. and Patterson, D. A. (1978). "X-tree--A Tree Structured Multiprocessor Computer Architecture," *Proc. 5th Symp. on Computer Architecture,* pp. 144-151.

D'Hollander, E. H. (1981). "Speedup Bounds for Continuous System Simulation on a Homogeneous Multiprocessor," *Proc. of Int'l. Conf. on Parallel Processing,* pp. 176-182.

Dias, D. M. and Jump, J. R. (1981). "Packet Switching Interconnection Networks for Modular Systems," *IEEE Computer,* December, pp. 43-53.

Dijkstra, E. W. (1965). "Solution of a Problem in Concurrent Programming," *Comm. of the ACM,* 8, September, 569-570.

Dijkstra, E. W. (1968). "Cooperating Sequential Processes," in *Programming Languages* (F. Genuys ed.), Academic Press, New York, pp. 43-112.

Dimopoulos, N. (1983). "The Homogeneous Multiprocessor Architecture — Structure and Performance Analysis," *Proc. of Int'l. Conf. on Parallel Processing,* pp. 520-523.

Dohi, Y., Suzuki, A., and Matsui, N. (1982). "Hardware Sorter and Its Application to Data Base Machine," *Proc. of 9th Ann. Symp. on Computer Architecture,* pp. 218-228.

Doran, R. W. (1982). "The Amdahl 470 V/8 and the IBM 3033: A Comparison of Processor Designs," *IEEE Computer,* Vol. 15, No. 4, pp. 27-36.

Dowsing, R. D. (1976). "Processor Management in a Multiprocessor System," *Electronic Letters,* Vol. 12, No. 24, November.

Dubois, M. (1982). "Analytical Methodologies for the Evaluation of Multiprocessing Structures," *Ph.D. Thesis,* Purdue University, West Lafayette, Indiana.

Dubois, M. and Briggs, F. A. (1982a). "Effects of Cache Coherency in Multiprocessors," *IEEE Trans. Computers,* C-31, No. 11, November.

Dubois, M. and Briggs, F. A. (1982b). "Performance of Synchronized Iterative Processes in Multiprocessor Systems," *IEEE Trans. Software Eng.,* July, pp. 419-431.

Duff, M. J. B. (ed.) (1983). *Computing Structures for Image Processing,* Academic Press, London.

Editor of FEN (1982). "CRAY Supercomputers and Finite Element Analysis," *Finite-Element News,* No. 5, October.

El-Ayat, K. A. (1979). "The Intel 8089: An Integrated I/0 Processor," *IEEE Computer,* Vol. 12, No. 6, pp. 67-78, June.

Emer, J. S. and Davidson, E. S. (1978). "Control Store Organization for Multiple Stream Pipelined Processors," *Proc. 1978 Int'l. Conf. on Parallel Processing,* pp. 43-48.

Enslow, P. H. (1977). "Multiprocessor Organization," *Computing Surveys,* Vol. 9, March, pp. 103-129.

Enslow, P. H., (ed.) (1974). *Multiprocessors and Parallel Processing,* Wiley-Interscience, New York.

Ercegovac, M. D. and Karplus, W. J. (1984). "On a Dataflow Approach in High-Speed Simulation of Continuous Systems," *Proc. of Int'l Workshop on High-Level Computer Architecture,* Los Angeles, California, May, pp. 2.1-2.8.

Ericsson, T. and Danielsson, P. E. (1983). "LIPP — A SIMD Multiprocessor Architecture for Image Processing," *Proc. of 10th Ann. Symp. on Computer Architecture,* pp. 395-401.

Eriksen, O. and Staunstrup, J. (1983). "Concurrent Algorithms for Root Searching," *Acta Informatica,* Vol. 18, pp. 361-376.

ETA Systems (1983). "The New Force in Supercomputing," *Announcement Note,* ETA Systems, Inc., St. Paul, Minn., December.

Evans, D. J. (ed.) (1982). *Parallel Processing Systems,* Cambridge University Press, England.

Evensen, A. J. and Troy, J. L., (1973). "Introduction to the Architecture of a 288 - Element PEPE," *Proc. Sagamore Conf. on Parallel Processing,* pp. 162-169.

Fabry, R. S. (1974). "Capability-based Addressing," *Comm. of the ACM,* Vol. 17, July, pp. 403-412.

Faggin, F. (1978). "How VLSI Impacts Computer Architecture," *IEEE Spectrum,* 15, May, pp. 28-31.

Fairbairn, D. G. (1982). "VLSI: A New Frontier for System Designers," *IEEE Computers,* January, pp. 87-96.

Farouki, R. T. et al. (1983). "Computational Astrophysics on the Array Processor," *IEEE Computer*, Vol. 16, No. 6, pp. 73-84.

Feierbach, G., and Stevenson, D. K. (1978). "The Phoenix Array Processing System," *Phoenix Project Memo. 7*, NASA Ames Research Center, Mountain View, California.

Feng, T. Y. (1974). "Data Manipulation Functions in Parallel Processors and Their Implementations," *IEEE Trans. Computers*, Vol. C-23, No. 3, March. pp. 309-318.

Feng, T. Y. (ed.) (1977). "Parallel Processors and Processing," Special issue, *ACM Computing Surveys*, Vol. 9, No. 1, March.

Feng, T. Y. (1981). "A Survey of Interconnection Networks," *IEEE Computer Magazine*, December, pp. 12-27.

Fennell, K. D. and Lesser, V. R. (1977). "Parallelism in Artificial Intelligence Problem Solving: A Case Study of Hearsay II," *IEEE Trans. Computers*, March, pp. 98-111.

Fernbach, S. (1981). "Applications of Supercomputers in the US: Today and Tomorrow," *Proc. of Symp. on Supercomputer Architecture*, Tokyo, Japan, October, pp. 33-79.

Ferrari, D. (1974). "An Analytic Study of Memory Allocation in Multiprocessing System," in *Computer Architecture and Networks*, (Gelenbe and Mahl, eds.), North Holland, New York.

Fichtner, W., Nagal, L. W., Penumali, B. R., Peterson, W. P., and D'Arcy, J. L., "The Impact of Supercomputers on IC Technology Development and Designs," *Proc. of IEEE*, January, pp. 96-112.

Fisher, A. L. and Kung, H. T. (1983). "Synchronizing Large VLSI Processor Arrays," *Proc. of 10th Ann. Symp. on Computer Architecture*, pp. 54-58.

Fisher, J. A. (1983). "Very Long Instruction Word Architectures and the ELI-512," *Proc. of 10th Ann. Symp. on Computer Architecture*, pp. 140-149.

Flanders, P. M. (1982). "A Unified Approach to a Class of Data Movements on an Array Processor," *IEEE Trans. Computers*, C-31, pp. 809-819.

Floyd, R. W. and Ullman, J. D. (1982). "The Compilation of Regular Expressions into Integrated Circuits," *Journal of the ACM*, Vol. 29, pp. 603-622.

Flynn, M. J. (1972). "Some Computer Organization and Their Effectiveness," *IEEE Trans, Computers*. Vol. C-21, No. 9, September pp. 948-60.

Flynn, M. J. (1977). "The Interpretive Interface: Resources and Program Representation in Computer Organization," in *High Speed Computer and Algorithm Organization* (edited by Kuck et al.), Academic Press, New York, pp. 41-69.

Fontao, R. O. (1971). "A Concurrent Algorithm for Avoiding Deadlocks in Multiprocess Multiple Resonance Systems," *Proc. 3rd Symp. Operating System Principles*, October

Forsstrom, K. S. (1983). "Array Processors in Real-Time Flight Simulation," *IEEE Computer*, Vol. 16, No. 6, pp. 62-72.

Fortes, J. A. B. and Moldovan, D. I. (1984). "Data Broadcasting in Linearly Scheduled Array Processors," *Proc. of the 11th Annual Int'l Symp. on Computer Architecture*, Ann Arbor, Michigan, June 5-7, pp. 224-231.

Foster, C. C. (1976). *Content-Addressable Parallel Processors*, Van Nostrand Reinhold Co., New York.

Foster, M. J. and Kung, H. T. (1980). "The Design of Special-Purpose VLSI Chips," *IEEE Computer*, Vol. 13, No. 1, pp. 26-40.

Franklin, M. A. and Wann, D. F. (1981). "Pin Limitation and VLSI Interconnection Networks," *Proc. of Int'l. Conf. on Parallel Processing*, pp. 253-258.

Franklin, M. S. and Soong, N. L. (1981). "One-Dimensional Optimization on Multiprocessor Systems," *IEEE Trans. Computers*, C-30, pp. 61-66.

Franta, W. R. and Houle, P. A. (1974). "Comments on Models of Multiprocessor Multi-Memory Bank Computer Systems," *Proc. of the 1974 Winter Simulation Conf.*, Vol. I, Washington, D.C., January.

Friedman, A. and Kershaw, D. (1982). "Vectorized Incomplete Cholesky Conjugate Gradient (ICCG) Package for the Gray-1 Computer," *Laser Program Ann. Report* UCRL-500021-81, Lawrence Livermore National Lab., Livermore, California.

Fritsch, G., Kleinoeder, W., Linster, C. U., and Volkert, J. (1983). "EMSY 85 The Erlangen Multiprocessor System for a Broad Spectrum of Applications," *Proc. of 1983 Int'l. Conf. on Parallel Processing*, August, pp. 325-330.

Fromm, H. et al. (1983). "Experiences with performance Measurement and Modeling of a Processor Array," *IEEE Trans. Computers*, C-32, pp. 15-31.

Fuller, S. H. and Harbison, S. P. (1978). *The C.mmp Multiprocessor*, Technical Report, Computer Science Dept., Carnegie-Mellon University, Pittsburgh, Pennsylvania.

Fuss, D. and Tull, C. G. (1984). "Centralized Supercomputer Support for Magnetic Fusion Energy Research," *Proc. of IEEE*, January, pp. 32-41.

Gaillat, G. (1983). "The Design of a Parallel Processor for Image Processing On-Board Satellites: An Application Oriented Approach," *Proc. of 10th Ann. Conf. on Computer Architecture*, pp. 379-386.

Gajski, D., Kim, W. and Fushimi, S. (1984). "A Parallel Pipelined Relational Query Processor: An Architectural Overview," *Proc. of the 11th Annual Int'l Symp. on Computer Architecture*, Ann Arbor, Michigan, June 5-7, pp. 134-141.

Gajski, D. D. (1981). "An Algorithm for Solving Linear Recurrence Systems on Parallel and Pipelined Machines," *IEEE Trans. Computers*, March, pp. 190-205.

Gajski, D. D., Panda, D. A., Kuck, D. J., and Kuhn, R. H. (1982). "A Second Opinion on Dataflow Machines and Languages," *IEEE Computer*, February, pp. 58-70.

Gajski, D., Kuck, D., Lawrie, D., and Sameh, A. (1983). "Construction of a Large Scale Multiprocessor," *Rept. No. UiUCDCS-R-(3-1123*, Dept. of Computer Science, University of Illinois, Urbana, February.

Gallopoulos, E. J. and McEwan, S. D. (1983). "Numerical Experiments with the Massively Parallel Processor," *Proc. of Int'l. Conf. on Parallel Processing*, pp. 29-35.

Gannon, D. (1981). "On Mapping Non-uniform PDE Structures and Algorithms onto Uniform Array," *Proc. of Int'l. Conf. on Parallel Processing*, pp. 100-105.

Gao, Q. S. and Zhang, X. (1980). "Another Approach to Making Supercomputer by Microprocessors -- Cellular Vector Computer of Vertical and Horizontal Processing with Virtual Common Memory," *Int'l. Conf. Parallel Processing*, August, pp. 163-164.

Gao, G. R. (1984). "Pipelined Mapping of Homogeneous Dataflow Programs," *Proc. of Int'l Conf. on Parallel Processing*, August.

Gaudet, G., and Stevenson, D. (1978). "Optimal Sorting Algorithms for Parallel Computers," *IEEE Trans. Computers*, Vol. C-27, January, pp. 84-87.

Gaudiot, J. L. (1982). "On Program Decomposition and Partitioning in Dataflow Systems," *Ph.D. Thesis*, Dept. of Computer Science, University of Calif. at Los Angeles, October

Gaudiot, J. L. and Ercegovac, M. D. (1982). "A Scheme for Handling Arrays in Dataflow Systems," *Proc. 3rd Int'l. Conf. on Distributed Computing Systems*, Hollywood, Florida, October.

Gecsei, J. and Lukes, J. A. (1974). "A Model for the Evaluation of Storage Hierarchies," *IBM System Journal*, No. 2, pp. 163-178.

Georgiadis, P. I., Papazoglou, M. P., and Maritsas, D. G. (1981). "Towards a Parallel SIMULA Machine," *Proc. of 8th Ann. Symp. on Computer Architecture*, pp. 263-278.

Ginsberg, M. (1977). "Some Numerical Effects of A FORTRAN Vectorizing Compiler on A Texas Instruments Advanced Scientific Computer," in *High Speed Computer and Algorithm Organization*, (Kuck, et al., eds.), Academic Press, New York, pp. 461-62.

Ginsberg, M. (1983). "Some Observations on Supercomputer Computational Environments," *10th IMACS World Congress on System Simulation and Scientific Computation*, Montreal, Canada, August 8-13.

Gloudeman, J. F. (1984). "The Anticipated Impact of Supercomputers on Finite-Element Analysis," *Proc. of IEEE*, January, pp. 80-84.

Gloudeman, J. F. and Hodge, J. C. (1982). "The Adaptation of MSC/NASTRAN to a Supercomputer," *10th IMACS World Congress on Systems Simulation and Scientific Computation*, Montreal, Canada, August 8-13.

Goke, R. and Lipovski, G. J. (1973). "Banyan Networks for Partitioning on Multiprocessor Systems," *Proc. 1st Ann. Symp. Computer Architecture*, pp. 21-30.

Goldschlager, L. M. (1982). "A Universal Interconnection Pattern for Parallel Computers," *Journal of the ACM*, Vol. 29, pp. 1073-1086.

Gonzalez, M. J. (1977). "Deterministic Processor Scheduling," *ACM Computing Surveys*, Vol. 9, No. 3, pp. 173-204, September.

Gonzalez, T. and Sahni, S. (1978). "Preemptive Scheduling of Uniform Processor Systems," *Journal of the ACM*, Vol. 25, No. 1, pp. 92-101, January.

Goodman, J. R. and Séquin, C. H. (1981). "Hypertree: A Multiprocessor Interconnection Topology," *IEEE Trans. Computers*, C-30, pp. 923-933.

Goodyear Aerospace Co., "Massively Parallel Processor (MPP)," Tech. Report GER-16684, July.

Gopal, G. and Wong, J. W. (1981). "Delay Analysis of Broadcast Routing in Packet Switching Networks," *IEEE Trans. Computers*, C-30, pp. 915-922.

Gosden, J. A. (1966). "Explicit Parallel Processing Description and Control in Programs for Multi and Uni-processor Computers," *AFIPS Fall Joint Computer Conf.*, Spartan Books, New York, pp. 651-660.

Gostelow, K. P. and Thomas, R. E. (1980). "Performance of a Simulated Dataflow Computer," *IEEE Trans. Computers*, October, pp. 905-919.

Gottlieb, A., Grishman, R., Kruskal, C. P., McAaliffe, K. P., Randolph, L. and Snir, M. (1983). "The NYU Ultracomputer-Designing an MIMD Shared Memory Parallel Computer," *IEEE Trans. Computers*, February, pp. 175-189.

Graham, R. L. (1972). "Bounds on Multiprocessing Anomalies and Packing Algorithms," *Proc. AFIPS 1972 Spring Joint Computers Conf.*, 40, AFIPS Press, Montvale, New Jersey, 205-217.

Gray, F. G., McCormack, W. M., and Haralick, R. M. (1982). "Significance of Problem Solving Parameters on the Performance of Combinatorial Algorithms on Multi-Computer Parallel Architectures," *Proc. of Int'l. Conf. on Parallel Processing*, pp. 185-192.

Greutz, M. (1983). "Doing Physics with Computers — High Energy Physics," *Phys. Today*, Vol. 36-No. 5, p. 35.

Grinberg, J., Nudd, G. R., and Etchells, R. D. (1984). "A Cellular VLSI Architecture," *IEEE Computer*, Vol. 17, No. 1, pp. 69-81.

Grit, D. H. and McGraw, J. R. (1983). "Programming Divide and Conquer on a Multiprocessor," *Lawrence Livermore National Lab. Rep.* UCRL-88710.

Grohoski, G. R. and Patel, J. H. (1982). "A Performance Model for Instruction Prefetch in Pipelined Instruction Units," *Proc. of 1982 Intl. Conf. on Parallel Processing*, August 24-27, pp. 248-252.

Gula, J. L. (1978). "Operating System Considerations for Multiprocessor Architecture," *Proc. of the Seventh Texas Conf. on Computing Systems*, Houston, Texas, November.

Gurd, J. and Watson, I. (1980). "Data Driven System for High Speed Parallel Computing," *Computer Design*, Parts I & II, June, July.

Gylys, V. B. and Edwards, J. A. (1976). "Optimal Partitioning of Workload for Distributed Systems," *Proc. Compson*, pp. 353-357.

Hagiwara, H. et al. (1980). "A Dynamically Microprogrammable Computer with Low-Level Parallelism," *IEEE Trans. Computers*, C-29, pp. 577-595.

Hambrusch, S. E. (1983). "VLSI Algorithms for the Connected Component Problems," *SIAM J. Computers*,

Händler, W. (1977). "The Impact of Classification Schemes on Computer Architecture," *Proc. 1977 Int'l. Conf. on Parallel Processing*, pp. 7-15.

Händler, W., Schreiber, H., and Sigmund, V. (1979). "Computation Structures Reflected in General Purpose and Special Purpose Multiprocessor Systems," *Proc. of Int'l. Conf. on Parallel Processing*, August, pp. 95-102. Vol. 12, pp. 354-365.

Hansen, P. B. (1975). "The programming language Concurrent Pascal," *IEEE Trans. on Software Engineering 1*, 2, June, pp. 199-207.

Hansen, P. B., (1977). *The Architecture of Concurrent Programs*, Prentice-Hall, Englewood Cliffs, New Nersey.

Harris, J. A., and Smith, D. R. (1977). "Hierarchical Multiprocessor Organizations," *Proc. 4th Symp. on Computer Architecture*,

Hayashi, H., Hattori, A., and Akimoto, H. (1983). "ALPHA: A High-Performance LISP Machine Equipped with a New Stack Structure and Garbage Collection System," *Proc. of 10th. Ann. Symp. on Computer Architecture*, pp. 342-348.

Hayes, J. P. (1978). *Computer Architecture and Organization*, McGraw-Hill Book Co., New York.

Haynes, L. S. et al. (1982). "A Survey of Highly Parallel Computing," *IEEE Computer*, Vol. 15, No. 1, pp. 9-26.

Hedlund, K. S. (1982). "Wafer Scale Integration of Parallel Processors," *Ph.D. Thesis*, Computers Science Dept., Purdue University, Lafayette, Indiana.

Hellerman, H. and Smith, H. J., Jr., (1970). "Throughput Analysis of Some Idealized Input, Output and Compute Overlap Configurations," *ACM Computing Surveys*, June, pp. 111-118.

Higbie, L. C. (1978). "Applications of Vector Processing," *Computer Design*, April pp. 139-45.

Hoare, C. A. R. (1972). "Towards a Theory of Parallel Programming," in *Operating Systems Techniques*, (Hoare, ed.). Academic Press, New York.

Hoare, C. A. R. (1974), "Monitors: an Operating System Structuring Concept," *Comm. of the ACM*, pp. 549-57, October.

Hobson, R. F. (1981). "Structured Machine Design: An Ongoing Experiment," *Proc. of 8th Ann. Symp. on Computer Architecture*, pp. 37-56.

Hockney, R. W. (1983). "Characterizing Computers and Optimizing the FACR (L) Poisson-Solver on Parallel Unicomputers," *IEEE Trans. Computers*, C-32, pp. 933-941.

Hockney, R. W. and Jesshope, C. R. (1981). *Parallel Computers: Architecture, Programming and Algorithms*, Adam Hilger Ltd., Bristol, England.

Hogenauer, E. B., Newbold, R. F., and Inn, Y. J. (1982). "DDSP — A Data Flow Computer for Signal Processing," *Proc. of Int'l. Conf. on Parallel Processing*, pp. 126-133.

Holgate, R. W. and Ibbett, R. N. (1980). "An Analysis of Instruction-Fetching Strategies in Pipelined Computers," *IEEE Trans. Computers*, C-29, pp. 325-329.

Holley, L. H., et al. (1979). "VM/370 Asymmetric Multiprocessing," *IBM Systems Journal*, Vol. 18, No. 1.

Holt, R. C. (1972). "Some Deadlock Properties of Computer Systems," *ACM Computing Surveys*, 4, September, pp. 179-195.

Holt, R. C., Graham, G. S., Lazowska, E. D., and Scott, M. A. (1978). *Structured Concurrent Programming with Operating Systems Applications*, Addison-Wesley.

Hon, R. and Reddy, D. R. (1977). "The Effect of Computer Architecture on Algorithm Decomposition and Performance," in *High-Speed Computers and Algorithm Organization*, (Kuck, et al., eds.), Academic Press, New York, pp. 411-421.

Hoogendoorn, C. H. (1977). "A General Model for Memory Interference in Multiprocessors," *IEEE Trans. Computers*, Vol. C-26, No. 10, October, pp. 998-1005.

Hopper, A. and Wheeler, D. (1979). "Binary Routing Networks," *IEEE Trans. Computers*, Vol. C-28, No. 10, pp. 699-703.

Horowitz, E. (1983). *Fundamentals of Programming Languages*, Computer Science Press, Rockville, Maryland.

Horowitz, E. and Zorat, A. (1981). "The Binary Tree as an Interconnection Network: Applications to Multiprocessor Systems and VLSI," *IEEE Trans. Computers*, Vol. C-30, No. 4, April, Pp. 247-253.

Hoshino, T. et al. (1983). "Highly Parallel Processor Array 'PAX' for Wide Scientific Applications," *Proc. of Int'l. Conf. on Parallel Processing*, pp. 95-105.

Houstis, C. E., Houstis, E. N., and Rice, J. R. (1984). "Partitioning and Allocation of PDE Computations in Distributed Systems," in *PDE Software: Modules, Interfaces and Systems* (B. Engquist, ed.), North-Holland, New York.

Houstis, E. N., Mitchell, W. F., and Rice, J. R. (1983). "Collocation Software for Second Order Elliptic Partial Differential Equations," *CSD-TR 446*, Computer Science, Purdue University, Lafayette, Indiana.

Houstis, E. N. and Rice, J. R. (1984). "Toward Vector ELLPACK," in *Advances in Numerical Methods for Partial Differential Equations* (Stapleton and Vishnevetsky, eds.) IMACS, Rutgers University, New Brunswick, New Jersey.

Hovesty, K. and Jenny, C. J. (1980). "Partitioning and Allocating Computational Objects in Distributed Computing Systems," *Proc. IFIP* 80, pp. 593-598.

Hsiao, C. C. and Snyder, L. (1983). "Omnisort: A Versatile Data Processing Operation for VLSI," *Proc. of Int'l. Conf. on Parallel Processing*, pp. 222-225.

Hsiao, D. K. (ed.) (1983). *Advanced Database Machine Architecture*, Prentice-Hall, Inc., Englewood Cliffs, New Jersey.

Hu, T. C. (1961). "Parallel Sequencing and Assembly Line Problems," *Oper. Res.*, Vol. 9, No. 6, November-December, pp. 841-848.

Huang, K. H. and Abraham, J. A. (1982). "Efficient Parallel Algorithms for Processor Arrays," *Proc. of Int'l. Conf. on Parallel Processing*, pp. 271-279.

Hufnagel, S. (1979). "Comparison of Selected Array Processor Architecture," *Computer Design*, March, pp. 151-158.

Hwang, K. and Yao, S. B. (1977). "Optimal Batched Searching of Tree-Structural Files in Multiprocess Computer System," *J. of Ass. of Computing Machinery*, Vol. 24, No. 3, July, pp. 441-454.

Hwang, K. (1979). *Computer Arithmetic: Principles, Architecture and Design*, Wiley, New York.

Hwang, K. and Ni, L. M. (1980). "Resource Optimization of a Parallel Computer for Multiple Vector Processing," *IEEE Trans. Computers*, Vol. C-29, September, pp. 831-836.

Hwang, K., Su, S. P., and Ni, L. M. (1981). "Vector Computer Architecture and Processing Techniques," in *Advanced in Computers*, Vol. 20, (M. C. Yovits, ed.), Academic Press, New York, pp. 115-197.

Hwang, K. and Chang, T. P. (1982). "Combinatorial Reliability Analysis of Multiprocessor Computers," *IEEE Trans. Reliability*, Vol. R-31, No. 5, December, pp. 469-473.

Hwang, K. and Cheng, Y. H. (1982). "Partitioned Matrix Algorithms for VLSI Arithmetic Systems," *IEEE Trans. Computers*, Vol. C-31, December, pp. 1215-1224.

Hwang, K. and Fu, K. S. (1983). "Integrated Computer Architectures for Image Processing and Database Management," *IEEE Computer*, Vol. 16, January, pp. 51-61.

Hwang, K. (1984). "VLSI Computer Arithmetic for Real-Time Image Processing," Chap. 7 in *VLSI Electronics: Microstructure Science*, Vol. 7, (Einpruch, ed.), Academic Press, New York.

Hwang, K. and Briggs, F. A. (1984). *Computer Architecture and Parallel Processing*, McGraw-Hill, New York.

Hwang, K. and Su, S. P. (1983a). "VLSI Architectures for Feature Extraction and Pattern Classification," *Computer Vision, Graphics, and Image Processing*, Vol. 24, November, pp. 215-228.

Hwang, K. and Su, S. P. (1983b). "Priority Scheduling in Event-Driven Dataflow Computers," *TR-EE 83-86*, Purdue University, West Lafayette, Indiana.

IBM Corp. (1974). *System/370 Principles of Operation*, Form No. GA22-7000-4.

IBM Corp. (1976). *IBM System/360 and System/370 I/O Interface Channel to Control Unit,* Form No. GA22-6974-3.

IBM Corp. (1976). *IBM 3838 Array Processor Functional Characteristics,* No. 6A24-3639-0, file no. S370-08, Endicott, New York, October.

IBM Corp. (1976). *IBM System/370 Model 168 functional characteristics.* Form No. GA22-7010-4.

IBM Corp. (1978). *3033 Processor Complex Theory of Operation/Diagrams Manual.* Vols. 1-5, SY22-7005, January.

Ignizio, J. P., Palmer, D. F., and Murphy, C. M. (1982). "A Multicriteria Approach to Supersystem Architecture Definition," *IEEE Trans. Computers,* C-31, pp. 410-418.

Irani, K. B. and Chen, K. W. (1982). "Minimization of Interprocessor Communication for Parallel Computation," *IEEE Trans. Computers,* C-31, pp. 1067-1075.

Ishikawa, Y. and Tokoro, M. (1984). "The Design of an Object Oriented Architecture," *Proc. of the 11th Annual Int'l Symp. on Computer Architecture,* Ann Arbor, Michigan, June 5-7, pp. 178-187.

Isloor, S. S. and Marsland, T. A (1980). "The Deadlock Problem: An Overview," *IEEE Computer,* Vol. 13, No. 9, September

Jain, N. (1979). "Performance Study of Synchronization Mechanisms in a Multiprocessor," *Ph.D. thesis,* Carnegie-Mellon University, Pittsburgh, Pennsylvania.

Ja'Ja', J. and Simon, J. (1982). "Parallel Algorithms in Graph Theory: Planarity Testing," *SIAM J. Computers,* Vol. 11, pp. 314-328.

Jenevein, R. M. and Browne, J. C. (1982). "A Control Processor for a Reconfigurable Array Computer," *Proc. of 9th Ann. Symp. on Computer Architecture,* pp. 81-89.

Jess, J. A. G. and Kees, H. G. M. (1982). "A Data Structure for Parallel L/U Decomposition," *IEEE Trans. Computers,* C-31, pp. 231-238.

Jesshope, C. R. (1980). "The Implementation of Fast Radix-2 Transforms on Array Processors," *IEEE Trans. Computers,* C-29, pp. 20-27.

Jin, L. (1980). "A New General-Purpose Distributed Multiprocessor Structure," *Proc. of Int'l Conf. on Parallel Processing,* August, pp. 153-154.

Johnson, O. and Paul, G. (1981). "Vector Algorithms for Elliptic Partial Differential Equations Based on the Jacobi Method," in *Elliptic Problem Solvers,* (M. Schultz, ed.), Academic Press, New York, pp. 345-351.

Johnson, P. M. (1978). "An Introduction to Vector Processing," *Computer Design,* February, pp. 89-97.

Jones, A. K. and Schwarz, P. (1979). "Experience Using Multiprocessor Systems: A Status Report," Dept. of Computer Science, Carnegie-Mellon University, *Tech. Report CMU-CS-79-146,* October.

Jones, A. K. and Gehringer, E. F. (eds) (1980). *The Cm* Multiprocessor Project: A Research Review,* Computer Science Dept., Carnegie-Mellon University, July.

Jordan, H. F. (1984). "Experience with Pipelined Multiple Instruction Streams," *Proc. IEEE,* Vol. 72, No. 1, pp. 113-123.

Jordan, H. F., Scalabrin, M., and Calvert, W. (1979). "A Comparison of Three Types of Multiprocessor Algorithms," *Proc. of the 1979 Int'l. Conf. on Parallel Processing,* Bellaire, Michigan, August, pp. 231-238.

Jump, J. R. and Ahuja, S. R. (1978). "Effective Pipelining of Digital Systems," *IEEE Trans. Computers,* September pp. 855-65.

Kapauan, A., Field, J. T., Gannon, D. B. and Snyder, L. (1984). "The Pringle Parallel Computer," *Proc. of the 11th Annual Int'l Symp. on Computer Architecture,* Ann Arbor, Michigan, June 5-7, pp. 12-20.

Kaplan, K. R. and Winder, R. V. (1973). "Cache-Based Computer Systems," *Computer,* March, pp. 30-36.

Karp, K. M. and Miller, R. E. (1966). "Properties of a Model for Parallel Computations: Determinacy, Termination, Queueing," *SIAM Journal of Applied Mathematics,* Vol. 24, November, pp. 1390-1411.

Karplus, W. J. and Cohen, D. (1981). "Architectural and Software Issues in the Design and Application of Peripheral Array Processors," *IEEE Computer*, September, pp. 11-17.

Kartashev, S.I. and Kartashev, S.P. (1980). "Problems of Designing Supersystems with Dynamic Architectures," *IEEE Trans. Computers*, December, pp. 1114-1132.

Kascic, M. J. (1979). *Vector Processing on the Cyber 200*, Control Data Corp., St. Paul, Minnesota.

Kashiwagi, H. and Miura, K. (1983). "Japanese Superspeed Computer Project," *Proc. of Advances in Reactor Computation*, American Nuclear Society, Salt Lake City, Utah, March.

Kaufman, M. T. (1976). "An Almost-Optimal Algorithm for the Assembly Line Scheduling Problem," *IEEE Trans. Computers*, November pp. 1169-1174.

Keller, R. M. (1975). "Look-Ahead Processors," *ACM Computing Surveys*, Vol. 7, No. 4, December, pp. 177-195.

Keller, R. M., Patil, S. S., and Lindstrom, G. (1979). "A Loosely Coupled Applicative Multiprocessing System," *Proc. of Nat'l. Computer Conf.*, AFIPS Press.

Kennedy, K. (1979). "Optimization of Vector Operations in an Extended Fortran Compiler," *IBM Research Report*, RC-7784.

Keyes, R. W. (1981). "Fundamental Limits in Digital Information Processing," *Proc. of IEEE*, Vol. 69, No. 2, pp. 267-278.

Kidode, M. (1983). "Image Processing Machines in Japan," *IEEE Computer*, Vol. 16, No. 1, pp. 68-80.

Kinney, L. L. et al. (1981). "An Architecture for a VHSIC Computer," *Proc. of 8th Ann. Symp. on Computer Architecture*, pp. 459-470.

Kinney, L. L. and Arnold, R. G. (1978). "Analysis of a Multiprocessor System with a Shared Bus," *Proc. of the 5th Ann. Symp. on Computer Architecture*, Palo Alto, California, April, pp. 89-95.

Kishi, M., Yasuhara, H., and Kawamura, Y. (1983). "DDDP: A Distributed Data Driven Processor," *Proc. of 10th Ann. Symp. on Computer Architecture*, pp. 236-242.

Klappholz, D. (1981). "The Symbolic High-Level Language Programming of an MIMD Machine," *Proc. of Int'l. Conf. on Parallel Processing*, pp. 61-53.

Knight, J. C. and Dunlop, D. D. (1981). "Measurements of an Optimizing Compiler for a Vector Computer," *Proc. of Int'l. Conf. on Parallel Processing*, pp. 58-59.

Kober, R. and Kuznia, C. (1978). "SMS — A Multiprocessor Architecture for High-Speed Numerical Calculations" *Proc. of Int'l. Conf. Parallel Processing*, pp. 18-23

Kogge, P. M. (1977). "Algorithm Development for Pipelined Processors," *Proc. 1977 Int'l. Conf. Parallel Processing*, August.

Kogge, P. M. (1981). *The Architecture of Pipelined Computers*, McGraw-Hill, New York.

Kogge, P. M., and Stone, H. S. (1973). "A parallel algorithm for the efficient solution of a general class of recurrence equations." *IEEE Trans. Computers*, C-22, pp. 786-93.

Koren, I. (1981). "A Reconfigurable and Fault-Tolerant VLSI Multiprocessor Array," *Proc. of 8th Ann. Symp. on Computer Architecture*, pp. 425-442.

Kowalik, J. S. and Kumar, S. P. (1982). "An Efficient Parallel Block Conjugate Gradient Method for Linear Equations," *Proc. of Int'l. Conf. on Parallel Processing*, pp. 47-52.

Kozdrowicki, E.W. and Theis, D.J. (1980). "Second-Generation of Vector Supercomputers," *IEEE Computer*, November pp. 71-83.

Kraley, M. F. (1975). "The Pluribus Multiprocessor," *Digest of Papers, 1975 Int'l. Symp. on Fault-Tolerant Computing*, Paris, France, p. 251, June.

Kroft, D. (1981). "Lockup-Free Instruction Fetch/Prefetch Cache Organization," *Proc. of 8th Ann. Symp. on Computer Architecture*, pp. 81-88.

Kronlöf, K. (1983). "Execution Control and Memory Management of a Data Flow Signal Processor," *Proc. of 10th Ann. Symp. on Computer Architecture*, pp. 230-235.

Kruskal, C. P. (1982). "Results in Parallel Searching, Merging, and Sorting," *Proc. of Int'l. Conf. on Parallel Processing*. pp. 196-198.

Krygiel, A. J. (1981). "Synchronous Nets for Single Instruction Stream-Multiple Data Stream Computers," *Proc. of Int'l. Conf. on Parallel Processing*, pp. 266-273.

Kuck, D. J. (1977). "A Survey of Parallel Machine Organization and Programming," *ACM Computing Surveys*, Vol. 9, No. 1, March, pp. 29-59.

Kuck, D. J. (1978). *The Structure of Computers and Computations*, Wiley, New York.

Kuck, D. et al. (1980). "The Structure of an Advanced Vectorizer for Pipelined Processors," *Proc. COMPSAC 80*, pp. 709-715.

Kuck, D. J., Kuhn, R. H., Padua, D. A., Leasure, B., and Wolfe, M. (1981). "Dependence Graphs and Compiler Optimizations," *Proc. 8th ACM Symp. Principles Programming Languages*, January, pp. 207-218.

Kuck, D. J., Lawrie, D. H., and Sameh, A. H., (eds., 1977). *High Speed Computer and Algorithm Organization*, Academic Press, New York.

Kuck, D. J. and Stokes, R. A. (1982). "The Burroughs Scientific Processor (BSP)" *IEEE Trans. Computers*, Vol. C-31, May, pp. 363-376.

Kuhn, R. H. (1980). "Optimization and Interconnection Complexity for: Parallel Processors, Single-Stage Networks, and Decision Trees," *Ph.D. Thesis*, University of Illinois at Urbana, Dept. of Computer Science, Report No. 80-1009, February

Kuhn, R. H. and Padau, D. A., (eds, 1981). *Tutorial on Parallel Processing*, IEEE Computer Society Press, Order No. 367, Los Angeles, California.

Kulisch, U. W. and Miranker, W. L. (eds., 1983). *A New Approach to Scientific Computation*, Academic Press, New York.

Kumar, M. Dias, D. M. and Jump, J. R. (1983). "Switching Strategies in a Class of Packet Switching Networks," *Proc. of 10th Ann. Symp. on Computer Architecture*, pp. 284-300.

Kumar, M. and Hirschberg, D. S. (1983). "An Efficient Implementation of Batcher's Odd-Even Merge Algorithm and Its Application in Parallel Sorting," *IEEE Trans. Computers*, Vol. C-32, pp. 254-264.

Kung, H. T. (1980). "The Structure of Parallel Algorithms," in *Advances in Computers*, Vol. 19 (ed, M.C. Yovits), Academic Press, New York, New York, pp. 65-112.

Kung, H. T. (1982). "Why Systolic Architectures," *IEEE Computers*, January, pp. 37-46.

Kung, H. T. and Leiserson, C. E. (1978). "Systolic Arrays (for VLSI)," in *Spare Matrix Proc.*, Duff, I. W. et al., (Eds.), Society of Indust. and Appl. Math., Philadelphia, Pennsylvania, pp. 245-282.

Kung, H. T. and Lam, M. (1984). "Wafter-Scale Integration and Two-Level Pipelined Implementations of Systolic Arrays," *Journal of Parallel and Distributed Computing*, Vol. 1, No. 1, August.

Kung, S. Y. (1984). "On Supercomputing with Systolic/Wavefront Array Processors," *Proc. of IEEE*, Vol. 72, No. 7, July.

Kung, S. Y., Arun, K. S., Galezer, R. J., Rao, D. V. B. (1982). "Wavefront Array Processor: Language, Architecture, and Applications," *IEEE Trans. Computers*, Vol. C-31, No. 11, November, pp. 1054-1066.

Kurtzberg, J. M. (1974). "On the Memory Conflict Problem in Multiprocessor Systems," *IEEE Trans. Computers*, Vol. C-23, No. 3, pp. 286-293, March.

Kushner, T., Wu, A. Y., and Rosenfeld, A. (1982). "Image Processing on ZMOB," *IEEE Trans. Computers*, C-31, pp. 943-951.

Lai, T. H. and Sahni, S. (1983). "Anomalies in Parallel Branch-and-Bound Algorithms," *Proc. of Int'l. Conf. on Parallel Processing*, pp. 183-190.

Lamport, L. (1977). "Proving the Correctness of Multiprocess Programs," *IEEE Trans. on Software Engineering*, Vol. SE-3, No. 2, pp. 125-143, March.

Lampson, B. W. (1974). "Protection," *Operating Systems Review* 8(1), January.

Lang, T. and Stone, H. S. (1976). "A Shuffle-Exchange Network with Simplified Control," *IEEE Trans. Computers*, Vol. C-25, January, pp. 55-56.

Larson, A. G. (1973). "Cost-Effective Processor Design with an Application to Fast Fourier Transform Computers," *Ph.D. Thesis*, Stanford University.

Lawrence Livermore Laboratory (1979). "The S-1 Project: Ann. Reports," Vol. 1 Architecture, Vol. 2 Hardware, and Vol. 3 Software, UCID-18619, University of California, Livermore, California.

Lawrie, D. H. (1975). "Access and Alignment of Data in an Array Processor," *IEEE Trans. Computers*, Vol. C-24, No. 12, December, pp. 1145-1155.

Lawrie, D. H. and Vora, C. R. (1982). "The Prime Memory System for Array Access," *IEEE Trans. Computers*, Vol. C-31, No. 5, October, pp. 435-442.

Lee, M. and Wu, C.-L. (1984). "Performance Analysis of Circuit Switching Baseline Interconnection Networks," *Proc. of the 11th Annual Int'l Symp. on Computer Architecture*, Ann Arbor, Michigan, June 5-7, pp. 82-90.

Lee, R. B-L. (1980). "Empirical Results on the Speed, Efficiency, Redundancy and Quality of Parallel Computations," *Int. Conf. Parallel Processing*, August, pp. 91-96.

Lev, G., Pippenger, N., and Valiant, L. G. (1981). "A Fast Parallel Algorithm for Routing in Permutation Networks," *IEEE Trans. Computers*, C-30, pp. 93-100.

Levy, H. M. (1983). *Capability-Based Computer Systems*, Digital Press, Bedford, Massachusetts.

Lewell, J. (1983). "Turning Dreams into Reality with Super Computers and Super Visions," *Computer Pictures*, January/February, p. 40.

Li, G. J. and Wah, B. W. (1984). "Computational Efficiency of Parallel Approximate Branch-and-Bound Algorithms," *Proc. of Int'l Conf. on Parallel Processing*, August.

Li, H. (1983). "A VLSI Modular Architecture Methodology for Real Time Signal Processing Applications," *Proc. of Int'l Conf. on Parallel Processing*, pp. 319-324.

Li, H. F. (1977). "Scheduling Trees in Parallel Pipelined Processing Environments," *IEEE Trans. Computers*, November, pp. 1101-1112.

Li, P. and Johnsson, L. (1983). "The Tree Machine: An Evaluation of Strategies for Reducing Program Loading Time," *Proc. of Int'l. Conf. on Parallel Processing*, Mich., August, pp. 202-205.

Lincoln, N. R. (1982). "Technology and Design Trade Offs in the Creation of a Modern Supercomputer," *IEEE Trans. Computers*, Vol. C-31, No. 5, May, pp. 363-376.

Lincoln, N. R. (1983). "Supercomputers = Colossal Computations + Enormous Expectations + Renowned Risk," *IEEE Computer*, Vol. 16, No. 5, pp. 38-47.

Lint, B. and Agerwala, T. (1981). "Communication Issues in the Design and Analysis of Parallel Algorithms," *IEEE Trans. on Software Engineering*, Vol. SE-7, No. 2 March, pp. 174-188.

Lipovski, G. J. and Malek, M. (1981). "A Theory for Multicomputer Interconnection Networks," *Tech. Report TRAC-40*, University of Texas, Austin, March.

Lipovski, G. J. and Tripathi, A. (1977). "A Reconfigurable Varistructured Array Processor," *Proc. 1977 Int. Conf. on Parallel Processing*, pp. 165-174.

Liu, J. W. S. and Liu, C. L. (1978). "Performance Analysis of Multiprocessor Systems Containing Functionally Dedicated Processors," *Acta Informatica*, Vol. 10, No. 1, pp. 95-104.

Liu, K. Y. (1981). "A Pipelined Digital Architecture for Computing a Multi-Dimensional Convolution," *Proc. of Int'l. Conf. on Parallel Processing*, pp. 109-111.

Lorin, H. (1972). *Parallelism in Hardware and Software*, Prentice-Hall, Englewood Cliffs, New Jersey.

Louie, J. (1981). "Array Processors: A Selected Bibliography," *IEEE Computer*, Vol. 14, No. 9, pp. 53-57.

Ma, P., Lee, E. Y. S. and Tsuchlya, M. (1981). "On the Design of a Task Allocation Scheme for Time-Critical Applications," *IEEE Proc. Real-time Systems*, pp. 121-126.

Maekawa, M. (1981). "Optimal Processor Interconnection Topologies," *Proc. of 8th Ann. Symp. on Computer Architecture*, pp. 171-186.

Mago, G. A. and Middleton, D. (1984). "The Progress Report," *Proc. of the Int'l Workshop on High-Level Computer Architecture*, Los Angeles, California, May, pp. 5.13-5.25.

Marathe, M., and Fuller, S. H. (1977), "A study of multiprocessor contention for shared data in C.mmp.," *ACM SIGMETRICS Conf.*, Washington, D.C., December.

Marczyński, R. W. and Milewski, J. (1983). "A Data Driven System Based on a Microprogrammed Processor Module," *Proc. of 10th Ann. Symp. on Computer Architecture*, pp. 98-107.

Maron, N. and Brengle, T. S. (1981). "Integrating an Array Processor into a Scientific Computing System," *IEEE Computer*, Vol. 14, No. 9, pp. 41-44.

Matick, R. E. (1980). "Memory and Storage," in *Introduction to Computer Architecture*, (Stone, ed), SRA Inc., pp. 205-274.

Mattson, R. L., Gecsei, J., Slutz, D. R., and Traiger, I. L. (1970). "Evaluation Techniques for Storage Hierarchies," *IBM Systems Journal*, 9, 78-117.

McDowell, C. E. (1983). "A Simple Architecture for Low Level Parallelism," *Proc. of Int'l. Conf. on Parallel Processing*, pp. 472-477.

McGraw, J. R. (1980). "Data Flow Computing--Software Development," *IEEE Trans. Computers*, December, pp. 1095-1103.

McGraw, J. R. and Skedzielewski, S. K. (1982). "Streams and Iteration in Val: Additions to a Data Flow Language," *The 3rd Int'l. Conf. on Distributed Computing Systems*, October, pp. 730-739.

Mead, C. and Conway, L. (1980). *Introduction to VLSI Systems*, Addison Wesley, Reading, Massachusettes

Mehra, S. K., Wong, J. W. and Majithia, J. C. (1980). "A Comparative Study of Some Two-Processor Organizations," *IEEE Trans. Computers*, C-29, pp. 44-49.

Milutinovic, V., Furht, B., Hwang, K., Lopez-Benitez, N. and Waldschmidt, K. (1984). "The VM-Architecture: A HLL-Microprocessor Architecture for Dedicated Real-Time Applications," *Proc. of the Int'l Workshop on High-Level Computer Architecture*, Los Angeles, California, May, pp. 7.20-7.27.

Miranker, G., Tang, L., and Wong, C. K. (1983). "A 'Zero-Time' VLSI Sorter," *IBM Journal of Research and Development*, Vol. 27, No. 2, pp. 140-148.

Miranker, G. S. (1977). "Implementation of Procedures on a Class of Data Flow Processors," *Proc. Int'l. Conf. Parallel Processing*, IEEE No. 77CH 1253-4C, pp. 77-86.

Misunas, D. P. (1977). "Workshop on Data Flow Computer and Program Organization," *Computer Architecture News*, j6, 4, October, 6-22.

Miura, K. and Uchida, K. (1983). "FACOM Vector Processor VP-100/VP-200," *Proc. NATO Advanced Research Workshop on High-Speed Computing*, Jülich, W. Germany, June 20-22, Springer-Verlag.

Moldovan, D. I. (1983). "On the Design of Algorithms for VLSI Systolic Array," *Proc. of IEEE*, January, pp. 113-120.

Montoye, R. K. and Lawrie, D. H. (1982). "A Practical Algorithm for the Solution of Triangular Systems on a Parallel Processing System," *IEEE Trans. Computers*, C-31, pp. 1076-1082.

Moto-oka, T. (1983). "Overview to the Fifth Generation Computer System Project," *Proc. of 10th Ann. Symp. Computer Architecture*, June, pp. 417-422.

Mowbray, T. J. (1983), "Language Features for a Static Data Flow Environment," *Ph.D. Thesis*, University of Southern California, Los Angeles, California., May.

Mrosousky, I., Wong, J. Y., and Lampe, H. W. (1980). "Construction of a Large Field Simulator on a Vector Computer," *Journal of Petroleum Tech.*, December pp. 2253-2264.

Mudge, T. N. and Abdel-Rahman, T. (1983). "Efficiency of Feature Dependent Algorithms for the Parallel Processing of Images," *Proc. of Int'l. Conf. on Parallel Processing*, pp. 369-373.

Mühlbacher, J. R. (1981). "Full Table Scatter Storage Parallel Searching," *Computing*, Vol. 27, pp. 9-18.

Mukai, H. (1981). "Parallel Algorithms for Solving Systems of Nonlinear Equations," *Computers and Math. with Appls.*, Vol. 7, pp. 235-250.

Muntz, R. R., and Coffman, E. G. (1969). "Optimal Preemptive Scheduling on Two Processor Systems," *IEEE Trans. Computers, C-18,* November, pp. 1014-1020.

Murakami, K. et al. (1983). "A Relational Data Base Machine: First Step to Knowledge Base Machine," *Proc. of 10th Ann. Symp. on Computer Architecture,* pp. 423-425.

Muraoka, Y. (1971). "Parallelism Exposure and Exploitation in Programs," *Ph.D. Thesis,* University of Illinois at Urbana-Champaign, Dept. of Computer Science Rpt. 71-424, February

Murata, T. and M. Y. Chern (1983). "Efficient Matrix Multiplications a Concurrent Data-Loading Array Processor," *Proc. Int'l. Conf. Parallel Processing,* August, pp. 90-94.

Myers, G. J., (1978). *Advances in Computer Architecture,* John Wiley, New York, New York

Nassimi, D. and Sahni, S. (1982). "Optimal BPC Permutations on a Cube Connected SIMD Computer," *IEEE Trans. Computers,* C-31, pp. 338-341.

National Science Foundation Report (1983). "Report of the Panel on Large-Scale Computing in Science and Engineering," NSF 83-13.

NEC Corp. (1983). "NEC Supercomputer SX-1/SX-2," *Tech. Note,* Cat. No. E51133, NEC Building, Minato-Ku, Tokyo, Japan, August.

Nessett, D. M. (1975). "The Effectiveness of Cache Memories in a Multiprocessor Environment," *Australian Computer Journal,* Vol. 7, No. 1, March, pp. 33-38.

Newan, I. A. and Woodward, M. C. (1982). "Alternative Approaches to Multiprocessor Garbage Collection," *Proc. of Int'l. Conf. on Parallel Processing,* pp. 205-210.

Newton, G. (1979). "Deadlock Prevention, Detection and Resolution: An Annotated Bibliography," *ACM Operating Sys. Review,* Vol. 13, No. 2, Apr., pp. 33-44.

Newton, R. S. (1974). "An Exercise in Multiprocessor Operating System Design," *Agard Conf. Proc. No. 149 on Real-Time Computer-based Systems,* Athens, Greece, May.

Ni, L. M. (1980). "Performance Optimization of Parallel Processing Computer Systems," *Ph.D. Thesis,* Purdue University, School of Electrical Engineering, Lafayette, Indiana.

Ni, L. M., and Hwang, K. (1981). "Performance Modeling of Shared Resource Array Processors," *IEEE Trans. on Software Engineering,* Vol. SE-7, No. 4, July, pp. 386-394.

Ni, L. M. and Hwang, K. (1984). "Vector Reduction Techniques for Arithmetic Pipeline," *IEEE Trans. Computers,* accepted to appear.

Nishimura, H. et al. (1983). "LINKS-1: A Parallel Pipelined Multimicrocomputer System for Image Creation," *Proc. of 10th Ann. Symp. on Computer Architecture,* pp. 387-394.

Nolen, J. S., Kuba, D. W., and Kascic, M. J., Jr. (1979). "Application of Vector Processors to the Solution of Finite Difference Equations," *AIME Fifth Symp. Reservoir Simulation,* February, pp. 37-44.

Nolen, J. S. and Stanat, P. L. (1984). "The Impact of Vector Processors on Petroleum Reservoir Simulation," *Proc. of IEEE,* January, pp. 85-89.

Norrie, C. (1984). "Supercomputers for Super-problems: An Architectural Introduction," *IEEE Computer,* March, pp. 62-74.

Nutt, G. J. (1977). "A Parallel Processor Operating System," *IEEE Trans. on Software Engineering,* Vol. SE-3, No. 6, November, pp. 467-475.

Oleinick, P. N. (1978). The Implementation and Evaluation of Parallel Algorithms on C.mmp, *Ph.D. Dissertation,* Carnegie-Mellon University, Pittsburgh, Pennsylvania.

Orcutt, S. E. (1974). "Computer Organization and Algorithms for Very High-Speed Computations," *Ph.D. Thesis,* Stanford University, California.

Owicki, S., and Gries, D. (1976). "Verifying Properties of Parallel Programs: an Axiomatic Approach," *Comm. of the ACM,* 19, 5, May, pp. 279-85.

Padegs, A. (1983). "System/370 Extended Architecture: Design Consideration," *IBM Journal of Research and Development,* Vol. 27, No. 2, pp. 198-205.

Pauda, D. A., Kuck, D. J., and Lawrie, D. H. (1980). "High-Speed Multiprocessors and Compiling Techniques," *IEEE Trans. Computers,* September, pp. 763-776.

Parker, D. S. and Raghavendra, C. S. (1982). "The Gamma Network: A Multiprocessor Interconnection Network with Redundant Paths," *Proc. of 9th Ann. Symp. on Computer Architecture,* pp. 73-80.

Parkinson, D. and Liddell, H. M. (1983). "The Measurement of Performance on a Highly Parallel System," *IEEE Trans. Computers,* C-32.

Patel, J. H. (1981). "Performance of Processor-Memory Interconnections for Multiprocessors," *IEEE Trans. Computers,* October, pp. 771-780.

Patterson, D. A. et al. (1983). "Architecture of a VLSI Instruction Cache for a RISC," *Proc. of 10th Ann. Symp. on Computer Architecture,* pp. 108-116.

Patterson, D. A. and Séquin, C. H. (1981). "RISC 1: A Reduced Instruction Set VLSI Computer," *Proc. of 8th Ann. Symp. on Computer Architecture,* pp. 443-458.

Paul, G., and Wilson, M. W. (1975). *"The VECTRAN Language: An Experimental Language for Vector/Matrix Array Processing,"* IBM Palo Alto Scientific Center Report 6320-3334, August.

Paul, G. (1982). "Vectran and the Proposed Vector/Array Extensions to ANSI Fortran for Scientific and Engineering Computations," *IBM Conf. on Parallel Computers and Scientific Computations,* Rome, Italy, March 3-5.

Paul, G. (ed, 1984). "Special Issue on Supercomputers — Their Impact on Science and Technology," *Proc. of the IEEE,* Vol. 72, January, pp. 1-144.

Pearce, R. C. and Majithia, J. C. (1978). "Analysis of a Shared Resource MIMD Computer Organization," *IEEE Trans. Computers,* Vol. C-27, No. 1, pp. 64-67, January.

Pease, M. C. (1977). "The Indirect Binary n-cube Microprocessor Array," *IEEE Trans. Comput.,* Vol. C-25, May, pp. 458-473.

Perrott, R. H. (1979). "A Language for Array and Vector Processors," *ACM Trans. on Programming Languages and Systems,* Vol. 1, No. 2, October, pp. 177-195.

Perrott, R. H. et al. (1983). "Implementation of an Array and Vector Processing Language," *Proc. of Int'l. Conf. on Parallel Processing,* pp. 232-239.

Preston, K., Duff, M. J. B., Levialdi, D. S., Norgren, P. E., and Toriwaki, J. I. (1979). "Basics of Cellular Logic With Some Applications in Medical Image Processing," *Proc. of IEEE,* May, pp. 826-856.

Peterson, J. L. (1977). "Petri Nets," *ACM Computing Surveys,* 3028: Computing Surveys, 9, September, pp. 223-252.

Peterson, V. L., (1984). "Impact of Computers of Aerodynamics Research and Development," *Proc. of IEEE,* January, pp. 68-79.

Peterson, W. P. (1983). "Vector Fortran for Numerical Problems on Cray-1," *Comm. of ACM,* Vol. 26, pp. 1008-1021.

Petersen, W. P., Fichtner, W., and Grosse, E. H. (1983). in Amorphous Solids," *IEEE Trans. Electron Devices,* Vol. ED-30, p. 1011.

Philipson, L. (1984). "VLSI Based Design Principles for MIMD Multiprocessor Computers with Distributed Memory Management," *Proc. of the 11th Annual Int'l Symp. on Computer Architecture,* Ann Arbor, Michigan, June 5-7, pp. 319-327.

Pleszkun, A. R. and Davidson, E. S. (1983). "Structured Memory Access Architecture," *Proc. of Int'l. Conf. on Parallel Processing,* pp. 461-471.

Potter, J. L. (1983). "Image Processing on the Massively Parallel Processor," *IEEE Computer,* Vol. 16, No. 1, pp. 62-67.

Pradhan, D. K. and Kodandapani, K. L. (1980). "A Uniform Representation of Single-and Multistage Interconnection Networks Used in SIMD Machines," *IEEE Trans. Computers,* September, pp. 777-790.

Prasad, N. S. (1981). *Architecture and Implementation of Large Scale IBM Computer Systems* Q.E.D. Information Sciences, Inc., Wellesley, Massachusettes

Preparata, F. P. and Vuillemin, J. E. (1979). "The Cube-Connected Cycles: A Versatile Network for Parallel Computation" *Proc. 20th Symp. Foundations of Computer Science*, pp. 140-147.

Priester, R. W. et al. (1981). "Signal Processing with Systolic Arrays," *Proc. of Int'l. Conf. on Parallel Processing*, pp. 207-215.

Purcell, C. J. (1974). "The Control Data STAR-100 - Performance Measurements," *AFIPS NCC Proc.*, pp. 385-387.

Radoy, C. H. and Lipovski, G. J. (1974). "Switched Multiple Instruction Multiple Data Stream Processing," *Proc. 2nd Ann. Symp. Computer Architecture*, pp. 183-187.

Ramakrishnan, I. V., Fussell, D. S., and Silberschatz, A. (1983). "On Mapping Homogeneous Graphs on a Linear Array-Processor Model," *Proc. of Int'l. Conf. on Parallel Processing*, pp. 440-447.

Ramamoorthy, C. V., Chandy, K. M., and Gonzalez, M. J. (1972). "Optimal Scheduling Strategies in a Multiprocessor System," IEEE Trans. Comput., C-21, February, pp. 137-146.

Ramamoorthy, C. V. and Li, H. F. (1977). "Pipeline Architecture," *ACM Computing Surveys*, Vol. 9, No. 1, March pp. 61-102.

Ramamoorthy, C. V. and Wah, B. W. (1981). "An Optimal Algorithm for Scheduling Requests on Interleaved Memories for a Pipelined Processor," *IEEE Trans. Computers*, C-30.

Rao, T. R. N. (1984). "Joint Encryption and Error Correction Schemes," *Proc. of the 11th Annual Int'l Symp. on Computer Architectures*, Ann Arbor, Michigan, June 5-7, pp. 240-241.

Rathi, B. D. et al. (1983). "Specification and Implementation of an Integrated Packet Communication Facility for an Array Computer," *Proc. of Int'l. Conf. on Parallel Processing*, pp. 51-58.

Raw, B. R. (1979). "Program Behavior and the Performance of Interleaved Memories," *IEEE Trans. Comput.*, Vol. C-28, No. 3, March, pp. 191-199.

Reeves, A. P. (1980). "A Systematically Designed Binary Array Processor," *IEEE Trans. Computers*, C-29, pp. 278-287.

Reilly, J., Sutton, A., Nasser, R., and Griscom, R. (1982). "Processor Controller for the IBM 3081," IBM Journal of Research and Development, Vol. 26, No. 1, January, pp. 22-29.

Requa, J. E. (1983). "The Piecewise Data Flow Architecture Control Flow and Register Management," *Proc. of 10th Ann. Symp. on Computer Architecture*, pp. 84-89.

Rice, J. (1981). *Matrix Computations and Mathematical Software*, McGraw-Hill, New York.

Rice, J. R. (1983). "Very Large Least Square Problems and Supercomputers," *Technical Report 464*, Dept. of Computer Science, Purdue University, December

Rice, J. R. (1984). "Software Parts for Elliptic PDE Software," in *PDE Software: Modules, Interfaces and Systems* (B. Engquist, ed), North-Holland, New York.

Robinson, J. T. (1977). "Analysis of Asynchronous Multiprocessor Algorithms with Applications to Sorting," *Proc. of the 1977 Int'l. Conf. on Parallel Processing*, Detroit, Michigan, pp. 128-135, August.

Robinson, J. T. (1979). "Some Analysis Techniques for Asynchronous Multiprocessor Algorithms," *IEEE Trans. on Software Engineering*, January, pp. 24-30.

Rodrigue, G., Giroux, E. D., and Pratt, M. (1980). "Perspective on Large-Scale Scientific Computations," *IEEE Computer*, October, pp. 65-80.

Rodrigue, G. (ed., 1982). *Parallel Computations*, Academic Press, New York.

Rosene, A. F. (1967). "Memory Allocation for Multiprocessors," *IEEE Trans. on Electronic Computers*, Vol. 16, No. 5, October, pp. 659-665.

Rosenfeld, A. (1983). "Parallel Image Processing Using Cellular Arrays," *IEEE Computer*, Vol. 16, No. 1, pp. 14-21.

Rosenfeld, A. and Wu, A. Y. (1981). "Reconfigurable Cellular Computers," *Information and Control*, Vol. 50, pp. 64-84.

Rudolph, L. and Segall, Z. (1984). "Dynamic Decentralized Cache Schemes for MIMD Parallel Processors," *Proc. of the 11th Annual Int'l Symp. on Computer Architecture*, Ann Arbor, Michigan, June 5-7, pp. 340-347.

Rumbaugh, J. (1977), "A Data Flow Multiprocessor," *IEEE Trans. Computers,* Vol. C-26, No. 2, pp. 138-146, February.

Russell, R. M. (1978). "The Cray-1 Computer System," *Communications of the ACM,* January pp. 63-72.

Sameh, A. H. (1977). "Numerical Parallel Algorithms — A Survey," in *High-Speed Computers and Algorithm Organization,* (Kuck, et al., eds). Academic Press, New York, pp. 207-228.

Sameh, A. H. (1983). "On Two Numerical Algorithms for Multiprocessors," *Proc. NATO Advanced Research Workshop on High Speed Computing,* Edited by Kawalik, W. Germany, June.

Sasidhar, J. and Shin, K. G. (1981). "Design of a General-Purpose Multiprocessor with Hierarchical Structure," *Proc. of Int'l. Conf. on Parallel Processing,* pp. 141-150.

Sastry, K. V. and Kain, R. Y. (1975). "On the Performance of Certain Multiprocessor Computer Organizations," *IEEE Trans. Computers,* Vol. C-24, No. 11, pp. 1066-1074, November.

Satyanarayanan, M. (1980a). "Commercial Multiprocessing Systems," *IEEE Computer,* Vol. 13, No. 5, pp. 75-96.

Satyanarayanan, M. (1980b). "Multiprocessing: An Annotated Bibliography," *IEEE Computer,* Vol. 13, No. 5, pp. 101-116.

Savage, J. E. (1980). "Area-Time Tradeoffs for Matrix Multiplication and Related Problems in VLSI Models," *Journal of Computers and System Science,* Vol. 27, No. 2, pp. 230-242.

Sawkar, P. S., Forquer, T. J., and Perry, R. P. (1983). "Programmable Modular Signal Processor — A Data Flow Computer System for Real-Time Signal Processing," *Proc. of Int'l. Conf. on Parallel Processing,* pp. 344-349.

Schaefer, D. H. (1982). "Spatially Parallel Architectures: An Overview," *Computer Design,* August, pp. 117-124.

Schwartz, J. T. (1980). "Ultra-Computers," *ACM Trans. Programming Languages and Systems,* Vol. 2, No. 4, pp. 484-521.

Séquin, C. H. (1981). "Doubly Twisted Torus Networks for VLSI Processing Arrays," *Proc. of 8th Ann. Symp. on Computer Architecture,* pp. 471-480.

Sethi, A. S. and Deo, N. (1979). "Interference in Multiprocessor Systems with Localized Memory Access Probabilities," *IEEE Trans. Computers,* Vol. C-28, No. 2, February.

Shar, L. E. and Davidson, E. S. (1975). "A Multiminiprocessor System Implemented Through Pipelining," *IEEE Computer,* February pp. 42-51.

Shen, J. P. and Hayes, J. P. (1980). "Fault Tolerance of a Class of Connecting Networks," *Proc. 7th Symp. Computer Architecture,* pp. 61-71.

Shin, K. G., Lee, Y. H., and Sasidhar, J. (1982). "Design of HM^{2}P — A Hierarchical Multimicroprocessor for General-Purpose Applications," *IEEE Trans. Computers,* C-31, pp. 1045-1053.

Shoshani, A. and Coffman, E. G. Jr. (1970). "Sequencing Tasks in Multiprocess, Multiple Resource Systems to Avoid Deadlocks," *Proc. 11th Ann. Symp. Switching and Automata Theory,* pp. 225-233, October.

Siegel, H. J. (1979). "A Model of SIMD Machines and a Comparison of Various Interconnection Networks," *IEEE Trans. Computers,* Vol. C-28, No. 12, December, pp. 907-917.

Siegel, H. J. (1980). "The Theory Underlying the Partitioning of Permutation Networks," *IEEE Trans. Computers,* Vol. C-29, No. 9, September, pp. 791-800.

Siegel, H. J. (1984). *Interconnection Networks for Large-Scale Parallel Processing: Theory and Case Studies,* D. C. Heath & Computers, Lexington, Massachusettes

Siegel, H. J., Siegel, L. J., Kemmerer, F. C., Mueller, P. T., Smalley, H. E., and Smith, S. D. "PASM: A Reconfigurable SIMD/MIMD System for Image Processing and Pattern Recognition," *IEEE Trans. Computers,* December 1981, pp. 934-947.

Siewiorek, D., Bell, C. G., and Newell, A. (1980). *Principles of computer structures.* McGraw-Hill, New York.

Siewiorek, D. P. et al. (1978). "A Case Study of C.mmp, Cm' and C.vmp, Part I: Experience with Fault-Tolerance in Multiprocessor Systems," *Proc. of the IEEE,* Vol. 66, No. 10, pp. 1178-1199, October.

Sintz, R. H. (1980). "Optimal Use of a Vector Processor," *COMPCON Proc.*, pp. 277-281.

Sites, R. L. (1978). "An analysis of the Cray-1 computer," *Proc. 5th Ann. Symp. on Computer Architecture,* Palo Alto, California, pp. 101-6.

Sites, R. L. (1980). "Operating Systems and Computer Architecture," in *Introduction to Computer Architecture* (Stone, ed), SRA Inc., Chicago, pp. 591-643.

Slotnick, D. L., Borck, W. C., and McReynold, R. C. (1962). "The SOLOMON Computer," *Proc. of AFIPS Fall Joint Computers Conf.,* Washington, D.C., pp. 97-107.

Smith, A. J. (1977). "Multiprocessor Memory Organization and Memory Interference," *Comm. of the ACM,* Vol. 20, No. 10, pp. 754-761, October.

Smith, A. J. (1982). "Cache Memories," *ACM Computing Surveys,* Vol. 14, No. 3, September, pp. 473-530.

Smith, B. J. (1978). "A Pipelined Shared Resources MIMD Computer," *Proc. 1978 Int. Conf. on Parallel Processing,* pp. 6-8.

Smith, B. J. (1981). "Architecture and Application of the HEP Multiprocessor Computer System," *Real Time Signal Processing IV,* Vol. 298, August. Smith, J. E. (1982). "Decoupled Access/Execute Computer Architecture," *Proc. of 9th Ann. Symp. on Computer Architecture,* pp. 112-120.

Snyder, L. (1982). "Introduction to the Configurable Highly Parallel Computer," *IEEE Computer,* January, pp. 47-64.

Sovis, F. (1983). "Uniform Theory of the Shuffle-Exchange Type Permutation Networks," *Proc. of 10th Ann. Symp. on Computer Architecture,* pp. 185-193.

Sowa, M. and Murata, T. (1982). "A Data Flow Computer Architecture with Program and Token Memories," *IEEE Trans. Computers,* C-31, pp. 820-824.

Sperry Univac (1982). *The Univac Series 1100 Announcement,* May.

Srini, V. P. and Asenjo, J. F. (1983). "Analysis of Cray-1S Architecture," *Proc. of 10th Ann. Symp. on Computer Architecture,* pp. 194-206.

Stanat, P. L. and Nolen, J. S. (1982). "Performance Comparisons for Reservoir Simulation Problems on Three Supercomputers," Paper SPE 10640.

Sternberg, S. R. (1983). "Biomedical Image Processing," *IEEE Computer,* Vol. 16, No. 1, pp. 22-34.

Stevens, K. (1975). "CFD - A FORTRAN-like Language for the Illiac IV," *SIGPLAN Notices,* March, pp. 72-80.

Stevenson, D. K. (1980). "Numerical Algorithms for Parallel Computers," *Proc. Nat'l. Computer Conf.,* AFIPS Press, Vol. 49, pp. 357-361.

Stone, H. S. (1971). "Parallel Processing with the Perfect Shuffle," *IEEE Trans. Computers,* Vol. C-20, February, pp. 153-161.

Stone, H. S. (1977). "Multiprocessor Scheduling with the Aid of Network Flow Algorithms," *IEEE Trans. on Software Engineering,* Vol. SE-5, January, pp. 85-93.

Stone, H. S. (1980). "Parallel Computers," Chap. 8 in *Introduction to Computer Architecture,* (Stone, ed), SRA, Chicago, pp. 363-426.

Stone, H. S. (1984). "Computer Research in Japan," *IEEE Computer,* March, pp. 36-32.

Stout, Q. F. (1983). "Sorting, Merging, Selecting, and Filtering on Tree and Pyramid Machines" *Proc. 1983 Int'l. Conf. Parallel Processing,* pp. 214-221.

Strecker, W. (1976). "Cache Memories for PDP-11 Family Computers," *Proc. 3rd Symp. on Computers Architecture,* pp. 155-157.

Stringa, L. (1983). "EMMA: An Industrial Experience on Large Multiprocessing Architecture," *Proc. of 10th Ann. Symp. on Computer Architecture,* pp. 326-333.

Su, S. P. (1982). "Pipelining and Dataflow Techniques for Designing Supercomputers," *Ph.D. Thesis,* School of E.E., Purdue University, Lafayette, Indiana, December.

Su, S. P. and Hwang, K. (1982). "Multiple Pipeline Scheduling in Vector Supercomputer," *Proc. of Int'l. Conf. on Parallel Processing*, pp. 226-234.

Sugarman, R. (1980). "Superpower Computers," *IEEE Spectrum*, April, pp. 28-34.

Sugimoto, S. et al. (1983). "A Multi-Microprocessor System for Concurrent LISP," *Proc. of Int'l. Conf. on Parallel Processing*, pp. 135-143.

Swan, R. J., Bechtholsheim, A., Lai, K. W. and Ousterhout, J. K. (1977). "The Implementation of the Cm* Multimicroprocessor," *Proc. AFIPS 1977 Nat. Computers Conf.*, 46, AFIPS Press, Montvale, New Jersey, pp. 645-655.

Swanson, J. A., Cameron, G. R., and Haberland, J. C. (1983). "Adapting the Ansys Finite-Element Analysis Program to an Attached Processor," *IEEE Computer*, Vol. 16, No. 6, pp. 85-94.

Swartzlander, E. E., Jr. and Gilbert, B. K. (1982). "Supersystems: Technology and Architecture," *IEEE Trans. Computers*, C-31, pp. 399-409.

Syre, J. C. et al. (1980). "The Data Driven LAU Multiprocessor System," in *Information Processing 80*, (Lavington, ed.), North Holland, New York.

Syre, J. C., Comte, D., and Hifdi, N. (1977). "Pipelining, Parallelism and Asynchronism in the LAU System," *Proc. 1977 Int. Conf. on Parallel Processing*, pp. 87-92.

Tadjan, M., Buehrer, R. E., and Haelg, W. (1982). "Parallel Simulation by Means of a Prescheduled MIMD-System Featuring Synchronous Pipeline Processors," *Proc. of Int'l. Conf. on Parallel Processing*, pp. 280-283.

Takahashi, N. and Amamiya, M. (1983). "A Dataflow Processor Array System: Design and Analysis," *Proc. of the 10th Int'l. Symp. on Computer Architecture*, June 13-17, pp. 243-251.

Takuhaski, Y. (1982). "Partitioning and Allocation in Parallel Computation of Partial Differential Equations," *Proc. 19th IMACS World Congress*, Vol. 1, 311-313.

Tanenbaum, A., (1978). "Implication of Structured Programming for Computer Architecture," *Comm. of ACM, 21,* March, pp. 237-246.

Tang, C. K., (1976). "Cache System Design in the Tightly Coupled Multiprocessor System," *Proc. AFIPS 1976 Nat. Computers Conf., 45,* AFIPS Press, Montvale, New Jersey, pp. 749-753.

Tanimoto, S. L. (1983). "A Pyramidal Approach to Parallel Processing" *Proc. 10th Ann. Symp. Computer Architecture,* pp. 372-378.

Tanimoto, S. L. (1984). "A Hierarchical Cellular Logic for Pyramid Computers," *Journal of Parallel and Distributed Computing,* Vol. 1, No. 1, August.

Tesler, L. G. and Enea, H. (1968). "A Language for Concurrent Processes," *Proc. SJCC,* AFIPS Press, Montvale, New Jersey.

Texas Instruments, Inc. (1971). "Description of the ASC System: Parts 1 to 5, *Manual* Nos. 934662 to 934666.

Texas Instruments, Inc., (1972). *ASC FORTRAN Reference Manual,* Pub. No. 930044.

Theis, D. J. (1974). "Special Tutorial: Vector Supercomputers," IEEE *Computer Magazine,* April, pp. 52-61.

Thomas, R. E. (1981). "A Dataflow Architecture with Improved Asymptotic Performance," *Ph.D. Thesis,* Dept. of Computer Science, University of California, Irvine, California, April.

Thompson, C. D. (1978). "Generalized Connection Networks for Parallel Processor Intercommunication," *IEEE Trans. Computers,* Vol. C-27, no. 12, December, pp. 1119-1126.

Thompson, C. D., and Kung, H. T. (1977). "Sorting on a Mesh-Connected Parallel Computer," *Comm. of the ACM,* Vol. 20, No. 4, pp. 263-271, Apr.

Thompson, S. D. (1980). "A Complexity Theory for VLSI," *Ph.D. Thesis,* Dept. of Computer Science, Carnegie-Mellon University, Pittsburgh, Pennsylvania, September.

Thurber, K. J. (1976). *Large Scale Computer Architecture - Parallel and Associative Processors,* Hayden Book Co., New Jersey.

Thurber, K. J. (1979a). "Parallel Processor Architectures - Part I: General Purpose System," *Computer Design,* January pp. 89-97.

Thurber, K. J. (1979b). "Parallel Processor Architectures - Part II: Special Purpose Systems," *Computer Design,* February pp. 103-114.

Tjaden, G. S. and Flynn, M. J. (1973). "Representation of Concurrency with Ordering Matrices," *IEEE Trans. Computers,* Vol. C-22, No. 8, August, pp. 752-761.

Tohru, M. O. (1983). "Overview to the Fifth Generation Computer System Project," *Proc. of 10th Ann. Symp. on Computer Architecture,* pp. 417-422.

Tokoro, M. (1983). "On the Working Set Concept for Dataflow Machine," *Proc. of 10th Ann. Symp. Computer Architecture,* June, pp. 90-97.

Tomasulo, R. M. (1967). "An Efficient Algorithm for Exploiting Multiple Arithmetic Units," *IBM Journal of Research and Development,* Vol. 11, No. 1, January, pp. 25-33.

Treleaven, P. C. (1979). "Exploiting Program Concurrency in Computing Systems," *IEEE Computer 12,* January, pp. 42-50.

Treleaven, P. C., Brownbridge, D. R., and Hopkins, R. P. (1982). "Data Driven and Demand-Driven Computer Architecture," *ACM Computing Surveys,* March, pp. 93-144.

Treleaven, P. C. and Lima, I. G. (1984). "Future Computers: Logic, Dataflow, ..., Control Flow?" *IEEE Computer,* Vol. 17, March, pp. 47-48.

Tripathi, A. R. and Lipovski, G. J. (1979). "Packet Switching in Banyan Networks," *Proc. of the 6-th Ann. Symp. on Computer Architecture,* New York, New York, April, pp. 160-167.

Uchida, S. (1983). "Inference Machine," *Proc. of 10th Ann. Symp. on Computer Architecture,* pp. 410-416.

Uhr, L. (1984). *Algorithm-Structured Computer Arrays and Networks,* Academic Press, New York.

Ullman, J. D. (1984). "Flux, Sorting, and Supercomputer Organization for AI Applications," Vol. 1, No. 1, August.

Ullman, J. D. (1984). *Principles of VLSI Computations,* Computer Science Press, Rockville, Maryland.

Ungar, D., Blau, R. Foley, P., Samples, D., and Patterson, D. (1984). "Architecture of SOAR: Smalltalk on a RISC," *Proc. of the 11th Annual Int'l Symp. on Computer Architecture,* Ann Arbor, Michigan, June 5-7, pp. 188-197.

Vajtersic, M. (1982). "Parallel Poisson and Biharmonic Solvers Implemented on the EGPA Multiprocessor," *Proc. of Int'l. Conf. on Parallel Processing,* pp. 72-81.

Valiant, L. G. et al. (1983). "Fast Parallel Computation of Polynomials Using Few Processors," *SIAM J. Computers,* Vol. 12, pp. 641-644.

VanAken, J. and Zick, G. (1981). "The Expression Processor: A Pipelined Multiprocessor Architecture," *IEEE Trans. Computers,* C-30, pp. 525-536.

Vick, C. R., Kartashev, S. P. and Kartashev, S. I. (1980). "Adaptable Architectures for Supersystems," *IEEE Computer,* Vol. 13, No. 11, pp. 17-35.

Vuillemin, J. (1983). "A Combinational Limit to the Computing Power of VLSI Circuits," *IEEE Trans. Computers,* C-32, pp. 294-300.

Wah, B. W., Li, G.-J. and Yu, C.-F. (1984). "The Status of MANIP — A Multicomputer Architecture for Solving Combinatorial Extremum-Search Problems," *Proc. of the 11th Annual Int'l Symp. on Computer Architecture,* Ann Arbor, Michigan, June 5-7, pp. 56-63.

Wagner, R. A. (1983). "The Boolean Vector Machine," *Proc. of 10th Ann. Symp. on Computer Architecture,* pp. 59-66.

Walker, L. L. (1972). "Multiprocessor Operating System Design," in *Operating Systems, Int'l. Computer State of the Art Report,* Infotech Ltd., Maidenhead, England.

Wallach, Y. and Konrad, V. (1980). "On Block-Parallel Methods for Solving Linear Equations," *IEEE Trans. Computers,* C-29, pp. 354-359.

Wann, D. F. and Franklin, M. A. (1983). "Asynchronous and Clocked Control Structures for VLSI Based Interconnection Networks," *IEEE Trans. Computers*, C-32, pp. 284-293.

Wang, R. Q., Zhang, X., and Gao, Q. S. (1982). "SP2I Interconnection Network and Extension of the Iteration Method of Automatic Vector-Routing," *Proc. of Int'l. Conf. on Parallel Processing*, pp. 16-25.

Waser, S. and Flynn, M. (1982). *Introduction to Arithmetic for Digital Systems Designers*, Holt, Rinehart and Winston, New York.

Watson, I. and Gurd, J. (1982). "A Practical Data Flow Computer," *IEEE Computer*, Vol. 15, No. 2, pp. 51-57.

Watson, R. W. (1970). *Timesharing System Design Concepts*, McGraw-Hill, New York.

Watson, W. J. and Carr, H. M. (1974). "Operational Experiences with the TI Advanced Scientific Computer," *AFIPS NCC Proc.*, pp. 389-397.

Weide, B. W. (1982). "Modeling Unusual Behavior of Parallel Algorithms," *IEEE Trans. Computers*, C-31, pp. 1126-1130.

Weiss, S. and Smith, J. E. (1984). "Instruction Issue Logic for Pipelined Supercomputers," *Proc. of the 11th Annual Int'l Symp. on Computer Architecture*," Ann Arbor, Michigan, June 5-7, pp. 110-118.

White, C. H. (ed., 1976). *Multiprocessor Systems, Int'l. Computer State-of-the-Art Report*, Infotech Ltd., Maidenhead, England.

Widdoes, L. C. Jr. (1980). "The S-1 Project: Developing High-Performance Digital Computers," *Digest of Papers: IEEE Compcon*, pp. 282-291.

Wilkes, M. V. (1972). *Time-Sharing Computer System*, 2nd ed., Elsevier, New York.

Wilson, A., Siewiorek, D. and Segall, Z. (1983). "Evaluation of Multiprocessor Interconnect Structures with the CM* Testbed," *Proc. of Int'l. Conf. on Parallel Processing*, pp. 164-171.

Wing, O. and Huang, J. W. (1980). "A Computational Model of Parallel Solution of Linear Equations," *IEEE Trans. Computers*, C-29, pp. 632-638.

Wittmayer, W. R. (1978). "Array Processor Provides High Throughput Rates," *Computer Design*, March, pp. 93-100.

Wu, C. L. and Feng, T. Y. (1980). "On a Class of Multistage Interconnection Networks," *IEEE Trans. Computers*, Vol. C-29, No. 8, August, pp. 694-702.

Wu, C. L. and Feng, T. Y. (1981). "Universitility of the Shuffle Exchange Network," *IEEE Trans. Computers*, Vol. C-30, No. 5, May, pp. 324-331.

Wu, S. B. and Liu, M. T. (1981). "A Cluster Structure as an Interconnection Network for Large Multimicrocomputer Systems," *IEEE Trans. Computers*, Vol. C-30, No. 4, April, pp. 254-265.

Wulf, W. A. et al. (1975). "Overview of the Hydra Operating System," In *Proc. of the 5th Symp. on Operating System Principles*, pages 122-131, ACM, November, Austin, Texas.

Wulf, W. A., Levin, R., and Harbison, S. P. (1981). *HYDRA/C.mmp: An Experimental Computer System*, McGraw-Hill, New York

Yao, A. (1982). "On Parallel Computation for the Knapsack Problem," *Journal of ACM*, Vol. 29, pp. 889-903.

Yasrebi, M. and Lipovski, G. J. (1984). "A State-of-the-Art SIMD Two-Dimensional FFT Array Processor," *Proc. of the 11th Annual Int'l Symp. on Computer Architecture*, Ann Arbor, Michigan, June 5-7, pp. 21-29.

Yasumura, M., Tanaka, Y., and Kanada, Y. (1984). "Compiling Algorithms and Techniques for the S-810 Vector Processor," *Proc. of Int'l Conf. on Parallel Processing*, August.

Yasuura, H., Takagi, N. and Yajima, S. (1982). "The Parallel Enumeration Sorting Scheme for VLSI," *IEEE Trans. Computers*, C-31, pp. 1192-1201.

Yau, S. S., and Fung, H. S. (1977). "Associative Processor Architecture—A Survey," *ACM Computing Surveys*, March, Vol. 9, No. 1, pp. 3-28.

Zadeh, L. A. (1984). "Coping with the Imprecision of the Real World," *Comm. of ACM*, Vol. 27, April, pp. 304-311.

Biography

Kai Hwang is a Professor of Computer Engineering at the School of Electrical Engineering, Purdue University. He received the BSEE degree from National Taiwan University, the MSEE degree from University of Hawaii, and the Ph.D. in EECS from the University of California at Berkeley. His specialty includes the areas of computer architecture, arithmetic processors, parallel processing, and machine intelligence. Dr. Hwang has authored and coauthored over 60 scientific papers and books in the computer area.

His current research and teaching interest lies mainly in vector supercomputers, multiprocessors, VLSI and dataflow computing structures, and image understanding systems. he is the author of Computer Arithmetic Principles, **Architecture and Design** (Wiley, 1979) and of **Computer Architecture and Parallel Processing** (McGraw-Hill, 1984). He edited the text **Supercomputer Design and Applications**, (Computer Society Press, 1984). He has been a Distinguished Visitor of IEEE Computer Society since 1981.

Dr. Hwang has lectured throughout Europe, Asia, and North America on topics on advanced computer architecture and parallel processing techniques. He is presently serving as the Co-editor-in-Chief of the **Journal of Parallel and Distributed Computing.** Dr. Hwang has served as a principal investigator, a consultant or a lecturer in studies on supercomputer architectures and large-scale scientific computations for U.S. National Science Foundation, IBM Fishkill Facilities, Fujitsu in Japan, Academia Sinica, NATO Advanced Study Institute, and several other research organizations.

6/12/84

BIOGRAPHY

Kai Hwang is a Professor of Computer Engineering at the School of Electrical Engineering, Purdue University. He received the BSEE degree from National Taiwan University, the MSEE degree from University of Hawaii, and the Ph.D. in EECS from the University of California at Berkeley. His specialty includes the areas of computer architecture, arithmetic processors, parallel processing, and machine intelligence. Dr. Hwang has authored and coauthored over 60 scientific papers and books in the computer area.

His current research and teaching interest lies mainly in vector supercomputers, multiprocessors, VLSI and dataflow computing structures, and image understanding systems. he is the author of **Computer Arithmetic Principles, Architecture and Design** (Wiley, 1979) and of **Computer Architecture and Parallel Processing** (McGraw-Hill, 1984). He edited the text **Supercomputer Design and Applications,** (Computer Society Press, 1984). He has been a Distinguished Visitor of IEEE Computer Society since 1981.

Dr. Hwang has lectured throughout Europe, Asia, and North America on topics on advanced computer architecture and parallel processing techniques. He is presently serving as the Co-editor-in-Chief of the **Journal of Parallel and Distributed Computing.** Dr. Hwang has served as a principal investigator, a consultant or a lecturer in studies on supercomputer architectures and large-scale scientific computations for U.S. National Science Foundation, IBM Fishkill Facilities, Fujitsu in Japan, Academia Sinica, NATO Advanced Study Institute, and several other research organizations.

6/12/84